The
Concinse Knowledge
Natural History

THE GORILLA.

The
Concinse Knowledge
Natural History

By

R. Lydekker

GYAN

Published by

GYAN

Gyan Publishing House
5, Ansari Road
Daryaganj, New Delhi-110002
Phone: 011-47034999, 9811692060
E-mail: books@gyanbooks.com

Distribution Network
gyanbooks.com
India, USA, Canada, UK, Australia, France

ISBN : 978-81-212-6705-2 (PB)
First Published, 1987

2nd Impression 2022

Printed at: Gyan Press, Delhi.

THE CONCINSE KNOWLEDGE NATURAL HISTORY
Author: R. Lydekker

The Concise Knowledge Natural History

BY

R. LYDEKKER, B.A., F.R.S., V.P.G.S.; R. BOWDLER SHARPE, LL.D.;
W. F. KIRBY, F.L.S., F.E.S.; W. GARSTANG, M.A., F.Z.S.;
B. B. WOODWARD, F.L.S., F.G.S.; F. A. BATHER, M.A., F.G.S.;
R. KIRKPATRICK; R. I. POCOCK; AND
H. M. BERNARD, M.A., F.L.S.

With 530 Original Illustrations by

J. KEULEMANS, F. H. MICHAEL, ERNALD W. MILES,
FRANK C. ALDWORTH, AND OTHER ARTISTS

1897

PREFACE

THIS work aims to be a concise and popular Natural History, at once accurate in statement, handy in form, and ready of reference.

The several departments of Zoological science are treated by specialists, all of whom are distinguished as authorities and as original investigators; and the text is illustrated by upwards of five hundred original drawings made and reproduced expressly for the work.

A concise systematic index precedes the work, and a full alphabetical index which contains about ten thousand references is given at the end. Great pains have been taken to render these both accurate and complete.

TABLE OF AUTHORS

MAMMALIA (*Mammals*)	R. LYDEKKER, F.R.S., V.P.G.S., &c.
AVES (*Birds*) - - -	R. BOWDLER SHARPE, LL.D., &c.
REPTILIA (*Reptiles*) - -	R. LYDEKKER, F.R.S., V.P.G.S., &c.
AMPHIBIA (*Frogs, Toads, &c.*)	R. LYDEKKER, F.R.S., V.P.G.S., &c.
PISCES (*Fishes*) - -	R. LYDEKKER, F.R.S., V.P.G.S., &c.
CYCLOSTOMATA (*Lampreys, &c.*)	R. LYDEKKER, F.R.S., V.P.G.S., &c.
PROTOCHORDA (*Lancelet, &c.*)	W. GARSTANG, M.A., F.Z.S., &c.
HEMICHORDA (*Balanoglossus*)	W. GARSTANG, M.A., F.Z.S., &c.
ARTHROPODA (*Insects, &c.*) -	W. F. KIRBY, F.L.S., F.E.S , &c.
MOLLUSCA (*Snails, &c.*) -	B. B. WOODWARD, F.L.S., F.G.S., &c.
BRACHIOPODA (*Lamp Shells, &c.*)	F. A. BATHER, M.A., F.G.S., &c.
ECHINODERMA (*Star Fish, &c.*)	F. A. BATHER, M.A., F.G.S., &c.
BRYOZOA (*Moss Animals*) -	R. KIRKPATRICK (British Museum).
VERMES (*Worms*) - -	R. I. POCOCK (British Museum).
COELENTERA (*Corals, &c.*)	H. M. BERNARD, M.A., F.L.S., &c.
PROTOZOA (*Animalculæ*) -	H. M. BERNARD, M.A., F.L.S., &c.

THE ANIMAL KINGDOM.

SUB-KINGDOM I.—VERTEBRATA.

CLASS I.—MAMMALIA.

MAMMALS.

CLASS II.—AVES.

BIRDS.

CLASS III.—REPTILIA.

REPTILES.

CLASS IV.—AMPHIBIA.

AMPHIBIANS.

CLASS V.—PISCES.

FISHES.

CLASS VI.—CYCLOSTOMA.

LAMPREYS AND HAG-FISHES.

CLASS VII.—PROTOCHORDA.

CLASS VIII.—HEMICHORDA.

SUB-KINGDOM II.—ARTHROPODA.

CRUSTACEA, INSECTA, &c.

CLASS I.—CRUSTACEA.

CLASS II.—ARACHNIDA.

SPIDERS, SCORPIONS, AND MITES.

CLASS III.—MYRIOPODA.

CENTIPEDES AND MILLEPEDES.

CLASS IV.—PROTRACHEATA.

CLASS V.—INSECTA.

SUB-KINGDOM III.—MOLLUSCA.

WHELKS, OYSTERS, SNAILS, &c.

CLASS I.—AMPHINEURA.

CLASS II.—PELECYPODA (*BIVALVES*).

CLASS III.—SCAPHOPODA.

CLASS IV.—GASTROPODA.

CLASS V.—CEPHALOPODA.

SUB-KINGDOM IV.—BRACHIOPODA.

LAMPSHELLS, &c.

SUB-KINGDOM V.—ECHINODERMA.

STAR-FISH, SEA-URCHINS, &c.

SUB-KINGDOM VI.—BRYOZOA [POLYZOA].

MOSS ANIMALS.

SUB-KINGDOM VII.—VERMES.

THE WORMS.

SUB-KINGDOM VIII.—COELENTERA.

SPONGES, CORALS, &c.

SUB-KINGDOM IX.—PROTOZOA.

ANIMALCULÆ.

THE ANIMAL KINGDOM.

SUB-KINGDOM I.—VERTEBRATA.

CLASS I.—MAMMALIA.

BY R. LYDEKKER, B.A., F.R.S., V.P.G.S., &c.

IT is a somewhat curious deficiency in the English language that it has no word of its own that will include all the animals forming the class known to zoologists as the Mammalia. It is true that the term Beasts properly belongs to the great majority of the members of the class, but it has also acquired another meaning, and expressly excludes man. Even more objectionable is the term Quadrupeds, since not only does this exclude man and the higher apes, but etymologically includes crocodiles, lizards, and turtles. Accordingly, as neither of these two words are suitable to designate the class as a whole, naturalists have long been in the habit of using an Anglicised version of its scientific designation, and at the present day the term "Mammals" has come so widely into use that no apology for its employment here is called for. Mammals, then, are the highest of the Vertebrata, and thus of all animals, and take their name from the general presence of prominent udders, furnished with teats, in the female, for the secretion of the milk, by which the young are invariably fed during the earlier stages of their existence, such udders being situated in the higher types on the breast, although in many of the lower forms they are abdominal in position. In the very lowest members of the class there are, however, no distinct teats, the milk-glands discharging by means of a number of small apertures in the skin of the lower surface of the body. It is thus the presence of these milk-glands, and the suckling of the more or less helpless young, that are the prime essential features of the class.

Characteristics of Vertebrates.

Before glancing at certain others of their distinctive features, a few words may be said in regard to the Vertebrata, which form a sub-kingdom, including the five classes of Mammals (Mammalia), Birds (Aves), Reptiles (Reptilia), Amphibians (Amphibia), and Fishes (Pisces). And here it may be noticed that certain low forms, such as the lampreys and lancelet (*Amphioxus*), commonly classed among Fishes, are now regarded as forming a portion of a lower group known as the Protochordata. Vertebrates take their name from the general presence of the structure termed the vertebral column, or backbone, although in some of the lower forms this is represented merely by a cartilaginous rod. Whether this structure be merely such a rod, or whether it be divided into the numerous bony segments known as vertebræ, it is invariably situated on the dorsal aspect of the body, or that from which the limbs are turned away. On that side of the primitive backbone lying nearest to the back, there runs a tube or canal, formed by arches of bone or cartilage arising from the bodies of the vertebræ, and containing the great nervous cord commonly spoken of as the spinal marrow or cord. This cord in the adult state of the higher forms being thus included within what are called the arches of the vertebræ. On the side of the primitive backbone opposite to that occupied by the spinal marrow is a much larger chamber, containing the heart and digestive organs ; so that, in cross-section, the body of a Vertebrate consists of a smaller nerve-tube lying above the primitive backbone, and of a much larger tube, containing the heart and digestive organs below the latter. Throughout the Vertebrates the limbs never exceed two pairs, and are always turned away from that aspect of the body containing the nerve-tube ; and the two jaws are upper and lower, and work against one another in a vertical plane.

Distinctive Features of Mammals.

In addition to the presence of milk-glands, and the suckling by the young of the fluid they secrete, the following structural features may be noticed as distinctive of the Mammalian class. A highly important feature is the mode of articulation of the lower jaw to the skull proper, or cranium ; this being effected by means of a prominence, or condyle, at the higher portion of the hinder extremity of the lower jaw, articulating with a special cavity—the glenoid cavity—in the cranium. On the other hand, in the lower Vertebrates this articulation is effected by means of a special separate bone—the quadrate—articulating above with the cranium, and below with the lower jaw ; this quadrate, as such, being absent in the Mammalia. Another peculiarity connected with the lower jaw is that it consists of a right and left branch—connected at the chin by a bony or cartilaginous union—each of which is formed of but a single bone; whereas in the inferior Vertebrates several distinct bones enter into the composition of the two branches. Externally, Mammals are further characterised by the possession of hair on the skin, although this may be represented merely by a few bristles in the neighbourhood of the mouth during the earlier stages of existence. Internally, that portion of the great body-cavity containing the heart and lungs is completely shut off from the chamber in which are placed the digestive organs by means of a transverse partition, known as the midriff or diaphragm. Existing Mammals, at any rate, have also a higher type of brain than the inferior classes, an especial feature being the presence of a transverse band of tissue on its lower surface, connecting together the main lateral halves or hemispheres.

Such are some of the leading characters by which the Mammalia may be distinguished from the whole of the other Vertebrates. From both Birds and Reptiles the class differs by the circumstance that the skull is movably articulated to the first vertebra of the neck by means of two knobs, or condyles, situated one on each side of the lower part of the aperture, or foramen, through which the spinal cord passes into the skull to join the brain. Two condyles are, however, present in the Amphibians (frogs and salamanders), which differ from Mammals in their cold blood. A second distinction from Birds and Reptiles is to be found in the structure of the ankle joint; the movable joint in Mammals being situated above the ankle, whereas in the other groups it is placed in the middle of the same. In common with Birds, Mammals differ from the three lower classes of the Vertebrata in having warm blood, driven by a four-chambered heart through a double circulatory system; one portion of the blood being propelled through the lungs for the purpose of re-oxygenation, while a second portion is sent through the body by means of the general circulation. Whereas, however, in Mammals, the aorta, or great vessel, by which the blood passes from the heart to the body, crosses the left branch of the windpipe, in Birds it crosses the right. At no stage of their existence do Mammals ever breathe by means of gills; lungs, even in the aquatic forms, being the sole respiratory agents. Neither do they ever pass through any kind of metamorphosis, such as takes place in the Amphibia. As a general rule, the young are born in a living, and frequently in a more or less helpless condition; but in the very lowest members of the class the female lays eggs.

With but very few exceptions, Mammals have seven vertebræ in the neck, and thereby present a remarkable contrast to Birds and Reptiles, in which the number is exceedingly variable. In all the terrestrial forms the two pairs of limbs are fully developed; but in the marine Cetaceans and Sirenians the front pair are modified into paddles, and all external traces of the hinder ones completely lost, while the body has assumed a fish-like form. In the Bats alone are the fore limbs structurally modified to subserve the purpose of true flight, like that of Birds.

Skeleton.

As in the following pages reference is often made to various bones of the skeleton, this part of the subject cannot be passed over without brief mention. The fully developed skeleton, as shown by the accompanying diagram, comprises a skull (1), a jointed breast-bone, or sternum (*b*), a still more numerously jointed backbone, the ribs (2), the limb-bones, and the girdles by which they are suspended to the backbone and its neighbourhood, and a pair of collar-bones, or clavicles (*c*). As already mentioned, the skull proper, or the skull without the lower jaw, is termed the cranium; this consisting of a number of (mostly paired) bones, articulated immovably together at their edges. The hinder portion of the cranium encloses the brain; while the front part, or facial region, contains the mouth and organs of smell. Of especial importance are the bones forming the upper jaw, which comprise in front a pair of premaxillæ, containing the front or incisor teeth; behind which are the maxillæ, containing the tusks and cheek-teeth. The lower jaw has been already mentioned sufficiently. In the backbone the cervical, or neck-vertebræ are recognised by having no ribs attached to them; behind these follow the dorsal vertebræ, each carrying a pair of movable ribs, of which the more anterior are connected with the breast-bone; and these in turn are succeeded by the lumbar, or loin-vertebræ, to which no movable ribs are articulated. Behind the lumbars comes the solid mass of several united vertebræ, known as the sacrum, to which are firmly articulated the haunch-bones, or ilia (*a*), forming the upper part of the pelvis (3). Behind the pelvis are the bones of the tail, or caudal vertebræ, which may be either very few or very numerous. In the higher Mammals the shoulder-girdle proper is formed only by the two blade-bones, or scapulæ, which overlie the anterior ribs without any attachment to the backbone, and have at their lower end a shallow cavity for the reception of the head of the uppermost bone of the arm or fore-limb. When fully developed, the collar-bones are articulated by one extremity to the blade-bones, and by the other to the upper segment of the breast-bone. Certain other bones entering into the composition of the shoulder-girdle of the lowest representatives of the class, will be noticed under that group. In the skeleton of the fore-limb, or arm, we have the upper

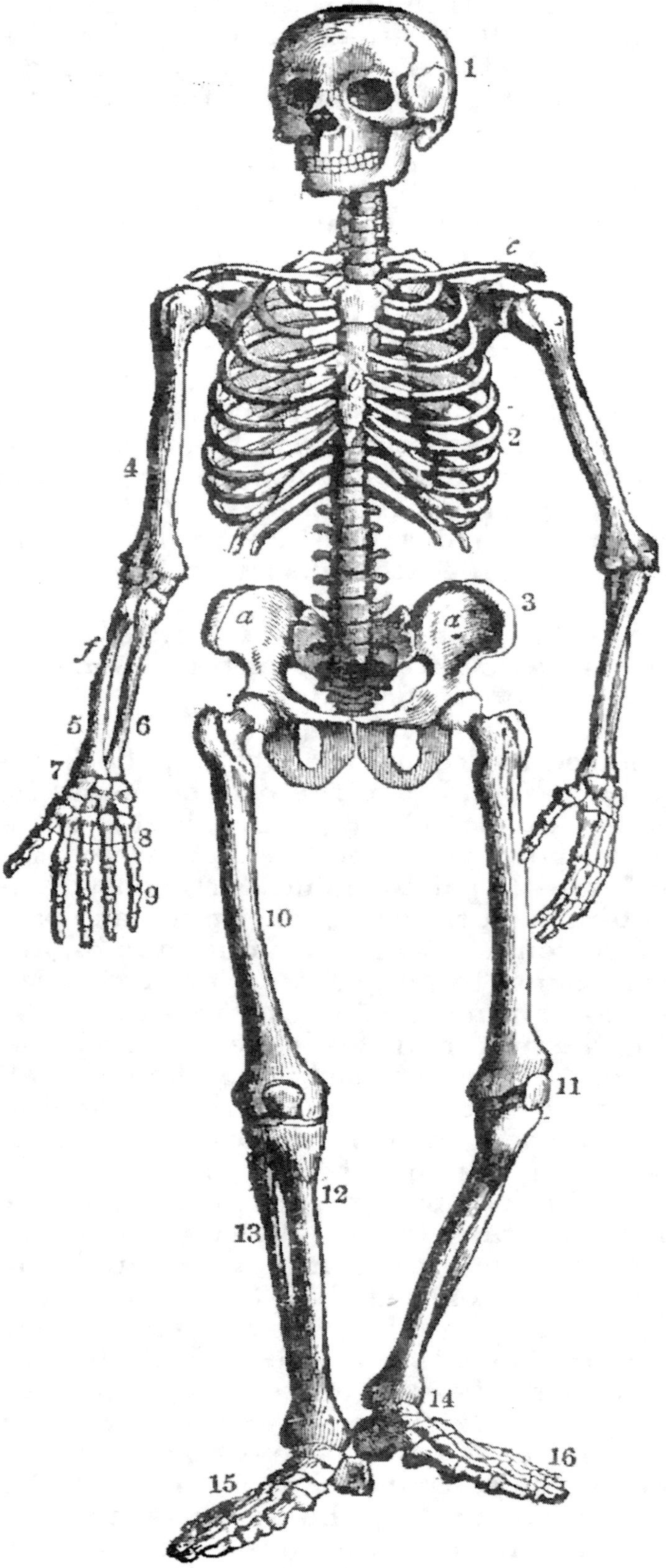

Fig. 1.—HUMAN SKELETON.

arm-bone, or humerus (4), articulating to the blade-bone. The fore-arm (*f*) comprises two bones, the radius (5) anteriorly, and ulna (*b*) posteriorly, both articulating with the lower end of the humerus, and the upper end of the latter forming the prominence of the elbow. At the lower end of the radius and ulna comes the wrist joint, or carpus (7), consisting of an upper and lower row of small massive bones, frequently having a central bone between them. To the upper row of bones, counting from the side of the thumb to the little finger, the names of scaphoid, lunar, and cuneiform are applied. When these three bones directly overlie the bones of the lower row, the carpus is said to be of the linear type; but when they overlap, it is said to be an alternating carpus. The wrist is followed by the metacarpal bones (8), which never exceed five in number, and these again by the phalanges, or bones of the digits; such digits (9) being likewise never more than five in number. Whereas in the first digit, or thumb, there are but two phalanges, in the other digits there are normally three. The pelvic-girdle (3), or that by which the hind-limb is supported, differs essentially from the shoulder-girdle, in that it is immovably fixed to the backbone at the sacrum. The pelvis, as the whole structure is called, is divided into a right and left innominate bone. In the higher Mammals, each innominate consists of a single bone, although it primarily consists of three distinct elements. The uppermost of these, and the one by means of which the attachment to the sacrum is made, is called the haunch-bone, or ilium (*a*), and corresponds to the scapula in the fore-limb. Inferiorly there are two elements, of which the first is the pubis, and the second the ischium. Each innominate bone on its outer side contains a cup-shaped cavity (into the composition of which enter alike the ilium, pubis, and ischium) known as the acetabulum; and with this articulates the femur, or thigh-bone (10), representing the humerus of the fore-limb. Toward the middle of the hinder surface of its shaft this bone frequently bears a bold projecting crest termed the third trochanter. As the humerus articulates with the two bones of the fore-arm, so the thigh-bone articulates with the two bones of the lower leg, of which the larger is known as the tibia (12), and the smaller as the fibula (13). Following these comes the ankle-joint, or tarsus (14), which, like the carpus, is formed of an upper and a lower row of small massive bones; the two uppermost bones being respectively known as the huckle-bone, or astragalus; and the heel-bone, or calcaneum. Inferiorly the tarsus is succeeded by the metatarsal bones (15), corresponding to the metacarpals in the fore-limb, these being followed by the phalanges of the toes (16), which are similar to those of the front limb. To the first toe of the hind foot the name hallux is often applied. It may be added that when (as in the ruminants) there are only two metacarpals, or metatarsals, which are completely joined together so as to form a single bone, or when (as in the horses) there is originally but a single metacarpal or metatarsal, such bone, whether of dual origin or primarily single, is called a cannon-bone. The knee-cap, or patella (11), is a bone in the tendon of the great muscle of the thigh.

With regard to the teeth, it has been already stated that in the upper jaw

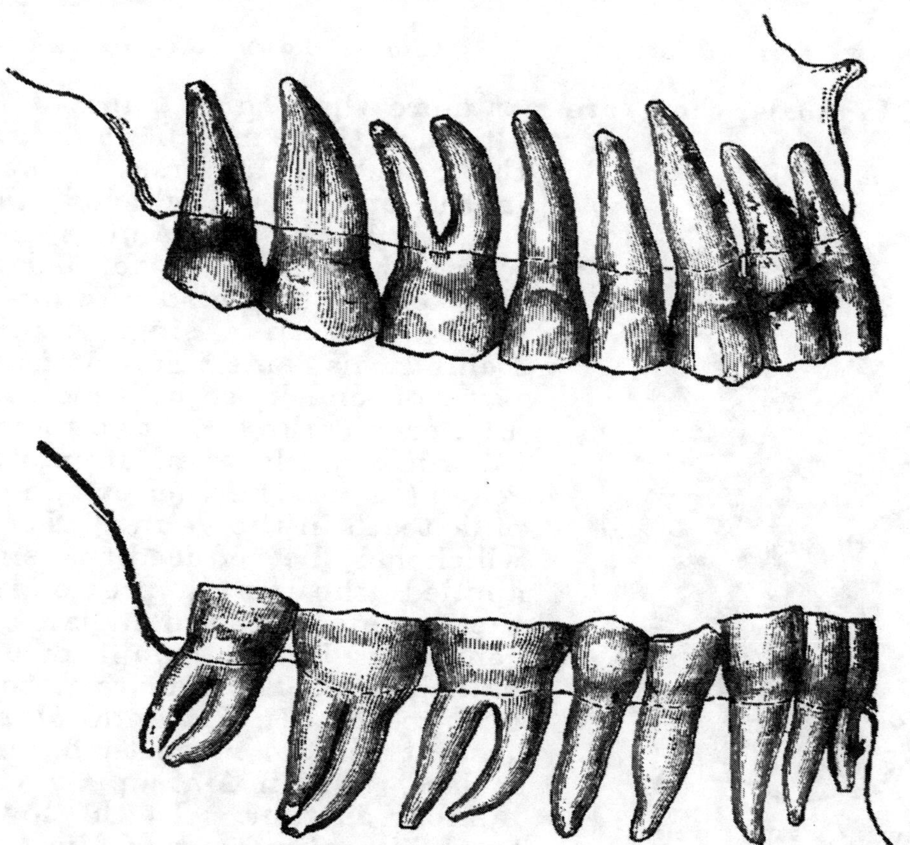

Fig. 2.—Side View of Upper and Lower Human Dentition, with the sides of the jaw removed to show the rests of the teeth. The three lower teeth with branched roots are the molars; in front of these are the two premolars, then comes the canine, and, finally, the pair of incisors.

the teeth implanted in the premaxillary bones, which are always of a comparatively simple type, with single roots, are termed incisors. In the great

Fig. 3.—UPPER JAW OF THE GORILLA.

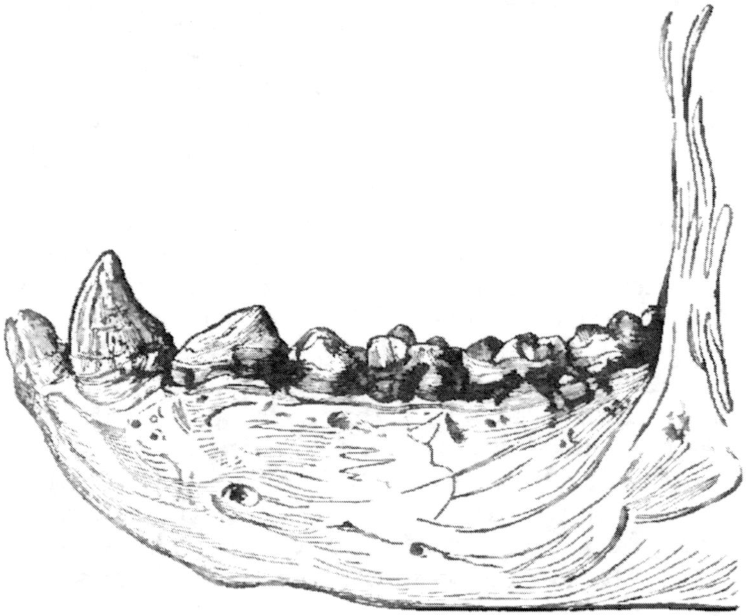

Fig. 4.—LOWER JAW OF THE GORILLA.

majority of Mammals, there are not more than three pairs of these teeth, although there may be four or five pairs in the Pouched Mammals. The first tooth in the upper jaw, which is implanted in the maxillary bone, and is very generally long and tusk-like, is termed the canine; this tooth being also of simple type, and generally with a single undivided root. Behind this come a series of, at most, four pairs of cheek-teeth, which have generally, except the first, two roots each, and, in ordinary Placental Mammals, are preceded (as are the incisors and canine) by milk-teeth in the young. To these teeth, which may be reduced to a single pair, is applied the term, premolars. Behind these come the true molars, which have generally broad complex crowns and branching roots, and are not preceded by milk-teeth. In Placental Mammals there are but seldom more than three pairs of molars, but in Marsupials the ordinary number is four. In the lower jaw the tooth biting in front of the upper canine is the lower canine, in front of which are the incisors. In the Placental Mammals these do not exceed three pairs, and are

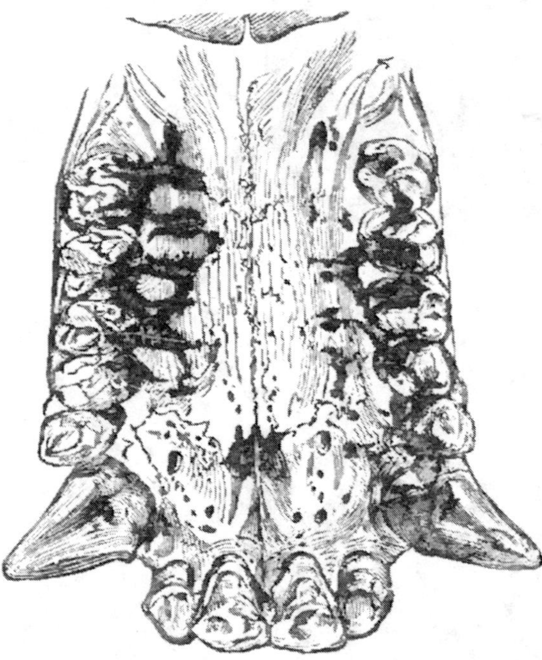

Fig. 5.—PALATE OF THE GORILLA.
In the palate the three hindmost teeth are the molars, in advance of which are the two premolars; the single large tooth on each side is the tusk, or canine, in front of which are the two pairs of incisors.

generally numerically the same as the upper incisors ; but in the Marsupials, where there may be four pairs, they are generally less numerous than the upper. Behind the lower canine come the premolars, which are followed by the molars, the latter being distinguished from the last premolar by having no deciduous predecessors.

Geographical Distribution.

A very important subject connected with the study of Mammals is their geographical distribution on the surface of the globe, but to understand this thoroughly, it is essential to have a knowledge of the extinct forms, and to be acquainted with the changes in the form of the continents and islands which have taken place during earlier epochs of the earth's history. Every traveller is aware that the Mammals of different regions of the globe differ more or less markedly, but this difference is by no means co-extensive with the distance of the various regions from one another. Thus, whereas the Mammals of Japan are very similar to those of Europe, while there is a marked resemblance between the former and those of North America, when we pass from the Malayan Islands to Australia, there is a very sudden and remarkable change.

As a whole, Mammals are a comparatively modern group, which have only attained their present great development during the Tertiary, or latest epoch, of the earth's history. It is true that they existed during the preceding Secondary Epoch, or the one in which the chalk, oolites, lias, etc., were deposited ; but all the forms were then small, and occupied a subordinate position in the fauna of the world, the continents being then peopled by various strange, and frequently gigantic, kinds of Reptiles, while, in the oceans, the place of the modern whales, porpoises, and Sirenians was taken by the Reptilian Ichthyosaurs and Plesiosaurs, It is in consequence of this comparatively late development that the geographical distribution of Mammals differs widely from that of Reptiles and Amphibians, although it coincides to a certain degree with that of Birds, which are likewise a relatively modern group.

From the evidence of Mammals alone, the globe may be divided into three main zoo-geographical realms, two of which may be further sub-divided into regions. These three primary divisions are respectively named the Notogæic, Neogæic, and Arctogæic realms, or Notogæa, Neogæa, and Arctogæa. The first of these includes Australia, New Guinea, New Zealand, and the islands as far east as New Ireland and New Caledonia, together with Celebes, Lombok, and the islands between these and Australia. From Borneo and Java, Celebes and Lombok are separated by a deep channel, and whereas all the islands to the west of this channel, which is known as Wallace's line, have their Mammalian fauna of an Oriental or Indian type, and are without any Marsupials, those on the west of the same show a more or less marked Australian type, Marsupials making their first appearance in Celebes, and becoming more numerous as we approach Australia and Papua, where that group is the dominant one.

The Austro-Malayan islands, as Celebes and the adjacent islands may be called, form, indeed, a transition, so far as Mammals are concerned, between the regions to the west and Australia and New Guinea, although it is on the whole most convenient to include them in the Notogæic realm. The typical part of that realm, as represented by Australia, New Guinea, and the adjacent islands, is characterised by the great preponderance of Pouched Mammals, or Marsupials, while it is here only that the Egg-Laying Mammals, or Monotremes, are met with. In Australia itself, in addition to Bats, which here and elsewhere need not claim our attention, the only Mammals except Marsupials and Monotremes are a certain number of Rodents belonging to the family *Muridæ*, and the Australian wild dog, or dingo. New Guinea, on the other hand, possesses a pig, which may possibly, however, have been introduced.

When Celebes and the other Austro-Malayan islands are reached, Monotremes are absent, and Marsupials form only a small moiety in the fauna. This realm is the sole home, not only of the Monotremes, but likewise of the typical Diprotodont Marsupials,[1] while the only other part of the world where Marsupials are now found is America, where they are represented among other forms by the opossums, which are quite unknown in Australia. As Marsupials of extinct types inhabited the Northern Hemisphere during earlier epochs, it is evident that the Notogæic realm received its Marsupial and Monotremes fauna at a date when such creatures were the dominant forms in South-Eastern Asia, which was then populated by but few other types of Mammalian life. When these ancestral Marsupials and Monotremes had effected an entrance into Australia and New Guinea, with the adjacent islands, they became more or less completely cut off from the rest of the world, and were enabled to develop apart from the competition of the higher forms of life. It is noteworthy that some of the Australian Rodents present a marked similarity to these of the Philippines, showing that the immigration has been from the northward. Notogæa may be divided into several regions. One of these is the New Zealand region, characterised by the absence of all terrestrial Mammals, and the abundance of flightless birds, nearly all of which are now extinct. Under the title of the Australian region may be included Australia, Tasmania, New Guinea, the Aru Islands, New Caledonia, New Britain, etc. ; this region being characterised by the preponderance of Marsupials and the presence of Monotremes. The Austro-Malayan region, which includes the islands mentioned above, has, on the other hand, only a small number of Marsupials among a preponderance of Placentals, so that this region forms a transition between Notogæa and Arctogæa.

Nearly as distinct from the rest of the world as the last, is the Neogæic realm, comprising South and Central America, together with the West Indian Islands. Now, however, the distinction of this realm, as a primary region, is much obscured by the union of South with North America, which has allowed many essentially Northern types to migrate into South America, while a certain number of Southern forms have penetrated into the Northern half of the continent. There is evidence that during the Cretaceous Period, or latest division of the Secondary Epoch, what is now Mexico was a sea, while in the Middle, or Miocene division of the Tertiary Epoch, the same was the case with Central America. It is thus evident that at two distinct periods, North and South America were disconnected ; although it is quite possible that during some other part of the Tertiary Period antecedent to the Miocene, there may have been a temporary connection either by way of the Isthmus of Darien, or by Florida and the West Indies. At the present day the Neogæic realm is practically the sole home of the Edentates,[2] of the New World monkeys (*Cebidæ*) and marmosets (*Hapalidæ*), as well as of many peculiar types of Hystricomorphous Rodents, such as the viscacha (*Lagostomus*), coypu (*Myopotamus*), carpincho (*Hydrochærus*), cavies (*Cavia*), agutis (*Daryprocta*),

[1] This and other terms are fully explained in the sequel.
[2] A few of these and other groups range into Texas.

pacas (*Cœlogenys*), etc., etc., several of them belonging to families which are confined to this realm. Here also the Marsupial opossums (*Didelphyidæ*) attain their maximum development, only a couple of species ranging into North America; while the camel-like llamas (*Lama*) are restricted to this realm. The peccaries (*Dicotyles*), again, are mainly South and Central American while among the Carnivora the coatis (*Nasua*) are exclusively so. In addition to the llamas and peccaries, the only other Ungulates are deer, mostly belonging to the American genus *Cariacus*. True deer (*Cervus*) are totally wanting, as are all Insectivora.

Here, it must be mentioned, that during the Pleistocene Period, or latest division of the Tertiary Epoch, South America was populated by a much more wonderful fauna. Among these were horses and mastodons (allies of the elephants), together with a giant Ungulate (*Toxodon*) typifying a distinct sub-order (Toxodontia) by itself, together with a second, known as the *Macrauchenia*, which is likewise the type of a sub-order (Litopterna.) Here also flourished the gigantic Glyptodonts, which are extinct allies of the armadillos of the present day. Deer, llamas, peccaries, coatis, and various cats were also present at the period in question. When, however, we go back to a still earlier era—the Lower Miocene—horses, peccaries, deer, llamas, coatis, and cats were entirely absent; and the fauna consisted solely of monkeys, marmosets, various peculiar extinct groups of Ungulates, and Hystricomorphous Rodents, together with certain peculiar extinct Marsupials, and some other groups which need not be mentioned. When this fauna flourished, Neogæa must have been quite isolated from the rest of the world. It is, however, clear that (although the Edentates may have originated there) the Ungulates and Hystricomorphous Rodents must have entered from other regions, although how they got there is at present a mystery, seeing that none of the latter occur in the earlier Tertiary strata of North America. At the close of the Miocene Period, South America became connected with North America, from whence it received its extinct horses, together with its existing deer, llamas, peccaries, mice, coatis, cats, dogs, etc.; while, at the same time, a certain number of essentially Neogæic types obtained a footing in North America.

Although fuller details would be necessary to make this very complicated subject clear, it is thus evident that previous to its latest and existing union with North America, Notogæa possessed a very peculiar and characteristic fauna which entitles it to form a primary realm by itself; but that this original distinction has been greatly obscured by later emigrations and immigrations. Of this primitive fauna the Edentates, monkeys, marmosets, Hystricomorphous Rodents, and certain Marsupials, are now remnants; while the coatis and llamas, which are at the present day confined to the realm, do not properly belong to it at all.

Arctogæa includes the whole of the rest of the world, and may be characterised by the absence of Monotremes, Diprotodont Marsupials, and Edentates,[1] and the presence of Insectivora; Marsupials occurring only in North America. This vast tract may be divided into a number of regions. First and most distinct comes the Malagasy region, including Madagascar and the Comoro Islands, which is specially characterised by the abundance of its lemurs, civet-like Carnivores, and Insectivora, coupled with the absence of

[1] The pangolins and aard-varks are here separated as a distinct order (Effodientia). The few Edentates straggling into North America may be disregarded.

all Ungulates except an African type of pig, and the paucity of Rodents, which are represented only by the rat tribe (*Muridæ*). Next in importance is the Ethiopian region, comprising Africa south of the Tropic of Cancer and Southern Arabia. Here one of the most distinctive features are the number of large Ungulates, among which the zebras, a host of antelopes, hippopotami, wart-hogs, and the giraffe are now peculiar; while deer are absent, and sheep and goats very scarce, and only represented in the northern portion of the region. Gorillas and chimpanzees are now solely Ethiopian, as are practically the dog-headed baboons (*Papio*), while certain other genera of monkeys are confined to the region. Elephants and rhinoceroses also occur, although these are markedly distinct from their Oriental cousins. Aard-varks are now solely Ethiopian; while pangolins are common to this and the Oriental regions. Bears are practically wanting.

Although in many ways nearly related to the Ethiopian, the Oriental region, which comprises India, Southern China and the Malayan countries as far as Wallace's line, is markedly distinct, having no hippopotami, giraffes, or wart-hogs, while its antelopes are far less numerous, and also generically distinct from those of Africa south of the Tropic. Instead of chimpanzees and gorillas, there are orangs and gibbons; dog-faced baboons are wanting, and there are several peculiar genera of monkeys, while the lemurs are quite distinct from those of Africa. True pigs, as distinct from bush-pigs, are abundant, as are also bears and deer, the latter mostly of a peculiar sub-generic type. There are no aard-varks, although pangolins are common: and the rhinoceroses and elephant are widely different from those of Africa. The region may be sub-divided into several sub-regions, which need not be mentioned here.

With the exception of Southern North America, the whole of the remainder of the Arctogæic realm may be included in the Holarctic region, which is characterised by the absence of man-like apes, lemurs, elephants, and rhinoceroses, the paucity of monkeys, the abundance of goats and sheep, and the presence of the two species of bison; marmots and beavers being also characteristic of this region, while pangolins are practically wanting. Finally, we have the Sonoran region, including Southern North America, to about as far north as latitude 45 deg., and especially characterised by being the home of the prong-buck (*Antilocapra*) and the family of pocket-gophers (*Geomyidæ*.)

MAMMALIA.

ORDER I.—PRIMATES.

Apes, Monkeys, and Lemurs.

The first ordinal group of Mammals is the one named by the great Swedish naturalist Linnæus, Primates, and includes not only apes, monkeys, baboons, and marmosets, but likewise man himself, as well as the infinitely lower creatures commonly designated lemurs, which differ from all the others in their expressionless, fox-like faces. Were the latter animals (as they not unfrequently are) separated as a distinct ordinal group, the Primates would be much easier of definition than is the case when they are included ; but as there is little doubt that the latter arrangement is the proper one, it is essential that it should be followed.

In the great majority of the members of the order, the hand, which is always a grasping organ, is furnished with five fingers, generally provided with more or less flattened nails, but in certain cases the thumb is wanting. The thumb itself in the higher forms is completely opposable to the other digits, but in certain of the lower representatives of the order its power of opposition is but very limited. In the five-toed hind-foot, except in man, the great-toe is similarly opposable to the other digits. With the exception of the second, or index finger of the lemurs, the terminal joints of the fingers and toes are expanded to form a support for the broad and flattened nails. In both the fore and hind-limbs all the component bones are separate from one another ; and perfect collar-bones or cavicles are invariably present. All the Primates are further characterised by the sockets, or orbits, of the eyes being surrounded by a complete bony rim. As regards the teeth, the molars have broad, flattened crowns, surmounted either by tubercles or a pair of transverse ridges, and are thus admirably adapted for the mastication of the fruits, leaves, or other vegetable substances on which the majority of these animals subsist. In number, the molar teeth form three pairs in each jaw, save only in the marmosets ; these teeth being always more complex and larger than the premolars.

The latter are reduced to two pairs in each jaw in all the higher forms, with the exception of one family of American monkeys ; and even among the lemurs no existing species has more than three pairs of these teeth. Moreover, in all the apes and monkeys the incisor teeth, which in many other animals form three pairs, are reduced to two pairs in both jaws; but among the lemurs the number of these teeth is subject to a considerable amount of variation. Save in the aberrant lemur known as the aye-aye, there are at least two teats on the breast of the females.

As a rule, the members of the order are forest-dwelling animals, inhabiting tropical and sub-tropical countries, although a few range into regions where in winter the boughs of the trees are enveloped in snow; but it is only in the hottest and dampest tropical forests that the largest members of the order are met with. Although many apes and monkeys are able to assume the upright position, it is very few that habitually use it; and even when they do, the aid of the arms is necessary to maintain the balance in walking.

The Primates may be divided into two great subordinal groups; the first (*Anthropoidea*) including man, apes, baboons, monkeys, and marmosets, whilst the second (*Lemuroidea*) embraces only the lemurs.

Man-like Apes.—Family *imiidæ.*

The first and highest group of the Primates includes the so-called man-like apes, such as the gorilla, chimpanzee, orang, and gibbons, collectively constituting the family *Simiidæ*. That these apes are our nearest cousins is well known ; but the degree and extent of this relationship, as well as the characters by which it is displayed, are probably less familiar. In the first place, it will be noticed that we speak of this relationship as one of cousinship, and not of ancestry ; and it is well that the reader should free himself from any idea that there is any vestige of direct ancestral kinship between these, for the most part, hideous creatures and himself. Such relationship as does exist is of a comparatively distant kind; and the common ancestor must have lived ages before the mammoth roamed over England, since at that date man was as distinctly differentiated from the apes as he is in the present century. Whether this "missing link" will ever be found, or in what country it is most likely to have lived, are questions impossible to answer; but from the extreme rarity with which fossil remains of man-like apes are found in countries where they are known to have existed for long ages, and from the probability that the distributional area of the aforesaid "link" was extremely limited, there is not much hope that the researches of palæontologists will ever be rewarded by such a discovery.

From their large bodily size, coupled with that hideous caricature of the human face and form characterising the more typical representatives of the man-like apes, no one would have any difficulty in distinguishing these creatures from their lower relatives. There might, however, be some hesitation with regard to the long-armed gibbons, and it is, therefore, essential to point out how the members of the man-like group may be distinguished as a whole from other monkeys.

Among the sub-order Anthropoidea there is an important distinction between the Old and New World forms. The whole of the Old World representatives of this division of the order are characterised by having teeth agreeing both in number and arrangement with those of man. Thus in all cases in each jaw there are two pairs of incisors, a single pair of tusks, or canines, and five pairs of cheek-teeth, of which the last, or "wisdom-tooth," is frequently very late in making its appearance (*see* fig. 5). Of these five cheek-teeth the first two on each side are simpler than the three hinder ones, and are preceded in the infant by milk-teeth, whereas the latter have no such predecessors. It is accordingly the custom to call the two simpler teeth premolars or bicuspids, and the three more complex ones molars. If, now, we examine an ordinary American monkey, we shall find six cheek teeth on each side of both the upper and lower jaws, of which half are premolars and half molars; while in the marmosets, which constitute a second American family, although the total number of cheek-teeth is the same as in the Old World forms, yet the proportion is different, there being three premolars and two molars. It may, therefore, be stated that all American monkeys differ from their Old World cousins in having three instead of two pairs of premolar teeth, whence it may be inferred that they belong to a lower and more generalized type, there being a universal tendency throughout the higher Vertebrates to a diminution, or disappearance of the teeth with the advance of specialisation. In the marmosets the loss of the last molar is unique in the higher division of the order, and is, indeed, a somewhat remarkable peculiarity to occur in a herbivorous Mammal, among which the reduction is usually confined to the front and premolar teeth.

As the teeth serve most readily to differentiate the Old World monkeys from their American allies, so the man-like apes are sharply distinguished from their relatives by the conformation of the same organs. Thus the molar teeth of the man-like apes closely resemble those of man, having the angles of their crowns rounded off, and carrying on their grinding-surfaces four very blunt tubercles, placed alternately to one another, as well as a somewhat smaller tubercle at the hinder end. On the other hand, in the lower monkeys the molar teeth are oblong in form, and carry four very prominent tubercles arranged in pairs at the two extremities of each tooth, and each pair being connected so as to form a couple of more or less well-defined transverse ridges extending right across the crown. Then, again, whereas in the man-like apes the last molar, or "wisdom-tooth," in the lower jaw is similar in form to the two teeth in front of it, in the great majority of the Old World monkeys this tooth has a large projecting heel at its hinder end. These dental characters afford very important evidence of the close kinship of the man-like apes to man himself, and undoubtedly outweigh the difference in the form of the whole dental series now to be noticed, which is largely due to adaptation. In both the upper and lower jaws of man the teeth are arranged in a regular horse-shoe series, with scarcely any interruption to the continuity by the tusks, which are but little taller than the other members of the series. On the other hand, in the adults (and especially the males of the larger species) of the man-like apes the cheek-teeth are arranged in a nearly straight line, and form a more or less angulated junction with the line of the incisors; the large canines, or tusks, occupying the angle between the two series, and thus forming a marked break in continuity. In these respects the man-like apes resemble their inferior kindred. If, however, a young individual of the larger man-like apes, and especially the chimpanzee, be examined, it will be found that the teeth, owing partly to the imperfect protrusion of the tusks, form a less interrupted and more regularly curved series. Indeed, with the exception that the whole jaw is longer and narrower, and the partially-protruded tusks are proportionately larger, the characters of such specimens make a marked approximation to the human type; and the jaw of a chimpanzee at this stage may be regarded as almost intermediate in structure between that of man and that of an adult male gorilla. Moreover, in this juvenile state the bony union of the two branches of the lower jaw partakes of the short and rounded form characterizing that of man; whereas in the adult it becomes longer and more deeply channelled, like that of the lower monkeys. In many respects the teeth and jaws of the gibbons, or smallest representatives of the present group, conform to the intermediate type. Not only are the human characteristics most developed in the teeth and jaws of the young of the larger man-like apes and the gibbons at all ages, but the same is true with regard to the skull of the former. The skull of the young gorilla, for instance, lacks the beetling crests over the eyes and the prominent ridge down the middle of the crown, which give such a forbidding and repulsive aspect to the cranium of tho full-grown male. This loss of human resemblances is due to specialisation taking two difficulty lines in man on the one hand, and in the larger man-like apes on the other; the development in the one case tending to increased size of brain, coupled with no marked increase in the size of the tusks, while in the other the brain grows at a less rapid rate, and the skull and tusks (more especially in the male) assume characters approximating them to those of the inferior animals. Both in men and apes the young condition may accordingly be regarded as the most generalised.

Among the other features in which the man-like apes differ from the lower monkeys and resemble man, are the absence of dilatable pouches in the cheeks for the storage of food, and the total loss of the tail, as well as the flattened, instead of laterally compressed, form of the breast-bone; the gibbons alone retaining the naked patches on the buttocks so characteristic of the monkeys, but only in a much reduced condition. The gorilla and chimpanzees further differ from the other members of the group, and thereby resemble man alone, in the loss of the so-called central bone of the wrist—a bone occupying a nearly central position between the upper and lower rows of small bones of which that joint is composed. What may be the object of the disappearance of this bone, it is not easy to say; but the fact that it is wanting in the two genera of apes just mentioned is very significant of their close structural affinity with man. In one respect the man-like apes stand apart both from the human and the monkey type, namely, in the great relative length of the arms as compared with the legs, the disproportion being most strongly marked in the gibbons, which are actually able to walk in the upright posture with their bent knuckles touching the ground.

So far, indeed, as their bodily structure is concerned, the man-like apes seem undoubtedly more nearly related to man than they are to the lower monkeys; and they constitute a family (*Simiidæ*) by themselves, which may be regarded as intermediate between the one (*Cercopithecidæ*) including the lower monkeys, and that represented by man himself. While at present the "missing link" between man and the apes is wanting, extinct forms tend to connect the latter very closely with the monkeys. For instance, a fossil ape (*Dryopithecus*) from the Miocene Tertiary strata of France has the bony union between the two branches of the lower jaw much longer than in any existing man-like ape, although it is approached in this respect by the gorilla; while from the corresponding beds of Italy another extinct form (*Oreopithecus*) appears to be in great part intermediate between the man-like apes and the lower monkeys.

The present distribution of the anthropoid apes clearly points to the existing species being the last survivors of a group which was once widely spread over the Old World, when warmer climatic conditions prevailed over what we now call the temperate regions. The gorilla, for instance, is confined to Western Equatorial Africa; where it is accompanied by the two species of chimpanzee, one of which ranges eastwards across the continent as far as Uganda. The orangs, of which there are probably two species, on the other hand, are confined to the great islands of Sumatra and Borneo; while the numerous species of gibbons have a wide range in South-Eastern Asia, attaining their maximum development in the Malayan Archipelago and the adjacent regions. This distribution is remarkably discontinuous, but the little known of the past history of the group tends somewhat to consolidate the present scattered distributional areas. For instance, a chimpanzee once inhabited Northern India; while it is most probable that an orang also was a contemporaneous dweller in the same country. This suggests that India may have been the original home of the larger man-like apes, from whence the chimpanzees and gorillas migrated south-westwards to Equatorial Africa, while the orangs travelled in an easterly direction to find a last home in the tropical islands to which they are now confined.

Chimpanzees (*Anthropopithecus*).

Of the four existing genera of the man-like apes, the chimpanzees (*Anthropopithecus*) are those which come nearest to man, this being especially shown by the shortness of the bony union between the two branches of the lower jaw, the form and mode of arrangement of the teeth (especially in the young), the relatively small development of the tusks of the male, the absence of the enormous bony crests on the skull so characteristic of the gorilla, and the slight difference in the size of the two sexes. The chimpanzees and the gorilla alone resemble man in having seventeen vertebræ between the neck and the sacrum, and likewise in the absence of the central bone in the wrist, although they differ in the comparatively unimportant feature of possessing an additional pair of ribs. It will be unnecessary to give a full description of these animals, and it will suffice to say that the common species (*A. troglodytes*), which ranges across Tropical Africa from the Gabun to Uganda, has the face, ears, hands, and feet, dark reddish flesh-colour, or more rarely blackish brown, while the general colour of the hair is wholly black, except on the lips, where it is short and white, and on the buttocks, where it has a dash of reddish brown. There has been some difference of opinion as to whether the so-called bald chimpanzee (*A. calvus*) of the West Coast of Africa is entitled to rank as a distinct species, but recent researches tend to show that it has no such claim. In size chimpanzees are much smaller animals than the gorilla. In walking, the palm of the hand can be applied to the ground, and the same is the case with the sole of the foot; but although chimpanzees can stand or walk erect on the soles of their feet, they much prefer to progress in a stooping posture, supporting themselves on their bent knuckles.

Fig. 6.—Common Chimpanzee (*Anthropopithecus troglodytes*).

In some districts living to a great extent on the ground, chimpanzees are more arboreal in their general habits than the gorilla, although much less so than the orang. They feed on wild or even cultivated fruits, and generally associate either in family parties or in small communities, although the males and females pair for life. For the protection of the female and young a kind of nest or resting-place is built in some tree, where they pass the night, the male remaining on ground below. In the early morning and evening, and less commonly during the night, chimpanzees give vent to a series of unearthly shrieks and howls; Dr. Pechuel-Lösche observing that "since they are really accomplished in the art of bringing forth these unpleasant sounds, which may be heard at a great distance, and are reproduced by the echoes, it is impossible to estimate the number of individuals who take part in the dreary noise, but often we seemed to hear more than a hundred."

Fig. 7.—The Gorilla (*Gorilla savagei*).

Gorilla.

The hideous creature forming the sole representative of the genus *Gorilla* differs from the chimpanzees in the great development of the tusks of the male as well as in the large size of the bony crests on the skull above the eyes, and likewise by the male being very much larger than the female. There are also certain differences in the conformation of the cheek-teeth, and the brain has a more oval contour, thereby approximating to the human type. In height the male gorilla (*G. savagei*) may exceed six feet, although the female does not measure more than four and a half feet. The general colour of the animal is black or blackish, the whole skin of the face being glossy black, scattered over with a few hairs. The geographical range of this gigantic ape is exceedingly limited, being confined to that part of the West Coast of Equatorial Africa lying between the Camerun mountains and the Congo River. Like chimpanzees, gorillas live in family parties, although these do not combine to form communities; and they are likewise stated to construct arboreal resting-places for the female and young. They walk in a shuffling manner somewhat similar to that adopted by chimpanzees, but as their arms are longer they are not compelled to stoop so much, and the open hand, in place of the bent knuckle, is stated to be put on the ground in this mode of progression. The yell of the male gorilla is described as a terrific sound; and these animals appear to be not only ferocious, but likewise extremely courageous, always advancing boldly to meet a foe, and never running away like a chimpanzee. As in all the man-like apes, the female produces but a single young at a birth, which is nurtured with tender solicitude, and defended to the last extremity. When at rest, the gorilla generally assumes a squatting posture, with the arms folded across the breast; and in sleep lies stretched out at full length either on the back or on one side, with an arm under the head. Extremely delicate in constitution when removed from its native haunts, this ape rarely survives captivity long even in Africa, while the climate of Europe soon puts an end to its existence.

Fig. 8.—THE ORANG-UTAN (*Simia satyrus*).

The first skeleton of the gorilla which reached England was presented to the Royal College of Surgeons by Captain Harris in 1851. This was followed in 1858 by an entire gorilla preserved in spirits, which was sent from the Gabun to the British Museum. Of the few live specimens which have reached Europe, none seem to have survived more than fifteen or eighteen months. The earliest to reach England appears to have been one which, in 1860, was the property of an itinerant showman, who mistook it for a chimpanzee, and did not discover his mistake until after the animal's death. Fifteen years later a young male gorilla was procured from the natives by the German Loango Expedition, and taken to Berlin. This animal was fed on fruits and goat's milk, and under kindly treatment became so tractable that he was allowed to wander about the ship with little or no restraint. He showed some cunning and a tendency to mischief, but no evil propensities. He would pay surreptitious visits to the store-room on occasion, and slyly help himself to the dainties he affected, making off with unmistakable signs of guilty consciousness when disturbed or caught in the act. Arrived at Berlin, he was placed in the Aquarium, where for fifteen months he was the object of much attention. He died of consumption, as did his successor, who arrived at Berlin in 1883, and died the following year. A young gorilla which reached the Zoological Gardens, London, a few years ago, lived but a few months.

Orang-Utan (*Simia.*)

The reduction of the number of vertebræ between the neck and the sacrum to sixteen, together with the retention of the central bone in the wrist, the great length of the arms, which in the upright posture reach to the ankles, and the peculiar upward prolongation of the vertex of the skull, serve at once to show that the orang (*Simia*) stands on a lower evolutionary platform than either of the preceding representatives of the family. Externally it is further distinguished by the rudimentary condition of the great-toe, the peculiarly flattened form of the almost dish-like leaden-hued face of the adult, and the red tinge of the long and shaggy hair, the latter being in marked contrast to the black hue of the gorilla and chimpanzees. Although in possessing only a dozen pairs of ribs the orang differs from both the latter and resembles man, yet this resemblance is greatly outweighed by the difference in the number of the vertebræ.

It is now generally admitted that there is but a single species of orang-utan (*Simia satyrus*), which is confined to the great islands of Sumatra and Borneo, and is known to the Dyak inhabitants of the latter by the name of Mias. A peculiar characteristic of the adult male is the presence of a large, smooth, soft, tumour-like, flexible expansion of the skin of the sides of the face, giving the remarkable breadth and flatness so characteristic of the whole countenance. In size, orangs are subject to considerable variation, large males reaching from four feet two inches to four feet six inches ; the females being much smaller.

The orang is a much more truly arboreal animal than either of the other large apes, and is likewise a solitary creature, the sexes only coming together at the pairing season. Females are generally to be seen accompanied by their young, sometimes only a single one, but in other instances with those of two births. The young cling with remarkable tenacity to the body of the mother as she climbs from tree to tree. Although most excellent climbers, orangs are exceedingly slow and deliberate in their movements, and are thus quite unlike the gibbons.

Mr. Brooke of Sarawak says, "The orangs, so far as I have been able to observe them, are as dull and as slothful as can well be conceived, and on no occasion, when pursuing them, did they move so fast as to preclude my keeping pace with them easily through a moderately clear forest ; and even when obstructions below (such as wading up to the neck) allowed them to get away some distance, they were sure to stop and allow us to come up. I never observed the slightest attempt at defence ; and the wood, which sometimes rattled about our ears, was broken by their weight, and not thrown, as some persons represent. If pushed to extremity, however, the pappan could not be otherwise than formidable ; and one unfortunate man, who with a party was trying to catch one alive, lost two of his fingers, besides being severely bitten on the face, whilst the animal finally beat off his pursuers and escaped. When hunters wish to catch an adult, they cut down a circle of trees round the one on which he is seated, and then fell that also, and close before he can recover himself, and endeavour to bind him. The rude hut which they are stated to build in the trees would be more properly called a seat, or nest, for it has no roof or cover of any sort. The facility with which they form this seat is curious ; and I had an opportunity of seeing a wounded female weave the branches together, and seat herself in a minute. She afterwards received our fire without moving, and expired in her lofty abode, whence it cost us much trouble to dislodge her. The adult male I killed was seated lazily on a tree ; and when approached, only took the trouble to interpose the trunk between us, peeping at me and dodging as I dodged. I hit him on the wrist, and he was afterwards despatched."

The last members of the family are the gibbons (*Hylobates*) which are restricted to the warmer parts of South-Eastern Asia, and are especially abundant in the Malay Peninsula and islands. They are the lowest and smallest representatives of the man-like apes, and although agreeing with those above described in the absence of a tail and cheek-pouches, and by the circumstance that their grinding-teeth are constructed on precisely the same plan as those of ourselves, they approximate to the lower monkeys in possessing small naked callosities on the buttocks. In habitually walking in the upright position, frequently with the assistance of their enormously elongated arms, they are peculiar in the ape world. This peculiarity, coupled with their apparently human-like skulls, might lead the uninitiated to suppose that these creatures were the most man-like of all apes. A moment's reflection would, however, show that in such highly-organised animals, a small species, in order to be able to carry on the functions necessary to its existence, must have a proportionately larger brain than its bigger relatives ; and a large brain implies, of course, a large skull. Moreover, in small and purely arboreal animals like the gibbons, there is no reason why the skull should be strengthened by the enormous frontal ridges which give such a repulsive aspect to the physiognomy of the male gorilla. Accordingly, we see that the somewhat human-like form of the skulls of the gibbons does not in any way indicate that they are more nearly related to ourselves than their larger kindred ; while the callosities on their buttocks, and several features in their anatomical structure, show that they are decidedly less so.

Gibbons (*Hylobates*).

Although in the confined space of a cage in the "Zoo" the gibbons have but little opportunity of displaying the marvellous activity by which they are characterised in their native woods, yet even there their engaging manners cannot fail to attract attention ; and many show the gentleness and docility so distinctive of these apes in a most marked manner. In the more congenial climate of Calcutta, which admits of gibbons being placed in the open air, their movements are, however, far more like those of the wild state ; and one of these creatures in the local "Zoo" showed its lightning-like activity by actually catching birds while on the wing. Not only is this bold activity characteristic of the gibbons, but they likewise exhibit a wonderful delicacy of touch. For instance, many gibbons display a marked *penchant* for spiders, which are captured with the long slender fingers ; but before devouring their prizes these animals will not unfrequently play with them for hours, allowing them to descend by spinning a thread from one of their captor's fingers, and then suddenly jerking them upwards into their hands. Not less noteworthy than their active movements are the loud, unearthly cries of the gibbons, in imitation of which the hulock (*H. hulock*) of Assam, Burma, etc., derives

Fig 9.—A Gibbon (*Hylobates*).

its name. These wailing cries, which are uttered hour after hour in the morning, and again, although less continuously, in the evening, may be heard for miles when a whole drove are shouting in concert; and even those of a solitary individual in the Calcutta Gardens made themselves audible at least a mile off.

Out of a total of eight species of the genus, the siamang (*H. syndactylus*) of Sumatra is the largest, measuring more than a yard in length; and it differs from all the rest by having the second and third toes of the hind foot united by a web as far as their terminal joints. In colour, the siamang is uniformly black throughout, and in this respect it agrees with the Hainan gibbon (*H. hainanus*); whereas, in all the other species there is a white band across the forehead. Among these latter, one of the best known is the hulock (*H. hulock*) from Assam and the countries immediately to the east. Writing of the cries of another species (*H. leuciscus*), Mr. H. O. Forbes observes that it "makes its presence known to the traveller in Java, when he reaches its upland forest-districts. In the evening just about sundown, and more especially in the early morning, commencing before sunrise and finally ceasing when the sun is above the tops of the trees, he will be surprised by a sudden outbreak of what appears to be now the plaintive wailings of a crowd of women, now the united howling of a band of castigated children."

Old World Monkeys.—Family *Cercopithecidæ*.

The whole of the remaining monkeys and baboons of the Old World form a second family, which, while agreeing with the man-like apes in the number of their teeth, differ by the crowns of the molars being surmounted by a pair of transverse ridges, each formed by the coalescence of two sub-conical tubercles. All the members of the family have naked callosities on the buttocks, and cheek-pouches are very generally present. The breast-bone differs from that of the man-like apes in being laterally compressed and narrow, instead of broad and flattened from back to front. The tail, which may be either wanting, short, or very long, is never endowed with the power of prehension; and the partition between the two nostrils is narrow. Eight existing genera are included in the family, some of which are Oriental, while others are confined to Africa south of the Sahara. None are known from Madagascar, New Guinea, or Australia, the eastern limits of the group being formed by Celebes and the Philippine Islands.

Fig. 10.—Proboscis-Monkey (*Nasalis larvatus*).

Proboscis-Monkey (*Nasalis*).

The most ludicrous in appearance of all the tribe is the well-known proboscis-monkey (*Nasalis larvatus*) of Borneo, easily distinguished from all its kin by the extraordinary length of its nose. This monkey, together with the two following genera, constitutes a sub-family characterised by the absence of cheek-pouches for storing food, the complex and sacculated structure of the stomach, the great length of the tail, and also by the front limbs being shorter than the hinder pair. All these monkeys feed largely or chiefly on young shoots or leaves; and it is in adaptation to this diet that their stomach is specially modified and cheek-pouches are wanting. The constitution of all the tribe is very delicate, so that these monkeys are ill-adapted to stand captivity.

The peculiar structure of the nose is sufficient to differentiate the proboscis-monkey from all its allies; but to this may be added the circumstance that the tail is shorter than the head and body.

The numerous species of langurs, which are nearly thirty in number, are confined to the Oriental countries, where one species ranges as far north as Kashmir, while a second is peculiar to the highlands of Eastern Tibet. All these monkeys have thin and slender bodies, elongated limbs, and a very long and whip-like tail; the head being rounded, and the muzzle short and thick. The thumb is rather short, but the great-toe well developed; and the callosities on the buttocks are relatively small. The hair is abundant, and generally long, soft, and frequently glossy; while there is usually a fringe of long, stiff hairs projecting over the eyes. Grey is the predominant hue in the pellage; but the face, hands, and feet are perfectly black.

Langurs (*Semnopithecus*).

The best known of all the group is the Hanuman, or sacred langur (*Semnopithecus entellus*) of India, which ranges from the Deccan northwards to the south bank of the Ganges, and is held sacred by the Hindus. Of this monkey a writer in the *Graphic* gives the following interesting account:

"Among the thousand or more temples and shrines with which the holy Hindu city of Benares is endowed, visitors generally find the great temple dedicated to the worship of the goddess Dûrga one of the most interesting. It is known to Europeans as the monkey-temple, because in and around its precincts many hundreds of sacred monkeys roam about without interference. The temple was erected during the last century by the Rani Bhawani of Natre in honour of Shiva's wife, the goddess who is supposed to delight in death and slaughter, and of whom the believers in the various attributes of the deities, comprising the Hindu Pantheon, stand in the greatest dread. The Dûrga Kund is conspicuous in this city of temples for the grace and simplicity of its architecture. It adjoins a tank which is the finest in Benares, and occupies the central portion of a quadrangle, the walls being stained red with ochre. The sacred portion of the temple consists of twelve finely-carved pillars standing on a marble platform, and supporting a heavy roof. This platform is about 4 ft. from the ground, and is ascended by a flight of low steps on each side of the square. The temple is well provided with the necessary instruments for creating the frightful noises which emanate from these abodes of idolatry all over India. Drums of huge dimensions, gongs, bells, and tom-toms are all at the service of the priests in performing the rites required of them. But the antics of the monkeys which make this temple their home are, next to its architecture, the most attractive feature of the place. The goat's blood with which the walls are sprinkled, and the sacrifices that are known to take place here to appease the wrath of Shiva and his terrifying spouse, are rather revolting to a Christian; but the grotesque play of the monkeys, their importunate begging, the pranks they enact on one another, and the graceful agility they are constantly displaying, supply a perpetual source of amusement which one is apt to think must prove rather distracting to the devout Hindus who come here to worship. A few years ago, as no one dared molest these animals, they not only increased rapidly in numbers, but, growing to be extraordinarily bold, developed alarming thieving propensities. The annoyance they caused amounted to a public nuisance, for no house in the place was safe from their depredations. At last the trouble grew so serious that some reduction in the number of these adept thieves became a necessity, although the prejudices of the people were against any such steps being taken. In the end the Government was requested to interfere, and, waving aside all other considerations but that of public polity, the authorities had many hundreds—report says thousands—captured and sent away. Nevertheless there are plenty of them left, and they certainly constitute one of the sights of a city that is probably in many respects the most interesting in the world."

Guerezas (*Colobus*).

In Africa south of the Sahara the place of the langurs is taken by the guerezas, of which there are nine species, easily distinguished by the total absence of the thumb. In the true guereza (*Colobus guereza*), ranging from Somaliland to the Niam-Niam country and Mount Kilima-Njaro, the hair of the back is developed into a beautiful, long silky mantle hanging down on the sides of the body, and likewise by the extremely bushy tail; the mantle and tail, as well as a ring round the face, being pure white, while the rest of the fur is jetty black. The pellage of this species is extensively used by the natives of Africa; while that of all the long-haired kinds is largely imported into Europe for manufacture into muffs and other articles of dress.

Guenons (*Cercopithecus*).

The guenons, or typical representatives of the family, which include considerably over thirty species, are likewise exclusively confined to Africa south of the Sahara desert. In common with the remaining members of the family, they constitute a sub-family distinguished from the last by the presence of cheek-pouches and the simple structure of the stomach. Their food is more varied than that of the langurs and their allies, and consequently these monkeys are much better adapted for captivity than are the latter. The guenons are specially characterised by the relative slenderness of their build, the more or less shortened muzzle, the moderate size of the callosities on the buttocks, and the long tail. From the two following genera they may be readily distinguished by the circumstance that the last molar tooth in the lower jaw has no projecting heel at its hinder end, but consists simply of two transverse ridges, like the teeth immediately in advance of it. Among the better known species may be mentioned the green monkey *(Cercopithecus callitrichus)*, the Diana monkey *(C. diana)*, so named from the white fillet above the eyes, and the mona monkey *(C. mona)*; all these being from West Africa.

Mangabeys (*Cercocebus*).

Differing from the guenons solely in the presence of the aforesaid heel to the last lower molar, the mangabeys, or white-eyelid monkeys, likewise form a genus confined to Africa, where they are represented by only half-a-dozen species. They form a group intermediate between the preceding and the following one.

Macaques (*Macacus*).

In the Oriental countries this group of monkeys is represented by the macaques, of which there are rather less than a score of species. The macaques resemble the mangabeys in the structure of the last molar tooth, but are readily distinguished by the considerable production of the muzzle, in which the nostrils are not terminal. While the cheek-pouches and the callosities on the buttocks are always well developed, the tail may be either long, short, or absent. Although these monkeys are mainly Oriental, one species, the

Barbary ape (*Macacus innus*), is found in North Africa and on the rock of Gibraltar; and one of the Asiatic species ranges as far north as Eastern Tibet, while a third is found in Japan. In the Barbary ape the tail is wanting, in the common Bengal monkey (*M. rhesus*) it is about half the length of the head and body, and in the crab-eating macaque (*M. cynomolgus*) it is considerably longer. The well-known Indian lion-tailed monkey (*M. silenus*) takes its name from the presence of a large terminal tuft to the tail; the head and neck being also furnished with a mane. Many of these monkeys are of comparatively large size, and are very savage in disposition, biting fiercely when annoyed.

Black Ape (*Cynopithecus*).

The black ape (*Cynopithecus niger*) of the island of Celebes is the sole representative of a genus forming a connecting link between the preceding and the following, the muzzle being more produced than in the macaques, and the fore part of the skull bearing longitudinal ridges, as in some of the dog-faced baboons. This monkey, which takes its name from the dark colour of the hair, has the tail reduced to a mere fleshy tubercle concealed among the fur. It is also found in the island of Batchian, in the Molucca group, where it has probably been introduced by the Malays.

Gelada Baboons (*Theropithecus*).

Two species of baboons, the one (*Theropithecus gelada*) from Southern Abyssinia, and the other (*T. obscurus*) from North-Eastern Africa—constitute a genus differing from the next by having the nostrils placed on the sides of the long muzzle, as in the macaques, instead of being terminal and opening on its truncated extremity. The true gelada is a most extraordinary-looking creature, having a long crest of dark brown hair above the eyes, and a mantle-like mane of the same descending from the neck and shoulders to the loins, and also reaching on the arms as far as the elbows; the chin, and a patch on the throat, as well as another on the chest, being bare, and, as are all the other naked parts, black in colour. In size this baboon measures 29 inches to the root of the tail; the latter appendage, inclusive of the tuft at the tip, being upwards of 32 inches.

Fig. 11.—A Dog-Faced Baboon (*Papio*).

Dog-faced Baboons (*Papio*).

The remaining members of the family *Cercopithecidæ* are all included in the genus *Papio*, and are commonly known as dog-faced baboons on account of the great elongation of the muzzle, in the truncated termination of which are pierced the nostrils in the same manner as in a dog. The callosities on the buttocks are very large and frequently brilliantly coloured; the muzzle is greatly swollen and often marked by longitudinal flutings; and the tail is more or less shortened. The dog-faced baboons, of which there are eleven different species, include the largest and most repulsive-looking members of the entire family; and are now confined to Africa south of the Sahara and Southern Arabia, although during the later geological periods they were represented in India.

The largest and most hideous of the tribe is the mandril (*Papio maimon*) of the forests of Western Equatorial Africa, remarkable for its robust build, stump-like tail, highly swollen and fluted muzzle, and the brilliant tints of blue and scarlet with which the naked portions of the face and buttocks of the adult males are decorated. In South Africa the genus is represented by the chacma (*P. porcarius*), which is a more soberly-coloured species, with a tail equal in length to half the body; while the yellow baboon (*P. babuin*) of West Africa may be taken as an example of species in which the tail is still longer. Although found in the upland forests of Mount Kilima-Njaro, the dog-faced baboons are more generally inhabitants of open, rocky districts, where they go about in large parties, inflicting severe damage on the products of the cultivated lands, and fiercely attacking all intruders on their domains. In their diet they are well-nigh omnivorous, feeding not only upon fruits and cereals, but likewise devouring large numbers of lizards and insects, in search of which they turn over stones with their fingers. The late Sir R. Burton wrote that in the jungles of Usukuma these baboons "are the terror of the neighbouring districts; women never dare to approach their haunts; they set the leopard at defiance, and, when in a large body, they do not, it is said, fear the lion."

New World Monkeys.—Family *Cebidæ*.

As already stated on page 12, the monkeys of the New World differ from their Old World cousins in having three in place of two pairs of premolar teeth in each jaw; the number of molars being the same in both. In consequence of these and other differences, the New World monkeys, which do not range to the north of tropical America, are referred to a separate family group, under the name of *Cebidæ*. These monkeys are further characterised by the absence both of cheek-pouches and of naked callosities on the buttocks, while the tail, when long, is frequently, although by no means invariably, prehensile. The thumb is quite incapable of being opposed to the other digits, but all the fingers and toes have flattened nails. In the nose the partition between the two nostrils is very broad, so that the nostrils themselves are widely separated, and frequently diverge to a great extent from each other. The upper molar teeth have very short crowns, with the four tubercles arranged obliquely, and the external surfaces of the outer pair flattened and fluted, while the inner ones are distinctly crescent-shaped.

So different, indeed, are the American monkeys—which attain their maximum development in the tropical forests of Brazil—from the Old World forms, that it is quite possible they may trace their origin to a totally independent source. They may be divided into ten genera, some of which comprise a very large number of specific representatives.

The Howlers (*Alouatta*).

The half-dozen species commonly called, from their loud nocturnal cries, howlers constitute a genus characterised by the massive, unwieldy body, the pyramidal head, long and somewhat dog-like muzzle, the massiveness of the angle, or hinder part of the lower jaw, and a remarkable thickening of the throat due to the enlargement of the so-called hyoid bones into a thin bony capsule of large size. It is owing to the development of this capsule that the howlers are enabled to utter the discordant yells with which they make night hideous to all travellers in the forests of Tropical America. All the species have a large beard and whiskers, but the colour of the hair is subject to great specific variation. In the red howler (*A. seniculus*), for instance, the head, neck, limbs, and tail are dark chestnut-brown, and the back and sides of the body golden yellow; whereas in the black howler (*A. nigra*) the whole of the long hair is deep black.

All the howlers are surly in disposition, and feed chiefly on fruits and leaves. When howling, two or three take up their position on the topmost branches of the forest trees, and commence their chorus. Mr. O. Salvin writes that their wonderful cry is certainly most striking, "and I have sometimes endeavoured to ascertain how far this cry may be heard. It has taken me an hour or more to thread the forest undergrowth from the time the cry first struck my ear to when, guided by the cry alone, I stood under the tree where the animals were. It would certainly not be over-estimating the distance to say two miles. When the sound came over the Lake of Yzabal unhindered by the trees, a league would be more like the distance at which the cry may be heard."

Capuchins (*Cebus*).

Agreeing with the howlers (which form a sub-family by themselves) in having the lower incisor teeth placed vertically, the capuchins, together with several allied genera, differ by the absence of any inflation of the hyoid bone. In all the group the tail is long and prehensile; although in some species, when its tip is haired, instead of bare and sensitive, the grasping power of this organ is much less well marked than in the rest. The thumb may be either present or wanting.

The capuchins, or typical representatives of the entire family, are somewhat stoutly-built monkeys, with the limbs of moderate length, the fur not woolly, the thumb fully developed, and the lower surface of the extremity of the tail covered with hair. Although the various species of capuchins are extremely difficult to distinguish, about eighteen different kinds are now recognised by naturalists; their range extending from Mexico to Paraguay. In constitution these monkeys are exceedingly hardy, and as they are easy to train, and gentle in disposition, they are more commonly carried about in England and other European countries by peripatetic organ-grinders than any other of their kindred. From its completely haired tip, the tail of the capuchins does not act so thoroughly as a fifth hand as it does in the spider-monkeys. The white-throated capuchin (*Cebus hypoleucus*) is a well-known representative of the genus.

Fig. 12.—A Woolly Monkey (*Lagothrix*).

Woolly Monkeys (*Lagothrix*).

Nearly allied to the capuchins, the two species of woolly monkeys take their name from the peculiar texture of their fur, which forms the most characteristic feature of the genus to which they belong. In addition to this character, these monkeys are distinguished by the clumsy build of the body, the rounded head, the much flattened muzzle—in which the nostrils are circular, but not approximated—and by the naked lower surface of the tip of the tail. The two species are both inhabitants of the forests of Amazonia, the best known being Humboldt's woolly monkey (*Lagothrix humboldti*). The barrigudos, as these monkeys are called by the Brazilians, live exclusively on fruits, and are of larger size and less active habits than the capuchins. They suffer considerably from the cold, and even at Bahia I have seen them on a wet day fall into a torpid condition, when they were relentlessly thrown into the sea by their captors. Mr. Wallace remarked that from their gentle disposition they are "most frequently seen in confinement, and are great favourites from their grave countenances, which resemble the human face more than those of any other monkeys, their quiet manners, and the great affection and docility they exhibit."

Woolly Spider-Monkey (*Brachyteles*).

The woolly spider-monkey (*Brachyteles arachnoides*), which is now considered to be the sole representative of its genus, is in many respects intermediate between the woolly monkeys and the true spider-monkeys, having the dense woolly pellage of the former, coupled with the long and slender limbs of the latter. The thumb is rudimental, and the nails of the other digits are compressed and pointed. These monkeys, which are confined to the dense forests of South-Eastern Brazil, from Cape San Roque to Rio Grande do Sul, appear to be very rare, and little is consequently known of their habits.

Spider-Monkeys (*Ateles*).

The last genus of this sub-family includes the half-score species of true spider-monkeys, constituting a genus distinguished from the preceding by the fur not being of a woolly nature, the complete absence of the thumb, and the slight compression of the nails. Both the tail and limbs are greatly elongated. These monkeys have a wide range, extending from Mexico to Paraguay; the variegated spider-monkey (*Ateles variegatus*) being one of the most familiar. In it the prehensile tail reaches its perfection. It is a remarkably sensitive organ, answering the purpose of a "fifth hand," being capable of use "for any purpose to which the hand could be applied," and for hooking out objects from places "where a hand could not be inserted." They wrap their tails about them to protect themselves from cold, to which they are very sensitive, and hold on by them to the branches of trees with such tenacity that they remain suspended after death. The prehensile part of the tail is naked and of extreme sensibility. The tail is also used to preserve balance when walking erect, for which purpose it is thrown up and curled over. The appearance of these monkeys, as they leap from branch to branch in their native woods, swinging by their tails, and often hanging on to those of each other, until a living bridge is formed from tree to tree, is exceedingly picturesque. Although they lack the extreme agility of the Oriental gibbons, the spider-monkeys are by far the most active members of the family to which they belong. Mr. Belt writes that he has often seen two or three together on the lower branches of the forest trees, "holding on to each other, and to the branch with their fore-feet and long tail, whilst their hind-feet hang down, all the time making threatening gestures and cries. Some-

Fig. 13.—A SPIDER-MONKEY (*Ateles*).

times a female would be seen carrying a young one on its back, to which it clung with legs and tail, the mother making its way among the branches, and leaping from tree to tree, apparently but little encumbered by its baby."

The beautiful little squirrel-monkeys are the first representatives of a third sub-family of the *Cebidæ*, which, while agreeing with the last in the vertical position of the incisor teeth, and the normal conformation of the hyoid bone, are distinguished by the tail, which is long, having no power of prehension. In all the thumb is well developed. From the allied forms the squirrel-monkeys, or saimiris, are specially distinguished by the soft, close, and erect fur, and the backward production of the head; the face being relatively small, the eyes very large and set close together, the partition between the nostrils very wide, and the rather long tail covered with comparatively short hair. There are four species of the genus, of which the common squirrel-monkey (*Chrysothrix sciureus*) is the type. These monkeys are some of the commonest of their tribe in America, where they range from Costa Rica to Brazil and Bolivia. In habits they are diurnal, feeding chiefly upon insects, although they will also kill and eat the smaller birds.

Squirrel-Monkeys (*Chrysothrix*).

The eleven representatives of this genus form a group which is to a considerable extent intermediate between the squirrel-monkeys and the under-mentioned douroucoulis. From the former the small head is distinguished by not being produced backwards, and the small size of the eyes; but the nostrils are similar in the width of the partition by which they are separated, and the fur has the same close and soft texture. The tail is, however, bushy, and the canine teeth are relatively small, while the angle, or hinder extremity, of the lower jaw is expanded somewhat after the same fashion as in the howlers, although to a smaller degree. The titis range from Panama to the southern limits of the great forests; a well-known species being the white-collared titi (*Callithrix torquata*). In habits, they are very similar to the squirrel-monkeys; insects, eggs, and small birds constituting their chief nutriment.

Titis (*Callithrix*).

From both the preceding genera the small monkeys commonly known as douroucoulis are distinguished by their nocturnal habits and the great size of the eyes, which are only separated from each other by a very narrow partition. The head is rounded, and the nostrils are placed closer together than in either of the allied genera; the moderately long tail being bushy, and the fur soft and close. In colour the eyes are yellowish, and they have a peculiar stare, communicating, in conjunction with their large size, a somewhat owl-like expression to the whole face. There are five species of the genus, several of which, like the three-striped douroucouli (*Nyctipithecus trivirgatus*), have three more or less distinctly defined longitudinal dark stripes running down the forehead. The range of the douroucoulis extends from Nicaragua to the Amazon and Eastern Peru. During the daytime, these somewhat lemur-like monkeys remain snugly coiled away in the holes or among the branches of trees, and only issue forth at night in search of prey. When on the prowl, they give vent to loud howls or cat-like cries; and their food includes insects, birds, and fruits. In constitution they are extremely delicate, only surviving capture for a brief period.

Douroucoulis (*Nyctipithecus*).

The last group of the family is formed by the uakari and saki monkeys, which constitute a sub-family distinguished from all the foregoing by the lower incisor teeth being inclined obliquely forward, somewhat after the manner of those of the lemurs, and separated by an interval from the canines. The tail, which may be either long or short, is never prehensile, and the thumb is well developed. Usually the nostrils are widely separated, and the ears are large.

Uakaris (*Uacaria*).

The uakaris, of which there are three species, each with a very small distributional area, are readily distinguished from all other American monkeys by the extreme shortness of the tail. The bald uakari (*Uacaria calva*) from the Rio Negro, and the red uakari (*U. rubicunda*) from the Upper Amazon, have a brilliant scarlet face, contrasting strongly with the long silky white hair of the body, whereas the black-faced species (*U. melanocephala*) has a dark countenance. All are timid, gentle creatures, of so delicate a constitution that it is almost impossible to keep them in confinement.

Sakis (*Pithecia*).

The sakis, of which there are five species, are readily distinguished from the last by the long bushy tail and the thick beard adorning the chin. In the lower jaw the angle is expanded in a manner approaching that of the howlers. A familiar type is the black saki (*Pithecia satanus*) of the Lower Amazon; and while in some species, like the hairy saki (*P. monachus*), long hair clothes the head, body, and tail, in others this is confined to the region of the head. In habits these monkeys appear to be very similar to the vakaris.

The Marmosets.—Family *Hapalidæ*.

The beautiful and delicate little creatures from Tropical America, commonly known as marmosets, form a family agreeing in many respects with the last, but distinguished by having only two pairs of molar teeth in each jaw, and also by the fingers and toes, with the exception of the shortened great-toe, terminating in carved compressed claws, instead of flattened nails. The long thumb lies parallel to the other digits, to which it is incapable of being opposed, so that the fore-limb terminates in a paw rather than a hand. The skin of the face is naked, the ears are large and frequently surmounted by a fringe of long hairs, and the long and bushy tail has no prehensile power. The family, which is represented by a large number of species, mostly inhabitants of the forests of Equatorial South America, has been divided into two genera according to the length of the lower canine teeth. Those forms in which these teeth are not longer than the incisors are known as true marmosets (*Hapale*), whereas those in which the former considerably exceed the latter have been termed tamarins (*Midas*). Marmosets vary considerably in colour, some having the fur mottled with grey, brown, and black, whereas in others it has a more or less uniformly golden or silvery tint. Marmosets are essentially forest animals, feeding chiefly on insects and fruit, and are so delicate that it is difficult to keep them alive out of the tropics. They are exceedingly gentle in disposition, and soon become tame and affectionate. In their organisation they are the lowest of the monkey tribe.

Fig. 14.—A MARMOSET (*Hapale*).

The Typical Lemurs.—Family *Lemuridæ*.

The typical lemurs, which attain their maximum development in the island of Madagascar, and are now found elsewhere only in Africa and the Oriental countries, are the first of three existing Old World families, collectively forming the second great division of the Primates, technically known as the Lemuroidea. From the first subordinal division, or Anthropoidea, the Lemuroids are distinguished by the following features. In the first place, their faces, instead of being more or less mobile and rounded, are long, fox-like, and quite devoid of expression; but in this respect they are not very different from the marmosets. More important are certain differences in the structure of the skull and the soft internal organs, but as these require a certain amount of anatomical knowledge on the part of the reader for their proper comprehension, they may be passed without further notice. A distinctive character of the group is to be found in the circumstance that the second toe in the hind-foot always terminates in a long curved claw. The thumb and great-toe are invariably present, but the second or index finger of the fore-paw may be wanting. With the exception of the aberrant aye-aye and tarsiers, which respectively form a family by themselves, the middle pair of upper front or incisor teeth are separated from one another by an interval or gap, whereas in all the monkeys they are in contact.

In appearance the various kinds of lemurs differ remarkably from one another, some looking not unlike monkeys, while others are characterised by their very long and slender limbs, enormous eyes, and somewhat ghostly form. Whereas some are furnished with long tails, others are devoid of these appendages; and the ring-tailed lemur of Madagascar differs from the rest in its tail being ringed with black and white. This species is, moreover, an exception in that it lives among rocks, whereas all the others are arboreal in their habits. None of the living lemurs are of large size, the length of the head and body in the largest being only about two feet, and many are not larger than a rat. All are excellent climbers, and the majority spend the day in sleep, either in the hole of a tree, in a nest, or rolled up in a ball and hanging to a bough. Their food comprises leaves, fruits, birds and their eggs, reptiles and insects, and, in one case, sugar-cane; and the majority rarely descend to the ground. Some of the larger Malagasy kinds are, however, an exception in this respect, as well as in their diurnal habits, and they may at times be seen jumping across the open spaces separating one wood from another in search of fresh feeding-places. The structure of their brains shews that lemurs are creatures of low organisation, and the existing forms are probably not very remotely related to the ancestral stock which gave rise both to monkeys and lemurs. Geologically the group is an ancient one; and the living forms attain their maximum development where they have been free from the competition of the larger and more highly organised Mammals.

In the typical lemurs constituting the family under consideration there are two pairs of upper incisor teeth separated from one another by a gap in the middle line; while there are three pairs of lower incisors inclined almost horizontally forwards. There are three pairs of molars in each jaw, but the premolars may be either two or three on each side, and in the lower jaw the first of these teeth assumes a tusk-like form, and thus plays the part of a canine. The family may be sub-divided into four sub-families, most of which contain a considerable number of genera.

The first and highest sub-family, which is restricted to Madagascar and contains the largest existing representatives of the group, is characterised by possessing thirty teeth in the adult, by the length of the hind-limbs, the normal structure of the ankle-joint, the large size of the opposable great-toe, and the union of the other toes by a web which extends as far as the end of their first joints. In the female two teats are on the breast.

Endrina (*Indris*).

The endrina (*Indris brevicaudata*), which is the sole representative of its genus, is the largest of the living lemurs, measuring about two feet in length. It may be easily recognised by its rudimental tail, large ears, and moderately elongated muzzle; its coloration being usually black with whitish spots and patches, but in some cases almost or entirely white. Like the sifakas, this lemur is diurnal in its habits.

Sifakas (*Propithecus*).

Nearly allied to the last are the three species of sifakas, easily recognised by the long tail, the rather short muzzle, and the partial concealment of the ears by the fur. The species are extremely variable in coloration, and while some inhabit the dense forests on the eastern side of Madagascar, others frequent the sparsely wooded, arid tracks on the west. Writing of the habits of the sifakas, Mr. Foster observes that "they live in companies of six or eight, and are very gentle and inoffensive animals, wearing always a most melancholy expression, and, as a rule, being morose, inactive, and more silent than other lemurs. They rarely live long in captivity. In their native state they are most alert in the morning and evening, as during the heat of the day they conceal themselves amid the foliage of the trees. When asleep or in repose, the head is dropped on the chest and buried beneath the arms, the tail rolled up on itself and disposed between the hind-legs. The sifakas live exclusively on vegetable substances—leaves, fruits, and flowers—their diet not being varied, as in the other groups, by small birds, eggs, or insects. Their life is almost entirely arboreal, for which the muscles of their hands and feet, as well as the parachute-like fold of skin between their arms and bodies, and their peculiarly hook-like fingers are most fitted. The young one is carried about by its mother on her back, its hands grasping her arm-pits tightly. The sifakas are held in great veneration or fear by the natives of Madagascar, and are never intentionally killed by them."

Avahi (*Avahis*).

The third and last generic representation of the sub-family is the woolly avahi (*Avahis lanigera*), distinguished from the last by the greater length of the tail, the short muzzle, and the total concealment of the ears by the fur, which is of a soft, woolly nature.

True Lemurs (*Lemur*).

The second sub-family of the *Lemuridæ*, which is likewise confined to Madagascar and the Comoro Islands, is typically represented by the true lemurs. It is distinguished from the last by the presence of 36 teeth in the adult, the shorter relative length of the hind-limbs, and the free hind-toes; all the former having long tails. As a genus the true lemurs are characterised by the elongated muzzle, the conspicuous, tufted ears, and the separation of the upper incisor teeth both from one another and from the canines; the two teats of the female being situated on the breast. The genus contains eight species, among which the ring-tailed lemur (*Lemur catta*) is peculiar on account of the character from which it takes its name, and likewise from its dwelling among rocks instead of in trees. Strictly nocturnal in habits, these lemurs feed on a mixed diet; and the females carry their offspring singly transversely across the lower part of their bodies.

The two species of gentle lemurs are separated from the last on account of their short, truncated muzzle, small and hairy ears, the small size of the upper incisor teeth, which are in contact with one another, and with the canine on each side, and likewise by the presence of four teats on the breast of the female.

Gentle Lemur (*Hapalemur*).

Fig. 15.—The Ring-Tailed Lemur (*Lemur catta.*)

A third generic group, with several species, is separated on account of the small size or absence of the upper incisor teeth, the bald ears, and the more elongated muzzle; the females having four teeth. One species (*Lepidolemur caniceps*) is by some referred to a genus apart, under the name of *Mixocebus*.

Sportive Lemur (*Lepidolemur*).

The galagos, which are confined to the forests of the warmer parts of Africa, are the typical representatives of a third sub-family, readily distinguished from the foregoing by the great elongation of two of the bones of the ankle-joint. The galagos themselves are characterised by the large naked ears being capable of folding at the will of their owner; the long tail being generally bushy, and the females having two teats on the breast and two on the abdomen.

Galagos (*Galago*).

Galagos vary in size from that of a rat to that of a small cat. In habits they are nocturnal and omnivorous; and when they descend to the ground, their progression is by hops, for which the structure of their hind-limbs is specially adapted. The Senegal galago (*Galago senegalensis*), which goes about the forest either singly or in pairs, makes a nest in the fork of a tree, and in the daytime either retires to that resort, or reposes on a branch, with its tail folded across its body and round its neck; always being unwilling to move, and staring with its great eyes at passing travellers.

The mouse-lemurs, which by many writers are divided into the genera *Chirogale*, *Microcebus*, and *Opolemur*, although here all included under the former name, are the Malagasy representatives of the galagos, and include a large number of small-sized species. From the galagos they may be distinguished by the large ears being hairy at the base, and incapable of folding. None of these lemurs exceed a rat in size, and several of the species pass the dry season in a state of torpor, which they are enabled to endure by previously accumulating a large store of fat at the root of the tail. Such sleeps usually take place in hollow trees, where the little animals carefully build a comfortable nest of grass and fallen leaves.

Mouse-Lemurs (*Chirogale*).

The remaining members of the *Lemuridæ* form a fourth sub-family, agreeing with the typical one in the number of the teeth, but distinguished by the second or index finger of the fore-paws being either very short or rudimental. While the fore and hind-limbs are of nearly equal length, the ankle-joint is not specially elongated, the thumb and great-toe diverge widely from the other digits, and the tail is short or rudimental. In the female there are only two teats, which are situated on the breast. So great is the divergence of the great-toe that it is commonly directed backwards. None of these lemurs are found in Madagascar.

Lorisis (*Nycticebus* and *Loris*).

The lorisis, or slow lemurs, which are confined to the Oriental countries, and have no external tail, but a perfect, although small, index finger, are divided into the two genera *Nycticebus* and *Loris;* the former being characterised by the inner pair of upper incisor teeth being considerably larger than the outer, and the comparative stoutness of the limbs ; whereas in the latter both pairs of incisors are very small and of equal length, and the limbs are very long and slender. The slow lorises, as the members of the first genus are called, range over the Malayan countries to Cochin-China, while the slender loris is confined to Southern India and Ceylon. Both types are small creatures, with very large eyes, slow in their movements, omnivorous in their diet, and purely nocturnal.

Pottos (*Perodicticus*).

In West Africa the lorisis are represented by two nearly allied animals known as pottos, in which the index finger is reduced to a mere tubercle without a nail ; the tail being sharp or rudimental. The larger of these is the true potto (*Perodicticus potto*), the awantibo (*P. calabarensis*) of Old Calabar being a rather smaller and more delicately made animal, with the index finger and tail more rudimental than in the former. In their movements the pottos are even slower than the lorises.

Tarsiers.—Family *Tarsiidæ*.

The second family of the Lemuroids is constituted by the two or three species of tarsier, all of which are included in the single genus *Tarsius,* and range from the Malayan countries to Celebes and the Philippines. Rather smaller than an ordinary squirrel, the tarsiers may be recognised by their enormous eyes and ears, long, thin, and tufted tail, and long, slender limbs, in which the ankle-joint is greatly lengthened. They have 34 teeth ; and their dentition differs from that of the typical lemurs in that the first pair of upper incisor teeth are in contrast with one another in the middle line, and that the anterior lower premolar is not tusk-like. Tarsiers live on insects and lizards, in search of which they may be seen on moonlight nights hopping on the boughs of trees in a curiously frog-like manner.

Fig. 16.—TARSIER (*Tarsius spectrum*)

Aye-Aye.—Family *Chiromyidæ*.

The last of the existing lemurs is the remarkable aye-aye (*Chiromys madagascariensis*) of Madagascar, which likewise constitutes a family by itself. It is about the size of a cat, and is distinguished from all the rest of its tribe by the structure of its teeth, which are singularly like those of the Rodents ; each jaw having a single pair of chisel-like incisors in front, followed after an interval by the blunt cheek-teeth. The fore-paws are very large, with all the fingers long and slender, but the middle, or third one, much more attenuated than the rest; and in the hind-foot all the digits except the great-toe have curved claws. The ears and eyes are large, the tail is bushy, and the two teats of the female are abdominal. The aye-aye feeds both upon sugar-cane and large wood-boring caterpillars; both its teeth and the slender third finger being employed to extract the latter.

Fig. 17.—THE AYE-AYE (*Chiromys madagascariensis*).

At the present day, the lemurs of Madagascar may be compared in point of size to small or medium-sized monkeys, the largest of them—the short-tailed endrina—not measuring much more than two feet in length. The investigation recently carried on by various explorers in the island have, however, revealed the fact that up to a very late period Madagascar was the home of a lemur vastly exceeding in size any of the existing representatives of the group, and which in this respect may be compared to the great West African baboon known as the mandril. This giant lemur (*Megaladapis*, as it is called) is known by the somewhat imperfect skull and lower jaw, which are about three times the dimensions of those of the endrina. The interest of this animal is, however, by no means confined to its comparatively gigantic proportions, since while its skull and teeth conform in their general structural features to those of the existing members of the group, they are specially modified in a manner altogether peculiar. The most striking peculiarity connected with the skull is the extreme slenderness of the hinder portion containing the brain in comparison with the great elongation of the face; the latter seeming out of all proportion to the former. In this respect, indeed, the skull presents a curious resemblance to the dog-faced baboons of Africa; as it also does in the strongly-marked ridges it bears for the attachment of powerful muscles. Such resemblances, however, it is almost needless to observe, are merely superficial, and must by no means be taken as indicative of any genetic relationship between the two groups; and if a young skull were forthcoming, it is probable that we should find this much less unlike ordinary lemurs. Another peculiarity of the giant lemur is to be found in the more lateral position and wider separation of the sockets of the eyes, which are also relatively smaller than in existing forms, thus indicating that the habits of the animal were less completely nocturnal than those of the latter. The molar teeth of the upper jaw are characterised by the presence of only three tubercles on the crown, owing to the fusion of the two inner ones of the four-columned molars of ordinary lemurs; a few of the smaller existing species having, however, teeth of a nearly similar type. Although in the type skull the front teeth are wanting, the form of their sockets shows that they must have been very similar in general form to those of living lemurs. In many respects the skull shows a marked resemblance to that of the European Tertiary lemur known as *Adapis*, a feature of especial interest in regard to the origin of the Malagasy fauna from that of the Eocene Period in Europe.

Giant Extinct Lemur (*Megaladapis*).

The remains of the giant lemur were discovered in the great marsh of Ambolisatra, and their slightly mineralised condition indicates their comparatively recent age. Indeed, there is but little doubt that the creature has been killed off within the human period, and in his history of Madagascar, published in 1658, De Flacourt writes in the following terms of an animal then inhabiting the island, which, if not actually the giant lemur, would appear to have been a closely allied form. He writes that "the *Trétrétrétré* or *Tratratratra*, is an animal of the size of a two-year-old calf, with a rounded head and human-like face; both fore and hind feet being like those of a monkey. It has the hair wavy, the tail short, and ears like those of a man. It resembled the *Tanache* described by Ambroise Paré. It was seen by the tank of Lipomani, in the neighbourhood of which was its abode. It is a solitary creature, held in great terror by the natives, who flee whenever it comes in sight." With the exception of the rounded head and the size (which is doubtless exaggerated), this description accords remarkably with the giant lemur, and when the head was covered with fur, it is probable that it would appear much less elongated than does the bare skull.

ORDER II.—CHIROPTERA.

The Bats.

The second ordinal division of the Mammalia is that of the bats, or Chiroptera, which is the one most easily defined of all, seeing that in no other members of the class are the limbs similarly modified for the purposes of flight, while it is in these animals alone among the class that the power of true flight is found. By true flight is meant the capacity of sustaining the body in the air for an indefinite period by the shortness of the wings; this being markedly different from the spurious flight of such creatures as flying-foxes, whose progress through the air is due merely to a leap from a height aided by parachute-like expansions of the skin of the limbs and the sides of the body.

In the fore-limb or wing of a bat, the humerus or upper-arm bone is only moderately elongated, but in the fore-arm the single bone corresponding to the human radius has become greatly lengthened; and this lengthening is much more strongly marked in the case of the bones of the fingers, exclusive of the thumb, all of which assume the form of very long and slender rods. The thumb, which terminates in a hooked claw used for climbing and suspension, remains free; but the other four fingers are connected together by the delicate, naked, leathery membrane of the wing, and mostly have neither claws nor nails at the tip; the longest of the whole five digits being the third or middle finger. The membrane of the wing, or, as it is often called, patagium, is continued up the arm and along the sides of the body to the hind-legs, down which it extends; while the two hind-legs are also connected by another extension, which may embrace a considerable portion of the tail. The membrane of the hind-legs is usually supported by a peculiar spur projecting from the foot; but the toes, which are of normal proportions, remain perfectly free from one another. Owing to the connection of the hind-limbs with the membrane of the wings, the knee-joint is directed backwards instead of forwards in the manner characteristic of all other terrestrial Mammals, and this structure renders the movements of these animals on the ground so awkward and shuffling. Bats always have very large and roomy chests, with well-developed collar-bones; but the hind-quarters are feeble and weak. In many bats the delicate sense of touch, by which they are enabled to avoid coming into collision with objects when flying in the dark, appears to be mainly situated in the wing-membranes and in the delicate skin of the frequently large ears, the latter often having an inner earlet, or tragus. In a large number of species there are, however, expansions of the skin in the region of the nose; these nose-leaves sometimes merely taking the form of a triangular single or double plate standing up above the muzzle, whereas in other cases they assume a marked appearance, covering a greater portion of the face. These organs appear to be entirely sensory in function; and it is quite possible that bats may possess some special sense of which we have no cognizance.

Ordinary bats have teeth very similar to those of the order Insectivora (the next in the series), and there is no doubt that these animals are derived from some early members of the latter group which have gradually become adapted for true flight; the transition having probably been effected by the development of a parachute-like expansion of the skin of the sides of the body and limbs. In habits all bats are nocturnal, and the majority are insectivorous, although a few have taken to blood-sucking. There is, however, one important group—the fruit-bats—which are entirely frugivorous, and in these the teeth have quite lost the cusped structure distinctive of ordinary bats, and have assumed an altogether peculiar conformation. All the fruit-bats are of comparatively large dimensions; and in this group are included the largest representatives of the entire order. A certain number of bats have acquired the habit of licking out the honey from the corollæ of flowers, and for this purpose their tongues have become modified into elongated protrusile organs, frequently terminating in a bush-like expansion of delicate filaments.

Although one bat, at least, extends as far north as the Arctic circle, the members of the order obtain their maximum development in tropical and subtropical countries; and it is to such regions of the Old World that the fruit-bats are confined, that group being entirely unknown in America.

The number of bats known to science is between four and five hundred, which are arranged in rather more than eighty genera, distributed under six family-groups. As bats are Mammals with which the ordinary student has but little to do, this large assemblage will be treated much more briefly than most of the other orders; such genera as are mentioned not having separate paragraphs to themselves.

Fruit-Bats.—Family *Pteropodidæ*.

Popularly known by the highly inappropriate title of flying-foxes, the fruit-bats form not only a family by themselves, but likewise a subordinal group differing from a second one, in which are contained all the members of the order. From other bats this group of Megachiroptera, as it is called, is chiefly distinguished by the characters of the molar teeth, which have low, rounded crowns, elongated in the antero-posterior direction, and divided by a distinct longitudinal ridge; such teeth being far better adapted for fruit-eating than are the cusped molars of ordinary bats. From other bats, fruit-bats are also distinguished by the structure of the wing, in which there are three joints in the second or index finger, whereas in the other members of the order the number of such joints is reduced to two, or even one. Another peculiarity of the group is to be found in the complete circle formed by the base of the conch of the ear; while the tail, if present, is short, and situated below the membrane between the hind-legs, with which it may have no connection. In all cases the ears are small, and unprovided with an inner tragus. Fruit-bats are confined to the warmer parts of the Old World.

The common fruit-bats, or fox-bats (*Pteropus*), forming the typical representatives of the family, are characterised by their long and fox-like faces, the presence of 34 teeth, the absence of a tail, and the thick coat of woolly fur on the neck; all being of large size. These bats inhabit the Oriental countries, Madagascar, New Guinea, and Australia, but are unknown in Africa. The long lines in which they wend their way to their feeding-grounds at evening are well known to all residenters in tropical countries. From this genus the tailed fruit-bats (*Xantharpyia*) may be distinguished by the presence of a short tail, which is connected with the membrane between the legs, as well as by their smaller size, duller colours, and the absence of any difference between the fur of the neck and that of the body. These bats are common to the Oriental countries, Syria, Africa, and Madagascar. In Africa south of the Sahara the place of the common fruit-bats is taken by the epauletted fruit-bats (*Epomophorus*), so called from the tufts of long hair on the shoulders of the males. Their large and elongated heads have a bluntly conical or truncated muzzle, large, flabby, and extensive lips, and a tuft of white hair on the margin of each ear. While some are tailless, others have a short tail, unconnected with the leg-membrane. The tufts of hair on the shoulders of the males arise from long pouches on the sides of the neck. These bats are most abundant on the West Coast, where the single species of the allied genus *Scotonycteris* is also found.

Fig. 18.—FRUIT-BAT (*Pteropus*).

Another genus is formed by the short-nosed fruit-bats (*Cynopterus*), ranging from India to the Philippine Islands, and distinguished by the short and rounded muzzle, marked by a vertical groove, the reduction of the teeth to 32 or 30, and their small size. Most of them have a short tail connected with the membrane between the legs. Very curious are the two species of tube-nosed fruit-bats (*Harpyia*), inhabiting the islands of Celebes, New Guinea, North Australia, and New Ireland, and taking their name from the production of the nostrils into a pair of tubes reaching a short distance in advance of the blunt muzzle. Even more interesting is the cusp-toothed fruit-bat (*Pteralopex*) of the Solomon Islands, since the cusps in its molar teeth serve to indicate that all the fruit-bats have been derived from insectivorous members of the order. Another group of the family, comprising seven genera, among which *Carponycteris* may be selected as an example, is distinguished by the great length of the extensile tongue, which terminates in a number of papillæ, and is probably employed for licking out the soft contents of tropical fruits. Save that one species is found in West Africa, these bats are confined to the Oriental and Australasian countries. They are all of comparatively small size, and have long and pointed faces, and the narrow molar teeth scarcely projecting above the surface of the gums.

This exclusively Old World family is the first group of the ordinary bats, or Microchiroptera, in which the molar teeth are usually surmounted by a number of sharp cusps, and the food generally consists of insects. The other leading characteristics by which the sub-order is distinguished from the fruit-bats have been already noticed under the heading of the latter. As a family, the *Rhinolophidæ* are characterised by the presence of a well-developed nose-leaf surrounding the nostrils, which are placed in a hollow on the muzzle, as well as by the large size of the ears, in which an inner tragus is wanting, and which are generally quite separate from one another at the base.

Horse-shoe and Leaf-nosed Bats.—Family *Rhinolophidæ.*

The greater horse-shoe bat (*Rhinolophus ferrum-equinum*) is a familiar British representative of a very widely-spread genus, in which there are 32 teeth, and the nose-leaf consists of two portions, namely a horse-shoe-like moiety immediately over the nose, and a pointed one behind. In the leaf-nosed bats (*Hipposiderus*), which have, likewise, a wide range, and are represented by a large number of species, the hinder portion of the nose-leaf is not pointed, and there is no median portion concealing the nostrils; while the teeth are reduced to 30 or 28 in number. There are no European representatives of these bats, which range over Africa, Asia, and Australia. The most curious member of the whole family is the flower-nosed bat (*Anthops ornatus*) of the Solomon Islands, in which the whole front of the face, save the eyes and lips, is covered with a complex and ornate membrane, forming a complete mask to the countenance.

Fig. 19.—HORSE-SHOE BAT (*Rhinolophus ferrum-equinum*).

The so-called false vampire bats (*Megaderma*) form one of two genera constituting a family distinguished from the last by the presence of a large inner tragus in the very long ears. In this genus, which is common to the Oriental countries and Africa, the muzzle is surmounted by a rather tall nose-leaf; whereas in the allied genus *Nycteris* this appendage is almost wanting, and the ears are not joined together to nearly such an extent as is the case in the former, where their union extends nearly half their height. With the exception of one Javan and Malayan species, and a second from Egypt, all the members of the second genus are confined to Africa south of the Sahara.

False Vampire Bats.—Family *Nycteridæ.*

The typical bats form an extensive family, with a large number of genera and species, ranging over both the Eastern and Western Hemispheres; and it is to this family that all the British bats, with the exception of the two species of the genus *Rhinolophus*, and likewise the majority of those inhabiting Europe generally, belong. In this family the nose-leaf is wanting, so that the nostrils form simple crescentic or circular apertures at the end of the muzzle; the comparatively long tail is included in the membrane joining the hind-legs, and extends to its free edge, and the ear has a distinct inner tragus. In the upper jaw the incisor teeth, of which there may be either one or two pairs, are of small size, and separated by a gap in the middle line; but, with one exception, there are three pairs of the corresponding lower teeth. Over one hundred and fifty species are known. The long-eared bats (*Plecotus*), of which there is one species from the northern portion of the Old World, and a second from North America, constitute a genus characterised by the great length of the delicate ears, which are united

Typical Bats.—Family *Vespertilionidæ.*

for a short distance above the forehead, and the presence of grooves, representing an incipient nose-leaf on the muzzle just behind the nostrils. When at rest, the long ears are folded back, leaving the tragus alone standing upright. In the allied genus (*Synotus*), of which the barbastelle is the British representative, there are also only two species, one of which is European and the other Asiatic. They may be easily distinguished from the long-eared bats by the shortness of the ears, which are united for some distance basally, and likewise by the reduction in the number of the teeth from 36 to 34.

Fig. 20.—LONG-EARED BAT (*Plecotus auritus*).

The pipistrelle, or common bat (*Vesperugo pipistrellus*), together with the much larger noctule (*V. noctula*) and serotine (*V. serotinus*), are British representatives of a third genus, differing in several particulars from the two preceding. There are, for instance, no traces of grooves or foldings in the skin of the nose, and the small ears are completely separate from each other. The genus, which apparently contains a greater number of species than any other in the order, has an almost cosmopolitan distribution, but is one somewhat difficult to define, as some of its representatives approximate more or less to other genera ; the number of teeth being either 30, 34, or 36. The more typical kinds may be recognised by the relatively stout body, the broad, flattened head and blunt muzzle, and the broad, short, and triangular ears, in which the tragus is generally thickened and somewhat inclined outwards. As a rule, the hind-legs are short, and the membrane connecting them with the tail nearly always has an additional portion on the outer side of the spur on the heel. Omitting notice of the genera *Nycticejus* and *Chalinolobus*, mention must be made of the American genus *Atalapha*, of which the hoary bat (*A. cinerea*) of the United States is a familiar representative. All members of this genus have but a single pair of upper incisor teeth, and are further characterised by the membrane between the hind-legs being more or less hairy. Like other bats living in cold climates, the hoary bat hibernates during winter ; this species selecting caves, to which it resorts in large numbers for the period of torpor. Many European bats prefer, however, church-towers and roofs, or outbuildings, while some select hollow trees, and it is a curious fact that in the case of certain species the males and females associate in separate colonies. An unusually warm day, even in mid-winter, will generally cause a certain number of bats to awake from slumber and issue forth, after which they again fall into the same torpor as before.

Among the numerous genera of this family, the tube-nosed bats (*Harpyiocephalus*), from hilly districts in the Oriental countries, Tibet and Japan, deserve special mention, on account of the remarkable similarity between the structure of their nostrils and those of the tube-nosed fruit-bats. In the present genus the tubes into which the nostrils are prolonged are, however, shorter and much more divergent than in the last-named group.

Of the typical genus (*Vespertilio*), which is only second in point of numbers, there are four British representatives, among which Daubenton's bat (*V. daubentoni*) is one of the best known. Those bats differ from the members of the family already noticed in having upwards of 38 teeth, there being two pairs of incisors in the upper jaw ; and they are specially distinguished by the circumstance that these latter are so fixed in the jaw as to diverge from one another, as well as by the cheek-teeth (that is to say premolars, and molars together) forming three pairs in each jaw. A further distinctive feature is to be found in the minute size of the second upper premolar tooth, while the ear has a characteristic elongated oval form, and its inner tragus is remarkably narrow. The genus has a wide geographical distribution, being spread over the temperate and tropical regions of both hemispheres. A bat belonging to this genus (*V. welwitschi*) from West Africa, closely allied to the British Bechstein's bat (*V. bechsteini*), is remarkable for the circumstance that the wing-membranes are coloured orange and black; the Indian *V. hodgsoni* also having a very similar type of coloration. Another Indian bat with black and orange wings belongs to the genus *Cerivoula*, distinguished from *Vespertilio* by the upper incisor teeth being vertical instead of divergent. A fourth peculiarly coloured species is the West African *Nycticejus albofuscus*, belonging to a genus closely allied to *Vesperugo*, and having the outer portions of the wing-membranes dazzling white. In these abnormally coloured bats it appears that those in which black and orange obtain are in the habit of reposing among the fruit and leaves of various tropical trees, in which an orange ground is frequently relieved by black spots.

Schreibers' bat (*Miniopterus schreibersi*), ranging from Germany to Japan and Australia, is the only member of a genus differing from all those hitherto noticed by the great elevation of the crown of the head above the face; the same feature also characterises the South American and West Indian bats forming the genus *Natalus*. Two very curious bats belonging to this family, and each forming a genus by itself, are remarkable for having the feet furnished with adhesive discs, by which they are enabled to climb smooth, polished surfaces. One of these is the tricolor bat (*Thyroptera tricolor*) of Brazil, in which the suckers form circular discs on the lower surface of the thumb and the sole of the hind-foot; the second being the golden bat (*Myxopoda aurita*) of Madagascar, in which the sucker on the thumb is in the form of a horse-shoe, while those on the feet are of smaller size. Both these bats are distinguished from all the other members of the family by having three joints to the third or middle finger of the wing, thereby resembling the undermentioned family *Phyllostomatidæ*.

Free-tailed Bats.—Family *Emballonuridæ*.

In the preceding families of the Microchiroptera the tail is enclosed in the membrane connecting the two hind-legs, but in the two families of this group still remaining for consideration, this appendage, when present, generally either perforates the membrane in such a manner that its free extremity appears on the upper extremity of the latter, or is produced considerably beyond the free hinder margin of the same. Another feature is that the inner, and frequently the only, pair of upper incisor teeth, are of large size and placed close together in the middle line; and a third characteristic is to be found in the circumstance that when the wing is at rest, the first joint of the third finger is folded back upon the supporting metacarpal bone instead of being extended forwards in the same line. In two species, each representing a genus by itself, the last-named characteristic is, however, wanting. Only a single species of these two families is met with in Europe, the second family being exclusively American. In the members of the family *Emballonuridæ* there are but two joints in the third finger of the wing, and there is no distinct nose-leaf; but, as a rule, the ear is furnished with a small inner tragus, and there is but a single pair of upper incisor teeth, which are inclined towards one another. An oblique truncation of the extremity of the snout causes the nostrils to project more or less in advance of the extremity of the lower jaw. These bats are most abundant in the zone lying thirty degrees on each side of the Equator; and among them are the only two indigenous Mammals found in New Zealand. Both in this and the next family only a small proportion of the more interesting types out of a very large number of genera will be noticed in this place.

The typical representatives of the family are the sheath-tailed bats (*Emballonura*), ranging from the Malayan countries to the Philippine Islands, and also found from Madagascar to the Navigator group. They belong to a group of several genera in which the free extremity of the slender tail perforates the membrane between the legs, while the legs are relatively long, and the upper incisor teeth are weak; two pairs of these teeth being present in this particular genus. Further distinctive characteristics of *Emballonura* are that there are 34 teeth, that the muzzle is more or less distinctly produced, the top of the head flat, the ears completely separate from each other, and their tragus somewhat oblong and expanded above. Tropical America is the home of the allied pouch-winged bats (*Saccopteryx*), all of which are small-sized creatures, with only a single pair of upper incisor teeth, and a peculiar glandular pouch on the under side of the wing in the neighbourhood of the elbow-joint. These pouches, which are rudimental in the females, appear to have a sexual function, and in one species a white frill of skin protrudes from the aperture of each.

The tomb-bats (*Taphozous*) form another large genus, with representatives in Africa, the Oriental countries, and Australia, and differ from other members of the group in having only two pairs of lower incisor teeth, and also in the shedding of the single upper pair in the adult condition. The males, and in some cases also the females, of many species have glandular pouches beneath the chin; and some forms which hibernate for a long period accumulate large deposits of fat about the root of the tail before retiring for their torpor. The typical representative of the genus is found in large numbers in the ancient tombs of Egypt.

The two species of white bats (*Diclidurus*) from Tropical America are worthy of notice, on account of the yellowish or creamy-white colour of the tips of the fur. Closely allied to the tomb-bats, they differ in having three pairs of lower incisor teeth, while they are distinguished from all other bats by the presence of a pouch on the under surface of the membrane between the hind-legs. Two other bats from the same region, known as the hare-lipped bats (*Noctilio*), take their name from the curious resemblance of their folded upper lips to those of the Rodents, while one species is remarkable on account of its diet, which consists mainly, if not exclusively, of small fish. Another peculiar member of the same sub-family is the long-tailed bat (*Rhinopoma microphyllum*), ranging from North-Eastern Africa through India to Burma, and is easily recognised by the very long, whip-like tail, which projects far beyond the hinder margin of the extremely short membrane joining the hind-legs.

The mastiff-bats (*Molossus*), so named on account of their very broad and wide-mouthed muzzles, are the first representatives of a second sub-family of the *Emballonuridæ* characterised by the thickness of the tail, which, save in one species, is produced a considerable distance beyond the free margin of the membrane joining the legs. All have short, strong legs, very broad feet, and callosities at the base of the thumbs, while there is only a single pair of incisor teeth in the upper jaw. The hind-feet have no attachment to the wings, the membranes of which can be folded away between the arms and legs, while the membrane joining the hind-legs can be drawn upwards along the tail; and it appears that all the members of the sub-family are better adapted for crawling than are any other bats. The mastiff-bats are confined to Tropical and Sub-Tropical America, and generally have 26 or 28 teeth, with two pairs of lower incisors. The large ears, in which there is generally a small tragus, are united at their bases; the lips, in common with those of two allied genera, are very large, and often thrown into pouches; while the wings are remarkably long and narrow.

The large Malayan naked bat (*Chiromeles torquata*) takes its name from the thick and puckered skin being almost entirely naked; and is further peculiar in that the large first hind-toe can be opposed to the other digits. But the most curious feature about the animal is the presence of a large pouch on the under surface of the body below the armpits, in which the young are carried during the period of suckling. The object of this special development is sufficiently apparent, since, owing to the absence of fur, the young would be quite unable to cling to the body of the parent in the usual bat fashion. The muzzle of this curious bat is remarkably long and pig-like; and the rather large ears are widely separated from one another. Although most abundant in Africa south of the Sahara, the wrinkled-lipped bats, constituting the genus *Nyctinomus*, are the most widely spread, and, at the same time, the most numerously represented group of the present sub-family, being found in India and Burma, China, Australia, New Guinea, Tropical America, and Madagascar; while a single species (*N. cestoni*) is found in Southern and Central Europe, where it is the sole representative of the entire family. Closely allied to the mastiff-bats, the members of the present genus may be distinguished by the gap dividing the upper incisor teeth in the middle line, and likewise by the greater development of the wrinkles on the full, fleshy lips.

The last member of the family that will be mentioned is the New Zealand bat (*Mystacops tuberculatus*), distinguished by having three joints to the third finger of the wing, the first of which, when at rest, is folded back beneath the metacarpal bone, instead of above it, as in the other members of the family. Owing to a peculiarity in the structure of the wings, this species is better suited for crawling than any other bat. The other species of bat inhabiting New Zealand (*Chalinolobus tuberculatus*) belongs to a genus nearly allied to *Vesperugo*, and is also found in Australia.

Vampire-Bats.—Family *Phyllostomatidæ*.

The great family of vampire-bats is exclusively confined to Tropical America and the West Indies, and bears nearly the same relation to the preceding family as is presented by the horse-shoe bats to the typical bats. In addition to the features common to the *Emballonuridæ*, all have three joints to the middle or third finger of the wing, while there is either a well-developed nose-leaf, or folds and warts are present on the chin. A distinct tragus in the moderately-sized ears will always serve to distinguish the numerous representatives of this family which have a nose-leaf from the horse-shoe bats, without the necessity of counting the number of joints in the middle finger of the wing. Vampire-bats are exceedingly numerous, both as regards genera and species, so that only a few of the former can be referred to here. All are strong flyers; but the various groups present great differences in the nature of their food, some devouring insects and fruits alike, while others are wholly frugivorous, and others again have taken to a blood-sucking habit.

In two small genera of the family (*Chilonycteris* and *Mormops*) the nose-leaf is wanting, and its place supplied by two or more lappets of skin hanging from beneath the skin. One of these chin-leafed bats (*M. blainvillei*) is remarkable for its bright orange fur, and likewise for the extremely fragile structure of the whole head and body. The harmless vampires (*Vampirus*) belong to a group of genera in which the tail, when present, perforates the membrane between the legs, while the nose-leaf is spear-shaped. The largest is the great vampire (*V. spectrum*), from Brazil, in which the expanse of wing is upwards of 28 inches; the tail being wanting. Apparently these bats feed exclusively on fruits. Nearly allied are the three species of javelin-bats (*Phyllostoma*), which may be distinguished from the harmless vampires by the shorter and broader form of the muzzle, as well as by the reduction in the number of the lower premolar teeth from three to two pairs. There is some degree of doubt whether any of the javelin-bats are addicted to blood-sucking propensities.

Fig. 21.—VAMPIRE-BAT (*Desmodus rufus*).

More remarkable than any of the family are the long-tongued vampires, which are referred to several genera, such as *Glossophaga*, *Chæronycteris*, *Phyllonycteris*, etc., easily recognised by the narrow muzzle and the long, slender, extensile tongue, tipped at the extremity with sensile papillæ, and capable of being protruded a long distance in advance of the tongue. Like the javelin-bats, these vampires have a small spear-shaped nose-leaf rising vertically from the muzzle immediately between the nostrils. The tongue appears to be used both to scoop out the soft interior of fruits, and likewise to extract small insects from tubular flowers.

Another well-marked assemblage is formed by the short-nosed vampires, of which there are no less than nine genera, and among which *Artibeus* and *Stenoderma* may be mentioned by name. All these bats, which are for the most part frugivorous in their diet, are distinguished by the extreme shortness of their muzzles, which are generally very wide, and are provided with a short nose-leaf; the fore-part of the latter being in the form of a horse-shoe, and the hinder moiety spear-shaped. One of these species (*Artibeus perspicillatus*) is very common in the plantations of Jamaica, where it feeds on mangoes, bread-fruit, etc.

The last representatives of this extensive family are the blood-sucking vampires, of which one species alone constitutes the genus *Desmodus*, while the latter represents another genus named *Diphylla*. Both these bats are characterised by the short and conical form of the muzzle, which carries a small nose-leaf, the shortness of the membrane between the hind-legs, the absence of a tail, and the small number and peculiar structure of the teeth. In the first-named genus the total number of teeth is 20, molars being wanting; but in the second it is 22, owing to the presence of a pair of rudimentary molars in the upper jaw. Both have a single pair of broad chisel-like incisor teeth in the upper jaw, which fill up the whole space between the tusks; and the two pairs of upper, and three pairs of lower premolars have sharp cutting edges. In correlation with the nature of their diet, the stomach of these bats is narrowed and elongated into a tube-like organ. The common vampire (*Desmodus rufus*), ranging from Central America to the south of Brazil, measures about three inches in length, and has reddish-brown fur on the upper parts. The second species (*Diphylla ecaudata*) is rather smaller, and confined to Brazil. These bats attack animals by shaving away the upper layer of the skin from some bare part with their incisor teeth, and then suck up the blood as it oozes from the capillary vessels.

ORDER III.—INSECTIVORA.

INSECT-EATING MAMMALS.

THE third order of Mammals comprises a large number of mostly small-sized insectivorous species, structurally nearly allied to the bats, but with the fore-limbs of normal structure. With the exception of the tree-shrews and a few aquatic species, they are all more or less completely nocturnal in their habits; but the group as a whole is one by no means easy of definition. As a rule, they have five toes to each foot, all of which are furnished with claws, and neither the thumb nor the great toe is capable of being opposed to the other digits. In walking the whole sole of the foot is applied to the ground, in what is termed the plantigrade manner. The crowns of their short upper molar teeth are surmounted by a number of minute, sharp cusps, which may be arranged either in the form of a W or a V; and the incisor teeth, of which there are not less than two pairs in the lower jaw, are never chisel-like, but the first pair is often larger than the others. The canines, or tusks, are very generally not distinctly larger than the other teeth; and there is never a pair of scissor-like cheek-teeth like those characterising the terrestrial Carnivora. Except in one or two species, perfect collar-bones are developed; and the lobes of the brain are nearly smooth, thus indicating very low mental powers. Externally, Insectivores very generally have long slender and narrow snouts, with the muzzle projecting considerably beyond the extremity of the lower jaw; and while many of them are coated with fur, which may be harsh and rough, others have a covering of spines, or spines mingled with fur.

As regards their geographical distribution, these Mammals present some very curious features. In the first place, they are totally wanting in South America, where their place is taken by the Marsupial opossums; but they are represented by a peculiar family, with one genus, in the West Indian Islands. A more or less closely allied family occurs in Madagascar, where there are also other peculiar types; and the order is distributed over North America and all the great continents of the Old World, although absent from Australia and Papua. From geological evidence, coupled with its abundance in Madagascar, the order is evidently an ancient one; and its existing members have probably been enabled to survive either by their small size and nocturnal habits, their protective armour of spines, or from dwelling in countries where the larger Carnivora are either absent or but few in number, or by having taken to a subterranean mode of life. Whereas the majority of the Insectivora are terrestrial, the flying-lemurs are arboreal, and able to take flying leaps from tree to tree; the tree-shrews are also arboreal; the moles and some of the shrews, on the other hand, are burrowers; and the desmans, certain shrews, and the African *Potamogale* are aquatic in their habits.

The Flying-Lemurs.—Family *Galeopithecidæ*.

From all other members of the order the so-called flying-lemurs, or cobegos, are at once distinguished by the presence of an expansion of the skin of the sides of the body connecting the fore and hind-limbs, and also by the toes of both feet being webbed right up to the sharp and curved claws. The hind-legs are likewise connected together in a similar manner; the connecting skin involving the whole of the long tail. Another remarkable feature is to be found in the conformation of the incisor teeth, which in both jaws are flattened from back to front, the upper ones being cusped, while the lower ones differ from those of all other Mammals in being of a comb-like structure.

Fig. 22.—THE FLYING-LEMUR (*Galeopithecums volans*).

The cobegos, of which there are two species belonging to the single genus *Galeopithecus*, range from Tenasserim through the Malayan Peninsula and Islands to the Philippines and Siam. Unlike the ordinary members of the order to which they are assigned, they subsist mainly on leaves and fruits. During the daytime they hang head-downwards in a bat-like manner from the boughs or stems of trees; but at dusk and during the night pass from tree to tree in long flying leaps, supported by the parachute, such leaps being at times as much as seventy yards in length. In size, the common Malayan species may be compared to an ordinary cat. Owing to their great structural differences from the other members of the order, the cobegos are regarded as forming a sub-order by themselves, under the name of Dermoptera; all the other forms constituting a second subordinal group known as the Insectivora Vera.

Tree-Shrews.—Family *Tupaiidæ*.

The tree-shrews, or tupaias, of the Oriental countries, are the first of a group of five families characterised by having broad upper molar teeth, upon the summits of which the numerous small cusps are arranged more or less in the shape of the letter W. In appearance the tree-shrews, except as regards their long, pointed muzzles, are so like small squirrels, that they might easily be mistaken for those animals; and this resemblance, together with their arboreal habits, is one of the features by which they are most easily recognised. From the next family they may be distinguished by the socket of the eye being completely surrounded by bone in the skull, and likewise by the metatarsus, or upper portion of the hind-foot, being of normal proportions. They are all animals of small size, with thick fur, short ears, and the long tail either bushy throughout or with a pen-like expansion near the end. Tree-shrews subsist on both insects and fruit, taking the latter in

Fig. 23.—TREE-SHREW (*Tupaia tana*).

their fore-paws and sitting up to devour it in a squirrel-like manner. Although chiefly arboreal, they at times seek their food on the ground.

The typical tree-shrews (*Tupaia*), which range from India to the Philippines, and are represented by a large number of species, have the long tail bushy throughout, although the longer hairs are arranged on the upper and lateral surfaces, the under side being short-haired. Two species, of which one is from Borneo and the other from Siam, have been separated as *Dendrogale*, although this scarcely seems necessary. Very distinct is, however, the beautiful little pen-tailed shrew (*Ptilocercus lowi*) of Borneo and some of the adjacent islands, in which the exceeding long tail is evenly short-haired for the greater portion of its length, although towards its extremity it bears a double row of long hairs, arranged like the vanes of a feather. This little creature measures between five and six inches to the root of the tail, which is considerably longer than the head and body.

Jumping-Shrews.—Family *Macroscelididæ*.

In Africa south of the Sahara the place of the tree-shrews is taken by the terrestrial jumping-shrews, one species of the typical genus ranging into Northern Africa. From the tree-shrews these animals differ not only by their terrestrial habits, but also by the elongation of the metatarsal segment of the hind-foot, which enables them to take the leaps from which they derive their name; and likewise by the bony rim of the socket of the eye being incomplete behind. The tail also is not bushy. In the typical genus the snout is elongated so as to form a short proboscis, on which account the name of elephant-shrew is applied to these creatures.

Fig. 24.—A JUMPING-SHREW (*Macroscelides*).

In the typical jumping-shrews (*Macroscelides*) the number of teeth is usually 42, and there are five toes on the fore-foot and generally the same number on the hind-foot; while the ears are large, and the tail is naked and rat-like. In one species (*M. tetradactylus*), from the Mozambique Coast, there are, however, but 40 teeth, while the number of toes on the hind-foot is reduced to four; and on this account the animal is generically separated by some as *Petrodomus*. A very distinct genus is formed by the long nosed jumping-shrews (*Rhynchocyon*) from the East Coast of Africa, in which there are only 36 teeth, and but four toes to both the front and hind-feet. The hind-legs are also relatively shorter. Unlike the tree-shrews, the members of this family are nocturnal in their habits.

Hedgehog Tribe.—Family *Erinaceidæ*.

In the three remaining families of the group with the cusps on the upper molars arranged in the form of the letter W, the brain-cavity is relatively smaller than in the two preceding families, and the union of the front portion of the lower part of the pelvis in the middle line of the body either shorter or altogether wanting, while not only has the socket of the eye no complete bony ring, but even the post-orbital process found in the jumping-shrews is totally absent. Although the hedgehogs themselves are easily distinguished from the other members of the group by their spiny covering, this is not the case with their more rat-like allies the gymnuras; and accordingly other characters have to be sought in order to define the family *Erinaceidæ*. In all save one species the feet are five-toed and furnished with claws adapted for digging; while the first and second upper molar teeth have five distinct cusps, the central one of which is minute and connected with the two inner ones by oblique ridges. The family is confined to the Old World.

The hedgehogs (*Erinaceus*) are sufficiently distinguished by the coat of spines covering the upper surface and sides of the body, and their power of rolling themselves up into a ball as a defence against attack, and are likewise such familiar animals, that but little in the way of description is necessary. The tail is extremely short; and the total number of teeth is 36. Hedgehogs are distributed over the greater part of Europe and portions of Africa and Asia, although unknown in the countries lying east of the Bay of Bengal, and likewise in Madagascar. The European species (*E. europæus*) differs from all the others by the coarser nature of the fur between the spines, and by the upper canine tooth being inserted by one instead of two roots. In habits, all hedgehogs are nocturnal and omnivorous, their diet comprising insects, molluscs, eggs, voles, fruits, and roots. In cold countries they hibernate in a nest made of leaves and grass, and well concealed among bushes.

The shrew-hedgehogs, which may be compared to large, coarsely-haired shrews, replace the hedgehogs in Burma and the Malay countries. They differ from the latter by being covered with coarse hair instead of spines, as well as in having 44 teeth. There are two species, of which Raffles's shrew-hedgehog (*Gymnura rafflesi*) is by far the commoner, and considerably the larger, measuring 12 or 14 inches to the root of the tail, which is long and rat-like. The smaller shrew-hedgehog (*Hylomys suillus*), on the other hand, measures less than 5 inches, with a tail of only an inch in length, and has the third upper premolar tooth much smaller than in the first species. The range of both is nearly co-extensive.

Fig. 25.—SHREW-HEDGEHOG (*Gymnura rafflesi*).

The Shrews.—Family *Soricidæ*.

The numerous representatives of this extensive family are mouse-like or rat-like creatures, with soft, short fur, long and pointed snouts, rounded ears, closely pressed to the sides of the head, and a very peculiar type of dentition. From ordinary rats and mice they may be distinguished by their typically insectivorous snouts; but it is remarkable that a peculiar rat recently discovered in the Philippines is curiously like a shrew in this respect, although it retains the characteristic rodent incisor teeth, which are, however, reduced to an exceedingly small size. As regards their dentition, shrews are specially characterised by the first pair of upper incisor teeth being long and generally sickle-shaped, with a more or less distinct projecting basal cusp on the hinder border, while those of the lower jaw are long, and projecting forwards, in some cases with an upward curve at the tip. With the exception of one African species, there are only six pairs of lower teeth. A peculiarity of the skull of the shrews is the absence of the bony zygomatic arch running beneath the socket of the eye, although the same deficiency is found in one species of hedgehog. The upper molars of the shrews lack the fifth cusp found in the first two of these teeth in the hedgehogs.

The shrews are not only more numerous in genera and species than any other family of the order to which they belong, but have likewise a much wider geographical distribution, being found over the greater part of Europe.

as well as in the temperate and tropical portions of Asia and North America, and also in Africa, although they are represented in Madagascar only by a single species, which is not improbably introduced. Although the majority of the shrews are terrestrial and nocturnal in their habits, a few have taken to an aquatic mode of life. They are all very shy and retiring, which is probably their chief protection; and their food is entirely composed of insects, worms, molluscs, and such like. Many shrews exhale a strong, musky odour; and at certain times of the year many of these animals are found lying dead in the open, the cause of this mortality not being at present clearly ascertained. Although it may seem a trivial character, the circumstance of the teeth being stained reddish-brown, or simply white, serves to divide the shrews into two groups.

The typical shrews, or those forming the genus *Sorex*, belong to the group with reddish teeth, and are specially characterised by having 32 teeth, the ear well-developed, and the long tail covered with hairs of equal or nearly equal length. The range of the genus includes North America, Europe, and Asia north of the Himalaya; its British representatives being the common shrew (*S. araneus*) and the lesser shrew (*S. pygmæus*). Although shrews hibernate, specimens have been occasionally seen running over the snow in mid-winter. The Oriental shrews (*Soriculus*), which are the only representatives of the red-toothed group in that region, are nearly allied; but they have generally only 30 teeth, and the first upper incisor has an inner cusp. Nearly allied are two Mexican species constituting the genus *Notiosorex*, and characterised by having only 28 teeth and no inner cusp to the first upper incisor, the tail being also shorter. A larger American genus is *Blarina*, which is mainly confined to the northern part of that continent, although a few forms descend into Central America. Here the number of teeth varies from 30 to 32, while the ear is truncated above and the tail short, the other characters being the same as in *Soriculus*. The water-shrews (*Crossopus*), which are the last representatives of the red-toothed section, have 30 teeth, small, non-truncated ears, the long tail fringed on its lower surface with elongated hairs, and the feet also fringed. The single species (*C. fodiens*) is thoroughly aquatic, and ranges from England to the Altai Mountains.

Certain shrews from Africa constituting the genus *Myosorex* are the first representatives of the white-toothed section, and are specially characterised by having well-developed ears, a long tail clothed with nearly or quite equal hairs, and either 30 or 32 teeth, one minute species being unique in having seven pairs of lower teeth. More numerous are the well-known musk-shrews (*Crocidura*), differing from the last in having 28 or 30 teeth, and the long tail covered with a mixture of long and short hairs. These shrews range from South and Central Europe to Africa and Asia, reaching as far east as Amurland, and being represented by one species in Madagascar. Out of some 80 species one of the best known is the Indian musk-shrew (*C. cœrulea*), commonly known as the musk-rat, of which the odour is so strong that every article of food is rendered uneatable by the mere passage over it of the animal. The Kirghiz shrew (*Diplomesodon pulchellus*) alone represents a genus differing from the last by the shorter tail, the hairy soles of the feet, and the presence of only 26 teeth. The two mole-shrews (*Anurosorex*), of which one is from Assam and the other from Tibet and China, are peculiar in being of fossorial habits, and may be distinguished by the absence of the external conch of the ear, the short tail, the naked soles of the scale-covered feet, and the velvety fur. The two remaining genera are aquatic, and thus occupy in this section a position similar to that held by the water-shrew in the red-toothed division of the family. Of these, the swimming shrews (*Chimarrogale*) are represented by one species from the Himalaya, the hills north of Burma, and the mountains of North Borneo, and by a second from Japan. They have 28 teeth, the long tail with a fringe of elongated hair beneath, small ears, and the toes free. On the other hand, the web-footed shrew (*Nectogale elegans*) of Tibet, while agreeing with the last in the number of its teeth, differs in the absence of external ear-conches, its webbed toes, and in the development of the pads on the soles of the hind-feet into adhesive suckers, the tail being longer than the body. Probably this shrew is more completely aquatic than any other member of the family. Its eyes are very minute, and the dark velvety fur of the upper parts displays a beautiful iridescent lustre.

The Desmans and Moles.—Family *Talpidæ*.

Although the common mole is sufficiently distinct from a shrew, other forms so closely connect the *Talpidæ* with the *Soricidæ* that internal characters have to be relied on to distinguish the two families. The present family may, however, be differentiated from the last by the presence of a bony zygomatic arch in the skull, and likewise by the development of a distinct auditory bulla in the same, as well as by the conformation of the teeth. The eyes are always small, and may be covered by the skin ; the short ears are buried in the dense fur ; the fore-limbs are generally modified either for digging or swimming ; there is no median union of the pubic portion of the pelvis on the under surface of the body ; in the lower leg the tibia and fibula are welded into a single bone ; and the first pair of incisor teeth in each jaw are of simple structure, and the lower pair do not project forwards. The range of the family includes the temperate portions of Europe, Asia, and North America, two moles only occurring south of the Himalaya. A few species are cursorial, and the desmans are aquatic, but the majority of the family are fossorial in their habits.

The two species of desman (*Myogale*) are the typical representatives of a section of the family in which the collar-bones and humerus or upper arm bone, are moderately elongated, and the front paws have no additional sickle-shaped bone. As a genus, the desmans are specially distinguished by the possession of 44 teeth, their webbed feet, the long, trunk-like snout, which projects far in advance of the upper lip, and the long scaly tail. The Russian desman (*M. Moschata*), which measures about 16 inches in length, has a compressed tail ; whereas in the much smaller Pyrenean species (*M pyrenaica*) the tail is cylindrical, and the snout relatively longer. Both inhabit the banks of rivers and lakes, are excellent swimmers, and live on water-insects and snails.

Fig. 26.—RUSSIAN DESMAN (*Myogale moschata*).

The shrew-moles, of which there are two genera, form a connecting link between the moles and shrews. In *Urotrichus*, of which there is one Japanese and one North American species (the latter being separated by some as *Neurotrichus*), there are 36 teeth, and the broad fore-paws are adapted for digging ; whereas in the single Tibetan species of *Uropsilus* there are 34 teeth, the fore-paws are narrow, and the tail is naked and scaly.

The North American web-footed moles (*Scalops*) belong to the second division of the family, in which the collar-bones and humerus are very short and wide, and the fore-paws are furnished with an additional sickle-like bone next the thumb. In this genus the tip of the snout is simple, the hind-foot webbed, the tail short and nearly naked, and the first upper incisor tooth longer than the second. Curiously enough, in spite of their webbed hind-feet, these animals are not aquatic, but subterranean in their habits, burrowing after the manner of the ordinary mole. The two North American hairy-tailed moles (*Scapanus*) differ in having 44 teeth, and the tail hairy. Having the same number of teeth as the last, the star-nosed mole (*Condylura cristata*) of North America is sufficiently distinguished by the curious star-like ring of appendages surrounding the extremity of the muzzle. The tail is nearly equal in length to the body ; and the front-paws are less powerful than in the true moles, and have no cleft in the bones of their terminal joints.

From all the American representations of the section the true moles (*Talpa*) of the Old World may be at once distinguished by the first pair of upper incisor teeth scarcely exceeding the second in size. As a rule, there are 44 teeth, and the fore-paws are characterised by their extraordinary width and power ; the tail being very short, and in a Nepalese species (*T. micrura*) concealed by the fur. With the exception of the common mole (*T. europæa*), the eyes are covered by a membrane ; and in all they are functionally useless. The appearance and habits of the moles are too well known to need description. The common species, although unknown in Ireland, ranges from England to Japan, and a second European species (*T. cæca*) is found to the south of the Alps. The other seven species are exclusively Asiatic, two only occurring to the south of the Himalaya, one of which inhabits Nepal and Assam. By some the Tibetan musk-mole (*T. moschata*) is generically separated as *Scaptochirus*. The only other member of the family is the yellow-tailed mole (*Scaptonyx fuscicaudatus*) of Eastern Tibet, which differs from the true moles in having only two pairs of lower incisor teeth, and also in the narrower fore-feet, thus approximating to the shrew-moles.

Family *Potamogalidæ*.

Two very remarkable Insectivores, the one from Western Africa, and the other from Madagascar, differ from all the preceding, and agree with the following families in having narrow upper teeth, with their cusps arranged in the form of the letter V ; this section being apparently less specialised than the one in which they form a W. In the skull the zygomatic arch is wanting, and the auditory bulla is represented by a simple ring ; collar-bones are wanting ; and the pubic portion of the pelvis is united inferiorly only by ligament.

Fig. 27.—Potamogale velox.

The African *Potamogale* is a thoroughly aquatic creature, measuring about two feet in length, with 40 teeth, a long cylindrical body, long and compressed tail, short legs, unwebbed feet, and the nostrils with protecting valves. In colour it is dark brown above, with violet reflexions, and whitish below. Very different is the small mouse-like *Geogale* of Madagascar, which has only 34 teeth, and also differs in having the lower ends of the tibia and fibula in the leg separate, although it is not known whether collar-bones are present.

Two curious Insectivores, one inhabiting Cuba and the other Hayti, form the genus *Solenodon*, which alone represents a family agreeing in the general characters of the teeth and skull with the last, but differing in that there is a short bony union between the pubic portion of the pelvis ; and also in that the teats are situated on the buttocks. These animals have a very long cylindrical snout, with the nostrils opening on its sides, a long naked tail, feet adapted for walking, and the fur long and coarse. They resemble *Potamogale* in having the second pair of lower incisor teeth much larger than the first, but are peculiar in that the crowns of the former are deeply excavated. These animals probably feed on flesh as well as on insects.

Family *Solenodontidæ.*

The tenrecs of Madagascar and the Comoro Islands, of which there are five genera and a considerable number of species, constitute another closely allied family, mainly distinguished from the last by the teats being situated on the breast and abdomen. The true tenrec (*Centetes ecaudatus*), which is the largest member of the order and the sole member of its genus, is characterised by the absence of a tail, and the possession of 40 teeth, among which there are four pairs of upper molars—the latter feature being almost unique among Mammals other than the Marsupials. The adult males differ from most Insectivores in possessing large tusks in both jaws ; and while the young have long rows of white spines along the back, these disappear in the adult. The total length of a full-grown specimen varies from 12 to 16 inches. The number of young produced at a birth is very great, upwards of twenty-one having been recorded in one instance. Nearly allied are the two species of streaked tenrecs (*Hemicentetes*), distinguished by having three in place of two pairs of upper incisor teeth, and probably only three of upper molars, as well as by the smaller dimensions of the canines, which scarcely exceed the incisors in size. In these animals, which may be compared in size to a mole, the rows of spines on the back are permanently retained. The small animals known as hedgehog-tenrecs (*Ericulus*) take their title from their resemblance to miniature hedgehogs, although it is probable that they are incapable of rolling themselves into such a complete ball-like form as are the latter. The whole of the back and sides are protected by a coat of parti-coloured short spines ; and these animals are further distinguished by the possession of a short tail. While in one species (*E. setosus*) the number of teeth is 36, in the second (*E. telfairi*) it is reduced to 34. By some the latter is made the type of a distinct genus, under the name of *Echinops*. The two mouse-like long-tailed tenrecs, forming the genus *Microgale*, differ from all tho foregoing in the absence of spines in the fur at all ages, and likewise by the extraordinary length of the tail, which in one of the two is double that of the head and body. The number of teeth is 40. Lastly, the two mole-like rice-tenrecs (*Oryzorictes*), while agreeing with the preceding genus in the absence of spines among the fur, differ by the shortness of the tail and their burrowing habits. Whereas in one species (*O. hova*) the fore-foot has the usual five toes, in the other (*O. tetradactylus*) the number is reduced to four, of which the three inner ones are armed with strong digging claws. These animals do much harm to the rice crops in Mada-

The Tenrecs. —Family *Centetidæ.*

Fig. 28.—Tenrec (*Centetes ecaudatus*).

gascar by burrowing beneath the roots of the plants in search of insects and grubs.

Golden Moles.—Family *Chrysochloridæ*.

The last family of the Insectivora is represented by the golden or Cape moles (*Chrysochloris*), which take their name from the iridescent golden, green, and purple metallic tints adorning the fur; and all of which are restricted to South and East Africa. From the preceding families of the present section of the order the golden moles are distinguished by the possession of a bony zygomatic arch and auditory bulla in the skull; and their triangular molar teeth are remarkable for the height of their crowns. In form, these animals are shorter and thicker than ordinary moles, with the head deeper, and the muzzle much more blunt. The eyes are covered with skin, and the ears completely buried in the fur. The fore-feet are modified into special digging instruments, and have but four toes, of which the middle pair are provided with large and powerful triangular claws. Usually there are 40 teeth, although in some species the number is reduced to 36, owing to the loss of the anterior premolars in each jaw. The golden moles burrow in much the same manner as the European mole, but their runs are made so little below the surface that the earth is raised as a continuous ridge, and no hillocks are thrown up. Like the common mole, they feed almost exclusively on earthworms.

Fig. 29.—Cape Golden Mole (*Chrysochloris*).

ORDER IV.—CARNIVORA.

Flesh-Eating Mammals.

This great and important order of Mammals includes all the terrestrial beasts of prey, together with the aquatic seals and walruses. Although their carnivorous propensities form one of the most distinctive features of the majority of the members of the order, it must not be assumed that by any means all the Carnivora are exclusively flesh-eaters, many of the bears feeding largely on fruits and roots, while some of the smaller forms subsist largely on insects. Whether the typical Carnivora are more highly organised animals than the Primates, is a matter regarding which different views may be entertained; but it is certain that for their particular mode of life these animals have attained the highest development of which the Mammalian type is capable, and the beauty of form and coloration of the larger cats, as well as their extreme agility, cannot but draw forth the admiration of all. A striking feature of Carnivora in general is the wide geographical range of families, genera and species, and the large number of specific types by which the former are represented; the order presenting in this respect a most marked contrast to the Insectivora, in which, as shown above, most of the families and genera have an exceedingly limited distribution, while the number of species contained in a genus is usually very small. The reason of this is obvious. Carnivora are enabled to obtain suitable prey in every part of the globe, and there is, in consequence, practically no limit to the range over which a species may extend itself; while being dominant forms, the number of species in a genus has naturally multiplied to a great extent. As might be expected in such a case, the different species of many large genera display a marked tendency to variation, so that there is frequently much difficulty in deciding as to what constitutes a species, and what a mere variety; this being remarkably exemplified among the great groups of the cats and foxes.

Although certain extinct forms, of which no further mention will be made in this volume, tend to connect them with the Insectivora, the modern Carnivora form a tolerably well-defined group, which would, however, be easier of definition were the seals and walruses referred to a separate order. Throughout the group the number of toes is very generally five, and never falls below four on each foot; and in all cases these toes are armed with claws, which are usually curved and sharp, and bear no resemblance to nails. Neither the equivalent of the thumb or the great toe of the Primates can be in any way opposed to the other digits. Very frequently collar-bones are wanting, and in no instance are they complete; that is to say, they never connect the blade-bone, or scapula, with the breast-bone, as they do in the Primates and Insectivora (except the *Potamogalidæ*). The teeth, which are divisible into the ordinary four series, are generally well-developed; the number of incisors being usually three on each side of both jaws, and the outer pair, especially in the upper jaw, is considerably longer than either of the other two. The canines almost invariably form large tusks; and the more anterior, or the whole of the cheek-teeth have compressed and pointed crowns, frequently consisting of one large central cone, supported by a smaller cusp in front and behind. In the terrestrial Carnivora the last premolar in the upper, and the first molar in the lower jaw, are specially modified to bite against one another with a scissor-like action, and are accordingly spoken of as the carnassial, or sectorial teeth. These teeth attain their maximum specialisation and perfection among the cats: whereas in the bears and some of the raccoon family their sectorial character is much less marked, although it is still noticeable. On the other hand, in the seals and walruses all the cheek-teeth are nearly alike, and are generally cusped and sharp-pointed throughout the series, although blunt in the latter family. The modification of the limbs into flippers affords, however, an easy method of distinguishing the whole of the seal group from other Mammals. As a rule, when the number of cheek-teeth is reduced below the normal, the reduction takes place at the hinder, or molar end of the series, whereas in most other Mammals it is the anterior premolars that tend to disappear.

In the skull of all Carnivores the lower jaw is articulated by a transversely-extended sub-cylindrical condyle, clasped in front and behind by two overlapping processes from the skull itself, which are sometimes so prominent as (in the badger) to prevent the dislocation of the lower jaw without fracturing the bone. Very generally, the socket of the eye is freely open behind, although in certain cats and the mungooses it is surrounded by a complete bony ring. The zygomatic arch, so frequently absent in the Insectivora, is almost invariably well developed in the present order. A peculiarity in the wrist-joint of all the Carnivora is that the two bones known as the scaphoid and lunar, forming the inner and upper elements of the upper row of this part of the skeleton in other Mammals, are here fused together to form but a single bone. Moreover, the central bone of the wrist, which is present in all the Primates, save man and some of the man-like apes in the Carnivora, is invariably lacking. From the Insectivora the Carnivora are further distinguished by the numerous convolutions on the surface of the large hemispheres of the brain.

The Cat Tribe.—Family *Felidæ*.

In common with the three following families of the terrestrial Carnivora, the cats are distinguished from the other members of the order by certain very important structural features connected with the hinder part of the base of the skull. In all these families that chamber of the inner ear known as the auditory bulla forms a thin bladder-like expansion, divided (except in the hyænas) into two compartments by a vertical bony partition; while the bony auditory meatus, or tube, leading into this bulla, is remarkable for its shortness. From their allies, existing cats are distinguished by the strong development of the canine teeth, by the molar teeth never exceeding one pair in both the upper and lower jaws, and also by the three pairs of incisors occupying the same transverse line, instead of the middle pair being pushed up above the level of the other two. The single upper molar is a flat functionless tooth, with its crown considerably wider than long, and placed on the inner side of the upper carnassial, which consists of three distinct lobes. The lower molar, or carnassial, is a highly specialised tooth, usually consisting solely of a two-lobed cutting blade, although in a few species a small ledge on its hinder surface represents the large heel characterising the same tooth in most other members of the order. There are three upper and two lower premolars; the last in the upper jaw being the carnassial, and the first small and functionless. The skull, in conformity with the shape of the head, is characterised by the shortness of its facial portion and the great width of the zygomatic arches. The general form of the cats is too well known to need description; but it may be mentioned that the fur is generally thick and close, and that its markings usually take the form either of dark transverse stripes, spots, rosettes, or dark-margined cloudings on a lighter ground. As a rule, the tail is long, cylindrical, and tapering; while it is very frequently marked with dark and light rings. In the extreme elongation of the body, a few cats, like the South American eyra, approximate to the civet-tribe; but, in most cases, the body is of moderate length, and the limbs by no means remarkably short. All cats have five front and four hind toes, the first front toe being raised above the others. They walk on the tips of their toes, in the digitigrade manner; and in the great majority the claws are capable of complete retraction within hollow horny sheaths, by specially arranged muscles, and are thus always kept sharp and fit for use. In the hunting-leopard this, however, is not the case, and that animal is accordingly referred to a genus apart from the one containing the whole of the other species. The tongue of cats is remarkable for the rough rasping papillæ with which its upper surface is coated; and in the eye the pupil, when contracted, frequently assumes the form of a vertical slit.

With the exception of New Guinea, Australia and New Zealand, cats have a world-wide distribution, and inhabit all climates and stations, save the extreme north.

The typical cats (*Felis*), which include about forty-six different species, and have a distribution co-extensive with that of the family, are characterised by the claws being capable of withdrawal into the aforesaid protecting sheaths, and likewise by the presence of a distinct tubercle on the inner side of the upper carnassial tooth. The largest and most powerful members of the genus are the lion (*F. leo*), common to Africa, Persia, and India, although rapidly disappearing from the latter country; the tiger (*F. tigris*), ranging from India to China and Siberia, although unknown in Ceylon; the leopard or panther (*F. pardus*), also common to Asia and Africa; the snow-leopard, or ounce (*F. uncia*) of Central Asia; the jaguar (*F. onca*) of South and Central America; and the puma (*F. concolor*), which has the widest range in latitude of any animal, extending from the south of Patagonia to the Great Slave Lake. Of these, the lion and puma are uniformly tawny-coloured species, although showing traces of spots in the young state and sometimes in certain lights even in the adult; the male lion being distinguished from all other members of the genus by the large mane (which may be dark coloured), covering the head, neck, and shoulders, and the tuft at the tip of the tail, in which is a small horny claw of unknown function. The tiger has double transverse black stripes on an orange or tawny ground; while all the other species named are marked by dark rosettes or rings on a light ground. In both the leopard and jaguar the central portion of the rosette is darker than the general ground colour of the fur; but whereas in the former the rosettes form simple rings, in the latter there is one or more solid black spots in the centre. On the head and limbs the spots are solid, and the tail is ornamented with rings. In the ounce the fur is much longer than that of the ordinary leopard, and the Siberian variety of the tiger differs in the same manner from Indian examples. Although the lion is a much noisier animal than the tiger, in power, size, and habits, the two are very similar. It would be out of place to enter into any detailed discussion as to the dimensions of either lions or tigers, as this has been fully investigated in other works. In regard to tigers, it may, however, be mentioned, that it is now generally admitted that males do occasionally reach, or even slightly exceed 12 feet in total length, measured along the curves of the body in what is termed sportsman's style; one shot by Colonel Boileau in 1861 being slightly over 12 feet, while General Sir C. Reid's tiger, exhibited in London stuffed in 1862, is recorded to have measured 12 feet 2 inches as it lay on the ground. Further information is required as to the maximum weights attained by male tigers. Sanderson gives the weight of a well-grown male shot by himself as 350 pounds; while Elliot has recorded examples respectively weighing 362 and 380 pounds. The late Captain J. Forsyth has, however, estimated the weights of tigers killed by himself at from 450 to 500 pounds, and these large weights have been confirmed of late years by Mr. Hornaday, who, in his work, "Two Years in the Jungle," records a tiger of 9 feet 11½ inches in length, which weighed upwards of 495 pounds; while the Maharajah of Cuch Behar has given weights varying from 540 to 481 pounds, and a tiger killed by Mr. F. A. Shillingford, measuring 9 feet 10 inches, weighed 528 pounds. One killed by Sir Samuel Baker weighed 437

Fig. 30.—THE LION.

pounds after losing about a gallon of blood, so that its whole weight was probably about 447 pounds. Of course, much depends upon how fat the animal is at the time of its death. Sir S. Baker estimating that, while a very fine tiger in average condition will weigh some 440 pounds, the same animal, when unusually fat, will scale 500 pounds. If, however, a tiger just under 10 feet in length will weigh about 500 pounds, it may be safely assumed that an 11 or 12 feet example in similar condition will considerably exceed this weight, and it is, therefore, probable that the maximum weight attained by the tiger has yet to be recorded. It is accordingly earnestly to be desired that sportsmen will not only measure, but will likewise weigh any unusually large tigers they may have the good fortune to kill.

Those who have the opportunity of seeing an attack by a tiger on large animals like buffalo or gaur, which he is unable to overthrow, will do good service if they can throw any light on the mode of attack in those instances where the prey is hamstrung. Mr. Blanford considers that in this occasional mode of attack the hamstringing is probably effected by a blow from the claws, and states that he has known two instances where buffaloes were left hamstrung by tigers. This mode of attack being apparently very rare, will of course be seldom seen by European eyes, so that should it come under notice a record will be of extreme value.

As a rule, however, it is believed that a tiger seizes large animals by the fore-quarters, throwing one paw over the shoulder, and attacking the throat with the jaws ; a sudden upward wrench, during which the destroyer often springs to the opposite side of his victim, serving to dislocate the neck. On the other hand, some writers are of opinion that the tiger first seizes the animal by the back of the neck. Thus Sir S. Baker writes that "the attack of a large tiger is terrific, and the effect may well be imagined of an animal of such vast muscular proportions, weighing between 400 and 500 pounds, springing with great velocity and exerting its momentum at the instant that it seizes a bullock by the neck. It is supposed by the natives that the tiger, when well fastened upon the crest, by fixing its teeth in the back of the neck at the first onset, continues its spring, so as to pass over the animal attacked. This wrenches the neck suddenly round, and as the animal struggles, the dislocation is easily effected ; the tiger then changes the hold to underneath the throat, and drags the body to some convenient retreat, where the meal may be commenced in security. With very few exceptions, the tiger breaks the neck of every animal it kills."

Fig. 31.—The Tiger.

Another observer, Mr. Mervyn Smith, who had the good fortune to see two buffaloes killed by a tiger, writes as follows :—"The animals, when first seen by me, were about a hundred yards off, and a little to my left front. There was a distance of perhaps ten yards between them. I noticed the farthest buffalo suddenly stumble and fall, as I thought, but it did not rise again ; its mate looked up and gazed in the direction of its companion, and then turned its head as if to flee, but before it could do so a dark object rose out of the ground, as it were, and seized it by the throat, and flung it on its side. My horse had also caught sight of the dark object, and instinct told him at once what it was, for he galloped like mad, and never stopped till he got to the bungalow. It was fully an hour before I could assemble the villagers and return to the spot, where we found both buffaloes stone dead. In both cases the bite was on the under part of the throat, so as to close the windpipe and prevent the animal making any cry. The necks also appeared to have been broken by a sudden wrench of the head to one side, by the tremendously powerful fore-arm of the tiger. There appeared to have been very little struggle, and death must have been almost instantaneous. Now, what I would particularly like to draw attention to, is the stealthy method of attack. There was absolutely no noise—no roar, scarcely a rustling of the bushes when the second animal was struck down—and very little of the tiger to be seen. Had not my eyes been on the buffaloes at the time, I hardly think I should have been disturbed at all. In fact, I should not have known that the buffaloes had been killed by a tiger within a few yards of me. I scarcely saw the tiger at all—only his head, which appeared to rise up out of the ground and seize the second buffalo by the throat." A tiger almost invariably commences his meal on the hind-quarters ; and neither this animal nor the lion are by any means averse to carrion. Both have a very similar roar, although that of the tiger is but rarely uttered ; and both differ from the majority of cats in their inability to climb trees. In common with cats in general, lions and tigers go about either singly, in pairs, or in small family parties, and although a few may, it is said, combine to drive their prey to one another, they never hunt in packs after the manner of dogs. The stealthy manner in which cats stalk, with their body elongated to its utmost extent and almost touching the ground, and the rigid tail occasionally twisting nervously, is well known to all.

Among the smaller species of the genus, the clouded leopard (*F. nebulosa*) and the marbled cat (*F. marmorata*), of the Oriental countries, may be cited as excellent examples of the clouded type of coloration. The Bornean Bay cat (*F. badia*) is one of the few uniformly-coloured species; a second being the South American eyra (*F. eyra*), which is more remarkable on account of its elongated and weasel-like form. One of the most variable of all is the Oriental leopard-cat (*F. bengalensis*). The African serval (*F. serval*) is a long-legged and short-tailed species, in which the dark spots are solid ; while the caffer cat (*F. caffra*) of the same country is generally regarded as the ancestral stock of the domestic cats of Europe, although there has probably been a considerable amount of crossing with the wild cat (*F. catus*), which has led to the prevalence of the tabby type of coloration. In South America the very variable ocelot (*F. pardalis*) exhibits a modification of the clouded type of coloration, while the tiger-cat (*F. tigrina*) is more distinctly spotted; the pampas cat showing a striped pattern. The jungle-cat (*F. chaus*), which is common to India and Africa, together with certain allied Asiatic species, forms a transition from the more typical cats to the lynxes, the latter being characterised by the long pencils of hairs terminating the ears and the moderately long or short tail. In the caracal (*F. caracal*), which is a uniformly-coloured species common to India and Africa, and connecting the jungle-cat with the true lynxes, the tail is of considerable length ; but in the latter group, all the members of which are confined to the Northern Hemisphere, it is very short, and the pellage is always spotted, at least during some portion of the year. Whether the **Canadian lynx** (*F. canadensis*) is distinct from the common lynx (*F. lynx*) of Europe and Northern Asia is a moot point; but the Spanish lynx (*F. pardina*) is a well-marked form.

The slender-bodied and long-limbed cat, known as the hunting-leopard (*Cynælurus jubatus*), is referred to a genus apart from the other members of the family on account of the claws being only partially retractile, although their extremities are protected by sheaths; while a further point of distinction is to be found in the rudimental condition of the tubercle on the inner side of the upper carnassial tooth. The hunting-leopard, which is found both in India and Africa, has the fur marked with solid black spots. In habits it differs somewhat from the true cats—two individuals hunting together, and making a simultaneous sudden rush when their prey comes within striking distance. These animals are kept for hunting in India.

Fig. 32.—SPANISH LYNX (*Felis pardina*).

Civet Tribe.—Family *Viverridæ.*

The nearest allies of the cats are the great tribe of civets, palm-civets, mungooses, etc., all of which differ from the *Felidæ* in that the auditory bulla of the skull is marked by a transverse external constriction, indicating the position of the internal bony septum, while the middle pair of lower teeth are raised above the level of the other two, as in all other land Carnivora. From the living *Felidæ* the *Viverridæ* are further distinguished by the more numerous series of teeth, the number of premolars varying from three to four on each side of the jaws; while there are generally two pairs of molars in each jaw, although occasionally these may be reduced to a single pair in the upper, and very rarely also in the lower jaw. The toes, which may be either digitigrade or plantigrade, are generally five in number on each foot, although they may be reduced to four in either the front or hind pair, or even in both. Considerable difference obtains in regard to the retractibility of the claws, and likewise as to the extent to which the sole of the hind-foot is clothed with hair. From ordinary cats civets differ externally in the more elongated form of the body, the longer head and sharper muzzle, and the shorter legs; although in these respects they are approached by the eyra. In coloration they are generally striped, spotted, or blotched; some of them having distinct longitudinal stripes, which are never seen in the cats. The family is strictly confined to the Old World, exclusive of Australia and Papua, and attains its maximum development in Africa and the Oriental countries—Europe having only a couple of species in its southern districts. Madagascar is the home of several peculiar genera. Upwards of twenty-three distinct generic types are now recognised.

Fossa (*Cryptoprocta*).

The most aberrant of all is the fossa (*Cryptoprocta ferox*) of Madagascar, which in the number and structure of its teeth approaches the cats, and is regarded by many authorities as entitled to constitute a family by itself. In the form of the auditory bulla of the skull this animal is somewhat intermediate between the civets and the mungooses; and each foot has five toes, with completely retractile claws. There are four pairs of premolar teeth, of which the first is shed at an early period, and a single pair of molars, which are cat-like in form, the lower one having only a small posterior ledge, as in the lynxes, and no inner cusp. The nose and upper lip have a median groove; and the feet are sub-plantigrade, the tarsus and metatarsus being naked. The fossa measures about five feet in total length, and is nearly uniform sandy brown in colour.

Fig 33.—THE FOSSA (*Cryptoprocta ferox*).

Together with several allied genera, the true civets (*Viverra*) are characterised by the conical form of the auditory bulla of the skull, in which the hinder border is broad, truncated, and not everted, while in front it is narrow and compressed, with the anterior chamber small. Usually there are highly odoriferous glands in front of the scrotum; and the curved claws are generally more or less retractile. In form and number the teeth come very close to those of the dogs, there being always four pairs of premolars in each jaw. The blade of the upper carnassial tooth differs from that of the cats in consisting of only two lobes, and there is a well-developed tubercle on the inner side of the same tooth; while the lower carnassial is composed of an anterior cutting blade, and a long posterior tuberculated heel. In shape, the upper molars are triangular; the first of the two being placed behind the carnassial tooth, and not on its inner side.

Civet Group.

From the allied genera the true civets are distinguished by the following characters. A vertical groove divides the middle of the upper lip; the rather long tail is ringed dark and light; the feet are completely digitigrade, with the tarsus and metatarsus fully haired; and there are no tufts of hair on the ears. The upper molar teeth are two in number on each side; a black gorget ornaments the throat; an elongated crest of erectile hairs usually runs down the back; and the whole hair is loose and long. The rather short and blunt claws can be only partially retracted; and the pupil of the eye contracts to a circular form. There are five species of civet, one of which (*Viverra civetta*) is African, while the other four are Oriental. Four are of nearly equal size, and may be compared in this respect to a large cat; but the rasse (*Viverra malaccensis*), which differs somewhat in the structure of the skull from the four others, and is referred by many writers to a distinct genus, under the name of *Viverricula*, is a much smaller animal. An inhabitant of India, China, and the Malayan countries, it has been introduced into Madagascar. All civets have comparatively short, stout, and rather compressed bodies, with the limbs proportionately longer than in the allied genera. Their coloration takes the form of black or blackish-brown streaks and blotches on a greyish ground. Most of them are non-arboreal; and all are strong-smelling creatures, one of their secretions being used in perfumery. For the purpose of collecting the perfume, tame civets are kept in cages by the Malays, and their secretion periodically scraped from the pouch with a wooden spoon. Daubenton's civet (*Fossa daubentoni*) of Madagascar closely resembles the above-mentioned rasse in general characters, but differs from all the species of *Viverra* in the presence of two small bare spots on the under surface of the metatarsus; and the scent-pouch is apparently wanting. The limbs are slender; and there is neither a dark line down the back, nor a black gorget on the throat. Nearly allied to the civets are the six species of genets (*Genetta*), five of which are exclusively African, while the ordinary genet is common to Northern Africa, Southern Europe, and Syria. From both *Viverra* and *Fossa* they may be distinguished by the presence of a bare, longitudinal strip along the lower surface of the metatarsus; a hairy space dividing this naked strip from the foot-pads. The absence of a scent-pouch forms a further distinction from *Viverra*, while the presence of a dark stripe down the back constitutes another difference from *Fossa*. All the genets are comparatively small animals, which live chiefly on the ground, where they prey upon small rodents, birds, and eggs. None have a black gorget on the throat, although there may be a short crest of erectile hairs down the back.

The beautifully-coloured Oriental viverroids known as linsangs (*Linsanga*) have the under surface of the tarsus and metatarsus as fully clothed with hair as in the true civets, but differ in possessing only a single pair of upper molar teeth. All the three species are very long-bodied and short-limbed animals, with the claws of the five-toed feet almost as retractile as in the cats; and the fur remarkably short, close, and erect, resembling, in fact, velvet-pile. There are no scent-glands corresponding to those which yield the perfume in the civets. Upon a white or greyish-white ground-colour the fur is beautifully marked with black or dark brown patches, such patches forming either a small number of large, dark areas extending transversely across the body, or being broken up into smaller quadrangle spots. Dark longitudinal streaks, some of which may break up into spots, traverse the neck and shoulders, while there are smaller ones on the head; and the long cylindrical is marked with alternate dark and light rings of considerable length. When contracted, the pupil of the eye is circular. The skull and teeth are very similar to those of the genets, but the heel of the lower carnassial tooth is relatively smaller. In West Africa the linsangs are represented by the closely allied *Poiana poënsis*, distinguished by having a naked strip on the under surface of the metatarsus, as in the genets. Linsangs are good climbers, feeding chiefly on small birds. They produce two litters in a year, giving birth to a pair of young at a time.

The two Malayan species of *Hemigale* differ from all the preceding members of the group except *Fossa* in the absence of distinct rings on the tail, except, at most, near the root; while they are further distinguished by the front of the auditory bulla of the skull being pointed instead of blunt. The carnassials are also relatively smaller and of a less trenchant type. A distinctive feature of the genus is the concentration of the pads of the hind-foot to form a naked space on the metatarsus, ending in a sharp point behind; the tarsus being fully haired. The hair on the back of the neck is peculiar in being directed forwards; and when there are any dark markings on the back they take the form of uninterrupted transverse bands. The claws on the five-toed feet are strongly curved; and the nose and upper lip, as in all the preceding genera, are grooved. Numerically, the teeth are the same as in *Viverra*. Hardwicke's hemigale (*H. hardwickei*), from the Malay Peninsula, Sumatra, and Borneo, measures about 15½ inches to the root of the tail, and has dark transverse bands on the back; whereas *H. hosei*, from the mountains of North Borneo, is uniformly dusky.

The palm-civets form three nearly allied genera, one of which is African, while the other two are Oriental. The two species of African palm-civets (*Nandinia*), one of which is from the west, and the other from the east side of the continent, agree with *Hemigale* in the form of the naked area on the metatarsus, but differ in the incomplete ossification of the auditory bulla of the skull. Otherwise the genus is very similar to the true palm-civets, the marking taking the form of spots, and the tail being ringed. The two species of small-toothed palm-civets (*Arctogale*), from Burma and the Malayan countries, differ from the preceding genus in the uniformly-coloured tail; and are further distinguished by the relatively small size of the teeth, the narrow palate, which is produced far behind the last molar, and the ossification of the bulla of the skull. The dark markings take the form of longitudinal rows of stripes or spots on the back. Represented by ten species, the true palm-civets (*Paradoxurus*) range throughout the Oriental countries from India to the Philippines and Celebes, and are distinguished from the last by their larger teeth, the less prolongation of the palate backwards, and the presence of a naked glandular area in front of the scrotum of the males, and in a similar position in the females. Like *Arctogale*, they have the whole of the metatarsus and a considerable portion of the tarsus bare, the hair extending in an evenly curved line across the hinder part of the heel. The claws of the five-toed feet are as curved and retractile as in the genets; the tail is long and generally not ringed; the markings are usually in the form of elongated streaks, although more rarely spots, but some species are uniformly coloured; and the pupil of the eye contracts to a vertical slit. The teeth are numerically the same as in *Viverra*, but the carnassials relatively shorter and less trenchant. In size these animals may be compared to an ordinary cat. Palm-civets are essentially nocturnal and arboreal creatures, feeding upon small birds, mammals, eggs, and lizards, and frequently taking up their abode among the leaves of palm-trees, From their habit of drinking the palm-juice, or toddy, from the vessels suspended from the trees for its reception, they are termed toddy-cats.

Fig. 24.—PALM-CIVET (*Paradoxurus*).

From all other members of the family, the binturong (*Arctictis binturong*), ranging from the Eastern Himalaya to the Malayan countries and Siam, differs by its prehensile tail and tufted ears, as well as by the tarsus and metatarsus of the plantigrade hind-feet being completely naked. The ears are short, the short claws only partially retractile, the hair very long, coarse, and loose, and the long tail very bushy; the general colour being black. The binturong, which may be compared in size to a cat, is a thoroughly nocturnal and arboreal creature.

Fig. 35.—THE BINTURONG (*Arctictis binturong*).

The last member of the sub-family is the peculiar Bennett's civet (*Cynogale bennetti*) from the Malay Peninsula, Sumatra, and Borneo, which is a grizzled grey animal, readily distinguished from all the foregoing by the absence of a groove on the nose and upper lip, the short tail, the partially webbed feet, and by the under surface of the metatarsus and tarsus being somewhat less naked. In size it may be compared to the larger civets, the length of the head and body being about 32 inches. Its habits are believed to be partially aquatic.

With the exception of the fossa, which forms a sub-family by itself, the whole of the foregoing members of the family constitute the sub-family *Viverrinæ*, characterised by the features noticed above.

The Mungoose Group. The mungooses, or ichneumons, are the first representatives of a second sub-family (*Herpestinæ*) presenting the following distinctive characters. The auditory bulla of the skull is pear-shaped, and its hinder margin distinctly everted, with the so-called paroccipital process not projecting beyond, but spread over it, and in the adult becoming merged in its hinder surface. The claws are long and non-retractile; and there are no glands in front of the scrotum. As a genus, the mungooses may be distinguished from their allies by the presence of five toes to each foot, a vertical groove on the nose, and usually four pairs of premolar teeth; the molars being, as usual, two in each jaw. The muzzle is sharply pointed, the body long and weasel-like, the legs very short, the ears short and rounded; and the tail generally long and tapering, with loose, elongated hair. The feet are plantigrade; but there is much variation in the extent of the bare portion of the soles of the hind ones; in some species this area extending back to the heel, while in others the lower surface of the tarsus is hairy. The coarse and loose fur has a peculiar speckled appearance, owing to the presence of dark and light rings on the hairs, and the tail is never ringed. The sharp cusps of the cheek-teeth are in marked contrast to the bluntly-cusped ones of the palm-civets; and the skull is remarkable for a sharp constriction behind the sockets of the eyes, and likewise for the circumstance that the latter generally have a complete bony ring. Mungooses range over Africa and the Oriental countries as far as the Philippines, the Egyptian species (*H. ichneumon*) entering Southern Europe. All these animals are terrestrial, and very active in their habits, generally living in holes. They are deadly enemies to rats and other Rodents, as they are to snakes. The most venomous serpents are attacked without hesitation, the immunity of the mungoose from harm in such encounters being apparently due to its extreme activity and watchfulness. From the majority of species of *Herpestes*, the African small mungoose (*Helogale parva*) differs in having only three pairs of premolar teeth in each jaw; the first of these being approximated to the canine, and thus distinguishing the genus from the few species of *Herpestes* with a similar number of teeth, in all of which there is a gap between the canine and the first tooth of the premolar series.

Africa is the home of several peculiar generic types of mungooses. First, there are the three species of four-toed mungooses (*Bdeogale*), distinguished by having but four toes to each foot; the soles of the hind-feet being hairy. The South African pencilled mungoose (*Cynictis penicillata*) is the sole member of another genus with five front and four hind toes; but more easily defined by the presence of a hole in the centre of the peculiarly-shaped auditory bulla of the skull, the soles of the hind-feet being hairy. A third genus is represented by the large red Meller's mungoose (*Rhynchogale melleri*)), easily distinguished from all the preceding members of the sub-family by the absence of a vertical groove on the nose and upper lip. Each foot is furnished with five toes, there are four pairs of premolar teeth in each jaw, and the under surface of the tarsus and metatarsus is hairy. The fourth African genus (*Crossarchus*) contains the five species of cusimanses, which while resembling the last in the absence of a groove on the muzzle, differ by having only three pairs of premolar teeth in each jaw, the flat bony palate of the skull, and the naked soles of the hinder portion of the hind-feet. Several of the species, such as *C. fasciatus*, have a number of dark transverse bands across the back. Lastly, the pretty little meerkat (*Suricata tetradactyla*) of South Africa differs from all the other smooth-nosed mungooses in having only four toes to each foot, and is further characterised by possessing three pairs of upper, and four of lower premolars, as well as by the naked under surface of the whole of the tarsus and metatarsus. The muzzle is sharp, the front claws are very long, and the profile of the face is convex. The general colour of the fur is light grizzled grey, with black bands across the hinder part of the back, and a black ring round each eye. Meerkats measure from 14 to 15 inches to the root of the tail; and are vivacious little animals, living in holes in colonies, and coming out to air themselves in the sun, when they survey passers-by with a peculiarly inquisitive expression.

Fig. 36.—BANDED MUNGOOSE (*Crossarchus fasciatus*).

Madagascar Mungooses.

The Island of Madagascar is inhabited by four peculiar genera of mungooses, three of which are more or less closely related to the *Herpestinæ*, while the fourth certainly forms a sub-family by itself. From all other members of the *Viverridæ*, the two species of striped mungoose are distinguished by the numerous continuous dark stripes running down the whole length of the back and sides. They have but three pairs of premolar teeth in each jaw, the first of which is placed close to the canine; and the canines themselves are of large size. The five-toed feet have longer claws than in the typical mungooses; the muzzle is grooved inferiorly; the tail is covered with elongated hairs; and the under surface of the tarsus is bare. From the last, the elegant mungoose (*Galidia elegans*) may be distinguished by the smaller size of the lower canine teeth, the presence of short sparse hairs on the lower surface of the tarsus and metatarsus, the uniform coloration of the body, and the ringed tail. The two species of brown-tailed mungoose (*Hemigalidia*) differ from the preceding by the presence of four pairs of premolars in each jaw, the larger size of the second upper molar, the uniformly-coloured tail, the more pointed form of the muzzle, and the smaller degree of curvature of the claws.

Finally, there is the small-toothed mungoose (*Eupleres goudoti*), distinguished from all other mungooses by the non-eversion of the hinder border of the auditory bulla of the skull, and from the rest of the family by its very remarkable dentition. The canines are minute, and like the first three premolars, which are widely separated from one another, and the molars are but little different from the premolars. Indeed, the whole dentition is strikingly like that of an Insectivore, and there can be little doubt that this highly modified mungoose subsists entirely or chiefly on insects.

The Aard-Wolf.—Family *Proteleidæ.*

A peculiar hyæna-like animal from Africa, known to the Dutch as the aard-wolf, and scientifically as *Proteles cristatus*, is regarded as representing a family by itself, distinguished by having the auditory bulla of the skull divided by a septum into two chambers, and by the small and degraded characters of the cheek-teeth, among which there is but a single pair of molars in each jaw. In the fore-feet there are five toes, but in the hinder pair the number is reduced to four; their claws being strong, blunt, and non-retractile. In appearance, the aard-wolf is curiously like a small striped hyæna, with a more pointed muzzle, longer ears, and a thick mane of elongated erectile hair along the neck and back. Common in South Africa, this animal has also been recorded from Angola and Somaliland. It feeds on carrion, grubs, and white ants.

Fig. 37.—AARD-WOLF (*Proteles cristatus*).

The Hyænas.-Family *Hyænidæ.*

From the two preceding families the hyænas, of which all the three existing species may be included in the single genus *Hyæna*, differ by the absence of any internal partition in the auditory bulla of the skull. In the living species there is only one pair of molar teeth in each jaw, the upper one being small, and placed on the inner side of the carnassial. The latter tooth resembles the upper carnassial of the cats in having three distinct lobes to the blade; and the lower carnassial has a bi-lobed blade and a very small posterior heel. All the teeth are very strong and powerful; the anterior premolars being in the form of blunt cones; and the skull, in which the sockets of the eyes are freely open behind, is remarkable for the great height of the crest on the middle of the upper part. The limbs are somewhat elongated, especially the front pair; the tail is relatively short; and the fur is loose and long.

In appearance, hyænas are the most ungainly of all Carnivora, and thereby present a marked contrast to the cats. They are nocturnal, gregarious, and cowardly, feeding chiefly on carrion and carcases; and being generally unable or indisposed to kill the larger animals for themselves, feast on the remnants of carcases left by lions and tigers. For cracking the bones of such derelicts their powerful teeth and strong jaw-muscles are most admirably adapted.

The striped hyæna (*H. striata*) of India, South-West Asia, and North and East Africa, is easily recognised by its transversely striped pellage, long fur, which forms a mane on the shoulders and back, and large pointed ears. The teeth are characterised by the relatively large size of the upper molar and by the lower carnassial having a heel of considerable size, and a cusp on the inner side of the blade. The brown hyæna (*H. brunnea*) of South

Africa, although nearly allied, has some points of resemblance to the third species. The largest and most powerful of all is the spotted hyæna (*H. crocuta*), now confined to South Africa, and characterised by the spotted coloration of the body, smaller proportionate length of the fore-limbs, large head, with moderate-sized and rounded ears, the presence of a mane on the neck and back, and the smoother and shorter tail. The last upper molar tooth is very small, or even wanting, and the lower carnassial has no inner cusp and a very small posterior heel, thus closely approaching the corresponding tooth of the cats.

Fig. 38.—SPOTTED HYÆNA (*Hyæna crocuta*).

The Dog Tribe.—Family *Canidæ*.

As regards the auditory bulla and adjacent regions of the skull, the Dog Tribe are in many respects intermediate between the preceding group of families and those which follow. The bulla itself is inflated and bladder-like, but has no internal partition; and the paroccipital process, although in contact with the bulla, is prominent, and not applied to it, as it is in the cats and civets. Another distinctive feature of the group is the presence of a long and coiled cœcum, or blind appendage, at the junction of the large and small intestine; that appendage being either very small or absent in the preceding families. The crowns of the upper molar teeth are triangular in shape; and these teeth, which are nearly always two in number, are situated behind the carnassial. The latter tooth, as in the civets, has two lobes to the blade; and the lower carnassial generally has a large tubercular heel behind the blade, and a well-developed cusp on its inner side. In most cases there are three lower molars (of which the carnassial is the first), whereas in the civets there are never more than two of these teeth; and there are always four pairs of premolar teeth in each jaw. Dogs, under which title may be included wolves, jackals, and foxes, have a cosmopolitan distribution, and differ markedly in their habits from the cats. Although a few will run up the stems of sloping trees, none are climbers; and many consort in packs to hunt their prey by scent. Many form burrows in the ground; and while they are more or less carnivorous, some will supplement a flesh diet with fruits, insects, or garbage. All walk on the tips of their toes, and are thus digitigrade; and the claws are short, blunt, slightly curved, and non-retractile.

Typical Genus.

By far the great majority of the members of the family may be included in the genus *Canis*, which has a geographical distribution equal in extent to that of the former. It is characterised by the general presence of 42 teeth, and there are five front and four hind toes. The tail is of moderate length or long, and generally more or less bushy; and the pupil of the eye may contract either to a vertical slit or a circle. The general form is too well known to require description. The genus may be divided, from the characters of the skull, into two primary series, the first typified by the wolves, and the second by the foxes.

This series includes the wolves, jackals, and wild dogs, together with the domesticated breeds, and is best characterised by the circumstance that the postorbital process of the frontal bone, that is to say the one forming the hinder boundary of the socket of the eye, has its superior surface smooth and convex, and its free extremity bent downwards.

Wolf-like Series. In this group the wolves are the largest wild representatives; the common wolf (*C. lupus*) ranging over the northern portions of both the Old and New Worlds. There are no wolves either in Africa or South America, although it is curious that the so-called Antarctic wolf (*C. antarcticus*) of the Falkland Islands appears to belong to the group. In Asia there are several wolves, although none are found in the countries to the east and south-east of the Bay of Bengal, and there is some difference of opinion as to their relationship to the common wolf. With regard to the wolf inhabiting the plains of India, most persons not specially versed in the mysteries of zoology would probably be unable to distinguish it from its European cousin, unless specimens were placed side by side, and even then would find some difficulty. It appears, however, that there are certain differences in the habits of the two animals, which suggest the probability of their specific distinctness from one another. For instance, the Indian wolf is remarkable for its silence, only very rarely, if ever, uttering the well-known howl of the common species; although it is stated that it will occasionally bark, after the manner of a pariah dog. Then, again, Indian wolves, although sometimes found in small family parties of half-a-dozen or so, are never known to collect in the enormous packs which make the European species so dreaded in winter. It is probable that these differences in habits would not by themselves alone be regarded as sufficient to establish the right of the Indian wolf to rank as a distinct species. When, however, it is found that there are in addition certain points by which the two animals can be distinguished from one another, these differences in habits become of importance in adding to their distinctness. The Indian wolf is, indeed, a somewhat smaller and slighter animal than the European species, the average difference in the length of the two animals being about six inches. Then, also, the hair is rather shorter, and there is little or no under-fur; while the colour is generally rather more inclined to brown than in the common wolf. The absence of under-fur in the Indian wolf might, we think, be well explained by the hotter climate in which it dwells; but, in spite of this, naturalists are probably right in regarding it as a distinct species, under the name of *Canis pallipes*.

Fig. 39.—Common Wolf.

The Indian wolf does not range into the Himalaya, neither is it found to the westward of the Indus, or in Ceylon. That island seems, indeed, to enjoy a happy immunity from the presence of several of the larger Indian Carnivora, as it has neither wolves, wild dogs, hyænas nor tigers. In the case of the tiger it has been attempted to account for this absence by the suggestion that this animal is but a comparatively recent immigrant into India from the north, and had not reached that country at the time Ceylon was united with the mainland. If this were so, it would seem, however, that the same explanation ought to hold good for hyænas and wolves; but as both the latter are known to have been well represented in India in the later geological epochs, some other reason must apparently be sought, at least, in their cases.

It is difficult to leave the Indian wolf without referring to the subject of wolf-nurtured children. Many of the stories relating to these have been brought together by Professor V. Ball, in his "Jungle Life in India," where it is related that in all the recorded instances the children were boys, and that the greater number of cases have occurred in Oude. Many persons refuse to attach any credence to such stories, but Mr. Ball strongly urges a suspension of judgment until further evidence be attained. If such stories be really based on fact, we can only look to Europeans who are stationed or travelling in the wilder parts of India to bring to light decisive evidence in support of any new cases that may occur.

Fig. 40.—INDIAN WOLF (*Canis pallipes*).

It has been already mentioned that the Indian wolf does not extend westward of the Indus; and in Sind, Baluchistan, and Gilgit its place is taken by the European wolf, which not improbably may also range into the northern part of the Punjab. Large wolves, distinguished by their long soft hair and pale colour, are common on the farther side of the snowy range in Ladak and Tibet, where they are known to the natives by the name of *Changu*. These Tibetan wolves have been generally regarded as a distinct species, described as *Canis laniger* or *chanco*, and considered to be more nearly allied to the Indian than to the European wolf. It seems, however, that this view is incorrect, and that the Tibetan wolf is nothing more than a pale-coloured and woolly-haired variety of the common wolf. Occasionally long-haired black wolves are met with in Tibet, which have been regarded as indicating yet another species (*C. niger*). There is, however, no doubt but that these are merely varieties of the ordinary Tibetan wolf, similar to the dark variety of the short-haired wolf of Europe. It is to a considerable extent for the purposes of protecting their flocks against the ravages of wolves that Tibetan villages and encampments are guarded by the huge mastiffs, which not unfrequently make themselves so extremely unpleasant to the European visitor.

The following interesting account of the habits of wolves in Norway, where these animals are still abundant, is given by a writer in the *Asian* newspaper of August 19th, 1893:—

"The pairing-season occurs in February, and in nine weeks the female brings forth her young. When the time of birth approaches, the mother retires to the most remote and unfrequented parts of the forest, where in some cleft or cave in the rocks, surrounded by close undergrowth, she conceals her offspring. These remain blind for ten or eleven days, and for six or eight weeks are nourished by the mother, but when only a month old they leave the den for short distances, and play about with one another like puppies. The she-wolf is a good mother, and as long as her young are small she never goes any great distance from them, and they remain with her till the pairing-season comes round again, when they themselves are capable of procreation. At first they are dark coloured, the end of the tail being black, but after they have got to be about a couple of feet in length they are of a yellowish-grey, of a darker shape on the back, and have a black muzzle.

"During the summer months wolves are partial to extensive woodland solitudes, especially those interspersed with mossy tarns and streams. In winter, on the other hand, especially during severe cold and rough weather, they tend towards the more inhabited and open districts. Wolves always make their excursions at night, and between sunset and sunrise they frequently cover great distances; while during the day they rest in close covert. When pressed by hunger, in extreme cold, when they leave or are returning to their young, or when they have been deprived of these, they send forth long-drawn and melancholy howls. In woods, and generally speaking, in narrow surroundings, wolves are cowardly and cunning; while on extensive plains or tracts of ice, where they can see about them, they are much more courageous, especially when in company; but even under such circumstances they rarely assume the offensive towards man. In districts frequented by these animals they have certain paths which they almost invariably follow, and so closely do they keep in one another's tracks it is difficult to say that more than one has passed. In going to and from the place where the young are concealed they invariably follow the same route, and so a regular beaten track is formed. Only when in droves will they attack the larger animals, such as the elk; at first they steal as near their victim as possible, and endeavour to seize it by making long bounds; failing in this, they set about running it down, two or three following the hunted beast closely, the rest trying to cut it off, or by lying in wait and springing at its throat. If captured when quite young, wolves remain comparatively tame for some time, but their savage nature generally breaks out ere long, and they cannot be depended on."

Of other species, the North American coyote (*C. latrans*) is a smaller form, with very long hair, which appears to connect the true wolves with the jackals. The latter animals are really nothing more than small wolves, and usually have the bushy tail equal to about one-third the length of the head and body. The common jackal (*C. aureus*) extends from Burma and India through South-Western Asia to South-Eastern Europe and North Africa; but is replaced in Africa south of the Sahara by several allied forms, such as the side-striped jackal (*C. adustus*) and the handsome black-backed jackal (*C. mesomelas*). The dingo (*C. dingo*) of Australia is generally reckoned as a domesticated species, but there is considerable evidence that it existed in Australia previous to the advent of men.

Most sportsmen who have shot in India, whether in the plains or in the hills, are probably more or less familiar with those animals commonly known as wild dogs. Although they are not often seen actually hunting their prey, yet they may not unfrequently be met with when shooting in or near forests; while in the hills the frightened and disturbed condition of ibex and other large game will often indicate their presence in a district where it would otherwise be unsuspected. Like many of the colloquial names applied to animals, the term wild dogs by which these creatures are generally known is an exceedingly inappropriate one, because it is just this particular group of dog-like animals which differs more from ordinary dogs than do most others of the larger *Canidæ*. It would indeed be far better if wolves and jackals were spoken of as "wild dogs," since it is those members of the family which come closest to our domestic dogs, of some of which they are probably the parent stock. In such cases, however, it is utterly hopeless for the naturalist to attempt to fight against popular usage, and we must accordingly be content to accept the ordinary names for the animals under consideration.

All who have ever seen an Indian wild dog, whether in the flesh or stuffed, will not be likely to mistake it for any other member of the canine family. In size it is somewhat larger than a jackal of average dimensions, and is characterised by the generally ruddy colour of the hair, and especially by the black tip of the moderately long and bushy tail. Moreover, the muzzle and legs are relatively rather short in comparison with the size of the head and body; while the profile of the face differs from that of other canine animals by being slightly convex instead of concave or straight.

The reader may ask whether such characteristics as the above offer any justification for the objection to the term wild dog as applied to these animals; and if it were these alone on which naturalists rely, he would be perfectly justified in so doing. To obtain, however, any true ideas as to the relationships of an animal, we are compelled not only to study its colour and proportions, but likewise to take into consideration its skeleton and other parts of its organisation. Now, if we take the skull of a wild dog and compare the number of teeth in the lower jaw with those of a wolf, jackal, or fox, we shall find an important point of difference. In the lower jaws of all the three animals last mentioned, and also in those of domestic dogs, we shall find that there are 11 teeth on each side; the eleventh being the smallest of all those situated behind the tusk. If, on the other hand, we examine the lower jaw of any wild dog, we shall find that the small eleventh tooth is wanting, so that there are only 10 lower teeth. A wild dog has, indeed, only 10 teeth on each side of both the upper and lower jaws, whereas in dogs, wolves, jackals, and foxes there are 10 upper and 11 lower teeth. We have here, therefore, an easily recognised point of distinction between a wild dog and most other members of the family. There are, however, two African and one South American representatives of the family, which, while differing from the ordinary type as regards the number of their teeth, have no intimate connection with the wild dogs. A difference of one tooth more or less in the lower jaws of different members of the family may not appear a very important one—and to a certain extent it is not so. But it at any rate serves to show that wild dogs cannot possibly be the parents of any of our domestic breeds of dogs, since it is a well ascertained fact that when once a tooth has been lost in any group of animals it never reappears (unless it may be as an occasional abnormality) in their descendants. Another point of distinction between wild dogs and other members of the family is that there are either 12 or 14 teats in place of the usual 10.

Relying on the two points of difference last noticed, many naturalists have considered that wild dogs ought not to be included in the same genus as wolves and jackals, and the former have accordingly been described under a separate generic title, as *Cuon*, or more correctly *Cyon*, from the Greek name for a dog. Such a distinction appears, however, unnecessary, and it is preferable to include wolves, jackals, foxes, and wild dogs under the common title of *Canis*.

As regards their distribution, wild dogs are found in India, Burma, Siam, and the Malayan Peninsula and islands; while in Central Asia they extend as far northwards as the Altai Mountains, which divide Mongolia from Siberia, and as far westwards as Amurland, and the Isle of Saghalien in the Sea of Okhotsk. It is, however, somewhat curious that, so far as our information goes, these animals are quite unknown both in Northern China and Japan. Wild dogs are, therefore, at the present day exclusively confined to Asia, where they do not appear to extend eastwards of the longitude of the Ural Mountains. This distribution will, however, only hold good for the present epoch, since there have been found in the caves of various parts of Europe lower jaws of canine animals agreeing with those of living wild dogs in having 10 instead of 11 teeth; and we shall, therefore, be justified in considering at or about the time when the mammoth flourished that wild dogs hunted over Europe as they do at the present day in Asia. The circumstances of the occurrence at a former epoch in Europe of a group of animals, now confined to Asia is by no means an isolated one, since there is evidence that at still earlier periods of the earth's history deer, like the muntjac and spotted deer of India, and long-snouted crocodiles akin to the garials of the Ganges and Borneo, flourished in various parts of Europe. All these facts in distribution seem, indeed, to point to the conclusion that Asia has served as a kind of refuge for groups of animals which, for some reason or another, were unable to exist any longer in Europe.

Naturalists have long been exercised as to whether the wild dog of the Himalaya was identical with that of the plains of India, and also whether one or both of these could be distinguished from the wild dog of Burma and the Malayan islands. In many works the wild dog of India and the Himalaya will be found alluded to by the name of *Cyon rutilans*—a name properly belonging to the Malayan form. These writers probably derived their information from the late Dr. Jerdon, who in his "Indian Mammals" included the Malayan, Indian, and Himalayan forms under this single name. Colonel Sykes had, however, long before separated the Indian wild dog under the name of *C. dukhunensis*, while for the Himalayan form Hodgson proposed the name of *C. primævus*. Mr. Blanford, who states that he can find no difference between the wild dog of the Himalaya and that of the plains of India, considers that these are probably distinct from the kind found in Burma and the Malayan region. The difference between the two is, however, very slight; but the Himalayan and Indian species (*C. deccanensis*) is a rather larger and stouter animal, with longer hair, and a woolly under-fur, and the general colour varying from a ferruginous red to tawny; while the Burmese and Malayan species (*C. rutilans*) is smaller and slighter, with shorter hair, no under-fur, and a brighter colour. The Indian species extends to the north-west as far as Gilgit and Hunza, from whence it ranges eastwards through Ladak into Tibet. Curiously enough, it is found that this wild dog is quite distinct from the species inhabiting the Altai (*C. alpinus*) which has much larger upper molar teeth. This, as Mr. Blanford well observes, is a most remarkable feature in distribution, for whereas most of the animals of the Himalaya, like the ibex and the great Tibetan sheep, are either identical with or closely related to those of the Altai and adjacent regions, here we have a case where the Himalayan form is identical with one inhabiting the plains of India, and perfectly distinct from the one found in the Altai. This may, however, be explained by the greater facility with which the Carnivora can adapt themselves to different surroundings, owing to the circumstance that wherever they go they are sure to meet with herbivorous animals, on which they can prey. Herbivorous animals, on the other hand, are generally more or less completely dependent on one or more particular kinds of plants for sustenance, and are consequently unable to exist in regions where such plants do not grow.

In the same series with the wolves and jackals are included a number of South American species, commonly spoken of as foxes, which they much resemble in external aspect, although having wolf-like skulls. Among these are Azara's dog (*C. azaræ*) and the crab-eating dog (*C. cancrivorus*). A much larger South American form is the so-called maned wolf (*C. jubatus*)—a large reddish-coloured animal. The so-called raccoon-dog (*C. procyonides*), which has been generically separated as *Nyctereutes*, is distinguished by its long loose fur, short ears, and abbreviated bushy tail, its general colour being dusky.

Fox-like Series.

Probably every Englishman thinks he knows a fox when he sees it; and it is not unlikely that he would be disposed to resent the suggestion that he could not distinguish between foxes and certain other members of the canine family, or that there could be any hesitation in deciding whether any foxes he might be shown were or were not specifically identical with the common English kind. Nevertheless, it is by no means easy to determine from external characters alone whether a given canine animal is or is not a fox; while the difficulty of deciding whether many of the larger foxes of Asia and America should be regarded merely as varieties of the common fox, or as distinct species, has long exercised the minds of naturalists. Indeed, the latter question has only recently been decided by the leading zoologists of England in favour of the former view; and we are by no means sure that their opinions are accepted by all American zoologists.

Probably most people would say that a fox is sufficiently characterised by his slight build, elongated body, short limbs, long ears, sharp muzzle, and long bushy tail, of which the length always considerably exceeds half that of the head and body. So far, indeed, as they go, these characteristics are excellent, and they will serve to distinguish a fox from a wolf or jackal. The whole of them are, however, not applicable to all foxes, the Arctic fox having comparatively short ears, while they will not serve to distinguish foxes from the above-mentioned South American representatives of the family, such as the so-called Azara's dog. The latter animals have, indeed, the general build and appearance of foxes, their muzzles being sharp, their ears long, and their tails of great length and thickly haired. The naturalist says emphatically, however, that they are not true foxes, and it is, therefore, evident that he has certain characteristics to rely on which are not included among those just mentioned.

A more careful examination of a fox will show that the pupil of the eye forms merely a narrow vertical ellipse when seen in a strong light, whereas that of wolves, jackals, and dogs is circular. Unfortunately, however, even this character will not serve to distinguish foxes from the above-mentioned South American species. Of more importance is the circumstance that vixen foxes have but 6 teats, whereas the females of wolves, jackals, and dogs generally have 10, but occasionally only 8 teats, while in the Indian wild dogs the number is increased to 12 or 14. As usual, however, when he wants to find a feature which shall be absolutely characteristic, the naturalist has recourse to the skull in order to definitely separate foxes from all other members of the family. If, indeed, we examine the skull of any kind of domestic or wild dog, of a wolf, or a jackal, we shall not fail to observe, as noticed above, that the triangular bony projection from the middle of the skull which forms the hinder border of the upper part of the socket of the eye—hence known as the postorbital process—is highly convex, and curves from above downwards. On the other hand, in the skull of any species of fox, the same process has a very distinct hollow on its upper surface, and it does not curve downwards in the smallest degree. A further examination will also show that in a dog, jackal, or wolf the middle portion of the skull is considerably elevated above the level of the extremities of these two processes; whereas in a fox the whole surface of this part of the skull lies nearly in a horizontal plane. If we were to make a vertical section of the two skulls, we should find that in the skulls of the dog, jackal, and wolf the bone forming the roof was honeycombed by a number of cells, whereas in the fox it is solid; and it is the presence, or absence, of these cells which causes the great difference in the contour of the skulls of a dog and a fox.

The above feature absolutely distinguishes the skulls of all species of foxes from those of all other members of the family, and we are accordingly now able to give a much more satisfactory definition of a fox, which will be somewhat as follows, *viz.*: A long-bodied, short-limbed member of the canine family, with a long and bushy tail exceeding half the length of the head and body, generally long ears, a sharp muzzle, elliptical pupils to the eyes, 6 teats, and the forehead of the skull not honeycombed by cells, and with the postorbital processes hollowed above. From these important differences some writers are inclined to separate the foxes from the genus *Canis* under the name of *Vulpes*.

There has been much discussion as to whether foxes and dogs will breed together. Thus, Mr. Bartlett, the superintendent of the Zoological Society's Gardens, whose wide experience entitles him to rank as a high authority on the point, writing in 1890, says that, "So far as my experience goes, I have never met with a well-authenticated instance of a hybrid between a fox and a dog, notwithstanding numerous specimens of supposed hybrids of this sort which from time to time have been brought to my notice." Since that date, several writers in *Land and Water* have, however, asserted the existence of such hybrids, but further evidence is still desirable on the subject. And if such a hybrid be proved to exist, it would be very desirable that the form of the pupils of its eyes, and the number of its teats, should be carefully recorded during life, while after death an examination of its skull by a qualified observer would be of the highest interest.

Turning to the numerous varieties of the common fox and their distribution, it is almost needless to observe that in England the fox is of a bright reddish-brown colour on the upper-parts, with the under-parts and the tip of the brush white, and the back of the ears and the lower portions of the limbs black. There are, however, some local or individual variations even in this country, which have given rise to the names of greyhound, mountain, and bush foxes; but all these are, at the most, of trivial import. Occasionally English foxes are killed with the tip of the brush grey or black, and there is one instance on record of a white English fox. Of far more importance is the circumstance that ome time previous to 1864 an immature fox was killed in Warwickshire with all the under-parts of a greyish black hue. Now, as a general rule, the foxes of Northern and Central Europe are similar in colour to the ordinary English form, but in Southern

Europe they are all paler above, with the under-parts dusky. There can, however, be no question but that these are all of one species, and it is therefore very interesting to find one instance of the occurrence of the Southern variety—assuming that the Warwickshire specimen was not an imported animal—in this country.

Proceeding eastwards into Asia, we find two large foxes differing very markedly from the ordinary English form. The first of these is the yellow fox of Central Asia, formerly regarded as a distinct species under the name of *C. flavescens*, and characterised by its general pale and yellowish colour, and the large size of its magnificent brush. It has, however, still the dark ears and white brush-tip of the English fox, and there can be no doubt that modern writers are right in regarding it merely as a pale variety of the latter. This variety inhabits open country, and lives in burrows, or among rocks or bushes.

The handsome animal known as the mountain-fox (the so-called *C. montanus*) of the Himalaya, although nearly allied to the last, is frequently so strikingly different, when in its winter dress, from the ordinary English fox, that most sportsmen would regard it as a distinct species. The fur of the back varies in colour from chestnut to iron-grey, and the shoulders are often marked by a conspicuous dark transverse stripe, while the under-parts, and especially the throat, are more or less dusky. The black outer surfaces of the ears and the white tip to the brush proclaim, however, the affinity of this fox to the southern variety of the European fox; and it appears to be merely another variety of the latter. This Himalayan fox differs from the Central Asian variety in that it does not excavate burrows, but lives in thickets or on cultivated land. When we add that the so-called Nile fox (*C. niloticus*) is but another variety of the same species, it will be evident that if he can but obtain a pack of hounds and suitable ground, the sportsman may hunt one and the same species of fox, whether he be in England, in the South of Europe, on the banks of the Nile, in the deserts of Central Asia, or in the vale of Kashmir.

This is, however, by no means all, for if the fox-hunter cares to cross the Atlantic he may again hunt the common fox in Virginia and other parts of North America. It is true, indeed, that these large North American foxes have been considered distinct species, under the names of the red fox (*C. fulvus*) and the cross-fox (*C. pennsylvanicus*). The cross-fox is, however, obviously but a variety of the red fox, distinguished by the presence of a more or less distinct dark stripe across the shoulders; and since both forms have the black ears and white tail-tip of the European species, there can be little hesitation, in spite of their variation in colour, in regarding them merely as local races of the same widely-spread form.

Fig. 41.—THE COMMON FOX.

Again the so-called silver or black fox (*C. argentatus*) from California and the Western United States, so valued on account of its beautiful fur, is only a melanistic (dark) variety of the red fox, and is therefore merely another race of *Canis vulpes*. The silver fox, we may observe in passing, is a comparatively rare animal, of which perfectly black skins, with only the characteristic white tip of the tail, are so scarce that they fetch from £50 to £70 in the market. It thus appears that an animal may vary in colour from foxy-red above, with white under-parts and tail-tip and black limbs and ears, to one in which the whole of the fur is black save the tip of the tail, and yet belong to one and the same species.

No account of the distribution of the common fox would be complete without some reference to the fact that it is one of the very oldest of our British Mammals, its fossilised remains having been dug up in the topmost beds of the so-called red crag of the Suffolk coast. These deposits far ante-date the river gravels and cavern-mud in which occur the remains of the mammoth and other gigantic extinct Mammals; and it will thus be evident that this extreme antiquity of the British fox will readily account for its present unusually wide geographical distribution.

Before taking leave of the common fox and its numerous varieties we may refer to the circumstance that there has been much discussion as to whether badgers are hurtful to young foxes. As the result of these it appears that the charge against the badger has been effectually disproved, more than one writer recounting instances where fox and badger-cubs have been brought up in amity as inhabitants of the same earth. In spite, however, of this, it appears that there is still, at least in some districts, war waged by sportsmen against the unfortunate badger.

With regard to North American foxes, it may be observed that in addition to the red and cross-fox, the so-called grey fox or Virginian fox (*C. virginianus*) is largely hunted with hounds in some parts of the States. This fox is much smaller than the European species, the length of its head and body being only about 19 inches, in place of some 24 inches. It is further distinguished by its relatively shorter muzzle, and also by the presence of a ridge of long stiff hairs running along the middle of the upper part of the tail. The general colour of this fox, as its common name implies, is some shade of grey; but there is considerable individual variation in this respect, and some specimens show a more or less marked reddish tinge. If an English huntsman were to see his quarry suddenly rush straight up the trunk of a tree in the midst of a run, his astonishment would certainly be great, yet we are assured by American writers that tree-climbing is a frequent habit of the grey fox. Thus Dr. Ellzey writes in Shields' "Big Game of North America," that "whether the greys ever climb trees in pursuit of prey I am uncertain; but they take to a tree as readily as a cat, when hard run by hounds. I think it nearly certain that they climb for persimmons, grapes, and berries. Red foxes never climb trees under any circumstances; when hard run they go to earth." If the above explanation of this curious habit is the true one, it would seem that grapes are not sour to the grey fox. Grey foxes afford but a poor run in comparison with the common species, their course only holding for a short distance, and that accompanied by many doublings; while the run usually terminates either by the capture of a fox within an hour, or by the animal either climbing a tree or taking refuge in a hole of the same. On the other hand, the American red fox runs as strongly as his European relative; his course, it is said, generally taking the form of a large parallelogram. The cubs of the grey fox have been compared to small black puppies, and are thus very different in appearance from those of our own species. A second North American species is the kit-fox (*C. velox*), which is still smaller than the grey, its brush being only about 11 inches in length, against 16 inches in the latter. Above, this fox is light grey, with an admixture of long white hairs, while the flanks are yellowish and the under-parts white, the brush having no white tip. This species lives in burrows, and takes its name from its extreme speed. Whether it is commonly hunted with hounds I am unaware. More distinct than either of the above is the long-eared fox (*C. macrotis*), of California, in which the ears are nearly as large as in the under-mentioned fennecs. Its general colour above is grizzled grey. South America has no true foxes.

In India the place of the common fox is taken by two small species—the Indian desert-fox (*C. leucopus*) and the Bengal fox (*C. bengalensis*). The former, which is somewhat the larger of the two, agrees with the common species in the white tip to the brush, and also in the dark brown or black outsides to the ears; while the latter has a black tip to the brush and greyish ears. The desert-fox, as its name implies, inhabits sandy wastes, and has a considerable turn of speed; Jerdon stating that it "gives a capital run sometimes, even with English dogs."

The Bengal fox, which only measures about 20 inches from the tip of the snout to the root of the tail, is found in more or less open country over the greater part of India, and may not unfrequently be seen by residents in Calcutta playing about the Maidan near Fort-William. Jerdon writes that "this fox is much coursed with greyhounds in many parts of India, and with Arab or country dogs, or half-bred English dogs it gives a most excellent course, doubling in a most dexterous manner, and if it is within a short distance of its earth, racing the dogs. Its numerous earths prevent in general much sport being had in hunting it with foxhounds, and its scent is poor." Another small Asiatic species, with a dark tip to the brush, is the Corsac fox (*C. corsac*), whose habitat extends from the shores of the Caspian through the Russian steppes to Mongolia. The skin of this species is an article of considerable commercial importance, an average of about 50,000 coming annually into the market. There are several other allied species of foxes inhabiting Asia, such as the Japanese fox (*C. japonicus*) and the Tibetan fox (*C. ferrilatus*), but as they are mostly but little known in Europe, it is unnecessary to make further allusion to them on this occasion. Mention must, however, be made of the Arctic fox (*C. lagopus*), characterised by its short ears, extremely bushy brush, and the long hair clothing the soles of the feet. As a rule, this fox is bluish-grey in summer (when it is known as the blue fox), but changes to pure white in winter; although in some cases, more especially in Iceland, the dark tint is retained throughout the year. This species is practically circumpolar, and on an average from 25,000 to 60,000 skins annually find their way into the market. The Arctic fox, in order to provide a supply of food for the long and dreary winter of its native habitat, is in the habit of laying up stores of lemmings and other small animals concealed in holes and fissures of the rocks.

South and Central Africa is the home of an entirely different group of small foxes, known as fennecs (*C. zerda*, *C. famelicus*, and *C. cama*), and characterised by the enormous length of their ears. These fennecs are more or less sandy-coloured animals, with a dark tip to the tail, and differ from the European fox in their social habits, dwelling together in small companies. A skin of an apparently allied species has been obtained from Afghanistan.

The Cape hunting-dog (*Lycaon pictus*) is the sole living representative of a genus differing from *Canis* in having but four toes to each foot. Its skull approximates to that of the wolves, but is somewhat shorter and broader, and there is a slight difference in the form of the teeth. This animal is of large size, and marked with unsymmetrical blotches of white, yellow, and black, the distribution of which shows considerable individual variation. Numbers combine in packs to hunt their prey. A second well-marked genus of the *Canidæ* is formed by the bush-dog (*Ictioyon venaticus*) of British Guiana and Brazil, which is a dark-coloured animal not larger than a fox, with a short, sparsely-haired tail, short limbs, very small ears, close hair, and a very aberrant dentition. In the first place, the number of molars is reduced to one pair in the upper and two in the lower jaw, while the lower carnassial has no cusp on the inner side of the blade, and its posterior heel is secant instead of tubercular, so that practically the entire tooth is reduced to a cutting blade. The last member of the dog family is Lalande's fennec (*Otocyon megalotis*) of South Africa, which, while agreeing in many respects with the true fennecs, has very much larger ears, but is specially distinguished by having four pairs of lower molar teeth, and either three or four pairs of the same in the upper jaw, the total number of teeth thus being either 46 or 48. Its habits are like those of the fennecs.

Other Genera.

Fig. 42.—Cape Hunting-Dog (*Lycaon pictus*).

In the three remaining families of the terrestrial Carnivora the auditory bulla of the skull possesses a simple undivided septum, and its bony external tube, or meatus, leading to the outer ear, has its lower margin considerably produced, while the triangular paroccipital process stands quite apart from the bulla. In the intestine the blind appendage or cœcum is entirely absent. The bears themselves are specially characterised by the broad, flat, tuberculated crowns of the molar teeth, of which there are two upper and three lower pairs; and likewise by the rudimentary development of the first three pairs of premolars in each jaw, which are in many cases entirely lost. The upper carnassial is very short and triangular, and both this tooth and the lower carnassial have but little resemblance to the true sectorial type, as shown in the cats and dogs. In the skull the auditory bulla is very flat, and scarcely at all inflated. The large feet are furnished with five toes each, and are completely plantigrade; while their long and slightly compressed claws are non-retractile. The body is very stout, the tail short, the ears moderate, the hair generally long and loose, and the gait clumsy and shambling. Bears go about either in pairs or in small family-parties, and are all excellent climbers. Most of them eat roots, fruits, and other vegetable substances, although they will also consume the flesh of dead animals and carrion; and in cold

The Bear Tribe. —Family *Ursidæ*.

Fig. 43.—Bush-Dog (*Icticyon venaticus*).

countries all hibernate during the inclement season, their hiding-places being frequently caverns, the clefts of rocks, or hollow trees. The typical genus *Ursus*, in which there are 42 teeth, and some of the premolars are deciduous, includes all the existing members of the family except two. Of these the polar bear (*U. maritimus*) of the Arctic regions stands apart from the rest on account of its relatively smaller head, small and narrow molars, more hairy soles, and creamy white colour. Its food consists mainly of flesh. The brown bear (*U. arctus*) is a very widely-spread species, ranging all over Europe and Northern Asia, and represented in Syria by one variety (*U. syriacus*), in the Himalaya by the pale isabelline bear (*U. isabellinus*), and in North America by the grizzly bear (*U. horribilis*) and the American black bear (*U. americanus*), both of which are now considered merely as varieties of the European species. The Himalayan black bear (*U. torquatus*), with shaggy black fur and a white gorget, is a very distinct species; as is also the small Malayan bear (*U. malayanus*), ranging from North-Eastern India to the Malayan countries, and distinguished by its long extensile tongue and short black fur, with a light gorget on the throat. Another well-marked form is the spectacled bear (*U. ornatus*) of the Chilian Andes. With the exception of *U. crowther*, of the Atlas range, which may be only a variety of the common species, Africa has no bear. The Indian sloth bear (*Melursus ursinus*) differs in having only two pairs of upper incisor teeth, small molars, large extensile lips, and a deeply hollowed palate; the black fur being very long, loose, and harsh, and the throat marked by the usual light gorget. It feeds chiefly on ants, other insects, fruit, flowers and honey. More different than all is the parti-coloured bear (*Æluropus melanoleucus*) of Tibet, with a total of 40 teeth, the premolars large and, except the first, two-rooted, and the first upper molar broader than long, instead of longer than broad, as in other bears. In colour it is black and white, with black rings round the eyes.

Fig. 44.—PARTI-COLOURED BEAR (*Æluropus melanoleucus*).

Raccoon Tribe. Family *Procyonidæ*.

Mainly American, the raccoon tribe includes small carnivores with two pairs of molars in each jaw, which may be either many-cusped or tuberculated, a short and broad upper carnassial tooth, plantigrade feet, and the tail ringed. The single Old World form is the panda or cat-bear (*Ælurus fulgens*) of the Eastern Himalaya, which is a reddish-coloured animal, of the size of a cat, with a long, ringed tail. It has a total of 38 teeth, very broad many-cusped upper molars, and a curiously rounded and vaulted skull. The face is cat-like, the ears are moderate and rounded, and the limbs stout, with large partially retractile claws. The panda is a good climber, and feeds chiefly upon vegetable substances. The American raccoons (*Procyon*) have 40 teeth, broad and tuberculated molars, and three lobes to the blade of the upper carnassial. The body is stout, the head broad, with a sharp muzzle, the whole sole of the foot not applied to the ground in walking, and the toes capable of being widely spread, with sharp non-retractile claws. The tail is rather short and ringed, and the fur thick and soft.

Raccoons are almost omnivorous animals, obtaining much of their food along the banks of lakes and streams, and swimming well. Much of their time is, however, spent in trees, in hollows of which the young are brought forth; and in North America they hibernate during the cold season. The cacomistles (*Bassariscus*), represented by one species from the Southern United States and Mexico and another from Central America, form a closely allied genus, distinguished by the more slender build, sharper nose, longer tail, and less completely plantigrade feet. Another genus is *Bassaricyon*, of Central America, which has raccoon-like teeth, but an external form very like that of the kinkajou. The coatis (*Nasua*), which range from Central America to Paraguay, are easily recognised by the prolongation of the muzzle into a long and somewhat upturned mobile snout; the long and tapering tail being ringed. The dentition is similar to that of the raccoons, with the exception that the upper canines are longer and more pointed, and the molars smaller. Coatis are arboreal animals, going about the forest in small parties, and feeding chiefly on birds, eggs, insects, lizards, and fruits. Lastly, the kinkajou (*Cercoleptes caudivolvulus*) differs from all the rest in its long and taper tail being prehensile; the number of teeth being 36. It is a pale yellowish-brown animal, of the size of a cat, entirely nocturnal, and arboreal in its habits.

Fig. 45.—The Panda (*Ælurus fulgens*).

The last family of the land Carnivora is the large and widely-spread one of the weasels, which includes the otters, badgers, shunks, etc. Except in the ratels (where there is but a single pair in each jaw), the members of this family may be distinguished from the two preceding ones by having one pair of upper, and two of lower molars, and by the inner portion of the upper molars being longer from back to front than the outer blade. The auditory bulla of the skull is but little inflated.

Weasel Tribe.—Family *Mustelidæ*.

Fig. 46.—Cacomistle (*Bassariscus astutus*).

Otters.

The otters (*Lutra*) form an aquatic group characterised by the short and rounded feet, the webbed toes, the small, curved, and blunt claws, and the broad and flattened head. The jaws are short, with large, closely packed teeth; the upper molar being especially large, quadrangular in form, and its inner tubercular portion much expanded from back to front; and all the cheek teeth sharply cusped. The body is very elongated, the ears are short and rounded, the limbs short, the tail long, thick, and tapering rapidly, and the fur very short and close. In certain species the claws may be rudimental or wanting. With the exception of Australia and New Guinea, otters are cosmopolitan in their distribution, the largest species being the Brazilian otter. They are expert divers and swimmers, feeding entirely on fish, for the capture and retention of which their powerful and sharply-cusped teeth are admirably suited. The total number of teeth is 36. Nearly allied to the otters is the sea-otter (*Latax lutris*), distinguished by having only 32 teeth, among which the lower incisors are reduced to two pairs, the blunt and rounded tubercles of the molars, and the flipper-like hind-feet, in which the toes are flattened, as in the seals, and the fifth toe is the longest and stoutest. The head is rounded, the ears very small, the tail short and bushy, and the pellage with a beautiful under-fur. The total length of the animal is about four feet. Naturalists have hitherto believed that the sea-otter when on land has the hind-toes turned forwards, but Mr. Snow, of Yokohama, states that this is incorrect, and that they are really doubled backwards, beneath the soles. The southern range of the sea-otter extends as far as Southern California and Mexico. On the Asiatic side, it occurs at the Komandorski Islands, Kamschatka, and the Kurile Islands. As a rule, only one is produced at birth, but occasionally two. Mr. Snow has seen two small pups with their mother, and has taken two from the inside of an otter he killed. It is not absolutely known at what age the otter arrives at maturity. Mr. Snow believes that it does so in the third year. Crabs and sea-urchins are the usual contents of the stomach, but occasionally small fish and spawn are also found. The crabs are crushed by the strong molar teeth, it being impossible that the crushing is produced by the striking of two shells together, as the form of the fore-feet will not allow of anything being grasped. The otter dives for its food, and returns to the surface with the prey held between its two fore-paws, in which it continues to hold it while eating it. On many occasions Mr. Snow has seen schools of from 10 to 50 or more otters together some 10 or 15 miles from any land, but not of late years. The mode of capture adopted by Europeans is to "run" the sea-otter with three boats, each manned by four or five men, a hunter being in the bow armed with a rifle. When an otter is "raised" (as it is called), the boats proceed to surround it, lying some 500 to 600 yards apart in the form of a triangle. The boats are so manœuvred that the otter is kept between them. Every time the animal makes its appearance above the water, it is shot at, until it is secured. When the sea-otter is netted, it becomes entangled in the meshes and drowned. The long white hairs of the fur are its chief beauty. They are not removed when it is prepared for use. A skin has sold for upwards of £225.

Fig. 47.—COATI (*Nasua rufa*).

Skunks.

The skunks of America are the first representatives of a second sub-family in which the feet are elongated, with straight toes, and non-retractile, slightly curved, somewhat compressed, and blunt claws, which are of very large size in the hind-foot; the form of the upper molar being variable. The typical skunks (*Mephitis*), which are confined to North and Central America, are easily recognised by their black fur, relieved on the back with broad longitudinal stripes of white, and the bushy black and white tail, which is generally carried over the back. They have 34 teeth, and are provided with special glands for the secretion of the noisome fluid to which they owe their name. The little skunk (*Spilogale putorius*) of the Southern United States and Central America is a much smaller animal, and the only member of the group that can climb. The South American skunk (*Conepatus mapurito*), ranging from Texas to Patagonia, differs in having only 32 teeth, and also in its heavier build, and by the nostrils opening downwards and forwards, instead of on the sides of the muzzle. Mr. Aplin, writing of this species, observes that "the scent-gland cannot be opened unless the tail is at a right angle, or something near it, with the line of the body; and that therefore when held by the tail the weight of the skunk's body keeps the tail more or less in a line with it, and the skunk is unable to discharge its vile secretion. To perform this operation it is of course necessary to catch the skunk asleep, or otherwise deeply occupied (digging roots, for instance), and to run the risk of its waking up or turning round and seeing you. I believe I could have easily done it myself, as I have more than once seen a skunk lying curled up asleep in the daytime. Indeed, while looking for a parrot I had shot among some bushes, I very nearly stepped upon one which was curled up on the ground; and there it remained until I put a revolver bullet through its body. However, I never cared to risk the loss of useful garments, it having been proved, I believe, that clothes once well dosed at close quarters may as well be burnt. The skunk passes the daytime in sleep, when undisturbed. In Soriano I used to find them laid up in holes and under clefts in the granite boulder rocks, in deserted ant-nests, among paja grass, or in the crown of a big hassock of this, and in one or two cases on the ground among bushes. In the latter case it lies on its side curled round. When roused in a hole by a dog, it presents a rather diabolical appearance as it pops its little vicious head out. Notwithstanding demonstrations of this kind, I have only once seen a skunk use its teeth. In this case one fastened on to Jim's flanks, and the old dog walked about with it hanging on for half a minute, looking round at it in much astonishment at this unusual and unseemly behaviour—the fact being that he could not get hold of his enemy, which turned with him. The skunk seems to be an omnivorous feeder. Its long strong claws are well adapted for digging, and places where they have been scratching are to be seen all about the camp. They probably feed on small mammals, reptiles, and insects, as well as roots, and are always credited with robbing hen-roosts. With regard to the distance at which you can smell a skunk, I cannot give an opinion; but you often smell them when you cannot see them, and just about sundown the smell is a usual and familiar one about the camp; at night, too, a strong whiff of it as you sit or stroll in the *patio* is a very common occurrence. At a hundred yards to leeward, with the slightest breeze the smell of a discharge

Fig. 48.—COMMON SKUNK (*Mephitis mephitica*).

would be very pungent. The smell is said to be a good *remedio* for the headache." Although skunks are essentially nocturnal animals, they may occasionally be seen walking about on the open Argentine pampas in broad daylight.

Badgers.

The next group of the sub-family includes the badgers, of which there are likewise several genera, none of which are found in South America. Of these the sand-badgers (*Arctonyx*), of the Oriental countries, form a genus characterised by having 38 teeth, of which the lower incisors project forwards, the anterior premolars are often rudimental or wanting, and the upper molar is much larger than the carnassial, and longer than broad. The naked mobile snout is pig-like, the ears are minute and rounded, the eyes small, the feet digitigrade when walking, the tail moderately long and tapering, and the fur bristly, with a soft under-fur. The Indian species is rather larger than the ordinary badger. Nearly allied is the Malayan badger (*Mydaus meliceps*), from Java, Sumatra, and Borneo, which is a small burrowing animal, distinguished from the last by the nostrils being inferior, instead of terminal in position, and by the extreme shortness of the tail, which is clothed with rather long bushy hair. In the true badgers (*Meles*) the number of the teeth is also 38, but the first premolar in each jaw is minute, and often shed at an early age, while the very large upper molar is quadrangular, as broad as long, and much surpassing the carnassial in size. Moreover, the lower jaw is so firmly articulated to the skull that it cannot be separated without fracture. The skull differs from that of the sand-badgers, and thereby resembles the Malayan badger, in that its bony palate is only produced a comparatively short distance behind the last pair of teeth. The muzzle is pointed, the body stout and broad, the ears and tail very short, and the limbs short and strong, with partially plantigrade feet. The coloration of the common badger is too well known to need description. The genus includes only a few species, which are confined to Europe and Asia north of the Himalaya, one kind inhabiting Persia and another Japan. Badgers are nocturnal, omnivorous, and burrowing animals, producing three or four blind young at a birth. In North America the group is represented by the American badgers (*Taxidea*), in which the first upper premolar appears to be always wanting, and the upper carnassial is nearly as large as the molar, and the tubercular heel of the lower carnassial relatively smaller than in the Old World badgers. The stout body is depressed, and the tail very short. Nearly allied to the badgers are the ratels (*Mellivora*) of India and Africa south of the Sahara, which differ from all other members of the family in having but a single pair of lower molars, and are further distinguished by the limbs and under surface of the body being black, while the upper-parts are greyish. In this genus the upper carnassial is a large tooth, with its inner tubercle at the front end, as in the remaining genera of the sub-family; the upper molar being short from back to front, with its inner portion much expanded. In the lower carnassial the posterior heel is very minute. Ex-

Fig. 49.—COMMON BADGER.

ternally, the ratels have a stout body, a flattened head, rather pointed nose, rudimental ears, stout and short limbs, and a very short tail. They subsist chiefly on honey-comb, which they dig out with their powerful claws. The so-called ferret-badgers (*Helictis*), from the Oriental countries, some of which are remarkable for their brilliant coloration, form a very distinct genus. They have 38 teeth, a long head, with a sharp naked muzzle, obliquely truncated at the tip, small ears, elongated body, short limbs, and a rather short or moderate bushy tail. All are small animals, climbing well, and subsisting on a mixed diet. The last genus of the sub-family is typified by the Cape polecat (*Ictonyx zorilla*); another species occurring in Egypt, and, it is said, Asia Minor. These animals have a dentition and bodily form very similar to those of the true polecats, from which they may at once be distinguished by their coloration, which is very similar to that of the skunks.

Weasels, etc.

The last sub-family of the *Mustelidæ* comprises the true weasels and their allies, and is characterised by the toes being short and partially webbed, the claws also short, sharp, compressed, curved, and frequently partially retractile; while the upper molar is of moderate size, and wide transversely. The first genus is *Galictis*, of which there are two well-defined South American species, locally known as the grison and the tayra. Both these have 34 teeth, among which the molars are small but stout, while the upper carnassial has its inner tubercle near the middle of its length, and the lower carnassial has a minute posterior heel, and either a very small or no inner cusp. The head is broad and flattened, the body elongate, the limbs short, with plantigrade feet, in which the claws are non-retractile and the soles naked, while the tail is long or moderate. Both species are found as far south as the Argentine pampas, and are noted for their savage disposition.

Fig. 50.—THE COMMON WEASEL.

In the typical genus *Mustela* may be included not only the martens, but likewise the smaller polecats and weasels. In the two latter the dentition is numerically the same as in *Galictis*, but in the former the number of teeth is increased to 38, owing to the presence of the first pair of premolars in each jaw, on which account these animals are frequently referred to a genus by themselves, under the name of *Putorius*. From *Galictis* they are all readily distinguished by the inner tubercle of the upper carnassial tooth being situated close to its front edge, instead of in the middle. All these animals have the characteristic long and slender weasel-body, short, digitigrade limbs, rounded feet, short toes, with sharp, compressed, and partially retractile claws, and the long or moderate tail more or less bushy. The larger forms, or martens, are restricted to the Northern Hemisphere, one species occurring as far south as Sumatra. They are all mainly carnivorous and arboreal, and generally produce from four to six young at a birth. The best-known species are the pine-marten (*Mustela martes*), ranging from Britain across Northern Europe and Asia; the beech-marten (*M. foina*), extending from Central and Southern Europe to the Himalaya and Turkestan; the sable (*M. zibellina*) of Siberia and Kamschatka; the closely-allied North American marten (*M. americana*); the very distinct Indian or yellow-throated marten (*M. flavigula*), ranging from India to Sumatra, China, and Amurland; and the large Pennant's marten (*M. pennanti*) of North America.

Of the forms with only three pairs of premolars and no inner cusp to the lower carnassial tooth, the largest are the nertz (*M. lutreola*) of Eastern Europe, and the nearly related North American mink (*M. vison*). Next come the five species of polecat, as typified by the common European polecat (*M. putorius*); while the smaller forms include the true weasels and stoats. Of these, the stoat or ermine (*M. erminea*) and the weasel (*M. vulgaris*) are common to Europe, North and Central Asia, and North America, while the assogue (*M. hibernica*), which is intermediate in size and coloration between the other two, is restricted to Ireland, being the only Mammal peculiar to the British Islands. The South African *Pœcilogale albinucha*, which has a coloration similar to that of the Cape polecat (*Ictonyx*), has been referred to a distinct genus, on account of there being only two pairs of premolar teeth in each, and by the lower molars being generally reduced to a single pair. The name *Lyncodon* has been proposed for a Patagonian weasel, in which the dentition is numerically the same as in the preceding.

The last genus of the mustelines is represented solely by the wolverene or glutton (*Gulo luscus*) of the northern districts of both hemispheres. In this comparatively large animal, which is an inhabitant of forests, there are 38 teeth, all of which are very stout and strong; the upper molar being much smaller than the carnassial, the lower carnassial large, with no inner cusp, and a small posterior tooth, and the third upper incisor so large as to resemble a second tusk. The form is more like that of a bear than a weasel, the body and limbs being stout, the latter long, with large, partially plantigrade feet, the small ears almost buried in the loose, coarse fur, the eyes, the tail short, thick, and bushy, and the soles of the feet covered with bristly hairs. The dark fur has a light saddle-shaped mark on the back. The wolverene is a good climber, and lives on large birds and mammals, killing animals even as large as the reindeer. It has a curious habit of carrying off and collecting articles for which it can have no possible use.

Eared-Seals.—Family *Otariidæ*.

The fur-seals, or eared-seals, are the first of three families of the aquatic Carnivora, all the members of which are modified for an aquatic life, and collectively constitute the sub-order Pinnipedia. In all these animals the upper-arm and fore-arm, and the corresponding segments of the hind-limb, are abnormally shortened, and to a great extent enclosed in the skin of the body, whereas the feet, and more especially the hinder pair, are elongated and expanded into large flippers, with the toes widely separated and completely united by webs. Five toes are present, of which the first and fifth in the hind-limb are stouter and usually longer than the three middle ones. The incisor teeth are always reduced below the typical number of three pairs in one or both jaws; and the cheek teeth, which usually consist of four pairs of premolars and a single pair of molars, are nearly alike, and lack the specially modified carnassials characteristic of the land Carnivora. The body is of a tapering,

Fig. 51.—Sea-Lion.

pyriform shape, admirably adapted for progression through the water, passing almost imperceptibly into the tail, which is always short. On land seals are awkward animals, progressing with a series of ungainly jumps, and most of them spend the greater part of their time in the water, although all come ashore for the purpose of breeding. The great majority are marine, although a few inhabit inland seas and lakes. Most feed on fish, crustaceans, and other marine animals.

The eared-seals, all of which may be included in the single genus *Otaria*, are distinguished as a family by the circumstance that when on land the hind-flippers are turned forwards beneath the body, and likewise by the presence of small external ears; the under surfaces of both flippers being naked. They have either 36 or 34 teeth, according to the presence or absence of the second pair of upper molars; and there are three pairs of upper, and two of lower incisors. The cheek teeth are sharp and compressed, consisting of one large central cusp, flanked by two much smaller ones. The head is separated from the body by a distinct neck, and the claws, especially those of the first and fifth toes, are small or rudimental. Many species have a very dense under-fur, constituting the "sealskin" of commerce, and these are known as fur-seals; while others, in which there is no under-fur, are termed hair-seals. Although absent from the shores of the North Atlantic, the eared-seals have a wide geographical distribution. Among the better-known forms may be mentioned the southern sea-lion (*O. jubata*) of the Falkland Islands and Patagonia, which differs remarkably from all the rest in the structure of its skull; the large northern sea-lion (*O. stelleri*) of the North Pacific, which may attain as much as 10 feet in length; Gillespie's sea-lion (*O. gillespii*) from California and Japan; the sea-bear (*O. ursina*) from the Pribyloff Islands and other parts of the North Pacific; *O. pusilla* of South Africa; and *O. fosteri* from Australia and New Zealand. All the eared-seals are peculiar for their habit of spending a long period on land during the breeding-season, where they form the well-known "rookeries." Here the males arrive first, and proceed to take up fixed stations, where they collect as many females as they are able to capture; and it is not a little remarkable that during their whole sojourn on shore, which may extend to a period of three months, they undergo a complete fast.

The following account of seals and sealing in Japanese waters is from the consular report on the trade of Hakodate, as given in the *Times* of May, 1895. The writer states that in the island of Yezo the "conditions, as regards space and time, are very similar on both sides of the ocean. The Russian rookeries of the Commander Islands are the exact counterpart (though smaller) of the American rookeries of the Pribyloff Islands; the two face each other, in about the same latitude, from the opposite sides of Behring Sea. From these centres the seals, after their four or five months' summer sojourn, start southwards for their immense swims in the Pacific, extending on the American side as far down as San Francisco, and on the Asiatic side as far down as Sendai Bay, and even the entrance of Yedo Bay. But there is one noteworthy difference between the two cases. While, on the American side, owing to the long sweep and turns of the coast-line, the range of the swim is quite 3,200 miles, on the Asiatic side it is a nearly straight run of less than half that distance. Hence the seal-herd, though larger, is more dispersed on the American side; and it is probable that hunters choosing the Asiatic side gain more through the concentration of the herd than they lose through its inferiority in numbers. Indeed, the effective hunting range—at all events, for the first stage of the hunting season—is not much more than 800 miles long, extending from Sendai Bay to Nemuro, the most easterly point of Yezo Island. On reaching Nemuro the seals suddenly disappear about the end of June, and no sealing craft as yet has followed them up, keeping them in sight, between this point and the rookeries on Behring and Copper Islands, or the still smaller rookery of Robben Island in the Okhotsk Sea. The explanation of this sudden acceleration of the seal's pace may be, as the hunters think, merely the quickening of the natural instincts, on the eve of the breeding-time. But it may also be due to a falling off in the food supply along the line of the Kurile archipelago. The fact, however, is undoubted that, beyond Nemuro, the schooners lose sight of the seals about the end of June, and this check of their pursuit serves as a mark to divide the hunting season into two distinct stages.

"The schooners, as a rule, leave Victoria or San Francisco at the end of December or early in January, and, after a two months' voyage across the Pacific, strike the Japanese coast about the latitude of Yokohama, where some of them put in to victual and refit. They begin hunting about the middle or end of March, first meeting large clusters of seals in about latitude 38 deg. N. off Sendai Bay, from about 30 to 250 miles off the shore. The seals are then proceeding northwards at a leisurely pace, travelling during the night and feeding and sleeping in the daytime, especially in bright, sunshiny weather. 'Sleepers,' as the hunters call them, are the easiest to shoot; 'travellers' are more difficult. A schooner with six or seven boats can take, on the average, close on 1,000 skins in the four months, March to June. That closes the first stage of the season, and they then either tranship their catches at sea into a collecting ship from Victoria and San Francisco, or else put into Hakodate and prepare their skins for shipment to London or America. This done, after a short stay and revictualling in port, they start northwards for the second stage of the hunting on the western side of Behring Sea and in the Okhotsk Sea. This part of the hunting season, lasting from the end of July till the end of October, yields a very much smaller catch than the first stage, and, with a protective zone established round the rookeries, the sealers will probably find it hardly worth while to continue it. At the rate at which the pelagic sealing schooners are increasing, and in the absence of more effective measures for the protection of the herd on the rookeries, no less than at sea, the industry cannot last long. The Canadian sealing fleet engaged in hunting on the western side of the Pacific has increased even more rapidly than on the American side. In 1891 only one schooner, in 1892 11 or 12, and in 1893 at least 30 hunted in Asiatic waters. In the first place, the advantage, as compared with the American side, of the shorter range and greater concentration of the herd, is now well known to the sealers. Secondly, the close season, and the limits prescribed by the award of the Behring Sea arbitrators, are sure to drive many to the western side. And, lastly, the fact that there is a considerable saving in freight and charges when the skins are packed in Japan and shipped *via* the Suez Canal to London, as compared with the charges and freight from the American side, will tell in the same direction."

Of the Alaskan seal-herd, Mr. H. W. Elliott writes, that "the fighting between the old males for the cows is mostly—or, rather, entirely—done with the mouth. The opponents seize one another with their teeth, and then, clenching their jaws, nothing but the sheer strength of the one, and the other tugging to escape, can shake them loose, and that effort invariably leaves an ugly wound, the sharp canines tearing out deep gutters in the skin and furrows in the blubber, or shredding the flippers into ribbon-strips. The bulls generally approach each other with comically averted heads, just as though they were ashamed of the rumpus which they are determined to precipitate. When they get near enough to reach one another, they enter upon the repetition of many feints or passes before either the one or the other takes the initiative by gripping. The heads are darted out and back as quick as a flash; their hoarse roaring and shrill piping whistle never ceases, while their fat bodies writhe and swell with exertion and rage; furious lights gleam in their eyes; their hair flies off into the air, and their blood streams down. All this combined makes a picture so fierce and so strange that, from its unexpected position and its novelty, this is one of the most extraordinary brutal contests man can witness."

The Walrus.—Family *Trichechidæ.*

The walrus or morse (*Trichechus rosmarus*) of the polar seas, although differing remarkably in its dentition from both, presents in many respects a connecting link between the preceding and following families. It agrees, for instance, with the *Otariidæ* in having the hind-flippers turned forwards beneath the body when on land, but resembles the *Phocidæ* in having lost all external traces of ears. As regards the dentition, the upper canines are developed into enormous tusks, projecting far below the lower jaw, but the whole of the other teeth are small, simple, and single-rooted, the molars having rounded, flattened crowns. The walrus is one of the heaviest and most bulky of all seals, old males not unfrequently measuring from 10 to 11 feet in length, while much larger examples are on record. In form the head is round, with rather small eyes, and the short, broad muzzle furnished with a tuft of stiff bristles on each side. The hair of the rest of the body is short and closely pressed to the skin, its general colour being yellowish. The tail is rudimental; in the front-flippers the toes are nearly equal in length, and furnished with small, flat nails, but in the hind-pair the nails of the three middle digits are large, and those of the two marginal ones minute. There is some difference of opinion as to whether the walruses of the Atlantic and North Pacific Oceans belong to the same or to distinct species, but, in any case, the difference between them is extremely slight. Walruses are social animals, collecting on the ice-fields in herds of considerable size, and being often found on detached ice-floes. The females produce one, or occasionally two calves in the spring or early summer, for which they display the most marked affection. Their food consists almost entirely of two species of bivalve molluscs, which are raked out of the mud with the tusks, and easily crushed by the flat molar teeth. Whether the tusks are also employed to drag the animals out of the water by being hitched on to the ice, is a disputed point. The cry of the walrus is a loud roar, which, when many are together, can be heard for a long distance.

Fig. 52.—WALRUS (*Trichechus rosmarus.*)

True Seals.—Family *Phocidæ*.

The true or earless seals constitute the last family of the fin-footed Carnivora, and are those best adapted for a thoroughly aquatic life, the hind-flippers being permanently directed backwards alongside of the tail, and external ears totally wanting. A further difference from the eared-seals is to be found in the circumstance that the under surface of the feet is hairy; and in no case is there any under-fur, the ordinary fur being short and closely pressed to the skin. All the species have five pairs of cheek teeth in each jaw, but the number of incisors is variable. On land, most of the true seals advance by a jumping movement, produced by the muscles of the body, assisted only by the front-flippers.

The common grey seal (*Halichœrus grypus*), of the coasts of the whole North Atlantic, is the type of the sub-family *Phocidæ*, characterised by having three pairs of upper, and two of lower incisor teeth, well-developed claws on all the toes, and the hind-toes of nearly equal length, with the webs not reaching beyond their extremities. In the grey seal the cheek-teeth, except the last one or two in the upper, and the last in the lower jaw, are single-rooted, and consist generally of a single compressed cusp, although additional cusps may be present in the two hinder pairs in the lower jaw. The typical seals (*Phoca*), all of which are confined to the Northern Hemisphere, differ from the last in that all the cheek teeth are of smaller size, and, with the exception of the first pair in each jaw, are inserted by double roots, and have accessory cusps to their crowns. As examples of this genus may be cited the bearded-seal (*P. barbata*), Greenland seal (*P. grœnlandica*), common seal (*P. vitulina*), the Caspian seal (*P. caspica*) from the Caspian and Sea of Aral, and *P. sibirica* of Lake Baikal. Like other members of their tribe, these seals resort to the coast to bring forth their young, which may be either one or two in number; and not the least remarkable fact in their life-history is the circumstance that the offspring have to be taught by their parents to enter the water. They usually congregate in large herds, and are especially fond of lying basking in the sun like so many pigs. Seals are regularly hunted for the sake of their hides and blubber, the latter yielding a valuable oil.

Fig. 53.—COMMON SEAL (*Phoca vitulina*).

A second sub-family of the *Phocidæ* is typified by the monk-seal of the Mediterranean and adjacent portions of the Atlantic, which, with the nearly extinct West Indian seal, constitutes the genus *Monachus*. In this sub-family there are but two pairs of incisor teeth in each jaw, the cheek teeth, with the exception of the first pair, are inserted by two roots, and the first and fifth toes of the hind-flippers much exceed the three middle ones in length, and have their claws rudimental or wanting. The monk-seal is characterised by the possession of 32 teeth, and by the crowns of the cheek teeth being hollowed on the inner side—where there is a strongly marked basal ledge—and their front and back accessory cusps very small. The first cheek tooth in both jaws, as well as the last in the upper, are considerably smaller than the rest; and all the claws are rudimental. The four other generic representatives of the sub-family *Monachinæ* are restricted to the southern seas; each genus including only a single species. First among these comes the beautifully spotted leopard-seal (*Ogmorhinus leptonyx*), in which all the cheek teeth have three large cusps; the central one being the largest, with its apex curved backwards, while the tips of the others incline towards the middle one. Writing of the seals of this and other species seen during a voyage undertaken in 1892-93, Mr. W. S. Bruce observes that from December to February they "are to be found on the pack-ice, where, during the day, they bask in the sun, digesting the meal of the previous night. Their food consists of fish or shrimp-like crustaceans, and sometimes of penguins. Stones, which were probably first swallowed by the penguins, may also be found in their stomachs. They become so lazy with sleep that a man may dig them in the ribs with the muzzle of his gun, and wondering what it is disturbing their slumbers, they raise their head, which quickly falls pierced with a bullet. There may only be one seal on a piece of ice, which is usually the case with the leopard-seals, but the smaller kinds lie in half-dozens and tens, and as many as forty-seven were seen on one piece during the recent cruise. On one occasion several seals were found upon a tilted berg; so high was the lowest edge above the surface of the water that the boat's crew with difficulty clambered up and secured their prey. Yet the seals must have made a leap from the water on to this their last resting-place. December seems to be their mating-season: about that time they are in very poor condition, and very much scarred. The females appear to be as freely scarred as the males. It was also noted that the seals were most numerous where the water was bluest and clearest—this in all probability meaning that they were more numerous on the outside of the pack, since the muddy olive-brown colour of the water, due to diatoms, seen so frequently in the south polar seas, seems to indicate proximity to the main pack. The males appear to be as numerous as the females, and, in the case of the leopard-seal and Weddell's seal at least, the males are perhaps rather smaller than the females. They move swiftly through the water, and can throw themselves eight or nine feet above the surface, covering distances of fully 20 feet. Their moaning in the gloaming of a calm grey day comes as a weird sound through the haze, and makes the icy solitude more lonely, adding awe to a scene already full of fascination. They seem to wonder at man, and not recognising him as an enemy they allow him to approach, only to be laid low with club or bullet. It is a matter of great regret that they should be so indiscriminately massacred; there is no regard for sex or age, and even females heavy with young do not escape. If fleets of sealers continue to visit the south, there should be some law of protection, otherwise there is no doubt that, like the southern fur-seals at the beginning of the century, these Antarctic seals will be exterminated."

The second genus is represented by the still more beautiful Antarctic white seal (*Lobodon carcinophaga*), distinguished from the last by the much compressed and elongated cheek teeth having one chief recurved cusp, with one anterior, and from one to three much smaller but distinct posterior cusps. Of this lovely seal Mr. Bruce writes that "its coat is of a beautiful creamy white, resembling that of the polar bear, but short-haired, the colour becoming somewhat more intense along the back. Looking at the animal face to face, its coat appears silvery, and the dorsal stripe almost vanishes; but when looked at from behind it assumes a deeper cream colour, and the broad stripe along the back becomes quite prominent. The full-grown animal may attain a length of about seven feet. The sea-leopard is a very striking animal, and, with the exception of the elephant-seal, is the largest of true seals. In the recent Antarctic expedition (1892-3) some were met with that measured over 13 feet in length. Their coat is a dark brown-grey and mottled, becoming paler grey below, and in some cases almost black on the back. A rather striking and not altogether inappropriate name was given to these seals by the sailors in the recent cruise; they called them 'serpents,' and they do really often look very serpent-like with their long necks and green eyes." Less common is Weddell's seal (*Leptonychotes weddelli*), in which the cheek-teeth are small, with simple, somewhat compressed, conical crowns, carrying a broad basal ledge, but no distinct fore-and-aft cusps. These seals are nearly as large as the leopard-seal, but of less graceful make, having a thicker coat of blubber, and the fur more woolly, and dark brownish-grey in colour. The last member of the sub-family is the rare Ross's seal (*Ommatophoca rossi*), characterised by the small size of all the teeth, the small posterior, and still smaller anterior cusps of those of the cheek series, and the very large size of the sockets of the eyes, as well as by the small size of the claws on the front-flippers, and their absence in the hinder pair. It is described as a beautiful animal, with large, affectionate-looking eyes, and resembling the white seal in form and size, but with a mottled grey pellage, darker above than below.

The third and last sub-family is represented solely by the hooded or bladder-seal (*Cystophora cristata*) of the Arctic Seas, and the gigantic elephant-seal (*Macrorhinus leoninus*) of the Southern Ocean and the coast of California. In this group the incisor teeth form two pairs in the upper, and one pair in the lower jaw, the total number of teeth thus being 30, in place of the 32 characterising the preceding sub-family; and as a rule the cheek-teeth are implanted by single roots. In the males the nose is surmounted by an appendage capable of being inflated at will; and the first and fifth toes of the hind-flippers are much longer than the others; all these toes having the claws rudimental or absent, and webs projecting beyond their tips. The hooded-seal takes its name from the large loose sac of skin over the nostrils of the full-grown males, which, when inflated with air, looks somewhat like a hood. Rudimental nails are present on the hind-feet; and the last molar in each jaw is generally implanted by two roots. In the elephant-seal, on the other hand, the old males have a kind of trunk-like prolongation of the nose, which, although ordinarily limp, can be distended under the stimulus of excitement. All the teeth are relatively small, those of the cheek series being all simple and single-rooted, and nails are totally wanting on the hind-flippers. The elephant-seal is the largest of all seals, the males attaining the enormous length of 20 feet, and the females about one-third less. Mr. Bruce writes that "the males are said to come ashore on the South Shetlands about the end of August and beginning of September, and in the first part of October are followed by the females. The males are very fat when they first arrive, but get lean towards the end of December, when they leave the islands. Another herd was said to visit the islands about the middle of January—when they renew their hair—and still another in March; by the end of April all returning to the sea. They are very difficult to kill, but, like the other species, allow themselves to be approached even with a club. This seal used to be highly valued for its blubber; in 1821 and 1822 alone as much as 940 tons of sea-elephant oil was taken from the South Shetlands; and it may here be mentioned that during these same two years at least 320,000 fur-seals were also taken from these islands."

ORDER V.—RODENTIA.

MAMMALS THAT GNAW.

NEXT to the Bats, the order of Mammals most easily defined is the one including the Rodents or Gnawing Mammals, all of which have a very similar and peculiar type of dentition specially adapted for rasping and gnawing hard vegetable substances. The order comprises a large number of families and genera, many of which are exceedingly numerous in species, so that the total number of its members is greater than that of any ordinal group in the whole class. As common and well-known examples of the Rodent order may be cited squirrels, dormice, marmots, beavers, rats, voles, porcupines, and hares and rabbits, all of which are characterised by possessing a pair of chisel-shaped teeth in the front of each jaw, which are worn by use into a sharp, cutting, transverse edge, and grow continuously throughout the life of their owners. It is with these chisel-like front or incisor teeth that the Rodents perform that gnawing action (so markedly developed in the beavers and porcupines) from which they derive their name ; and it is owing to the circumstance that the front of each tooth is faced with a plate of hard enamel, while the remainder consists of soft ivory, that these beautiful instruments maintain their cutting-edges. These two pairs of front teeth are absolutely characteristic of all Rodents; and in by far the greater majority of the order there are no other teeth in this region of the jaw. As if, however, for the purpose of hinting how these animals were originally related to Mammals provided with a fuller set of teeth, the hares and rabbits, together with their near allies the picas or tailless hares, have a minute pair of somewhat similar teeth placed immediately behind the large pair in the upper jaw. Being perfectly useless to their owners, this second pair of upper front teeth evidently comes under the category of rudimental or vestigiary structures. Behind the front teeth of all Rodents comes a long gap in each jaw, after which is the series of grinding or cheek teeth, which are never more than six in number, and are frequently reduced to four, or even three. Consequently, no member of the order ever has canine teeth. Were it not that there are two groups of animals with a dentition of a similar type, these peculiarities in the teeth would absolutely distinguish Rodents from all other members of the Mammalian class. Of the groups in question, the one contains the wombats of Australia, which are broadly distinguished by the presence of a pouch for the young, while the second group is represented solely by the curious aye-aye of Madagascar, which agrees in its internal anatomy with the lemurs, and is accordingly assigned to that group. With these exceptions the dentition is absolutely characteristic of the Rodent order ; and as the student is not likely to confound with them either of the creatures named, he may rely on the nature of the teeth in identifying the members of the order. A curious feature in the anatomy of Rodents is that the mouth is divided into two chambers communicating by a narrow orifice ; the first containing the incisors, and the second the cheek teeth, and the hair being continued inwards behind the former. The object of this arrangement is evidently to prevent the intrusion of foreign objects into the mouth. As a rule collar-bones are well developed, although they may be wanting. There are generally five toes to the fore-feet, but in the hind-feet the number may be reduced to four, or even three; the claws being usually sharp and curved. A single species of *Spermophilus* has a ringed tail.

The order has a cosmopolitan distribution, being fairly well represented even in Australia, New Guinea, and Madagascar; but it is in South America that it attains its maximum development, the number of family types peculiar to that region being very large. In size, Rodents vary from that of a rather small pig to that of the smallest shrew, the harvest-mouse being one of the most minute of Mammals. The carpincho (*Hydrochœrus capivara*) of South America is the largest of the Rodents. As regards habits, all feed almost exclusively upon vegetable substances (except perhaps one rat from the Philippines, and a second from South America), but in other respects they present great diversity. The flying-squirrels, for instance, are flying, arboreal, and nocturnal, whereas the ground-squirrels are terrestrial. Others again, such as the marmots, form large colonies, the members of which live in burrows, and are to a great extent diurnal; while others, like the beaver and coypu, have taken to an aquatic life. In structure, Rodents are so much alike that somewhat obscure osteological characters have to be relied upon in order to divide them into groups.

Fig. 54.—THE CARPINCHO (*Hydrochœrus capivara*).

African Flying-Squirrels.—Family *Anomaluridæ*.

Agreeing with the great bulk of the order in the possession of only a single pair of upper incisor teeth, the members of this and the three following families constitute a group (*Sciuromorpha*) chiefly characterised by certain peculiarities in the structure of the skull. In this portion of the skull the cheek or zygomatic arch (that is to say the long slender bar of bone running along the lower border of the socket of the eye) is chiefly formed by the bone known as the jugal, which is not supported by a backwardly-directed process from the upper jawbone, or maxilla; postorbital processes arising from the frontals to define the hinder margin of the sockets of the eyes may or may not be developed; and in the lower jaw the hinder, or angular portion arises from the socket of the lower incisor tooth.

Although flying-squirrels are abundant in the Oriental countries, in Africa south of the Sahara their place is taken by a separate family, comprising two distinct genera. These African flying-squirrels differ from their Asiatic cousins in that the parachute, by means of which they take their long flying leaps, is supported in front by a rod of cartilage projecting from the elbow, instead of from the wrist; and an additional peculiarity is the presence of a row of overlapping horny scales on the under surface of the tail, which are believed to be of use in climbing. The typical representatives of the family are the short-tailed flying-squirrels (*Anomalurus*), most of the species inhabiting West Africa, although one is found in Equatoria, and a second near

Zanzibar. The smallest is the equatorial flying-squirrel (*A. pusillus*), in which the length of the head and body is 11 inches, and that of the tail just over five inches. The second genus (*Idiurus*) is represented only by a single species from the Cameruns district, which is not larger than a small house-mouse, the length of the head and body being only just over two and a half inches, and that of the tail four inches. Agreeing with the ordinary African flying-squirrels in the general form and mode of support of the parachute, as well as in the presence of rows of scales on the under surface of the tail, this species is at once distinguished by the short, knob-like nose, and the thinly-haired tail; the latter terminating in a pencil of hairs, and being nearly double the length of the head and body, instead of shorter. In place of being uniformly and thickly covered with fur, the tail is short-haired on its upper surface, with three longitudinal rows of elongated sparse hairs, while beneath it is naked, with three rows of scales near the base. An important difference is also to be found in the structure of the fore-foot, in which the thumb is reduced to a mere knob-like rudiment, while in the hind-foot the first toe is much smaller than the other four, which are of approximately equal length. There are likewise structural differences in the skull, into the consideration of which it will be unnecessary to enter on this occasion. In colour, the fur of the back and upper surface of the parachute is pale whitish-brown, the hairs being blackish-grey at the base; while on the under surface the general hue is a mixture of yellowish and dark grey, with a tinge of silver-grey on the parachute.

Fig. 55.—LONG-TAILED AFRICAN FLYING-SQUIRREL (*Idiurus*).

Writing of the habits of Pel's flying-squirrel (*Anomalurus peli*) of West Africa, Mr. W. H. Adams observes that "these squirrels come out of their holes in the trees some hours after sunset, returning long before daybreak. They are only to be seen on bright moonlight nights, and, in fact, the natives say they do not come out at all in stormy weather or on very dark nights. They live on berries and fruits, being specially fond of the palm oil-nut, which they take to their nests to peel and eat. They pass from tree to tree with great rapidity, usually choosing to jump from a higher branch to a lower one, and then climbing up the tree to make a fresh start. The temperature on the hills varies considerably. During the time I was there—the rainy season, from the middle of April to the middle of June—it was never very hot, one night the thermometer going down to 44 deg. on the ground. Of course, in the dry season it is much hotter, but the natives say these animals are much more plentiful in the rains, and that the rainier the season the more they see. They litter twice a year, once about September, the young remaining in the nest for about nine weeks, during which they are fed by the old ones on such food as shoots and kernels; they do not attempt to jump till the end of that period, extending the length of their jumps with their growth. I do not know the other time of breeding, or whether they have a regular season. The hunters told me that two or three were usually born at one birth, and never more than four."

This extensive family includes not only ordinary squirrels, but likewise the typical, or northern flying-squirrels, together with marmots, chipmunks, etc. The family is distinguished from the last by the absence of scales on the bushy tail, and the presence of postorbital processes defining the hinder border of the socket of the eye; while if a parachute is developed, it is supported by a cartilaginous rod arising from the wrist. The palate is broad, and there are usually two pairs of upper and one of lower premolar teeth, although the first pair in the upper jaw, which are always small, may be shed at an early age, or even wanting. The cheek teeth are rooted, and in the young always bear tubercles on their crowns, although in the adult these may be converted into deep plates separated by clefts extending partially across the crown. With the exception of Madagascar and Australasia, the family has a cosmopolitan range.

Squirrel Tribe.—Family *Sciuridæ*.

The first genus is represented only by the large groove-toothed squirrel (*Rhithrosciurus*) of Borneo, easily recognised by the numerous vertical grooves on the upper incisor teeth. Next come the Ethiopian spiny squirrels (*Xerus*), typically characterised by the coarse spiny fur, the small size or absence of external ears, and the comparatively straight and long claws; while they are further distinguished by certain features of the skull and teeth. This group ranges all over Africa from Abyssinia southwards. The numerous species of true squirrels (*Sciurus*) differ from the last by the shortness of the skull, in which the postorbital processes are more elongated. The tail is very long and bushy; the ears are generally large, and in some instances tufted; there are only four functional toes to the fore-feet; the claws are long, curved, and sharp; and the females have either four or six teats. The cheek teeth have low tuberculated crowns. The genus has a very wide distribution, but attains its maximum development in the Malayan countries. Whereas, with the exception of the muzzle and chest, the common squirrel (*S. vulgaris*) is nearly uniform brownish-red, the little Indian palm-squirrel (*S. palmarum*) is marked with longitudinal dark and light stripes on the back, and many species have two or three conspicuous bright-coloured and white bands on the flanks, while one American form is peculiar among Mammals in assuming a special brilliant breeding-dress. All the squirrels are arboreal, but their habits are too well known to need special mention. From the true squirrels the ground-squirrels, or chipmunks (*Tamias*), of the northern portions of both hemispheres, differ by having pouches inside the cheeks for the storage of food; and are also characterised by the presence of distinct white or greyish-white longitudinal stripes bordered by black bands on the sides, or sides and back. Chipmunks, which are among the most common of North American Rodents, are terrestrial in their habits, and chiefly remarkable for the accumulations of food which they collect for winter use; such supplies being carried to the place of storage in the capacious cheek pouches.

The susliks, or gophers (*Spermophilus* [1]), which have a geographical distribution nearly similar to that of the chipmunks, although most of them are found in desert regions where the latter never go, are readily characterised by their somewhat slender and squirrel-like form, the presence of cheek pouches, and the rudimental first toe of the fore-foot, which may, however, be provided with a nail. In the skull the first upper premolar is larger than in the true squirrels, and the two series of cheek teeth are nearly parallel. The ears may be either minute, or relatively large and tufted; and the tail

[1] The earlier name *Anisonyx* is used by American authors.

may be either of medium length, or reduced to a stump. The coloration, which is never like that of the chipmunks, may be either uniform or striped. In habits, the susliks are social and burrowing animals, selecting dry sandy soil for their underground habitations; and in the colder portion of their range hibernating during the inclement months of the year. The common American species is the striped gopher (*S. tridecemlineatus*). Susliks agree with the two following genera in that the incisor teeth lack the compressed form characterising those of the squirrels and their immediate allies, and also in the simple structure of their molars. The prairie-marmots, or prairie-dogs (*Cynomys*) of North America form in some respects a connecting link between the susliks and the true marmots, being intermediate in size between the two, and having stouter bodies than the former. Their ears are small, and the tail is generally short, while their cheek pouches are less capacious than those of the susliks, and the first toe of the fore-feet is well developed, and carries a large claw. The massive skull has the large postorbital processes directed nearly outwards, and the stout molar teeth, which form two series converging behind, differ from those of both the susliks and marmots in having three, in place of two grooves, on their crowns. In habits the prairie-marmots very closely resemble the true marmots, but the mounds of earth they throw up from their burrows have a very distinct crater-like form.

From the prairie-marmots the true marmots (*Arctomys*) may be distinguished by their stouter form, the absence of cheek pouches, the rudimental first toe of the fore-foot, which carries only a small flat nail, and the above-mentioned differences in the form and direction of the upper molar teeth. Marmots are common to the northern half of both the Old and New World, ranging as far south as the Pyrenees, Alps, and Himalaya. They are among the larger members of the order, the common Alpine marmot measuring more than 20 inches in length, exclusive of the tail. In appearance they are stoutly built, with short legs, powerful claws, a broad and short head, small and rounded ears, and a bushy tail, usually less than half the length of the body. Their fur is moderately long, and somewhat stiff; while their colour exhibits various tints of golden or reddish-brown, shading, more or less markedly into black along the back and tail, the tip of the latter being always blackish. As regards their habits, marmots live in extensive societies, their large and deep burrows forming warrens, and communicating with one another underground. All the regions they inhabit experience a very severe winter climate, during which the marmots hibernate securely in the depths of their burrows, only waking from their long sleep at the melting of the snows. Those that dwell in the mountains of Europe and Asia generally select open valleys or uplands, where the soil is more or less sandy, for the construction of their burrows, the neighbourhood of water being essential. In Russia and Siberia they inhabit the open and barren steppes. Extreme wariness, especially where they dwell on frequented routes, is characteristic

Fig. 56.—COMMON MARMOT (*Arctomys marmotta*).

of all marmots. During the daytime they may be seen playing around their burrows, at the mouths of which they sit upright when the least alarmed. In this situation, the moment they catch sight of a suspicious object, they throw themselves down their burrows, which are often situated at the root of a rhubarb plant, with the well-known shrill scream, at the sound of which any other animal that may be in the vicinity immediately takes alarm. It is almost superfluous to observe that, in order to secure them when thus sitting, it is necessary to shoot marmots dead; for, even with the slightest kick left in them, they will often manage to tumble into their holes before they can be seized. When disturbed for the first time, they will usually reappear after a short interval; but after a second fright they generally sulk, and seldom show again. Wishing to secure a number of skins for rugs, the writer and his party, after much toil, once succeeded in turning a small rivulet into a marmot warren on one of the plateaus of Little Tibet, but, to their dismay, were unable to "bolt" a single marmot—the whole colony preferring to perish miserably by drowning in their burrows rather than face their foes in the open.

In Europe there occur two species of marmot—namely, the Alpine marmot (*A. marmotta*) and the somewhat smaller bobac (*A. bobac*). The former is an exclusively European form, only found in the three disconnected mountain chains of the Pyrenees, Alps, and Carpathians, at elevations varying between 5,000 and 1,000 feet, where it meets with a climate suitable to its existence. The second species, in which the head and body measure about 15 inches in length, has its western limit on the German frontier, and thence ranges eastward through Galicia and Poland, right across the steppes of Southern Russia, and thence to Amur, Kamschatka, and Siberia—the climate of these regions being sufficiently rigorous to admit of the existence of these animals at ordinary elevations. It is noteworthy that marmots do not extend to the north-westward either into Lapland or the Scandinavian peninsula, where the country does not present the character of the Russian steppes, which in summer are scorched by a burning heat, and in winter form a trackless expanse of snow. The southern limits of the bobac do not appear to be yet definitely known. When, however, we reach the mountains of Yarkand and other parts of Turkestan, and thence proceed southwards to the northern districts of Ladak in Western Tibet, we meet with a very similar, although somewhat larger, short-tailed species known as the Himalayan marmot (*A. himalayanus*), the range of which appears to extend eastward into Tibet proper, where this species has been described under other names. The Himalayan marmot is another species which, at all events in the southern portion of its range, can only find a suitable climate at great elevations, the height at which it is usually found in Ladak and Turkestan varying between 12,000 feet and something over 17,000 feet. Another species is also met with in the neighbourhood of Yarkand and the Pamir, at elevations of about 13,000 feet, known as the golden marmot (*A. aureus*), and is distinguished from the last by its more golden colour, and shorter and thicker tail. Examples of this species were also obtained in Turkestan during Przewalski's expeditions. To the south-west the writer, when crossing the elevated plateau of Deosai, or "Devil's Plains," situated between the town of Skardo on the Indus in Western Tibet and the mountains north of Kashmir, the elevation of which is between 12,500 feet and 13,000 feet, found marmots exceedingly abundant, although he was unable to determine to which of the two preceding species they belonged, or whether they were more nearly allied to the Cabul species to be immediately mentioned. The Deosai plateau, it may be mentioned, is one of the most desolate and dreary regions that can well be imagined, consisting of rolling hills and dunes of sand and gravel, with a sparse coating of vegetation, where almost the only living things to be seen are marmots and mosquitoes. The climate is most rigorous; the sun's rays beating down with terrific power through the dry and rarified atmosphere during the day in the summer months, but the temperature rapidly falling, and often sinking below the freezing point after sunset. In winter this region is absolutely impassable; so that its climate may be regarded as an intensification of that of the steppes.

The Cabul marmot (*A. dichrous*), which is also met with in Turkestan, is a smaller species than the golden marmot, from which it is further distinguished by its duller coloration, and the absence of any black on the back. The regions whence it is obtained have a climate of the general character mentioned above. The last species to be mentioned is known as the red or long-tailed marmot (*A. caudatus*). This appears to be the largest of all those found in the Old World, attaining a length of nearly two feet, exclusive of the tail, which measures about one foot. It is readily recognised, not only by its size and long, bushy tail, but also by the full rufous tinge of the hair, and the large extent of black found on the back of many individuals, the skins being handsomer than those of any of the other kinds.

The distribution of this Himalayan marmot is extremely interesting as showing that these animals can only exist in an arid climate more or less nearly approaching that of the steppes or of Tibet. To understand this, it must be mentioned that the immense mountain-barrier lying to the northward of the valley of Kashmir, the lowest gap in which has an elevation of 11,500 feet, cuts off almost completely the clouds coming up from the plains of India from the more or less arid regions to the northward. Now, whereas marmots are totally unknown on the great range of mountains south of the Kashmir valley, where the rainfall is excessive, directly the traveller reaches the summits of the passes of the northern range, and thence far down on the northern side, the shrill cry of the red marmot strikes his ear. This is very noticeable in travelling on the Central Asian high road up the Sind Valley, when he crosses the Zogi Pass into the Tibetan area. This marmot may likewise be met with on crossing the passes leading to our distant frontier station of Gilgit; and it also appears to range into many parts of Ladak, although its exact limits are not yet accurately defined. It is thus evident that marmots now exist only at such elevations or in such regions as possess an extreme continental climate—that is to say, one where the summers are hot and the winters excessively cold. It has been shown that in Europe the Alpine marmot inhabits three distinct and isolated ranges, separated from one another by low-lying areas possessing a climate entirely different from the type above referred to; and it is thus clear that it could not have crossed these unsuitable low areas while the climate of Europe was the same as at the present day. That there must have been at some time or other a direct communication between these isolated marmot areas is, therefore, self-evident.

The next section of the *Sciuridæ* is formed by the true, or northern flying squirrels, of which there are three well-marked generic groups. In all these animals the parachute is supported by a rod of cartilage projecting like a yard-arm from the outer side of the wrist, and there is another expansion of skin connecting the fore-limbs with the neck, while there may be a third between the hind-legs and the root of the tail. The whole of these flying-squirrels are characterised by the complex structure of their molar teeth ; and as their skulls differ considerably from those of other members of the family, they must be regarded as constituting a sub-family group by themselves.

Flying-squirrels of this group have existed since a comparatively early epoch in the Tertiary period, and it is consequently impossible to affiliate them with any of the genera of ordinary squirrels ; so that it is quite likely that they have originated from a totally extinct genus or genera. Hence, it is impossible to say whether the three genera into which they are divided have all taken origin from one non-volant form, or whether the power of flight has been separately evolved in each of the three generic groups. Of the three genera, the one known as *Sciuropterus* includes the lesser flying-squirrels, all of which have the crowns of their molar teeth comparatively low, and the parachute of moderate width, and not including any portion of the tail. Having one representative in North America, and a second in North-Eastern Europe and Siberia, the lesser flying-squirrels are mainly characteristic of India and the Malayan countries. While some of the larger kinds measure as much as 12 inches from the nose to the root of the tail, in the pigmy flying-squirrel of Cochin-China and Arakan the length of the head and body scarcely exceeds five inches. These squirrels collect in numbers in hollow trees, where they remain in slumber during the daytime, to issue forth at night for the purpose of feeding. Climbing to a coign of vantage on some tree, they take their flying leaps to the bough or trunk of another at a lower level, not unfrequently covering a distance of some 30 or 40 yards. The length of the leap is, however, still greater among the members of the next genus, reaching from 60 to nearly 80 yards. The larger flying-squirrels (*Pteromys*) form an exclusively Asiatic group, represented by some ten species, and extending from the Malayan countries as far north as Eastern Tibet. In addition to their superior dimensions, these flying-squirrels are distinguished from the preceding group by the greater width of the parachute along the sides of the body, and the enclosure of the base of the tail in the portion connecting the two hind-legs. The tail itself is, moreover, completely cylindrical, instead of slightly compressed ; and the molar teeth have rather taller and more complex crowns than in the lesser flying-squirrels. In some of the larger species the head and body may measure as much as 18 inches in length, while the tail may reach to 24 or 25 inches. The last member of the sub-family is the woolly flying-squirrel (*Eupetaurus*) —a large species from the neighbourhood of Gilgit, distinguished by the very tall molar teeth, which have flat, instead of ridged, masticating surfaces.

Finally, the five species of pigmy squirrels (*Nannosciurus*), of which one is West African, a second from the Philippines, while the other three are Bornean, constitute another sub-family, c aracterised by certain peculiarities in the skull and the complex structure of the molar teeth.

The Sewellels.—Family *Haplodontidæ*.

An unimportant family is constituted by two North American Rodents known as sewellels (*Haplodon*), which differ from the *Sciuridæ* by the absence of postorbital processes in the skull and the rootless molars. According to Dr. Merriam, they are aquatic in their habits.

The last family of the squirrel-like group of the order is represented only by the beavers (*Castor*), easily distinguished by the broad, flattened, and scaly tail. The skull is massively made and devoid of postorbital processes, with the angle of the lower jaw rounded; the cheek teeth do not develop roots, and have their crowns marked with re-entering folds of enamel; the premolars are limited to a single pair in each jaw; and the hind-feet are webbed.

The Beavers.— Family *Castoridæ.*

Beavers, which are the largest Rodents in the Northern Hemisphere, and are thoroughly aquatic in their habits, are confined to certain parts of that hemisphere, being found only in Europe, Northern Asia, and North America. The actual extent of their range in the Old World is not so clearly defined as could be wished. There is, however, ample evidence that this range originally extended from the British Islands in the west, to France, and perhaps Italy, Spain, and Greece, in the south, thence eastward to Asia Minor, and possibly Persia, and to the north-eastward as far as the Yenesei and Lena in Siberia, and thence to Amur, Scandinavia, and Russia; but there does not appear to be any good evidence as to the eastern limits of beavers in the direction of Northern China, although it may not be improbable that in this region these animals only inhabited the rivers flowing northwards into the Caspian Sea and the Arctic Ocean. On the Continent, beavers were finally exterminated in Holland in 1825. In France a number of names, such as Bièvre, Beuvron, and Beuvray, or Beuvry, as well as the ancient Bibrax and Bibracte, point to the originally wide distribution of beavers. Fossil remains of these animals occur in many places, such as Abbeville, in the valley of the Somme, the neighbourhoods of Paris and Clermont, and the cavern of Lunel-Viel, in Hérault. The Rhone and its tributaries, especially the Gardon and the Cèse, appear to have been the great stronghold of these creatures within the historic period. Even, however, in the last century they had become exceedingly rare, owing to the incessant persecution to which they had been subjected. Still, they have been met with at intervals even up to the present day. Thus Gervais records the capture of a specimen in 1846, close to the port of Avignon, and mentions having seen two others near Arles. The floods of 1840 doubtless led to the destruction of a considerable number, so that after this date they were much more rare than formerly. The circumstance that the monks of a monastery on the right bank of the Rhone at Villeneuve-les-Avignon included beavers among their *plats maigres*, indicates that in earlier days they were probably abundant. M. St. Hilaire, in the *Bulletin de la Societé d'Acclimatation* for 1888, records the capture of three specimens during that year in the Rhone, and a recent writer concludes that from 25 to 30 beavers are still annually killed in that river and its tributaries. There does not appear to be evidence that these animals linger in any other of the French rivers.

Fig. 57.—BEAVER (*Castor fiber*).

It is mentioned in some of the old writers that beavers occur rarely in Italy, Spain, and Greece, but it is difficult to find on what evidence these statements rest ; but since remains of the existing species are found in the superficial beds in the neighbourhood of Rome, there is a considerable likelihood that its alleged occurrence in Italy within the historic period may be based on fact. The lake-cities or "phalbauten" of Switzerland afford evidence of the abundance of beavers in that country during the pre-historic period, and in the last century a few were still to be found in the Aar, Limmat, Reuss, and other tributaries of the Rhine. That some lingered on into the present century is proved by a specimen from the Rhine exhibited in the Jardin des Plantes in 1829 ; and there is evidence of their presence in the early part of this century both in the Rhine and the Rhone basins.

In Germany fossil remains of beavers are found in several of the great caves, more especially in that of Gailenreuth in Franconia. As late as the closing decades of the last and the early ones of the present century, colonies of these animals were abundant on many of the German rivers, remnants of which still exist here and there up to the present time. In North-Western Germany the Moselle and the Maas were formerly noted habitats of these animals, although we have no record of the date of their disappearance, even if this has yet taken place. The Lippe, which, like the Moselle, is a tributary of the Rhine, was likewise a well-known haunt. Thus at Ketlinghausen, and still higher up the river at Padderbun, beavers were abundant, and formed regular colonies, like their Canadian cousins, at the beginning of the present century, and it is probable that some few still exist. Proceeding northward to the basin of the Elbe, the account by Meyernick, published in 1829, of a colony on one of the tributaries of this river near Magdeburg, is too well known to need repetition. Lower down the river at Wittenberg, and also at Kähnert, they were also comparatively abundant in 1801 ; and at the former locality there is evidence of their occurrence in 1848, and again as late as 1878, when no less than eight individuals were observed in an old river channel. Again in Bohemia, the valley of the Moldau, with its numerous affluents, which forms the upper reaches of the extensive basin drained by the Elbe, abounded in beavers up to the year 1848, since which date, in spite of strict precaution, they have probably been greatly reduced in numbers. The basin of the Danube, in South-Eastern Germany, is, however, probably the greatest stronghold of German beavers at the present time. In 1837 the small river Amper, a tributary of the Isar, situated some distance to the north of Munich, was occupied by several colonies, which were preserved as a valuable commercial property. There is also good evidence of the existence of the last-named colonies, as well as of others on the Isar, Iller, and Salzach—tributaries of the Danube—up to 1846, since which date I have been unable to come across any records of them.

There is a dearth of information with regard to the presence of beavers lower down the Danube valley in Austria-Hungary and Turkey ; but it is certain that they did, or do still, exist in the former regions ; and they have also been recorded from the Lower Danube on well-authenticated evidence. That beavers may have existed, or still exist, in other parts of European Turkey, is suggested by the fact of their appearance in Asia Minor. They have been recorded in the upper Euphrates valley by Helfer in a book published in 1879 ; while Eichwald long since mentioned their occurrence in the rivers of the Caucasus; and Smarda included them in his list of the Mammals of Mesopotamia. Messrs. Danford and Alston observe that trustworthy authorities at Kaisariyeh (a town in Rumelia, on the Kizil river, flowing into the Black Sea) stated "that in the marshes between that place and Sudjesu there existed an animal like an otter, but which had a broad, hairless tail." And there can be no reasonable doubt that these authors are right in identifying this creature with the beaver. The possible eastward extension of the beaver into Persia is suggested by Mr. Blanford.

From the Caucasus the range of the beaver may be traced through Russia, Poland, and Livonia, to Lapland, and thence to the Scandinavian Peninsula. Immediately to the north of the Caucasus, Oken recorded their abundance in the valley of the Tereck in 1842. In Central Russia there is no definite evidence of their occurrence, but in the Baltic provinces of Livonia the record is again ample. Many places in this district take, indeed, their name from beavers, and about the middle of the last century these animals appear to have had populous colonies on most of the streams of the country. In 1724, so common were they, that their dams were a serious inconvenience to the district, owing to the floods caused by them. It appears, however, from the researches of Loewis, that beavers are now completely exterminated from Livonia, the last specimen having been shot in 1841. In 1889 the existence of a few beavers in the river Svislotch, Government of Mink, and also in the Dnieper, was recorded. In North Russia the rivers Dwina and Petchora, flowing respectively into the White Sea and the Arctic Ocean, were the resorts of beavers as late as 1842, but it is probable that they are now completely extinct. Passing eastward into Silesia, there is evidence of the former wide distribution of these animals, it being stated that they extended as far as Amur. In the basin of the Obi, in Western Siberia, they appear to be extinct in the valley of the Irtsh, where they were formerly abundant; but at least up to 1876 they continued to be found in the small affluent of the Obi known as the Pelyin. Beavers have long since completely disappeared from the Yenesei, in Eastern Siberia, but information is still required with regard to the more easterly valley of the Lena. In Poland and Lithuania beavers may still linger on; but, as already observed, there is a want of evidence as to the limits of their original range in the region lying eastward of a line connecting the Baltic with the Black Sea. Reverting to the neighbourhood of the White Sea, and pursuing a course towards the north-east, it appears that Lapland lost its beavers early in the present century. The skull of the last specimen known to have been killed in these regions was obtained about 1830.

In Scandinavia, although beavers were widely distributed in the last and early part of the present century, it appears that they have now totally disappeared from Sweden but still exist in at least three remote spots in Norway. The number of specimens living in the latter country in 1880 was estimated at not more than 60; but Collett placed their number at about 100, and, as they were strictly preserved, he did not consider that they were decreasing. Completing this survey of the range of the European beaver with Denmark, evidence of its former existence is found in the shape of skulls and bones from the mosses and turbaries, while it is also known to have lived there within the historic period. As to the precise date of its extermination, there appears no definite record.

With regard to the range of the American beaver, few words will suffice. It may be observed, in the first place, that, although some writers are indisposed to regard this beaver as specifically distinct from the European one; yet, from the constant difference in the form of the bones of the nasal region of the skull, it seems to be a valid species, the proper name of which is *Castor canadensis*. The earliest epoch of its occurrence is in the Pleistocene deposits of South Carolina, New Jersey, Tennessee, and other localities, as well as in the cavern-deposits of Virginia and Pennsylvania. Within the historic period its range extended from Alaska and the Hudson Bay territories in the north, along the Atlantic seaboard as far south as Georgia and Northern Florida, and thence along the Gulf of Mexico as far as the Rio Grande in Texas, and for some distance into Mexico itself, while on the Pacific Coast it is known to have extended as far south as California and Arizona. In the interior of the continent beavers were naturally confined to the neighbourhood of the great lakes and river valleys. Writing in 1877 of the American beaver, Dr. Allen observes that "its present range, however, is much less extended, very few being found east of the Mississippi River south of the great lakes, and it is everywhere less numerous than formerly. Some still remain in Northern Maine and in the Adirondack region of New York, and probably some still survive thence southward in the sparsely settled districts to Alabama and Mississippi. A recent article states that they are still abundant in portions of Virginia. Their existence in great abundance throughout the Atlantic States, and thence westward to the Pacific, is thoroughly attested. They having been less persistently hunted during recent years than formerly, they are reported to be slowly on the increase in most localities where they still remain."

The Dormouse Tribe.—Family *Myoxidæ*.

The dormice are the first representatives of the second section of the Rodents, or Myomorpha, which presents the following characteristics. In the skull the zygomatic arch is slender, and usually has the jugal bone extending but little forwards, being supported by a long backwardly directed process of the upper jaw-bone, or maxilla. There are no postorbital processes defining the hinder border of the socket of the eye; and, except in one sub-family of the *Spalacidæ*, the angle of the lower jaw takes origin from the inferior surface of the sheath of the lower incisor. All the members of the section differ from the Sciuromorpha in that the tibia and fibula, or bones of the lower leg, are welded together.

Resembling the true squirrels in shape and habits, the dormice form an Old World family of small arboreal Rodents characterised by their long hairy tail, the large size of the ears and eyes, and the shortness of the fore-limbs. There is but one pair of premolars in each jaw, and the molars are rooted with transverse re-entering foldings of enamel on their crowns. The dormice may be divided into two main groups, according to the structure of the stomach. In *Myoxus*, as typified by *M. glis* of continental Europe, the stomach is simple, but the different species, which have been arranged under several generic heads, differ considerably in other respects. In the typical species the bushy tail has the hairs arranged in a row on each side, while the molars are large, with flat crowns and complex enamel-foldings. In a second group (*Eliomys*), typified by the European *M. nitella*, and extending over Europe, Asia, and Africa, the tail has the hairs arranged in two rows, but is tufted at the end, while the molars are small, with concave crowns, and the folds of enamel indistinct. The third group of the genus (*Graphiurus*) is solely African, and is distinguished by the tail being short, cylindrical, and tufted, while the enamel-foldings on the small molars are almost wanting. A West African form (*Claviglis*) differs by the shorter and more distinctly tufted tail. On the other hand, the common dormouse of England and the rest of Europe (*Muscardinus avellanarius*) differs from all the foregoing in the thickened glandular walls of the anterior portion of the stomach; the molars having flat crowns, with complicated foldings of enamel, and the somewhat bushy tail being cylindrical. The more northern representatives of the family take their name from the long winter torpor they undergo.

From the *Myoxidæ* the very extensive and cosmopolitan family of the *Muridæ*, which includes rats, mice, and voles, may be distinguished by the total absence of premolar teeth in both jaws. The group is, however, better characterised by the structure of the skull, in which the frontal bones are markedly constricted, while in the zygomatic arch the short and slender jugal bone is in most cases reduced to a small splint connecting a backwardly-directed process from the upper jaw-bone, or maxilla, with a forward projection from the squamosal bone at the hinder end of the skull. Still more characteristic is the expansion of the lower part of the first-named process into a large, flattened descending plate; and in most cases the large aperture in the skull for the passage of nerves situated beneath the anterior root of the zygomatic arch is elevated, and much wider above than below. The first toe of the fore-foot is rudimental, and in most cases naked and scaly. This family, which includes more than a third of the members of the entire order, is the only one among the Rodents represented either in Madagascar or in Australia. Although a few species are aquatic, and some arboreal, the great majority of the *Muridæ* are terrestrial, a considerable number of them living in burrows. Some fifty genera have been described.

The Mouse Tribe.—Family *Muridæ*.

The first sub-family is confined to Australia, New Guinea, and the island of Luzon, in the Philippines, where it is represented by three genera. In this group the molars, which are frequently reduced to two pairs in each jaw, develop roots, and have their crowns divided into alternating oblique lobes, partially splitting up into tubercles. In the typical genus *Hydromys*, of Australia and New Guinea, the molars are two in number, and the external form is modified for the needs of an aquatic existence, the feet being webbed, the tip of the muzzle thickly clothed with hairs, by means of which the nostrils can be clothed; while the skull differs from that of other members of the family in that the aperture beneath the socket of the eye is nearly circular, instead of pear-shaped, and the descending vertical plate at the front of the zygomatic arch is absent. In habits the two species of this genus resemble water-voles. The genus *Chrotomys*, of which there is one species from Luzon, differs from the other two in having three pairs of molars; its skull being intermediate between that of the first and third genus, and its external form mouse-like, the toes being devoid of webs. In *Xeromys*, which occurs typically in Australia, but is taken to include a rat from Luzon, the molars resemble those of *Hydromys* in structure and number, but the skull and external form are nearly similar to those of an ordinary mouse. In size this species is not larger than the common mouse, whereas the other members of the group are much bigger.

The Australasian Group.—Sub-Family *Hydromyinæ*.

The second sub-family is represented only by the beautiful little Malabar spiny mouse (*Platacanthomys lasiurus*) of Southern India, which is an arboreal form easily distinguished by the long bushy tail, which exceeds the head and body in length, and also by the presence of flattened spines mingled with the hairs. The rooted molars have their crowns divided into complete transverse laminæ.

Malabar Spiny Mouse (*Platacanthomyinæ*).

The Gerbil Group (*Gerbillinæ*).

The beautiful little large-eyed murines, known as gerbils, typify a third sub-family, characterised by the narrowness of the incisors, the sub-division of the crowns of the molars into transverse laminæ, the generally large size of the auditory bulla of the skull, and the elongation of the hind-limbs. From the other genera, the gerbils (*Gerbillus*), which range over Southern Europe, Asia, and Africa, are distinguished by the deeply grooved upper incisors, and the circumstance that the first molar has one, the second two, and the third three transverse laminæ; the long tail being tufted at the tip Gerbils are inhabitants of desert districts, where they burrow in the sandy soil. Some writers separate certain species as *Meriones*. The short and club-like form of the fleshy tail, as well as the very large size of the auditory bulla of the skull, serve to distinguish the African genus *Pachyuromys*, in which the narrow incisors are faintly grooved. Three other small genera from Africa, namely, *Mystromys*, *Otomys*, and *Dasymys*, differ from the gerbils and from one another in the structure of the molars; they are all typically South African, but the second has also been recorded from East Africa and the Congo. A fifth genus (*Malacomys*), represented by a single species from the Gabun, connects the gerbils with the rats, having the teeth and limbs of the former, but the long scaly tail of the latter.

The Philippine Rats (*Phlæomyinæ*).

Two genera of very large long-haired rats from the Philippine islands represent a sub-family in which the incisors are very broad, the molars divided into transverse laminæ, and the claws large. In *Phlæomys*, of which there is but a single well-defined species, the ears are small and hairy, the tail moderate and sparsely haired, and the auditory bulla very small; the first molar having three, and the others two laminæ. The second genus (*Crateromys*) includes one very large greyish species from Luzon, which may be compared in size to a small marmot, and has a totally different type of molars.

The Tree-Mice (*Dendromyinæ*)

This group, which is confined to Africa south of the Sahara, is typified by the two species of *Dendromys*, and is characterised by the convexity of the incisors, the rooted and tuberculated molars, hairy ears, and long claws. The members of the typical genus have the habits of dormice a slender build, grooved incisors, and a long, scaly, thinly-haired tail. *Steatomys* also has grooved incisors, but of stouter form, and a rather short, thickly-haired tail; while *Lophuromys* differs by its smooth incisors, and the fine flattened bristles which replace the hair. The fourth genus is *Limacomys*.

Cricetine Group (*Cricetinæ*).

The large, generalised, and almost cosmopolitan group of the cricetine *Muridæ* is characterised by the rooted upper molars carrying two longitudinal rows of tubercles. It is typified by the hamsters (*Cricetus*) of the Old World, which are confined to Europe and Asia, and are characterised by having six tubercles on the first upper molar, large cheek pouches, and a very short tail. The true hamster (*C. frumentarius*) is a burrowing species, well known on the Continent from the large amount of food it accumulates in its subterranean dwelling. The white-footed mice (*Sitomys*) of the New World form a very large, closely allied group, in which cheek pouches may be present or absent. They are divided into a number of sub-genera, according to habits, bodily form, dentition, etc., which have been named *Rhipidomys*, *Oryzomys*, *Calomys*, *Vesperimus*, *Onychomys*, *Scapteromys*, *Phyllotis*, *Acodon*, and *Oxymycterus*. *S. hydrobates* is peculiar on account of its fringed feet and aquatic habits;

while another species has spines mingled with the fur. The Brazilian genus *Holochilus*, which includes the largest American rats, differs by the relatively larger last upper molar and the stouter skull. Another allied type are the fish-eating rats (*Ichthyomys*) of South America, characterised by the webbed and fringed hind-feet, and their aquatic and probably fish-eating habits, while *Nectomys* is another allied Peruvian form. The rice-rat (*Sigmodon hispidus*), ranging from the United States to Ecuador, differs markedly from *Sitomys* in the pattern of the tubercles on the molar teeth. Writing of these rats, Mr. G. Lincecum, in the *American Naturalist* for 1872, states that they dwell together on the prairies of Texas in families in much the same manner as the prairie-marmot. "They prefer light sandy soil on the prairie, where the shivered limy sandstone crops out; but where the prairie is enclosed and cultivated they take possession of the fencing, and burrowing under the bottom rail, excavate sufficient cells, and construct their copious grassy beds there. Out on the prairie, in the wild state, they make one principal burrow, in front of which they pile up the earth that comes from all their subterranean galleries. They rarely extend their main burrow more than eight or nine inches in depth, while their underground passages are seldom more than four or five inches below the surface. They also construct several secret outlets, opening 10 or 12 inches from the main hole, which opening they very ingeniously conceal by strewing a few grass blades over it; and so, when the rat-hunter attacks the citadel, the inmates escape through some of the concealed passages. Eight or nine inches deep, and turned a little to one side in the main hole, is a cavity, seven or eight inches in diameter, filled with fine, soft grass blades, which must be quite warm and pleasant, serving the family for winter-quarters. During the hot months they construct nice grass beds in a basin-like cavity, which they dig out under the sides of tufts of grass, or heaps of bush." From all the above the South American genus *Rhithrodon*, with five rat-like species, and the North American *Rhithrodontomys*, containing three species of the size of large mice, differ in their grooved upper incisors. Another well-marked type of the group is presented by the North American wood-rats (*Neotoma*), in which the molars simulate the prismatic pattern characteristic of the voles. Certain species in which the tail is very bushy have been separated generically as *Teonoma*; while *N. alleni* has been referred to a distinct genus under the name of *Hodomys*. The next five genera of cricetines are confined to the island of Madagascar, where they are the sole representatives of the Rodent order. Of these, *Hypogeomys* is a large fawn-coloured rat, with large ears and feet and a long tail; *Nesomys* includes two long-haired rufous species; *Brachytarsomys* contains a single rat with velvety fawn-coloured fur, short feet, and a long tail; the single species of *Hallomys* differs from *Nesomys* by the much longer hind feet; while the two dormouse-like representatives of *Eliurus* are easily recognised by the short and nearly naked ears, and by the long tail being bushy, except on its basal third, where it is scaly. The last representative of the subfamily is the crested rat (*Lophiomys imhausi*) of North-Eastern Africa, so named on account of the crest of long hair running along the back. This very large rat, which is arboreal in its habits, differs from all other members of the family in the first toe of the fore-foot being opposable, the rudimental collar-bones, and by the bony roof covering the muscles of the hinder part of the skull. All the hair is long, the long tail bushy, and the colour black and white. The animal has quite unnecessarily been made the type of a distinct family.

The Vole Group (*Microtinæ*).

Closely allied to the cricetines, of which they may be regarded as a specialised branch, the large group of voles are distinguished by their generally rootless, or imperfectly rooted molars being composed of two longitudinal rows of alternating triangular prisms. Externally they differ in most cases from the typical rats and mice by their heavier and less elegant form, less active movements, smaller eyes, blunter muzzle, smaller ears, and shorter limbs and tail. They are restricted to Europe, Asia north of the Himalaya, and North America. An annectant form between the cricetines and typical voles is the North American genus *Phenacomys*, in which the molars develop roots. The typical genus *Microtus*, which includes nearly half a hundred species ranging over Europe, Northern Asia, and North America, is sufficiently characterised by its rootless molars and the naked soles of the feet; the British forms being the water-vole (*M. amphibius*), the field-vole (*M. agrestis*), and the red, or bank-vole (*M. glareolus*). Each of these is the representative of a distinct sub-generic group, severally characterised by the number of prisms in the molar teeth, and to which the names *Paludicola*, *Agricola*, and *Evotomys* have respectively been applied. The extraordinary hordes in which some species of land voles make their appearance at certain seasons, and the damage they then inflict on agricultural produce, are matters of common knowledge. The round tailed musk-rat of Florida, which has been regarded as constituting a genus (*Neofiber*) by itself, is considered by Dr. Merriam to be not more than a sub-genus of *Microtus*. Nearly allied is the true musk-rat, or musquash (*Fiber zibethicus*), of North America, which is the largest member of the group, and measures nearly a foot in length to the root of the tail. Heavily built, it is characterised by its broad head—which joins the body without any well-defined neck,—short limbs, small eyes, ears nearly concealed in the thick, beaver-like fur, and the rudimental first toe of the fore-foot: the long tail being laterally compressed, scaly, and sparsely haired. The general colour is dark brown, tending to black on the back, and grey on the under-parts. Both sexes have a gland secreting the musky substance from which the animal derives its name. Although its toes are not webbed, the musk-rat is an aquatic creature, feeding on a mixed vegetable and animal diet. Its fur is of considerable value; and the skull is very similar to that of *Microtus*. Another distinct generic type is presented by the groove-toothed vole (*Synaptomys*) of the United States, in which the upper incisors are grooved, while the external form resembles that of the true voles, and the molars are like those of the lemmings. The latter Rodents (*Myodes*), of which there is one Old World and one North American species, differ from the voles by their heavier build, the blunt convex head, very short tail and ears, the hairy soles of the small feet, the bevelled upper incisors, and the pattern of the molar teeth.

The common lemming (*M. lemmus*), which measures about five inches in length, and has yellowish-brown fur with darker spots, is remarkable for the periodical migrations undertaken by its countless swarms; these hordes passing over every obstacle in their course till they finally reach the sea, in which they perish. Nearly allied to the last genus, the circumpolar banded lemming (*Cuniculus torquatus*) may be easily distinguished by the absence of external ears, the shortness of the feet, which are thickly haired beneath, the rudimental first toe of the fore-foot, and the great length of the claws of the third and fourth toes of the same. The molars approximate to those of the voles, but the first in the upper jaw differs from that of all the other members of the sub-family in having seven prisms.

Although frequently regarded as representing a sub-family by themselves, the mole-voles, of which there are two genera, may be considered merely as voles specially adapted for a subterranean existence ; the limbs and tail being very short, and the body somewhat mole-like, while the eyes are small. In the genus *Ellobius*, with one species from Russia, and a second from Afghanistan, the claws are short, whereas in *Siphneus*, of which there are several representatives from Central and Northern Asia, those of the fore-feet are enormously powerful.

Typical Group (*Murinæ*).

In the typical rats and mice and their allies, forming the murine group of the family, the molars are rooted and tuberculated, with three rows of tubercles on at least the anterior ridge of the first one in the upper jaw. Indeed, with one exception, there are three longitudinal rows of tubercles on all the upper molars ; while, save in one genus, there are two such rows in the corresponding lower teeth. The whole group is restricted to the Old World, being represented in Australia and New Guinea, but unknown in Madagascar. The great majority of forms are very similar in external appearance, their build being light, their eyes large and bright, their tails long and scaly, their movements active, their coloration sombre, and their habits generally burrowing and nocturnal.

The least specialised member of the family is a small mouse from the Congo Valley, known as *Deomys*, which differs from all the others in that only the first ridge of the anterior upper molar has three rows of tubercles, the other two ridges of this tooth and all those of the other molars having but two such rows, as in the cricetines. On the other hand, Berdmore's rat (*Hapalomys berdmorei*), from Burma, appears to be the most specialised of all, the lower as well as the upper molars having three longitudinal rows of tubercles. Another peculiar genus (*Vandeleuria*) is represented by a species extending from India to Yunnan, and characterised by having flat nails on the first and fifth digits of both feet, as well as by the great length of the tail. North-Eastern India and some of the countries to the east of the Bay of Bengal are the home of the pencil-tailed tree-mouse (*Chiropodomys*), distinguished by having flat nails on the first digit of both feet, whereas all other members of the family, except one species of *Mus*, have a flat nail only on the first toe of the fore-foot. The next for notice are three genera restricted to the mountains of Luzon, in the Philippine group, two being represented only by a single species. By far the most remarkable of these is the shrew-rat (*Rhynchomys*), distinguished by the shrew-like prolongation of the muzzle, the short and feeble incisors, and the reduction of the molars, which are very small, to two pairs in each jaw. Not improbably this species, which is of the size of the black rat, and of a uniform olive-grey coloration, subsists on insects or larvæ, as the incisors appear too weak for gnawing. The second genus, *Carpomys*, is represented by two somewhat dormouse-like rats, with thick, woolly fur, and the long tail well haired ; while the single species of *Batomys* differs by the hind-feet being wider and shorter, and the fore-feet more elongated.

The true rats and mice constitute a genus (*Mus*) having a distribution coextensive with that of the sub-family, and including nearly 150 species. In these Rodents the incisors are narrow and smooth, the molars of the typical murine structure, the foramina at the anterior end of the bony palate elongated, both the eyes and ears large, the extremity of the muzzle naked, the fur soft, occasionally mixed with spines, a flat nail on the first toe of the fore-foot, the long and nearly naked tail covered with overlapping rings of scales, and cheek pouches absent. The species found in Britain are the common rat (*M. decumanus*), which appears to have been originally a native of Western China, but has now been introduced into all parts of the habitable globe; the smaller and sharper-nosed black rat (*M. rattus*), which is likewise an Eastern form; the common house-mouse (*M. musculus*), also hailing from the East; the wood-mouse (*M. sylvaticus*), together with a larger variety known as *M. flavicollis;* and the tiny harvest-mouse (*M. minutus*). The latter, it is well known, builds small globular nests between several corn-stalks, and is itself able to ascend a single one of such stalks, aided in climbing by its partially prehensile tail. It will be unnecessary here to refer to the habits of mice in general, but some reference may be made to the so-called "singing" and "waltzing mice." Singing mice are ordinary house-mice, which, owing to some disease of the vocal organs, are enabled to produce musical notes. Waltzing mice are a Japanese product, of which the following account is given by Mr. E. R. Waite:—"At first," he writes, "a visitor probably regards the mice as mere colour varieties of the common white race. A moment's observation reveals the peculiarities of the breed, and attention is riveted by their strange performances. Early in life they exhibit the tendency which has earned for them the name above employed. When a nursling leaves the nest its gait consists of an evident attempt to proceed in a straight line; this is frustrated by a tremulous movement of the head, which is nervously shaken from side to side. Shortly, a tendency is exhibited to turn; this develops into a rotatory motion, performed with extraordinary rapidity, which constitutes the peculiarity of the waltzing mouse. The ordinary routine of daily life is constantly interrupted by this mad disposition to whirl, frequently indulged in for several minutes, and, with an occasional stoppage of a few seconds, continued for hours. The floor of one cage being somewhat rough, the mice actually reduced their feet to stumps before it was noticed. Like ordinary mice, they sleep during the day, but apparently waltz the whole night long. If, however, they are disturbed during daylight, they leave their bed and work off some superfluous energy. The rotation is so rapid that all individuality of head and tail is lost to the eye, only a confused ball of black and white being recognised. Very often they spin in couples, revolving head to tail at such a speed that an unbroken ring only is perceived. . . . An individual generally spins in one direction only, and the majority turn to the left." Although probably due in the first instance to brain-disease, the peculiarity, like the "tumbling" of tumbler-pigeons, is now hereditary in the breed.

The longitudinally-striped Barbary mouse (*M. barbarus*), together with certain other more or less variegated African species, are frequently separated from *Mus* as a distinct genus, under the name of *Arvicanthis.* Nearly allied are the numerous species of bandicoot-rats (*Nesocia*), ranging in Southern Asia from Palestine to Formosa, and from Ceylon to Kashmir, but also extending into Turkestan and the Lob-nor district of Central Asia. They differ from the typical genus by the wider incisors and molars; the tubercles on the latter being partially connected by transverse ridges so as to produce a semi-laminated type of structure. The two species of groove-toothed mice (*Golunda*), one of which is Indian and the other African, are easily distinguished by having a groove down each of the front incisors. In addition to having a species of *Mus*, Australasia is the home of four peculiar genera of the sub-family. Of these, the mosaic-tailed mice (*Uromys*), ranging from the Aru Islands to Queensland, may be distinguished from *Mus* by the scales on the tail being united by their edges so as to form a mosaic-like pavement, instead of overlapping. The prehensile-tailed mouse (*Chiruromys*), of which there is but a single species inhabiting the mountains of New Guinea, is characterised by the naked tip of the tail being endowed with prehensile power; the scales of the rest of the tail being arranged in diagonal rows. The upper molars have their tubercles very numerous, and arranged in a complex manner; while there are several peculiarities connected with the structure of the skull. The numerous Australian species of jerboa-rats (*Conilurus*) are easily recognised by their elongated hind-limbs, and long ears and tail. They are inhabitants of desert districts, where they hop after the manner of jerboas. The fifth genus (*Mastacomys*) is known only by a single Tasmanian species, and differs from *Mus* by the great width of the molars, and the reduction of the number of teats to four; the fur being noticeable for its length and softness. Differing remarkably as regards the latter feature, the spiny-mice (*Acomys*), of which there are about seven small-sized species, take their name from the fur being almost entirely replaced by flattened spines. The skull and dentition are very similar to those of the type genus, but the ascending process of each branch of the lower jaw is much smaller. These mice range from Syria through East Africa as far south as Mosambique, generally frequenting deserts, where some, at least, feed on bulbs. The long-nosed rat (*Echinothrix*) of Celebes takes its name from the elongation of the face, and is further characterised by the faint grooving of the incisors, and the thick admixture of spines among the fur. The small blind-mouse (*Typhlomys*) of China is sufficiently characterised by the minute size of the eyes, which are almost concealed by the long lashes. Except that it has smaller ears, it is otherwise very similar in appearance to a house-mouse. The African pouched rats (*Cricetomys* and *Saccostomus*) differ from all the other members of the sub-family in being provided with cheek pouches, the single West African species of the former having grooved upper incisors, while in the two representatives of the latter these teeth are plain. The last member of the family is a mouse from Sumatra and Java, described as *Pithechirus*, and presenting a considerable external resemblance to *Chiropodomys*.

The Mole-Rats.—Family *Spalacidæ*.

The mole-rats constitute a small family confined to the Old World and characterised by their generally mole-like build, cylindrical bodies, short limbs, furnished with large claws, small or rudimental eyes and ears, usually short or rudimentary tail, large incisors, and rooted molars with re-entering enamel-folds on their crowns. Premolars, varying in number, are present in some forms but wanting in others; the palate is narrow; and the anterior part of the zygomatic arch of the skull lacks the descending vertical plate so characteristic of the *Muridæ*. The great mole-rat (*Spalax typhlus*) of South-Eastern Europe, South-Western Asia, and North-Eastern Africa, which is the sole member of its genus, is the type of a sub-family characterised by the angular portion of the lower jaw arising from the lower part of the sheath of the incisor in the manner characteristic of the Myomorpha generally; and also by the absence of premolars. It is a subterranean animal, driving tunnels in the earth in search of the bulbs which form its food, and has the eyes completely covered by skin, and rudimental ears and tail. In the nearly allied bamboo-rats (*Rhizomys*), of which there are several species from the Oriental countries, Tibet, and Abyssinia, the minute eyes are open ; there are small naked external ears, and the short tail is partially covered with hair. The other four genera, all of which are confined to Africa south of the Sahara, differ from other Myomorpha, and thereby resemble the undermentioned Hystricomorpha, in that the angle of the lower jaw arises from the side of the sheath of the incisor. Of these, the great sand-mole (*Bathyergus maritimus*) of the Cape, which attains a length of 10 inches, has grooved upper incisors, a single pair of premolar teeth in each jaw, no external ears, and extremely powerful claws. In the allied *Georychus* and *Myoscalops* the incisors are smooth; the members of the former genus usually have a single pair of premolars, and the single species of the latter three pairs of these teeth in both jaws, while the second toe of the hind-foot is the longest. In both, the first pair of premolars may be absent. The curious little naked sand-rats (*Heterocephalus*), of which the two species are confined to Somaliland, are degraded forms, with no premolars, either two or three pairs of molars, an almost completely bare skin, small eyes, no external ears, a tail of moderate proportions, and a pair of large pads on the powerful fore-feet. These tiny little animals make shallow tunnels in the hot sand of the desert, throwing up at intervals small heaps resembling miniature volcanic craters.

Fig. 58.—BAMBOO-RAT (*Rhizomys badius*).

The Pocket-Gophers.—Family *Geomyidæ*.

This comparatively small family is exclusively confined to North and Central America, where it ranges from the plains of the Saskatchewan, in Canada, southwards to Costa Rica, although attaining its maximum development in the Western United States and Mexico, and being unknown in the region east of the Mississippi, save the Gulf States. The essential characteristic of these Rodents is the possession of large pouches opening externally on the cheeks at the sides of the mouth. In addition to three pairs of molars, they have a single pair of premolar teeth in each jaw; all the cheek teeth in the more typical forms being rootless, and consisting of simple prisms, without any unfolding of the enamel. The premolars consist of a double prism, but all the molars, with the exception of the last pair in the upper jaw of some species, comprise but a single prism, whose summit presents an oval disc of ivory bordered by a ring of enamel.

"All the members of the family," writes Dr. Merriam, "spend their entire lives underground, and their whole organisation is modified in accordance with the needs of a subterranean existence. The species, though numerous, are very much alike externally They are short-legged, thick-set animals, without any appreciable neck, without noticeable external ears, and with very small eyes. The feet are largely developed for digging. The fore-paws in particular are very strong, and armed with long curved claws, and the sides of the toes are lined with rows of bristles that evidently serve in preventing the dirt from passing between the fingers, thus completing a more effective arrangement for keeping the tunnels clean, and for pushing the earth out of the openings of the burrows. The tail, which is of moderate length, is thick, fleshy, and usually devoid of hair, and is endowed with tactile sensibility.

"The pocket-gophers in working their way through the earth in the construction of their tunnels, use the powerful upper incisors as a pick to loosen the ground. At the same time the fore-feet are kept in active operation, both in digging and in pressing the earth back under the body, and the hind-feet are also used in moving it still further backwards. When a sufficient quantity has accumulated behind the animal, he immediately turns in the burrow, and by bringing the wrists together under the chin with the palms of the hands held vertically, forces himself along by the hind-feet, pushing the earth out in front. When an opening in the tunnel is reached, the earth is discharged through it, forming a little hillock that resembles in a general way the hills thrown up by moles. In many species there is a naked callosity over the front half of the nose, which must be of great assistance in the construction of the tunnels. When this callosity is largely developed, the nasal bones underneath are highly arched or inflated."

The same writer then goes on to observe that he was much surprised to see a captive example of one of the species run as rapidly backwards as forwards. "This method of progression was particularly noticeable when the animal was in his own quarters, where he could follow a runway or an accustomed route. When carrying food to one of his store-houses he rarely turned round, but usually ran backwards to the place of deposit, returning for more, and repeating the operation again and again, the to-and-fro movement suggesting a shuttle on its track."

The cheek pouches, which are clothed internally with fur, according to the same author, "are used exclusively in carrying food, and not in carting dirt, as often erroneously supposed. They reach back as far as the shoulder, and are so attached that they cannot be completely averted without rupture of their connections." Writing of a tame specimen, Dr. Merriam observes that "the manner of eating was peculiar and interesting, and showed an ability to use the huge fore-feet and claws in a way previously unsuspected. After satisfying the immediate demands of hunger, it was his practice to fill one or both cheek pouches. His motions were so swift that it was exceedingly difficult to follow them with sufficient exactness to see just how the operation was performed. If a potato was given him, or a piece too large to go into the pouch, he invariably grasped it between the fore-paws, and proceeded to pry off a small piece with the large lower incisors. He would then raise himself slightly on his hind-legs and hold the fragment between his fore-paws while eating, for he usually ate a certain quantity before putting any into the pouches. If small pieces were given him he took them promptly, and passed them quickly into the pouches. Some pieces were thus disposed of at once; others were just trimmed by biting off projecting angles. As a rule, one pouch was filled at a time, though not always, and the hand of the same side was used to push the food in. The usual course is as follows:—A piece of potato, root, or other food is seized between the incisor teeth, and immediately transferred to the fore-paws, which are held in a horizontal position, the tips of the claws curving toward one another. If the food requires reduction in size, the trimming is done while held in this position. The piece is then passed rapidly across the side of the face with a sort of wiping motion which forces it into the open mouth of the pouch. Sometimes a single rapid stroke with one hand is sufficient; at other times both hands are used, particularly if the piece is large. In such cases the long claws of one hand are used to draw down the lower side of the opening, while the food is poked in with the other. It is obviously impossible for the animal to pass food from the mouth to the pouches without the aid of its fore-claws. The most remarkable thing connected with the use of the pouches is the way they are emptied. The fore-feet are brought back simultaneously along the sides of the head until they reach a point opposite the hinder end of the pouches; they are then pressed firmly against the head and carried rapidly forward. In this way the contents of the pouches are promptly deposited in front of the animal. Sometimes several strokes are necessary. I am not prepared to say that the animal cannot empty the pouches by means of the delicate investing muscles; but I have never seen them emptied in any other way than that here described."

According to American writers, the typical members of the family may be divided into no less than nine genera; but by English zoologists they have hitherto been included in only two. Of these, *Geomys*, as typified by the common pocket-gopher (*G. bursarius*), is characterised by having either one or two grooves on the upper incisors. In the typical species there are two of these grooves, and the same is the case with another form which has been separated as *Zygogeomys;* the latter being peculiar in that the jugal, or cheekbone, does not enter into the formation of the upper border of the zygomatic arch. In all the other forms, which have received the names of *Pappogeomys*, *Orthogeomys*, *Cratogeomys*, *Platygeomys*, *Heterogeomys*, and *Macrogeomys*, there is but a single groove on each incisor; the groups being distinguished by the conformation of the skull, and the extent to which the cheek teeth are covered with enamel. From the above the species of *Thomomys* are distinguished by the upper incisors being either perfectly smooth, or marked only by a single fine streak on the inner side.

Fig. 59.—POCKET-GOPHER (*Geomys bursarius*).

The kangaroo-rats (*Dipodomys*), together with the two following genera, are referred by American writers to a different family, and are distinguished by their narrow incisors, moderate or large ears and eyes, and the elongated hind-limbs and tail. In the kangaroo-rats the molar teeth are rootless; the typical forms having four toes, whereas others, which it has been proposed to separate as *Perodipus*, possess five. These small Rodents inhabit open sandy districts, and have habits very similar to those of jerboas. From the foregoing, the genera *Perognathus* and *Heteromys* differ by their rooted molars; the latter being distinguished by the admixture of flattened spines in the fur, and having species ranging into South America. All the forms are small and mouse-like; the common *D. phillipsi* being from South Mexico.

Jerboa Tribe. —Family *Dipodidæ*.

The jerboas and their allies form a small, widely-distributed family, by no means easy of definition. Usually there is a pair of upper premolars, the incisors are narrow, the molars are divided by transverse folds of enamel into laminæ, the vacuity in the skull below the anterior root of the zygomatic arch is large and rounded, and the hinder part of the auditory bulla is very large. The rat-like Rodents of the genus *Sminthus*, which range over Eastern and Northern Europe, Central Asia, Kashmir, and Kansu, differ from the other members of the family in the equality of the length of the fore and hind-limbs; the upper jaw having a single pair of premolars, while there are none in the lower. The North American jumping-mice (*Zapus*) are distinguished by the elongation of the hind-limbs, and the presence of a pair of premolars in both jaws; the hind-feet being furnished with five toes, and the metatarsal bones separate from one another. The common species ranges from Hudson Bay to Colorado. Agreeing with the last in their elongated hind-limbs, the next four genera differ in having only three functional hind-toes, and by the union of the metatarsal bones of the hind-foot. Of these four genera *Dipus* has only three hind-toes, while *Euchoretes*, *Alactaga*, and *Platycercomys* have five, of which the first and fifth do not touch the ground. The first three of these have a long, cylindrical and tufted tail; *Dipus* being distinguished from the other two by its grooved incisors, and the frequent absence of premolars. *Euchoretes* is represented only by the Yarkand jerboa, characterised by its elongated muzzle and large ears; while *Platycercomys*, of which there are several species, ranging from Siberia to Nubia, differs by its flattened and lancet-shaped tail, and the invariable absence of premolars, the incisors being smooth. The true jerboas (*Dipus*), of which there are several species, extend from Algeria through Egypt and North Arabia to Eastern Persia and Central Asia. *Alactaga* is best known by the Kirghiz jerboa (*A. decumana*) of the Kirghiz steppes. All the jerboas are essentially desert-haunting animals, living in the open, and progressing by long leaps. The last and largest member of the family is the so-called Cape jumping-hare (*Pedetes caffer*), ranging from the Cape to Angola and Mozambique, and differing from all the other genera in having rootless molars. The hind-limbs are elongated, the metatarsal bones separate, and the hind-feet furnished with four toes; while the ears are long and narrow, and the very long tail is clothed with elongated hair.

Fig. 60.—A JERBOA (*Dipus*).

Fig. 61.—CAPE JUMPING-HARE (*Pedetes caffer*).

With the exception of the hares and picas, which form a group by themselves, the whole of the remaining members of the order are included in a section known as the Hystricomorpha, which embraces six families. As a whole, this section is characterised by the stoutness of the zygomatic arch of the skull, in which the jugal bone forms the whole of the central portion without any support from a process of the maxilla, while the angle of the lower jaw arises from the outer side of the bony sheath of the socket of the incisor. The collar-bones may be either complete or imperfect; in the lower part of the hind-leg the fibula is distinct from the tibia; and there is almost always a single pair of premolar teeth in each jaw. The members of this section are particularly characteristic of Central and South America

Octodont Tribe.—Family *Octodontidæ*.

(including the West Indies), the whole of the six families being represented there, while four are confined to these countries, and one is met with elsewhere only in Africa.

By far the largest of these families is that of the *Octodontidæ*, which has some representatives in Africa, although the majority of the forms are confined to South and Central America and the West Indies. All have complete collar-bones; the vacuities in the front of the bony palate of the skull are greatly elongated; the crowns of the molar teeth are marked by infoldings of enamel on both sides; there are generally five toes to each foot; and the teats are placed high up on the sides of the body. In form, these Rodents are usually more or less rat-like, and most are terrestrial in their habits.

The first group of the family is African, and is represented by two genera, both easily distinguished by having the two inner toes of the hind-foot furnished with a horny comb and bristles for the purpose of cleansing the fur. Each genus has but a single species. The gundi, *Ctenodactylus*, is an inhabitant of North Africa, near Tripoli, and is peculiar among the family in having no premolars, the tail being reduced to a stump; whereas in *Pectinator*, of Somaliland, premolars are present, and the tail is moderately long and bushy. Both are about the size of a water-vole.

The second group comprises six genera, five of which are South American, and the other African. They have partially rooted or rootless molars, with simple enamel-folds and soft fur. The typical form is the degu (*Octodon*) of Chili and Peru, which is a rat-like animal, with a rather long brush-tipped tail, medium-sized ears, and the upper and lower molars alike. Other species of the same genus inhabit Bolivia, which is also the home of the two species of *Habrocoma*, characterised by the lower molars being more complex than the upper, the large ears, and the extreme softness of the fur. Nearly related are the burrowing tuco-tucos (*Ctenomys*) of South America, deriving their popular name from the bell-like cry uttered underground. They have broad incisors, kidney-shaped crowns to the rootless molars, small eyes, moderate ears, long claws, and bristles on the hind-feet. The one species of the genus *Aconæmys*, from the Southern Andes, differs from the last by its larger ears and shorter claws, and is further characterised by the enamel-folds of the upper molars meeting in the middle.

From *Ctenomys*, the two Chilian species of *Spalacopus* differ by their rudimental ears; they are noticeable on account of their laying up a winter store of food. The very similar African genus *Petromys*[1] may be distinguished from the last by its harsher fur, the shortness of the first toe of the fore-foot, and more thickly-haired tail.

The coypu, or nutria (*Myopotamus*), of South America, which is the only member of its genus, is the typical representative of the last sub-family, which has one African and ten American genera. In this group the molars, which may be rootless or partially rooted, have deep and curved folds of enamel, more or less harsh fur, which may be mingled with spines, and the tail generally long. As a genus, the coypu, which attains a length of about two feet, has very large red incisors, two inner and two outer enamel-folds in the upper molars, and three inner and one outer in the lower ones, moderate-sized ears, a rather long, scaly, and sparsely haired tail, and webbed hind-feet. Mr. Aplin writes that in Uruguay "it inhabits the larger permanent lagunas. I have heard it stated that if a laguna is inhabited by

[1] Some writers place this genus in the first sub-family.

nutrias it is a sign that it never dries up in a drought. But during the drought which prevailed during the time I was in the country, some places inhabited by nutrias did dry up, but it was probably many years since they had done so previously. In the steep banks of the lagunas the nutrias make drives, the mouths of the tunnels being half in and half out of the water when it is at its normal height. The nutria is not a very shy animal. Some of them inhabited a little water-course by the side of which the sheep-dipping place was situated; they were probably attracted by the head of water kept up by a small dam. The nutria swims with hardly a ripple, and disappears noiselessly in the dive at the water-line. The body is dull brown, muzzle greyish, and there is a little warm brown on the side of the head. It swims with the nose, the top of the head, and a narrow line of the back out of water, all on a dead level, or almost so; the nostrils being very high up in the line of the skull, they are kept out of the water without the nose being poked up towards the sky. A half-grown one brought to me alive ate green maize readily."

Fig. 62.—Coypu (*Myopotamus coypu*).

In the West Indies the family is represented by the large arboreal Rodents known as hutias, most of which are included in the genus *Capromys*, although, on account of the more complex structure of its molars, one species from Hayti and Jamaica is separated as *Plagiodon*. They may be compared to gigantic rats, one of them measuring 22 inches to the root of the tail. Their incisors are narrower than those of the coypu, the first genus having one inner and two outer folds of enamel in the upper molars. From both the above the two species of cane-rat (*Thrynomys*)[1] from Southern Africa are at once distinguished by the presence of three deep grooves in each of the upper incisors. The small American forms constituting the genera *Echinomys* and *Loncheres* are sufficiently characterised by generally having flat, lance-shaped spines intermingled with the fur; most of the species being inhabitants of Brazil and Guiana, although one of the second genus is found in Central America. The South American *Mesomys* differs from *Loncheres* in having a short, curved claw on the first toe of the fore-foot, as well as in the absence of spines. The single and rare species of the Brazilian genus *Dactylomys* is characterised by its short ears, long scaly tail, the rudimental first toe of the fore-foot, the very long third and fourth toes of the same, which are furnished with short, convex nails, the flat incisors, and the division of the molars into two complete lobes, each of which has a single enamel-fold, forming a fork-shaped grinding surface; as well as by the two series of upper cheek teeth converging so much as to meet in front. A smaller Brazilian form known as *Cannabateomys* differs by the union of the two lobes of the molars by means of a bridge of enamel, and the slight convergence of the teeth. Another South

Fig. 63.—Hutia (*Capromys*).

[1] To replace the preoccupied name *Aulacodus*.

American genus is *Carterodon*, which includes small rat-like animals differing from all the other members of the family inhabiting the same country in its broad and grooved upper incisors; the upper molars having one inner and two outer enamel-folds, and the lower ones the reverse of this arrangement. Lastly, the South American *Cercomys* differs from the foregoing by its pointed muzzle and smooth incisors.

Porcupine Tribe. —Family *Hystricidæ*.

The number of long, sharp spines with which the skin of "the fretful porcupine" and its allies are protected sufficiently distinguish the *Hystricidæ* from all other Rodents. These animals are of stout build with the fore and hind-limbs of nearly equal length, the front portion of the skull very short and broad, and the molars, which may be either completely or partially rooted, with folds of enamel on both sides. The family may be divided into two groups, one of which is confined to the New World, and the other to the Old. In the American porcupines the molars are fully rooted, the collar-bones complete, the upper-lip undivided, the soles of the hind-feet covered with rough tubercles, the first digit of the fore-foot wanting, and numerous long hairs mixed with the spines; while the females have only four teats. The numerous species of tree-porcupine (*Synetheres*) are confined to the forest districts of tropical America, and are specially characterised by their long, prehensile tails, short, many-coloured spines, light build, and the presence of only four toes to the hind-feet; these toes grasping against a fleshy pad on the inner side of the foot. In habits these porcupines are thoroughly arboreal, and also less nocturnal than their Old World allies. A Brazilian species (*Chætomys*) is generically distinguished on account of the different conformation of its skull and more complex pattern of its molar teeth. The Canadian porcupine (*Erethizon*) forms a kind of connecting link between the New and Old World members of the family, the build being heavy, and the tail stumpy and non-prehensile. The spines are almost buried in the long hairs, and there are four toes in front and five behind.

In the three Old World genera of the family, the molars are only partially rooted, the collar-bones incomplete, and the soles of the hind-feet smooth, while there is a rudimental first toe to the fore-foot, and the female has six teats. In no case is the tail prehensile. The true porcupines (*Hystrix*), which are spread over the warmer parts of Europe and Asia, as well as Africa, are best characterised by their large size, highly inflated and convex skull, and the short tail, terminating in a number of hollow quills, which produce a rattling noise when the creatures move. These porcupines are burrowing and nocturnal in their habits. The brush-tailed porcupines (*Atherura*), of which one species is Malayan and the other two West African, differ by their inferior size and long tails, the latter surmounted with a tuft of flattened spines. A third genus (*Trichys*) is represented by a single Bornean species, differing from the last in the structure of the skull; the spines being also shorter, and the bristles on the tail narrower and parallel-sided.

Chinchilla Tribe. —Family *Lagostomatidæ*.

This and the following families of the group are exclusively confined to South and Central America and the West Indies. In the present family the hind-limbs are elongated, the tail is bushy, the fur extremely short, the collar-bones complete, the bony palate of the skull narrowed in front and deeply excavated behind, the incisors short, and the molars separated into isolated transverse laminæ by continuous folds of enamel. This family is typically represented by the beautiful little chinchillas (*Eriomys*) of the

Andes, so much esteemed on account of the marvellous softness of the pearly-grey fur, and characterised by having five toes in front and four behind, as well as by the bushy tail. The larger Cuvier's chinchilla (*Lagidium*), which is likewise an inhabitant of the Andes, has only four toes both in front and behind; whereas in the viscacha (*Lagostomus*), of the Argentine pampas, there are but three toes to the hind-feet; the fore-feet having the same number as in the last genus.

As regards its external appearance, the viscacha may be not inaptly compared in point of form and size to a marmot, although its hind-limbs are proportionately longer, and the head is inordinately large. The tail, which is bushy throughout, is about one-third the length of the head and body, which varies from about 19 inches to 23 inches; and the short ears are distinctly notched behind. Almost as soft as that of the chinchilla, the fur (which is unfortunately useless for commercial purposes) is of a greyish hue above, with some dusky mottlings and black markings on the upper-parts, while beneath it is white, or white tinged with yellow, the tail being blackish-brown. The head has some very characteristic markings, which render the animal so conspicuous from a distance. Thus a blackish stripe extends across each cheek from the muzzle, while above this is a broad white stripe, ending in front of each eye, this being followed by a third band of a dark colour across the lower part of the forehead. Essentially burrowing and nocturnal in their habits, and seldom issuing from their hiding-places before dusk, viscachas live in companies numbering from about 20 to 30 head. The viscacheria forms a dome-shaped elevated mound on the pampas, perforated here and there by the numerous apertures of the burrows. The burrows themselves are excavated for a great depth in the soft black mould of the pampas; and as they frequently diverge near their extremities, or open out into a large common chamber, it may be easily imagined that the task of digging out a warren in ordinary circumstances is an almost impossible one. Carefully cleared of all vegetation, the mound of the viscacheria is kept scrupulously clean; but the viscachas have the curious habit of collecting on this spot not only the *débris* of their food, but likewise any objects they may come across in their wanderings. Consequently the summit of the mound is littered over with bones of cattle and ostriches, thistle-stalks, maize-cobs, clods of earth, and masses of the hard calcareous rock, locally known as tosca. Moreover, if a passer-by happen to lose any of his smaller belongings, such as a knife or a watch, he will be pretty sure to come across it by searching all the viscacherias in the neighbourhood. The object of this remarkable habit it is almost impossible to conjecture, although it is probably analogous to that of the Australian bower-birds. For some distance round the viscacheria the grass of the camp, through continual nibbling, is much finer than that of the pampas in its original condition; and before the introduction of sheep, and the consequent refining of the turf, the viscachas were undoubtedly in this respect of service to the farmer. When about to issue from their holes, or when driven in by the intrusion of a visitor after they have come forth, viscachas make a most unearthly growling and snarling deep down in their holes—the sound, which may be best compared to the booming of a bear in its lair, giving the impression to the uninitiated that the dwelling is tenanted by animals of much larger size and fiercer disposition than is really the case. In spite of the refining of the herbage already alluded to, viscachas are an unmitigated pest to the farmer, not only on account of the large area covered by their burrows, but likewise by the enormous quantity of fodder consumed by the animals themselves, which in former days absolutely swarmed on the pampas. Consequently for years the estancieros have waged incessant war against these Rodents, with the result that in the parts of Argentina which have been longest under cultivation one may ride for miles without coming across a warren.

Agutis and Pacas.—Family *Dasyproctidæ*.

The two genera of this South and Central American and West Indian family include a small number of relatively large, terrestrial Rodents, characterised by the fore and hind-limbs being of nearly equal length, and having their toes furnished with hoof-like claws, by the short or rudimental tail, the very imperfect collar-bones, the broad palate, long incisors, and the partially rooted molars, in which the foldings of enamel form notches on the two sides of the crowns. The agutis (*Dasyprocta*) are rather delicately built animals, with long limbs and three hind-toes, ranging from the confines of Mexico to Paraguay, and represented by a single outlying species in the West Indies. On the other hand, the pacas (*Cœlogenys*), which are found from Ecuador to Brazil and Paraguay, are larger and more heavily-built animals, with five toes to the hind-feet, and further characterised by the longitudinal rows of light-coloured spots on the fur, and the enormous hollow, bony capsules formed by the expanded bones of the cheeks. Branick's paca (*Dinomys*), of which only a single specimen from Peru has hitherto been obtained, is distinguished from the *Dasyproctidæ* by the cleft upper-lip, somewhat long and bushy tail, the presence of four toes to each foot, and the complete collar-bones; and is accordingly regarded as the representative of a separate family.

Fig. 64.—AGUTI (*Dasyprocta*).

The Cavies.—Family *Caviidæ*.

The next of these South American families is that of the cavies, and includes large or small heavily-built Rodents, with four front and three hind-toes, rudimental or short tails, and the cheek teeth divided by transverse folds of enamel into a number of thin plates lying parallel to one another. The typical representatives of the family are the true cavies (*Cavia*), of which the guinea-pig is a domesticated descendant, having assumed a coloration quite different from the uniform olive-brown tint characteristic of its wild ancestors. Quizos, as these animals are called in the Argentine, may be found not only among aquatic plants in marshy districts, and skulking in the tufts of coarse grass on the pampas, but also in the neighbourhood of human habitations, where they will not unfrequently take up their residence under the floors of outbuildings, whence they issue forth to feed at night. All the true cavies are small and short-legged creatures, with no tail, and short ears; but the Patagonian cavy, representing the genus *Dolichotis*, is a much larger and taller animal, measuring nearly a yard in length, and standing over a foot at the shoulder, with tall ears and a short tail. An inhabitant of the open districts of Patagonia and Argentina, the mara, as it is called by the natives, much resembles a hare in its movements. Unfortunately, the spread of cultivation has well-nigh exterminated this handsome Rodent from most parts of the Argentine. Largest, not only among South American Rodents, but in the order, is the aquatic carpincho or capivara (*Hydrochœrus*), figured on p. 89, and attaining a length of four feet. The most remarkable peculiarity of this animal is the large size and complex structure of the last molar tooth, which in the upper jaw may have as many as twelve plates, and is comparable in structure to the corresponding tooth of the Indian elephant. The carpincho is an inhabitant of the more tropical districts, not extending southwards of Uruguay. Writing of the habits of the carpincho, Mr. Aplin observes that "a favourite locality is a broad laguna in the river, furnished with open water, and also beds of 'camelotes,'—a sloping, open, grassy bank on one side, where the carpinchos can lie in the daytime in the cooler weather, sleeping and basking in the sunshine; on the other a low, shelving bank, clothed with 'sarandi' scrub growing out into the black, reeking mud and shallow water beyond. The stems of the sarandi in the festering mud have a gloomy appearance, sometimes brightened in spring by the large, pink flower of a convolvulus climbing up the stems. In one or two places of this description, I could almost always make sure of seeing some carpinchos—sometimes a herd of a dozen or fifteen together, for they are sociable. You might meet with them at any part of the rivers where there was plenty of water, or in the *montè* on the banks, and I have put one up in thick dry grass fifty yards or more from a river. At night they are said to wander for some distance to visit maize-fields. When alarmed, they snort violently, and rush impetuously into the river with a great splash and noise. It is said that a frightened carpincho making for the river will not turn out of its way for anything, and that if you are between them and the river they will knock you over. The paces of the carpincho are a walk and a hurried gallop, reminding one of that of a pig, but most likely differing little in character from that of a guinea-pig, which the carpincho resembles in shape and make. Probably their habit of rushing impetuously into the rivers is the reason why some horses are so frightened at these animals; the horses may have been scared when they went down to drink, or perhaps even charged by two or three lumbering brutes. Sometimes carpinchos are much more tame than at others. If they are on the opposite side of a small river, they often take no notice at all; and I have watched them in the autumn sitting up on their haunches like dogs, sunning themselves, or lying asleep on their bellies, with their fore-paws stretched out in front of them, and their heads in some cases laid on their paws, a little on one side. I have also on more than one occasion walked up within half a dozen yards of them. Sometimes when you approach a little herd of them, they sound their alarm and merely watch you, walking slowly down to the water as you get nearer. At other times they rush impetuously into the water at the first sign of danger. They are said to be much wilder on the larger rivers, the Rio Negro for instance, probably because they are less accustomed to seeing any people except those who hunt them. No doubt the protection they were afforded in the Santa Elena camp contributed largely to their tameness there, but I always noticed they were less tame on the Arroyo Grande than on its tributary the Saúce. When disturbed and rising to their feet, carpinchos get upon their fore-legs first. The hair of the carpincho is scanty, not much more plentiful than some pigs' bristles, which it greatly resembles. Their colour varies from dull brown to bright chestnut, and this irrespective of age, or size, or season either, for I have noticed all colours from spring to late autumn; smaller animals are, however, generally of the dull brown colour, and *vice versâ*. Their skins tan into splendidly thick, soft leather, which is used for belts, slippers, saddle-covers, etc. Like other thick-skinned animals, they like to wallow in mud. They work out hollows in the ground, in which they wallow; these are known as carpincho-baths. The carpincho does not go to ground, but lives on the banks of the rivers in such cover as it can find. It is capable of remaining under water and of proceeding for some distance under the surface; but when a herd has been disturbed at a laguna, the members probably lie low by putting just their noses above water under the shelter of a bed of camelotes or other water-plants. I am puzzled to say how many young they have at a birth. On the 8th May I saw two females, each with a young one, about 18 inches long, at her side. I have never seen more than one young one with a female, but this I have often seen; the young one keeps close to its mother's side, and they plunge into the water together. I am aware that the supposition that the carpincho has only one young one at a birth is contrary to what has been written about this animal; but I merely give my own observations for what they are worth."

Picas.—Family *Lagomyidæ*.

The two last families of the order, constituting the group Lagomorpha, differ from the rest in having a small second pair of upper incisors behind the large ones of the upper jaw; the latter being also peculiar in that the coating of enamel, instead of being confined to the front surface, extends round to the back. Young animals have three pairs of upper incisors. The small Rodents known as picas, or tailless hares, all of which are included in the single genus *Lagomys*, are characterised by the equality in the length of the limbs, the absence of a tail, the short ears, complete collar-bones, and rootless molars, divided into transverse laminæ by complete folds of enamel. The living species have two pairs of premolar teeth in each jaw, and the skull has no postorbital processes. Represented by about a dozen species, the picas are chiefly inhabitants of the Himalaya and the highlands of Central and Northern Asia, although one outlying form inhabits South-Eastern Europe, and a second the Rocky Mountains. These little creatures dwell in the chinks and crevices of rocks, from which they dart out with remarkable celerity, uttering at the same time their peculiarly shrill cry.

Fig. 65.—A Pica (*Lagomys*).

Hares and Rabbits.—Family *Leporidæ*.

From the picas, the hares and rabbits (*Lepus*) are at once distinguished by their elongated hind-limbs, long ears, short, upwardly-bent tail, and imperfect collar-bones; while the skull differs in possessing large postorbital processes, and there are three pairs of premolar teeth in the upper jaw and two in the lower. Whereas there are five toes to the fore-limbs, the hind pair has but four, and the soles of all four are as fully haired as the rest of the limbs; the inside of the cheeks being also hairy. There are rather more than a score of species belonging to the genus, which has an almost cosmopolitan distribution, although more numerous in the northern hemisphere than elsewhere, being absent from Madagascar and Australasia, and represented only by a single species in South America. All are very much alike in external appearance. Of the European species, the common hare (*L. europæus*), distinguished by the very long ears and hind-legs, inhabits the whole of Europe with the exception of Northern Russia, Scandinavia, and Ireland. In the latter countries its place is taken by the mountain hare (*L. timidus*), which ranges eastwards to Japan, and is found on several of the mountain ranges of Southern Europe, namely the Pyrenees, Alps, and Caucasus. Smaller than the common hare, it has shorter ears and hind-legs; and in the colder portions of its habitat changes to pure white in winter, with the exception of the black tips to its ears. The rabbit (*L. cuniculus*) is a smaller and shorter-limbed form, with the black tips to the ears much reduced in size, or absent; it was originally a native of the countries bordering the western half of the Mediterranean, but has been introduced into Northern Europe and many other parts of the world. It differs from the hares in its burrowing habits.

ORDER VI.—UNGULATA.

The Hoofed Mammals.

This extensive order, which includes hyraces, elephants, horses, rhinoceroses, oxen, antelopes, pigs, etc., is one by no means easy of definition, although its existing members are characterised by having the toes enclosed either in hoofs, or furnished with broad, flattened nails. The number of toes varies from five (in the elephants) to one (in the horses); in the fore-arm the radius and ulna may be united; in the wrist the scaphoid and lunar bones (united in the Carnivora) are always separate; collar-bones are wanting in all the existing forms; and the condyle, or knob, by which the lower jaw articulates with the skull, is always more or less elongated transversely, and never from before backwards in the manner characteristic of the Rodents. The cheek teeth have broad and flattened crowns—often interpenetrated by deep foldings of the enamel from the summits and sides—adapted for grinding; and when these teeth are reduced below the typical number of seven, the reduction always takes place from the anterior portion of the series, or, in other words, in the premolars, so that there are constantly three pairs of molars in each jaw. The limbs are always adapted for terrestrial progression, so that there is no power of supining the fore-foot; and when the first toe is present it has no power of opposition to the others.

Although a few are omnivorous, the great majority of the Ungulates subsist entirely on a vegetable diet; and, with the exception of these sufficiently protected by their great bodily size, most depend upon their swiftness of foot to escape their enemies. While a small number are not larger than hares, the great majority of the members of the order are animals of large size, and they include among them the most gigantic of all existing terrestrial creatures. The living Ungulates may be divided into four well-marked subordinal groups, while there are others which are now extinct.

The Proboscidea or first subordinal group of the Hoofed Mammals, is now represented solely by the two existing species of elephants, both of which are included in the genus *Elephas*. In addition to their huge bodily size, elephants differ externally from all other animals by the production of the nose into a long, flexible proboscis, or trunk, and likewise by the large tusks normally present in the males, and often in both sexes. Their huge and massive limbs are less enveloped superiorly in the skin of the body than is the case with the great majority of Ungulates; and their component long-bones are remarkable in being placed almost vertically one above the other, so as to form straight columns for the support of the body. From all other living members of the order elephants differ in having five perfect toes to each foot; while they are further distinguished from all, except the little hyraces, by the arrangement of the bones of the wrist-joint in the fore-foot. In this joint the two horizontal series of quadrangular bones are placed almost directly over one another, and likewise above the supporting meta-carpal bones, in such a manner that the whole foot could be completely cleft in twain between the third and fourth toes. The rounded feet are supported on large, flat cushions, on the front edge of which the position of the toes is indicated by large, broad nails. As regards the teeth, the upper tusks correspond to one of the three pairs of incisors characterising more typical Mammals; but there are no other incisors, nor any traces of canines. The tusks always remain open at the base, and grow continuously throughout the life of their owners. The cheek teeth, of which there are six pairs in each jaw, are peculiar in that they are not all in use at the same time, the small anterior ones coming into use first, and being in turn shed as they are worn out and replaced by the larger hinder ones, which make their appearance in the jaws in an arc of a circle, so that very old individuals are left with only a single huge molar on each side of each jaw. Equally peculiar are these teeth in structure. They consist of a great number of tall, parallel, thin, transverse plates growing from a common base, and consisting of a core of comparatively soft ivory, covered with a thin layer of flint-like enamel; the interspaces, or valleys, left between the plates being filled up with a still softer substance known as cement. When such a tooth is worn by grinding against its fellow in the opposite jaw, the summits of the enamel-covered plates are cut through so as to expose elongated ellipses of ivory; and the roughened, flat surface thus produced is made of vertical transverse layers of three substances, arranged in the order of cement, enamel, ivory, enamel, cement. Since each of these constituents differs in hardness, it will be sufficiently apparent that the millstone-like apparatus formed by the teeth is admirably adapted for triturating vegetable substances of all kinds to a pulp.

The Elephants. —Family *Elephantidæ*.

Of the two existing species, the Indian elephant (*E. indicus*) is best distinguished by the structure of the molar teeth, in which the constituent plates are very numerous and very thin, with their investing enamel, which is also thin, thrown into a number of fine crimpings. Tusks are usually present in the male sex only, and may even be wanting in that. The ears are relatively small; and the finger-like process on the upper margin of the tip of the trunk is much more developed than the one on the lower edge. As a rule, there are four nails on the hind-foot, and five on the front. The Indian elephant is an inhabitant not only of the country from which it takes its name, but likewise of Ceylon, Burma, the Malay Peninsula, Cochin-China, Sumatra, and Borneo, although it may have been introduced into the island last named. Associating in herds of variable size, it is fond of cool, shady forests in the neighbourhood of water, avoiding as much as possible the full glare of the sun, and feeding chiefly upon leaves, fruits, and small branches. So much has been written on the subject of the habits of this species that this may be passed over here; but as much misapprehension obtains as to the height attained by the animal, a somewhat full notice may be given.

With all his large experience of Indian elephants, the late Mr. Sanderson, in his "Thirteen Years among the Wild Beasts of India," stated that the largest male he had at that time ever seen measured 9 feet 10 inches at the shoulder; while two others with which he was acquainted touched 9 feet 8 inches. He adds, "There is little doubt that there is not an elephant 10 feet at the shoulder in India." Next comes Sir Samuel Baker, who, after mentioning in "Wild Beasts and their Ways" that the well-known African elephant "Jumbo" measured 11 feet at the shoulder, and weighed $6\frac{1}{2}$ tons, declared that no Indian elephant approaches these dimensions. It is further set down in the same book that "9 feet at the highest portion of the back is a good height for an Indian male, and 8 feet for the female, although occasionally they are considerably larger. There are hardly any elephants that measure 10 feet in a direct perpendicular." Later on Mr. Sanderson was forced to admit that his statement as to there being no elephants of 10 feet in height in India required modification, for he himself subsequently measured a male standing 10 feet $7\frac{1}{2}$ inches. Those dimensions are, however, reported by Colonel D. Hamilton to have been exceeded in a male killed in 1863 by the late Sir Victor Brooke, of which the height is given as 11 feet, or the same as that of "Jumbo." Moriom Kelaart, whose observations are generally most trustworthy, records having seen an elephant in Ceylon of upwards of 12 feet in height. That such a stature may occasionally be reached by a few giants of the tribe seems to be supported by an enormous skeleton of a tusker mounted in the Indian Museum, Calcutta, which, as now articulated, stands 11 feet 3 inches at the shoulder, thus indicating a height of about 12 feet when in the flesh. This skeleton is believed to have belonged to the tusker of a small herd that haunted the district to the north of the Raniganj Coal Field from Soory and the southern spurs of the Rajmehal Hills to Jamtara. In our opinion this skeleton is correctly mounted, so that its height would appear to be truly 12 feet, although it has been stated that the thigh bone is not perceptibly larger than one belonging to an elephant known to have been less than 10 feet in height. The elephant of 10 feet $7\frac{1}{2}$ inches measured by Mr. Sanderson is, however, still the tallest actually known with absolute certainty; although we by no means venture to assert that Colonel Hamilton's estimate of the height of the one shot by Sir Victor Brooke may not be perfectly accurate. Be this as it may, it is certain that the Indian elephant is, on the average, a considerably smaller animal than its African cousin; and individuals attaining a height of even 10 feet are so rare that each case is deserving of record. That elephants vastly exceeding 10 feet in height formerly lived in India is proved by the occurrence

Fig. 66.—INDIAN ELEPHANT.

in the gravels of the Narbada Valley of limb bones beside which those of the skeleton last mentioned appear almost puny, many of these fossil bones being exhibited in the geological galleries of the Calcutta Museum. These elephants belonged, however, to an extinct species.

From the height of the Indian elephant we turn naturally to the largest dimensions and weight of its tusks. Mr. Sanderson states that the largest tusks he ever obtained measured 5 feet along the curve, with a circumference of 16 inches at their junction with the gum; while the weight of the pair was 74½ pounds. The single perfect tusk of the elephant shot by Sir V. Brooke, to which allusion has been made, measured 8 feet, with a maximum girth of 16·9 inches, and weighed 90 pounds. Mr. Blanford mentions, however, that a somewhat shorter tusk weighed upwards of 100 pounds; and two pairs from the Garo Hills, mentioned in *The Asian* newspaper in October, 1888, are stated to have been respectively of 155 and 157 pounds weight. The tusks of the large skeleton in the Calcutta Museum have unfortunately been removed, but the size of their sockets indicates that they must have been immense. All these dimensions are, however, comparatively small when set against those of unusually large African elephants; Sir Samuel Baker referring to single tusks of that species, which weighed respectively 149, 172, and 188 pounds; while Sir E. G. Loder has a tusk of 184 pounds in weight. Huge as are the tusks indicated by such weights, they must, however, have been small by the side of those of an extinct Indian elephant from the Siwalik hills, of which the skull is preserved in the British Museum. The tusks of this monster have a total length of about 12 feet 9 inches, with a girth of 26 inches near the base; and the weight of each in the living state may be safely estimated at considerably over 200 pounds. While on the subject of elephants' tusks, we may take the opportunity of mentioning that, as we learn from Mr. Sanderson's book, there appears to be a widespread belief that elephants have no milk or deciduous tusks. Nevertheless, such tusks are developed in all young elephants, and may be seen in place in skulls of suitable age. They may be at once distinguished from the permanent tusks by the circumstance that their lower extremities are completely closed, whereas those of the latter always remain open. These milk-tusks are, however, so small, and are shed at such an early age, that their fall is not likely to be noticed by the *mahouts*, even when they have under their charge animals sufficiently young for this change to take place.

In India, elephants, as a rule, do not breed in captivity, but in Burma they not unfrequently do so; and a writer in *The Asian* newspaper of April, 1895, states that in the Chindwin division, there were kept a male and "five female elephants; four out of the five female elephants have calved since last September, and these calves will go and suck any elephant they like without the elephant objecting. I have seen two calves go and suck one elephant at the same time, then go off to another and suck her. Elephants, without a calf, will allow another's calf to suck them. This I noticed down in Pyinmana, where one of the elephants calved; the calf used to go round and suck three of the females. Again, with the elephants up here, one calved in September, another in October, a third in February, and the fourth in March. The calf that was born in September used to regularly suck the elephant that calved in October, and this before her calf was born; in fact, it used to follow the one that had not calved more than it did its own mother, and the female seemed to be as fond of the calf as if it had been her own. When No. 2 calved in October it did not make any difference, both the calves sucked either

No. 1 or No. 2 just as they liked, and they invariably sucked the same elephant at the same time; then they used to go off and suck the other two that had not calved then. These six elephants have now been in the Forest Department for at least six years to my knowledge, and how long they were in it before I don't know. It shows how absurd it is people in India saying elephants will not breed in captivity; here, in Burma, our elephants are always fettered and turned out into the forest to graze, and elephants in better condition it would be hard to find; our elephants get no flour, paddy, or any other kind of rations, and no tree-fodder. After the day's work is done, they are hobbled and turned out to feed themselves; when they are not wanted, they remain out in the jungle, the *mahout* going and seeing them once or twice a day. In this way they can eat just what they like." The teats of the female elephant are placed between the hind legs; and the young calf sucks with its mouth, and not with its trunk.

There are many methods by which elephants are captured, among which the following, as detailed in *The Asian* newspaper, may be selected for notice: —"Elephant-capturing operations by the pit-fall systems were set in working order in the locality of the forest station at Mount Stuart on the Anaimalai Hills in the season of 1890. For the past five years, during each of the working seasons which commence in June and end in December, elephant-captures have been attempted. Places were selected in the known runs of the elephants, and the pits were dug in groups of three. To commence with, about 21 pits were dug in different parts, all, however, being within a two-mile radius of the Mount Stuart forest station. Since 1890, some 20 pits more have been dug out. The dimensions of the original pits were 12 feet by 9 feet, with a depth of 10 feet. These are too large, and a pit 10 feet by 10 feet by 10 feet is amply big enough. The sides of the pits were made vertical and not sloping downwards, as are the pits in Malabar; and some 2 or 3 feet of brushwood was placed in the bottom of each to act as bedding to break the fall of the animal. The pits were then covered by means of bamboos placed across them, and on these were spread grass, leaves, etc. The pits are visited every morning by a forest-guard or watcher deputed for the purpose, and these report to their superior officers whenever a fall takes place. During the first year, one animal, to which the name of Juno was given, was captured. This subsequently died. In the second year, 1891, four animals were captured, two of which subsequently died, and two of which are now living. In the third year, 1892, two extraordinary falls took place by which seven animals were captured in five pits. Out of these seven animals, four are still living. During 1893 two animals were captured, and during the present year, 1894, four animals have been caught, all of which are living. Out of a total of 17 captures, 12 are now living. It may be remarked, moreover, that the casualties took place amongst the first three years' captures, when the attendants, who are local hillmen, called Mulcers, were entirely inexperienced concerning elephants. During the last two years the bed of brushwood has been increased considerably so as to reach to within 4 feet of the top of the pit. The results speak for themselves: not a single animal has since been injured in the fall, although two of the latest captures are the largest animals caught since operations were commenced. The removal of a capture to the kraals, which are within two or three miles from the pits, is a very simple matter, provided everything is in readiness beforehand. The size of the animal's neck is estimated, and a peg is put in the rope so as to prevent the noose going smaller than the neck-size as estimated. This noose is then thrown over the elephant's neck and pulled tight to the peg, the end of the rope being bound round a neighbouring tree; next, one of the elephant's hind-legs is noosed, and the end of this rope, for the time being, bound round a neighbouring tree. The neck-rope at the peg then has to be tied with twine or fibre to prevent the noose being loosened by the elephant. This operation is, taking it all round, the most risky one connected with the capture. But if proper care is taken there is nothing to fear. The pit is then filled up by means of billets of wood being thrown in, and as the animal rises nearer the surface of the ground, the two ropes fastening him are pulled tighter around the trees. Eventually he gets out of the pit somewhat fatigued; the ropes which secure him are then fastened to two tame elephants, and the animals are marched in single file (the captured one being of course in the middle) to the kraal, and all the ropes are removed. He is watered three times a day, and soon made tame by kindness, given sugarcane, etc. Somewhat large animals are generally in the kraal three months before they can be taken out; the little ones of 4 feet or 5½ feet high are, however, removed within three weeks of capture. The work of capturing elephants is an exceedingly interesting one, and only needs care and constant supervision to render it successful; and certainly the more one has to do with these animals the more one is bound to recognise what intelligent, useful beasts they are."

The African elephant (*E. africanus*), which, as already stated, is a larger animal than the Indian, has large tusks in both sexes, and is broadly distinguished by the structure of the molar teeth, in which the plates are fewer and lower, with the ivory-spaces wider and more lozenge-shaped, and the enamel thicker and only slightly crimped. The finger-like processes on the upper and lower edges of the tip of the trunk are more nearly equal in size; the ears are enormous, forming large flaps extending over the shoulders, and there are only three nails on the hind-foot. As in the Indian species, the rugged, naked skin bears only a few sparse hairs, but there are a number of stout bristles on the edges of the end of the tail. Until decimated or exterminated in many districts by human greed, this species ranged over the whole of Africa south of the Sahara, and frequently occurred in enormous herds. It is less impatient of the sun than its Indian cousin, and subsists largely on the soft roots of trees, which are dug up by the tusks; one tusk being generally employed in this service, and thus more rapidly worn away than its fellow.

The Hyraces —Family *Procaviidæ*.

The second sub-order of the Ungulates—the Hyracoidea—is formed by the small Rodent-like animals known as hyraces, all of which are confined to Africa and Syria, and may be comprised in the single genus *Procavia*. In the structure of the wrist-joint of the fore-foot these animals resemble the elephants, from which they differ in having only three toes on the hind-foot, and but four functional ones in the fore-foot, where the first is rudimental, as well as in the characters of the dentition. As regards their front teeth, the hyraces make a curious approximation to the Rodents, the upper jaw having a single pair of curved incisors, which grow throughout life, and are separated by a long gap, without the intervention of a canine, from the cheek-teeth. In the lower jaw there are, however, two pairs of the former teeth, in place of the single pair characterising the Rodents, while the upper incisors differ from those of the latter in being sharp-pointed instead of chisel-shaped, and also in their triangular section, two of their surfaces being coated with enamel. The cheek teeth, which include four pairs of premolars and four of molars in each jaw, are singularly like those of the rhinoceroses, and thus quite different from those of the Rodents. With the exception of the second toe of the hind-foot, the toes are protected by short, broad nails; and the tail is remarkable for its extreme shortness. In general appearance, hyraces (which are the conies of Scripture) are very like large cavies. While the majority live in colonies among the cracks and crannies of rocks, some of the African species are arboreal in their habits, climbing the stems and larger branches of trees, and sleeping in their holes; in this respect they are unique among the Ungulate order.

Fig. 67.—A HYRAX (*Procavia*).

The primitive and ancient group of animals commonly known as tapirs are the first representatives of the third sub-ordinal section of the Ungulates, technically termed the Perissodactyle section. The essential feature of the members of this section is to be found in the structure of the feet, in which the toe corresponding to the third or middle digit of the human hand or foot is always larger than the one on each side of it, and symmetrical in itself; the total number of toes on the hind-foot never exceeding three, and on the front-foot four. It is in consequence of this special development of the third toe that the group is spoken of as the Odd-toed or Perissodactyle Ungulates. In addition to this essential feature, the Perissodactyla differ from the two preceding sub-orders in the structure of the wrist-joint of the fore-foot, in which the two horizontal rows of small bones not only interlock with one another, but are likewise not disposed in vertical lines immediately above the supporting metacarpals. Hence in these animals it would be impossible to cleave the foot between any two of the toes without cutting through solid bone. A further difference from the elephants is to be found in the circumstance that the huckle-bone, or astragalus, of the ankle-joint of the Perissodactyles is a vertically elongated bone terminating above in a deeply grooved, pulley-like surface for articulation with the larger bone of the leg, instead of being shallow, with a flat upper surface. All these animals walk in the digitigrade fashion on the summits of their toes, which are more elongated than in the elephants. At the present day the Perissodactyla are represented by only three families, each containing a comparatively small number of species; but in former epochs of the earth's history they were much more numerous.

The Tapirs.—Family *Tapiridæ.*

Fig. 68.—MALAYAN TAPIR (*Tapirus indicus*).

From the other members of the sub-order, tapirs, which are somewhat pig-like and antediluvian-looking animals, are readily distinguished by the production of the muzzle into a short, mobile snout, and the presence of four toes on the front-feet, the hind pair having three. They have low-crowned cheek-teeth; the upper molars having an outer wall formed by the union of two conical tubercles, from the inner side of which a pair of transverse crests run obliquely across the grinding surface of the crown. In the lower molars there is simply a pair of transverse ridges to each; the total number of teeth being 42. The skin of all the tapirs is sparsely haired; and in size these animals may be compared to a large donkey.

The whole of the five living species of tapirs may be included in the single genus *Tapirus*, to which special interest attaches on account of its remarkable geographical distribution. Thus, whereas one of the five species is found in the Malayan countries, the whole of the other four are restricted to the forest-region of Tropical America, some of the latter ranging high into the Andes. This, however, is by no means all, since the Malayan species is much more nearly related to two of the American species than are the latter to their compatriots. Had we the existing forms alone to deal with, this discontinuous distribution would be very difficult to explain; but we learn from geology that these animals were formerly widely spread over the Northern Hemisphere, whence they have migrated southwards to their present isolated habitats.

The Malayan species (*T. indicus*), which is the largest of the five, differs from all the others in having the middle of the body white; the remainder of the skin being uniformly black, as is the whole of that of the American species. In all the five kinds the skin of the young is, however, striped and spotted with white. As regards their mode of life, tapirs are essentially shy, harmless, and nocturnal forest animals, always frequenting the neighbourhood of water, in which they often swim.

The Rhinoceroses.—Family *Rhinocerotidæ*.

The rhinoceroses, which include by far the largest representatives of the Perissodactyle sub-order, may be best distinguished from the tapirs by the form and number of their teeth. These are always numerically less than 42 in the living species; and the upper molars differ from those of the tapirs in that their outer surface forms a continuous wall, undivided into lobes, while the grinding surface, although consisting primarily of two oblique transverse ridges, presents a much more complicated pattern. In the lower molars, the ridges, instead of being simply transverse, are curved into crescents. Another point of distinction, so far as the existing kinds are concerned, is the presence of only three toes on both the front and hind-feet. Rhinoceroses derive their name from the presence of either one or two horns arising from the middle line of the fore-part and middle of the head; these horns consisting entirely of an agglutinated mass of hair-like substances, having no connection with the bones of the skull.

In appearance, rhinoceroses are huge, ungainly brutes, with an enormous head, much elevated and expanded posteriorly, short, massive limbs, large, tubular, upright ears, often fringed with hairs, a moderately long, tapering tail, and very thick skin, which is generally but sparsely covered with hair, and may be thrown into a number of massive folds. They have always the full number of seven pairs of cheek teeth; but canines are wanting, and the incisors, if present at all, are reduced below the typical number of three pairs.

Rhinoceroses are restricted to the Oriental countries and Africa; but there is some difference of opinion whether they should be divided into several genera, or all included under the single generic term *Rhinoceros*. Adopting the latter alternative, the five existing species may be arranged in two divisions, of which one includes the three Oriental forms, and the other the two African. The Oriental rhinoceroses are characterised by possessing incisor teeth in both jaws, one (or the only) pair in the lower jaw forming sharp, triangular, projecting tusks, capable of inflicting terrific gashes when their owners charge. By far the largest of these is the great Indian rhinoceros (*R. unicornis*), which is confined to the great grass-jungles of North-Eastern India, and is characterised by its massive but short, single horn, the large bosses on the deeply-folded skin, the numerous pleats round the neck, and the complicated structure of the upper molar teeth. The Javan rhinoceros (*R. sondaicus*), which is a much smaller animal, ranging from Eastern Bengal and the Sandarbans to Burma, the Malay Peninsula, and the islands of Sumatra, Borneo, and Java, differs in the arrangement of the folds of the skin, which lacks the great bosses of the larger species, and likewise by the lower and simpler crowns of the upper molar teeth. The third representative of the Oriental group of the genus is the Sumatran rhinoceros (*R. sumatrensis*), which ranges from Assam, Chittagong, and Burma, to the Malay Peninsula, Siam, Sumatra, and Borneo, and is the smallest of the three. Having upper molar teeth of the same type as those of the Javan species, it differs from both that and the Indian rhinoceros in having two horns on the head, the foremost of which is often much larger than the single one of either of the other Asiatic species.

Fig. 69.—INDIAN RHINOCEROS (*Rhinoceros unicornis*).

The two species of African rhinoceroses differ in that the incisors of the adults are rudimental or wanting in both jaws, and likewise in the absence of foldings in the skin, which covers the body uniformly; both having two horns. The largest of these is the square-mouthed, or Burchell's rhinoceros (*R. simus*), frequently inappropriately spoken of as the white rhinoceros. This animal, which was formerly met with in enormous numbers to the north of the Orange River, but is now well-nigh exterminated, if, indeed, it be not actually extinct, takes its name from its square and truncated upper-lip. In addition to this, it is characterised by the tall and complex crowns of the upper molar teeth, which present a pattern very similar to that obtaining in the Indian species, as well as by the great length of the front horn, which is frequently found with its tip obliquely abraded, on account of having been pushed along the ground as its owner walked. The general colour of the skin is slaty-grey. On the other hand, the common African, or so-called black rhinoceros (*R. bicornis*), has the prehensile lip characteristic of the other members of the genus, while its front horn does not attain the enormous length reached in *R. simus*, and the upper molars are of simpler structure. This rhinoceros ranges from Abyssinia to the Cape, and differs considerably in habits from the other African species. Possibly a third species may exist in North-Eastern Africa.

The third and last family of the Odd-toed Ungulates is that of the horses, under which title are included not only horses proper, but also zebras and asses, all of which may be comprised in the single genus *Equus*. From all other living Mammals the members of this genus differ by the reduction of the number of toes to a single one in each foot; but as there are certain extinct horses provided with three perfect toes on each foot, we learn that this essential peculiarity of the existing forms is a feature of comparatively late acquisition. Indeed, evidence of this descent from a three-toed ancestor is afforded by the so-called splint-bones which are found in the horse, lying on each side of the upper half of each cannon-bone, and correspond to the metacarpals and metatarsals of the second and fourth digits of the typical five-toed foot, the cannon-bone representing the third or middle one. In the case of such well-known animals as the horses, it would be quite superfluous in a work of the present nature to describe them in any detail, and it will accordingly suffice to point out a few of the features which indicate that they form a family by themselves. More important than the single digit of the feet is the peculiar structure of the molar and premolar teeth, which form tall quadrangular prisms, in which the enamel is thrown into a number of deep foldings and plications, the intervening depressions and flutings being completely filled with cement. Although the resemblance is at first not very easy to make out, a careful study of the pattern on the crowns of the upper molar teeth of a horse will show that it is really essentially the same as in the rhinoceroses, of which it may be regarded as a specialised modification. The upper premolar teeth, which are generally three in number, although occasionally a small anterior one is present, are as complex as the molars, and are peculiar in being larger than the latter; similar features occurring in the lower jaw. There are thus normally six pairs of cheek teeth in each jaw; the total number of teeth in the adult male being 40, although in the female it may be reduced to 36, as the canines, or tusks, which are always rudimental in that sex, are in some cases altogether wanting. The canines occupy the centre of a long gap between the premolars and the incisors; the three pairs of the latter forming a semi-circle at the extremities of the jaws. The incisors of the horses are peculiar in having the summits of their crowns deeply infolded, like the finger of a glove with the tip pushed in; and it is according as to how much of this infold, or "mark," remains in the teeth of a horse that its age is approximately determined. The skull of a horse, which is of an exceedingly elongated form, differs from that of either a tapir or a rhinoceros in having the socket of the eye completely surrounded by a ring of bone; and in the limbs the bones known as the ulna in the front pair, and the fibula in the hind, are incomplete, and respectively united with the radius and the tibia. A special feature of the horses is the great elongation of the cannon-bone (metacarpal and metatarsal) in each foot, which gives them their characteristic length and slenderness of limb, and enables the upper parts of both the fore and hind-legs to be enclosed in the skin of the body. It is almost superfluous to observe that the so-called knee of a horse represents the human wrist, and the hock the ankle; the whole of the limbs situated below these joints corresponding to the middle finger or toe of the human hand or foot, with the supporting metacarpal or metatarsal bone. The toe of each foot is enveloped in a solid hoof, which is broader in the front than in the hind-limb; and the inner sides of the fore-limb always has a naked wart-like callosity above the wrist-joint, while there may be a similar pair of callosities on the hind-limb.

The Horse Tribe. —Family *Equidæ*.

The ears are elongated ; the long and tapering tail may be either long-haired throughout its length, or only at the tip; and the neck is ornamented with an upright or flowing mane. Horses are now restricted to the Old World, although they formerly existed both in the northern and southern halves of the New World.

The common or true horse (*Equus caballus*) is now best known in a domesticated or half-wild condition, although it is probable that the wild horses, or tarpans, of the Russian stěppes, are the direct descendants of the original primitive stock, and have never been domesticated. From the other species of the genus the horse is distinguished by the tail being covered with abundant long hair from root to tip, by the presence of a warty callosity on each hind-leg, just below the inner side of the ankle-joint, the longer and pendant mane, shorter ears, more elongated limbs, smaller head, and wider hoofs. Some doubt exists whether the horse from Central Asia described as *E. prezevalskii* is a valid species ; but if it be, it appears to be intermediate between the horse and the asses, having callosities on both limbs, an erect mane, no forelock, small ears, and the upper part of the tail short-haired.

The zebras of Africa south of the Sahara form a group closely allied to the asses, but distinguished by their more or less completely striped coloration. Of these the true, or mountain zebra (*E. zebra*) formerly inhabited the mountains of the Cape Colony in large herds, but is now greatly reduced in numbers. It is a rather small species, standing about four feet at the withers, with rather long ears, the lower part of the tail somewhat thinly clothed with long hairs, and a short mane ; the ground colour being white, with broad, black, transverse stripes, extending over the whole skin, except that of the under-parts and the inner surface of the thighs, and the lower part of the face chestnut brown. On the hind-quarters short transverse stripes extend from the longitudinal one running down the spine towards or to the oblique ones of the haunches. Grevy's zebra (*E. grevyi*), of the Galla country, differs by the much narrower and more numerous stripes, especially those of the head, the spine-stripe being disconnected from the others. More distinct is the larger Burchell's zebra (*E. burchelli*), from the open plains to the north of the Orange River, characterised by the pale yellowish-brown ground-colour of the hair, and the broad brown or black stripes ; a dark stripe, to which the lateral stripes may be united, traversing the middle line of the under-surface of the body, and the spinal stripe being isolated from the uppermost haunch-stripe parallel to it. Very generally faint stripes occupy the middle of the broad intervals between the dark stripes of the haunches ; and the limbs and tail may be either fully or partially striped, or uniform. Upon such variations several nominal species have been established, but it appears preferable to look upon all these in the light of mere varieties of a single variable species. Many attempts have been made, with more or less marked success, to break this zebra to harness.

Fig. 70.—BURCHELL'S ZEBRA (*Equus burchelli*).

According to a newspaper report, recent experiments in the Transvaal have been "successful, in so far as the training is concerned, but the trials with these animals have wofully disappointed those who fancied they might be advantageously utilised for draught purposes. Most people in South Africa, in districts where zebras abound, have hitherto regarded these animals as impervious to that human control that would be necessary to render them reliable between the shafts or in traces, and it is only lately that efforts have been directed towards their domestication. Teams of them, comprising ten or more, have been broken in and 'inspanned' to coaches and other vehicles, by way of testing their amenability to the bit and the whip, and their behaviour in harness has been in some respects most satisfactory and promising, though their peculiarities sometimes rather out-mule the mule, their shyness being particularly pronounced, and their disinclination to start gently another characteristic, resulting often in jumps out of harness, or other antics, such as those practised by a jibbing or highly-nervous horse. These faults, however, cure themselves in time, simply by the punitive lessons they teach the zebras; but the stamina of the animals is not of a nature to stand the strain of either the lessons so acquired, or the burden of the draught for any length of time, and looking at the conformation of the zebra one is hardly surprised. Resembling the mule in many points, he yet lacks that essential inherited by the latter from both his progenitors—toughness of bone and muscle, prescribed by generations of usage as a beast of burden. It is admitted by all who have seen zebras in harness that, from a spectacular point of view, they are worth the trouble spent upon their training, and as mounts for children they are certainly more respectable-looking and dignified than the donkey, and in chaises, too, they would probably be found equal to very light work. As draught animals, in the ordinary sense of the term, however, they are not successes. Whether a breed could be manufactured from the zebra, in the same way as the mule has been, and whether with similar success, are questions that an intermingling of blood at the present time might satisfactorily answer in the future."

The fourth species is the quagga (*E. quagga*) of South Africa, which forms a connecting link between the others and the asses, having the head, neck, shoulders, and the middle of the body striped, but the hind-quarters, tail, and limbs uniformly coloured. This animal always had a very restricted distribution, and is now nearly, if not quite, exterminated.

The leading characters by which the uniformly-coloured asses differ from the horse have been already pointed out. The Asiatic wild ass (*E. hemionus*) is a variable species, of an isabelline rufous tint, with a dark, longitudinal stripe down the spine, but none across the withers, and comparatively small ears. Its three leading varieties are the Syrian wild ass, the onager of Persia, Baluchistan, the Punjab, Sind, and Kach, and the kiang of Mongolia and the Tibetan highlands, which is the largest and most horselike of the three. All these wild asses inhabit more or less completely desert districts, and are exceedingly fleet of foot, passing over the roughest ground at a gallop. The African wild ass (*E. asinus*), from Abyssinia, Nubia, and Somaliland, differs from the preceding by its greyer coloration, much longer ears, and the general presence of a dark stripe across the withers. It is evidently the ancestor of the domestic breed, but its speed and endurance must not be judged by those of the latter. The late Sir Samuel Baker wrote that "those who have seen donkeys only in their civilised state can have no conception of the beauty of the wild or original animal. It is the perfection of activity and courage. It has a high-bred tone in his deportment, a high-actioned step when it trots freely over the rocks and sand, with the speed of a horse when it gallops over the boundless desert. The specimens now in the Zoological Gardens will enable any one to perceive the character of the animal as it was before being altered by generations of captivity." The bray of the Abyssinian is identical with that of our common ass, and Darwin notes the marked aversion to walking across a brook, which characterises the domestic donkey, as indicating its derivation from a desert-haunting animal; as also does its pleasure in rolling in the dust. The Somali ass differs from the ordinary African form in its more greyish colour, the absence of the cross-stripe over the shoulders, the very slight indication of the spinal stripe, and more especially in the numerous black markings on both front and hind-legs. It has, likewise, smaller ears and a longer mane. It may be a matter of doubt whether these differences are of specific value, but they probably only indicate a variety. Of this form Mr. Lort Phillips writes that "on March 22, 1884, when about 20 miles to the west of Berbera, we fell in with a small herd of wild asses. After a long and tedious stalk I succeeded in bagging one, which turned out to be of quite a new species to me, having no mark whatever on the body, which was of a beautiful French grey colour. On its legs, however, it had black stripes running diagonally. I have, unfortunately, lost the book in which I put its measurements, but it was a superb creature, and stood quite 14 hands at the shoulder; our Berbera horses looked quite small in comparison."

The Hippopotami.—Family *Hippopotamidæ*

The two species of hippopotamus, both of which are now confined to Africa, and may be referred to the genus *Hippopotamus*, bring us to the fourth and last sub-ordinal division of the Hoofed Mammals, which far outnumbers the whole of the other three put together, both as regards families, genera, and species. From the fact that the two toes corresponding to the third and fourth digits of the human hand and foot are of equal size, and symmetrical to a vertical line drawn between them, this group has been appropriately named the Artiodactyla, or Even-toed Ungulates. Whereas, however, in some species, such as the giraffe, only these two digits are present; in others, like the hippopotami, there are four functional digits; while in yet others, as the oxen, the middle pair alone are functional, and the lateral ones much reduced in size, and of no functional importance. In the peccaries the hind-foot is unique among the sub-order in having only three toes. Although the structure of the feet forms the prime distinction between the Artiodactyla and Perissodactyla, there are many other points of difference between the two groups, a few of which may be mentioned. As regards the teeth, the premolars of the Artiodactyla are almost invariably of simpler structure than the molars; while the last lower molar is nearly always composed of three transverse lobes, whereas in all the living representatives of the Perissodactyla it is two-lobed. The femur or thigh-bone of the latter group is always provided with a large projecting process in the upper half of the shaft known as the third trochanter, which is invariably absent in the one under consideration. Again, in the ankle-joint the huckle-bone, or astralagus, of the Artiodactyla has its lower articular surface divided into two nearly equal facets, whereas in the Perissodactyla such surface is single. There are many other minor points of difference, but those given are amply sufficient to distinguish between the two sub-orders.

The hippopotami are the most primitive and least specialised of the existing members of the Artiodactyla, and are characterised as a family by the following features. Having a very bulky, clumsily-built body, and short limbs, these animals possess a very broad and obtuse muzzle; the feet are short and broad, each having four toes of nearly equal size, invested in rounded hoofs, and all applied to the ground in walking; the incisor teeth, which grow throughout life, are curved downwards in the upper jaw, and project straight forwards in the lower; and the canines, which also grow continuously, are very large and curved, those of the upper jaw being directed downwards. The molar teeth are tuberculated, and have four columns, the summits of which show trefoil-shaped surfaces of ivory, bordered by a broad rim of enamel, when worn by use. In the head, the great elongation of the face causes the small eyes and still more minute ears to be situated very far backwards; the legs are so short that the lower surface of the body is scarcely raised above the ground in the standing posture; and the round tail is likewise extremely short. The thick skin is almost entirely naked. The common hippopotamus (*H. amphibius*) is an animal too well-known, both as regards form and habits, to require any detailed description; its most distinctive feature being the possession of two pairs of incisor teeth in each jaw. On the West Coast of Africa there exists, however, in Liberia, a second species of the genus, known as the pigmy hippopotamus (*H. liberiensis*), differing not only in size, but likewise in habits, from the one with which all are familiar. In place of attaining a total length of about 11 feet, measured in a straight line, and weighing probably some three or four tons, the pigmy hippopotamus is not larger than a good-sized wild boar, although it has the short and stout limbs of its gigantic cousin, with which it also agrees to a certain extent in the relatively large size of its head. As regards its mode of life, this species differs, however, *in toto* from the common one. Instead of passing at least as much of its time in the water as on the land, and never living away from rivers or lakes, the pigmy hippopotamus is an inhabitant of the dense tropical forests of that part of Western Africa which is its home, where it apparently leads a life very similar to that of wild pigs, wallowing in swamps after the manner of those animals, but apparently not habitually frequenting rivers, though it is doubtless, like almost all Mammals, able to swim well when the necessity arises. Moreover, in place of associating in large herds after the manner of the common species, and never moving far from one particular locality, the Liberian hippopotamus is a comparatively solitary creature, going about at most only in pairs, and wandering long distances through the woods. It differs essentially from the common species in usually having only a single pair of lower incisors, on which account it has been generically separated by some under the name of *Chœropsis*. Specimens are, however, occasionally

Fig. 71.—COMMON HIPPOPOTAMUS (*Hippopotamus amphibius*).

met with having two pairs of these teeth on one side of the jaw. If fossil species be taken into consideration, other variations will be found in the number of these teeth; but before proceeding farther, it is necessary to remark that, since in ordinary Mammals the typical or full complement of incisor teeth consists of three pairs, it is natural to suppose that one pair has been lost in the common species. That such is the case is demonstrated by the extinct Siwalik hippopotamus (*H. sivalensis*) of the Himalaya, in which, between the two large tusks, there are three pairs of incisors, differing from those of the common species in being all of nearly equal size; and if we were to examine the upper jaw, we should find the same number of teeth. In the presence of these three pairs of incisors the Siwalik hippopotamus resembles the pig, from which it departs less widely than does the common species, in that these teeth are relatively smaller, and also of nearly equal size. The Siwalik hippopotamus must accordingly be regarded as a less specialised species than either of its living cousins; and since, together with an allied species from Burma (*H. iravaticus*), it is the oldest representative of the genus, its generalised features are precisely what evolutionary considerations would have led us to expect. There is, however, yet another point in connection with these teeth demanding notice. From the evidence of the common species, it is impossible to determine which of the three pairs of lower incisors found in the Siwalik hippopotamus have dissappeared in the former; but in the gravels of the Narbada Valley in Central India, there are found two extinct members of the genus, *H. namadicus* and *H. palæindicus*, in the former of which the lower incisors are similar in size and number to those of the Siwalik species; but in the latter, while the inner and outer pairs are very large, there occurs on each side between them a minute and rudimentary tooth, squeezed out from the general line to the upper margin of the jaw, and evidently about to disappear altogether. There is thus evidence that the missing pair of lower incisor teeth in the common hippopotamus is the second; and a complete transition can be traced, as regards the number of these teeth, from the Siwalik species through the common one to the Liberian hippopotamus. While it is quite possible that the African hippopotamus may have been derived from the Siwalik species, it is clear that the pigmy hippopotamus is not the descendant of its giant existing cousin.

With regard to the geographical distribution of the genus, while there is no evidence that the pigmy species ever ranged beyond its present habitat of Liberia, the case is very different with regard to the range of the common species. At the present day this animal is found from the Cape Colony northwards to the cataracts of the Nile, and it extends westwards to Senegal; but while for several centuries it has been very seldom met with on the Nile below the entrance of the Atbara and Blue Nile, there is abundant evidence that in the time of the Pharaohs it was common in Egypt, where in the temple of Edfu, as well as several other buildings, there are frescoes representing the mode in which it was hunted and speared. That the hippopotamus is the animal indicated in the book of Job under the name of behemoth is undoubted, but there is no evidence that the Jews were acquainted with it otherwise than during their sojourn in Egypt. It is true it has been suggested that its range may have extended eastwards as far as Palestine, but this is conjecture, and, had the creature ever lived there, some of its remains should have been found. In the superficial deposits of Southern and Central Europe there occur, however, numerous remains of a hippopotamus which cannot be specifically distinguished from the existing African form, although it was generally of rather larger size. This difference in size was once thought to indicate that the fossil form was a distinct species, but the discovery of a half-fossilised jaw in the alluvium of the Nile near Kalabshi, in Nubia, showed that in former times the African hippopotamus attained dimensions as large as the European form. In England the hippopotamus ranged at least as far north as Leeds, and it is a remarkable circumstance that in many places its remains have been found in association with those of the reindeer. In Algeria, where the genus is now unrepresented, a small species (*H. hipponensis*) flourished during the Pleistocene period; this being distinguished by having three pairs of lower incisor teeth, which differed from those of other members of the genus in having their enamel smooth and their extremities somewhat expanded, thus approximating to the corresponding teeth of the pigs. Equally noteworthy is the occurrence of another species (*H. lemerlei*) in Madagascar, where its remains are common in the great marsh of Ambulisatra. Somewhat intermediate between the common and the Siwalik species, this rather small hippopotamus had sometimes three and sometimes two pairs of incisors in the lower jaw. One or two small species, which may have been partially terrestrial in their habits, dwelt in Italy, Malta, and some of the other Mediterranean islands in past times.

The Pig Tribe. —Family *Suidæ*.

From the hippopotami the members of the great pig tribe, all of which are confined to the Old World, are at once distinguished, not only by their lighter build and longer limbs, but likewise by the peculiar form of the snout, which always terminates in an oval, fleshy disc, in which are perforated the nostrils. The feet, although severally furnished with four toes, are also different in that they are much narrower, and that the middle pair, which are alone functional when the animals are walking on firm ground, are much larger than the lateral ones, and have flat adjacent surfaces, so as to form a so-called divided hoof. In the teeth, the incisors, which are somewhat variable in number, are rooted, and thus only grow for a brief period, while the canines are rootless, and distinguished by the upper pair being directed more or less markedly outwards or upwards. The molar teeth, which are tuberculated, do not wear into the distinct trefoils characterising the corresponding teeth of the hippopotami.

The true pigs (*Sus*) differ from all the other members of the family in having the typical number of 44 teeth, although in certain African representatives of the genus the anterior premolars are frequently shed in the adult. The canines of the upper jaw are curved outwards and upwards, and in the males are very large, and project far beyond the lips; they are worn on their outer convex surfaces to a sharp edge by the attrition of the longer and more slender lower tusks. In the upper incisors, which are directed downwards, the first is considerably larger than the second, which, in turn, succeeds the third in size; and the three pairs of lower incisors are directed almost horizontally forwards. The skull is characterised by the great elevation of its hinder or occipital portion. The external form of the pigs is too well known to need anything in the way of description; but it may be remarked that whereas in many of the domesticated breeds the skin is nearly naked, in the wild boar it is covered with a thick coat of bristly hair. Whereas the adults of all the species are more or less uniformly coloured, the young of the wild breeds are longitudinally striped and spotted with yellow or white. The typical representative of the genus is the wild boar (*S. scrofa*) of Europe,

North Africa, Asia Minor, and Central Asia, replaced in India by the closely allied *S. cristatus.* India is the home of the smallest species, the pigmy hog (*S. salvanius*) of the Bhutan terai, which scarcely exceeds a hare in size. Numerous species inhabit the Malayan countries and islands as far east as Celebes and the Philippines, while one, which may, however, have been introduced, is found in New Guinea. Africa south of the Sahara has but one of the more typical representatives of the genus, which inhabits the Senhaar districts. Elsewhere in that continent, as well as in the adjacent island of Madagascar, the place of the typical swine is taken by the bush-pigs, which are frequently regarded as representing a distinct genus, under the name of *Potamochœrus.* The bush-pigs have long, pencilled ears, and tend to lose the anterior premolar teeth in both jaws, while their molars are of simpler structure than those of the other members of the genus. Of the two African species, *S. africanus*, ranging from South to Central Africa, has grey hair, whereas in the West African *S. porcus* the colour is red, and the pencilled ears are of great length.

Fig. 72.—Bush-Pig (*Sus africanus*).

The other two genera of swine differ from the foregoing in having uniformly coloured young, both being remarkable for the extraordinary development of the tusks of the males. This feature attains its maximum in the babirusa (*Babirusa alfurus*) of the island of Celebes, in the males of which the upper tusks pierce the skin of the face, and curve backwards over the eyes in a manner recalling the horns of the chamois. The lower tusks, which are equally long and slender, curve backwards in a somewhat similar manner, but do not wear against the upper pair. There are but two pairs of upper incisors, and only two pairs of premolars in each jaw. In appearance, the babirusa is a rather short-bodied and long-limbed pig, with small ears, a very wrinkled skin, and the upper edge of the extremity of the snout overhanging the lower. By far the most hideous and repulsive-looking members of the family are the two African species of wart-hogs (*Phacochœrus*), characterised by large conical warty growths projecting from the sides of the face. The whole head is much flattened and expanded, and the muzzle very broad. The huge tusks, which are nearly as large in the sows as in the boars, curve upwards, outwards, and forwards; the upper ones, which are tipped with enamel only at the apex, being of great thickness, and abraded on their convex surfaces by the more slender lower pair. In the adult there is but a single pair of upper incisor teeth,

Fig. 73.—Wart-Hog (*Phacochœrus æthiopicus*).

although, as in all the pigs, the normal three pairs of these teeth are retained in the lower jaw. The premolars are reduced to three pairs in the upper, and two in the lower jaw; but in aged animals not only all these teeth, but likewise the first two pairs of molars, are generally shed, so that there is only the last pair of molars left in each jaw behind the tusks. These last molars are of great size and very peculiar structure, being composed of a number of narrow cylindrical columns arising from a common base, and closely packed together, so as to form a long, narrow, tall crown. Different as such a tooth looks at first sight from the corresponding molar of an ordinary pig, a closer inspection will show that it is nothing but a highly specialised modification of the same general type.

All pigs are more or less nocturnal in their habits, associating in droves, or "sounders," of variable size, and inflicting much damage on crops by their habit of grovelling in the soil in search of roots with their snouts. In diet they may be said to be omnivorous, scarcely anything edible coming amiss to them. The females produce a large number of young at a birth, and thereby differ very remarkably from the ruminants, in which the number very seldom exceeds two, and is more generally one. Boars attack with their lower tusks, and the wounds inflicted by these formidable weapons are terrific, a horse being not unfrequently ripped open by one sweep from the tusk of a charging boar.

Peccaries.—Family *Dicotylidæ*.

Although nearly allied to the pigs of the Old World, with which they appear to be still more intimately connected by means of certain extinct types, the small American swine known as peccaries (*Dicotyles*) are generally regarded as indicating a family group by themselves. They are specially distinguished by the circumstance that the canine teeth of the upper jaw have their points directed downwards in the ordinary manner, with their hinder edges sharpened to a cutting edge; and likewise by the toes on the hind-feet being reduced to three. In the skeleton the third and fourth metacarpal and metatarsal bones are united at their upper ends. Another peculiarity is to be found in the circumstance that the last premolar in the upper jaw is as complex as the first molar, its crown carrying four distinct tubercles. The stomach also is of a more complicated construction than that of the true pigs; and the back is provided with a peculiar gland, from which these animals derive their scientific title. The total number of teeth is 38, there being only two pairs of incisors in the upper jaw, and three pairs of premolars in each. Peccaries, which range from the Red River of Arkansas to the Rio Negro of Patagonia, much resemble small blackish pigs in general appearance. They are forest-haunting animals; and although of small size individually, the large droves in which they collect render them foes by no means to be despised by the lonely traveller in the Brazilian or Paraguayan forests.

Camel Tribe.—Family *Camelidæ*.

The three preceding families of the sub-order Artiodactyla constitute a sectional group known as the Suina, and are collectively characterised by the tuberculate molar teeth and the circumstance that the third and fourth metacarpal and metatarsal bones of the feet (that is to say those corresponding to the third and fourth digits of the human hand and foot) are never completely united together, and are in most cases entirely separate. The remaining members of the sub-order are divided into three other sections, all of which differ from the Suina, and agree with one another in that the molar teeth, instead of being simply tubercular, have the columns on their crowns bent into the form of crescents, of which there are four in those of the upper jaw. Technically, this type of tooth is known as the selenodont; and all the animals possessing it are characterised by their power of ruminating, or chewing the cud. Moreover, in all cases the third and fourth metatarsal bones of the hind-feet are completely fused together to form a cannon-bone, terminating inferiorly in two pulley-like surfaces, or trochleæ, which carry the two middle toes; the same condition also obtaining in the corresponding metacarpal bones of the fore-foot, except in one species of chevrotain. All these animals are thus more specialised than the Suina; the tubercular type of molar, and the separate metacarpal and metatarsal bones of the foot, being evidently the more primitive type.

The first section of these selenodont Artiodactyles is known as the Tylopoda, or cushion-footed group, and includes only the single family of the *Camelidæ*, now represented by the camels of the Old World and the llamas of South America. Having selenodont molars and complete cannon-bones in both feet, the camel tribe are specially distinguished by retaining incisor teeth in the upper jaw, and by the lower canines being tusk-like and separated from the incisors, which always form three pairs. The limbs are long, with the thigh of the hinder pair less enclosed in the skin of the body than is the case in the following families; while the feet have but two toes, which are embedded in a large pad-like cushion, and have only small nails on the upper surface of their extremities. In the cannon-bones the two trochleæ of the lower extremity are widely divergent, and lack the median longitudinal ridge found in all other members of the sub-order. The neck of these animals is long and flexible, and its component vertebræ present a peculiarity unknown in any other living Mammals. As regards their soft internal parts, the camels have a less complex stomach than the true Ruminants; two of its chambers having special honeycomb-like cells for the retention of water.

From their allies the llamas, the two species of camel (*Camelus*) are readily distinguished not only by their much larger bodily size, but likewise by the presence of one or two fatty humps on the back, which diminish or increase in size according to the physical condition of the animal. The head is large, with relatively short and rounded ears; the broad feet have the toes very slightly separated; the moderately long tail terminates in a tuft; and the nearly straight hair is not woolly. Adult camels have a total of 34 teeth, with but one pair of upper incisors, although in the young there are three pairs of the latter. The camels are among the few animals of which there are now no wild representatives; the so-called wild Bactrian camels of Turkestan being now pretty conclusively proved to be the descendants of a domestic race which escaped long ago from captivity. Of the two species, the Arabian camel (*C. dromedarius*), which is found in a domesticated state from Africa to India, is characterised by the single hump; while in the stouter-built and more shaggily-haired Bactrian camel (*C. bactrianus*) there are two of these excrescences. The latter species is kept as a beast of burden from the Crimea to Turkestan and Pekin. From the large loads they are capable of carrying, as well as their power of enduring deprivation from water for a considerable period, camels are invaluable as a means of transport in dry countries, where the roads are not too rocky. They are, however, best suited for traversing sandy deserts; but where the ground is wet, especially on inclined roads, they are almost useless. The Bactrian camel, which is doubtless a native of Asia, is much better suited for traversing high mountains and enduring cold than the Arabian species. Regarding the two-humped camels of the neighbourhood of Yarkand, it has long been a disputed point whether these are really wild, or whether they are the descendants of an originally domesticated race. Something towards clearing up this question has been done by Major C. S. Cumberland, who had the good fortune to shoot one of these animals. Its skin and skull were submitted to Mr. Blanford, who reports that they belonged to a two-humped camel, in which the humps were represented by large tufts of hair. The skull agreed fairly well with that of a domestic Bactrian camel (*C. bactrianus*), and differed from that of the single-humped Arabian camel (*C. dromedarius*). Whether, however, such differences, as presented by the former, were indicative of the existence of a distinct race, the materials at hand were insufficient to determine. In regard to these camels in their native home, Major Cumberland writes as follows :—" The habitat of the wild camel is the Gobi steppe from Khotan to Lob-Nor. Except when snow lies on the ground, these animals may be met with here and there along the old bed of the Yarkand and Tarim Rivers, which they frequent for the pools of brackish water that are to be found here and there. But as soon as the snow falls they move off into the desert, as if then independent of the water-supply. They prefer the snow, I imagine, as being less salt than the water, although it also is impregnated to a certain extent soon after it falls. The camel is very shy in its habits, and, so far as I could ascertain, has never been caught or domesticated. The natives told me that no horse in the country could catch the camels in the deep sand of the region they frequent. They appear to me to be distinct from the Bactrian camel; they are less stumpy in build, the hair is finer, closer, and shorter. They vary in colour, like the domestic species, from dark brown to lightish dun. Their origin has yet to be traced. I take it that they have sprung

Fig. 74.—THE ARABIAN CAMEL.

Fig. 75.—THE BACTRIAN CAMEL.

from camels when the district known as Takla Makan was buried in a great sandstorm some centuries ago. Tradition relates that no human beings survived, but it is likely enough that some of the camels and horses did so, and that this was the origin of the wild camels and ponies that are found in this district."

Camels have been successfully introduced into North America; and for some years, according to a writer in *The Asian* newspaper, have been largely employed as a means of transport in South Australia and Queensland, while recently the Swan River colonists have followed the example there set them; a large number of superior Rajputana camels, which had been marched down from Bikanir to Calcutta, having been shipped to Western Australia to be used in carrying supplies from Perth to the newly discovered gold fields at Coolgardie. The utility of the camel being thoroughly recognised in the Antipodes, the fact that an agitation against the animal is being raised in Queensland is rather a surprise. "Such, however, is the case, as a petition was recently presented by the residents of the Charleville district to the Governor of Queensland, praying that something should be done to prevent the introduction of camels into the colony. In it the petitioners pointed out the urgent need that some constitutional means should be adopted to prevent an imminent and dangerous invasion of Western Queensland by camels, as their employment would tend to deprive the present carriers of their means of livelihood. It was stated that the rates of carriage were low, the teams plentiful, and that the carriers were willing to travel on all roads, while the low standard of living among the camel-drivers must result in loss of trade to the district. It was further said that many of the Western carriers were settlers on the land, and the colony would suffer if such a class of men were forced to emigrate; that the value of the Western lands would be depreciated, and the welfare of the community injuriously affected. In reply the Premier, to whom the petition was forwarded by the Governor, expressed the opinion that the agitation against the camels was rather hasty. The cause of their presence in the colony was the drought in the South-Western districts. It was impossible for teams to travel at all times, and as the Warrego Rabbit Board could not get their netting brought by the ordinary methods, an officer was sent to South Australia, and the required quantity of netting carried to its destination by camels. Then a squatter in the district, whose wool could not be taken away by the carriers in consequence of the want of water on the route to be travelled, had had it forwarded by the camels to Charleville. The forty camels carried altogether eighty bales of wool—two bales to each animal—or just about the quantity that is sometimes taken by one team of bullocks."

Although the name llama properly belongs only to the domesticated forms, it is commonly applied to all the South American representatives of the family, which differ from the camels by their greatly inferior size and lighter build, the want of any hump, the longer and more pointed ears, the short and bushy tail, the narrower feet, with more distinctly separated toes, and the long and woolly hair. They have two teeth less than the camels, owing to the upper premolars in the adult being reduced from three to two pairs. Of the two wild species, the vicuña (*Lama vicuna*) is the smaller and more lightly-built animal of the two, and is restricted to the high Andes of Peru, Ecuador, and part of Bolovia, where it associates in large herds in the coldest and most inhospitable districts. On the other hand, the guanaco (*L. guanacus*) ranges from the Peruvian Andes through the open pampas of Argentina to Patagonia and Tierra del Fuego; although it has now been exterminated from most parts of the pampas. In size it may be compared to a red-deer; and its fur is of beautiful, light fawn-brown colour. The llama and alpaca are domesticated varieties of the guanaco, kept by the inhabitants of the Peruvian highlands; the former and larger of the two being employed as a beast of burden, while the latter is bred for the sake of its valuable wool. All these animals have a peculiar cry, with some resemblance to the neigh of a horse; and in the domesticated state they are disagreeable associates, on account of their unpleasant habit of spitting, apparently as a means of defence. Extinct members of the family are common in the Tertiary rocks of North America, while fossil camels occur in Northern India; and it is by these lost types that we are enabled to account for the present anomalous geographical distribution of the group, which is evidently of northern origin.

Fig. 76.—GUANACO (*Lama guanacus*).

The Chevrotains. —Family *Tragulidæ*.

Among the smallest of all Ungulates are the graceful little Oriental animals commonly known as chevrotains, or mouse-deer, which in coloration, form, and habits, more nearly resemble the Rodent agutis than ordinary Hoofed Mammals. Together with a nearly-allied African genus, these animals constitute a third section of the selenodont Artiodactyles, known as the Tragulina. From the camel tribe they differ in the total absence of incisor teeth in the upper jaw, and also by the circumstance that in the lower jaw the canines are approximated to the incisors, which they resemble in form, as well as in the structure of the feet. From the true Ruminants they may be distinguished by the stomach having only three in place of four distinct compartments, as well as by the fibula, or outer and smaller bone of the lower half of the hind-leg, being complete and quite distinct from the larger bone, or tibia. Another point of distinction is to be found in the form of the so-called odontoid process projecting from the lower part of the front surface of the second vertebra of the neck, which in the present group is conical, whereas it is spout-like in the true Ruminants. A resemblance to the latter group, and at the same time a distinction from the camel tribe, is to be found in that the two bones of the ankle-joint, respectively known as the cuboid and the navicular, are welded together to form a single bone. As in the true Ruminants, the toes are enclosed in solid hoofs; four complete toes being developed in each foot.

The smallest representatives of the family are the true or Oriental chevrotains (*Tragulus*), of which there are four or five species, ranging from India and Ceylon through the Malayan countries, as far east as the island of Palawan in the Philippine group. They have a total of 34 teeth, and are mostly uniform in coloration. The somewhat larger West African chevrotain (*Dorcatherium*) differs by the shorter and stouter feet, and the separation of the third and fourth metacarpal bones; the latter feature distinguishing it from all other selenodont Artiodactyles. In colour, it is deep brown, with longitudinal white stripes on the flanks, spots of the same on the back, and a white chest and throat. Both in this animal and the true chevrotains the upper canines of the males form tusks projecting below the lip. In appearance they are very like minute deer, having moderate-sized ears and a short tail, but the head has no bony or horny appendages.

Fig. 77.—A CHEVROTAIN (*Tragulus*).

The deer tribe is the first of four families constituting the true Ruminants, or Pecora, and including the whole of the remaining members of the order. They derive their name of Ruminants from their power of chewing the cud—a feature which they possess in common with the camel tribe and chevrotains; and they agree with the latter group in lacking upper incisors, and in having the lower canine approximated to and resembling the lower incisors as well as in the union of the cuboid and navicular bones in the ankle-joint, and in the covering of the toes taking the form of horny hoofs. From the chevrotains they may be distinguished by the stomach being divided into four distinct compartments, by the anterior, or odontoid process of the second vertebra of the neck assuming the form of a spout, or half-cylinder, and by the fibula of the hind-leg being reduced to a mere nodule representing the lower extremity of the complete bone, and articulated to the tibia. Another point of distinction is that the lateral metacarpal and metatarsal bones of the feet are never complete, but are represented only by their upper or lower ends. Very generally the skull is provided with a pair of laterally placed appendages, which may be either unbranched, covered with horn, and permanent, or branched, bony, and deciduous. When such appendages are present, the upper canines are generally small or wanting; but when the former are absent, the latter are frequently large. As a source of food, the true Ruminants are by far the most important of all animals to the human race. Unknown in Australia and New Guinea, they attain their maximum development in the continents of the Old World proper; in North America, except the *Cervidæ*, they are poorly represented, while in the southern half of the New World the only members of the group are deer.

The Deer Tribe. —Family *Cervidæ.*

As a family, the deer tribe are generally distinguished by the heads of the males being ornamented with the branching deciduous appendages properly known as antlers, although often wrongly termed horns; these when fully developed consisting simply of lifeless bone, and being nearly always shed annually, to be reproduced in a somewhat more complex form the following season. Both sexes usually have well-developed upper canines, which may attain very large dimensions in the males, especially in the few instances where antlers are wanting. The face is always provided with the so-called larmiers, or tear-pits, below the eyes; and the underlying region of the skull always has a very large unossified vacuity. As a general rule, both fore and hind-feet carry four toes; and very often the lower ends of the lateral metacarpal and metatarsal bones persist. With the single exception of the musk-deer, the liver is provided with a gall-bladder.

It would require too much space to describe the mode in which antlers are formed and subsequently shed, but it may be mentioned that the annual formation of such an enormous amount of bone as is contained in the antlers of the wapiti, for instance, is one of the most extraordinary phenomena to be met with in the whole animal kingdom. As regards their distribution, it is remarkable that deer are totally absent from Africa south of the Sahara, as they are from Madagascar. Although the more northern deer inhabiting the New World are either generically or specifically identical with Old World forms, the majority of the American forms, and all those inhabiting South America, are perfectly distinct from those of other regions.

The most aberrant members of the family are the well-known musk-deer (*Moschus*) of Asia, which constitute a sub-family by themselves, and are represented by one species (*M. moschiferus*) ranging from the Himalaya and Cochin-China to Siberia, and by a second (*M. sifanicus*) from Kansu, in North-Western China. One of the peculiar features of these deer—the presence of a gall-bladder in the liver—has been already referred to ; a second, although less peculiar character, is the absence of antlers in both sexes. To compensate for this deficiency, the upper jaw of the male is provided with a pair of long scimitar-like tusks, which may project as much as three inches below the margin of the lips. The musk-deer has moderately long and somewhat pointed ears, a short tail, very large lateral hoofs to the feet, and the fur of a peculiarly coarse and brittle nature, its general colour being a speckled brownish-grey. The most peculiar feature about the animal is, however, the presence on the abdomen of the male of a large gland, discharging by a small orifice, and secreting the highly odoriferous substance known as musk, which is much used in perfumery, and commands a high price in the market. For the sake of obtaining this precious product, musk-deer are regularly hunted by the natives of the countries they inhabit ; one plan being to drive them against nets. In the Himalaya they are met with either singly or in pairs ; and during the early spring may be seen traversing the snow-clad birch and pine forests.

Fig. 78.—MUSK-DEER (*Moschus moschiferus*).

Of the more typical deer, the first group is that of the Oriental muntjacs (*Cervulus*), all of which are comparatively small species characterised by the short antlers arising from long bony pedicles on the skull, which rapidly converge as they descend the face. From this peculiarity these animals are often called rib-faced deer. The males have large tusks ; and the antlers consist of a beam, or shaft, with a small tine at the base. In the lateral toes all traces of the bones have disappeared. There appear to be three well-marked species of muntjacs, the range of the genus extending from India to Eastern Tibet and China. In common with most of the deer of the Old World, the muntjacs are characterised by the retention of the upper extremities of the lateral metacarpal and metatarsal bones of the feet. Nearly allied to the muntjacs are two small deer from China and Eastern Tibet, constituting the genus *Elaphodus*, and commonly known, from the presence of a tuft of hair between the antlers, as tufted deer. They differ from the muntjacs in that the pedicles of the antlers converge, instead of diverging, as they ascend on the face ; while the very small and simple antlers have no basal knobs representing a brow-tine. The males have large upper canines, and the hairs are coarse and almost quill-like.

By far the greater number of the deer of the Eastern Hemisphere belong to the typical genus *Cervus*, of which the most familiar examples are the red-deer and the fallow-deer. From the muntjacs and their allies all these deer are easily distinguished by the absence of the bony ridges which form the bases of the long pedicles of the antlers of the former. As a rule, the antlers, which, as in most members of the family, are confined to the male sex, are of large size, considerably exceeding the whole skull in length, and they do not branch in the regular forked manner characteristic of the American deer. While, in the majority of the species, the antlers are rounded, or slightly flattened, in a few they are flattened, or palmated. Unlike those of the muntjacs, the upper canine teeth are of comparatively small size, and in the lateral digits of the feet the bones are present. Although the genus is mainly confined to the Old World, it is represented in North America by the magnificent wapiti. In the main, deer are forest-haunting animals, the old bucks going about with several does during the breeding season, which they have obtained by driving away younger competitors, or by vanquishing rivals of their own age. Generally but a single offspring is produced by the hinds at a birth, and these, as is the case with almost all Ungulates, are able to run by the side of their dam in the course of a few days. Whereas the adults may be either uniformly coloured, or spotted with white for a portion or the whole of the year, the young are very generally spotted, although those of the Indian sambar are usually an exception in this respect. Many of the uniformly coloured species of the genus display a conspicuous white blaze on the buttocks, and in all the muzzle is naked and narrow, while the antlers of the males arise at a sharp angle to the middle line of the face. The European species are very regular in their times of feeding and repose ; and, like other members of the family, the males during the breeding season utter a peculiar "belling" cry, which is both a challenge to rivals of their own sex, and likewise a call to the female. The genus may be divided into several more or less well defined groups according to the form of the antlers, and other structural features.

Fig. 79.—MUNTJAC (*Cervulus muntjac*).

Of these the first for consideration is the Rusine group, which is exclusively confined to the Oriental countries, ranging as far eastwards as the Philippine Islands. In this group the antlers are rounded and frequently marked by strong vertical grooves, while they lack the so-called bez-tine (the one arising immediately above the first, or brow-tine), and the upright and slightly curved beam terminates in a simple fork, so that the number of points to each antler is only three. The brow, or basal-tine, rises close to the thickened rugose ring forming the base, and known as the burr, and makes an acute angle with the beam, or main shaft. In the more typical forms, the colour is uniformly brown, the tail is of medium length in all, and the neck is generally maned. The largest and best known representative of this group is the sambar (*C. unicolor*), which stands nearly five feet in height, and, with its numerous varieties, ranges from India and Burma, through the Malay Peninsula, Borneo, and Samatra to China. As a rule, the young are not spotted. In Formosa there is the nearly allied *C. swinhoei*, while *C. philippinus* and *C. alfredi* are smaller forms inhabiting the Philippine Islands, the last being distinguished by its spotted coat. Still smaller is the Indian hog-deer (*C. porcinus*), easily distinguished by the absence of a distinct mane on the neck, and the comparatively simple antlers, the young being spotted till they attain an age of about six months. A second Oriental assemblage is the Rucervine group, typically represented by the Indian swamp-deer (*C. duvauceli*), and the closely allied *C. schomburgki* of Siam. In these the beam of the antlers is rather flattened and more curved than in the first group, while the large brow-tine arises at an obtuse angle from the beam, with an upward curvature. To the same group belongs the remarkable Eld's deer, or tameng (*C. eldi*) of Burma, Cambodia, and the Island of Hainan, in which the whole antler forms a continuous curve from its extreme summit to the tip of the brow-tine. In all the three species the tail is sharp, and the neck provided with a mane, the young being spotted. David's deer (*C. davidianus*) of Northern China may be regarded as representing a third group by itself, the antlers rising straight from the brow, and then giving off a long back-tine. Each antler is forked at the summit, but the prongs of the fork may again divide. The brilliantly coloured axis, or spotted deer (*C. axis*) of India, in which the coat is permanently spotted with white, likewise forms a group by itself. It has antlers of the same general type as those of the Rusine group, the brow-tine usually arising at an acute or right angle from the beam, but it differs in the absence of a mane on the neck, and the greater length of the tail. The molar teeth are characterised by the great height of their crowns. The pretty little Japanese deer (*C. sica*), which has been successfully introduced into several English parks, is the typical representative of a small assemblage of species, chiefly from North-Eastern Asia, which constitute the Pseudaxine group. When fully developed, the antlers have a brow and trez-tine (the second, or bez-tine, being absent), and terminate in a fork, of which the hinder-tine is the smaller, so that the total number of points on each is four. In summer the coat is spotted, but it becomes uniformly coloured in winter; the tail is of medium length, and the neck slightly maned.

The typical or elaphine group, which includes the red-deer (*C. elaphus*) of Europe, and the North American wapiti (*C. canadensis*), is characterised by the presence of a second, or bez-tine, to the antlers, when these attain their maximum development; the beam of each antler being rounded, and near its summit splitting up into a larger or smaller number of points, which in some species form a cup. The tail is short, and included within a large light-coloured patch on the buttocks; the remainder of the body being uniformly brown. The red-deer, which ranges over Europe, Western Asia, and North Africa, has the antlers, when fully developed, as in a "royal hart," forming a distinct cup at the summits. The deer of Northern Asia, from the Caucasus to Siberia, and thence to North China, has been separated as *C. xanthopygus*; but its right to specific distinction seems rather doubtful. Other members of this group are the Persian maral (*C. maral*); the Kashmir stag or hangul (*C. cashmirianus*), represented by a variety in Yarkand; the shou (*C. affinis*) of Tibet; Thorold's deer (*C. thoroldi*), which is also a Tibetan form, easily distinguished by its white muzzle; the great Thian Shan stag (*C. eustephanus*);

and the closely-allied wapiti (*C. canadensis*) of North America. In all these species, which include the largest members of the genus, the antlers do not form a distinct cup at the summit. The Barbary variety of the red-deer does not develop the bez-tine.

The common fallow-deer (*C. dama*), whose native home appears to be the Mediterranean countries, and the Persian fallow-deer (*C. mesopotamicus*), are the sole existing members of the last, or Damine, group of the genus, characterised by the palmation of the antlers, and by the fur being generally spotted, although there is a uniformly brown variety of the common species. These deer have no upper canine teeth, and the tail is of moderate length. To this group may be referred two very fine species, which have only become extinct comparatively recently. Since the year 1697, when certain of its remains were described by a Dr. Molyneux in the Philosophical Transactions of the Royal Society of London, the gigantic extinct deer of the Irish peat-bogs had been known to science; while the magnificent proportions attained by its antlers have given it a notoriety not shared by most other animals of a past epoch. Although found more abundantly, and generally in a better state of preservation, in the bogs of Ireland than elsewhere, the Irish deer is by no means confined to the island from which it takes its name. On the contrary, its remains have been obtained from many of the caverns and superficial deposits of both England and the Continent, and its continental range extended from Italy in the south to Russia in the north. In popular language, this deer is generally spoken of as the Irish elk; but, as is the case with a number of popular terms, this is a misnomer, the animal really being a true deer, referable to the genus *Cervus*. It is true, indeed, that its broad, palmated antlers present a superficial resemblance to those of the elk; but this no more indicates any close affinity with that animal than do the somewhat similarly palmated antlers of the fallow-deer. Like many other animals, both living and extinct, the Irish deer rejoices in a number of scientific names; but its proper title is *Cervus giganteus*. It is almost superfluous to mention that the antlers of this magnificent deer are larger than those of any other known species, having a span in some cases of over 11 feet from tip to tip. In form, the antlers have a short and nearly cylindrical beam, given off in a nearly horizontal plane at right angles to the axis of the skull. Near their origin from the skull, there arises a descending brow-tine, which is flattened, and generally forked. As soon as the beam expands, it gives off from the front, or lower edge, a trez-tine, nearly opposite to which is a third, or posterior tine on the hinder or upper margin, both these tines being seen fully from the front. Beyond these tines, the antlers expand to their fullest width, and usually terminate in five or six snags, of which the topmost are directed nearly upwards. The second of the extinct species is Ruff's deer (*C. ruffi*), hitherto only found in Germany. In place of the outward horizontal extension characteristic of the Irish deer, the antlers of Ruff's deer are directed upwards and outwards, nearly after the fashion of a fallow-deer, so that their innermost terminal snags are separated only by a comparatively small interval. That this deer is closely allied to the Irish deer, and has no such close kinship with the fallow-deer, is, however, proved by the flattened and expanded form of the brow-tine. A further difference from the ordinary Irish deer is exhibited by the different position of the plane of the expanded portion of the antlers. Thus, whereas in the former the whole of their inner surface and the entire trez and posterior tines are visible from the front, in Ruff's deer we see, instead of the inner surface, the front edge and a part of the outer surface, while only the tips of the posterior tines are visible, and the trez-tine (which is much longer than in the normal form) is foreshortened. The position of the plane of the expanded portion of the antlers is another point in which Ruff's deer approximates to the fallow-deer.

The reindeer (*Rangifer*), together with all the remaining members of the family, differ from the foregoing in that the lateral metacarpal bones of the fore-feet and the corresponding metatarsals in the hind-limbs are represented by their lower, instead of their upper, extremities. From all other deer, the reindeer are at once distinguished by having antlers in both sexes; these being very large, with the cylindrical beam suddenly bent forwards near the middle of its length, and having a brow-tine which is generally branched and palmated on one side, and simple on the other. Above the brow-tine comes a large bez-tine. In form, reindeer are heavily-built animals, with short limbs, in which the main hoofs are widely separable, and the lateral pair unusually large, the muzzle being broad and hairy. The young, like their parents, are uniformly coloured. The ordinary reindeer (*R. tarandus*) ranges from Norway and Sweden over the northern regions of the Old World; and it is probable that the North American variety known as the caribou is not specifically distinct. The uses to which reindeer are put by the Lapps and the inhabitants of other northern countries are too well known to require mention.

Fig. 80.—REINDEER (*Rangifer tarandus*).

The largest of all living deer is the elk or moose (*Alces machlis*), which is the only living member of its genus, and has a circumpolar distribution, ranging in the Old World as far south as Prussia and the Caucasus. It is a long-legged, ungainly-looking animal, with the large, overhanging, broad muzzle covered with short hairs, except a small, naked triangular spot below the nostrils. The tail is rudimental, and the hair of the young uniformly coloured. In the males the enormous antlers arise from a cylindrical beam directed at right angles to the middle line of the skull, and then expand into a huge basin-shaped mass, consisting primarily of an upper and lower moiety, and having the free edge bordered by a number of irregular snags. Elk feed chiefly upon the leaves and twigs of trees; and during the winter collect in small parties, keeping open a small patch of ground by continually trampling down the snow. Frequently the hind gives birth to a pair of fawns. The ant-

Fig. 81. —ELK (*Alces machlis*).

lers may weigh as much as sixty pounds. The two remaining genera of Old World deer are represented by small forms. Of these, the roe-deer *(Capreolus)* have comparatively short cylindrical antlers with three tines each; the front tine rising from the front of the upper half of the beam and inclining upwards. There are no upper canines, the naked portion of the muzzle is small, and does not extend below the nostrils, the tail is very short, and the fur of the young spotted. In addition to the common roe (*C. caprea)* of Europe and Western Asia, a second species *(C. pygargus)* inhabits Turkestan and the mountains dividing Russia from China, while a smaller variety is found in Manchuria. Roe-deer usually inhabit more or less open country, and go about in pairs. From all other members of the family except the musk-deer, which it resembles in the long tusks of the males, the small Chinese water-deer *(Hydropotes inermis)* differs in the absence of antlers from both sexes. The muzzle has a rather large naked portion, and the young are spotted. As in the roes, there are large glands in the hind-feet, and small ones in the front pair. In form, these deer have long bodies and short limbs, and they are remarkable for producing from three to six fawns at a birth.

Agreeing with the genera just described in the structure of the metacarpal and metatarsal bones, the American deer, exclusive of the wapiti, reindeer, and elk, are, with two exceptions, included in a genus (*Cariacus*) characterised by the antlers, when fully developed, dividing in a more or less regularly fork-like manner. Whereas, however, in some species the antlers are large and branching, in certain of the smaller forms they form simple spikes. The muzzle resembles that of *Cervus*, the tail is of variable length, and the fur of the adults is uniformly coloured. The genus ranges over almost the whole of the American Continent, but attains its maximum development in the south. The brockets, of which the red brocket (*C. rufus*) is a well-known example, are a southern group, easily recognised by their unbranched, spike-like antlers. They have a tail of moderate length, and the fawns are spotted. The Costa Rica deer (*C. clavatus*) of Central America differs from the brockets in having the hair of the face directed upwards, instead of radiating from two points. The Andes is the home of two species (*C. chilensis* and *C. antisiensis*) known as guemels, and characterised by their simply forked antlers, of which the front prong is the longer. There are tusks in the upper jaw, and the young are uniformly coloured. The pampas-deer (*C. campestris*) is the typical representative of another South American group of the genus, in which the antlers are regularly forked, with the hinder prong, and occasionally also the front one, again forking. There are no upper canines, the tail is very short, and the coloration of the fawns is uniform. The last group of the genus is typified by the Virginian deer (*C. virginianus*), and comprises not only the largest species, but likewise all those inhabiting North America. In this group the antlers are very large and complex, and distinguished by the presence of a larger or smaller basal snag near the base of the front surface. Upper tusks are absent, and the fawns are spotted. Whereas in the Virginian deer the basal snag is very large, and directed upwards, in the large-eared mule-deer (*C. macrotis*) of North America it is much smaller. Of the former Mr. Parker Gilmore writes, that "this splendid animal has still a very wide habitat. Its boundaries, however, originally were from the Atlantic Ocean to the Rockies, and from the Gulf of Mexico to about 47° N. latitude, and although eagerly sought by everyone deeming himself a hunter, it can be found in greater or less numbers near the oldest settlements. As an article of food the meat of this deer is unsurpassed, especially when the animal has fattened upon Indian corn. For grace and contour of outline they are incomparable. Their horns have a most peculiar and graceful outline, receding at first backwards from the burr, then coming forward with a bold sweep It is extremely timorous and wary, but if wounded and unable to escape it will fight gallantly for its life. In such encounters its horns are not, in my experience, so much to be dreaded as its fore-feet." Finally, the two pudu-deer (*Pudua*) of the Chilian Andes and Ecuador, although nearly related to the brockets, differ sufficiently to form a genus by themselves. In size they scarcely exceed a hare ; and they have a pair of very minute simple antlers rising from the middle of the forehead, while they exhibit certain peculiarities in the structure of the skull and ankle-joint.

The Giraffe.—Family *Giraffidæ*.

The African giraffe (*Giraffa camelopardalis*), which is the sole existing representative of its genus and family, enjoys the proud distinction of being the tallest of all Mammals, and is easily recognised by its extremely elongated neck and limbs, as well as by its dappled coloration. In many respects intermediate between the deer and the hollow-horned Ruminants, although more nearly allied to the former than to the latter, it is chiefly entitled to form a family by itself on account of the peculiar structure of the appendages on the skull, which, properly speaking, come under the designation neither of antlers nor horns. Between the large ears are a pair of short horns, as they may be called, which are completely covered with skin, and are formed of bones, which in the young state can be easily detached from the skull. Lower down on the forehead is a single median dome-like bone, which is likewise detachable in the young. In general conformation the skull of the giraffe is very like that of the deer ; but the cheek teeth have very short crowns, and a peculiarly rugose enamel. There are no upper tusks ; the lateral hoofs are totally wanting in both limbs ; the tail is long and tufted at the end ; and there is generally no gall-bladder to the liver. In colour, the South African giraffe differs from the North African variety by the darker tint and larger size of the chestnut blotches, and the narrower buff lines by which they are divided. The giraffe, however, has attained its towering stature without any important departure from the general structure characterising its nearest allies, and thus preserves all the essential features of an ordinary quadruped. It owes its height mainly to the enormous elongation of two of the bones of the legs, coupled with a corresponding lengthening of the vertebræ of the neck. As in all its kindred, the lower segment of each leg of this animal forms a cannon-bone, the nature of which has been explained above, and in the fore-limb it is the bone below the wrist (commonly termed the knee), and the radius above the latter, which have undergone an elongation so extraordinary as to make

Fig. 82.—THE GIRAFFE.

them quite unlike, as regards proportion, the corresponding elements in the skeleton of an ordinary Ruminant, although retaining precisely the same structure. Similarly, in the hinder-limb, it is the cannon-bone below the ankle-joint, or hock, and the tibia above, which have been thus elongated. To one unacquainted with anatomy, it might appear that a giraffe and a hippopotamus would differ greatly in regard to the number of vertebræ in the neck; but, nevertheless, both conform in this respect to the ordinary Mammalian type, possessing only seven of such segments.

Other noticeable features in the organisation of the giraffe are the large size and prominence of the liquid eyes, and the great length of the extensile tongue; the former being designed to give the creature the greatest possible range of vision, while the extensibility of the latter enhances the capability of reaching the foliage of tall trees afforded by the lengthened limbs and neck. In comparison with the slenderness of the neck, the head of the giraffe appears of relatively large size; but this bulk, which is probably necessary to the proper working of the long tongue, is compensated by the extreme lightness and porous structure of the bones of the skull. Somewhat stiff and ungainly in its motions—the small number of vertebræ not admitting of the graceful arching of the neck—the giraffe in all its organisation is admirably adapted to a life on open plains dotted over with tall trees, upon which it can browse without fear of competition by any other living creature. Its wide range of vision affords it timely warning of the approach of foes; from the effect of sand-storms it is protected by the power of automatically closing its nostrils; while its capacity of existing for months at a time without drinking renders it suited to inhabit waterless districts like the northern part of the great Kalahari desert. Although capable of withstanding the want of water for a long period during the summer, the giraffe, when opportunity offers, will drink long and frequently; but it is certain that for more than half the year, in many parts of Southern Africa at least, it never takes water at all. In certain districts, as in the Northern Kalahari, this abstinence is, from the nature of the country, involuntary; but according to Mr. Bryden, the giraffes living in the neighbourhood of the Botletli River—their only source of water—never drink therefrom throughout the spring and winter months. When a giraffe does drink, unless it wades into the stream, it is compelled to straddle its fore-legs far apart in order to bring down its lips to the required level, and the same ungainly attitude is perforce assumed on the rare occasions when it grazes.

Absent from the countries to the north of the Sahara, as well as in the great forest regions of the west, which are unsuitable to its habits, the giraffe at the present day ranges from the North Kalahari and Northern Bechuanaland in the south, through such portions of Eastern and Central Africa as are suited to its mode of life, to the Southern Sudan in the north. Unhappily, however, it is almost daily diminishing in numbers throughout a large area of Southern and Eastern Africa, and its distributional area as steadily shrinking. Whether it was ever found to the south of the Orange River and in the Cape Colony may be doubtful, although there are traditions that it once occurred there. Apart from this, it is definitely known that about the year 1813 these animals were met with only a little to the north of the last-named river; while as late as 1836 they were still common throughout the Transvaal, and more especially near the junction of the Marico with the Limpopo River. Now their last refuge in these districts is the extreme eastern border of the Transvaal (where only a few remain), and the district lying to the north of Bechuanaland and known as Khama's country, or Bawangwato, together with the Northern Kalahari. Even here, however, their existence is threatened, as there is a proposal to put down tube-wells in the Kalahari, which, if successfully accomplished, will open up the one great stronghold of the animal to the hunter. Unless, therefore, efficient and prompt measures are taken for its protection, there is much reason to fear that the giraffe will ere long be practically exterminated from this part of Africa, although it will doubtless long survive in the remote districts of the Sudan and Kordofan.

The Prongbuck.—Family *Antilocapridæ*.

Although closely allied to the typical hollow-horned Ruminants, the prongbuck, or prong-horned antelope (*Antilocapra americana*) is regarded as representing a distinct family, on account of the circumstance that not only are the sheaths of the horns branched, but that they are annually shed, and their place taken by new sheaths, which have been growing up beneath the old ones. In size, the prongbuck may be compared to a fallow-deer, although its form is lighter and more elegant. It has no lateral hoofs; the horns are present usually only in the males; the ears are rather long and pointed; and the tail is short. There is a thick mane of long hair on the neck, and the general colour is chestnut; but there is a white patch on the rump, and white bars on the throat, while the lower portion of the flanks, together with the under-parts, are likewise white; the compressed and scimitar-like horns being black. Prongbucks are inhabitants of the open plains of Eastern-Central North America, where they associate in herds, which may frequently be of large size.

Hollow-horned Ruminants.—Family *Bovidæ*.

The last, and at the same time by far the largest family group of the Ungulates, is that of the hollow-horned Ruminants, or *Bovidæ;* under which title are comprised antelopes, goats, sheep, oxen, etc. Almost the whole of the members of this great assemblage are inhabitants of the Old World, the only American forms being the Rocky Mountain goat, the bighorn sheep, musk-ox, and American buffalo, and all these confined to the northern half of that continent. Indeed, there is little doubt that the ancestors of at least three of these were immigrants from the Eastern Hemisphere; and there is no evidence that South America was ever the home of any member of the group. The essential feature of the hollow-horned Ruminants is the presence, in one sex at least of all the existing forms, of a pair of unbranched horns on the upper part of the head, composed of an underlying core of bone, covered with a hollow, horny sheath, which is never shed. None of these animals ever have upper canine teeth; and the lateral metacarpal and metatarsal bones of the feet are invariably absent, although lateral hoofs are not unfrequently present. In many cases the tear-pits, or larmiers, so characteristic of the deer, are

Fig. 83.—Prongbuck (*Antilocapra americana*).

absent from the face ; and in such cases the underlying region of the skull is fully ossified, while, when those glands are developed, the unossified space in the skull below each eye is generally of less extent than in the *Cervidæ*.

Fig. 84 —Bubaline Antelope (*Bubalis*)

The first and least specialised group of the family includes the animals commonly known as antelopes, which are arranged, under a very large number of genera, and pass imperceptibly into the goats. Although no definition can be given of an antelope, as a rule these animals have comparatively long necks, and are of more or less light and graceful build, while their bony horn-cores are generally solid throughout. By far the great majority of antelopes inhabit the open plains of Africa south of the Sahara, but there are none in Madagascar, while Burma and the Malayan countries only possess a few forms, which may be regarded as intermediate between the true antelopes and the goats. The well-known hartebeests (*Bubalis*), so remarkable on account of their long, solemn-looking faces, are the typical representatives of a section comprising two genera, all of which, with the exception of one species of hartebeest, which is Syrian, are confined to Africa, and mostly to the regions lying south of the Sahara desert. All are of comparatively large dimensions, and generally have the withers considerably taller than the rump. Horns of moderate length are present in both zones, and are either lyre-shaped or recurved, with their bases more or less closely approximated ; the muzzle is naked; there is a small, tufted gland below each eye; and the tail is comparatively long. In the skull there are no large pits in the forehead, nor any unossified spaces below the eye-sockets ; and the upper molar teeth have very tall and narrow crowns. The typical hartebeests, of which there are several species, ranging from Syria and Algeria to the Cape, are characterised by the great height of the withers, the great length of the head, which has the horns placed on a kind of crest at its summit, and the sudden backward flexure of the extremities of the horns. The horns themselves are compressed and ringed at the base; the muzzle is narrow, and the tail hairy. In certain other species the abovementioned features are less strongly developed; and in the blesbok (*B. albifrons*) and bontebok (*B. pygargus*) the horns are lyrate, the crest on the top of the head much less strongly marked, and the withers lower. In consequence of these differences many writers separate the latter animals under the name of *Damaliscus.* The strange-looking wildebeests, or gnus (*Connochœtes*), differ from the hartebeests by their shorter head and broad and bristly muzzle, as well as by the heavily-maned neck, and in the conformation of the horns. The latter, which are situated on the vertex of the skull and approximated at their bases, are nearly smooth and cylindrical, and curve outwards, or outwards and downwards, with their tips bent upwards. The hoofs are remarkable for their extreme narrowness, and the elongated sweeping tail is clothed with a mass of long hairs. Whereas the females of the hartebeests resemble sheep in having but two teats, those of the wildebeests agree with cows in possessing four. The two species of wildebeests are chiefly remarkable for the strange gambles and antics in which they indulge, especially when the herd is approached by travellers. They are frequently found in company with zebras.

The African duikerboks (*Cephalophus*), most of which are exceedingly diminutive and graceful little creatures, although two species from the west coast are of much larger dimensions, form the typical representatives of the second section. In all these the horns are short and simple, without ridges, and are developed only in the males. There is a more or less elongated gland beneath each eye; the muzzle is large and naked; the tail is short; and the teats of the females are always four in number. The upper molar teeth have broad, square crowns; and in the skull there are no pits on the forehead, and no fissure beneath the socket of the eye, although there is a deep depression in the bones of this region. The duikerboks are characterised by having a tuft of long hairs between the small horns, which are situated far back on the forehead, the gland below the eye taking the form of a narrow slit or a row of pores, and the tail being very short. The nearly allied four-horned antelope (*Tetraceros quadricornis*) of Peninsular India is sufficiently distinguished by the males generally carrying two pairs of horns, of which the front ones are very minute.

More numerously represented is the *Cervicaprine* group of antelopes, which comprises several genera, with species of large or medium size, confined to Africa south of the Sahara. In these the horns are confined to the males; the gland below the eye may be either large, rudimental, or wanting; the muzzle is either hairy or naked; the tail is short; and the upper molars are narrow. There is usually a large unossified space in the skull below the eye, and also distinct pits on the forehead.

According to the recent classification of Messrs. Sclater and Thomas, a number of small African antelopes generally included in the *Cervicaprinæ* are entitled to form a section by themselves (*Nanotraginæ*). Of these the six species of the genus *Madoqua*—among which the Abyssinian Salt's antelope (*M. saltiana*) has been longest known—are very small antelopes characterised by the production of the hairy muzzle into a more or less marked proboscis, and the presence of a tuft of hair on the crown of the head. In three of the species, among which is the one named, the last lower molar has no third lobe at its hinder end, and the proboscis is relatively short. Nearly allied is the royal antelope (*Nanotragus pygmæus*) of Guinea, the smallest member of the entire family, sufficiently distinguished by the smooth crown of the head, the presence of a small naked area on the muzzle, and the minute horns. Another genus, which includes the Zanzibar steinbok (*Nesotragus moschatus*) and *N. livingstonianus*, differs from the last by the larger horns. The true steinbok (*Raphiceros campestris*) agrees with the two last genera in the absence of lateral hoofs and of tufts of hair on the knees, but differs by other characters which are regarded as entitling it to form a genus apart. More distinct is the South African oribi (*Oribia scoparia*), which has both lateral hoofs and tufts of hair at the knees. From all these the well-known klipspringer (*Oreotragus saltator*), which ranges along the east coast from the Cape to Abyssinia, and has the habits of a chamois, differs in the form of the skull, the thick, brittle hair, resembling that of the musk-deer, and the clumsy hoofs. In the skull of both genera there is a deep pit below the eye. Among the typical Cervicaprines, the rehbok (*Pelea capreola*) of South Africa is a larger uniformly-coloured animal, with small, compressed, upright, and scarcely diverging horns placed over the eyes, a large bare part to the muzzle, and no depression in the skull below the latter. It is an inhabitant of open, sandy districts, and may be compared in size to a fallow-deer. Still larger is the handsome water-buck and its allies, constituting the genus *Cobus*, characterised by the long sub-lyrate horns of the males, which are ringed nearly throughout their length, the large portion of the muzzle that is devoid of hair, the deep hollow in the forehead of the skull and the absence of a depression below the eye, the gland being rudimental. The tail is long, ridged with hair above, and tufted at the end; and the colour of the fur uniform. In most species the hair is long and coarse; and all frequent the neighbourhood of water. The three representatives of the allied genus *Cervicapra* may be distinguished by the short and bushy tail; and also by the circumstance that the premaxillary bones, which from the extremity of the muzzle, do not extend upwards to join the nasals. The best known of these is the South African reitbok (*C. arundineum*), which stands nearly a yard at the withers, and is of grizzled ochre colour.

The typical, or *Antilopine*, section is also a large one, and includes the gazelles and certain allied forms which are mostly inhabitants of sandy or desert districts. The horns, which are usually restricted to the males, are generally either compressed and lyrate or recurved, or cylindrical and spiral, with well-marked rings on their lower portion. The muzzle is covered with short hairs; the short or moderate tail is compressed and hairy on its upper surface; and the upper molars are narrow, and resemble those of the sheep. In the skull there are generally large pits in the forehead, and a depression below the eye. Perhaps the handsomest member of the group is the Indian black-buck (*Antilope cervicapra*), which is the sole representative of its genus, and easily recognised by the deep blackish hue of the back and head of the adult males, and the beautiful spirally-twisted and ringed horns; the gland below the eye being very large. The pala (*Æpyceros*) and its other African allies have the horns compressed, widely divergent, and ringed only at the base; and differ from the black buck by the absence of a gland on the face, and of lateral hoofs to the feet. A clumsily-built and somewhat sheep-like antelope from the Asiatic steppes, known as the saiga (*Saiga tatarica*), is one of two genera characterised by the large and puffy muzzle, this feature being most developed in the present form, in which the nostrils open downwards. There is a small gland on the face, lateral hoofs are present, and the female has four teats. In the males the horns are short, lyrate, ringed, and yellow in colour. The Tibetan chiru (*Pantholops hodgsoni*) differs from the last in the nostrils opening anteriorly, and in the form of the horns; the latter being very long, erect, compressed, sublyrate, and ringed in front for two-thirds in length, while their colour is deep black. There is no gland on the face, and the female has only two teats. These beautiful antelopes are found in herds on some of the most elevated regions in the world. The largest genus of the group (*Gazella*) is represented by the beautiful gazelles, which are mainly confined to the desert regions of Africa and Asia, although the aberrant springbok is found on the plains of the Cape Colony and adjacent districts. All the gazelles are noticeable for their elegant build, and their more or less sandy coloration, while the majority differ from the foregoing members of the section in that horns are developed by both sexes. Nearly all the species are characterised by having a white streak, bordered by a dark line, running down the face from each horn to the nostril, so as to isolate a dark central patch on the muzzle. The gland below the eye is small and concealed by hair, and the knees generally carry tufts of long hair. The springbok (*G. euchore*), remarkable on account of its habit of taking leaps in the air, and also from the enormous herds in which it was formerly found, differs from all the rest of the gazelles in having an erectile crest of long, stiff, white hair running down the back. Clarke's gazelle (*Ammodorcas clarkei*), from Northern Somaliland, is distinguished by the regular upwards and forwards curvature of the horns of the males, which are ringed in part at the base; the females being hornless. The skull is intermediate between that of the preceding and following genus. Waller's gazelle (*Lithocranius walleri*), which is an East African form ranging from the Kilimanjaro district to Somaliland, represents another genus by itself. The females are hornless, but in the males the horns are erect and curved forwards in a hook-like manner; while both are characterised by the extraordinary neck, which gives to the animal almost the appearance of a small giraffe. The genus is, however, best characterised by the solid structure of the skull. The small Somali *Dorcatragus* seems to be another aberrant gazelle.

The next group of antelopes, which are common to Africa and Arabia, are best characterised by the upper molar teeth being structurally similar to those of the oxen. In these teeth the crowns are very tall and broad, so as to form an almost square section, while, on their inner side, they have a narrow additional column superadded to the four large normal crescentic ones. All these antelopes are of very large size, and both sexes are provided with long horns, which are placed immediately over or behind the eyes, and are recurved, straight, or subspiral in form. The muzzle is hairy, there is no gland below the eye, and the long, cylindrical tail is tufted at the extremity. In the skull there are no distinct pits on the forehead, there is no depression below the eye, and only a very small unossified slit in the same region. The handsome recurved horns, rising vertically from a crest above the eyes and sweeping backwards in a scimitar-like sweep at an obtuse angle to the profile of the face, serve at a glance to distinguish the sable-antelope (*Hippotragus niger*) of South Africa and its near ally the roan antelope (*H. equinus*). In both these large and splendid animals, as well as in a kindred species from the Sudan, the horns are ringed nearly to their tips, the sable-antelope being one of the few members of the tribe which have the whole upper-parts, save some white streaks on the face, a deep, full black. In all these antelopes the neck is furnished with an erect or curving mane, and the tip of the tail is strongly tufted. The gemsbok of South Africa is the type of an allied genus (*Oryx*), ranging not only over the whole of Africa south of the Sahara, but also found in Syria and on the shores of the Persian Gulf. Here the horns are long, slender, and ringed at the base, but may be either straight or somewhat curved backwards, although in all the species they arise behind the eyes with their direction at first in the plane of

Fig. 85.—SABLE-ANTELOPE (*Hippotragus niger*).

the face. The mane on the neck is shorter and the tail longer and more hairy than in the last genus. The general hue of the hair in the oryx is grey or tawny, with black markings on the face and legs; and, although somewhat ungainly in build, they are all decidedly handsome animals, the typical species standing about 4 ft. at the withers, and its horns often exceeding a yard in length. Oryxes are inhabitants of open sandy plains, where they associate in small herds. The third genus of the group is the addax (*Addax nasomaculatus*) of the deserts of North Africa and Arabia, which differs from the last by the horns being subspiral and lyrate, and also by the heavy mane of long hair on the neck and throat, and the presence of a tuft of hair on the throat, the general colour of the hair being whitish.

The last, or *Tragelaphine*, section of the true antelopes comprises several genera of large-sized forms, all of which, save one, are inhabitants of Africa south of the Sahara. The horns, which are usually confined to the male sex, are not ringed, but have a ridge at least on the basal portion of the front surface, and are generally twisted in a spiral, with the front ridge curving outwards from the base. The muzzle is naked, and there is a small gland below each eye. The skull has a small unossified fissure, but no depression below the eye, and there is very generally a pair of pits on the forehead. The upper molar teeth are broad, but may have either tall or short crowns. A very characteristic, although by no means universal, feature of the group is the marking of the body by vertical white stripes. In India the group is represented solely by the well-known nilgai (*Boselaphus tragocamelus*), characterised by having the hind limbs much shorter than the front pair, the short horns—which are placed behind the eyes—ridged and triangular at the base, and nearly straight, the naked portion of the muzzle large, the ears small, and the upper molars tall, with an additional column on their inner sides; the body being uniformly coloured. Nilgai, which may be found either in jungle or open country, generally associate in small herds, although the bulls are often found singly. In all the other members of the group the fore and hind limbs are of approximately equal length; the horns are long, ridged throughout, and twisted into a spiral; while the naked portion of the muzzle is of small extent, and the size of the ears large. The molar teeth are short-crowned, and the body is generally striped. Perhaps the handsomest of all are the two African species of kudu, constituting the genus *Strepsiceros*, in which the horns of the males are situated behind the line of the eyes, rising in the form of an open spiral, with their front ridge very strongly marked, at an obtuse angle to the plane of the face. The neck is fringed with a mane, the tail relatively short, the body marked with vertical white streaks descending from a spinal stripe of the same colour, and the hoofs short. In the skull there is a deep hollow, with pits, on the forehead, and a large unossified space below each eye. Of the two species, the true kudu (*S. kudu*) ranges from South Africa to Abyssinia, while the much smaller, lesser kudu (*S. imberbis*) is confined to Somaliland and the Kilimanjaro district. Of the former splendid animal, Mr. Bryddon, in the *Asian* newspaper of November, 1894, writes as follows:—"The kudu bull stands 5 ft. or a little more at the withers. Its general colour varies from rufous grey to almost blue, and especially in the older animals this bluish colouring will be found predominating. Along the spine runs a white streak, and from this thin white stripes extend transversely across the body towards the belly. Just under the eye on either side is a clear white band which meets on the front of the face; while upon the cheeks two or three circular white spots are to be found. The head is neat, game-like, and altogether beautiful, and is surmounted by tall spreading spiral horns of great weight and size, which diminish in corkscrew-like formation to sharp points. The greatest recorded length of a kudu's horns appear to be 3 ft. $9\frac{3}{8}$ in. in a straight line ; over the curve 5 ft. $\frac{5}{8}$ in. The greatest length of the horns of a lesser kudu in a straight line is 2 ft. $1\frac{1}{4}$ in. ; over the curve 2 ft. $7\frac{1}{2}$ in. There are often great and striking differences in the spread of kudu horns. Fine specimens will sometimes spread between the tips as much as nearly 3 ft. 9 in. Other and equally fine horns will only spread a little over 2 ft. But whether widespread or closer in growth, the effect of these magnificent spiral horns is equally grand. The eyes are large and very beautiful. The ears are of a light brown colour, and very large and spreading. The hearing of this antelope is marvellously acute, and the great, yet delicate, ears are manifestly exactly fitted for the arrest of the slightest vibration of sound. The senses of smell and sight are also excessively fine, and, united to its preternaturally sharp hearing and general suspiciousness, render the kudu usually a very difficult animal to approach or surprise. The neck of the male is strong, shapely, and well fitted to support the weight of the immense horns. The chin is white. From the throat to the dewlap extends a long and handsome fringe of white and blackish-brown hair, which adds not a little to the handsome appearance of the antelope. The neck also is slightly maned. The legs are strong yet slender, clean, and beautifully formed, terminating in shapely feet, which give a dainty spoor, shaped like the ace of hearts. The kudu spoor is, indeed, one of the most perfect imprints of all African beasts of chase. In length this animal extends some 9 ft. The withers, as in so many other examples of African game, are high ; the body is stoutly formed, and in general contour not unlike that of a Highland stag. The hair is, however, much closer and finer than the red deer's. The tail is about 2 ft. long, terminating in a point. The general port and demeanour of this antelope is exceedingly noble ; and the magnificent carriage of the head, surmounted as it is by the great spiral horns, is one of the finest things in nature. The female, lacking as she is in horns, cuts a much poorer figure than her lord ; and her ears, unrelieved by the fine spiral horns, appear far more prominent and remarkable. The calves are beautiful little creatures, of a bright rufous colour, strongly lined with white. The cows have only one calf at a time, usually between September and November—the favourite calving period with most South African antelopes. The kudu feeds more upon the young leafage and sprouting greenery of bushes, shrubs, and trees, than upon grass. Its favourite browsing-ground is bush and woodland, the stony slopes of hills, and well-bushed mountain-sides. In these haunts this antelope is difficult of approach, and offers very excellent stalking. In countries not much shot over, however, the kudu may be occasionally surprised at quite close quarters. In woodland and bushy country the pace of the kudu, considering the weight and size of its horns, and the difficulties and obstacles of covert, is surprising. In hill country it is wonderfully active and will jump magnificently ; upon open ground, however, where it occasionally strays, it may be ridden down without much trouble, and upon the flat its gait is laboured and somewhat slow. This antelope is gregarious, and runs usually in parties of from five to eight ; occasionally, however, larger troops, numbering as many as twenty individuals, are encountered. In the dense forest south of the Botletli river, while hunting giraffe, I startled a troop of fifteen upon one occasion. The hide of the kudu is one of the most valuable of all South

African antelopes; it commands a high price and is much sought after. From it are manufactured velschoens (shoes), leather thongs, whip-lashes, and even harness. The hide is thinnish, but excessively tough. I have seen a complete set of Cape cart harness made of kudu hide, which was smart-looking, serviceable, and of everlasting wear. The flesh is excellent and well-tasted, and the marrow bones are esteemed a very great dainty by hunters and natives in the interior. The kudu is widely distributed. Its range extends beyond the Zambesi into Central Africa, and it is found as far north as Somaliland and even Abyssinia. It has a variety of native names even in South Africa. The Bechuanas call it tolo; the Matabele, e-balabala; the Makalakas, e-zilarwa; the Makobag, unzwa; the Masarwa bushmen, dwar; the Mashunas, noro. In North-east Africa the Somali name is godir; while upon the Lower Zambesi it is goma."

Nearly allied to the kudus are the numerous African species of harnessed antelopes (*Tragelaphus*), most of which are distinguished by the smaller number of spiral turns in the horns, although one species comes so close in this respect to the kudus, that it may be a question whether all should not be included in a single genus. The harnessed-antelopes take their name from the white stripes or rows of spots with which the bodies of nearly all are adorned, some of them being remarkable for the extreme brilliancy of their coloration. Whereas the splendid *T. euryceros* of West Africa, conspicuous for the brilliant chestnut ground colour of its coat, is only second in size to the kudu, the guib (*T. scriptus*) does not exceed a goat in height. Two of the species, one of which is the well-known sitatunga or nakong (*T. spekei*) of South Central Africa, have their hoofs remarkably elongated, and spend their time in marshy situations, where they will conceal themselves by submerging the whole body except the tip of the muzzle. The largest of all antelopes are the two African species of eland (*Orias*), which differ from the other members of the present section by having horns in both sexes, while they are further distinguished by the close, corkscrew-like spiral of these appendages. Although in one variety of the common species they are fairly well marked, as a rule the white stripes on the body are indistinct or absent. There are few handsomer antelopes than a large eland bull, with its fine dewlap, full tuft of dark brown hair on the forehead, slight mane, and generally pale tawny hair.

Fig. 86.—HARNESSED-ANTELOPE (*Tragelaphus angasi*).

The well-known chamois, gemze, or izard (*Rupicapra tragus*), which inhabits all the higher mountain ranges of Europe, and is locally known by the above-mentioned names, is the typical representative of a section of the hollow-horned ruminants, in many respects intermediate between the true antelopes and the goats. Accordingly, they are often spoken of as the caprine, or goat-like antelopes. As a rule, the horns, which are nearly equally developed in both sexes, and rise behind the line of the eyes, are short and wrinkled at their bases, and conical or somewhat compressed in form, with a more or less divided backward curvature. Although it may be much reduced in size, there is generally a gland beneath each of the eyes; the short and tapering tail is well-haired above, the hoofs are relatively large, and the whole build is heavy and clumsy. In form the molar teeth resemble those of the goats; and the skull generally has a depression, but no fissure, below each eye. From its allies, the chamois is readily distinguished by the peculiar hooked form of the horns, which rise close together almost vertically from the forehead, and then curve suddenly back in the well-known hook. The muzzle is hairy, and the gland beneath the eye small. In height, a chamois does not stand more than a couple of feet at the withers. Chamois are inhabitants of the high Alpine regions immediately below the snow-line; and although they were formerly met with in large herds, in most of their habitats their numbers have been greatly reduced by constant persecution, while from some districts they have completely disappeared. Their marvellous powers of leaping are familiar to all. In the Himalaya, Malay countries, parts of China, and Japan, the place of the chamois is taken by the allied but larger and more clumsily-built animals known as serows (*Nemorhœdus*), of which there are several species. From the former they are readily distinguished by the finely-wrinkled and sharply-tapering black horns having no distinct hook at the extremities. The ears are large, the fur is coarse and long, and the gland below the eye small. The Himalayan species is found in thick bush at moderate elevations, and is a marvellous adept at getting over the roughest ground at a rapid pace. Nearly allied are the smaller animals known as goral (*Cemas*), of which the typical representative is met with in the outer ranges of the Himalaya, while other forms occur in Eastern Tibet, Northern China, and Amurland. They differ from the serows in lacking a gland beneath the eye, and also in the conformation of the skull. One of the most remarkable members of the group is the takin (*Budorcas taxicolor*) of the Mishmi Hills in Assam, and Eastern Tibet, which may be compared to a very large, rough-haired, and reddish-coloured serow, with greatly developed smooth horns, whose size and curvature strongly recalls those of the gnus. Scarcely anything is known of these animals in a wild state, although they are probably sufficiently common in their native haunts. Another nearly allied form is the so-called Rocky Mountain goat (*Haploceros montanus*) of North America, which is one of the very few American representatives of the hollow-horned ruminants. It is likewise one of the few animals which are permanently white at all seasons of the year, its coat being very long and shaggy, and forming a most striking contrast to the jet-black horns and hoofs. The horns, which are set close together and curve somewhat backwards, are distinctly compressed at their bases; the ears are small, and there is no gland below the eyes. The most remarkable structural peculiarity about the animal is, however, the extreme shortness of the cannon-bones in both the fore and hind feet, which in this respect are quite unlike those of any other ruminants.

Fig. 87.—ROCKY MOUNTAIN GOAT (*Haploceros montanus*).

The next group of the *Bovidæ* is formed by the goats and sheep, which are so nearly allied that it is very difficult to distinguish between them. In this *Caprine* section both sexes are provided with horns, but those of the females are much inferior in size to those of the males. They are usually compressed, triangular in cross section, and marked with bold, transverse ridges or wrinkles, while they may either curve backwards or outwards, or may be spirally twisted. The muzzle is usually completely covered with hair; the gland below the eye is either very small or totally absent; the tail is generally short and flattened; and glands are often present between the hoofs. With the exception of one species of goat, the females have but a single pair of teats. The molar teeth are characterised by the great height of their crowns, those of the upper jaw having only four crescentic columns. In the skull a depression below each eye may or may not be developed. In the true goats, constituting the genus *Capra*, the long horns are laterally compressed, and either curve backwards in a bold sweep, with an outward inclination at the tips, or are spirally twisted. There is neither a gland beneath the eye nor a depression of the skull in the same region; the chin is more or less distinctly bearded; the males emit a powerful and characteristic odour; and, if glands are developed between the hoofs, these are confined to the fore feet. The true goats are mainly confined to the mountains of Europe and Asia, although sparingly represented in Abyssinia, Egypt, and Palestine. In Europe there are two species, viz., the ibex (*C. ibex*) and the Spanish ibex (*C. pyrenaica*), of which the former was confined to the Alps, but is now extinct in its pure form, although a half-breed between this and the domestic goat exists in certain districts. The ibex is easily recognised by the bold transverse ridges or knobs on the front of its scimitar-like horns, whereas in the Spanish ibex these are much less developed, and the curvature tends to become spiral. Mr. A. Chapman writes that this goat survives in some of the secluded valleys on the Spanish side of the Pyrenees, and finds a congenial home in the elevated cordilleras of Central Spain, especially in the Sierra de Gredos—the apex of the long range which forms the watershed between the Tagus and the Douro, and continues to Portugal as the Sierra de Estrelha. In the south of Spain the ibex occurs in the Sierra Morena, and especially in the Sierra Nevada, as well as the Sierra Bermeja, which runs parallel with the Mediterranean; but examples from these localities differ somewhat from those of the northern and central ranges, and Schimper distinguished the southern race as *Capra hispanica*. In the Gredos and Nevada ranges the ibex leave the vicinity of the snow, or, at least, the most rugged and inaccessible ground, after sunset only, when they descend to feed; and under no circumstances are they found, even in winter, amongst forest or covert of any kind; but in the lower ranges of the Bermeja and Palmitera, which do not exceed 4800 feet in height, and where the scrub and even pine trees attain the summit, they are found comparatively low down, and may be hunted over ground that looks far more suitable for roe-deer. But wherever found, the races have one habit in common: they take refuge on the narrowest ledges, where it seems hardly possible that their bodies can pass, and still further avail themselves of crevices and recesses in the wall of rock. In the Caucasus there are at least two species of goats, one known as *C. cylindricornis*, in which the horns in curvature, smoothness, and colour are so like those of certain wild sheep as to render it almost impossible to draw any valid distinction between the two groups. Of wild goats five well-defined species are recognised from India, four of which are not found southwards of the Himalaya. Three out of these are included in the genus *Capra;* while the other two have much shorter horns, and are referred to a second genus. The pasang or Persian wild goat (*C. ægagrus*) is a western form only extending into India on its western side, where it is met with in Baluchistan and Sind. It is easily recognised by the sharp edge of its scimitar-like horns; and is considered to be the ancestral stock from which the domesticated breeds of goat have been derived. The Himalayan ibex is generally regarded as identical with the ibex of Siberia and the Thian Shan (*C. sibirica*), although it has been thought that it may be distinct. It differs from the pasang by the front of the horns of the bucks being flattened and marked by bold knots. Further information is required about a dark-coloured ibex from Baltistan, which has been considered to be merely the common species in its winter dress, but this is not yet ascertained with certainty. There is also much uncertainty about an ibex of which three specimens have been obtained—probably from the upper Kishanganga Valley in Kashmir territory—characterised by the marked outward curvature of the horns, and the absence of knobs except near their tips. The markhor (*C. falconeri*) is easily recognised by its spirally twisted horns; and zoologists are now satisfied that, in spite of the great difference in the form of the spiral of their horns, all the varieties belong to a single species. The two remaining Indian wild goats are the Himalayan tahr (*Hemitragus jemlaicus*) and the so-called Nilgiri ibex (*Hemitragus hylocrius*). Both differ from the true goats by their comparatively short horns; and they are further distinguished by having a small naked area at the end of the muzzle. The Nilgiri wild goat differs from the tahr by having the outer side of its horns convex, and not passing into a sharp ridge in front; while the latter is distinguished from all other goats and sheep by the presence of four teats in the females. A third species of the same genus inhabits the Muscat district of Southern Arabia. The sheep (*Ovis*) are connected with the sheep-like goats, such as *Capra cylindricornis* of the Caucasus, by means of the bharal of Tibet and the North African arui, or Barbary sheep, both of which differ from the more typical representatives of their genus by the absence of a gland below the eye, and their smooth, olive-coloured horns; although they resemble other sheep in having glands between the hoofs of both the fore and hind feet. As a group, sheep are characterised by the massive horns of the rams curving backwards and downwards in a bold sweep, with the tips generally turned inwards, while they are usually marked with more or less prominent transverse ridges. Except in the two species named, their colour is brownish, and there is a small gland on the face below the eye, with a corresponding shallow depression in the skull. All the feet have glands between their hoofs; the chin is devoid of a beard, although there may be a ruff of long hair on the throat; and the rams have not the unpleasant odour characteristic of the males of the goats.

Fig. 87.—THE MARKHOR (*Capra falconeri*).

Sheep are mainly inhabitants of Central and North-Eastern Asia, one species just entering the Punjab. In Europe two or three kinds are found in the Mediterranean regions, and there is one in the north of Africa, but no other throughout the whole extent of that continent; while a single species inhabits North America. The largest and finest of the group are the argalis of Central Asia, and amongst these the most magnificent is the Pamir-sheep (*O. poli*), whose horns are characterised by their double twist and outward direction. In the true argali (*O. ammon*) of the Altai, and the closely-allied *O. hodgsoni* of Tibet, the horns, although more massive, are shorter, and form but a single curve. In these species the wrinkles on the horns are strongly marked, but in the bighorns, of which one species (*O. canadensis*) inhabits the highlands of western North America, while the second (*O. nivicola*) is found on the opposite side of Behring Straits in the Kamschatkan Peninsula, these wrinkles are much less developed, and the depression below the eye in the skull is less deep. Another group, in which the horns, although well wrinkled, are smaller than in the argalis, is represented by the sha (*O. vignei*) of the inner Himalaya, Persia, and certain ranges of the Punjab (where it is known as the urial), as well as by the Armenian sheep (*O. gmelini*) of Asia Minor and Persia, the smaller but closely allied *O. ophion* of the island of *Cyprus*, and the mouflon (*O. musimon*) of Sardinia and Corsica, easily distinguished by the saddle-shaped mark on the back; the three last-named kinds being further characterised by the absence of horns in the ewes. The two remaining species, as already said, differ from all the foregoing in their comparatively smooth and olive-coloured horns, and the absence of a gland below the eye and a depression in the skull for its reception. Of these the bharal (*O. nahura*) is a Tibetan form, with short, bluish-grey fur ornamented with black markings; while the arui (*O. tragelaphus*) of the mountains of Northern Africa differs from all the others in possessing a fringe of long hair on the fore-quarters, and likewise by the greater length of the tail. It is a remarkable fact that nearly all the wild sheep are short-tailed animals, and have fur instead of wool; but, although it is difficult to explain the origin of the long tail of the domesticated breeds, it is noteworthy that certain African races have the fleece partaking more of the nature of fur than of wool. In habits sheep much resemble goats, the young males and females associating in large flocks, from which the old males often disassociate themselves, except during the breeding-season. Both groups are exceedingly wary animals, and both are inhabitants of mountain regions; but whereas goats always restrict themselves to rocky and more or less precipitous districts, wild sheep may be often found on open, undulating, grassy ground like the Pamirs.

Fig. 89.—PAMIR-SHEEP (*Ovis poli*).

Nearly allied to the sheep is the somewhat larger ruminant commonly known as the musk-ox (*Ovibos moschatus*), which may be compared roughly in point of size to Highland cattle, although its coat is still more shaggy. The musk-ox is now restricted to Arctic America and the north of Greenland, although in a past epoch it ranged over northern Asia and Europe as far south as Britain. With the sheep this ruminant agrees in its hairy muzzle and the general structure of the molar teeth; but the horns are quite peculiar, those of the adult males being greatly flattened and expanded at their bases, where they almost meet in the middle line of the forehead, after which they bend downwards by the sides of the face, and then curve sharply upwards. While they are whitish and fibrous at the base, at the tips they are smooth and black, with a nearly circular section. The small and pointed ears are almost buried in the long hair; the general colour is brown, and the short and sheep-like tail is completely lost among the hair. In winter a woolly under-fur is mingled with the long hair to form an efficient protection against the intense cold of the regions inhabited by this animal. A peculiar feature of the feet of the musk-ox is that the two hoofs of each are not symmetrical; these being partially covered with hair on the lower surface. In general habits musk-oxen much resemble sheep, collecting in flocks of considerable size, among which the proportion of old rams is comparatively small. The musky odour from which the animal derives its name does not appear to be due to the secretion of any special scent-gland.

Fig. 90—MUSK-OX (*Ovibos moschatus*).

The last, or bovine section of the family, is represented by the buffaloes, bison, and oxen, all of which may be included in the single genus *Bos*. All are animals of very massive build, with a short neck, and the head carried nearly in the line of the back, the largest members of the whole family being included among them. From the sheep, the oxen, as the group may be collectively termed, are markedly distinguished by the conformation of the tall crowns of the molar teeth. In the upper jaw these have a nearly square cross section, with a well-defined additional fifth column on the inner side, and the whole of the valleys and clefts completely filled up with cement. The horns, which are massive, and nearly as large in the females as in the males, are placed on the summit of the skull with their bases far apart, and may be cylindrical or triangular in section, their direction being at first more or less outwards, after which they turn upwards at and near the tips. They always lack the transverse knobs of the goats and the wrinkles of those of the sheep, so that the surface is comparatively smooth, the colour being dark. Internally the bony cores of the horns, like those of the goats and sheep, are much honeycombed. In all cases the broad muzzle, in which the nostrils are placed wide apart, is more or less completely naked and moist; there is no gland beneath the eye, and consequently no depression in this region of the skull; the bulls usually have an ample dewlap beneath the throat, the long and tapering tail is generally tipped with a large bunch of long hair, and there are no glands between the hoofs of either foot. The udders of the cows are provided with four teats. As in the sheep and goats, small lateral hoofs are retained. The majority of the oxen are confined to the continents of Europe, Asia, and Africa, but one species of bison inhabits North America, and a small aberrant form is found in the Island of Celebes.

The latter species, which is known as the anoa (*B. depressicornis*), is the smallest and most antelope-like member of the whole group, having the short angulated horns directed nearly upwards from the forehead, and the colour black, with a few white spots on the hind quarters. Another small but more buffalo-like form (*B. mindorensis*) inhabits the Philippine Islands, where it is locally known as the tamarao, but it is not certain whether this may not prove to be a hybrid between the anoa and the Indian buffalo. The true buffaloes are characterised by their more or less angulated horns and convex forehead. Of these, the Indian buffalo (*B. bubalus*) has its home in the Oriental countries, but has been introduced as a domesticated animal into Egypt and the South of Europe. It is a huge, ungainly brute, with the long horns flattened and angulated throughout their length; those of the bulls being very thick and curving upwards in a crescentic form, while those of the cows are slender and directed more immediately outwards. In their habits these buffaloes are essentially marsh-haunting animals, loving to wallow in the soft, warm mud of such situations. The skin of old animals is almost devoid of hair. The Cape buffalo (*B. caffer*) is a very different-looking animal, with a shorter skull and horns than the Indian species; the bases of the horns growing together in a kind of helmet-like mass on the forehead, where they nearly meet in the middle line; these appendages curving downwards at their origin from the skull, and then taking an inward direction, while their tips are almost cylindrical. The black skin is nearly naked, but the ears are margined with a fringe of elongated hairs. In certain forms from Central Africa the hairs on the skin are reddish in colour, and the horns smaller and less expanded and approximative on the forehead. This form grades almost imperceptibly into a smaller variety or species known as *B. pumilus*, in which the small horns are very widely separated from one another at their bases.

Fig. 90.—CAPE BUFFALO (*Bos caffer*).

The bisons differ from the buffaloes by their cylindrical horns, which are placed rather low down on the forehead; the latter being very wide and convex, and the whole skull comparatively short and wide. In the skeleton the number of pairs of ribs may be either fourteen or fifteen. In place of the nearly-naked or sparsely-haired hide of the buffaloes, the bisons have an abundant coat of short, thick, crisp, curly brown hair over the greater part of the body, while the head, neck, shoulders, and fore limbs are clothed with a massive mane of longer and darker hair, almost hiding the ears, and concealing the bases of the horns, as well as shading the eyes. The great elevation of the withers, as compared with the hind quarters, gives the appearance of a large hump behind the neck. Of the two species, the European bison (*B. bison*) is now confined to the Caucasus, Lithuania, and some of the adjacent districts, running completely wild in the former area, but artificially protected in the latter. It appears to be essentially a forest-haunting animal. The American bison (*B. americanus*), locally known as the buffalo, is very closely allied, but is of rather smaller dimensions, with lower and weaker hind-quarters, but a stronger and more massive shoulder, a greater abundance of long hair on the fore-quarters, and a rather shorter tail. The range of this splendid animal extended from a short distance north of the Gulf of Mexico to beyond the Saskatchewan in Canada, and probably reached almost from the Atlantic to the Pacific sea-board. For seventy years, at least, the Mississippi may, however, be regarded as its extreme eastern boundary. The countless millions in which bison formerly roamed over the open prairies are known to all; but incessant pursuit and the opening up of the country by railroads, slowly, but too surely, tended to its complete extermination from the open country. According, however, to Mr. Theodore Rooseveldt, there are still, and always have been, small numbers of bison inhabiting the Rocky Mountains northwards from Colorado, and the depths of the great forests in the sub-Arctic regions beyond the Saskatchewan River, and these, though locally called mountain-buffalo or wood-bison, are only a variety of the bison of the plains. For some years there have been reports of a small herd of bison inhabiting the remote corner of Val Verde county, Texas, near the Rio Grande border; and some time ago a shepherd came upon the herd and counted it to comprise fifty individuals. Commenting on this, a writer in the *Asian* newspaper of June 15th, 1895, observes that, "when we consider the enormous area of the country and the sparse population in the more mountainous and wooded districts, we find no difficulty in believing that the animal survives in small numbers, as a denizen of the forest, varying, in accordance with his new conditions of life, from the bison which roamed the prairies in tens of thousands a quarter of a century ago. And when we consider the physical peculiarities of the animal, there is reason to think that in the woods the species may hold its own against man and other enemies with better success than it did on the plains. His eyesight is not keen—a defect gravely against him in the open, but for obvious reasons of much less consequence in the forest. His acute hearing, of little service on the plains, is invaluable in the woods; and his excellent nose is equally serviceable in either case. It would seem as though the bison had been primarily designed for a sylvan existence. Mr. Rooseveldt observes that the so-called mountain-buffalo or wood-bison is rather heavier in body and shorter of limb than his brother of the prairie; but in regard to this we have to remember what a recent writer has said of the prairie-bison in his latter days. Living in a state of perpetual flight from mounted hunters he became specialised with wonderful rapidity. His heavy body became lighter, his legs developed in length, and his whole appearance acquired a certain 'ranginess,' indicative of the effort of nature to adapt herself to changed conditions; flight was the refuge of the bison in the last days of his existence as a beast of the plains, and his formation in a few generations underwent the change compelled by the struggle for life. It is possible that Mr. Rooseveldt, when comparing the bison of the Rockies with that of the plains, may have had in mind this latterly specialised animal; but, nevertheless, we can well believe that forest existence, more sedentary than prairie life even in its past peaceful days, is calculated to develop greater weight of body and brevity of limb. There is no good reason for believing that the bison now dwelling in the Rockies, sub-Arctic regions, Texas, and, we venture to hope, elsewhere, in inaccessible cornèrs of the continent, varies very markedly from the prairie form. There always have been woodland-dwelling members of the species. Bison were indigenous to the tract of country known as the Yellowstone Park, when it was proclaimed a national reserve. The park is admirably adapted for a sanctuary. Embracing an area of some 3300 square miles, and forming, roughly speaking, an oblong of about 70 miles by 50, not less than 84 per cent. of the whole is forest-clad mountain, valley, and plateau. The central portion forms a plateau varying from 7000 to 8500 feet in elevation, and averaging 8000 feet. Here the indigenous bison finds comparative security, and is steadily increasing in numbers. In 1884 the bison population of the Yellowstone Park was estimated at 200; in the winter of 1891-92 a snow-shoe party, exploring for the purpose, found various small herds, which by actual count gave nearly 300 animals, each herd containing a proportion of well-grown calves."

Somewhat intermediate between the bison and the true oxen is the Tibetan yak (*B. grunniens*), so invaluable to the inhabitants of the highlands of the inner Himalaya as a means of transport across those arid and inhospitable regions. While the horns are not unlike those of the bison in form and position, and the general conformation of the skull is also similar in the two groups, the yak has the long hair disposed as a fringe from the fore legs along the flanks to the hind limbs, the tail being also invested with similar elongated hairs from root to tip. The ribs are fourteen in number; and the colour of the wild race is uniformly blackish-brown, although many of the hybrid domestic breeds are more or less variegated with white. The male lacks the distinct dewlap characteristic of almost all the other oxen. Another peculiarity of the yak is to be found in the strange grunting cry from which its scientific name is taken.

Three species of oxen confined to the Oriental countries constitute what is termed the Bibovine group. These are characterised, like the true oxen, by possessing only thirteen pairs of ribs, but are peculiar in having a more or less well-marked ridge running down the anterior half of the back, produced by the unusual height of the spines of the vertebræ in that region. The horns, which occupy the highest portion of the skull, are somewhat flattened, more especially at the base, and after inclining outwards for some distance are then directed upwards. The tail is relatively short, not reaching below the hocks; the lower portions of the legs are white, and the general colour of the males is blackish, and those of the females either amber or blackish-brown. The largest and handsomest of the three species is the well-known gaur (*B. gaurus*)—the bison of Indian sportsmen—which inhabits hilly forests throughout India, and is also found in the Malay peninsula. The most characteristic feature of this splendid animal, which attains a height of fully six feet at the withers, is the large, convex, and forwardly-curving crest between the bases of the horns, communicating a concave profile to the forehead. The ridge on the back is very strongly developed, and stops very sharply with a sudden step-like descent; and the colour of the female is nearly similar to that of the male. As in the other members of the group, the thick coat of hair is short, fine, and remarkably sleek. From this species the gayal, or mithan (*B. frontalis*), differs by the straight line formed by the ridge of the skull between the widely-sundered horns, and the consequently straight profile of the forehead. The horns differ from those of the gaur in being shorter, rounder, and less curved, their tips having no distinct inward curvature, while their colour is uniformly black, instead of being of a greenish tinge at the base. In the males also the dewlap is more developed, while in both sexes the limbs are relatively shorter and the colour is blacker. Gayals are kept in a semi-domesticated state in Assam, Chittagong, and other parts of north-eastern India, but occur wild in the interior of the Tenasserim provinces of Burma. From both the above, the smaller animal from Burma, Java, Balli, and Lombok known as the banteng (*B. banting*), differs by the more rounded horns, the slight development of the ridge on the back, the white patch on the rump of both sexes, and the reddish-brown colour of the body of the cows.

Lastly, the true, or Taurine oxen are represented by the common ox (*B. taurus*) and the Indian humped cattle (*B. indicus*), both of which are now known only in the domesticated state, although it is possible that the half-wild cattle of certain British parks may be the more or less modified direct descendants of the old English aurochs, as the wild ox was originally called. In this group the spinal ridge characterising the gaur and its allies is absent; the horns are cylindrical, with their tips inclined backwards, and are placed at the very extremity of the highest ridge of the skull; while the forehead is flat, and the whole skull much elongated. The tail also is larger, reaching below the hocks; and the hoofs are large and rounded, instead of being narrow and pointed. Probably the original colour of the aurochs was reddish.

ORDER VII.—SIRENIA.

THE MANATIS AND DUGONGS.

THIS and the following order of mammals differ from all those hitherto described in that all their members are adapted for a permanently aquatic life—that is to say, they never voluntarily leave the water, as do the seals during the breeding-season. Accordingly, their bodies have assumed a more or less completely fish-like form, with little or no traces of a distinct neck; while the fore-limbs are modified into paddle-like flippers, the hind-limbs are completely wanting externally, and the tail forms a flattened paddle lying horizontally in the water. Structural evidences clearly show that both groups are descended from terrestrial mammals; and as these creatures have to come to the surface periodically for the purpose of breathing, the horizontally-expanded form of the tail-fin is sufficiently obvious; such an organ being admirably adapted, by means of a few powerful strokes, to bring its owner rapidly to the surface. In fishes, on the other hand, which breathe the atmospheric air contained in water by means of their gills, there is no necessity for such periodical visits to the surface, and the tail-fin is accordingly expanded in the vertical direction, thus forming a most efficient propeller for progression in a horizontal plane.

The manatis and dugongs, forming the present order, constitute a very small group of mammals, all of which may be included in the single family *Manatidæ*. Having the general fish-like bodily conformation alluded to above, the sirenians, as members of the present group are collectively termed, differ in many important respects from the whales and porpoises. One marked point of distinction is to be found in the circumstance that the body, instead of being laterally compressed, is flattened from above downwards. The head, again, is of an ordinary type, being relatively small in comparison to the body, with the nostrils placed at the extremity of the muzzle, and the summit rounded. To meet the exigencies of an aquatic life, external ears are, however, wanting, and the nostrils are capable of being closed at will by means of tightly-fitting valves, so as to prevent the ingress of water. In no case is the back furnished with a fin; and the fore flippers may retain traces of nails, although the whole of their toes are enveloped in a common skin, while the skeleton of these parts contains no more than the normal complement of bones to the toes—that is to say, each toe, except the first (where there are but two), has three joints. The backbone, or spinal column, differs from that of land mammals, in that none of the vertebræ in the region of the haunches are welded together to form a sacrum, such a structure being unnecessary in an animal devoid of hind limbs, while its presence would hinder the supple movements of the body so essential in purely aquatic creatures. From those of whales and porpoises, the vertebræ of existing sirenians differ by the absence of thin bony plates at the extremity of each end of the body, or lower portion of the same; although these were well developed in certain extinct members of the order. The manati is remarkable for the circumstance that the seven vertebræ of the neck, which are so remarkably constant in the class, are reduced to six. Neither of the genera have collar-bones, or clavicles, but in all the members of the group the bones of the skeleton are remarkable for the extreme solidity and denseness of their structure. Great variability is displayed in regard to the dentition; the recently extinct species from Behring Strait having no teeth at all; whereas in the manatis there is a very full series of masticating organs, which present a certain resemblance to the molars of the hippopotamus. In no case do the teeth resemble those of the toothed cetaceans; and although in the recent forms milk-teeth are not developed, rudiments of these have been detected, and in certain extinct kinds such teeth were functional. Similarly, nasal bones, or those roofing the cavity of the nose in ordinary mammals, have disappeared in the existing representatives of the group, although they were well developed in the earlier forms. From these peculiarities it is evident that the existing sirenians are specialised creatures evidently derived from land mammals of a more ordinary type. To fit them for long periods of submergence, both manatis and dugongs have the lungs much elongated, and extending almost the whole length of the back; while the blood-vessels are expanded in certain parts of the body into net-like structures, known as *retia mirabilia*, in which pure blood can be held back for a considerable time, instead of immediately passing onwards to the heart.

As regards their mode of life, the sirenians are inhabitants of large rivers, estuaries, sheltered bays, and shallow seas generally; never ploughing through the water of the open ocean in the manner so characteristic of the whales and porpoises; and seldom, indeed, wandering out of sight of shore. Moreover, instead of having the carnivorous habits so characteristic of the cetaceans, all the sirenians are exclusively vegetable feeders; tearing up the sea-weed and tangle when in the ocean, and other aquatic plants when they frequent fresh-waters, and masticating them after the manner of a pig either by means of their powerful molar teeth, or, when these are wanting, with the aid of horny plates which then invest the surface of the mouth. Both manatis and dugongs produce but a single offspring at a birth, which is tended with great care and affection by the mother. When suckling, the young is held between the flippers of the female parent and pressed close to her breast, upon which are situated the single pair of teats; and as both parent and offspring hold their rounded and somewhat human-shaped heads above water, there is no reasonable doubt that it is these animals that have given rise to the old legends of mermaids and mermen. The representatives of both the existing genera are usually found associating in small herds, their range including the coasts of the warmer portions of the Atlantic Ocean, the Red Sea, Indian Ocean, parts of the Bay of Bengal, and the seas of Australia. The northern sea-cow was, however, an inhabitant of colder regions, being only found in Behring Strait.

Manatis.

The manatis (*Manatus*), of which there appear to be three well-defined species from the tropical coasts of the Atlantic, are chiefly fluviatile creatures, seldom venturing into the ocean, but ascending long distances up the larger rivers, and being especially abundant in the Amazon. They grow to a length of about twelve feet, and are heavy, ungainly-looking creatures, with the thick and almost bark-like skin traversed by a number of fine wrinkles. Although in old age the skin may be nearly naked, in early life it is sparsely covered with soft hairs. Externally these animals are specially distinguished by the position of the nostrils at the extremity of the muzzle, the rounded form of the rudder-like tail, and the usual retention of three rudimental nails on each of the flippers. In the front of the jaws no incisor teeth are visible, although in the young state rudiments exist beneath the horny plates investing this region; but the cheek-teeth, of which eleven pairs are developed in each jaw, are fully developed and approximate in structure to those of the hippopotamus. As a rule, however, only six pairs of the latter teeth are in use at any one time, the anterior ones falling out before those at the hinder end of the series have cut the gums. In the skeleton the extremity of the skull and lower jaw are comparatively short and but slightly bent downwards, while, as already mentioned, there are only six vertebræ in the neck.

The triangular muzzle of the manati is remarkable for the circumstance that the extremities of the upper lip are developed into a pair of large fleshy flaps, which can be either brought into apposition with one another or widely separated, so that the animal can, when they are in the former position, seize and retain a leaf between them. Commercially, manatis are valued for their thick hides and the abundant supply of oil yielded by their fat; and they have in consequence of late years been greatly reduced in numbers.

Dugong.

The dugong (*Halicore dugong*), which ranges from the Red Sea along the Indian and Malayan coasts to Australia, may be distinguished externally from the manatis by the nostrils being situated on the superior aspect of the muzzle, the concave hinder border of the tail, and the total disappearance of all traces of nails from the flippers. In the skull the front extremity of both of the upper and lower jaws are extremely massive and deep, with a very marked and sudden downward flexure, while the dentition is of a totally different type from that of the manatis. None of the teeth develop roots, and consequently grow throughout the life of their owner; the number in the adult condition including a pair of upper incisors and five pairs of cheek-teeth in each jaw. In the males the upper incisors take the form of large downwardly-directed tusks, partially invested with enamel; but in the female these teeth never pierce the gums. The cheek-teeth, which are quite devoid of enamel, and equally developed in both sexes, form simple cylinders, increasing in size from the first to the last, the latter being more complex than those in advance, and consisting of two cylinders united by a narrow bridge. Although usually measuring from 5 to 7 feet in length, dugong grow to as much as from 8 to 9 feet. In colour they are generally bluish-grey throughout, but in some examples the under-parts are more or less decidedly lighter. The essential difference between the dugong and manatis in the matter of habits is that the former is essentially a marine animal which never attempts to ascend rivers, and its food consequently consists entirely of seaweed of various kinds. In former days dugong were met with in herds comprising hundreds of individuals, which were remarkable for their extraordinary tameness and fearlessness of man. Human greed has, however, done the usual work, and now their haunts are tenanted only by solitary individuals or pairs, which are shy and difficult of approach. Dugong oil is valued for its extremely limpid character; and in Timor-Laut these animals are hunted by the natives for the sake of their tusks, from which ear-rings and other ornaments are manufactured.

Fig. 92.—DUGONG (*Halicore dugong*).

To their comparatively wide geographical distribution may be attributed the escape of the manatis and dugong from complete extermination; but the rhytina, or northern sea-cow (*Rhytina gigas*), which, at the time of its discovery in 1741, existed in numbers on the shores of the Commander group of islands in Behring Strait, soon fell a victim to the persecution of man. Indeed, it appears that within less than thirty years from the date when its haunts were first invaded by Behring's party, the rhytina had ceased to exist; and it is now known to us only by certain descriptions and a number of more or less well-preserved skeletons which have been disinterred from its former haunts. In size the northern sea-cow vastly exceeded all its allies, being stated to attain a length of between 20 and 30 feet, with a weight in some cases of upwards of eight thousand pounds. It was evidently the most specialised member of the group, teeth being entirely wanting, and their function discharged by horny plates on the surfaces of the mouth, while the extremities of the flippers were blunted, and the bones of the digits apparently wanting. The head was small in proportion to the size of the body, and the tail was more deeply forked than in the dugong. So rough and ragged was the thick epidermis of the naked skin, that it has been compared to the bark of an oak tree, and could only be cut by an axe. While one account states that the colour of the skin was generally uniform brown, although occasionally flecked with white, a drawing taken from life shows alternate dark and light transverse bandings.

Northern Sea-Cow.

ORDER VIII.—CETACEA.

Whales, Porpoises, and Dolphins.

Before the doctrine of the adaptation of animals to their natural surrounding had become understood, no creatures were a greater puzzle to naturalists than the cetaceans, under which title are included whales, sperm-whales, porpoises, and dolphins. Their fish-like form and marine habits seemed indicative of their fish-like affinities; whereas their internal structure, breathing, and mode of reproduction proclaimed their mammalian kinship. The latter features ought to have shown at once what their real position in the zoological scale really was; but, nevertheless, they long occupied a place among the fishes. We read, for instance, in an abridged English edition of Buffon's "Natural History," published in the year 1821, that all these creatures "resemble quadrupeds in their internal structure, and in some of their appetites and affections. Like quadrupeds, they have lungs, a midriff, a stomach, intestines, liver, spleen, bladder, and parts of generation; their heart also resembles that of quadrupeds, with its partitions closed up as in them, and driving red and warm blood in circulation through the body; and to keep these parts warm, the whole kind are also covered between the skin and muscles with a thick coat of fat or blubber. As these animals breathe the air, it is obvious that they cannot bear to be any long time under water. They are constrained, therefore, every two or three minutes, to come up to the surface to take breath, as well as to spout out through their nostril—for they have but one—that water which they sucked in while gaping for their prey. But it is in the circumstances in which they continue their kind that these animals show an eminent superiority. Other fish deposit their spawn, and leave the success to accident; these never produce above one young, or two at the most, and this the female suckles entirely in the manner of quadrupeds, her breasts being placed, as in the human kind, above the navel. Their tails also are different from those of all other fish; they are placed so as to lie flat on the surface of the water; while the other kinds have them, as we every day see, upright or edgeways. This flat position of the tail enables them to force themselves suddenly to the surface of the water to breathe, which they are continually constrained to do."

With such a generally admirable account of the leading features of their organisation, it is marvellous how naturalists could have failed to recognise the true affinities of the cetaceans, and continued to class them among fishes, instead of transferring them to mammals. Indeed, almost the only error in the foregoing account is the portion relating to the "spouting" of cetaceans; this error being by no means extinct among non-zoological persons even at the present day. Instead of the water thrown up in the air when a whale "spouts" having been taken in at the mouth and expelled through the nostrils, it is mainly the condensed vapour from the creature's breath, although when a whale commences to spout or blow before it has quite reached the surface, a certain quantity of the superincumbent water is thrown up with the breath.

Cetaceans, then, are neither more nor less than highly specialised mammals which have assumed a fish-like form in correlation with the needs of a purely aquatic mode of existence. Although a few are found in large rivers, the majority are thoroughly pelagic in their habits, never coming to shore even for the purpose of breeding, and, in consequence, their fish-like characters are even more pronounced than is the case with the sirenians. The tail, or "flukes," which is always more or less distinctly forked, is, however, as we have seen, expanded in a horizontal, instead of in a vertical, plane, and in place of the two paired fins of most fishes, cetaceans have only a single pair of flippers, corresponding to the fore limbs of ordinary mammals. Although these flippers are completely invested in a continuous skin without any nails or external traces of digits, internally they contain the same skeletal elements—albeit, highly modified—as their terrestrial kindred. There is, however, the important exception that the bones of the digits are greatly more numerous than in other mammals, although the number of digits themselves never exceeds the normal five; this peculiarity offering an important distinction between cetaceans and sirenians. Like fishes, many members of the present order have a back-fin; although this differs from that of the former group in lacking an internal skeleton. Unlike most fishes, cetaceans have, however, a perfectly naked skin; although the general presence of a few scattered bristles, especially in the young state, around the mouth, proclaims their origin from fully haired mammals. And here may be mentioned the very remarkable circumstance that certain extinct members of the order were furnished with a bony armour, somewhat comparable to that of crocodiles; although this does not permit of our saying that all cetaceans are descended from armoured ancestors. In coloration, whales and porpoises resemble most fishes inhabiting the surface of the sea, such as mackerel and herrings, in that the upper surface of the body is dark, and the lower light—this being obviously a protective resemblance, as the dark upper surface, when viewed by reflected light, harmonises with the dark waves; while the light under surface, when viewed from below by transmitted light, must be scarcely distinguishable from the bright sky above. As in the sirenians, the external conchs of the ears are totally wanting, and the aperture of the ear itself is extremely minute. The eyes also are relatively small, and placed far back on the sides of the head, which is always large in proportion to the size of the body. An important difference from the sirenians is to be found in the position of the nostrils, which may open externally by either a double or a single aperture; these being invariably situated on the very summit of the head, and thus enabling the creatures to commence breathing the very moment they reach the surface, without altering their normal horizontal position. To prevent the ingress of water while beneath the surface, the nostrils can be completely closed by a valve or valves. Reference has already been made to the essential difference between the skeleton of the flipper of a cetacean and a sirenian; and it may be added that the vertebræ of the former have the terminal plates, or epiphyses, which are practically or entirely wanting in the existing members of the latter group, very strongly developed. The coat of fat, or blubber, lying beneath the skin, so characteristic of all cetaceans, has been already alluded to; but it must be also mentioned that these animals have net-works—*retia mirabilia*—of blood-vessels for the retention of oxygenated blood during their descent, which can be used gradually, and thus enable them to stay below for a longer period than would otherwise be the case. The two teats of the female differ from those of the sirenians in being placed far back on the abdomen.

Although none of the porpoises and dolphins attain very large dimensions, and some of them are comparatively small creatures, the cetacean order includes not only the largest of all mammals, but likewise of all living animals. That they trace their origin back to terrestrial mammals may be considered beyond all doubt, although from what particular group they are descended cannot at present be determined. As a rule, the various pelagic representatives of the order enjoy a very wide geographical range, although certain species, such as the Greenland-whale of the Arctic Ocean, and the pigmy-whale of the Southern Seas, are confined to a relatively small area. Almost all cetaceans are carnivorous.

Cetaceans are divisible into two great divisions, or sub-orders, known as the whalebone-whales (*Mystacoceti*), and the toothed whales (*Odontoceti*); the former group comprising only the single family (*Balænidæ*), whereas the latter is divided into three families. As their names imply, the most obvious distinction between these two groups relates to the absence or presence of functional teeth; the absence of teeth in the first group being compensated by the development of the peculiar substance known as whalebone, or baleen. In the young of the whalebone-whales, rudiments of true teeth are, however, developed beneath the roots of the incipient whalebone, although these subsequently wither without having ever cut the gum. As the nature and structure of whalebone is a matter of some interest and importance, a small space must be devoted to its consideration before entering upon the leading characteristics of the Mystacoceti. Whalebone, then, is a horny substance attached to the roof of the mouth, from which it hangs by a broad, transversely-arched base, in the form of a series of parallel, narrow, elongated triangular plates, placed transversely to the long axis of the mouth, with their external edges firm and straight, but the inner ones frayed out into a kind of fringe. The longest plates of whalebone are situated near the middle of the jaw, from which point the length gradually diminishes towards the two extremities, where they become very short. Whereas, however, in the Greenland-whale the length of the longest plates varies from some 10 to 12 ft., and the total number of plates in the series is about 380, in the great rorquals or fin-whales, the length is only a few inches, while the number of plates is considerably less. To accommodate the enormous whalebone-plates of the Greenland-whale, the bones of the upper jaw are greatly arched upwards, and the slender lower jaw is bowed outwards, thus leaving a large space—both in the vertical and horizontal directions—the transverse diameter of which is much wider below than above. When the mouth is closed, the plates of whalebone are folded obliquely backwards, with the front ones lying beneath those behind them; but directly the jaws are opened, the elastic nature of this substance causes it to spring at once into a vertical position, and thus form a sieve-like wall on both sides of the mouth, the thin ends of the plates being prevented from pushing outwards by the stiff lower lip which overlaps them. By elevating its enormous fleshy tongue within the cavity thus formed, the whale causes the enclosed water to rush out between the plates, leaving such small creatures as it contained lying dry on the surface of the tongue ready for swallowing. In structure, whalebone, which, although black in the Greenland-whale, is white in some of the other species, is of a horny nature, and grows from transverse ridges on the mucous membrane of the roof of the mouth; being, in fact, nothing more than an extreme development of the ridges on the palate of a cow, hardened and lengthened by an excessive growth of a horny superficial or epithelial layer. The whole of this vast

Whalebone-Whales.

horny growth takes place, however, after birth, young whales having smooth palates, with no trace of the horny plates.

Apart from the presence of the distinctive and characteristic whalebone, the members of the present group have the following characteristic features in common. In the first place, the nostrils open externally by two distinct longitudinal slits, or "blow-holes;" while the internal region of the nose retains traces of an organ of smell—this, by the way, being another proof that cetaceans are descended from terrestrial mammals. Distinct, although small, nasal bones partially roof over the nose-cavity of the skull; and the whole region of this part of the skull retains the normal symmetry. In order to accommodate the whalebone, the two branches of the lower jaw are curved outwards in a bow-like form; while at their front extremities they are only loosely connected together by ligament. The breast-bone, or sternum, consists of only a single piece, to which but one pair of ribs articulate; and all the ribs have but a slight connection with the vertebræ, articulating only with the horizontal transverse processes, and not touching the bodies of the vertebræ. Although the whalebone-whales are represented by a comparatively small number of species, all these are of large bodily dimensions, the smallest of them—the pigmy-whale—attaining a length of some 20 ft.

The most specialised representatives of the sub-order and family are the true, or right-whales, constituting the genus *Balæna*, of which there appear to be two well-defined species. Externally, the right-whales are easily recognised by the enormous relative size of the head, the perfectly smooth throat, the absence of a back-fin, and the moderate length of the flippers. Their whalebone, which is black in colour, is proportionately longer and more elastic than that of any other species, with the exception of the pigmy-whale; and for its accommodation the palate of the skull is much narrower and more highly arched than in other whales, while the branches of the lower jaw are more bowed outwards. The skeleton of the flippers contains five fully-formed digits; the vertebræ of the neck, which are reduced to the condition of thin plates, are completely welded together into a solid, immovable mass, and the tympanic bone of the internal ear is squared. In conformity with the arched form of the skull, the margin of the lower lip runs high up on the sides of the head and is highly convex; while the size of the opened mouth is enormous. In spite, however, of the huge dimensions of this cavity, the calibre of the throat is so small that it is a common saying among sailors that a herring is sufficient to choke a whale. Of the two existing species, the Greenland-whale (*B. mysticetus*) of the Arctic seas is the more specialised, the head being larger and the whalebone longer than in its southern cousin. The latter (*B. australis*) is commonly known as the southern right-whale, and although formerly abundant in the Atlantic, is nowadays a rare creature. From the right-whales the single species of pigmy-whale (*Neobalæna*), from the South American and Australasian seas, differs in having a small, hooked back-fin, as it does in its white whalebone. Whereas the Greenland species grows to a length of from 45 to 50 ft., the pigmy-whale does not appear to exceed 20. A connecting link between the right-whales and the under-mentioned rorquals is afforded by the great Pacific grey-whale (*Rhachianectes*), in which the throat has a single fold, and the back is devoid of a fin, while the whalebone is even shorter and more coarse than in the rorquals, the palate showing but a slight degree of vaulting, and the head being relatively small, and the body elongated. The vertebræ of the neck are thicker than in the right-whales, and mostly free from one another. In length the female varies from 40 to 44 ft., but the male is rather smaller.

The other members of the family are the humpback (*Megaptera*) and the rorquals or finners (*Balœnoptera*), in both of which the skin of the throat is marked by a number of longitudinal flutings or grooves, while the back carries a fin; the whalebone being short and coarse, and usually of a yellowish colour. The vertebræ of the neck are of considerable thickness, and totally separate

Fig. 93.—A FIN WHALE (*Balœnoptera*).

from one another; and the tympanic bone of the internal ear is much more rounded and globular than in the right-whales, its shape somewhat recalling that of a large cowri shell. In the skeleton of the flippers the number of digits is reduced to four; and the head is comparatively small in proportion to the body, with the palate but slightly arched, and the branches of the lower jaw little bowed outwards. Another character of the group, as compared with the right-whales, is the smaller degree of expansion of the tail-fin or flukes. From the finners, the single species of humpback (*Megaptera boops*) is distinguished by the relative shortness and depth of the body, which rises above the level of the back-fin behind the shoulders, and likewise by the extraordinary length of the flippers, which is nearly one-fourth that of the entire animal. In length the female is about the same as the Greenland-whale. As a rule humpbacks have the flippers of a pure glistening white; and when one of these animals is gambolling, as they often do, it will frequently lie on its side just below the surface of the water, so that the whole body is concealed. In this position one white flipper will be seen sticking straight up some 9 or 10 ft. above the water, and when first viewed from the deck of a passing vessel appears a most extraordinary object, which may well puzzle the beholder.

The rorquals, or finners, on the other hand, are characterised by the elongation and slenderness of the body and the comparative shortness of the flippers, which are pointed at their extremities. The largest member of the group, as indeed it is of all whales, is the blue, or Sibbald's rorqual (*Balœnoptera sibbaldi*), commonly known to the American whalers by the name of "sulphur-bottom," which reaches the enormous length of from 80 to 84 ft. The common rorqual (*B. musculus*), frequently stranded on the British coasts, is also a huge animal, frequently measuring from 65 to 70 ft.; but the other two species are of inferior dimensions, the smallest being the lesser fin-whale (*B. rostrata*), of which the length does not exceed from 30 to 35 ft. While some of the species feed largely on cod, others subsist chiefly on cuttle-fish.

On account of the length and elasticity of the whalebone, and the abundance of oil yielded by their blubber, from a commercial point of view, the right-whales are of far greater value than the humpback and finners; while their inferior speed, as compared with the latter, renders them far more easy to overtake and capture. The southern right-whale was, however, long ago practically exterminated from the Atlantic by the old Basque whalers; and incessant persecution has so diminished the numbers of the Greenland-whale that comparatively few are now to be met with on the old whaling-grounds. Consequently, whalers have been compelled to turn their attention to the less valuable finners and humpback; and the use of steam vessels and explosive harpoons fired from guns has rendered their capture far less difficult than in the days of rowing-boats and harpoons and lances thrown by hand. Till recently the "fishing" has been mainly carried on in the northern and sub-tropical seas, but a few years ago four ships were fitted out for whaling in the Antarctic; and the following account of what was observed is condensed from a newspaper report. It is there stated that the right-whales always come north to the grounds eastward of New Zealand early in October, and remain till near the end of December. Then they collect in "schools," and start on a south-east course with a speed of about five knots an hour night and day. Several ships have followed them in this course until they met with the ice-drift in lat. 50 deg. south and long. 160 deg. west, where the chase was abandoned. The whales always arrive on the ground in schools of ten or fifteen, and then separate and pair off—or at most one bull and two cows. It is not thought that the whales, with the exception of the humpbacks, come north to calve, as they are never seen with any young. Of late years right-whales have been seen north of 35 deg. 30 min. south lat. Finners and humpbacks are always to be found on the "ground," apparently travelling in a south-easterly direction. The humpbacks come up from the southward along both the east and west sides of Australia and New Zealand about the end of May, and continue their course northerly to about lat. 18 deg. south, when they disperse. About the first week of October they begin to work their way back south until lost amidst the ice. Experienced whaling-masters are of the opinion that there must be some place to the southward, as yet unknown, where the whales assemble in large numbers. A vessel fitted with an auxiliary screw, it is stated, could follow the whales to their destination without danger of being blocked by the ice. The right-whale, according to men who are engaged in the trade at the present time, must be very numerous in the Antarctic Ocean, as the fishery has never been carried on there with any constancy and vigour; whereas in the Arctic Ocean the whales are looked upon as almost extinct. The southern-whale is not so large as the Greenland, only yielding from 800 lbs. to 1200 lbs. of bone—the length of which varies from 8 ft. to 15 ft.—valued at £1600 to £1800 a ton, while the oil, averaging from 8 to 14 tons, brings £28 per ton. The humpbacks are very numerous off Norfolk Island of late. These whales measure from 60 to 70 ft. in length and yield from 50 to 70 barrels of oil.

The Australians interested in the success of the trade are confident that a large industry in whale and seal-fishing could be developed in the Antarctic seas by auxiliary screw-whalers, which could be fitted out at the comparatively small cost of £6000 each.

Toothed Whales.

The essential characteristic of the toothed-whales, or *Odontoceti*, is a negative one, and consists in the entire absence of whalebone. Very generally, indeed, teeth are developed, at least in the lower jaw, but these may be reduced to a single pair, or even in the male narwhal to a solitary tooth, while in the female of the latter species there are none of any functional importance. Another very well-marked point of distinction is the single external aperture of the nostrils, which very frequently takes the form of a transverse crescentic slit, closed by a flap-like valve. Then, again, the skull is always more or less unsymmetrical in the region of the nostrils, and in the existing members of the sub-order the nasal bones are reduced to mere rounded nodules, taking no share in roofing the nasal cavity. In certain extinct forms, however, these bones are of more normal character, and partially cover the chamber of the nose. No trace of an organ of smell is retained by any of the toothed-whales. In the skeleton the breast-bone, or sternum, is usually composed of several distinct portions, to which the extremities of several of the ribs are articulated by the intervention of cartilages; and a certain number of the anterior ribs are articulated at their upper ends to the bodies of the vertebræ, as well as to the transverse processes of the same. The lower jaw of a toothed-whale may always be distinguished from that of a whalebone-whale by the two branches being nearly straight, of great depth at the hinder extremity, and in front uniting with one another by a bony union of larger or smaller extent. In all the members of the group the skeleton of the flippers exhibits five complete digits. Throughout the sub-order the teeth are always of a simple structure, having conical or compressed crowns and undivided roots; and only a single series is ever developed, the replacement of the anterior teeth, so common among mammals, being wanting. In number the teeth of many species greatly exceed the ordinary mammalian series. Observations on fœtal cetaceans have indeed shown that rudiments of a second series of teeth are developed in the gums, which serve to show that the functional teeth correspond in the main to the milk-series of ordinary mammals.

Although in the development of whalebone and the loose articulation of the ribs to the backbone the whalebone-whales are clearly more specialised than the toothed-whales, yet as regards the single nostril and the structure of the nasal bones the latter group is decidedly more aberrant than the former. Hence it may be inferred that neither of the two sub-orders is derived from the other, but that both have grown up side by side quite independently. It has generally been considered that they are divergent branches from a common ancestral stock; but it is possible that they have no sort of genetic affinity with each other, and have respectively originated from two totally distinct mammalian groups. More decisive evidence than any yet adduced is, however, required before the latter view can be definitely accepted.

The largest of all the toothed-whales is the gigantic sperm-whale (*Physeter macrocephalus*), the sole member of its genus, and the typical representative of a family (*Physeteridæ*) characterised by the absence of teeth in the upper jaw of the adult, and the variability, both as regards size and number, of those of the lower jaw. In all the members of the family the hinder portion of the skull is much elevated, so as to form either a semi-circular wall, or a pair of crests behind the nasal aperture. All these cetaceans are entirely pelagic in their habits, and feed exclusively or chiefly on cuttles and squids. In the sperm-whale the number of teeth in the lower jaw varies from twenty to twenty-five pairs; the teeth themselves being of large size, with pointed and somewhat curved crowns, upon which there is no trace of enamel. The head is of enormous dimensions, measuring about one-fourth the total length

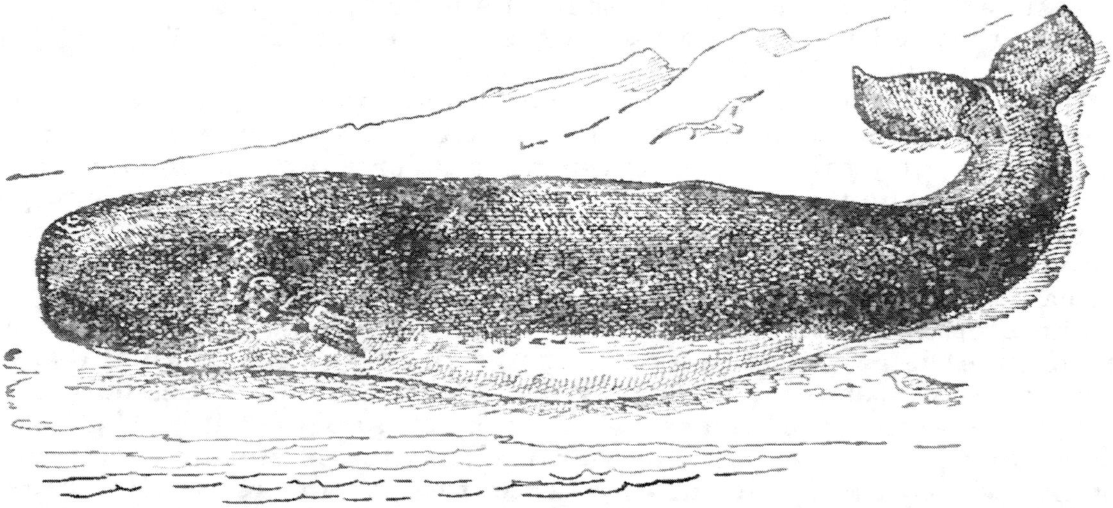

Fig. 94.—THE SPERM-WHALE (*Physeter macrocephalus*).

of the animal, and characterised by the abrupt truncation of the enormous muzzle, the S-like form of the blow-hole, which is situated somewhat to the left of the middle line, and the long mouth opening below, and somewhat behind, the extremity of the muzzle. The skull behind the nostrils has an enormous cavity, bounded behind by a semi-circular wall of bone of several feet in height, and containing during life the oily substance which yields, when refined, the valuable spermaceti. An even more precious product of this cetacean is ambergris, which, although generally found floating on the surface of the ocean, is really a concretion formed in the intestines of the sperm-whale. It is an amber-coloured substance, generally containing a number of the horny beaks of the squids on which sperm-whales feed. Although the female is a much smaller animal, the male cachalot, as the sperm-whale is often called, grows to a length of between 50 and 60 ft. In the sperm-whale the two branches of the lower jaw are united in front for about half their length, but in the much smaller and somewhat porpoise-like animal known as the lesser sperm-whale (*Cogia breviceps*) the union between the two branches of the lower jaw is less than half the total length of the jaw, and the number of lower teeth is reduced to from nine to twelve pairs. This whale attains a length of about 10 ft., and differs from the cachalot in carrying a large back-fin. The flippers, moreover, which in the sperm-whale are remarkably small in proportion to the size of the body, are here relatively longer. It is interesting to notice that fossil sperm-whales (*Physodon*) have been discovered possessing a full series of enamel-capped teeth in both the upper and lower jaw.

Nearly allied to the preceding are the bottled-nosed and beaked-whales, belonging to a group distinguished by the reduction of the lower functional teeth to a single pair, the others being rudimentary and concealed in the gum. None attain a large size, and all are pelagic, subsisting almost exclusively on squids and cuttle-fish. The bottle-noses, as typified by the common *Hyperoödon rostratus*, so frequently stranded on the British coasts, take their name from the extreme convexity of the crown of the head in the adult male, which rises abruptly above the base of the short beak. They have but a single pair of teeth in front of the lower jaw, but even these are invisible in the living state; and the back, like that of the beaked-whales, bears a fin. Although the common bottle-nose, which has a very wide geographical distribution, does not exceed about 30 ft. in length, it is valued not only on account of its oil, but likewise for the spermaceti contained in the head. In addition to the large overhanging and unsymmetrical crests above the nostrils, the skulls of old males have another pair of longitudinal crests on the sides of the base of the beak, which come almost into contact, and have their front surfaces broad, flat, and rugose. Cuvier's whale (*Choneziphius* cuvieri*) differs from the bottle-nose in possessing a pair of large forwardly and upwardly directed teeth at the extremity of the lower jaw. From both the preceding the beaked-whales (*Mesoplodon*) are readily distinguished by the production of the anterior portion of the skull into a long cylindrical beak, composed of massive, ivory-like bone; while they are further characterised by the pair of lower teeth being generally situated near the middle of the jaw. These teeth are generally of large size, and more or less compressed latterly. In one species (*M. layardi*) they are enormously developed, and of a strap-like form, curving over the beak to such an extent as in some cases actually to prevent the mouth from being fully opened. The beaked-whales appear to be solitary creatures, avoiding the neighbourhood of the coasts, and thus but seldom stranded. During the Pliocene epoch they must, however, have been abundant in the English seas, as their solid fossilised beaks are of common occurrence in the so-called crag deposits of the East Coast. Arnux's whale (*Berardius arnuxi*), from the seas of New Zealand, which is the last member of the family, differs from the true beaked-whales in possessing two pairs of lower teeth. Whereas the beaked-whales usually measure about 15 or 16 ft. in length, this species reaches as much as 30 ft.

Freshwater-Dolphins.

A small family of the Odontoceti known as the *Platanistidæ* is represented solely by three small species, two of which are exclusively freshwater, while the third is an estuarine form. While resembling the members of the next family in the possession of a numerous series of teeth in both the upper and lower jaw, they are distinguished by the length of the bony union between the two branches of the latter, and likewise by the mode of articulation of the ribs with the backbone. None of the vertebræ of the neck are welded together. The typical member of the group is the well-known susu, or Gangetic dolphin (*Platanista gangetica*), which may often be seen sporting in the Ganges, Indus, or Bramaputra. This species usually attains a length of 7 or 8 ft., and is characterised by the long and compressed beak, in which are crowded a very numerous series of sharply-pointed teeth, the rudimental back-fin, the fan-shaped flippers, the slit-like form of the blowhole, and the minute size of the eye, which is perfectly useless as an organ of vision. The skull may be recognised by the enormous curving longitudinal crests arising from the base of the beak, and almost meeting above it. The food of the susu appears to consist almost exclusively of prawns and bottom-

* This name—originally applied to an allied fossil form—is used by Cope to replace *Ziphius*, on account of the pre-occupation of the latter.

haunting fish, which are raked up from the mud by the long beak. The other two existing members of the family are South American. One of these is the inia or Amazonian dolphin (*Inia geoffroyensis*), inhabiting the upper portions of the river-system from which it derives its name, and being more porpoise-like in form than the last. The long cylindrical beak has a number of sparse bristly hairs; and its numerous teeth have a tubercle at the base. Unlike the susu, the eye is fairly large, and the flippers are not fan-shaped. Seven feet is the maximum length of the male inia; and the general colour is blackish above and reddish beneath. From both the preceding the small La Plata dolphin (*Stenodelphis blainvillei*), from the estuary of the Rio de La Plata, may be at once distinguished by its uniformly buff coloration, which is admirably suited to harmonize with the colour of the stained water of the Plate river, and at once proclaims that the species is not of pelagic habits. In size, this dolphin seldom, if ever, exceeds 5 ft., and is often considerably less. Unlike both the other species, it has a well-developed back-fin, and the beak is of great length, and furnished on each side with from fifty to sixty teeth; the number in the other genera being about thirty. Another distinctive feature is to be found in the form of the blow-hole, which forms a transverse crescent, instead of a longitudinal slit. At certain seasons of the year enormous numbers of these elegant little cetaceans are captured in the Bay of Monte Video by the fishermen, who detest them on account of the large quantities of fish they consume.

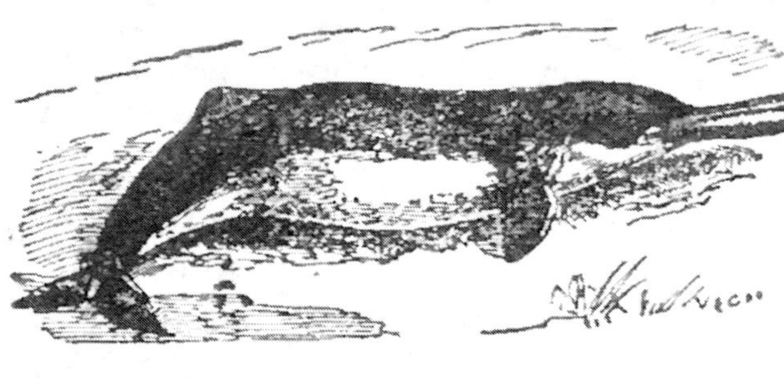

Fig. 95.—Gangetic Dolphin (*Platanista gangetica*).

Porpoises, Dolphins, etc.

The whole of the remaining members of the order are included in the single family *Delphinidæ*. The majority of the species are of comparatively small size; and while most are found in the neighbourhood of coasts where they frequently ascend tidal rivers, a few are of exclusively fluviatile habits. Many of the genera are very closely allied, and distinguished mainly by the structure of the skull, so that in a popular work it is by no means easy to indicate their distinctive peculiarities. While the majority resemble the *Platanistidæ* in possessing a numerous series of teeth in each jaw, in two species this is not the case. From that family they may be distinguished by the shorter union between the two branches of the lower jaw, and also by a difference in the mode of articulation of the ribs to the backbone. In all cases the blow-hole is in the form of a transverse crescent, with the two horns pointing forwards; and very generally from two to four of the anterior vertebræ of the neck are welded together into a solid mass. One of the most aberrant, and at the same time one of the most beautiful, members of the family is the spotted-narwhal, or sea-unicorn (*Monodon monoceros*), the males of which carry the well-known spirally-twisted "horn," or tusk, from which several of the names of the species are derived. Exclusively confined to the Arctic seas, where it associates in small "schools," the narwhal belongs to a group of dolphins characterised by the blunt and rounded form of the head and the total absence of a beak. There is no back-fin; the wide and rounded flippers are short; and the colour is dusky, with dark-grey mottlings. The single tusk of the males is always the left one, the right remaining, as a rule, undeveloped in the gum; but occasionally specimens are found with two tusks. Besides these tusks there are no other functional teeth in the males, and the females are toothless. The length of the head and body varies from 12 to 16 ft. and that of the tusk between 7 and 8 ft. Allied to the narwhal is the beautiful white-whale or beluga (*Delphinapterus leucas*), which is likewise a northern form, and also the sole representative of its genus. It may be recognised by its pure glistening white skin, the absence of a tusk, and the presence of numerous teeth in the front of the jaws. The beluga, which congregates in troops of considerable size, is regularly hunted for the sake of its hide, blubber, and flesh; the latter being dried and eaten by the Greenlanders and Eskimos, as well as by the sledge-dogs of the latter.

In ordinary language the term porpoise is applied to many of the members of the present family, but in a scientific sense it is confined to the members of the small genus *Phocœna*, all of which are comparatively small-sized cetaceans, characterised by possessing from sixteen to twenty-six pairs of small, short, somewhat spade-shaped teeth. In the common porpoise (*P. communis*) of the European seas the back is furnished with a well-developed fin; but in the Indian species (*P. phocœnoides*) this appendage is wanting. Porpoises are the most common and familiar of all cetaceans, their rolling gambols being well known not only to all those who have made a voyage, but likewise to visitors to the sea-side. The allied genus *Cephalorhynchus* is typified by Heaviside's dolphin (*C. heavisidei*), and includes four species from the Southern seas. They have a conical head, without any distinct beak, and from twenty-five to thirty-one pairs of small and sharp teeth. The back-fin is triangular or ovate; and in three out of the four species the flippers have a characteristic elliptical shape. Externally their most distinctive feature is the coloration, the upper-parts being black, and the under surface of the body white, with the white area terminating on the under side of the tail in a trident, the lateral prongs of which run obliquely upwards on the flanks a little behind the back-fin. The Irawadi dolphin (*Orcella fluminalis*), of which a variety, or perhaps an allied species, occurs in the Bay of Bengal and some of the neighbouring seas, represents a genus distinguished by the globose, beakless head, and the small size and number of the teeth, the latter occupying nearly the entire length of the jaws, and including from thirteen to seventeen pairs in the upper, and from twelve to fifteen in the lower jaw. They are set close together, and are conical and pointed in shape, those in the front of the jaws of the adult males being inclined outwards. The moderate-sized flippers are broad at the base, and of a subovate contour; while the back-fin is small and hooked. From 7 to 7½ ft. is the usual length of these dolphins, which are either blackish or slaty in colour.

From all the preceding the large and strikingly-coloured cetaceans known as killers, or grampuses (*Orca*), differ by the large size of their powerful conical teeth, which are crowded together, and usually form twelve pairs in each jaw. And they are further characterised by the great vertical height of the back-fin. As regards colour, the upper-parts and flippers are black and the lower surface whitish; the white area ending on the under side of the tail in a trident, very nearly the same as in the above-mentioned genus *Cephalorhynchus*. Above and behind the eye is a white streak, and there is a purplish band across the back behind the fin. Killers, of which there is but a single well-defined species, grow to a length of at least 20 ft., and enjoy an almost cosmopolitan distribution. They derive their popular name from their rapacious habits, and are the only cetaceans which prey on other members of their own order. One killer has been known to swallow several entire seals one after the other; and not unfrequently several individuals combine forces to attack and kill one of the larger whales, hunting with the perseverance of a pack of hounds. When swimming near the surface of the water, killers may be easily recognised by the great size of the nearly vertical back-fin. The lesser killer (*Pseudorca crassidens*), which is also cosmopolitan, and attains a length of about 14 ft., differs from its larger relative by the smaller size of the back-fin, the pointed flippers, and the cylindrical (instead of angulated) roots of the teeth, as well as by the uniformly black colour of the skin. There are generally eight pairs of upper and ten of lower teeth.

Fig. 96.—KILLER (*Orca gladiator*).

Although the name of black-fish would apply equally well to the foregoing, it is given to the cetacean known scientifically as *Globiocephalus melas.* The black-fish is characterised by the extremely short and rounded head, the almost uniformly black colour of the skin, and the presence of from eight to twelve pairs of small conical teeth in the front portion of the jaws. The back-fin is long, low, and thick, and the flippers are relatively long and narrow. Generally there is a lance-shaped white patch on the throat. In length, the black-fish, or, as it is often called, pilot-whale, grows to a length of 20 ft. Whether there is more than one species is somewhat uncertain; but, at anyrate, a form inhabiting the Bay of Bengal is distinguishable by the reduction in the number of the teeth. As regards habits, this cetacean is the most sociable of its order, and since all the members of a herd always blindly follow their leader, enormous numbers are frequently slaughtered at a time. The last of the beakless group of the family is the rare Risso's dolphin (*Grampus griseus*), which differs from all the other *Delphinidæ*, save the female of the narwhal, by the absence of upper teeth, while the lower jaw carries only from three to seven small teeth towards its anterior end. In general appearance this species is very similar to the black-fish, although the head is less decidedly globular, and the flippers are rather shorter. It is easily recognised by the peculiar grey striping and mottling of the skin; scarcely any two individuals being quite alike in this respect. This species is almost cosmopolitan, specimens being stranded from time to time on the British coasts.

Intermediate, between the beakless and beaked members of the family, is a genus known as *Lagenorhynchus,* which includes the various species of short-beaked dolphins. Noticeable on account of their strongly-contrasted black and white coloration, the short-beaked dolphins are characterised as a whole by the short, ill-defined and somewhat ploughshare-like beak of the skull, the moderate size of the back-fin and flippers, and the distinct ridges on the tail. The teeth vary considerably both in size and in number; but, as in the black-fish, the bony union between the two branches of the lower jaw is short. The sides of the body are always marked by two light-coloured areas, between which is a band, or a series of streaks of black.

The second group of the family includes the true dolphins and their allies, in all of which there is a distinctly defined beak, generally exceeding the brain-cavity in length, and marked off from the hinder portion of the head by a V-shaped groove. By sailors dolphins are indifferently spoken of either as porpoises or bottle-noses, which frequently leads to a confusion between them and either true porpoises or the bottle-nosed whales. They are divided into numerous genera, according to the number of the teeth, the relative length of the beak, and the conformation of the bones of the palate. They are all comparatively small animals, but few exceeding a length of about 10 ft.; and while most of them are marine, some ascend the larger rivers temporarily, and others are permanent inhabitants of fresh-waters. Fish of various kinds constitute the usual prey of dolphins, but it is believed that one species of the genus *Sotalia* from the Cameruns district subsists on sea-weed. In the true dolphins (*Delphinus*), of which there are several species, the beak is of considerable length; the flippers and back-fin are long and slightly hooked; there are from about forty to sixty-five pairs of sharp teeth in each jaw, which have an oval section at the base; and the union between the two branches of the lower jaw is short. In the bottle-nosed dolphins (*Tursiops*) the beak is shorter and more tapering, and the number of teeth less, there being generally from twenty-two to twenty-six pairs. A third genus is typified by the rough-toothed dolphin (*Steno frontatus*), from the Atlantic and Indian Oceans. Here the beak is greatly elongated, and the bony union between the two branches of the lower jaw very long; the rather large teeth varying from twenty to twenty-five pairs, and being often marked by rough groovings. Nearly allied are the long-beaked river-dolphins forming the genus *Sotalia*, which may be distinguished by their fluviatile or estuarine habits, and the smaller number of vertebræ in the backbone; the teeth being always smooth, and the base of the flippers very wide. Several of the species inhabit the Amazon-system, while one is found in some of the Chinese rivers, and another in the estuaries and rivers of the Cameruns district.

ORDER IX.—EDENTATA.

Sloths, Ant-Eaters, and Armadillos.

The three families of mammals named above, all of which are practically confined to South and Central America, although one or two wander as far north as Texas, are the representatives of an order in which all the existing forms are devoid of front teeth, while the cheek-teeth have no external coating of enamel, but consist solely of ivory, or of ivory with a layer of cement. In consequence of this poor development of the teeth, the group is known by the name of Edentata. To the same group have been commonly referred the pangolins of the warmer parts of the Old World and the aard-varks of Africa, but it is nearly certain that these cannot rightly be included in the same order, and they are accordingly referred here to a group by themselves. It is rather difficult to give many other characters in addition to the absence of front teeth common to all members of the order, but it may be stated that the cheek-teeth grow throughout life and thus never develop roots; while it is but very rarely that milk-teeth are present, and in only a single instance do these cut the gum. With the exception of the sloths, in which they have probably been lost, the hinder vertebræ of the trunk have additional articular surfaces. In their whole organisation the edentates display a low type, as is exemplified by the generally small size of their brains, in which there are usually but few convolutions on the surface.

Sloths.

The sloths, or *Bradypodidæ*, form a small family of edentates specially characterised by their adaptation to an arboreal life, and differing from nearly all other mammals by their habit of hanging back-downwards from the branches of the trees on which they dwell. They are comparatively small, slenderly-built animals, with a peculiarly rough, shaggy coat, a short, rounded, and almost sperical head, and inordinately long and slender limbs—especially the front pair—terminating in huge, hook-like claws. The small ears are completely buried among the long fur covering the head; and the tail is rudimental. The cheek-teeth, which comprise five pairs in the upper and four in the lower jaw, form short cylinders, of which the external layer is harder than the central core, so that by use their grinding surfaces become slightly cupped. Whereas, however, in the three-toed sloths the whole of the teeth are of this simple type, in the two-toed species the first pair in each jaw are taller than the rest and assume a somewhat tusk-like form, with their summits obliquely bevelled by mutual wear. In the limbs the narrow and curved feet are reduced to the condition of little more than hooks; the three-toed forms having three claws on each foot, whereas in the other group the number of claws in the fore feet is reduced to two. Although admirably adapted for suspending the animal back-downwards from a branch, the feet of the sloth are but poor instruments for progression on the ground, and when walking, a sloth advances awkwardly and slowly, with the soles turned inwards. Externally the fur of the sloth is of a dull brownish or ashy colour, the individual hairs having a fluted outer surface. The most extraordinary feature about the fur is, however, the growth of a vegetable substance on the surface of the hairs, thus increasing the resemblance of the animal, when hanging at rest from a bough, to a rough lichen-clad knot. Beneath the outer coat of long grey hairs is a finer under-fur marked by longitudinal stripes of chocolate-brown and orange; a patch of this under-fur being frequently exposed in the middle of the back by the habit these creatures have of rubbing or resting this part of their bodies against the trees. In conformity with the shape of the skull, the soft tongue is very short. The female has the single pair of teats situated on the breast. Internally sloths are specially characterised by the complexity of their stomachs, and a peculiar folding of the windpipe. Sloths are divided into two distinct generic groups. Of these, the three-toed sloths (*Bradypus*) are characterised by having three toes to each foot, and all the teeth short and cupped, whereas in the two-toed sloths (*Cholœpus*), there are only two toes on the fore feet, and the front pair of teeth in each jaw are taller than the others and obliquely bevelled at the summits. Very exceptional among mammals are the sloths in regard to the number of vertebræ in the neck. Thus, whereas in one of the two-toed kinds there are the normal seven, in a second the number is reduced to six; while in the three-toed group there are invariably nine of these segments.

By the natives of the tropical forest-regions of South and Central America, where sloths are alone found, the three-toed kinds are spoken of as aï, while the name of unau is applied to the members of the two-toed group. Mainly nocturnal in their habits, sloths appear to be sluggish creatures, passing the daylight hours curled up with the head safely tucked between the fore-limbs, and at night wandering about slowly in search of food, which consists solely of leaves and other vegetable substances. Caution is a great characteristic of their movements, a fresh branch being firmly seized before hold is relaxed of the one they are about to leave. They are usually found either singly or in small family parties; and the females produce but a single offspring at a birth, which is fully developed, except in the matter of size, when it makes its appearance in the world.

Fig. 97 —Three-Toed Sloth (*Bradypus tridactylus*).

Ant-Eaters.

The second family of the edentates is formed by the South American or true ant-eaters (*Myrmecophagidæ*), of which there are three species, referable to as many genera; one of these being strictly terrestrial, while the other two are more or less arboreal in their habits. So unlike are these creatures, both as regards external character and the structure of their skeleton, to the sloths, that it is at first sight difficult to believe that there is any very intimate relationship between the two groups. And, indeed, were it not that in the superficial deposits of South America there occur remains of certain extinct edentates known as ground-sloths (of which the gigantic *Megalotherium* is a familiar example in our museums), forming to a great extent a group intermediate between the sloths and the ant-eaters, it would be difficult even for zoologists to fully realise how intimate this relationship really is. Taking the existence of these extinct connecting links for granted, it may be noticed that in place of the short and rounded head of the sloths, the ant-eaters have the head and skull more or less elongated and narrow, while the slender jaws are entirely toothless, and the tongue is long, cylindrical, and capable of being protruded far in advance of the lips. The degree of elongation of the skull is, however, by no means the same in all the members of the group, the maximum development in this respect being exhibited in the case of the great ant-eater. Still more striking is the difference in the structure of the feet in the two groups. In the great ant-eater, for instance, the fore-foot is furnished with five complete toes, the middle one of which is much larger and more powerful than the rest; and all but the fifth, or outermost, are furnished with strong claws. In this genus there are also five toes to the hind-feet; but in the third representative of the family there are only four claws to each foot. When the great ant-eater is walking, only the extreme outer side and part of the upper surface of the fore-foot is applied to the ground; but in the hind-foot, which has the fourth toe the largest, and claws to all five, the whole of the short and wide sole touches the ground in the ordinary manner. An important point of distinction from the sloths is that the bones of the terminal joints of the fore-feet have a longitudinal slit in the middle of the upper surface; and in all cases the limbs are relatively short and stout. Unlike the sloths, the ant-eaters have a very long and powerful tail, which in two of the species is endowed with the power of prehension, as indeed is the case with so many of the animals inhabiting the dense forest-regions of tropical America. In correlation with their insectivorous habits, the stomach of the ant-eaters is perfectly simple in structure, and the brain is more convoluted than in the sloths. Two out of the three species have the fur of the body marked by dark and light longitudinal bands or patches, and it is noteworthy that this type of coloration approximates to that obtaining in the under-fur of the sloths. In order to procure their insect-food, which mostly comprises ants and termites, the long worm-like tongue, which can be protruded with great rapidity from the tubular mouth, is provided with a viscid secretion.

The largest and most specialised member of the family is the great ant-eater, or tamahoa (*Myrmecophaga jubata*), which is terrestrial in its habits, and is easily recognised by the exceedingly long and slender head, passing almost imperceptibly into the neck, the minute ears, the fringe of long hair clothing the fore-limbs and flanks, and the huge mass of still more elongated hairs covering the tail. This ant-eater, which attains a length of about 4 ft. to the root of the tail, is distributed over the whole of the tropical districts of South and Central America, frequenting either damp swampy forests or the margins of rivers. Like the other species, it is strictly nocturnal in its habits, and but a single offspring, which is carried for some time on the back of its parent, is produced at a birth. Next in point of size is the lesser ant-eater, or tamandua (*Tamandua tetradactyla*), which scarcely attains half the dimensions of its larger cousin, and is distinguished by the uniformly short fur, shorter head, the much longer ears, and the cylindrical prehensile tail, which is naked both at the tip and along the whole of the lower aspect. In the fore-feet the claw of the fifth digit is rudimental and concealed beneath the skin, while that of the third is much larger than either of the others, the hind-foot being generally similar to that of the larger species. The tamandua has approximately the same geographical distribution as the latter, from which it differs in being mainly arboreal in its habits. The most sloth-like, and at the same time the most diminutive member of the group is the two-clawed ant-eater (*Cyclotnrus didactylus*), which does not exceed a rat in size, and has the sloth-like habit of hanging back downwards from the boughs of trees, to which it clings by its long, hook-like claws. In the shortness of the head this species likewise presents a decided approximation to the sloths. While the front paws have four toes, only the first and second of these—that is to say, those corresponding to the index and middle fingers of the human hand—are furnished with claws; but the four toes of the hind-foot are all clawed, and as they are

Fig. 98.—Great Ant-Eater (*Myrmecophaga jubata*).

placed close together and the claws are of nearly equal length, they collectively form a hook-like organ not unlike the foot of a sloth. From the other ant-eaters this species differs in the uniformly foxy-red hue of the short silky fur. In its skeleton it differs from the other two members of the group in possessing collar-bones, in which respect this species once again approximates to the sloths. In other ant-eaters the ribs are unusually broad, but in the present species this character is so exaggerated that they almost come into contact with one another, and thus nearly enclose the body in a solid bony casque. Thoroughly arboreal in its mode of life, and furnished with a highly prehensile tail, the two-clawed ant-eater is restricted to the hottest regions of America, ranging from Northern Brazil through Peru and the Guianas to Central America.

Armadillos.

The development of a bony shield composed of isolated plates welded together by their edges, or overlapping like tiles on a roof over more or less of the upper surface of the body, serves to differentiate the armadillos and their tiny relative the pichiago not only from all other existing edentates, but likewise from other mammals. All these animals collectively constitute the family *Dasypodidæ*, which is sufficiently distinguished by the aforesaid bony armour. In ordinary armadillos the armour is divided into two solid shields, one of which protects the shoulders, and the other the haunches, while between these are a variable number of movable transverse bands, permitting the animal to bend its back to a smaller or greater extent, and in one case even allowing the assumption of a completely ball-like form. Both in the front and hind shield the constituent plates are polygonal in form, and articulate with one another immovably by their edges; but in the movable bands they are tile-like and overlapping. The fixed shields and movable bands collectively constitute the carapace. The component plates are marked by a characteristic sculpture, which varies much in the different genera, and may consist either of raised pustules or minute punctures; and each plate is overlaid by a thin horny shield. More or less abundant hairs grow from the skin at the junction of the plates of the carapace; and occasionally these are so abundant and luxuriant as practically to conceal the latter from view. A small shield of polygonal bony plates, with their edges in apposition, serves to protect the upper surface of the head; while the tail is usually defended by a similar type of armour, which may either take the form of oblique rows of plates or tubercles, or of a series of rings of gradually decreasing diameter, severally composed of the same plates. Irregular bony plates likewise protect the short and powerful limbs, of which the front pair are provided with strong claws adapted for digging. In the fore-limbs the claws may vary in number from three to five, whereas the much smaller and weaker ones of the hind-foot are always the latter number. Armadillos have moderately long and more or less depressed heads, sharply pointed in front, and armed with a rather small number of simple peg-like teeth. They have long tails, fully developed collar-bones; and the bones of the arm and fore-arm are specially expanded and modified for the purpose of digging. Their tongues, although relatively long, have not the extreme elongation characterising the ant-eaters. Armadillos have a much more extensive geographical range than either of the preceding families of edentates, ranging from Patagonia to Central America, and one species at least reaching as far northwards as Texas. Although different species or genera are confined to different localities and situations, members of the group are to be met with alike on the grassy pampas of Buenos Aires, the sandy plains of Mendoza, and the tropical forests of Brazil. While a few are diurnal, the majority are nocturnal in their habits, and all are burrowers. In many districts the Argentine pampas is perfectly honeycombed with the long burrows of various kinds of armadillos. Armadillos live chiefly upon insects, worms, and molluscs, but one species at least feeds largely upon carrion, although this is probably an acquired habit, due to the large number of carcases of horses and cattle which nowadays strew the pampas. In their movements they are extremely swift, starting off with a tremendous rush when disturbed while feeding at night, and requiring a good dog to keep pace with them. Whereas some species run on the tips of their claws, with the body raised high above the ground, others carry the carapace lower. The rapidity with which an armadillo will bury itself in the soft ground of the Argentine pampas must be witnessed to be credited. Most of the true armadillos have medium-sized or rather large ears, placed far apart from one another; the first and second claws of the fore-foot are, if present at all, slender; and the breast of the female bears a single pair of teats.

The first genus (*Dasypus*) includes the typical armadillos, of which the six-banded species (*D. sexcinctus*) of Brazil, and the Argentine peludo, or hairy armadillo (*D. villosus*), are well-known examples. These animals have from six to eight movable bands in the carapace, which is more or less depressed with strongly serrated margins. The ears are small or moderate, and the head is very broad and much depressed, with the muzzle comparatively blunt. The tail, which is shorter than the head and body, is plated with distinct rings near the root. In the fore-foot the first toe is the slenderest of all, and the second the longest. The teeth, which are relatively large, are generally nine above and ten below, the first upper pair being usually implanted in the premaxillary or anterior jaw-bones. Some of the species are of considerable size, the head and body in the typical one measuring as much as 16 inches. In the Argentine the peludo is now mainly nocturnal, and feeds largely upon the carcases of cattle, beneath which its burrows are frequently formed. The much smaller pichi (*D. minutus*) of the same districts is, however, chiefly a diurnal animal. In spite of having but two teats, the female produces from two to four young, which are born blind, with the armour already developed, but in a soft and flexible condition. The second genus, of which the broad armadillo or tatouay (*Lysiurus unicinctus*) of Brazil, Paraguay, and Surinam is the typical representative, differs from the last by the greater number of movable bands in the carapace, which are either twelve or thirteen. The teeth, of which there are either eight or nine pairs in each jaw, are relatively smaller than in the first genus, and in the upper jaw do not extend so far backwards on the sides of the palate. The tail, also, is almost devoid of bony plates, of which it has only a few on the under side and near the tip. The chief characteristic of the fore-foot is the great size of the curved claw borne by the third toe; the fourth and fifth toes having similar but smaller claws, while those of the first and second are long and slender. In the hind-foot

Fig. 99.—HAIRY ARMADILLO (*Dasypus villosus*).

the claws take the form of short and blunt nails. The plates of the carapace are ornamented by an indistinct granular sculpture. In size the tatouay is intermediate between the six-banded armadillo and the next species. The great number of the teeth—of which there are from twenty to twenty-five pairs—at once serves to distinguish the giant armadillo (*Priodon gigas*) of Brazil and Surinam from all its relatives. It is also the largest living member of the family, the head and body measuring about 3 ft. in length. The number of movable bands in the carapace is thirteen ; and in the anterior and posterior shields of the carapace the plates are arranged in rows very similar to those of the movable bands which they resemble in sculpture. Structurally the feet are very similar to those of *Lysiurus*, but the claw of the third toe in the front foot is relatively larger, while that of the fifth is very small. The tail, which is nearly equal in length to the carapace, is, however, of a totally different type, being completely invested with large plates arranged in spiral rows. Very different are the three small species of three-banded armadillos (*Tolypeutes*), in which the fore and aft shields of the carapace are very greatly developed and the movable bands reduced to three. The plates on the carapace are small and tuberculated, the shield on the head is very large and flat, and the extremely short tail is covered with prominent tubercles. As the borders of the carapace, which are smooth, are much produced on either side of the fore and hind limbs, these animals are enabled to roll themselves up into a complete although somewhat flattened ball ; the shield of the head, by one side of which lies the tail, almost completely filling up the front and hinder notches in the carapace. The head is long and narrow, with the rather large ovate ears placed somewhat low down ; while the jaws carry eight or nine pairs of upper and nine of lower teeth, which are of relatively small size and reach backwards to the hinder end of the palate. In the fore-foot the third claw is more developed than in any other species, the claws of the first and fifth toes being either rudimental or absent. The common species grows to a length of about fifteen inches, and is found in the pampas of Argentina, where, however, it now seems extremely rare. Trusting to their impassive power of defence, all the armadillos of this genus are diurnal and non-burrowing animals, generally lurking in the large tussocks of pampas-grass. When running they go on the extreme tips of their claws, and scuttle along at a great pace. The last genus of the true armadillos is represented on the Argentine pampas by the mulita (*Tatusia hybrida*), and there are other species in different parts of the continent, one of which ranges into Texas, while another from Peru is remarkable for the thick coat of fur which entirely conceals the carapace. These pretty little armadillos differ from the whole of the foregoing by the close approximation of the long mule-like ears (whence the name of mulita for the Argentine species), as well as by the presence of an additional pair of teats on the abdomen of the females, and also by the development of a set of milk-teeth. The seven or eight pairs of permanent teeth are very minute, and do not make their appearance till comparatively late in life. The long and narrow head is produced into a cylindrical and obliquely-truncated, somewhat pig-like snout. Extreme elongation and compression is the leading characteristic of the carapace, which has from seven to nine movable bands ; the plates of the latter being marked by a V-shaped line of punctures, while the smaller ones of the solid shields have an elevated oval central area surrounded by an incomplete ring of small tubercles. The tail is surrounded by a series of bony rings, decreasing in size from root to tip, and thus recalls a partially opened telescope. In the fore-feet there are four long claws, of which the innermost are the largest; while in the five-clawed hind-feet the third is the longest and the fourth and fifth the shortest. About 11 in. is the average length of the head and body of the mulita, but another species is somewhat larger. The mulita may be often found skulking among the tussocks of pampas-grass during the daytime, when, with the aid of a dog, it can generally be captured before it has time to make good its escape into its burrow. Not unfrequently when a Gaucho captures a mulita he crops its ears and turns it loose, such crop-eared specimens being at first rather a puzzle to the naturalist. In spite of the circumstance that carrion forms a considerable portion of the diet of these animals, roasted mulita is a favourite dish in the Argentine.

Quite different from the true armadillos are the beautiful little pichiciagos, or fairy pink armadillos, of which one species (*Chlamydophorus truncatus*) is locally distributed over the sandy districts of Western Argentina, while the second (*C. retusa*) is from the Bolivian highlands. From the armadillos these tiny little creatures differ by having the upper surface of the head and body covered by a continuous mantle, formed of quadrangular horny shields underlain by thin bony plates, and gradually widening from the front of the head to the hinder end of the body, where it is abruptly truncated. In the Argentine species this mantle is attached to the body only along the line of the backbone, its under surface being hairy; but in the Bolivian form (which is referred by some writers to a separate genus, under the name of *Burmeisteria*) it is joined to the skin throughout its whole extent. The truncated hinder end of the body is protected by a solid bony shield with overlying horny scales; the short tail protruding through a notch in its lower border. The whole of the rest of the body is covered with long silky hair, which in the Argentine species is pure glistening white, while the mantle is pinkish. The minute ears are completely concealed by this fur; and both fore and hind feet have five claws, the front toes being connected to the base of the latter, while those of the hinder pair are free. In length the Argentine species measures only about 5 in., but the Bolivian form is somewhat larger. Pichiciagos inhabit sandy districts, where they excavate burrows with marvellous rapidity; and it is believed that the hinder shield is used as a rammer to close the burrow when tenanted, the creatures apparently making their exit by digging a fresh passage.

ORDER X.—EFFODIENTIA.

Aard-Varks and Pangolins.

Although, as stated above, the animals known as aard-varks and pangolins are generally included among the Edentata, they have little in common with the typical representatives of that order. Hence they are assigned to a distinct ordinal group termed the Effodientia. That group is typified by the aard-varks, and is only provisionally regarded as comprising the pangolins, which are perhaps entitled to constitute an order by themselves. The Effodientia resemble the Edentata in never having front teeth; but differ from all the latter in the absence of additional articular facets to the hinder trunk-vertebræ. More definitely they may be distinguished from the edentates as follows. When teeth are present these are of a totally different type to those of the latter, and when teeth are absent the hinder trunk-vertebræ lack the aforesaid additional articulations which are present in the toothless edentates.

Aard-Varks.

The aard-varks, or ant-bears (*Orycteropodidæ*), forming the typical members of the order, are now represented by two closely allied species of the genus *Orycteropus*, both of which are confined to the Ethiopian region. There is, however, evidence that during the Tertiary period aard-varks existed in the south of Europe. The existing forms are uncouth and strange-looking animals of large size, with the skin nearly naked, or sparsely covered with bristly hairs. The long and narrow head is furnished with greatly elongated, slender, and pointed ears, and terminates in a somewhat pig-like snout, in which are perforated the circular nostrils, while the mouth is tubular. The neck is short, the fore-quarters are comparatively short, the back is much arched, and the tail, which is nearly as long as the body, is thick, cylindrical, and tapering. In the short but powerful fore-limbs, the four toes are furnished with medium-sized strong nails ; while the hind-feet have five nearly equal toes, each bearing a nail. When walking, the entire soles are applied to the ground. Adult aard-varks usually have five pairs of cheek-teeth in each jaw, although from eight to ten pairs of upper teeth, and eight of lower ones are developed. Of these all but the last three have milk-predecessors, which never cut the gum. These teeth have no enamel, and are composed of a number of adherent polygonal denticules, traversed by a series of radiating tubes ; such a structure being quite unparalleled in the mammalian class. The tongue is cylindrical and extensile. In total length these animals may measure as much as 5 ft. In habits, aard-varks are nocturnal, burrowing, and insectivorous, feeding chiefly on ants and termites. Their powers of digging are very great, and in South Africa their burrows are generally constructed in the neighbourhood of termite hills.

Fig. 100—AARD-VARK (*Orycteropus capensis*).

Pangolins.

Very different both in external appearance and internal structure are the pangolins, or scaly ant-eaters, of the warmer parts of the Old World, constituting the family *Manidæ*, and all included in the single genus *Manis*. The most peculiar and striking feature of the animals is the investiture of the head, body, tail, and limbs in a complete coat of overlapping horny scales, so that the general appearance is much like the cone of a spruce-fir. Teeth are wanting ; and the skull is long, conical, and devoid of a zygomatic or cheek-arch, with a very slender lower jaw. The eyes are minute, and the external conchs of the ears rudimental. A few bristly hairs often occur between the scales, and the latter do not extend on to the under surface of the body, or the inner sides of the limbs. The long and worm-like tongue can be protruded a great distance in front of the tubular mouth. Each of the limbs is furnished with five toes, terminating in long powerful claws, of which the supporting bones are longitudinally split at their extremities; the front claws being much larger than the hinder ones, and the third toe in each foot superior in size to the rest. In walking, the front claws are bent beneath the soles, so that the weight of the body is mainly borne on the upper and outer sides of the third and fourth digits; but in the hind-limbs the whole sole of the foot is applied to the ground in the ordinary manner. The tail may be either long or medium. Collar-bones are wanting in the skeleton. Pangolins are confined to south-eastern Asia, and Africa south of the Sahara; the largest species, which measures upwards of 6 ft. in total length, being an inhabitant of West Africa. They resemble the aard-varks in feeding on ants and termites, which are licked up by the extensile tongue, after their hillocks have been laid open by the powerful claws of these animals. They are likewise nocturnal, and have the power of rolling themselves up into a ball, when they are completely secure from most enemies. Some of the African forms are more or less arboreal, but all the rest are purely terrestrial. Apparently only a single young is produced at a birth, for the nourishment of which the breast of the female carries a pair of teats.

Fig. 101.—A. Pangolin (*Manis*).

ORDER XI.—MARSUPIALIA.

Pouched Mammals.

The whole of the ten mammalian orders treated of above are collectively characterised by the circumstance that, during intra-uterine life, the blood-vessels of the fœtus are connected with those of the parent by means of a vascular organ known as the placenta. And it is due to this communication between the fœtal and maternal circulations that the young are born in the more or less highly-developed state characteristic of the whole assemblage. Collectively, the whole ten orders form a sub-class, known indifferently as the Eutheria or Placentalia. On the other hand, in the mammals forming the subject of the present section, a placenta is never developed, and there is consequently no direct connection between the circulatory systems of the parent and offspring, so that the young are produced in an exceedingly imperfect state of development. To this group, which forms a second sub-class, the name of Metatheria, or Implacentalia, is applied, while it is sometimes known as the Didelphia, on account of the completely double uterus or womb, and thereby contrasts with the Eutheria, in which the uterus is either single, or its two branches are united at their outlet. Hence the name Monodelphia is not unfrequently given to the first of the two sub-classes.

Whereas the Placentals, as already indicated, are split up into the ten orders described above, no such division seems practicable in the case of the Implacentals. Consequently the whole of them may be included in the single order Marsupialia, which may be popularly known either as Marsupials or Pouched Mammals.

Both the technical and popular names of the group are derived from the very general presence of a more or less fully-developed pouch on the abdominal surface of the body of the female, into which the imperfectly-developed young are transferred at birth, and where they remain until sufficiently advanced to take care of themselves. This pouch is, however, by no means universally present in the order, and cannot, therefore, be taken as its distinctive character. The imperfect state of development of the young at birth is, however, absolutely distinctive of all Marsupials; and when born the fœtuses resemble helpless and nearly motionless sacs of flesh, which are extremely small in proportion to the size of the parent, those of the large kangaroos being no larger than a man's thumb. These helpless little abortions are transferred by their parent immediately after birth to her teats, which are always situated within the pouch whenever that appendage is developed. Of course such ill-developed creatures can do nothing in the way of sucking by themselves, and Nature has accordingly provided a special arrangement by means of which their wants can be supplied. This arrangement takes the form of special muscles surrounding the milk-glands of the female, which by a spontaneous contraction compress the glands, and thus force the nourishing fluid down the throats of the immovable, naked young. In order to prevent the helpless young from being choked as they hang to the teats of the mother, the upper part of the larynx, or superior extremity of the windpipe, is so elongated as to project through the fauces, or hinder apertures of the mouth, and thus reach the internal nostrils. In consequence of this arrangement a closed passage is formed from the nostrils to the lungs, so that the fœtus can breathe while the milk flows down its throat. The young Marsupials thus nourished hang on to the nipples of the mother until their bodies and limbs are sufficiently developed to enable them to move about by themselves; but, as in the case of the kangaroos, they frequently resort to the pouch as a haven of refuge from danger for a long time after they have made their appearance in the outer world, and it is by no means uncommon for the pouch to be tenanted by helpless fœtuses and half-grown young. Except in the thylacine, where they are reduced to a rudimental condition, the pouch is supported by a pair of marsupial or epipubic bones attached to the front edge of the lower part of the pelvis; these bones being also present in the male.

In all the Pouched Mammals the brain is characterised by its proportionately small size, and the slight development of the convolutions on its surface. As already mentioned, the womb or uterus is double throughout its entire length; and in most cases the lower border of the angle, or hinder extremity of the inferior margin of each branch of the lower jaw is more or less strongly bent inwards. Although there is great variation, both numerically and structurally, in the dentition, yet there is one feature in regard to the teeth characteristic of the order generally. This relates to the mode of succession and replacement of the teeth. Whereas in the great majority of terrestrial Placentals the whole or the greater number of the teeth in advance of the true molars (which in that group are typically three in number on each side of each jaw) are preceded by milk or baby-teeth, in the Pouched Mammals only one tooth on each side of the jaws has such deciduous predecessor, and even this is not invariably developed. Regarding the dental succession in the order, the writer may quote the following passage from a work he has devoted to the group:—"The tooth thus replaced has been hitherto generally regarded as corresponding to the last or fourth milk-molar of the higher mammals, while the apparently replacing tooth has consequently been identified with the last or fourth pre-molar of the same. Recent researches have, however, tended to show that this is not a case of true replacement at all, and that the tooth, which makes its appearance late in life, is really a retarded pre-molar, which will consequently be the fourth of the full series, while the apparently replaced tooth is really the fifth. Be this as it may, the mode of succession is peculiar and unique; and it may be still convenient to speak of the replacing tooth as the fourth pre-molar, and the one it replaces as the fourth milk-molar." It should be added that some authorities consider the whole of the teeth of a Marsupial in advance of the molars as corresponding to the milk-series of the Placentals; and also that, when the full series is developed, there are four pairs of molars in each jaw in the present order.

That the Pouched Mammals are inferior in their organisation to the Placentals, is admitted by all; and they are also, as shown by their history in past times, among the oldest, if not actually the oldest, representatives of the entire class. There is, however, some difference of opinion among zoologists as to whether this group includes the ancestors from which the higher mammals have originated.

In regard to their geographical distribution, the Marsupials present some very curious features. At this present day their head-quarters are the Notogæic realm, comprising Australia, Papua, Celebes, and the other islands lying to the eastward of Wallace's line. And it is here that they attain their maximum development. Whereas, however, they form the great bulk of the mammalian population of Australia and Papua, in Celebes and the adjacent islands they constitute only a small minority of the fauna. Elsewhere, Pouched Mammals are found only in America, where they are represented by the opossums and selvas; and here they are chiefly restricted to South and Central America, constituting the Neogæic realm, only a single species, which is evidently an immigrant from the south, inhabiting the northern half of the continent. During the Secondary epoch of geological history, Marsupials of extinct generic types were abundant in the northern hemisphere, while in the succeeding Tertiary epoch opossums flourished in Europe and North America. It is thus evident that the ancestral Marsupials were driven from the northern hemisphere by the incoming of the higher forms of mammalian life to find a secure refuge in southern islands. And it further appears that while in South America they have had to compete with numerous types of Eutherians, in Australasia they have had the land pretty much to themselves, and have there been enabled to attain the wonderful development so especially characteristic of that region.

Kangaroo Tribe.

The kangaroos and their immediate allies form a large family (*Macropodidæ*) belonging to the first of the two great subordinal divisions of the Pouched Mammals, technically known as the Diprotodontia. This division, which is mainly confined to the Notogæic realm, is specially characterised by the number of the front or incisor teeth, of which there are never more than three pairs; the usual complement being three pairs in the upper jaw and one in the lower. The innermost, which are in some cases the only pair of incisors in both jaws, are always large, with sharp, cutting edges, while generally the upper canines, if present at all, are small, and the lower ones are absent. Among the cheek-teeth, the four pairs of molar-teeth have broad, quadrangular crowns, generally surmounted either by a pair of transverse ridges or by four blunt and rounded tubercles. Such a type of dentition is adapted for a vegetable diet, which is characteristic of the diprotodonts generally.

From the allied families the kangaroo tribe are specially distinguished by possessing rooted teeth, among which are three pairs of upper and one of lower incisors, the upper incisors being nearly vertical, while the large lower pair project nearly horizontally forwards, and in some cases are capable of working against one another like the blades of a pair of scissors. A small upper canine may or may not be present. The five-toed fore-limbs are in general much shorter and weaker than the hinder pair, while the latter are generally four-toed, and have the digit corresponding to the fourth of the typical series of five greatly developed at the expense of the other three, and forming the sole axis of support for the limb. Of the smaller toes, the second and third, or those on the inner side of the enlarged digit, are enclosed in a common skin, from which feature the hind-foot of this family is termed syndactylous. The great relative size and strength of the hind-limbs of the more typical members of the family is correlated with the upright position of the body, and the mode of progression is by enormous leaps. In repose the body is swung on a kind of pivot supported by the thigh-bones, the feet resting on the ground, and the large and thick tail serving to form the third leg of a tripod. Among the smaller forms the tail may be prehensile; and there are a few arboreal types in which the disproportion between the fore and hind limbs is very much less strongly marked than is the case with the typical kangaroos. All feed entirely on grass or leaves; and the stomach, as is so frequently the case with vegetable feeders, is of a somewhat complex type. In the females the opening of the pouch is forwards, so that when it contains young, these are in an upright position. The members of the family are confined to Australia, Tasmania, and New Guinea, with some of the neighbouring islands, such as the Aru group; the true kangaroos, which generally associate in large herd, or "mobs," and frequent either open grassy plains or timbered districts, being the largest existing members of the order.

The true kangaroos and wallabies, constituting the genus *Macropus*, are the typical representatives of a sub-family (*Macropodinæ*) characterised by the sub-equality of the claws of the fore-feet, which are never very large, and the generally elongated and pointed ears. In the dentition the last upper pre-molar is placed either immediately in the line of the molars, or is at most but slightly everted; and the molars, which increase regularly in size from the first to the fourth, are transversely ridged. As a rule, the upper canine is either very small or wanting, and the central pair of upper incisors are but slightly larger than the other two. From the other members of the sub-family the numerous species contained in the genus *Macropus* have the nose naked, the ears large, and the fur on the nape of the neck nearly always directed downwards. The disproportion between the length of the fore and hind limbs is very strongly marked; and the large claw of the hind-foot is always larger than the naked terminal pad on the sole of the same. The tail is thick, tapering, and evenly haired throughout; and there are four teats in the pouch of the females. There are upwards of twenty-three species included in the genus, which may be arranged under the heading of kangaroos proper, and larger and lesser wallabies. While the great grey kangaroo (*M. giganteus*) has the stature of a man, some of the smaller wallabies are no bigger than a rabbit. The great majority of the species are confined to Australia and Tasmania, but the agile wallaby (*M. agilis*) is common to Australia and New Guinea, while the Aru Island wallaby (*M. brunii*) is restricted to the Aru and Kei Islands, and the sombre wallaby (*M. browni*) is common to New Guinea and the New Britain group. From the true kangaroos the larger wallabies differ by their more brilliant coloration, and the presence of a longitudinal external bridge connecting the anterior ledge of the molars with the first of the two transverse ridges, coupled with the absence of a median longitudinal bridge between the same ledge and ridge. The habits of kangaroos and wallabies have been so often described as to render a repetition unnecessary.

Fig. 102.—BENNETT'S WALLABY (*Macropus ualabatus*).

From the preceding genus the six species of rock-wallabies (*Petrogale*) are distinguished by the shortness of the large claw of the hind-foot, which only slightly exceeds the naked pads on the sole in length, and by the long cylindrical tail being thinner, more thickly haired, and tufted at the tip. These wallabies are restricted to the Australian mainland, and differ from the true wallabies by inhabiting rocky districts instead of open plains. Their climbing and leaping powers are highly developed ; but the tail is employed solely as a balancing organ, and never as a support to the body. The presence of a horny spur or nail of unknown function at the tip of the long, tapering, and short-haired tail is a sufficiently distinctive feature of the three nail-tailed wallabies constituting the genus *Onychogale*. In addition to this, these animals have the nose hairy (with the exception in some cases of the base of the partition between the two nostrils); while the large claw of the hind-foot is long, narrow, compressed, and sharply pointed. There is also a difference in the form of the upper incisor teeth. Like the rock-wallabies, the members of this genus are restricted to continental Australia. The same is the case with the three species of hare-wallabies (*Lagorchestes*), in which the nose is entirely or partially covered with hair, the large claw of the hind-foot is long, stout, and not concealed by hair, while the rather short tail is evenly haired throughout its length. In some respects forming a connecting link between the genus *Macropus* and the under-mentioned tree-kangaroos, the three species of dorca kangaroos (*Dorcopsis*) are confined to New Guinea, and present the following distinctive features. The excess in the length of the hind over the fore-limbs is much less strongly marked than in the true kangaroo and wallabies ; there is a large and broad portion of the nose completely naked ; the head is long and narrow, with small ears ; the fur on the nape of the neck is entirely or partially reversed, so as to be directed forwards towards the head. In both jaws the fourth pre-molar is a compressed cutting tooth, greatly elongated, from before backwards, and having its surfaces marked by upright grooves, and a distinct ledge on the base of the inner side. The direction of the two series of cheek-teeth is nearly parallel. Although it is known that they are not arboreal, nothing definite has been ascertained in regard to the habits of these rather small kangaroos.

More remarkable than all are the tree-kangaroos (*Dendrolagus*), of which three species are known from New Guinea, and two from Queensland. In general build these animals are of fairly normal proportions, and quite unlike ordinary kangaroos, the fore-limbs being strong, stout, and nearly equal in length to the hinder pair. The naked portion of the nose is broad and covered with sparse hairs; and the fur on the nape of the neck is reversed, as is sometimes also that of the back. In the broad hind-foot the two united inner toes are not very markedly smaller than the other two; while the stout and strong claws of the latter are nearly as curved as those of the fore-foot. The elongated tail is thickly and evenly haired. One of the species measures 26 in. to the root of the tail. Regarding the habits of one of the Queensland species, Mr. E. R. Waite, writing in the "Proceedings of the Linnæan Society of New South Wales," observes that "the native name is mapi, and the animals are difficult to procure, as the blacks esteem them as a delicacy, and only surrender their captures when compelled. When a mapi is discovered, a fence 5 or 6 ft. in height and several feet in diameter is built of rattan and bushes round the tree. Some of the blacks enter the enclosure, ascend the tree, and drive the animal down. It usually jumps to the ground, often from a height of 20 ft. Should it elect to descend the trunk, it does so tail-foremost. On reaching the ground the animal is eventually caught by the men surrounding the enclosure, generally by the tail, which member is dragged through the fence, the unfortunate mapi being despatched with blows from a nulla-nulla. The blacks will not venture within the fence on account of the dread in which they hold the powerful claws of the animal. The natives who hunted for Dr. Lumholtz [the discoverer of the first example of this species made known to science] called the animal bungary, and adopted a somewhat different method of capture." Regarding the second Queensland species of the genus (*D. bennettianus*), a correspondent wrote to Mr. Waite as follows:—"The native name of the climbing kangaroo is charibeena. The blacks hunt them with dogs and are very fond of the flesh. I had often heard the blacks talking about them, but though I have been here nearly ten years it was only about three years ago that I succeeded in obtaining one. In the daytime they are found among the top branches of the trees and come down in the evening to feed upon creepers, ferns, and fruit. I have found several down on the flat land, but as a rule they seem to be most numerous on or near the top of the hill ridges here, which are about 1500 to 2500 ft. high. When found in the daytime, the animals generally sleep with the heads

Fig. 103.—TREE KANGAROO (*Dendrolagus*).

hanging on the breasts between the fore-limbs, and the tail is used as a balancing pole. At first I could not induce the blacks to catch any of the charibeenas, as they said that a full-grown one would show fight, but when I went with them and caught the first one myself with a lasso they saw how easy it was, and have since always caught them in this manner, except when out of reach ; in this case they make the animal jump; as soon as it reaches the ground one boy holds its head down with a forked stick while another passes a bag over its hind-quarters and slips it over its head. The best time to hunt them is early in the morning while the scent is fresh. A dingo, or mongrel—the former preferred—is used, and follows the scent to the foot of the tree which the kangaroo has climbed to camp for the day. If the tree be a low one, it is tolerably easy to find the animal, but it often happens that they go from one tree to another before they find a suitable 'camp,' and then it becomes necessary for a native to ascend a high tree in the vicinity so as to be able to look down on the surrounding trees, as the kangaroo sits right out in the sun and is more easily seen from above than from below. If one approaches quietly, it is quite easy to catch the animal by the tail and slip it into a bag while up the tree ; but the least noise rouses them, and it is surprising how quickly they can travel, jumping sometimes 20 to 30 ft. from one tree to another, and I have seen one jump fully 60 ft. from a high tree to the ground and not hurt itself at all. When jumping it seems always to land on its fore-feet, and though I have repeatedly shaken them down from great heights, I have never seen one injured, as they always, like a cat, fall on their feet. The tail is never used to hang by, only to balance with, though I have often seen one bend its tail over a branch while it reached down below the branch upon which it was sitting to secure some berries. These kangaroos can stiffen the tail so that it stands straight out like a rod. When caught and kept in captivity they soon become quiet and take readily to eating bread, sweet potatoes, apples, oranges, mangoes, and the rinds of sweet potatoes and yams ; also the leaves of several of the eucalypti, white cedar, and many other trees, the names of which I do not know. In the scrub they seem to have a partiality for the bird's-nest fern, the moustera, and a small climber like the pepper-plant, and eat almost any of the wild fruits which are so plentiful here. The males are very pugnacious, and if two of them be put into an enclosure together will often fight until one is killed. They spar with the fore-paws in quite a scientific manner, uttering grunts all the time, till one sees an opportunity of closing with the other, when he makes straight for the back of the neck, and if he succeeds in getting a grip with his teeth, he shakes the other like a dog does a rat. Some of the old males have quite a harem, and keep their wives from straying apart, and do not let any other males go near them. I have found several of these families numbering from three to five females and one male. The young males, and also the very old ones, are generally found by themselves, or two or three of them together without any females. I think they breed twice a year, and have only one young one at birth. The kangaroos are most plentiful among rocky hills, where the scrub is thick and stunted, and though they feed both on the ground and in the trees and among rocks, I fancy that they feed mostly in the two latter places." With the single species of banded-wallaby (*Lagostrophus fasciatus*) from Western Australia, we again come to a genus in which the general build is the same as in *Macropus;* the nose being naked, the hind-feet covered with long bristly hairs by which the claws are completely hidden, and the back marked by dark cross-bands. The banded-wallaby is a comparatively small species, measuring only about 18 in. to the root of the tail.

Still smaller are the rat-kangaroos, of Australia and Tasmania, of which there are several distinct generic types, collectively constituting the sub-family *Potoroinæ*. Of this group the distinctive characteristics are as follows:—In size all the forms are small, and may be compared to hares or rabbits, the ears being usually small and rounded. In the fore-feet the claws are greatly elongated, those of the three middle toes being disproportionately larger than those of the other two; as in the *Macropodinæ*, there are only four toes to the hind-foot; and the long tail is hairy. In the dentition the upper canines are invariably present and generally well-developed; the central pair of upper incisors have taller crowns than either of the other two; the fourth pre-molar, which is a compressed and trenchant tooth of great antero-posterior length, may either be set in the same line as the molars, or somewhat bent outwards in front; and the molars, which decrease in size from the first to the fourth, have tuberculated crowns. The three species of typical rat-kangaroos forming the genus *Potorous* vary somewhat in size, and have the nose naked, the ears very short and rounded, the front claws long and somewhat slender, the hind-limbs not very much larger than the front ones, the hind-feet very short, with naked and coarsely-granulated soles, and the tapering hairy tail devoid of a crest. In the dentition the fourth pre-molar has from two to four vertical grooves. These rat-kangaroos, which generally inhabit scrub-jungle, have their leaping powers much less strongly developed than in the allied genera. In running, both fore and hind limbs are brought into action. Nearly allied in external character is the South Australian plain rat-kangaroo (*Caloprymnus campestris*), which is an animal of comparatively large size, with the nose and ears as in the typical genus, the front claws long and strong, the hind-feet relatively long, with coarsely-granular soles, and the tail thin, cylindrical, and covered evenly with short hair. While the last pre-molar is similar to that of the preceding genus, the skull is generally like that of the next. The four species of prehensile-tailed rat-kangaroos (*Bettongia*) are sufficiently distinguished by the feature from which they take their popular name. The hair on the tail is long, and forms a more or less distinct crest; the last pre-molar is much elongated, with from seven to fifteen distinctly-marked, oblique grooves on the sides; and the squared molars, of which the fourth is much the smallest, carry four tubercles. These little animals are completely terrestrial and nocturnal, using their prehensile tails solely for the purpose of carrying bundles of grass and twigs to their nest; such bundles being held by the tail being bent down over and round them. Three of the species are Australian, and the fourth Tasmanian. The last member of the sub-family is the rufous rat-kangaroo (*Æpyprymnus rufescens*) of New South Wales, in which the nose is partially hairy, the ears are somewhat elongated, the hind-feet long, with narrow, granulated soles, and the tail evenly-haired. The long and narrow last pre-molar has from seven to eight vertical grooves, but no inner ledge; and the molars are oblong, with the tubercles less distinct and tending more to form ridges than in the other genera, while the decrease in size from the first to the last is less marked. Like the other members of the group, this animal is nocturnal, but it is remarkable for its speed and the great length of its leaps when disturbed.

Of especial interest is the tiny musk-kangaroo (*Hypsiprymnodon moschatus*) of Northern Queensland, since it forms a connecting link between the kangaroo tribe on the one hand, and the phalangers on the other. Indeed, it is chiefly owing to the presence of a pocket like pit on the outer side of the hinder part of the bone of the lower jaw that it is referred to the present rather than to the following family. It is regarded as representing a distinct sub-family (*Hypsiprymnodontinæ*) of the *Macropodidæ*, characterised by the small, weak, and nearly equal-sized claws, the presence of five toes in the hind foot (the first of which can be opposed to the rest), the naked and scaly tail, and the oblique position of the short last pre-molar tooth. In size this creature is very small, with a rat-like bodily form, a completely bare nose, large, thin, and naked ears, the hind and fore limbs of nearly equal length, and adapted for walking, the first toe of the hind-foot elongated and without a claw, the fourth toe of the same not abnormally large, and the tail cylindrical and tapering, with some hair at the root. The musk-kangaroo is a partially arboreal animal, which is mainly diurnal, and frequents scrubs on the banks of rivers and in the coast-range. Either one or two young are produced at a birth; and the characteristic musky odour is more pronounced in the female than in her partner.

Phalanger Tribe.

Owing to the intermediate characters presented by the musk-kangaroo, the differentiation of the phalanger tribe (*Phalangeridæ*) from the *Macropodidæ* is by no means so easy as would be the case were that creature non-existent. There are, however, two leading features which may be regarded as absolutely distinctive of the former group. In the first place, each branch of the lower jaw-bone lacks the deep pocket-like pit on the outer side of its hinder extremity so characteristic of the kangaroo tribe; and, secondly, the aperture of the pouch of the female is directed backwards instead of forwards. Among other more or less distinctive features, the following may be enumerated:—Five toes are present in both the hind and fore feet, those of the latter being usually of nearly equal size; while in those of the former the second and third are syndactylous, the fourth is the largest, the fifth but little smaller, and the first large, opposable to the rest, and terminating in a broad, clawless pad. With the exception of the koala, the tail is long and generally prehensile; and the stomach is simple. The dentition is extremely variable, owing to the frequent presence of a number of small functionless teeth in the front portion of the jaws. It may be said, however, that, as a general rule, there are three pairs of upper, and one of functional lower incisors, and that the latter never have the scissor-like action characteristic of the kangaroos. The last of the two or three pre-molars usually present is generally furnished with a rather sharp-cutting edge, and is placed obliquely to the line of the molars, with its front edge everted; and the molars, of which there are usually four pairs, have either blunt tubercles, or sharp-cutting crests. The family includes not only the animals properly known as cuscuses and phalangers (the mis-called opossums of the Australian colonists), but likewise the flying-phalangers, the koala or native bear, and the long-snouted pouched mouse. The geographical range of this extensive family includes not only Australia, Tasmania, and Papua, but likewise Celebes, and some of the other Austro-Malayan islands. The koala and long-snouted pouched mouse are, however, exclusively Australian. All are essentially arboreal and nocturnal in their mode of life, most using their prehensile tails to assist in climbing, while a few are enabled to take (like the flying squirrels) long flying leaps by the aid of parachute-like expansions of skin from the sides of the body. The great majority of the phalanger tribe are vegetable feeders, subsisting mainly on fruits and leaves; but a few consume insects, which form either the whole or a portion of their diet, and some are carnivorous.

The peculiar animal known as the koala (*Phascolarctus cinereus*), which presents some external resemblance to a small bear, is the sole representative of a sub-family (*Phascolarctinæ*) characterised by the following distinctive features:—The tail is absent, the muzzle short and broad, the tongue non-extensile, the cheeks furnished with pouches for the storage of food, the intestine provided with a cæcum, or blind appendage, the teeth relatively large, and only a single pair of pre-molars in the upper jaw. In size the koala is a rather large animal, measuring about 32 in. in length. Its build is stout and clumsy, and the thick woolly fur is generally greyish above and whitish below. The large ears are thickly haired and ragged at the edges; the front toes are sub-equal in length, the fourth being the longest and the first the shortest, while both the first and second can be opposed to the other two. The strong claws are thick and sharp, and in both the fore and hind limbs the soles of the feet are simply granulated, and have no striated pads. The female has a single pair of teats. In the skeleton there are eleven pairs of ribs, and the upper molar teeth have short, broad, and squared crowns, bearing curved longitudinal crests, of which the convexity is directed outwards. The koala, which is confined to Eastern Australia, is a dull, sluggish creature, addicted to crawling on the stems and branches of gum-trees in a deliberate lazy manner, and feeding mainly on leaves and flowers. During the daytime it generally lies asleep in the hollow of some forest giant, but at night prowls among the topmost branches in search of food, the females carrying their offspring securely perched on their backs, where the woolly fur affords them a secure foothold. Only a single young one is produced at a birth, and the adults seem to be more or less completely solitary animals.

Fig. 104.—KOALA (*Phascolarctus cinereus*).

The second sub-family (*Phalangerinæ*), which includes all the other members of the family save one, may be defined as follows:—The tail, which is always well-developed, is generally prehensile, the muzzle is short and broad, the tongue is incapable of extension, there are no cheek-pouches, the intestine has a cæcum, the stomach is simple, and the teeth are comparatively large. The first and typical genus (*Phalanger*) is represented by the cuscuses, of which there are five species, ranging from Celebes and the Moluccas to Australia and New Guinea. They are rather large, or medium-sized, somewhat cat-like animals, of stout build, with thick and woolly fur, which may be either coarse and wiry, or fine and silky, and moderate-sized or small ears. In the fore-feet the toes are nearly equal in length, their relative lengths being in the order 4, 3, 5, 2, 1. The long claws of all the feet are stout and curved, and the naked soles are striated, with large and ill-defined cushion-like pads. The prehensile tail is stout and strong, with its terminal portion naked, and either smooth or granulated. Two pairs of teats are borne by the female. Cuscuses are slow and sleepy animals, completely arboreal and mainly herbivorous in their habits, passing the day curled up asleep among the densest foliage of forest trees, and only becoming active as the shades of evening approach. A great amount of variation obtains in the coloration of the different sexes and individuals of the same species, while there is frequently some difference in the teeth. Whereas in the black cuscus of Celebes (*P. ursinus*) both sexes are of a uniformly dark blackish brown colour; in the widely distributed spotted cuscus (*P. maculatus*) the sexes are generally different, and the coloration takes the form of various combinations of white, rufous, and black, the females being generally grey and black, while the smaller males are usually spotted, although occasionally they resemble an ordinary grey female, save for a few indistinct whitish spots on the flanks and back. Nearly allied to the cuscuses are the true phalangers (*Trichosurus*)—the opossums of the colonists—of which the two species are restricted to the Australian mainland and Tasmania. These also are large, stoutly-built cat-like animals, with thick, woolly fur, and short or medium ears. The front toes may be distinguished from those of the cuscuses in that relative lengths follow the order 4, 3, 2, 5, 1; the claws being large and strong, and the soles of the hind-feet densely haired beneath the heel, but elsewhere naked, and furnished with low, rounded, ill-defined pads. In the powerful prehensile tail the terminal third or half is bare inferiorly, and the extreme tip devoid of hair all round. A peculiar gland is situated in the centre of the chest. Among the teeth, the molars have four cusps, tending to unite into a pair of transverse ridges; and the last pre-molar, which closely approximates to the corresponding tooth of *Hypsiprymnodon*, is large, placed obliquely, and marked by vertical groovings. The common phalanger (*T. vulpinus*) takes up its habitation in the branches of the tallest red and blue gum-trees of the Australian and Tasmanian forests, passing the day in slumber, and wandering forth at night to brouse on their leaves, bulbs, and seeds. In climbing, they are much aided by their highly prehensile tails; and on the rare occasions when they descend to the ground, it is probably for the purpose of drinking. In the breeding season, and less commonly at other times, phalangers utter a loud cry; and, as a rule, but one offspring is produced at a birth, although there may occasionally be a pair. More numerous, and at the same time more widely distributed than the preceding, are the ring-tailed-phalangers (*Pseudochirus*), of which there are eleven specific representatives, whose

Fig. 105.—SPOTTED CUSCUS (*Phalanger maculatus*).

Fig. 106.—COMMON PHALANGER (*Trichosurus vulpinus*).

geographical range includes New Guinea, as well as Australia and Tasmania. While some are as large as the true phalangers, others are considerably smaller; but all possess short and rather woolly fur, and stout and medium sized ears, which are well haired on the hind aspect. The relative lengths of the toes of the fore-foot hold the same order as in the cuscuses; but the first and second toes resemble those of the koala in being markedly opposable to the other three. In both feet the claws are of moderate length, and the bare soles are provided with large striated pads. The long and tapering tail has the lower surface of the extremity devoid of hair for a variable distance, and is highly prehensile. Four teats are present in the female. The upper molars are large and oblong, with the tubercles modified into sharp cusps, from which proceed crescentic ridges; the corresponding lower teeth having a nearly similar structure. In habits the common ring-tailed-phalanger differs from the true phalangers in that it prefers the so-called tea-scrub to the gum-trees; and also in that it generally associates in small colonies. These animals construct small nests, not unlike the drey of a squirrel; and whereas usually but a single young one is produced at a birth, occasionally as many as three may be found in the pouch. Nearly allied in the structure of its skull and teeth to the preceding genus is the taguan flying-phalanger (*Petauroides volans*), which is the first of three genera provided with a parachute for the purpose of taking flying leaps from tree to tree. This species is of comparatively large size, measuring about 17 in. to the root of the tail, while the latter is about 20 in. in length. The fur of the body is remarkable for its long, soft, and silky character; the unusually large ears are oval in form, and bare internally, but hairy on the outside; and the skin of the flanks is expanded to form a parachute. The long claws are much curved and sharply pointed; and the tail is long, cylindrical, and evenly covered with bushy hair, its extreme tip being prehensile and destitute of hair on the lower surface. The habits of this and the other flying-phalangers are very similar to those of the flying-squirrels; and in Australia these animals are commonly known by the latter name. The present species is confined to Eastern Australia.

Two species of rather small phalangers, ranging from Northern Australia to New Guinea and the Aru Islands, constitute a genus (*Dactylopsila*) distinguished by the great elongation of the fourth digit of the front paws, and the conspicuous black and white longitudinal striping of the fur of the body. In these striped-phalangers, which are devoid of a parachute, the oval ears have nearly naked tips. In the front paws the length of the digits follows the order 4, 3, 5, 2, 1, the inequality in their lengths, as in the hind-feet—where the fourth and fifth are much elongated—being very marked. A prominent soft pad is situated on the wrist; and the claws are long. The long and cylindrical tail is evenly bushy throughout, except the under surface of the tip, which is bare. The oblong molars bear four simple tubercles. Some degree of doubt exists as to the reason for the elongation of the fourth digit of the fore-paws. The suggestion has, indeed, been made that the elongation is for the purpose of extracting insects and grubs from beneath the bark and from crevices in trees, and consequently that these phalangers are largely, if not exclusively insectivorous; but other writers consider that they subsist on leaves. From the striped-phalangers the little Leadbeater's-phalanger (*Gymnobelideus leadbeateri*) of Victoria, which measures only 5½ in. to the root of the long tail, differs by the normal proportions of the toes; the length of those of the fore-feet following the order 4, 3, 5, 2, 1. The claws are rather short; the large ears entirely naked and untufted; and the tail, which exceeds the head and body in length by about an inch, is cylindrical and bushy. With the exception of the last, which is triangular, the upper molars are square, with rounded corners, and carry four tubercles. Several peculiarities characterise the skull. From their similarity in cranial and dental characters to the last, it is believed that the three species of flying-phalangers forming the genus *Petaurus* have been evolved either from an ancestral form of *Gymnobelideus*, or some nearly allied type. These animals, which are of small or medium size, have a soft and silky fur, rather large, oval, and almost naked ears, and a broad parachute-like expansion of the skin of the flanks. In the fore-foot the toes gradually increase in length from the first, the fifth attaining the maximum elongation in the largest species, and the fourth in the two smaller ones. The claws, which are longer than in the preceding genus, are strong, sharp, and highly curved; and the long tail is evenly bushy throughout. Both the chest and the crown of the head bear a gland. The range of the genus includes New Guinea and part of Australia, extending from Victoria to the islands of the Halmahera group. All the three species are inhabitants of Australia; a variety of one (*P. breviceps*) being peculiar to New Guinea, New Britain, the Halmahera group, and certain other islands. Writing of one of the species, Bennett observes that "it retires either between the forked branches or in the hollow cavities of the trees during the day to sleep, and at night passes from one to another by flying leaps, aided by its parachute-like membrane, descending to the ground only from unavoidable necessity, such as when the trees are so far apart as to render it impossible to traverse the space by leaping."

Fig. 107.—FLYING-PHALANGER (*Petaurus breviceps*).

With the pretty little dormouse-phalangers (*Dromicia*), of which there are four species, ranging over New Guinea, Western Australia, and Australia, we revert to a genus unprovided with a parachute. In addition to this feature and their small dimensions, the dormouse-phalangers are characterised by their large, thin, and almost naked ears; the normal proportions of the toes, which in the fore-limb follow the order 3, 4, 2, 5, 1, as regards relative length; and the short and rudimental fore-claws. The cylindrical tail is well furred only near the root, being elsewhere scaly and sparsely covered with short hairs, except at the extremity, where it is roughened and completely naked beneath, and endowed with the power of prehension. With the exception of the last, which may be wanting, the molars have regularly rounded crowns, carrying four tubercles each. These little animals, one of which is rather smaller than the British dormouse, are purely nocturnal creatures, living on fruits, honey, and insects, and hiding during the daytime in the hollows, or beneath the dead strips of bark which hang down from the stems of gum-trees. One species undergoes a partial hibernation during the colder months of the year. A curious resemblance is presented by the pretty little pen-tailed-phalanger of New Guinea (*Distœchurus pennatus*) to the pen-tailed tree-shrew (*Ptilocercus*) among the Insectivora described on page 44, in that both have the long hairs of the elongated tail arranged in two opposite lateral rows like the vanes of a feather. Whereas, however, in the shrew these vanes occupy only the terminal portion of the tail, in the phalanger they extend uninterruptedly throughout its length. In addition to this very important feature and the absence of a parachute, the pen-tailed-phalanger is characterised by its rather short and thinly-haired ears, which have several tufts near the base, the normal length of the toes, and the sharp and curved claws. The molars, of which there are invariably but three pairs, are small and rounded, with smooth, unridged cusps, and the last pre-molar is very small in the upper jaw, and wanting in the lower. Only a single pair of teats is present in the female. The third genus in which a parachute is developed is *Acrobates*, comprising the two species of pigmy-flying-phalangers, one of which is Australian and the other Papuan. And since these beautiful little animals, although considerably smaller, resemble the pen-tailed-phalanger, not only in the structure of their skulls and teeth, but likewise in their vaned tails, it is pretty evident that they are derived from the same ancestral stock. The pigmy-phalangers have moderate-sized ears, a narrow parachute-like expansion of skin along the flanks, and the toes—which are of normal proportions—terminating in a broad striated pad. In the fore-foot the length of the digits follows the general order of 4, 3, 5, 2, 1, and the claws, although not very prominent, are sharp and well developed. Additional differences from *Distœchurus* are to be found in the larger size of the upper pre-molar, and the presence of the corresponding tooth in the lower jaw, and likewise in the existence of two pairs of teats in the pouch of the female. The Australian species, which measures 3 in. to the root of the tail, is a far less brilliantly-coloured animal than its Papuan ally. It is commonly known as the flying-mouse, and was formerly abundant about Port-Jackson, but nothing very definite has been ascertained in regard to its mode of life.

The last sub-family (*Tarsipedinæ*) of the tribe under consideration is represented only by the elegant little long-snouted-phalanger (*Tarsipes rostratus*) of Western Australia. The sub-family is characterised by the elongation of the tail, the long and slender muzzle, the extensile tongue, the absence of a cæcum, or blind appendage to the intestine, and the minute size and rudimental character of the cheek-teeth. As a genus, the animal, which measures about 3 in. to the root of the tail, may be characterised as follows:—The size is small and the form light and graceful; while the long and narrow head is furnished with ears of moderate size, which are but thinly covered with hair; and the soles of the feet are naked and granulated. With the exception of those of the united second and third toes of the hind-foot, the claws are rudimental; and the tail, which exceeds the head and body in length by about an inch, is thinly haired and prehensile. Four teats are present in the pouch of the female. Although the upper canine and the lower incisor teeth are fairly well developed, there are at most but three pairs of molars, and the pre-molars are reduced to a single pair in the upper jaw. A remarkable feature is the absence of any inflection of the angle of the very slender lower jaw. The long-snouted-phalanger appears to be an exceedingly rare animal, inhabiting flowering shrubs, from the blossoms of which it extracts honey by the insertion of its highly extensile tongue.

The three species of wombat, all of which are confined to Tasmania and Australia south of the tropics, and are included in the single genus *Phascolomys*, are the sole representatives of the third and last family of

Australian diprotodont marsupials (*Phascolomyidæ*). They are clumsily-built animals, differing from all the members of the group hitherto mentioned by their burrowing habits; and they may be regarded as occupying among the Australian fauna the position held in other regions by the burrowing rodents. Curiously enough, they also approximate to the latter order in the nature of their dentition, the incisors being reduced to a single cutting pair in each jaw, behind which comes a long gap, without any canines, till the cheek-teeth are reached. Stout and clumsy in form, the wombats have a short and broad muzzle; thick, short, and strong limbs of nearly equal length in front and behind; the fore-feet with five nearly sub-equal and powerfully-clawed toes; the first hind-toe short and clawless, the remaining toes of the same foot having strong and curved claws, and the second and third imperfectly united by a common skin; and the tail rudimental. Internally, the stomach is simple, and the intestine is furnished with a cæcum. The teeth are rootless throughout life; the large, curved, and chisel-like incisors having enamel only on the front and sides; and the five pairs of cheek-teeth are strongly curved, the molars consisting of two lobes, but the pre-molars with only one. As regards their habits, it will suffice to say that wombats are harmless, inoffensive animals, burrowing deeply in the ground, and subsisting on the roots which they thus disinter. They are entirely nocturnal, never issuing from their holes till evening, and returning to them with the first rays of morning.

Wombats.

A distinct family (*Epanorthidæ*) is now represented solely by two small rat-like South American animals, which, from the estate where the second example was obtained, may be known as the selvas. One was originally described and referred to the present order under the name of *Hyracodon fuliginosus*, in the year 1863, upon the evidence of a specimen obtained in Ecuador; but the description was so insufficient that naturalists had no clue to its affinities. In the autumn of 1895 a second example was obtained from Colombia, which showed that it indicated a type of marsupial hitherto known only from fossil forms occurring in the Tertiary rocks of Patagonia, which have been described under the names of *Epanorthus, Abderites,* etc. As the name *Hyracodon* had been previously employed for an extinct genus of mammals, the selvas were at the same time re-christened *Cœnolestes.*

Selvas.

The selvas have an elongated skull somewhat like that of the Australian-bandicoots, with four pairs of upper incisor teeth and a large pair of canines, and thus resemble the Polyprotodont type. In the lower jaw there is, however, a single pair of horizontally-projecting lower incisors, not unlike those of the kangaroo, behind which are several pairs of small functionless teeth representing the other incisors, canine, and earlier pre-molars. In both jaws the four pairs of molars are oblong teeth, with four blunt cusps, and thus totally unlike the corresponding teeth of the opossums and other members of the Polyprotodont sub-order. The feet are of normal type, with five toes each, of which the first appears to be opposable in a limited degree to the others; and the rat-like tail is partially prehensile towards the extremity. Externally, the selvas look very like small, blackish rats, with a sharp nose.

In all probability, these animals and their extinct allies are descendants from a group of Polyprotodont Marsupials whose remains are found in the Tertiary deposits of Patagonia, and whose ancestors reached South America by means of a land connection—perhaps by way of the Antarctic continent—with

Australia. Unlike the opossums, which are comparatively recent immigrants from the North, the selvas, like the edentates, belong to the original primitive fauna of South America, which was first developed when that country was completely cut off from North America by a sea occupying the site of the Isthmus of Panama and Mexico.

Bandicoot Tribe.

The bandicoots (*Peramelidæ*) are the first representatives of the second great subordinal division of the pouched mammals, technically known as the Polyprotodontia. This name is assigned from the circumstance that these animals differ from the preceding group by the larger number of incisor teeth, of which there are never less than three pairs in each jaw, while more generally there are four or five pairs of these teeth in the upper, and three or four in the lower jaw. These incisors are always relatively small and of subequal size, and they are flanked by large, tusk-like canines, close behind which are the anterior cheek-teeth. Nearly always the cusps of the molars are numerous and sharp; and the whole dentition is of a markedly carnivorous type. In all their characters, the Polyprotodonts are a less specialised group than the Diprotodonts; and they have at the present day a wide geographical distribution, being represented not only in the Notogæic realm, but likewise in South America, and, more sparingly, in North America. They were also living in various parts of the world during the Tertiary and Secondary epochs. In Australasia, and to a certain extent in South America, the members of the present group—all of which are either flesh or insect eaters—take the place of the Carnivora and Insectivora of other parts of the world.

From the other three families included in the sub-order the bandicoots are broadly distinguished by the circumstance that the second and third toes of the hind-foot are reduced in size, and enclosed in a common skin in the same manner as among the Diprotodonts. In addition to this very striking and characteristic feature, the members of the present family have the hind-limbs markedly longer than the front pair; in the fore-limbs the three middle toes, or occasionally only two, are long and furnished with claws, the others being rudimental or wanting; and the hind-foot has either four or five toes of very unequal lengths, the first toe being rudimental or absent, the second and third small and united, and the fourth the stoutest. As in the phalangers, the opening of the pouch of the female is directed backwards. Internally, there is a cæcum to the intestine; and in the skeleton collar-bones are lacking. In the upper jaw there may be either four or five pairs of incisor teeth, whereas in the lower jaw there are invariably three. The tail, which is always relatively long, is never prehensile. Bandicoots are restricted to Australia, Tasmania, New Guinea, and certain of the adjacent islands, such as the Aru, Kei, and Duke of York group. In habits they are mainly fossorial and insectivorous, although a few are more or less completely omnivorous. Among the more aberrant forms are the rabbit-bandicoots (*Peragale*), of which there appear to be two species, both restricted to the Australian mainland. Their most distinctive feature, and the one from which they derive their name, is the great length of the ears. In form these animals are light and delicate, with a long and narrow muzzle. The three middle toes of the fore-foot are long and furnished with stout, curved claws, and in the hind-foot all trace of the first toe is wanting externally. The hind-limbs greatly exceed the front ones in length; the soles of the hind-feet are hairy; and there is a distinct crest of hair on the upper surface of the terminal half of the tail. The upper jaw carries five pairs of incisor teeth; and the molars have a quadrangular or rounded section. In size and habits, these bandicoots, which are omnivorous, may be compared to a rabbit, which they resemble in their habit of constructing burrows in places where the soil is suitable. The true bandicoots (*Perameles*), of which there are about a dozen different species, are comparatively small animals, ranging over Australia, Tasmania, Papua, and some of the neighbouring islands. While some are heavy and ungainly, and others light and elegant in bodily form, all have long and pig-like snouts, but the length of the ears is variable. The three middle toes of the fore-foot are nearly equal in length, and furnished with strong, curved claws; while in the hind-foot there is a clawless first toe, the second and third digits having flat twisted nails, the fourth exceeding all the rest in length, and carrying a stout pointed claw, and the fifth being similar but smaller. The tapering tail may be either clothed with short hair or almost bare; and there are three pairs of teats in the pouch of the female. In the dentition there are usually five pairs of upper incisors; and the upper molars, which may be either squared or triangular in form, carry sharp cusps. They are exclusively terrestrial and nocturnal in their habits; and apparently feed chiefly on earth-worms, although they also consume insects, grubs, bulbs, roots, and fallen berries and fruit. Bandicoots make sleeping-nests of dried grass, leaves, and sticks; and, in spite of ridding them of worms and insects, do much harm to gardens and corn-fields. The third and last genus of the family is represented only by the pig-footed bandicoot (*Chœropus castanotis*) of Australia, which, although allied to Gunn's bandicoot (*Perameles gunni*), is clearly distinguished by the very peculiar structure of the feet. In the fore-foot, the first and fifth toes are absent, the fourth is rudimental, while the second and third are alone fully developed and furnished with long, slender claws. Considerably different is the structure of the hind-foot, in which the first toe is wanting, and the fifth rudimental, the fourth being very large. Of a grizzled grey colour, and measuring about ten inches to the root of the tail, the pig-footed bandicoot is an animal of light and slender build, with a short and narrow muzzle, long and slender ears, and a short, cylindrical tail, slightly crested on its upper surface. There are five pairs of upper incisors; and the pouch of the females contains eight teats. In its habits this animal closely resembles the other members of the family, burrowing holes in the ground, and being omnivorous in diet, although feeding chiefly upon insects. In spite of the number of its teats, the female only produces two young ones at a birth.

Fig. 108.—A Bandicoot (*Perameles*).

Dasyure Tribe.

The second of the four families of the Polyprotodonts is characterised by having a simpler type of foot-structure than obtains in the *Peramelidæ*, the second and third digits of the hind-foot being completely separate. Hence, it is probable that the *Dasyuridæ* (as the present family is termed) constitute the original stock from which the *Peramelidæ* have branched off. In addition to this primary feature in the structure of the limbs, it may be noticed that there are five toes to the fore-foot, and that in the hind-foot the first toe is either small or wanting, while the other four are pretty equally developed. The long and hairy tail is never prehensile; and the pouch, when developed, opens forwards and downwards. Internally, the stomach is simple, and the intestine devoid of a blind appendage. There are four pairs of incisor teeth in the upper jaw, and three in the lower; the entire dentition being of an essentially carnivorous type, the upper molars having more or less distinctly triangular crowns bearing a number of sharp cusps. Indeed, although a few of the smaller kinds are more or less completely insectivorous, the present family includes all the truly flesh-eating Australian Marsupials, as it does the largest members of the entire sub-order. Geographically, the range of the group embraces Australia, Tasmania, and New Guinea, together with many of the adjacent islands, exclusive of the Austro-Malayan group.

Fig. 109.—TASMANIAN-WOLF (*Thylacinus cynocephalus*).

Its large size, generally wolf-like form, and striped body are sufficient to distinguish at a glance the thylacine or Tasmanian-wolf (*Thylacinus cynocephalus*) from all its kindred. This animal, which measures about 44 in. to the root of the tail, has a large wolf-like head, with moderate-sized ears, a long and slender muzzle, and the elongated jaws armed with very powerful teeth. The long tail is covered with close, short hair. All the feet are markedly digitigrade, the five toes of the front pair being armed with short, thick, conical claws, while the hind-feet have but four toes each. The back is marked with transverse black bands on a tawny ground. Only four teats are present in the pouch of the female, and the marsupial bones are rudimental. The full marsupial number of three pairs of pre-molar teeth are present. Although this ferocious animal appears to be now restricted to Tasmania, the genus was represented at a comparatively recent epoch on the Australian mainland. It is a nocturnal creature, inhabiting caves and hollows among rocky fastnesses; and, if seen abroad by daylight, is dull and sluggish. It never hunts in pack, and its sole cry appears to be a dull guttural growl. At the present day sheep are the chief prey of the thylacine, as these are both more numerous and easier to capture than the diprotodont marsupials upon which it formerly lived. Four is the number of young produced in a litter. Although but little more than half its size, the Tasmanian devil (*Sarcophilus ursinus*) is an even more sanguinary and destructive creature, killing sheep and fowls, apparently for the mere pleasure of slaughter, long after its appetite is satiated. In form this animal is very stout and powerful, having

Fig. 110.—TASMANIAN-DEVIL (*Sarcophilus ursinus*).

a short and broad muzzle, wide and rounded ears, an evenly-haired tail of medium length, and plantigrade feet, in the front pair of which the toes are armed with strong, curved claws; while in the hind pair the first digit is absent, and the naked soles lack well-defined pads. In colour the body is blackish, flecked with white. As regards the dentition, this differs from that of the thylacine in that there are only two pairs of pre molars in each jaw; while the upper molars, with the exception of the fourth pair, are strong, triangular, and much shorter and wider. The distribution of the Tasmanian devil, both now and in the past, is precisely similar to that of its cousin the thylacine.

Under the common title of native cats are included, in Australia, a number of considerably smaller predaceous marsupials, usually showing a slender, weasel-like form of body, although a few are more stoutly built. These constitute the genus *Dasyurus* of zoologists, of which the leading characteristics are as follows:—The ears are elongated and narrow; the bare nose is marked by a deep, vertical groove running down to the upper lip; the long tail is uniformly and thickly haired throughout its length; the feet are plantigrade, with sharp, curved claws, the first toe in the hinder pair being either rudimental or absent, and the partially or wholly naked soles of the hind-feet are granulated. In all cases the body is marked with spots. The pouch, which opens vertically downwards, contains either six or eight teats. The teeth are numerically the same as in *Sarcophilus*, but much less strongly developed. Dasyures are found alike in Australia, Tasmania, New Guinea, and some of the neighbouring islands. They differ from the two preceding genera, in that the majority are more or less completely arboreal in their habits; and they feed not only on flesh, but likewise on insects, being especially destructive to birds and their eggs. The largest among the six species is the spotted-tailed dasyure (*D. maculatus*), from east and south-east Australia, and Tasmania, which may be compared roughly in size to a cat, and differs from the rest by having the tail, as well as the body, spotted. It is further characterised by having well-defined, transversely striated pads on the soles of the feet, from which it may be inferred that its habits are largely arboreal. The pouched-mice (*Phascologale*), of which no less than thirteen species are recognised, are smaller animals, differing from the dasyures in the absence of spots on the fur, and the practical want of the pouch in the female. In all, the form is slender and graceful; the ears are rounded; the tail is long, but may be either bushy, crested, or nearly bare, and the broad and short feet terminate in sub-equal toes furnished with sharp, curved claws. In the hind-foot the first toe is, however, short and clawless, and the soles of the feet are naked and smooth, with five transversely striated pads, the first toe frequently having its pad divided. Except in one species, where the first lower pair are wanting, there are three pairs of pre-molars in each jaw. The pouched-mice, which range over Australia, Tasmania, New Guinea, the Aru Islands, etc., are thoroughly arboreal animals, feeding exclusively on insects, and

Fig. 111 —SPOTTED-DASYURE (*Dasyurus viverrinus*).

thus taking the place of the tree-shrews of the Oriental region. Whereas the largest is not bigger than an ordinary rat, the others are considerably smaller. In all the Australian species the fur of the back is uniformly coloured, and the same is the case with a few of the forms inhabiting Papua, although the majority from that area are longitudinally striped. Four nearly allied animals, which may be known as the narrow-footed pouched-mice, and constitute the genus *Sminthopsis*, are easily distinguished from the foregoing by the narrow feet which are either partially haired or naked, with the bare portion granulated, and with or without pads, the latter, when present, being either smooth or but faintly striated. These pouched-mice are restricted to Australia and Tasmania, and differ from the members of the preceding genus in being strictly terrestrial, so that in this respect they are comparable to ordinary shrews. More markedly distinct is the long-legged pouched-mouse (*Antechinomys laniger*), from the interior of New South Wales and southern Queensland, which is a mouse-like, leaping animal specially characterised by the great elongation of the hind-limbs and the loss of the first toe in the hind-foot. The fur is uniformly coloured, the tail is long and tufted, and the ears are of large size. These little creatures, which subsist exclusively on insects, inhabit open sandy districts. As the members of the two preceding genera respectively represent the tree-shrews and ordinary shrews, so the present form may be likened to the African jumping-shrews.

One of the most remarkable of all the pouched mammals is the banded ant-eater (*Myrmecobius fasciatus*) of south and west Australia, which presents a curious approximation in the number and structure of its teeth to some of the extinct Secondary marsupials of Europe. By many writers it is regarded as the representative of a distinct family by itself, and it certainly constitutes a sub-family (*Myrmecobiinæ*) of the *Dasyuridæ*, which may be distinguished from the whole of the foregoing genera (*Dasyurinæ*) by the following features :—In place of being of normal proportions, the tongue is long, cylindrical, and extensile; the nose is naked and grooved below; the pointed lower lip projects in advance of the teeth; and there is a gland on the chest opening on the exterior by means of several apertures. The cheek-teeth are small and delicate, the molars forming more than four pairs, and being separated from one another by intervals, while those of the lower jaw have their inner cusps larger than the outer ones. In general appearance the banded ant-eater is a graceful squirrel-like animal, with the hinder part of the back marked by a series of narrow white stripes on a bright rufous ground. The ears are rather long and narrow, and the tail is elongated and bushy. All external trace of the first toe of the hind-foot is wanting, and all the functional toes are armed with claws adapted for digging; the soles of the fore-feet being partially naked, while those of the hinder pair are completely so, their pads being small and granulated. The pouch is obsolete, and the number of teats appears to be four. The cheek-teeth usually comprise three pairs of pre-molars and five of molars in each jaw, but occasionally there is a sixth pair of lower molars. As a rare abnormality,

Fig. 112. —BANDED ANT-EATER (*Myrmecobius fasciatus*).

four pairs of lower incisors may be developed. The banded ant-eater feeds mainly on ants, which are licked up by the tongue, but it will also consume insects of other kinds. It proceeds in a series of hops, with the tail uplifted; and when pursued, or for sleeping, retires to a hollow log or tree. It is stated to produce from seven to nine young at a birth, although it is difficult to reconcile this with the alleged presence of only four teats. After birth, the young are protected solely by the long hair on the abdomen of the mother.

A separate family (*Notoryctidæ*) of polyprotodont marsupials is represented solely by the curious marsupial mole (*Notoryctes typhlops*), from the sandy deserts of central South Australia. Among the essential characteristics of the family the following are the most important:—There are only three pairs of incisor teeth in each jaw, and there are neither ear-conchs or eyes visible externally. The limbs, which are sub-equal in length, are stout, strong, and each furnished with five toes; the hind-foot having a clawed first toe, not opposable to the other digits which are of unequal size. Collar-bones are present; and the under surface of the skeleton of the tail carries the so-called chevron-bones so commonly present in reptiles. The upper molar teeth have triangular crowns bearing three cusps only. Externally, the marsupial mole is a somewhat peculiar-looking animal, of a pale golden-red colour, and measuring about 5 in. to the root of the stumpy tail. A hard, horny shield, divided into two parts by a transverse ridge, serves to protect the upper surface of the blunt muzzle; and the apertures of the ears are well-nigh hidden by the fur. In both feet the four inner toes are clawed, but the fifth carries a short, broad nail; the claws of the third and fourth front toes are very large and powerful, while those of the corresponding hind toes curve outwards and backwards, the toes of these feet decreasing in size from the second to the fifth. In both pairs of limbs the soles of the feet are naked and covered with a tough leathery skin. The short, stumpy tail is also hard and leathery, decreasing rapidly in diameter from the base, and terminating in a blunt, knob-like extremity. The pouch opens backwards, and contains only two teats. The creature spends most of its time burrowing in the sand of the Australian deserts in search of its insect-food, occasionally making its appearance on the surface. Its enormously-powerful front claws enable it to bury itself in the sand with extraordinary rapidity.

Marsupial Mole.

Fig. 113 —MARSUPIAL MOLE (*Notoryctes typhlops*).

The last family of the marsupials is an American one, and is represented solely by the opossums (*Didelphyidæ*). In spite of the remoteness of their habitat, these animals are very closely allied to the *Dasyuridæ*, from which they may be distinguished by having four (instead of three) pairs of lower incisors, and by the first hind toe being opposable to the other digits. There is no claw to the first hind toe; and the number of pairs of upper incisor teeth is five, or the same as in the *Dasyuridæ*. As a rule, the tail is long, scaly, naked, and prehensile, although rarely it may be short, and more or less covered with hair. Internally, the stomach is simple, and the intestine has a blind appendage.

Opossums.

In most species the pouch is wanting, although it may be represented by two lateral folds of skin, while more rarely it is complete. There are three pairs of pre-molar teeth in each jaw. The females have from five to twenty-five teats. Opossums, which vary in size from that of a cat to that of a mouse, include more than a score of species, all but two of which are restricted to the Neogæic realm, whence the northern forms are probably comparatively recent wanderers. With the exception of the water-opossum, the members of the family are mainly arboreal animals, although some of the smaller kinds are more or less terrestrial. Arboreal species have, however, extended their range to the open Argentine pampas. Whereas the larger kinds are very destructive to poultry, the smaller species subsist exclusively on insects. In those opossums in which the female has no pouch, the young are borne on the back of their parent, generally curling their own tails round that of the latter, which is purposely bent forwards over the back and head. Nearly all the species may be included in the typical genus *Didelphys*, which may, however, be split up into several sub-generic groups. The first of these is represented solely by the common opossum (*D. marsupialis*), with its numerous varieties, which is four to five times the dimensions of any other kind, and may be compared, in this respect, to a cat. Its range extends from the United States to Chili, South Brazil, Uruguay, and Argentina, and it is the only species entering North America above Mexico. As the representative of a sub-genus, it may be characterised as follows:— The very long tail is naked, scaly, and highly prehensile; elongated bristle-like hairs are mingled with the fur; and the fifth hind toe is much shorter than the fourth, which is of nearly the same length as the first and second. The female has a well-developed pouch for the reception of the young, which at birth are extremely minute. They develop, however, very rapidly, and soon become as large as mice, when they leave the pouch, although returning for the purpose of sucking, or in order to escape from impending danger. Of the habits of this species Mr. C. Lincecum, in the *American Naturalist* for 1872, writes as follows:— "They dwell in hollow logs, stumps, and in holes at the roots of the trees. They do not burrow or prepare dens for themselves, but find such as are ready-made. I have seen them carrying into their holes, at the approach of cold weather, considerable bundles of dry leaves rolled up in their tail; they understand the signs of the coming spells of bad weather, and they prepare for it by making for themselves good comfortable beds. They do not hibernate, but are found out hunting in frosty weather. They possess but little caution. Hence they are often found in the poultry-houses, chicken-coops, smoke-houses, and even in our dining-rooms, rustling about for something to eat. I have often seen their tracks in the roads and paths where they had travelled three or four miles to a farmyard, to which they had no doubt been attracted by the crowing of the roosters. They will catch a grown hen and carry her off squalling at the top

Fig. 114. —COMMON OPOSSUM (*Didelphys marsupialis*).

of her voice, and will not abandon her till the dogs, which have been aroused by the uproar, have overtaken them and commenced cracking their bones. They will eat bacon, dry beef, carrion, any kind of fowl, rabbits, any sort of small game, almost all the insects, and fruits of every variety. They voraciously devour the musk-melon, and several species of mushrooms; in short, they are nearly omnivorous. The only case in which the opossum manifests any respectable degree of cautiousness is when it is hunted at night in the forest; on hearing the din and noise of the hunters it with some difficulty makes shift to climb a small tree or sapling, where, wrapping the naked, rasp-like tail round some convenient limb, it quietly awaits the approaching dogs and hunters. By many people the flesh is considered delicious. Its flavour resembles that of the flesh of a young hog, but is sweeter, less gross, and is, no doubt, a more healthy food for man. A dog will starve sooner than eat the flesh of an opossum; negroes and many other persons are exceedingly fond of it. During their breeding season, the males are very rampant and belligerent. Numbers will collect round a female and fight like dogs. Twenty or thirty years ago I witnessed a fight myself in the forests of Mississippi. The female was present; there were three males; two of them were fighting, while the third one was sitting a little distance off, looking as though he felt he had seen enough. They were fighting hard, and had been, from the signs in the wallowed-down grass, for three or four days, kicking over the female, who immediately went into a spasm when I examined the pouch. Opossums are exceedingly tenacious of life. I have many times seen the dogs catch them and chew and crack, seemingly, all the bones in their skin, leaving them to all appearance entirely lifeless; and, going out the next morning for the purpose of removing the dead thing, would find that it had left its death-bed, and putting the dogs on its track, trail him a mile or more before overtaking him. He would, to be sure, be found in a bad fix, but at the same time he lacked two or three more bone-crackings of being dead. They cannot, like the raccoon, be so far domesticated as to form any attachment for persons or their houses, though I have two or three times found them under the floors of dwelling-houses, where they had been for some time, and had evidently taken up winter-quarters, but they did not remain there long." Of the South American variety known as Azara's opossum, Mr. Aplin, in the "Proceedings of the Zoological Society for 1894," observes that in Uruguay, "where it is known by the name of *Comadréja*, this opossum lives in a nearly treeless country, the river *monté* in South Soriano being the only natural wood (composed of low thorny trees and big willows), and the Comadréja preferring to live on the higher camp, where it lies up in clefts and holes among the granite boulder-rocks; among these a few low thorny bushes are found in some cases. I have never seen a Comadréja in the *monté* or up any native tree, but have no doubt they often climbed the trees at the *estancias*, which they are all well able to do. Yet this animal has a very prehensile tail, naked and scaly. Having hauled one out of a cleft by the tail, I found that it twined the latter tightly round my fingers, the muscular power being considerable. They run up the boulder-rocks with great agility. At bay, whether in rocky holt or old ants'-nest, laid up in a soft bed of dead grass, or drawn and facing a dog with arched back and grinning teeth, they make a snarling, grunting growl and a hiss. It is necessary to kill those taking up their quarters near houses, but they are often very difficult to kill. I have hammered one with a stick and thrown its heavy body against a rock time after time, and then, after carrying it by the tail for some distance, discovered that it was still alive. Much of the difficulty arises from their habit of shamming. Once I smoked out a female and two one-third grown young ones. A young one came first and was apparently laid out with a blow from my stick; I had to run round the rock after the next, and when I came back (in less than half a minute) the first had come to life again and departed. An old buck, worried by a dog and finished off with a shot in the head from a collecting-gun and left for dead, was found an hour or so after partly recovered. A female was brought in with ten young, naked, pink, and blind; head and body 2 in., tail 1½ in. long. Inside the mother's pouch were nine teats only."

As a representative of the second sub-genus (*Metachirus*) may be mentioned the quica-opossum (*D. opossum*), ranging from Mexico to the Argentine. The three representatives of this sub-genus are medium-sized species, with the relative lengths of the hind-toes the same as in the common-opossum—that is to say, the three middle toes are sub-equal in this respect, and considerably exceed the outermost. The fur is short and straight, without any admixture of bristles; and the pouch may be either well developed or rudimental. Of the thick-tailed-opossum (*D. crassicaudata*) from Guiana, South Brazil, Uruguay, and Argentina, which is another member of the same sub-genus, Mr. Aplin writes as follows:—"The Comadréja-colorada, as this species is called, is rare in the part of Soriana where I was living, only one having been killed there during my stay so far as I know. It is said by the residents to be excessively savage for so small an animal. Responding to a suggestion, I inquired whether the female had a pouch capable of carrying her young, and one rather sharp and observant *puestero's* boy declared that it had. Although the adults are so savage, a lady of my acquaintance had a young one, taken from the body of its dead mother in the camp south of the Rio Negro in February, which was perfectly tame. It unfortunately shared the fate of so many ladies' pets and was slain by a large cat belonging to a house at which she was staying on her way to the coast, a day or two before I went over there. The fur of this animal is very beautiful. It is of a warm, light chestnut, paler and yellower on the sides and lower parts. The upper-parts have a flush on them of what can only be described as crimson." As a matter of fact, this species has no pouch, which in a fully developed condition is present only in the common and quica-opossums. The third sub-genus (*Philander*) is represented by two South American species of medium size, in which the fourth hind-toe is the longest, while the third and fifth are about equal and next in size, and the second is somewhat the shortest of the four. In both the pouch is rudimental, while externally these species are characterised by their woolly fur and the presence of a dark longitudinal stripe down the middle of the face. A considerable number of small-sized opossums from Central and South America constitute the sub-genus *Micoureus*, in which the form is slender, the fur generally straight, although occasionally slightly woolly, and there is no dark face-stripe. The relative lengths of the hind-toes are generally the same as in the last group, but in some cases the fifth digit is not longer than the second. A pouch is always wanting, and the tail is generally longer than the body, and highly prehensile. In the velvety-opossum (*D. velutina*) the tail is, however, much shorter, and thereby serves to connect this group with the following one. In the last group (*Peramys*), which is likewise confined to South and Central America, and contains about eight very small species, the tail is generally only about half the length of the head and body, and more or less covered with short, fine hairs, while it has but little or no prehensile power. In the hind-foot the fifth toe is considerably shorter than the second, and the third and fourth digits are equal, and but little longer than the latter. From the absence of prehensile power in the tail, it has been inferred that these tiny little opossums are mainly terrestrial in their habits. A small opossum recently described from Chiloe Island, off the coast of Central Chili, is regarded as representing a separate genus under the name of *Dromiciops*. A third genus contains only the water-opossum, or yapock (*Chironectes minimus*), ranging from Guatemala to the south of Brazil, and distinguished by its parti-coloured fur and aquatic habits. Structurally it is characterised by the presence of a projecting tubercle on the inner side of the fore-foot, giving the appearance of a sixth digit; and likewise by the webbing of the hind-toes as far as their terminal pads, whereby the first digit is much less opposable than in other opossums. In size the yapock may be compared to the common-opossum.

Fig. 115.—YAPOCK (*Chironectes minimus*).

ORDER XII.—MONOTREMATA.

EGG-LAYING MAMMALS.

THE third and last sub-class of mammals—variously known as the Prototheria, or Ornithodelphia, and containing only the single order Monotremata—differs much more widely from the other two than do the latter from one another, and thereby approximates to the lower vertebrates. These strange mammals, which are confined to the Notogæic realm, are especially characterised by laying eggs, after the manner of birds and reptiles; although the young subsequently developed from such eggs are nourished by milk from the mammary glands of the female parent. Instead, however, of opening into teats, these milk-glands discharge their secretion upon the porous skin of the inside of a more or less developed temporary pouch by means of numerous small apertures. After hatching, the head of the young, which develops a special suctorial mouth, is thrust into the pouch, and the milk forced into its mouth by the contraction of special muscles. Structurally, the milk-glands of the Monotremes correspond to the ordinary sweat-glands of other mammals, and not to their milk-glands. From the other two sub-classes of mammals, Monotremes differ in that the hinder extremity of the body possesses but a single orifice, from which are discharged both the waste-products and the reproductive elements; the two egg-passages, or oviducts, opening into the extremity of this cloaca, as the single excretory passage is termed. In these respects the egg-laying mammals resemble birds and reptiles. Similar resemblances are presented by the portion of the skeleton known as the shoulder-girdle, or that serving for the support and articulation of the bones of the fore-limb. In all the higher mammals, with the exception of some of the Edentates (where the coracoids may be distinct), the shoulder-girdle comprises, at most, only a pair of collar-bones (*clavicles*) and two shoulder-blades (*scapulæ*), of which the latter bear a so-called coracoid process at the lower extremity. On the other hand, in the egg-laying mammals, as in lizards, an unpaired additional T-shaped bone known as the inter-clavicle overlies the collar-bones and breast-bone (*sternum*); while the coracoid processes are represented by a pair of separate coracoid bones situated on the lower surface of the chest, and connected with the blade-bones to form the articular cavity for the head of the upper arm-bone, or humerus. Behind these, on the same aspect of the body, are a second pair of bones known as the meta-coracoids, and representing the bones commonly called coracoids in birds, which are articulated inferiorly to the breast-bone. The brain is also of a lower and simpler type than in the higher mammals; the same being also the case with the small bones of the internal ear. Another feature (which at present appears to have been verified only in the first of the two families) indicative of inferior organisation is the low temperature of the blood as compared with that of other mammals.

In both the families of Monotremes the males are furnished on the inner surface of the heel with a perforated horny spur, connected with a gland behind the thigh; and it is not improbable that during the breeding season this gland may secrete a poisonous fluid which flows into any wound inflicted by the spur. As in the Pouched Mammals, the Monotremes have a pair of marsupial bones affixed to the front edge of the lower part of the pelvis. Both families have the skull produced into a beak, which may be either cylindrical or flattened; and in the adult state at least, teeth are wanting. There are no traces of external ear-conchs; the two pairs of limbs, which are of nearly equal length, are modified for burrowing or digging; and the tail is either rudimental or short and wide. As in the case of the Edentates, there is no clue to the origin of the Monotremes, but there can be no doubt that the existing forms are highly modified and specialised descendants from some extremely ancient stock.

The strange Australian creature, known as the duck-bill or duck-mole (*Ornithorhynchus anatinus*), is the sole representative of the first family (*Ornithorhynchidæ*) of the Monotremes. As distinctive of the family, the following features appear the most important:—In the head the muzzle is produced and expanded to form a broad, depressed beak, covered with a delicate sensitive skin, which, in the dried state, assumes the appearance of horn. The tongue is of normal proportions, and non-extensile. In the fur there is no mixture of spines; the tail, although short, is broad and flattened; and the feet are large and wide, with the toes webbed, and the soles bare and without pads. In the young and adolescent condition, each jaw bears three pairs of many-cusped molars, of which the first is the smallest in the upper jaw, and the last in the lower; but in the adult these teeth are shed, and their functions discharged by horny plates growing up around and beneath them. In the male the horny spur on the hind-foot is very large; while in the female the pouch is rudimental. The brain has smooth hemispheres. The duck-bill has a somewhat elongated and depressed body, covered with dark-coloured fur of two kinds. In both limbs the five-toed feet have long claws to all the digits, although those on the fore-feet are broad and blunt, while those behind are compressed and

Duck-bill.

pointed. The beak is smooth, short, and evenly-rounded in front, with a flap of skin marking its junction with the head; and the cheeks have pouches for the storage of food. In length the adult male measures about 18 in. to the root of the tail, which is one-third the length of the head and body; but the female is considerably smaller. The duck-bill is confined to the fresh-waters of Tasmania and Australia, where it especially frequents still and deep pools in rivers with banks suitable for the construction of its long and tortuous burrows; these burrows generally having two entrances, the one situated above, and the other below the level of the surface of the water. In length a burrow may be as much as 20 ft., and at its extremity it expands into a capacious chamber, which is lined at the breeding season for the reception of the white eggs—usually two in number. Here in due course they are hatched, the female sitting upon them in the same manner as a bird, since the pouch is not sufficiently large for their reception. When first hatched, the young are completely naked and helpless, and are fed with milk in the manner indicated above. As soon as they are able to feed, they are supplied with fresh-water snails and insects such as form the chief nutriment of their parents. Duck-bills are mainly nocturnal animals, passing the day rolled up asleep in their burrows.

Fig. 116.—DUCK-BILL (*Ornithorhynchus anatinus*).

Very different, both in appearance and their mode of life, to duck-bills are the echidnas, or spiny ant-eaters, constituting the family *Echidnidæ*. In place of being aquatic, these Monotremes are terrestrial and nocturnal in their habits, while the sexes lack that discrepancy in size which forms such a marked feature in the preceding group. In place of the duck-like beak of the *Ornithorhynchus*, the muzzle of the echidnas forms a long, slender beak, which is completely devoid of teeth at all ages, and is suited to the long, extensile, worm-like tongue characteristic of all ant-eating mammals. The fur is so thickly intermingled with short and stout spines, not unlike those of the hedgehogs, that sometimes little more than the latter are visible. The tail is quite rudimental; the short, sub-equal limbs have unwebbed toes, furnished with broad, powerful, nail-like claws, and, although the soles of the feet are provided with soft, fleshy cushions, there are no pads. A peculiar feature connected with the mouth is the presence of spines on both the palate and the tongue. During the breeding season the pouch of the female is much more developed than in the duck-bill; and the hemispheres of the brain differ from those of the latter in being well convoluted. The smooth surface and bird-like form of the skull is very characteristic of the family, and the lower jaw is remarkable for its extreme slenderness. These animals subsist exclusively on ants, which are dug out by the powerful claws and licked up by the extensile tongue. The large size of the pouch enables the female to carry about with her the two eggs, which in due course are hatched by the heat of her body. The echidnas have a wider geographical distribution than the duck-bill, and are represented by two genera, one of which ranges from

Echidnas.

south-eastern New Guinea to Australia and Tasmania, while the second is exclusively Papuan. All the echidnas have stout and depressed bodies, which when the creatures are in repose rest flat on the ground, although in walking the legs raise the body some distance above the surface. In the typical genus of which there appears to be only one very variable specific representative (*Echidna aculeata*), the whole of the five digits of each foot are furnished with claws, which in the fore-feet are broad, slightly curved, and directed forwards, while in the hinder pair they are more slender, and curved outwards, the second, or the second and third, considerably exceeding the fourth and fifth in length, and that of the first toe being short, blunt, and rounded. The beak, which is of about the same length as the rest of the head, may be either straight or slightly curved upwards; and the tongue tapers at the tip, and has the spines confined to its basal portion. Of this species there are three well-marked local races or varieties. The ordinary or typical form, which is confined to the Australian mainland, is of medium size, measuring about 17 in. to the root of the tail. Next comes the variety from south-eastern New Guinea, measuring only about 14 in. in length, and with the spines of the back shorter. The largest and most distinct of all is the Tasmanian form, which grows to 20 in., and has the fur so long as almost to conceal the spines, while the claw of the third toe of the hind-foot is almost as much elongated as that of the second. In Australia the common echidna is generally met with in sandy or rocky districts and is especially abundant in the mountains. When on level ground, it proceeds with an unsteady, shuffling gait, the short and broad front feet being turned outwards, and the claws of the hind-feet bent outwards and backwards in such a manner as to cause the inner border of the sole to rest on the ground. These animals do not venture abroad till evening, but during the night they are very active, burrowing with great activity in search of their favourite ants. When suddenly attacked or surprised, echidnas roll themselves up into a ball-like form, but if time be allowed, they invariably endeavour to make their escape by burrowing.

Fig. 117.—Five-Toed Echidna (*Echidna aculeata*).

The second genus of the family (*Proëchidna*[1]) is distinguished by the feet usually carrying only three claws each, although the first and fifth toes are represented by two or more joints, and may occasionally be clawed. The length of the claws of the hind-foot diminishes regularly from the second to the fourth toe; and the beak, which is markedly curved downwards, is much longer than in the typical echidna, being nearly as long as twice the length of the remainder of the head. In the Arfak mountains of north-western New Guinea the genus is represented by Bruijn's echidna (*P. bruijni*), which measures about 19 to 20 in. in length, and has dense woolly fur, with but few spines. In western New Guinea it is replaced by a larger form with stouter limbs, shorter claws, and longer, more sparsely distributed, and more hairy fur, but whether it is anything more than a local variety may be doubtful.

[1] It has recently been proposed to substitute the name *Zaglossus*, which is stated to be earlier.

SUB-KINGDOM I.—VERTEBRATA.

CLASS II.—AVES.

BY R. BOWDLER SHARPE, LL.D., F.L.S., &c.

STRUCTURALLY the skeleton of a bird differs very remarkably from that of an ordinary mammal, although it is considerably less unlike that of the egg-laying mammals. In all the features in which the bird's bony framework departs from the mammalian type, it approximates to the reptilian conformation in general features. Still, it must not be supposed that in this respect birds are exactly like any living reptiles. Although in their general structural plan their skeletons are similar, that of the bird has become modified and specialised from the original type, which renders it markedly different from that of either a crocodile or a lizard. One of the chief points in which the skeleton of a bird resembles that of a lizard, and thereby departs from the mammalian type, is the mode in which the skull is articulated to the first joint of the backbone. Whereas in a mammal the articulation takes place by means of a pair of knobs on the hinder part of the skull, which are received into corresponding cups in the first joint of the backbone, in the bird and reptile there is but a single knob, or condyle, fitting into a cup in the first vertebra. Then, again, while in the mammal the lower jaw articulates directly with the solid wall of the true skull, or cranium, in the bird and reptile there is on each side an intervening separate bone, known as the quadrate. A third feature in which the skulls of birds and reptiles resemble one another, and differ from those of mammals, is the complex structure of each branch of the lower jaw—each branch consisting in the two former groups of several distinct bones, whereas in the latter it is formed of a single bone.

In order to give strength to the back in flying, the vertebræ of the hinder part of the backbone are fused together into a solid mass, forming the so-called sacrum, which is much more extensive than in mammals. To either side of this sacrum are firmly attached the bones of the pelvis, all of which are very unlike the corresponding bones of mammals, and of which the upper elements, or ilia, are by far the largest. In all living birds the bones of the tail are aborted, and terminate in a triangular piece known as the "ploughshare bone." In all birds the ribs are few in number, and in most cases these differ from the mammalian type by the presence of an oblique process on the hinder border. These uncinate processes, as they are called, are met with in some reptiles.

Perhaps the most extraordinary feature in the skeleton of an ordinary flying bird is the excessive development of the bones of the breast, which in some cases cover almost the whole of the under surface of the body. By far the largest of these elements is the breast-bone, or sternum, corresponding with the element similarly named in mammals. Whereas in flying birds this sternum is strongly keeled, in order to afford a firm basis of origin for the pectoral muscles, in the ostrich and its kindred it is flattened. At the sides the sternum is attached to the true ribs by the intervention of so-called sternal ribs. Superiorly it bears a pair of bones commonly known as coracoids, but more properly termed metacoracoids. Superiorly these metacoracoids join the scimitar-like scapulæ, or shoulder-bones, and at their junction form the cavity for the reception of the head of the upper wing-bone, or humerus. Joining the upper ends of the metacoracoids, and extending downwards towards the sternum, is the well-known merry-thought, or furcula; although in this modification peculiar to birds, the furcula really represents the united collar-bones, or clavicles, of man. In ordinary mammals there are no separate representatives of the metacoracoids; but such occur in the egg-laying mammals, although differing widely from those of birds. Before leaving this region of a bird's skeleton, it is important to mention that in the backbone—at least in the neck—the individual joints, or vertebræ, are articulated together by saddle-shaped surfaces, such a mode of articulation being unknown in any other class of vertebrate animals.

As regards the structure of the bones of the wing, very few words will suffice. The two upper segments of this part of the skeleton are essentially similar to the same part in mammals. The bones of the wrist, or carpus, are, however, reduced to two in number; while those of the metacarpus and fingers are flattened and otherwise modified, the number of digits never exceeding three. The three digits respectively represent the thumb, index, and middle fingers of the human hand. Of these, the thumb has either one or two joints, the index two, and the third digit one. The metacarpals of the index and third fingers are united together by a thin plate of bone, which may be perforated.

In a bird's leg the general plan of structure is a specialised modification of that obtaining in reptiles. The grand distinction between the leg of a reptile and that of a mammal, lies in the fact that, whereas in the latter the ankle-joint occurs at the top of the two rows forming the ankle, or tarsus, in the former the joint is situated between the two rows. A bird's leg is formed on the latter plan, but has undergone the further modification that the two rows of tarsal bones are respectively welded to the bones above and below them. We have first of all the thigh-bone, or femur; next comes the tibia (with the aborted fibula at its upper end), to the lower extremity of which are attached the upper row of tarsal bones, thus forming a tibio-tarsus. Below this comes a compound bone, formed by the lower row of tarsal bones and the three middle metatarsal bones of the typical five-toed foot, this compound bone being termed the tarso-metatarsus. Usually this bone terminates below in three pulley-like surfaces, to which are attached the bones of the toes; but in the ostrich there are only two of these pulleys, and likewise only two toes. When the first toe, or halhex, is present, it is attached to the hinder surface of the lower end of the tarso-metatarsus. No trace of the fifth toe ever remains. Whereas in mammals each of the toes, save the thumb, has three joints, in a bird (as also in a reptile) the number of these joints increase from the second to the fourth toe.

The chief character which distinguishes the class Aves from the other classes of vertebrate animals is *the possession of feathers.* The production of the young from an egg is not confined to the birds, but is shared by some mammals and reptiles; nor is the power of flight a sole prerogative of the birds, but their feathery covering is a really distinctive characteristic.

That birds existed on the earth in very remote times is undoubted, and that they were very different in form and structure from those which we have around us now, is equally certain. As the special character of the class

Aves is the possession of feathers, the earliest creature which can be determined to have possessed this special prerogative of the birds is the *Archæopteryx.* The remains of this curious animal were first discovered in the sand-stone formation of Solenhofen in Bavaria, whence comes the bulk of the stone used for lithographic purposes in the present day. The original slab containing these priceless remains is now in the British Museum, and with it we commence the study of the class Aves. The head is, unfortunately, missing in this specimen, but the imprint of the tail is clear enough, and shows a structure quite different from that which is to be seen in any bird of modern times. It is longer than the body of the bird itself, and, instead of the feathers being placed side by side, and capable of being spread like a fan, we find in the *Archæopteryx* the tail consisting of a series of vertebræ, upon which the feathers were disposed laterally, while there must evidently have been quills upon the wings. The digits of the latter terminated in little claws or hooks, a condition which exists in some of our present-day birds, though the exact structure is modified. A second specimen of an *Archæopteryx* was afterwards discovered in the same formation at Solenhofen, and has passed into the possession of the Berlin Museum. In this individual the head has been preserved, and shows us a reptilian-looking skull with actual teeth. Thus we know that *Archæopteryx* possessed teeth and feathers, but of a kind unlike those of any bird of modern times. It introduces the first sub-class of birds, *viz.*, the *Saururæ.*

Among the numerous other members of the class Aves, which we shall have to pass in review, will also occur several birds with teeth; but these will all be found to belong to a much earlier age than our own, so that we may safely say that at the present day no really toothed bird exists.

At the same time, there are found on the earth to-day many types of birds which must be considered to be the survivors of very ancient bird-life; and if these do not belong exclusively to one type, or to any single order or family of existing birds, we shall yet have little difficulty in assigning to most of them their proper position in the natural system. The idea that all toothed birds must belong to one group is now held to be erroneous, and the notion that the diving *Hesperornis* of the New World was allied to the *Archæopteryx* of the Old World, simply because they both possessed teeth, is not admitted at the present day.

Granting, however, that our Passerine birds are the highest development of the Avian form at present existing, it naturally follows that we must look to a totally different type if we desire to connect the bird-life of the present day with that of the past; and the flightless birds, the ostriches, and their kin, are admitted by all ornithologists to be the modern survivors of ancient forms. Like the huge mammals and reptiles, which were the fore-runners of the modern representatives of these classes, the birds of the Struthious order of Madagascar (*Æpyornis*) and the Moas of New Zealand were enormous. A singular interest attaches to the ancient *Struthiones,* which were immensely larger than their descendants of our own epoch. Thus the moas of New Zealand attained a huge size, and, as far as recent researches carry us, they must have been alive on the earth not so very long ago. The moas live in the traditional history of the Maories; specimens have been unearthed with the skin still attached to the bones; moa-feathers have been found in some number; and much controversy has been excited as to whether they have become extinct within the last hundred, or five hundred, years. That they were living within historic times is certain. Of the *Æpyornis* of Madagascar we know less, but though its bones are not so often discovered as those of the moa, its eggs, unearthed from the tombs of buried chiefs, are not unfrequently found

The Ratite Birds, as these great flightless creatures of the ostrich tribe are usually called, derive their name from the fact that they have a "ratite" or "raft"-like breast-bone. On the latter there is no keel, to which a pectoral muscle may be attached for the purposes of flight, and they have now no mechanism by which they can propel their huge bodies through the air like ordinary birds. That ostriches and their allies will ever fly is simply impossible, as their numbers are being annually decreased, and the necessary ages requisite for them to develop the means of flight as an escape from their enemies will never be allowed to them, as man, with his spreading civilisation and his deadly rifle, gradually encircles the poor birds in their last havens of rest. The probability is, judging from the well-developed wings of the early *Archæopteryx*, that ancient birds could fly, and that the ostriches and moas are the descendants of birds perfectly capable of flight, but which from the lack of natural enemies in ancient times, have gradually lost their power of flying, and ultimately developed into the flightless birds of the present day, wherein safety is secured by their excellent power of running, or by their nocturnal habits, where concealment and swiftness of foot play the most important part in their preservation.

Sub-class *Ratitæ*.

The Struthious or Ratite Birds (Sub-class *Ratitæ*) may, therefore, be divided into six Orders, *viz.* the Rheas (*Rheiformes*), the Ostriches (*Struthioniformes*), the Emus and Cassowaries (*Casuariiformes*), the extinct Moas (*Dinornithiformes* and *Æpyornithiformes*), and the Apteryges (*Apterygiformes*). Of these the moas are extinct, but members of the other orders still survive.

Fig. 1.—The Common Rhea (*Rhea americana*).

The ostriches may be distinguished by having only two toes instead of three. The moas had three toes, and, therefore, they belonged to the great group of three-toed Struthious Birds, of which so many have perished. Of those that survive, the rheas (*Rheiformes*) are distinguished by the following characters: the absence of any keel to the breast-bone, no hind-toe, and three toes in front. They are to all intents and purposes ostriches, and generally go by the name of the "South American Ostrich," as they are entirely confined to the South American Continent. Of the rheas, four species are recognised. One of these may be considered an unknown species as yet, as *Rhea nana* (Lydekker) has only been characterised from its egg, which is remarkably small, and on this evidence, which is certainly self-evident, Mr. Lydekker has separated the small Patagonian species as distinct. The common rhea (*Rhea americana*) is the best-known species, and the most widely distributed, being found from Southern Brazil and Paraguay to the province of Matagrosso, westwards to Bolivia, south to the Rio Negro in Patagonia, and even beyond. In the provinces of Bahia and Pernambuco it is replaced by the great-billed rhea (*R. macrorhyncha*), and in Chili and Patagonia by Darwin's rhea (*R. darwini*), which is said to range north of the Rio Negro, where it may be coterminous with the range of *R. americana.*

The nandu, as the rhea is called in Argentina, is, according to Mr. W. H. Hudson, doomed to speedy extinction, the republican governments of South America apparently being too much occupied in other business to trouble their heads about bird protection, which appears to be only an outcome of extreme civilisation. Mr. Hudson, the recorder of so much that is interesting in the habits of the birds of Argentina, has given the results of his acquaintance with the rhea, and we regret that space forbids us to quote more than a brief extract. It seems that the male takes upon himself the duties of incubation, and Mr. Hudson's story is as follows :—" In the month of July the love season begins, and it is then that the curious ventriloquial bellowing, booming, and weird-like sounds are emitted by the male. The young males in the flock are attacked and driven off by the old cock-bird ; and when there are two old males, they fight for hens. Their battles are conducted in a curious manner, the combatants twisting their long necks together like a couple of serpents, and then viciously biting at each others' heads with their beaks ; meanwhile, they turn round and round in a circle, pounding the earth with their feet, so that where the soil is wet or soft, they make a circular trench where they tread. The females of a flock all lay together in a natural depression of the ground, with nothing to shelter it from sight, each hen laying a dozen, or more, eggs. It is common to find from thirty to sixty eggs in a nest, but sometimes a larger number, and I have heard of a nest being found containing one hundred and twenty eggs. If the females are many, the cock usually becomes broody before they finish laying, and he then drives them away with great fury, and begins to incubate. The hens then drop their eggs about the plains ; and from the large number of wasted eggs found, it seems probable that more are dropped out of, than in, the nest. The egg when fresh is of a fine golden yellow, but this colour grows paler from day to day, and finally fades to a parchment-white.

" After hatching, the young are assiduously tended and watched over by the cock, and it is then dangerous to approach the rhea on horseback, as the bird, with neck outstretched and outspread wings, charges suddenly, making so huge and grotesque a figure that the tamest horse becomes ungovernable through terror. Eagles and the large caracarà are the enemies which the rhea most fears when the young are still small ; and at the sight of one flying overhead, he crouches down and utters a loud, snorting cry, whereupon the scattered young birds run in the greatest terror to shelter themselves under his wings."

The Ostrich.

Although at present only to be found in Africa and Arabia, there is no doubt that in former times the range of the ostrich was much more extensive. It is now practically extinct in Mesopotamia and in Syria, but, according to Mr. Lydekker, fossil remains of an ostrich have been found in North Western India, while an egg, supposed to belong to one of these birds, has been described from Southern Russia.

Three species of ostrich are recognised in Africa, of which the common one,

Struthio camelus, and the South African form, *S. australis*, have flesh-coloured thighs, whereas the Somali-land ostrich, *S. molybdophanes*, has black thighs. It is not a little vexatious that no one has yet determined how many species of ostrich really exist at the present day. Their plumes are classified by dealers, and those of the Barbary form are supposed to be different from those of the South African form, but at present no museum contains a series which illustrates the life history, or the number of species existing of these well-known birds.

Fig. 2.—The Ostrich (*Struthio camelus*).

The ostriches have only two toes, the first and second being absent. The quills and tail-feathers are well-developed for this class of bird, but no after-shaft is present. The male is larger than the female, and he undertakes the care of bringing up the family after he has hatched out the eggs. He especially looks after the nest at night, and broods over the eggs, though in many tropical countries the latter are covered over with sand, and left to the heat of the sun during the day. The cock-bird has more than one wife, generally three or four, who make common cause in the laying of the eggs, and deposit them in the same nest, sometimes as many as twenty eggs being found together.

The Emus.

These birds comprise the order *Casuariiformes*, with two sub-orders, *Dromeæ* (Emus) and *Casuarii* (Cassowaries). Both are inhabitants of the Australian region, the cassowaries being confined to the Papuan sub-region of the latter. Of the emus, three species are known, and it is quite possible that a fourth existed within recent times, as the Tasmanian emu was apparently distinct from the Australian form, but is now quite extinct. The small black emu of Kangaroo Island is known only from two specimens in the Paris Museum, and is also extinct. Thus we have but the common emu (*D. novæ hollandiæ*) and the spotted emu (*D. irroratus*), the former inhabiting Eastern and the latter Western Australia. The birds of this sub-order all have three toes, and are further distinguished from the ostriches by their rudimentary wings and apparent absence of a tail, while the body feathers have an after-shaft, which is as long as the actual plume itself, so that the latter appears as if it were a double feather.

The habits of the emu can now be studied in parks and public menageries in this country, where they not unfrequently nest. The bird is said by travellers to be good eating. As with the other Struthious Birds, constant persecution is making it rarer year by year, and it has now entirely disappeared from haunts where it once was quite numerous. The female is smaller than the male, and on the latter devolves the principal part of the duties of incubation. It has a curious note, which Gould has described as follows :—"The note of the emu is a low booming or pumping noise, which we know to be produced in the female by means of the expansion and contraction of a large membranous bag, surrounding an oblong opening through the rings of the trachea." The nestlings are beautifully striped little creatures. The egg is of a rich dark green, but this colour fades in course of time, and gives place to a dull black.

The Cassowaries.

These are curious birds, which commence their life in a mottled plumage, with no visible casque on the skull, and grow to an adult black plumage with an elevated casque of varying shape and generally some highly coloured wattles on the throat and neck. Eleven species are known, all of them met with in the Papuan group of islands, with the exception of one species, the Australian cassowary, which occurs in the Cape York Peninsula and extends as far south as Rockingham Bay. Most of our information regarding these curious flightless members of the class Aves is derived from the study of specimens sent alive to Europe, and many of us are familiar with the great turkey-like heads and black bodies of the cassowaries, with their five spiny quills in lieu of wings, their helmets and ornamental throat-wattles. Like the emus, the long after-shaft to the body-feathers gives these the appearance of being a double plume. Some of the New Guinea species apparently inhabit the same districts of that great island, while others are peculiar to Ceram, the Arn Islands, and New Britain respectively. The colour of the eggs of the cassowaries is dark green, and the young are brown, when full-grown, and have no casque. As in the case of the other Struthious Birds, the duties of incubation fall upon the male, who looks after the young ones when they are hatched.

Extinct forms, allied to the emus and cassowaries, have been found in Australia (*Dromornis*), in India (*Hypselornis*); while the moas of New Zealand (*Dinornithidæ*) and Madagascar (*Æpyornis*) belong to the same group.

The Kiwis.

Although the kiwis are recognised as belonging to the Struthious Birds, they are decidedly aberrant members of the sub-class, and are very like gigantic rails in their ways, being excellent runners and chiefly nocturnal in their habits. Like the emus and their kindred, they are great hands at kicking, and at a meeting of the British Ornithologists' Club, when the Hon. Walter Rothschild exhibited living specimens of every known species of kiwi, the birds made known their resentment by vigorous and lightning-like kicks on the walls of their cages, some assaulting the wires front-ways, and some kicking backwards.

Fig. 3.—THE APTERYX (*Apteryx australis*).

These curious birds will, doubtless, become extinct within a short period. There are only five species of kiwi now to be met with in New Zealand, though there is no doubt that the genus *Apteryx* was more widely distributed over the southern lands in past times. The kiwis have four toes, but there is no visible wing, and the nostrils are placed near the tip of the long bill. There is no tail visible, and the long after-shaft of the emus and cassowaries is absent. In the kiwis the hind toe, or hallux, is present, so that all four toes are represented. The egg is white, and may be considered enormous for the size of the bird which lays it. There is no marked difference in the size of the sexes, but the female appears to be slightly larger than the male. The observations on the ways of the kiwis in a state of nature are singularly deficient, and it is to be feared that the members of the genus *Apteryx* will disappear from the face of the globe without their life-history being thoroughly recorded. The eggs, judging from those laid in captivity, never appear to exceed two in number, and they are incubated in true Struthious manner by the male. Those which have been kept in our zoological gardens in this country have been seldom seen in daylight, as they go to sleep all the day and conceal themselves in the straw of their dens. When taken out, they run round in a dazed manner, and quickly return to their concealment. It is even said that when poked with sticks they will not rouse themselves, and quickly go to sleep again. An extinct form of *Apteryx* has been discovered in New Zealand (*Pseudapteryx*, Lydekker).

Carinate Birds.

All the rest of the birds belong to the order *Carinatæ*, or birds with a keeled sternum. Thus they ought to be all capable of flight, but as a matter of fact there are many exceptions, and there are not a few which have lost this power. The vast majority, however, have a deep keel or ridge to the breast-bone, which distinguishes them from the *Ratitæ*, of which we have just spoken. The nearest allies to the *Apteryges*, in a natural series, would be, in our opinion, the rails (*Rallidæ*), but we are bound to take notice of the curious partridges of South America, the tinamous, because they possess a remarkable palate, the bones of which are very like those of the Struthious Birds, and hence we commence our study of the *Aves Carinatæ* with the order *Tinamiformes*.

The Tinamous.—Order *Tinamiformes*.

In general appearance they resemble partridges, and they have much the habits of the latter birds, excepting the fact, that many of them are inhabitants of the forests, whereas the partridges are, essentially birds of the open country. Sixty-five species of tinamous are enumerated by Count Salvadori in his recent treatise on the order, and they are all inhabitants of the neo-tropical region, *i.e.* Central America, south of Mexico, and South America generally. Some of them are of large size, as big as an ordinary hen, but with the feathering much closer set, and with very little of the tail visible. The most remarkable feature of the tinamous is, perhaps, the colour of their eggs, which varies from a purplish brown or red to a bluish green, but whatever the colour may be, the eggs are always remarkable for their gloss. As Count Salvadori observes, they are "curiously unlike those of other birds, and the shell looks like highly burnished metal, or glazed porcelain, presenting also various colours, which seem to be constant in the particular species, varying from pale primrose to sage green, or light indigo, or from chocolate brown to pinkish orange."

Fig. 4.—THE GREAT TINAMO (*Rhynchotus rufescens*).

The species of tinamou vary very much in size, some being no larger than an ordinary quail, while others are as big as a good-sized fowl. The plumage of many of them is mottled and barred, and none exhibit any decorative ornament beyond the occasional presence of a chestnut breast. While some of them inhabit the open pampas, others are strictly forest birds, and the conclusion forced upon us is that tinamous are struthious partridges,

Game-Birds of the partridge type, which have retained some of the osteological characters of their struthious ancestors. Of the great tinamou (*Rhynchotus rufescens*) of Argentina, Mr. W. H. Hudson writes:—"This species is solitary in its habits, conceals itself very closely in the grass, and flies with the greatest reluctance. I doubt if there is anywhere a bird with such a sounding flight as a tinamou; the whirr of its wings can only be compared to the rattling of a vehicle driven at great speed over a stony road. From the moment it rises until it alights again, there is no cessation in the rapid vibration of the wings; but, like a ball thrown from the hand, the bird flies straight away with extraordinary violence until the impelling force is spent, when it slopes gradually to the earth, the distance it is able to accomplish at a flight being from 800 to 1,500 yards. This flight it can repeat when driven up again, as many as three times, after which the bird can rise no more."

The Game-Birds. —Order *Galliformes*.

This is a very large order of birds, and may be divided into four big sub-orders, *viz.* the *Megapodii*, or mound-builders; the *Craces*, or curassows; the *Phasiani*, consisting of the grouse, pheasants, partridges, guinea-fowls, and turkeys; and, lastly, the bustard-quails, or hemipodes (*Hemipodii*). Everyone is familiar with the appearance of an ordinary Game-Bird, such as the common fowl, or the turkey, the pheasant, the partridge, or the grouse. The mound-builder, the curassow, and the bustard-quail are less known, because in Great Britain we have no representative of these sub-orders, though occasionally examples of each of them may be seen in captivity. The palate in the Game-Birds is cleft, or, as it is usually called, "schizognathous," and another peculiar character is the perforation of the episternal process of the breast-bone, or sternum, so that the feet of the coracoid-bones meet through the opening thus afforded.

The Mound-Builders. —Sub-Order *Megapodii*.

These curious birds have a somewhat remarkable distribution, as they extend from Australia throughout the Malayan Archipelago to the Island of Labuan and the Philippine Archipelago. They are not found in Java or Sumatra, but have recently been discovered in the Kangean group of islands; and a species is also known from the Nicobar Islands in the Bay of Bengal. Thus it will be seen that the distribution of the megapodes is restricted to the south-east of Asia and Australia.

Professor Huxley separated the megapodes of the Austro-Malayan sub-region and the curassows of the neo-tropical region into a sub-order, *Peristeropodes*, in contrast to the *Alectoropodes*, or true Game-Birds, because they have a smaller inner notch of the sternum, this inner notch being less than half the length of the entire sternum, whereas in the ordinary Game-Birds the inner notch of the sternum is more than half the length of the entire sternum. Again, in the megapodes and curassows, the hallux, or hind-toe, is on the same level as the other toes, whereas in the *Alectoropodes* the hallux is raised above the level of the other toes. Of the mound-builders there are seven genera, of which the most striking types are the true mound-builders (*Megapodius*), the brush-turkeys (*Talegallus*), and the maleo-bird (*Megacephalum*).

The maleo is confined to the Island of Celebes, and is the only one of this dull-coloured group of Game-Birds which shows any pretension to colour. It has a breast of a delicate pink, and an ornamental bare knob on the crown, but is otherwise of a dusky colour like the rest of the group. Dr. A. R.

Wallace, during his celebrated expedition to the Malay Archipelago, found the maleo practising all the usual nesting devices of the mound-builders. The female lays eggs at intervals, and he says that the size of the latter precludes the female bird from having more than one fully-developed egg at the same time. The eggs are, therefore, laid at an intervening period of ten or twelve days, and are deposited in a mound of loose, hot, black sand. "In the months of August and September," he writes, "they come down in pairs to the nesting-place, and scratch holes three or four feet deep, just above high-water mark, where the female deposits a single large egg, which she covers over with about a foot of sand, and then returns to the forest." Each female is supposed to lay six or eight eggs during the season, the male assisting her in making the hole, coming down and returning with her. Many birds, according to Dr. Wallace, lay in the same hole, as a dozen eggs are often found together.

Fig. 5.—THE MALEO (*Megacephalum maleo*).

The Brush-Turkeys.

Some of these birds gain their name of brush-"turkeys" from the wattle which is seen on the base of the neck in the genera *Catheturus* and *Æpypodius*. Though devoid of these fleshy wattles, which are turkey-like, the remaining genus, *Talegallus*, is of large size, and, in a country which possesses no real Game-Bird of the kind, might pass for a near approach to a turkey in size and general appearance. Of the habits of the Australian brush-turkey (*Catheturus lathami*), Gould gives the following account:—"At the commencement of spring, this species scratches together an immense heap of decaying vegetable matter as a depository for its eggs, and trusts to the heat engendered by the process of fermentation for the development of its young. The heap employed for this purpose is collected by the birds during several weeks previous to the period of laying; it varies in size from that of two to that of many cart-loads, and in most instances is of a pyramidal form. The construction of the mound is either the work of one pair of birds, or, as some suppose, the united labours of several; the same site appears to be resorted to for several years in succession, the birds adding a fresh supply of materials each succeeding season. The material composing these mounds is accumulated by the bird's grasping a quantity of earth in its foot and throwing it backwards to one common centre, the surface of the ground being so completely scratched over, that scarcely a leaf or a blade of grass is left. The mound being completed, and time allowed for a sufficient heat to be engendered, the eggs are deposited in a circle at the distance of nine or twelve inches from each other, and buried more than an arm's depth, with the large end upwards; they are covered up as they are laid, and allowed to remain until they are hatched. I have been credibly informed, both by natives and by settlers living near their haunts, that it is not an unusual event to obtain half a bushel of eggs at one time from a single mound. Some of the natives state that the females are constantly in the neighbourhood of the mound about the time when the young ones are liable to be hatched, and that they frequently uncover and cover them up again, apparently for the purpose of assisting those that may have appeared; while others have informed me that the eggs are merely deposited, and the young allowed to force their way out unassisted. One point, however, has been clearly ascertained, *viz.* that the young, from the hour they are hatched, are clothed with feathers, and have their wings sufficiently developed to enable them to fly on to the branches of trees, should they need to do so to escape from danger; they are equally nimble on their legs. In fact, as a moth emerges from its chrysalis, dries its wings, and flies away, so the youthful brush-turkey, when it leaves the egg, is sufficiently perfect to be able to act independently and procure its own food."

Of the habits of the Papuan and Moluccan genera, *Talegallus* and *Æpypodius*, little is known; but the ways of the species of *Lipoa* and *Megapodius* have been more carefully studied. *Eulipoa* from the Moluccas has but one species, *E. wallacii*, with a more rounded wing than in the ordinary megapodes, and further remarkable for its brighter colours. Of the ocellated megapode (*Lipoa ocellata*) Sir George Grey sent to Mr. Gould a most interesting account of the habits, from which it appears that the birds first scratch a hole in the sand, fill it up with dead leaves and grass, and then build a mound of dried grass, etc., over it. The hole is then opened and an egg deposited in the sand, and as many as eight are placed at intervals, an egg being deposited every day, or at least every few days; and the male bird helps the female to uncover the hole. The eggs are placed upright, and several mounds are found within a short distance of each other, each being the property of a single pair of birds. All the megapodes are very shy birds, and escape to the trees when pursued, roosting in these during the heat of the day, and being then apparently stupid birds they can be shot down in succession without attempting to fly, so that the whole party is soon cleared off.

The true megapodes (*Megapodius*) are the most widely distributed of any of the group, but are best known from the studies which have been made of the habits of the Australian species, *M. tumulus*. Gilbert found many nests of this bird in the Cobourg Peninsula, and dug out a young bird, which he kept alive for a few days. It was, however, very wild and intractable, and made its escape; but it is interesting to learn that this little chick employed its time in continually scratching up sand, for which purpose it only used one foot. Eggs were taken by Gilbert from a depth of six feet in the mound, but as the holes ran down obliquely from the centre, towards the outer slope of the hillock, the eggs might be six feet deep from the summit but only two or three feet from the side of the mound. One mound that Gilbert found in Knocker's Bay in a thicket was fifty feet in height and sixty feet in circumference; and the late Mr. Davison met with a mound of the Nicobar megapode (*M. nicobariensis*) which was eight feet in height and quite sixty feet in circumference. Mr. John Whitehead, in the course of his famous explorations in the Malay Archipelago, visited the Island of Palawan, and there made the acquaintance of Cuming's megapode (*Megapodius cumingi*), which he found nesting from June to August. The note of this species is a most doleful "mew," exactly like that of a cat in distress, and is heard many times towards evening, adding to the melancholy of the forest. The nest he describes as a most wonderful structure, and no doubt the result of the labour of several pairs of birds. The eggs were placed so deep that it was impossible to reach them, and he says that he dug out a young bird so far grown that it looked like the adult of another species, and yet, although fully feathered and able to fly well, he was convinced that it had never seen daylight.

The curassows form the second sub-order of Professor Huxley's Peristeropodes, and like the megapodes have the hind-toe not elevated, but on the same level as the other toes. They have also a tufted oil-gland, and their whole appearance is more like that of the pheasants and true Game-Birds, and quite different from that of the megapodes. The wind-pipe is long and convoluted. They likewise nest in trees and lay two white eggs, and the nestlings have a patterned downy stage, like that of true Game-Birds. Mr. Ogilvie-Grant, who has made a special study of all the Gallinaceous Birds, recognises eleven genera of curassows, and he divides them into two sections, the true curassows with a very deep bill, and the guans with a more elongated and widened bill, the upper mandible being broader than it is high. Very little has been recorded of the habits of the curassows in their wild state, but they are often to be seen in menageries, where they walk about like great turkeys, or sit on the branches of the trees provided for them.

The Curassows. —Sub-Order *Oraces.*

Fig. 6.—THE CRESTED CURASSOW (*Crax alector*).

One of the most curious of the curassows is Lord Derby's guan (*Oreophasis derbianus*), or the Derbyan mountain-pheasant, as it is also called. It has the top of the head almost bare, and an elevated kind of cylindrical casque on the crown, situated between the eyes. This remarkable bird is found only in Guatemala, where it is apparently restricted to the forests on the Volcan de Fuego. Here Mr. Osbert Salvin found it feeding on fruits in the higher branches of the forest-trees in the early morning, and descending to the underwood as day advances, remaining there all the day-time, basking or scratching among the leaves. This, says Mr. Salvin, is pretty much what the curassows and guans of the lowlands do. The Indian name for the mountain-guan is "khannanay," and it is apparently very rare even on the mountain which is its sole habitat.

All the rest of the Game-Birds, comprising by far the greater number of known species, belong to the sub-order *Alectoropodes*, and have the hind-toe elevated, and raised above the level of the other toes. Mr. Ogilvie-Grant recognises two large families, the *Tetraonidæ* or grouse, and the *Phasiandæ* or pheasants and partridges. In the grouse the nostrils are hidden by feathers. The toes are mostly feathered, and there are never any spurs on the legs.

The Grouse. —Family *Tetraonidæ.*

Eleven genera are recognised as constituting the family *Tetraonidæ*, and among them are the genera *Lagopus*, *Lyrurus*, and *Tetrao*, which are represented in Great Britain by our red grouse and ptarmigan, the black grouse, and the capercailzie.

The willow-grouse or "Ripa" of Scandinavia (*Lagopus lagopus*) is the most wide-spread of all the group, for it inhabits the northern regions of both hemispheres, varying slightly in different localities, so that many races are recognised by modern ornithologists. These forms, however, all belong to one type, and they are characterised by a common character, the assumption of three different styles of plumages, in summer, autumn, and winter respectively, their plumage thus varying in accord with the colour of the country which they inhabit. Thus, in summer, when their surroundings are darkest, the plumage is of a dark colour; in autumn, when the tint of the country is grey, they become grey; and, lastly, when the land becomes white from its covering of snow, the willow-grouse again changes its plumage into snowy white. In our red grouse (*Lagopus scoticus*), which is an insular form of the "Ripa," the changes of plumage are quite different, and the bird always remains dark-coloured throughout the year, the necessity for change on the ground of protective resemblance to its surroundings having become removed in our island climate. It is to be noticed as a curious fact that the willow-grouse, throughout its changes, never loses its white wings. The nest of the red grouse is always upon the ground, and the birds are subject to the attacks of many enemies, of which the carrion and hooded crows are perhaps the most active. Unlike some of the other grouse, our British species has but one mate, and is monogamous, the nesting season being in April and May, though sometimes lasting into the early days of June, as grouse are much affected by the mildness or inclemency of the season, and when the latter is wet, the number of eggs laid is much smaller than in favourable summers. The red grouse is essentially a bird of the moors, and its place on the higher mountains is taken by the ptarmigan (*Lagopus mutus*), which also inhabits the higher mountains of Scotland and Europe generally as far east as the Urals.

The True Grouse.

Fig. 7.—The Black Grouse (*Lyrurus tetrix*).

The black grouse (*Lyrurus*) are represented by two species only, one of which, *L. tetrix*, is our British species, and extends in suitable localities across Europe and Northern Asia to Eastern Siberia, being represented in the Caucasus by a second species, the Georgian black grouse (*Lyrurus mlokosiewiczi*).

The Capercailzies.

These woodland grouse are the largest representatives of the family, and rank, indeed, among the largest of Game-Birds. They are peculiar to the Old World, where they inhabit the pine-forests of Europe and Asia. Four species are known, our British capercailzie (*Tetrao urogallus*) inhabiting certain parts of Scotland and extending its range through the pine-covered mountains of Europe and Asia as far as Lake Baikal. In the Ural Mountains it is replaced by *T. uralensis*, and again in Eastern Siberia by *T. parvirostris*, which is represented in Kamtchatka by *T. kamtchaticus*. They are woodland birds, and our own species feeds on the tender shoots of larch and spruce, as well as on various ground-fruits, in pursuit of which it sometimes quits its favourite fir-woods for the more open country. Like the black grouse, the capercailzie has several wives, and desperate fights take place amongst the males, who, at the commencement of the nesting season, are often shot by the hunter, as they are engaged in "laking," as it is called. The male resorts to some particular spot to utter his love-song, and becomes so absorbed in his "spell" as to be utterly oblivious to anything going on around him.

In America several peculiar forms of grouse are found, the dusky capercailzies (*Dendragapus*) having a naked air-sac on the sides of the neck, which they are able to inflate at will. Mr. Gale describes the nesting habits of *D. obscurus* in Colorado, and says that the male, during the nesting season, performs some curious evolutions. "If," he says, "you are anywhere near the haunts of a pair, you will surely hear the male, and most likely see him. He may interview you on foot, strutting along before you, in short, hurried tacks, alternating from right to left, with wide-spread tail tipped forward, head drawn in and back, and wings dragging along the ground, much in the style of a turkey-gobbler. At other times you may hear his mimic thunder overhead again and again in his flight from tree to tree. As you walk along, he leads, and this reconnoitring on his part, if you are not familiar with it, may cause you to suppose that the trees are alive with grouse. He then takes his stand upon a rock, stump, or log, and distends the lower part of his neck, opens his frill of white, edged with the darker feather tips, showing in the centre a pink narrow line, describing somewhat the centre of a circle; then with very little apparent motion he performs his growling or groaning, I don't know which to call it, which has the strange peculiarity of seeming quite distant when quite near, and near when distant; in fact, appearing to come from every direction but the true one." The pinnated grouse (*Tympanuchus*) have an elongated tuft of feathers on each side of the neck, as well as an air-sac. These and the ruffed grouse (*Bonasa*) are also North American, being replaced in Europe and Northern Asia by the hazel-hens (*Tetrastes*), which inhabit hilly and wooded districts.

The Partridges.

In the family *Phasianidæ*, which includes all the partridges, quails, and pheasants, we meet with the most typical of the Game-Birds. Mr. Ogilvie-Grant proposes to divide them into three sub-families—partridges (*Perdicinæ*), pheasants (*Phasianinæ*), and *Odontophorinæ*, or American tooth-billed partridges. The latter may be at once distinguished by having the cutting edge of the lower mandible serrated or toothed. The partridges may be recognised by their short and stumpy tails, which never exceed the length of the wing, and there are other minor differences, which the above-mentioned author has pointed out. Unfortunately for the classification of the Game-Birds, many forms are intermediate, while the characters assigned to the partridges hold good only to a certain extent, the character which should separate partridges from pheasants, *viz.* the proportion of the primaries and the secondaries, breaks down, as Mr. Ogilvie-Grant has pointed out, in the important genus *Phasianus*, which has the wing of a partridge, but the long tail of a pheasant. Thus the two groups, the partridges and the pheasants, to outward appearance so different, appear to be inseparably connected, and it is difficult to find any line of demarcation between them. Pheasant-like partridges and partridge-like pheasants fill the gap between the true partridges and the true pheasants.

The Snow-Partridges.—Genus *Lerwa*.

The snow-partridges of the Himalayas are represented by the genus *Lerwa*, which has the upper half of the tarsus covered with feathers, indicating an inhabitant of high elevations. Thus we find the genus *Lerwa* only in the upper ranges of the Himalayan system, from Koteghur to Sikkim, and again in Moupin and the mountains of Szechuen in Western China. It is found near the snow-line in summer, and is somewhat local in its distribution, inhabiting rocky situations, where its plumage blends with its surroundings, and makes the bird difficult to identify. It nests in the Himalayas at an elevation of from 12,000 to 15,000 feet, and is very tame, probably on account of its habitat being only reached by a most adventurous sportsman, whose visits are few and far between.

These large and handsome birds are readily distinguished by their large size and by the number of their tail-feathers, which are 20 or 22 in number.

The Snow-Cocks.—Genus *Tetraogallus.*

The snow-cocks, or snow-pheasants as they are called (*Tetraogallus*), are the largest of the partridge-group, and are only found in high ranges, from the mountains of Asia Minor, the Caucasus, and Persia, to the Himalayas, Turkestan, the Altai, and the higher hills of Moupin and North-Western China. In the Himalayas, the snow-pheasant (*T. himalayensis*) is an inhabitant of the snowy ranges, from which it only migrates to somewhat lower altitudes on the approach of the winter snow. These birds are generally found in packs of from five to ten, but sometimes twenty or thirty are in a single flock ; and even during the nesting-season a good many are found in company. Snow-pheasants are birds of the open, rocky hill-country, frequenting grass-lands, and never entering the forest or perching on trees. They are, therefore, evidently gigantic partridges in their ways, and it is a mistake to call them snow-"pheasants," as is so often done.

The red-legged partridges differ from the true partridges in having only 14 feathers in the tail. They are also easily recognisable by the beautiful barring of red, grey, and black of the sides of the body. The most familiar of all the group is the red-legged partridge of England (*Caccabis rufa*), which is confined to South-Western and Western Europe. In North-West Africa, Sardinia, and Southern Spain it has a near ally in the Barbary red-legged partridge (*C. petrosa*), while the rock red-legged partridge (*C. saxatilis*) takes its place in the mountains of Southern Europe, from the Pyrenees to the Balkans. A paler form, known as the Chukar or Greek partridge (*C. chukar*), extends from Greece through Central Asia to China, and is a well-known bird in the Himalayas. In Tibet and Kokonoor a large species, Prjevalski's red-legged partridge (*Caccabis magna*), is met with ; but the largest of all is the black-headed red-legged partridge (*C. melanocephala*), which lives in Southern Arabia, and is a very fine bird, approaching even some members of the genus *Tetraogallus* in size.

Fig. 8—THE RED-LEGGED PARTRIDGE (*Caccabis rufa*).

The distribution of these species of *Caccabis* is most interesting, and there is no doubt that climate exercises considerable influence on their plumage, those which inhabit dry and sandy localities being paler than those of the more cultivated country. This is especially true of the chukars ; but considerable variation in tint is also seen in the common red-leg from different areas. The chukars inhabit dry and stony situations, and never go into the forests, preferring in the Lower Himalayas the grassy hill-sides to the cultivated fields. In summer they are met with in pairs, or in small parties ; but in winter they assemble in loose, scattered flocks, sometimes to the number of forty or fifty, or even a hundred.

In the bare portion of the countries between North-Western India, Persia, and North-Eastern Africa, is the home of the see-see partridges (*Ammoperdix*), of which two species, *A. bonhami* and *A. heyi*, are known; and then we leave the true partridges for the francolins, which are a very large group, principally African. They may be divided into two genera, *Francolinus* and *Pternistes.* Both these genera have 14 tail-feathers; but the former has a feathered throat, while in *Pternistes* the throat is bare. More than forty species of francolin are known, of which all but four are peculiar to Africa. They inhabit all kinds of country: some the open grass-lands, some bare and desert situations, while others are found in forest-lands.

The Common Francolin.—*F. francolinus.*

This interesting species (*F. francolinus*) has now been practically exterminated in its former haunts in Sicily and other parts of Southern Europe, but is still found in Cyprus, Palestine, and Asia Minor, whence it extends eastwards to the Indian Peninsula, as far as Assam and Manipur. It is familiarly known as the black partridge, by Indian sportsmen, and is a favourite Game-Bird in the north-west provinces of India, though it is much less common in many places than it was formerly. This is partly owing to the persecution it receives, while from the accounts published by Mr. Allan Hume and his friends, the francolin is not a prolific breeder, and the young birds suffer from the depredations of stoats, jackals, etc. It is, like most of its kind, a ground bird, but Mr. Greig says that the cock will at times get on to a stump or ant-hill, when calling, and he has even seen them high up in fir-trees. The natives are very fond of keeping the francolin as a pet, and numbers are netted by them. Some of the African species are quite small, scarcely larger than a quail, whilst others are of large size and heavy build, and they are sometimes so disinclined to fly, that after being flushed a second time, they will allow themselves to be taken with the hand rather than rise again.

The Bare-throated Francolins.—Genus *Pternistes.*

These birds have all the appearance of francolins, but differ from them in having the throat naked. Nine species are known, and they are all peculiar to the Ethiopian region. *Pternistes swainsoni* is one of the best-known species, and is the "pheasant" of Matabeleland. Mr. T. E. Buckley says that the coveys are extremely difficult to flush, and they prefer to escape by running. In the day-time they come out into the open, and frequent the neighbourhood of small streams; they pass the night in the brushwood, and roost on trees. They feed on bulbs, seeds, berries, and insects. The eggs of Swainson's bare-throated francolin are six or more in number; they are rounded in shape, of a pinkish cream-colour, finely speckled with chalky-white.

In the Malayan Archipelago the francolins of Africa and India are represented by the genus *Rhizothera,* distinguished by its long bill. The typical species, the long-billed francolin (*R. longirostris*), is an inhabitant of the southern portion of the Malay Peninsula, Sumatra, and the lowlands of Borneo. In the highlands of the latter island, on Mount Dulit, at an elevation of 4,000 feet, it is replaced by Hose's long-billed francolin (*Rhizothera dulitensis*).

Of these birds our common partridge (*P. perdix*) is the type, and the best-known species. In illustration of the curiosities of bird-life, especially in species the most familiar to us, I may mention that Mr. Ogilvie-Grant, who has made the game-birds his special study, has recently discovered differences in the coloration of the sexes of the partridge hitherto unrecorded.

The male, as might be believed, has a large horse-shoe shaped mark of chestnut on the breast. This is either feebly developed or entirely absent in the adult female, which can always be recognised by the barred wing-coverts, of which the ground colour is black, with widely set buff cross-bars. Young birds of both sexes can be told by the pointed, not rounded, end to the first primary, while the yellowish horn-colour of the feet is also a distinguishing character. Then comes the curious fact that the young female has a horse-shoe mark on the breast, which is not seen in the immature male. Many ornithologists recognise certain races of the common partridge in Europe, and a small form, supposed to inhabit the higher ground in summer and to descend to the lower ground in winter, is known as *Perdix damascena.* A still more curious hill race from the mountains of Lorraine, which crops up occasionally in certain parts of England, is the mountain partridge (*Perdix montana*), a bird almost entirely rufous, with a creamy buff head. It cannot be considered more than a variety of the ordinary partridge, but at first sight would seem to be a perfectly distinct species.

The True Partridges.—Genus *Perdix*.

In Eastern Siberia our common partridge is represented by the bearded partridge (*P. daurica*), which has tufts of feathers on the throat, forming a kind of "beard." In Tibet and Kansu two species of true partridge are encountered, *P. hodgsoniæ* and *P. sifanica*, both of which have sixteen tail feathers, instead of eighteen, as in our common species.

The Tree Partridges.—Genus *Arboricola*

Passing by several small genera of bush quails (*Margaroperdix* of Madagascar, *Perdicula* and *Microperdix* of India), we come to the tree partridges (*Arboricola*) which inhabit the hill ranges of the Himalayas, Assam, and the Burmese provinces, and those of Sumatra, Java, Borneo, Hainan, and Formosa. This distribution is interesting as showing the Himalayan element in the mountain fauna of the last-named islands. In the lower hills of Burma, Malacca, Sumatra, and Borneo occurs the allied genus *Tropicoperdix*, which contains a couple of species very like those of *Arboricola*, but distinguished by the absence of the supra-orbital chain of bones, which is one of the features of *Arboricola.* Closely allied to these tree-partridges are the genera *Hæmatortyx* of Mount Kina Balu, in North-Western Borneo, remarkable for its three-spurred leg and crimson head, and *Caloperdix*, the latter genus containing three species, inhabiting respectively the mountains of Tenasserim and the Malay Peninsula, Sumatra and Java, and North-Western Borneo. The crested wood-partridges (*Rollulus*), which have a tuft of long hair-like bristles on the middle of the forehead, are represented by a single species (*R. rouloul*), which is found in the Indo-Malayan sub-region from Southern Tenasserim and the Malay Peninsula to the Sunda Islands. It is accompanied in the greater part of its range by the black wood-partridge (*Melanoperdix nigra*).

The Quails.—Genus *Coturnix*.

These little birds are only found in the Old World, the common or migratory quail (*Coturnix coturnix*) being found in Europe and Northern Asia in summer, and migrating in vast hosts. The numbers which appear in the winter quarters of the species, in Northern Africa, in Egypt, and, above all, in North-Western India, are sometimes incredible. Colonel Tickell, in one of his shooting experiences, speaks of them as like locusts in number. In South Africa our European quail is replaced by the Cape quail (*Coturnix capensis*), which extends northwards to the Azores, and the Canary Islands; and in Japan, Mongolia, and China, *C. japonica* replaces *C. coturnix*. The female of *C. japonica* is bearded, which is a curious fact, when one remembers that a bearded partridge of Siberia replaces our own western partridge (*P. perdix*). In India, Africa, and Australia are peculiar species of the genus *Coturnix*, and New Zealand formerly possessed a species of its own (*C. novæ zealandiæ*). The New Zealand quail is now extinct, and specimens are valued at nearly £100, and yet fifty years ago it was so common that twenty brace in a day's shooting was not considered a large bag! If the sportsmen of those days had known of the impending extinction of the species, and had preserved the skins of the birds they shot for the table, a small fortune might have been their lot.

The Swamp and Painted Quails.

These small birds are peculiar to the Australian region, inhabiting Australia, New Guinea, and the islands of Timor and Flores. They closely resemble the true quails, and only differ in their short grey axillaries. The eggs, however, are not so boldly marked as in those of the quails, and are of a pale bluish white, with a number of light brown spots. The painted quails (*Excalfactoria*) are birds of small size, but of many colours. They inhabit India, the Indo-Chinese countries, and the entire Malayan Archipelago to Australia, while one species, *E. adansoni*, is found in Africa.

The Pheasants.—Sub-Family *Phasianinæ.*

Under this sub-family are also included the turkeys and the guinea-fowls, and it contains the most widely distributed and the most highly decorated of the Game-Birds. The bamboo-pheasants and the spur-fowl of the Indian region have rather the aspect of partridges than true pheasants. Another intermediate form between the two sub-families is seen in the blood-pheasants (*Ithagenes*) of the Himalayas and the allied chains of mountains in North-Western China. They are forest birds, living at a great altitude near the snows, affecting the clumps of mountain-bamboo, and feeding at some seasons on the tops of pine and juniper, when their flesh is somewhat rank to eat, and at others on seeds and small fruits, when their flesh is quite palatable.

The Horned Pheasants.—Genus *Tragopan.*

These splendid birds, generally called "Argus" pheasants by Indian sportsmen, on account of their white-spotted plumage, are found in the Himalayas and the hills of Assam and South-Eastern China. They are remarkable for the adornments of the males, which have fleshy horns and a bare gular lappet of bright colours. The latter is displayed during the breeding-season, but is scarcely distinguishable in the winter, when the birds are most easily observed, as they descend to the lower grounds and are often snared by the natives. In summer they frequent the forests near the snow-line.

The Moonals.—Genus *Lophophorus.*

The moonals or impeyan pheasants are some of the handsomest of all known birds, their plumage being metallic, and of divers colours of green, purple, and blue, and they carry a crest of light spade-shaped plumes or curled feathers. They inhabit the higher ranges of the Himalayas and the mountains of Assam and Western China, descending to lower elevations as the winter comes on. Mr. Hume, speaking of the common moonal, says:—

"There are few sights more striking, where birds are concerned, than that of a grand old cock shooting out horizontally from the hillside just below one, glittering and flashing in the golden sunlight, a gigantic rainbow-tinted gem, and then dropping stone-like, with closed wings, into the abyss below."

The fire-backed pheasants (*Acomus* and *Lophura*) are inhabitants of the mountains of the Indo-Chinese provinces and the Malayan Peninsula and Islands. On the high mountains of North-Western Borneo, on the Lawas River and the region of Mount Dulit occurs one of the most remarkable of all game birds, the lobed pheasant (*Lobiophasis*), which has no less than thirty-two feathers in the tail, which, as Mr. Ogilvie-Grant says, is "by far the largest number of tail-feathers in the *Phasianidæ*. One of the eared pheasants (*Crossoptilum auritum*) has twenty-four, and the smallest number occurs in the painted quails (*Excalfactoria*), which have only eight!" The female of the lobed pheasant, however, has twenty-eight feathers only. The horns and wattles on the head show some sort of likeness to the naked ornaments found in the tragopans, but the style of plumage is in other respects entirely different. Like the tragopans, the lobed pheasant inhabits the mountains, but does not extend beyond 2,000 feet, and, according to Mr. C. Hose, it lives in the forest, and has the ways of a jungle-fowl.

Fig. 9.—LOBED PHEASANT (*Lobiophasis bulweri*).

The Eared Pheasants.—Genus *Crossoptilum.*

In these birds, which are remarkable for the long white tufts on the side of the head, whence the name of "eared" pheasants, the sexes are alike in colour. They are large birds, inhabiting the high mountains of Tibet, Western China, and Manchuria. They live in the woods at high elevations, and assemble in large flocks.

The Kalij Pheasants.—Genus *Gennæus.*

The best-known species of *Gennæus* is the silver pheasant, so often seen in aviaries. The kalijes inhabit the Himalayas and the hills of Assam and Burmah. In the Himalayas they are found at different elevations, from 1,000 up to 9,000 feet. They are easily reared in captivity, and large numbers are snared by the natives. The black-backed kalij is described by Mr. Gammie, a well-known Himalayan naturalist, as being very tame when it is found away from its native forests, which it does not often quit. He says:—"In fine weather, the male often makes a sharp, drumming noise by beating his wings against his sides, somewhat after the style of the wing-flapping of a domestic cock, preparatory to crowing from some elevated place; but instead of the cock's few leisurely flaps, the kalij strikes oftener and smarter, producing a sound more like drumming than flapping. This noise is heard at all seasons of the year, but most frequently before the setting in of the rainy season; at other times just before a fall of rain. Hence the natives look on the drumming of the kalij as a sure sign of approaching rain." The Himalayan kalijes, even in a wild state, interbreed, while in the species from the Burmese provinces, intermediate forms also occur, which render it difficult to draw the line between the different species.

The koklass or pucras pheasants (*Pucrasia*) are found in the Himalayan chain from Afghanistan eastwards to Tibet, and the mountain ranges of

Southern China to Fokien and Manchuria. They are birds of the forests like the kalijes, and of a somewhat retired and solitary disposition, according to Mr. F. Wilson, who writes of *P. macrolopha*:—"In the remote forests of the interior of the Himalayas, on the report of a gun, all the koklass pheasants within half a mile or so will often crow after such a report. They will also crow after a clap of thunder or any loud or sudden noise, and this peculiarity seems to be confined to those which live in the dark shady woods of the interior, as I never noticed them acting thus in the lower hills. The food of the koklass pheasants is varied, like that of the kalijes, and consists, according to Mr. Wilson, of leaves and buds, roots, grubs, acorns, seeds, berries, moss, and flowers. The nest of *P. macrolopha* is described as a hole scraped in the ground, and sheltered by a tuft of grass, or a bush, or rock. The species is found nesting at an elevation of from 5,000 to 11,000 feet in the Himalayas."

The Koklass Pheasants.—Genus *Pucrasia*.

The Common Pheasant.—*Phasianus colchicus*.

To the genus *Phasianus* belong the birds which we all know familiarly as pheasants, and it is interesting as representing one of the few types peculiar to the Palæarctic region. There are a great many species of the genus *Phasianus* scattered through Europe, Central Asia, and China, most of them being of the form and general coloration of our common pheasant (*P. colchicus*), which is supposed not to be a native of Western Europe, but to have been imported from the Caucasus or from Asia Minor. Recent discoveries of fossil remains, however, tend to prove that pheasants of some kind were ancient inhabitants of the western Palæarctic region, and it is quite possible that the pheasant of our own day is a descendant of these old forms, and that the story of its introduction into England by the Romans is a myth. At the present time it is very difficult to find a pure-bred pheasant in the British Islands, as by far the greater number of those birds killed in the autumn have white rings round their necks, owing to the introduction of the Chinese ring-necked pheasants, with which our native birds have freely crossed. The genus *Phasianus* is one of the few typical forms of birds peculiar to the Palæarctic region, for in the Himalayas it is represented by the cheer pheasant (*Catreus wallichii*). Thus the true pheasants are found in temperate Europe, where *P. colchicus* is the only representative species of the genus, to Central Asia and China, where the species are many, though in these countries the pheasants have either white rings on their necks or white patches on the upper part of their wings. Of *P. colchicus* there are several representative races, as for instance *P. talischensis*, from Talisch, on the south-western border of the Caspian Sea; *P. persicus*, from the south-eastern shores of the Caspian; and *P. principalis*, from North-Western Afghanistan. Thence in the Oxus Valley, Zarafshan, and other localities in Central Asia, our common pheasant is represented by various species and races, for a description of which students must search the writings of Mr. Ogilvie-Grant and others. The ring-necked pheasants are found from Turkestan to Kuldja, Eastern Siberia,

Fig. 10.—THE COMMON PHEASANT (*Phasianus colchicus*).

China, and the island of Formosa. In Japan a splendid species is resident, *P. versicolar*, remarkable for its dark green breast, and in the same country are found the copper pheasants (*P. sœmmeringi* and *P. scintillans*), birds of a different type altogether from our ordinary pheasant. The finest of all, however, is Reeves' pheasant (*Phasianus reevesi*), which lives in China, and is remarkable for its white crown and the length of its tail, which, in fully adult birds, attains to the dimensions of five feet!

The barred-backed pheasants (*Callophasis*) are represented by two species only, *C. ellioti*, from the mountains of South-Eastern China, and *C. humiæ*, from the Shan States and the Lushai Hills and those of Manipur.

The Caped Pheasants.—Genus *Chrysolophus*.

The best-known species of the genus *Chrysolophus* is the golden pheasant (*C. pictus*), and the name is commonly used to designate the genus, and is perfectly appropriate to the golden pheasant, but is a misnomer for the Lady Amhersts' pheasant, which has no golden colour on its neck, but carries a "cape" of white, barred with steel-blue. The golden pheasant inhabits Southern and Western China to Kokonoor, and *C. amherstiæ* replaces it in the mountains of Western China and Eastern Tibet.

The Jungle-Fowl.—Genus *Gallus*.

These birds have a special interest, as it is from them that all our breeds of poultry have been derived, although it is difficult to believe that a cochin-china, a dorking, or a Spanish fowl can have originated in these spangled, many-coloured denizens of the forests of the East. The nearest approach to the wild stock that domestic variation produces is found in the "Game" fowl, and a very interesting group is to be seen in the Natural History Museum of some birds shot wild in the Fiji Islands by Mr. E. L. Layard, C.M.G. In the early voyages in the Pacific by Captain Cook and other navigators, fowls were turned loose on some of the islands, to provide food for any unfortunate sea-faring folk who might be shipwrecked on them. At the present day these birds have taken to their original habits as jungle-fowl, and have to be hunted and shot. They have, moreover, reverted to the plumage of true jungle-fowl, and though the cocks still show traces of a domestic strain, the hens, as well as some of the cock-birds, have assumed once more the coloration of the wild stock from which they were originally derived. The true jungle-fowl are found at the present day in the Indian Peninsula and Ceylon, the Indo-Malayan region to Cochin-China and the island of Hainan, south to the Philippines, Java, Sumatra, Borneo, Celebes, and other islands of the North Moluccas.

The Peacock Pheasants.—Genus *Polypectrum*.

These are birds of grey coloration, but remarkable for the metallic green, purple, or blue spots or "eyes" which adorn their plumage. Five species are known, inhabiting the Himalayan system of mountains from Sikkim to Tenasserim and Cochin-China, and thence through the Malayan Peninsula to Sumatra, Borneo, and the island of Palawan in the south of the Philippine Archipelago. They are found from the lowlands up to 6,000 feet in Tenasserim. They seem to affect forest country, feeding on fruit, insects, worms, and small land-shells. The call of *P. chinquis*, the Himalayan species, is said by Mr. Clark to be something like a laugh—"*ha—ha—ha*—ha." Mr. John Whitehead says that in Palawan he found the species of the island, *P. napoleonis*, very local, and his specimens were all collected in one district of the forest. It is not known for certain whether the peacock pheasants are polygamous, and Mr. Whitehead inclines to the idea that they are not; but

Mr. Clark once came across a party of four, consisting of one male and three female birds. In Palawan Mr. Whitehead found that Napoleon's peacock pheasant had a "showing-off" ground, like that of the argus pheasants, a bare space cleared in the forest, kept scrupulously clean, "with a small hump of earth in the middle, where, no doubt, the male birds show off their splendid plumage, and perhaps do battle." He adds that the fights, if they have any, must be very short and decisive, as the double spurs of the cocks would be sufficient to cut his adversary into bits. In the Himalayan species, *P. chinquis*, which ranges into Cachar and Tenasserim, as many as four spurs are sometimes found on the legs of the male.

The Argus Pheasants.—Genus *Argusianus*.

Of these extraordinary pheasants, three species are known: the common argus (*A. argus*) of the Malay Peninsula, Gray's argus (*A. grayi*) of Borneo, and *A. bipunctatus*, the habitat of which is at present unknown. In Tonquin the crested argus (*Rheinhardius ocellatus*) occurs. The argus pheasants are remarkable for "the hundred metallic eyes" on the wings, the feathers of which are prolonged in an extraordinary manner, while the tail-feathers exceed in length the dimensions of any of the Game-Birds. Like the giraffe, which most people would think to be incapable of threading its way through jungle, the apparently clumsy argus makes its escape by darting into the thicket, and it is one of the most difficult of birds to force into flight. So says the greatest of modern collectors of birds, the late Mr. W. R. Davison, who spent years in the jungles of Tenasserim and the Malayan Peninsula, engaged in forming that wonderful collection of Oriental birds presented to the nation in 1885 by Mr. Allen Hume, C.B. In Tenasserim he paid great attention to the habits of the argus, and is perhaps the only white man who has seen the bird in its native haunts. He found them extremely shy and difficult of observation, never rising, but seeking safety in running away through the thick jungle. The males themselves do not seem to engage in combat, though they will answer each other's call. The note is "how-how," repeated ten or a dozen times, though the report of a gun in the neighbourhood, or the passing of a troop of monkeys, will set every male calling. The cry of the female is different, "how-o-woo," repeated ten times or more. The males clear an open space in the forest, which Mr. Davison believed to be a "dancing-ground," though he never caught a bird *in flagrante delicto*. Not a leaf is allowed to soil the hallowed spot, though occasionally a male of the fire-back pheasant will intrude, and take a savage delight in driving the argus from his carefully-prepared "arena."

The Pea-Fowl.—Genus *Paro*.

Two kinds of pea-fowl are known, the common *Paro cristatus* of India and Ceylon, and *P. muticus* of Indo-China and the Malayan Peninsula. These birds do not ascend the mountains, as a rule, but are plentiful in the plains of North-Western India, and in Rajputana they are held sacred by the natives. Near Jeypur, for instance, the number of pea-fowl is very large, and they can be observed from the windows of the passing train, walking about in the grass near the sides of the line, or perching on the fences. They are very well-known birds in confinement, and the "train" of eyed plumes, formed by the elongated upper tail-coverts of the male bird, is one of the most extraordinary developments of plumage in the Class *Aves*.

Two very aberrant forms of guinea-fowl, *Phasidus* and *Agedastes*, inhabit West Africa, from Liberia to the Congo; but the true guinea-fowls (*Numida*) are found over nearly the whole of Africa, to which continent and Madagascar they are peculiar. Seven species are recognised, each with a kind of horn or helmet on the head, and they are all birds of the open country, in contradistinction to the crested guinea-fowls, which are forest-haunting birds. The true guinea-fowls (*Numida*) go in flocks, and frequent the scrubby bush on the borders of streams. They escape by running, but when hotly pursued by a dog, they take to the trees, and are so occupied with taking stock of their canine pursuer, that they can be shot down, one after the other. That they can be easily tamed is proved by the way in which they are domesticated in nearly every country. In Damara Land, the late Mr. C. J. Andersson says that he has seen a thousand together. When the birds assemble in search of water, and when a pool is discovered, the first-comers act in a most civilised manner, approaching and drinking their fill, and retiring in an opposite direction, that the next in order may have room to file in and slake their thirst.

The Guinea-Fowls.—Genus *Numida.*

Of the crested guinea-fowls (*Guttera*) four species are known, all inhabitants of the bush-country and forests. One of them is peculiar to West Africa (*G. cristata*), one to South-East Africa (*G. edouardi*), and one to East Africa (*G. pucherani*). Like the ordinary guinea-fowls, when hunted with a dog, they take to the trees, and are easily shot. One of the most beautiful of the group is the vulturine guinea-fowl (*Acryllium vulturinum*), with a bare head like a vulture, whence its name, and remarkable for the bright cobalt-blue colour on the wings and flanks. The bare portions of the head and neck are also cobalt-blue. It is an inhabitant of Eastern Africa, from the Pangani River to Somali Land.

The Turkeys.—Genus *Meleagris.*

The common turkey of our farmyards is descended from the Mexican turkey (*Meleagris galloparo*). Many races of wild turkeys are known in the Southern United States and Florida, each of which has a separate and definite range; but the most beautiful species of all is the Honduras turkey (*M. ocellata*). Though they feed on different kinds of seeds during the day, the turkeys betake themselves at night to the trees to roost. They even ascend the mountains to a height of 8,000 to 10,000 feet, descending to the lower valleys in autumn, when they congregate in great flocks. They are polygamous, and the male leaves to the female the entire duty of rearing the young.

Fig. 11.—THE TURKEY (*Meleagris gallopavo*).

The Toothed Partridges.—Sub-family *Odontophorhinx.*

These are all birds of the New World, and are remarkable for having the edge of the lower mandible serrated and toothed. They are a somewhat large group, and include all the colins and tufted and painted partridges. Two of the best known species are the Californian quail (*Lophortyx californiana*) and the Virginian quail (*Ortyx virginianus*).

The Hemipodes. —Genus *Turnix*.

At the end of the series of Game-Birds are found some tiny birds, which look like dwarf partridges. These are the bustard-quails or hemipodes, which were formerly associated with the true quails (*Coturnix*). The differences between the hemipodes and the Game-Birds are chiefly osteological, and need not be detailed here; but the absence of the hind-toe distinguishes the genus *Turnix* at a glance, though the Australian genus *Pedionomus* has four toes like an ordinary Game-Bird. One of the most curious facts connected with the hemipodes is the superior size and colour of the female. In some cases she is nearly twice the size of her mate, and on the latter devolves the duty of hatching the eggs out and taking care of the young. It is curious that these little birds should have such an ostrich-like peculiarity, but there is otherwise nothing struthious about them, for the hemipodes have the bones of the palate more like those of Passerine-Birds than those of Game-Birds. They frequent the open plains and grass-country, but are also found in some places on the outskirts of cultivation. Hemipodes are entirely birds of the Old World, and are distributed over Africa, Madagascar, India, and China, and extend throughout the Malayan Archipelago to Australia.

The Sand-Grouse—Order *Pterocletes*.

The sand-grouse are peculiar birds, half Pigeons, half Game-Birds, of which the English people are not ignorant. Although the sand-grouse are birds of the desert, and are found throughout Africa, Central Asia, India, and the Tibetan and Mongolian plateaux, there is one species, Pallas' sand-grouse (*Syrrhoptes paradoxus*), which makes regular irruptions from its Eastern home in the Kirghis deserts into Western Europe, and at times visits England in swarms. Doubtless these immigrations have occurred for ages at regular intervals, but in the Middle Ages our ancestors were too much occupied in fighting and cutting each others' throats to notice a swift-flying bird like the sand-grouse, which their weapons would have been powerless to capture. And thus it happens that our first great record of the occurrence of Pallas' sand-grouse in England took place in 1863, and then again in 1888 another great irruption took place, when not only a large number were seen in Western Europe, but they actually stayed and even nested in Great Britain. In some places the flocks were protected by intelligent land-owners; but they ultimately disappeared, having apparently migrated back to their Eastern home.

Fig. 12.—THE PIN-TAILED SAND-GROUSE.
Pterocclurus alchata

The sand-grouse are certainly desert birds, their very plumage being of a sandy colour, and assimilating to their surroundings. In many of their osteological characters they resemble the pigeons, but in the digestive organs they resemble Game-Birds, so that their natural position is as a distinct order between these two well-marked groups. They have feathered legs, but never carry a spur like Game-Birds, and they have either three toes, or, if the fourth toe is present, it is only rudimentary. The egg is, however, peculiar, being neither white like that of the pigeons, nor uniform like that of the pheasants and partridges, nor richly mottled like that of the grouse, but *double-spotted*, with brown spots mostly in evidence, and underlying spots of pale purple. The eggs are, moreover, oval in shape, but equally rounded at each end.

Although the sand-grouse are not often observed during the day-time, they are to be obtained in the mornings and evenings, when they assemble at the water-pools to drink. Of Pallas' sand-grouse the late General Prjevalski writes :—' At the drinking-places, as well as at the feeding-places, these birds never settle on the ground without first describing a circle, in order to assure themselves that there is no danger. On alighting, they hastily drink and rise again ; and, in cases where the flocks are large, the birds in front get up before those at the back have time to alight. They know their drinking-places very well, and very often go to them from distances of tens of miles, especially in the mornings between nine and ten o'clock, but after twelve at noon they seldom visit these spots." Sometimes the sand-grouse are driven south by an unexpected fall of snow, and by clearing the snow from a patch of ground, Swinhoe tells us that the natives sometimes manage to net an entire flock of birds. It may be such a sudden snow-storm that forces the sand-grouse of Central Asia to make the unexpected invasion into Western Europe to which we have referred.

The Pigeons.—Order *Columbiformes.*

The Pigeons are a large order of birds, and are divisible into two sub-orders, *viz.* the *Columbæ* or True Pigeons, and the Dodos (*Didi*). Pigeons have a swelling of the bill near the tip, similar to the bill of the plovers, which we shall discuss presently. At the base of the bill is a soft bare skin, or cere, which is very prominent in some of the fruit-pigeons, and is generally of a bright colour. The osteological and anatomical characters which separate them from the Game-Birds (which some of the ground pigeons greatly resemble) are numerous, the chief one, perhaps, being that the fore-part of the sternum or breast-bone is never perforated to receive the feet of the coracoids, as is the case in the Game-Birds. The nest which pigeons build is one of the simplest structures known among birds, for it consists of a slight cradle of sticks, and is generally placed in a tree. The eggs are white, and two in number, though there are many species which lay but a single egg, and in this order of birds we meet with the great exception to the rule in the Class *Aves*, *viz.* that birds which lay white eggs usually nest in holes or burrows, so that the eggs are concealed from view. Not only, however, are the eggs of the pigeons white, but the frail platform on which they are placed renders them easily visible from above, and often from below. The young are hatched naked, but after a little while become clothed with hairy down ; they remain helpless in the nest for a long time after they are hatched, and are fed by the old birds.

The True Pigeons, of which our ring-dove or wood-pigeon, and the ordinary dove-cote pigeons may be taken as representatives, constitute the order *Columbæ*, and they are divided by Count Salvadori, the latest monographer of the order, into five families.

The Fruit-Pigeons.—Family *Treronidæ.*

The first family of the pigeons consist of the fruit-pigeons (*Treronidæ*) with three sub-families, *Treroninæ*, or green fruit-pigeons, painted fruit-pigeons (*Ptilopodinæ*), and true fruit-pigeons (*Carpophaginæ*). The green fruit-pigeons are found in Africa, India, and the Indo-Chinese sub-region, through the Malayan sub-region to the Molucca Islands. All the members of the sub-family *Treroninæ* have the tarsus short, exceeded in length by the middle toe, and the tail feathers vary from 12 in number to 16, while the chief peculiarity is the broadening of the toes beneath, and having the skin expanded on the soles, as Count Salvadori has pointed out. The green fruit-pigeons are accustomed to assemble in flocks of comparatively large size, and feed, as a rule, on small fruit.

The Painted Pigeons.—Sub-Family *Ptilopodinæ*.

The *Ptilopodinæ* include some of the most beautiful birds of the world among their number. Although they are mostly birds of small size, the exquisite blending of their bright coloration renders their combination of plumage extremely beautiful, and there is no more wonderful bird in the world than the golden fruit-pigeon of the Fiji Islands (*Chrysœnas victor*).

The true painted pigeons (*Ptilopus*) are nearly all highly-coloured birds, and have generally the first primary narrowed to a slender point. They are among the smallest of all the pigeons, many of them scarcely exceeding the bulk of a thrush, but they are ornamented, as a rule, with a patch of bright colour on the fore part of the crown, which may be rose-colour, pink, or even pale lavender. Very little has been written about their habits, but of the allied genus, *Megaloprepia*, which has not the attenuated ending to the first primary-quill, and has a somewhat longer and more rounded tail than *Ptilopus*, we learn from Gould that the magnificent fruit-pigeon (*Megaloprepia magnifica*) is found in the bushes of the interior of South-Eastern Australia, where it feeds on wild figs and the nut-like fruit of the large palms. It is a shy bird, and is not easily discovered, unless it betrays its presence by the hoarse, loud, and monotonous note, which is frequently uttered by the male during the pairing season. The note is so extraordinary, and so unlike that of any other bird, that it causes the utmost surprise and wonderment as to what it can proceed from, in the minds of persons who hear it for the first time. Five species of *Megaloprepia* are known, ranging from the Northern Moluccas to New Guinea and to South-East Australia; whereas no less than 75 of the painted pigeons (*Ptilopus*) are known. They are distributed over the Malayan Archipelago, from the Malay Peninsula to Australia, and even to the Pacific Islands. In Madagascar and the neighbouring islands they are represented by the species of wattled fruit-pigeons (*Alectrœnas*), of which four kinds only are known, that from Mauritius, *A. nitidissima*, being now extinct.

The Large Fruit-Pigeons.—Sub-Family *Carpophaginæ*.

In this sub-family are found some of the largest of all the existing pigeons, and many of them are beautifully ornamented with bright patches of colour. Even where ornamental plumage does not obtain, the tones of rufous and grey and bronzy-green render them very lovely birds. Some have a fleshy knob at the base of the bill, as in the genus *Globicera*; others carry a conspicuous crest, as in *Lopholaimus*. They are found from India and the Indo-Chinese countries throughout the entire Malayan Archipelago to Australia. One of these great fruit-pigeons, *Carpophaga œnea*, is a very well-known-bird in certain parts of India and Burma. In the last-named province Mr. Eugene Oates says that the imperial green fruit-pigeon, as he calls *C. œnea*, is generally distributed throughout the forests and well-wooded parts of the country, wherever, in fact, there are trees which yield edible fruits. It is entirely arboreal, going about in parties, and occasionally in couples, and feeding on fruits. It makes its nest in thickets and bamboo bushes, and lays but one egg, though in India two young birds have been found in a nest.

In the true pigeons, of which our wood-pigeon and rock-pigeon may be considered the types, the tail is always composed of twelve feathers. The soles of the feet are not so broad as in the fruit-pigeons, and, according to Count Salvadori, only the hind-toe has any expansion on the sides. Only four genera of *Columbidæ* are admitted by the above-named author, *viz. Gymnophaps*, represented by a single species from South-Eastern New Guinea, *G. albertisi*, named after the famous Italian naturalist, D'Albertis, who discovered it; *Columba*, with fifty-eight species and a cosmopolitan range; *Nesænas*, from Mauritius, with its single species, *N. mayeri*; and *Turturæna*, peculiar to Africa, with five species.

The True Pigeons.—Family *Columbidæ*.

It is not necessary to dilate on the characteristics of the ordinary pigeons, In the woods, the wood-pigeon or ring-dove is, in many parts of its range, the mildest and shyest of birds, but in confinement it makes the tamest of pets, and can be fed by children in the gardens of Paris, and is now so civilised that it is one of the features of St. James' Park in London. The stock-dove (*C. œnas*) is a more retiring bird, and nests in holes of trees or of old buildings, while the rock-dove (*C. livia*) frequents caves on the sea-coast. From the latter are believed to have sprung all our numerous forms of domestic pigeon. All the species of the African genus *Turturæna* are somewhat rare, and little is known of their habits.

All these are Eastern birds, with a very long tail, exceeding the wing in length. Only four genera are known: *Turacœna*, of Celebes and Timor; *Macropygia*, the dominant form, with about thirty species, mostly of a rufous coloration, with many bands; *Reinwardtœnas*, with its three species, inhabiting the Moluccas from Celebes, south to the Bismarck Archipelago; and lastly, *Coryphœnas* of the Solomon Islands. Both the latter genera have short and somewhat hooked bills.

The Long-Tailed Pigeons.—Sub-family *Macropygiinæ*.

The *Macropygiæ* are commonly called cuckoo-doves, on account of their barred plumage. They are forest-birds, feeding on fruits, and building a slight nest, in which two eggs are laid.

This sub-family is peculiar to North America, and only one species (*E. migratoria*) is known. It has occasionally visited Great Britain. In its native country it is remarkable for the enormous flocks which pass on migration, and occupy a breeding area of great extent. One observer states that he saw a flight of these pigeons five miles long and a mile in breadth, while their nests were found in nearly every tree for a distance of twenty-eight miles. As with the Carolina parrot, however, constant persecution is rapidly diminishing the numbers of this interesting bird. and its nesting-area is no longer so widely extended as in former times.

The Passenger-Pigeons.—Sub-family *Ectopistinæ*.

This family of pigeons has rather a longer leg than those we have been previously discussing, the length of the tarsus being equal to, or exceeding, that of the middle toe. The tail-feathers vary in number from 12 to 20, according to the different genera. The *Zenaidinæ* are exclusively American, the *Peristerinæ* are American and African; the *Geopeliinæ* are American, Australian, and Indo-Malayan; while the *Phabinæ*, *Geotrygoninæ*, and *Calænadinæ* are Malayan and Australian. There is nothing very peculiar about the habits of these ground-doves, but the remaining sub-family *Turturinæ*, or turtle-doves, is one of the largest in the whole family of pigeons, and contains about thirty species, of which our British turtle-dove,

The Ground-Pigeons.—Family *Peristeridæ*.

(*T. turtur*), and the cream-coloured turtle-dove (*T. risorius*) so often kept in cages, are the best-known examples. The sub-family *Calœnadinæ* is represented by the single genus *Calœnas*, the Nicobar pigeons, as they are called, remarkable for their metallic plumage and the long hackles on the neck, like those of a fowl. The crowned pigeons (*Goura*) which are only found in the Papuan Islands, are remarkable for their beautiful crests of diffused plumes. Six species are known, all of them inhabiting different areas of the great island of New Guinea, or the islands immediately adjacent to it.

Fig. 13.—THE CROWNED PIGEON (*Goura coronata*).

The Tooth-Billed Pigeons.—Family *Didunculidæ*.

This interesting form of pigeon, represented by a single genus only, *Didunculus*, is an inhabitant of Samoa or the Navigator's Islands. It has a large hooked bill, which has also some notches or toothed serrations near the tip of the lower mandible. It is remarkable for the similarity of its form to that of the dodo, though, of course, it is on a much smaller scale. Hence the name *Didunculus*, or little dodo, of which the single species, *D. strigirostris*, was, a short time ago, threatened with the same extinction as that which has overtaken its larger relative. The dodo, not having wings capable of flight, was unable to save itself when danger threatened ; but the *Didunculus*, though a ground-bird, and formerly nesting on the ground, so that it was fast diminishing in numbers, owing to the attacks of wild cats, appears suddenly to have resumed its arboreal habits, and now both roosts and nests in trees, so that of late years its numbers have greatly increased.

The sub-order, *Didi*, consists of two genera, *Pezophaps* and *Didus*, both now extinct, but living on the earth less than three hundred years ago. The solitaire (*Pezophaps solitarius*) inhabited the island of Rodriguez, and was about the size of a turkey. The old traveller, Leguat, has given a description of the bird as follows :—"They never fly ; their wings are too little to support the weight of the bodies ; they serve only to beat themselves and flutter when they call one another. They will whirl about for twenty or thirty times together on the same side during the space of four or five minutes. The motion of their wings makes a noise very like that of a rattle, and one may hear it two hundred paces off. The bone of their wing grows greater towards the extremity, and forms a little round mass under the feathers as big as a musket ball. That and its beak are the chief defence of this bird. Some of the males weigh forty-five pounds. The females are wonderfully beautiful, some fair, some brown ; I call them fair, because they are of the colour of fair hair. They have a sort of peak, like a widow's, upon their breasts (*lege* beaks), which is of dun colour. No one feather is straggling from the other all over their bodies, they being very careful to adjust themselves, and make them all even with their beaks. The feathers on their thighs are round like shells at the end, and being there very thick, have an agreeable effect They have two risings on their craws, and the feathers are whiter than the rest, which lively represents the fine neck of a beautiful woman. They walk with so much stateliness and good grace, that one cannot help admiring and loving them; by which means their fine mien often saves their lives. We find in the gizzards of both male and female a brown stone, of the bigness of a hen's egg; 'tis somewhat rough, flat on one side, and round on the other, heavy and hard. We believe that this stone was there when they were hatched, for let them never be so young, you meet with it always. They have never but one of 'em, and besides, the passage from the craw to the gizzard is so narrow, that a like mass of half the bigness could not pass. It served to whet our knives better than any other stone, whatsoever."

The dodo lived in Mauritius, and more is known of its appearance than of the solitaire, as several drawings of it were made from life, and now exist in various libraries. A foot of the bird is in the British Museum, and another is in the Ashmolean Museum at Oxford, along with a head, these being the last relics of an embalmed specimen which was destroyed by the authorities at Oxford in 1855. Another head of the dodo is in the Museum at Copenhagen, but the actual remains of the body of this wonderful bird are very few, and the species is principally known from the skeletons which have been unearthed during the last few years. The heavy body of the dodo, with its feathery tail, and wings represented by a few plumes only, have led some authorities to consider it as a kind of struthious bird, from the similarity of its wings to those of an ostrich, but recent researches have shown that the dodo was a gigantic pigeon.

Fig. 14.—The Dodo (*Didus ineptus*).

We have now followed the Class *Aves* from the Ratitæ, through the Tinamous to the Game-Birds, and thence through the Sand-Grouse to the Pigeons. We now come to a sudden stop in the continuity of the series of orders of birds, and take up the thread of connection a little further back, it being absolutely impossible to follow a direct linear arrangement in a scheme of classification.

The hoatzin has the appearance of a Game-Bird, and especially of a guan. Like the latter birds, it is an inhabitant of South America, where it is found on the Amazon and the rivers of Guiana, Venezuela, Colombia, Ecuador, Peru, and Bolivia. For all its guan-like appearance, the bird is more of a rail than a Game-Bird, and its curious nest, suspended in the branches overhanging the water, is like that of a rail, while its eggs greatly resemble those of the *Rallidæ.* Many of its anatomical characters, its osteology, and the peculiarities of the young birds, show that the genus *Opisthocomus* is an isolated form, probably the survival of some ancient stock of birds, of which it is the only survivor. Fossilized remains of a bird like the hoatzin have been found in France, so that the type may have been far more widely spread in ancient times, and have been distributed over certain portions of the Old World.

One curious feature about the hoatzin is the size of its crop, which is situated in a deep cavity in the upper half of the pectoral muscles. It occupies the upper part of the chest, and is so enormous as to distort the furcula and sternum. The nestling is hatched naked, and has a well-developed claw on the pollex and index fingers of the wings, so that it is able to crawl about by their means. Mr. J. J. Quelch, the Director of the Museum at Georgetown in British Guiana, has written a most interesting account of the hoatzin, from which we have extracted the following notes :—"Soon after the hatching of the eggs, the nestlings begin to crawl about by means of their wings and legs, the well-developed claws on the pollex and index being constantly in use for holding and hooking on to the surrounding objects. If the birds are drawn from their nest by means of their legs, they hold on firmly to the twigs both with bill and wings ; and if the nest be upset by means of a rod pushed up from below, they hold on to all objects with which they come in contact by means of bill, feet, and wings, making considerable use of the bill, not only to reach objects above them, but also with the help of the clawed wings to raise themselves to a higher level. One curious feature noticed with a nestling which had been upset in the river, was its power of rapid swimming and diving when pursued. As soon as the hand was placed close to it, it rapidly dived into the dark water, in which it was impossible to see it, and would rise at distances of more than a yard away. Owing to this power, the little creature managed to evade all my attempts to seize it, taking refuge eventually under the bushy growth, where it was impossible to pursue it. The prolonged immersion which a nestling will thus instinctively and voluntarily undergo, or which an adult bird will bear in an attempt to drown it, seems to me to be quite remarkable.

Fig. 15.—THE HOATZIN (*Opisthocomus cristatus*).

"The nestlings, when resting on the bare sticks of the nest, are observed to rest the weight of the body, as in the adult birds, on the bare and thickened integument of the *carina sterni*, the toes being spread out and the wings generally drawn up to the side."

The food of the adult hoatzin consists of leaves or fruit, and the birds after death have a very unpleasant odour, which prevents them being eaten as food. They are incapable of sustained flight, and in this fact we see another rail-like characteristic. Mr. Quelch observes :—"Whether from the fact of their occupying situations where they are but seldom disturbed, or but little likely to be pursued, or from a natural weakness of wing, the birds are but seldom seen in flight ; and when they take to the wing during disturbance, they do so for but a very short distance—a very exceptional flight being once observed of a length of about 40 yards, with the wind, across a creek, from a high growth on one bank to a lower level on the other. Usually they rise almost with a jump from the branch, seldom in a straight line, but with a marked convex curve to the point where they alight. The flight of the birds, in spite of their great expanse of wings, in relation to the weight of the body, is thus extremely awkward, and the body presents a peculiarly humped appearance. During their longer courses, the wings are rapidly and violently flapped. The apparent awkwardness in placing themselves when they alight, is chiefly due, I believe, to the smallness of the branches on which they usually settle, and which they are unable firmly to grasp with their long toes, balancing themselves meanwhile by the expanded wings and tail; but it is also attributable, I think, though to a much less degree, to a certain weakness in their legs—even though they are thick and apparently strong-looking—since when they alight on a thick limb, a certain amount of instability is still manifest.

"This weakness of limbs seems to be still more evidenced by the method of perching characteristic of the birds. At any time during the heat of the day they will be found resting on the branches, two or more together, the body directly applied to the wood, and supported on the bare, thickened, and hardened patch of skin which covers the flattened and broadened surface of the posterior determination of the *carina sterni*."

From the game-like rail, or rail-like Game-Bird *Opisthocomus*, we now pass to the true rails. Only one family can be admitted, which bears the name of *Rallidæ*. At first sight it would seem more natural to divide the rails into three families—true rails (*Rallidæ*), water-hens (*Gallinulidæ*), and coots (*Fulicidæ*); but after a prolonged study of the family, we have come to the conclusion that there is no separation to be drawn between these apparently natural groups, and the most that can be done is to recognise two subfamilies, rails and water-hens (*Rallinæ*), and coots (*Fulicinæ*), the latter having lobate webs on the toes like the grebes.

The Rails.—Order *Ralliformes*.

That the rails are birds of an ancient origin is undoubted. Their feeble powers of flight are compensated for by their swiftness of foot and power of concealment, and at the present day there are many flightless rails, descendants of an ancient stock. At the same time there are species, like our corn-crake (*Crex crex*), which are capable of long migrations, as are also others of the crakes; but, as a rule, the rails are stay-at-home birds, and do not care for long journeys across the seas. With the exception of the blue water-hens (*Porphyrio*), they are birds of rather sombre coloration.

Numerous fossil species of rails have been described from the Miocene and Eocene formations, and in America extinct forms (*Telmatornis*) have been found in the Cretaceous.

Fifty-three genera of rails have been admitted by me in the twenty-third volume of the "Catalogue of Birds," and the following are the most remarkable, and call for special notice. The *Rallidæ* may be divided into three great groups—true rails (*Rallinæ*), crakes (*Crecinæ*), and coots (*Fulicinæ*). As before mentioned, on account of their lobed toes, the coots may be even further separated from the rails and crakes.

In the rails the bill is long and slender, so as to exceed in length the middle toe and claw. The crakes have a shorter and stouter bill. The true rails may be divided into two groups, water-rails and wood-rails. Of the former four genera are recognised, and our English water-rail is the type of this section. The water-rail is certainly not a bird to be observed every day. It is the impersonification of shyness and retiring habits. A coot or a moor-hen is often seen in the open, and may be observed from the windows of a railway train, swimming about on lakes or pools of water, the coot easily discernible by its waxy-white shield on the forehead, the moor-hen by its red frontal shield and the bright red garter above the hock, which is easily in evidence as it swims. The water-rail, on the contrary, is never seen, nor can its voice be heard, like that of the noisy corn-crake. It is a bird of the reed-beds and the marshes, and is so disinclined for flight, that even when pursued by a dog, it will double and turn and twist, rather than fly, and is often caught by the dogs before it can bring itself to use its wings. The eggs are numerous, from seven to eleven in number, of a creamy white, double-spotted, with reddish-brown overlying spots and ashy-grey underlying ones. The nest is well concealed among coarse herbage, of which it is composed, and the young are covered with black down, and can take care of themselves soon after they are hatched, swimming and diving, and managing to conceal themselves from danger in a marvellous manner.

The Rails.—Sub-Family *Rallinæ.*

Fig. 16 —WATER-RAIL (*Rallus aquaticus*).

The water-rails are found all over the New World, and also in the Old World, except in the Indo-Malayan sub-region and the whole of the Australian region, where their place is taken by the barred rails (*Hypotænidia*). In the tropical regions of South America, *Limnopardalus* replaces the genus *Rallus*, and in the islands of the Australian region, the dusky rails (*Cabalus*) are one of the most curious forms of bird-life. In the Chatham Islands is, or rather was, found *C. dieffenbachii*, now believed to be extinct, and in these islands also occurs *C. modestus*, a dusky-brown species, which cannot fly, and is also on the verge of extinction, while a third species, *C. sylvestris*, is peculiar to Lord Howe Island.

The Wood-Rails.

These are birds of the bush and forest, though showing considerable likeness to the water-hens. They are found in both hemispheres, and one genus at least, *Megacrex*, from Southern New Guinea, is incapable of flight. The black wood-rail (*Habroptila wallacii*) was discovered by Dr. A. R. Wallace in the island of Halmahéra in the Moluccas, and when sent home by him, the species was described and figured in the "Proceedings of the Zoological Society," as an ordinary rail standing in the water. Consequently, when the Dutch travellers received instructions from Professor Schlegel to be sure and find *Habroptila*, they searched for the bird in the marshes, but ultimately discovered it in the bush. It is altogether a curious form, black like a water-hen, and having a small frontal shield.

Perhaps one of the most interesting genera of this group of rails are the wood-rails of the neo-tropical region (*Aramides*), which have a somewhat ornamental plumage of rufous and grey, with a bright yellow bill and red legs. Of late years they have been seen in the aviaries and zoological gardens of Europe, and have even been known to nest in captivity.

Of the ypecaha wood-rail of Argentina (*Aramides ypecaha*) Mr. Hudson, the biographer of Argentine birds, has given many amusing details, and he credits the species with considerable intelligence, repudiating the idea that this wood-rail is to be considered an ideal member of what has been called a "stupid family" of birds. He writes :—"On spying an intruder, it immediately utters a powerful cry, in strength and intonation not unlike that of the pea-fowl. This note of alarm is answered by other birds at a distance as they hastily advance to the spot whence the warning was sounded. The cry is repeated at irregular intervals, first on one side, then on the other, as the birds change their position to dog the intruder's steps and inspect him from the reeds. I have surprised parties of them in an open space, and shot one or more ; but no sooner had the survivors gained their refuge, than they turned about to watch and follow me, sounding their powerful alarm the whole time. I have frequently been followed half a mile through the rushes by them, and by lying close and mimicking their cries, have always succeeded in drawing them about me. But the ypecaha's loudest notes of alarm are weak compared with the cries he utters at other times, when, untroubled with a strange presence, he pours out his soul in screams and shrieks that amaze the listener with their unparalleled power. These screams, in all their changes and modulations, have a resemblance to the human voice, but of the human voice exerted to its utmost pitch, and expressive of agony, frenzy, and despair. A long piercing shriek, astonishing for its strength and vehemence, is succeeded by a lower note, as if in the first one the creature had well-nigh exhausted itself. The double scream is repeated several times ; then follow other sounds, resembling, as they rise and fall, half-suppressed cries of pain and moans of anguish. Suddenly the unearthly shrieks are renewed in all their power. This is kept up for some time, several birds screaming in concert ; it is renewed at intervals throughout the day, and again at set of sun, when the woods and marshes resound with the extravagant uproar. I have said that several birds unite in screaming ; this is invariably the case. I have enjoyed the rare pleasure of witnessing the birds at such times, and the screams then seem a fit accompaniment to their disordered gestures and motions. A dozen or twenty birds have their place of reunion on a small area of smooth, clean ground surrounded by reeds ; and by lying well concealed and exercising some patience, one is enabled to watch their proceedings. First one bird is heard to utter a loud metallic-sounding note, three times repeated, and somewhat like the call of the guinea-fowl. It issues from the reeds, and is a note of invitation quickly responded to by other birds on every hand as they all hurriedly repair to the customary spot. In a few moments, and almost simultaneously, the birds appear, emerging from the reeds and running into the open space, where they all immediately whirl about and begin the exhibition. Whilst screaming, they rush from side to side as if possessed with frenzy, the wings spread and agitated, the beak wide open and raised vertically. I never observed them fight or manifest anger towards each other during these performances ; and, knowing the pugnacious spirit of the ypecahas, and how ready they are to seek a quarrel with birds of other species, this at first surprised me, for I was then under the mistaken impression that these gatherings were in some way related to the sexual instinct. Whilst watching them I also remarked another circumstance. When concealing myself amongst the rushes I have been compelled to place myself so disadvantageously, owing to the wet ground, that any single bird straying accidentally into the open space would have discovered my presence immediately; yet the birds have entered and finished their performance without seeing me, so carried away are they by the emotion that possesses them during these moments. But no sooner has the wild chorus ended than, aware of my presence, they have fled precipitately into the reeds."

The Crakes.—Sub-Family *Crecinæ*.

These are rails with a stout bill, the culmen being shorter than the middle toe and claw. They may be divided into two sections, distinguished by the presence or absence of a bare frontal shield. Those which possess the latter characters are the moor-hens.

Among the largest of the crakes are the weka rails of New Zealand (*Ocydromus*), of which there are three species. These birds are remarkable for their pugnacious disposition, and also for the tameness with which they will wander from their homes in the bush, even entering camps and houses. They are heavy-bodied birds, with feeble wings, which are insufficient to carry them through the air, and they are consequently incapable of flight. Like their distant relative, the *Apteryx*, they serve themselves by running only, and are also protected by their crepuscular habits, being more lively at night than in the day, and calling throughout the dark hours. These birds evince a curious antipathy to anything of a red colour, and this is the more interesting as remains of extinct forms of weka rails have been found in the Mascarene Islands, one of which is known as *Erythromachus*, "the fighter of red." The former distribution of forms of flightless rails in New Zealand and the Chatham Islands, almost, if not absolutely, identical with each other, has given rise to some very interesting speculations as to whether there was an ancient continuation of land area between these two portions of the globe. Certainly the discovery of the remains of an extinct genus, *Aphanapteryx*, in Mauritius and in the Chatham Islands, is very remarkable.

The Smaller Crakes.

Of these, the most typical form is our corn-crake or land-rail (*Crex crex*), whose harsh voice is heard in the hay-fields during the summer, often far into the night. Like all of its kind, the corn-crake loves seclusion, and is seldom seen on the wing, except during the shooting season, when the birds are driven up by the dogs. Even then they only take short flights, and drop into cover again. Everything points to the wing-power of the corn-crake being of the feeblest description and yet we know that it must be a bird capable of covering considerable distances, as it reaches South Africa on its winter migration. The little crake (*Zapornia parva*), the spotted crake (*Porzana porzana*), and Baillon's crake (*Porzana intermedia*), are all species which visit England, and the genus *Porzana* may be said to be cosmopolitan in its range. In the Sandwich Islands were found two curious flightless crakes of small size, *Pennula ecaudata* and *P. sandwichensis*, and in the island of Kushai also lived till recently a small black crake (*Aphanolimnas monasa*). All these interesting little birds are now believed to be extinct, and as they could not fly, they were doubtless exterminated by cats and rats. In the island of Laysan in the Pacific, however, there still exists one of these curious little crakes, *Porzanula palmeri*.

Numerous genera of small crakes are known, of which space does not permit us to give a detailed description; but the distribution of the white-winged crakes (*Ortygops*) is deserving of special mention. There are four species, each of which is peculiar for having some white quills, which are very conspicuous when the bird flies. The distribution of the four species is very interesting. One, *O. noveboracensis*, is only found in North America ; a second, *O. exquisita*, in Eastern Siberia and China ; a third, *O. notata*, in Uruguay ; and a fourth, *O. ayresi*, in South-Eastern Africa.

Passing from the crakes to the water-hens, we find many varied forms, some of them flightless, as *Pareudiastes pacificus*, the black water-hen of Samoa, and the isolated water-hens of Tristan d'Acunha (*Porphyriornis nesiotis*) and of Gough Island (*P. comeri*). All rails, isolated on any island, appear to become rapidly incapable of flight. They seem to be birds which are always averse to taking wing, and doubtless for this reason the power of flight soon disappears ; but they are, as a rule, perfectly able to take care of themselves by running, or by concealing themselves in the grass.

The Water-Hens.—Genus *Gallinula*.

The water-hens are found all over the world, and are all very similar to our own species, the "moor-hen," as it is frequently called (*Gallinula chloropus*). They are birds of black plumage, and have a bare red shield on the forehead. The most brilliant of all the rails are the blue water-hens (*Porphyrio*), which are found all over the Old World, from the Mediterranean over Africa, and from India and China to Australia, They are very handsome birds, with bright red bills and red legs, contrasting with their blue and green plumage, and in many places they are kept in confinement as ornamental fowl ; they are, however, somewhat destructive and mischievous. The largest of the blue water-hens is the famous *Notornis* of New Zealand, which is a giant form, incapable of flight, and believed to have become extinct during recent years. A fossil form of rail, *Aptornis*, also from New Zealand, was at first believed to be a small kind of moa, which will give some idea of its large size.

The Coots.—Sub-family *Fulicinæ*.

These birds are remarkable for their stout bodies, bare frontal shield of ivory-white or yellow, and, above all, for their curiously lobed toes. They are found in nearly every part of the globe, and several species are met with in South America. One of the most curious of the ancient forms was the extinct *Leguatia gigantea* of Mauritius.

Fig. 17.—THE FINFOOT. (*Heliornis fulica*).

The Finfeet.—Family *Heliornithidæ*.

These curious birds are intermediate between the rails and the grebes, and are chiefly remarkable for their lobed toes, which in the South American finfoot (*Heliornis fulica*) are banded with black and yellow. Whereas all the rails, as well as the water-hens and coots, have the nestlings clothed in black down, the young finfoot is said to be hatched naked. At present very little is known about these birds and their habits, and the above statement may turn out to be incorrect. It certainly seems to be very unlikely that birds so obviously connected with the rails and grebes should have anything but downy young. There are three genera of the *Heliornithidæ*—*Podica* from Africa, *Heliopais* from Burma and Malacca, and *Heliornis* from South America. All the species are very shy and difficult of observation. The Senegal finfoot (*Podica senegalensis*) was found by Mr. Büttikofer in Liberia, and his is apparently the only record of the habits of the birds. They swim about in pairs, and do not seek to escape by diving, like the rails or grebes, but simply by concealing themselves in the foliage on the banks. When flying, which they seldom do, they go heavily, striking the water with their bill and feet.

The Grebes.—Order *Podicipedidiformes*.

These birds are familiarly known on account of the use made of their beautiful white breasts for muffs or the trimming of dresses, but in a wild state they are not easy to observe, as they are among the shiest of birds. Although the species are not very numerous, there is scarcely a portion of the globe which grebes do not inhabit. The feet are lobed, and there is never any visible tail, the broad rectrices of other birds being represented in the grebes by a tuft of downy plumes.

The Sclavonian Grebe (*Podicipes auritus*).

The Sclavonian Grebe is one of the most beautiful of the order, and is an inhabitant of the northern portions of both hemispheres. It is not an unfrequent visitor to Great Britain in winter. The great-crested grebe (*Podicipes cristatus*) is almost cosmopolitan in its range, and is the largest of the British species. It is still to be found nesting on some of the Norfolk broads and inland lakes of England, building, like all grebes, a nest of the dampest description, composed of weeds and rushes. The eggs are at first white, but become stained in a very short time, as the bird generally covers them up with weeds on leaving the nest. All the grebes are splendid divers, and even the little nestlings take to the water soon after they are hatched, and escape either by diving or by hiding themselves in the weeds and rushes. The nestlings are very pretty little creatures, covered with soft down of a zebra-like pattern in streaks of white and black or brown.

Fig. 18.—THE SCLAVONIAN GREBE (*Podicipes auritus*).

There are not many genera of the grebes, most of the species belonging to the genus *Podicipes*, but in America the thick-billed grebe belongs to a distinct genus, *Podilymbus*, while on Lake Titicaca, in Bolivia, is found a large form, *Centropelma*, which has such small wings that it is apparently incapable of flight.

The dabchick of our English waters (*Tachybaptes fluviatilis*) is one of the smallest grebes, and is distributed over the greater part of the Palæarctic region, but is replaced by an allied species in Africa (*T. capensis*), and in India by *T. albipennis*.

In the summer the dabchick frequents rivers, lakes, and even ponds and small sheets of water, where it builds a nest of weeds, which are always in a moist condition, and the nest always resembles a small heap of refuse more than anything else. A dabchick is a pretty object to watch, but it is so shy a bird that a near approach is impossible, and it is only at a distance that they can be seen swimming about on the water. On the first sign of danger, it disappears like magic, and comes to the surface again for a second, only to dive again out of sight on the instant. If one of them be surprised in the open, it will dive immediately, and if there be a bed of reeds or other shelter, it makes for them under the water, and one never knows at what distance its head will reappear. Twenty and thirty yards is by no means an uncommon dive for a dabchick to make, and it uses its lobed feet as propellers and steerers, not making much use of its wings, which are held close to the body, the stumpy and soft tail being of no sort of use to it as a steering apparatus.

The downy nestlings are striped, and in the first plumage the dabchicks are brown above. In the autumn they are to a certain extent migratory, and are shot in our tidal harbours ; but in mild winters they do not desert their native homes. In summer, both sexes don a nuptial plumage, with a yellow patch on the bill and a black breast, against which the rufous colour of the face and neck forms a striking contrast. In all the grebes, the brighter colours and the ornamental tippets and crests are dropped during the winter season.

Fig. 19.—The Little Grebe or Dabchick (*Tachybaptes fluviatilis*).

The Divers.—Order *Colymbiformes.*

The divers are birds of the Northern Hemisphere, few in number and arctic in habitat. Four species are known, all of which are found in Great Britain, two of them nesting within our limits. The red-throated diver (*Colymbus septentrionalis*) is one of them, and the black-throated diver (*C. arcticus*) is the second. The great northern diver (*C. glacialis*) is a more or less frequent visitor in winter, and the white-billed diver (*C. adamsi*) has occurred a few times.

The Great Northern Diver (*Colymbus glacialis*).

This is chiefly known as an inhabitant of North America and Iceland, as the great northern diver which breeds in the Old World will probably be found to be *C. adamsi.* The habits of all the divers are much the same. On the water they are at home, swimming about and diving with the greatest of ease ; but on land they are very awkward, and the backward position of their legs seems to make it impossible for the birds ever to stand upright. In fact, they seem to shuffle along the ground with a snake-like motion, and never walk. They excel all the grebes in their power of flight, though, as a rule, they trust to their swimming and diving powers to escape from danger, and are often to be seen swimming in the sea far away from land ; and they are also able to submerge their bodies, so that only the head and neck is exposed, and they can remain under water for an astonishing time, the great northern diver having been known to remain below the surface for eight minutes. The nesting-place is on some inland loch or secluded lake, and the nest is a poorly constructed affair. The eggs are two in number, of a russet-brown or olive-brown colour, with black spots and fainter black underlying markings.

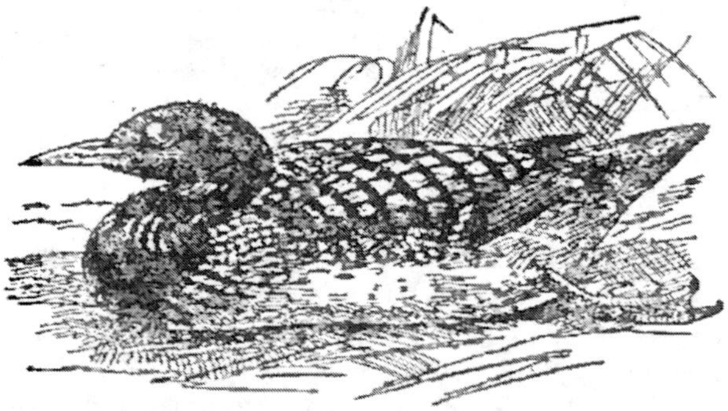

Fig. 20.—The Great Northern Diver (*Colymbus glacialis*).

The divers differ from the grebes in having webbed feet and a well-developed tail. The young birds are covered with down, and are able to dive and shift for themselves shortly after they are hatched. The sexes are alike in plumage, and they have a distinct summer and winter dress, as with the grebes.

The Penguins.—Order *Sphenisciformes*.

The penguins are birds of the Southern Hemisphere, the most northerly ranging species occurring in the Galapagos Islands, off the coast of South America. They are chiefly remarkable for their close-set plumage, unlike that of any other birds, and the flipper-like character of their wings. The feathers, which are harsh and scaly, and generally devoid of barbs, are distributed over the whole body, so that there are no bare spaces between the feather-tracts, as in most birds. Penguins are found in astonishing numbers in the Southern Seas, especially at their breeding-places, which are selected on rocky islands, such as Kerguelen, Tristan d'Acunha, the islets round New Zealand, and the Falklands. As they cannot fly, great havoc is worked among them on their island homes during the nesting season, when thousands are killed for the sake of their oil.

Fig. 21.—The King Penguin (*Aptenodytes longirostris*).

The penguins vary very much in size, from the diminutive *Eudyptila minor* to the gigantic emperor and king penguins (*Aptenodytes patachonica*) of the Antarctic Seas. They always walk or hop in an erect position, and they are assisted in the support of their heavy bodies by the unusual strength of their tarsi, the metatarsal bone being very short and wide. The scapular bone is also of unusual width for a bird. The nestlings are covered with dense down, which is retained for a considerable period, until, in fact, the birds are nearly full-grown.

The habits of all the penguins are very similar, and the following account of the "Johnnie" (*Pygoscelis tæniata*), by the Rev. A. E. Eaton, who observed the species on Kerguelen Island, during the "Transit of Venus Expedition," is very characteristic of the order, and we therefore give the following extracts :—

"It builds in communities, some of only a dozen, others from 70 to 150 families. A more populous colony was visited by six officers from the ships, who estimated the number of nests in it to amount to 2,000 or more. These larger communities are approached from the sea by regular paths, conspicuous at a distance, like well-worn sheep tracks, which lead straight up the hill from the water. Their formation is due to the penguins being very particular about where they land and enter the sea. A small party of the birds occupied a position upon the neck of a low promontory within an hour's walk of Observatory Bay. Their nests were nearest to the farther side of the isthmus ; but when they were approached, the male birds used to run to the water, not by the shortest route where it was deep close to the rocks, but by the longest to a place where the shore was shelving. It was amusing to see them start off in a troop as fast as their legs could carry them, holding out their wings and tumbling headlong over stones in their way, because as they ran they would keep looking back instead of before them, and to hear their outcries. Panic and consternation seemed to possess them all ; but the females (possibly because they could not keep up with their mates) seldom went far from their nests, and, if the intruder stood still, soon returned and settled down again upon their eggs. Not many weeks had passed before a change was effected in their conduct. The young were hatched, and now the mothers anxiously endeavoured to persuade them to follow the example of their fathers, and run away to sea. But the nestlings preferred to stay in their nests; they did not mind if the stranger did stroke them, although their anxious mothers ran at him with open mouths whenever he dared to do so. Only a few of the older chicks could be prevailed upon to stir, and they, after waddling a few yards, became satisfied with their performance, and turned to go home again. The mothers, who had straggled to a greater distance, began to return too. It was now that the more tardy youngsters began to experience the ills of life. Every penguin that had reached its place before them aimed blows at them as they passed by towards their own abodes. One of the little birds certainly did seem to deserve correction. It saw its neighbour's nest empty, and sat down in it. The old female Johnnie, the rightful occupier, presently returned in company with her own chick, to whom, having put her head well into his mouth, she began to administer refreshment after his run. Seeing them so pleasantly engaged, the small vagrant, thoughtlessly presuming upon her generosity, went nearer and presented himself to be fed also, as if he had a right to her attention and care. She looked at him while he stood gaping before her with drooping wings, unable for the moment to credit what she saw. But suddenly the truth flashed upon her, and, provoked by his consummate audacity, she gave vent to her indignation, pecked his tongue as hard as she could, chased him out of the nest, darting blows at his back, and croaked ominously after him as he fled precipitately beyond the range of her beak, leaving trophies of down upon the scene of his unfortunate adventure. The whole of this community of penguins was subsequently boiled down into 'hare soup' for the officers of H.M.S. *Volage*, and very nice they found it. The nests were composed of dried leaf-stalks and seed-stems of pringlea, together with such other suitable material as happened to be at hand. There were two eggs in every nest, and one of them was invariably larger than the other. Most likely the birds hatched from the larger eggs are of the opposite sex to those which are produced from the smaller. Whether the big or the little egg is the first to be laid was not ascertained.

"As is the case with many other kinds of birds, Johnnies are very regular in their habits. Every afternoon at nearly the same time they repair to the shore when they have done fishing, landing in small parties at their accustomed places at the heads of shallow inlets. On issuing from the water they dispose themselves to rest, seldom proceeding beyond the verge of the shore. Those which are inclined to sleep put their heads behind their flippers; the others stand amongst them with their neck shortened so as to bring the head down close to the body, with the beak slanting upwards and forwards, somewhat in the manner of a very young thrush during repose. Their eyes present a rather tearful appearance, and resemble bits of dull black glass set in their heads,—perhaps the nictitating membrane may be kept drawn over them. At frequent intervals a kind of watery fluid is ejected from their mouth by a shake of the head."

The Petrels.—Order *Procellariiformes*. The petrels are also often called the *Tubinares*, on account of their tubular nostrils. They are generally associated with the gulls, but there is really little in common between the two groups, beyond the fact that they are both marine orders of birds. The petrels differ from the gulls in many important anatomical and osteological characters, but we need go no further here than to specialize their peculiar nostril and bill, the covering of the latter consisting of several horny pieces separated by deep grooves.

The albatroses are the largest of the petrels, and, indeed, possess a wider spread of wing than any known bird. On the other hand, some of the storm-petrels are hardly larger than a swallow. All of them have a peculiar odour, a sort of musky smell, which clings to the person after handling a number of these birds. The eggs, too, are impregnated with this smell, which adheres to them for years after they have been in a cabinet.

The petrels lay but one egg, and this is generally concealed under a rock or boulder, the nest being of the flimsiest description, though the albatroses make a rough nest in the open. The young are covered with down, and remain helpless for some time in the nest; the down is generally of a sooty colour, but is white in the case of some of the larger albatroses. Mr. Osbert Salvin, in his recent work on the group, recognises four families—*Procellariidæ* or storm-petrels, *Puffinidæ* or shearwaters, *Pelecanoidæ* or diving-petrels, and *Diomedeidæ* or albatroses.

There are two sub-families of the *Procellariidæ*, the short-legged petrels (*Procellariinæ*), and the long-legged petrels (*Oceanitinæ*). In the former we find the storm-petrel of the British coast (*Procellaria pelagica*), which is the typical form of the group. It inhabits the North Atlantic Ocean as far south as West Africa, and enters the Mediterranean Sea. At the nesting time it visits the islands and western coasts of Great Britain, but has not been found breeding on the east coasts of England or Scotland. Another well-known member of the storm-petrels is the fork-tailed or Leach's petrel, which is found throughout the North Atlantic, and also occurs in the Japanese Islands. It is a larger bird than the storm-petrel, and is easily known by its forked tail. It breeds on some of the Outer Hebrides and also on the islands off the coast of Kerry. A curious instance of the way in which petrels are distributed over the ocean, and how very little we really know of their range, has lately been noted in England, where in December, 1895, a specimen of the Canarian fork-tailed petrel was obtained for the first time, at Littlestone in Kent. It is only fourteen years ago that this species was described by Mr. Ridgway from the Sandwich Islands in the Pacific, to which it was believed to be confined. In 1895 Mr. Ogilvie-Grant discovered it on the Salvage Islands in the Atlantic, and now the British Museum contains specimens from Madeira and the Desertas group, as well as from St. Helena. It has also been recently discovered as an inhabitant of the Galapagos Islands off South America. Another remarkable case occurred a few years ago, when a petrel from the Fiji Islands and the New Hebrides, *Œstrelata brevipes*, one of the rarest of all petrels, turned up unexpectedly in Wales. It had never been heard of before away from the Pacific Ocean.

Fig. 22.—FORK-TAILED PETREL (*Oceanodroma leucorrhoa*).

This family is numerously represented in all the great oceans of the world, with the exception of the Indian Ocean, where there are not so many species. The British Islands are visited by several species of *Puffinus*, and one, the manx shearwater, is resident and breeds on St. Kilda, as well as in other places in the west of Europe. Like all other members of their family, the shearwaters are birds of rapid flight, and may be seen in flocks far out at sea, apparently revelling in the rough weather.

The Shearwaters and Fulmars.—Family *Puffinidæ.*

The fulmar-petrels (sub-family *Fulmarinæ*) are also very widely distributed over all the oceans, and some of them are as large as gulls, one species, *Ossifraga gigantea*, from the Southern Seas, being as large as some of the albatroses. The common fulmar-petrel (*Fulmarus glacialis*) is a well-known inhabitant of the seas of Arctic Europe, and nests on St. Kilda and the Shetland Islands.

The diving-petrels (*Pelecanoididæ*) are curious little birds from the Southern Seas, which have much the appearance of the little auk (*Mergulus alle*) of the Northern Hemisphere. Mr. Eaton says that, like that species, the diving-petrels have a hurried flight, and dive into the sea without any interruption of the action of their wings; both also emerge from beneath the surface flying, and they both swim with their tails rather deep in the water. This resemblance, he says, does not extend to other particulars of their habits. The little auk, when breeding, usually flies and fishes in small flocks of six or a dozen birds, and nests in communities of considerable size, which are exceedingly noisy. Diving-petrels, on the other hand, are more domestic in their mode of living, fishing and flying for the most part in pairs or alone, and nest sporadically. Their burrows are about as small in diameter as the holes of bank martins or kingfishers. They are made in dry banks and slopes where the ground is easily penetrable, and terminate in an enlarged chamber, on the floor of which the egg is deposited. There is no specially constructed nest. Some of the burrows are branched, but the branches are without terminal enlargements, and do not appear to be put to any use by the birds.

The family of albatroses or *Diomedeidæ* contains three genera, *Diomedea* with nine species of true albatroses, *Thalassogeron*, or culminated albatroses, with five species, and *Phœbetria*, or sooty albatroses, with a single species. Most of the members of this family are birds of wide range, whence the common species gets its name of "wandering." They are remarkable for their wide extent of wing and their graceful and sustained flight. At certain periods of the year they resort to the islands in the Southern oceans to breed, and the gatherings which take place are sometimes incredible. Thus on the island of Laysan, in the Pacific, thousands upon thousands of eggs of the white albatros (*Diomedea immutabilis*) are collected. Mr. Palmer, who visited this island on behalf of the Hon. Walter Rothschild, says that the birds literally covered

Fig. 23.—The Wandering Albatros (*Diomedea exulans*).

the surface of Laysan, the young in some places being as thick as they could stand. He writes :—"It is very curious to watch the love-making antics of the birds. First they stand face to face, then they begin nodding and bowing vigorously, and then rub their bills together with a whistling cry ; after this they begin shaking their heads and snapping their bills with marvellous rapidity, occasionally lifting one wing, straightening themselves out, and blowing out their breasts ; then they put their bill under their wings or toss it in the air, with a groaning scream, and walk round each other, often for fifteen minutes at a time. They are quite fearless, and do not move out of the way. When Mr. Freeth was going to the guano-field on his tram-way-line, he had to send a boy ahead to clear the tracks of the young albatroses."

Mr. D. le Souef gives a very interesting account of a visit to Albatros Island in Bass' Straits, Australia :—"The nests of the cautious albatros (*Thalassogeron cautus*) are situated at varying distances one from the other, from a foot upwards, some on the ground, and others again on the uneven side or top of a point of rock. Some of the birds had come on shore to rest only, while a few of them had their heads turned back and partially under their wings, and were asleep. When one wished to fly it had to walk to the edge of the cliff, and go off with a downward sweep ; but when the wind was blowing very strong the bird could then rise, facing it, from a point of rock. One bird I found in a depression about 60 feet across and 30 feet deep, with steep sides, and as it could neither climb or fly out I caught it and climbed up the bank with the bird under my arm, and took it back to the "rookery." On approaching very close to the birds, they would partly stand up on their nest, leaning backwards and apparently resting the tail on the edge of the nest, and then facing the intruder. When one was within two feet of them, they would utter a loud cackling noise, shaking their heads up and down, and opening and shutting their beaks rapidly. A considerable noise was made by the mandibles coming together, and at the same time a strong-smelling oily secretion was thrown up. In order to secure an egg, the beak of the bird was caught hold of with one hand and the egg taken up with the other, and on stepping back the beak was let go again. The bird would then sit or stand on its nest for some time afterwards. The birds often had difficulty in alighting on a particular spot, when the wind was blowing strongly on to their breeding-ground from the sea, as they always flew against the wind when desiring to alight, and I have watched them sometimes try seven or eight times before they could successfully accomplish their object. They came up with considerable force, holding their heads well back, and stretching out their expanded feet at the same time, and the fact of having their wings half-closed gave them a very ungainly appearance when alighting."

The Auks.—Order *Alcæ*.

The auks are birds of the Northern Seas. They form a peculiar group, and are usually associated with the gulls, from which birds, however, they differ in many important characters, though in their osteology the two orders have many points in common. Externally, however, the differences are apparent at a glance. The gulls are splendid flyers, but are no great divers, while diving is one of the chief features of an auk's economy. Again, the gulls make a nest of some sort, the auks seldom or never, for the latter birds select a bare ledge or cleft of a cliff, or the broken rocks, on which to lay their egg, the colour and markings of which are entirely different from those of any gull or tern.

One of the most interesting of all the *Alcæ* is the great auk, which was a kind of gigantic razorbill, but possessing such diminutive wings that the power of flight was denied to it. It has become extinct during the first half of the present century, and specimens of the bird and the egg fetch large prices whenever they come into the market. The great auk, as Professor Newton has pointed out, owes its extinction entirely to the agency of man, who hunted the bird to its destruction. It seems to have had a comparatively limited range, having been abundant in Newfoundland and the adjacent shores of North America and Iceland, ranging in smaller numbers to the Hebrides and the shores of Northern Britain.

Fig 24.—The Great Auk (*Plautus impennis*).

The razorbill (*Alca torda*) and the guillemot (*Uria troile*) are well-known British birds, which breed in vast numbers on our coasts, the best-known nesting colonies being on the cliffs of Flamborough and on the Farne Islands, Here large numbers of the eggs are taken every year, those of the guillemot presenting an endless variety of colour and marking. The black guillemot (*Uria grylle*) nests in the Arctic regions, and in the north of Scotland and Ireland, and the rotche or little auk (*Mergulus alle*) is a winter visitor to Great Britain, being often driven far inland by stress of weather. The breeding-places of the little auk have been described as tenanted by countless thousands, Admiral Beechey having stated that he saw a column of these birds on the wing at one time which he estimated at four millions!

Our English puffin, or sea-parrot, is a representative of the group of the auks which are most numerous in the North Pacific Ocean, where several crested species are found. They are remarkable for the coloration of the bill, which is grooved in a curious fashion, and exhibits bright colours, while there is also a blue excrescence above the eye. These ornamental features of the bird's bill are a sign of the breeding-season, and are shed as by a moult in the winter, to be resumed in the following spring. The birds of the year have quite a small bill, without any of the grooving or coloured ornamentation which characterises the adults. Puffins differ from the other auks in their nesting habits, the egg, which is white, with occasionally a few indistinct markings, being placed in a rabbit burrow, or in a hole tunnelled by the birds themselves.

Fig. 25.—The Puffin (*Fratercula arctica*).

The gulls are divided into two families, the true gulls, or *Laridæ*, and the skuas, or *Stercorariidæ*. The general appearance of gulls is too well known to detain us long with the characters which define the order, which is admitted to be closely related to the order *Charadriiformes*, the great group of plovers and snipes, with which the Gulls possess many anatomical characters in common, though they differ from the plovers and their allies in having webbed feet. The *Laridæ*, or true gulls, differ from the skuas in having no "cere" on the bill, which is a feature in the latter family. The cere is a wax-like bare space at the base of the bill, a common characteristic of Hawks and Parrots, but rare in every other order of birds, and it is decidedly interesting that it should reappear in a family of gulls, especially as it is combined with a decidedly rapacious disposition in the skuas.

The Gulls—Order *Lariformes.*

The family *Laridæ* is divided by Mr. Howard Saunders into three subfamilies: the terns, or sea-swallows (*Sterninæ*); the skimners (*Rhynchopinæ*); and the gulls (*Larinæ*).

The sea-swallows are found all over the world, from the high north to the extreme south. They are mostly marine, but many of them are birds of the marshes, especially during the nesting season, while others frequent rivers and inland lakes. It is, however, on the sea that these graceful birds are generally seen to the greatest advantage, as they hover over the water, or glide along above its surface, occasionally dropping down to capture some small fish or other prey. They often follow shoals of small fry, and we remember seeing a flock of large terns in the Red Sea, evidently engaged in decimating a shoal of fish on the surface of the water, and keeping up such a cackling all the time that they could be heard at least a mile off.

Fig. 26.—Arctic Tern (*Sterna macrura*).

In the British Islands we have thirteen different kinds of terns, five of which breed with us, the best known being the common tern (*Sterna fluviatilis*), the arctic tern (*S. macrura*), and the lesser tern (*S. minuta*). The sandwich tern (*S. cantiaca*) now only nests in a few localities; and a few pairs of the beautiful roseate tern (*S. dougalli*) are believed to still breed in one or two places off our coasts. Among the visitors to the British Islands are the three species of marsh tern. belonging to the genus *Hydrochelidon*, which have only moderately forked tails, the outer feather or "streamer" not being prolonged, as in most of the terns. The black tern (*H. nigra*) is the commonest of the three species which visit England, the white-winged black tern and the whiskered tern being of very rare occurrence. These marsh terns nest in swamps and marshes throughout temperate Europe, Asia, and North America, and they are plentiful in the marismas of Southern Spain and the Danube. The nests are made of weeds, and are placed on tussocks, or on floating vegetation.

The largest of the terns is the Caspian tern (*Hydroprogne caspia*), a large red-billed species, which measures nearly two feet in length, and is found over the greater part of the globe. The common and Arctic terns are species which breed in colonies on many parts of the British coasts, laying their eggs on the shingle, and making scarcely any attempt at a nest. The eggs have a great resemblance to those of some of the plovers, and, like the latter are difficult to distinguish on the ground. This is especially the case with the eggs of the lesser tern (*Sterna minuta*).

One of the rarest visitors to Britain is the sooty tern (*Sterna fuliginosa*). This is the species which breeds in such enormous numbers on certain islands, such as Laysan in the Pacific, and Ascension Island in the Atlantic. In the latter the assemblage of these birds is known as "Wideawake Fair." On Ascension, according to Mr. Howard Saunders, the sooty terns lay but one egg, and this was also found to be the case by Mr. Palmer on Laysan, the birds being perfectly fearless, and not moving off their nest, but pecking and biting at anyone that approached them. As many as two hundred dozens of eggs have been collected on Ascension Island in the course of a morning, and this will give some idea of the numbers frequenting that spot.

In the tropical islands of the southern oceans is found a curious form of tern, snowy-white in plumage, with a pointed black bill. This is the snowy tern (*Gygis alba*), which possesses a very wide range over the islands of the Pacific and South Atlantic. It lays but a single egg, which is placed carelessly among the rocks or scrub, but is also often found in a cavity of a branch or on the fork of a tree.

The Skimmers.—Sub-family *Rhynchopinæ*.

These curious river terns are called scissor-bills, on account of the remarkable disparity in the length of the two mandibles of the bill and their extreme sharpness of the ridges, which is compressed like the blade of a pair of scissors. The name given to the American species by one of the old writers in 1731 is "cut-water," a very good title for the bird, as these scissor-bills fly along the top of the water, cutting the latter with their blade-like under mandible, which is considerably longer than the upper one. The skimmers frequent rivers in the tropical countries of the Old and New Worlds, being found nesting as far north as Virginia in North America, and Egypt in the Old World. The eggs, which resemble those of the true terns, are laid on sand-banks in the rivers frequented by the birds. Five species are known, each with a separate range, *Rhynchops nigra* being found in the Southern United States to Central America, *R. intercedens* in Brazil, and *R. melanura* in the northern part of South America. *R. flavirostris* is an inhabitant of Africa, and *R. albicollis* of India.

The Gulls.—Sub-family *Larinæ*.

Their heavy build and square tails, as a rule, distinguish gulls from terns, but it must be remembered that some of the gulls are small, and many are not so big as the Caspian tern, for instance. The forked tail of the terns is seen in one genus of gulls, *Xema*, which contains two species, Sabine's gull (*X. sabinii*), and the large fork-tailed gull (*X. furcata*). The former is an inhabitant of the Arctic Seas, but sometimes straggles as far as the coasts of Britain, while *X. furcata* is only known from the Galapagos and the coasts of Western America. Ross's gull (*Rhodostethia rosea*) is another Arctic species, which on rare occasions visits Europe, but is one of the rarest of all the gulls, and is remarkable for its wedge-shaped tail and the beautiful rosy blush on its white breast, which is like that seen in the roseate tern.

Of the true gulls (*Larus*), of which the common gull (*L. canus*) may be considered the type, there are more than forty species known, and these are distributed, like the terns, throughout the greater part of the globe, from the Arctic regions in the north to the extreme south. The gulls may be divided into two groups, those with a hood and those without. The hooded gulls comprise such species as our black-headed gull (*Larus ridibundus*) and its allies, another British species being the little gull (*L. minutus*). The other gulls with which we are familiar in this country, such as the greater black-backed gull (*L. marinus*), the lesser black-backed gull (*L. fuscus*), the herring gull (*L. argentatus*), have white heads and white tails. The habits of gulls are much the same all the world over. They feed mostly on fish ; but some of the larger kinds are not only great robbers, but will eat almost anything, and will devour young birds and even sickly mammals. The little black-headed gull, on the other hand, is a most useful bird, as it frequents and breeds in inland districts, where it often follows the plough, and devours large numbers of grubs and insects. The other gulls breed on the rocky coasts, mostly in the north, sometimes in vast numbers together. This is especially the case with the kittiwake (*Kissa tridactyla*), which is separated from the true gulls on account of the absence of a hind toe.

Fig. 27.—The Common Gull (*Larus canus*).

The skuas are often called the parasitic gulls, from their habit of robbing the smaller gulls of their food, instead of catching it for themselves. They differ from the true gulls in having a cere, or bare wax-like base, to the bill. The latter is very strongly hooked at the tip, and in the posterior portion of the sternum, or breast-bone, there is only a single notch, instead of two, as in the gulls.

The Skuas.—Family *Stercorariidæ.*

Four species of the great skuas are known, of which one, *M. catarrhactes*, is an inhabitant of the North Atlantic, where it breeds in a few scattered localities, such as Iceland, the Faeroes, and Norway, and a few pairs still nest in the Shetland Isles, where great pains are now taken to preserve them, as they had become nearly extinct there. They not only feed on fish and carrion, but rob other gulls of their prey, and even kill and eat some of the smaller species. The eggs are two in number, and the birds become very bold in defence of their nests. A second species of great skua (*M. chilensis*) inhabits both the Atlantic and Pacific coasts of South America, from Peru on the west, to Southern Brazil on the east. From the New Zealand seas to Kerguelen, and thence to the Falkland Islands, occurs *M. antarctica*, while in Victoria Land and the frozen countries of the Antarctic Continent is found a peculiar pale form of great skua, *M. mac-*

The Great Skuas.—Genus *Megalestris.*

Fig. 28.—Buffon's Skua (*Stercorarius parasiticus*)

cormicki. The long-tailed skuas (*Stercorarius*) differ from the members of the preceding genus in having more or less elongated central tail-feathers, these being developed in some of the species to a great length. The members of the genus *Stercorarius* are three in number, all of them breeding in the high north, and visiting more southern localities in winter. With the exception of the Pacific coast of South America, where only the pomatorhine skua (*S. pomatorhinus*) has been known to occur, the whole of the other Southern oceans appear to be visited by these skuas. They all nest on the tundra of the Arctic regions, and the pomatorhine skua and Buffon's skua are only winter visitors to the British Islands, but Richardson's skua (*S. crepidatus*) nests in the Orkneys and Shetland Isles, as well as in some of the Hebrides and on the north-west of Scotland. Like their larger relatives, these smaller skuas live principally by robbing the terns and smaller gulls of the fish they capture. They will also devour young birds and eggs, as well as lemmings and small rodents, crustacea, etc., while the young of Buffon's skuas are said to be fed on crowberries in the summer.

The Plovers and Bustards.—Order *Charadriiformes*.

As has already been mentioned, there are many characters which the *Charadriiformes*, or Limicoline birds, as they are often called, share with the gulls, the principal one being the cleft, or schizognathous palate. The nostrils are almost entirely schizorhinal, or in the form of a slit, though there are exceptions to this in the seed-snipes, the bustards, and the thick-knees. The eggs of most of the *Charadriiformes* are peculiar to the group, being generally pear-shaped, four in number, and double spotted, having the overlying markings black, arranged in lines, blotches, or spots, and the underlying spots grey. The young are covered with down, and can take care of themselves very shortly after their birth, running with great swiftness, and being able to escape capture by their protective coloration, which effectually conceals them in the midst of their natural surroundings.

The Crab-Plovers.—Sub-order *Dromades*.

There is but a single species to represent this sub-order, and it is one of the most peculiar of birds. While possessing anatomical characters which show that it is an aberrant kind of plover (though many observers have considered it to be rather an aberrant kind of tern), it differs from all gulls and plovers in laying a pure white egg. Its nesting habits are in fact altogether peculiar. Not only does it lay a white egg, but only one, and that is placed in a tunnel hollowed out in the sand, as described below. The crab-plover is a handsome black and white bird, the mantle being black, and having the plumes elongated, so as to form a swallow-tailed patch when the bird is flying. It is long-legged, like a thick-knee or stone-plover, and inhabits the coast-land of Eastern Africa and Arabia, the Persian Gulf, and the eastern shores of the Indian Ocean, as far as Ceylon, reappearing in the Andamans and the Nicobar Islands in the Bay of Bengal. It probably breeds in most of the above localities, but the headquarters of the species seem to be in the Persian Gulf, and the coasts of Arabia and Mekran. Mr. Nash, who visited one of the islands off Bushire, found that the birds burrowed into the sand-hills to the distance of about four feet, and in the shape of a bow, the passage being about a foot below the surface of the ground, and the entrance usually near or under tussocks of grass or low shrubs, the single egg being laid on the bare soil at the end of the hole, without any sign of a nest. The birds nest in colonies, and the young, which are covered with greyish down, remain in the holes during the day, like young petrels, and they are apparently night-feeders.

Like *Dromas*, the sheathbills are very aberrant members of the Limicoline group, and are only found on the islands of the Atlantic, such as the Crozettes, Kerguelen, Marion Island, and the Falklands. The species of the latter islands is *Chionis alba*, the yellow-billed sheathbill, which is also found in Southern Patagonia, and extends to the island of South Georgia and the land of the Antarctic Continent. The species inhabiting Kerguelen and Marion Islands is *Chionarchus minor*, which has a black bill, and does not exhibit the wattles on the face found in *Chionis alba*. The form of the sheath is also somewhat different, though both show a tube-like opening on the base of the bill, something like that of a petrel. In the bird from the Crozettes (*Chionarchus crozettensis*) this petrel-like opening to the sheath is absent, and the bird is smaller than *C. minor*, and has darker legs.

The Sheathbills. —Sub-order *Chionides.*

Fig. 29.—THE YELLOW-BILLED SHEATHBILL (*Chionis alba*).

The Rev. A. E. Eaton gives an amusing account of the habits of the sheathbills in Kerguelen Island during the visit of the "Transit of Venus Expedition" to that place. They were common where the coast was rocky and sheltered, and were seen in flocks of as many as thirty, but during the breeding season they were met with only in pairs. They were very tame and inquisitive, and suffered considerably in consequence during the stay of the expedition, as they could often be knocked on the head with a stick. Mr. Eaton writes.—"They were also very assiduous in their attendance on the colonies of shags and crested penguins, whose eggs they greedily devoured. The sitting birds stretched out their necks and croaked at the sheathbills sauntering past their nests; but the marauders, keeping just out of reach of their bills, paid little regard to them, and proceeded in a business-like manner to eat up the first eggs they chanced to find unguarded. It occasionally happened that while an old shag was gesticulating violently at a *Chionis* in front of her, his friend pecked from behind at the eggs, which, in the excitement of the moment, were not completely covered by her. When she found out what was taking place she drove him away with a croak, and, true to her sex, affected to have won her point in the affray. Reseating herself upon the nest with great dignity of deportment, and gently replacing with her bill the broken eggs under her feathers, she resigned herself to the task of trying to hatch them. Some time after the sheathbills have gone away the broken eggs are inspected, and if there is only a small hole pecked in each of them they are kept in the nest. Their appearance and manner of caressing one another led the blue-jackets to call sheathbills 'white pigeons.' In their gait and flight they closely resemble ptarmigan; and like these they utter their cry when starting on the wing, as well as during flight. After they have attained a fair rate of speed, they sail along from time to time with outstretched wings. On alighting at their destination they often greet one another with a gentle chuckle, nodding their heads the while."

The eggs of the sheathbills are plentifully marked, and resemble those of oyster-catchers among the plovers. The nest is a rough affair, placed in a hole behind or between rocks, sometimes an old burrow of a petrel being used and enlarged by the sheathbill. Enough has been said to show that the sheathbill is a very remarkable form of bird. Its inquisitiveness and tameness reminds us of the weka rails, while its habit of devouring eggs is also one of the bad propensities of the larger rails. In some other respects, as Mr. Eaton remarks, it resembles a ptarmigan, and that it is a bird of considerable power of flight is proved by a specimen in the British Museum, which was shot whilst flying round a ship 200 miles from land.

The Seed Snipes.—Sub-order *Attagides.*

These birds are only found on the Andes and in the southern portion of South America, from Argentina to Tierra del Fuego and the Falkland Islands on the east, and from Chili to Ecuador on the west. There are but two genera, *Attagis* and *Thinocorus*, the former birds being as large as grouse, the latter of the size of a quail. Despite their game-like plumage, they are allied to the plovers, though they differ from these in having a palate much like that of a passerine bird, while the nostrils are holorhinal, not schizorhinal. The nest is a mere depression in the ground, sometimes lined with a few blades of grass, and the eggs are pale stone-colour, very thickly speckled with light and dark brown.

The Plovers.—Sub-order *Charadrii.*

This is a very large group, and contains all the plovers, snipes, and sandpipers. The palate throughout is cleft or schizognathous, the nostrils split or schizorhinal, basipterygoid processes are present, and the spinal feather tract is forked on the upper back. The eggs are nearly always pear-shaped, four in number, and are deposited point to point. The plovers and snipes form one large family, *Charadriidæ*, but there are no less than ten sub-families.

The Phalaropes.—Sub-family *Phalaropinæ.*

These are small Arctic birds, which exhibit certain grebe-like characters, for they have the toes lobed, swim well, and have also a serrated edge to the hinder margin of the *planti tarsi*, the hind portion of the exposed leg being exactly as in the grebes. The phalaropes are likewise remarkable for their bright coloration, in which the female excels the male, and is the handsomer bird of the two; she is also larger than the male, and does all the courting. There are three genera of phalaropes, each containing a single species—*Crymophilus*, with the grey phalarope (*C. fulicarius*); *Phalaropus*, with the red-necked phalarope (*P. hyperboreus*); and *Steganopus*, with Wilson's phalarope (*S. tricolor*), as the representatives of the three respective genera. The two former breed in the Arctic regions of both hemispheres, but Wilson's phalarope inhabits temperate North America. All of them migrate far south in winter, and are found off the coasts of South America as well as in the Indian and Australian seas.

Some of the details of the nesting habits of phalaropes, as observed by Mr. E. W. Nelson in Alaska, are very amusing. Speaking of the red-necked phalarope (*P. hyperboreus*), he remarks:—"As the season comes on, when the flames of love mount high, the dull-coloured males move about the pool, apparently heedless of the surrounding fair ones. Such stoical indifference usually appears too much for the feelings of some of the latter to bear. A female coyly glides close to him and bows her head in pretty submissiveness, but he turns away, picks at a bit of food, and moves off; she follows, and he quickens his speed, but in vain; he is her choice, and she proudly arches her neck, and, in mazy circles, passes and repasses close before the harassed bachelor. He turns his breast first to one side, then to the other, but there is his gentle wooer ever pressing her suit before him. Frequently he takes flight to another part of the pool, all to no purpose. If, with affected indifference, he tries to feed, she swims along side by side, almost touching him, and at intervals rises on wing above him, and, poised a foot or two above his body, makes a half-dozen quick, short wing-strokes, producing a series of sharp whistling noises in rapid succession. In the course of time, it is said, water will wear away the hardest rock, but it is certain that time and importunity have their full effect upon the male phalarope, and soon all are comfortably married, while *materfamilias* no longer needs to use her seductive ways and charming blandishments to draw his notice. About the first of June the dry rounded side of a little knoll, near some small pond, has four dark heavily-marked eggs, laid in a slight hollow or whatever lining the spot affords, or, more rarely, upon a few dry straws and grass-blades, brought and loosely laid together by the birds. Here the captive male is introduced to new duties, and spends half his time on the eggs, while the female keeps about the pool close by."

The Snipes.—Sub-family *Scolopacinæ*.

Snipes and sandpipers differ from plovers in having a long bill, with no "dertrum." The latter name is applied to the swelling of the end of the bill, which makes this portion higher than the middle or the basal part. Similar swellings are seen in pigeons. The bill in many of the snipes is widened at the tip and is pitted, but it is not deeper at the end than at any other part of its length. The nasal groove or depression in which the nostrils are placed is continued through nearly the whole line of the bill. The snipes and sandpipers, moreover, differ from the *Totaninæ* or *Tatlers* in having their long toes cleft to the bases, without any connecting web between the basal joints.

The Painted Snipes.—Genus *Rostratula*.

The sub-family *Scolopacinæ* may be divided into two main groups, the snipes and woodcocks, which have the eye placed far back in the head, almost on the ear-opening, while the sandpipers have the eye placed as in other ordinary wading birds. One of the most curious genera belonging to this sub-family is that of the painted snipes (*Rostratula*), which contains three species, one, *R. semicollaris*, being confined to South America, while *R. capensis* is found in Africa and India as far north as Japan, *R. australis* taking its place on the Australian continent. In these painted snipes, which resemble ordinary snipes in their habits, we meet with the same peculiarity as in the phalaropes, *viz.* that the female is handsomer in plumage than the male. The latter is a grey bird, with rounded spots of golden buff on the wing-coverts and quills, while the female is not only larger, but has chestnut on the hind neck, and in the hen of *R. capensis* on the throat also. The South American *R. semicollaris*, however, does not differ in the plumage of the sexes. In Chili and Peru occurs the curious *Phegornis mitchelli*, which has a chestnut neck like *Rhynchæa*, but has no hind toe.

The true woodcocks (*Scolopax*) are only two in number, our own well-known species, and a dark form resident in the mountains of Java and New Guinea, called *S. saturata*. In North America, however, there is a small form called *Philohela minor*, which is distinguished by its attenuated outer primaries; and in the island of Bourou, in the Malay Archipelago, occurs a peculiar woodcock

The Woodcocks.—Genus *Scolopax*.

Neoscolopax rochusseni. All the woodcocks differ from the snipes in having successive broad bars of black and buff on the hinder head and neck, whereas the snipes always have a buff band down the centre of the crown. They are likewise birds of the woods and forests rather than the open marshes, which the snipes love to frequent. The jack snipe (*Limnocryptes gallinula*) differs from the true snipes in having four notches in the hinder margin of the sternum instead of two.

The true snipes (*Gallinago*), of which our common snipe (*G. gallinago*) is the type, differ from the woodcocks in having much more pointed wings, the long inner secondaries equalling the primaries in length, while the markings on the head are longitudinal, not crosswise. They are lovers of the marshes, as a rule, but some of them occur only on the high lands, and appear to have the habits of woodcocks. Such are the wood-snipe (*G. nemoricola*) of the Himalayas, and the imperial snipe (*G. imperialis*) of the Andes of Colombia, and Jameson's snipe (*G. jamesoni*) from the Andes of Ecuador in South America. In the Auckland and Chatham Islands are found peculiar tawny-coloured species (*G. aucklandica* and *G. pusilla*), which run like rails, and do not take to flight, unless very hard pressed. With the exception of these few resident species, snipes are migratory birds, nesting in the temperate and sub-Arctic regions of the north, and going to the far south in winter. Thus Latham's snipe (*G. australis*) nests in Japan and winters in Australia, and the North American Wilson's snipe wanders south to British Guiana and Brazil, and the great snipe (*G. major*), which breeds in the north of Europe, winters in South Africa. Snipes vary very much in the number of the tail-feathers, our own snipe having only 14, though sometimes it is found with 16, but in the wire-tailed snipes, *G. stenura* and *G. megala*, as many as 26 and 20 are found. These two species nest in Eastern Siberia, and visit India and China in great numbers on migration. The outer tail-feathers in *G. stenura* are reduced to wire-like plumes, the eight feathers on the outside measuring less than 0·2 inch in width. The largest of the snipes are *G. gigantea* from Southern Brazil, and *G. undulata* of British Guiana, which are from 15 to 20 inches in length.

Fig. 30.—The Common Snipe (*Gallinago gallinago*).

A curious habit of the common snipe during the nesting season is known as "drumming." "The male may then be seen," says Mr. Seebohm, "in broad daylight, high in the air, wheeling round and round in enormous circles, and flying diagonally upwards with rapid beats of the wings, then swooping down an imaginary inclined plane with half-expanded and visibly-vibrating wings, but with outspread tail-feathers, uttering a sound which is technically called 'drumming.'" The sound is heard only when the bird is descending, but some observers assert that they have heard it proceeding from a snipe on the ground or perched on a dead branch. It has been likened to the bleating of a goat, and bears some resemblance to the suppressed gobble sometimes heard from a turkey. Many naturalists believe that the sound is produced by the vibration of the wings or the action of the air on the outspread tail ; but others,

Mr. Seebohm among the number, believe that it is effected by the vocal organs.

The sandpipers differ from the snipes in having the position of the eye normal, and not reaching to the ear-opening, as in the snipes and woodcocks. In this group of the sub-family *Scolopaeinæ* we find some of the most interesting of the waders, the purple sandpipers (*Arquatella*), the dunlins (*Pelidna*), the knots (*Tringa*), the curlew sandpipers (*Ancylochilus*), the stints (*Limonites*), and the sanderlings (*Calidris*). They are mostly birds which breed in the Arctic regions, and go to the southern continents of the globe to pass the winter. Of the curlew sandpiper no egg has yet been found; of the knot no really authentic egg is known; and of the sanderling but very few. In this group of sandpipers occurs the spoon-billed sandpiper *Eurynorhynchus pygmæus*), a little stint with a spoon-shaped bill, which nests in the arctic regions of Eastern Siberia, where Nordenskjold met with it during the voyage of the *Vega*, and passes along the coasts of Japan and China to winter on the shores of Burma.

The Tatlers.—Sub-family *Totaninæ*.

These birds are very closely allied to the foregoing, but are distinguished by having the outer toes connected with the middle one by a web at the base. In the *Totaninæ* are included all the curlews and whimbrels (*Numenius*), the godwits (*Limosa*), the tatlers (*Totanus*), the green sandpipers (*Helodromas*), the summer snipes (*Tringoides*), the wood sandpipers (*Rhyacophilus*), and the ruffs (*Pavoncella*). They are mostly birds which build in northern climes and in the temperate portions of the Palæarctic and Nearctic regions. The nest is usually placed in a marsh, the eggs being pear-shaped and four in number, laid with the pointed ends directed towards each other; the green sandpiper (*Helodromas ochropus*), however, nests in trees, utilising the old nest of a thrush or some other bird in which to deposit its eggs. The tatlers frequent the sea-shores on their journey south, and their musical notes enliven the dreary expanse of mud-flats on many parts of the British coasts during the autumn. In the breeding season many of the stints have a musical trill or song, which they utter as they mount into the air above their nests.

One of the most remarkable of the tatler group is the ruff, no two males of which are alike in plumage. The female, called the reeve, is smaller than the male, and of a plainer brown plumage. In winter both sexes don a plain-coloured dress, much like that of any other tatler, and the male can only be distinguished from the hen by his larger size. On arriving at their breeding-places in Europe and Siberia, the males have a large ruff or shield on the neck, and a tuft of occipital plumes on each side of the head. These ruffs are sometimes plain without bars, and may be white, rufous, or black, while every kind of variation is seen in the colour of the ruffs and occipital ornaments. Sometimes they are white barred with black, or rufous with black bars; in fact,

Fig. 31.—THE RUFF (*Pavoncella pugnax*).

the variation is endless. They are pugnacious birds, and fight for the females, before whom they dance and pirouette, always ending by placing the bill on the ground, so as to display the beauty of the ruff to the chosen lady.

Close to the true curlews comes the pearl-grey curlew (*Ibidorhynchus struthersi*), which is found on the inland streams of the mountains of China, Central Asia, and the Himalayas. It is the sole representation of the sub-family *Ibidorhynchinæ*, and has a curlew-like bill, but differs in having the metatarsus reticulated both in front and behind. In outward appearance it much resembles the small ibises, but an examination of the skull shows that it is really an aberrant Limicoline bird.

The Stilts and Avocets.—Sub-family *Himantopodinæ*.

These birds are remarkable for their long legs and for the shape of their bills. In the stilts (*Himantopus*) the bill is slender and straight, and the legs are extremely long, and when the birds are flying these are carried out behind them, and from their bright red colour are very conspicuous. The stilts are mostly black and white birds, distributed through the marshes of the temperate and tropical portions of both hemispheres, while a completely black species (*H. melas*) is found only in New Zealand.

The avocets have the bill upturned, and the lower edge of the under mandible is broad and flattened, the bird using it to scoop aside the sand in search of food. The range of the avocets is very similar to that of the stilts, and though they pass southwards in winter, they nest in Africa and India in places suitable to their marsh-loving habits. One species, *Recurvirostra andina*, is only known from the Andes of Chili, and in Australia the chestnut-breasted avocet is found (*Cladorhynchus leucocephalus*), a bird with webbed toes and devoid of a hind toe like the avocets, but with a very slightly up-curved bill, and with longer and more stilt-like legs.

The sub-family *Peltohyatinæ* is represented by a single genus, *Peltohyas*, which again has but one species, *P. australis*. This bird has usually been considered to be a kind of dotterel, and it has a dertral swelling towards the end of the bill, as in these birds, but the tarsus has transverse scutes both in front and behind, and the species is more like a courser in appearance. I fully expect that an examination of its osteology and general anatomy will prove that it is allied rather to the latter birds than to the plovers.

The True Plovers.—Sub-family *Charadriinæ*.

In this sub-family we find the majority of the plovers, which are distinguished by having both aspects of the tarsus covered with hexagonal scales. They may be divided into two groups, the lapwings and the dotterels, the former with broad and rounded wings, mostly resident in the countries they inhabit; the latter with sharp and pointed wings, with the secondaries nearly as long as the primaries, and accustomed to long migrations. Some of them are known, like the American golden plover (*Charadrius dominicus*), to be capable of immense flights, such as from Labrador to the Bermudas, without touching land.

Two genera have longer bills than any of the rest, *Thinornis* and *Anarhynchus* of New Zealand. The latter is known as the wry-billed plover, and has its bill twisted to the right. Then comes the long array of dotterels, such as *Ægialitis*, of which our common ring-dotterel is the type. The members of the genus *Ægialitis* are found nearly over the whole world, and perform long migrations to the South in the winter. Their four pear-shaped eggs are laid in a little depression in the sand or shingle, and the nestlings are difficult to capture, on account of their resemblance to the surroundings in which they are hatched ; the same may be said of the eggs, which closely resemble the adjacent shingle. Some of the other dotterels, such as the members of the genus *Ochthodromus*, are handsome birds, with a chestnut collar across the chest. The true dotterels (*Eudromias*) are mountain-breeding birds, and our English species, *E. morinellus*, is the only one of the group with any black on the belly. This, however, is not assumed as a breeding-dress, as is the case with the grey and golden plovers.

The latter birds have a spangled plumage, and don a black breast in summer, passing into a white-breasted livery in winter. The grey plover (*Squatarola helvetica*) differs from the golden plover (*Charadrius pluvialis*) in having a hind toe. It nests on the tundra or barren grounds in the Palæarctic and Nearctic regions beyond the limit of forest growth, and until recently its eggs were amongst the rarest in collections. Mr. Seebohm and Mr. Harvie Brown, however, have obtained them on the Lower Petchora River, and Mr. Trevor-Battye and Mr. H. J. Pearson on Kolguev Island.

Another group of the broad-winged lapwings is represented by our common pewit (*Vanellus vanellus*), which has no wattle on the face or spur on the wing, like many of the other genera of the *Charadriinæ*, such as the spur-winged plovers of Africa (*Hoplopterus*), which have a formidable spur on the bend of the wing, with which they fight. *H. spinosus* is said to be the species which attends on the crocodile, and enters its mouth to clean the teeth of the monster. Some of the other genera of this group of plovers have a facial wattle, but no spur on the wing, while in the genus *Xiphidiopterus* we have two species, one Javan, and the other West African, which have a large wing-spur and a conspicuous facial lappet as well.

Fig. 32.—The Common Lapwing (*Vanellus vanellus*).

All the wattled plovers (sub-family *Lobivanellinæ*) have the metatarsus transversely scaled in front, but reticulated behind. They are nearly all broad-winged birds like the pewits or lapwings, and most of them have spurs on the wings, and wattles or lappets on the face.

We now come to a group of the *Charadriinæ*, where there is no swelling at the end of the bill, and in this section of the plovers are the oyster-catchers (*Hæmatopodinæ*) and the turnstones (*Arenariinæ*).

The Oyster-catchers.—Sub-family *Hæmatopodinæ*.

All the oyster-catchers have the metatarsus reticulated both in front and behind, and the angle of the lower mandible is placed very far back, the end of the bill being compressed, and having a somewhat sharp ridge. Twelve species of oyster-catchers are known, most of them being black or black and white in plumage. They are found in all parts of the globe, but do not extend very far north. They breed on the shores and on the sandy beds of rivers, and the nest is a little depression in the sand or moss. The eggs are not unlike those of the stone-plovers or thick-knees, being of a clay-brown with blackish spots or scribblings.

Only one genus, *Arenaria*, represents this sub-family of plovers, which is a very distinct one. There is no dertral swelling to the end of the bill, and the metatarsus is transversely sealed in front, but reticulated behind, while there is no connecting web between the toes, as in the oyster-catchers. Two species of turn-stone are known.

The Turn-stones.—Sub-family *Arenariinæ.*

The common turn-stone (*A. interpres*) is one of the most cosmopolitan of birds, nesting in the Arctic regions of both hemispheres, and ranging south almost as far as land extends. The male is a very handsome bird in the nesting plumage, though the females and young birds are not so brightly coloured. It gains its name of "turn-stone" from its habit of turning over stones, often of considerable size, in order to reach the insects underneath. A second species is found in Western North America, the black turn-stone (*A. melanocephala*).

Fig. 33.—THE COMMON TURN-STONE (*Arenaria interpres*).

The Pratincoles. Sub-order *Glareolæ.*

These are curious birds, peculiar to the Old World, where they are found from Southern Europe and Central Asia to China, south to India and Australia. They have all long wings and a swallow-like flight, and they nest in companies, laying eggs which are unlike those of plovers or snipes, being so thickly scribbled over that the ground-colour is almost invisible. One of them, the common pratincole (*Glareola pratincola*), has occurred in England on a few occasions. The pratincoles have the claw of the middle toe pectinated, as in the coursers, from which they are distinguished by their long wings.

The Coursers.—Sub-order *Cursorii.*

Although allied to the plovers and pratincoles, and, like these birds, possessing slit or schizorhinal nostrils, the coursers differ from them in having no basipterygoid processes, and they may be differentiated from the former by their pectinated middle claw. They have both aspects of the metatarsus transversely scaled. Of true coursers (*Cursorius*) there are five species, the best-known of which is the cream-coloured courser (*C. gallicus*), which has occasionally wandered to England, though its natural habitat is the desert country to the south of the Mediterranean, where it is found from the Azores and the Canary Islands eastwards to North-Western India. On the island of Fuerteventura it breeds in large numbers, and the eggs, till lately very rare, are now in the collection of every oologist. Two eggs only are laid, on the bare ground, without any attempt at a nest; they are stone-coloured, with numerous dots and scribblings of brown, and are scarcely distinguishable from the surrounding soil. Three species are found in

Fig. 34.—THE CREAM-COLOURED COURSER (*Cursorius gallicus*).

Africa, and one, the coromandel courser (*C. coromandelicus*), is plentiful in the Indian Peninsula. Of the allied genus *Rhinoptilus*, eight species are known, all Ethiopian, excepting one, *R. bitorquatus*, which is a bush-frequenting species in a restricted area of Central India.

The Stone-Plovers.—Sub-order *Œdicnemi*.

These birds, with their great yellow eyes and stout legs, form the connecting group between the plovers and the bustards. They have holorhinal nostrils like the latter, and in many anatomical characters are more like the latter sub-order than the *Charadrii*. They are found throughout the temperate and tropical portions of the Old World, and re-occur in Central and South America.

The common stone-curlew, thick-knee, or Norfolk plover, is found on barren wolds and shingly portions of the coast in many parts of England. It occurs in similar situations throughout Central and Southern Europe, as far east as India. It is a particularly shy bird, and on the approach of danger, it sinks its body on the ground, and lies quite flat, with its neck stretched out. The little nestlings, which are clothed with greyish-buff down, also endeavour to conceal themselves in like manner. The eggs, two in number, are laid on the bare ground, without any attempt at a nest, and are stone-coloured, with brown and grey markings, and so closely resemble stones that they are very difficult to find. Of the seven other species of stone-curlew known, four are African and three American. In Australia the long-legged thick-knee (*Burhinus grallarius*), and in India and the Malay Archipelago two gigantic species, *Esacus recurvirostris*, and *Orthorhamphus maginrostris*, occur.

Fig. 35.—THE STONE-CURLEW (*Œdicnemus œdicnemus*).

The Bustards.—Sub-order *Otides*.

Like the stone-curlew, the bustards have holorhinal nostrils, as well as a split or schizognathous palate. The breast-bone has two notches on its posterior margin, there is no oil-gland, and the feathers have a distinct after-shaft. In the males of some of the species there is a gular pouch, and the throat is capable of being inflated to an enormous extent.

The bustards differ very much in size, some of them being scarcely larger than stone-curlews, though they are always heavier in build. The male of the great bustard measures more than three feet and a half in length, and the great kori bustard of Africa is over four feet in length, while some of the small forms, such as the crested bustards of Africa (*Lophotis*), only measure a foot and a half in length.

They are all birds of the deserts and open wolds, and are strictly confined to the Old World, the larger number being found in Africa, which is the home of six genera out of the twelve which are known. India has two genera of florikins, *Houbaropsis* and *Sypheotis*, while the genus *Otis*, of which the great bustard is the type, and *Tetrax*, containing the lesser bustard (*T. tetrax*), are found only in Europe and Northern Asia.

The great bustard (*Otis tarda*) is now extinct as a British species, but was one of our indigenous birds in the early part of the present century, inhabiting Salisbury Plain and other open wolds in England from the borders of Scotland to Dorset. It now occurs only as a rare visitor, and it is not known whether the native British bustards occurred in former times as migrants or were resident in this country. The former supposition is probably correct, as the species is known to be migratory to most of the European countries in which it still breeds. In the nesting season it retires to the fields of tall grass and corn, where it is able to conceal its great bulk, and it is said that at this season of the year the birds moult their quills, and are unable to fly.

The male of the great bustard is much larger than the female, and has, besides his brighter coloration, more conspicuous whiskers. His method of showing off, when courting the female, is one of the most curious sights in the whole of nature. He commences by shivering his wings and lowering his quills, and his next action is to turn up his tail and lay it flat on his back, so that the snow-white under tail-coverts form a sort of frill. Across the flattened tail he disposes his primary quills so that the ends of these cross each other, and keep the tail out of sight, the whole proceeding being hidden by ruffling up the scapular feathers till nothing can be seen of the tail or the primary quills. The act of crossing the latter across the back naturally brings the fore-part of the wing into an extended position, and the inner secondaries, which are pure white, are thrown up as a frill on each side of the back, while all the wing-coverts are more or less inverted, as if the bird were trying to turn himself inside out, the long parapteral wing-coverts being thrown back, so as to secure an uninterrupted view of the white frill caused by the elevation of the inner secondaries and the halo of the under tail-coverts. The bird then lays its head deep down between the shoulders, so that the whiskers stand up on each side, and then proceeds to inflate his throat and chest, which become distended to an enormous degree. He then shows himself to his lady-love, and paces slowly in front of her, now and then springing round to exhibit the white under tail-coverts. This curious performance was witnessed in the Zoological Gardens by Mr. Pickhardt, who has mounted the group of bustards for the gallery in the Natural History Museum.

The eggs of the bustards are two or three in number, of an olive-brown colour, spotted or blotched with brown, the underlying spots being grey, the eggs being never very strongly marked. No nest is made.

The Cranes.—Order *Gruiformes.*

In this assemblage we have birds of very varied form and the Cranes were considered in former times to be allied to the herons. The difference in the structure of the palate, however, shows that they are not really related, as the herons have a bridged or desmognathous palate, whereas in the cranes and their allies the maxillo-palatine bones do not coalesce with each other or with the vomer. The young, likewise, are hatched covered with down, and can take care of themselves soon after leaving the egg, while the nestlings of herons have to remain for a long time helpless, and are fed by the parent birds in the nest. There are also many other anatomical and osteological characters which separate the cranes.

The True Cranes.—Sub-order *Grues.*

They are stately birds, with long legs and generally some bright ornamental colour on the head, while the inner secondaries are developed into handsome drooping plumes. With the exception of South America, cranes are found in every part of the world, and Africa possesses three out of the nine known genera. The sarus cranes (*Antigone*) are found in India and Burma, and one species, the well-known "native companion" (*A. australasiana*), in Australia. This is a peculiar and interesting distribution, as there is a large Indian bustard (*Eupodotis edwardsi*), which has its nearest ally (*E. australis*) in Australia. As a rule, however, the cranes are Northern birds, five species nesting in the Palæarctic region. In many of them the trachea is convoluted, and enters a cavity in the fore-part of the sternum.

The common crane (*Grus grus*) is now only an occasional visitor to Great Britain, but there is no doubt that it formerly bred in England, before the drainage of the meres deprived it of its favourite breeding haunts, and the discovery of fossil remains in Ireland shows that it was once still more widely distributed in the British Islands. The nesting-home of the crane is at present in the forest morasses of North and Central Europe, and in the marshes of Southern Spain. It is a summer visitor to Europe, and sometimes large numbers of cranes are observed on migration, flying in a V or Y formation, and trumpeting loudly. Colonel Irby records that he must on one occasion have seen, at least, four thousand pass overhead near Gibraltar. The food of the crane consists of corn and seeds of all kinds, as well as lizards and frogs, and in India the cranes, which arrive from the North to winter, do great damage to the water-melons. The eggs are two in number, brown, with a few spots or smudges of darker brown and underlying spots of grey. The nest is often a large structure, as much as five feet across, and is built among sedge and rushes, sufficiently short to enable the bird when standing up to catch sight of any intruder.

Fig. 36.—THE COMMON CRANE (*Grus grus*).

The Limpkins.—Sub-order *Arami*.

The limpkins are long-billed birds, having the appearance of large rails, of a brown colour, spotted with white. In osteological characters, however, they most resemble the cranes, and, like the latter birds, they have no notches in the hinder margin of the sternum. The wings are rounded, and the secondaries are as long as the primaries, the first of the latter quills being sickle-shaped, narrowed and incised for the basal two-thirds, with the tip spatulate. Two species of the genus *Aramus* are known, the Florida limpkin (*A. pictus*) extending from Southern Florida to Central America and the West Indian Islands, while the South American limpkin (*A. scolopaceus*) is found from Paraguay to Guiana and Venezuela. Mr. W. H. Hudson, the chronicler of bird-life in Argentina, says that the limpkins, or caraus, as they are called in that country, are more nocturnal than the rails, and take wing more readily, as they have greater powers of flight. In their gestures and motions on the ground they resemble rails, but differ strikingly from all Ralline birds in their habit of flying, when disturbed, to some open place, where they walk about conspicuously, watching the intruder. "By day," writes Mr. Hudson, "the carau is a dull bird, concealing itself in dense reed-beds in streams and marshes. When driven up he rises laboriously, the legs dangling down, and mounts vertically to a considerable height. He flies high, the wings curved upwards and violently flapped at irregular intervals; descending, he drops suddenly to the earth, the wings motionless, pointed up, and the body swaying from side to side, so that the bird presents the appearance of a falling parachute. On smooth ground he walks faster than a man, striking out his feet in a stately manner, and jerking the tail, and runs rapidly for ten or twelve yards before rising. At the approach of night he becomes active, uttering long, clear, piercing cries, many times repeated, and heard distinctly two miles away. These cries are most melancholy, and together with its mourning plumage and recluse habits, have won for the courlans several pretty vernacular names. It is called the "lamenting bird" and the "crazy widow," but is more familiarly known as the carau. As the breeding season draws near they become exceedingly clamorous, making the marshes resound day and night with their long wailing cries. The nest is built among the rushes, and contains ten or twelve eggs as large as turkeys', slightly elliptical, sparsely marked with blotches of pale brown and purple on a dull white ground, the whole egg having a powdery or floury appearance."

The Kagus.—Sub-order *Rhinochetides*

In New Caledonia is found the singular bird known as the kagu (*Rhinochetus jubatus*), the only representative of the sub-order *Rhinochetides.* It is an elegantly coloured grey bird, with a large crest, and is nocturnal in its habits. In internal structure, it has much that is crane-like; but it differs from the latter group of birds by possessing powder-down patches on each side of the rump. When in captivity, the kagu exhibits considerable dancing powers, in which feature he also resembles the cranes.

The Madagascar Kagus.—Sub-order *Mesitides.*

This sub-order is represented by a single species, *Mesites variegata*, a bird peculiar to the eastern slope of the mountain-chain which traverses the island of Madagascar. Its plumage is of a reddish-brown, and it looks like an aberrant kind of rail. Like the kagu, it possesses powder-down patches, but instead of two, there are five: two on the side of the back, one on the sides of the body, and two on the belly. It is said to build its nest on the ground, but little is known of its habits.

The Sun-Bitterns.—Sub-order *Eurypygæ.*

These remarkable birds are confined to South and Central America. They are also very rail-like in appearance, and resemble the kagus in having powder-down patches. Two species are known, the South American sun-bittern (*Eurypyga helias*), inhabiting Amazonia, Brazil, and Guiana, and the large sun-bittern (*E. major*) being found in Central America and Colombia.

Fig. 37.—THE SUN-BITTERN (*Eurypyga helias*).

The plumage of the sun-bittern is curiously variegated; the wings are beautifully spotted, and the bird is fond of sitting with its wings outspread, as if sunning itself. The nest is placed in a tree, and the bird has another heron-like character in having to feed the young birds in the nest for some time, though the nestlings are covered with down, as in true cranes. The eggs are said to resemble those of a woodcock.

The members of this sub-order are five in number, all confined to South America. They possess many crane-like features, but differ from all the aberrant *gruiformes* which we have been considering, in their domesticity, as they are often tamed by the natives of Brazil.

The nest is on the ground, the eggs being white, a peculiar colour for a Crane-like bird, and the nestling is covered with down, and is able to provide for itself soon after it is hatched. The birds gain their name "Trumpeter" from their peculiar trumpet-like note, and no doubt the modification of the trachea has something to do with this, as the windpipe is enormously long, and is continued under the skin of the abdomen nearly to the anus. The Trumpeters differ from the Cranes in having oval or holorhinal nostrils, and their plumage, instead of being firm and harsh, is particularly soft. They are residents in the parts of South America they inhabit, and have not any great powers of flight. They live at large in the forests, and often assemble in flocks of considerable size.

The Trumpeters. —Sub-order *Phosphiæ*.

Fig. 38.—THE COMMON TRUMPETER (*Psophia repitans*).

In associating the Seriamas with the Cranes, we are following the most recent conclusions of anatomists; but it must be conceded that they are very aberrant members of the *Gruiformes*. In some respects they resemble the bustards, and, like them, have holorhinal nostrils, but in the possession of four toes, and in other characters, they differ so much from those birds that in our opinion there is really no real affinity between them. Like the Cranes and the other allied forms we have just been considering, the Seriamas have a cleft or schizognathous palate, and their mode of life presents some features in common with the Secretary-Bird (*Serpentarius secretarius*) of Africa. Recognising this fact, some ornithologists, myself among the number, have considered the Seriama to be an aberrant accipitrine bird. The common Seriama is an inhabitant of South-Eastern Brazil; and in Argentina another species occurs, Burmeister's Seriama (*Chunga burmeisteri*). These two represent the only known species of the sub-order. The resemblance in appearance to the secretary-bird is remarkable, and in its mode of walk, its crested head, and its long legs, there is much that reminds us of the latter bird, which has a curious method of pounding its food. If the latter be a rat, it springs into the air, and brings down both feet with all its force, till it has reduced its prey to a pulp. This is also done by the Seriama. Mr. Hudson says that these birds live on the ground among the high grasses of the Campos, where the traveller frequently hears their loud screaming cry as he rides along the tracks. Their food consists principally of insects and caterpillars, but they also devour berries

The Seriamas.—Sub-order *Dicholophi*.

Fig. 39.—THE SERIAMA (*Cariama cristata*).

and reptiles. They nest in low bushes, the eggs being two in number, rounded and spotted, resembling those of Cranes and Rails.

The Extinct Birds of Patagonia (*Stereornithes*).

Somewhere in the neighbourhood of the Seriamas and the Cranes and Rails must apparently be placed some extraordinary forms of bird-life which have been discovered in the Miocene deposits of Patagonia, and described by Dr. Ameghino under the order *Stereornithes*. These peculiar creatures are only known from their fossil remains, and they were at first supposed to be Struthious Birds, and akin to the Rheas. Further information is required concerning them, but at the present time, my colleague, Mr. Andrews, considers that they are totally different from any ostrich-like birds, and were probably gigantic fore-runners of the Seriama and the Crane-like birds of modern times.

The Heron.—Order *Ardeiformes*.

All the members of this order have a bridged or desmognathous palate, and the nestlings are hatched helpless, and are fed in the nest by the parent birds for a considerable period. Thus they differ from the Cranes, with which they were associated in the older classifications. The Heron-like birds may be divided into three great groups, viz., the Storks (*Ciconiidæ*), the Spoonbills and Ibises, and the Herons.

The Storks.—Family *Ciconiidæ*.

Although in outward appearance Storks and Herons look very much alike, there are several characters which render them easily separable. For instance, no Stork has the claw of the third or middle toe pectinated; that is, furnished with a comb-like process, as is the case with all Herons. Again, the hind toe is not on a level with the other toes, but is elevated above it; and the furcula, or "merry-thought," bone shows no median projection in the angle, as is seen in the true Herons. There are other anatomical and osteological characters which can be adduced for the separation of the Storks from the Herons which it is not necessary to enumerate in detail.

The Storks.—Sub-order *Ciconii*.

In this Order are included the true Storks (*Ciconiidæ*), the Marabous, or Adjutants (*Leptoptilus*), the Open-bills (*Anastomus*), and the Wood-Storks or Wood-Ibises (*Tantalus*), the latter being generally admitted as a distinct sub-family, *Tantalinæ*. All these birds have no "powder-down" patches on the sides of the rump, thus differing from the true Herons and the Hammer-heads (*Scopi*) and the Shoe-billed Storks (*Balænicipitidæ*).

Fig. 40.—The White Stork (*Ciconia ciconia*).

The best-known representative of the *Ciconii* is the White Stork (*Ciconia ciconia*) of Europe, a bird which occasionally visits England, but is to be more easily studied on the opposite shores of the Continent. It is always interesting to take a country walk in Holland in the spring and see the Storks' nests, which are plentifully distributed in the Dutch gardens, where the birds are encouraged to nest by the erection of cradles or other accommodation (often an old cart wheel) erected for their benefit. In most places frequented by the Storks it is considered lucky to have a nest on the premises, and the latter increases in bulk year by year as the birds return to their nesting-places, which are often on the tops of houses. They have a curious habit of sitting motionless for hours together, often on one leg, as if absorbed in contemplation, uttering occasionally their single exclamation, which is produced by the snapping of the mandibles, for they apparently have no true note or call.

Before migrating to spend the winter months in Africa the Storks often assemble in large flocks, returning to Europe in January and February, and their first halting-place to nest seems to be in the Mediterranean countries, especially in Morocco, where they are strictly protected. Colonel Irby states that he was told by a Frenchman that "in the City of Morocco, as well as at Fez and some other large towns in the Moorish Empire, there are regular Storks' hospitals, and that should one be injured, or fall from the nest, it is sent to this institution, or rather enclosure, which is kept up by subscription from wealthy Moors, who consider the Stork a sacred bird." The late M. Favier, who lived for some years in Morocco, writes the following note, which gives a very good idea of the migrations of the Stork and its habits in this favoured country. He says:—"The Stork is seen on migration in vast numbers around Tangier passing to Europe during January and February, some of the birds terminating their journey by remaining to breed in Morocco. These are the first to depart south, returning again year after year to the same places, and apparently by the same route as that taken in their gradual departure.

"Some large flights pass on without stopping; those which migrate in August rest awhile on their way south; so during the autumnal migration (which lasts, like the spring, for about a month—the latter half of August and the first part of September) this species is extremely numerous, and is seen round the environs of Tangier in all directions; they are very tame, and often follow close behind the plough.

"The superstition which shelters this bird from molestation by the natives is the belief that the Storks were inspired by Allah to protect the harvest and the country from noxious insects and reptiles, and that the birds themselves (knowing the benefits they confer on man) ask in return protection for their offspring by building their nests on the walls of towns and houses, and that, therefore, anyone who kills them must be a Kaffir, *i.e.*, not a true believer of the Prophet, especially as the birds would only be killed for mischief, and not for food. It may be added that some of the Arabs believe that the Storks originate from a wicked Kadi and his family, who, as a punishment for their great cruelty, were all changed into these birds, and that these *miserables* humble themselves to appease Allah, and in the hope of some day regaining their human form, pray without ceasing day and night, and, whenever they rest, prostrate themselves and clean their bills."

The White Stork of Europe has a red bill, and is represented in Eastern Siberia and Japan by the Black-billed White Stork (*Ciconia boyciana*), and in America by the Maguari Stork (*Euxenura maguari*), which has a greenish bill. The Black Stork (*Ciconia nigra*) is another European bird which has occasionally visited England. It winters in Africa and in the Indian Peninsula, and, like its white relative, only visits Europe in the summer, when it is also found over Northern Asia. It differs from the White Stork in being a forest bird, but in habits and food it resembles that species. Indeed, in these respects all Storks are very similar.

In India and Africa a curious species occurs, viz., the White-necked Stork (*Dissura episcopus*), which, on examination, would seem to have a double tail, whence its Latin name. The white under tail-coverts are longer than the black tail-feathers, and are stiffened so as to appear like rectrices rather than coverts. The same curious formation occurs in one of the American Storks (*Euxenura maguari*).

The Jabirus are the largest of the Storks, standing higher on their legs than even the Adjutants. There are two species of Jabiru besides the American one mentioned above, viz., *Mycteria senegalensis* of Africa and *M. australis* of Australia. They have a very peculiar bill, which is slightly upturned at the end, and of a black and red colour.

Of a more ungainly form, and with a bare and scabious head, are the Adjutants (*Leptoptilus*). They are very large birds, and as fossil remains have been found in the Miocene deposits in France, we may conclude that they were at one time much more widely distributed than they are now. At present one species of *Leptoptilus* is African, another Indian, and a third Javan. They all possess the beautiful soft under tail-coverts known as "Marabou" feathers, and on the neck they have a bare pendulous pouch which they are able to inflate; and from the way in which this is done by the birds in confinement, it would appear as if it was considered an ornamental appendage, though from its livid colour the protrusion of this naked bag is anything but ornamental. In India the Adjutants are protected on account of their usefulness as scavengers, as they will devour almost anything, and they may often be seen in the streets of the towns. In aviaries they often stand on one leg for hours motionless, or, with their legs stretched forward under them, they will go to sleep with their heavy heads resting on their crops. Mr. Eugene Oates says that he noticed enormous numbers of Adjutants in Pegu. "Along with the Pelicans," he says, "breeding in the same trees, were innumerable Adjutants. One can hardly realise the number of these birds that visit Pegu in October, unless, as I have done, one has seen the vast armies which settle on the plains on their first arrival. I have stood on a bund where I could see for about two miles around me, and the whole area was literally covered with them. Some fifty birds stand huddled together, then there is a bare spare of about 100 ft., and then another group of birds. Their numbers are incredible. They all arrive suddenly in the Pegu plain on the same day, and after resting for about two days, they betake themselves to the forest, where I had the pleasure of visiting them. Certainly almost all the Indian Adjutants must come to Pegu to breed. These birds utter only one sound, and it resembles the lowing of a cow when separated from her calf. It was the only sound heard in these gloomy forests." Colonel Bingham found the nests of the Indian Adjutant on the Nedong Hills in Tenasserim, and only succeeded in reaching the rocks on which they were built after a stiff and difficult climb.

The Open-billed Storks.—Genus *Anastomus*.

These birds are generally known as the "Shell-Ibises," though they have no connection with the true Ibises, but are Storks of a peculiar type; Mr. Leydecker calls them "Shell-Storks," which is a much more appropriate name for them, as their food consists principally of molluscs, for the breaking of which the bird's "nut-cracker"-like bill is distinctly well adapted. The peculiar gap in the bill is not seen in the young birds, but seems to develop as the birds get older.

These birds have also generally been called "Wood Ibises," and they seem to be a kind of connecting link between the Storks and the Ibises, though in structure they resemble the former. Three species are known—the American Wood-Stork (*Tantalus loculator*), the African *Pseudotantalus ibis*, and the Indian species, *P. leucocephalus*. Of the nesting of the latter bird Lieut. Burgess has given the following account:—"In a village about ten miles from the Godavery river, where there are a great number of large banian trees both outside and inside the walls, I found a community of these birds, which had built their nests on them, probably to the number of fifty. The trees inside the walls were as thickly covered with nests as those outside, and the birds, which appeared docile and tame, did not mind the noise of the people passing beneath them. When I visited the village, the young birds were all well fledged and most of them able to fly. The villagers informed me that the old birds move off to the river in the very early dawn, and having caught a sufficient supply for their young, return at about eight or nine o'clock; a second expedition is made in the afternoon. Some idea of the quantity of fish caught by these birds may be gathered from what the people told me, that numbers of fine fish were dropped by the old birds when feeding their young and were eaten by them. A young bird of this species, which I shot in Sind, disgorged a large quantity of small eels. The nest is composed of small sticks, and is placed at the top of the trees, and if there are many on the same tree, they are placed pretty close together."

The Wood-Storks.—Family *Tantalidæ*.

In many of its characters the African genus *Scopus*, which represents this sub-order, is intermediate between the Storks and the Herons. In the form of the furcula, without any median projection, it resembles the former, and it also wants the pectinated claw of the Herons, while the absence of powder-down patches likewise allies it to the Storks. In some points of its anatomy *Scopus* is Heron-like, but in external appearance it is unlike any member of the above-mentioned sub-orders. The colour of the plumage is a sombre brown, but the bird has a fine crest and a curiously-compressed bill, with a strong dertral hook at the end. Both the inner and the outer toe are connected together by a distinct basal web.

The Hammer-headed Storks.—Sub-order *Scopi*.

But it is in its nesting habits that the Hammer-head is so peculiar. The nest is the work of a pair of birds, and is placed either on rocks or trees, sometimes six or eight being found within a short distance of each other. Sir John Kirk found one on the Zambesi, 6 ft. in diameter, with small openings on one side. The nest is a mass of sticks, and the bird has been said to make three distinct chambers; but in South Africa the nests are described as being for the most part a solid mass of sticks, sometimes to the extent of a cart load, the nest being often decorated with bones, bits of crockery, or other rubbish, or any bright thing which the bird can collect, after the manner of a Bower Bird (*Ptilonorhynchus*).

Fig. 41.—THE HAMMER-HEAD (*Scopus umbretta*).

These extraordinary birds are represented, as in the preceding instance, by a single genus *Balæniceps*, which, like *Scopus*, is confined to the Ethiopian region, but instead of being widely distributed like the Hammer-head, the Shoe-bill is confined to the districts of the Upper Nile. The shape of the bill, with its dertral hook, is sufficient to distinguish *Balæniceps* at a glance. The genus further possesses two powder-down patches like the Herons, but differs from the latter birds in the absence of any pectination on the middle claw, and in its Stork-like furcula. Taking all points of its anatomy into consideration, the balance of evidence seems to be in favour of the alliance of *Balæniceps* with the Storks.

The Shoe-billed Storks.—Sub-order *Balænicipitides.*

Fig. 42.—The Shoe-billed Stork (*Balæniceps rex*).

Von Heuglin considered the "Abu-maskup" or Shoe-bill to be a kind of Marabou, and an inhabitant of the Upper Nile regions, such as the Saraf River, the Lower Kir district, and the Gazelle River, and the countries lying between. It is everywhere a shy bird and decidedly scarce, its habits being Stork-like, standing on one leg and feeding on fish. Its only note seems to be a snapping of the bill like that of a Stork.

One of the chief differences between the Herons and the Storks is the pectinated claw on the third or middle toe, and another difference is the position of the hind toe, which, in the Storks, is elevated above the level of the other toes, and in the Herons is on the same level as the latter. The median process on the furcula has been already alluded to. The *Herodiones* may be divided roughly into the Herons and the Bitterns. The former have *twelve* tail-feathers, and the latter *ten*.

The Herons.—Sub-order *Herodiones.*

Fig. 43.—The Common Heron (*Ardea cinerea*).

The true Herons comprise a large number of genera, all more of less closely connected together, but differing in certain constant peculiarities, which warrant their being separated as genera, or, at least, as sub-genera. Thus the Purple Heron of Europe is remarkable for its long middle toe, which is as long as the tarsus, and hence it is known as *Phoyx purpurea*.

The genus *Ardea*, on the other hand, has the proportions of the toes different, the middle toe being shorter, and the tarsus longer than the middle toe and claw. Besides the pectinate or comb-like claw on the middle toe, our Common Heron (*A. cinerea*) has the tip of the bill serrated or furnished with saw-like notches along the cutting edge at the end of the upper mandible.

The Common Heron is now to be found nesting in England only in certain heronries where the bird is protected. The havoc which the bird plays among the fish in preserved waters is sufficient excuse for its slaughter, and many are killed on account of the damage they do. Nevertheless, the Heron is an extremely handsome ornament to our waters, and it is always a beautiful sight to see one of these birds standing motionless by a pool of water, or flying with its heavy wings and outstretched legs high above us in the air. The nests of the Common Heron are bulky structures, and, as a rule, are built on trees, though occasionally, where trees are absent, they will be built on bushes or even on the ground. The eggs are of a beautiful greenish-blue colour.

When in full nesting plumage, our own *Ardea cinerea* dons some long crest feathers and some elongated feathers on the back, but in these features it is entirely eclipsed by some of the Egrets, such as the species of *Herodias* and *Garzetta*, which have beautiful ornamental plumes on the breast and lower back during the breeding season. The long dorsal train of the Little Egrets (*Garzetta garzetta*) forms the material with which the English ladies of the present day decorate their bonnets and hats. Every one of these plumes, sold as "osprey" feathers by the dealers, has been taken from the body of a bird killed while bringing food to its nestlings, which are in consequence left to starve. It is scarcely possible that, in the present day, when so much publicity has been given to the fact that the wearers of these plumes are responsible for the slaughter of numberless beautiful Egrets, and the death of the young ones by starvation, any Englishwoman can plead immunity from complicity in the crime of consenting to the murder of these pretty birds; and one is forced reluctantly, seeing that the plumes are obtained solely for the English market, to believe that our people love to have it so, and that they would rather that thousands of Egrets were killed than that their bonnets should be without an "osprey" plume.

The Night-Herons. Genus *Nycticorax*

Passing from the true Herons and the Egrets to the Night-Herons, we find several intermediate forms, such as the lovely Agami Heron of Guiana (*Agamia agami*), and the Reef-Herons (*Demiegretta*). In the latter birds we meet with a curious fact, viz., that they have two forms, a white and a grey one, and, as far as one can say at present, the white form goes through all the changes of the grey one, assuming the ornamental plumes of the breeding season; and yet, when the two forms cross, as they often seem to do, the result is seen in any amount of pied birds. The same phenomenon is exhibited in an American Heron (*Dichromanassa rufa*), where one form of the species is white and the other rufous. The two forms breed together, and some of the nestlings will be white and others rufous.

The Night-Herons are found nearly everywhere on the globe, and the European species, *Nycticorax nycticorax*, occurs in the temperate and tropical portions of the Old and the New Worlds. These birds breed in colonies, and build a nest of a framework of sticks, in which the eggs lie in a sort of cradle. One may travel for miles through a marsh without suspecting the presence of the Night-Herons, and suddenly come upon the breeding place, when the air becomes full of the noisy cries of the birds, as they hover over their nests, and evince the greatest concern at the invasion of their retreat.

One of the most curious of the Night-Herons is the American Boat-bill (*Canchroma*). At first sight the remarkably wide and shoe-shaped bill would suggest an affinity with the Shoe-billed Stork (*Balæniceps rex*), but the characters of the bird are absolutely Heron-like, and there is no doubt that the bird is an exaggerated form of Night-Heron, its plumage also suggesting the propriety of this alliance. The genus stands, in fact, between the true Night-Herons (*Nyctieorax*) and the Mottled Night-Herons (*Gorsachius*) of the Indian Region.

Fig. 44.—THE BOAT-BILLED HERON (*Canchroma cochlearia*).

Two species of Boat-billed Herons are known—the South American species *C. cochlearia*, which is found from Brazil to Guiana, Colombia, and Ecuador, and the Central American species, *C. zeledoni*, which takes its place from Panama to Mexico, and has a tawny-coloured breast instead of a white one. They are nocturnal birds, and Mr. Richmond says that in Costa Rica he found *C. zeledoni* in colonies, and the note of the species was a "squawk," something like that of the Night-Heron.

The Bitterns have ten tail-feathers and the end of the bill serrated. In this group are contained the Little Bitterns (*Ardetta*), the Dwarf Tiger Bitterns of South America (*Zebrilus*), and the Asiatic Bitterns (*Ardeirallus* and *Dupetor*), as well as the True Bitterns (*Botaurus*). Of the Little Bitterns ten species are known, and the distribution of the genus is almost cosmopolitan. The most typical species is the Little Bittern of Europe (*Ardetta minuta*), a bird which still occasionally finds its way to England, and doubtless formerly bred in the British Islands. One of the most remarkable of the Little Bitterns is, however, the Argentine species (*Ardetta involucris*), concerning which Mr. W. H. Hudson tells a remarkable story, one of the most interesting of all histories of bird-life. Most of the Bitterns have the curious faculty of concealing themselves from observation by their faculty of "reed-simulating," and many of our readers must have noticed some of these birds in the Zoological Gardens standing stock-still, and evidently imagining that by so doing they were invisible to the intruder. The Common Bittern (*Botaurus stellaris*) will not only do this, but will gradually and slowly turn his breast to any observer if the latter only walks slowly away from him, under the evident impression that by so doing he renders himself invisible, as, indeed, the bird would be if he were in his native reed-bed;

Fig. 45.—THE LITTLE BITTERN (*Ardetta minuta*).

but, as he has a background of green bushes or wood-work, his efforts at concealment are vain.

The notion of concealment in relation to natural surroundings is, however, thoroughly explained by Mr. Hudson's experiences. He writes :—"One day in November, 1870, when out shooting, I noticed a Variegated Bittern stealing off quickly through a bed of rushes thirty or forty yards from me. He was a foot or so above the ground, and went so rapidly that he appeared to glide through the rushes without touching them. I fired, but afterwards ascertained that in my hurry I missed my aim. The bird, however, disappeared at the report, and, thinking I had killed him, I went to the spot.

"It was a small isolated bed of rushes I had seen him in ; the mud below, and for some distance round, was quite bare and hard, so that it would have been impossible for the bird to escape without being perceived ; and yet, dead or alive, he was not to be found. After vainly searching and re-searching through the rushes for a quarter of an hour, I gave over the quest in great disgust and bewilderment, and, after reloading, was just turning to go, when, behold ! there stood my Heron on a reed, no more than eight inches from, and on a level with, my knees. He was perched, the body erect, and the point of the tail touching the reed grasped by its feet, the long, slender, tapering neck was held stiff, straight, and vertically; and the head and beak, instead of being carried obliquely, were also pointing up. There was not, from his feet to the tip of his beak, a perceptible curve or inequality, but the whole was the figure (the exact counterpart) of a straight, tapering rush ; the loose plumage arranged to fill inequalities, and the wings pressed into the hollow sides, made it impossible to see where the body ended and the neck began, or to distinguish head from neck or beak from head. This was, of course, a front view ; and the entire under-surface of the bird was thus displayed all of a uniform dull yellow, like that of a faded rush. I regarded the bird wonderingly for some time, but not the least motion did it make. I thought it was wounded or paralysed with fear, and, placing my hand on the point of its beak, forced the head down till it touched the back ; when I withdrew my hand, up flew the head, like a steel spring, to its first position. I repeated the experiment many times with the same result, the very eyes of the bird appearing all the time rigid and unwinking, like those of a creature in a fit. What wonder that it is so difficult—almost impossible—to discover the bird in such an attitude. But how happened it that, while repeatedly walking round the bird through the rushes, I had not caught sight of the striped back and the broad, dark-coloured sides? I asked myself this question, and stepped round to get a side view, when, *mirabile dictu*, I could still see nothing but the rush-like front of the bird. His motions on the perch as he turned slowly or quickly round, still keeping the edge of the blade-like body before me, corresponded so exactly with my own that I almost doubted that I had moved at all. No sooner had I seen the finishing part of this marvellous instinct of self-preservation (this last act making the whole complete), than such a degree of delight and admiration possessed me as I have never before experienced during my researches, much as I have conversed with wild animals in the wilderness, and many and perfect as are the instances of adaptation I have witnessed. I could not finish admiring, and thought that never had anything so beautiful fallen in my way before, for even the sublime cloud-seeking instinct of the White Egret and the typical Herons seemed less admirable than this, and for some time I continued experimenting, pressing down the bird's head and trying to bend him by main force into some other position; but the strange rigidity remained unrelaxed, the fixed attitude unchanged. I also found, as I walked round him, that as soon as I got to the opposite side, and he could no longer twist himself on his perch, he whirled his body with great rapidity the other way, instantly presenting the same front as before.

"Finally I plucked him forcibly from the rush and perched him on my hand, upon which he flew away; but he flew only fifty or sixty yards off, and dropped into the dry grass. Here he again put in practice the same instinct so ably, that I groped about for ten or twelve minutes before refinding him, and was astonished that a creature, to all appearance so weak and frail, should have strength and endurance sufficient to keep its body rigid and in one attitude for so long a time."

This habit of concealing themselves among surroundings to which their plumage assimilates in colour seems to be a characteristic of all the Bitterns, as I have seen our Common Bittern (*Botaurus stellaris*) attempting to perform this feat in an aviary, and the Tiger Bitterns (*Tigrisoma*) also remain in a rigid position for hours together.

It should be mentioned that nearly all the Herons lay eggs of a beautiful greenish-blue colour, while those of many of the Bitterns are white, and that of the Common Bittern is yellowish brown.

The Spoon-bills and Ibises.—Sub-order *Plataleæ*.

Although agreeing with the Storks in the form of the furcula, the members of this sub-order differ from them and from the Herons in several important osteological characters, the principal one being the schizorhinal or "split" nostril. The Spoon-bills are such extraordinary looking birds, that there is no possibility of their being mistaken for any of the other long-legged Herons or Storks, from all of which they are distinguished by their flattened and spoon-shaped bill. They are found in nearly every part of the globe, but do not extend very far north, and six species are known, viz., four species of *Plataleæ*, one of *Platibis*, confined to Australia, and one of *Ajaja*, viz., the Rosy Spoon-bill of the New World (*Ajaja ajaja*).

Fig. 46.—THE COMMON SPOON-BILL (*Plataleæ leucerodea*).

The Common Spoon-bill used to breed in the marshes of our eastern counties, but has not been known to do so for the last three hundred years. Now the species is only an accidental visitor, but it still nests on the Horster Meer in Holland, where its breeding places are strictly protected. The nests are made of dead reeds lined with dry grass, and are placed on the tussocks of grass with a few sticks as a foundation; a few nests being built low down in the alder trees. On the Danube the Spoon-bills nest in company with Egrets and other Herons, and the following interesting account of a visit to one of these breeding-places is given in Mr. Barkley's work, "Bulgaria Before the War." He found a colony on an island a few miles below Rustchuk, and he describes the scene as follows:—"Pushing our small boat into a narrow creek, we took off our shoes and stockings, and, turning up our trousers, picked our way through the tangled boughs in the direction of the sound, which evidently proceeded from the centre of the island, and I shall not easily forget the sight we beheld when we reached it.

"There, on the pressed-down boughs of the willows, only a few feet above the water, were hundreds of great flat nests of the various kinds of Herons, Spoon-bills, Egrets, Bitterns, etc., all huddled together in one confused mass, and the entire colony reeking with the most indescribably filthy smell.

"It was rather late for eggs, as most of them were hatched off; but was just the time to observe the doings of the children of these sedate, quiet, peaceful-looking birds, and I must say that I never yet beheld such a collection of little fiends, nor a more hideous set.

"Their bodies were of the smallest proportions, while every other part of them—their wings, legs, necks, and beaks—were of the longest. Most of them had no feathers, and all seemed possessed with one idea, and that was either to limb a small brother or swallow him whole, and all kept up either a shriek of fear or pain or a yell of rage. Floating on the top of the putrid water were masses of dead birds, some with legs torn off, others without heads or wings. Most of them were dead, but others were dragging their maimed carcases about in a ghastly manner. So intent were they on their fiendish pastime that they took little notice of us, and dragged and clawed themselves about after their weaker brethren at our very feet, whilst the old parent bird sat looking on from the topmost twigs as if fratricide were the proper moral pastime of the young. A big Spoon-bill would chase a small Egret from bough to bough till at last he tired it out, and then seizing it with one claw, would take hold of its leg or wing and tear it from the poor victim, or else, getting its head in its mouth, would try to swallow it whole, and gulp and gulp till so much of the little one was down its throat that it was itself choked, and would turn over on its back, kicking and struggling, to be in turn seized by a brother and torn limb from limb.

"All uttered up some hideous scream, and all kept clambering and dragging themselves about from bough to bough, either hunting or being hunted, and from what we saw I am sure that nine-tenths of all hatched in that colony came to an untimely end before they could fly. We did not stay long to watch them, but quickly securing some eggs from the few nests that were not hatched off we beat a retreat, with our opinions of the beautiful, gentle-looking birds greatly changed."

The Ibises.—Family *Ibididæ*.

The Ibises are easily distinguished from the Spoon-bills by the shape of their bills, which are long and curved, and have the nasal groove extending nearly the whole length of the bill, which is soft, excepting at the extreme tip. The bill in some of the Ibises is indeed very like that of a Curlew (*Numenius*), and one genus of the Charadriiformes, *Ibidorhynchus*, is so like an Ibis, that externally its characters would ally it to the latter group of birds rather than to the Waders, to which, as its internal structure shows, it actually belongs.

The most interesting of all the Ibises is undoubtedly the Sacred Ibis of the Egyptians. As the ancient paintings show, the bird was a great feature in Egyptian life, and the mummies of these birds which are found in the temples show that it was regarded with great veneration by the ancient Egyptians. The species still inhabits the Upper Nile regions, and many writers state that it is never found in Egypt at the present day. This, however, is not the case, as the British Museum has several specimens procured in Egypt, one of them having been shot near Damietta about twelve years ago. We know also that the species extends to the Persian Gulf, its winter home being in Eastern and Southern Africa.

There are no less than twenty different genera of Ibises, and many of them are remarkable for highly developed crests and ornamental plumes, while in the Sacred Ibis and its allies the head and neck are bare. The Glossy Ibises (*Plegadis*) are among the commonest and best known of the whole family, as one of them, *P. falcinellus*, has visited England on many occasions. This species breeds in numbers on the marshes of the lower Danube, as well as in similar places in Africa and India, and the egg is one of the most beautiful of any of the Heron-like birds, being of a deep greenish-blue, darker and richer in tint than the eggs of any species of Herons.

Fig. 47.—THE SACRED IBIS (*Ibis æthiopica*).

We now approach the great group of swimming birds, such as the Ducks, the Pelicans, and their allies; but, before arriving at the consideration of these well-marked orders, there intervenes a remarkable form of bird, the Flamingo. In its long legs and long neck it might well be taken for a kind of Heron or Stork; and, indeed, until recent years, the position of the Flamingoes was considered to be in close proximity to the last-named birds. They are, however, more nearly allied to the Ducks and Geese, having a desmognathous or "bridged" palate; while the young are hatched covered with down, and are able to run about in a few hours and obtain food for themselves. These features they possess in common with the Ducks and Geese and the Screamers, and these three groups were united by Huxley into one natural order, *Chenomorphæ*.

The Flamingoes.—Order *Phœnicopteriformes*.

The Flamingoes resemble the Ducks and Geese in having the sides of the bill laminated, an arrangement which enables them to sift their food in the way which every one of our readers must have seen tame Ducks do in a farmyard or on a lake. Besides many osteological characters, the Flamingoes present an external appearance unique among birds. The legs are abnormally long, the metatarsus being three times as long as the femur, and the anterior toes fully webbed. The neck is also extremely long, the cervical vertebræ being eighteen or nineteen in number. The bill is decurved in a remarkable manner; but in the nestling, which is covered with greyish-white down, the bill is straight, as in any other Duck-like bird.

Fig. 48.—THE COMMON FLAMINGO (*Phœnicopterus roseus*).

The most curious feature in the economy of the Flamingo is its nest, which is built of mud. For a long time it was supposed that the birds sat upon their single egg, with the legs straddled on each side of them. This idea was, however, dissipated by Mr. Abel Chapman in 1883, when he visited the Marismas of the Guadalquivir, in Spain, and found out the nesting habits of the Flamingo. He writes :—"One cannot go far into the Marisma without seeing that extraordinary fowl the Flamingo, certainly the most characteristic bird of the wilderness. In herds of 300 to 500, several of which are often in sight at once, they stand feeding in the open water, all their heads under, greedily tearing up the grasses and water-plants from the bottom. On approaching them, which can only be done by extreme caution, their silence is first broken by the sentries, who commence walking away with low croaks, then the whole five hundred necks rise at once to the full extent, every bird gaggling his loudest as they walk obliquely away, looking back over their shoulders as though to take stock of the extent of the danger. Pushing a few yards forward, up they all rise, and a more beautiful sight cannot be imagined than the simultaneous spreading of their thousand crimson wings, flashing against the sky like a gleam of rosy light. Then one descends to the practical, and a volley of slugs cuts a lane through their phalanx.

"In many respects these birds bear a strong resemblance to Geese. Like them Flamingoes feed by day, and great quantities of grass, etc., are always floating about the muddy water where a herd has been feeding. Their cry is almost indistinguishable from the gaggling of Geese, and they fly in the same catenanan formations. In size Flamingoes vary greatly. The largest I have measured was fully 6 ft. 5 in., whilst others (old red birds) barely reached 5 ft." He thus describes the finding of the nests :—"On reaching the spot we found a perfect mass of nests; the low mud plateau was crowded with them as thickly as the space permitted. These nests had little or no height; some were raised 2 or 3 in., a few might be 5 or 6 in.; but the majority were merely circular bulwarks of mud, with the impression of the bird's legs distinctly marked on it. The general aspect of the plateau was not unlike a large table covered with plates. In the centre was a deep hole full of muddy water, which, from the 'gouged' appearance of its sides, appeared to be used as a reservoir for nest-making materials. Scattered all round this main colony were numerous single nests rising out of the water, and evidently built up from the bottom. Here and there two or three or more of these were joined together—'semi-detached,' so to speak. These separate nests rose 6 or 8 in. above the water level, and were about 15 in. across. The water was about 12 or 15 in. deep. None of these nests as yet contained eggs, and though I returned to the 'pajarera' on the latest day I was in its neighbourhood (11th May), they still remained empty. On both occasions many hundreds of Flamingoes were sitting on the nests, and on the 11th we had a good view of them at close quarters. Linked arm in arm with Felipe, and crouching low in the water, to look as little human as possible, we approached within some 70 yds. before their sentries showed signs of alarm, and, at that distance, we observed the sitting birds as distinctly as one need wish. Their long red legs doubled under their bodies, the knees projecting as far as, or beyond, the tail, and their graceful necks neatly curled away among their back feathers, like a sitting swan, with their heads resting on their breasts—all these points were unmistakable. Indeed, it is hardly necessary to point out that in the great majority of cases (the nest being hardly raised above the level of the flat mud) no other position was possible."

Of Flamingoes six species are known, and they are found in the temperate and tropical portions of both the Old and New Worlds. Three species belong to the genus *Phœnicopterus*—*Phœniconaias* has one species, *P. minor*, found in Africa and North-Western India; and *Phœnicoparrus* inhabits the Andes of Chili and Peru and has two species, *P. andinus* and *P. jamesi*.

In Miocene times several forms of birds allied to the Flamingoes existed in Europe, and have been classed by Mr. Lydekker under the extinct genus *Palæolodus*. He states that they were smaller than the Flamingoes of the present day, and had shorter and stouter legs, while it is probable also that their bill was not deflected.

The Screamers.—Sub-order *Palamedeæ*.

Although agreeing in many characters with the Ducks and the Geese, the Screamers have one peculiarity which separates them from all chenomorphine birds, in that they have no uncinate processes to the ribs, and no laminæ on the sides of the bill. The toes are long and almost devoid of web, and the general appearance of the birds is gallinaceous. Two genera are known, *Palamedea* and *Chauna*. The genus *Palamedea* is recognised by the long horn which it carries on its forehead. Beyond this it has no crest on the head, and has fourteen tail-feathers. Only one species, *P. cornuta*, is known, and this is an inhabitant of Guiana, Amazonia, Venezuela, Ecuador, and Bolivia. The general plumage is black, with a white belly, and the wing carries two spurs, the anterior one of which is much the longer. Very little has been recorded of the habits of the Horned Screamer, but Mr. Edward Bartlett noticed the species about the lakes in the Upper Amazons, and the habits are probably very similar to those of the next species.

Fig. 49.—THE HORNED SCREAMER (*Palamedea cornuta*).

The Crested Screamer (*Chauna cristata*).

The genus *Chauna* differs from *Palamedea* in having a crested head, naked lores, no horn on the forehead, and in possessing twelve tail-feathers instead of fourteen. Two species of *Chauna* are known—the Crested Screamer (*C. cristata*) and the Derbian Screamer (*C. chavaria*). The latter is found in Venezuela and Colombia, while the Crested Screamer inhabits Argentina and the neighbouring provinces of Southern Brazil. In Mr. Hudson's well-known work on Argentine ornithology we find the following notes on the species:—

"The Crested Screamer, like most of the larger Birds and Mammals in every part of the globe to which European emigration is attracted, is probably doomed to rapid extermination. My observations of the bird in that portion of the Pampas where it is most abundant date back some years, to a time when the inhabitants were few and mainly of Spanish race—never the destroyers of bird-life. The conditions had become extremely favourable to this species. It is partially aquatic in its habits, and in desert places is usually found in marshes, wading in the shallow water, and occasionally swimming to feed on the seeds and succulent leaves of water-loving plants. After the old giant grasses of the Pampas had been eaten up by the cattle, and the sweet grasses of Europe had taken their place, the Screamers took kindly to that new food, preferring the clovers, and seemed as terrestrial in their feeding habits as Upland Geese. Their food was abundant, and they were never persecuted by the natives. Their flesh is very dark, coarse-grained, but good to eat, with a flavour resembling that of the Wild Duck; and there is a great deal of meat on a bird with a body larger than that of a Swan. Yet no person ever thought of killing or eating the Chajá, and the birds were permitted to increase to a marvellous extent. It was a common thing a few years ago in the dry season to see them congregated in thousands, and so little afraid of man were they, that I have often ridden through large scattered flocks without making the birds take wing. A curious thing about the Screamer is that it pairs for life, and yet is one of the most social of birds. But if a large flock is closely looked at, the birds are invariably seen methodically ranged in pairs. Another curious thing is that, notwithstanding the formidable weapons they possess—each wing armed with two large spurs—they are extremely pacific in temper. I have never been able to detect even the slightest approach to a quarrel among them; yet it is hard to believe that they do not fight sometimes, since weapons of offence are usually found correlated with the disposition to use them. Captive birds, however, can be made to fight; and I have known Guachos take them for the pleasure of witnessing their battles. They are very easily tamed, and in that state seem to show greater docility and intelligence than any of our domestic birds, and become so attached to their home that it is quite safe to allow them to fly about at will. They associate, but do not quarrel, with the poultry. They are quick to distinguish strangers from the people of the house, showing considerable suspicion of them, and sometimes raising a loud alarm at a stranger's approach. Towards dogs and cats they are often unfriendly; and when breeding it is dangerous for a strange person to approach the nest, as they will sometimes attack him with the greatest fury.

"The Screamer is a very heavy bird, and rises from the ground laboriously, the wings, as in the case of the Swan, making a loud noise. Nevertheless, it loves soaring, and will rise in an immense spiral circle until it wholly disappears from sight in the zenith, even in the brightest weather; and considering its great bulk and dark colour, the height it ultimately attains must be very great. On sunny windless days, especially in winter and spring, they often spend hours at a time in these sublime aerial exercises, slowly floating round and round in vast circles, and singing at intervals. How so heavy and comparatively short-winged a bird can sustain itself for such long periods in the thin upper air to which it rises has not yet been explained. The voice is very powerful. When disturbed, or when the nest is approached, both birds utter at intervals a loud alarm-cry, resembling in sound the anger-cry of the Peacock, but twice as loud. At other times its voice is exercised in a kind of singing performance, in which male and female join, and which produces the effect of harmony. The male begins, the female takes up her part, and then with marvellous strength and spirit they pour forth a torrent of strangely-contrasted sounds—some bassoon-like in their depth and volume, some like drum-beats, and others long, clear, and ringing. It is the loudest animal sound of the Pampas, and its jubilant martial character strongly affects the mind in that silent, melancholy wilderness. The Screamer sings all the year round at all hours, both on the ground and when soaring; when in pairs, the two birds invariably sing together, and when in flocks they sing in concert. At night they are heard about nine o'clock in the evening, and again just before dawn. It is not unusual, however, to hear them singing at other hours. The nest is a large fabric placed among the low rushes and water-lilies, and is sometimes seen floating on the water, away from its moorings. The eggs are five, pointed at one end, pure white, and in size like the eggs of the domestic Goose. The young are clothed in yellow down like Goslings, and follow the parents about from the date of hatching."

Mr. Lydekker, when in Argentina, found the Screamer nesting on a lagoon, and saw the parent birds swimming about amongst the Ducks. On his approach they fled to the banks, but soon returned to the water. They had evidently young birds on the lagoon. This aquatic feature in the Screamers is of the highest interest, as confirming the anserine affinities which their anatomy demonstrates.

The Geese and Ducks.—Sub-order *Anseres*.

These well-known birds are easily recognised by their external characters, their semi-flattened bills, shortish legs, and fully-webbed feet distinguishing them from the Screamers and Flamingoes, while, like the latter birds, they have uncinated processes to the ribs. Count Salvadori, who has recently monographed the sub-order *Anseres* in the "Catalogue" of the Birds in the British Museum, divides it into no less than eleven sub-families belonging to the single family *Anatidæ*. To these we can only refer in passing.

The Swans.—Sub-family *Cygninæ*.

The Swans are such well-known birds that very little description of them is necessary. Among the Duck tribe they are easily recognisable by their abnormally developed neck, which equals, or even exceeds, the body of the bird in length. There is no lobe to the hind toe, a feature which allies the Swans to the Geese, but separates them from the majority of the Ducks. There are three genera of Swans, viz., *Cygnus*, containing the Swans with which we are most familiar; *Chenopis*, the Black Swan of Australia, with ornamental scapulars and inner secondaries; and *Coscoroba*, the Chilian Swan, which has feathered lobes, and is as much a Goose in appearance as it is a Swan in reality.

The Mute Swan is the familiar species which swims about on our rivers and lakes. In most parts of the British Islands the Swan may be regarded as a semi domesticated bird, but in many places on the Continent it is an absolutely wild species. It is to this Swan that the Polish Swan (*Cygnus immutabilis*), with its white cygnets, must be referred, as Count Salvadori, and all the best of recent observers, consider it to be only a domestic variety of the Mute Swan. Other well-known species of *Cygnus* are the Whooper (*C. musicus*) and Bewick's Swan (*C. bewicki*), the latter bird nesting in Arctic Europe, where it makes a large nest composed entirely of moss. It visits us in some numbers during the winter months. These British species of Swans are distinguished by the size and the colour of their

Fig. 50.—THE MUTE SWAN (*Cygnus olor*).

bills. Australia has one species, the Black Swan (*Chenopis atrata*), and finally we have the Coscoroba Swan (*Coscoroba candida*) which is found from Chili and Patagonia to Argentina and Uruguay. Of this species Mr. W. H. Hudson writes:—"In their habits, language, and flight they differ much from the Black-necked Swan, and the country people call them *Ganso* (Goose), probably on account of their Goose-like habit of sometimes feeding away from the water, or because their flesh has the flavour of Wild Goose. As a rule, they go in small parties of five or six individuals, but sometimes flocks numbering two or three hundred are seen in the cold season. Their migrations are very irregular, and sometimes they are exceedingly abundant in a certain district one year and absent from it the next. When disturbed they utter a loud, musical, trumpeting cry in three notes, the last with a falling inflection; and, their wings being much longer proportionately than in the black-necked species, they rise with greater ease, and have a much freer and an almost soundless flight."

The Semipalmated Goose (*Anseranas semipalmata*) is the sole representative of a distinct sub-family *Anseranatinæ*, with the toes only half-webbed, and the hind toe very long, and on a level with the other toes. It is an inhabitant of Australia and Tasmania, and is still plentiful in some districts, though it has disappeared from many places where it once was numerous. Gould says that, in Northern Australia "it occurs in such countless multitudes that it forms one of the chief articles of food of the aborigines, and was of the utmost value to Leichardt and his party during their adventurous journey from Moreton Bay to Port Essington, as shown in numerous parts of his interesting account of the expedition. So dense are the flocks that occur in the northern parts of the country, that the natives are able to procure numbers of them by spearing," and, says Leichardt, "it seemed that they only spear them when flying, and always crouch down when they see a flight of them approaching; the Geese, however, know their enemies so well that they immediately turn when they see a native rise and put his spear into his throwing-stick; some of my companions asserted that they had seen them hit their object at the almost incredible distance of 200 yds."—an assertion which Gould says he could readily believe, from what he has himself witnessed. This Goose has a very remarkable trachea, nearly 5 in. in length, and mostly lying outside the pectoral muscle under the skin.

The next sub-family of the Geese consists of the Spur-winged Geese (sub-family *Plectropterinæ*), and several allied forms. They have fully webbed feet, a very long hind toe, and long tail-feathers. The true Spur-winged Geese (*Plectropterus*) have the lores naked and caruncles on the forehead and base of the bill, while on the wing they carry a formidable spur, from which feature they derive their popular name. There are four species of Spur-winged Geese, all confined to Africa, admitted by Count Salvadori, the best authority on the *Anseres*, but even he is obliged to allow that there may really exist but a single species after all.

Only one other genus with bare lores and caruncles on the face is known, and this is the genus *Cairina*, with the single species *C. moschata*, the Muscovy Duck of Tropical America. Another prominent form of the *Plectropterinæ* is the Knobbed Goose (*Sarcidiornis*), of which there are two species, *S. melanonota* of India and Africa, and *S. carunculata* of Southern Brazil and Argentina.

We remember seeing the "Comb Duck," as Indian naturalists call the Indian *Sarcidiornis*, on one occasion during our journey through the

North-West Provinces, and that was at Futtehpur Sikri, near Agra, where a male was perched on the lofty entrance gateway. The testimony of Mr. A. O. Hume and other Indian naturalists is to the effect that the "Comb Duck" breeds principally in trees, and the late Mr. A. Anderson states that the eggs are generally to be found in holes of old desiduous trees, but he has also found the birds frequenting old ruined forts. He says:—"I was present at the capture of a female Nukta on her nest, which yielded the extraordinary number of forty eggs. Of course it is just possible, though highly improbable, that this may have been the joint produce of two birds; but the emaciated condition of the one captured, coupled with the fact that one egg was an abnormally small one, and evidently her last effort, does not favour the supposition. The tree selected was an ancient banyan (*Ficus indicus*), which overlooked a large sheet of water several miles round. The nest-hole was at an elevation of some 20 ft., 3 ft. deep and 2 in circumference." One of the genera of the *Plectropterinæ* is a very interesting form, viz., the Pink-headed Duck (*Rhodonessa caryophyllacea*). The appearance of a delicate pink head in such a family as the *Anatidæ* is one of the most curious phenomena in the whole class of birds. Its range is confined to Behar and Bengal, to the north of the Ganges and west of the Brahmapootra, whence it ranges north to Nepal, east to Burma, and south to Madras.

Some of the most interesting of the present sub-family are the Dwarf Geese (*Nettopus*) or "Cotton-Teal," as they are generally called. They are little Geese of about the size of a Bantam fowl, only found in the tropics of the Old World, in Africa, India, and China, and thence south to Australia. The Indian species, *N. coromandelianus*, nests generally in holes of trees, but sometimes it is said to make "a semi-floating nest on the water, among the rushes or lotus-leaves, of weeds, grass, etc., all together, filled up several inches above the water-line." The late Mr. A. Anderson observes:—"I once had the opportunity of watching a pair in the act of selecting their habitation. They invariably flew into the tree together; and while the female used to enter the hole, to reconnoitre as it were, the male sat on a bough watching for her exit. No sooner did she make her appearance than they both flew away together, giving utterance to a peculiar cackling sound, which has been pronounced to be like the words 'Fix bayonets.' Their visits used to be repeated at intervals of every fifteen or twenty minutes. The Drake never went into the hole; and I am therefore inclined to believe that he does not lend his aid in the performance of the duties of incubation." One nest taken by Mr. Spry at Bredaon in August contained twelve eggs. It was in a hole at no great height, but it was 3½ ft. deep, and only large enough to admit of ingress and egress; the contents had to be removed by means of an iron spoon, something like a soup-ladle with an extra long handle.

The Summer Duck (*Æx sponsa*) of North America, and the beautiful Mandarin Duck (*Æx galericulata*) of China compose the genus *Æx*, which is the last of the *Plectropterinæ*.

The Cereopsis Geese.—Sub-family *Cereopsinæ*.

The genus *Cereopsis* is the sole representative of this sub-family, and is distinguished by its shorter hind toe and shorter tail-feathers. The bill is high at the base, and there is no metallic wing-speculum. The chief peculiarity of the Cereopsis Goose is the possession of a cere at the base of the bill, which character separates it from the true Geese. It is an inhabitant of Australia, and is often seen in captivity; and it has been known to breed in our Zoological Gardens. As Mr. Gould says, however, it is by no means a desirable addition to the farmyard, for it is so pugnacious that it not only drives all other birds before it, but readily attacks pigs, dogs, or any other animal that may approach it, and often inflicts severe wounds with its hard and sharp bill.

Remains of an extinct Goose (*Cnemiornis calcitrans*) have been discovered in New Zealand, and Count Salvadori has placed it in the vicinity of *Cereopsis.* It was a larger bird than the latter, and was apparently flightless, as there is no keel to the sternum.

The characters of this sub-family are almost exactly the same as those given for the sub-family *Cereopsinæ*, excepting that there is no cere. There are at least six well-marked genera, of which the most beautiful are perhaps the Snow-Geese (*Chen*), though some of the Brent Geese are also handsome birds. The true Geese (*Anser*) are found in all the northern parts of the Old and New Worlds, breeding in the high north, and migrating south in winter, often in vast numbers. The Grey Geese (*Anser*) are nearly all of them British, the best-known being the Grey Lag-Goose (*A. anser*), the White-fronted Goose (*A. albifrons*), the Bean Goose (*A. fabalis*), and the Pink-footed Goose (*A. brachyrhynchus*). All the true Geese have the serrations or saw-like edges of the upper mandible visible from the outside, and the cutting edge of the mandible is sinuated, whereas in the Brent Geese (*Branta*) the cutting edge is straight, and the serrations are not visible from the outside.

The True Geese.—Sub-family *Anserinæ.*

These are, like the True Geese, also birds of the Arctic portions of the Old and New Worlds, where they breed in large numbers; and, as they moult their quills before coming south, they are trapped by the natives in numbers. Mr. Trevor-Battye describes the capture of more than three thousand Brent Geese on the island of Kolguev, the birds being driven by the Samoyeds in boats towards the shore, where a large circle of net is prepared for them, and the birds are thus trapped and killed.

The Brent Geese.—Genus *Branta.*

Fig 51.—THE RED-BREASTED GOOSE (*Branta ruficollis*).

One of the handsomest of the Geese, and, indeed, of all water-fowl, is the Red-breasted Goose (*Branta ruficollis*), which breeds in Siberia, winters in great numbers on the Caspian Sea, and has occasionally come over to England. It is remarkable for having been drawn on their monuments by the ancient Egyptians, and even at the present epoch it seems to be met with sometimes in Egypt.

Count Salvadori's next sub-family is the *Chenonettinæ*, containing the Magellanic Geese and their allies, the Blue-winged Geese (*Cyanochen*) and the Maned Goose (*Chenonetta*).

The Upland Geese.—Sub-family *Chenonettinæ.*

In this group of Geese the hind toe is narrowly lobed and the bill is rather short and Goose-like, as opposed to the somewhat flat and broad bill of the Ducks which form the next sub-family *Anatinæ*. The Upland Geese (*Cloephaga*) are all inhabitants of South America, where they range from Peru, Bolivia, and Southern Brazil to Chili, Patagonia, and the Falkland

Islands. Mr. Hudson describes *C. inornata*, the Barred Upland Goose, as migrating northwards along the eastern coast of Argentina in April and May. "Their great camping-grounds," he writes, "are the valleys of the rivers Negro and Colorado, where they are often so numerous as to denude the low grounds of the tender winter clovers and grasses, and to cause serious loss to the sheep-breeders. They also visit the cultivated fields to devour the young wheat, and are intelligent enough to distinguish between a real human enemy and the ragged men of straw, miscalled scarecrows, set up by the farmers to frighten them. While committing their depredations they are exceedingly wary and difficult to shoot; but at night, when they congregate by the waterside, they give the sportsman a better chance. They are social birds, always going in large flocks, and are very loquacious, the female having a deep, hanking note, while the male responds with a clear whistling, like that of the Sanderling etherialised."

No less than nineteen genera are admitted by Count Salvadori as belonging to this sub-family. Among them are the Tree-Ducks (*Dendrocygna*), the Sheld-ducks (*Tadorna* and *Casarca*), the Wild Ducks (*Anas*), the Wigeons (*Mareca*), the Teal (*Nettion* and *Querquedula*), the Pin-tails (*Dafila*) and the Shovelers (*Spatula*), besides many less-known forms of Duck.

The True Ducks.—Sub-family *Anatinæ*.

The ways of the Ducks are all very similar, and there is not much to say in detail about their habits, beyond the fact that some are frequenters of inland waters, while others are more maritime in their haunts.

The Sheld-ducks are very handsome birds, of varied plumage, and with a metallic patch or speculum in the wings. This is a character which is found in most of the Ducks, and many species are determined by the colour of the wing-speculum. Another curious feature of the Ducks is that, after the young are hatched, the males put off their bright plumage and assume a dull-coloured brown dress like that of the hen birds. This plumage is very difficult to determine, as the male birds during the moult are practically helpless, and have no quills to fly with, so that they retire into privacy, and very few specimens are procured at this stage of a Duck's existence. I am unable to say from direct observation whether this hen-like summer plumage, which only lasts a few weeks, is assumed by all Ducks; but I have reason to suspect that there are few species which do not possess such a stage.

Fig. 52.—The Common Sheld-duck (*Tadorna tadorna*).

The beautiful Sheld-duck is a burrower, sometimes having its nest as far as 5 ft. from the mouth of the hole, while it has been known to penetrate as far as 12 ft. into the earth. These holes are often burrowed by the birds themselves, but quite as frequently a rabbit-burrow is made use of. The Sheld-duck often builds upon cliffs at such a height that it is evident the parent bird must carry the young ones down to the water, as must be the case also with the Common Mallard when it builds its nest in a tree, as it often does.

Of these Ducks there are four sub-families, all with the hind toe broadly lobed. The Scoters (*Fuligulinæ*) have the bill more or less depressed and the tail-feathers not stiffened. A large number of genera is represented in this sub-family, which includes such forms as the Pochards (*Nyroca*), the Scaups (*Fuligula*), the Steamer Ducks (*Tachyeres*), the Golden-Eyes (*Clangula*), the Long-tailed Ducks (*Harelda*), the Harlequins (*Cosmonetta*), the Scoters (*Œdemia*), and the Eiders (*Somateria*), and their allies. They are mostly sea-ducks, and some of them, like the Harlequin Duck and Steller's Eider (*Heniconetta stelleri*) are very handsome birds. The stiff-tailed Diving Ducks (sub-family *Erismaturinæ*) differ from the *Fuligulinæ* in their narrow tail-feathers, which are much stiffened. Only four genera are admitted, *Thalassiornis*, *Nomonyx*, *Erismatura*, and *Biziura*. The latter is a curious Australian form, with a pendant lobe on the chin, and twenty-four tail-feathers.

The Diving Ducks.

In these birds the tail is long and stiffened, and the general look of the birds is very much like that of the Mergansers, but they have no serrations on the edges of the mandibles. They are found only in the Andes from Ecuador to Chili, frequenting the torrents of the high mountains, and being very difficult of observation.

The Torrent-Ducks—Sub-family *Merganettinæ*.

In this last sub-family we find only the Smew (*Mergus albellus*) and the Mergansers (*Lophodytes* and *Merganser*). In the latter birds the tooth-like serrations are very different from those of any other of the Ducks, being strongly inclined backwards at the tips. These are not, however, real teeth, though they have the appearance of so being, but are merely serrations along the edge of the mandible, so that in the skeleton there is no appearance of any indentation on the bone of the bill. Thus they are very different birds from the extinct *Hesperornis*, which had real teeth, though they are interesting as being the nearest approach which we can show at the present day to the toothed birds of ancient times.

The Mergansers.—Sub-family *Merginæ*.

Fig. 53.—THE RED-BREASTED MERGANSER (*Merganser serrator*).

Seven species of the genus *Merganser* are known, and they are found in the Palæarctic and Nearctic regions, but are absent in the Ethiopian and the greater part of the Indian Region. One species is isolated in the Auckland Islands, viz., *M. australis*, and another in South-Eastern Brazil, *M. brasilianus*. The Red-breasted Merganser is smaller than the Goosander (*M. merganser*), and nests in Scotland and Ireland. Like the other Mergansers it is an expert diver, and it feeds principally on fish. On this account they are somewhat persecuted.

These birds, often called the *Steganopodes*, have the hind toe or hallux united to the second toe by a web, so that all four toes are webbed. All the Pelecanoid birds have the palate bridged or "desmognathous," and there are no basipterygoid processes in the palate. There are five sub-orders, viz., the Tropic-Birds (*Phaethontes*), the Gannets (*Sulæ*), the Cormorants and Darters (*Phalacrocoraces*), the Pelecans (*Pelecani*), and the Frigate-Birds (*Fregati*). As their name implies, the Tropic-Birds are inhabitants of the tropics. They are often an interesting feature of a sea-voyage, as they fly, high in the air, round and round the steamer, with a beating flight, as if everything depended on the haste they made. The osteological and anatomical characters which distinguish them from the other Pelican-like birds are many, but their external form sufficiently distinguishes them, their lengthened tail being especially remarkable. The bill is nearly straight, and not hooked as in the allied forms, neither is there any perceptible pouch. One of the best accounts of the habits of the Tropic-Birds is that given by Mr. W. E. D. Scott on *P. flavirostris*, as observed by him in Jamaica. He writes:—"Of fifteen specimens procured on the 27th of February five were shot, eight were taken in a cave which opened by a small mouth from the cliff, and two were secured in holes in the cliff. The cave where the birds were found had a very small entrance, about large enough for a man to crawl into, in the face of the cliff. This was approachable only in the calmest weather, in a boat. The entrance led at once into a spacious chamber of irregular shape. Going directly back from the mouth the cavern was some 60 ft. deep. It was at its widest point some 70 or 80 ft., and oval in shape as a whole. The bottom was covered with coarse sand and gravel, and boulders of varying size, evidently having fallen from above, were scattered thickly over this floor, except at the extreme back of the cavern furthest from the sea. The height of the roof or ceiling, which was of an uneven, rough surface, was about 25 ft., and many bats were hanging wherever the projections or inequalities afforded them opportunity. Toward the back of this chamber five birds were secured, each one sitting on a single egg. The place chosen for the nesting site—for this is all it can be termed—was in all these cases where two boulders on the gravelly floor lay close together, just leaving room on the ground for the birds to crawl between them. Two birds were obtained in like situations that had not laid, and may have been simply resting. The females were, in every case, the birds that were sitting on the eggs, and it was quite evident, upon dissection, that the single egg forms the complement in these cases. The birds taken from the holes in the cliff, and also those taken in this cave, were very tame, and were captured readily without attempting to escape. Later on the same day a bird was found, with a single egg laid at the bottom of one of the holes in the face of the cliff.

The Pelicans and their Allies.—Order *Pelecaniformes.*

Fig. 54.—THE YELLOW-BILLED TROPIC-BIRD (*Phæton flavirostris*).

"In breeding the birds seem eminently gregarious, and the colonies at different points often reach an aggregate of at least fifty pairs. At sea, far out of sight of land, the birds are much more solitary in their habits, single birds being frequently met with, and it has been rare in my experience to meet with more than four individuals together in such locations."

The Gannets are distributed over the seas of the greater part of the world, and are easily recognisable both from their internal and external characters. Like the Tropic-Birds, they have a nearly straight bill without any hook in it, and there is a small and scarcely perceptible pouch, though much of the face and throat is bare.

Fig. 55.—The Common Gannet (*Dysporus bassanus*).

The Gannets.—Sub-order *Sulæ*.

During the breeding season the Gannets leave their fishing grounds to a great extent, and our own species resorts to certain rocky places on our coast, of which Ailsa Craig and the Bass Rock are the best known, and there builds a rough nest of sticks and seaweed, and lays a single chalky-white egg. This chalky egg is a peculiarity of nearly every member of the Pelican-like birds, and in the Gannets and Cormorants it is a distinct feature. On scrubbing the egg, however, with a brush, the chalky surface can be removed, and the egg appears of a delicate blue, like that of a Heron. The flight of a Gannet is very fine, and the birds are capable of covering great distances in a very short space of time, while it is certain that during the nesting season the parent birds have to go far afield to their fishing grounds to procure food for the young. Only one egg is laid, and the young birds are at first naked, and of a slaty-black colour. They then become covered with a thick coating of white down, and afterwards attain their first full plumage, which is greyish-brown with white spots, but it is believed that five moults are required before the birds attain their full white plumage.

The Cormorants.—Sub-order *Phalacrocoraces*.

Although agreeing in osteological characters with the preceding groups, the Cormorants and Darters have certain evident peculiarities which separate them from the Gannets and Tropic-Birds. The bill is more raptorial, and is furnished with a hook at the end, and the tail-feathers are more stiffened than in these birds. This is especially the case with the Darters. There is, however, no perceptible pouch externally.

In the British Islands we have two representatives of the sub-order, the Common Cormorant (*Phalacrocorax carbo*) and the Shag (*P. graculus*). The former is the larger bird of the two, and has fourteen tail-feathers; while the Shag is smaller and greener, and has only twelve tail-feathers. In this way the young birds of the two species, which are brown, can always be distinguished. Cormorants are found nearly everywhere on the face of the globe, and are particularly numerous in New Zealand and the adjacent islands.

Cormorants are great fish-eaters, and they are consequently excellent swimmers and divers. They often nest on trees in inland places, but as a rule their nest is placed on the rocks adjoining the sea. The young are hatched perfectly naked, and are ugly little black morsels, like the nestlings of the Gannet; but they are afterwards covered with dense down of a sooty-brown colour, and their first full plumage is brown, with a white under-surface. In the breeding plumage the old birds generally don a crest, and our Common Cormorant has white filamentous plumes distributed over the head and neck, as well as an ornamental white patch just above the thighs.

Fig. 56.—THE COMMON CORMORANT (*Phalacrocorax carbo*).

The way in which Cormorants and Shags feed their young is very curious, and is well described by Sir Walter Buller. Writing of the Pied Shag of New Zealand (*P. varius*), he says :—

"We found the Shags in great force, and it was most interesting to watch the operations of both old and young birds. There were 80 or 100 nests, many of which were vacant owing to the lateness of our visit, the breeding having commenced in October. The nests are large, round structures, composed, as already mentioned, of dry sticks and twigs and other loose materials, bound together by means of a peculiar kind of Kelp, for which the Shags may be observed diving in the sea, sometimes in four fathoms of water. They have a somewhat compact appearance, and are usually placed in a thick fork among the branches or between two limbs of a tree lying close together. In each of those still tenanted there were two fully-fledged young birds, and these youthful Shags kept up a constant 'squirling' noise, accompanied by a perpetual swaying of the head from side to side in an impatient sort of way. The old bird comes up from the sea with her gullet full of small fish, and takes up her station on a branch adjoining to or overlooking the nest. The young birds, after craning their necks almost to dislocation, quit their nest and mount up alongside the parent, when the peculiar feeding operation commences. The mother bends down her head in a loving way, opens wide her mandibles, and the young Shag, with an impatient guttural note, thrusts his head right down the parental throat and draws forth from the pouch, after much fumbling about, the first instalment of his dinner. No sooner has he swallowed this than he begins to coax for more, caressing the mother's throat and neck with his bill in a very amusing fashion. The old bird waits till she has recovered the discomfort of the last feed, then opens her mouth again, and the action is repeated, first by one young Shag, then by the other. When the pouch is emptied, the mother spreads her ample wings and goes off for a fresh supply of *anas*, whilst her offspring shuffle themselves back again into their nests to await her return. But this feeding process and the squirling cries which herald it are going on at the same time all over the camp, and as a consequence there is a perfect din of voices. In the midst of these may be heard deep guttural cries; but these are probably the occasional scoldings of the old birds to repress the inconsiderate eagerness of their young ones, for during the operation of feeding there is a good deal of apparent squabbling among the young fraternity for the first attention, accompanied by a vigorous fluttering and flapping of the wings. In one of the nests, where the young birds were not sufficiently advanced to leave it, I observed that the occupants, during the intervals when their parents were absent, kept up an incessant flapping of their wings and swaying of their long necks, first to one side, then to the other, with a never-ceasing cry as if in great bodily distress."

Although at first sight bearing considerable resemblance to the Cormorants, the Darters present many striking differences. They are often called "Snake-Birds," as they are able to submerge their bodies and swim along with only their snake-like heads and necks protruding above the water. Cormorants, it may be remarked, are said to be able to do the same. Then the Darters have a "kink" in the neck, which the Cormorants have not; and this "kink" is arranged in a sort of set spring-like manner, so that when the bird spears a fish, its neck goes off with a jerk, and the fish is transfixed by its bill in a second. We were much interested in watching a Darter and a Cormorant in the "Fish-House" at the Zoological Gardens, and it was curious to see the way in which these two birds differed in their mode of catching fish. The Darter, when let out of his cage, plunged into the water and swam about for a little time, then he sank his body below the surface, keeping his head and neck above it, but, perceiving some fish swimming at the bottom of the tank, it simply sank below the water and then went for them with a few rapid strokes. No fish had a chance. The Darter simply let the spring on his neck go, and unerringly speared his victim as with a lance. It was curious to notice that, whereas the Cormorant often swallowed his fish under water, the Darter invariably brought them to the surface, shook them off his bill, and then swallowed them.

The Darters.—Family *Plotidæ*.

Fig. 57.—THE DARTER (*Plotus anhinga*).

The Darters are tropical birds, being found in America, Africa, India, and Australia, and one species penetrates the Palæarctic region; for the African Darter (*Plotus levaillanti*) breeds on the Lake of Antioch, where Canon Tristram found the nests. The bird, he says, merely seems to tread down a tuft of coarse grass or rushes, or press down the centre of a little bush. A curious habit of the Darter, and likewise of the Cormorants, is to sit motionless in the sun with extended wings, as if the bird were "hanging itself out to dry." A captured Heron or Bittern is an awkward customer to carry home, if not dead, for the bird will reserve all its strength for a final effort to lance its bill at the eye of its captor, as I once had occasion to experience when carrying home a young Heron, which did its best to make a deadly thrust at my face. So with the Darter and its formidable bill, for Mr. Thomas Ayres writes that a wounded African Darter (*P. levaillanti*) made a sudden dart at his eye, and it was only by the merest instinct of self-preservation that he put up his hand to receive the thrust. The upper mandible pierced with great force the bone of his thumb, and the bill, being serrated, stuck among the muscles, and he had a hard job to pull it out.

It is not necessary to enumerate the characters, osteological and otherwise, which distinguish Pelicans, because their external appearance is so peculiar that they are easily recognisable birds. The bulky body, the long bill, hooked at the end and having an enormous gular pouch, are sufficient external characters to distinguish the Pelicans, so that we need not waste many words on them. In ancient times they were even more widely distributed, and lived in England, like the Flamingoes to which we

The Pelicans.—Sub-order *Pelecani*.

have alluded above (p. 288). They are birds which are found in the temperate and tropical portions of both hemispheres, and in America the Knob-billed Pelican (*P. erythrorhynchus*) has a remarkable bony excrescence on the upper mandible, which is put on during the breeding season, and afterwards falls off. Nearly every species assumes a patch of yellow or brown colour on the chest during the nesting season, at which time, too, a crest is generally donned.

Fig. 58.—The Roseate Pelican (*Pelecanus onocrotalus*).

On the habits of the Roseate Pelican in the delta of the Danube the following note has been published by Messrs. Sintenis :—

"The islands where they breed are more or less composed of reed-fragments, often without any fresh vegetation, often also bordered by green rushes and other high plants. The aspect of the large white eggs shining through the green all round is very charming when seen from the middle of the lake; but when closely inspected, the places look very dirty and slovenly. The smell was bearable, the process of fermentation and putrefaction being generally over—a sign that the birds had not laid since the 7th instant. Generally there were two eggs in a nest; but there were also plenty of single ones. Nearly half as many eggs as were lying on the islands were floating on the surrounding water. The latter keeps sending up air-bubbles, by which it is kept in constant commotion, no doubt caused by the substances putrefying at the bottom. The eggs were in all stages of hatching; but in most of them the young birds were fully developed, so that we had a trouble to find a number which could yet be blown. The eggs which our *chasseur* had taken on the 7th were, on the average, far less advanced; and it does not seem to us at all improbable that the heat of the sun may have had some influence upon the abandoned eggs, at least to a certain extent."

Of the breeding of the spotted-billed Pelican in Burma (*P. manillensis*), Mr. Eugene Oates gives a very interesting account :—"The whole forest consisted of very large trees, but a portion—about one in twenty—was made up of wood-oil trees, gigantic fellows 150 ft. high and more, and with a smooth, branchless trunk of 80 to 100 ft. These are the trees selected by the Pelicans. I was out one day till 3 P.M., continually moving, and must have walked at least twenty miles in various directions, but never from first to last was I out of sight of either a Pelican's or Adjutant's nest. From what I saw, and from what the Burmans told me, I compute the breeding-place of these birds to extend over an area about twenty miles long and five broad.

"With regard to the Pelicans, I noticed that no tree contained less than three nests, and seldom more than fifteen. Some birds select the upper branches, placing their nests on the nearly horizontal branches of the tree, not far from the trunk. In all cases the nests on one branch touch each other, and when these nests are on a horizontal branch they looked like an enormous string of beads.

"Judging from the size of the bird, I should say the nest is about 2 ft. in diameter, and, when in a fork, to be 18 in. deep. Others on flat branches are shallower. They are composed entirely of twigs and small branches, and I could detect no lining in those nests which were thrown down to me.

"The eggs are invariably three in number, and on the 11th November all I took were either fresh or only slightly incubated. The female bird sits very closely, and frequently I found that the bird would not fly off her eggs till I fired a gun. It was a most ludicrous sight to see the sitting birds stretch neck and head out of the nest to have a look at us, as often happened.

"Notwithstanding the millions of birds which breed in this forest, a most wonderful silence prevails. The Pelican seems to be perfectly mute, and the Adjutants only bellow at intervals. The only sound which is consequently heard—and after a time even this sound passes unnoticed—is a sort of Æolian harp caused by the movement of the wings of innumerable birds high in air."

The Frigate-Birds.—Sub-order *Fregati*.

In certain particulars the Frigate-Birds, of which there are only two, are closely allied to the Pelicans. Like the latter birds, they have the clavicle anchylosed to the sternum, and other osteological characters in common, while they also have a large gular pouch. Besides this, they are remarkable for their hooked and almost raptorial bill, and their habits partake of those of the Birds of Prey to a great extent. The flight of the Frigate-Birds is wonderful, and can be sustained for an extraordinary length of time; while the birds have a complete arrangement of air-cells beneath the skin which they are able to inflate at will. Mr. Palmer, who collected birds for the Hon. Walter Rothschild in Laysan and the adjacent islets, has given some interesting notes on the habits of the Frigate-Birds. In his diary of 20th June he writes:—"While walking in Laysan I turned some of the Frigate-Birds which had young off their nests. Scarcely had I pushed one off when another Frigate-Bird would rush up, seize the young one, fly off, and eat it. Sometimes the parent bird would give chase, but it always ended in one or the other eating the young bird. I could scarcely believe my own eyes, so I tried several; but they would even take young birds out of the nest which were almost fully feathered." Again from Liasinsky Island he writes:—"The Frigate-Birds have their nests on the scrub round the lake. It is very interesting to watch them getting their food. In the daytime they soar about all over the island, and every now and then one of them picks up a young Tern. Then a number of others chase him, and keep taking the prey one from the other till at last it is eaten or drops to the ground. But they generally make for the sea with their prey, as it is easier for them to pick up on the sea than on land. When soaring they hardly seem to move a wing, and sometimes I have seen them cleaning and picking their feathers as they floated along in the air. In the evening, just before sunset, they hover close round the island, waiting for the Petrels and other birds to come

Fig. 59.—THE GREAT FRIGATE-BIRDS (*Fregata aquila*).

home with food, when they give chase, and do not leave the unfortunate bird until it has disgorged some, if not all, of its food. I have seen a Petrel when thus chased drop on the water from sheer exhaustion; but even then the Frigate-Bird would not leave it till it had disgorged."

These very aberrant kinds of Birds of Prey are strictly American, being represented in both North and South America by the Turkey Vultures, and in the Andes by the Condors. They differ so much from ordinary Accipitrine birds in their anatomy and osteology that they are now by common consent kept separate from the latter, and some ornithologists have even gone so far as to suggest that they are more nearly allied to the Storks, and even to the Hornbills. Although not true Birds of Prey, I think that there can be no doubt that they find their nearest allies in the Vultures of the Old World, which they much resemble in their habits. They have, however, a very peculiar nostril, the septum of which is perforated, so that it can be seen through. The hind toe is small, but is raised above the level of the other toes, and it is connected with the *flexor perforans digitorum* tendon.

The Turkey Vultures.—Order *Cathartidiformes.*

The great Condor of the Andes is the largest and most striking of the Turkey Vultures, but the best-known are the smaller kinds such as the *Cathartes aura* of North America. In Captain Bendire's work on the Life-histories of North American Birds, we find the following notes on the habits of the species from Dr. W. L. Ralph:—"In Florida they are abundant and appear to decrease but little in numbers. When not molested they become very tame, and in many of the Southern cities and villages they can be seen walking around the streets or roosting on the house-tops with as little concern as domestic animals.

"Although they eat carrion, these birds prefer fresh meat, and the reason of their eating it when decayed is that they cannot kill game themselves and their bills are not strong enough to tear the tough skin of many animals until it becomes soft from decomposition. I have often had Ducks and other game, which I had hung in trees to keep from carnivorous animals, eaten by them. When they find a dead animal they will not leave it until all but the bones and other hard parts have been consumed, and if it be a large one, or if it have a tough skin, they will often remain near it for days, roosting by night in the trees near by. After they have eaten—and sometimes they will gorge themselves until the food will run off their mouths when they move—they will, if they are not too full to fly, roost in the nearest trees until their meal is partly digested, and then commence eating again. Many times I have seen these birds in company with the Black Vulture floating down a stream on a dead alligator, cow, or other large animal, crowded so closely together that they could hardly keep their balance, and followed by a number on the wing. I have never seen them fight very much when feeding, but they will scold and peck at one another, and sometimes two birds will get hold of the same piece of meat and pull against each other until it breaks, or until the weaker one has to give it up."

The Birds of Prey.—Order *Accipitriformes.*

In this order are included the Secretary Birds, the Vultures, Hawks, and Ospreys. The characters of the Secretary Birds are detailed below, and their peculiarities emphasised, but the Ospreys (*Pandiones*) form a well-characterised intermediate group between the Vultures and Hawks (*Accipitres*), and the Owls (*Striges*), possessing certain features which are characteristic of the latter, especially in the proportions of the skeleton.

The Secretary Birds.—Sub-order *Serpentarii.*

That these are Birds of Prey there can be little doubt, but they are decidedly aberrant, and were separated from the rest of the *Accipitres* by Professor Huxley. They have abnormally long legs, and an equally abnormal tail, with the centre feathers much elongated, while from behind the head rises the crest of pointed feathers, from which the bird gets its name of "Secretary," on account of some fancied resemblance to a secretary, who is supposed to carry quill pens behind his ear. There are other peculiar anatomical and osteological features which separate the Secretary from the other Raptorial birds. Several ornithologists, amongst them myself, have perceived certain characteristics in the Seriama (*antea*, p. 277) which suggest an affinity with the Secretary; and, if the Seriama is admitted to be a kind of Crane, it is also certain that it possesses certain Accipitrine characters which are difficult to account for. The external appearance of the two birds is not unlike, and there is one very curious habit which they possess in common, viz., the way in which they attack their prey, by striking it with rapid beats of their long legs, both of which are brought down with terrific force, until the object is beaten to a pulp. Another character which those birds possess in common, is the fact that both the outer and inner toe are connected by a web, which is one of the features of the Caracaras, to which, in my opinion, the Secretary is distantly related.

Fig. 60.—THE SECRETARY BIRD (*Serpentarius secretrius*).

Serpentarius is an African genus, and the single species is therefore strictly Ethiopian, but in ancient times the Secretary lived in Central Europe, as its remains, like those of the African Touracous, have been found in France.

The Secretary is a pugnacious bird, so that frequently serious fights take place between two males for the possession of a female, and the bony knob which they carry on the carpal joint of the wing is doubtless an offensive weapon. When attacking a Cobra, the Secretary defends itself by holding its wing in front of it as a shield, and strikes the snake down by vigorous blows of its feet. On account of its usefulness in destroying venomous snakes it is protected in all parts of Africa, and as many as three large snakes have been taken from the stomach of one of these birds, besides lizards and tortoises, and a quantity of grasshoppers and other insects; while it will frequently kill a large snake by carrying it high in the air and dropping it to the ground. The eggs are two, rarely three, in number, and white.

The Birds of Prey.—Sub-order *Accipitres.*

These are the true Raptorial or Accipitrine Birds of authors. They may be divided into two great families, the Vultures (*Vulturidæ*) and the Hawks (*Falconidæ*). The Vultures are mostly carrion-eaters, and are found in the tropical portions of the Old World, the so-called "Vultures" of the New World having been already separated off as the

Cathartidiformes (*anteà*, p. 304). Although so different from their American allies, the habits of the Old World Vultures are very similar. They have a bare head and neck, scantily clothed with down or plumes; but these parts are never fully clothed with feathers as in the true Birds of Prey.

The genera of the *Vulturidæ* are six in number, viz., the Black Vultures (*Vultur*), the Griffons (*Gyps* and *Pseudogyps*), the Eared Vultures (*Otogyps*), the White-headed Vultures (*Lophogyps*), and the Scavenger Vultures (*Neophron*).

The Black Vulture is the only representative of the genus *Vultur*. It is found in the Mediterranean countries, whence it ranges through Central Asia to the Himalayas, and even to China. It is a large bird, nearly 4 ft. in length, and is entirely black or dark brown, with a pad of thick, velvety down on the crown and a ruff of brown down on the neck. It is more solitary in its habits than the Griffons; and in Spain, according to Colonel Irby, the species breeds in trees, and not in colonies, laying only one egg about the beginning of April. It acts the part of a King Vulture towards the Griffons, and drives the latter away from any carcase which they may be feeding upon.

Fig. 61.—The Black Vulture (*Vultur monachus*).

The Griffon Vultures.—Genus *Gyps*.

Four, or perhaps five, species of Griffons are known, the most familiar being the *Gyps fulvus* of Southern Europe. Colonel Irby gives an interesting account of the species in Spain. It is very plentiful near Gibraltar, and nests in colonies, not exceeding thirty-five pairs, in holes, or rather in caves in the perpendicular crags or "lajas" which are found in many of the Sierras. The eggs, according to Captain Willoughby Verner, are white when fresh laid, but soon become stained and often covered with mud and blood. He says:—"Anyone who has seen a party of Griffons on damp soil, churning up the ground with their feet around a carcase, can easily understand the eggs becoming soiled." Colonel Irby observes:—"How the numbers which inhabit Audalucia get sufficient to eat is a puzzle to me. They must be able to fast for some days, or else travel immense distances for their food, as in the winter and spring it is unusual to see dead animals about; but in the hot parching months vast quantities of cattle die of thirst and want of pasture. A bull fight is a sort of harvest to Vultures, which flock in great numbers to revel on the carcases of the unfortunate horses that have been so cruelly killed."

The Scavenger Vultures.—Genus *Neophron*.

Of the Scavenger Vultures there are four species, the best-known being the Egyptian Vulture (*Neophron percnopterus*). The members of this genus are smaller than the generality of Vultures, and have a long curved bill with a longitudinal nostril. The Egyptian Vulture is an inhabitant of the Mediterranean countries and Africa. In India it is replaced by a nearly allied form with a yellow bill, known as *N. ginginianus*. In Africa two brown species, *N. pileatus* and *N. monachus*, occur.

The Egyptian Scavenger Vulture is a more than ordinarily foul feeder, even for one of its kind, and frequents human habitations, where it devours all kinds of offal and excrement, but it will at other times devour lizards, snakes, and small rodents, as well as worms, insects, and even fruit. According to the late C. J. Andersson, it is said to devour ostrich eggs, by carrying a stone up into the air and dropping it upon them. The nest is generally placed on cliffs, but sometimes on trees.

Of the True Hawks there are five sub-families, the Caracaras (*Polyborinæ*), the Long-legged Hawks (*Accipitrinæ*), the Buzzards (*Buteoninæ*), the Eagles (*Aquilinæ*), and the Falcons (*Falconinæ*).

Of the Caracaras there are but two genera, *Polyborus* and *Ibycter*. They are distinguished from the other Hawks by having the outer and inner toe connected to the middle one by a membrane or web. In all the other sub-families there is a web only between the base of the outer and middle toes. *Polyborus* has but two species, *P. tharus*, of South America, which is found from the Straits of Magellan to Amazonia, and *P. cheriway*, which occurs from Ecuador and Guiana, through Central America, into the Southern United States.

Fig. 62.—The Brazilian Caracara (*Polyborus tharus*).

Mr. W. H. Hudson has given a long and interesting account of the habits of the "Carancho," as the *Polyborus* is called in Argentina. It is too long to be given in its entirety, but we cannot refrain from making a few extracts:—"The Caranchos pair for life, and may therefore be called social birds. They also often live and hunt in families of the parents and young birds until the following spring, and at all times several individuals will readily combine to attack their prey, but they never live or move about in flocks. Each couple has its own home or resting-place, which they will continue to use for an indefinite time, roosting on the same branch and occupying the same nest year after year; while at all times the two birds are seen constantly together, and seem very much attached. Azara relates that he once saw a male pounce down on a frog, and, carrying it to a tree, call his mate to him and make her a present of it. It was not a very magnificent present, but the action seems to show that the bird possesses some commendable qualities which are seldom seen in the Raptorial family. Without doubt it is a carrion-eater, but only, I believe, when it cannot get fresh provisions; for, when famished, it will eat anything rather than study its dignity and suffer hunger like the nobler Eagle. I have frequently seen one or two or three of them together on the ground, under a column of winged ants, eagerly feasting on the falling insects. To eat putrid meat it must be very hungry indeed. It is, however, amazingly fond of freshly-killed flesh; and, when a cow is slaughtered at an estancia-house, the Carancho quickly appears on the scene to claim his share, and, catching up the first thing he can lift, he carries it off before the dogs can deprive him of it. When he has risen to a height of five or six yards in the air he drops the meat from his beak, and dexterously catches it in his claws without pausing or swerving in his flight. It is singular that the bird seems quite incapable of lifting anything from the ground with the claws, the beak being invariably used, even when the prey is an animal which it might seem dangerous to lift in this way. I once saw one of these birds swoop down on a rat from a distance of about 40 ft., and rise with its struggling and squealing prey to a height of 20 ft., then drop it from its beak and gracefully catch it in its talons. Yet, when it pursues and overtakes a bird in the air, it invariably uses the claws in the same way as other Hawks. This I have frequently observed, and I give the two following anecdotes to show that even birds, which one would imagine to be quite safe from the Carancho, are on some occasions attacked by it. In the first case, the bird attacked was the Spur-winged Lapwing, the irreconcilable enemy of the Carancho and its bold and persistent persecutor. The very sight of this Hawk rouses the Lapwings to a frenzy of excitement, and springing aloft, they hasten to meet it in mid-air, screaming loudly and continuing to harry it until it leaves their ground, after which they return, and, ranged in triplets, perform their triumphal dances, accompanied with loud drumming notes. But if their hated foe alights on the ground, or on some elevation near them, they hover about him, and first one, then another, rushes down with the greatest violence, and gliding near him, turns the bend of its wing so that the spur appears almost to graze his head. While one bird is descending, others are rising upwards to renew their charges; and this persecution continues until they have driven him away, or become exhausted with their fruitless efforts. The Carancho, however, takes little notice of his tormentors; only when the Plover comes very close, evidently bent on piercing his skull with its sharp weapon, he quickly dodges his head, after which he resumes his indifferent demeanour until the rush of the succeeding bird takes place.

"While out riding one day a Carancho flew past me attended by about thirty Lapwings, combined to hunt him from their ground, for it was near the breeding season, when their jealous irascible temper is most excited. All at once, just as a Lapwing swept close by and then passed on before it, the Hawk quickened its flight in the most wonderful manner and was seen in hot pursuit of its tormentor. The angry hectoring cries of the Lapwings instantly changed to piercing screams of terror, which, in a very short time, brought a crowd numbering between two and three hundred birds to the rescue. Now, I thought, the hunted bird will escape, for it twisted and turned rapidly about, trying to lose itself amongst its fellows, all hovering in a compact cloud about it and screaming their loudest. But the Carancho was not to be shaken off; he was never more than a yard behind his quarry, and I was near enough to distinguish the piteous screams of the chased Lapwing amidst all the tumult, as of a bird already captive. At the end of about a minute it was seized in the Carancho's talons, and, still violently screaming, borne away. The cloud of Lapwings followed for some distance, but presently they all returned to the fatal spot where the contest had taken place; and for an hour afterwards they continued soaring about in separate bodies, screaming all the time with an unusual note in their voices as of fear or grief, and holding excited conclaves on the ground, to all appearance as greatly disturbed in their minds as an equal number of highly emotional human beings would be in the event of a similar disaster overtaking them."

The Long-Legged Hawks.—Sub-family *Accipitrinæ*.

Only the outer and middle toes are united by a membrane in this subfamily, but the legs are very long, the thigh (*tibio-tarsus*) and the leg (*tarso-metatarsus*) being nearly as long as one another. The birds included in this group are the Gymnogenes, Harriers, Gos-Hawks, and Sparrow-Hawks.

The Gymnogenes.—Genus *Polyboroides*.

These curious crested Hawks are Ethiopian, one species being found in tropical Africa and another in Madagascar. They are grey birds with a well-developed crest, and a bare face of a light yellow colour. The structure of the leg is peculiar, for the tibio-tarsal joint is flexible, and the bird has the power of putting its leg out of joint, as it were, and placing the tarsus at a backward angle, instead of forwards, as in ordinary Birds of Prey. The Neotropical genus *Geranospizias* is also said to possess the same faculty. In the Gymnogene this power of twisting its leg about, as on a pivot, is said by observers to be of use to the bird in drawing out frogs from the marsh holes. Its food appears to consist chiefly of lizards and frogs, and also of insects; and Mr. Ayres says that in Natal it frequents lands on which the grass has been recently burnt, stalking over the ground like a Bustard.

The Harriers.—Genus *Circus*.

The Harriers are long-legged birds, differing from the Sparrow-Hawks and Gos-Hawks in having the hinder aspect of the tarsus reticulate and in having an oval nostril. They have also a ruff round the face similar to that of the Owls, and on this account they have often been considered to be a connecting link between the Hawks and the Owls. This character, however, is of secondary importance compared with the development of their long legs, which, in our opinion, allies them to the Sparrow-Hawks. Some sixteen species of the Harriers are known, and they inhabit the temperate and tropical portions of both hemispheres. They do not range into the arctic regions, and those which breed in northern localities migrate south in winter, often in large numbers. The habits of all the Harriers are very much the same in different countries. The nest is built on the ground, and the eggs are white, with occasionally a few brown markings; they appear bluish inside when held up to the light. They are not birds of bold and rapid flight like the Sparrow-Hawks or Eagles, but are great robbers of other birds' eggs and young, feeding also on small mammals, reptiles, fish, and insects. Mr. Seebohm speaks of the Marsh Harrier (*Circus æruginosus*) as being "usually seen passing slowly over its swampy haunts a few feet from the earth, quartering the ground much as a well-trained dog searching for game. Its flight is somewhat slow and laboured, performed with measured beats of the wings, varied by gliding motions as it surveys the ground below. It will beat over its hunting-ground, returning backwards and forwards, as if diligently searching every spot likely to contain its prey. Now and then it is seen to drop somewhat slowly to the earth to secure a frog or a mole, which it will either eat at once or convey to some distance."

Of Montagu's Harrier (*Circus pygargus*) Colonel Irby records the finding of a regular colony near Lixus, in Morocco. With his telescope he could see the sitting hen birds dotted about the marsh. The North American Hen-Harrier (*Circus hudsonius*) has similar habits to those of the European species, but is not such an egg-destroying bird, and is looked upon as a beneficial Hawk, as it devours great quantities of meadow-mice and ground squirrels, as well as noxious insects, such as locusts and destructive ground-crickets. The flight of this Harrier is described as graceful, and at certain times the males perform aerial evolutions. The male never assists the female in the duties of incubation, but diligently supplies his mate with food. Mr. John Clark informed Captain Bendire that he has seen the female rise from the nest to welcome the male with shrill cries when he came in sight, and then take the prey from his talons and fly back with it to the nest.

Intermediate between the Harriers and the Gos-Hawks comes the genus *Micrastur*, containing the Harrier-Hawks of Tropical America. These are birds which have the stout build of a Gos-Hawk combined with the facial ruff of the Harriers, and, as in the last-named genus of birds, the tarsus is reticulated behind. Then follow several genera of Gos-Hawks, such as *Geranospizias* of Tropical America, *Urotriorchis* of Africa, and *Erythrocnema*, again a New World form, so closely allied to the Chanting Gos-Hawks of Africa (*Melierax*) that the two genera are scarcely distinguishable.

The Red-thighed Gos-Hawks.—Genus *Erythrocnema*.

Two species of this genus are known, one, *E. unicincta*, inhabiting South America from Brazil to Chili, and the other, *E. harrisi*, being found in Central America, north to the Southern United States. Little has been recorded of the habits of the Red-thighed Gos-Hawks, but Captain Bendire says that they appear to be lazy and sluggish birds, with a slow and not graceful flight. They build in low trees, and the nest is a poorly constructed affair, so that on one occasion Captain Bendire declares that he could see the eggs through the bottom of the nest.

The Chanting Gos-Hawks.—Genus *Melierax*.

These birds are confined to the Æthiopian Region, and they are called "Chanting" Gos-Hawks on account of their supposed utterance of a song. Le Vaillant is the principal authority for this statement, but like many other records of this traveller's, it is open to doubt; and Mr. Layard says that he never heard anything of the sort in South Africa.

The preceding genera possess a bony tubercle in their nostrils, but the true Gos-Hawks (*Astur*) have not this peculiarity. On the contrary, they have an oval nostril with no tubercle. They are remarkable for their stout and heavy bill, accompanied by stout legs and short toes. They are of all sizes, some of them being as big as a Buzzard, while others are scarcely larger than a Thrush.

The Common Gos-Hawk.—*Astur palumbarius*.

The Common Gos-Hawk is a bird of the woods and forests, where it builds a nest of great size, which it lines with roots and moss, but does not use green leaves as many birds of prey do. The great size of the nest is probably due to the additions made by the birds from year to year. The eggs are pale greenish white, and are only very rarely marked with faint brown spots. The Gos-Hawk is a most useful bird to the falconer, as it is an adept at taking rabbits, but it belongs to the group of short-winged Hawks and cannot fly down its prey like an Eagle or a Falcon. Seebohm observes:—"In spite of his comparatively short wings, he is a bird of very powerful flight, and of undaunted courage. He disdains to eat carrion, and will scarcely stoop to catch a sitting bird. He hunts on the wing, and nothing is safe from his attacks, from a sparrow to a grouse, or from a mouse to a young roe. In summer he confines himself principally to the woods and the open places in their immediate neighbourhood; but late in autumn and winter he extends the range of his hunting-grounds, pursuing partridges and hares, and making raids on the pigeons belonging to the farmers, and sometimes snatching the game from under the very nose of the sportsman."

The Gos-Hawks are about forty in number, and many of them, though small, are of beautiful plumage, such as the Fijian *Astur torquatus* and its allies, which are pale grey birds with a rufous collar round their necks and vinous coloured breasts. This group inhabits the Australian region, more especially the Moluccas, and the Papaan Islands. Another group is that of the Indian Shikra (*Astur badius*), which has allied species in Burma, Africa, and South-Eastern Europe. They are all small birds with prettily barred breasts. One of the most interesting, however, is the White Gos-Hawk of Australia, a pure white species, which looks like an albino. *Astur novæ hollandiæ*, as it is called, is confined to the Australian continent, with a representative species, *A. leucosomus*, in New Guinea.

The Sparrow-Hawks.—Genus *Accipiter*.

This is also a numerously represented genus of Hawks; the difference between the Sparrow-Hawks and the Gos-Hawks consisting principally in the smaller bills and longer toes of the former birds. Like the Gos-Hawks, the members of the genus *Accipiter* are found over the greater part of the world, and both small and large species are met with. They are generally of slight build, but use their short wings with great dexterity, doubling in their flight in the most rapid manner, and snatching their prey with a sudden plunge, seldom attempting to seize it in the open.

In our English Sparrow-Hawk the female is a much larger bird than the male, and is much the more powerful bird of the two, though nothing can well exceed the spirit and dash of the little male Sparrow-Hawk. The chief food of the species consists of small birds, but it takes Blackbirds, Partridges, and, according to Mr. Seebohm, even Wood-Pigeons. It is a very determined marauder on the Pheasant coops, and catches a number of young birds of all sorts, feeding its own young on these. The nest is somewhat large, and, unlike that of most of the smaller Birds of Prey, which generally appropriate the nest of some other bird, the Sparrow-Hawk builds its own nest. The eggs of the species of *Accipiter* are invariably more handsome than those of the Gos-Hawks, and some of the eggs of our own species are beautifully marbled with reddish brown.

Fig. 63.—THE FEMALE SPARROW-HAWK (*Accipiter nisus*).

The largest of the Sparrow-Hawks is the Pied Sparrow-Hawk of Africa, which is nearly 2 ft. in length.

The Buzzards.—Sub-family *Buteoninæ*.

With this sub-family we commence the description of the shorter legged Hawks, wherein the tibio-tarsus is always longer than the tarso-metatarsus. The first of the three sub-families is that of the *Buteoninæ* or Buzzards. And here we find a character which runs through them all, and is very constant, viz., that the hinder aspect of the tarsus is *scaled*, and not reticulated. This we believe to be the principal characteristic of the Buzzards, which on the one hand are allied to the Gos-Hawks, and on the other to the Eagles, the difference between the latter and the Buzzards being by no means strongly marked.

At the head of the *Buteoninæ* we find the genus *Erythrotriorchis*, or Rufous Buzzard-Hawks, of which there are two species, one, *E. radiatus*, found in Australia, and the other, *E. doriæ*, inhabiting New Guinea. They are very rare birds, and but little has been recorded concerning their habits.

Of the succeeding genera, *Buteogallus* and *Tachytriorchis*, also very little is known. They are Neotropical forms; but *T. abbreviatus* and *T. albicaudatus* occur in the Southern United States, and some good accounts of their nesting have been published by Captain Bendire in his excellent work on the "Life-Histories of North American Birds." The latter species visits Southern Texas during the summer, and migrates south in winter, visiting South America as far as Argentina in companies. In the winter Mr. W. H. Hudson has known them to become so reduced in flesh that, after every cold rain or severe frost, numbers would be found dead under the trees where they roosted, and in that way most of them perished before the return of spring. Captain B. F. Goss found the species breeding abundantly near Corpus Christi, in Texas, in the spring of 1882. His note to Captain Bendire is as follows:—"I found the favourite breeding-places of the White-tailed Hawk to be a strip of open bushy land, lying between the thick line of timber and chaparral along the coast and the open prairie. Any bush rising a little above the surrounding level seemed a suitable nesting site, and no attempt was made to conceal the nest. In most places it was very prominent, and could be seen for a long distance. I examined fifteen, and they were all placed in low bushes, generally not higher than 6 ft. In a few cases I had to stand upon the waggon to reach them. They were composed of sticks, dry weeds, and grasses, a coarse, dry grass entering largely into the composition of most of them. They were poorly constructed, but moderately hollowed, and usually lined with a few green twigs or leaves. Taken as a whole, the nests looked ragged in outline and slovenly in finish. About one nest in four contained three eggs; the rest but two. These Hawks are wary, and difficult of approach at all times. They would leave their nests as soon as we came in sight, sometimes when still half a mile away, and generally they kept entirely out of sight. An occasional pair sailed high over our heads, uttering a faint cry while we were at their nest. Only a single one came within reach of our guns." Both of the genera *Heterospizias* and *Tachytriorchis* differ from the typical Buzzards in their shorter tails, the wings reaching beyond the tip of the latter.

The True Buzzards. —Genus *Buteo*.

The genus *Buteo* contains about twenty species, of which our European Common Buzzard (*Buteo buteo*) is the type. They are almost identical in their mode of life one with another, and mostly resemble small Eagles in their habits. They are, as a rule, useful birds, as they feed upon rats and mice, insects, and small reptiles, which they pounce upon from a sitting position; hence they do not often capture birds, as they do not take their prey on the wing. The nest of the Common Buzzard is a somewhat large structure, built in a tree, and is flat at the top and lined with fresh green leaves. The eggs are three or four in number, white, or bluish white in colour, the markings being blotches or streaks of a rich brown colour, which are often absent.

Of the utility of the Buzzards to the farmer and agriculturist very good proof is given in Dr. A. K. Fisher's work on the "Hawks and Owls of the

United States in relation to Agriculture," where tables of the food found in the stomachs of the Buzzards are given, from which it appears that large numbers of small mammals and insects, especially locusts, are devoured by these Birds of Prey, and that very few small birds are captured by them, though the larger kinds of Buzzards will occasionally take a Duck or a Partridge.

In the *Buteoninæ* are also contained some other forms of Buzzards, such as the genera *Asturina* and *Urubitinga*, the habits of which call for little special notice here, though some of the latter are very handsome birds of nearly pure white plumage. They are neotropical in habitat, as are also the Harpies, with which the Buzzards conclude. It is generally the fashion to speak of the Harpies as Eagles, instead of Buzzards, but the way in which the hinder aspect of the tarsus is plated, instead of being reticulated, is sufficient to show that these great birds are really members of the sub-family *Buteoninæ*.

The Harpy (*Thrasætus harpyia*).

There are three genera of Harpies — *Harpyhaliaetus*, with one species, *H. coronatus*, a grey bird found in South America; *Morphnus*, also with a single species, *M. guianensis*, found in Amazonia and Guiana as far west as Panama; and *Thrasaetus*, with the true Harpy, *T. harpyia*, as its type, a species found over the greater part of Southern and Central America as far north as Mexico. The Harpy is one of the most splendid, as it is the most powerful, of all the Birds of Prey. Like the other Harpies it possesses a very long crest, which it usually keeps raised, adding to its fierce appearance. It is said to kill calves and animals of far greater bulk than itself, and Dr. Felix Oswald says that "in the Oaxaca district in Mexico, the 'Lobo volante,' or 'Winged Wolf,' attacks and kills heavy old turkey-cocks, young fawns, sloths, full-grown foxes and badgers, middle-sized pigs, and even the black Sapajou monkey (*Ateles paniscus*). The nest is built in the highest forest-trees, especially the *Adansonia* and the *Pinus balsamifera*. The more inaccessible rocks of the foot-hills are also commonly chosen for a breeding place, and it is not easy to distinguish the compactly-built eyrie on the highest branches of a wild fig tree from the dark-coloured clusters of the Mexican mistletoe (*Viscum rubrum*) which are seen in the same tree-tops. The process of incubation is generally finished by the middle of March, if not sooner, and from that time to the end of June the rapacity of the old birds is the terror of the tropical fauna, for their hunting expeditions, which later in the year are restricted to the early morning hours, now occupy them the larger part of the day."

The Eagles.—Sub-family *Aquilinæ*.

In this sub-family the tibio-tarsus is much longer than the tarso-metatarsus, as it was in the *Buteoninæ*, but in all the Eagles the hinder aspect of the tarsus is reticulated, not plated. The bill is festooned but not toothed, as it is in the Falcons, which follow later. There are two genera with wedge-shaped tails, *Gypaetus* and *Uroaetus*. In the former genus is found the species generally called the Bearded "Vulture," on account of the tuft of bristly feathers which is grown on its chin. The Bearded Eagle (*Gypaetus barbatus*) extends from Southern Europe throughout Central Asia to the Himalayas, but has become very rare, if, indeed, not wholly extinct, in Switzerland, where it was once a well-known bird. The Læmmergeier, as it is also called, is still found in some of the other mountain ranges of Southern Europe, and in the

Himalayas it is by no means uncommon. I have myself more than once seen one of these magnificent birds flying over within 30 yds. of my head, and turning his head down from side to side, taking stock of everything below him. His pale yellow eye, which is surrounded by a red ring, and his bearded chin were plainly seen. The flight of a Læmmergeier is grand in the extreme. The bird, however, has many of the habits of a Scavenger Vulture, and resembles *Neophron* in some of its ways, though it does not seem to be such a foul feeder. The species has been known to follow camps, and it is not infrequently to be met with in the neighbourhood of villages in the north-western Himalayas and Tibet. Not only in the Mediterranean countries, but in the Himalayas also, the bird is known as the "bone-breaker," and it undoubtedly has the curious habit of devouring bones. Von Tschudi says that five bullock's ribs 2 in. thick and from 6 to 9 in. long, a lump of hair, and the leg of a young goat, from the knee to the foot, were found in the stomach of one of these Bearded Eagles, while in another the large hip-bone of a cow, the skin and fore-quarters of a chamois, many smaller bones, etc., were discovered. It is also said to drive the chamois and goats over the precipices, and devour the bodies when they have fallen below. The weak feet and claws of the Læmmergeier are vulturine, and not like those of True Eagles, and it is certain that the bird could not capture any large prey with its talons. Its method of breaking the bones which it delights in, is to take them up in the air to a great height and then let them drop on a rock, and it was doubtless in this way that Æschylus was killed more than 2000 years ago, an "Eagle," *i.e.*, a Læmmergeier, having dropped a Tortoise on his bald head, mistaking the latter for a rock. "Marrow bones," says Mr. Hudleston, "are the dainties the Læmmergeier loves the best; and when the other Vultures have picked the flesh off any animal, he comes in at the end of the feast and swallows the bones, or breaks them and swallows the pieces, if he cannot get the marrow out otherwise. I once saw a mature bird of this species which had evidently swallowed a bone, or something uncommonly indigestible, close to the *abattoir* at Athens. He was in a very uncomfortable attitude, and appeared to be leaning on his long tail for support." A second species of Læmmergeier (*Gypaetus ossifragus*) is found in the mountains of North-Eastern Africa.

We now come to the true Eagles (*Aquila*) of which our Golden Eagle is the type, while the Bearded Eagles are connected with the typical Eagles by means of the Wedge-tailed Eagle of Australia (*Uroaetus audax*), a bird which has the aspect of a true Eagle, but has at the same time the wedge-shaped tail of a Læmmergeier.

The True Eagles.—Genus *Aquila*.

In this genus occur some of the best-known Birds of Prey, such as the Golden Eagle (*Aquila chrysaetus*), the Imperial Eagle (*A. heliaca*), the Tawny Eagle (*A. rapax*), and the Spotted Eagle (*A. maculata*). When on the wing it cannot be denied that the Eagles are birds of magnificent appearance, and I have seen nothing grander in my experience of bird-life than a pair of Eagles circling above the Himalayas and screaming in protest against an approaching storm, as it made its way up the valley. On the other hand, in many ways Eagles are little more than large Buzzards, and a great deal of unnecessary romance has been shed around them. Of the Imperial Eagle, Mr. A. O. Hume writes that he considers it no better than a great hulking Kite. In India, he says, it is an ignoble feeder, and he has generally found the birds gorged with carrion. After a good meal, they will sit stupidly on a tree, or any little mud pillar, and permit you to walk within thirty yards of them, but, before feeding, they are somewhat wary, and can by no means always be secured, even when seen sitting. On more than one occasion he found desert rats (*Gerbillus erythrurus*) in their crops, and he once shot one of a pair, which were busy on the line of rails at Etawah, devouring a Bandicoot rat (*Mus bandicota*), which some passing train had cut in two. Occasionally, but rarely, they had eaten snails and other birds. Once he shot a male, which was dancing about on the ground in such an astounding fashion that he killed it to see what the matter was. The bird proved to have been choking, and it had swallowed a whole dry shin-bone and foot of an antelope. The bone, apparently, could not be got down altogether, and in trying to void it, the sharp points of the hoof had stuck into the back of the palate.

There are many other kinds of Eagles, such as the Buzzard-Eagles (*Archibuteo*), and the members of the genus *Eutolmaetus*, of which Bonelli's Eagle (*E. fasciatus*) is the type, and the Booted Eagle of Southern Europe (*E. pennatus*) is another well-known member of the genus. *Lophotriorchis* is another remarkable form, with a well-developed crest. It has one species, *L. kieneri*, found in India and the Malay Archipelago, while the only other species occurs in the mountains of Colombia in South America, a very interesting fact in geographical distribution. One of the most curious of Eagles is the Birds'-nesting Eagle (*Neopus malaiensis*) of India and the Malayan countries and islands. It is a black bird, with powerful talons which are nearly straight. It spends its time hunting for eggs and nestlings, and is continually on the wing, like a Kite. "It subsists," says Colonel Legge, "as far as can be observed, entirely by birds'-nesting, and is not content with the eggs and young birds, which its keen sight espies among the branches of the forest trees, but even seizes the nest in its talons, decamps with it, and often examines the contents as it sails lazily along." Part of a bird's nest has been found in this Eagle's stomach.

The Crested Eagles (*Spizaetus*) of the Indian Region and the Black Eagle of Africa (*Lophoaetus occipitalis*) complete the list of feathered-legged Eagles. All the rest belong to the bare-legged section which have the tibio-tarsus unfeathered. To this section belong the Sea-Eagles and their allies, the Serpent-Eagles. Of the latter there are many species in Africa and in the Indian Region, the best-known being the members of the genus *Circaetus* and *Spilornis*. Of the former we have one species in Southern Europe, *Circaetus gallicus*, but the true Serpent-Eagles (*Spilornis*) are inhabitants of India. The amount of good which they do may be calculated by the statement of Mr. A. O. Hume, who has shot numbers of these birds, that he found fifty little serpents in the stomach of one individual, and on another occasion he knew of a Cobra, 2½ ft. in length, being taken out of a Serpent-Eagle's stomach. *Butastur* is another oriental genus, and the Bateleur-Eagles (*Helotarsus*) are confined to Africa. The true Sea-Eagles (*Haliaetus*) are nearly world-wide in distribution, but they are absent in South America. In Europe and North America we have the White-tailed Eagle (*Haliaetus albicilla*) and the Bald Eagle (*H. leucocephalus*), the latter remarkable for its pure white head. The Ethiopian region contains a beautiful species, *H. vocifer*, and one of the most widely distributed Birds of Prey in Australia and the East is *H. leucogaster*, the white-bellied Sea-Eagle.

From the Sea-Eagles we pass to the Kites, which are also members of the sub-family *Aquilinæ*. At first sight they would seem to have no connection with Eagles, but they are connected with the latter birds through the Brahminy Kites (*Haliastur*). These birds inhabit India and Burma, and extend through the Malay Archipelago to Australia. The Brahminy Kite of India (*Haliastur indus*) makes a nest in a tree very much like that of a Kite, and lays a white egg, mottled with dots and hieroglyphics of reddish-brown.

From the genus *Haliastur* is an easy transition through the African Swallow-tailed Kite (*Nauclerus riqcouri*) and the American Swallow-tailed Kite (*Elanoides furcatus*) to the typical Kites (*Milvus*). The Swallow-tailed Kite of America is a lovely and most graceful bird, the back and tail being black, and the head and underparts pure white. It nests in the Southern United States, and winters in Brazil. Florida is one of its breeding grounds, and the following account of its habits is given by Dr. William L. Ralph in Captain Bendire's "Life-History of North American Birds." He writes:—"Excepting, perhaps, the Turkey Vulture, I think that this bird is the most graceful of any when on the wing. It has the same easy floating motion, but at times it flies very rapidly and turns very quickly, which is something I have never seen the former bird do. Their motions are very 'Swallow'-like, and this, with their forked tail, makes them look like gigantic Barn-Swallows; and like the Chimney-Swifts they have a habit of travelling together in small companies, usually consisting of three individuals, especially when they first return from the South. During the breeding season flocks, consisting of from two to three to ten or twelve birds, but oftener of three, may be seen following one another around, frequently uttering their calls and circling in and out among the tree-tops so fast as to make one dizzy to look at them. Except during this season one seldom sees one of these birds unless it is flying, and I have often wondered if they did not at times sleep while on the wing. At least I know that they usually, if not always, eat while flying, for I have many times seen one sailing leisurely along, occasionally bending its head to tear a piece from a small snake that it held in its talons, and I have never seen one alight to eat its food, like other Birds of Prey."

There are many other forms of Kite, such as the Hooked-billed Kites (*Rosthramus*), the Black-shouldered Kites (*Elanus*), and other small genera, but the best known are, of course, the true Kites of the genus *Milvus*. In the towns and villages of tropical countries of the Old World these birds are nearly always in evidence, flying about with a continuous squeaking cry. The Common Kite is nearly extinct in England, but there are many places on the Continent where it is still plentiful; and Mr. Seebohm gives the following account of its habits:—"In the manner of taking its prey the Kite very much resembles the Buzzards, and even the Harriers. It is by no means a bold and powerful bird, for a clucking hen has been known to put it to flight, and the fiery little Sparrow-Hawk mobs it with impunity. The Kite takes its food upon the ground, and usually catches young or weakly birds or mammals, and also does not even refuse to make a meal on carrion. Like all rapacious birds, the Kite appears to have some favourite spot which serves as a dining-table or larder, where the food brought to feed its hungry young is also plucked and otherwise prepared for them. The nest in the breeding season is also a well-stocked larder, far more food being conveyed thither than is really consumed. In these places may be seen the remains of Grouse, Plovers, and young Curlews and Wild Ducks. In addition to this food the Kite also takes young hares and rabbits, mice and rats, frogs, lizards, more rarely snakes, and the larger coleopterous insects

—creatures that are taken without much exertion or power. In former days, when the Kite was more abundant in these islands than it is now, it was said to be a great enemy to the poultry, young chickens forming a favourite object of its pursuit. At the present day, however, the Kite need cause the poultry-keeper no alarm. Its haunt now, where but a remnant of its former numbers find a last retreat, is in the wildest districts of Scotland, or Wales, where the Red Grouse is probably its favourite fare. How the Kite manages to take so large and strong a bird as a cock Red Grouse is surprising; and it is most probably only the young and weakly ones that fall victims to its swoop. Mr. Booth also suggests that the Peregrine ofttimes unwittingly finds the Kite a meal, and puts a bird in its way that would never be secured unless weakly or wounded. As is well known, that bold, rapacious Falcon often strikes a bird for mere sport, and will leave it where it lies; and there, no doubt, it is sometimes found by the less active Kite and conveyed away. The note of the Kite may be compared to a wild plaintive scream or 'mew,' and is but rarely heard, save in the breeding season. Unmusical as its cry may be, still it appears to be full of wild harmony with the rugged scenery of its haunts, imbues them with life, and, when heard as the bird is flying far overhead, lends a charm to districts where other bird life is wanting."

The Kites which most approach the Falcons are the Perns or Honey-Kites. These have a peculiarly soft plumage, unmistakable to the touch of a practised ornithologist; and this is shared by many of the Falcons, showing that it is practically impossible to draw distinctive characters between the sub-families of Accipitrine birds. Thus the Buzzards merge into the Eagles, and thence through the Sea-Eagles and the Brahminy Kites we reach the true Kites, and from them the Perns, which are half Falcons, and thence the transition is easy to the true Falcons. So it may be affirmed that there is scarcely any order of birds in which the natural connection of the families, sub-families, and genera are better maintained and exemplified than in the *Accipitriformes*.

Some of the most curious of the Perns, and, one may say, of all Birds of Prey, are the Black Perns (*Machœrhamphus*). They are nocturnal birds, coming forth in the twilight to feed on bats and small swifts. One species, *M. anderssoni*, is Ethiopian, being found in Tropical Africa and Madagascar; while the second species, *M. alcinus*, inhabits Southern Burma, the Malayan Peninsula, Borneo, and extends to New Guinea.

The Honey-Kites.—Genus *Pernis*.

These birds are generally called Honey-"Buzzards," but it is certainly wrong to think of them as Buzzards. Their habits, their outward form, and, above all, their curious soft plumage, all point to their affinities with the Kites. There are three species of Honey-Kite, *Pernis apivorus* of Europe, *P. ptilonorhynchus* of Tropical Asia, and *P. celebensis* of Celebes.

The True Falcons.—Sub-family *Falconinæ*.

The Falcons differ from the Kites, which immediately precede them, and from the other Birds of Prey in having a toothed or notched bill. In some of the genera there is a distinct double tooth, as in the Cuckoo-Falcons (*Baza*). These are very interesting Hawks on account of their geographical distribution. They are all birds of the forest districts, one species being found in West Africa, another in Natal, a third in Madagascar, and thence eastwards the species are distributed through the Indian Region and the Moluccas to the Bismarck Archipelago and North-

Eastern Australia. These birds get their name of Cuckoo-Falcons from their large Cuckoo-like yellow eyes and the barred plumage of the lower surface of the body, which is like that of a Cuckoo.

In Central and South America the Cuckoo-Falcons are represented by the Double-toothed Falcons (*Harpagus*), and in the same parts of the Neotropical region occur the Grey Kite-Falcons (*Ictinia*), one of which, *I. mississipiensis*, ranges into the Southern United States. All these genera which we have recently mentioned belong to the borderland between the Kites and the Falcons. They have the characteristics of the latter birds, united to Kite-like plumage and habits, and they further differ from the true Falcons in having an oval nostril, with no central tubercle, whereas the latter birds have a rounded nostril with a central tubercle. The habits of the Mississippi Kite-Falcon have been well described in the works of Captain Bendire and Dr. A. K. Fisher. The latter writes:—"The food of this species, like that of the Swallow-tailed Kite, consists of insects, such as the larger beetles, grasshoppers, and locusts, lizards, small snakes, and frogs. It never has been known to molest birds or mammals, except to drive the larger species away from the vicinity of its nest. Three specimens which Wilson examined at Natchez, Miss., contained the remains of beetles; and he saw them flying about the trees feeding on cicadas. Dr. Coues mentions one shot at Bluffton, S.C., whose stomach was crammed with the same insects, together with a few Katydids. It is wonderful at what a distance its keen eyes can detect a comparatively small insect. Mr. E. W. Nelson says:—'I saw them repeatedly dart with unerring aim upon some luckless grasshoppers from an elevation of at least 100 yards.' (Bull. Essex Inst., Vol. IX., 1877, p. 58.) As regards the economic value of this Kite much the same statement may be made as of the previous species. It does little or no damage, but much good. Soon after arriving in its summer home it begins to remodel its old nest or the deserted nest of some other bird, and more rarely, when these are not available, it builds a new one. The remodelling consists in patching up the sides with a few sticks and adding a sparse lining of Spanish moss or green leaves. The nest is usually situated in the tops of the tallest trees, among the smaller branches, where it is well concealed by the foliage. The full complement of eggs, usually two or three in number, is deposited by the middle of May, though in some cases it must be much earlier, for the writer once secured a young bird in southern Louisiana at the end of May which had already acquired nearly the adult plumage. This Kite is not at all shy, and may be secured easily as it sits on some tall stub; in fact, Col. N. S. Goss tells of shooting a pair from the same tree, as the second one did not move at the report of the gun, but looked down with surprise on its fallen companion. It is said to be morose and irritable in captivity, and very difficult to tame. A specimen which the writer once wounded was the very picture of rage, as with flashing eyes and erect crest it threw itself on its back and prepared to repel the aggressor with its talons. This species is fully as gregarious as any of the other Kites, and oftentimes may be seen in flocks of twenty or more circling over a favourite hunting ground. It is observed most frequently around the border of woods in the vicinity of water, and is particularly fond of half-cleared ground where dead trees still stand, these being used for perches. Its flight is as varied and graceful as that of the Swallow-tailed Kite, is long protracted, and the birds often ascend to so great a height as to be barely visible. While soaring high in the air its flight simulates that of the turkey-buzzard very closely, and as the two birds are often seen together the Kite looks like a miniature of the other."

A curious little genus of true Falcons is *Microhierax*, the members of which are little larger than sparrows. They inhabit the Indian region, especially the Indo-Malayan islands. An allied genus, *Poliohierax*, is found in the Burmese Provinces and in the desert regions of Africa, and the two species known present this unique peculiarity among the true Falcons, that the sexes differ remarkably in colour, the males being grey, while the females have a maroon-coloured beak. One of the chief characteristics of the Falcons is that the males and females are alike in colour, but the latter differ markedly in their superior size.

The Falconets.—Genus *Microhierax*.

The true Falcons (*Falco*) are typified in our Peregrine Falcon (*F. peregrinus*), and various races of this type are distributed over the Old and New Worlds, whilst the Lanner (*F. feldeggii*), and the Juggur Falcon are well-known representatives of the same type.

These birds are really gigantic Kestrels, the form and habit of the birds being those of the true Falcons, while the formation of the foot is that of a Kestrel, the outer and inner toe being about equal in length, whereas in the genus *Falco* the outer toe is much longer than the inner one. Hence the latter birds with their powerful foot are the Falcons *par excellence*. It is the Peregrine and its allies which are the chosen bird of the falconer, while the noble Falcons are not thought much of by them.

The Noble Falcons.—Genus *Hierofalco*.

As I have said before, the members of the genus *Hierofalco* ought to be considered as gigantic Kestrels. They have the same proportions of the toes, but they are very much larger than any Kestrel. They are principally inhabitants of the Arctic regions, the Greenland Jer-Falcon being, like the Snowy Owl and other inhabitants of the snow-clad regions of the high north, almost entirely white, like their snowy surroundings. Thus the Greenland Jer-Falcon is an inhabitant of Labrador and Greenland, occasional stragglers, mostly young birds, finding their way to Great Britain and various countries of Europe. The Iceland Jer-Falcon (*Hierofalco islandus*) inhabits Iceland, and also occasionally wanders to parts of the European Continent, while in Southern Greenland its place is taken by Holboell's Jer-Falcon (*H. holboelli*). In Scandinavia, and thence across Siberia to North America, occurs the Norwegian Jer-Falcon (*H. gyrfalco*). Two other species complete the genus—one the Saker Jer-Falcon (*H. saker*) inhabiting South-Eastern Europe and Central Asia to North-Western India, while Henderson's Jer-Falcon (*H. hendersoni*) is found in Thibet. The plumage of these last two species is rufous, rather than grey or white, and they look like large Kestrels.

Fig. 64.—The Greenland Jer-Falcon (*Hierofalco candicans*).

Besides the Peregrine Falcon, we find in the genus *Falco* a large assemblage of smaller Falcons, such as the Hobby (*F. subbuteo*) and its allies, the Merlin (*F. æsalon*) and kindred species, the Lanner (*F. feldeggii*) and several other Falcons peculiar to the tropical portions of the Old and New Worlds.

The Kestrels.—Genus *Cerchneis*.

The Kestrels differ from the true Falcons in having the outer toe short, and about equal to the inner toe in length. They are birds of small size, and are chiefly insectivorous, many of them catching their prey on the wing, and devouring it as they fly. They catch a large number of field mice, and are everywhere a real friend to the agriculturist. In Dr. Fisher's report on the American Kestrel and its food, it is interesting to observe that in the stomachs of a large series (320) examined, few remains of birds were found, but a considerable number of mice. The chief food of the species was, however, grasshoppers, locusts, and caterpillars.

The Ospreys.—Sub-order *Pandiones*.

The Ospreys, or Fishing Hawks, as they are often called, hold an intermediate position between the Hawks and the Owls. The skeleton very closely approaches that of the latter birds, and the Ospreys have another character in common with the Owls, viz., that the outer toe is reversible, and can be turned backwards or forwards at will. The soles of the feet are likewise furnished with spicules, thus enabling the bird, with its toes distributed nearly at right angles and its spiked soles, to seize and drag from the water the large fish on which it preys.

The Osprey is now a very rare bird in Great Britain, and is only found in certain parts of Scotland, where it is protected, though a few stragglers, mostly young birds, are shot in other parts of the United Kingdom from time to time. The Osprey is a cosmopolitan species, and is found nearly over the whole of the world, the birds from the Australian region being slightly smaller than those from Europe or North America. The nest of the Osprey is an enormous structure, and is placed on a tree, or on a ruined building. The eggs are among the handsomest of those of Birds of Prey.

Fig. 65.—THE OSPREYS (*Pandion haliætus*).

The Owls.—Sub-order *Striges*.

In addition to the reversible toe alluded to above, a character which they share with the Ospreys, the Owls are further distinguished by their soft plumage, and by the absence of a cere or waxlike skin at the base of the bill, which is seen in almost all the true Accepitres. Owls have also a facial disk, which is surrounded by a ring of short, crisp feathers reaching from below the chin, and extending above the eye to the base of the bill. The nostrils are also generally hidden by bristles, and the eyes are directed forwards instead of sideways.

The Horned and Wood-Owls.—Family *Bubonidæ*.

The sub-order *Striges* contains but two families—*Bubonidæ*, comprising the Owls generally, and the Barn-Owls (*Strigidæ*). In these birds the hind margin of the sternum or breast-bone has two distinct clefts, and the furcula or "merry-thought" bone is free, and not united to the keel of the sternum. There is also no serration or pectination of the claw on the middle toe, such as is seen in the Barn-Owls.

In the *Bubonidæ* there are two sub-families—the Horned-Owls (*Buboninæ*) and the Wood-Owls (*Syrniinæ*). In the former the facial disk is not so distinct, and fails in intensity above the eye, whereas in the *Syrniinæ* or Wood-Owls this disk is fully developed, and extends as far above the eye as it does below it. In the Horned-Owls, again, the ear-conch, always a striking feature in the sub-order, is smaller than the diameter of the eye itself, and is not shut in by an opercular fold. In the Wood-Owls the ear-conch is very large, exceeding the diameter of the eye, and is shut in by a very distinct opercular fold.

The Fishing-Owls. —Genus *Ketupa*.

It is interesting to notice that we find in the Owls a group of fishing species, which remind us of the Ospreys. Like the latter birds, these Owls have spicules on their feet, and they have likewise bare tarsi, which is doubtless a convenience to the birds in lieu of their plunging their soft downy plumaged legs into the water; though it must not be forgotten that some of the feathered-legged species, such as the Tawny-Owl (*Syrnium aluco*), and the Barn-Owl (*Strix flammea*), do not hesitate to catch fish on occasion. The members of the genus *Ketupa* are found in India, China, and the Malayan Peninsula and Islands. They have feathered tufts or horns on their head, and are represented in Africa by the genus *Scotopelia*, which has three species very similar to those of *Ketupa*, but without the feathered tufts on the head. Mr. Hume says that the Brown Fish-Owl of India (*K. ceylonensis*) feeds on birds and small Mammals, and it is also known to eat crustacea. They build a large nest on the cleft of a rock, or on a broad shelf of a cliff, or in the hole of a tree, while sometimes they repair a nest of Pallas's Sea Eagle (*Haliaetus leucoryphus*), and appropriate it.

Pel's Fishing-Owl (*Scotopelia peli*).

Pel's Fishing-Owl is a very handsome bird, discovered by Governor Pel on the Dutch Gold Coast in West Africa. He saw it sitting on a bough overhanging the Rio Boutry which he was traversing in his boat. Afterwards it was re-discovered in the Gambia, and an amusing account of this "fetish" bird is given by Colonel O'Connor, who had one alive:—"During seven years' exploration of Western Africa, I only met with one specimen of the Owl 'Nero.' He was brought as a chicken, full of pen-feathers, or rather down, of a delicate straw-colour, and very thick, from a lagoon in the Bawa country. No native would admit 'Nero' as a visitor; and when the bird was installed in Government House, the servants and the head people came in a body to remonstrate, asserting 'he was a "Gumbi Owl," a "Fettish"!!! and would destroy and kill whatever object he looked on.' The chief groom (an old soldier, who had charge of the poultry) insisted that every cock and hen would go dead. Strangely enough, an epidemic broke out, and carried off fifty to sixty head of fowls; and each day the groom placed the defunct birds on the steps of Government House to meet the eye of Mrs. O'Connor, seeming to exult in the mortality amongst the feathered tribe. 'You see wid your own eye, Missus, dat debil jumbi bird, he go kill all de fowls: Governor tink he hab long head, but he no takey owl: suppose you put him in de stable, he see Nelly' (Mrs. O'Connor's favourite mare), 'de horse he go tumble down dead.' Death at last ceased to reign amongst the poultry population, and Nero became my principal pet. He ranged over the Piazza, perching on the branch of a tree; he was fed regularly by the orderly on roasted fish, but he often came to the dinner-table and flew down for scraps of meat or bread-and-butter, which he took gently from myself or Mrs. O'Connor, permitting us to rub his head, crest, neck, and back, seemingly enjoying the caressing. But he would snatch meat or bones from the cat or dog, and when the eagle was introduced into his company, he beat him in a most unmerciful manner away from his peculiar and original portion of the Piazza—the eagle being one of the fiercest and most pugnacious of African birds, brought from the upper parts of the Sabia River near 'Wallie,' and, when in vigour, able to carry away a kid or small lamb. Nero luxuriated in a tub of water, frequently washing himself and perching himself on the rim until dry. He was wont to go out to the garden or fields, where instantly an immense commotion arose among all the birds; the larger ones flew round the owl, keeping a very civil distance—the smaller birds flew away; but Nero treated both alike with sovereign contempt; he would return of his own accord to the roosting-place in the Piazza, and when put out and confined for some days, rejected all food, and pined until restored to his perch. With me he was as tame as any canary, and after an absence of two months recognised my voice when I went to his cage, at Oatlands (Devon), appearing much pleased by my taking him out for a walk on the grass. Many natives from the interior told me they had not seen such a bird before; but they considered him unlucky."

The Eagle-Owls.—Genus *Bubo*.

These are some of the largest of all the Owls, and they are found in nearly every part of the globe except Australia. The Eagle-Owl of Europe (*Bubo bubo*) is a magnificent species, with very large ear-tufts, and is such a powerful bird that it even kills fawns, as well as rabbits and hares, and is very destructive to game. It is an inhabitant of the forests of Europe, nesting in a tree, though in some places it has been known to nest on the ledge of a cliff. The eggs, like those of all Owls, are pure white.

The Eagle-Owl of North America (*Bubo virginianus*), according to Dr. A. K. Fisher, devours a good quantity of poultry, but feeds chiefly on rats, mice, and other rodents, with an occasional beetle or other insect.

The Tufted-Owls.—Genus *Scops*.

These are little birds, seldom exceeding the size of a Thrush, and having the appearnce of diminutive Eagle-Owls. Like the latter they have a strongly mottled plumage and conspicuous ear-tufts. They are found in nearly every part of the world, excepting in the extreme south of America and in Australia and the Pacific Islands. The species of Europe (*Scops scops*) is distributed over the greater part of the continent below the line of the Baltic, and is a migratory bird; it occasionally visits Great Britain.

The Snowy-Owl.—*Nyctea nyctea*.

This large Owl is of the size of the Eagle-Owls, and like them it has ear-tufts, though these are very small, and are often difficult to trace. It is distinguished by its snowy-white plumage, and is an inhabitant of the Arctic regions, both in the Old and New Worlds, keeping above the limit of forest-growth and never nesting in the latter districts. It is a day-flying Owl, and feeds principally on mice and lemmings, but in winter, when this food fails it, the Snowy-Owl will catch grouse, hares, ducks, and it has even been known to capture fish. It makes its nest on the ground on the tundra or on a ledge of a bank, and it lays six or eight white eggs. Sometimes as many as ten are found in a nest, and they are generally laid at intervals, so that young of all sizes are to be met with, and there can be no doubt that the warmth of the downy young, which are first hatched, contributes to the hatching of the eggs laid later on.

The Hawk-Owl (*Surnia ulula*).

From its long tail and short wings, as well as from its barred under-surface, this Owl bears considerable resemblance to a Hawk, whence its popular name. The soft plumage and the noiseless flight, however, distinguish it as an Owl at once. It is a diurnal bird in its habits, like the Snowy-Owl, and is often seen sitting on the top of a tree on the lookout for its prey. It is also a very courageous bird, and will often attack anyone who attempts to rob its nest. The latter is placed in a tree, either in a cavity or in old nests among the branches. The eggs are white, and vary in number from four to eight. As with the Snowy-Owl, they are laid at intervals, and are found in various stages of incubation.

The Burrowing-Owls.—Genus *Speotyto.*

In the Old World are found the group of Little Owls (*Carine*) and the Brown Hawk-Owls (*Ninox*), and these are replaced in America by the curious Burrowing-Owls. These little birds associate with the prairie-dogs, and their eggs have been found at a distance of 10 ft. from the mouth of the burrow, which is seldom made by the birds themselves. It has often been recounted how the Owls and the prairie-dogs live in harmony together, and, as Professor Elliot Coues says, "the case is further complicated by the introduction of the rattlesnakes." And no little pure bosh is in type respecting the harmonious and confidential relations imagined to subsist between the trio, which, like the "happy family" of Barnum, lead Utopian existences. He disposes of the myth as follows:— "First, as to the reptiles, it may be observed that they are, like other rattlesnakes, dangerous, venomous creatures. They have no business in the burrows, and are after no good when they do enter. They wriggle into the holes partly because there is no other place for them to crawl into on the bare, flat plain, and partly in search of Owl's eggs, owlets, and puppies to eat. Next, the Owls are simply attracted to the villages of the prairie-dogs as the most convenient places for shelter and nidification, where they find eligible, ready-made burrows, and are spared the trouble of digging for themselves. Community of interest makes them gregarious to an extent unusual among rapacious birds, while the exigencies of life in the plains casts their lot with the rodents. That the Owls live at ease in the settlements and on familiar terms with their four-footed neighbours is an undoubted fact, but that they inhabit the same burrows, or have any intimate domestic relations, is quite another thing. It is no proof that the quadrupeds and the birds live together that they are so often seen to scuttle at each other's heels into the same hole when alarmed, for in such case the two simply seek the nearest shelter independently of each other. The probability is that young prairie-dogs often furnish a meal to the Owls, and that, in return, the latter are often robbed of their eggs; while certainly the young of both and the Owl's eggs are eaten by the snakes." The principal food of the Burrowing-Owl consists of insects, and they devour large numbers of locusts and grass-hoppers, though the birds also eat a great many rodents; and at times a great quantity of food has been found stored up in their burrows.

These little Owls are scarcely bigger than Sparrows, and none of them exceeds a Thrush in size. They are widely distributed in both the eastern and western hemispheres, but are absent in Australia and the Austro-Malayan and Pacific Islands. They have a very rounded wing, and a swollen cere like the Little Owls (*Carine*) and the other members of the *Buboninæ* we have just been considering. Their food consists mostly of insects, and the flight of *Glaucidium brodiei* of the Himalayas, which is the only species I have seen alive, was very swift, and the bird appeared to be perfectly at home in daylight. The European species is the Pigmy Owlet (*Glaucidium pygmæum*), and in North America, where more than one form occurs, we learn that one of the species, *G. gnoma*, an inhabitant of the Western States as far south as the highlands of Mexico, is not only an insect-feeder, but also devours small birds and rodents, as well as lizards. It is diurnal in its habits like the little species which I saw in the Himalayas, and, like others of its kind, breeds in old Woodpecker's holes.

The Owlets.—Genus *Glaucidium*.

We have already alluded to the characters of the ear-conch and the operculum which separate the members of the sub-family *Syrniinæ* from those of the *Buboninæ*. Three genera are recognised in the *Syrniinæ*, viz., the Horned-Owls (*Asio*), the Wood-Owls (*Syrnium*), and the Downy-Owls (*Nyctala*).

The Eared- and Wood-Owls.—Sub-family *Syrniinæ*.

The Horned, or Eared, Owls, as they are generally called, are found nearly all over the world, and our Short-eared Owl (*Asio accipitrinus*) is one of the most cosmopolitan of all birds, nesting in the north and migrating south in winter. It is one of the most useful of all the Owls, and on the occasions when Voles have proved such a plague to agriculturists, the Short-eared Owls have appeared in the stricken districts, and have devoured numbers of the mischievous rodents. It also follows the hordes of lemmings and preys upon them. It is a day-flying bird, and nests on the ground, often in small colonies. The Long-eared Owl (*Asio otus*), on the contrary, is a forest-loving bird, and comes out chiefly in the gloaming and at night, when it catches large numbers of mice and other small rodents. Several pairs are often found in the same neighbourhood, and in America the species has been recorded as nesting in company, the nest being generally the deserted one of a hawk or crow of some sort, with a slight lining added. It very rarely nests, like so many of the other Owls, in hollow trees.

The Horned-Owls.—Genus *Asio*.

The Wood-Owls differ from the Horned-Owls in having no ear-tufts of feathers on the head, and in having much less of a cere than the last-named birds. The typical species is the Wood-Owl or Tawny-Owl of Europe (*Syrnium alueco*), which is entirely a woodland bird, nesting in holes of trees, in which it also passes the greater part of the day. At night it is more lively, and its hooting note is often heard throughout the night. Although generally nesting in the hollow of a tree, this Owl has been known to annex a Wood-Pigeon's nest or a squirrel's "drey," or the deserted nests of a Crow or Magpie, while a rabbit's burrow has also been known to be occupied by the Tawny-Owl. The eggs are three or four in number and are white.

The Wood-Owls.—Genus *Syrnium*.

Of the Downy-Owls (*Nyctala*), the best known species is Tengmalm's Owl (*N. tengmalmi*), an inhabitant of Northern Europe and North America, and in the latter country a second species, *N. acadica*, occurs.

The White Owls.—Family *Strigidæ*.

These birds differ from the *Bubonidæ* in having a pectinated claw to the middle toe. The hinder margin of the sternum or breast-bone is without notches, and the furcula or "merry-thought" bone is joined to the keel of the sternum. There is but one genus in the family, viz., *Strix*, of which our own Barn-Owl or White Owl is the type.

The present species is nearly world-wide in its distribution, but does not occur very far to the north. The Barn-Owl appears to follow man and his civilisation, doubtless from the fact that where farms are settled, rats and mice will follow. The number of mice which a Barn-Owl will consume is really wonderful, shrews and voles being also taken in great numbers; and Waterton tells us that a mouse is brought to the nest every twelve or fifteen minutes, while we ourselves have found more than forty field-mice, freshly caught, in the nest of one of these Owls. They will also catch bats in small numbers, and occasionally birds form part of their diet, but the principal food of the Owl consists of small rodents; and it may confidently be said that the Barn-Owl is one of the farmer's best friends. Dr. A. K. Fisher, in his report on the "Hawks and Owls of the United States in relation to Agriculture," says that he scarcely found anything but mice in the stomachs of thirty-nine Barn-Owls he examined. Four birds had been captured, as well as locusts and other insects, but the staple food was mice and rats. Besides the Barn-Owls, which have a mottled plumage, there are a couple of brown-backed species, known as Grass-Owls. One inhabits Africa, and bears the name of *Strix capensis*, while in India and the Malay countries to Australia and the Pacific Islands, a second species (*S. candida*) occurs. Both these birds have longer legs than the Barn-Owl, and live in the open grassy country.

Fig. 66.—THE BARN-OWL (*Strix flammea*).

The Parrots.—Order *Psittaciformes*.

We are shortly coming to the Picarian birds—the Trogons, the King-fishers, and such-like forms. Between them and the birds which we have hitherto passed in review there would seem to be but little connection, and at first sight none but the Parrots afford a connecting link. They have been placed in all sorts of different positions in the schemes which have been propounded for the classification of birds, and they have been recently pushed to the end of the series by a well-known anatomist, because he did not know where else to place them. There was reason in making them the head of all the birds, as was done by Blyth and Bonaparte, on account of their superior intelligence, for the same reason that the monkeys were placed at the head of the Mammalia, and there was also sense in associating them with the climbing birds on account of their zygodactyle foot, with two toes directed forwards and two backwards. They have, however, certain characteristics which isolate them from the majority of birds, and it requires a little consideration to determine their position in the natural system. Nowhere does their place appear better in a linear arrangement of birds than after the *Accipitres* and *Striges*, leading on to the *Picariæ*. Like the latter birds they nest in holes, and lay white eggs, but so do most of the Owls. The Parrots have a cere which is distinctly an Accipitrine character, and the Owls have semi-zygodactyle foot, not very different in outward appearance from that of the Parrots. Indeed, it was one of the most curious of my experiences to see a Little Owl (*Carine noctua*) catch a black beetle and eat it. It held the beetle between its toes, exactly like a Parrot takes its food, and munched it up, holding its foot like a hand to take the insect to its mouth.

In the Parrots the palate is bridged or "desmognathous," and the upper mandible is movable and loosely articulated to the skull, while the plantar tendons are like those of the Game-Birds. The nestlings of Parrots are decidedly curious, and differ from those of Owls, and also of Picarian birds. They are covered with a dense coating of down of a dusky colour, but appear to be completely naked when first hatched. The feathers are encased in sheaths, like those of Picarian birds, and these sheaths last for a considerable time, being thrown off only when the feather itself is nearly perfect, so that the young bird, from being covered with bristly spines, becomes all at once fully feathered.

Count Salvadori, who has monographed the Parrots in the twentieth volume of the British Museum "Catalogue of Birds," divides them into six families, the Kaka Parrots (*Nestoridæ*), the Lories (*Loriidæ*), the Lorikeets (*Cyclopsittacidæ*), the Cockatoos (*Cacatuidæ*), the true Parrots (*Psittacidæ*), and the Owl-Parrots (*Stringopidæ*).

The Kaka Parrots.—Family *Nestoridæ*.

In this family the tongue is fringed, and the culmen of the bill is grooved along the middle. The species are now confined to New Zealand; but *Nestor productus* and *N. norfolcensis*, from Philip Island and Norfolk Island respectively, though now extinct, show that the genus extended, in former times at least, as far as the above-mentioned localities. The Nestors are forest-loving birds, and the following are Sir W. Buller's notes on the habits of the Kaka:—"This is one of our highly characteristic forms, and is met with, more or less, in every part of the country. Far away in the depths of the forest, where the trees are clad with rich mosses, cryptograms, and lycopods to their very tops, where, as if to hide the mouldering decay of Nature, huge masses of green vines and creeping plants cover the aged trunks and bind the bush together—where the sunlight, struggling through leafy tops, discloses here and there a feathery tassel of *Asplenium flaccidum* hanging from the branches or a clump of the scarlet-flowered mistletoe—there the Kaka is at home, and may be seen twisting and turning among the sprays, hopping Cockatoo-fashion along a branch, then climbing higher with graceful agility; resting for a moment to whistle for his mate and, when he has joined him, expressing his pleasure in a sharp chuckling note, like the striking together of two quartz pebbles; then, as if suspecting some treachery below, he suddenly takes wing with loud cries of '*Kaka*,' and glides smoothly through the leafy maze, closely followed by his spouse. On a rear view the brilliant plumage under the wings is very conspicuous when the bird is flying; but when the bird is climbing or hopping, in the manner habitual to it, the wings are kept closed. Then on the outskirts of the forest you meet with him again—more generally in the early morning—hunting diligently for his insect food, or regaling himself on ripe berries of various kinds in the thick underwood; and towards evening three or more of them may be seen in company, flying high above the forest level; then alighting on the withered, naked top of some lofty kahikata or kauri tree—always perching on the highest points—resting a few moments, and taking wing again till they are fairly out of sight. In the early watches of the night, too, especially during the breeding season, and just before the break of dawn, its peculiar cry betrays its wakeful restlessness."

The same author writes of the Kea Parrot (*Nestor notabilis*):—"When hunting for food in its wild mountain home, it may be seen perched for a few moments on a jutting rock; then, descending to the ground to hunt for grubs and insects, or to gather the ripening seeds from certain Alpine plants, it disappears for a time and then mounts to the summit of another rock, just as I have seen the Common Raven doing in the higher parts of the Bernese Alps. On the level ground their mode of locomotion is similar to that of the Kaka, consisting of a hopping rather than a walking movement. Like that bird also, they are semi-nocturnal, exhibiting much activity after dusk and in the early dawn. The cry of the Kea, as generally heard in the early morning, has been aptly compared to the mewing of a cat; but it likewise utters a whistle, a chuckle, and a suppressed scream, scarcely distinguishable from the notes of it noisy congener. But the most interesting feature in the history of this bird is the extraordinary manner in which, under the changed conditions of the country, it has developed a carnivorous habit—manifesting it, in the first instance, by a fondness for fresh sheep-skins and other station offal, and then, as its education progressed, attacking the living sheep for the purpose of tearing and devouring the kidney-fat, and inflicting injuries that generally prove fatal. This habit, confined at first to only a few of the more enterprising birds, soon became general, and it is a common thing now for whole parties of them to combine in this novel hunt after live mutton! So destructive, indeed, have they become on some of the sheep-runs, that the aid of Parliament has been invoked to abate the nuisance by offering a subsidy to Kea-hunters. Before the full development of the raptorial habit described above, the penchant for raw flesh exhibited by this Parrot in its wild state was very remarkable. Those that frequented the sheep stations soon manifested a distaste for all other food and lived almost exclusively on flesh. They took possession of sheep's heads that were thrown out from the slaughter-shed, and picked them perfectly clean, leaving nothing but the bones. An eye-witness thus described this operation:—"Perching itself on the sheep's head, or other offal, the bird proceeds to tear off the skin and flesh, devouring it piecemeal, after the manner of a Hawk, or at other times holding the object down with one foot, and with the other grasping the portion it was eating, after the ordinary fashion of Parrots."

In these Parrots the tongue is furnished with a kind of brush, and the culmen is smooth and not grooved along the middle. The Lories are birds of brilliant plumage, and since Count Salvadori's review of the family in the "Catalogue of Birds," Professor St. George Mivart has published a monograph of the *Loriidæ*, beautifully illustrated by Keulemans. Following Salvadori's arrangement, Professor Mivart recognises fourteen genera of Lories, which are strongly represented in the Moluccan sub-region, and extend west to Celebes, and eastwards to the Australian and Pacific sub-regions. Although many of the Lories are well known as cage-birds, and the species are well represented in most museums, it is extraordinary that so little information is forthcoming as to their habits. Of several genera,

The Lories.—Family *Loriidæ*.

such as *Chalcopsittacus*, *Eos*, and others, scarcely anything is known, and we have only been able to gather the following scanty notes from Professor Mivart's "Monograph" to give us some idea of the habits of the *Loriidæ*. Of *Eos rubiginosa*, from the Caroline Islands, Dr. Otto Finsch observes:—"This Parrakeet makes itself known by its continued noise, uttered both on the wing and when resting in the foliage of high trees. It is not at all a shy bird, approaching fearlessly the neighbourhood of houses and plundering the fruit trees, notwithstanding all the means taken to destroy them. They keep mostly in pairs, or in small companies of from three to five; and often, when I had shot one of a flock, the remainder would come down to their dying comrade and share the same fate."

Of the Green-tailed Lory of the Solomon Islands (*Lorius chlorocercus*), an account is given, by Mr. James Marler, of a pair of young birds:—"For a long time we apprehended that they would starve rather than go to the ground for their food; so I hit on the device of hanging it to the wire swinging loose in the cage. To this they instantly resorted, holding it steady with one foot, and tearing it with their bills. They hang and feed in any position, holding sometimes by one foot and twisting round in every direction. Often in their play, or battles, they would simultaneously grasp claws and struggle to upset each other." In the Pacific we find the genus *Vinia* confined to the Navigator's Islands and the Friendly and Fanning groups. Dr. Streets gives an account of the way in which Kuhl's Lory (*Vinia kuhli*) is taken on Washington Island:—"When the islander wishes to take the Lories alive, he provides himself with two pieces of bamboo, each about a yard long. On the end of one he perches a tame bird, and from the extremity of the other suspends a short running noose made of cocoa-nut fibres. The decoy bird, as it is carried about among the cocoa-nut trees, utters a harsh, rasping sound, and the wild birds fly down from the trees and alight alongside it on the bamboo-stick, when, by means of the other stick, they are skilfully noosed. When caged aboard ship, they exhibited as pretty a picture of love as one can imagine. They sat billing and smoothing each other's feathers for hours, and as night came on, two would get together, and sleep with their heads turned towards each other. They lived in confinement but a very short time, and bore it badly. At times, even while we stood watching their lively antics, one would tumble off its perch and die, apparently in convulsions." The most numerously represented genus of the *Loriidæ* is *Trichoglossus*, which is distributed over the greater part of the Australian Region, and the Papuan sub-region also presents us with a group of small pointed-tailed Lories, such as *Hypocharmosyna* and *Oreopsittacus*, some of which are not much larger than a sparrow.

Count Salvadori's next family, the *Cyclopsittacidæ*, contains only two genera, *Neopisttacus* and *Cyclopsittacus*, from Papuasia and the Molucca Islands, as well as Australia. The bill is deeper than in the other two families noticed above, and the size of the birds is small.

The Cockatoos.—Family *Cacatuidæ*.

In this family the under mandible has a series of ridges producing a file-like surface. They embrace at once the largest and the smallest of the Parrots, among the former being the Cockatoos, of which the Great Black Cockatoo (*Microglossus aterrimus*) is an immensely powerful bird, while the members of the genus *Nasiterna* do not possess the bulk of a sparrow. The White Cockatoos are generally seen in this country in a state of captivity, but they form an interesting feature of wild Australian bird-life, as may be seen from the following note given by Gould:—"The crops and stomachs of those killed were very muscular, and contained seeds, grain, native bread (a species of fungus), small tuberous and bulbous roots, and in most instances large stones. As may be readily imagined, this bird is not regarded with favour by the agriculturist, in whose fields of newly-sown grain and ripening maize it commits the greatest devastation; it is consequently hunted and shot down wherever it is found, a circumstance which tends much to lessen its numbers. It evinces a decided preference for the open plains and cleared lands, rather than for the dense brushes near the coast; and, except when feeding or reposing on the trees after a repast, the presence of a flock, which sometimes amounts to thousands, is certain to be indicated by their screaming notes, the discordance of which may be easily conceived by those who have heard the peculiarly loud, piercing, grating scream of the bird in captivity, always remembering the immense increase of din occasioned by the large number of birds emitting their harsh notes at the same moment; still, I considered this annoyance amply compensated for by their sprightly actions and the life their snowy forms imparted to the dense and never-varying green of the Australian forest—a feeling participated in by Sir Thomas Mitchell, who says, 'amidst the umbrageous foliage, forming dense masses of shade, the White Cockatoos sported like spirits of light.' The situations chosen for the purpose of nidification vary with the nature of the locality the bird inhabits; the eggs are usually deposited in the holes of trees, but they are also placed in fissures in rocks wherever they may present a convenient site; the crevices of the white cliffs bordering the Murray in South Australia, are annually resorted to for this purpose by thousands of this bird, and are said to be completely honeycombed by them. The eggs are two in number, of a pure white and rather pointed at the smaller end."

The True Parrots.—Family *Psittacidæ*.

This family comprises the majority of the species of the order *Psittaciformes*. They differ principally from the *Cacatuidæ* in having the orbital ring generally incomplete, while the head is not crested as in the Cockatoos and their allies. These are small distinctions, and, as Count Salvadori has pointed out, the two families above named can scarcely be separated. In the family *Psittacidæ* are comprised all the Macaws (*Ara*), the Conures (*Conurus*), the Amazons (*Chrysotis*), the Long-tailed Parrakeets (*Palæornis*, *Platycercus*, etc.), as well as the true Parrots (*Psittacus*).

Numerous other genera, including the Love-Birds (*Psittacula*, *Agapornis*, etc.), likewise belong to this section, and one of the most curious of all is the genus *Nasiterna*. It consists of some little birds, less than a sparrow in size, inhabiting New Guinea and the neighbouring groups of islands. Their small size renders them difficult of observation, and little has been recorded of their habits. Baron von Rosenberg found the Pigmy Parrot of Mafoor Island in Geelvink Bay (*N. maforensis*) nesting in holes of trees, the eggs being white, and not larger than those of the Bottle-Tit of Europe. Of the Pigmy Parrot of New Guinea (*N. pygmæa*) Dr. Meyer writes:—"I got this bird only near the foot of the Arfak Mountains, in New Guinea, where, at Andai, I procured specimens in the middle of the day. There this lovely little Parrot was sleeping on the lower branches of the trees, and could be whipped off with a stick. This is also the case with other Parrots which are allied to the *Cacatua* group. I may mention *Cyclopsitta lunulata*, from the Philippine Islands, the individuals of which species sleep in the middle of the hot tropical day in rows under the shade of the foliage, when one after another can be shot down without the survivors attempting to fly away. It may be imagined how soundly they sleep when the noise of the shot does not disturb them; and it is the same with *Nasiterna*. At other times of the day it is difficult to procure, as it lives in the high trees, where its small size and green plumage form a sufficient protection."

Space does not permit of a full discussion of the habits and ways of all the Parrots, which are, after all, very similar; but, as the Grey Parrot is a typical representative of the family *Psittacidæ*, I give a few extracts from the account published by Mr. J. G. Keulemans, who studied the habits of the species in Prince's Island, in the Bight of Benin. In this West African island the Grey Parrot is very common, and does a great deal of mischief to the maize fields. The birds resort in great numbers to certain parts of the forest to roost. Although he ultimately discovered the nesting-place of the Parrots, it was not easy to find the actual nests, though the cries of the birds convinced him that hundreds were concealed in the dense foliage around him. His servant at last found a nest, but as darkness was coming on fast, the tree was marked for operations on the following morning. "While thus occupied," says Mr. Keulemans, "troops of Parrots approached from different sides and settled among the trees. As for ourselves, we found capital shelter under a clump of bushes, where we concealed ourselves, and thence we observed the doings of the Parrots around us. Some were climbing and hanging on branches, others flying and scampering through the foliage. We saw them perching close to each other, and afterwards five or six settled just above our shelter. Numbers came from all sides, and the chattering which we had previously heard at the distance was by this time close to us. There was a noise of whistling, screaming, quarrelling, and the breaking of dead branches. We saw them pass before us and settle on the trees. At this time we must have been surrounded by hundreds of Parrots. Being now almost dark, and having to pass the night in the open air, it was time to take steps to make our sojourn in the forest as comfortable as possible. A fire being the first necessity, we left our shelter in order to gather some of the dead palm-leaves that lay about. As we emerged from our covert the Parrots perceived us, and in a moment the whole place was ringing with their deafening screams. The fire was soon made, and, burning up quickly, it cast a cheerful light and warmth around the spot, rendering our bivouac more agreeable; and the Parrots, attracted by the unusual sight, kept flying over and around the place thus illuminated. An hour afterwards, quiet being restored, we proceeded to get our supper, consisting of roasted bananas. This being finished, we dried some moss to serve for a bed, and retired; but the night was so cold, and the mosquitos kept stinging my face so pertinaciously, that it was impossible to sleep, so I got up and roasted some more bananas, smoked a pipe, and then felt quite ready to go in pursuit of the birds. As it wanted

Fig. 67.—The Grey Parrot (*Psittacus erithacus*).

some three hours to daylight, I occupied myself in preparing lime sticks and making snares. On the appearance of the first streak of dawn, we proceeded to the tree where a nest was suspected to be. My black man, being a capital climber, went up to the hole, and looking in found two young Parrots, which he carefully tied up in a pocket handkerchief and lowered down to me; the little things seemed to be about a fortnight old, and readily took some banana I offered them. The old birds were absent, probably seeking food; at least, we did not see them. The two young ones we fastened with string to the trunk of the tree, and placed some lime sticks round about them. In this way we caught one of the parent birds, the securing of which was a matter of some difficulty, owing to the resistance it made. We put the freshly caught old bird in a linen bag, and fastened it beside the young ones. In a few minutes our captive began to turn round and round, at the same time screaming vociferously; this quickly attracted the attention of the Parrots in the neighbourhood, which came near, gazing with astonishment at the bag which contained their mysteriously hidden comrade. One, more bold than the rest, flew down and settled on a limed stick, but its struggles were so violent that it succeeded in getting away. I then took my gun and shot two individuals, the others immediately taking flight."

The Owl-Parrot.—*Stringops habroptilus.*

The last genera of the *Psittacidæ* are the Ground Parrots (*Pezoporus* and *Geopsittacus*) of Australia, and these lead us to the remarkable Kakapo or Owl-Parrot of New Zealand. This is a large bird, of green, moss-like plumage, which is remarkable for having fully developed wings, but which, like other New Zealand birds, is incapable of flight. This is shown by the sternum of the bird, which has become so reduced that a keel no longer exists, and the bird can no longer fly. Of the habits of this curious Parrot, Sir Walter Buller, the historian of New Zealand birds, writes as follows:—"During the day it remains hid in holes under the roots of trees or rocks, or, very rarely, perched on the boughs of trees with a very dense, thick foliage. At these times it appears stupid from its profound sleep, and if disturbed or taken from its hole, immediately runs and tries to hide itself again, delighting, if practicable, to cover itself in a heap of soft, dry grass. About sunset it becomes lively and animated, and playfully issues forth from its retreat, and feeds on grass, weeds, vegetables, fruits, seeds, and roots. When eating grass it rather grazes than feeds, nibbling the grass in the manner of a rabbit or wombat. It sometimes climbs trees, but generally remains upon the ground, and only uses its short wings for the purpose of aiding its progress when running, balancing itself when on a tree, or in making a short descent, half jump, half flight, from a higher to a lower bough. When feeding, if pleased with its food, it makes a continued grunting noise. It is a greedy bird, and choice in its food, showing an evident relish for anything of which it is fond. It cries repeatedly during the night, with a noise not very unlike that of the Kaka (*Nestor meridionalis*), but not so loud. The Kakapo is a very clever and intelligent bird; in fact, singularly so; it contracts a strong affection for those who are kind to it, shows its affection by climbing about and rubbing itself against its friend, and is eminently a social and playful bird. Indeed, were it not for its dirty habits it would make a far better pet than other bird with which I am acquainted, for its manner of showing its attachment by playfulness and fondling is more like that of a dog than a bird. It builds in holes under trees and rocks, and lays two or three white eggs, about the size of a pullet's, in the month of

February, and the young birds are found in March. At present (1884) the bird is known only to exist in the Middle Island of New Zealand, on the West Coast, between Chalky Harbour and Jackson's Bay, and in the Northern Island, about the sources of the Waganui, and in part of the Taupo countries. It was, within the recollection of the old people, abundant in every part of New Zealand ; and they say it has been exterminated by the cats introduced by the Europeans, which are now found wild and in great numbers in every part of the country. They say also that the large rat introduced from Europe has done its part in the work of destruction. The natives assert that, when the breeding season is over, the Kakapo lives in societies of five or six in the same hole, that it is a provident bird, and lays up in the fine season a store of fern roots for the bad weather."

The Picarian Birds.—Order *Coraciiformes.*

This large order contains a number of sub-orders, which will be treated of below in detail. They are very different in outward form from each other as well as in habits and in structure, but they have one striking character in common, which separates them from the Perching birds or Passeriformes, and that is the arrangement of the deep plantar tendons of the foot. In the Picarian birds the hallux or hind toe is connected with the *flexor perforans digitorum* and not with the *flexor longus hallucis.* In all other birds an exactly opposite arrangement takes place.

The Oil-Birds.—Sub-order *Steatornithes.*

These curious birds cannot be reckoned to be Nightjars, although they have the outward appearance of being members of the latter group. Their habits are crepuscular like those of the *Caprimulgidæ*, but there are many characters which show that they are not true Nightjars, but constitute a sub-order apart. They lay white eggs, which no Nightjar ever does, the sternum has two notches on its hinder margin, and there are other osteological features which distinguish the Oil-Bird.

The colour of this singular species is reddish brown inclining to chestnut, with small triangular white spots on the head and neck, and cross-barrings of blackish on most of the upper parts, and white spots on the median wing-coverts ; the under surface is pale chestnut, suffused with greyish.

The Oil-Bird (*Steatornis gariepensis*), or Guacharo, as it is usually called, is an inhabitant of South America, from Guiana to Venezuela and Co ombia, and thence south to Ecuador and Peru. The best account of the habits of this curious bird is that given by Mr. Jean Stolzmann, the celebrated explorer of Northern Peru. He states that the Guacharo passes "the whole day in the caves, hiding itself in the inaccessible ledges, and if startled by a cry or by a shot they make for the roof of the cave, uttering piercing cries. A promiscuous discharge among the flying birds is usually attended with no result, as it is impossible to take aim in the darkness, and out of sixty shots which he fired in the Ninabamba grotto, the result was only eleven birds. After they become tired they return to their holes, one by one, and it is afterwards impossible to make them budge by any noise whatever. Scarcely has twilight

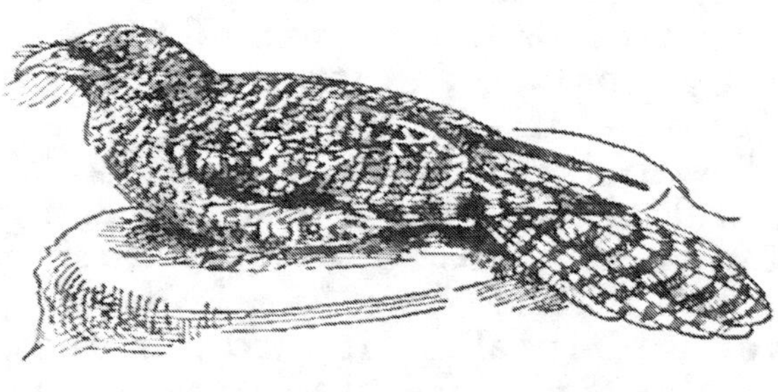

Fig. 68.—The Oil-Bird (*Steatornis cariepensis*).

set in, and while still the west is lit up by the setting sun, the Guacharos come out of their caves and fly over the forests at a considerable height, their movements being very much like those of Nightjars, but they never utter any note. They feed later on in the darkness on the fruits of Nectandra trees, and those fruits they seize while in full flight." The stones of the fruit are afterwards rejected, and Dr. Bevan Rake found large quantities of such stones on the floor of the caves in Trinidad, which he visited in order to procure some nests and young birds. The eggs are two in number, as a rule, but three and even four have been found ; as before recorded, they are white. The nest is a round pile, about a foot in height, and a little more in diameter, looking like a mass of grey clay in the form of a cheese, and when the young are about a fortnight old, they become very fat, so much so that the birds appear as if entirely hidden under a thick layer of yellow grease. It is from this peculiar development of its young that the Guacharo gets its name of "Oil-Bird." The Indians are in the habit of visiting the caves at the time when the young are sufficiently grown, and of killing the latter by hundreds, melting down the fat into earthern jars, and this fat is known by the name of guacharo-butter. Stolzmann says that the note of the Guacharo is very disagreeable, being a loud *cri-cri-coori?*

The Frog-Mouths.—Sub-order *Podargi.*

These thick-headed birds, with their soft owl-like plumage, might well pass for relations of the *Striges*, and, like the latter birds, they are strictly nocturnal in their habits. They are oriental in habitat, being found only in the Indian and Australian regions. The palate is desmognathous or bridged, and the absence of any pectination or comb-like process on the claw of the middle toe, shows that they are not very closely allied to the Nightjars, notwithstanding their external resemblance. The *Podargi* contain but one family, with two sub-families, *Podargince* and *Ægothelinæ*. In the first-named powder-down patches are present, and the nostrils are linear and hidden by bristles, while in the *Ægothelinæ* there are no powder-downs, and the nostrils are open and exposed.

The sub-family *Podargince* contains but two genera, *Podargus* and *Batrachostomus*.

Fig. 69.—THE TAWNY-SHOULDERED FROG-MOUTH (*Podargus strigoides*).

The Frog-mouths are birds of mottled plumage, the genus *Podargus* being confined to Australia and the Papuan Islands. Of the habits of the Tawny-shouldered Frog-mouth (*Podargus strigoides*), Gould gives the following account :—"Like the rest of the genus, this species is strictly nocturnal, sleeping throughout the day on the dead branch of a tree, in an upright position across, and never parallel to, the branch, which it so nearly resembles as scarcely to be distinguishable from it. I have occasionally seen it beneath the thick foliage of the *Casuarinæ*, and I have been informed that it sometimes shelters itself in the hollow trunks of the *Eucalypti*, but I never could detect one in such a situation. I mostly found them in pairs, perched near each other on the branches of the gums, in situations not at all sheltered from the beams of the mid-day sun. So lethargic are its slumbers that it is almost impossible to arouse it, and I have frequently shot one without disturbing its mate sitting close by; it may also be knocked off by sticks or stones, and sometimes is even taken with the hand. When aroused, it flies lazily off with heavy flapping wings to a neighbouring tree, and again resumes its slumbers until the approach of evening, when it becomes as animated and active as it had been previously dull and stupid. The stomach of one I dissected induced me to believe that it does not usually capture its prey while on the wing, or subsist upon nocturnal insects alone, but that it is in the habit of creeping among the branches in search of such as are in a state of repose. The power it possesses of shifting the position of the outer toe backwards, as circumstances require, is a very singular feature, and may also tend to assist it in its progress among the branches. A bird I shot at Yarrundi, in the middle of the night, had the stomach filled with fresh-captured mantis and locusts (*Phasmidæ* and *Cicadæ*), which seldom move at night, and the latter of which are generally resting against upright holes of the trees. In other specimens I found the remains of small coleoptera, intermingled with the fibres of the roots of what appeared to be a parasitic plant, such as would be found in decayed and hollow trees. The whole contour of the bird shows that it is not formed for extensive flight or for performing those rapid evolutions that are necessary for the capture of its prey in the air, the wing being short and concave in comparison with those of the true aerial Nightjars, and particularly with the Australian form to which I have given the name *Eurostopodus*. Of its mode of nidification I can speak with confidence, having seen many pairs breeding during my rambles in the woods. It makes a slightly-constructed flat nest of sticks carelessly interwoven together, and placed at the fork of a horizontal branch of sufficient size to ensure its safety; the trees most frequently are the *Eucalypti*, but I have occasionally seen the nest on an apple-tree (*Angophora*) or a swamp-oak (*Casuarina*). In every instance one of the birds was sitting on the eggs and the other perched on a neighbouring bough, both invariably asleep; that the male participates in the duty of incubation I ascertained by having shot a bird on the nest, which, on dissection, proved to be a male. The eggs are generally two in number, of a beautiful immaculate white. The night-call of this species is a loud hoarse noise, consisting of two distinct sounds which cannot be correctly described."

The Frog-mouths of the genus *Batrachostomus* are smaller birds, as a rule, than the *Podargi*, and inhabit the Indo-Malayan region. Some, like the Eared Frog-mouth of the Malay Peninsula, have long ear tufts, and many of them have the mouth beset with long bristly hairs. The Owlet-Nightjars (*Ægotheles*) are the sole representatives of the sub-family *Ægothelinæ*. They inhabit Australia and the Papuan Islands and the Moluccas. Gould describes the Australian species as being somewhat Owl-like in their carriage and in the way in which they turn their head round. They live in the holes of trees, and come out at night in pursuit of insects, flying in a straight line, and not turning and twisting about like Nightjars. They differ from the latter birds, also, in their method of sitting across, and not lengthwise, on a branch.

These curious birds form a kind of connecting link between the Rollers and the Frog-mouths, but they really constitute one of those peculiar forms in which Madagascar abounds. The bill is something like that of a Roller, but the base is hidden by recurved plumes, while the nostril is linear, and is placed in the middle of the upper mandible, a quite peculiar position for that of a Picarian bird. The fourth toe is partly reversible, a character peculiar to the Climbing Birds. The affinity with the Frog-mouths is remote, but is shown by the possession of powder-down patches. The sexes differ in plumage, the male being glossy green above and grey below, while the female is rufous above, with a black head, and bars on the sides of the head and back of the neck, the under-surface being fawn colour. Like the Rollers, the Kiroumbo has a habit of playing in the air, ascending to a great height, and then descending in a curve nearly to the tops of the trees by almost closing its wings, at the same time uttering a whistle so like that of an eagle, that Sir Edward Newton says he was some time before he could satisfy himself that the note was that of the Kiroumbo.

The Kiroumbos.—Sub-Order *Leptosomati*.

The Rollers.—Sub-order *Coraciæ*.

In these beautiful birds we find a single family, only known from the Old World, but there almost universally distributed. The palate is "desmognathous," or bridged, and the soles of the feet are flat, the toes being united together for nearly their entire length. In Madagascar three forms of Ground-Rollers occur, constituting the sub-family *Brachypteraciinæ*, and remarkable for their long legs. Little is known of their habits; but the Pitta-like Ground-Roller (*Atelornis pittoides*) is known to frequent the ground, and only to perch on the lowest branches of the trees. They have a direct and straight flight, and jerk their tails in a curious way whenever they alight on a branch.

The true Rollers, of which the Common Roller (*Coracias garrulus*) is the type, consist of two genera, *Coracias* and *Eurystomus*, forming the sub-family *Coraciinæ*. These are birds of bright colours, and are more arboreal in habit than the Mascarene Rollers of the sub-family *Brachypteraciinæ*. Not being ground-runners, we find the metatarsus much shorter in *Coracias* than in the last-mentioned birds. The Rollers build in holes of trees, laying white eggs, but not making much nest, the latter consisting of a few roots, straws, or feathers. Both sexes incubate, and during the breeding-season the male ascends to a considerable height in the air, and then descends to where the nest is situated by a series of somersaults and jerks, uttering a harsh note, which Naumann describes as "räh-rähäh-rräh-rrâ," etc., changing to "rock" as the bird throws a somersault.

Fig. 70.—The Common-Roller (*Coracias garrulus*).

The genus *Coracias* has a longish bill, not unlike that of a crow, and nearly all the species have bright greenish-blue on the wings and tail, which colour is very conspicuous when the birds are flying. They are found in Europe, thence to Central Asia, throughout Africa, India, and the Burmese provinces, reappearing in Celebes, where one species, *C. temmincki*, occurs.

The Broad-billed Rollers (*Eurystomus*) occur in Africa, India, Australia, and one species, *E. calonyx*, actually goes to Eastern Siberia during the nesting season.

The Kingfishers.—Sub-order *Halcyones*.

The Kingfishers agree with the Rollers in most of their anatomical characters, having a desmognathous, or "bridged," palate, and the hallux connected with the *flexor perforans digitorum* tendon; but they differ from them in having the spinal feather-tract not forked on the back, and in other characters. The eggs are white, and are always concealed in the hole of a tree or bank, no nest being made.

Kingfishers may be divided into two sub-families, *Alcedininæ* and *Daceloninæ*. The former contain the "fishers," and the latter the omnivorous feeders, whose food consists of crustacea, insects, reptiles, etc.

The Fish-Eating Kingfishers.—Sub-family *Alcedininæ*.

In these birds the bill is long and slender, much compressed, and with an evident keel along the culmen. There are five genera comprised in this sub-family, of which the genus *Alcedo*, which contains our Common Kingfisher, is the type. There are, however, two long-tailed genera of fish-eating species, the Pied and Green Kingfishers (*Ceryle*) and the Stork-billed Kingfishers (*Pelargopsis*), which have the tail longer than the wing. The three other genera, *Alcedo*, *Corythornis*, and *Alcyone*, have short tails, in no case as long as the wings.

The Stork-billed Kingfishers (*Pelargopsis*) are large birds with long red or black bills, and they are inhabitants of the Indian and Indo-Malayan sub-regions. They are mainly piscivorous, but Mr. Stuart Baker records that in Cachar he has known the species of the country (*P. burmanica*), to devour lizards and other small reptiles, while he once saw one attack a nest of young Mynas in a hole of a tree, and drag one of them out and swallow it.

The Pied Kingfishers—Genus *Ceryle*.

The genus *Ceryle* is remarkable among the Kingfishers for the difference in the markings of the sexes, the male in some species having a double pectoral band, whilst in others the contrary is the case, and the males or the females have a band, while the opposite sex has none at all. The Pied Kingfishers are inhabitants of Africa, India, China, and Japan, and the best-known species is *Ceryle rudis* of Africa, over the whole of which continent it is distributed, while it ranges east as far as the Persian Gulf. The colour above is black, varied with white, and the under-surface is white, with two black bands across the chest in the male, and a single band in the female. It is a familiar bird to travellers in the Nile Valley, as it hovers above the water like a Kestrel, and falls on its prey with a stoop like that of the latter bird. In India and China it is replaced by the Indian Pied Kingfisher (*Ceryle varia*), which has no black spots on the white base of the tail. In the Himalayas and the mountains of China, as far as those of the southern island of Japan, the Pied Kingfishers are represented by *Ceryle lugubris*, a large species with the hovering habits of *C. rudis*, and equally a fish-eater. In Africa there are also some large species of *Ceryle*, with grey backs, and in America a similar section of the genus is met with, of which the Ringed Kingfisher (*Ceryle torquata*), and the Belted Kingfisher (*C. alcyon*), are well-known representatives. The latter species has a pectoral band of grey in the male, while the female has an additional band of rufous. In the rest of the South American species of *Ceryle* the back is green, and in this section occurs one of the smallest of all Kingfishers, *C. superciliosa*, which is only 5 inches in length.

The genus *Alcedo* is found over the greater part of the Old World, and eleven species are known, of which Africa claims three, Europe and

Northern Asia one, and the remaining seven are Indian and Malayan. Our Common Kingfisher (*A. ispida*), is the brightest of our indigenous birds, and forms the most beautiful ornament of our rivers and lakes. It is 7½ inches in length, with a chestnut under-surface and a brilliant cobalt-blue back, which shows vividly when the bird flies. It nests in holes, mostly in banks of sandy soil, where the tunnel is hollowed by the birds themselves, or in holes of trees, sometimes at a considerable distance from water.

Fig. 71 —THE COMMON KINGFISHER (*Alcedo ispida*).

In Africa and Madagascar occur the Crested Kingfishers (*Corythornis*), small birds with a long drooping crest, and in Australia and the Moluccas, the three-toed Kingfishers (*Alcyone*), which have the shape and fish-catching habits of our own *A. ispida*, but are of a dull purple colour, and have only three toes instead of four, the hind-toe being absent.

In this sub-family the bill is shorter and wider, the tail generally long, and the food of the species consists less of fish than of insects, small crustacea, reptiles, and even small rodents.

The Insectivorous Kingfishers.—Sub-family *Daceloninæ*.

The first genus is *Ceyx*, a small form of Kingfisher which frequents forests rather than streams. The members of this genus have a wider and less compressed bill than those of *Alcyone*, but like the latter genus they have only three toes. They are found in India and the Malayan sub-region, being very abundant in the Philippines and extending to the Moluccas. They are mostly bright-coloured birds, some being of a beautiful red all over, whilst others have a blue back and resemble species of the genus *Alcedo*. In Africa they are represented by a genus of tiny Kingfishers (*Ispidina*) which are also insect-eaters, as are also the allied genera *Ceycopsis* of Celebes and *Myioceyx* of Western Africa.

Fig. 72.—THE LAUGHING KINGFISHER (*Dacelo gigas*).

From these small forms we pass to the Reptilivorous Kingfishers, the Crested Kingfishers of Malacca and Borneo (*Carcineutes*), the Hook-billed Kingfisher (*Melidora*), and Shoe-billed Kingfisher (*Clytoceyx*) of New Guiana, and the Laughing Jackasses of Australia (*Dacelo*). Of the common Laughing Kingfisher, the "Jackass" of the Australian colonists, we have the following account of Mr. Gould's:—"In its disposition it is by no means shy, and when any objects are presented to its notice, such as a party traversing the bush or pitching their tent in the vicinity of its retreat, it becomes very prying and inquisitive, often perching on the dead branch of some neighbouring tree, and watching with curiosity the kindling of the fire and the preparation of the meal; its presence, however, is seldom detected until it emits its extraordinary gurgling, laughing note, which generally calls forth some exclamation according with the temper of the hearer, such as 'There is our old friend the Laughing Jackass,' or an epithet of a less friendly character. So remarkable are the sounds emitted by the bird that they have been noted by nearly every writer on New South Wales and its productions. Mr. Caley states that its 'loud noise, somewhat like laughing, may be heard at a considerable distance, from which circumstance, and its uncouth appearance, it probably received the extraordinary appellation given to it by the settlers on their first arrival in the colony.' Captain Sturt says, 'Its cry, which resembles a chorus of wild spirits, is apt to startle the traveller who may be in jeopardy, as if laughing and mocking at his misfortune;' and Mr. Bennett, in his 'Wanderings,' says, 'Its peculiar gurgling laugh, commencing in a low, and gradually rising to a high and loud tone, is often heard in all parts of the colony, the deafening noise being poured forth while the bird remains perched upon a neighbouring tree; it rises with the dawn, when the woods re-echo with its gurgling laugh; at sunset it is again heard; and as that glorious orb sinks in the west, a last "good-night" is given in its peculiar tones to all within hearing.' It frequents every variety of situation — the luxuriant brushes along the coast, the more thinly-timbered forest, the belts of trees studding the parched plains, and the brushes of the higher ranges being alike favoured with its presence; over all these localities it is rather thinly dispersed, being nowhere very numerous. Its food, which is of a mixed character, consists exclusively of animal substances; reptiles, insects, and crabs, however, appear to be its favourite diet; it devours lizards with avidity, and it is not an unfrequent sight to see it bearing off a snake in its bill to be eaten at leisure; it also preys upon small mammalia. I recollect shooting a Great Brown Kingfisher in South Australia in order to secure a fine rat I saw hanging from its bill, and which proved to be a rare species. The *Dacelo gigas* breeds during the months of August and September, generally selects a hole in a large gum-tree for the purpose, and deposits its beautiful pearl-white eggs, which are one inch and nine lines long by one inch and five lines broad, on the decomposed wood at the bottom. When the young are hatched, it defends its breeding-place with great courage and daring, darting down upon any intruder who may attempt to ascend the tree."

The large genus *Halcyon* contains more than fifty species, which are found over Africa, India, and China, to Japan, and thence south to Australia, and over the greater number of the Pacific Islands. They are mostly insect-eaters, and are often found far away from water. The last genus of the Kingfishers is *Tanysiptera*, which includes some elegant birds with only ten tail-feathers, the middle ones being produced beyond the others, and generally ending in a spatula or racket. These are birds of the Moluccas and the Papuan Islands, one species, *T. sylvia*, being found in the Cape York Peninsula of North-Eastern Australia. On the habits of this species a short notice has been published by the late John Macgillivray, the original discoverer of the species:—"This pretty *Tanysiptera* is rather plentiful in the neighbourhood of Cape York, where it frequents the dense brushes, and is especially fond of resorting to the small sunny openings in the woods, attracted probably by the greater abundance of insect food found in such places than elsewhere. I never saw it on the ground, and usually was first made aware of its presence by the glancing of its bright colours as it darted past with a rapid, arrow-like flight, and disappeared in an instant among the dense foliage. Its cry, which may be represented by *whee-whee-whee* and *wheet-wheet-wheet*, is usually uttered while the bird is perched on a bare, transverse branch or woody, rope-like climber, which it uses as a look-out station, and whence it makes short dashes at any passing insect or small lizard, generally returning to the same spot. It is a shy, suspicious bird, and one well calculated to try the patience of the shooter, who may follow it in a small brush for an hour without getting a shot, unless he has as keen an eye as the native to whom I was indebted for first pointing it out to me. According to the natives, who know it by the name of 'Quatăwur,' it lays three white eggs in a hole dug by itself in one of the large ant-hills of red clay which form so remarkable a feature in the neighbourhood, some of them being as much as 10 ft. in height, with numerous buttresses and pinnacles. I believe that the bird also inhabits New Guinea; for at Redscar Bay, on the south-east side of that great island, in Long. 146° 50' E., a head, strung upon a necklace, was procured from the natives." We now know that the New Guinea bird is distinct, and is *T. salvadoriana*.

The Hornbills.—Sub-order *Bucerotes.*

The Hornbills are remarkable birds, not only on account of their form, but from the singular habit which every one of the species affects, so far as we know, of imprisoning the female while she is engaged in incubating. The Hornbills vary immensely in size, from the great Rhinoceros Hornbill (*Bucerus rhinoceros*), which is nearly 4 ft. long, to the tiny *Lophocerus hartlaubi* which is only just over a foot in length. The Ground-Hornbills (*Bucorax*) are natives of Africa, where they are generally distributed in the Ethiopian region. They are thoroughly terrestrial birds, of black plumage, with a little red or blue decoration on the bill, or the bare portion of the throat. Walking about on the ground, they have the appearance of black Turkeys, and are considered "omen"-birds among the Kaffirs. They will devour almost any food, and eat numbers of beetles, worms, small rodents, etc., and they also kill large snakes, against which they generally advance in company, holding their wings before them like a shield.

The Great Hornbill (*Dichocerus bicornis*) is a native of the Western Ghauts of India and the Himalayas, and thence through the Burmese Provinces to the Malayan Peninsula to the mountains of Sumatra.

The Pied Hornbills (*Anthracocerus*) are found in India and the Burmese Provinces to Cochin China, and south to the Malayan Peninsula to the Sunda Islands. These birds are generally found in family parties, consisting of five or six individuals. They inhabit well-wooded countries and forests, especially near rivers, where they have been known to feed on fish. Their chief food, however, consists of fruits and berries.

Fig. 73.—THE MALABAR PIED HORNBILL (*Anthracocerus coronatus*).

The habits of the Hornbills seem to be alike in their method of nidification, but in some species the act of enclosing the female is performed by the male, whereas in some instances the female assists in her own imprisonment. Some explanation for this curious custom may be found in the circumstance that when the female has laid her egg in the hollow tree, she commences to moult, and would therefore be entirely defenceless and at the mercy of her enemies, if she were not fenced in, and in the closing of the fortress she herself assists. A narrow opening is left, through which the male is able to supply her with food.

The Hoopoes.—Sub-order *Upupæ.*

At first sight there would appear to be little connection between the Hornbills and the Hoopoes, but in our brief account of the *Bucerotes* we were unable to illustrate all the smaller genera such as *Lophocerus*, *Ocycerus*, etc., which are much more like the Crested Hoopoes than the larger forms of Hornbills. Like the latter birds, the Hoopoes have the fore-part of the sternum perforated, so as to receive the feet of the metacoracoids. There are two families of *Upupæ*, the true Hoopoes (*Upupidæ*), and the Wood-Hoopoes (*Irrisoridæ*). The former are sandy-coloured birds, with a large crest and a square tail. The latter are black with a metallic blue or bronze gloss, and a long graduated tail.

The Hoopoe is an inhabitant of temperate Europe and Asia, being represented in certain portions of the Indian Peninsula and the Burmese provinces by the Indian Hoopoe (*U. indica*). Two other species are found in Africa only, and one is peculiar to Madagascar. The Hoopoe nests in a hole, generally in a tree, and the female and young birds are fed by the male. The nest is often made of very filthy materials, but the young do not seem to suffer, and have the same delicate, soft plumage as the adults, which they resemble even to the possession of the crest. In North-Western India I saw the Hoopoes in small flocks in the open fields, and in such places they are great devourers of grubs and insects. They usually keep their crests depressed, but raise them when alarmed or excited. The note resembles the syllable *hoop*, uttered two or three times; and the late Consul Swinhoe states that from his observations in China, the bird produces its note by puffing out the sides of the neck and hammering on the ground at the production of each note, thus exhausting the air at the end of the series of three notes, which make up its song. The eggs, four to seven in number, when fresh laid, are pale greenish-blue, but fade to a dull olive or yellowish-brown.

Fig. 74.—The Common Hoopoe (*Upupa epops*).

The Bee-Eaters.—Sub-order *Mesopes.*

The Bee-eaters are birds of bright plumage, and, as a rule, of slender form, with long tails. They resemble the Kingfishers and Hornbills in the form of the feet, the toes being joined together, the fourth toe being united to the third toe as far as the last joint, and the second toe being united to the middle one for the basal joint only. The palate is "bridged" or desmognathous, and the breast-bone has four notches in its hind margin, while the episternal process is perforated to receive the feet of the metacoracoids. The Bee-eaters are found in the temperate and tropical portions of the Old World.

In Africa we find the Swallow-tailed Bee-eaters (*Dicrocercus*), and the Square-tailed Bee-eaters (*Melittophagus*), while *Merops*, which has the central tail-feathers elongated, has seventeen species, which are found in Africa, India, China, the Malayan Archipelago, and Australia, one species,

M. apiaster, visiting Southern Europe every summer, extending even to Central Asia and Kashmir. The bird generally tunnels a hole into the bank of some river, and the white eggs are deposited in a chamber at some distance, sometimes of several feet from the opening. Occasionally the birds have been known to bore downwards through the sandy soil, and Mr. E. L. Layard records one instance which came under his own observation in Cape Colony, where the ground was "perforated with numberless holes, into which the birds were diving and scrambling like so many rats." He found the species breeding on the Berg river in September and October, so that the bee-eater may be considered one of the few species which are known with certainty to nest in their winter quarters. In certain parts of Spain the bee-eater commits great havoc among the bees as they fly out of the hives, and the bird is, in consequence, detested by the peasants.

Fig. 75.—THE COMMON BEE-EATER (*Mesops apiaster*).

In the Indian and Malayan sub-regions occur the bearded bee-eaters, remarkable for an ornamental tuft of plumes on the chest. One species, *Meropogon forsteni*, with the central tail-feathers produced, is confined to the island of Celebes; while the genus *Nyctiornis*, which has a square tail, is represented by two species, *N. athertoni*, of the Himalayas, with a blue throat, and *N. amicta*, of the Malayan Peninsula, with a scarlet throat. These birds are of stouter build than the rest of the bee-eaters, and are believed to nest in holes of trees.

The Motmots.—Sub-order *Momoti*.

The motmots are exclusively neo-tropical in habitat, and contain but a single family, the *Momotidæ*. They represent to a great extent the *Meropidæ* of the Old World. The palate is desmognathous or "bridged," the sternum has four posterior notches, and the hind-toe or hallux is always present, and is connected with the *flexor perforans digitorum* tendon. Seven genera are recognised, *Urospatha*, *Prionirhynchus*, *Eumomota*, *Momotus*, *Baryphthengus*, *Aspatha*, and *Hylomanes*, the last being dwarf motmots, and akin to the todies (*Todi*).

Fig. 76.—LESSON'S MOTMOT (*Momotus lessoni*).

One of the chief features of the motmots is the long tail, *Hylomanes* being the only genus with a short tail. In most of the true motmots the central tail-feathers are elongated, and generally end in a racket, which is preceded by a bare shaft. This racket is produced by the bird itself, as it nibbles off the web of the feather with its bill, which has a serrated or saw-like edge to the mandibles. Instances have been recorded of motmots, probably young and inexperienced birds, imbued with the instinct that they have to trim certain of their tail-feathers, but, as the latter grow at first all of the same length, not knowing on which rectrices to commence action. Consequently they begin to nibble feathers to right and left, until the development of the two central tail-feathers beyond the rest teaches the birds that these are the two specially designed by nature to carry the "racket"!

The motmots are green birds, generally with a black patch on the crown, which is surrounded by blue; the under-side is paler, and generally of a fawn-coloured shade. They nest in holes, often tunnelling to a distance of six feet, and the eggs are laid in a rounded chamber at the end of the tunnel, as is the case with the kingfishers and bee-eaters of the Old World. With the kingfishers, however, there is no nest beyond the remains of the fish-bones which are cast up by the parent birds, whereas in the nest-hole of the motmots a few dry twigs are sometimes present. The nesting-place, according to Mr. Zeledon, is a foul-smelling habitation, in which the young remain till they are able to fly pretty well. It should be noted that young birds have the edges of the mandibles quite smooth, and without any serrations.

The Todies.—Sub-order *Todi*.

The todies are also represented by a single neo-tropical family, the *Todidæ*, which is peculiar to the West Indian sub-region. Only four species are known, and these are from the islands of Jamaica, Cuba, San Domingo, and Porto Rico. The long, flattened bill, with its evident rictal bristles, suggests that of an exaggerated flycatcher, and in many of its habits a tody resembles a flycatcher, though it will at times search for its food like a warbler. The todies have a desmognathous palate, showing their true affinity to the motmots and kingfishers, and they nest in holes in banks excavated by the little birds themselves, though they appear likewise to avail themselves of holes and depressions already made. The eggs, like those of other picarian birds, are glossy white, and are laid on a bed of earth in a chamber at the end of the tunnel.

Fig. 77.—THE JAMAICA TODY (*Todus viridis*).

The Nightjars.—Sub-order *Caprimulgi*.

This is a very interesting group of birds, of which we have one representative in England, the common nightjar, or "goatsucker," as it is often foolishly called, *Caprimulgus europæus*. In the *Caprimulgi* we meet with both ægithognathous forms, such as *Caprimulgus* and the allied genera, and schizognathous forms, such as *Chordeiles* of the New World. The presence of two types of palatine characters in one family raises grave doubts as to the value of this formation of the palate, which has been so much insisted upon by osteologists. There are eighteen genera of the sub-family *Caprimulginæ*, and they all have the middle toe furnished with a kind of comb. They possess no powder-down patches.

Our common nightjar (*Caprimulgus europæus*) is crepuscular in its habits, a bird of the twilight. During the day it rests, and only flies when suddenly disturbed; but, as dusk comes on, it comes forth in pursuit of insects, and is often to be seen flying by the light of the moon, soaring above with a sailing flight, and occasionally producing a "clacking" noise by flapping its wings together above its head. The singular jarring noise which the creature makes seems to be its love-song, and in a heathy country, which is the usual habitat of the goatsucker, this "churring" utterance is heard as twilight commences, and even far into the night.

From their mottled and soft plumage, the goatsuckers have been generally associated with the owls, but there is no real affinity between these moth-catching birds and the rapacious birds of the night. Their nocturnal habits are really the only character which they have in common. The young goat-suckers differ from those of other picarian birds in the fact that they are not hatched naked, but are covered with down, though they are not able to provide for themselves like most of the downy nestlings of other birds. The eggs, also, are not white, but are double-spotted, an unusual feature in picarian birds. No caprimulgine bird makes a nest, the eggs being laid upon the bare ground.

The Leona Nightjar (*Macrodipteryx longipennis*).

Africa possesses two curious genera of nightjars, which, in the breeding-season at least, carry ornamental plumes. These are *Macrodipteryx longipennis* of West Africa, and *Cosmetornis vexillarius* of South-eastern Africa. In the former genus, the ninth primary-quill is enormously elongated, and ends in a "racket." In *Cosmetornis*, the seventh and eight primaries are elongated, the ninth enormously, so as to produce a train when the bird is flying. Round Lake Nyassa and on the Zambesi, this bird is a well-known object as it flies over the water in the evening. I have received the following note from Miss Alice Werner, who was connected with the Blantyre Mission. Having read some notes of mine on *Cosmetornis* published elsewhere, she comments on them as follows:—

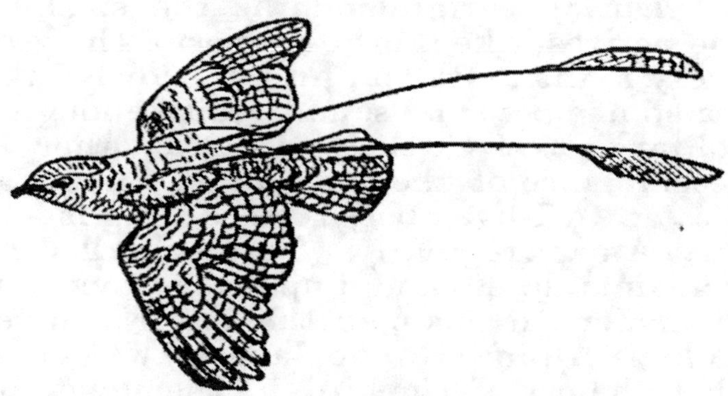

Fig. 78.—LEONA GOATSUCKER (*Macrodipteryx longipennis*).

"I have frequently seen the bird —at Blantyre, in Angoniland (*i.e.* on the Ntumbi plain, about thirty miles west of the Upper Shiré), and in the neighbourhood of Mount Milanje. The Manganja call it 'lumbe,' the Angoni 'gumbe.' I see that Sir John Kirk says that it was only from October to January that the singular prolongation of the wing feathers was observed.

"By a note in my diary, I find that I saw one at Blantyre on September 25th. I had seen another previously to this—perhaps a fortnight before, but, unluckily, I did not make a note of it, and cannot remember the date—*certainly* it was *before* the 25th of September, and I distinctly remember the long wing feathers on both occasions. Seeing the bird outlined in black against the sky (just after sunset, when the light was not quite gone) I took it for a huge and grotesquely-shaped bat with an exaggerated, claw-like, prolongation at the end of the wing. I have never seen them in flocks—only singly, or, at most, one rising shortly after the other, so that they might have been a pair. While I was at Mr. John Moir's plantation of Lauderdale (at Mount Milanje) last November, one of the natives brought up to the house three young 'Lumbi' which had been found (I think) in a hollow tree. They were about the size of newly-hatched chickens, and nearly fledged—they could not fly, but raised their wings (which were of immense length in proportion to their bodies) straight above their heads, and ran along the floor very quickly. We tried to feed them on chopped egg, soaked bread and flies, but could not keep them alive more than a day or two.

"I see you give no description of the feathers, but your figure gives the impression that the long wing-feathers are white, or, at least, distinctly light-coloured. I would not be positive, but am almost sure, that in a specimen shot by Mr. E. Laidlaw Thomson at Lauderdale (which was the only one I ever had the opportunity of examining closely), these feathers were mottled black and brown like the rest of the plumage. I remember seeing two, if not three, in the bush near the Chinunka River, along the road to Fort Anderson.

"The first time I ever came across them was in Angoniland, passing through the bush in the dark. I could not see them distinctly, and at first from their noiseless flight took them to be bats, and was rather puzzled when assured that they were not bats (melemi) but birds. As far as I can remember, they *always* flew out of trees or bushes, and never from the ground."

The Mottled Nightjars. —Sub-family *Nyctibiinæ*.

In these South-American nightjars there is no pectination of the middle claw, but powder-down patches are present on the sides of the body and on the breast. In this character they show an affinity to the *Podargi*, and like the latter birds they lay their egg on an exposed branch or stump of a tree, as is proved by the interesting notes of Dr. Goeldi on *Nyctibius jamaicensis*. He observed the nesting habits of this species in the province of Rio de Janeiro, and writes as follows:—

"During certain months the smaller *N. jamaicensis*, called 'Uratáo' by the natives, like all the species of the group, is heard at Colonia Alpina almost every night. Its 'pu-hu-hu' slowly pronounced, but with much energy, is a constant nocturnal sound, quite enough to frighten a timid wanderer in the solitary forest-patches. On the other hand, I was often astonished at the resemblance of the voice of the large greyish *N. grandis* to the mewing of a cat. In November, 1895, during moonlight nights, I had occasion to hear it at Amapá regularly. The bird called continuously in the adjacent 'sirinbal' (the inundated and impassable avicenna-forests) which borders in a most characteristic manner the lower course of the coast-rivers of Guiana. At Colonia Alpina (Rio de Janeiro) we got so well acquainted with *N. jamaicensis* that the cry of the bird in the neighbourhood on moonlight nights was the regular signal for us to take up our guns and go forth on our nocturnal hunting-trips. The bird is easily deceived by imitating its voice. Supposing the call to be that of a rival, it leaves some inaccessible and invisible standpoint in the interior of the forest, and is drawn nearer to a post on some isolated dry gigantic tree, which, being in better light, offers more chance of a successful shot. Even here, however, its wonderful protective colour, its singular manner of perching in the direction of the axis of the branch and appearing like a mere protuberance of it, while it retains a motionless position for a quarter of an hour or more, render it very difficult to discern, except to very practised eyes. My cousin, Andreas Goeldi, after long experience, is a perfect *Nyctibius* hunter. Notwithstanding our familiarity with the habits of the species of *Nyctibius*, for three years we were never lucky enough to discover its breeding-place, though we made all possible efforts. Before I left Colonia Alpina I strongly recommended the continuation of these efforts to my cousin, and likewise as regards *Hydropsalis*. At length, some months after my arrival on the Amazons, I received the agreeable news,—the discovery of an authentic nest of *N. jamaicensis*. My cousin's letter was accompanied by detailed notes and photographs, and when, in August, 1895, I made a journey back to Rio de Janeiro, I had, on a short visit to Colonia Alpina, the opportunity of seeing the localities and studying the facts, which were as follows: —On the 24th November, 1894, the son of one of our neighbours and colonists brought to us a dead male *Nyctibius jamaicensis* and a fresh egg, telling us that he had shot the 'Uratáo' standing upright on the top of a stump. After having killed the bird he climbed up the stump and found, as he had supposed, that the bird had its breeding-place there. In a slight depression on the top he found the egg, which he carefully brought to my cousin, together with the bird itself. My cousin immediately went to the spot pointed out by the boy, and inquired minutely into every detail.

"The locality is on a sloping hill on the left side of a brook, tributary of the Rio Alpina, which runs through a valley parallel to that of the centre of the colony. In 1891 and 1892 one of our colonists, now dead, had a maize plantation there, but since that time the ground has become what in Brazil is called 'capocira,' *i.e.* a hill covered with shrubs and small trees of about 2 inches in height. Along the declivity of the right side of the brook, at a distance of about 30 mètres from the latter, is a path of communication between the different colonial lots of the valley and the forest-slopes on both sides. The stump in question is about 20 mètres distant from the brook, surrounded by shrubs and easily visible from the path on the other side, and was evidently put there three years ago by the former colonist. The nearest human residences are distant from five to six minutes only.

"The stump, still partly covered with its original bark, has a height of 1·8 mètres above the level of the ground. Its diameter at top is 9·5 centimètres. The top has in the centre a small depression, caused by decomposition, and scarcely presents sufficient room for a rather large egg. There was no trace of a softer substratum or nest material.

"The egg measures 41·5 millimètres in the longitudinal axis, and 30·5 millimètres in the transverse axis. Its general colour is white. On the blunt pole, however, are some very delicate pale violet spots, and regularly distributed over the whole surface, are some large ones of brownish-rufous colour resembling drops of dried blood. Neither the former nor the latter markings can be effaced by washing with spirit; they belong properly to the egg, which is of a very elegant shape."

The Swifts.—Sub-order *Cypseli*.

The swifts are some of the most rapid in flight of all the birds in the world. "Greased lightning" is a term often applied by naturalists in the East to the flight of some of the species, notably the spine-tailed swifts of the genus *Chætura*. Like some of the goatsuckers alluded to above, the palate of the swifts is ægithognathous, but here the resemblance between the swifts and the Passeriformes ends. Of course, the most swift-like of the perching birds are the swallows, and until recent years these birds were classified together, because they were long-winged, of swift flight, and had the same habit of hawking insects on the wing. In reality, however, the swallows are highly modified flycatchers, and have little in common with the *Cypseli*, which are more nearly related to the humming-birds of America (*Trochili*). Like most picarian birds, the swifts have ten tail-feathers, while the swallows have twelve. The latter have two notches in the posterior end of the sternum, while there are no notches in that of the swifts, which further have a very high keel, indicating that they are birds of extremely developed powers of flight. The proportions of the wing-bones are likewise very different in the two groups, being directly opposite to each other, for, whereas in the swifts the humerus is very short, the forearm longer, and the manus extremely long, in the swallows the relative proportions are exactly the contrary.

Mr. Ernst Hartert, the latest exponent of the *Cypseli*, divides the single family which the sub-order contains, the *Cypselidæ*, into three sub-families, *Cypselinæ* or true swifts, *Chæturinæ* or spine-tailed swifts, and crested swifts (*Macropteryginæ*). From the recent researches of Mr. F. A. Lucas, it seems that the last-named birds are very distinct from the true swifts, and probably constitute a distinct family, their singular mode of nidification, *viz.* the placing of their egg in a diminutive nest on a branch or a stump, being very similar to that observed in the frogmouths (*Podargi*) and the *Nyctibiinæ* (*antea*, p. 344). Mr. Hartert characterises the sub-family *Cypselinæ*, which contains the true swifts, by the form of their toes, the outer and middle toes having only three phalanges, while the metatarsus is distinctly feathered. In one species, the pied swift of Central America (*Aeronautes melanoleucus*), the toes are also covered with plumes. The genus *Micropus*, of which our common swift (*M. apus*) is the type, has all the toes directed forward, but in the palm swifts (*Tachornis* and *Claudia*) the toes are arranged in pairs.

The common swift is migratory, like most of the family, arriving in Europe early in May, and being one of the first of our summer birds to disappear to its winter quarters in Africa. The mode of flight in a swift is more like that of a bat than that of a bird, especially in the gloaming, when the swifts chase each other at an incredible speed, uttering shrill screams. The rapidity of their flight far exceeds that of any swallow. About sixteen species of the genus *Micropus* are known.

Fig. 79.—THE COMMON SWIFT (*Micropus apus*).

The sub-family *Chæturinæ* consists of the spine-tailed swifts and the edible swiftlets. In these birds the toes are normal, and the metatarsus is not feathered. The spine-tailed swifts (*Chætura*) are found in both hemispheres, and have the shafts of the tail-feathers produced into a point or spine. Some of them are birds of considerable size, the needle-tailed swift (*Chætura caudacuta*), which has occasionally been seen in England, measuring nearly a foot in length to the end of its long wings, which in this group of swifts always protrude beyond the tail. It nests in Siberia, and migrates to Australia in the winter.

The swifts of the genus *Collocalia* are tiny birds, which inhabit the Indian and Australian regions. Some fourteen species are known. The birds build in caves, affixing, to the walls of the limestone, cup-shaped nests, which are formed principally of the bird's own saliva, though in some species there is some moss mixed up in the nests, while others are almost entirely made of moss. These "moss" nests, however, are of no commercial value, while the pure white nests are sold for making soup to the Chinese.

The Edible Swiftlets.—Genus *Collocalia*.

The tree-swifts are beautiful birds, often ornamented with a large crest or with long white whiskers. They have the metatarsus bare, and it is shorter than the middle toe, whereas in the *Chæturinæ* the tarsus is as long as the middle toe, or even longer, and there are two foramina in the hinder margin of the sternum, whereas in the other sub-families of swifts there are no such notches. There is but a single genus, *Macropteryx*, with five species, and the most singular feature about the tree-swifts is their mode of nesting. Nearly twenty years ago, Sir Hugh Low's native collector brought to him in Labuan a tree-swift's nest, which he said he had found lying under the bird's body when he shot it. The nest was of about the size of half-a-crown, and contained one white egg, which had been broken in the fall. From what we know now of the nesting of the genus *Macropteryx*, it is evident that in the above instance the shot must have carried away the top of the stump on which the nest had been placed, as Mr. Hume has presented to the British Museum a similar nest obtained by Mr. K. Thompson, who found one in India. Mr. Hume says :—"The stem to which the nest was attached is about 0·8 inch in diameter ; against the side of this the nest is glued, so that the upper margin of the nest is on a level with the upper surface of the branch. The nest itself is half of a rather deep saucer, 1·75 inches in diameter, and about 0·6 inch in depth internally. The nest is entirely composed of thin flakes of bark, cemented together by the bird's saliva, and is about an eighth of an inch in thickness." Only one white egg seems to be laid.

The Tree Swifts. —Sub-family *Macropterygince.*

The humming-birds are exclusively a New World group. The species described up to the present time are nearly 500 in number, and among them are found some of the tiniest birds in the world, some of them not being larger than a bumble-bee. The bulk of the species are from South and Central America, a few only reaching to the southern United States, and only a small number migrating north in summer to Canada, and even as far as Alaska.

The Humming-Birds.— Sub-order *Trochili.*

The plumage of the humming birds is usually of a brilliantly metallic nature, and they are admitted to be some of the most beautiful and interesting of all birds. Their classification is extremely difficult, for the characters blend from one genus into another, until it is almost impossible to say where the series should begin and where it should end. So much so is this the case, that Mr. Osbert Salvin, when he wrote the sixteenth volume of the British Museum "Catalogue of Birds," was forced, for want of more definite characters, to divide the humming-birds into three sections, those with a well-defined saw-like edge near the margin of the tip of the upper mandible, those with this serration faintly marked, and those without any serration at all.

It is impossible in the space at our disposal to pass in review all the genera and species of humming-birds, for they are of every size, shape, and variety of metallic plumage. The largest of all is the giant humming-bird (*Patagona gigas*), from the Andes of Ecuador to Chili. This bird measures about 8½ inches in length, whereas some of the smallest species, such as *Calypte helenæ* of Cuba, and *Chætocercus bombus* of Ecuador, only measure 2½ inches.

The tongue in this order of birds is very peculiar, and its structure is only equalled by that of the woodpeckers (*Pici*) and sun-birds (*Nectariniidæ*). The structure is thus described by Sir William Flower in the "Bird-Gallery" of the British Museum :—"The tongue is slender, and very long and extensile. As in the woodpeckers, the two branches of the hyoid bone which support its base, curve, when the tongue is drawn within the bill, upwards around the back of the skull, and then forward over the top of the head. Instead of the tongue being, as in the woodpeckers, solid and ending in a barbed horny point, it is hollow, and divided at the free end into two slender branches, each of which bears a thin membranous fringe on its outer margin."

The wings of the humming-birds are strong, and the primaries are ten in number, while the secondaries are only six. The first primary-quill is sometimes attenuated (*Atthis*, *Aglæactis*, etc.), while in some genera, such as *Campylopterus*, the shafts of the primaries are broad and stiffened. The tail is of various shapes, sometimes square, sometimes rounded, or, as in the genus *Phæthornis*, graduated, with the two central rectrices elongated and pointed. Many genera have forked tails, with the outer tail-feather elongated, especially in the male. The racket-tailed humming-birds have a forked tail, with the outer rectrix ending in a spatule or racket. In some genera, like the shear-tails (*Thaumastura*) or the stars (*Chætocercus*), all the tail-feathers are pointed and spine-like, and in the king humming-birds (*Topaza*), the central feathers are elongated and curved, crossing each other at the same time. The most remarkable, however, of all the humming-birds, as regards its tail, is *Loddigesia mirabilis* from the Upper Amazons. In the female and young male, ten rectrices are present as usual, but in the adult male there are only four, a very small pair in the middle, and an elongated pair on the outside, which cross each other and end in a "boss" or "racket." Some of the upper tail-coverts are so lengthened that they appear to be part of the tail. The flight of humming-birds is more like that of a hawk-moth than that of an actual bird, for the little creatures hover in front of a flower, suspended, as it were, in the air, with their wings vibrating so rapidly as to appear simply like a film. Their food consists of the tiniest insects, and in the case of the sword-bill hummer (*Docimastes ensiferus*) the bill is elongated to an enormous proportion, so that the bird is able to probe long tubular flowers for its food. The nest of the humming-birds is always beautiful, and is generally composed of the down of plants, felted, and covered with spiders' webs or soft lichens. It is generally round, but is occasionally purse-shaped, and is placed on a branch or at the end of a leaf. The eggs are white, and two in number.

Fig. 80.—A HUMMING-BIRD.

The Colies.—Sub-order *Colii*.

The colies form a separate sub-order, which contains but a single genus, *Colius*, with nine species, all peculiar to Africa. There are only ten tail-feathers, and the hind-toe is connected with the *flexor perforans digitorum* tendon. The bill is something like that of a finch, and the birds have a slight crest. The palate is bridged or desmognathous, and the sternum has four notches on the posterior margin. The position of the colies in the class *Aves* has been much debated, and it seems to us that their place in the natural system must always be open to some comment, but they must be placed somewhere near the trogons and the touracoes.

Fig. 81.—THE CAPE COLY (*Colius colius*).

The colies have curious feet, all the four toes being directed forward, the first one being perhaps reversible; the birds use their feet for climbing, and they hang in peculiar positions. They make an open nest, of grass and twigs, lined internally with soft grass, placed in a fork of a tree, and the eggs are white.

The trogons are all birds of bright plumage, even the hens having brilliant colours in many of the species. They are often called *Heterodactyli* on account of their peculiar feet, which constitute the chief structural feature of the order. The palate is schizognathous or slit, and the second toe is turned backwards. The front plantar tendon (*flexor perforans digitorum*) is split into two, and leads to the two front toes, while the hind plantar (*flexorlongos hallucis*) is again split, and leads to the two hind toes. The plumage of the trogons is of the softest description, and the skin is so thin that we have often heard travellers say that it has no more substance than tissue-paper, and every one admits that trogons are the most difficult birds in the world to prepare.

The Trogons.—Order *Trogones.*

At the present day the order is distributed over Africa, a great part of India and the Malayan sub-region, but they are most numerous in Central and Southern America. In ancient times they occurred in France, as fossil remains have been found there along with those of touracoes and secretary-birds.

One of the most splendid of birds is the long-trained trogon or quezal, which has been adopted by the republic of Guatemala as its national emblem, and figures on the postage stamps of that country. It has a tail of eight inches in length, but the upper tail-coverts are enormously developed, the central ones extending into a train four times as long as the actual tail itself. The quezal is found in Guatemala and Costa Rica, but is not so plentiful as formerly; it is entirely a bird of the forests, and has a rapid flight. Mr. Stolzmann noticed the Peruvian quezal clinging to the trunks of trees like a woodpecker.

The American trogons (*Trogon*) are chiefly fruit-eaters, like the African species of *Hapaloderma.* They are entirely forest birds, and are said to be rather stupid, not even flying away at the report of a gun, so that a whole party may be shot down one after the other. They are generally seen in pairs, but occasionally assemble in small flocks. The note is variously described as being harsh, or clucking, as well as soft and low. Of the Peruvian species, *Trogon caligatus*, Mr. Stolzmann gives the note as "*cou-cou-cou-cou-co-co-co-co,*" the second half being uttered in a lower tone than the first. The Indian trogons (*Harpactes*) are more insect-feeders than their American allies. The eggs of trogons are white or pale-buff (that of the quezal being said to be greenish-blue), three or four in number, and deposited on the dry wood in the hole of a tree.

Fig. 82.—The Large-tailed Trogon (*Trogon macrurus*).

Two sub-orders are represented in this order, *viz.* the cuckoos (*Cuculi*) and the touracoes (*Musophagi*), the former being a cosmopolitan group, and the latter being confined to Africa, though there is evidence that in ancient times touracoes inhabited Europe, as fossil remains of these birds have been found in France. The cuckoos and the touracoes have the following characters in common, which differentiate the *Coccyges* from all other orders of birds. The first and fourth toe are turned backwards, and the second and third forwards, the hallux being always developed, and served by the *flexor*

The Cuckoo-like Birds.—Order *Coccyges.*

longus hallucis tendon, and not by the *flexor perforans digitorum.* The palate is "bridged" or desmognathous. In the cuckoos the oil-gland is nude, and the feet thoroughly zygodactyle, with two toes directed forwards and two backwards, whereas in the *Musophagidæ* or touracoes the fourth toe is not so completely turned backwards as in the *Cuculidæ*, and the foot is therefore termed semi-zygodactyle.

The *Cuculidæ* are divided by Captain Shelley into six sub-families, of which the first contains the true cuckoos or *Cuculinæ.* In these birds the tail is composed of ten feathers, the upper tail-coverts are not unduly prolonged, the wing is long and pointed, showing that most of the species are migrants, therein differing from the wing in the bush-cuckoos, which has a rounded and concave wing, indicating that they are not birds of strong flight.

In this sub-family are found the crested cuckoos (*Coccystes*), the typical cuckoos (*Cuculus*), the hawk-cuckoos (*Hierococcyx*), the golden cuckoos (*Chrysoeoccyx*), the American cuckoos (*Coccyzus*), the koels (*Eudynamis*), the channel-bills (*Scythrops*), and several other genera. In the genus *Coccystes* we find the first instance of the curious parasitic nature of the cuckoos, but in the case of the great spotted cuckoo (*Coccystes glandarius*) there is not the same remarkable variation in the colour of the egg that we find in the common cuckoo (*Cuculus cdnorus*). On the contrary, the egg of *C. glandarius* is very crow-like, and it is deposited in the nests of crows and magpies. The Indian crested cuckoo (*C. jacobinus*) lays blue eggs, and places them in the nests of birds which also lay blue eggs, such as babbling-thrushes, etc.

The True Cuckoos.—Genus *Cuculus*.

Ten species of true cuckoo are known, and the type of the genus *Cuculus* is our common cuckoo (*Cuculus canorus*). The genus is distributed over the whole of the Old World, excepting in the Pacific Islands.

In a concise work like the present there is not space to give in detail the habits of a bird like the cuckoo, whose life-history would require a volume to itself. It will be, however, known to most of my readers that the female cuckoo makes no nest of its own, but deposits its egg in the nest of some other bird, and leaves to the latter the task of hatching the eggs and bringing up the young cuckoo. The latter, while still blind and naked, ejects the other little occupants of the nest, and receives thereafter the undivided attention of the foster-parents. The latter are of many kinds, flycatchers, warblers, finches, etc., preference, however, being given to the warblers and pipits and other insectivorous birds. In the Western Palæarctic region alone the egg of *C. canorus* has been found in nests of 120 different species, and another curious fact in connection with the economy of the species is that the cuckoo's egg is remarkably small for the size of the bird, and is, in many cases, almost an exact copy of the egg of the foster-parent. Each female cuckoo is believed to lay the same type of egg during its life, so that a bird which lays blue eggs, to be inserted in the nest of a blue-egged species like the redstart or pied flycatcher, always lays blue eggs. The cuckoo ranges all over Europe and Northern Asia, and winters in Africa, India, and Australia.

Fig. 83.—THE COMMON CUCKOO (*Cuculus canorus*).

Many genera of the *Cuculinæ* have a good deal of metallic colour about them, and the golden cuckoos of Africa and India, with their emerald-green and purple plumage, are among the most beautiful of all birds. In America, the black-billed cuckoo (*Coccyzus erythrophthalmus*) and the yellow-billed cuckoo (*C. americanus*) build their own nests, and are most affectionate parents.

The Lark-heeled Cuckoos.—Sub-family *Centropodinæ*.

In the *Centropodinæ*, the hind-claw is straight, and like that of a lark. There is but one genus, *Centropus*, which is distributed over the Ethiopian, Indian, and Australian regions, and no less than thirty-two species are known. They have a hooting note, like "*whoot-whoot*," and on the Gold Coast the species is known as the "Scotchman." In India, Mr. Hume says that *C. sinensis* follows up the hooting note by "*kurook-kurook-kurook-kurook*," after an interval of a few seconds. It makes a nest in thick thorny bushes or trees, about six inches in height and twelve inches across, composed of grass or twigs, and in the form of an oblate spheroid; it is too small for the size of the bird, so that the tail of the latter is generally seen sticking out.

The Bush Cuckoos.—Sub-family *Phænicophæinæ*.

The bush cuckoos have a rounded and concave wing like the lark-heels, but want the spur-like claw of the latter birds. In this sub-family are found the rain-cuckoos (*Saurothera*, *Hyetornis*, *Piaya*, etc.) of America, the steel-blue cuckoos (*Ceuthmochares*) of Africa, the bush-cuckoos (*Phænicophaes*, *Rhinococcyx*, etc.) of the Indian region, and the couas of Madagascar. The members of this sub-family build their own nests and lay white eggs. They are mostly bush-haunting birds and thread their way through the jungle and the trees with great facility.

The most round-winged of the bush-cuckoos are the members of the genus *Neomorphus*, which represents the sub-family *Neomorphinæ*. Only three other genera are contained in the latter, *Carpococcyx*, with the pheasant-cuckoo of Borneo (*C. radiatus*), and the road-runners (*Geococcyx* and *Morococcyx*) of the New World. The species of *Neomorphus* are all neo-tropical, being found in the southern countries of Central America and the tropical portions of South America. Five species are known, all of which are very rare, and nothing has been recorded of their habits.

The *Diplopterinæ*, which constitute the fifth sub-family of cuckoos, are entirely American and are remarkable for the extreme length of their upper tail-coverts, and the sixth sub-family, the *Crotophaginæ*, is also American. In the latter there are only eight tail-feathers, instead of ten, and some of the Savana cuckoos (*Crotophaga*) have very curious habits, several females apparently laying in the same nest, so that sometimes as many as twenty eggs have been found in one nest. The egg, too, is very peculiar in the *Crotophaginæ*, as it appears at first sight to be blue covered with white scratchings and marblings, but the true colour of the egg is white, and the blue is only an overlying colour, which gets rubbed and scratched off through contact with the lining of the nest.

The Touracoes.—Family *Musophagidæ*.

In appearance these birds are very different from cuckoos, and their semi-zygodactyle foot has already been alluded to (p. 350). They are forest-birds, confined to Africa, where nearly thirty species have been described. In ancient times they appear to have inhabited France, as fossil remains have been discovered in that country. Some of the species are crested and of a dull coloration, but the majority are brilliantly plumaged birds, and are generally called "Lowries" by the colonists of South Africa.

In the true touracoes (*Turacus*) the nostrils are hidden by bristles; in all the other genera they are exposed. In the genus *Musophaga*, of which *M. rossæ*, from Angola and the Congo basin, is an example, there is not only an ornamental frontal shield of red, but the primary quills are of a deep crimson, as they are in all the members of the genus *Turacus*. From the wing-feathers of these birds has been extracted a kind of copper called turacine. The nest of the touracoes is an open one, made of sticks, and the egg is white.

Fig. 84.—LADY ROSS TOURACOE (*Musophaga rossæ*).

The Climbing Birds.—Order *Scansores*.

In all the *Scansores* the foot is typically zygodactyle, the first and fourth toes being turned backwards, the second and third forwards, and the arrangement of the plantar tendons is as curious. The *flexor perforans digitorum* tendon leads to the third digit only, while the *flexor longus hallucis* first sends a tendon to the other plantar tendon, and a second to the fourth digit, after which (if the hallux be present) it splits into two tendons, one leading to the hallux, the other to the second digit.

The Toucans.—Sub-order *Rhamphastides*.

Of the three sub-orders of the *Scansores* the toucans are exclusively neotropical. They are very plentifully represented in Central and South America, and are remarkable for their long, generally particoloured bill, and for their curious feathery tongue. The palate is desmognathous or "bridged," and the vomer truncated.

The toucans are about sixty in number, and are contained in five genera, *Rhamphastos*, *Andigena*, *Pteroglossus*, *Selenidera*, and *Aulacorhamphus*. The long bill, which at first sight appears so clumsy and awkward, is really a very light structure, full of empty cellules, and the colours of the bill are usually those of the adjoining bare skin of the face. The birds inhabit the forests and feed on fruit, and are often found in company. Though they have a scansorial foot, they do not climb like woodpeckers, but proceed by great hops, like the hornbills, from branch to branch.

Fig. 85.—THE TOCO TOUCAN (*Ramphastos toco*).

The Barbets.—Sub-order *Capitones*.

The barbets are small birds with zygodactyle feet, which are found in the neo-tropical, Ethiopian and Indian regions, but do not extend into the Australian region, nor are they found in the temperate regions of the Northern Zone of either hemisphere. Some have a bridged palate, but others have the palate ægithognathous or passerine. The vomer is bifid, the oil-gland tufted, and there are other internal characters which separate them from the rest of the climbing birds. They feed chiefly on fruit, but many species are insectivorous, and their curious monotonous notes have gained for them the names of "Tinker or Coppersmith," the little Indian species (*Xantholæma hæmacephala*) nodding its head sideways as it utters its metallic call. Like woodpeckers they bore a hole in a tree, and lay their eggs, which are white, on the chips of wood. Of the Peruvian species of *Capito*, Stolzmann says that he has found them in small parties on high trees, feeding on fruits in company with toucans, chatterers, and other birds.

Fig. 86.—THE GOLDEN-GREEN BARBET (*Capito aurovirens*).

The Honey-Guides.—Sub-order *Indicatores*.

The honey-guides have an interesting distribution over the earth's surface. They are mostly confined to Africa, but one species occurs in the Himalayas, and another in the mountains of Malacca and Borneo. The palate is ægithognathous, and the bill is not unlike that of a finch. The colouring of the birds is generally sombre, though some African species have white lower backs and the Indian honey-guide (*I. xanthonotus*) has a yellow back. The name of "honey-guide" is derived from the fact that several of the African species will lead men to a bee's nest, sitting on the trees and uttering a piping note. If followed, they will fly on in advance a little way, and, as a rule, the bird is rewarded with a little piece of the comb, from which it extracts the grubs. The food of all the species, as far as is known, consists of hymenoptera.

Fig. 87.—THE GREAT HONEY-GUIDE (*Indicator*).

The Woodpecker-like Birds.—Order *Piciformes*.

The *Piciformes* resemble the *Scansores* in having the plantar tendons peculiar in their arrangement as already described by Seebohm. The *flexor perforans digitorum* leads to the third digit only. The *flexor longus hallucis* first sends a tendon to the other plantar, then a second to the fourth digit, after which (if the hallux be present) it splits into two tendons, one leading to the hallux, the other to the second digit.

The Woodpeckers.—Sub-order *Pici*.

In the woodpeckers the palate is peculiar, and has been termed "saurognathous" by the late Professor W. Kitchen Parker, the vomer being slender, pointed, and split, the lateral halves separate. The bill is formed for the hammering of trees, which these birds are famous for, and is, in the majority of woodpeckers, strong and chisel-shaped, though weaker and more curved in the ground-feeding species. The tongue is very peculiar, for here we meet with a similar arrangement to that noticed in the humming-birds (*antea*, p. 347). The tongue is long and worm-like, and is capable of being protruded to an enormous length by means of the hyoid bones, the cornua of which extend backwards over the skull. The tongue is furnished with a pointed, horny, barbed tip. This arrangement, so far as is known, obtains in all woodpeckers excepting *Sphyropicus* and *Xenopicus*.

The late Mr. Edward Hargitt divided the family *Picidæ*, at which he laboured unceasingly for fourteen years, into three sub-families, woodpeckers (*Picinæ*), piculets (*Picumninæ*), and wrynecks (*Iynginæ*). The latter birds have a soft and mottled plumage like that of a nightjar. They have a long tail, the feathers of which are soft and not pointed like those of the woodpeckers. Three species are resident in Africa, but our common wryneck (*I. torquilla*) is a migrant to Europe and Northern Asia, wintering in Africa, India, and Southern China.

The Piculets.—Sub-family *Picumninæ*.

The piculets are tiny little birds without the stiffened tail of the woodpecker, but otherwise resembling them in the form of the bill and the bristles around the nostrils. In the neo-tropical region the piculets are represented by the genus *Picumnus* with thirty-five species, and *Nesoctites* with a single species, their place being taken in Africa by the genus *Verreauxia* with one species, *V. africana*, and in the Himalayas and throughout the Indo-Malayan region by the genus *Sasia*, which has only three toes. Both the last-named genera have a bare orbital patch round the eye.

Of the habits of the species of *Picumnus* very little has been recorded, but Stolzmann says that in Peru he has seen them on the borders of the rivers, tapping the small branches of the trees, and running along the horizontal limbs, sometimes above the branch, sometimes below.

The True Woodpeckers.—Sub-family *Picinæ*.

All the true woodpeckers have the tail spiny, with the shafts of the tail-feathers stiffened. They may be divided into two groups, the feathered-necked section and the narrow-necked section. In the first section are found the ground woodpeckers (*Geocolaptes*), the yellow-winged woodpeckers (*Colaptes*), and all such forms as the green woodpeckers (*Gecinus*) and their allies, the pied woodpeckers (*Dendrocopus*), the three-toed woodpeckers (*Picoides*), and, in fact, the bulk of the sub-family. The narrow-necked woodpeckers are principally tropical, but they inhabit both the Old and the New Worlds, being, however, much more plentiful in the former, and they are represented in Europe by the great black woodpecker (*Picus martius*).

The distribution of the woodpeckers is interesting from the following fact, that they are universally distributed over North and South America, the whole of Africa, Europe and Asia, until we approach "Wallace's Line" in the Moluccas, and there we find that a few species extend beyond the limits of the Indo-Malayan sub-region, into Flores and Celebes. In fact, the woodpeckers coincide in distribution with the monkeys, and do not extend beyond the last-named island.

Woodpeckers.

In habits they are singularly alike, excavating holes in trees, which they drill with the utmost precision and with such accuracy that the hole appears as if it had been made by the most skilled of carpenters. No nest is made, and the white eggs are deposited on the chips of wood at the end of the hole, which is often of considerable depth. The note of our green woodpecker, or yaffle, is a resounding laugh, while the pied woodpeckers call to each other by a series of taps on the slender boughs of the tallest trees, their ordinary note being harsh and unmusical.

An interesting genus of the section of narrow-necked woodpeckers is seen in *Thriponax*, which is found in the Indian region, and extends through the Indo-Malayan sub-region and the Burmese provinces to the Philippines on the one hand, and to South India and the Andaman islands on the other. Then the genus, of which Hargitt's woodpecker is one of the most typical species (fig. 88), reappears in Corea and the Japanese islands of Tsu-shima, thus proving that in the Eastern Hemisphere the same introduction of tropical forms unexpectedly occurs in the palæarctic area as it does in the Western Hemisphere.

Fig. 88.—Hargitt's Woodpecker (*Thriponax hargitti*).

The Puff-Birds.—Sub-order *Buccones*.

The puff-birds are neotropical, and are only found in Central and South America. They differ from the woodpeckers in having a nude oil-gland and in the possession of cæca, and their pterylography is different. The palate is bridged or desmognathous, and a vomer is present. The feet are zygodactyle, and the *flexor perforans digitorum* tendon leads to the third digit only, the other plantar tendon serving the three other toes, as in the woodpeckers. The bill is stout and curved, and in the genus *Bucco* is hooked at the end, the base being well furnished with rictal bristles. The plumage of the puff-birds is mostly of a sombre character.

Forty-three species of puff-bird are known, divided by Dr. Sclater into seven genera, *Bucco* with twenty species, *Malacoptila* with seven, *Micromonacha* with one, *Nonnula* with five, *Malacoptila* with one, *Monacha* with seven, and *Chelidoptera* with two. The accounts of the habits of these birds represent them to be sluggish and apathetic ; they inhabit the forests and feed on insects, after which they fly from their perch, apparently in a manner similar to that of a bee-eater or a flycatcher. Very few notes have been published on their habits or nesting, but the eggs are believed to be white, and deposited in the holes of hollow trees.

Fig. 89.—The Greater Pied Puff-Bird (*Bucco macrorhynchus*).

The Jacamars.—Family *Galbulidæ*.

The jacamars are a small family of neo-tropical birds, mostly of metallic plumage, resembling the puff-birds in much of their internal structure and their zygodactyle feet. The bill, however, is not heavy, as in the latter birds, but is long, slender and pointed, and they usually have a long and pointed tail.

The jacamars feed on insects, which they dart after from a perch, like a flycatcher. *Jacamerops aurea* is said to be casually met with as solitary individuals or in pairs, preferring trees on the banks of streams to more open places in the forest. Here they watch for passing insects, which they catch on the wing, and return to their position. They often remain almost motionless for hours without stirring a feather. The jacamars are said to tunnel a small hole in a bank and to lay white and nearly round eggs. Of the black-cheeked jacamar (*Galbula melanogenia*) more has been published about the habits, and we learn from Messrs. Salvin and Godman in their "Biologia" that it is a solitary bird, frequenting deep ravines overhung with trees; it has a quick, darting flight, utters no cry, and feeds on insects. Mr. Richmond says that, on the Escondido River in Nicaragua, he noticed the bird jerking its tail like a kingfisher, and he describes the cry as piercing, and resembling the syllables "keé-u," with the first syllable very shrill and strongly accentuated.

Fig. 90.—The White-bellied Jacamar (*Galbula leucogastra.*)

Before commencing the account of the true perching birds or *Passeriformes*, there remain two orders which have generally been placed with the latter, but which, in our opinion, should be kept distinct. These are the broad-bills (*Eurylæmi*) and the lyre-birds (*Menuræ*).

The broad-bills are only found in the Himalayan region in India, whence they extend through the Burmese provinces to the Malayan peninsula and islands to Borneo and the Philippines. They have a passerine or ægithognathous palate, but the structure of the deep plantar tendons is strikingly different from those of the typical passerine foot, as the *flexor longus hallucis* tendon sends out a strong band or "*vinculum*" to join the tendon of the *flexor profundus digitorum*. The trachea is also peculiar, and the sternum has no forked manubrial process. In the first subfamily of the *Eurylæmidæ* Dr. Sclater places but one genus, *Calyptomena*, which is distinguished by the frontal plumes covering the nostrils. It contains but three species, which are, however, the finest of the broad-bills. Their principal colour is emerald-green, varied with velvety black, and *C. whiteheadi* from Kina Balu Mountain in Northern Borneo, is the largest of the family, measuring nearly a foot in length. It builds a good-sized nest, according to Mr. John Whitehead, who discovered this splendid species, which it "suspends from the end of a slender bough about fifty feet from the ground. The outside is composed of fresh green moss bound over the bough, and worked into the sides, ending in a long streamer, which assists in assimilating the nest to the long dripping streamers of mess and lichens which hang from every bough in this continual rainy season. The inside of the nest is very solid, lined with dry bamboo-leaves above and below, forming a well-sheltered pocket. The eggs are glossy creamy-white." A second species of *Calyptomena*, *C. hosii*, a green bird with a blue breast, has been discovered in the mountains of Savawak by Mr. Charles Hose, while the small species, *C. viridis*, is found everywhere in the low country throughout the Malayan peninsula and islands.

The Broad-Bills. —Order *Eurylæmi*.

Fig. 91.—Horsfield's Broadbill (*Eurylæmus javanicus*).

Of the *Eurylæmine*, which have bare nostrils, there are six genera, *Psarisomus* with one species, *Serilophus* with two, *Sarcophanops* with two, *Eurylæmus* with two, *Corydon* with one, and *Cymborhynchus* with two. *Psarisomus dalhousiæ* of the Eastern Himalayas and the hills of Assam and Burma is a very handsome bird, being green, with a black head and a blue patch on the crown. Another fine species is Horsfield's broadbill (*E. javanicus*), which is found in Java and the Malayan islands and peninsula as far north as Tenasserim. The food of the broadbills appears to consist of insects, but occasionally of small reptiles. They are inhabitants of the forests, and are said to be sluggish and somewhat stupid birds. The nests are suspended from the boughs of trees, and are of a purse-like shape, being composed of fibre and grass. Unlike the eggs of *Calyptomena*, those of the true broadbills are spotted with black or brownish-red on a cream-coloured ground.

The Lyre-Birds.—Order *Menuræ*.

The lyre-birds have always been considered aberrant passerine birds, but they cannot in any way, according to our ideas, be associated with the *Passeriformes*, on account of their curious nesting-habits and downy nestling. In addition to this, the lyre-birds have other anatomical features, which separate them from the true perching birds, and we believe that our separation of the *Menuræ* as a distinct order will be followed by future systematists, as the young lyre-bird looks more like the nestling of a petrel than that of any other bird, and such a nestling plumage is unknown in any species of passerine bird, the young of which are mostly hatched naked. The adult lyre-bird is a very remarkable creature. It has legs like those of a megapode, and altogether looks more like a Game-Bird than anything else, but it must be looked upon, we think, as a kind of gigantic wren, though in effect it is, like so many of the Australasian birds, a form by itself. We have heard it suggested that the lyre-birds are allied to the birds of paradise, but the only warranty for such a proposition is that the plumage of the tail in *Menura* is fantastic, as is the decorative plumage of the birds of paradise. Three species of *Menura* are known, all peculiar to the continent of Australia. They are very shy birds, inhabiting the brush country, and living solitary or in pairs. The food consists of insects, chiefly beetles and centipedes, occasionally varied with snails. Their strong feet give them the power of making enormous leaps, and Gould states that they will jump from the ground to a bough ten feet above it. The nest of the lyre-bird is domed like that of a wren; it is of large size, formed of sticks, and lined with feathers, and it has a kind of outer rough covering, composed of sticks, moss, and leaves. Only one egg is laid, of a purplish-grey colour, spotted and blotched with purplish brown.

Fig. 92.—The Lyre-Bird (*Menura superba*).

The Perching-Birds.—Order *Passeriformes*.

The principal character which distinguishes the *Passeres* or perching-birds is the form of the palate, which is ægithognathous or passerine, with the vomer truncated in front. The hind toe is always present, and is connected with the *flexor longus hallucis* tendon and not with the *flexor perforans digitorum*. The bulk of the *Passeriformes* belong to the division *Acromyodi*, in which the intrinsic muscles of the syrinx are fixed to the ends of the bronchial semi-rings. Much discussion has taken place between ornithologists as to which is the highest form of bird, and many are inclined to think that preference should be given to the thrushes and warblers, on account of their powers of song, just as the monkeys are placed at the head of the Mammalia on account of their man-like aspect; but in our opinion, the crows (*Corvidæ*) are at the head of the *Passeriformes*, being, with the exception of their want of song, the most perfectly developed of birds. The wing of a crow exhibits in its fullest perfection the power of flight, every wing-covert and quill being shown in the most complete development. The same is seen in the feet of a crow, where all the scales on the tarsi and toes are more strongly indicated than in any other passerine bird.

The Crows.—Family *Corvidæ*.

The colour of the crows is black or decidedly sombre, as a rule, only relieved by brighter plumage in the case of the magpies (*Pica*), jays (*Garrulus*), and the beautiful blue jays of America (*Cyanocorax*, *Xanthura*), etc. All these forms belong to the true crows (*Corvinæ*), of which our rook (*Trypancorax frugilegus*), carrion crow (*Corone corone*), magpie (*Pica pica*), and jay (*Garrulus glandarius*) are typical examples. They all have the nostrils placed high in the mandible, whereas the choughs (sub-family *Fregilinæ*) have the nostril placed low in the mandible, nearer to its lower margin than to its upper one. In the *Fregilinæ* we find four genera: *Graculus*, with our own red-billed chough (*G. graculus*), *Pyrrhocorax*, with its single species, *P. pyrrhocorax*, the Alpine chough, and *Corcorax*, with a single Australian species, the white-winged chough (*C. melanorhamphus*). The most interesting of this group of birds, however, are the desert-choughs (*Podoces*). Of these there are four species, all confined to the desert regions of Central Asia from Buchara to Turkestan and Thibet. They are sandy-coloured birds, like most desert-haunting creatures, but with brighter heads and wings: *P. panderi* from Buchara was the first species of the genus to be described, but nothing has been recorded of its habits. *P. hendersoni* from Yarkand is better known, and Dr. Henderson says that they always kept in pairs, and moved about from one sand-hill to another, seemingly searching for insects in the sand. The stomachs, however, were filled with grain, picked out of the horse-dung in the road. The eggs of *P. panderi* are like those of crows, but one species, *P. humilis*, lays white eggs.

Fig. 93.—PANDER'S DESERT-CHOUGH (*Podoces panderi*).

The Birds of Paradise.—Family *Paradiseidæ*.

The crows are all ambulatores or walkers, but there is no proof that the birds of paradise progress by walking steps, when on the ground. On the contrary, the *Paradiseidæ* are entirely forest birds. They differ from the true crows in the structure of the feet, the outer toe being longer than the inner one but shorter than the middle one. Their fantastic plumage is their chief characteristic, but the nest and eggs are corvine, and the paradise birds are really nothing but gaudy-coloured crows.

They include the rifle-birds (*Ptilorhis*), and other sickle-billed forms like the twelve-wired birds of paradise (*Seleucides*) and the superb birds of paradise (*Epimachus*). In all the sickle-billed species, composing the sub-family *Epimachinæ*, the bill is long and curved, and exceeds the tarsus in length. In *Ptilorhis* the plumage is velvety black, with a metallic head and a metallic green shield on the breast. The nest of Queen Victoria's rifle-bird (*P. victoriæ*) is described as a loosely constructed structure of dead leaves and green branchlets, the eggs being of a flesh-colour, with streaks and spots of reddish-brown. The rifle-birds are found in Australia and New Guinea.

Fig. 94.—THE RED-PLUMED BIRD OF PARADISE (*Paradisea raggiana*).

The Papuan Islands and the Moluccas are also the home of the true birds of paradise, which compose the sub-family *Paradiseinæ*, which have a stouter bill, with the culmen not so long as the tarsus. Some eighteen genera are to be found in this sub-family, including not only the true paradise-birds, but many others of varied form and decorated plumage. They inhabit the forest country at different altitudes, and in some localities, such as the Aru Islands, they are very abundant, the insensate fashion of decorating ladies' hats with the plumes of these lovely birds having, wonderful to relate, not yet succeeded in exterminating them. They feed chiefly on fruit.

The Bower Birds.—Family *Ptilororpynchidæ*.

The bower birds are undoubtedly closely allied to the birds of paradise, and it is difficult to say where one family ends and the other begins. Such forms as the golden bird of paradise (*Xanthomelus aureus*) have been placed with the *Paradiseidæ*, but this genus and its allies are probably bower-builders, and it is certain that some of the allied forms, like *Prionodura newtoniana* and *Amblyornis inornata*, undoubtedly construct large bowers.

The satin bower-bird of Australia (*Ptilonorhynchus holosericeus*) builds an arched bower of sticks, decorated with snail-shells, bleached bones of small mammals, and the bright feathers of parakeets. But one of the most extraordinary of all these fantastic bowers is that erected by the gardener bird of North-Western New Guinea. Dr. Beccari, who discovered the bower of this species in the Arfak Mountains, describes it as follows:—"The *Amblyornis* selects a flat even place round the trunk of a small tree, which is as thick and as high as a walking-stick of middle size. It begins by constructing at the base of the tree a kind of cone, chiefly of moss, of the size of a man's hand. The trunk of the tree becomes the central pillar, and the whole building is supported by it. On the top of the central pillar twigs are then methodically placed in a radiating manner, resting on the ground, leaving an aperture for the entrance. Thus is obtained a conical and very regular hut. When the work is completed, many other branches are placed transversely in various ways, to make the whole quite firm and impermeable. A circular gallery is left between the walls and the central cone. The whole is nearly three feet in diameter. All the stems used by the *Amblyornis* are the thin stems of an orchid (*Dendrobium*), an epiphyte forming large tufts on the mossy branches of great trees, easily bent like straw, and generally about twenty inches long. The stalks had the leaves, which are small and straight, still fresh and living on them—which leads me to conclude that this plant was selected by the bird to prevent rotting and mould in the building, since it keeps alive for a long time, as is so often the case with epiphytical orchids. Before the cottage there is a meadow of moss. This is brought to the spot and kept free from grass, stones, or anything which would offend the eye. On this green turf, flowers and fruit of a pretty colour are placed so as to form an elegant little garden. The greater part of the decoration is collected round the entrance to the nest; and it would appear that the husband offers there his daily gifts to his wife. The objects are very various, but always of a vivid colour."

The Starlings.—Family *Sturnidæ*.

The starlings are a widely distributed group, peculiar to the Old World. Our common starling (*Sturnus vulgaris*) is an exceedingly plentiful bird in England, where it stays all the year, receiving an additional host of migrants in the autumn and winter. Like the crows, the starlings are walking, not hopping, birds like sparrows and finches. They differ from the crows, however, in having a streaked nestling, and they have no rictal bristles. Besides the members of the genus *Sturnus*, which contains the true starlings of Europe and Asia, and of which our own starling is the representative, the family embraces many allied genera, chiefly Asiatic, such as the field-starlings and mynas (*Sturnia* and *Temenuchus*), and the rose-coloured pastor (*Pastor roseus*). The latter is an extraordinary bird, on account of its nidification. It appears in certain districts of South-Eastern Europe in vast swarms, hurriedly rears its young, and departs again with such rapidity that its absence has hardly been noticed from its winter quarters. The starlings have the first primary very short, and have on that account been associated with the swallows and wagtails, but with these families they have nothing to do. Their eggs are always bluish or white, and the nest is a rough structure, placed in a hole of a tree or wall. The starlings are principally insect-feeders, and they do an immense amount of good to the agriculturist, though it must be admitted that at certain times they commit some depredation among the fruit.

Fig. 95.—The Common Starling (*Sturnus vulgaris*).

The Tree Starlings.—Family *Eulabetidæ*.

This family is for the most part Indian and Moluccan, but there are several African and Australian forms. It contains the wattled grakles (*Eulabes*) of the Indian region, the glossy starlings of Africa (*Lamprocolius*), and the genus *Calornis* of the Indian and Australian regions. These birds are arboreal in their habits, and differ from the true starlings in having distinct rictal bristles, and in laying spotted eggs. In Madagascar the *Eulabetidæ* are represented by the genus *Euryceros*, a chestnut bird with a huge bill of a blue colour. Only one species, *E. prevosti*, is known.

The *Dicruridæ* are black crow-like flycatchers, inhabiting Africa, India, and China, south throughout the Malayan Archipelago to Australia. They sit on exposed branches of trees, whence they fly out and capture insects. Their nest is a cradle suspended between the fork of a branch, and the eggs are whitish, with red markings. In nearly all the species the tail is very plainly forked, especially in *Buchanga*, and in some genera, such as the Himalayan *Chibia*, the outer feathers are curved upwards. Some of the drongos, such as *Dissemurus* and *Bhringa*, have the outer tail-feathers greatly prolonged, and ending in a racket.

The Drongos.—Family *Dicruridæ.*

Fig. 96.—THE BLACK DRONGO (*Buchanga atræ*).

The orioles are an Old World family of birds, the plumage being of a bright yellow or orange colour, though some of the Moluccan and Australian forms, such as *Mimeta*, are dingy enough in colour, and resemble honey-suckers (*Meliphagidæ*). The orioles build a nest like the drongos, a cup-shaped cradle between the fork of a branch.

The Orioles.—Family *Oriolidæ.*

The golden oriole winters in Africa, and comes to Southern and Central Europe in the spring. It not only visits the British Islands pretty frequently, but has certainly bred there. The note of all the orioles is very rich and flute-like, and their habits are arboreal, their food consisting of insects and fruit. The young birds are streaked below, showing an affinity to the starlings; and the eggs are white, with black spots.

Fig. 97.—THE GOLDEN ORIOLE (*Oriolus galbula*).

These birds are usually called orioles by American naturalists, chiefly on account of their black and yellow colour, which recalls the plumage of the orioles of the Old World. They are, however, structurally distinct, and differ in their habits. The family contains many well-known genera, such as the bobolink (*Delichonyx oryzivora*) and the cow-birds (*Molothrus*), those curious parasitic creatures of which Mr. W. H. Hudson gives such an interesting account in the "Argentine Ornithology." He gives details of the way in which the Argentine cow-bird (*M. bonariensis*) victimises many other small birds by placing its eggs in their nests; and he also tells us that when the young cow-bird is hatched, the other occupants of the nest soon disappear, though whether this massacre is the result of interference on the part of the old birds, or is the work of the nestling cow-bird itself, as with our common cuckoo, has not yet been proved.

The Hang-Nests.—Family *Icteridæ.*

Another well-known member of the family is the red-winged hang-nest (*Agelæus phæniceus*), popularly known amongst us as the red-winged starling, and the meadow starlings (*Sturnella*) also belong to the family.

The true hang-nests or troupials of the genus *Icterus* are widely spread over the New World. The chief element in their coloration is a bright yellow or orange, but they differ from the orioles of the Old World, with which they are often confused, by having only nine primaries. Nearly 140 species of *Icteridæ* are known, and some species of the genus *Cassidix* appear, from the recent observations of Mr. A. Schulz, to be parasitic on each other, for Dr. Kuschel of Breslau informs us that *Cassidix oryzivorus* deposits its eggs in the nest of *C. persicus*. The meadow-larks (*Sturnella*) are ground birds, as their name implies.

Fig. 98.—THE BLACK-HEADED HANG NEST (*Icterus melanocephalus*).

Intermediate between the hang-nests and the finches come the weaver-birds. Although they resemble the finches in their food and in many of their habits, they mostly build domed and hanging nests like the *Icteridæ*.

The Weaver-Birds.—Family *Ploceidæ.*

Weavers are found in all parts of Tropical Africa and Madagascar, as well as in India and Burma, as far south as the Malayan Peninsula. The weaver-finches, which are an integral portion of the family *Ploceidæ*, consist of the wax-bills, such as *Estrilda*, *Lagonosticta*, *Poephila*, etc., are found in the Australian region, as well as all over Tropical Africa and throughout the Indian region. The weaver-birds build a substantial nest, purse-like in shape, often with a long stocking-like entrance. As the nests are generally suspended from the ends of palm-branches, or from trees which overhang the water, it is supposed that this stocking-like appendage is added to the nest to prevent the attacks of monkeys or snakes, both of which are enemies of the young weaver-birds. The weavers have no pretensions to singing powers, and can only keep up an incessant chattering, which does duty for a song. When kept in captivity, and supplied with dried grass for weaving, a baya weaver (*Ploceus baya*) will make a nest in a cage, and the industry of the birds is simply remarkable. The eggs of weaver-birds vary to a great extent, being pure white, or bluish or greenish, with deeper markings of the same colours.

Fig. 99.—THE BLACK-HEADED WEAVER-BIRD (*Hyphantornis melanocephalus*).

The Tanagers.—Family *Tanagridæ.*

These are brilliantly-coloured birds of the New World, resembling finches in appearance, but distinguished by having a notch in the upper mandible. They are very numerous in the neotropical region, and several species visit North America in summer.

The American Creepers.—Family *Cærebidæ.*

These curious little birds are allied to the *Tanagridæ*, but have nevertheless the habits of the creepers, and their creeper-like eggs, white with red spots, point to an alliance with the tree-creepers (*Certhiidæ*). The principal genera of the family are *Certhiola* and *Cæreba*, the latter containing the well-known blue-creeper (*Cæreba cyanea*).

From these families which lie on the borderland of the finches, we pass to the family *Fringillidæ*. The latter family is one of the largest in the whole series of the *Passeriformes*. It is almost universal in its distribution, and comprises three sub-families: the grosbeaks (*Coccothraustinæ*), the true finches (*Fringillinæ*), and the buntings (*Emberizinæ*).

The Finches.—Family *Fringillidæ*.

The Grosbeaks.—Sub-family *Coccothraustinæ*.

In these birds, of which our common hawfinch (*Coccothraustes coccothraustes*) is the type, the bill is large and swollen, and the nasal bones are produced backwards beyond the front line of the bony orbit. There are no less than twenty-three genera of grosbeaks, and they are represented in nearly every quarter of the globe. The northern forms are *Coccothraustes* in the Old World, and *Ligurinus*, of which our common greenfinch (*Ligurinus chloris*) is the type. In North America *Hedymeles* is the prevailing form, while in the Himalayas we have *Mycerobas* and *Pycnorhamphus*. The smaller grosbeaks are principally neo-tropical, and are represented by the genera *Spermophila*, and in the Galapagos Islands by *Geospiza* and *Camarhynchus*. The cardinal grosbeaks (*Cardinalis*) are inhabitants of the Southern United States as far as British Honduras in Central America, and species of the genus are also found in Venezuela and Trinidad.

The Finches.—Sub-family *Fringillinæ*.

This family embraces all the best known of the finches. The type may be said to be our common chaffinch (*Fringilla cœlebs*), but all the linnets, siskins, goldfinches, and other familiar birds are part and parcel of this sub-family. The bill is less massive than in the grosbeaks, and the upper mandible is not produced backwards beyond the front line of the orbit; otherwise the angle of the genys is much the same as in the grosbeaks.

Fig. 100.—The Chaffinch (*Fringilla cœlebs*).

The finches constitute a very numerous sub-family, and many beautiful birds are embraced within its limits. Besides our own European forms mentioned above, there are many interesting tropical genera, such as the rose-finches (*Carpodacus*), which are found in North America, as well as in Northern Europe and Asia, being especially abundant in the Himalayas. The sparrows all belong to this group of finches, as well as the canaries, which are principally African, and the saffron-finches (*Sycalis*) of South America, the bullfinches (*Pyrrhula*) and the crossbills (*Loxia*).

The Buntings.—Sub-family *Emberizinæ*.

In the buntings there is generally a gap between the two mandibles, and the angle of the lower mandible is much more acute than in the finches and grosbeaks. The buntings are grain and insect-eating birds, often of bright colours, and distributed over the greater part of the globe, excepting the Australian and Polynesian regions. In most of the buntings, as with the finches, there is a complete winter plumage, and the summer dress is gained, not by a thorough moult, but by a shedding of the edges of the winter feathers, so that the underlying pattern comes into prominence. One of the best examples of this phenomenon is the snow-bunting (*Plectrophenax nivalis*), which arrives in England in the winter in a rufescent dress. The summer plumage is gradually assumed by the shedding of the pale edges to the feathers; the black tips to the primary coverts disappear by abrasion, and the white bases of the primaries extend by degrees, as the rufous colour of the upper parts is gradually shed, allowing the underlying black and white plumage to predominate, so that the summer dress of the snow-bunting is pure black and white.

Fig. 101.—THE SNOW-BUNTING (*Plectrophenax nivalis*).

Besides the genus *Emberiza*, which contains our yellow-hammer (*E. citrinella*), cirl-bunting (*E. cirlus*), and ortolan (*E. hortulana*), the buntings likewise embrace the corn-bunting (*Miliaria miliaria*), the Lapland bunting (*Calcarius lapponicus*), and a large number of American genera (*Zonotrichia, Poospiza, Junco, Spizella, Ammodronus, Melospiza, Hæmophila, Pipilo, Spiza, Pseudochloris, Phrygilus, Paroaria,* etc.).

The Larks.—Family *Alaudidæ*.

Larks are chiefly denizens of the Old World, though North America claims a number of species of horned-larks (*Otocorys*), which represent a circumpolar genus, of which the European horned-lark (*O. alpestris*) occurs in Northern Europe and Northern Asia, as well as in North America. In America the horned-larks are more numerous, and even extend into Colombia in South America. The *Alaudidæ* are distinguished from all other passerine birds by the scutellations on the hinder side of the tarsi (*planta tarsi*). They are especially numerous in Africa, and also in the plains of India, the dominant genus *Mirafra* extending to the Malayan Islands and even to Australia. The sky-larks, of which our own familiar species, *Alauda arvensis*, is the best known representative, are chiefly palæarctic, though similar species occur in the Indian region. The larks are, without exception, ground-builders, and the eggs are generally dark brown, or whitish, with brown mottlings and speckles. Some twenty genera are known, among which are the desert larks (*Certhilauda*), remarkable for their long curved bill, the calandra larks (*Melanocorypha*), the short-toed larks (*Calandrella*), the crested larks (*Galerita*), the wood-larks (*Lullula*), and the finch-larks (*Pyrrhulauda*).

Fig. 102.—THE SKYLARK (*Alunda arvensis*).

The Wagtails and Pipits.—Family *Motacillidæ*.

Like the larks, the wagtails and pipits are "ambulatores," or walking birds. They do not hop like sparrows and finches. They resemble the larks in one peculiarity, *viz.* the extreme elongation of the inner secondaries, which are as long as the primary quills. The *Motacillidæ* have not the *planta tarsi* scutellated as in the larks, and they have only nine primaries, the first one being absent. In many of the larks, however, the bastard-primary is present, but is so tiny as almost to defy detection.

The pipits are generally birds of sombre brown coloration, more like that of the larks. They build their nests on the ground, generally under some sheltered portion of a bank. The true pipits (*Anthus*) are thirty-five in number, and are found in almost every part of the world. The common meadow pipit (*Anthus pratensis*) is one well-known species, and the tree-pipit (*A. trivialis*) is another. The eggs of these two pipits are much more richly coloured than those of wagtails, and are often of a pinkish-red or purplish colour, with darker spots and blotches. The brightest of the pipits are the members of the African genera *Macronyx* and *Tmetothylacus*, the species of *Macronyx* having yellow breasts, while one species, *M. ameliæ*, has a beautiful pink breast.

Fig. 103.—THE PIED WAGTAIL (*Motacilla lugubris*).

The wagtails are divisible into two sections, the "water" wagtails and the "field" wagtails, the latter being less frequenters of the river banks than of the inland pastures. The most thoroughly river-haunting species in our own islands is the grey wagtail (*Motacilla melanope*), while the pied wagtail (*M. lugubris*) is a typical "water"-wagtail, just as Ray's wagtail (*M. campestris*) is a typical "field"-wagtail. All these little birds, as well as the pipits, feed on insects, which they catch on the wing or on the ground, and they all have a graceful mode of running and walking, keeping up the whole time a constant up-and-down waving of the tail.

The American Warblers.—Family ***Mniotiltidæ*****.**

The *Mniotiltidæ* embrace a number of small warblers, entirely confined to the American region, where they fulfil the same functions as our own warblers (*Sylviidæ*) of the Eastern Hemisphere, feeding on insects. They differ, however, from the *Sylviidæ* in having nine primaries, nor is there any proof that the *Mniotiltidæ* have a double moult, in autumn and again in spring, like the warblers of the Old World. The principal genera of the *Mniotiltidæ* are *Dendrœca* and *Parula*, both of which are also denizens of South America. Some genera, like *Mniotilta*, appear to have an affinity with the creepers, while the genera *Basileuterus*, *Setophaga*, *Myiodioctes*, etc., have well-developed rictal bristles, and are like flycatchers in their external appearance.

Fig. 104.—THE TREE-CREEPER (*Certhia familiaris*).

The Creepers.—Family ***Certhiidæ*****.**

A typical creeper is easily distinguished from the other passerine birds by its stiffened tail-feathers, which resemble those of a woodpecker, and are of the same use to the birds in supporting themselves during their climb up an upright trunk. Unlike the woodpeckers, which only ascend the trunk, the tree-creepers often move along a bough horizontally. They have a long and curved bill, different from the conical bill of the tits, which they resemble in nesting habits and in the colour of the eggs, which are white, with rufous or reddish-brown spots. The genus *Certhia* contains about ten species, of which our tree-creeper (*Certhia familiaris*) is the typical one, but members of the genus are found throughout Europe and Northern Asia, as well as in the Himalayan mountains. They occur also throughout North America and extend into Central America.

Just as in the climbing birds like woodpeckers, there are stiff-tailed species and soft-tailed species, so we find in the creepers the spiny-tailed *Certhiæ*, and some soft-tailed genera like *Salpornis* of India and Africa, *Climacteris* of Australia and New Guinea, and the crimson-winged creeper (*Tichodroma muraria*), a species which inhabits the mountainous regions from China to the Himalayas, and from Turkestan to the Alps and the Pyrenees. It is a beautiful little bird of a delicate grey colour; in this it resembles a nut-hatch, but the bill is curved like that of a creeper. Like a nut-hatch, it has white spots on the outer tail-feathers, but has the wing-coverts crimson.

Fig. 105.—THE CRIMSON-WINGED CREEPER (*Tichodroma muraria*).

The Honey-Suckers. —Family *Meliphagidæ*.

The honey-suckers are one of those curious Australasian families which stand apart by themselves, and for which it is difficult to estimate the correct relationship. Gould wrote in 1865 a very excellent note on these birds, the habits of which he had studied himself in nature:—"The honey-eaters are unquestionably the most peculiar and striking feature in Australian ornithology. They are, in fact, to the farmer what the *Eucalypti*, *Banksiæ*, and *Melalencæ* are to the flora of Australia. The economy of these birds is so strictly adapted to those trees that the one appears essential to the other; for what can be more plain than that the brush-like tongue is especially formed for gathering the honey from the flower-cups of the *Eucalypti*, or that their diminutive stomachs are especially formed for this kind of food, and the peculiar insects which form a portion of it." The brush-tongue is the chief character of the honey-suckers, which are very numerous in Australia and New Guinea, and extends into the Moluccas and Polynesia.

The Sun-Birds. —Family *Nectariniidæ*.

The sun-birds are very similar in outward aspect to the neo-tropical humming-birds (*Trochili*, antea, p. 347). They are richly decorated in metallic colours, but instead of hovering in front of flowers, suspended in the air with a vibrating flight, they are more like tits in their ways; at least, so we gathered from watching a little troup of *Cinnyris asiatica* in a garden at Delhi, where they crept about through the bushes, uttering a little tit-like chirp, and picking off small insects from the leaves.

The Malachite sun-bird (*Nectarinia famosa*) is one of the largest of the *Nectariniidæ*, and is found in Southern Africa. Most of the species of sun-birds have square tails, but *N. famosa* and a few other African species have the central tail-feathers elongated. The sun-birds have an extensile tongue similar to that of the humming-birds and woodpeckers, and Mr. Eugene Oates has shown that the bill is serrated for the terminal third of both mandibles. They build pensile-like nests, made of fine grass or rootlets, and generally with a kind of hood, made of fine grass, above the entrance. The nest is usually attached to the end of a branch, but is sometimes found on the under-side of a broad leaf, such as that of a plantain.

Fig. 106.—THE MALACHITE SUN-BIRD (*Nectarinia famosa*).

The Flower-peckers.—Family *Diceidæ.*

The flower-peckers are small birds, allied to the sun-birds, but differing in their shorter bills, both mandibles being serrated along their cutting-edges. Their plumage is mostly brilliant, and they are found in the Indian and Malayan regions and throughout the Moluccas, New Guinea and Australia. Their food consists of insects and small berries, and they are remarkable for the beauty of their nests, which are purse-like, made of the cotton from plants, fine grass and vegetable-down, the nests being suspended from the end of a twig, often at a great height from the ground. The two principal genera of the flower-peckers are *Dicæum* and *Prionochilus*.

The White-eyes.—Family *Zosteropidæ.*

The white-eyes are found in Africa, the Mascarene islands, throughout India and Ceylon, to the Burmese provinces, China and Japan, and again throughout the whole of the Malayan region to Australia and Polynesia. They are nearly all birds of the same pattern of coloration, green or yellowish-green above, mostly with a yellow forehead, sometimes with a black one, while the majority of species are yellow below, or white with yellow throats. The name of "white-eye" is given to the *Zosteropidæ*, on account of a white ring of feathers which encircles the eye, and not because the eye itself is white. They feed upon small insects, which they seek for among the trees; and Mr. Oates says that the Indian species are generally seen in flocks, and utter a constant twitter as they search for food. The nest is cup-shaped, very neatly and delicately made of vegetable fibres or fine grass, moss or wool. The eggs are blue, and two or three in number

The Tits.—Family *Paridæ.*

The tits are a numerous family, most strongly represented in the northern parts of the Old and New Worlds, reaching in the latter to Central America, and in the former occurring throughout Europe, Africa, and Asia, but being absent from the Australian region. They have stout and conical bills, and have the nostrils covered with bristles, and strongly scutellated tarsi, which have suggested to some ornithologists their affinity to the crows (*Corvidæ*). There is, however, in our opinion, no relationship between these families, for the nesting habits of the two are entirely different, and the character of the eggs suggests no possible connection. The tits are all small birds, assembling in flocks and family parties in winter, when they associate with creepers, nut-hatches, and other small birds, in traversing the woods in search of insect food. The genera of tits are not many, and they are mostly represented in the avi-fauna of Europe. Thus *Parus* contains our great tit (*P. major*) and blue tit (*P. cœruleus*), *Pœcile*, the marsh tit (*P. palustris*) and its allies, *Lophophanes*, our crested tit (*L. cristatus*), and *Ægithalus*, our long-tailed tit (*Æ. vagans*). Nearly all of these build rough nests in holes of walls or of trees, and lay white eggs spotted with rufous, from five to ten in number. The long-tailed or bottle tit, on the other hand, lays white eggs, seldom with any spots, in an oval nest composed of moss, covered with lichens and lined with feathers. It is one of the most beautiful of all known nests, and is suspended in a tree or bush, generally at no great height from the ground.

Fig. 107.—The Bearded Reedling. (*Calamophilus biarmicus*).

The bearded reedling (*Panurus biarmicus*) is often called the bearded tit, but it is not a true tit, being a marsh-haunting bird, building a cup-shaped nest at the base of a bunch of reeds. The eggs are white, with reddish dots and streaks. It occurs still in the Norfolk broads in England, and extends throughout Europe to Central Asia in suitable localities. There is more difference in the colour of the sexes in the genus *Panurus* than there is in the tits. The males and females are alike in colour in the latter birds, whereas in the reedling the male is a handsome bird, with a grey head and a black moustache, while the female is quite a plain coloured bird.

The Nut-Hatches. —Family *Sittidæ.*

The nut-hatches are principally palæarctic and nearctic in their range. No species is found in South America, Africa (south of the Sahara), or in the Australian region. They are mostly grey-coloured birds, with conspicuous white spots near the end of the tail-feathers. In those parts of the world where true nut-hatches do not occur, their places are taken by birds of similar appearance and habits, though of brighter coloration. Thus, in the Himalayas south to the Burmese provinces and the Malayan sub-region occurs the genus *Dendrositta*, represented far away in Madagascar by *Hypositta*, and in Australia and New Guinea by *Sitella*.

The true nut-hatches (*Sitta*), of which our common nut-hatch is the type, are birds with the appearance of a small woodpecker, and they climb up trees with the same facility, using their wedge-shaped bill to prize off pieces of bark to feed on the insects which their prowess discovers. They have, however, soft-plumaged tails, not spiny tails like the woodpeckers and creepers, but they run along boughs exactly as these birds do, with the exception that nut-hatches often run down a trunk, which the other birds above-mentioned do not do.

Fig. 108.—The Common Nut-Hatch (*Sitta cæsia*).

The Gold-Crests. —Family *Regulidæ.*

The gold-crests form a little family of northern birds, intermediate between the tits and warblers, catching tiny insects like both of these, but differing from them in their structure and mode of nidification. They are very tiny creatures, our common gold-crest (*Regulus regulus*) being the smallest of our native birds. Gold-crests are found only in the northern parts of the Old and New Worlds, our own *R. regulus* and the fire-crest (*R. ignicapillus*) being palæarctic, with a smaller race in the Himalayas (*R. himalayensis*), and distinct forms in Madeira (*R. maderensis*), the Canaries (*R. teneriffæ*), and the Azores (*R. azorensis*), while North America has the ruby-crest (*R. calendula*).

Although such a small bird, the common gold-crest is a regular migrant to England across the North Sea, and sometimes migrations have taken place which have lasted from eighty to ninety days. The nest which the bird builds is slung like a hammock under the branch of a yew-tree or a fir: it is made of moss, and is generally well concealed, and lined with feathers, the eggs being from five to eight in number, of a creamy white colour, with a darker ring round the larger end.

The Shrikes or Butcher-Birds.—Family *Laniidæ*.

The shrikes are one of the most cosmopolitan families of birds, for, with the exception of South America, where they are absent, they are everywhere distributed. The true shrikes (*Lanius*), of which the great grey shrike (*L. excubitor*) is the type, are chiefly northern birds, but are distributed also over Africa, India, and the Indo-Chinese sub-region, but in the Malayan, Australian, and Oceanic sub-regions they are represented chiefly by the genus *Pachycephala*. The red-backed shrike (*Lanius collyrio*) and the wood-chat (*L. senator*) are two of the commonest of the European species, and the former visits Great Britain in the summer. The members of this family have gained their name of "butcher birds" from their habit of impaling their food on sharp thorns in the hedges near their nests, mice, frogs, grasshoppers, beetles, and other insects being often found in the "larders" of these birds.

The Swallow-Shrikes.—Family *Artamidæ*.

The swallow-shrikes or wood-swallows constitute a small assemblage of birds, containing the genus *Artamus*, of the Indian and Australian regions, with seventeen species, and *Pseudochelidon* of West Africa, with one species, *P. eurystomina*. The swallow-shrikes are grey or brown birds, with a pointed blue bill and very long wings, and Gould says that no one who has seen them in life can fail to notice how closely they resemble the swallows in the actions and general mode of life. The nest of *A. sordidus* is placed in the fork of a branch, or on the side of a tree, and is made of fine twigs neatly lined with fibrous roots. The eggs are white, spotted with umber brown.

Fig. 109.—The Wax-wing (*Ampelis garrulus*).

The Chatterers.—Family *Ampelidæ*.

The waxwings are a nine-primaried family, chiefly northern in their habitat, and possessing tropical genera only in North and Central America, where the crested chatterers (*Phainopepla* and *Ptilogonys*) occur.

The waxwing (*Ampelis garrulus*) is found in North America and in Northern Europe and Asia, and occasionally visits Great Britain, occurring at irregular intervals in some numbers. It gains its name from the wax-like tips which are developed on the secondary quills in the adult bird. These are also found in the American cedar-bird (*Ampelis cedrorum*), but in the Japanese waxwing (*A. japonicus*) the secondaries and tail are tipped with crimson. The nest of *A. garrulus* is a large and compact structure, made of twigs and moss, and lined with feathers, the eggs being stone-grey, spotted with black or blackish-brown.

The Greenlets.—Family *Vireonidæ*.

The *Vireonidæ* constitute a small family of about sixty birds, peculiar to the New World. They are mostly of a green colour, and in many respects resemble warblers, especially in the fact that the young birds scarcely differ from the adults, whereas in the shrikes, to which the greenlets are undoubtedly also allied, the young are cross-barred. The species of the genus *Vireo* build a pendent nest covered with lichens and mosses, and they lay white eggs, speckled with red.

The Warblers.—Family *Sylviidæ*.

The warblers were, until recent years, considered to be a part of the family of thrushes; but in 1881, they were separated by the late Henry Seebohm on characters which have been admitted to be of deep-seated importance, *viz.*, that the warblers had a double moult, one in spring and one in autumn, and the young were plain-coloured and resembled the adults, whereas the thrushes have only an autumnal moult, and have spotted young, differing from the plumage of the adult.

The warblers are denizens of the Old World, and are everywhere distributed. Unfortunately we have not space to describe the many forms of *Sylviidæ*, which include some of the finest songsters in the world, such as the nightingale (*Daulias luscinia*), the blackcap (*Sylvia atricapilla*), and other familiar summer migrants, such as the willow warbler (*Phylloscopus trochilus*), the chiffchaff (*P. minor*), etc. In the *Sylviidæ* are also placed reed warblers, like our own species (*Acrocephalus streperus*), and sedge warblers (*A. phragmitis*); as well as all the grass-warblers (*Cisticola*, *Prinia*, and *Sutoria*). Some of the latter group build very interesting nests, as they take a couple of leaves and sew the edges together, so as to form a purse, in which they build their nest, which is made of fine grass, cotton down, and hair. The eggs are three or four in number, white or bluish-green, boldly marked with brownish-red. The warblers are insectivorous birds, though most of them, at certain times, feed on small fruits and berries. In autumn many of them migrate for very long distances.

Fig. 110.—The Indian Tailor Bird (*Satoria satoria*).

The Thrushes.—Family *Turdidæ*.

As explained above, the thrushes have only one moult in the year, and that in the autumn, and they have the young birds thickly spotted and different from the adults. Thus in the family *Turdidæ* are placed the robin (*Erythacus rubecula*) and its allies the blue-throats (*Cyanecula*) and redstarts (*Ruticilla*), as well as the chats (*Saxicola*), and numbers of tropical genera, such as the chat-thrushes (*Cossypha*) of Africa, the shámas (*Cittocincla*), and the dhayal birds (*Copsychus*) of India.

The thrushes may be roughly divided into three groups: the ground-thrushes (*Oreocicla* and *Geocichla*), the true thrushes (*Turdus*), and the blackbirds (*Merula*).

One of the largest and handsomest of the ground-thrushes is White's thrush

(*Oreocicla varia*), a species which comes from its home in Siberia to visit Western Europe and the British Islands occasionally.

All the thrushes are insectivorous birds, but feed also on worms and small molluscs, while in the autumn and winter their food consists principally of berries. Most of the northern species are migratory, such as the fieldfare (*Turdus pilaris*), and the redwing (*T. iliacus*), which come to us from Scandinavia in the winter, while even our song-thrush (*T. musicus*) is to a great extent a migrant.

Fig. 111.—WHITE'S THRUSH (*Oreocincla varia*).

In the blackbirds (*Merula*), the sexes are different in colour, the female being always of a duller plumage than in the male, as is evidenced by our common blackbird (*M. merula*). The ground-thrushes are distinguished by a patch of white under the wing. There is scarcely any part of the world from which thrushes are absent.

The Dippers.—Family *Cinclidæ.*

The dippers, or water ouzels, are aquatic wrens. They are generally associated with the thrushes, but they have the front of the tarsus without any scutellæ, and only covered with a plain tarsal envelope. Like the wrens, they have no rictal bristles, and they build a round nest of moss under the shelter of a stone or the root of a tree, and lay white eggs.

The name of dipper is not attached to this bird because it dips under the water, but on account of the curious bobbing motion which the bird continually keeps up. Every time that it bobs its head, it flirts its wings and slightly erects its tail. The bird is ranked as "vermin" by ignorant people, who suppose that it devours the ova of trout, but it is generally allowed that the evidence of this crime on the part of the bird is open to doubt, and its food consists of caddis-worms, water-beetles, and small molluscs. The flight of the dipper is extremely rapid, and resembles that of a kingfisher. It flies with rapid beats of the wings above the surface of the water, and will disappear suddenly beneath the stream, but more often it settles on a rock and deliberately walks into the water, searching for its food among the stones at the bottom of the river.

Fig. 112.—THE COMMON DIPPER (*Cinclus aquaticus*).

Of the dippers about a dozen species are known, inhabitants of the mountain-streams of the northern parts of both hemispheres, extending to the Himalayas and China; while in the New World the genus is found in the highlands of Central America, and throughout the Andes of Colombia Ecuador, and Peru.

The Wrens.—Family *Troglodytidæ.*

The *Troglodytidæ* embrace a number of small birds such as our common wren (*Anorthura troglodytes*), which are spread over the greater part of the globe, being very abundant in the New World, but absent in the Australian and Ethiopian regions. They have no rictal bristles, and build domed nests. Many of them have a remarkable power of song.

The Mocking-Birds.—Family *Mimidæ*.

The mocking-birds are an American family, of which *Mimus polyglottus* and the cat-bird (*Galeoscoptes carolinensis*) are prominent examples. The *Mimidæ* are found throughout temperate North America, Central America, the West Indian islands, and the greater part of South America, even to Chili, Patagonia, and the Galapagos Islands. Their powers of song and mimicry are proverbial.

Fig. 113.—THE MOCKING-BIRD (*Mimus polyglottus*).

The Babblers.—Family *Timeliidæ*.

The *Timeliidæ* are short-winged, non-migratory birds, with the habits of thrushes and the rictal bristles of flycatchers. They are mostly ground birds, many of them, like *Crateropus*, proceeding through the bushes in flocks, while others, like *Ptilocichla* are clothed in dense plumage, resembling the *Formicariidæ* of South America. The characters and limits of this large Old World family are still imperfectly understood.

The Bulbuls.—Family *Pycnonotidæ*.

The bulbuls are another family peculiar to the Old World, thrush-like in character, but differing from the thrushes in their short tarsi, and stronger rictal bristles. They are birds of quiet habits, but possess a sweet song. The *Pycnonotidæ* are found all over Africa, and one species is an inhabitant of Algeria and Morocco. They are strongly represented throughout the Indian region, and extend into the entire Malayan region.

The Cuckoo-Shrikes.—Family *Campophagidæ*.

The chief character which distinguishes this Old World family of birds is the spiny character of the rump-feathers. They are found throughout the Ethiopian, Indian, and Australian regions, and constitute a link between the flycatchers and the shrikes.

The Flycatchers.—Family *Muscicapidæ*.

The flycatchers are mostly broad-billed, insect-catching birds, with abundant rictal bristles, entirely confined to the Old World, over the whole of which they are distributed. They have spotted young like the thrushes, and on this account it is often very difficult to determine whether some of the genera should be referred to the *Turdidæ* or the *Muscicapidæ*.

Fig. 114.—THE COMMON FLYCATCHER (*Muscicapa grisola*).

Our common flycatcher (*Muscicapa grisola*) is a late summer migrant to England, and arrives from Africa in May. The last-named continent is also the home of a number of resident species of the genus *Muscicapa*, which is also well represented in the Indian and Chinese regions by species similar to *M. grisola*. The nest of the latter species is often placed in a crevice of bark on a tree and decorated with lichens and spiders' webs, which help to conceal it. The eggs are greenish-white or stone-colour, with reddish-brown spots. The pied flycatcher (*Ficedula atricapilla*) represents another section of the *Muscicapidæ*, and lays blue eggs, the nest being in the hole of a tree. The fan-tailed flycatchers (*Rhipidura*) of India and Australia build a cup-shaped nest on a bough; and besides these few forms there are many others which we have not space to enumerate, such as the paradise flycatchers (*Terpsiphone*) of Africa and India, remarkable for their long tails, which form a kind of streamer.

The Swallows.—Family *Hirundinidæ*.

The swallows, so often associated with the swifts, because of their similar manner of flight and mode of living, are now recognised by all ornithologists as being true *Passeres*. They have, however, a different arrangement of the feather-tracts to the rest of the perching birds, in having the spinal tract forked on the back. Swallows are found all over the world, and in summer penetrate very far north, our common swallow (*Hirundo rustica*) having been seen near Spitsbergen, and wintering as far south as the Cape Colony and the Indian Peninsula. In America the cliff-swallow (*Petrochelidon pyrrhonota*) and the purple martin (*Progne purpurea*) also perform migrations almost equal in extent to those of the American barn-swallow (*Hirundo erythrogaster*), which is the counterpart of our *H. rustica*. Many of the swallows build in barns and outhouses or in holes of trees, and make rough nests of mud and straw, lined with feathers, but some, like the house-martins (*Chelidon*) build their mud nests under the eaves of houses, and lay white eggs. The nest of our house-martin (*Chelidon urbica*) is an instance of this method, and in this genus the eggs are white, not spotted as in the case of the true swallows. The bank-martins (*Cotile*) also lay white eggs, which are deposited at the end of a tunnel excavated by the birds themselves.

Fig. 115.—THE COMMON SWALLOW (*Hirundo rustica*).

Section *Mesomyodi*.

All the birds contained in this section of the passeriformes have the intrinsic muscles of the syrinx fixed to the middle of the bronchial semi-rings. The first sub-division of the *Mesomyodi* have the lower end of the trachea not modified, the syrinx as in the oscines, but with a lesser number of singing-muscles. This sub-division is called the *Acromyodæ*. There are eight acromyodian families, of which mention is made below, and they are distinguished by the different scutellation of the tarsi. In the first division occur the *Tyrannidæ*, *Oxyrhamphidæ*, and *Pipridæ*; in these the tarsus is what is called "exaspidean." In the second division, where the tarsus is "pycnaspidean," are the *Cotingidæ* and *Phytotomidæ*. In the third is the family *Philepittidæ*, with a "taxaspidean" tarsus; and lastly, the fourth division, with an "ochreate" tarsus, containing the *Pittidæ* and *Xeniscidæ*. The last three families inhabit the Old World, but all the others belong to the New World.

The Tyrants.—Family *Tyrannidæ*.

In the tyrants the "exaspidean" form of tarsus prevails, *i.e.*, the scutellation of the fore part of the tarsus is continued over the whole outer side of it, and includes also the hinder aspect or the *planta tarsi*. The family is divided by Dr. P. L. Sclater into four sub-families, the *Tæniopterinæ*, *Platyrhynchinæ*, *Elæniinæ*, and *Tyranninæ*. The tyrants number more than 400 species, a certain portion of which are migratory, breeding in North America, and wandering to Central and South America in winter. By far the greater majority of species are neotropical in habitat. They are insect-feeders, and resemble our flycatchers in habits, so much so that they are commonly known as "flycatchers" in America.

The Sharp-Bills.—Family *Oxyrhamphidæ.*

In the *Tyrannidæ* and *Oxyrhamphidæ* the toes are nearly free, according to Dr. Sclater, as in the *Oscines* or ordinary passerine birds. They differ from the members of the foregoing family in having a straight and pointed bill, instead of the flattened and hooked bill of the *Tyrannidæ*. As Mr. Salvin well observes, the position of the genus *Oxyrhamphus* is obscure, and it may turn out, when its anatomy is known, that it is not allied to the tyrants at all. In the male bird, according to Mr. Salvin, "the barbs of the central portion of the outer web of the outermost primary have their extremities destitute of barbules, and these bare points turned rather abruptly backwards and slightly inwards, the margin of the wing thus forming a strongly serrate edge. In the female the outer web of this feather is normal." Nothing has been recorded of the habits of the species of *Oxyrhamphus*, which are three in number.

The Manakins.—Family *Pipridæ.*

The *Pipridæ* differ from the two foregoing families in having the toes united at the base. They are mostly brightly-coloured birds, about seventy in number, strictly neotropical in habitat, and dwelling in the forests. A curious habit of one of the manakins, *Chiroxiphia linearis*, of Central America, is recorded by Mr. Nutting. Instead of fighting for the female, as is the case with most birds, this manakin dances himself into her favour. Mr. Nutting once saw two males dancing upon a bare twig about four feet from the ground. The two birds were about a foot and a half apart, and were alternately jumping about two feet into the air, and alighting exactly upon the spot whence they jumped. They kept time as regularly as clock-work, one bird jumping up the instant that the other bird alighted, each bird accompanying himself to the tune of *tolédo, tolédo, tolédo*, sounding the syllable "*to*" as he crouched to spring, "*lé*" while in the air, and "*do*" as he alighted.

The American Chatterers.—Family *Cotingidæ.*

In the *Cotingidæ* the tarsus is "pycnaspidean," with the scales of the hinder aspect of the tarsus (*planta tarsi*) separate, small in size, and generally arranged without any order. The bill is elongated, compressed, and not serrated. Six sub-families are recognised by Dr. Sclater, and all the species are neotropical. They comprise very varied forms, but the most striking are the cocks-of-the-rock (*Rupicola*) and the bell-birds (*Chasmorhynchus*).

Fig. 116.—THE BELL-BIRD (*Chasmorhynchus niveus*).

The Plant-Cutters.—Family *Phytotomidæ.*

The plant-cutters are only four in number, and are found in Western South America from Peru to Chili, thence to the Argentine Republic and Northern Patagonia. There is only one genus, *Phytotoma*, which agrees with the *Cotingidæ*, as regards the scaling of the tarsus, but is distinguished by its short, conical, and serrated bill.

In the following small family the tarsus is "taxaspidean," with the spaces on the soles of the tarsus close together, rectangular, and arranged in regular series. The *Philepittidæ* are ground birds, found only in Madagascar. Two species are known, one black, the other olive above, yellow below, but both having a bluish fleshy carbuncle above the eye.

The Wattled Ant-Thrushes.—Family *Philepittidæ.*

The *Pittidæ* differ from all the families we have been recently considering in having the tarsus "ocreate," or covered with an entire scale. With the exception of one species, *Pitta angolensis,* which inhabits West Africa, the whole of the family are denizens of the tropical regions of the Indian and Australian regions. The pittas are birds of bright coloration, inhabitants of the forests, and in many cases migratory. The Burmese genus *Anthocincla* has long superciliary tufts, which are absent in the other genera.

The Pittas.—Family *Pittidæ.*

Fig. 117.—The Purple Pitta (*Pitta granatina*).

The *Xeniscidæ* agree with the *Pittidæ* in the scaling of the tarsus, but have only ten tail-feathers, whereas the pittas have twelve. Three genera are known of these tiny wren-like birds, *viz. Acanthidositta, Traversia,* and *Xenicus,* all from the New Zealand sub-region.

The arrangement of the voice-organs in the *Tracheophonæ* is exactly opposite to that of the *Oscines* or ordinary passeres, and the lower end of the trachea is specially modified in order to form an organ of voice, and the bronchi are not involved in the arrangement at all.

Section *Tracheophonæ.*

The four families composing the *Tracheophonæ* are all neotropical, the *Dendrocolaptidæ* and *Formicariidæ* having only one pair of notches in the hinder margin of the sternum, while the *Conopophagidæ* and *Pteroptochidæ* have two pairs of posterior notches.

The Wood-Hewers.—Family *Dendrocolaptidæ.*

Fig. 118.—Bridges' Wood-Hewer (*Drymornis bridgesi*).

The wood-hewers are about three hundred in number, and are contained in six sub-families, three of which, the *Furnariinæ* (oven-birds), *Synallaxinæ*, and *Philydorinæ* have soft-plumaged tails, while the other four, consisting of the true wood-hewers and their allies, have spiny tails. The species we have figured comes from North and West Argentina, is somewhat gregarious, and Mr. Barrows says that its habits are somewhat like those of a woodpecker, but it spends much of its time on the ground searching for insects.

These are forest birds, inhabiting Central and South America, and numbering about 300 species. Mr. Osbert Salvin divides the family into two groups, those which frequent the trees and bushes and have short tarsi, and those whose habits are terrestrial, and feed on insects on the ground. The habits of the *Formicariidæ* are not very well

The Ant-Birds.—Family *Formicariidæ.*

known, but they appear to make their nests in trees and bushes, some of them being pensile, and suspended in a forked branch near the extremity of a bough. The eggs, according to Mr. Salvin, vary greatly, from rich dark-greenish blue to a mottled mahogany colour, and many are pure white, or are white with few or many spots. Although commonly known as "ant"-birds, whence also their scientific name, it is now believed that the *Formicariidæ* do not eat ants, but only feed on the insects driven up by the swarms of foraging-ants (*Echiton*).

The *Conopophagidæ* consist of a couple of genera, with eleven species, found in South America, from Colombia to South-Eastern Brazil and Bolivia. They bear a general resemblance to the *Formicariidæ*, but have four posterior notches in the sternum.

The tapacolas, or *Pteroptochidæ*, are a family of small wren-like birds, occurring in the Andes of Ecuador and Colombia, but more plentifully represented in Chili and Patagonia.

The Scrub-Birds.—Family *Atrichiidæ*.

In the *Atrichiidæ* the sternum is single-notched, and they have a rudimentary furcula or "merry-thought." The wings are so small that the power of flight must be very limited, and the *planta tarsi* is scaled like that of a lark. Only two species are known, both from Australia. Of the noisy scrub-bird (*Atrichia clamosa*), whom Gilbert discovered in Western Australia, Gould says that it is a very difficult bird to find among the tangled beds of dwarf-ferns and dense thickets, and is only detected by its peculiar and noisy note.

SUB-KINGDOM I.—VERTEBRATA.

CLASS III.—REPTILIA.

By R. Lydekker, B.A., F.R.S., V.P.G.S., &c.

From both mammals and birds, reptiles are broadly distinguished by the coldness of their blood, which has a temperature but little, if at all, raised above that of the surrounding air. Probably to the popular mind this is the most obvious distinction of reptiles ; and, in the ordinary acceptation of the term, it does serve to differentiate the group from all other vertebrates except fishes—with which these creatures are not likely to be confounded. But it must be remembered that the popular and scientific conceptions of what constitutes a reptile are totally distinct. Under that title the ordinary observer includes frogs, salamanders, and newts ; and, in fact, all terrestrial, cold-blooded vertebrates. From certain structural peculiarities the naturalist, on the other hand, separates the creatures just named from reptiles, and includes under that title only crocodiles, tortoises, turtles, lizards and snakes, with a number of extinct forms with which we are not concerned in this volume.

Although some reptiles, such as lizards, agree very closely with the egg-laying mammals (Monotremata) in the structure of the bones forming the shoulder-girdle, while this resemblance is still more markedly displayed by certain extinct members of the reptilian class, yet the relationships of modern reptiles are decidedly closer with birds. Both groups, for instance, agree in that the young are not nourished with milk ; while as regards structure there are several points in which they are identical, and at the same time differ from mammals. Notably, each branch of the lower jaw in birds and reptiles is composed of several distinct bones ; and the whole jaw is jointed on each side to the skull by means of a separate ossification known as the quadrate-bone. In both groups the ankle-joint is situated between the two horizontal rows of bones constituting the tarsus ; although in birds, as well as in some extinct reptiles, these bones are welded respectively with the long bones of the leg and of the metatarsus. A further distinction is the articulation of the skull to the first vertebra by means of a single knob-like condyle, instead of by the two condyles characterising mammals.

Such are some of the features common to birds and reptiles, as distinct from mammals. From birds, reptiles are broadly distinguished by the absence of feathers, the protective structures developed in the outer layer of the skin taking the form either of overlapping horny scales, or of large shield-like plates united by their edges. As already said, reptiles are further distinguished by their cold blood ; but this is obviously a feature of much less importance, for even among mammals the Monotremata have the temperature of the blood perceptibly lower than is the case with the higher members of the class. An important difference is, however, found in the great blood-vessel, or aorta, by which the blood passes from the heart to the body ; since, whereas in birds this is single and bends over the left branch of the windpipe, in reptiles it is double, and passes over both branches of the latter. Then, again, no reptiles are known in which the number of digits in the fore-limb is reduced to three; while in no case are the two collar-bones fused together to form the forcula, or merrythought, which constitutes such a striking feature in the skeleton of a bird. Other minor differences might be pointed out, but the foregoing are amply sufficient to distinguish a bird from a reptile. In common with the egg-laying mammals, both groups produce their young from eggs; but in certain reptiles the young are retained so long within the body of the parent that they are born alive into the world.

From the lower vertebrates, that is to say frogs, salamanders, newts, and fishes, reptiles differ in that they are never provided with gills at any period of life, and when first hatched are similar in general form and structure to the adult, or, in other words, do not undergo a metamorphosis.

Whereas birds are remarkably alike in general appearance and internal structure, reptiles present great diversity in these respects, and the distinction between the various orders of the latter are much more strongly marked than is the case with those of the former. If extinct types be taken into account, these diversities are still more strongly accentuated, and there are certain fossil forms which walked on their hind legs alone, while others were capable of flying in the same manner as a bird. For this reason the presence or absence of the power of flight is not given as one of the distinctions between birds and reptiles.

Geologically, reptiles are much older than either mammals or birds, and consequently a large number of their orders are extinct, while one is represented only by a solitary survivor. The existing orders are as follows:—

I. CROCODILIA (Crocodiles, Alligators, and Garials).
II. CHELONIA (Tortoises and Turtles).
III. SQUAMATA (Lizards, Chamæleons, and Snakes).
IV. RHYNCHOCEPHALIA (New Zealand Tuatera.)

In consequence of their greater antiquity, and the numerous migrations which they have undergone during early periods of the earth's history, reptiles do not agree with mammals in respect to their geographical distribution; so that the realms and regions into which the earth is divided from the evidence of the present and past distribution of mammals do not hold good for reptiles. Some of the leading features in the distribution of the orders and sub-orders of the present class are mentioned in the sequel.

ORDER I.—CROCODILIA.

CROCODILES, ALLIGATORS, AND GARIALS.

NOBODY can mistake a crocodile or alligator, or even their long-snouted allies, the garials, for any other reptile; and consequently, although they are nearly allied to certain extinct forms, there is no necessity here for giving an elaborate and detailed definition of the order. Great lumbering brutes, lying like logs in the water, but waking into sudden and unexpected activity directly living prey comes within their reach, crocodiles and alligators are specially characterised by the rows of large shield-like horny plates covering the back and parts of the neck, and in some cases also the under surface of the body. These shields, which do not overlap, but join one another by their edges, are often marked on the back by more or less distinctly developed longitudinal ridges, and, at least on the back, are underlain in the deep layer of the skin by solid bony plates. In the case of the ridged shields, the underlying plates are similarly ridged ; and in every instance the plates are marked by a peculiar honey-comb-like sculpture. A somewhat similar sculpture, although taking more the form of irregular branching ridges and grooves, is likewise developed on the outer surface of the bones of the head ; and in this respect the skull of every living member of the order differs from that of any other existing reptile. All crocodilians—as the members of the order may be collectively designated—are huge ungainly reptiles, with large flat heads, depressed and lizard-like bodies, short limbs, and long, compressed, and powerful tails, bearing on the upper surface a crest of horny lobes, which is double in the basal half of that appendage. The toes, which are five in number in the fore-limbs, but are reduced to four in the hinder pair, are more or less completely united by webs to form efficient paddles for swimming ; and on each foot the three toes on the inner side are furnished with strong and sharp claws. In the huge, ugly head, the apertures of the ears can be closed by means of movable lids, so as to prevent the ingress of water ; and the nostrils open at the very tip of the muzzle—whether this be short or broad, as in the alligators, or long and narrow, as in the garials. The vast and cavern-like mouth is armed with a formidable series of sharp, conical teeth, some of which are enlarged into tusks, while all are implanted in separate sockets, and form a single row on the summit of each jaw. To keep this terrible armament in repair, the teeth are being consequently shed and renewed, the new ones coming up beneath the hollow bases of the old ones and gradually pushing them out. Sometimes three or four teeth may be seen, one beneath the other, packed together like a nest of thimbles.

If the dried skull of one of these reptiles be examined, it will be found that the whole of the palate is formed by a solid roof of bone, and also that the quadrate-bone is firmly and immovably wedged in between the adjacent elements of the skull. Later on, we shall see that this type of structure differs very markedly from that which obtains among the lizards, and thus forms a most essential feature in the definition of the order. A more detailed examination of the skulls of all existing crocodiles will also show that the posterior, or internal, nostrils open on the palate right at the hinder end of the skull, close to where it joins the backbone. And it is by means of this arrangement that these reptiles are enabled to hold and drown their prey in their open mouths beneath the surface of the water without any danger of being suffocated themselves. This is effected by means of the production of the upper extremity of the windpipe well into the mouth, where it enters the internal nostrils, and thus forms a closed tube from the external nostrils to the lungs.

Another peculiarity in the structure of a crocodile which has much effect on its movements, is to be found in the vertebræ of the short neck. From the development of long processes on the sides of this portion of the backbone, a crocodile is totally unable to turn its head. Consequently, if a man be attacked on land by one of these monsters, he has but to await its rush, and then leap suddenly aside, when his aggressor will continue its course until able to turn its whole body.

Members of the order are found in all the warmer regions of the globe, but are happily absent from European rivers. ·They frequent alike rivers, marshes, and ponds; and, although never found far removed from water, will at times travel long distances on land. In periods of drought, some of them, at least, bury themselves deep in the mud, where they remain in a semi-torpid condition until awakened by returning moisture. They are the most thoroughly carnivorous of all reptiles; and their huge size and powerful teeth render them capable of seizing and killing almost all kinds of living prey. Animals coming to drink are seized by the nose, and pulled under water, to be ruthlessly drowned in the manner already indicated.

All crocodilians lay eggs, which are furnished with a hard white shell, and comparable in size to those of a goose. In number they usually vary from one to three score. They are buried by the female parent in the warm sand, where in due course they hatch. It appears, however, that in some instances, at least, the female opens the pit when the young are ready to burst their prison, being attracted by the cries uttered by the little crocodiles while still within the shell. The young ones are introduced to the water by the mother.

Although all living crocodilians are included in the single family *Crocodilidæ*, they are divided into several genera, some of which have a more or less limited geographical distribution, while others have a very extensive range. Of those with a restricted range, the first we have to notice are the caimans (*Caiman*) of Tropical America. Caimans are broad and short-snouted crocodilians, with a bony armour developed on the under, as well as the upper, surface of the body. In the skull, the nasal bones only extend as far forwards as the hinder aperture of the external nostrils; and, as a rule, both the first and fourth lower teeth, which are enlarged and tusk-like, are received into pits in the upper jaw, so as to be concealed when the mouth is closed. The upper teeth bite on the outer side of the lower ones; and the two branches of the lower jaw have but a very short union in the middle line at their front extremity. A peculiarity of the genus is to be found in the circumstance that the bony plates on the back are articulated together. There are several species of caiman, one of which ranges as far south as the La Plata River. Their true home is, however, the tropics, and in the Orinoco and Amazon they occur in thousands. In Brazil they are known as jacares, and one species from that country measures from eighteen to twenty feet in length. In capturing these ferocious and bloodthirsty monsters, the native Brazilians display great daring.

Caimans (*Caiman*).

The alligators are so closely allied to the caimans that they can only be distinguished by anatomical features. The most easily detected distinction is to be found in the skull, in which the nasal bones extend right across the aperture of the external nostrils, instead of stopping short at their hinder border. The bony plates on the back differ by the absence of any articulation between them; while those on the lower surface are either very thin or wanting. Of the two well-known species, the Chinese alligator (*A. sinensis*) is a comparatively small form, approximating to the caimans in the retention of thin bony plates on the under surface, and having the front toes free. In the gigantic North American alligator (*A. mississippiensis*), on the other hand, there are no plates beneath the body, and the front toes are webbed; while there are also differences in the number of plates on the neck and back, as well as in the number of teeth, which aid in distinguishing between the two kinds. The habits of alligators are very similar to those of other members of

Alligators (*Alligator*).

the order; but the female buries her eggs—which may reach a hundred in number—among leaves and other decaying vegetable matter, in order to hasten the process of hatching; and during the pairing-season the males spend much of their time on land. The Chinese species feeds largely upon fish.

True Crocodiles (*Crocodilus*).

The typical or true crocodiles are readily distinguished from both the foregoing genera by the circumstance that the upper teeth interlock with the lower ones, and likewise by the fourth lower tooth generally biting into a notch in the upper jaw. In the skull the nasal bones extend only as far forwards as the hinder margin of the nostrils; and whereas there are from seventeen to nineteen upper teeth, in the lower jaw the number is constantly fifteen. In all, the under surface of the body is devoid of bony plates. Crocodiles are represented by about eleven species, which are distributed over the south of Asia, Africa, Madagascar, the north of Australia, and Tropical America, and it is not a little remarkable that one of these (*Crocodilus porosus*) extends from India to Queensland, being also found in some of the islands of Polynesia, such as the Solomons and Fiji. This wide distribution is, however, readily explained by this species being largely estuarine in its habits, and taking readily to salt water, whereas all the others are fresh-water reptiles. Great difference obtains in the form of the skull in the various representatives of the genus, the Oriental magar (*C. palustris*) having a short and broad alligator-like snout, whereas in the sharp-nosed crocodile (*C. americanus*) of Central America, the muzzle is comparatively long, narrow, and pointed. Even in this species, however, the short front union between the two branches of the lower jaw is retained. In its still more elongated snout, the West African long-nosed crocodile (*C. cataphractus*) forms a connecting link between the more typical species and the under-mentioned garials. The species longest known is the Egyptian crocodile (*C. niloticus*), which is one of those with a snout of medium proportions.

Fig. 1.—NORTH AMERICAN ALLIGATOR (*A. mississippiensis*).

As a rule, the favourite haunts of crocodiles are sandbanks in rivers, where they lie basking for hours in the full sun, frequently with their ponderous jaws widely gaping. They appear to live for a great number of years—during the whole of which they continue to grow—and often frequent the same spot for long periods of time. Their ferocity is too well known to need mention; and many incautious bathers have lost their lives through these hideous reptiles. On the Hugli it is stated that women coming down to the river's edge to draw water have occasionally been seized and dragged under while stooping down on the marge. Although specimens are now seldom recorded of more than twelve or thirteen feet in length, there is good evidence that formerly the Indian magar grew to at least eighteen feet.

Stumpy Crocodile (*Osteolæmus*).

A small short-snouted species (*Osteolæmus tetraspis*) from Sierra Leone has been referred to a genus by itself, on account of the nasal bones extending right across the aperture of the nostrils. Although agreeing in this respect with the alligators, in all other features this species is a true crocodile.

Garials (*Rhynchosuchus* and *Garialis*).

Two members of the order differ from all the foregoing in having the edges of the very long and slender muzzle nearly straight, instead of more or less distinctly festooned, and likewise by the circumstance that the nasal bones stop considerably short of the hinder border of the external nostrils. A further marked difference is to be found in the great length of the bony union between the two branches of the lower jaw, which extends at least as far back as the fifteenth tooth. The teeth themselves are also much more slender than in the preceding genera, the fish-eating habits of the garials rendering a more powerful type of dentition unnecessary. Of these two species, Schlegel's garial (*Rhynchosuchus schlegeli*) inhabits the Malay peninsula and Borneo, and has the snout of medium elongation and slenderness. Its claim to generic distinction is due to the circumstance that the nasal bones extend forwards on the upper surface of the snout to reach the premaxillæ or anterior jawbones. It has twenty or twenty-one upper, and eighteen or nineteen lower, teeth; and its length varies from twelve to fourteen feet.

On the other hand, the true garial (*Garialis gangetica*), which inhabits the Ganges, Bramaputra, Indus, and Mahanadi, together with a river in Arakan, is distinguished by the much greater length and slenderness of the snout, in which the nasal bones stop short of the premaxillæ, so that the maxillæ, or hinder upper jawbones come into contact with one another on the upper surface of the snout between the other two pairs of bones. The almost uniformly sized teeth are very numerous, varying from 27 to 29 in the upper, and from 25 to 26 in the lower jaw. None of the lower ones bite into pits in the upper jaw, whereas some of the former are so received in the other species. All the toes are fully webbed. In the adult the general colour is dark olive on the head and back. The male garial may be distinguished by the development of the expanded extremity of the muzzle into a kind of hump, in the centre of which are situated the nostrils. The garial grows to a length of about twenty feet, and feeds entirely on fish. For the capture of its finny prey, the numerous slender, sharply pointed, and somewhat curved teeth are admirably suited; and the highly developed swimming powers of this species are also correlated with the nature of its food. The female deposits her eggs in the sand of the river-banks, these being generally laid in two distinct layers, one above the other. When the young first make their appearance in the world, they have the snout propor-

Fig 2.—TRUE GARIAL (*Garialis gangetica*).

tionately much longer than in the adult; but, owing to the more rapid growth of the body, this becomes gradually shorter. Young garials have the body and tail ornamented with a number of oblique dark bands on a lighter ground. Although the garial is commonly looked upon with suspicion, it does not appear that it ever attacks man or the larger mammals.

ORDER II.—CHELONIA.

Tortoises and Turtles.

The presence of a bony shell, in a more or less fully developed state—sometimes enclosing the whole body in a solid case, and in other cases reduced to a kind of dish-cover on the back—is the grand distinguishing feature of the tortoises and turtles, which collectively constitute the second great order of reptiles. Indeed, so far as their bony framework is concerned, these strange creatures may almost be described as reptiles turned inside out. For the ribs, which are generally united with bony plates in the skin to form the upper shell, or carapace, are actually placed outside both the blade-bones and the haunch-bones; while, when a shell is developed on the under surface of the body, its front portion is formed by the equivalents of the collar-bones.

The presence, in some form or other, of such a shell serves at once to distinguish the Chelonians from all other living reptiles. In ordinary tortoises and turtles the upper shell is firmly welded to the backbone; but the under shell, or plastron, which may or may not be joined by its edges to the sides of the carapace, is generally free from the internal skeleton. Externally the shell is covered by a number of longitudinal rows of horny shields, which can be stripped off without much trouble, and then reveal the underlying bony plates. Unfortunately for the ordinary student of natural history, the form and mode of arrangement of these hidden bony plates are of the utmost importance in the classification of many of these reptiles. And as they are not shown in figures taken from specimens in the ordinary condition, he must either refer to special works on the subject, or must visit a good museum. Both the superficial horny shields and the underlying bony plates have received special names; and as some acquaintance with their general mode of arrangement is absolutely essential to the study of these reptiles, a brief reference to the subject must be made in this place.

Taking any ordinary Chelonian, such as the common Greek tortoise of our gardens, we find the following general arrangement obtaining in the horny shields. Along the middle of the upper shell runs a single series of five large symmetrical shields known as the vertebrals. On each side these are flanked by a series of still larger shields, usually also five in number, termed the costals. The edges of the upper shell are formed by a numerous series of much smaller marginal shields, which in those forms with a complete shell overlap the middle of the sides, and thus come on to the plastron. At the middle of the front edge of the carapace there is very generally a small unpaired shield known as the nuchal; while the term caudal is applied to the corresponding single or double shield at the opposite end of the shell. On the under surface, or plastron, we find six pairs of large shields, respectively named, from front to back, the gular, humeral, pectoral, abdominal, femoral, and anal shields; while in some cases an unpaired intergular is interposed between the two gulars. Certain small shields on the borders of the slits for the fore and hind limbs need not be further referred to.

If we now strip off the horny shields, we shall find that the underlying bony plates conform to a great extent with the arrangement of the former, although presenting certain well-marked differences. In the middle line of the upper shell runs a single series of small many-angled plates termed the neurals, all attached below to the back-bone. A larger unattached nuchal plate in front, and one or two similarly detached pygals behind, complete this median unpaired series. The sides of the carapace are formed by the eight pairs of costal plates, which are firmly welded to the underlying ribs; while its borders are composed of the marginal plates, which resemble the corresponding horny shields in being angulated, and some of which join the plastron, when the latter is fully developed. Exclusive of these marginals, the lower shell or plastron generally consists of one unpaired and four paired elements. The front pair, corresponding to the collar-bones of other vertebrates, are the epiplastrals, behind or between which is the single entoplastral. Then follow the hyoplastrals, hypoplastrals, and xiphiplastrals; the latter forming the hinder extremity of the lower shell, and being frequently more or less deeply notched in the middle line. In addition to these elements, a few tortoises have a pair of mesoplastral bones intercalated between the hyo- and hypoplastrals, thus bringing up the total number of bones in the lower shell to eleven.

Scarcely less peculiar than their shells are the jaws of the Chelonia, which are invariably cased in horny sheaths, with sharp cutting edges, like the beaks of birds, and show no vestiges of teeth at any period of life, Generally the head is relatively short and wide; but there is a considerable amount of diversity in this respect, as there is in regard to the structure of the skull. In all cases, however, the quadrate-bone is firmly fixed between the adjacent bones of the skull, to which its relations are somewhat different from those obtaining in the Crocodilia. There are many other peculiarities connected with the bony framework of these reptiles; but those mentioned are amply sufficient to distinguish them from all other groups.

The order is divided into three sub-orders, respectively known as the Cryptodira, Pleurodira, and Trionychoidea; and these divisions are important, not only on account of indicating structural differences, but also on distributional grounds. Thus, whereas the first group attains its maximum development in the countries to the north of the Equator, the second group is now entirely restricted to the Southern Hemisphere, and is the only one represented in Australia. No members of the order are found in New Zealand; and the third group is unknown in both Australia and South America, as indeed it is in Europe, although this is probably due to temperature.

Great differences are observable in the mode of life of the different members of the order, the typical tortoises being almost or quite exclusively terrestrial, the soft tortoises fresh-water, and the turtles marine. All are, however, fond of water, and even the most exclusively terrestrial species are fond of an occasional bath. Many of the so-called terrapins may be regarded as amphibious creatures, spending much of their time in the water, but often dwelling for a considerable period on dry land. Between the land tortoises and the ordinary fresh-water terrapins there is not much difference in the structure of the feet; but in the turtles these are modified into paddles, adapted solely for swimming, and forming poor organs of progression on land. Even these purely marine forms are, however, in the habit of coming on shore for the purpose of depositing their eggs. It is important to remember that in ordinary language the term turtle is often applied to many of the fresh-water forms, although it is preferable to restrict it to the marine species. Whereas all the other members of the order lay hard-shelled eggs, those of the turtles are soft-shelled. In the matter of diet, Chelonians present as much diversity as in their other habits, some kinds being exclusively carnivorous, while others feed on vegetable substances.

Sub-Order I.—Cryptodira.

The members of this group are primarily characterised by their power of withdrawing the head within the margins of the shell by an S-like bending of the neck in a vertical plane; but as the same feature is to be found in the third group of the order, supplemental characteristics are necessary to define the present sub-order. With the exception of the abnormal leathery turtle, the shell of all the forms—no matter what be its degree of development—is furnished with a complete set of marginal bones, some of which are articulated to the extremities of the ribs. Accordingly, the Cryptodira may be defined as Chelonians which retract the head by means of a vertical S-like flexure of the neck, and either possess a complete set of marginal bones attached to the ribs, or have the limbs converted into flippers. These are, however, by no means the sole distinctive features of the group. An important structural peculiarity is to be found in the circumstance that none of the bones of the pelvic girdle have any attachment to the lower shell or plastron. Then, again, as a general rule, the latter bears only six pairs of horny shields, an intergular shield being but very rarely developed. If the dried skull be examined, it will be found that the ring of bone surrounding the aperture of the ear—technically termed the tympanic ring—is interrupted by a distinct notch in its hinder border; while the quadrate-bone articulates with the hinder end of the lower jaw by means of a convex knob or condyle, received into a pit in the latter.

With the exception of the soft tortoises, this group includes all the land and fresh-water Chelonians of the Northern Hemisphere, as well as the marine turtles and the leathery turtle. It is, however, by no means wanting in the Southern Hemisphere, as there are numerous forms—both of terrestrial and fresh-water habits—in Africa and South America, although none are known from Australasia. There are such a large number of genera—to say nothing of species—included in this group, that limitations of space permit of reference only to some of the more important types.

Land-Tortoises and Terrapins. —Family *Testudinidæ*.

This extensive family group is probably best known in the shape of the common Grecian tortoise and European pond-tortoise, both of which are commonly exhibited for sale in London shops, although neither are native denizens of the British Islands. In this family are also included the giant tortoises of the Mascarene and Galapagos Islands. There are no marine forms; but while some are terrestrial, others are more or less amphibious, spending a large portion of their lives in fresh water. Without going into abstruse and wearisome anatomical details, it is by no means easy to give a concise definition of the family. It may be observed, however, that while the head is capable of complete retraction within the margin of the shell, the limbs are never converted into paddles, and the shell itself is never heart-shaped. Both the upper and lower halves of the shell are well developed; and they may be connected together at the sides either by flattened surfaces, or they may give off minute interlocking processes, so as to be united by what are termed sutures. In no instance is there an intergular shield on the front of the plastron. Certain features connected with the bones of the carapace and internal skeleton by which this family is distinguished from those that follow may be best mentioned under the heading of the latter. Geographically the *Testudinidæ*—like the typical genus *Testudo*—have a range equivalent to that of the sub-order, of which they form by far the largest family. As regards diet, they are as diverse as in other habits, some feeding exclusively on vegetable substances, while others are carnivorous. It is not an uncommon belief that the Greek tortoise—which is mainly a vegetarian—will live upon black beetles; and I have known an instance where one of these reptiles was installed in a kitchen—*vice* a hedgehog deceased—to prey upon these troublesome insects, with results sadly to the disappointment of the purchaser.

The typical representatives of the family are the land-tortoises of the genus *Testudo*, most of which, like the common Grecian species, are comparatively small creatures, although some of those from the Mascarene and Galapagos Islands have a shell measuring considerably over a yard in length, and are capable of trotting off gaily with a load of three full-grown men on their capacious backs. In a work like the present the reader must not expect to find all the characters by which the tortoises of this genus are distinguished from their kin. In all cases the stout club-like limbs are adapted for walking on land, and are covered with horny scales or tubercles, while the unwebbed toes terminate in strong claw-like nails. The tail is always short. In a shell from which the superficial shields have been stripped, it will be seen that the neural bones are wide and short, with a quadrangular one generally alternating with an octagonal, although sometimes most are hexagonal. Of the costal bones, one is wide above and narrow below, and the next the reverse of this. As already said, these tortoises have a distribution practically coextensive with that of the family to which they belong; and all are herbivorous. In South and South-Eastern Europe the genus is represented by the well-known Grecian tortoise (*T. græca*), and also by the nearly-allied margined tortoise (*T. marginata*), which appears to be confined to Greece, and is distinguished by the absence of an enlarged tubercle on the thigh. Certain Indian and South African species, such as *T. elegans* and *T. geometrica*, are distinguished by the extreme convexity of the shell, which is beautifully painted either with narrow yellow lines radiating on a dark ground from the centre of each of the shields, or with similar black lines on a light ground. Giant tortoises formerly existed in Aldabra Island, to the north-west of Madagascar; the Mascarenes (Reunion, Rodriquez, and Mauritius); and the Galapagos group, off the Pacific coast of South America. From the second group they have, however, been exterminated, and have been greatly reduced in numbers in the others, where they formerly lived in thousands.

Fig. 3.—GRECIAN TORTOISE (*Testudo græca*).

and formed a valuable food supply for the crews of ships. Some of these tortoises are remarkable for the extreme tenuity and relatively small size of the shell, which is but little stouter than leather, and can be easily pierced with a knife. This is very notably the case with *T. ephippium* of the Galapagos Islands, fine examples of which are now preserved in the British Museum. Some of these monsters measure over four feet along the curve of the shell, and have been known to yield close upon four hundred pounds weight of excellent meat. In the Galapagos Islands these tortoises make regular tracks to their drinking-places in the hills, and feed chiefly upon the succulent stems of the cacti, so common there. During the breeding season, the males, according to Darwin's well-known account, utter a loud roar, audible at a great distance. The ordinary tortoises of South Europe, Algeria, and Egypt, frequent dry sandy localities, where they have full opportunity of basking in the rays of the sun. In Europe, at least, they hibernate during the cold season, by burying themselves deep in the earth, reappearing with the returning warmth of spring. In addition to their normal vegetable food, these tortoises are not averse to an occasional snail or insect. Four peculiar tortoises from South Africa are referred to the distinct genus *Homopus*, on account of the fore part of the palate lacking the distinct median ridge, characteristic of all the species of *Testudo*. Moreover, the neural bones of the carapace are never alternately quadrangular and octagonal, but always irregularly hexagonal, with the shorter of the two lateral surfaces at the hind end. The typical *H. areolatus* has but four toes on the front foot, whereas in another species there are five.

The three species of hinged tortoises from Tropical Africa, forming the genus *Cinixys*, are easily and broadly distinguished by the presence of a ligamentous hinge across the hinder third of the carapace, by means of which the posterior opening of the shell can be completely closed. These tortoises are small reptiles, not exceeding some nine inches in length; and in habits the majority are amphibious, thus connecting the land tortoises with the terrapins. Madagascar is the sole habitat of a single peculiar tortoise (*Pyxis arachnoides*), distinguished by having the front part of the plastron articulated to the remainder by a transverse hinge. In this species, therefore, the front aperture of the shell is capable of being closed at the will of its owner.

Coming to the terrapins, we find that these are distinguished from the foregoing by the toes being either webbed, or having rudiments of such webbing, as well as by the presence of three (instead of two) joints in the middle toe of both the front and hind-foot. In the fore-foot the metacarpal bones are also much longer and more slender than in the preceding group. Foremost among these come three small Oriental genera, respectively known as *Geoëmyda*, *Nicoria*, and *Cyclemys*, all of which differ from those which follow by having the shorter lateral surface of the hexagonal neural bones of the carapace placed at the hinder end—a feature in which they agree with *Homopus*. Of these forms it will suffice to mention that the species of *Cyclemys* differ from the others in having the hinder half of the plastron movably articulated by means of a transverse bony hinge, in consequence of which they are commonly spoken of as hinged terrapins.

In all the other members of the family, the hexagonal neural bones of the carapace have the shorter of the two lateral surfaces on each side situated in front. It is unfortunate that this important characteristic is hidden from view by the superficial bony shields—unless in the rare instances where they are sufficiently transparent to allow of the underlying bones being seen through them—but so it is, and the student must make the best of it. If we were making animals ourselves, we should doubtless give the members of each genus a characteristic mark by which they could be recognised at a glance. Foremost in this group are the true box-tortoises (*Cistudo*) of North America, which agree with *Cyclemys* in having a transverse hinge across the plastron, the posterior moiety of which consequently forms a movable flap, capable of closing the hinder aperture of the shell. As special features of the genus, may be noted the hooked beak, the smooth skin covering the top of the head, the imperfect webbing of the toes, and the extreme shortness of the tail. These tortoises have a vaulted carapace, and, as is usual in such cases, are mainly terrestrial in their habits. From this genus the depressed form of the shell serves at once to distinguish the European pond-tortoise (*Emys orbicularis*), which, with an allied North American species, alone represents the genus. There is no hook to the beak; the upper and lower shells are united only by ligament, and the hinder part of the plastron is movably articulated by a transverse hinge. The European species not only inhabits South and South-Eastern Europe, but ranges into Persia and Algeria. Its shell, which grows to a little over seven inches in length, is prettily speckled on the upper surface with golden flecks on a blackish ground. The pond-tortoise is a carnivorous species, living upon small fish, worms, and insects, and inhabiting both running and stagnant waters, in which it swims and dives with great facility. It is an interesting and easily-kept denizen of an aquarium.

Fig 4.—POND-TORTOISE (*Emys orbicularis*).

Of the remaining genera of the *Testudinidæ*, a very brief mention must suffice. The terrapins of the genus *Clemmys* form a somewhat important group, ranging over South Europe, North-Western Africa, and North America. In common with the four following genera, *Clemmys* is characterised by the absence of a median ridge on the front portion of the palate of the skull; and all the species are carnivorous in their habits. As in all the remaining genera of the family, the upper and lower shells are firmly united by suture, and there is no bony hinge in the plastron. The two species of the Oriental genus *Bellia* may be distinguished by the stronger vertical buttresses connecting the plastron with the carapace, and the small horny shields covering the hinder part of the head; the toes being completely webbed. The more or less decided balloon-shape of the anterior vertebral shields of the carapace is likewise a noteworthy feature of these small terrapins. Another allied Oriental genus is typified by *Damonia hamiltoni*, the shell of which is conspicuous for its yellow markings on a black ground, and the three longitudinal ridges traversing the carapace. The North American terrapins of the genus *Malacoclemmys* are also nearly allied, and have the whole head covered with a smooth skin. One species frequents brackish water; and it is members of this genus that afford the dish so well known to epicures in the United States under the name of terrapin.

The other members of the family are mainly vegetarian in their diet, and differ from the foregoing by the front portion of the broad palate bearing one or two longitudinal ridges. To this group belong the exclusively American terrapins of the genus *Chrysemys*, some of which range as far south as Brazil and Uruguay. Burma and Bengal are the respective habitats of two allied terrapins constituting the genus *Morenia*, distinguished by certain features in the conformation of the skull; while the single representative of *Ocadia* is Chinese. The four other genera, all the members of which are known as batagurs, are confined to the Oriental countries, and include the largest fresh-water members of the whole family, the shell of one of them measuring as much as twenty inches in length. The batagurs, which are divided into the genera *Cachuga*, *Callagur*, *Batagur*, and *Hardella*, are specially characterised by the excessive development of the vertical bony buttresses connecting the carapace with the plastron, which project as walls into the interior of the shell in such a manner as to divide it into three imperfect compartments. The different genera are chiefly distinguished by the contour of the vertebral horny shields of the carapace; the fourth shield in one genus narrowing anteriorly almost to a point in a manner quite unknown in any other members of the order. The batagurs have shells of extraordinary strength and solidity; and the larger species are almost exclusively aquatic, and very numerous in the rivers of India and Burma. In spite of their herbivorous habits, they are said to be dangerous to bathers; and it is certain that a snap from their powerful jaws would cause a very serious wound.

Family *Platysternidæ*.

A strange-looking aquatic tortoise (*Platysternum megalocephalum*) from the countries lying between Burma and the south of China demands special notice as being the sole representative of a family. Externally, its most conspicuous features are the enormous size of the head; the hooked beak; the extreme flatness of the shell, which looks as if it had no room to contain the internal organs of the creature; the great length of the scaly tapering tail; and the rather long and powerfully-clawed legs. The skull differs from that of the *Testudinidæ* in having the whole of its hinder portion covered over by a bony roof; and most of the vertebræ of the long tail articulate with one another by means of a cup behind and a ball in front, instead of in the reverse manner. These afford ample grounds for referring this tortoise to a family apart. The whole length of the shell is only about six inches. Of the habits of this remarkable reptile naturalists are ignorant.

Mud-Terrapins.—Family *Cinosternidæ*.

The mud-terrapins (*Cinosternum*), of which there are eleven species, all inhabitants of America to the north of the Equator, alone represent a third family, easily distinguished from all other Chelonia by the absence of the unpaired entoplastral bone of the plastron, thus reducing the number of elements in the lower shell from nine to eight. The shell is depressed, with its two portions firmly united; and the plastron has its two extremities movable, and its gular shields either united or absent. The tail is very short; and the webbed toes, save the fifth hind one, terminate in strong claws. In habits, these terrapins resemble ordinary fresh-water species.

Family *Dermatemydidæ*.

Three small genera of terrapins from Central America, respectively named *Dermatemys*, *Staurotypus*, and *Claudius*, form the fourth family. Together with the *Cinosternidæ*, these differ from the *Testudinidæ* in that each of the two lateral angles of the nuchal bone of the carapace gives off a long bony stay projecting backwards to underlie the marginal bones. The skull is of ordinary form; the plastron has the usual nine bones, and the tail is short. As in the *Cinosternidæ* and *Chelydriaæ*, an additional series of small horny shields is interposed between the marginal shields and those of the plastron. Whereas in the single representative of the genus first mentioned, the plastron is fully developed, in the other two genera it is cruciform, and connected on each side with the upper shell only by a very narrow bridge.

Snappers and Alligator-Terrapins.—Family *Chelydridæ*.

Far better known than the members of the last family are the large Chelonians commonly termed snappers and alligator-terrapins, all of which are now confined to the northern portion of America, one species ranging as far south as Guatemala and Ecuador. In their relatively large head and long scaly tails, these terrapins resemble the *Platysternidæ*. They differ, however, in the presence of long, rib-like processes, running backwards from the nuchal bone of the carapace to underlie the marginals, and likewise by the imperfect bony roof to the lateral regions of the hinder part of the skull. The vertebræ of the tail have, on the other hand, the same structure, the articular cup being on the hinder surface in the majority. The small, cross-shaped plastron is but very loosely attached to the upper shell; and it is not till a late period of life that the shell becomes fully ossified, large spaces long remaining in both the upper and lower halves. The long tail bears on its upper surface a crest, and all the toes, except the fifth hind one, are clawed. The front border of the carapace is notched in order to receive the ponderous head, which cannot be withdrawn into the shell. The largest member of the family is Temminck's snapper (*Macroclemmys temmincki*), which is generally to be seen in the reptile-house at the "Zoo," and ranges from Missouri to Florida. The very large head has the eyes lateral; and the tail is not so long as in the members of the second genus. In some specimens the shell measures twenty-four inches in length. The two species of alligator-terrapins, or snapping turtles (*Chelydra*), have the eyes directed upwards, and the tail exceeding the shell in length. The members of both genera are common denizens of the fresh-waters of the United States, where they are found in rivers, swamps, and ponds. In habits they are very active, rushing on their prey with extraordinary speed, and feeding entirely on animal food. The extraordinary power of their jaws (of which the upper one is hooked) renders their bites very severe; and bathers should always keep a good look-out to see that none of these reptiles are in their vicinity before venturing on a plunge. In captivity they are dull and sluggish creatures. Several females lay their eggs in the same spot.

Fig 5.—TEMMINCK'S SNAPPER (*Macroclemmys temmincki*).

The Turtles.—Family *Chelonidæ*.

The excellence of the flesh of one species, and the commercial value of the tortoise-shell yielded by a second, render the turtles a family of special importance and interest. From all the families yet mentioned the turtles are easily distinguished by the modification of their limbs into oar-like flippers, adapted solely for swimming, and also by the heart-shaped form of the shell. There are never more than two claws on each limb, the head cannot be completely retracted within the shell, and the tail is very short. The whole of the hinder region of the skull is covered by a bony roof. There is no bony union between the upper and lower shells; and in the carapace numerous unossified spaces remain for a long time, if not permanently. Except during the breeding season, when the females resort to shelving sandy shores for the purpose of laying their eggs, turtles are inhabitants of the open sea, where in calm weather they may at times be seen floating placidly on the surface. When on shore, they shuffle along in an awkward manner; and if turned on their backs are utterly helpless. Their eggs, unlike those of other Chelonians, have soft shells. Like most denizens of the open sea, the three common species of turtles have an almost world-wide distribution. Of these, the green turtle (*Chelone mydas*) is the one whose flesh is used for culinary purposes. Nearly allied is the hawksbill (*C. imbricata*), distinguished at all ages by the strongly hooked beak, and also by the circumstance that, for a considerable portion of life the horny shields of the shell overlap one another like the slates in a roof, instead of meeting at the edges. It is this species alone that yields the tortoise-shell of commerce. More distinct is the loggerhead (*Thalassochelys caretta*), in which the head is of proportionately greater size, and there are five, instead of four, pairs of horny costal shields on the carapace. The loggerhead is the largest of the three. It is somewhat remarkable that whereas the green turtle is an herbivorous animal, feeding chiefly upon sea-weeds, both the hawksbill and the loggerhead are carnivorous; the food of the latter consisting largely of cuttle-fish.

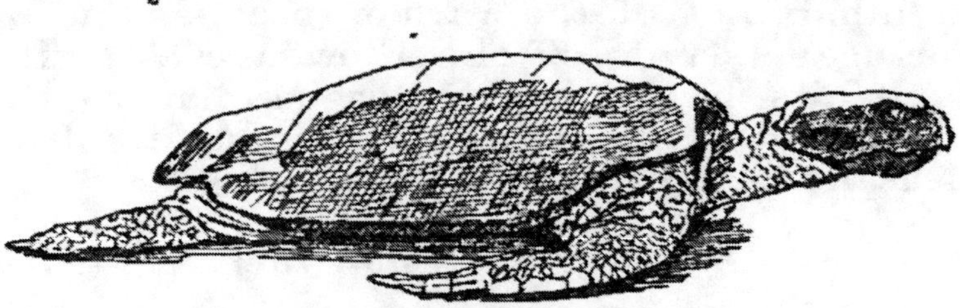

FIG. 6.—LOGGERHEAD TORTOISE (*Thalassochelys caretta*).

During the egging-season turtles come ashore in immense numbers, the Seychelles and Bahamas being two of their favourite resorts. While the females are busily engaged in the occupation of laying, and of covering up their eggs in the sand, the males generally pass the time by quarrelling among themselves. Moonlight nights are those usually chosen for resorting to the coast; and these, of course, are most favourable to the turtle-catchers, whose object is to intercept their victims before they can scuttle back to the sea. Not only are the eggs largely used as an article of food, but they also yield an excellent oil. Tortoise-shell, when heated, has the peculiar property of welding like iron, so that plates of almost any size can be obtained by uniting a number of shields. It can also be pressed into moulds, and beautiful amber-like necklaces and other ornamental articles are manufactured from the scraps and fragments.

Leathery Turtle.—Family *Dermochelyidæ*.

Although the huge leathery turtle (*Dermochelys coriacea*)—the giant of the tribe—is a marine species with flippers for limbs, yet it differs so markedly from the other turtles in the structure of its shell and the conformation of its skull, that it unquestionably represents a separate family by itself. Indeed, as regards its shell, not only does the luth (as this species is sometimes called) differ from other turtles, but likewise from all other living Chelonia. In place of the carapace being formed by a series of large regularly-shaped bones, some of which are firmly attached to the backbone and ribs, and all invested with separate horny shields, in the leathery turtle it is composed of a vast number of minute irregular ossifications, fitting together like mosaic, and having no sort of connection with the internal skeleton, while its investiture takes the form of a continuous leathery skin. Seven bold longitudinal ridges traverse the upper shell from end to end, and there are five similar ridges on the under shell, which is less fully developed. Claws are totally wanting on the flippers, of which the front pair greatly exceed the hinder in length. Although the structural peculiarities of the skull are of the highest importance in determining the systematic position of the creature, they need not be further alluded to in this place. In length this turtle frequently exceeds six feet. The leathery turtle, which is now rapidly diminishing in numbers, is an inhabitant of the warmer oceans, one of its favourite haunts being the Tortugas Islands off the Florida coast. It is known to be carnivorous, and its habits are probably very similar to those of the true turtles. Commercially this species is of no value, its flesh having a strong and highly unpleasant taste of musk.

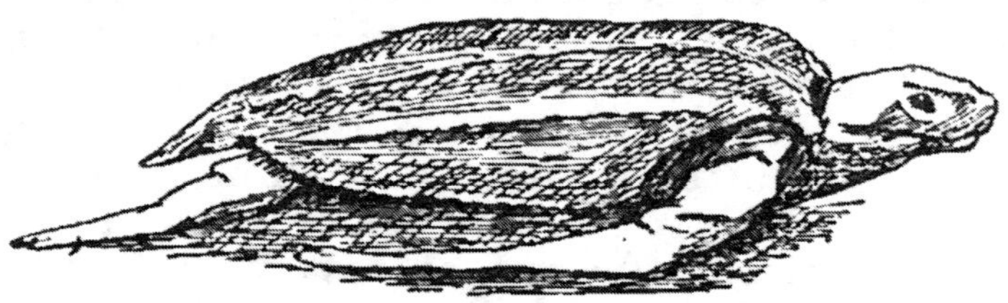

Fig. 7.—LEATHERY TURTLE. (*Dermochelys coriacea*).

Sub-Order II.—Pleurodira.

The members of the second sub-ordinal group of the Chelonia are best distinguished externally by the mode in which they withdraw the head and neck into the shell. In place of the **S**-like movement characterising the preceding group, these tortoises always bend the neck to one side in a horizontal plane, so that instead of occupying the middle of the front aperture of the shell, the head when retracted lies more or less on one or the other side, according to the relative length of the neck. This very obvious characteristic is, however, by no means the sole claim of the group to distinction. If the dried skull be examined, it will be found that the bony ring surrounding the aperture of the ear is entire instead of being notched behind, and also that the lower surface of the quadrate-bone is hollowed in order to receive a knob on the articulating portion of the lower jaw. In all cases the upper and lower shells are fully ossified and closely joined; and both have a firm union with the bones of the pelvis. When horny shields are present at all, there is invariably an intergular between or behind the two gulars. The Pleurodira are now restricted to the Southern Hemisphere, and are the only tortoises inhabiting Australia and Papua.

Family *Chelyidæ*.

The first family of the sub-order is represented by eight generic types, all of which are restricted to South America and Australasia. As distinctive features of the family, may be mentioned the presence of only nine bones in the lower shell, the incapacity of completely retracting the neck within the margin of the carapace, and the absence of the so-called temporal bony arch on the sides of the skull. The typical member of the family is the grotesque matamata (*Chelys fimbriata*) of the Guianas and North Brazil, a species easily recognised by its flattened triangular head, the peculiar tuft-like filaments on the sides of the broad and long neck, and the great bosses formed by the shields of the carapace, which is serrated on its margins. In length the shell of the matamata reaches fifteen inches. In habits this tortoise is a fresh-water and chiefly carnivorous animal; and it is probable that the tufts on the neck are for the purpose of attracting its prey within easy reach of its jaws. In addition to its other characteristics, the matamata has a proboscis to the snout, but this is wanting in the other South American long-necked members of the family, which form the genus *Hydromedusa*. These tortoises also differ in the comparative smoothness of the shell, and in having only four claws to each foot. The remaining three South American genera, namely *Hydraspis*, *Rhinemys*, and *Platemys*, have the neck proportionately shorter. Three generic types of the family are met with in Australia and Papua, one of which (*Chelodina*) has the neck very long, while in the other two (*Elseya* and *Emydura*) it is relatively shorter.

Fig. 8.—MATAMATA (*Chelys fimbriata*).

Family *Pelomedusidæ*.

The largest member of the whole sub-order is the great fresh-water tortoise of the Amazons (*Podocnemis expansa*), whose shell often measures two-and-a-half feet in length. Together with its allies, this species belongs to the second family of the sub-order, characterised by the presence of a pair of mesoplastrals between the hyo- and hypoplastral bones, the total number of elements in the lower shell thus being brought up to eleven. The neck can be fully withdrawn into the shell, and the skull has a lateral bony arch. The genus *Podocnemis* affords a remarkable example of discontinuous geographical distribution, six of the species being inhabitants of South America, whereas the seventh is found in the distant island of Madagascar. In this genus the hinder part of the skull is completely roofed over by bone; but this is not the case in the other two genera of the family. Of these, *Pelomedusa*, which has only a single species, inhabiting both Madagascar and Africa, resembles *Podocnemis* in that the two mesoplastral bones only show themselves on the sides of the lower shell, and are thus widely separate in the middle line. On the other hand, in *Sternothærus* the same two bones are as fully developed as the other elements of the plastron, in the median line of which they come into contact with one another. The whole of the species of this genus are African, but one extends its range into Madagascar. The great Amazonian species of *Podocnemis* is of considerable value to the natives of some parts of tropical America, on account of its eggs, which are collected in vast quantities, mainly for the sake of the oil they yield.

Fig. 9.—AMAZONIAN FRESH-WATER TORTOISE (*Podocnemis expansa*).

Family *Carettochelyidæ.*

A fresh-water turtle from one of the Papuan rivers described under the name of *Carettochelys*, resembles the true marine turtles in having the limbs modified into flippers, although displaying all the other characteristics of the present sub-order. Only two claws occur on each flipper; and the shell is remarkable for having a continuous leathery skin in place of the usual horny shields. There are certain other structural features in this little-known and rare Chelonian by which it differs from its allies.

Sub-Order III.—Trionychidæ.

The third and last sub-order of the Chelonia includes only the soft tortoises, represented by six genera, all of which are comprised in the single family *Trionychidæ*. All these tortoises have very long necks, which can be completely withdrawn within the margins of the shell by an S-like flexure in the same manner as in the Cryptodira. The jaws are hidden by the fleshy lips, and the muzzle is prolonged into a short proboscis. The feet are fully webbed, and only the three outermost toes are furnished with claws—a peculiarity from which the scientific name of the group is derived. None of these features are, however, of sufficient importance to justify the separation of the group as a distinct sub-order; but the shell is very peculiar. In place of the usual horny shields, both the upper and lower shells are invested with a thin, continuous leathery skin, through which can be seen and felt the raised sculpture ornamenting the surface of the underlying bones. Marginal bones, if developed at all, are restricted to the hinder border of the upper shell, and elsewhere the margins of this shell are continued into a wide, soft expansion of skin, so that the shell itself only occupies the region of the back. There is no attachment between the upper and lower shells, and the latter is only very imperfectly ossified. A greenish olive ground-colour, upon which are yellow or orange spots, is the general type of coloration, the spots being replaced by streaks on the under surface of the head. At the present day the soft tortoises are restricted to the fresh waters of the warmer regions of North America, Asia, and Africa. In habits, these very peculiar Chelonians are purely aquatic, and although the majority are confined to fresh waters, some frequent estuaries. They are all carnivorous; and, being extremely bold and fierce, are highly dangerous to bathers. All are mainly nocturnal, and when basking on a mud-bank, or on shore, for the purpose of laying their eggs, extend their long necks after any sudden surprise in a peculiarly cautious and stealthy manner. The spherical eggs are buried in the mud by the female as soon as laid.

The typical, and at the same time the widest spread, genus is *Trionyx*, which has a geographical distribution as extensive as that of the family, and is the only one found in America, fifteen distinct species being known. In this genus, the sculpture on the surface of the shell usually takes the form of irregular wavy ridges; while in the lower shell the hyoplastral and hypoplastral bones of each side are separate. A distinctive feature is the want of a fold of skin on the hinder part of the plastron, which in some of the allied forms conceals the hind-leg. The head is relatively short and broad, with the eyes situated far back. The shell and leathery disc of some of the members of this genus not unfrequently measure as much as a couple of feet in length, and the species are arranged in groups according to the number of bones entering into the composition of the upper shell, and the absence or presence of a longitudinal ridge on the palatal surface of the fore part of the lower jaw. Nearly allied to *Trionyx* are the general *Pelochelys* and *Chitra*, each represented by a single species from the Oriental countries. In the former—which extends from India to the Malayan Islands—the eyes have a more forward position than in the type genus, this feature being still more marked in the gigantic Indian *Chitra*, where they are situated close up to the snout, the whole skull being very long and narrow. The foregoing genera constitute a sub-family by themselves; and a second group of equivalent value is formed by the other three genera. The two essential characteristics of the second group are to be found in the presence of a skinny flap beneath the under shell—behind which the hind-foot can be withdrawn—and the complete union of the hyoplastral and hypoplastral elements of the lower shell. Externally the shell is distinguished by the pustular form of the sculpture. Of the three types of the sub-family, the Indian *Emyda* is specially distinguished by possessing a series of marginal bones round the hinder portion of the carapace. There are but three species, and in the largest of these the shell does not grow to more than about ten inches in length. Of the two African genera, the one known as *Cycloderma* has a complete series of neural bones running down the middle of the carapace; whereas, in the nearly related *Cyclanorbis* the series is incomplete, so that some of the costal bones of opposite sides come into contact with one another in the middle line.

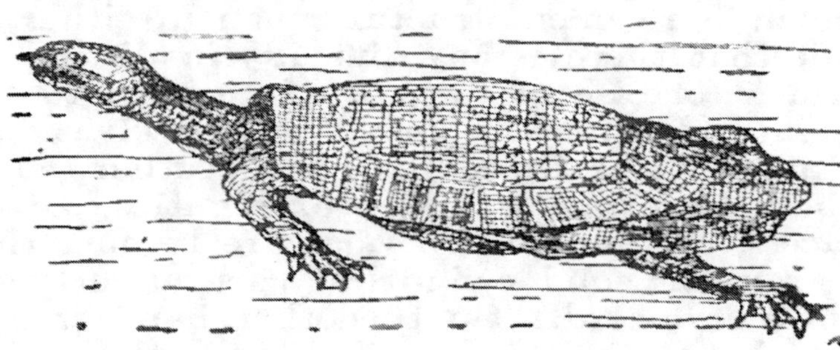

Fig. 10.—A Soft Tortoise.

It may be added that in the absence of any connection between the bones of the pelvis and the lower shell, as well as in the mode of articulation between the upper and lower jaws, and the notch in the ring round the aperture of the ear, the soft-tortoises resemble the Cryptodira. In certain forms and certain structural features of the skull they are, however, more like the Pleurodira.

ORDER III.—SQUAMATA.

Scaled Reptiles.

By far the largest of all the four orders of existing reptiles is the one including the lizards, chamæleons, and snakes; each of those groups forming a sub-order by itself. And here it may be remarked how unimportant is the external form of reptiles in regard to their zoological affinities. The New Zealand tuatera, for instance, which externally is like a lizard, has nothing whatever to do with the Squamata, but forms an order by itself; whereas ordinary lizards and serpents are comprised in one and the same order. Moreover, the blindworms, which in external appearance are like snakes, form a portion of the sub-order typified by the lizards. A general, but by no means invariable, feature of the Squamata is the covering of overlapping horny scales on the head, body, and limbs; but more important and constant structural peculiarities are to be found in the internal skeleton. Of the highest import is the fact that in all the members of the present order the quadrate-bone is movably jointed to the other elements of the skull, from which its lower extremity projects. Secondly, there is no bony rod running forwards from the outer side of the lower extremity of this bone to join the upper jaw; such a rod being always developed in the Crocodilia. The palate, again, has a much more open structure than in either the Crocodilia or the Chelonia;—not that there is any difficulty in distinguishing between a lizard or a snake and a tortoise or turtle. If we turn to the backbone, equally well-marked points of difference present themselves between the Squamata on the one hand and the Crocodilia on the other. In the former group the ribs of the chest have single upper extremities, or heads, which are articulated to facets, on the sides of what are termed the bodies of the vertebræ—that is to say, the solid cylindrical part underlying the arch through which passes the nerve-cord. On the other hand, in the Crocodilia the majority of the ribs have two heads; and those in the region of the back are articulated to a long horizontal transverse projection arising from the sides of the arch of each vertebræ. In the majority of the order the bodies of the vertebræ are movably united by means of ball-and-socket joints: the ball being situated behind and the socket in front. Neither in lizards or in serpents are the teeth ever implanted in the jaws by means of distinct sockets. In all cases the teeth are firmly welded to the substance of the jaw itself; but whereas in some forms they are affixed to the summits of the jaws, in others they are attached to the sides of the same. To the former mode of attachment, the name *acrodont* is applied, whereas the latter is termed *pleurodont*. Although the foregoing features are amply sufficient to distinguish the Squamata from the Crocodilia, it may be added that when the shoulder-girdle is fully developed, there is a breast-bone, a pair of collar-bones, and an unpaired median element, with the form of the letter T, known as the interclavide.

Sub-Order I.—Lacertilia.

Lizards.

Since it has been already mentioned that the blind-worm belongs to the present sub-order, it will be obvious that the presence of limbs will not suffice to distinguish between the lizards and the serpents, although the majority of the former are four-limbed creatures, and none of the latter have four fully developed and functional legs. In the limbless snake-like lizards the tongue cannot, however, be withdrawn into a basal sheath, as it is in serpents; and whereas the former are generally furnished with eyelids or external openings to the ears, both these are invariably wanting in the latter. The examination of the skeleton will also show that whereas in all lizards the two branches of the lower jaw are joined by bone where they meet at the chin, in the serpents such union is ligamentous; and it should further be observed that the limbless lizards always retain vestiges of the shoulder-girdle. As important points of distinction between the lizards and the chamæleons, it must be mentioned that such of the former as retain limbs have well-developed collar-bones, and that the tongue is flattened and not dilatable.

At the present day somewhere about seventeen hundred different species of lizards are known; these forming no less than twenty distinct families, mostly including a large number of genera. Hence it will be obvious that only some of the leading types can be even alluded to in this volume. Although lizards are found everywhere save the polar regions, the group attains its maximum development—both as regards bodily size and the number of forms—in the tropical and sub-tropical zones. They inhabit both dry and moist situations, although the majority prefer the former. Most are terrestrial, but many are arboreal, while a few are aquatic, one species at least venturing into the open sea. The so-called flying lizard can take long leaps in the air by the aid of a parachute-like expansion of skin supported by the elongated ribs ; and an Australian species is stated to walk on its hind-limbs like a bird. Sucker-like pads enable the geckos to climb vertical panes of glass like flies ; and some of the arboreal species resemble the American monkeys in having the tail endowed with prehensile power. Whereas the majority lay eggs, a few bring forth their young into the world alive. In spite of the popular dread attaching to the blind-worm, no lizards, with the exception of the few species belonging to the American family *Helodermatidæ*, are poisonous. A few members of the order are vegetable-feeders, but the great majority live on animal food, especially insects and other invertebrates. The facility with which many lizards part with a considerable portion of the tail when handled is a familiar fact ; but it is perhaps less well-known that the missing fragment can be speedily reproduced. As regards geographical distribution, the Lacertilia are widely different from the Chelonia. Thus, whereas Australasian lizards are unlike those of South America, between the lizards of Australia and those of India there is a most marked resemblance, while the Indian forms differ decidedly from those of Africa.

Geckos.—Family *Geckonidæ*.

The peculiar cry of some of its Asiatic members has given rise to the name by which the first family of the Lacertilia is both familiarly and scientifically known. From nearly all other members of the sub-order geckos are distinguished by the fact that the bodies of their vertebræ are cupped at both ends, instead of articulating by a ball and socket, while most of them have sucking discs on the extremities of the five-toed feet. In form they are depressed, and in coloration dull, and whereas the head is covered with bony granules or small scales, the body is generally invested with granules above and with overlapping scales beneath. In no case are the scales underlain by plates of bone. There are no movable eyelids, and the opening of the ear, and generally also the pupil of the eye, is in the form of a vertical slit. The tongue, which is short and devoid of a sheath at the base, may be either smooth or covered with shaggy prominences. The small teeth are attached to the jaws in the pleurodont manner, and in many cases the tail is more or less distinctly prehensile, although in some instances it is rudimental. Most numerous in the Oriental and Australasian countries, the geckos range over all the warmer parts of the world, and present a considerable number of generic modifications. Among these the genus *Ptyodactylus* is familiar to travellers in Palestine in the form of the little lobe-footed gecko. In common with its immediate kindred, this species has the toes expanded into circular lobes, upon the under surface of which are two rows of plates. *Hemidactylus*, as represented by the little Turkish gecko, is an allied genus, ranging over all the warmer parts of the world except Australasia, with dilated toes terminating in compressed claws, of which the tips are free. Very aberrant is the single and considerably larger species of the Oriental genus *Ptychozoum*, in which the skin of the flanks forms a large expansion, while there is also a fringe of lobes running along the two sides of the tail, and likewise on the hinder borders of the legs. The toes also are completely connected by web-like dilations, the first in each limb being clawless. A peculiarly marked type of coloration further aids in the recognition of this species. The countries bordering the Mediterranean are the chief habitat of another genus known as *Tarentola*, of which the common wall-gecko is the most familiar representative, all the species having the toes moderately dilated, but only the third and fourth clawed. The genus ranges as far south as the west coast of Africa, and is likewise represented by a species from the West Indian Islands. Whereas a large number of geckos frequent trees, walls, or buildings, some are found in open sandy districts, and these latter naturally have feet of ordinary type, as adhesive discs would be useless. In countries where these lizards abound, almost every house is tenanted by at least a pair. When undisturbed, such denizens will scamper over the walls with the greatest speed in search of flies, uttering now and then their shrill cries. It is, doubtless, owing to these vocal powers that geckos are so dreaded by the uneducated in all parts of the world—an analagous instance of the inspiration of a similar dread being afforded by the death-watch insects.

Fig. 11.—Fringed Gecko (*Ptychozoum*).

A second family of geckos (*Eublepharidæ*), of which there are only three genera, differ from the foregoing in being furnished with eyelids, and also in having cup-and-ball joints to the backbone.

The third family of the sub-order includes the three species of the Malagasy genus *Uroplates*, and is termed the *Uroplatidæ*. While resembling the true geckos in the doubly-cupped vertebræ, as well as in many other structural features, these lizards agree with the following nine families in that the inner ends of the collar-bones lack the loop-shaped expansion characteristic of the geckos.

Scale-footed Lizards.—Family *Pygopodidæ*.

The next family is that of the scale-footed lizards, or *Pygopodidæ*, which are confined to Australia, and appear to present a considerable resemblance to the *Geckonidæ*, with which they agree in the general conformation of the skull. All these lizards have assumed a snake-like form of body, with the complete loss of all external vestiges of the front limbs, although the hinder pair are represented by two large, flap-like scaly expansions, without any sign of division into toes externally. The commonest species grows to a length of about twenty inches, and is coppery-grey in colour, sometimes having three or five rows of blackish spots or streaks.

A very large proportion of the lizards of the eastern and southern countries of the Eastern Hemisphere pertain to the very extensive and important family

Family *Agamidæ*.

of the *Agamidæ*,—a family which includes at least a couple of hundred species ranged under thirty distinct generic groups. These lizards have a tongue of the same type as that of the geckos, no dilation of the inner extremities of the collar-bones, and no bony plates beneath the overlapping scales with which the head and body are invested ; but they differ from all the foregoing groups in their acrodont dentition. The eyes, which are relatively smaller than in the geckos, are furnished with movable eyelids, and have circular pupils. Small scales cover the crown of the head, and the scales on the lower aspect of the body are likewise not enlarged. Many of the species develop large ornamental crests or pouches, either in both sexes or in the male alone. These lizards generally have a long tail, which is not brittle ; and they always possess well-developed fore-limbs, which, with one exception, are five-toed. As a rule, the teeth are unequal in size, those at the corners of the jaws being developed into tusks. As in other lizards, the arboreal species have compressed bodies, while in those that dwell on the ground the trunk is more or less depressed. Although, as already said, agamoids are widely spread in the Old World, they attain their maximum development in the Oriental countries, only three generic groups inhabiting Africa. Perhaps the most remarkable members of the family are the flying lizards (*Draco*) of the Oriental countries, in which the hinder ribs are expanded to support a kind of parachute-like expansion of the skin of the flanks. These folds can be closed in a fan-like manner, and there are other expansions on the throat. The entire body is much depressed, and the tail is very long and tapering. The coloration of the upper surface of the body is metallic, with dark spots and bands, the parachute of the common species being bright orange with black markings. These lizards live high up on the trees, and pass from bough to bough by taking flying leaps with the support of the parachute. At times the expansions of skin on the throat are erected. The Oriental region is likewise the home of the beautiful tree-lizards of the genus *Calotes*, which are also thoroughly arboreal, although unable to take flying leaps. They have the drum of the ear visible externally, a crest running down the neck and back, the large keeled scales on the back of equal size, a long, whip-like tail, and no distinct fold of skin on the throat. Many of them have the power of rapidly changing their brilliant colours, and some measure as much as sixteen inches in length. More curious are the arboreal horned lizards (*Ceratophora*) of Ceylon, easily recognised by the presence of a horn on the nose of the males, and sometimes also in the females. There is no crest on the neck, and the drum of the ear is concealed. Next on our list are the numerous species of the typical genus *Agama*, which range from South-Eastern Europe over South-Eastern Asia, although absent from the greater part of India and Ceylon. These lizards are terrestrial in their habits, and accordingly differ from all the foregoing, with the exception of the flying-lizard, in having the body markedly depressed. They have the drum of the ear exposed, large thickened scales in front of the vent in the males, a fold of skin across the throat, and a pit on each side of the same part, while if the back is furnished with a crest, this is of small size. In parts of Asia these lizards are some of the most common representatives of their tribe, and may be seen in hundreds basking in the sun.

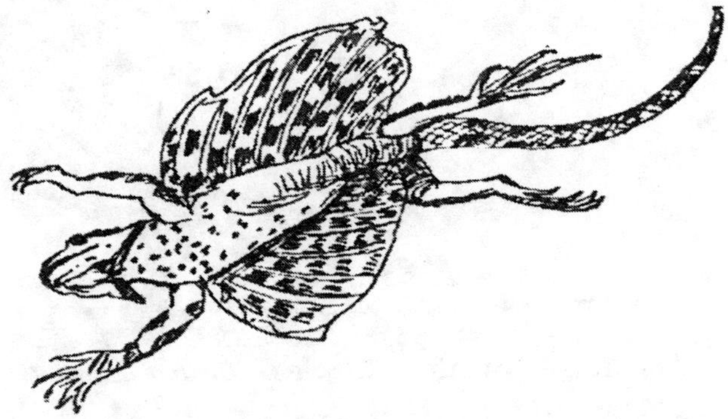

Fig. 12.—Flying Lizard (*Draco volans*).

Many of the genera of lizards are far from easy to distinguish from one another, but there is no difficulty in recognising the extraordinary Australian frilled lizard (*Chlamydosaurus kingi*), which has the throat surrounded by a large frill-like expansion of skin extending on to the sides of the neck.

This long-tailed lizard, which grows to a length of over thirty inches, is an inhabitant of open sandy deserts, and is peculiar in that it habitually walks on its hind-legs alone. It does not, however, hop, but walks with a bold, swinging gait. Probably the frill is given to the creature for the purpose of terrifying its enemies, as when alarmed this lizard sits up on its hind-limbs, expands the frill to its fullest extent, and shows its teeth; its appearance is then distinctly alarming, although the creature is perfectly harmless to large animals. From the preceding forms this lizard and a number of allied genera differ by having pores on the under surface of the body near the vent, or on the thighs, or in both of these situations. A closely related species is the sail-tailed lizard (*Lophurus amboynensis*) of the Malayan and Philippine Islands, in which the upper surface of the basal portion of the tail carries a huge vertical crest, while the nape and back are ornamented with a ridge of enlarged scales. This lizard, which has a compressed body, and an olive-green ground-colour with irregular black markings, is an inhabitant of wooded districts near water, and if frightened, immediately plunges into the latter element. It is a vegetable feeder, and its flesh is stated to be tender and well-flavoured.

Fig. 13.—FRILLED LIZARD (*Chlamydosaurus kingi*).

The tail is an important part in distinguishing many of the lizards of this family, and its characters form an easy means of recognising the thorny-tailed lizards of Northern Africa and South-Western Asia, which constitute the genus *Uromastix*. Whereas the body is smoothly scaled, the whole of the rather short tail is invested with a series of rings of large scales each armed with a thorn-like spine. They have very short and rounded heads; the drum of the ear is visible, and there are pores in front of the vent as well as on the thighs. A feature in which these lizards differ from all those noticed above is the large size of the front teeth, which in the adult are separated from those on each side of the jaws by a gap. Thorny lizards are abundant in the sandy plains of Arabia, Persia, and the Punjab, where they live in burrows. Probably the thorny tail is a means of defence, as if one of these lizards can but get its head and body well within its retreat, it seems to be pretty safe from attack. The writer once tried to drag one from its hole by seizing hold of the projecting tail, but the appendage gave way, leaving the creature secure from further harm. Their food is entirely of a vegetable nature; and the Arabs—by whom these lizards are frequently kept in captivity—are very partial to their flesh. The last member of the family that can be noticed is the moloch lizard (*Moloch horridus*) of South and West Australia, a creature which looks more like some monster in a pantomime

Fig. 14.—THORNY-TAILED LIZARD (*Uromastix*).

than a living animal. Measuring about eight inches in length, and having a depressed toad-like body and rather short tail, the moloch is covered all over above with large conical spines, which attain their greatest development immediately over the eyes and on the forepart of the back. It frequents sandy districts, is slow in its movements, and may be frequently seen abroad in the full sunlight. That its spiny armour renders it perfectly safe from all ordinary attacks, may be considered perfectly certain; and it is clear that the creature's motto is defence and not defiance, as it is perfectly harmless. It has the power of slowly changing its colour to a certain extent in accordance with its surroundings; and its chief nutriment is formed by ants, although it will also eat vegetable substances. Thorny devil or spiny lizard is the name given to this reptile by the colonists.

The Iguana Tribe.—Family *Iguanidæ*.

The name iguana is one of those terms constantly misapplied in popular zoology, and it is very frequently given to the monitors of India and Australia. As a matter of fact, most of the members of the great iguana tribe are confined to the New World, where they take the place of the Old World *Agamidæ*, which are wanting. There are, however, a few outlying iguanas in the Old World, two genera being found in Madagascar, while a third occurs in the Friendly Islands and Fiji. In many points of their organisation the *Iguanidæ* are closely related to the *Agamidæ;* but a ready means of distinction between the two groups is afforded by the dentition. Whereas the latter have the dentition of the acrodont type, in the former it is pleurodont; and a further difference is to be found in the nearly uniform size and form of all the teeth in the iguanas. Very frequently the teeth have lancet-shaped crowns, with serrated edges; but in some rare instances they are divided into three distinct cusps. Iguanas—of which there are fifty different generic modifications—present a curious parallelism to the *Agamidæ* in their structure and habits, doubtless due to the fact that they have to fill all the situations in the New World occupied by the different members of the latter in the Eastern Hemisphere. Whereas, however, there is no flying iguana, this group contains a marine type, which has no representative among the allied family. Nearly all the American forms are inhabitants of the warmer regions of the New World; most are insect-eaters, a few are vegetarians.

The beautiful iguanas of the American genus *Anolis* may be regarded as the western analogues of the Oriental tree-lizards. These are long-tailed arboreal species, with a pyramidal head, moderately long neck, a slender body of variable form, elongated hind-limbs, and large feet with toes of unequal length, in which the middle joints are expanded, and the claws long and elevated. The throat is ornamented with an appendage, which is generally brightly coloured in the males; but there is no crest on the back and neck. The teeth are distinctly three-lobed. More than a hundred different kinds of these lizards are known to science, many of which take up their residence in human dwellings, where they hunt for their insect prey, quite undisturbed by the proximity of the owners. Like their Oriental representatives in the *Agamidæ,* they have the power of changing the colour of their skin even more rapidly and decisively than the chamæleons. As the species of *Anolis* represent *Calotes* in the Old World family, so the basilisks (*Basiliscus*) simulate the sail-tailed lizard of the Malayan Islands. The American forms have, however, gone one better than their Old World prototype, for whereas in the latter the sail-like membranous expansion is confined to the upper surface of the tail, in the males of the former a similar vertical expansion of skin runs from the nape of the neck to the loins, where it is separated by a short interval from the one on the tail. In the back the crest is supported by the elongation of the spines of the back-bone; and in some cases the expansion on the tail is strengthened in a similar manner. The males have in addition a helmet-like elevation on the hinder part of the head. Basilisks are tree-dwelling reptiles, nearly always found in the neighbourhood of water. They generally repose on a bough overhanging some pool or river; and when frightened, immediately throw themselves into the water, in which the males swim with facility by the aid of the crested tail, which acts as a rudder. How the female manages to get along without the crest is not stated.

From a group so extensive as that of the iguanas it is difficult to select the forms best deserving of special notice. There is, however, no doubt that two curious lizards from the Galapagos Islands demand recognition here. Each of these is the sole representative of a genus by itself; but whereas one (*Amblyrhynchus cristatus*) lives to a great extent in the sea and feeds on seaweed, the other (*Conolophus subcristatus*) is a terrestrial creature subsisting on a more ordinary vegetable diet. Having pores on the thighs, and the fourth toe of the hind-foot longer than the third, these lizards are specially distinguished by the circumstance that both the front and lateral teeth are three cusped. The marine species, which measures over fifty inches in length, and is considerably the larger of the two, takes its scientific name from the extreme shortness and bluntness of the head; both the body and tail being markedly compressed, and the toes furnished with incipient webs. The upper surface of the head is ornamented with a number of conical bosses; and a strong serrated crest runs from the nape of the neck to the tip of the tail. The habits of these remarkable lizards have been well described by Darwin. He states that these reptiles are seldom found farther inland than a few yards distance from the shore; and that when in the water they swim strongly and easily with a serpentine movement by the aid of the powerful tail alone. On the volcanic rocks forming the coasts of their native islands these lizards are met with in large droves, which from time to time proceed to sea in search of food. In spite, however, of this fondness for the sea, they never take to the water when attacked as a means of escape. The smaller terrestrial species is easily distinguished by the cylindrical form of the tail and the absence of any trace of webbing on the toes. The head, too, is somewhat longer, and the dorsal crest fully developed only in the region of the neck. In weight, they scale from ten to fifteen pounds. On the central islands of the Galapagos group these lizards are, or were, found in such numbers that there is sometimes a difficulty in discovering a space of any size free from them. They live in burrows, and in the daytime love to lie basking in the sun for hours at a stretch in a dull, listless manner. Even when disturbed, they are slow to get out of the way; and in

Fig. 15.—GALAPAGOS SEA-LIZARD. (*Amblyrhynchus cristatus*).

all their movements they are very unlike ordinary lizards. Nearly allied to the Galapagos forms are the two species of the typical genus *Iguana*, which are restricted to Tropical America and the West Indies. From the former they are distinguished by the simple, conical front teeth; the lateral teeth being serrated. They have the body long and compressed, the quadrangular and large head covered above with enlarged shields, and the long tail invested with uniform and keeled scales. The neck, back, and upper surface of the tail are ornamented with a continuous spiny crest, and there is an appendage on the throat which is incapable of dilation. These iguanas are essentially arboreal lizards, living in forests in the neighbourhood of water, and frequently descending at night to the ground to feed. They readily take to water, in which they swim with facility; and although their diet is mainly of a vegetable nature, they will freely eat insects and other invertebrates. The common species measures as much as four and a half feet in length. By the natives of the countries they frequent, iguanas are highly esteemed, and they are regularly hunted in some districts for food. Their eggs are also much sought after for the same purpose. Nearly allied is the ring-tailed iguana (*Cyclura carinata*) of the West Indies, in which the crowns of the lateral teeth are tricuspid, and the throat is furnished with a pouch, the back and tail being strongly crested.

As the *Agamidæ* possess a spine-clad type in the form of the moloch lizard, so a similar type occurs in the present family. These creatures are generally called horned lizards, although in the States they are known by the title of Californian toad. The genus to which they belong (*Phrynosoma*) includes about a dozen species, which have a geographical range extending over the United States and Mexico. From all other members of the family they are at once distinguished by the numerous spines studding the skin of the body, head, and tail; while they are further characterised by their short, rounded head, general toad-like form of body, and abbreviated tail. About five inches is the ordinary length of these lizards. As regards habits, these lizards are inhabitants of sandy districts, where they prey upon beetles and such other insects as they are able to capture. Some of them are among the few members of the *Iguanidæ* which give birth to their young in a living condition. This peculiarity, coupled with their remarkable external appearance, would be sufficient to give these lizards a claim to distinction above their fellows. But they have another peculiarity. They spit blood; and this not from their mouth, but from their eyes. Incredible as this statement may appear, it is attested by several trustworthy observers. When handled, they have been known to squirt a jet of blood to a distance of more than a foot from one eye, and soon after to emit a similar stream from the other. And this not only once, but several times. Doubtless this most remarkable action is for defensive purposes; and American observers would do good service if they would describe in detail the mode in which the operation is performed.

A peculiar lizard from Mexico is the representative not only of the genus *Xenosaurus*, but likewise of the family *Xenosauridæ*. Passing this by as being worthy only of the attention of specialists, we come to the girdled lizards, of which there are four genera from Africa south of the Sahara, and the island of Madagascar. To a great extent the group is intermediate between the preceding family of the *Iguanidæ* and the following one of the *Anguidæ*. From the former it is distinguished by the hinder lateral regions of the skull being roofed over by (dermal) ossifications in the skin, and likewise by the

Girdled Lizards. —Family *Zonuridæ*.

interclavicle being cruciform instead of T-shaped; while, from the latter, it is differentiated by the conformation of the tongue—which, as in the *Iguanidæ*, is not divisible into an interior and posterior portion—as well as by the hollow bases of the teeth, and by the structure of the bony plates, which in one genus underlie the scales. All have a fold of skin covered with small scales along the sides of the body, by which the upper surface is defined from the lower. The head is invested with large and regular shields; but the back may be covered either with shield-like scales, which are frequently provided with keels, and are arranged in regular transverse zones, or with granules. As in the *Iguanidæ*, the teeth are pleurodont, and the bases of those in use are hollowed out by the tips of their successors, which rise vertically from beneath. In the three genera *Zonurus*, *Pseudocordylus*, and *Platysaurus*, both pairs of limbs are well developed, but in *Chamæsaura*, the general form is snake-like, the fore-limbs being absent, and the hind ones rudimentary, while the tail is remarkable for its excessive relative length. The only Malagasy form is a species of the genus first named.

Snake-like Lizards.—Family *Anguidæ*.

Although in several groups of the sub-order the limbs have more or less completely disappeared, in no case is the assumption of a serpent-like form more strongly marked than in the family typically represented by the common British blind-worm. It is to this family, accordingly, that the name of snake-like lizards is most applicable. While all these lizards resemble the members of the preceding family in having the hinder lateral regions of the skull roofed by bony plates developed in the deep layer of the skin, they differ in the structure of the teeth. It is true that the teeth are often attached in the pleurodont manner, but instead of having the base hollow, this is solid, the new teeth coming up between two of the old ones, instead of beneath the crown of the one immediately above. Whereas in most of the genera the teeth are either tubercular or in the form of short cones firmly attached to the sides of the jaws, in the blind-worms they are long, slender, highly curved, and very loosely fastened to the bone. In these respects the blind-worms come very close to the snakes, and also to the poisonous lizards of the family *Helodermatidæ*. And it is not a little remarkable that traces of a groove have been detected along the front surfaces of the teeth of the blind-worms which appear to correspond to the poison-grooves of those of the family in question. It seems, therefore, as if the popular dread of the blind-worm was instinctive, and that the creature is either descended from poisonous ancestors, or would be poisonous if it could. All the members of the family have bony plates developed in the deep layer of the skin beneath the scales, these plates, when viewed under the microscope, displaying a system of canals. Very peculiar is the tongue, which is divided into a large thick hinder portion, thickly covered with shaggy papillæ, and a small thin emarginate front moiety, of which the covering takes the form of small, scale-like papillæ. This front portion is extensile, and also capable of more or less full retraction into a

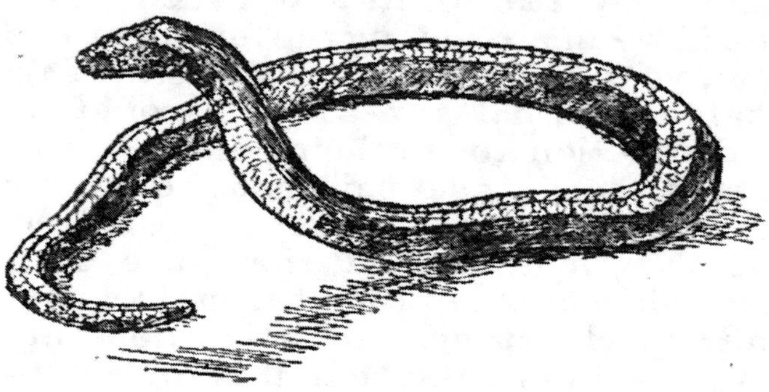

Fig. 16.—Blind-Worm (*Anguis fragilis*).

sheath formed by a transverse fold at the front of the hinder portion. A further resemblance to snakes is to be found in the circumstance that these lizards cast their skins in a single piece. As regards the limbs, great variety is presented by the seven genera included in the family, some having the feet fully developed, and terminating in five toes, whereas in others all external traces of limbs have disappeared. It is noteworthy that all the limbed forms are American, and that Central America and the West Indian Islands are the head-quarters of the group. Beyond the New World, two species are found in Europe and North Africa, while a third inhabits Burma and the Himalaya. Of the seven genera, *Gerrhonotus* and *Ophisaurus* are peculiar in having a lateral fold on the body; the former, which is exclusively American, having two pairs of five-toed limbs, while the latter has, at most, external representatives of the hinder pair. This genus includes the well-known scheltopusik (*O. apus*) of South and Eastern Europe, as well as one Oriental, and other American types. Of those without folds, the genera *Diploglossus*, *Sauresia*, and *Panoplus* are American and four-limbed, differing from one another in the number of the toes, which vary from one or two to five on each foot. *Ophiodes* is likewise American, but has only external rudiments of the hind-limbs. Lastly we have *Anguis*, represented solely by the familiar blind-worm of Europe, Western Asia, and North Africa, which lacks all vestiges of limbs externally, and has the lateral teeth large and fang-like. This species is also peculiar in giving birth to living young, all the other members of the family laying eggs in the ordinary manner. All the *Anguidæ* live on animal food, the larger kinds killing and eating small mammals, birds, and reptiles, whereas the smaller species confine themselves to worms, insects, slugs, and such like. As a rule they are strictly terrestrial, although some species of *Gerrhonotus* will climb up low bushes.

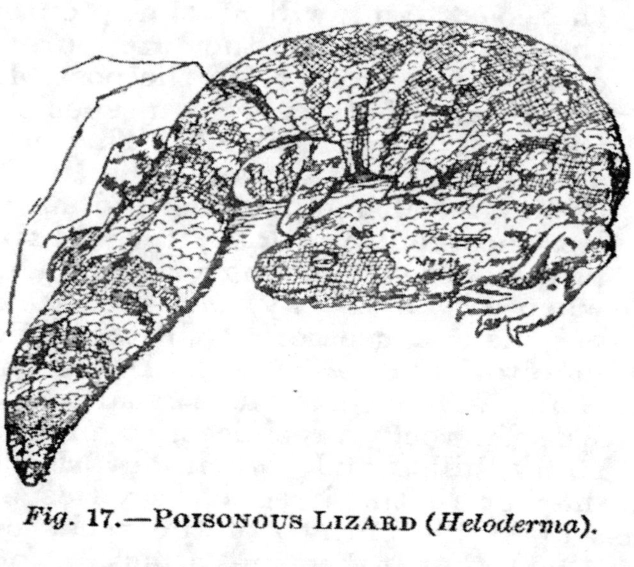

Fig. 17.—POISONOUS LIZARD (*Heloderma*).

The family *Anniellidæ*, as containing only a single Californian genus with two species, may be passed over without notice, and we accordingly proceed to the family *Helodermatidæ*, which also comprises only two species, and ranges from Central America to New Mexico and Arizona.

Poisonous Lizards.—Family *Helodermatidæ*.

In common with many of the poisonous snakes, these lizards are distinguished by their brilliant coloration, one kind having an orange or yellow ground-colour, with an irregular net-work of dark markings on the head and body, and dark rings round the tail. These lizards possess a tongue and teeth of the same general type as in the blind-worm, but have the upper surface covered with transverse rows of small granular tubercles, the under-parts being invested with squared scales. From those of the blind-worm the teeth differ by having grooves on the front and back surfaces for the transmission of the poisonous fluid, and there are certain structural differences in the skull. Both species are included in the genus *Heloderma*, and the one from Arizona is rather the larger of the two, its total length being about twenty inches. Both have the head broad and depressed, the body rounded and thick, the tail moderately long and cylindrical, and the limbs relatively small, with the third and fourth toes the longest. The poisonous lizards are sluggish and nocturnal, inhabiting sandy districts, with the soil of which their coloration is in admirable harmony. They are most commonly seen abroad in the rainy season, and are carnivorous in their diet. Small mammals are speedily killed by their bite, which is stated occasionally to have fatal effects on human beings.

Monitors.—Family *Varanidæ.*

A third family of the sub-order with only a single genus, is that of the monitors; the range of the numerous species extending from the Caspian through Southern Asia to Australasia, and likewise embracing all Africa, as well as the Pacific Islands. They are all of large size, one measuring between six and seven feet in length. As compared with the preceding families, their essential characteristic is to be found in the snake-like structure of the tongue, which is long, deeply forked at the tip, extensile, and capable of being withdrawn into a sheath at the base. They all have well-developed, five-toed limbs, a long and often compressed tail, small scales on the head, and the drum of the ear exposed. Owing to the presence of marginal rows of granules, the scales on the back do not overlap, and in no case is there a median longitudinal crest in this region. The different species of *Varanus* may be arranged in four groups, the distinctive features of which need not be noticed here. They are generally found in the neighbourhood of water, and one Indian species frequents the coast, and will at times enter the sea. In habits, they are purely carnivorous; and, with the possible exception of the Papuan species, they are also terrestrial. They are among the most active of the lizard tribe, and although generally harmless and avoiding attack, it would appear from the following account that, when driven to bay, they will turn on their aggressors. Of the Nile monitor (*V. niloticus*), Dr. Abel Smith writes that "it is usually met with in rocky precipices, or in low stony hills, and, when surprised, seeks concealment in the chinks of the former or in the irregular cavities of the latter, and when any projections exist upon the surface of the rocks or stones, it clasps them so firmly with its toes, that it becomes a task of no small difficulty to dislodge it, even though it can be easily reached. Under such circumstances, the strength of no one man is able to withdraw a full-grown individual, and I have seen two persons required to pull a specimen out of a position it had attained, even with the assistance of a rope fixed in front of its hind-legs. The moment it was dislodged it flew with fury at its enemies, who by flight only saved themselves from being bitten. After it was killed it was discovered that the points of all the nails had been broken previously, or at the moment it lost its hold. It feeds upon frogs, crabs, and small quadrupeds; and, from its partiality to the two former, it is often found among rocks near to springs or running streams, which fact having

Fig. 18.—A Monitor (*Varanus*).

been observed by the natives, has led them to regard it as sacred, and not to be injured without danger of drought." All lay eggs, and many, if not all the species, feed largely upon the eggs of birds.

Greaved Lizards.—Family *Teiidæ*.

A much larger assemblage is that of the greaved lizards of the New World, which there occupy the position held in the Old World by the allied family of the *Lacertidæ*. From all the preceding forms, the *Teiidæ* and following families are broadly distinguished by the circumstance that their cleft and often spear-like tongues are covered either with overlapping scale-like papillæ, or are marked by oblique folds. Then, again, in place of the small scales of the *Varanidæ*, the head is invested with large symmetrically arranged shields; and in the skeleton the inner extremities of the collar-bones are expanded, and not unfrequently assume a looped form. The *Teiidæ*—of which there are five-and-thirty genera, and more than a hundred species—have the head-shields free from the bones of the skull, no bony plates underlying the scales, and no bony roof to the hinder lateral regions of the skull, while the scales are arranged in transverse rows. The teeth are very variable in form and structure, but are always solid at the base, owing to the circumstance that their successors come up alongside. The teeth in the front of the jaws are always conical; but both these and the lateral series may be attached either on the acrodont or pleurodont plan. Distinct eyelids are generally present; the drum of the ear is always visible externally; and the tongue is in most cases covered with overlapping scales, and may be capable of retraction within a basal sheath. Although most of these lizards have five-toed limbs, in certain cases each foot has but four toes, while in other instances the limbs are represented only by stumps, and even all external traces of the hinder pair may disappear. The numerous representatives of this important family have their headquarters in equatorial America, although some forms may be met with throughout the warmer portions of that continent. Like the monitors, they are active in their habits, and feed upon animal substances; but they may be found in all sorts of situations, some living in holes in dry sandy districts, while others prefer the dense herbage of moist localities. The number of genera is far too great to admit of even mention in this place. It will accordingly suffice to take as our representative of the family the large and handsome species commonly known as the tegu (*Tupinambis tequexin*), which is a common and widely-spread species, ranging from the Guianas in the North to Uruguay in the South. Measuring about three feet in length, this lizard has a bold and striking bearing, owing to the elevation of the fore-quarters. Its general colour is some shade of olive above, ornamented with blotches and bars of black, and indistinct longitudinal rows of light spots. It is met with in great numbers among the virgin forests of Amazonia, where, with its forked tongue in rapid motion, it may be seen either sitting quietly upon a branch, or running rapidly over the ground. As is the case with some of the other members of the family, its flesh is esteemed as food by the natives.

Fig. 19.—The Tegu (*Tupinambis tequexin*).

As already mentioned, certain members of the preceding family have lost all external traces of the hinder pair of limbs, and as such species possess burrowing habits, they may be regarded as forming a connecting link between the *Teiidæ* and the degraded *Amphisbænidæ*. The latter, which take their name from the fact that most of them are able to advance with equal ease in either a forward or a backward direction, may, indeed, in all probability, be considered as derivatives from the ancestral stock of the former, which have little by little accustomed themselves to a subterranean mode of life, till the majority have acquired an almost completely worm-like form and habit. One American species, alone representing the genus *Chirotes*, still, however, retains minute though well-developed fore-limbs, which are placed close up to the head, and followed by the long worm-like body. And to the zoologist this form is of the highest importance, as indicating that all the other members of the family trace their origin to fully-limbed ancestors. With the exception of this solitary species, the amphisbænas are all limbless, worm-like creatures, in which even the bones of the pelvis and shoulder-girdle are reduced to the condition of rudiments. In all, the ears are wanting, the functionless eyes are buried deep down in the skin, and the minute mouth is often situated on the lower aspect of the head. The tail is always short; and the few and large teeth, as in the preceding family, may be either acrodont or pleurodont. Indeed, it is chiefly by certain degraded features of the skull that the *Amphisbænidæ* are distinguished from the *Teiidæ;* and as such differences are obviously produced by adaptation to their environment, the amphisbænas are but little removed from their nearest allies. Not the least interesting feature in connection with these strange creatures is their peculiar geographical distribution—a distribution which can only be understood by taking extinct forms into consideration.

Family *Amphisbænidæ*.

Of the existing types, the true home is Tropical America, although two species—one representing *Chirotes*—are found above the northern tropic; but a considerable number of species are inhabitants of Africa, and a few occur in the Mediterranean countries. Most remarkable is the circumstance that the extensive and typical genus *Amphisbæna* has representatives both in Tropical America and Africa south of the Sahara. This, however, is but one out of many instances showing a community between the faunas of South Africa and South America. The family is divided into two groups, according to the mode of attachment of the teeth. In the first group, or *Prosphyodontes*, which includes *Chirotes*, *Amphisbæna*, and six other genera, the teeth are welded to the inner edges of the jaws; whereas in the second group, or *Emphyodontes*, which is represented by *Trogonophis*, *Pachycalmus*, and *Agamodon*, they are affixed to the edges of the same. Regarding the mode of life of the amphisbænas, Mr. G. A. Boulenger writes as follows:—"All the members of this family are burrowers, and many live in ants' nests. They bore narrow galleries in the earth, in which they are able to progress backwards as well as forwards. On the ground they progress in a straight line, by slight vertical undulations, not by lateral movements, as in other limbless reptiles. The tail of many species appears to be more or less prehensile. The food of these lizards consists of small insects and worms. Little has been published on their habits, and all that is known about their mode of propagation is that *Anops kingi* is oviparous, and deposits its eggs in the nests of ants." It may be added that the *Amphisbænidæ* are peculiar among vertebrates in having the right lung rudimental or absent, whereas the left is elongated. In other snake-like lizards, and in snakes, it is the right lung that is functional.

The typical family of the sub-order is exclusively an Old World one, and is spread over the three great continents, although unknown in the island of Madagascar and likewise in the Australasian countries.

Family *Lacertidæ*.

From their New World cousins the *Teiidæ*, these lizards may be readily distinguished by the circumstance that a complete roof of bones developed in the deep layer of the skin covers the hinder lateral regions of the skull, and also by the fact that the shields of the head are attached to the bones of the skull. They further differ—and thereby resemble the *Amphisbænidæ*—in having the two anterior upper jaw-bones, or premaxillæ, immovably united in front. In none are the limbs aborted; and in all cases the feet terminate in five complete toes. The general form is too well known to require mention; and it is in these lizards that the long tail breaks off so readily at or near the middle. The teeth have hollowed bases, and are attached to the jaws in the pleurodont manner; and the tongue has the form of an arrow-head. Distinct eyelids, which can generally be closed, are developed; and the drum of the ear is visible from the outside. In none of these lizards are bony plates developed in the skin beneath the scales; and while the scales of the back may either overlap one another or have their edges in contact, those on the under surface of the body are arranged in transverse and longitudinal series, and are usually superior in size to those above. The family, which includes seventeen generic types and somewhere about a hundred species, attains its maximum development in Africa, being but poorly represented in the Oriental countries. While several species are met with in the south of Europe, two only are found in Britain, where, with the blind-worm, they are the sole representatives of the sub-order Lacertilia. All are fond of sunny localities, where their brisk movements and beautiful metallic tints render them attractive to all who do not possess an instinctive dislike to everything in the shape of a reptile. Flies, beetles, and slugs form their chief food; and as in the colder parts of Europe and Asia, these are not to be seen abroad in winter, lizards are perforce compelled to follow suit and pass the dull winter months in a state of torpor, either buried beneath the ground, or safely ensconced in clefts and crannies. Although one species produces its young alive, the rest lay eggs.

Both the British species belong to the typical genus *Lacerta;* and of these the smaller is the viviparous lizard (*L. vivipara*), which grows to a length of seven inches, and takes its name from the aforesaid peculiarity in its domestic arrangements. The second is the sand-lizard (*L. agilis*), which may measure between eight and ten inches in length, and ranges as far north as Sweden and Norway. More beautiful and considerably larger than either of the foregoing is the green lizard (*L. viridis*), ranging from Southern Europe through the Mediterranean countries to Persia. The northern limits are Germany, where this lizard never reaches the dimensions it attains in more favoured climes. Yet another South European species is the pearly lizard (*L. ocellata*), easily recognised by the presence of a row of large blue spots on each side of the body, the general colour of the upper-parts being in some cases green, with dots or a network of black, but in others dark olive with yellowish markings. This species is larger than any of the foregoing, sometimes measuring as much as twenty-three inches in length. It would be impossible in the space available to give the names and characteristics of all the seventeen genera included in the family. It may, however, be mentioned that in Southern Europe there occur three lizards belonging to a closely allied genus known as *Algiroides*, differing from *Lacerta* by the larger size of the scales on the back. Another South European genus, also extending into the north of Africa, is *Psammodromus*, the members of which differ from both the genera above-mentioned by the slight development or complete absence of a collar or gorget round the throat.

Skink Tribe. —Family *Scincidæ*.

A small neatly-made lizard, commonly known as the skink (*Scincus officinalis*), which inhabits the Sahara desert and the countries bordering the Red Sea, is the type of the last large and important family of the Lacertilia. It should, however, be mentioned that the small African family of the *Gerrhosauridæ* includes five genera, which, to a certain extent, serve to connect the *Lacertidæ* with the *Scincidæ*. They have, for instance, the scales of the body underlain by bony plates of peculiar internal structure, as is the case with the latter family, whereas in the union of the two premaxillary bones and the presence of pores on the thighs, they are like the former. The presence of such bony plates beneath the scales, the distinctness of the two premaxillæ, and the invariable absence of pores on the limbs, are characters amply sufficient to differentiate the *Scincidæ* from the *Lacertidæ*. There are twenty-five genera included in the family under consideration, in one of which (*Lygosoma*) no less than one hundred and fifty-nine distinct species are recognised by zoologists. With such a number of different forms, it is not surprising to find that the family is cosmopolitan. Its head-quarters are, however, the Australasian and Oriental countries, together with the islands of the Pacific and Africa. Skinks are essentially terrestrial lizards, all loving dry sandy deserts, where many burrow in the soil ; and it is probably largely due to such habits that the lower eyelid is furnished with a transparent window in the centre, so that the eye can be used when protected by its covering. A peculiar feature of the family is to be found in the circumstance that the young are almost invariably born in a living condition. Whereas, in all cases the limbs are relatively short, in certain instances one, and in others both pairs are wanting. Many of the above-mentioned features clearly indicate that they are a highly specialised group. Since the number of young produced at a birth may be as low as two, and does not seem to exceed half a score, the rate of increase of these lizards is comparatively slow.

The common skink (*Scincus officinalis*) which is a smooth-scaled, parti-coloured lizard of about eight inches in length, owes its scientific name to the circumstance that its flesh was formerly employed in European medicine, as it still is in the East. It is a creature common enough in Syria and Palestine, where it burrows in the sandy soil. Its flesh is stated by European travellers to be by no means unpalatable if properly cooked. The most extraordinary-looking member of the entire family is the Australian stump-tailed lizard (*Trachysaurus rugosus*), which is covered with large rough browny scales, underlain by thick bony plates, in such a manner as to give it the appearance of an extremely elongated pine-cone. The short and broad head is triangular in form ; the limbs are very short, the front and hind pair being widely separated from each other; and the tail is reduced to a very short, wide, rounded stump. In its habits the lizard is slow

Fig. 20.—COMMON SKINK (*Scincus officinalis*).

and lethargic, as if existence were somewhat of a bore, and although its chief food is of an animal nature, it is stated also to consume vegetable substances.

Certain worm-like burrowing skinks from the tropical and sub-tropical regions of the globe are degraded types, regarded as constituting two families by themselves. In both these families—the *Anelytropidæ* and the *Dibamidæ*—the degradation shows itself not only in the loss of limbs, but likewise in the simplification of the skull, which has lost all its lateral arches; while the eyes are buried beneath the skin, and the ears have no external opening. In the first family—which contains the Mexican genus *Anelytropsis* and the African *Feylinia* and *Typhlosaurus*—the bony plates beneath the skin are retained, but the two premaxillæ have coalesced into a single bone. On the other hand, in the *Dibamidæ* the premaxillæ remain distinct, but the bony plates in the skin have disappeared. This second family is represented only by the genus *Dibamus*, of which one species ranges from the Moluccas through Celebes to New Guinea, while the second is restricted to the Nicobar Islands.

Sub-Order II.—Rhiptoglossa.

CHAMÆLEONS.

In their slow and deliberate movements, as well as by their peculiar revolving eyes and generally grotesque appearance, chamæleons suggest the idea that they do not properly belong to the present order of things, but are survivors from some ancient epoch in the earth's history, when strange and uncouth monsters were to the fore. Nevertheless, we have no evidence that such is really the case, since such fossil chamæleons as are known belong to a comparatively late era, and the extreme specialisation of these strange creatures is, perhaps, rather in favour of their modern origin. Although in popular language chamæleons come under the designation of lizards, they are structurally so different from the Lacertilia that there can be no hesitation in regarding them as the representatives of a distinct sub-order. Apart from the peculiarities of their external appearance, they are broadly distinguished from lizards by the conformation of the tongue. Anyone who has seen a tame chamæleon harpoon a fly at a distance of half a dozen inches from its lips, will not readily forget the appearance of the long extensile, worm-like organ which is shot out from the mouth with the speed of an arrow, to be withdrawn immediately after with the hapless victim adhering to its viscid and club-shaped tip. The feet, too, are as unique in their way as is the tongue, some of the toes turning in one direction and the remainder in the other, so as to form a grasping organ of unrivalled power. Whereas in the front feet three toes go to form the inner half of the grasping organ, and two to the outer, in the hind-limbs this arrangement is reversed. The large revolving and prominent eye is in the form of an egg, with most of the exposed portion invested by a thick continuous lid of a granular texture, in the centre of which is the minute perforation for the pupil. Each eye can be moved independently of its fellow; and these movements serve to heighten the general grotesqueness of the creature's appearance. Owing to the frequent development of three tall backwardly-projecting ridges on the hinder part of the skull, the head often assumes a casque-like form; and the small triangular and compressed teeth are affixed to the jaws in the acrodont manner. In all the species the body is so much compressed as to be much deeper than wide, while, owing to the great relative length of the lanky limbs, it is raised high above the ground. The long tapering tail is as good a grasping organ as that of an American monkey. Externally, the whole surface is covered with granules, or small tubercles, so that, properly speaking, chamæleons do not come under the title of Squamata. In their skeleton, chamæleons differ from all lizards with fully-developed limbs by the complete loss of their collar-bones.

Chamæleons are all so closely related to one another that a single family—the *Chamæleontidæ*—suffices for the group. Moreover, with the exception of three Malagasy species forming the genus *Brookesia*, and two others from Africa, which are separated as *Rampholeon*, all the forms may be included in the typical genus *Chamæleon*, of which forty-four specific representatives are recognised. As regards their geographical distribution, chamæleons are chiefly characteristic of Africa south of the Sahara and Madagascar; but the common *Chamæleon vulgaris* is an inhabitant of many of the Eastern Mediterranean countries, and is also found in Andalusia and Algeria. India and Ceylon likewise possess a representative of the same genus, while South Arabia is the home of a third, and Socotra of a fourth. Great difference exists in the bodily size of the various members of the family; the smallest being a species of *Brookesia* measuring less than three inches in length, while many of the larger kinds grow to considerably more than a foot.

Fig. 21.—A Chamæleon.

Chamæleons are essentially arboreal animals, mostly living in trees or bushes abundantly clothed with leaves, and in localities where moisture is plentiful. Although these reptiles have long been celebrated for their power of changing the colour of their skins, yet it appears that the phenomenon is by no means so strongly marked in this group as it is among certain lizards. Still there is considerable change; and whereas most chamæleons are generally of an apple-green colour in daylight, it is stated that during the night the tint of the skin fades to a greyish-white. If during the daytime a chamæleon passes from a leaf to a bough, its skin soon assimilates to the sombre hue of the latter; and if seized in the hand the change is even more rapid. In spite of the partiality of nearly all the species for dense tropical or sub-tropical vegetation, a few have betaken themselves to spots in desert districts where they find herbage enough for their needs. All are insectivorous, their favourite food being flies; and the rapidity with which one of these insects is seized by the tongue forms a strange contrast to the otherwise sluggish and deliberate movements of these reptiles.

Sub-Order III.—Ophidia.

Snakes.

The leading structural features by which snakes are distinguished from the limbless lizards having been already given under the heading of the sub-order Lacertilia, these need not be recapitulated, and attention may accordingly be directed to some of the other characteristics of the former group. Everybody is aware that snakes are scaly reptiles, crawling on the ground without the aid of limbs; but it is probably less widely known that certain members of the group retain vestiges of the hind-legs in the shape of two spur-like projections from the body in the neighbourhood of the vent. And in such forms, if the skeleton be examined, it will be found that there are remnants of the bony framework of the pelvis and upper part of the hind-limbs. All these facts clearly show that snakes trace their descent from reptiles endowed with four complete limbs. Under the heading of the Lacertilia it has been mentioned that the two branches of the lower jaw of a snake are united at the chin by a ligament, so as to be capable of wide separation from one another; and in many members of the group the capacity of the mouth can be further augmented by a similar arrangement in the upper jaw, the bones of both the jaws themselves, and likewise those of the palate, being movably joined together. This arrangement permits these reptiles to devour a prey of considerably larger size than the normal calibre of their mouth and throat. In place of movable eyelids, snakes have a continuous transparent skin stretched over the eyes, which is periodically cast with the slough; and in no case is there any external opening to the ears. A peculiar feature in a serpent is the enormous number of vertebræ contained in the backbone, not less remarkable being the number of pairs of ribs. In fact, from the head to a long way down the tail, each joint of the backbone carries a pair of these appendages, which increase gradually in length from the head to the fore-part of the trunk, and thence as gradually diminish to the tail. There being no vestiges of collar-bones or breast-bone, each rib terminates below in a free point.

In order to give extra flexibility, and at the same time strength, to this exceedingly elongated backbone, the vertebræ of serpents are provided with extra articulations, a wedge-like projection from one fitting in to a corresponding hollow in the next. Such additional articulations are, however, by no means confined to snakes, but also occur in some lizards, notably the monitors. In ordinary land vertebrates the ribs are largely connected with the function of breathing; but in snakes—in addition to supporting the walls of the trunk, and thus keeping open the cavity of the chest—their chief function is in progression, so that these reptiles may really be described as rib-walkers. On the under surface of the body the majority of snakes have a series of large transverse horny shields, which are much wider than long, and in the trunk-region extend right across the lower surface; these shields, it may be remarked, being absent in the limbless lizards. In the tail the enlarged shields not unfrequently form a double longitudinal series. Each of the complete transverse shields corresponds to the termination of a pair of ribs. By holding on to the inequalities of the surface they are traversing by the free edges of the shields—which project backwards—and then by drawing closer together the ribs of one side of the body, and afterwards those of the other, a snake produces the well-known lateral undulations of its body. By straightening out the front part of the body when a firm hold is obtained, and then drawing after it the hinder portion, progression is effected. On a smooth surface movement is impossible, and no snake ever produces vertical undulations of its body. All snakes have a prehensile forked tongue, capable of retraction within a basal sheath, and during their waking hours kept in constant movement. Usually the head of a snake, both above and below, is invested with a number of large and symmetrically-arranged polished horny shields, to each of which a distinctive name is given. Internally, snakes are remarkable for the great elongation of the lungs, or rather lung, since, as a rule, only the one on the right side is functional.

As regards their biting organs, harmless snakes generally have two rows of teeth in the upper, and a single row in the lower jaw, such teeth being slender, sharp, and comparatively short. In some, however, either one or two pairs of teeth of the outer upper series may be larger than the rest, and provided with a groove, or completely tubular, such a type probably always indicating more or less developed noxious properties. In some of the most deadly members of the sub-order, the arrangements for the injection of the poison are of a more complicated nature. Here the short maxillary bones are capable of being moved so as to become at right angles to the bones of the rest of the palate, while each carries a large channelled tusk, which, at the moment of biting, assumes an erect position. Through this pair of tusks, or fangs, the poison is conveyed from the secreting glands, which are placed below and behind the eyes. In some kinds these glands are short, those of the cobra being of the size of an almond; but in others they extend far down the body. Regarding the mode of operation, an Australian writer observes that "the curious structure of the fang makes it almost certain that the poison shall be injected under the skin. The opening of the groove is not at the very tip, where it would be liable to get plugged up with skin or flesh, and so prevent the passage of the poison, but a little way up from and in front of this, so that the sharp point goes in first, and makes a little hole into which the poison flows. In fact the poison fang is the model of the medical injecting syringe, and is exactly adapted to its purpose. The secretion of the gland varies in different snakes in quantity and in quality. It is a clear viscid fluid, which can retain its deadly properties for long, and does not even lose them when dissolved in water or alcohol. Sir J. Fayrer, the great authority on Indian snakes, found that the blood of an animal killed by snake poison was itself poisonous, and he transmitted the venom through a series of three animals with fatal results."

It was long supposed that harmless and noxious serpents were broadly distinguished from one another by definite external characters, but this is now known to be incorrect; and it is only by an examination of the teeth that it can be determined whether or no any particular serpent is hurtful. The destruction of human life by snake-bite in India is something appalling, as may be gleaned by a recent return of the Indian Government. It is there stated that, whereas in 1892 the deaths caused by snake-bite in the lower provinces of Bengal were 9,510, in 1893 the number rose to 10,797. Though the deaths in Bengal, as might be supposed from its larger area, exceeded those in the other provinces, there was apparently nothing permanent in the rise, as the number fell to 9,856 in 1894. The decrease of mortality during 1894 is ascribed in Bengal and Assam to the low flood-levels, the snakes not having been dislodged from their usual haunts, as happens when the water is high. In Assam the mortality is the lowest recorded in the last ten years. The loss of life from snake-bite was highest, in proportion to the population, in Bengal, Ajmir, the North-Western Provinces, and Oudh and the Central Provinces. If all the provinces be taken together, one person was killed in this manner among every 10,267 of the population in 1894, as compared with one in every 10,424 in 1893. The apparent increase in Assam is ascribed to more accurate reporting. In the Central Provinces the same explanation has been offered for a continuous increase; but the statistics in general are viewed with distrust. The number of venomous snakes reported to have been destroyed, and the rewards granted on this account shown in the return, fell respectively from 117,120 to 102,210, and from Rs.12,607 to Rs.10,150.

Anything that can check this frightful mortality must be welcomed; and, after the trial of many so-called remedies, it appears that a real antidote is the blood-serum of animals which have been previously immunised to snake-poison or in that of venomous serpents themselves. Regarding the former method, Dr. J. G. M'Pherson writes that its discoverer—Professor Fraser of Edinburgh—first proved that there is a certain amount of toleration for snake-poison in animals. "Having ascertained the minimum dose required to cause the death of an animal, he started below that amount and gradually increased the dose after intervals of ten days. By this process of gradual increases in the dose of the snake-poison, he found the animal receiving as much at one time as fifty times the amount of the minimum lethal dose without it causing any perceptible bad effects. In fact, its general health seemed to improve, as he had the animals weighed once and sometimes twice every day; and all the time he was administering the venom there was a steady increase in weight. In the meantime Professor Fraser has not carried his experiments of quantity further than fifty times the minimum lethal dose at one time; but still, when he had got to that point, the animal was receiving in a single dose, without being affected, enough to kill fifty animals of the same size and weight. One of the animals which he had treated by this gradually increasing quantity had, in two months, received enough poison to kill three hundred and seventy fresh animals of equal size and weight, supposing that each just got the minimum lethal dose. He then described a second series of experiments in which he used the blood-serum of these animals which had been immunised as an antidote for the venom. He mixed an equal part of this blood-serum and venom together, and injected the mixture into a fresh animal. This produced no effect, the serum counteracting the action of the poison. Next he injected some of the immunised blood-serum, which he has named *antivenine*, into a fresh animal, and then some venom afterwards, but the serum hindered any action of the venom. Then he took another fresh animal and injected the venom, waiting till symptoms of poisoning were manifest; at once he injected his *antivenine*, and put a stop to any further progress of the poisoning. The same results took place after many experiments. All this points to the conclusion that this *antivenine*, or blood-serum, in an animal that has been able to stand with impunity fifty lethal doses at a time by the increasing dose process is really an antidote to the poison of snakes." Subsequent experiments have shown, as was not unanticipated, that the blood-serum of venomous snakes is likewise an antidote to their own poison.

Nearly all snakes feed upon the bodies of animals that they have killed themselves, the few exceptions to this rule subsisting on eggs. Owing to the extensile structure of the mouth and jaws, already mentioned, as well as to the separation of the lower ends of the ribs, and the power of extension existing in the stomach, snakes can devour animals of larger circumference than the ordinary girth of their own bodies. Both absolutely and proportionately the largest animals are swallowed by the pythons and boas; and as these snakes kill their prey by encircling it in the folds of their bodies, and thus crushing it to death, the carcase is rendered soft and plastic, and thus more easily swallowed than would otherwise be the case. Occasionally these serpents will swallow members of their own species, as happened not long ago in the menagerie of the Zoological Society of London. In this instance, two large boas occupied the same compartment in the reptile-house, the one measuring nine and the other eight feet in length. One night the two were seen all safe at closing time, but when the house was opened next morning, "only one boa was found in the cage; the other had disappeared. Though the survivor was only a foot longer than the other snake, there was no reason to doubt that it had completely swallowed its companion. It was so distended that the scales were almost separated, and it was unable either to coil itself or to move. There is every reason to believe that in accomplishing this almost incredible feat the snake acted by mistake, and that it devoured its companion by what deserves to be called an accident. The larger boa was fed with a pigeon before the house was closed for the night. It swallowed the bird, and the other boa was then given a pigeon, which it had begun to swallow when the snakes were left for the night. It is believed that the larger snake then caught hold of the part of the pigeon which projected from the other's mouth, and gradually enveloped not only the bird, but the head of the other snake. Once begun, the swallowing process would go on almost mechanically. As the swallowed snake was only one foot less in length than the swallower, and of nearly equal bulk, weighing about fifty pounds, the gastric juices must have dissolved the portion which first entered the snake's stomach before the remainder was drawn into the jaws. Though still rather lethargic, the surviving boa is not injured by its meal. It coils itself up without difficulty, and its scales have the beautiful iridescent bloom peculiar to the skin of snakes when in perfect health." Within about a fortnight the cannibal had completely recovered its usual condition. The majority of snakes swallow their prey while still living, as may be often witnessed when a common English water-snake seizes an unfortunate frog. Vipers and cobras, on the other hand, first kill their prey by the injection of venom. But few meals suffice for a snake, in spite of the circumstance that these reptiles digest their food with great rapidity.

In their general mode of life serpents show much variation, some living in sandy deserts, others haunting swampy localities, while yet others spend a large portion of their time in fresh water. Some, again, are mainly arboreal, and the members of one group are marine, and may be met with swimming in the open sea far away from land. The aquatic snakes—both fresh-water and marine—as well as vipers, give birth to living young; whereas the others lay soft-shelled eggs. Generally these are left to hatch by themselves, aided sometimes by such heat as may be produced by the decomposition of the heaps of leaves and other vegetable substances in which they are not infrequently deposited; but pythons actually brood their eggs. It might be thought that incubation by a cold-blooded creature would not aid development; but it is a remarkable fact that at such seasons the temperature of the blood of these snakes is raised slightly above the normal.

Serpents attain their maximum development, both as regards numbers and size, in the steamy tropical and sub-tropical zones; and it is here also that the most venomous forms are met with. Even in such localities there is, however, great variation in the relative proportions of noxious and innocuous kinds; and in the large proportion of the former the Oriental countries bear an evil reputation, as they also do in respect to the abundance of snakes in general. Next to these countries comes Tropical America in point of numbers; whereas Africa has only about half as many snakes as inhabit the Indian and Malayan countries. The African serpents are, as a whole, unlike those of Madagascar; while the latter show a considerable resemblance to South American types. The Australian snake-fauna is allied to that of India and the Malayan countries, as is well exemplified by the occurrence in both of pythons. In temperate regions snakes become gradually less common as we proceed north in the one hemisphere and south in the other; but, with the exception of New Zealand and the polar regions, the group may be considered to enjoy practically a world-wide range. Nine families of snakes are recognised by zoologists; and these include a very large number of genera, and probably more than fifteen hundred distinct species. With such a vast assemblage, it is of course impracticable in our limited space to do more than notice the leading and most important types. And even treating the group in this manner, there is considerable difficulty in giving the student a proper idea of the subject, on account of the close structural similarity between many of the families. To understand snakes thoroughly requires an intimate acquaintance with a mass of structural details, and the acquisition of a host of technical terms; and these can only be acquired by a patient practical study of the group.

Blind-Snakes.—Families *Typhlopidæ* and *Glauconiidæ*.

At the head of the sub-order are now placed the two comparatively unimportant families of blind-snakes, which differ from all the rest in lacking teeth in either the upper or the lower jaw. In form, these snakes are cylindrical and worm-like, with relatively short heads and tails; while in habits they likewise resemble worms, passing most of their lives in tunnels driven by themselves beneath the surface of the ground. Here they subsist by feeding upon such insects or their larvæ as they happen to encounter, ants being apparently a very favourite dish. Dull, rainy weather will occasionally tempt them above ground. Living in such subterranean haunts, the large inferior transverse shields of ordinary serpents would be useless, and we accordingly find the bodies of the blind-snakes covered all round with scales of equal size, although there are some large shields on the fore part of the head, beneath a pair of which are buried the rudimental and useless eyes. Unlike most of their kindred, these snakes cannot expand their jaws; and the small aperture of the mouth is placed on the under side of the head. That these snakes are nearly related to limbed reptiles is proved by the retention in the skeleton of more or less distinct vestiges of the pelvis. An important feature in the structure of the bony palate, which need not be considered in detail here, suffices to distinguish them from all the other members of the sub-order, to which it seems likely that they have no close relationship. Indeed it is quite probable that whereas the blind-snakes are descended from one group of lizard-like reptiles, all other ophidians may trace their origin to a second. In the first of the two families into which the blind-snakes are divided, it is the lower jaw which has lost its teeth, and the pelvis is represented by a single pair of bones. The family, which includes three distinct genera, with about a hundred species, ranges over all the warmer countries; one species of the large typical genus *Typhlops* occurring in Southern and Eastern Europe. On the other hand, in the *Glauconiidæ* it is the upper jaw that has no teeth, while two pairs of bones remain to represent the pelvis. The family includes only the genus *Glauconia*, of which there are nearly thirty species ranging over Africa, the south-west of Asia, and America.

Of far more importance than the last is the great family of boas and pythons, which include the largest of all living snakes, and are characterised by their habit of killing their prey by crushing it in the folds of their bodies. Like the blind-snakes, these huge serpents retain external vestiges of the hind-limbs, and likewise internal traces of the pelvis; but as they differ considerably from the former in the conformation of the bony palate of the skull, it is most probable that they have a totally distinct origin. Since they agree in this respect with the other seven more specialised families included in the sub-order, it is not improbable that these snakes are the survivors of the ancestral stock from which all the latter have originated. The jaws, too, are unlike those of the blind-snakes in that both are armed with a complete series of teeth. The vestiges of the hind-limbs usually take the form of a pair of spurs in the neighbourhood of the vent. The other distinctive features of the family are mainly connected with the structure of the skull; and as the only other snakes with vestiges of limbs are the small *Ilysiidæ*, which are not likely to be confounded with the members of the present family, it will be superfluous to allude further to these peculiarities. The family, which ranges over all the warmer regions of both hemispheres, is divided into the two subfamilies of the pythons or rock-snakes (*Pythoninæ*), and the boa-constrictors and sand-snakes (*Boinæ*). All the species included in the former are restricted to the Old World; but whereas the typical boas are solely American and Malagasy, some other members of the second group are widely distributed in the Eastern Hemisphere. The first sub-family is particularly characterised by the presence of an additional pair of bones—the supraorbitals—in the roof of the skull, which enter into the composition of the margins of the eye-sockets. The members of the genus *Python* are all large serpents, having teeth in the premaxillary or front upper jaw-bones, and a double series of shields on the lower surface of the tail, the latter being distinctly prehensile. Still more important is the presence of pits in two of the shields on each side of the fore part of the head; while other distinctive features are to be found in the characters of the teeth, as well as in the vertical slit formed by the pupil of the eye. There are nine different species of pythons recognised by zoologists; and these range over Africa and the Oriental countries, together with Australia and New Guinea. Fifteen and even twenty feet is by no means an uncommon length for the larger kinds, such as the Indian *P. molurus;* and occasionally specimens grow to between twenty and thirty feet.

Boa Tribe.— Family *Boidæ*.

A python, after having suffocated its victim by enveloping it in the coils of its body, proceeds to swallow it by seizing it by the head and gradually drawing it down. Greatly exaggerated notions are prevalent as to the size of the animals which can be swallowed by pythons and boas; and the stories of whole buffaloes and large deer are obviously unworthy of credence. Indeed, it seems probable that even a full-grown sheep is too large for the capacity of the leave of even the biggest of the tribe; and a sheep of half the full size would seem to be about the limit. In habits, pythons are chiefly nocturnal, and they are partial to damp forest districts where water is easy of access. In such situations they not unfrequently take up their residence in the roofs of houses when made of straw or other vegetable substances; and a well-known account of the discovery of such an unwelcome intruder into his temporary abode is narrated by Mr. Wallace. Perhaps the most peculiar circumstance in the life-history of these serpents is the incubation of the eggs. These, which comprise a large number, are arranged in a pyramidal heap, round which the parent coils her body; this posture being in some instances maintained for nearly two months. Regarding the appetite of a python (miscalled a boa) formerly in his possession, Captain Heyland writes as follows:—"The animal was brought to me early in January, and did not taste food from that time until the July following. During this period he generally drank a quart of water daily. The man who brought him stated that he had been seen to eat a hog-deer the day before he was taken. One evening early in July, hearing a noise, I went out, and discovered that the snake had left his harbour under the boards of a stable where he generally lay, and having entered a small shed in which some fowls were roosting, had swept eleven from the perch, and destroyed them by pressing them between his folds. Then taking them one by one head foremost into his mouth, swallowed the whole down in twenty minutes. The largest animal that he ate while in my possession was a calf, which he killed and gorged in two hours and twenty minutes. He never attacked dogs, cats, or pigs. Of these last, indeed, he seemed to be in dread, for whenever one was presented to him, he retired to a corner and coiled himself up with his head undermost. If fed with animals not larger than a duck, he ate readily every day, but after the meal of a goat refused food for a month." In Australia the genus is represented by *P. spilotis*, of which one variety is commonly termed the diamond-snake, the other the carpet-snake.

An Australian writer observes that "of our two pythons or rock-snakes, one, the diamond-snake, does not occur farther south than New South Wales, whilst the carpet-snake has a wider range, extending from Queensland to even as far as Southern Victoria. These pythons may reach the length of sixteen feet, but a more usual length is eight feet to ten feet. The diamond-snake has a yellow spot in the centre of each of its black scales, whilst the carpet-snake has a series of lighter patches with dark centres along each side, producing a fancied resemblance to the pattern of a carpet. They are really nocturnal animals, feeding on birds and small mammals, whilst in turn the blacks will eat their flesh with avidity." Krefft thus describes the way in which they secure their prey:—"Coiled on the branch of a tree, the reptile moves only the head and part of the body, advancing and retreating, in fact measuring its distance, with its head and neck bent into the form of a horizontal S. When pretty sure of its aim, the snake darts forward with open jaws, fastens upon its victim, and in an instant brings it within a loop formed by a portion of the body, which gradually tightens till the prey is suffocated. In this position the snake will remain for twenty minutes or half an hour, holding the body of the animal tightly. It then gradually uncoils, and, if inclined to feed, begins the process of swallowing with the head." In Africa the best known representative of the genus is *Python sebæ*, commonly termed the Natal rock-snake in the southern parts of that continent. Nearly allied to the pythons are the genera *Laxocemus*, *Nardoa*, and *Liasis;* the first including a single small species from Mexico, the second one inhabiting New Ireland, while the third has several representatives ranging from Timor to New Guinea and Northern Australia. All these resemble the true pythons in having the premaxillæ toothed, but in the Papuan *Chrondropython*, as well as in the North Australian *Aspidites* and the West African *Calabaria*, those bones carry no teeth.

The absence of premaxillary teeth is likewise characteristic of the members of the sub-family *Boinæ*, which are, however, specially distinguished by the want of the aforesaid supraoccipital bone in the skull. All have teeth on the palate, and likewise most of the shields on the lower surface of the tail arranged in a single series; but in these respects they resemble some of the three genera last mentioned. Most of the boa tribe have the head well marked off from the neck, and the tail with a certain amount of prehensile power. Foremost among these are the tree-boas of the genus *Epicrates*, in all of which the teeth in the fore part of the jaws are superior in size to those behind, while the head is covered with shields, the scales on the body are smooth, and there are, at most, but shallow pits in the so-called labial shields of the muzzle. All the members of the genus are inhabitants of Tropical America, the largest not exceeding seven feet in length. The presence of deep pits in the labial shields serves to distinguish the species of the nearly allied genus *Corallus*, of which four are from Tropical America, while the fifth is found in Madagascar. Four other snakes from the Moluccas, New Guinea, and Oceania, constitute the genus *Enygrus*, which differs from both the preceding in having ridges on the scales of the body. These boas do not appear to molest human beings, but the case is different with the anaconda (*Eunectes murinus*) of Tropical America, which grows to thirty feet or more in length.

In common with three other genera from the same countries, two of which are respectively represented by a single species, while the third includes several, the anaconda differs from all the foregoing in that the front teeth are not greatly enlarged, the whole series gradually diminishing in height from before backwards. Among the distinctive generic characters of the anaconda may be noticed the small size of the scales. Its general colour is olive or greyish-brown on the upper surface, upon which are one or two rows of large, dark, transversely-elongated blotches, and one or two of eye-like spots on the sides. The anaconda is essentially a water-snake, and in those parts of its habitat which are subject to a long period of drought, it buries itself in the dried river mud till the return of moister conditions. In the anaconda one of the pairs of shields on the head, technically known as nasals, come into contact with one another in the middle line behind the muzzle, but in the nearly-allied snakes forming the genus *Boa* a median line of small scales separates all the nasal shields. Of the seven species of true boas, five are from the warmer parts of Central and South America, whereas the other two are met with in far distant Madagascar. The common boa-constrictor (*Boa constrictor*) has a wide geographical range, being found from Venezuela to the inland districts of the Upper Argentine. Although marvellous stories are current as to the rapacity of this species — whose maximum length is about a dozen feet —it appears that its usual food consists of the smaller mammals, while even eggs are sometimes swallowed. It will, however, occasionally attack and kill deer or peccaries. All its victims are destroyed by the crushing effect of the compression of the encircling folds of the body. A snake from a small island near Mauritius, forming the genus *Cásarea*, differs from the true boas in having distinct keels on its scales, as well as in the greater relative length of the tail.

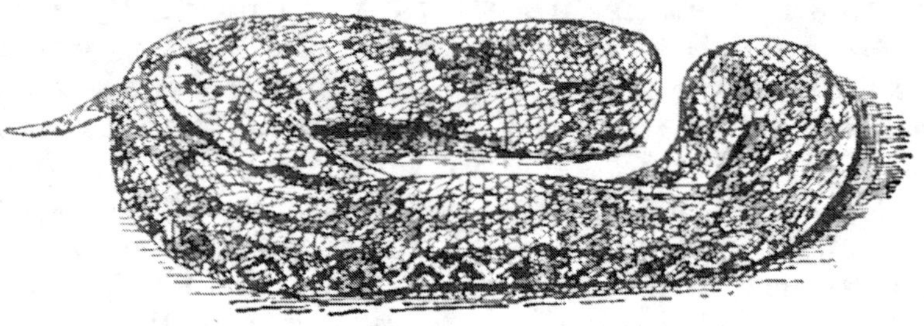

Fig. 22.—Boa Constrictor.

The only other members of the family that can be noticed are the sand-snakes (*Eryx*) of South-Eastern Europe, Asia, and North and East Africa, which differ from the boas in the want of any distinct line of demarcation between the head and neck. These snakes derive their name from frequenting open sandy districts, where they frequently enter the burrows of small mammals and lizards for the purpose of preying on their rightful occupants.

Cylinder-Snakes and Shield-Tails.—Families *Ilysiidæ* and *Uropeltidæ*.

Two small and comparatively unimportant families of the sub-order claim a few lines. The first of these, which includes but three genera, with a total of five species, is that of the *Ilysiidæ*, all the members of which resemble the pythons and boas in the retention of external vestiges of the hind pair of limbs, but differ in the conformation of the skull. The typical form is the coral cylinder-snake (*Ilysia scytale*), a small species from the upper part of the valley of the Amazon and the Guianas, the others being the various species of *Cylindrophis* from South-Eastern Asia, and the one representative of the nearly-allied *Anomalochilus*, which is Sumatran. The *Uropeltidæ*, which, in common with all the remaining snakes, have lost all external traces of limbs, form an allied family agreeing with both the preceding in the structure of the lower jaw, and taking their name from the peculiar conformation of the tail. Although in one genus it has a coating of keeled scales, in all the rest this appendage terminates in a bare roughened disc, and is thus quite unlike that of all other snakes. In all cases the tail is very short, the body is cylindrical, and there is no distinct neck, while both the mouth and the eyes are relatively small. These snakes, which are all of small size, and frequently brightly and handsomely coloured, are found only in the mountains of India proper and Ceylon, where they generally spend their time in tunnels channelled at a considerable depth below the surface, although in rainy weather they frequently skulk beneath stones and wood, and sometimes even venture out among grass and other herbage. In addition to the typical *Uropeltis*, they include six generic types, the total number of species recognised in 1893 being forty-one, of which only one pertains to the type genus. It may be added that a snake from South-Eastern Asia known as *Xenopeltis unicolor* is regarded as representing by itself the family of the *Xenopeltidæ*, the reason for this reference being that in the structure of the skull it exhibits distinct indications of relationship with the *Boidæ*, although agreeing with the next family in the number of bones entering into the composition of the lower jaw.

Colubrine Tribe.—Family *Colubridæ*.

Together with the aforesaid *Xenopeltis*, the snakes included in the two great and important families of the *Colubridæ* and *Viperidæ* are broadly differentiated from the *Boidæ* and their allies by having one bone less in each lateral branch of the lower jaw, the missing bone being termed the coronoid. It is unfortunate that this important distinctive feature is not visible in the living animal; but so it is, and the student must make the best of it. As already said, none of these snakes retain external vestiges of limbs. The colubrine tribe is an extremely large group, embracing as it does many more snakes than any of the other families into which the sub-order is divided. All are characterised by the circumstance that the maxillæ of the upper jaw are horizontal, and incapable of movement. Whereas, however, some, such as the common water-snakes, are perfectly harmless—except to the small creatures upon which they prey—others, like the sea-snakes and cobras, are among the most deadly of all serpents. In such a vast assemblage it is impossible to do more than notice some of the leading types.

As an example of the first of the three great sections into which it has been found advisable to divide the family, we may take the water-snakes of the genus *Tropidonotus*, of which the common British ringed-snake (*T. natrix*) is the most familiar representative. From the fact that all the teeth are completely solid throughout, showing no traces of either an external groove or a deeper channel, the section to which this genus belongs is technically known as the Aglypha. And this fact alone is sufficient to indicate that all the members of the section are innocuous. It will be superfluous to point out all the characteristics by which the water-snakes differ from their immediate allies—more especially as many of these are deep-seated, and require a considerable amount of anatomical knowledge for their proper apprehension. It may be mentioned, however, that teeth are present throughout both the upper and lower jaws, and that those in the hinder part of the upper series exceed in size those near the muzzle, while all those in the lower jaw have approximately the same dimensions. The relatively large eye has a circular pupil, the scales are arranged in regular series running lengthwise, and between the openings of the nostrils are placed a pair of internasal shields.

Of water-snakes there are forty or fifty species; and the range of the genus embraces the greater portion of the globe, with the exception of South America and Australia south of the tropic. The species are, however, less numerous in Africa than in the other countries of the Old World. All are fond of water, in which they swim well, and their favourite haunts are damp situations where access to a river or pond is easy. They live on frogs and other small animals, which are seized in the mouth and swallowed as rapidly as possible, without being killed by crushing in the folds of the body. In addition to the ringed snake, several other species of the genus inhabit Europe. Another familiar European species is the smooth snake (*Coronella lævis*), which belongs to a rather large genus. The so-called fierce snakes (*Zamenis*) are also well represented on the Continent, among such being the dark green snake (*Z. gemonensis*) and the horseshoe-snake (*Z. hippocrepis*). To the same genus belongs the well-known Indian rat-snake (*Z. mucosus*). Although many or all of the foregoing will at times ascend trees in search of their prey, the section includes others which are truly arboreal, and in coloration resemble the foliage among which they dwell. Such are the American wood-snakes of the genus *Herpetodryas*, and their Old World cousins included in the genera *Dendrophis* and *Dendrelaphis*. In all these, the eyes are proportionally much larger than in the water-snakes, and the body is more or less strongly compressed. Some are remarkable for being able to change the colour of their skin to harmonise with their surroundings after the manner of the chamæleons and certain lizards. Far more interesting than any other member of the family is the small South African egg-eating snake (*Dasypeltis scabra*). It may well be asked how a snake, with its long pointed teeth, manages to seize and swallow the eggs of birds without losing their savoury contents. And if the egg-eating snake had the ordinary dental armature, it would doubtless find this a very difficult task. But special arrangements have been made to suit its particular diet. Whereas teeth are wanting in the fore part of the jaws, the upper surface of the throat is provided with a long series of tooth-like organs formed by the elongation of the lower spines of the joints of the backbone, which project through the membranes into the throat. Taking an egg into the nearly toothless mouth, the snake gradually passes it downwards into the throat, where it is split by the pressure of the mill-like teeth, and its contents safely swallowed. Although this snake is a very small creature, it will at a pinch cram a hen's egg into its mouth, when it looks somewhat like a football with a tail to it. How it manages to force such a huge object into its throat, and still more, how it cracks it when once there, we are not told.

The second section into which the family *Colubridæ* is divided takes its name of Opisthoglypha from the circumstance that either one or several pairs of teeth in the hinder part of the upper jaw are traversed by a longitudinal groove for the purpose of conveying poison from the secreting gland. Whereas all are more or less noxious, many are deadly. In habits and form many of these curiously simulate the members of the first section of the family. The group is but poorly represented in Europe, but among the Continental species is the so-called cat-snake (*Tarbophis vivax*), forming a genus by itself. This snake belongs to a sub-family of the section—the *Dipsadomorphinæ*—in which the nostrils are always situated on the sides of the muzzle. It frequently grows to a yard or so in length, and is grey or brownish-yellow in general colour, with various dark spots and blotches, and a chestnut patch on the head-shields. It is fond of warm sunny spots among rocks, where it feeds chiefly on lizards, which it kills by the injection of poison. The typical representatives of the sub-family are the arboreal snakes of the genus *Dipsadomorphus* which are widely spread through the warmer regions of the Old World, where they have precisely the same mode of life as the arboreal forms included in the section Aglypha. In colour they incline to black and brown, while in length they may exceed a couple of yards. Many of them, at least, are purely nocturnal snakes, and whereas some feed on birds, others prey almost or quite exclusively on the smaller kinds of mammals. Occasionally they descend from their leafy haunts to wander on the ground. Of similar habits are the Indian whip-snakes (*Dryophis*), in which the somewhat compressed body and tail are remarkable for their extreme length and slenderness. This habit of body enables these snakes to curl their tail tightly round a bough, whence they strike to a long distance at any passing prey. Here, too, belongs the Tropical American and West Indian genus *Philodryas*, which includes a considerable number of arboreal species, characterised by the green tone of their coloration. This genus is also represented in Madagascar. The number and arrangement of the teeth form important features in the distinction of these genera of tree-snakes. In the present section the place of the water-snakes among the section Aglypha is taken by the fresh-water snakes of the genera *Homalopsis* and *Cantoria*, which range from India to New Guinea and the North of Australia. These snakes, few of which grow to more than a yard in length, are far more aquatic in their habits than the species of *Tropidonotus*, and but seldom leave the water at all; and some of them even descend rivers to enter the sea. Their food consists of fish and other aquatic creatures; and they give birth to living young while in the water. A considerable number lie in wait for their prey by anchoring themselves to roots or sunken branches by means of the prehensile tail.

Fig. 23.—The Coral-Snake (*Elaps corallinus*).

In snakes, beauty and venom frequently go together, and an excellent instance of this association is afforded by the coral-snake (*Elaps corallinus*) of South America and the West Indies. Together with the remaining members of the colubrine family here noticed, the coral-snake belongs to the section

Proteroglypha. The essential feature of that section is to be found in the circumstance that it is the front, instead of the hinder, upper maxillary teeth that are grooved for the transmission of the poisonous secretion. Needless to say, all are venomous—some highly so. The genus in which the coral-snake is included comprises many other species, of which the majority inhabit the warmer parts of America, although a few are found in Southern Africa. They typify a sub-family (*Elapinæ*) in which the tail has a cylindrical form, and all the members of which live either on the ground or in trees. The coral-snake, which grows to rather more than a couple of feet in length, is easily recognised by its brilliant coloration, the whole body and tail being divided into a number of segments of cinnabar-red, separated by shorter segments of black, with indistinct borders of greenish - white. The coral - snake, which frequents wooded districts, is a strictly terrestrial species, feeding upon other reptiles and insects. Nearly allied are the resplendent adders (*Callophis*) of the warmer parts of Asia, distinguished by the presence of a groove traversing the whole front surface of the upper fangs, and likewise by the scales forming thirteen rows. These slender snakes are generally found in rocky districts.

The dreaded crait (*Bungarus cæruleus*), and its relative the banded adder, or raj-samp (*B. fasciatus*), are well-known Indian representatives of a genus whose geographical range extends from India and Ceylon to the south of China. From *Callophis*, in which all the teeth behind the fangs are channelled, this genus differs in that from one to three of the same teeth are solid throughout; a connecting link being formed by the genus *Hemibungarus*, in which there is one unperforated tooth in the hinder portion of each side of the upper jaw. Although the banded adder is larger than the crait, it does not appear to be so fatal to human life in India as the latter, owing to the circumstance that it mainly keeps to the open country. The crait, on the other hand, is one of the snakes most commonly met with in human dwellings, where it is fond of hiding in all kinds of unsuspected places. In colour, the crait is very dark brown above, marked with narrow rings, bars, or streaks of white.

Fig. 24.—INDIAN COBRA (*Naia tripudians*).

Whereas the crait and its immediate allies have the head passing imperceptibly into the neck, and lack the power of inflating the latter, the cobras (*Naia*) possess a distinctly defined neck, the lower part of which can be dilated at will; while they further differ by the equality in the size of the scales of the back with those of other parts. Cobras are represented by half a score of species, some of which are Oriental, while the others are African; the best known being the Egyptian asp (*N. haie*) and the common Indian cobra (*N. tripudians*). The latter is familiar as being the species commonly exhibited by Indian snake-charmers, and as it has been described in so many popular works, while newspapers are always giving accounts of its ravages, nothing in the way of description need be given in this place. Ordinarily this species does not exceed six feet in length; but Capt. F. Hawkins writes in the *Asian* newspaper of August 5th, 1892, that in Sangor a specimen was killed measuring seven feet three inches. The giant cobra (*N. bungarus*) of the Oriental countries is, however, a considerably larger species. Mr. P. A. Bulkley, writing from Burma, observes that "it may interest your readers to know that about ten years ago, while shooting in the jungle, I came upon a fine specimen of the snake in question over 12½ feet long, and, after an exciting chase, succeeded in capturing it alive and uninjured. I kept it in captivity for some months at Castle Rock in a large case, giving an occasional exercise in the spare room of my bungalow, and eventually took it to England for the reptile-house at the Zoological Gardens. At Brindisi I had to leave the snake to complete its journey by steamer to London, and upon opening its case on arrival at the Zoo, it was, unfortunately, found to be dead. The body, however, was in good preservation, and may be seen in a large case of alcohol in the reptile-room of the Natural History Museum at South Kensington." Although there are no cobras in Australia, that country is the home of an equally deadly serpent known as the death-adder (*Pseudechis porphyriacd*). In this snake the cylindrical body is extremely long and slender, the head is but imperfectly defined from the neck, and the scales are smooth. The species, which grows to as much as seven feet in length, is commonly known in its native country as the black snake.

The last group of the present section of the *Colubridæ* is that of the sea-snakes, which form the sub-family *Hydrophiinæ*. They differ from the *Elapinæ* by the compressed and oar-like form of the tail, and also by the scales on the under surface being either nearly similar to those on the upper parts, or if enlarged into shields, by their being much smaller than in ordinary terrestrial snakes. As their name implies, the sea-snakes are peculiar in the sub-order for their marine habits. Most of them, indeed, pass the whole of their time in the open sea, where they produce their young alive without the intervention of eggs ; but there are certain species which are partly terrestrial, and serve to connect the more typical representatives of the sub-family with the crait and its allies. Sea-snakes are most abundant in the tropical portions of the Western Pacific and the Indian Ocean, although a few enjoy a much more extensive range. They are all highly venomous, and most are handsomely and brilliantly tinted, the coloration being always variegated. They feed on fish and other marine creatures, and frequently associate in companies of considerable size. When cast on shore by the waves, the majority are utterly helpless, lying where they are thrown until they die. Unlike other members of the sub-order, sea-snakes change their skins piecemeal instead of entire ; the renovation taking place very frequently. They also differ from ordinary snakes in the shortness of the tongue ; and while at sea only the extreme tips of this organ are thrust out through a couple of small notches from the closed mouth. The three species constituting the genus *Platurus* are those which serve to connect the rest with the crait group, and are distinguished by having the under surface of the body and tail covered

Fig. 25.—BANDED SEA-SNAKE (*Platurus laticaudatus*).

with transversely elongated shields, while the upper surface is invested with smooth overlapping scales. One of the most common kinds, which grows to a length of about three feet, is met with from the Bay of Bengal to Oceania. These snakes can crawl with ease on land, and specimens have been from time to time met with at considerable distances inland. In addition to certain features connected with the nostrils, the more typical members of the sub-family—which are arranged under several separate genera—differ from the preceding in having the under surface scaled like the back, although in some forms more or less distinct vestiges exist of the enlarged shields. These genera are to a great extent distinguished from one another by the characters of the teeth, the most important among them being *Hydrus*, *Hydrophis*, and *Distira*. Emerson Tennent writes that "sea-snakes are found on all the coasts of Ceylon. I have sailed through large shoals of them in the Gulf of Manaar, close to the pearl-banks of Aripo. The fishermen of Calpentyn, on the west, live in perpetual fear of them, and believe their bite to be fatal. In the course of an attempt which was made to place a lighthouse on the great rocks of the south-east coast, known by seamen as the Basses or Baxos, the workmen who first landed found the portion of the surface liable to be covered by the tides honeycombed and hollowed into deep holes filled with water, in which were abundance of fishes and some molluscs. Some of these cavities also contained sea-snakes from four to five feet long, which were described as having the head hooded like the cobra de capello, and of a light grey colour slightly speckled. They coiled themselves like serpents on land, and darted at poles thrust in among them. The Singhalese who accompanied the party said that they not only bit venomously, but crushed the limbs of any intruder in their coils."

Blunt-Heads.—Family *Amblycephalidæ.*

A small group of snakes, the members of which are externally very similar to those of the sub-family *Dipsadomorphinæ* in the *Colubridæ*, are considered to form a family by themselves. From the *Dipsadomorphinæ* they are distinguished externally by the absence of a groove on the chin. They resemble the *Colubridæ* in having the maxillæ fixed in a horizontal position, but differ both from that family and from the *Viperidæ* by the shortness of those bones in the hinder part of the palate known as the pterygoids, which do not extend sufficiently far back to reach either the hinder ends of the lower jaw or the quadrate bone. Both jaws are provided with teeth, all of which are solid, so that these snakes are non-venomous. The slight expansibility of the mouth indicates that they prey upon small animals, while the relatively large dimensions of the eye, in which the pupil is vertical, proclaim nocturnal habits. Five genera of these snakes are known, two, namely, *Amblycephalus* and *Haplopeltura*, being confined to the Oriental countries, whereas *Dipsas*, *Pseudopareus*, and *Leptognathus* are from Tropical America.

The Viper Tribe.—Family *Viperidæ.*

The last family of snakes is a large one, and includes the vipers, pit-vipers, puff-adders, and rattle-snakes; all being highly venomous. The essential distinctive feature of the *Viperidæ* is to be found in the fact that the short maxillæ of the upper jaw are armed with a pair of large perforated fangs, and can be erected so as to become situated at right angles to the plane of the hinder portion of the palate. Obviously, this gives to the fangs the most favourable position for inflicting severe wounds. In the viperine snakes the head is always more or less flattened, and is frequently triangular in shape; while the body is plump and thick, and the tail abbreviated. In accordance with their chiefly nocturnal habits, the eye has its pupil in the form of a vertical slit. Only a few vipers climb, and none are aquatic ; while, so far as present information goes, all give birth to their young in a fully developed state without laying eggs. In almost all countries popular report declares that the females of many species receive their young into their mouth when alarmed, whence they apparently pass down the throat ; and although many attempts have been made to discredit such statements, it is difficult to believe that they have not some foundation of truth.

Of the two sub-families into which these snakes are divided by zoologists, the typical vipers, or *Viperinæ*, are confined to the Eastern Hemisphere, and are characterised by the absence of pits or depressions in the pair of head-shields known as the loreals. The common British viper (*Vipera berus*) is the most familiar representative of the typical genus, all the members of which have two longitudinal series of shields on the under surface of the tail, while the scales on the body are keeled and arranged in from nineteen to thirty-one straight longitudinal rows, and the upper surface of the head is invested either with relatively small shields or with scales. There are about twenty different kinds of true vipers, and these are distributed over the greater part of the Old World, although there are none in Australasia or Madagascar, and only one in India. The common viper enjoys a very wide geographical distribution, extending from the Arctic Circle to Spain and Portugal, and from the latter country eastwards to Siberia. It not unfrequently grows to ten inches in length, and, like its kindred, is partial to warm sandy heaths. The sand-viper (*V. ammodytes*) of Southern and Eastern Europe is remarkable for having a flexible horn-like and scaly appendage surmounting the tip of the muzzle, the use of which has not yet been explained. To the genus *Bitis* belongs the dreaded African puff-adder (*B. arietans*), in which the head is broader and more distinctly triangular than in any of its kindred. As this noxious serpent has a habit of lying with only its head exposed, it is frequently not noticed by men and animals until too late ; and it is consequently responsible for many deaths. Even large mammals are said to succumb very speedily to the bite of this loathsome monster. The name of puff-adder is derived from the habit possessed by this snake of blowing itself out with air when excited. Nearly allied to the true vipers are the horned vipers of the genus *Cerastes*, so named from the presence of a pair of scaly horns situated above the eyes of the males, and in some species in the females also. The scales, too, are arranged in oblique instead of straight series. Both species of the genus are inhabitants of those parts of Northern Africa lying to the eastward of Morocco, but one is also found in Arabia. They grow to about a couple of feet in length, and assimilate remarkably in coloration to the sandy deserts they frequent. They may be often seen so deeply buried in the sand that only the head and a portion of the neck project above the surface. Another nearly allied genus is that of the saw-vipers, or *Echis ;* these snakes being distinguished from the last by the absence of

Fig. 26.—PUFF-ADDER (*Bitis arietans*).

horns on the head, and by the shields on the lower surface of the tail forming a single instead of a double series. This genus is likewise represented by two desert-haunting species, but one of these has a much wider geographical range than either of the horned vipers, extending from Northern Africa to India, whereas the second is restricted to Palestine and Arabia. Whereas the puff-adder produces a prolonged hissing sound by the expulsion of the air which has been drawn in to blow out the body, the Indian saw-viper gives rise to a somewhat similar sound in a totally different manner. In this species the keels on the scales of the sides of the body are distinctly serrated; and by rubbing the folds of the body together the contact of these saw-like keels gives rise to a kind of grating, or even hissing noise. This snake is a very fierce species, often attacking without provocation; and a large percentage of the deaths from snake-bite in India may be attributed to this species and to the equally deadly Russell's viper (*Vipera russelli*).

The second sub-family, or *Crotalinæ*, the members of which may be collectively termed pit-vipers, are typified by the well-known rattle-snakes of the New World, although several other genera belonging to the same sub-family are found in various parts of Asia. There are, however, no representatives of this group in Africa, where, on the other hand, the typical vipers, or *Viperinæ*, attain their maximum degree of development. The distinctive feature of the pit-vipers, and the one from which they take their name, is the presence of a pair of deep pits in the fore front of the head, situated between the eyes and the nostrils in the so-called loreal shields. Doubtless these pits have some special function in the economy of these reptiles, but what this may be naturalists do not seem to have hitherto discovered. The peculiar jointed horny appendage to the tail known as the rattle gives to the snakes of the typical genus *Crotalus* their distinctive name, and at the same time serves to distinguish them at a glance from all the other members of the sub-order. This rattle increases in size by the intercalation of new joints between its terminal button and the scaly portion of the tail, young specimens having only the button. The longer a rattle-snake lives, the more joints it has to its rattle; and formerly specimens with as many as twenty rings were by no means uncommon, although at the present day, owing to the war of extermination waged against these noxious reptiles, such are very rare. Very diverse views have been entertained as to the precise use of the rattle to its owner, and since the question is by no means even yet decided, it need not be discussed in this place. All rattle-snakes are characterised by the unusually large size of their venom-glands, and they are consequently among the most deadly of serpents. Most of the eleven representatives of the genus are North American, although one species extends to South America. In their general habits they are very similar to vipers, frequenting dry sandy districts; but in parts of North America rattle-snakes frequently take up their abode in the warrens of the prairie-marmot, where they prey on the young of the rightful owners. In the colder parts of their habitat, these snakes become torpid during the

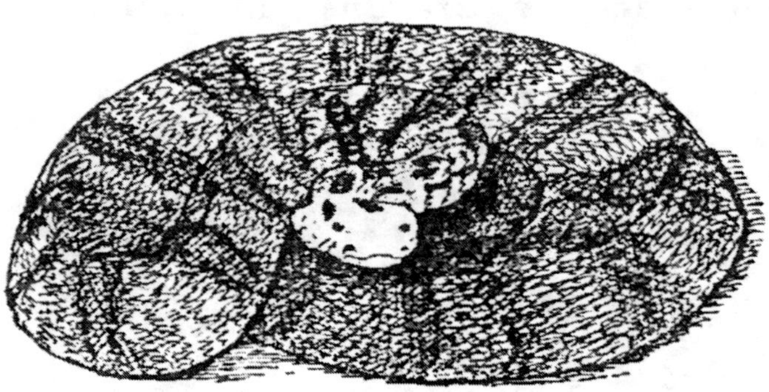

Fig. 27.—A Rattle-Snake (*Crotalus*).

winter months ; and in certain rocky districts they were formerly wont to assemble in enormous numbers, passing the winter huddled up together in caves, where they kept one another warm. At the approach of the cold season, thousands of these snakes might be seen travelling from all points of the compass to their own special cave ; and marvellous stories have been told of attacks made upon these haunts when the hapless reptiles were sleeping in fancied security. It is somewhat curious that rattle-snakes lack the power of hissing ; and it is highly probable that this disability has some connection with the presence of the rattle. Nearly allied to the rattle-snakes is the equally deadly bushmaster (*Lachesis mutus*) of tropical South America, which has a spine in place of a rattle at the tip of the tail, while the lower surface of the latter bears a number of spiny scales. There is often a well-marked keel running down the middle of the back, of which there is no trace in the typical genus. This snake is one of the few serpents which do not flee at the presence of man, always standing its ground and endeavouring to inflict a blow. Since it frequently grows to ten feet and over, and its bite is rapidly fatal even to large mammals, it is one of the most dangerous of its tribe, and were it more common than it actually is, fatalities would be very numerous. By Mr. Boulenger the serpents formerly designated *Trigonocephalus* and *Trimeresaurus* are now included in *Lachesis*. These differ from the typical forms in having the whole of the top of the head covered with small scales, instead of large scales. Some species are arboreal, and have the tail prehensile ; some of these inhabiting Tropical America, and others South-Eastern Asia. Whereas the species from the latter area have two rows of shields beneath the tail, those from the former have only a single row. Among the American forms with a non-prehensile tail, one of the most formidable is the jararaca (*L. lanceolatus*).

The so-called halys vipers, forming the genus *Ancistrodon*, have representatives alike in the northern half of the American Continent and Asia, while one kind is found in the Ural Mountains. Although none have a rattle, in some kinds there is a small spine at the tip of the tail, which appears to be a vestige of that organ. Of the Transatlantic species one of the most dreaded, and at the same time one of the handsomest, is the so-called copper-head (*A. contortrix*). It takes its name from the metallic coppery hue of the upper surface of the body ; this ground-colour being ornamented with a number of brown bands with darker edges. The copper-head, which frequents damp situations, has a wide geographical distribution. It is one of the species furnished with a spine-like horny appendage to the tail ; and differs from some of its kindred in having a single instead of a double series of shields on the under surface of the tail.

ORDER IV.—RHYNCHOCEPHALIA.

If we were to trust solely to external features a lizard-like reptile inhabiting certain small islands to the north-eastward of New Zealand, and locally known as the tuatera, would almost certainly be included in the order Squamata. When, however, the internal structure of this creature is examined, differences so important are observable that there can be no question of its total distinctness from that order. Accordingly, the tuatera, which is technically known as *Sphenodon punctatus*, not only represents by itself the family *Sphenodontidæ*, but also a distinct order. This, however, is only true at the present day, for in past epochs of the earth's history there flourished a number of reptiles evidently belonging to the same ordinal group, several of which lived in Britain. The tuatera, which grows to a length of about twenty inches, is characterised by the presence of a ridge of spines extending from the back of the head to the base of the tail, and represented on the latter by a less distinct crest. Superiorly, the body is covered with a mixture of small tubercles and granular scales ; but the lower aspect is invested with somewhat quadrangular large scales forming regular transverse bands. The toes, which are five in number on each foot, are partially webbed, and terminate in claws. In the eye the pupil takes the form of a vertical slit, and there is no external opening to the ear. None of these features are, however, sufficient to distinguish the tuatera from the lizards ; and to understand the distinction the skull must be examined. In the description of the Squamata it was stated that in all the members of that order the quadrate-bone is loosely connected with the other bones of the palate, and there is no bony arch connecting the former with the maxilla. On the other hand, in the tuatera the quadrate is firmly and immovably wedged in between the other bones, and is connected with the upper jaw by the aforesaid arch. There are likewise important differences in the structure of the bony palate, which is of a more primitive type than that of the lizards. Indeed, in many respects the skull is more like that of a crocodile, or even a tortoise, than that of a lizard. The teeth, too, are very peculiar. In the front of the jaws are a pair of chisel-like teeth, giving the form of a beak to this part of the skull : while the sides of the upper jaw and palate bear a double row of closely approximated teeth separated by a groove, and in that groove are received the single row of lower teeth, which are attached to the jaw in the acrodont manner. Although there are many peculiar features in this strange reptile, it will suffice to mention that within the skin of the hinder part of the under surface of the body are a number of abdominal ribs, forming a structure which corresponds anatomically with the plastron of a tortoise.

Fig. 28.—Tuatera (*Sphenodon punctatus*).

Although now becoming scarce, tuateras were formerly abundant in their native islands, where they might be seen in parties basking in the sun within easy reach of the sea. In captivity, where they flourish well, tuateras eat freely of meal-worms and other insects, but it is probable that vegetable substances form a part of their diet. Perhaps the most remarkable feature about this reptile is the vestige of an unpaired median eye situated deep down among the tissues of the head, and now totally functionless. Doubtless, however, in its ancestors this eye was functional, so that the original form may have been a veritable cyclops.

SUB-KINGDOM I.—VERTEBRATA.

CLASS IV.—AMPHIBIA.

By R. Lydekker, B.A., F.R.S., V.P.G.S., &c.

In popular natural history nearly every cold-blooded verebrate that breathes atmospheric air by means of lungs is commonly spoken of as a reptile, whether it crawls or creeps on the ground like a lizard, a frog, or a snake, or swims in the water like a newt; and if we take their adult condition alone into consideration, there is a good deal to be said in favour of regarding frogs and salamanders as reptiles, since they agree in many of their essential characters with the creatures to which the naturalist restricts that term. The case is, however, very materially altered when the developmental history of frogs and salamanders is taken into consideration. As every one knows, these creatures—with a few exceptions—commence their active existence after leaving the egg in the form of a tadpole. And as a tadpole is an aquatic creature, breathing the air dissolved in water by means of gills, and being provided with a fish-like tail, it is obvious that we have here a very important distinction from reptiles, which, at the commencement of life, are mere miniatures of the adult. It may be said, indeed, that frogs and salamanders commence life as fishes, but turn into reptiles when they become adult, and the existence of this remarkable change or metamorphosis serves to differentiate these creatures from reptiles as a distinct class, for which the name Amphibia is now usually adopted, although the alternative term Batrachia is also extant. It is true that in certain cases no such metamorphosis exists, the egg developing at once into a perfect air-breathing frog, while in some other instances the gills of the larval state are retained throughout life. In the former of these instances it is, however, evident that the larval stage has been suppressed owing to the exigencies of abnormal conditions in the life-history of the particular species. In the latter case, either the creature has now ceased to develop into the air-breathing adult form, or it has never advanced beyond the larval stage at any period of its history.

Amphibians, then, may be defined as cold-blooded vertebrates usually furnished with external gills at the commencement of life, but before becoming adult passing through a metamorphosis—during which the gills are exchanged for lungs;—and such of them as possess limbs having these structurally similar to those of reptiles. This change from a fish-like to a reptile-like animal is one of the most marvellous phenomena to be met with among vertebrates, and it is not a little remarkable that while everybody has the opportunity of witnessing this transformation each year of their lives, so many still refuse to believe in the evolution of animal life in general.

The metamorphosis is, however, by no means the sole feature by which amphibians are distinguished from reptiles. There are many structural peculiarities by which the adults of the former differ from the latter, although these are, unfortunately, deep-seated, and not externally apparent. Comparing the skull of a reptile with that of an amphibian, it will be found that whereas the former has a single knob-like prominence, or condyle, by means of which it is movably articulated to the first joint of the backbone, in the latter there are two such condyles. The embryo, too, of amphibians has a less complex type of enveloping structures, lacking the membranes respectively termed the allantois and the amnion.

Bearing in mind these important points of distinction, the student will readily see the propriety of separating the Amphibia as a class apart from the Reptilia. In the adult condition, the members of the present class show great differences of external form. The frogs and toads, for instance, are tailless, four-limbed creatures, in which the hind-legs exceed the front pair more or less markedly in length. On the other hand, the salamanders and newts, although likewise furnished with two pairs of limbs, have a long tail, and thus present a lizard-like form. In the newts, the tail, and sometimes also the back, is furnished with a longitudinal vertical fin, somewhat like that of a fish, although differing from the latter in the absence of any bony supports. Other forms have the body eel-like, and the limbs—of which the hinder pair may be wanting—small and rudimental ; while in some of these, like the olm, the external tuft-like gills are permanently retained. In yet another group, the whole form is worm-like, without any external vestiges of limbs.

In spite, however, of this great variation in external form, all the existing members of the class present the common feature of having the head, body, limbs, and tail covered with a soft skin, although in a few scales are buried beneath its surface. The outer skin, or epidermis, which is from time to time cast in a single piece, is always transparent, and the colour is consequently situated in the deeper layer. Various shades of black, brown, red, and yellow, are the predominant colours of amphibians, and these are very generally arranged in large irregular blotches, or in streaks ; but more rarely blues and greens are present. Peculiar glands, which may be either distributed over the whole surface, or confined to the region of the neck, secrete a milky fluid of a poisonous nature, which is poured out under the influence of rage or excitement. And that this secretion serves as a means of defence, will be evident to all who have watched a dog seize a toad. When this secretion reaches its highest development, the apertures of the glands open in the form of warty protuberances on the skin, as is the case in all toads and many salamanders. There are many peculiarities connected with the anatomy of the skeleton and soft internal parts of the Amphibia, but it will suffice to mention two. Unlike that of all the higher vertebrates, the tongue, when present, is attached to the front extremity of the lower jaw, so that it is protruded by being turned right over as if on a hinge ; and when in repose its tip is directed down the throat. It is always of a thick and fleshy nature, and thus quite unlike the same organ in snakes and lizards. The second peculiarity is connected with the skeleton, in which the ribs are either completely wanting, or represented merely by small rudiments affixed to the extremities of the long horizontal transverse processes of the joints of the backbone. This lack of functional ribs prevents amphibians from breathing in the same manner as the higher vertebrates, in which the cavity of the chest is alternately expanded and contracted by the movements of the ribs ; and they are, in consequence, compelled to take in air in large gulps by a swallowing action. In the presence of a large, thin, flattened bone, lying on the under surface of the hinder part of the skull, and known as the parasphenoid, amphibians differ from the existing forms of the higher vertebrates, and thereby approximate to fishes. In certain extinct reptiles, this bone appears, however, to be well developed, so that its importance in classification is less than has been supposed.

To describe in detail the developmental history of amphibians would require nearly as much space as is allotted in this volume to the entire class; and it is possible to give only the merest outline. Premising that all the members of the class lay eggs, and that in certain special cases some of the stages of development are abbreviated, the ordinary life-history of an amphibian is as follows. The eggs are generally deposited by the female in fresh water and are usually of small size and enveloped in a large jelly-like mass, among which the yolks are conspicuous as dark balls. When these eggs are ripe for hatching, the larvæ burst their investing membranes to make their appearance in the world as free-swimming fish-like creatures, provided with a long laterally compressed tail, but devoid of limbs or external gills. They still retain a portion of the yolk, which serves for a short time as nourishment. Soon a couple of pairs of feather-like gills make their appearance on the sides of the neck, and give the creature somewhat the look of bearing two pairs of fins. Although in those forms which permanently retain the tail these external gills persist for a considerable period, or even throughout life, in those of which the adults are tailless they soon disappear, and are replaced by internal gills comparable to those of fishes. These external gills are enclosed in a special gill-chamber, from which the water that has been taken in through the mouth is discharged through a single tube or a pair of tubes; the aperture of the latter being generally single, and situated either on the left side of the body or on its lower surface. With the sprouting of the external gills, the tail rapidly increases in relative size, and soon forms the greater portion of the creature. About this time small bud-like processes indicate the appearance of the limbs, the hinder pair first showing in the frogs and toads, but the front pair being the earlier in the tailed forms. In the earlier stages the jaws are furnished with horny teeth, but later with a kind of beak composed of the same substance. At this time the tadpole subsists on vegetable substances, and, consequently, has a long and much convoluted intestine. It, of course, breathes the air dissolved in the water in which it lives in the same manner as a fish, and has a two-chambered fish-like heart. In the tadpole stage the large tail has no backbone; and in the frogs and toads this appendage, after the limbs are well developed, is gradually absorbed, and finally disappears entirely. In the permanently tailed forms, on the other hand, this appendage develops vertebræ in its internal axis, when it becomes similar to the tail of a land reptile. About this time the jaws lose their horny beak, and develop teeth, and the intestine becomes shortened. Equally remarkable changes are at the same time taking place in the respiratory and circulatory organs. From the œsophagus a bag-like projection grows out, which, subsequently, divides into two, and eventually forms lungs, which little by little come into use, until the creature is able to breathe both in air and in water. Finally, the gills wither, and the adult frog or salamander appears as an air-breathing, insectivorous or carnivorous reptile-like creature, which has been developed from the fish-like tadpole. During the development of the lungs the heart has changed from a two-chambered to a three-chambered organ; so that even in this respect the adult amphibian is indistinguishable from a reptile. In most cases, when all these changes have been completed, the animal emerges from the water to pass a considerable portion of its time on land, although nearly always returning to its original element for the purpose of breeding. It has been said that the external gills usually form two pairs, but it should be added that, in some instances, these are increased to three, while in one case they are reduced to a solitary pair.

As regards their mode of life, amphibians are especially characterised by their partiality for moisture, some passing the whole of their time in the water, while none are found in absolutely desert districts. To their soft sensitive skins moisture is, indeed, an absolute necessity; and it seems that they imbibe such moisture as they require through the skin. In countries where one season of the year is especially dry, terrestrial amphibians are consequently compelled to undergo a period of more or less complete torpor. To a certain extent this is the case even in Britain, where a sudden shower after a dry spell brings out numerous frogs and toads at the commencement of evening in gardens where not one had been visible previously. In some parts of Argentina the effect of a shower after a drought is much more startling. There a garden may appear for weeks or months absolutely devoid of amphibian life, but after a single shower it will appear literally alive with huge frogs and toads of various kinds. Probably all the terrestrial amphibians are essentially nocturnal creatures, and, indeed, their skins soon become parched and withered by exposure to sunlight. Few objects are more pitiable than a belated frog or toad attempting to cross a dusty high-road in the full glare of the summer sun. Cloudy or wet days will, however, generally tempt these creatures from their hiding-places. Although the tailed forms are entirely or mainly silent creatures, frogs and toads during the breeding season utter their well-known croaking cries, and in moist tropical and subtropical countries life is rendered at times almost unbearable by their nocturnal choruses. In the breeding season frogs and toads become exceedingly bold, and they may be seen sitting within a few feet of the spectator, alternately dilating and contracting their capacious throats, as they give vent to their discordant cries. In order to make their sounds more intense, the males of many kinds are furnished with large sacs projecting on either side of the throat, which can be dilated till they resemble miniature balloons. Most members of the class subsist chiefly or entirely on insects and other small invertebrates, but some of the aquatic kinds consume fish, and some of the larger toads and frogs will readily attack not only other reptiles, but even the smaller birds and mammals. Thus a newspaper correspondent, writing from Nagpur, in India, observes that in the garden adjoining his house was a small pond, which was the home of a huge kind of frog. One afternoon he heard a myna making a great noise, and screaming as though it had been caught by some creature, so he went down the garden to ascertain what was the matter, and was just in time to see the bird disappearing down a big frog's throat. There were only a few feathers left, and the bird had been swallowed feathers and all. Now the common myna is quite as large as our English starling, and the frog certainly looked as though he had dined, so he was left in peace to enjoy his meal. On another occasion a big rat appeared in the house, and was being chased by himself and servants from room to room, when it dashed through a disused bathroom. A large frog which happened to be there made a most determined rush, but missed the rat, which disappeared down the waste water-pipe.

In conformity with their fondness for warmth and moisture, amphibians are most abundant in the tropical and sub-tropical portions of the globe, gradually diminishing, both in size and numbers, in the temperate zones, and being unknown in the polar regions, as indeed they are in deserts. Although members of the class are found in all regions except those named, the orders are by no means evenly distributed. In the Northern Hemisphere, for instance, salamanders and newts are abundant, and the burrowing forms, known as cæcilians, are wanting; whereas in the Southern Hemisphere cæcilians occur, but salamanders and newts are totally unknown. Among the frogs and toads certain families are confined to particular areas, but it is remarkable that there are indications of distinct relationship between certain groups respectively restricted to South America and Africa south of the Sahara.

ORDER I.—ECAUDATA.

Frogs and Toads.

The frogs and toads constitute one Order, all the members of which are easily recognised when adult by the short and often plump form of the body, the total absence of a tail, and the presence of four fully-developed limbs, the hind pair being generally much longer than the front ones. Even more striking features are displayed by the skeleton. Instead of continuing to the end of the body, the backbone proper stops short about the middle of the back, and never comprises more than eight vertebræ. Beyond this it is continued as a long, tapering, unjointed rod. To the extremities of the horizontal transverse processes of the last, or sacral vertebra, are articulated the anterior ends of the greatly elongated ilia of the pelvis, these bones running as far backwards as the hinder end of the aforesaid rod, where they bear the sockets for the articulation of the uppermost bone of the hind-legs. By this very peculiar, and indeed unique arrangement, the setting-on of the hind-limbs is carried far behind the sacrum. The radius and ulna in the fore-limb, and the tibia and fibula in the hind-limb, are respectively united to form a single bone, and the elongation of the hind-legs is produced by the lengthening of those bones in the ankle-joint known as the astragalus and calcaneum, so as to form a pair of parallel long bones. Like all other living members of the class in which both limbs are fully developed, frogs and toads have four front and five hind-toes. In the tadpole stage—which is occasionally suppressed—the hind-limbs bud before any trace of the front pair is visible. Usually this stage of existence is passed entirely in the water, but there are some very peculiar forms in which the young are produced in the moist foliage of leaves. On land the adults of the tailless batrachians progress either by taking long leaps from the hind-legs or by dragging forwards first one and then the other of these, and thus pushing the body along. In swimming, the hind-legs are alone employed for propulsion, the front pair being pressed close to the chest. The total number of species of the tailless amphibians probably does not fall far short of a thousand, and representatives of the group are found in all countries suitable to the existence of amphibian life- Curiously enough, the largest forms are found in some of the islands of the Pacific. Whereas the majority are terrestrial, a considerable number have adopted an arboreal life. The group is divided into twelve families, of which the two last differ from all the rest in the absence of the tongue. Unfortunately, the characters by which the first ten of these families are divided into two larger groups are taken from the skeleton, and are consequently somewhat difficult to explain to readers not specially versed in anatomy.

Sub-Order I.—Firmisternia.

The five families constituting this subordinal group are characterised as follows:—The tongue is present, and the large plate-like bones on the chest termed the metacoracoids are united together by a large median cartilage, attached to their free inner margins.

Typical Frogs.—Family *Ranidæ*.

In the family typified by the common British frog teeth are developed in the upper jaw, and the horizontal transverse processes of the sacral vertebra have, at most, only a slight terminal expansion, and are frequently cylindrical throughout. The frogs of this family display remarkable diversity in the form of the tips of the terminal bones of the toes, which may be either rounded, pointed, forked, T-shaped, or, more rarely, claw-like. The family—which includes a large number of genera and a host of species—has a wide geographical distribution. With the exception of a species of the typical genus from the extreme north of Australia, and another belonging to the genus *Cornifer* from New Guinea, there are no members of the family in Australasia. South America, too, is poorly off, having, in addition to certain species belonging to the typical genus *Rana*, only five genera, and about a dozen species. Moreover, since none of these latter range farther south than Ecuador and Colombia, while *Rana* does not apparently extend southward of Amazonia, the more southern parts of that continent are characterised by the total absence of the present family. In a group so extensive, it is difficult to select genera for special notice, although the typical *Rana* must of course be mentioned. In the numerous frogs of this genus the tongue is free and more or less deeply notched at the tip, the pupil of the eye forms a horizontal slit, and the toes of the fore-feet are free, whereas those of the hind-feet are more or less fully webbed. By putting the finger into the mouth of any frog of this genus, it will be readily felt that teeth are present on the vomers, occupying the middle region of the palate. Whereas in some forms the tips of the toes are simple, in others they are dilated. The genus has a distribution nearly coextensive with that of the family, one species being found in the extreme north of Australia, although there is none from Papua. There are several species of the genus inhabiting Europe, such as the common frog (*R. temporaria*), the edible frog (*R. esculenta*), the agile frog (*R. agilis*), the Spanish frog (*R. iberica*), and Lataste's frog (*R. latastei*). Of these, the only one indigenous to Britain is the common frog, in which the hind feet are incompletely webbed, and the males are unprovided with the dilatable throat-sacs characterising those of the edible species. Although the latter—of which

Fig. 1.—COMMON FROG (*Rana temporaria*).

there are two varieties, differing from one another in colour—is properly a native of the Continent, it has been introduced into the fens of Cambridge and Norfolk, where it seems to flourish. It has a very extensive geographical range, being found as far south as North-Western Africa, and as far east as Japan. Although the species is the only one eaten in Europe, other members of the sub-order are sent to table in distant lands, and the writer has partaken of a dish of frogs in Argentina which belonged to a totally different family. The great relative length of the hind-legs and generally slender form of the body serves to distinguish the agile frog; while the fourth and fifth of the species mentioned above differ from the rest by their spotted bellies. All these frogs are comparatively small creatures, which are greatly exceeded in size by species from more distant lands.

Among these, the bull-frog (*R. catesbyana*) of Eastern North America occupies an intermediate position in this respect; the largest member of the whole genus being the Solomon Island frog (*R. guppyi*), which grows to nine inches in length, exclusive of the limbs. The habits of the common frog are too familiar to need description; and it is probable that like this species, all the members of the genus take to the water at the time of breeding. Some are, however, more aquatic than others; and there are also certain frogs of this genus which are partially arboreal in their habits, while others have taken to burrowing in the ground. The climbing species have the tips of the toes expanded into discs, but smaller expansions may be present in the aquatic kinds. An Indian species (*R. breviceps*) makes burrows in the ground to a depth of about eighteen inches. Omitting mention of most of the other numerous genera of this extensive family, attention must be concentrated on the curious flying-frogs constituting the genus *Rhacophorus*. These frogs—of which there are more than forty species from the Oriental countries and the island of Madagascar—have the tips of both pairs of feet expanded into large discs, and very generally the front pair are as fully webbed as the hinder, although in some kinds the webs of the former are less fully developed. The eyes are remarkable for their fulness and brilliancy; and the general hue of the skin is bright green. Some species, are, however, stated to have the power of changing their hue to harmonise with their surroundings. In the skeleton of many of the species the tips of the terminal joints of the toes are in the form of the letter Y. Except during the breeding season, when they doubtless take to the water, these frogs are arboreal in their habits. They derive their name of flying frogs from a statement to the effect that one species at least has been observed to take a long flying leap from a tree, apparently supported by the large webs between the toes. Although it does not appear that such a feat has ever been witnessed by a European observer, it is almost incredible that the sole use of these huge webs is for swimming, more especially since these frogs pass but a comparatively small portion of their existence

Fig 2.—Flying Frog (*Rhacophorus*).

in water. One member of a Tropical American genus of this family—namely *Phyllobates trinitatis*, of Trinidad and Venezuela—is remarkable on account of its curious nursing habits. The tadpoles are provided with sucking-discs on the mouth, by means of which they attach themselves to the back of their female parent, and are thus carried about in safety. As many as from twelve to eighteen tadpoles may sometimes be found thus clinging to one frog. A similar mode of attachment occurs in one species of the under-mentioned genus *Dendrobates*, but in this case this mode of locomotion seems to be resorted to only when the ponds in which the individuals have bred dry up.

Family *Dendrobatidæ*.

In addition to the members of the genus *Rhacophorus*, there are many other frogs which have taken to an arboreal life, and so much do these resemble one another in external appearance that it is probable any non-scientific observer would regard all of them as being very closely allied. Not so that dreadful personage the anatomist, who tells us that while the members of one family conform in the structure of the bones of the chest to the sub-order now under consideration, all those of another family to be mentioned later have a totally different conformation of this region. Accepting this distinction, we must regard the Tropical American tree-frogs of the genus *Dendrobates*, and those belonging to the nearly allied Malagasy genus *Mantella*, as forming a family by themselves. From the frogs of the family *Ranidæ* the *Dendrobatidæ* are distinguished by the absence of teeth both in the upper jaw and on the bones of the palate. In both genera the toes are unwebbed, and terminate in small adhesive discs, but whereas in *Mantella* the tongue is notched at the tip, in *Dendrobates* it is entire. One species of the latter genus (*D. tinctorius*) is remarkable for the brilliancy and variability of its coloration; while it is further noticeable as being less arboreal than its congeners, generally frequenting low herbage or ground strewn with dead leaves. As already mentioned, another species carries its tadpoles clinging to its back from pool to pool in seasons of drought.

Family *Engystomatidæ*.

Another nearly allied family of frogs is distinguished from the last by the expansion of the extremities of the horizontal transverse processes of the sacral vertebra; both groups agreeing in the absence of teeth in the upper jaw. These frogs present great variation in the structure of the bones and cartilages forming the chest; the typical genus *Engystoma*, together with *Cacopus* and several others, showing the absence of the bones known as precoracoids—a feature rare in the sub-order. This family may be regarded as essentially a southern one, its geographical range embracing Africa, Madagascar, the Malayan Peninsula and Islands, India, the south of China, New Guinea, and South and Central America. Two species of the typical genus extend, however, into North America as far as Mexico and Carolina. Nearly a score of genera are included in the family. Among these, a considerable number are characterised by the extremely small relative width of the opening of the mouth; and it is probable

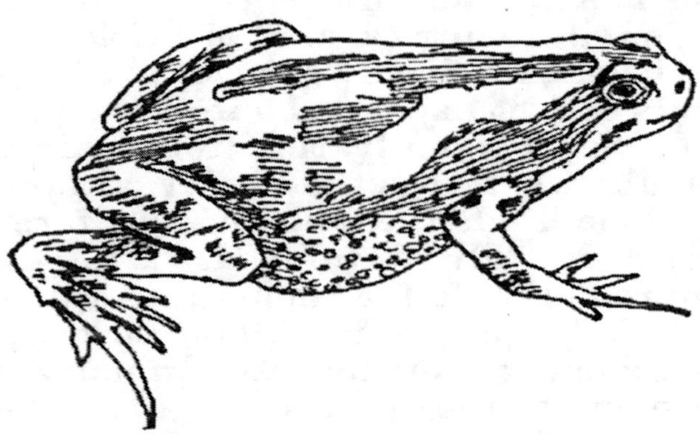

Fig. 3.—Cacopus systema.

that all these subsist more or less exclusively on ants and termites. A large proportion of these frogs are nocturnal in their habits, and these may be recognised by the vertical pupil of the eye. Although many have discs at the tips of the toes, none of these are tree-haunting species. A considerable number of members of the family are, however, burrowers; and in these the hind-limbs are unusually powerful, and are also specially protected by horny sheathings. Others, again, pass a large portion of their time in the water. It would be profitless to give in this place the distinctive characteristics of all the genera included in this extensive family; and attention may accordingly be confined to a few which are noteworthy on account of some peculiarity in the habits of their representatives. Foremost among these is the Chilian Darwin's frog (*Rhinoderma darwini*), in which the female has transferred the task of carrying and tending the eggs and young to her partner. Whereas there is nothing remarkable about the structure of the female of this frog, the male has a capacious pouch underlying the whole of the lower surface of the body, which communicates with the exterior by means of a pair of apertures opening into the mouth on each side of the tongue. As soon as his partner has deposited her eggs, the male frog takes them in his front paws and transfers them to his mouth, whence they pass into the great nursing pouch, where they remain in perfect security till hatched into young frogs, which make their way into the world by the same passages. The tadpoles never develop gills, and this frog is the sole member of its genus. Equally noteworthy are the African frogs constituting the genus *Breviceps*. These species, which take their name from the small size and shortness of the head, would almost seem to have given rise to the fable of the ox and the frog, since they have the singular habit of puffing out the body till the head and limbs are nearly buried, and the creature looks almost like a ball. What may be the object of this curious habit does not appear to have been ascertained.

Fig. 4.—Darwin's Frog (*Rhinoderma darwini*)

Family *Dyscophidæ*.

This family of frogs includes eight genera, all of which are confined to the island of Madagascar, with the single exception of the one species constituting the genus *Calluella*, which inhabits Burma and Tenasserim. The essential distinctive features of the frogs of this family are the presence of teeth in the upper jaw, coupled with the expansion of the extremities of the transverse processes of the sacral vertebra, the latter feature serving to distinguish them from the members of the family *Ranidæ*, in which there is no such expansion. These frogs are very closely allied indeed to those of the preceding family, and as their chief interest lies in their peculiar geographical distribution, they need no further notice on this occasion.

Family *Ceratobrachidæ*.

A large frog from the Solomon Islands technically known as *Ceratobatrachus guentheri*, and easily recognised by the extremely sharp point formed by the tip of the nose, is regarded as forming a family by itself. From all the members of the sub-order under consideration, this frog differs by having both the upper and the lower jaw armed with a full series of teeth; and it is further characterised by the absence of expansion of the extremities of the transverse processes of the sacral vertebra. It is an ugly-looking creature at best, the large triangular head bearing ridges, and the pointed nose being surmounted with a loose flap of skin, and similar flaps covering the eyes. The mouth, too, is of enormous capacity, and thus adds to the generally repulsive appearance of this frog. The sharp-nosed frog is evidently a highly specialised species, since it lays very large eggs, from which young frogs emerge in a highly developed condition, the tadpole stage being compressed and passed in the eggs. Mr. Guppy writes that "during the descent from one of the peaks of Faröe Island, I stopped at a stream some 400 feet above the sea, where my native boys collected from the moist crevices of the rocks close to the water a number of transparent, gelatinous balls, rather smaller than a marble. Each of these balls contained a young frog about a third of an inch in length. On my rupturing the ball, the tiny frog took a marvellous leap into existence, and disappeared before I could catch it."

Sub-Order II.—Arcifera.

The remaining families of the order in which the tongue is present constitute a second subordinal group, differing from the first by the conformation of the bones and cartilages of the chest. Instead of the two metacoracoid bones being connected together in the middle line by a single cartilage attached to their free inner edges, each of the metacoracoids is expanded on the same side into a plate of cartilage, one of which overlaps the other.

Family *Leptodactylidæ*.

Having the above-mentioned type of chest-structure, the large and important family of the *Leptodactylidæ*—the *Cystignathidæ* of many authors—are spread over Central and South America and Australia. In all of them only the upper jaw is furnished with teeth, and the extremities of the horizontal transverse processes of the sacral vertebra are either cylindrical, or only slightly expanded. In both these respects these frogs resemble the *Ranidæ*, so that they may be regarded as holding the same relative position in the present sub-order as is occupied by the latter in the Firmisternia. More than a score of genera and a very large number of species are included in the family, and it may be noted that whereas in the majority of the Australian genera the pupil of the eye is vertical, this is but seldom the case in the American forms. The family may be divided into three groups, in the first of which the breast-bone terminates below in a rod-like process. To this group belongs the typical genus *Leptodactylus*, of which all the numerous species are American. These frogs, in which the pupil is horizontal, are much like the *Ranidæ* in external appearance, but the hind-toes are not webbed. They are peculiar in that during the breeding season the fore-limb becomes much swollen, and in the skeleton the humerus bears a conspicuous bony ridge. All these frogs possess a very powerful voice, and in parts of the Argentine their croaking is a dreadful nuisance. Many of them burrow holes in the ground for their eggs. As an example of the second group, in which there is no bony rod to the breast-bone, and the hind-toes are nearly or completely free, we may take a West Indian species (*Hylodes martinicensis*) belonging to a large American genus, all the species of which are arboreal. This particular kind has the peculiar habit of laying its large eggs singly in the axils of leaves, where a few drops of water may from time to time collect after a shower. From these eggs the young frogs emerge with only a small remnant of the tail, which is soon absorbed ; and it appears that during development no gills are produced, but that the tail, which is richly supplied with blood-vessels, acts as a breathing organ. A third American genus is *Ceratophrys*, which includes the well-known horned-frogs of Brazil and Argentina, and belongs to a group in which there is no bony rod to the breast-bone, and the hind-toes are more or less fully webbed. The Brazilian *C. boiei* is a huge creature, growing to as much as eight inches in length, and furnished with a pair of large horn-like outgrowths on the upper eyelids. In the Argentine esquerzo (*C. ornata*) these processes are less developed, and the whole size is less. Like its kindred, furnished with an enormous mouth, this species is beautifully mottled with green, olive, and gold, and in this respect is really a handsome creature, although its shape is hideous. All the larger kinds are very fierce in disposition, and carnivorous in their habits, killing and eating small mammals, birds, reptiles, and other members of their own order. They are much dreaded by the natives of the districts they inhabit, who tell wonderful stories as to their flying at men, and even at the noses of horses and cattle. Their bite is stated to produce very extensive swellings. When attacking a large animal, they utter a cry more like a bark than anything else ; but their ordinary note is bell-like. I once brought several of these frogs in a box to Buenos Aires by rail, and during the journey the guard and some of the passengers were considerably alarmed by the noises proceeding from the cage, many of them wondering what kind of noisome beasts were therein enclosed.

Fig. 5.—Horned Frog (*Ceratophrys ornata*).

Nearly allied to the preceding are the two South American genera *Dendrophryniscus* and *Batrachophrynus*, forming a small family differing from the *Leptodactylidæ* merely by the absence of teeth in the upper jaw, and thus serving to connect them with the next group.

Family *Dendrophryniscidæ*.

The Toads.—Family *Bufonidæ*.

Of far more importance is the almost cosmopolitan and large toad family, in which teeth are absent in both jaws, while the extremities of the transverse processes of the sacral vertebra are expanded. That the family is closely allied to the *Leptodactylidæ* is indicated by the approximation of two of its genera to two of the latter. Thus the Australian *Pseudophryne* resembles *Crinia* of the same country, while *Engystomops* is like *Paludicola*, both these latter being South American. Again two other genera exhibit resemblances to the *Engystomatidæ*. Most of the members of the family are crawling creatures, but the Javan *Nectes* is completely aquatic in its habits, and the members of the Oriental and African genus *Nectophryne* appear to be arboreal. The members of *Rhinophrynus*—which is one of the two genera approximating to the *Engystomatidæ*—feed on ants. Whereas in some forms the extremities of the terminal bones of the toes are simple, in others, such as *Nectophryne*, they are shaped like the letter T. Our remarks must be restricted to the typical genus *Bufo*, of which there are a very large number of species distributed over the greater part of the world, with the exception of Oceania, Australasia, and Madagascar. In this genus the pupil of the eye forms a horizontal slit, the tip of the tongue is not notched, the toes of the fore-feet are free, but the hinder ones are partially webbed. Occasionally the ends of the toes are expanded into small discs; the head may bear bony ridges, and in many cases the skin is covered with warts, which under excitement secrete a milky acrid fluid. Two species are met with in Britain, namely the common toad (*B. vulgaris*), and the natterjack (*B. calamita*); the latter being very local in our islands, and easily recognised by the whitish or yellow streak on the middle of the back. Although not found in Britain, a third European species is the handsome green toad (*B. viridis*), which also ranges into the north of Africa and Asia. The males differ from those of the common species in possessing a vocal sac beneath the throat.

Fig. 6.—NATTERJACK TOAD (*Bufo calamita*)

Family *Hylidæ*.

Although many of the tree-frogs belonging to this family are very similar externally to the *Dendrobatidæ*, they agree with the toads in the conformation of the skeleton of the chest. From the *Bufonidæ* they may be readily distinguished by the possession of upper teeth; while a still more distinctive peculiarity is to be found in the claw-shaped terminal joints of the toes. The frogs of this family, which are mostly arboreal in their habits, and are ranged under a considerable number of generic divisions, attain their maximum development in America (especially its tropical regions) and Australasia, but also occur in Europe and Northern Asia, while a single representative of the typical genus Hyla is found in India. The genus just named includes more than a hundred and fifty species, and has a distribution coëxtensive with that of the family. Whereas the European *H. arborea* is a tiny little creature, some of the Brazilian species measure as much as three inches in length. These frogs have the tips of the toes expanded into discs, and the hind-feet more or less fully webbed. In the eye the pupil is horizontal; and the hinder end of the tongue may be either adherent or partially free. The males of the European species, and likewise those of some other kinds, have a huge vocal sac on the throat. In order to assimilate them to their surroundings, tree-frogs are of a brilliant green colour. Except during the breeding season—when they descend tem-

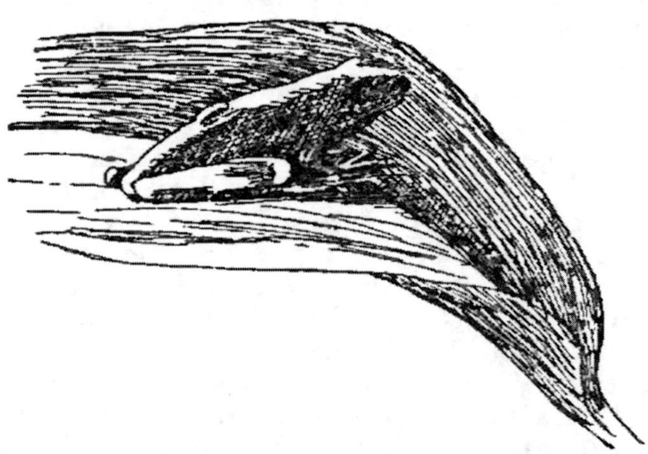

Fig. 7.—EUROPEAN TREE-FROG (*Hyla arborea*).

porarily to the water—they pass their whole time in trees or shrubs, and are enabled to absorb the moisture from leaves by means of special glands on the skin of the under surface of the body. Some of the species inhabiting the hottest parts of Brazil construct basin-shaped nests of mud in ponds for the protection of the eggs, this task falling entirely to the share of the female. As an example of a non-arboreal species, the North American grasshopper-frog (*Acris gryllus*) may be mentioned. This species, which is the sole member of its genus, and is very closely allied to *Hyla*, spends its time among herbage in moist situations. More remarkable are the pouched frogs (*Nototrema*), with several species from Central and Western Tropical America, and one from Pernambuco. These frogs are also closely allied to *Hyla*, but the females have a large pouch in the skin of the back, with its aperture near the hinder end of the body. In this pouch the eggs—to the number of about fifteen—are deposited by the male, and there they develop into tadpoles. The gills of the tadpoles are protected by a special bell-like organ: and the young do not leave the chamber until they have assumed the adult form.

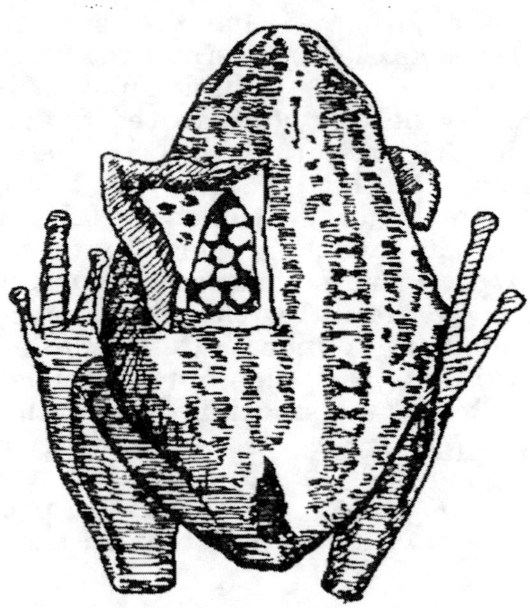

Fig. 8.—Pouched Frog (*Nototrema*.)

A small number of genera constitute a family distinguished from the *Hylidæ* by the much greater expansion of the extremities of the horizontal transverse processes of the sacral vertebra, and also by the simple terminations of the end joint of the toes. The genera have a small geographical range, but the family occurs in North America, Europe, the Oriental countries and Papua. In the country first named it is represented by several species of *Scaphiopus*, nearly allied to which are the two Central and South European species of *Pelobates*. The members of both these groups are burrowing frogs, with the hind-toes largely webbed, and in their movements they are somewhat intermediate between the true frogs and the toads. The eggs of the European forms are laid in long strings, which are twined by the males round the stems of aquatic plants. Another European species (*Pelodytes punctatus*), together with the other genera of the family, differs from the foregoing in the mode by which the rod forming the hinder termination of the back-bone is articulated with the last vertebra.

Family *Pelobatidæ*.

Fig. 9.—Midwife Frog (*Alytes*).

Family *Discoglossidæ.*

The sixth family of the present sub-order includes four genera, with a very small number of species, and is confined to the northern half of the Eastern Hemisphere and New Zealand. These frogs, which have teeth in the upper jaw, and the extremities of the transverse processes of the sacral vertebra expanded, are specially distinguished by the retention of rudimental ribs. To this family belong the painted frog (*Discoglossus pictus*) from the south of Europe and Algeria, and the fire-bellied frog (*Bombinator igneus*) of Europe and Asia, the latter having a triangular pupil to the eye, an adherent tongue, and no drum to the ear. The under-parts are mottled with orange or yellow, and the croak is very loud. The two European species of midwife-frogs (*Alytes*) are so named from the circumstance that the male takes the chains of eggs laid by the female and winds them round his hind-legs. After remaining concealed in a hole till the eggs are mature, he enters the water, when the tadpoles burst their shells.

Families *Hemiphractidæ* and *Amphignathodontidæ.*

These two small Tropical American families differ from all the other members of the sub-order in possessing teeth in both jaws, the first of the two having the extremities of the horizontal transverse processes of the sacral vertebra cylindrical, whereas in the second they are expanded.

Sub-Order III.—Aglossa.

The two genera and families by which alone this sub-order is represented differ from both the other subordinal groups in the complete absence of the tongue.

Family *Xenopodidæ.*

The three African species of spur-toed frogs (*Xenopus*) are sufficiently distinguished by possessing teeth in the upper jaw and the presence of spur-like nails on three of the toes of the hind-feet, which are fully webbed. Their tadpoles, which are born of large size, and without external gills, are furnished with a pair of barbels to the upper jaw.

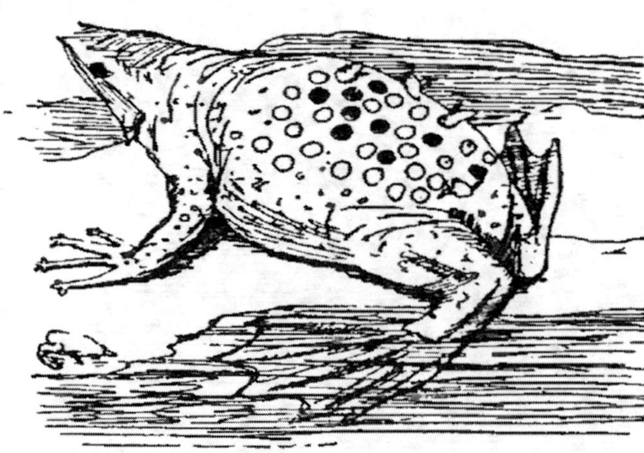

Fig. 10.—Surinam Water-Toad (*Pipa americana*).

Family *Pipidæ.*

The well-known Surinam water-toad, or pipa (*Pipa americana*), of the Guianas and Brazil, is the only member of this family, which is characterised by both jaws being toothless. Externally, the pipa may be recognised by its short and triangular head, which is furnished with a large flap of skin at each corner of the mouth, and has very minute eyes. The four front toes are quite free, and terminate in expanded star-like tips, but a large web unites all the five toes of the hind-foot. In any state the creature is ugly, but when the female is carrying her nursery about with her she is repulsive. Soon after they are laid, the eggs are taken up by the male and pressed, one by one, into the cells in the thickened skin of his partner's back, where they grow till they fit closely to the hexagonal form of their cells, each of which is closed above by a kind of trap-door. After some eighty-two days the eggs reach their full development and produce, not tadpoles, but perfect little toads. The reason of this is that tadpoles, which require to breathe the air dissolved in water by means of their external gills, could not exist in the cells, and, consequently, this stage of the development is passed through very rapidly within the egg. When ready to come forth, the young toads, which are usually from sixty to seventy in number, although there may sometimes be more than a hundred, burst open the lids of their cells, and, after stretching forth their head or a limb, make their appearance. When free from her charge, the mother rubs off what remains of the cells against any convenient stone or plant-stem, and comes out in a new skin. After breeding, these toads become much flattened, and pass the whole of their time in water.

ORDER II.—CAUDATA.

NEWTS AND SALAMANDERS.

THE ordinary British newts and the black-and-yellow salamander of the Continent are familiar representatives of an order of amphibians broadly distinguished from the frogs and toads by the permanent retention of the tail. In the skeleton they differ by the more normal structure of the bones of the limbs, in which there is no elongation of any of those in the ankle joint, while the ulna and fibula are respectively distinct from the radius and tibia. The more typical representatives of the order are lizard-like in external form, having a comparatively short body and two pairs of well-developed limbs. There are, however, certain aberrant types in which the body becomes more or less elongated in form, with a diminution in the size of the limbs, and in some instances the disappearance of the hinder pair. From the permanent retention of the tail, it is obvious that even in the more typical forms the metamorphosis is a much less marked feature among these amphibians than it is in the frogs and toads. And in certain instances there is no metamorphosis at all—the external gills persisting throughout life. In another case we have the peculiar condition that whereas certain individuals may retain their gills permanently, and breed while in this condition, other individuals of the same species lose their gills, and develop into the proper adult terrestrial form before breeding. It is thus evident that these amphibians are in a state of unstable equilibrium as regards their transformation; and it may be a question whether those kinds with permanent gills are not really larvæ, which for some reason have ceased to develop into the proper adult form.

Numerically, the tailed amphibians form a small group, containing probably less than one hundred and fifty species, arranged under four families. They are chiefly confined to the Northern Hemisphere—where they attain their maximum development in North America—and are unrepresented in Australasia, the intra-tropical districts of South America and Africa south of the Sahara. The true newts are, however, chiefly an Old World group. The Oriental region is very poorly furnished with these amphibians, having only three species altogether. Of these, one is an axolotl from Siam, belonging to the American genus *Amblystoma*, while the other two constitute the genus *Tylotriton*, one inhabiting the Liu Kiu Islands, and the other the eastern part of the Himalaya and Yunnan. All the tailed amphibians are nocturnal creatures, the great majority of which pass some portion of their time in water, while others are permanently aquatic. Such as develop lungs and lose their gills have to rise periodically to the surface of the water in order to breathe. Their tenacity of life forms a striking feature in the physiology of these creatures; species inhabiting tropical regions, subject to periodical droughts, becoming torpid at such seasons, while those from colder regions hibernate. Even envelopment in ice is not always sufficient to destroy life. The same low organisation is indicated by their power of reproducing the tail and limbs. Whereas the majority of species have large and well-developed eyes, a few which inhabit underground waters have lost the power of sight, and have the rudimental eyes deeply buried beneath the skin. The aquatic species swim chiefly or entirely by means of a tail, and thus differ markedly from the frogs, in which the hind-limbs alone are employed. Most of the terrestrial forms are slow-moving creatures, although a few dart about with the rapidity of lizards. Certain members of the order are peculiar in producing living young, the tadpoles being in some cases retained within the body of the female until considerably developed.

The greater number of the members of the order are included in the family typified by the common yellow and black salamander, although the genera may be arranged in four sub-families. As a family, the *Salamandridæ* are distinguished by undergoing a full metamorphosis, with the consequent loss of the gills in the adult condition, as well as by the presence of teeth in both jaws, of eyelids, and of maxillary bones. In the typical sub-family *Salamandrinæ*, the teeth on the palate are arranged in the form of a pair of posteriorly diverging rows, such rows being situated on the inner margins of two long processes running backwards from the palatine bones. No teeth are developed on the bone forming the hinder part of the inner surface of the skull, and known as the parasphenoid; and in the backbone the bodies of the vertebræ have a cup at the hinder end, and a ball in front. The common black and yellow salamander (*Salamandra maculosa*) is the best-known representative of the typical genus of the sub-family, which includes two other species, and is confined to Central and Southern Europe, Algeria, and Syria. From the newts, the typical salamanders may be distinguished by the following features. In form the tail is cylindrical and tapering; there are five toes to each of the hind-feet; the two rows of the teeth on the palate are curved; and the tongue, which is of rather large size, and nearly oval in form, is free at the sides, and to a certain extent behind. The black ground-colour, marked with a double row of longitudinal yellow blotches on the head and back, and similar markings on the upper surface of the tail and limbs, sufficiently distinguish the salamander from the other

Family *Salamandridæ.*

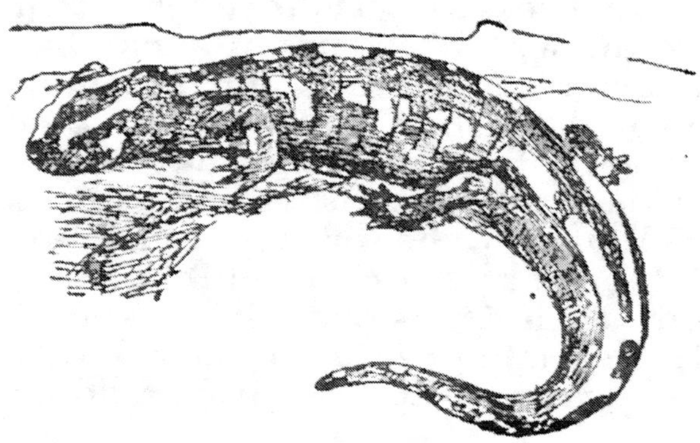

Fig. 11.—COMMON SALAMANDER (*Salamandra maculosa*).

members of the same genus. This species is a somewhat solitary and sluggish creature, spending most of the year on land, but resorting to the water during the spring, when breeding takes place. Usually the young are born alive, but occasionally eggs are laid, when they almost immediately hatch.

A large number of tadpoles come into the world at once, and these, in the ordinary mode of development, have already lost their gills. Formerly, highly poisonous properties were attributed to this salamander—as they, doubtless, still are among the uneducated peasantry of various parts of Europe,—and the creature was believed to be capable of being cast into a furnace without suffering harm. Beyond secreting an acrid fluid, it is, however, perfectly harmless. The range of this species includes a considerable part of Europe, as well as Syria and Algeria. Nearly allied is the somewhat smaller black salamander (*S. atra*) of the Alps. Although many eggs may be found in the body of the female, it appears that only a pair of tadpoles are produced, these being nourished by the eggs which never develop. While within the body of the parent, these tadpoles have very long external gills, which are shed previous to birth. Many years ago some tadpoles in the gilled condition were taken from the parent and placed in water. Almost immediately the large gills were cast off, and their place taken by much smaller ones, which remained for a long period. As remarked by Professor Mivart, "the curious and noteworthy point in this experiment is the fact that, after the original gills (which were unadapted for free external life (have perished, new and suitable gills become developed, and this not in a struggle for existence against rivals, but directly and spontaneously from the innate nature of the animal." The third and last species is *S. caucasica*, from the Caucasus, which differs from the other two in that the tail is shorter than the head and body. Its colour is black, with rows of roundish yellow spots on the back. It may be remarked here that in both the spotted species the young are uniformly dark-coloured, the yellow markings being only gradually acquired. Hence the ornamentation may be regarded as a lately acquired feature. On the other hand, where—as in the lion and deer—skin-markings occur only on the young, such ornamentation is very ancient, and tending to disappear. The Spanish salamander (*Chioglossa lusitanica*) differs by the tongue being fixed on a protrusile pedicle.

From the true salamanders, the newts (*Molge*) are distinguished by the laterally compressed form of the powerful tail, as well as by their permanently aquatic mode of life. Many of the species, too, are furnished with an upright longitudinal fin on the back, such fin generally attaining a special development during the breeding season in the males. Newts range over the three great continents of the Northern Hemisphere, although they are unknown to the south of the Himalaya, and are much more abundant in the Old World than in the New. They are the only members of the order inhabiting Britain, where the common species in many districts is to be met with in every pond. The handsomest and largest of the British species is the crested newt (*M. cristata*), which belongs to a group characterised by the presence of a fin-like crest on the back of the males, and in some cases of the females also, where,

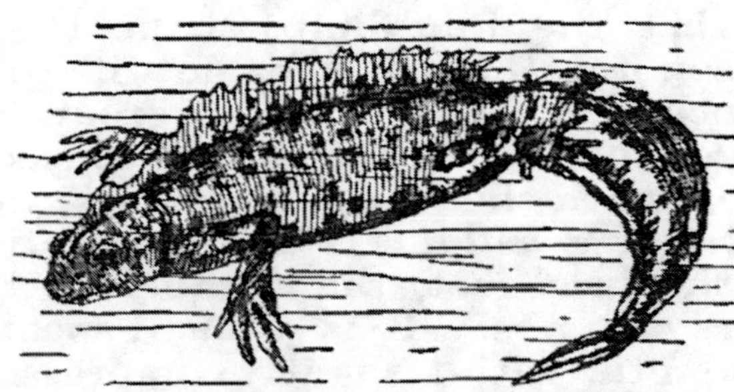

Fig. 12.—CRESTED NEWT (*Molge cristata*).

however, it is always considerably lower. In the males of the crested newt the crest is scalloped; and in both sexes the under surface of the body is orange with black marblings. When in full breeding-dress, a male of this species is indeed a beautifully-coloured creature. In size it grows to five inches or rather more. From Sweden southwards, this newt is spread over the greater part of Europe, with the exception of Italy. It is distinguished from all other members of the genus by a peculiarity in the structure of the skull. Far more abundant in this country is the much smaller common newt (*M. vulgaris*), in which the crest of the male is likewise festooned, while the hind-toes of the same sex are lobed during the breeding-season, the under surface of the body being yellowish, with large black spots in the male, and small dots in the female. In the latter, the back carries either a simple crest or a mere ridge. It is only in the breeding season that the crest of the male assumes its full development; and at this time the tail-fin is also festooned.

With the exception of Western Europe, this species is widely distributed on the Continent, and also ranges into Asia. The last and smallest of the British representatives of the genus is the webbed newt (*M. palmata*), which, in addition to a peculiarity in the structure of the skull, is distinguished by the hind-toes of the male being fully webbed during the breeding season. The crest of the male is straight; and that of the female either very small, or represented by a ridge. The lower surface of the body is more or less nearly uniformly coloured, although there is a narrow streak of orange in the middle line.

Several species found in the south of Europe have no crest in either sex. The habits of newts are so familiar to all who have lived in the country, that but little need be said on the subject. During the breeding-season, all are inhabitants of the water; but later on many of them forsake that element for a longer or shorter period, and become terrestrial. While some hibernate in holes or beneath stones, others retire to the mud at the bottom of ponds. The eggs are generally deposited on the stems of aquatic plants; and when the tadpoles first make their appearance, they have small, simple gills, behind which are a pair of small projections, representing the future fore-limbs. In the course of time the gills become branched, the fore-limbs show their four toes, and the hind-legs make their appearance. Soon after, the gills begin to shrink, and finally disappear, while lungs are developed, and the limbs acquire their full adult proportions, when the creature ceases to be a tadpole, and becomes a newt. It has been already mentioned that the tadpoles of the frogs and toads differ from those of the newts and salamanders in that the hind-limbs make their appearance before the front pair. The reason for this remarkable difference is doubtless to be found in the circumstance that in the former group the hind-limbs are proportionately much larger than in the latter, and consequently require a longer period for growth. From both the foregoing genera the Italian spectacled salamander (*Salamandrina perspicillata*) is at once distinguished by having only four toes to each of the hind-feet, the number of toes being consequently the same in both pairs of limbs. It is a small species, varying between three and four inches in length, with a slightly compressed and keeled tail, and a rough warty skin. The under surface of the tail and of the hinder end of the body is of a brilliant carmine red. This salamander inhabits moist, rocky districts, where its rapid movements render it liable to be mistaken for a lizard. True to its amphibian nature, it resorts, however, to the water in spring for breeding purposes. The warty salamander, *Tylotriton verrucosus*, of the Eastern Himalaya and Siam, together with the allied *T. andersoni* of the Liu-Kiu

Islands, constitute a genus confined to the Oriental region, and differing from all those mentioned above in the conformation of the skull, in which the pterygoid bōnes extend forwards to touch the maxillæ, instead of being separated from them by an interval. These salamanders have five hind-toes, and the tail strongly compressed. They are inhabitants of mountain districts. Nearly allied is the single species of *Pachytriton*, from South Kiansi, China, in which the tail is cylindrical at the root, although compressed near the tip.

In the second sub-family — *Amblystomatinæ* — of the *Salamandridæ* the teeth on the palate form either a transverse or posteriorly converging series, and are attached to the hinder margin of the posterior portion of the vomers, instead of to processes of the palatine bones. The vertebræ, too, differ from those of the first group in that both terminal faces of their bodies are slightly cupped ; this being a lower type of structure than the ball-and-socket articulation. The type of this group is the creature known in Mexico as the axolotl, which is the permanent larval form of a salamander from the United States described as *Amblystoma tigrinum*. It was long thought that these two forms were totally distinct animals ; but the identity of the two was conclusively proved by some Mexican axolotls kept many years ago in Paris. One of these layed eggs, which in due course developed into axolotls, but these latter ultimately assumed the form of the adult salamander. The most curious fact about the matter was that whereas the axolotls bred freely, none of the adult salamanders could be induced to propagate their kind. There are several species of the genus inhabiting North America, and a single outlying form in the mountains of Siam. With the single exception of the Mexican race of *Amblystoma tigrinum*, all these appear to pass from the tadpole to the salamander stage in the usual manner. The reason of the Mexican race retaining the larval stage appears to be that the country is very arid, and unfit for amphibian life. Consequently the axolotls remain permanently in the large lake by which the city of Mexico is surrounded. In this larval condition they have a long compressed tail, with a crest above and below, which is continued as a ridge on the back ; and on the sides of the neck are abundant bushy external gills. The limbs are rather small, and the general hue of the skin is mottled olive. On the other hand, the adult—which is normally developed in the United States—is an ordinary-looking salamander, with a relatively large head, good-sized limbs, and a sub-cylindrical tail ; the colour of the skin being blackish or brown, with numerous yellow spots. As special characteristics of the genus *Amblystoma*, it may be mentioned that the teeth on the palatines are arranged either in nearly a straight line or in an angle without any wide gap in the middle, and that the tongue bears a series of radiating pleats. Very closely allied is the genus *Linguælapsus*. A specimen of *L. annulatus* has been taken in Arkansas from a hot spring. Of the other

Fig. 13.—ADULT AXOLOTL (*Amblystoma tigrinum*).

genera included in the sub-family now under consideration, *Ranidens* from the north-eastern provinces of China and the east of Siberia, *Batrachyperus* from Tibet, and *Dicamptodon* from California, constitute a group characterised by the teeth on the palate forming a pair of arches, separated from one another in the middle line, and with the convexity forwards. The second of these genera differs from the other two in that the hind-feet are four-toed. A third group is formed by the Japanese *Onychodactylus*, in which the palatal teeth form a double arch, without any medium gap, while the claws are black. In the last group, represented by the Japanese and Chinese *Hynobius*, and *Salamandrella* of Eastern Siberia and Kamschatka, the palatal teeth converge backwards in a somewhat V-shaped figure ; the first genus having five hind-toes, and the second only four.

The other two sub-families are small. In the first, or *Plethodontinæ*, the parasphenoid bone differs from that of the two preceding sub-families in bearing teeth; the vertebræ being of the same type as in the *Amblystomatinæ*. Of the genera included, *Autodax* (*Anaides*), *Plethodon*, and *Batrachoseps* form a North American group characterised by the tongue being attached along the medium line as far as its front margin ; the first genus having very few teeth in the jaws, while in the second the hind-toes are five in number, and in the third only four. The second group, which is likewise North American, although its first genus ranges into Central America and the West Indies, includes *Spelerpes* and *Manculus*, and differs from the last in that the tongue is attached only by a pedicle from the middle of the lower surface, so that all its edges are free.

The fourth and last sub-family, *Desmognathinæ*, is also North American, and while agreeing with the third in having teeth on the parasphenoid, differs in that the bodies of the vertebræ are cupped behind and convex in front. In the typical genus *Desmognathus* the tongue is attached all along the middle line, whereas in *Thorius* it has a central pedicle, and is thus mushroom-like. *Haptoglossa*, from Costa Rica, is nearly allied to the latter, but differs in that the tongue is adherent in front. Of more interest is the single species of *Typhlotriton*, which inhabits a cave in Missouri, and is totally blind, the rudimental eyes being buried beneath the continuous skin of the head.

Although very small, the second family of the tailed amphibians is noteworthy on account of containing the largest members of the entire order.

Family *Amphiumidæ*.

Most of the few species are North American, but the giant salamander is an inhabitant of Japan and China. In their general structural characters the members of this family agree with the *Salamandridæ*, from which they are sharply differentiated by the absence of eyelids. All of them have the bodies of the vertebræ cupped at both ends, and in all the body is much elongated, and the relatively small front and hind-limbs widely sundered from one another. These features are clearly indicative of a closer relationship with fishes than obtains in the case of the true salamanders and newts. The same affinities are indicated by the aquatic habits of these creatures, and likewise by the permanent retention of internal gills; and, owing to the presence of the latter, respiration can be effected without the necessity of coming to the surface, at any rate for a considerable time. It is interesting to note that remains of a fossil species belonging to the same genus as the giant salamander occur in the Tertiary rocks of the Continent, from which it may be inferred that the family has migrated westward. The giant salamander (*Megalobatrachus maximus*) is a huge sluggish creature, frequently growing to as much as a yard in length.

and occasionally considerably more. With its flat, oval head, depressed body, warty skin, short, splay-toed limbs, and highly compressed tail, its appearance is by no means prepossessing, and when lying almost motionless in a tank of slimy green water in the reptile-house in the London Zoological Gardens, the attention it attracts from the general public is probably but slight. Nevertheless it is one of the most interesting of living animals, and our notions of zoological affinities would be much less clear than they are had this salamander and its allies become extinct. Externally this salamander is distinguished by having four toes in front and three behind, and likewise by the absence of gill-openings on the sides of the neck. Internally it will be found that there are two arches for the support of the gills on each side. If the mouth be opened, it will be seen that its floor is completely covered by the closely adherent tongue, and also that the teeth on the palate form a series running parallel to those on the edge of the upper jaw, these teeth being situated on the vomers. These salamanders, which, as already said, are common to Japan and China, inhabit clear mountain streams, where they feed on such aquatic creatures as they are able to capture; in captivity, at least, they are known to be cannibals, but this depraved taste was probably developed owing to lack of a sufficiency of other food. In autumn the female lays a number of small eggs; but the early stages of development are unknown, although it is probable that at first the young tadpoles are provided with external gills. The much smaller Mississippi salamander, or hell-bender (*Cryptobranchus lateralis*), is distinguished by the retention of a gill-opening on one or both sides of the neck, and the free front edge of the tongue, as well as by the presence of four pairs of arches for the support of the internal gills. Less than twenty inches seems to be the maximum size of this salamander. Geographically the range of the species extends from the Mississippi basin and the streams of the Louisianian district to North Carolina.

Fig. 14.—GIANT SALAMANDER (*Megalabatrachus maximus*).

Very different in appearance and structure from both the preceding is the species representing the genus *Amphiuma*, which has a somewhat more extended range than the hell-bender, since it is found in South Carolina. It is an exceedingly elongated eel-like creature, with very minute limbs, of which the front pair are situated close to the head, while the hinder ones are placed very far back at the commencement of the tail, which is much shorter than the body. It is a rather curious circumstance that whereas in some examples each foot is furnished with three toes, in others the number is reduced to two; but in organs which are either about to disappear, or are in the course of development, similar variations are by no means of unfrequent occurrence. In the nature of its food this creature is very similar to the Mississippi salamander; but whereas the latter occasionally leaves the water for a stroll on the bank, it does not appear that the former ever quits its native element. The female *Amphiuma* deposits a string of eggs resembling a rosary, round which she subsequently coils herself, after arranging the string in a mass.

According to the system of classification now favoured by zoologists, the tailed amphibians constitute a series regularly descending in their grade of organisation; and with the present family we reach a group in which the external gills of the young are permanently retained, while there are two pairs of rudimental limbs. An additional peculiarity is to be found in the absence of the maxilla in the scull. As in the preceding family, the bodies of the vertebræ have cupped terminal faces, and eyelids are wanting. The typical member of the family is the famous olm (*Proteus*) from the subterranean waters of Carniola, Carinthia, and Dalmatia. No better description of this creature is extant than one by Sir Humphry Davy, which runs as follows:—"At first sight you might suppose this creature to be a lizard, but it has the motions of a fish. Its head and the lower part of its body and its tail bear a strong resemblance to those of an eel; but it has no fins; and its curious bronchial organs are not like the gills of fishes; they form a singular vascular structure, almost like a crest round the throat, which may be removed without occasioning the death of the animal, which is likewise furnished with lungs. With this double apparatus for supplying air to the blood, it can live either below or above the surface of the water. Its fore-feet resemble hands, but they have only three claws or fingers, and are too feeble to be of use in grasping or supporting the weight of the animal. The hinder feet have only two claws or toes, and in the larger specimens are found so imperfect as to be almost obliterated. It has small points in place of eyes, as if to preserve the analogy of nature. It is of a fleshy whiteness and transparency in its natural state, but when exposed to light, its skin gradually becomes darker, and at last gains an olive tint. Its nasal organs appear large; and it is abundantly furnished with teeth, from which it may be concluded that it is an animal of prey; yet in its confined state it has never been known to eat, and it has been kept alive for many years by occasionally changing the water in which it was kept." From the olm the North American genus *Necturus* is at once distinguished by the possession of well-developed eyes, and likewise by the presence of four toes to each foot. In form, too, it is more lizard-like, the body lacking the eel-like elongation characteristic of the olm, while the limbs are less rudimental. There are two species of the genus, one of which is not uncommon in the rice-fields of the Southern United States. Although both breathe almost entirely by means of their plume-like external gills, it is stated that they will occasionally venture on land, when the lungs of course become the respiratory organs. In sinking a well recently in Texas, a third generic representative of the family was discovered at a depth of 180 feet in a subterranean stream. This form is related both to *Proteus* and *Necturus*, and has been named *Typhlomolge rathbuni*. It is characterised by the great length and slenderness of its limbs, and the broad, flattened, and squared muzzle.

Family *Proteidæ.*

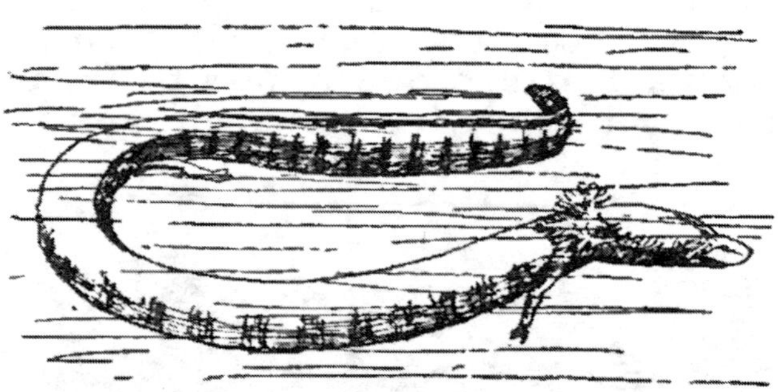

Fig. 15.—OLM (*Proteus anguineus*).

The last family of the tailed amphibians is confined to North America, where it is represented by *Siren lacertina* of the South-Eastern United

States and *Pseudobranchus striatus* of Georgia. Both these lowly creatures have long eel-like bodies, external gills, and a small pair of front legs. The hind-legs are, however, totally wanting, and there are no teeth in the margins of the jaws. In the species first named—which may measure nearly twenty inches in length—there are three pairs of gill-openings on the sides of the neck, and each of the fore-feet is furnished with four toes. From this genus *Pseudobranchus* is distinguished by the presence of only a single pair of gill-apertures, and the reduction of the front toes to three. These salamanders frequent damp situations and pools, and occasionally ascend the aerial roots or stems of trees. They are carnivorous in their habits, and are able to breathe either by their gills or their lungs. During the colder months of the year they hibernate.

Family *Sirenidæ.*

Fig. 16.—TWO-LEGGED SALAMANDER (*Siren lacertina*).

ORDER III.—APODA.

CÆCILIANS.

THE third and last order of Amphibia is represented by the blind, burrowing creatures commonly known as cæcilians. In appearance they are so worm-like that by the non-scientific observer they might readily be mistaken for Invertebrates. In the adult state they show no trace of limbs; but bud-like remnants of hind-legs have been detected in the embryos of *Ichthyophis glutinosus.* This clearly shows that they are a degraded form, but whether they are descended—as has been considered the case—from the tailed amphibians may, perhaps, be doubtful, seeing that they differ from that group in an important feature connected with their reproduction. They have either a rudimental tail or none at all, and they are further characterised by certain structural peculiarities in the osteology of the skull. The eyes are generally deeply buried beneath the skin, or placed beneath the bones of the skull, and in certain members of the group overlapping scales are concealed deep down in the skin. The head is provided with a tentacle, which may be capable of protrusion and retraction. Cæcilians present a very remarkable geographical distribution, being restricted to South and Central America (with the West Indies), Africa south of the Sahara, the Seychelles, and the Oriental countries. Their absence from Madagascar, coupled with their existence in the Seychelles, is a very noteworthy circumstance, and seems to indicate a connection between those islands and either Africa or India after Madagascar was insulated. The adults burrow in moist earth, like worms, where they lay large eggs, from which, in due course, are developed tadpoles furnished, at least before birth, with gills. Soon after hatching, the tadpoles take to the water, where they appear to remain until they assume the adult condition.

All the members of the order are so similar in structure that they are included in a single family group. The first genus, *Ichthyophis,* includes two species, ranging from India to the Malayan Islands; but whereas one (*I. glutinosus*) is also found in Ceylon, the second (*I. monochrous*) is unknown there. In these species overlapping fish-like scales are embedded in the skin, the eyes are distinguishable, the lower jaw is furnished with a double series of teeth, and the tentacle, which is capable of protrusion, is situated near the upper lip between the eye and the nostril. The first-named species grows to a length of about fifteen inches, but has a diameter of only half an inch. Writing of this species in Ceylon, the late Sir J. Emerson Tennent wrote as follows:—"The rocky jungle, bordering the higher coffee estates, provides a safe retreat for a very singular animal, first introduced to the notice of European naturalists by Linnæus, who gave it the name *Cæcilia glutinosa,* to indicate two peculiarities manifest to the ordinary observer, an apparent defect of vision, from the eyes being so small, and embedded as to be scarcely distinguishable, and the power of secreting from minute pores in the skin a viscous fluid, resembling that of snails, eels, and some salamanders. Specimens are rare in Europe, owing to the readiness with which it decomposes, breaking down into a flaky mass in the spirits in which it is attempted to preserve it. The creature is about the length and thickness of an ordinary round desk-ruler, a little flattened before and rounded behind. It is brownish, with a pale stripe along either side. The skin is furrowed into 350 circular folds, in which are embedded minute scales. The head is tolerably distinct, with a double row of fine curved teeth for seizing the insects and worms on which it is supposed to feed." More recent observations—especially those of Dr. Sarasin—have largely increased our knowledge of the mode of life of these strange and interesting creatures, which are generally found in soft mud. As already mentioned, rudiments of hind-limbs have been detected in the embryos. The large globular eggs are laid in a burrow near water, and are brooded by the female, who coils her body round the mass. The tadpoles are not hatched until after the loss of their external gills, and when they take to the water they breathe through a pair of gill-openings on the sides of the neck. These tadpoles have a very fish-like head, in which the eyes are much more distinct than in the adult, while they have also a well-defined and highly-compressed tail, furnished below and above with a fin, after the manner of a frog's tadpole. A nearly-allied Oriental genus is *Epicrinops,* with a single species. From *Ichthyophis* the genus *Uræotyphlus* is readily distinguished by the tentacle being situated

Family *Cæciliidæ.*

Fig. 17.—A Cæcilian Brooding its Eggs (*Ichthyophis glutinosus*).

below the nostril. The genus is represented by two species from Southern India, a West African form which has been referred to it having been shown to belong to *Geotrypetes.* In the foregoing genera the tentacle has a conical form, but in the typical genus *Cæcilia,* which is confined to Tropical South America, it becomes flap-like, with a horse-shoe shaped groove at the base, its situation being below the nostril. On the other hand, in the nearly-allied *Hypogeophis,* the same organ is placed below the nostril. This genus is specially interesting on account of its geographical distribution, having two species from Africa, and two from the Seychelles. A West African species formerly included in the same genus is now distinguished as *Geotrypetes petersi.* Still more remarkable is the distribution of the genus *Dermophis,* which has several species from Tropical America, one from West Africa, and another from the eastern side of the latter continent. From the preceding kinds this genus is distinguished by the globular form of the tentacle, which is surrounded by a circular groove, and situated below and in front of the eye.

In addition to the presence of scales in the skin, all the preceding genera are characterised by the eyes being either distinct or buried only in the skin. From these, *Gymnopis* and *Herpele* differ in that the same organs have sunk so deep as to be actually beneath the bones of the skull. In the former genus, which is confined to Tropical America, the globular tentacle is surrounded by a circular groove, and placed close to the muzzle, whereas in the latter—which is West African—it is nearer the nostril.

In the remaining genera of the family, the skin is devoid of scales. Of these, *Gegenophis,* as represented by a single Indian species, is remarkable on account of its extremely restricted range, being apparently recorded only from the Peria peak, in the Wynad district, at an elevation of about five thousand feet. Even there it is stated to be of rare occurrence. Unlike most of its kind, it lives under stones. As a genus, this cæcilian is characterised by the eyes being beneath the bones of the skull, and by the tentacle being globular, and surrounded by a circular groove. From this genus, *Siphonops,* with three species inhabiting Tropical South America, differs by the distinct eyes, and the flap-like tentacle, which has a horse-shoe shaped groove at the base, and is placed much nearer to the eye than to the nostril. The allied genus *Typhlonectes,* from the same regions, may be distinguished by the tentacle, which is of similar shape, being nearer to the nostril than to the eye, as also by the compression of the hinder end of the body. Lastly, we have the South American *Chthonerpetum,* which differs from all the other scaleless forms in the arrangement of some of the bones of the skull. It has a flap-like tentacle, situated mid-way between the eye and the nostril. One species of this genus is found in the neighbourhood of Buenos Ayres, and is thus more southern than any other American member of the family.

SUB-KINGDOM I.—VERTEBRATA.

CLASS V.—PISCES.

By R. Lydekker, B.A., F.R.S., V.P.G.S., &c.

In the preceding section it has been shown that the tadpoles of the Amphibia make a very close approximation in structure—and to a certain extent also in form—to fishes. The resemblance, however, stops suddenly short in regard to the structure of the limbs. In all amphibians the limbs resemble those of the higher vertebrates in being composed of a definite number of segments, and terminating in distinct digits, which are normally five in number. On the other hand, although in fishes there are distinct segments in the upper portion of the limbs, these do not correspond exactly with those of the higher animals, and there are no structures corresponding with fingers and toes. The limbs are, in fact, fins, and terminate either in a fringe of rays, or, more rarely, in a jointed cartilaginous rod, bordered on one or both sides with a smaller number of somewhat similar rays. In some fishes, it is true, limbs are wanting; but then this is also the case among the higher vertebrates, and does not impair the classificatory value of these appendages. Another important distinction from amphibians is to be found in the circumstance that the median fins of fishes—which are always present in some form or other—have rays similar to those of the paired fins. Accordingly, in a popular way, fishes may be defined as aquatic, cold-blooded, back-boned animals, breathing the air in water by gills (sometimes supplemented by lungs), and furnished with paired nostrils, paired and median fins, the former of which (when present) differ essentially from the limbs of higher animals. This definition will suffice to distinguish the class Pisces from all the preceding classes, but as it fails to differentiate the group from the lampreys (now regarded as a class apart), it must be added that all Pisces have a functional lower jaw.

Whether the earliest ancestors of fishes were as purely aquatic in their habits as their descendants is a question somewhat difficult to answer, although the reply should probably be in the affirmative. Anyway, it is certain that we have at present no indications of a direct transition between fishes and the classes immediately above and immediately below them, so that they stand out as one of the best defined of all groups; and there is very considerable uncertainty whether the paired fins of fishes can be regarded as the ancestral type from which the limbs of higher animals were evolved. In spite of certain minor variations—as exemplified by the difference in shape between an eel and a flat fish—all the members of the class are characterised by the adaptation of their bodily form to an aquatic life, a feature in which they resemble whales and porpoises among mammals. As is well observed by Dr. Bashford Dean, this adaptation to aquatic existence "has stamped them in a common mould, and has prescribed the laws which direct and limit their evolution ; it has compressed their head, trunk, and tail into a spindle-like form ; it has given them an easy and rapid motion, enabling them to cleave the water like a rounded wedge. It has made their mode of movement one of undulation, causing the sides of the fish to contract rhythmically, thrusting the animal forward." Very beautiful indeed are the lines of a typical swift-swimming fish, such as the common mackerel ; and in a front view the sectional outline will be found to form a perfect ellipse, from which project the fins as thin vertical or oblique ridges.

Interesting and important as is the structure of fishes in general, our remarks on this subject must be the briefest. Here it is important to mention that the ordinary bony fish of the present day, such as a mackerel or a roach, are very specialised forms, and afford but little idea of the general or primitive structural type of the class, a shark or a lung-fish being far preferable in this respect. Among the special organs of many, although by no means all fishes, is the air-bladder, which has the power of altering the specific gravity of the body to accord with that of the surrounding water. Frequently this bladder is connected by means of a duct with the œsophagus, and in the lung-fishes it assumes the characters of a lung. Of the external coverings of fishes, the most characteristic are the scales, although these are wanting in some groups and in certain members of others. The ordinary over-lapping scales are classified as cycloid or ctenoid, according as to whether the free margin is entire or pectinate. When they are coated with a highly polished enamel-like structure, and at the same time are more or less rectangular in form, they are termed ganoid. The lateral line found on the sides of many fishes is formed of scales, modified partly for the purpose of supplying mucus. The terminal portions of the fins—namely, the fin-rays—are likewise structures formed in the skin ; and these rays are articulated below with the interspinal bones in the bony fishes, and with the radial cartilages in the sharks and rays. The paired fins comprise the pectoral and pelvic ; and the median or unpaired, the dorsal, caudal, and anal. When the pelvic pair are situated in advance of the pectorals, they are said to be jugular in position ; when in the same line, thoracic ; and when far back, abdominal. Of the internal structure of the paired fins, such observations as are necessary may be deferred till the different groups are treated of ; but it may be mentioned that when the rays of the caudal fin surround the hinder extremity of the back-bone symmetrically, the tail-fin is said to be diphycercal. When, on the other hand, the upper lobe is greatly developed at the expense of the lower, while the rays are unsymmetrically, as in the sharks, it is termed heterocercal. More specialised than either of the foregoing is the so-called homocercal or completely forked tail, in which, although the back-bone terminates in an abbreviated unsymmetrical manner, the arrangement of the rays is symmetrical. Whereas in some fishes the notochord persists in its original form, in others it is partially surrounded by rudimental vertebral arches, and in the higher forms is completely replaced by bony vertebræ. Much the same may be said with regard to the primitive cartilaginous skull, which is retained in its original form in the sharks, but is completely bony in the higher fishes, in which, in addition to bones developed from cartilage, a number of investing so-called dermal bones likewise arise. Dermal bones, too, are developed in the pectoral girdle of the latter group. Very important in the skull of the bony fishes is the gill-cover or operculum, which when fully developed comprises the bones respectively known as the pre-, sub-, and interopercular, and the opercular proper. The gill-membrane aids the operculum in closing the gill-cavity in the higher fishes, and in this may be developed the so-called branchiostegal rays. In the membrane joining the two branches of the lower jaw may be certain large jugular plates. The teeth of fishes need not engage our attention further than to notice that they may be developed not only in the jaws and on the bones of the palate, but likewise also on the tongue and the pharyngeal bones of the throat. The soft internal parts must likewise be passed over almost without notice, although it may be mentioned that whereas the heart generally comprises only two chambers, in the lung-fishes it is furnished with three. The false gills, or remnants of a former gill situated in front of the permanent pair, and represented in the adult by a plexus of blood-vessels, are likewise too important not to be named. Then, again, there are the spiracles of the sharks, which are situated on the head, and are the openings of canals leading into the pharynx, and representing the first visceral clefts of the embryo. It is likewise important to notice that certain fishes, such as the bichir of the Nile and some of the lung-fishes, develop during the earlier stages of their existence pectinate external gills, and thus serve to connect the class with the larval forms of the Amphibia. As regards reproduction, it must suffice to say that whereas most fishes lay eggs—it may be of very small size, when they are collectively known as roe, or comparatively large—in certain kinds these are retained within the body of the parent till hatched. The interesting subject of distribution—both in depth and in horizontal extent—must be passed over without mention.

Excluding lampreys and lancelets, which are here assigned to distinct classes, very different views have been entertained even by modern systematists as to the proper classification of fishes. By Dr. Günther the following scheme for the existing forms was followed even as late as 1880, *viz.* :—

Sub-class I. PALÆICHTHYES.
- Order i. CHONDROPTERYGII.
  - Section 1. Plagiostomata.—Sharks and Rays.
  - ,, 2. Holocephala.—Chimæroids.
- Order ii. GANOIDEI.
  - Section 1. Dipnoi.—Lung-fishes.
  - ,, 2. Chondrostei.—Sturgeons.
  - ,, 3. Polypteroidei.—Bichir.
  - ,, 4. Lepidosteoidei.—Bony Pike.
  - ,, 5. Amioidei.—Bow-fin.

Sub-class II. TELEOSTEI.—Bony Fishes.
- Order i. ACANTHOPTERYGII.
- ,, ii. ACANTHOPTERYGII PHARYNGOGNATHI.
- ,, iii. ANACANTHINI.
- ,, iv. PHYSOSTOMI.
- ,, v. LOPHOBRANCHII.
- ,, vi. PLECTOGNATHI.

The defects in this classification, are the wide separation of the Ganoidei from the Teleostei, which, through the intervention of extinct forms, pass completely into one another, and the association of the Chimæroids with the Sharks and Rays to form a single subordinal group.

A far better scheme is the one just published by Dr. Bashford Dean, which is as follows :—

Sub-class I. Elasmobranchii.—Sharks and Rays.
,, II. Holocephali.—Chimæroids.
,, III. Dipnoi.—Lung-fishes.
,, IV. Teleostomi.—Ganoids and Bony Fishes.
Order i. Crossopterygii.—Fringe-finned Group.
,, ii. Actinopterygii.—Fan-finned Group.
Section 1. Chondrostei.—Ganoids.
,, 2. Teleocephali.—Bony Fishes.

Even this system has, however, certain disadvantages, and the following arrangement appears preferable. This is as follows, *viz.* :—

Sub-class I. Dipnoi.—Lung-fishes.
,, II. Holocephali.—Chimæroids.
,, III. Teleostomi.—Bony Fishes and Ganoids.
Order i. Actinopterygii.—Fan-finned Group.
,, ii. Crossopterygii.—Fringe-finned Group.
Sub-class IV. Elasmobranchii.—Sharks and Rays.

With these preliminary remarks, we may proceed to a brief systematic review of the various groups of the class. It must, however, be remembered that the number of existing fishes is so vast that it is quite impossible to notice even all the family types, while of the genera only a small percentage are selected for mention. It must also be born in mind that the true relationships of the sub-classes cannot be properly grasped unless the fossil forms are also studied.

SUB-CLASS I.—DIPNOI.

Lung-Fishes.

Like the next, the present group is now represented by a very small number of species, and as it was abundant in earlier epochs, it is evidently one that is on the wane. Whereas in many respects the lung-fishes approximate to the amphibians, in others they show affinity to the earlier sharks; and it has been suggested that they ought to form a class intermediate between Amphibia and Pisces. Regarding them, however, merely as a subclass of the latter, they agree with the Chimæroids in the essential feature that there is no movable separate suspending arrangement for the lower jaw; and from this peculiarity the name of Autostylica has been suggested for the two sub-classes in question. In the existing members of the group, which form the order Sirenoidei, the body is thick and spindle-shaped, its covering consisting of large overlapping horn-like scales, and the tail forming a diphycercal fin. In form, the head approximates to that of amphibians, as it does in its slimy integument. The paired fins are of the fringed type, their skeleton consisting typically of a jointed cartilaginous rod, fringed on both sides with divergent rays. In the skull the original cartilaginous cranium is roofed over with dermal membrane-bones, and the nostrils have posterior apertures opening into the back of the mouth to form true posterior nostrils, the latter feature distinguishing these fishes from all other members of the class. The small and compressed gills open externally by a single aperture which is protected by an operculum, from beneath which may protrude stunted and rudimental external gills. The nerves supplying the eyes, where they cross one another, have an interlacing of their fibres, and the short digestive tract exhibits the shark-like feature of a spiral valve in the membrane of the intestine. Not only is the elongated and sacculated air-bladder provided with a duct, but it acts in all respects as a lung, with which indeed it is in every sense comparable. The backbone is mainly notochordal, true vertebræ being developed only in the caudal region. The dentition is of a very peculiar type, and consists of a few very large and strongly-ridged plates, most of which are paired, and divided by a distinct median line.

Fig. 1.—AUSTRALIAN LUNG-FISH.

Lung-fishes are now represented only by three species, belonging to as many distinct genera, but all included in the single family *Lepidosirenidæ.* Of these, the least specialised is the Australian lung-fish (*Ceratodus*), which in the form of its paired fins retains more of the primitive type than does either of the other two. The scales are very large, and the paired fins are broad and lobate, consisting of a central scaled portion bordered by a fringe. Marginal teeth are wanting in the jaws ; but the palate contains a pair of large dental plates behind, and a couple of smaller chisel-like teeth in front, the lower jaw having a single pair of large plates. Long before it was known to science, the Australian lung-fish was familiar to the settlers on the banks of the two great rivers of Queensland, on account of the excellent quality of its salmon-coloured flesh ;—whence the name of Burnett salmon commonly applied to it. The fish, which grows to a couple of yards in length, lives among mud and leaves, and rises at times to the surface to breathe. Its food consists of both vegetable and animal substances ; and the large eggs are deposited singly. In the two remaining forms—one of which (*Lepidosiren*) inhabits the rivers of Tropical South America, and the other (*Protopterus*) those of Africa—the body is more eel-like, the limbs are reduced to whip-like filaments, and the anterior teeth are situated in the margins of the jaws. In many parts of the country the African lung-fish during the dry season envelops itself in a kind of shell or cocoon of mud, and in this state it can be dug up and exported, reviving when placed in warm water. Dr. Dean observes that "lung-fishes

Fig. 2.—AFRICAN LUNG-FISH.

have unquestionably many structures which may have been derived from the more generalised conditions of the sharks; and as a group they may not unreasonably be looked upon as descended from the primitive elasmobranchian stem."

SUB-CLASS II.—HOLOCEPHALI.

CHIMÆROIDS.

THE group typically represented by the spook-fish or chimæra is, as already mentioned, now a small and waning one, which agrees with the last in the structure of the skull. In spite of their many marked resemblances to the sharks, the writer last quoted is of opinion that they cannot be closely associated with that group. This external resemblance to the Elasmobranchii, coupled with the total absence of membrane-bones from the cartilaginous skull, at once serves to differentiate the chimæras from the lung-fishes; from which they also differ by the absence of true posterior nostrils, although there are nasal passages. Further differences are to be found in the form and structure of the paired fins, and the absence of an air-bladder. The optic nerves and intestine are similar to those of the lung-fishes and sharks; and the accessory reproductive organs of the males, known as claspers, are found elsewhere only in the latter group. Unlike the lung-fishes, the skin is generally naked, and when (as in the young) hard structures are developed therein, these agree with teeth, whereas such plates as are found in the lung-fishes are bony. Although the paired fins are not very unlike those of modern sharks, consisting of an abbreviated base and numerous rays arranged in a fan-like manner, their dermal margins are very large, and terminate in a sharp point. A large spine protects the front of the first dorsal fin, which is capable of being folded so as to lie in a groove in the back. The gill-arches are closely packed, and open by one aperture on each side, which is slit-like, and protected with a dermal fold containing an operculum of cartilage. The teeth are in the form of large plates closely affixed to the jaws, and are thickly studded with roughened grinding facets termed tritors. In the cartilaginous skeleton the axis of the back-bone remains notochordal, its sheath lacking distinct vertebræ, but being strengthened in the fore-part of the column by rings of cartilage. A lateral line is present on the sides of the body, and the tail gradually tapers away, to terminate in a diphycercal fin. Like sharks, chimæroids deposit large eggs, which are completely separate from one another.

Fig. 3.—COMMON CHIMÆRA.

Existing chimæroids are classed under three genera, all included in the family *Chimæridæ*. The first of these is *Harriotta*, which comprises two deep sea forms, one from the Atlantic and the other from Japanese waters. It appears to be the most shark-like type, and is characterised by the long slender beak, and the absence of an appendage on the forehead of the males. From the small size of the claspers in the same sex, it has been inferred that the eggs are fertilised after extrusion. The second genus, *Callorhynchus*, is represented by the bottle-nosed chimæra of the Southern Seas, and, together with the next, has an erectile spine on the forehead of the males. In form it is very shark-like, with the tail inclined upwards and without a fin on its upper surface; the muzzle being of moderate length, with a cartilaginous prominence terminating in a flap of skin. *Chimæra*, of which there are three species, is less shark-like than the other two, with the extremely abbreviate muzzle devoid of any appendage, and the whip-like tail forming a continuation of the longitudinal axis of the body, and finned for some distance both above and below. These fishes appear to be rare and local, and are generally taken in fairly deep water. Little is known of their life-history, but immature examples have been captured at great depths. Although some writers have considered the chimæroids as degenerate types allied to the Dipnoi, Dr. Bashford Dean is of opinion that they are more nearly related to the primitive sharks. If this should prove to be well founded, the autostylic type of skull must have been independently acquired in the Dipnoi and Holocephali, and cannot, consequently, be of much classificatory value.

SUB-CLASS III.—TELEOSTOMI.

Bony Fishes and Ganoids.

The passage between the modern bony fishes and the ancient ganoids having been discovered to be complete, there is no possibility of assigning these two nominal groups to distinct sub-classes, or even orders, and, accordingly, all the fishes which come under the designation either of Dipnoi, Holocephali, or Elasmobranchii, are now classed as Teleostomi. Indeed, the terms bony fishes and ganoids, as Dr. Bashford Dean well remarks, can only be used in a popular and convenient sense—the latter to denote the old-fashioned type, with its rectangular ganoid scales and cartilaginous internal skeleton, and the former to designate the modern type, with its rounded horny scales and fully calcified skeleton. The group is a very vast one, including by far the great majority of existing forms, and a host of extinct ones; and the range of variation is so great that a concise definition is by no means easy. All the members of the sub-class are, however, broadly distinguished both from Dipnoi and Holocephali by the existence in the skull of a movable apparatus for the suspension of the lower jaw, this type of skull structure being known as the hyostylic. In the internal skeleton, calcification exists to a greater or lesser degree, and membrane-bones are always present on the jaws. Moreover, the membrane-bones of the pectoral girdle, like the scapula and the various clavicular bones, form a chain connected with the posterior region of the skull. Very important is the close crowding of the gill-arches, and their complete protection by a fully-developed operculum. The external skeleton, when present, consists either of rounded horn-like scales, or of quadrangular bony plates. All the living forms deposit a vast number of minute eggs, crowded together into a mass. Whereas in the higher types the optic nerves simply cross one another, and there is no spiral valve to the intestine, in the ganoids the latter is present, and the fibres of the optic nerves interlace where they meet, to form what is known as a chiasma by the complete fusion of the two nerves. Very generally an air-bladder is present, and the less specialised bony fishes and all the ganoids are provided with a duct to the gullet. In the higher types the rays of the fins are entirely of dermal origin, their cartilaginous supports being abbreviated and enclosed within the body. In addition to the features already noticed, the ganoids have a larger number of gill-arches, a spiracle, an arterial cone furnished with many valves to the heart, a cellular air-bladder, and several shark-like features in other organs.

Order I.—Actinopterygii.

SUB-ORDER I.—ACANTHOPTERYGII.

The first great order of the sub-class includes what may be termed the Fan-finned Teleostomes, in which the fins are entirely supported by dermal rays, the primitive cartilaginous supports being greatly reduced and enclosed in the body-wall. A single paired series of transversely elongated rays—to which an unpaired anterior element may be added—are developed in the branchiostegal membrane between the two branches of the lower jaw. The caudal fin is variable. The spiny-finned fishes, forming the sub-order Acanthopterygii, together with the six following sub-orders,[1] are collectively distinguished by the supporting bony elements of the dorsal and anal fins being equal in number to the dermal rays, and by the tail being generally of the homocercal or abbreviate-heterocercal type although occasionally diphycercal. In the Acanthopterygii and four following sub-orders the skeleton is fully ossified, the optic nerves simply cross, and there is no spiral valve to the intestine. In common with the three following sub-orders, they have generally no duct to the air-bladder, the two parietal bones of the skull separated by the supra-occipital, and the pelvic fins usually jugular or thoracic. The chief distinction of the Actinopterygii themselves is that usually some of the rays of the dorsal and anal fins are not articulated, and form spines.

Section 1. Perciformes.—Family *Centrarchidæ*.

In this section the lower pharyngeal bones are generally distinct, and the scales ctenoid; while the preopercular bone is not connected by a bony stay with the orbit, the spinous dorsal is large, and the pelvic fins are thoracic, and usually furnished with five branched rays, although sometimes with only four. Certain other features connected with the skeleton are too complex to be noticed here. The *Centrarchidæ* form a comparatively small family, containing ten genera, and typified by the single species of *Centrarchus*, from the fresh waters of the United States; one of their distinctive characters being the presence of three or more spines in the anal fin. In habits these fishes are carnivorous; and many of them resemble the stickle-backs in building nests.

[1] The following are the sub-orders of the Actinopterygii—*viz.*, (1) Acanthopterygii, (2) Lophobranchii, (3) Plectognathi, (4) Anacanthini, (5) Physostomi, (6) Ætheospondyli, (7) Protospondyli, (8) Chondrostei.

Family *Percidæ.*

Of far more general interest are the twelve genera constituting the family *Percidæ*, in all of which there are never more than two spines in the anal fin, while there are two pairs of external nostrils. Like their nearest allies, the perches generally have a complete lateral line, no scales on the median fins or barbels to the mouth, and the teeth conical. Six to eight pairs of branchiostegal rays are present, as well as four pairs of gills, the last of which is followed by a slit; and the rayed portion of the dorsal fin does not much exceed the anal in length. Although *Lucioperca* (*Stizostedion*) and *Percarina* enter salt water, the family is essentially a fresh-water type, its members being spread over North America, Western Asia, and Europe. Among the generic types of the family are the true perches (*Perca*), with a distribution equivalent to that of the family; the aforesaid *Lucioperca*, or pike-perches, with a similar range; the three small species of the Danubian genus *Aspro*; *Percarina*, with two species from the neighbourhood of the Sea of Azov and the Black Sea; and the ruffes (*Acerina*), of which the three representatives are restricted to Europe and Asia.

Fig. 4.—COMMON PERCH.

Family *Serranidæ.*

Nearly allied to the last is the family of *Serranidæ*, or sea-perches, distinguished by the development of an internal lamina from the second suborbital bone supporting the globe of the eye, the number of spines in the anal fin being variable. In this extensive family the genus *Centrogenys* is noteworthy, on account of the union of the lower pharyngeal bones. It would be tedious to mention the distinctive characters of even the commoner and best known genera, and only a few will be referred to at all. As an example of the group of the sub-family *Serraninæ*, with two dorsal fins, we may take the South American *Percichthys*, which is one of the few fresh-water types. In this and four other allied genera the tongue is smooth, but in the bass, *Morone*, which have likewise two dorsals, that organ is covered with patches of teeth. Whereas some bass are marine, others are fresh-water in habitat. They all have nine dorsal and (like the other members of the sub-family) three anal spines. Among the group with a single dorsal fin, especial interest attaches to the widely-spread sea-perches of the genus *Serranus*, on account of the vast number of species and the large bodily size to which some of them attain. Although the tongue is edentulous, teeth are developed on the palate, and large tusks occur at intervals among the small teeth in the margins of the jaws. *Centropristes* is an allied genus. In another group of the same sub-family Mr. Boulenger includes the genera *Plesiops* and *Trachinops*, which were formerly referred to the *Nandidæ*. In these the lateral line is double, consisting of an upper portion, which disappears posteriorly, and a lower running along the middle of the side of the tail. Whereas the first genus is from the coral-reefs of the Indo-Pacific, the second is Australian, both being marine. To another sub-family—*Centropominæ*—distinguished by the extension of the lateral line on to the caudal fin, belong the two species of *Lates*, one of which is Nilotic, while the other is Oriental and Australian. The Oriental species grows to a length of five feet, and is probably as dangerous to bathers as are the larger kinds of *Serranus*.

Among the most gorgeously coloured of all the class, are the tropical chætodonts or scaly-finned fishes, readily distinguished from the foregoing families by the extension of the scaling on to the median fins. All are deep-bodied fishes, with cycloid or ctenoid scales, on which a continuous lateral line runs nearly to the caudal fin. Their mouth, which may be tubular, is armed with bands of minute teeth. Of the fins, the pelvic are thoracic, with a single spine and five rays; three or five spines are found in the anal; and the spinous portion of the dorsal is shorter than the rayed part. Stripes or spots are distinguishing features in the coloration of these fishes, which are mostly inhabitants of coral-reefs, where they feed on such animals as they can capture, although some ascend large tidal rivers. In the typical *Chætodon* the palate is devoid of teeth, the dorsal fin is not deeply notched, and has spines of nearly uniform length, while the muzzle is short or moderately produced. Some kinds have the body ornamented by fine lines, while others have on each side a large eye-like spot. *Chelmon* merits notice, on account of the elongation of the muzzle into a tube, from which the fish ejects a drop of water with such force and accuracy of aim as to disable any insect that may be resting on the foliage near the shore, and thus secure it for food. Both the species of shooting fish are Oriental, and are found both in rivers and near the coast. Other well-known genera are *Heniochus* and *Holacanthus*, the latter best known by the gorgeously coloured emperor-fish of the African and Oriental seas. In this fish the body is coloured a brilliant blue, ornamented with about thirty narrow gold stripes. Even more resplendent is the Oriental zebra-fish, in which the ground-colour of the body is yellow, marked with numerous vertical bands of blue margined with brown.

Family *Chætodontidæ*.[1]

Fig. 5.—CHÆTODON.

That epicurean delicacy, the red mullet (*Mullus barbatus*), typifies a small family distinguished from other Perciformes by the possession of a pair of barbels on the lower jaw. In this family the number of pairs of branchiostegal rays is only four; and the somewhat low body has large, thin, finely serrated scales, with a continuous lateral line. The dentition is weak. As regards the fins, there are two dorsals, in the first of which the spines are thin, while the second is placed above, and is similar to the anal, the pectorals being short, and the pelvics being furnished with five rays and a single spine. Mullets are comparatively small fish, of which the adults are marine. What appears to be the male of the common red mullet is uniformly carmine-red above, although the presumed female is marked by a few longitudinal yellow stripes. Tropical forms have been assigned to distinct genera. To preserve the brilliant red coloration, the fish should be scaled immediately after death.

Family *Mullidæ*.

[1] Although the chætodonts are included by Dr. Günther in the Perciformes, it is not improbable that they may be separated by Mr. Boulenger, when his Catalogue of Fishes is completed. For the present they may remain here.

The numerous representatives of the sea-breams are perhaps best characterised by the dentition, which takes the form either of cutting teeth in the fore-part of the jaws, or of grinding teeth on the sides of the same, the palate being in most cases edentulous. The dorsal fin is single, with its spinous and rayed portions of nearly equal longitudinal extent, and there are always three spines to the anal. The pelvics, which are thoracic in position, include five rays and a single spine, and although simple in one genus, in the other the rays of the pectorals are branched. The scales may be either very slightly serrated or simple, and the mouth is situated at the tip of the snout, with its cleft lateral. In form, these fishes may be described as normal, while in coloration they are dull. Although none grow to large dimensions, nearly all are eaten. The coasts of the temperate and tropical zones are their favourite resorts, but some kinds are found in brackish waters, while a few enter rivers. They may be divided into several sub-families, of which the *Cantharinæ* are typified by the British species of *Cantharus*, locally known by the name of old wife, but more generally as the black sea-bream. In this sub-family, to which also pertain the Mediterranean *Scatharus*, and the Oriental *Tropterodon* and *Crenidens*, there are no teeth on the vomers, but the front of the jaws carries trenchant incisors, which in some cases are lobed. On the other hand, in the *Haplodactylinæ*, there are teeth on the vomers, and flat, generally tricuspidate teeth in the jaws, the single genus *Haplodactylus* being the one with simple lower pectoral rays. *Sargus*, of which there are about a score of species from the Atlantic, Mediterranean, and Oriental seas, represents by itself a third sub-family (*Sarginæ*), characterised by the presence of a single series of incisors in the front of the jaws, and of several rows of grinding teeth, adapted for crushing, on the sides. Whereas *Haplodactylus* subsists on a vegetable diet, the sargi lives by grinding up molluscs and crustaceans. Another sub-family (*Pagrinæ*) of shell-crushers is well known in the form of the gilt-heads (*Chrysophrys*), which take their name from the gold spots on the forehead. In this sub-family there are also grinding teeth in the sides of the jaws, but the front teeth are conical. Other genera of this group are *Lethrinus*, *Sphærodon*, *Pagellus*, and *Pagrus*.

Family *Sparidæ*.

Fig. 6.—Common Sargus.

Still continuing the almost endless series of the Perciformes, we now come to a small and unimportant family including only the genus *Hoplognathus*, species of which have been discovered on the coasts of Japan, Australia, and Peru. The most essential feature of the group is the sharp cutting edges of the jaws, to which such teeth as are present are closely adherent, and thereby render the margin slightly serrated. The first dorsal fin, although low, has strong spines, and is separated only by a very short interval from the taller soft dorsal, the latter being very similar to the anal, above which it is situated. The three spines of the anal are very low.

Family *Hoplognathidæ*.

More important are the genera constituting the family *Cirrhitidæ*, these being best recognised by the thickened and undivided lower rays of the pectoral fins, which in some cases appear to be modified into organs of touch, and in others assist in locomotion. These fishes have deep, compressed bodies, cycloidal scales, and very generally six branchoistegal rays. The dorsal is single, and divided into a spinous and rayed half; and the pelvics, which are separated by an interval from the pectorals, are thoracic, and provided with a single spine and five rays, the anal being three-spined. The typical group includes several genera of small and frequently spotted fishes from the Indo-Pacific and Australasian seas, such as *Cirrhitichthys*, *Cirrhites*, and *Chorinemus*, in all of which there are teeth on the vomerine bones of the palate. In the second group, on the other hand, there are no teeth on the vomers; and among the genera are *Latris*, represented by two New Zealand and Tasmanian species, one of which (the trumpeter-fish) is of large size, and affords excellent food, and the more widely-spread *Chilodactylus*. The latter, which may be easily recognised by the great elongation of one of the rays of the pectoral fins, is likewise valuable as a food-supply, both in South Africa and at the Antipodes.

Family *Cirrhitidæ.*

Although the *Scorpænidæ* are included in Dr. Günther's classification among the Perciformes, they differ from the foregoing families by the presence of a bony stay connecting the preoperculum with the ring of bones beneath the orbit. If the absence of such stay be taken—as it is here—as a distinctive feature of the Perciformes, the present family must typify a section by itself. There are many genera included in the family, which ranges over nearly all oceans and seas. All the species are carnivorous, but whereas some approximate in external form and their mode of life to the *Serranidæ*, others are deep-sea types, with the skin expanded into appendages resembling sea-weeds. In some genera, such as *Scorpæna* and *Sebastes*, well-developed scales are present; this being also the case with the species of *Pterois* from the warmer parts of the Indo-Pacific, all of which are characterised by the height of the pectoral and dorsal fins. On the other hand, there are other types, such as *Choridactylus* and *Pelor* of the Indian seas, and the so-called *Micropus* of the Pacific, in which the scales are rudimental or wanting; *Choridactylus* being one of those with leaf-like expansions to the skin, while *Micropus* is notable on account of containing the smallest of all the Acanthopterygians, certain kinds being considerably less than a couple of inches in length.

Section Scorpæniformes.—Family *Scorpænidæ.*

Passing over without mention a few small and unimportant families, we come to the group known technically as *Berychidæ*, and popularly as slime-heads, which constitute not only a family, but likewise a sectional group by themselves. The essential feature of these fishes is the presence in the head of slime-bearing, or muciferous cavities, which are protected by a skin of great thickness. The body is compressed, and oblong or deep in shape; and the pelvic fins are thoracic, and almost always supported by five rays and a single spine. Generally the body is covered with ctenoid scales, although rarely there may be a naked skin; but there are never scales on the head. Nearly all these fish have large goggle eyes; and the obliquely cleft mouth is armed with minute teeth, while the palate is nearly always toothed, and the opercular bones are likewise armed. Except rarely, the number of rays in the branchiostegal membrane is eight. All the *Berychidæ* are marine, and nearly all live at considerable depths, although there are a couple of

Section Berychiformes.—Family *Berychidæ.*

genera—namely *Myripristis* and *Holocentrum*—most or all of whose members are found near the surface. Like other deep-sea forms, these fish have a wide distribution in species. Among the numerous genera, the single small Japanese species of *Monocentris* is remarkable on account of the large size of the vertically elongated scales, which form a kind of protective cuirass to the body; the opercular bones being unarmed. *Anoplogaster* of the Atlantic may be cited as a genus with a naked skin; whereas in the allied *Trachichthys* there are minute scales, from which the lateral line stands out in great prominence, both having the eye very large. In this genus, too, as well as in the typical *Beryx*, the dorsal fin is single, but in *Holocentrum* and certain other genera it is double.

Section Curtiformes.—Family *Curtidæ.*

The small family of the *Curtidæ* likewise represents a section by itself, distinguished by the possession of only a single dorsal fin, which is much inferior in length to the many-rayed and elongated anal, and likewise by the absence of the structure known as the suprabranchial organ. This family includes the Indian *Curtis* and the Oriental and Tropical Pacific *Pemperis.* In both these fishes the body is oblong, narrowing rapidly towards the tail; and, if present at all, the spines of the dorsal fin are very few. The body is covered with small or medium-sized scales; and minute teeth are developed both in the jaws and on the bones of the palate.

Section Polynemiformes.—Family *Polynemidæ.*

This section, also, includes only a single family, of which the three generic representatives—*Polynemus Pentanemus* and *Galeoides*—are easily recognised by the presence of a number of long filaments arising from below the pectoral fins. There are two somewhat short dorsal fins, separated from one another by a considerable interval; and mucus-producing canals are well developed in the head. These fishes are well represented on tropical coasts, and also enter estuaries and even fresh waters. They generally prefer muddy water, where their exceedingly elongated pectoral filaments doubtless act as efficient feelers.

Section Sciæniformes.—Family *Sciænidæ.*

The Mediterranean umbrine (*Umbrina*), the meagre (*Sciæna*), and the drum (*Pogonias*) of North America are three fairly well-known fishes, representing as many genera of the *Sciænidæ.* As a section, the group is distinguished by the great length of the soft dorsal fin, which exceeds to a greater or less extent both the spinous dorsal and the anal in this respect. Whereas these fishes resemble those of the last family in the development of mucus canals in the head, they differ by the absence of elongated pectoral filaments. In the skull there is no bony connection between the preopercular bone and the orbit; and the pelvic fins are situated thoracically, and furnished with one spine and five soft rays. In form, the body is somewhat elongate and compressed, and the scales are of the ctenoid type, with the lateral line continuous, and often extending on to the tail-fin. The mouth is terminal, and armed with bands of small teeth, among which enlarged tusks may be interspersed, but there are no teeth on the palate. The medium-sized eyes

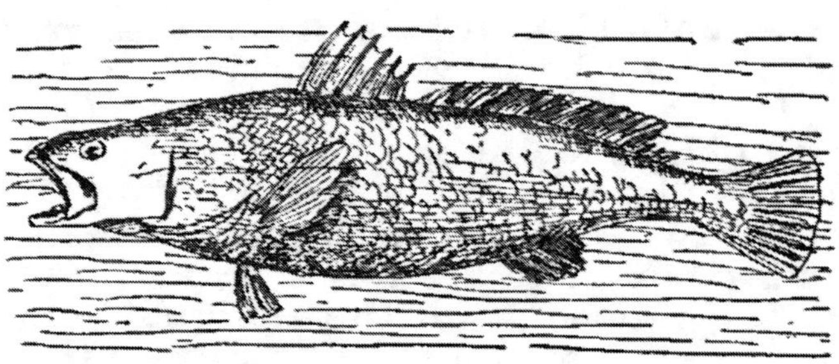

Fig. 7.—THE MEAGRE.

are lateral in position. The members of the family are in the main frequenters of the coasts of the Indian Ocean and the warmer parts of the Atlantic, many of them resorting to the mouths of the larger rivers, and some having taken to a completely fresh-water existence. The largest form is the common meagre, which sometimes reaches a couple of yards in length. Nearly all the species are fit for food; and the air-bladders of many are employed as a source of isinglass. The drum derives its name from the loud sound the fish is capable of producing; this sound being apparently due to the striking together of the upper and lower pharyngeal bones, which are heavily armed with flattened teeth.

Section Xiphiiformes.—Family *Xiphiidæ*.

Although there appears occasionally to be some confusion between sword-fishes and the very different saw-fishes, there ought to be no difficulty in distinguishing the former at a glance from any other fish that swims. This distinctive feature is the production of the upper jaw into the well-known "sword," which is wedge-shaped in form, and may exceed half the length of the rest of the head and body. Spear would, perhaps, have been a more suitable title for this formidable weapon, with which its owner can transfix an unfortunate cod or tunny, or drive it home in the side of a whale as easily as we can thrust a table-fork into a cheese. Not only so, but sword-fishes have often been known to drive their weapon deep into the planking of a ship's bottom, probably from having mistaken the vessel for a whale. Bathers, too, are by no means safe from the onslaughts of these ruthless monsters, which occasionally grow to over a dozen feet in length. The kinds of sword-fishes are numerous; and they are divided into the two generic groups of *Histiophorus* and *Xiphias*, according to whether long and narrow pelvic fins are present or absent. The dorsal fin, which may be either single or divided, has no distinct spinous portion; it is always of considerable height, and in some cases is so elevated as to project high above the water when the fish is swimming near the surface, and there are stories current that it is occasionally used as a sail. The skin of a sword-fish is either completely naked, or furnished with minute rudimental scales. These fishes are chiefly surface-swimmers, and are fond of lying in the sun to bask. According to Scoresby, the sword of one of these fishes, found embedded in the hull of a ship at Liverpool, had penetrated a sheet of copper, an oak plank two and a half inches in thickness, a solid oak timber of seven and a half inches, and another plank of a couple of inches. "The position of the bone was at the distance of four feet horizontally from the stern, and two feet below the surface of the water when the vessel was afloat. Hence it appeared that when the ship had been in rapid progress through the water, she had been met and struck by a sword-fish advancing in the opposite direction, by the shock of which, or by the action of the water forced past the body of the animal by the vessel's progress, the snout had been broken off and detached. The blow, though it must have been singularly forcible, was not observed by any person in the ship." As a further example of the power of the impact of these fish, it may be mentioned

Fig. 8.—COMMON SWORD-FISH.

that, according to Mr. Wood, a sword-fish, in striking a whaling vessel, drove its weapon "through the copper sheathing, an inch-board sheathing, a three-inch plank of hard wood, the solid white oak timber of the ship twelve inches thick, through another two-and-a-half-inch hard oak ceiling plank, and lastly, perforated the head of an oil-cask, where it remained immovably fixed, so that not a drop of oil escaped."

Section Trichiuriformes.—Family *Trichiuridæ*

The so-called scabbard-fish (*Lepidopus*) and the hair-tails (*Trichiurus*), together with the barracudas (*Thyrsitis*), may be cited as well-known examples of a family and section presenting the following leading characteristics. All have very long and compressed bodies, which sometimes assume a band-like form; and the skin is either naked or with rudimental scales. Both the dorsal and anal fins are elongated, with their spinous and soft portions of nearly equal extent; and when the pelvics and caudal are present, the former are thoracic in position, and the latter is distinctly forked. In some forms a portion of the median fins is split up into finlets. The mouth is wide, and there are some large and powerful teeth either in the jaws or on the palate. In all the forms there is an air-bladder. These fishes are carnivorous and predatory in their habits. They have a wide range in space; but whereas some are surface-dwellers, others are found at considerable depths. None afford a very high-class food, although the flesh of several is eaten. In the scabbard-fish, which grows to a couple of yards in length, the body is riband-like, the pelvic fins are wanting, as are scales; but there is a small caudal fin. The flesh is largely consumed in New Zealand, where the species is known as the frost-fish. On the other hand, the hair-tails take their name from the circumstance that the tail terminates in a tapering whip-like extremity, without trace of a caudal fin, the pelvics being wanting, or reduced to a pair of scales, and the anal rudimental, with its spinous portion represented by a number of very short isolated spines. From three to four feet is a common length for these fishes. Barracudas—also locally known as "snoek"—are still larger, and are extensively caught for food in New Zealand and at the Cape. They are characterised by the presence of minute scales in the skin, and of from two to six finlets behind the dorsal and anal, while the palatine bones are toothed. Although essentially coast-fishes, they are occasionally found far out at sea.

Section Cotto-Scombriformes.—Family *Acanthuridæ.*

For some time we have been dealing with sectional groups represented only by a single family each; but we now come to one including several families. In the present group the dorsal fin is either single, or, if divided, has its two portions closely approximated. When normal, the spinous portion is short; but it may be modified either into separate spines, tentacles, or a sucker. The anal resembles the soft dorsal, the hinder part of both these fins being sometimes split up into finlets. When present, the pelvics may be either jugular or thoracic in position, and the region of the vent is never furnished with papillæ. Most of the members of the section are marine fishes. The popular name of surgeons is given to the representatives of the family *Acanthuridæ* [1] on account of the circumstance that in the typical genus *Acanthurus* each side of the tail of the adult is furnished with a spine somewhat resembling a surgeon's lancet, and capable of inflicting a severe wound. In other kinds the spines may be two or three

[1] The family is commonly known as *Acronuridæ*, but *Acronurus* is now ascertained to be a synonym of the type genus.

in number, or replaced by keeled plates, and in all the dorsal fin is single, with but few spines. In form, the compressed body is deep or oblong, the scales with which it is invested being minute, while the eyes are lateral and of moderate size. The mouth is small, and armed with compressed incisor-like teeth, which may be either serrated or pointed, but teeth are never developed on the palate. The pelvic fins are situated thoracically. Internally, a peculiarity is to be found in the forked hinder extremity of the air-bladder. These fishes, which also include the genera *Naseus* and *Prionurus*, are inhabitants of tropical seas, and specially frequent coral-reefs. Here they feed partly on the growing coral and partly on vegetable substances.

Family *Carangidæ.*

The second family of the section under consideration includes—among other forms—the horse-mackerels (*Caranx*), the pilot-fish (*Naucrates*), and the so-called sea-bats (*Platax*). In all of these the body is more or less compressed in form, while the teeth, when developed, are conical, and there is no bony connection between the preopercular bone and the orbit. The skin may be either naked or covered with small scales, and the eyes are placed on the sides of the head. The spinous dorsal fin is shorter than the anal or soft dorsal, from the latter of which it is sometimes separated, while in other cases the two are continuous. In some cases the spinous portion is rudimental, and the hinder part of both the soft dorsal and anal may form finlets, while the pelvics, if developed at all, are thoracic. It is important to notice that the back-bone comprises ten vertebræ in the region of the trunk, and fourteen in that of the tail, although in one case the number of the latter is sixteen. Frequently shield-like plates distinguish the lateral line. An air-bladder is invariably developed. The horse-mackerels—as typified by the common scad—are too well known to require description, while the pelagic pilot-fish may always be recognised by the dark vertical stripes with which the body is ornamented. This fish derives its name from its habit of accompanying sharks or ships. In the preceding genera there are two anal spines remote from the soft portion of the fin ; but in the sea-bats the anal spines are continuous with the soft part, when present. These fish have the body very deep, and rhomboidal in form, and the great development of the median fins, which are often nearly similar above and below. In common with the great majority of the family, the three genera mentioned have the soft dorsal and anal fins of nearly equal extent, but in *Curtus* and *Pempheris* there is only a single dorsal, which is much shorter than the anal.

Family *Cyttidæ.*

The ugly but excellently flavoured John-dory (*Zeus faber*) is the best known representative of a small family distinguished from the other members of the section by the deep and highly compressed body, the double dorsal fin, and the presence in the backbone of more than ten trunk and more than fourteen caudal vertebræ. In the fishes of the genus named one series of bony plates runs along the base of the dorsal and anal fins, and another on the abdomen, but in the species of *Cyttus*—which inhabit the seas of New Zealand, South Australia, and Madeira—these plates are wanting, and the body is scaled.

Family *Stromateidæ.*

The small family of the *Stromateidæ* resembles the last in the absence of a bony stay between the preopercular and the eye, and likewise in the large number of thoracic and caudal vertebræ. They have the body compressed, more or less oblong, and covered with minute scales, the eyes lateral, the dentition very slightly developed, and a number of horny barbed processes in the gullet, while the long and single dorsal fin has no distinct spinous portion. The two genera are *Stromateus* and *Centrolophus;* one species of the latter occasionally reaching the southern shores of Britain, where it is known as the black-fish. Of more importance is the family *Coryphænidæ*, which differs from the last by the absence of spines in the gullet; the teeth, when present, being small and conical. The typical members of the family are the pelagic coryphænas (*Coryphæna*), commonly but incorrectly known as dolphins. These are large brightly-coloured fishes, with the body rather elongated and somewhat compressed, the dorsal fin occupying nearly the whole length of the back, the caudal very deeply forked, and the moderately long anal without any distinct spinous portion. In the adults the head is ornamented with a kind of crest. In the coryphænas beauty is even less than skin-deep, the exquisitely lovely colours being fugitive and transitory immediately the fishes are removed from their native elements. The coryphænas are highly predaceous fishes, and in the Mediterranean and other warm seas may often be seen in large companies pursuing the shoals of flying-fish. The only other genus that can be mentioned here is *Lampris*, represented by a single very beautiful fish from the Mediterranean and North Atlantic. Unfortunately, this fish is commonly known as the sun-fish, a title also applied to the members of the genus *Orthagoriscus*, mentioned in the sequel. Another instance of such synonomy occurs in the use of the name barracuda, which is applied indifferently to the species of the genera *Thyrsites* and *Sphyræna*. In the sun-fish, the whole body is very much compressed, short, and deep, the scales being minute and deciduous, the mouth narrow and toothless, the fore-part of the dorsal fin elevated to a point, and the pelvic fins including a number of rays. In colour, the body has a bluish ground, upon which are a number of silvery spots, while the fins are scarlet. In size, this splendid fish grows to about four feet.

Family *Coryphænidæ.*

From the allied families the small group of the *Nomæidæ* is distinguished by the differentiation of a distinct spinous portion, separated by a short interval from the soft portion of the dorsal; the caudal fin being forked, while finlets are sometimes developed, and the scales are cycloid and of moderate size. Four genera are included in the family, of which the typical *Nomæus* has representatives in the Indian and tropical portions of the Atlantic Ocean, while *Gastrochisma* has one species from the New Zealand seas.

Family *Nomæid.*

Nearly allied to the last is the valuable family of the mackerels, in which there are likewise two dorsal fins and generally finlets; the body being either scaled or naked. The best distinctive features of the family are to be found in the conformation of the fins; some forms having the spinous dorsal modified either into separate spines or into a large sucker; while when the former is normal the soft dorsal and anal are split up into finlets. In form, the body is either spindle-shaped or oblong; and, internally, the air-bladder may be present or absent. The mackerels are among the most highly organised of all fish, the loss of the air-bladder in some forms being probably due to the exact correspondence between the specific gravity of their bodies and that of the water, which renders any adjustment unnecessary. They are mostly pelagic forms, and their coloration is exactly in harmony with their environment, the mottled greens and blacks of the back rendering them invisible from above as they swim in the rippled waters, while their glistening silvery under-

Family *Scomberidæ.*

surface is equally inconspicuous when viewed from beneath against the clear sky above. Their blood has a temperature several degrees above that of the surrounding water, and their flesh receives a larger supply of this fluid than is ordinarily the case, and thus assumes a more or less distinctly red colour. So thoroughly are these fishes pelagic in their mode of life, that they even spawn in the open sea. In diet they are carnivorous; and at the time of year when the various members of the herring-tribe seek the shore for the purpose of depositing their ova, they are pursued by the different kinds of mackerel, which prey either upon the fry or upon the adult. The typical mackerels, or those constituting the genus *Scomber*, have a continuous first dorsal fin, furnished with weak spines, five or six finlets behind both the dorsal and anal fins, and the scales small and evenly distributed all over the body, the teeth being small, and each side of the caudal fin bearing two short ridges. There are several kinds of mackerel—some with and some without an air-bladder—and the distribution of the genus includes nearly all seas, although none are found on the Atlantic coast of the temperate portions of South America. Of larger size are the various fishes known under the names of tunny, albicore, and bonito, which collectively constitute the genus *Thynnus*, and differ from *Scomber* by the number of finlets reaching to from six to nine, the presence of one ridge on each side of the caudal fin, and the concentration of the scales on the fore-part of the body, where they form a kind of corselet. By far the most remarkable and interesting members of the family are, however, the sucking-fishes (*Echeneis*), characterised by the presence of a large, plate-like, adhesive disc, occupying the whole upper surface of the head. This sucker is formed by a structural modification of the first dorsal fin, and in the allied *Elacate* of the tropical Atlantic, which has no sucker, the fin in question is still represented by a few short isolated spines. Sucking-fishes have minute teeth, both on the jaws and on the palate, and in some cases also on the tongue; but they all lack an air-bladder. As they generally pass much of their time attached to the under-surface of the body of a shark or a turtle, or the hull of a ship, the back is less exposed to the light than the under-surface, and consequently becomes less darkly coloured than the latter. The smaller sucking-fishes grow to a length of about eight inches, whereas the larger kinds may measure as much as three feet.

Fig. 9.—COMMON MACKEREL.

Fig. 10.—SUCKING-FISH.

Family *Trachinidæ*.

The eighth family of the Cotto-Scombriformes includes the star-gazers (*Uranoscopus*, *Leptoscopus*, etc.), the weavers (*Trachinus*), the Atlantic tile-fish (*Lopholatilus*), and a host of other types too numerous to mention. All these fishes have a more or less elongated and narrow body, which has sometimes a naked skin, but in other cases is clothed with scales. There are one or two dorsal fins, of which the spinous portion is much less developed than the soft part, which is like the anal. Finlets are always wanting; and the pelvic fins comprise five soft rays and a single spine. The mouth is armed with small conical teeth. In regard to the number of vertebræ and the preopercular bone, the family agrees generally with those that immediately precede, but *Pseudochromis* is stated to possess a stay connecting the bone mentioned with the orbit. Most of the members of the family are small fishes living near the bottom of shallow seas; and all are carnivorous. The group is divided into several sub-families, the first of which is typified by the aforesaid star-gazers, which are ugly-looking fishes, easily recognised by the small mobile eyes being situated on the front of the head and looking upwards, the cleft of the mouth having likewise an upward direction; the lateral line being uninterrupted, and the caudal fin more or less rounded. On the other hand, in the weavers (*Trachinus*)—of which the common English species is known to fishermen by the name of sting-bull—the eyes retain to a greater or less extent the normal lateral position; the dorsal fin being either single or divided. The members of this genus are found in European waters, and on the Pacific coast of South America, although not on the Atlantic side. Wounds inflicted by the spines of the dorsal fin are dangerous on account of being injected with the secretion from a neighbouring poison-gland. Mention must be made of the large and handsomely-coloured tile-fish (*Lopholatilus*) of the American North Atlantic, not only on account of its being an exception among the family from its size and deep-water habitat, but likewise from the fact of having been met with in great profusion a few years ago, and then suddenly disappearing. It is remarkable for possessing a small, pointed fatty fin in front of the long single dorsal.

Families *Malacanthidæ* and *Batrachidæ*.

Since the first of the two families now to be considered contains only the tropical genus *Malacanthus*, it may be dismissed with the bare mention that it is characterised by the possession of not more than ten thoracic and fourteen caudal vertebræ, and the great length of the single dorsal and anal fins. Almost equally brief must be our reference to the frog-fishes (*Batrachidæ*), which include two genera in addition to the typical *Batrachus*, and are for the most part small fishes of carnivorous habits frequenting tropical coasts. They have the head broad and thick, with the eyes more or less inclined upwards; the long body compressed posteriorly; and either a coating of small scales or a bare skin. They have small or medium-sized conical teeth; and there is no connection between the orbit and the preopercular. There are only two or three spines in the first dorsal, but the soft dorsal and anal are elongated and similar; while the pelvic fins are jugular in position and furnished with a pair of soft rays, and the pectorals are not produced. Many of the species are poisonous, having a gland situated at the base of the pectoral fin, from which a noxious fluid is poured forth; the genus *Thallassophryne*, of the Pacific coast of Central America, being stated to rival many of the poisonous snakes in its venom.

Family *Lophiidæ*.

The familiar but hideous angler-fish (*Lophius piscatorius*) of the British coasts typifies a somewhat extensive family belonging to the section Cotto-Scombriformes, and possessing the following distinctive features. In these fishes the head and fore-part of the body are enlarged and covered with a naked skin, and the spinous dorsal fin is placed very far forwards, and consists of either a few more or less isolated spines, or is modified into tentacles, while in some cases it is altogether wanting. The pelvic fins—which may be wanting—comprise four or five rays, and are jugular in position, and the pectoral fins are supported by a prolongation of some of the bones of the internal skeleton. The teeth are rasp-like or villous, and there is no connection between the preopercular and the orbit. The apertures of the gills are very minute, and situated near the root of the pelvic fins, the gills varying from two-and-a-half to three-and-a-half in number, and false gills being usually absent. The family has an almost cosmopolitan distribution, and all its members are but poor swimmers, those which are of pelagic habits drifting about attached to floating bodies, while the littoral forms cling to submarine bodies by means of their pectoral fins, which serve the function of arms. The great size of the wide, flat, and rounded head, which carries the small eyes near the middle of the upper surface, the capacious mouth, and the modification of the first three dorsal spines into tentacles, serve to distinguish the species of the typical genus *Lophius*, which are not numerous. Rarely the common British species, which is often known as the fishing-frog, grows to five feet, although its ordinary length does not exceed three. The first tentacle bears a filamentous appendage, which by its movement serves to attract prey within reach of the capacious jaws. Another interesting member of the family is the pelagic tentacle-fish—*Antennarias*—often found in the gulf-weed, and remarkable for building a silken nest attached to the weed for the reception of the eggs, which are suspended within their receptacle in a cluster, like a bunch of grapes. Even more curious are the two Atlantic species of *Melanocetus*, which are small fishes, looking as if they consisted mainly of jaws and stomach.

Fig. 11.—ANGLER FISH (*Lophius piscatorius*).

Family *Cottidæ*.

The *Cottidæ*, of which the best known representatives are the mostly fresh-water bull-heads (*Cottus*) of the Northern Hemisphere and the marine-gurnards (*Trigla*), are well characterised by the presence of a bony stay connecting the preopercular with the suborbital ring of bones; a feature found among the preceding families of the section only in *Pseudochromis* and some allied genera. These fishes have the body lengthened, and more or less nearly cylindrical; the mouth being transverse, and bearing feeble teeth generally arranged in bands. Whereas in some forms the skin is naked, in others it is scaled, and the armature may consist of a single row of plate-like scales. Generally the dorsal fin is divided, when the soft portion—which is elongated like the anal—exceeds the spinous in extent. The number of rays in the thoracically-placed pelvics never exceeds five; and in some cases the pectorals have filamentous prolongations. The bull-heads, which comprise a very large number of species, a few of which are marine, are noted for their habit of lying sluggishly in the beds of rivers, with their heads concealed beneath the pebbles. The elongated and finger-like three anterior pectoral rays serve to

Fig. 12.—COMMON GURNARD (*Trigla*).

distinguish the gurnards; which are further characterised by their great ugly, bony heads, and the brilliant hues of scarlet or blue with which many of them are adorned. They inhabit all temperate and tropical seas, and are predacious fish, living chiefly on crustaceans. Their habitat is the sea-bottom, on which they crawl by means of the elongated pectoral rays; those appendages apparently also acting the part of feelers. When seen crawling on the bed of a glass tank in an aquarium a gurnard presents a peculiarly ghost-like appearance, reminding the beholder of some monster in a pantomime.

Family *Dactylopteridæ.*

Nearly allied to the last is the family typified by the flying-gurnards (*Dactylopterus*), which rival the true flying-fish in their power of skimming over the surface of the waves by means of their greatly expanded pectoral fins. All are easily recognised by the investiture of the body in a complete cuirass of keeled bony plates or scales. In Britain the group is represented by the so-called armed bull-head, which belongs to the genus *Agonus;* and the family also includes the beaked-gurnards, distinguished by the prolongation of some of the bones of the skull in the form of a flattened process on each side of the snout. The flying-gurnards themselves inhabit the Mediterranean and tropical seas. Here, too, may be placed the curious little dragon-fishes (*Pegasus*), which inhabit the seas of Australia, China, and India, and have a long beak and the body protected by very large plates; the coloration taking the form of small dark spots.

Section Gobiiformes.—Family *Cyclopteridæ.*

Very different in appearance to the last are the clumsy-looking fishes known as lump-suckers (*Cyclopterus*), which are the typical members of a family belonging to another sectional group. In this section the dorsal fin may be single or double, but its spinous division or portion is always short, and may consist of flexible spines; the soft dorsal being equal in extent to the anal. There is no bony connection between the preopercular and the suborbital ring; but there is a prominent papilla in the region of the vent. When pelvic fins are retained, they usually comprise a spine and five rays, although exceptionally the number of the latter may be reduced to four. In addition to their clumsy build, the lump-suckers are distinguished as a family by the presence of a sucker on the lower surface of the body supported by the rudiments of the pelvic fins. By means of their sucker these fishes affix themselves firmly to rocks or stones, and are thus safe from the buffeting of the waves. There are two generic modifications of the family, namely *Cyclopterus* and *Liparis*, in the former of which the skin is tuberculated and viscous, whereas in the latter it is entirely bare. All the members of the family are confined to the colder northern seas, some of them even entering the Arctic Ocean.

Family *Gobiidæ.*

From the lump-suckers, the gobies (*Gobius*) and their allies the mud-skippers (*Periopthalmus*) are sufficiently distinguished by the presence of well-developed rays to the pelvic fins, which may, however, be united together in the middle line of the body. The group is a very extensive one, both in respect to genera, species, and individuals; and it is represented on the temperate and tropical coasts of all parts of the globe. It is, of course, impossible to characterise the various genera; and, as regards the gobies, it must suffice to say that they are small fishes with a geographical range as extensive as is that of the family, and that, in many cases, the males build a cleverly constructed nest for the reception of the eggs. Of greater interest are the mud-skippers, or hopping-fish, on account of their strange habits, and the long time they can remain out of water. They are found on the coasts and estuaries of West Africa, and the countries bordering the Indo-Pacific Ocean. Owing to their remarkably prominent eyes, they look very much like tadpoles; the common species having its dorsal fins spotted with brilliant blue. The pectoral fins are very strongly developed, and are used, when the fish is out of water, for walking or climbing on the roots of mangrove trees. Dr. H. O. Forbes writes that "if the observer remain quite still, the *Periophthalmus* will sit motionless, staring at him with his great eyes, except that every now and then it will wink apparently, sometimes with one eye, and sometimes with both together. What seems to be winking, however, is the inversion of the eye into a depression immediately under it, for the purpose of lubricating the organ when it begins to become dry. The habit that most impresses the naturalist encountering these fishes for the first time is the long period which they can remain out of the water. The writer has timed individuals, both in their native state and in the aquarium, to sit for more than half an hour without a bath. They would then walk slowly into the water, immerse themselves over the head for a second, emerge and remain resting for a short time, with the head and shoulders above, and the mouth under the surface, and walk slowly out again on to the margin. This fish rarely if ever, goes beyond its depth, and only for a few seconds does it at any time completely submerge itself. Their usual habit is to sit propped up on their stiff ventral and strong pectoral fins, with the fore-part of the body elevated, and their quick mobile eyes conspicuous and inquiring; either, as already remarked, entirely away from the water, or with only the extremity of the tail dipping in. When out of the water and sitting still, the mouth is kept closed, and no motion can be detected in the gills or gill-covers. Every now and then the eyes are moistened as described above, and the fish flaps its pectoral fins across the gill-covers and the hind-part of the head. When the tide has just receded and the small marine animals are beginning to follow it, they are very busy darting here and there in pursuit, and gobbling them up voraciously. They will even attack and eat smaller members of their own species. When moving forward, they oar themselves on their strongly muscular pectorals, which they use simultaneously when hopping, or alternately in their more deliberate 'walking,' which leaves a curious triple track on the soft mud which they have traversed. When in the water the *Periophthalmus* sits on the bottom in the same attitude as on shore, with its upper-lip submerged, but with the rest of the head and upper part of the back exposed, the water being driven over its gills very slowly and deliberately as compared with the common trout in an adjoining tank. Its eyes are better adapted for sight out of than under water, and are capable of seeing all round."

Section Blenniiformes.—Family *Cepolidæ*.

The curiously-shaped marine band-fishes form the first representatives of a section which includes five other families. In this section the body is low, elongate, and either subcylindrical or compressed; the dorsal fin being very long, with its spinous portion—when distinct—equal to, or exceeding the soft part in extent. Indeed, in some cases the whole dorsal is composed of spines. The anal is more or less elongated; the caudal—when present at all—is rounded or somewhat truncate; and when the pelvic fins are developed, they may be either jugular or thoracic in position. The band-fishes (*Cepola*) —all of which are of small size—take their name from the long compressed body, which is covered with small scales ; the laterally-placed eyes being relatively large.

Family *Blenniidæ.*

Omitting all mention of the unimportant families *Trichonotidæ* and *Chiridæ*, except the statement that some members of the former, like the New Zealand *Hemerocoëtes*, have a continuous rayed and spineless dorsal fin running nearly the whole length of the back, with a very similar anal beneath, we come to the widely-spread and numerous family of the blennies. In these the body is more or less cylindrical in form, with its skin either naked or covered with scales, which are generally small. There may be from one to three dorsal fins, which occupy nearly the whole length of the back, but vary much in the relative proportion of spines, which in some cases constitute the entire structure. The anal is long, with few or no spines, and the pelvic pair, when developed, are jugular, and comprise less than five soft rays. Usually the head is furnished with false gills, and this character helps to distinguish the blennies from the cod tribe, which they resemble in the structure of the pelvic fins. Although a few attain large dimensions, the great majority of the blennies are small fish, and they include some of the most diminutive of their class. While some are estuarine or fluviatile in their habits, many more are marine and littoral, ranging over all the temperate and tropical coasts of the globe. The true blennies (*Blennius*), which have a naked skin, enjoy a wide geographical range, some being found far out in the open ocean among masses of floating weed, while others inhabit rivers, or even lakes. Whereas these blennies produce spawn in the ordinary way, the two species of the allied genus *Zoarces*—one of which is British—give birth to living young. In these fishes rudimental scales are developed in the skin, and the dorsal fin is only separated by a notch from the caudal, with which the anal is continuous. A remarkable contrast in point of size to the ordinary blennies is afforded by the various species of wolf-fish (*Anarrhichas*), which inhabit all the northern seas, and some of which grow to as much as a couple of yards in length. They have their mouths crammed with a number of very powerful tuberculated teeth, admirably adapted for grinding the hard shells of the shell-fish, crabs, and lobsters, on which these voracious fish subsist.

Family *Rhynchobdellidæ.*

No mention at all can be made of the fifth family (*Acanthoclinidæ*) of the blenniform section, and but a very brief one of the sixth, which includes the so-called spiny eels (*Mastacembelus* and *Rhynchobdella*) of West Africa and the Oriental countries. These are inhabitants of both brackish and fresh waters, and are chiefly remarkable for their resemblance in general appearance to the true eels (*Murænidæ*), from which they may, however, be at once distinguished by the presence of low spines in the fore-part of the elongated dorsal fin. Here, too, may be mentioned the curious oil-fish (*Comephorus*) of Lake Baikal, in regard to whose systematic position naturalists appear to be still in some degree of doubt, although it probably forms a family by itself.

Section Mugiliformes.—Family *Sphyrænidæ.*

The large fishes forming the family *Sphyrænidæ* are commonly known as barracudas, but since that name is applied to the members of a family already noticed, it is better to term them barracuda-pikes. They are the first representatives of a sectional group in which the back bears two fins, the first of these being composed either of feeble spines, or short, like the second, while the pelvic fins are abdominal in position, and comprise five rays and a single spine. The barracuda-pikes, which sometimes grow to as much as eight feet in length, and weigh forty pounds, are all included in the one genus *Sphyræna*. As a family, they are characterised by the long and somewhat eel-like form of the body, the small cycloid scales, continuous lateral line, the wide cleft of the mouth, which is armed with formidable teeth, and the moderate-sized and laterally-situated eyes. They are fierce and voracious fishes, inhabiting tropical and sub-tropical coasts. Although extensively used as food, their flesh is at times apt to develop poisonous properties.

Family *Mugilidæ*.

Passing by the small family of the *Atherinidæ*, of which the most familiar representatives are the so-called sand-smelts (*Atherina*) of the Mediterranean, with the bare mention that the lateral line is feebly and indistinctly developed, we come to the more important group of the grey mullets, most of which are included in the genus *Mugil*, and all of which lack the structure last mentioned. They have the same number (24) of joints in the backbone as the *Sphyrænidæ*, whereas in the *Atherinidæ* these are considerably more numerous. Grey mullets have a narrow cleft to the mouth, none or feeble teeth, and a very sharp, but rather tall first dorsal fin, which is composed of four stiff spines only. The members of the genus are numerous, and common on temperate and tropical coasts, where, according to Dr. Günther, "they frequent brackish waters, in which they find an abundance of food, which consists chiefly of the organic substances mixed with mud or sand. In order to prevent larger bodies from passing into the stomach, or substances from passing through the gill-openings, these fishes have the organs of the pharynx modified into a filtering apparatus. They take in a quantity of sand or mud, and, after having worked it for some time between the pharyngeal bones, they reject the roughest and indigestible portion." Most of the species grow to about four pounds weight, although some reach as much as ten.

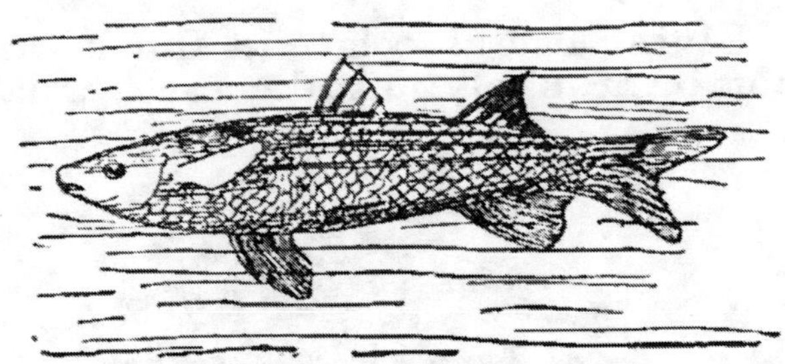

Fig. 13.—GREY MULLET.

Section Scombresociformes.—Family *Scombresocidæ*.

The garpike (*Belone*), the sauries (*Scombresox*), and the flying-fish (*Exocœtus*), collectively constitute a section and family characterised by the feeble development of the spines of the fins. They have the pelvic fins abdominal in situation, and are especially distinguished by the union of the pharyngeal bones, the absence of a spiny dorsal fin, and the forked tail-fin; the rayed dorsal being placed in the caudal region immediately over the anal. Although false gills are present, these are concealed and glandular. As a rule, the air-bladder is retained. A peculiar feature of the family is the simple structure of the stomach, which forms a mere expansion of the intestinal tract. Members of the family are to be met with in all temperate and tropical seas, some of them, like the flying-fish, being truly pelagic in their habits. Fresh-water forms, although few, are, however, by no means wanting; and it is somewhat remarkable that most of these—unlike their marine relatives—give birth to living young, instead of depositing spawn. The garpike, of which one species is commonly met with in the British seas, are specially characterised by the elongation of the jaws to form a long tubular beak, and the connection of all the rays of the anal and dorsal fins (which are precisely similar) by membrane. Young garpike are, however, much more ordinary-looking fishes than their parents, as the beak is not developed till late in life. During the growth of the beak the lower jaw is considerably longer than the upper one, although in the fully adult condition the two are equal in length. So much has been written about the habits of flying-fish (*Exocœtus*), and their form is so familiar, especially to those who have made a voyage in the warmer seas, that we may be well excused from saying much about either point in this place. The only other inhabitants of the deep which indulge in similar flights are the flying-gurnards, with which the true flying-fish are not likely to be confounded. To support them in the air, the pectoral fins of the flying-fishes are greatly elongated. In shape they are less elegant than many fishes, the head being blunt and almost truncated in front. There are numerous species of the genus, some of which appear to range over all seas suited to their existence, while others have a curiously circumsuited habit. A foot is about the usual maximum length, although specimens of eighteen inches are from time to time met with.

Flying-fish associate in shoals, and when disturbed by a vessel, which they not improbably mistake for a whale, rise one after another from the waves like a flock of swallows driven from their shelter. Although it is highly probable that their pectoral fins may vibrate for a few seconds after leaving the water, the flight of these fishes is due entirely to the initial velocity of the leap with which they leave the water; and how great this velocity is, may be inferred from the circumstance that sometimes the flight may cover a distance of at least three hundred yards. Probably attracted by the lights, flying-fish not unfrequently leap on board the deck of small vessels, while they occasionally make their entrance on to those of larger tonnage by way of the open port-holes. On one occasion during a voyage home from South America, such an unbidden visitor entered in this manner the cabin of a passenger, who at the time was shaving, and received a severe blow in the face from the newcomer.

Fig. 14.—FLYING-FISH.

The next section of the Acanthopterygii is typified by the stickle-backs of our streams and ditches; and common and familiar as these little fishes are, they are nevertheless highly interesting to the naturalist, both on account of their structure and their habits. Unfortunately, in our limited space, little can be here said on either. As a sectional group, the Gastrosteiformes are characterised by the circumstance that when a spiny dorsal fin is present at all, this takes the form of a variable number of isolated spines. Although in some forms the pelvic fins are thoracic, in others they assume an abdominal position, owing to the prolongation of the bones of the pelvic girdle, which are attached to the pectoral arch. The snout is generally more or less produced, with the small mouth at its extremity. It will be unnecessary to characterise the stickle-backs (*Gastrosteus*) in full, and it will therefore suffice to say that their somewhat compressed and elongate bodies are either naked, or protected by large plates on the sides, and that the number of spines on the back may vary from as few as

Section Gastrosteiformes.—Family *Gastrosteidæ*.

three to as many as fifteen. All are comparatively small fishes, and whereas the majority are inhabitants of fresh waters, a few are marine. What they lack in size, they make up for in fierceness, stickle-backs being perfect demons for fighting among themselves, while they are terribly destructive to the spawn and fry of larger and better fishes. They have, however, the redeeming quality of taking most excellent care of their own eggs and young, for the reception of which the male builds a nest, which he guards with vigilance, and, if necessary, with his life. Not only is this nest-building habit found in the fresh-water species, but it is likewise common to the sea stickle-back of the British coasts, which selects for its site of operations shallow brackish water, where sea-weeds are abundant. Among many anecdotes relating to the voracity and pugnacity of stickle-backs, we select one from the pen of Mr. J. Stark. On one occasion this gentleman placed in the water inhabited by a stickle-back a number of leeches. Thereupon the fish "darted round the tumbler with lively motions till it found a leech detached and in a proper situation for being seized. When the leech was very small, say about half an inch in length, it was often swallowed at once, before it reached the bottom of the vessel; but when a larger one, about an inch or an inch and a half in length in its expanded state, was put in, and had fastened itself by its mouth to the glass, the efforts of the stickle-back to seize and tear it from its hold were incessant, and never failed to succeed. It darted at the loose extremity, or, when both ends were fastened, at the curve in its middle, seized it in its mouth, rose to near the surface, and after a hearty shake (such as a dog would give a rat), let it drop. The leech, which evidently wished to avoid its enemy upon its release, again fastened itself by its mouth to the glass; but again and again the attack was repeated, till the poor leech became exhausted, and ceased to attempt to hold itself by its disc. The stickle-back then seized it by the head in a proper position for swallowing, and after a few gulps the leech disappeared. The flattened leech being of an oval form, and having a hard skin, was not attacked, unless when very young and small; and leeches of the other species, when pretty well grown, or larger than himself when expanded, were killed in the manner above mentioned, but not swallowed. In one of his attempts to seize a leech, the stickle-back having got it by the tail, the animal curled back, and fixed his disc upon his snout. The efforts of the stickle-back to rid himself of this encumbrance were amusing. He let go his hold of the leech, which then hung over his mouth, and darting at the sides and bottom of the glass with all his strength, endeavoured to rub off this tantalising morsel. This lasted for nearly a minute, when at last he got rid of the leech by rubbing his back upon the bottom of the vessel. The leech, perfectly aware of the company he was in, no sooner loosed his hold than he attempted to wriggle away from his devourer; but before he had reached mid-way up the tumbler, the stickle-back had turned, and finished the contest by swallowing him up."

Family *Aulostomatidæ*.

The second family of the section, which comprises the flute-mouths (*Aulostoma*, *Auliscops*, and *Fistularia*), is readily characterised by the production of the muzzle into a long flute-like tube, at the extremity of which is situated the small mouth; and, likewise, by the pelvic fins, which may be either thoracic or abdominal, comprising six (rarely five) soft rays and no spine. When they are abdominal they have no connection with the pelvis, which is always attached to the pectoral girdle. Whereas in some forms the body—which is always much elongated—is completely naked, in others minute scales are developed. The first dorsal-fin may either be wanting or composed of a few feeble isolated spines. The backbone contains a very large number of joints, and presents the peculiarity that many of those at the front end are united together to form a solid tube. The flute-mouths are confined to the warmer temperate and tropical seas. In spite of their large dimensions —their length being frequently as much as from four to six feet—they can only be regarded as highly developed stickle-backs.

Section Centrisciformes.—Family *Centriscidæ*.

We now come to the first of three sectional groups, each of which is represented only by one family. The first section is characterised by the presence of two dorsal fins, of which the spinous is very short, whereas the soft one—like the anal—is of moderate length. Of more importance is the fact that the pelvic fins are truly abdominal, and have no sort of connection with the pectoral girdle. These fish constitute the two genera *Centriscus* and *Amphisile;* one species of the former being popularly known as the bellows-fish or trumpeter-fish. They are small, short-bodied fishes, with a tubular mouth similar to that of the *Aulostomatidæ;* and as their powers of swimming are of the very feeblest, they are often carried by currents far out to sea, although their proper haunts are the shallows.

Section Gobioesociformes.—Family *Gobioesocidæ*.

Although the members of this section and family are likewise of small size, they differ from the last in the more normal conformation of their mouths and bodies. Having no spiny dorsal-fin, these fishes are easily recognised by the possession of a sucker on the lower surface of the body, placed between the pelvic fins, which are nearly jugular in position. Both the soft dorsal and anal fins are situated on the caudal region of the body, and are of small or medium extent. There are numerous genera of sucker-fishes, such as the West Indian and South American *Gobioesox*, the European *Lepadogaster*, and the New Zealand *Diplocrepis;* the latter being distinguished by the presence of incisor-like teeth in the front of the jaws. The group attains its maximum development in the temperate seas; all its representatives being marine and littoral.

Section Channiformes.—Family *Ophiocephalidæ*.

The so-called serpent-heads (*Channa* and *Ophiocephalus*) are inhabitants of the fresh waters of Africa and the Oriental countries, although more abundant in the latter than in the former area. They are long-bodied, flat-headed fishes, fond of grovelling in the mud, and often leaving their native element to travel some distance on land, where they progress by the aid of their pectoral fins. In these fish the head and body are covered with scales of moderate size, and the fins are without spines, the single dorsal, which is similar to the anal, being low and elongated, and the pelvic pair, if present, thoracic in position, and comprising six soft rays. The most characteristic feature in the structure of the serpent-heads is, however, the presence of a supplemental cavity on each side of the head above the gill-chamber; and it is probable that this aids in keeping the gills moist while the fish are on land. One yard is no uncommon length

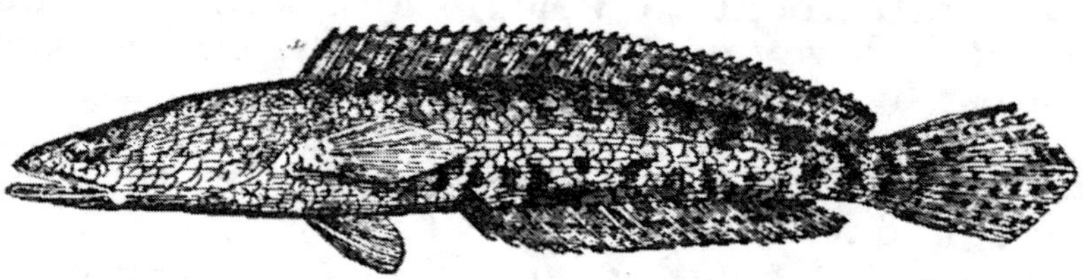

Fig. 15.—Serpent-Head.

for fishes of this group. During seasons of drought the serpent-heads bury themselves in mud; and when living in muddy waters they are in the habit of coming from time to time to the surface to gulp down a mouthful of air.

Section Labyrinthici.—Family *Anabantidæ.*

The famous climbing-perch (*Anabas scandens*) of the Oriental region, which has given rise to so many stories, true and false, is the type of a small section characterised by the possession of an accessory breathing-organ situated in a cavity on each side of the head above the gill-chamber. In both families of the section the body is compressed, and oblong or deep in form, with the investing scales of moderate size. In the first of the two families spines are present in the dorsal and anal fins, although their number is variable; while the lateral line is either interrupted or altogether absent, and the aperture of the gills is small. Like those of the next family, these fishes are inhabitants of fresh or brackish waters, and are able to exist for a considerable time out of water, where they breathe by means of the special organ. There are several genera, such as *Anabas* (climbing-perch), *Polyacanthus*, *Osphromenus* (gurami), and *Betta*, all of which are confined to the Oriental region and Tropical and South Africa. The Malayan gurami is a deep-bodied fish marked with vertical stripes, and with one of the rays of the pelvic fins greatly elongated. On account of the excellent quality of its flesh, it has been introduced into several districts in India, where it thrives well. The climbing-perch is a less deep and more uniformly coloured fish, with no elongation of the pelvic rays, and a taller dorsal fin. During dry seasons it will bury itself in the mud, but more frequently appears to migrate to ponds which are capable of withstanding the drought. On land it travels by using its pectoral fins as legs, fixing these on the further side of such objects as are capable of affording a sufficient fulcrum. One instance at least is on record of these fishes having been taken high up on a palm tree. The reader may well wonder as to the object of such an ascent, but it appears the fish make for the moisture often to be found in the hollows of such trees. The Oriental genus *Polyacanthus* is best known by the domesticated and beautifully coloured Chinese paradise-fish, which, from long cultivation has altered considerably from the original parent form. Another member of the family which has long been domesticated is the Siamese fighting-fish (*Betta pugnax*). In common with the Malays, the Siamese are inveterate gamblers, and in this instance they stake their money on the fighting endurance of their favourite fish. The fish themselves are by no means loth to afford their masters as much sport as possible, and whereas when alone their colours are dull, directly an opponent is seen, the whole body assumes a brilliant metallic lustre. Even a mirror is stated to be sufficient to arouse the pugnacious propensities of these fish, which will then dart forwards against their own image.

Family *Luciocephalidæ.*

The second family of the section is represented by the small fresh-water Malayan fish known as the pike-head (*Luciocephalus pulcher*), and sufficiently distinguished from the preceding family by the presence of a complete lateral line, the protruded jaws, and the general pike-like form of the head and body. The tail is rounded, the dorsal fin is single, and, like the anal, devoid of spines; the pelvic fins comprise one spine and five rays, and the eyes are large.

The fishes of this and the next section are amply characterised by their elongated and riband-like bodily form. This conformation gives them much the appearance of sea-snakes ; and although they are ordinarily inhabitants of deep water, they are sometimes driven to the surface. On such occasions it is highly probable that they are responsible for some of the alleged appearances of the "sea-serpent." Moreover, when cast on shore, they are extremely likely to be mistaken, by persons unacquainted with zoology, for that mysterious monster ; and not many years ago a telegram in the papers announced the discovery in Australia of a dead sea-serpent, which subsequently turned out to be a gigantic stranded riband fish. Here it may be well to remark that the writer by no means refuses to believe in the possibility of the existence of "sea-serpents," but at present contents himself with considering that the evidence is not yet sufficiently convincing. To return to the Lophotiformes, this section, in addition to the riband-like body, is characterised by the vent being situated near the hinder extremity of the latter, and closely followed by the anal fin ; the dorsal fin running along almost the entire length of the body, and commencing in an enormous backwardly-curved spine, which arises from an elevated crest on the summit of the short head. To the presence of this spine, or horn, the one representative of the section and family (*Lophotes cepedianus*) owes its popular name of unicorn-fish. Rhinoceros-fish would, however, be a better title. The unicorn-fish grows to a length of between five and six feet, and has been taken at considerable depths in widely distant parts of the ocean. That it is indeed a fairly deep-sea monster is apparent from its large eyes ; but this feature indicates that it is not an inhabitant of the deepest abysses, where ordinary visual organs would be of no use. Although we can never hope to acquire such knowledge, it would be matter of extreme interest to discover the use of the enormous horn of this strange fish.

Section Lophotiformes.—Family *Lophotidæ.*

Fig. 16.—Unicorn Fish.

Section Tænii-formes.—Family *Trachypteridæ.*

The riband-fishes differ from the *Lophotidæ* by two characters connected with the fins. In the first place, the anal is absent ; and in the second, the caudal fin is either rudimental, or is so placed as not to form a direct continuation of the longitudinal axis of the body, being then directed upwards in a fan-like manner. Very generally, however, this caudal appendage is lost in full-grown specimens. Young riband-fishes are so totally unlike their parents that no one would dream they belonged to the same group. Dr. Günther observes that such young fish, of from two to four inches in length, "are not rarely met with near the surface. They possess the most extraordinary development of fin-rays observed in the whole class of fishes, some of them being several times longer than the body, and provided with lappet-like dilatations. There is no doubt that fishes with such delicate appendages are bred and live in depths where the water is absolutely quiet, as a sojourn in the disturbed water of the surface would deprive them at once of organs which must be of some utility for their own preservation." Ribandfishes are classed under three genera, respectively known by the names of *Regalecus*, *Stylophorus*, and *Trachypterus*. Of these, the first includes the largest known species; Banks' riband-fish (*R. banksi*), which is occasionally cast on the shores of England, where it is known—most inappropriately—as the "king of the herrings," exceeding a score of feet in length. In place of the horn of the unicorn-fish, this riband-fish has a crest of curving spines on the crown of the head, which recalls the feathery crest of a cockatoo. In this genus the pelvic fins, which are placed almost immediately behind the extremely short pectoral pair, are reduced to long tapering filaments, without rays; the caudal fin being rudimental or absent. On the other hand, in the rare *Stylophorus*, the pelvic fins are totally absent, and the caudal forms a very long appendage like a whip-lash. In the typical *Trachypterus*, however, the pelvic pair of fins still retain their rays. The best known member of this genus is the northern one commonly known as the deal-fish, which is not unfrequently cast ashore after gales on the mainland and islands of the north of Britain.

Section Notacanthiformes.—Family *Notacanthidæ*.

An aberrant group of the sub-order is formed by the long-bodied deep-sea fishes, commonly known as thorn-backs, all of which may be included in the single genus *Notacanthus*. In these fishes the dorsal fin has no soft portion, and is composed of a great number of low tooth-like spines, separated from one another by comparatively long intervals, and extending over nearly the whole length of the back, the long anal being of somewhat similar structure. The muzzle is produced some distance in advance of the snout. The pectoral and pelvic fins are widely separated from one another, so that the latter are truly abdominal in position; but in spite of this the caudal region extends a long distance behind the pelvics, the tail terminating in a sharp point, without a distinct fin.

Section Pharyngognathi.—Family *Pomacentridæ*.

The members of the last sectional group of the great sub-order Acanthopterygii are distinguished from nearly all the forms hitherto mentioned by the coalescence in the median line of the lower pharyngeal bones. On this account the group has been regarded as of subordinal value, although it seems preferable that it should rank only as a section. That it is a specialised group is indicated, not only by the union of the pharyngeals, but also by the loss of the air-bladder. The group includes four families, of which the first is represented by the coral-fishes, forming the genera *Dascyllus*, *Heliastes*, *Pomacentrus*, etc. Most of these are inhabitants of the tropical seas, where, as their name implies, they frequent coral reefs. In form and coloration, as well as in habits, they are very similar to the *Chætodontidæ* (p. 465), many of them having alternate dark and light bands on the body. The absence of scales on the fins in the present family serves, however, to distinguish them at a glance from the members of the other group. In these fishes the body is deep and compressed; the scales are of the ctenoid or comb-like type; the lateral line is either interrupted, or stops short of the caudal fin; and false gills are developed in the head. The number of species is very large. In habits these fish are carnivorous, some of them being provided with powerful incisor teeth, for the purpose of feeding on coral.

Family *Labridæ.*

More familiar than the last is the extensive and important family of the wrasses, or thick-lipped fishes, in which the scales have smooth margins (cycloid), and the pouting lips are often greatly thickened. As in the preceding family, the dorsal fin is single, with the spiny portion at least as well developed as the rayed, which is similar to the anal; and the pelvic pair are thoracic in position, and comprise five rays and a single spine. Whereas in some of the wrasses the body is deep, in others it is of a more elongated shape. Wrasses are coast fishes, mostly of carnivorous habits, which attain their maximum development in the tropical and temperate seas. Although their palates are unarmed, their jaws are provided with a number of powerful teeth admirably suited for crushing the shell-fish on which these fishes chiefly subsist. Sea-anemones or corals afford, however, a preferable diet to some of the species, while a few are strict vegetarians. Wrasses are divided into a number of genera, which may be arranged in larger groups in correspondence with the conformation of the front teeth. In the typical *Labrax*, of which the headquarters is the Mediterranean, the jaw-teeth are conical and arranged in a single series. The two British forms are the ballan (*L. maculatus*) and the striped wrasse (*L. mixtus*), of which the latter exhibits great sexual differences in coloration. The gold sinny represents in Britain a genus (*Crenilabrus*) differing from the true wrasses in having the edge of the preopercular bone serrated at all ages, instead of only in the young.

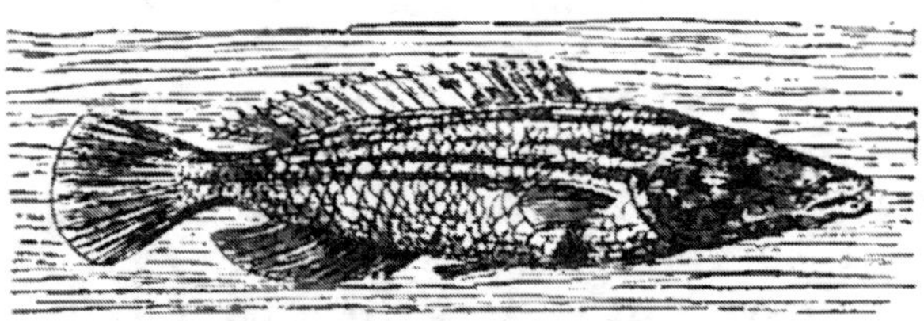

Fig. 17.—Striped Wrasse.

Family *Diatrematidæ.*

Passing by many other types, brief reference must be made to the parrot-wrasses (*Scarus*), deriving their name from the confluence of the anterior teeth to form a cutting beak. One species is common in the Mediterranean, where it was well known to the ancients. The viviparous wrasses (*Ditrema* and *Heterocarpus*) are noteworthy on account of their peculiar reproduction, and are accordingly referred to as a family by themselves. These fishes, which do not attain to a large size, are very characteristic of the temperate portions of the North Pacific, where the majority of the species are confined to the American side, although a few occur on the Asiatic.

Family *Chromididæ.*

The last group of the Acanthopterygii is the somewhat important family of the chromids, which have a very remarkable geographical distribution. From the other members of the group with the lower pharyngal bones united, they are distinguished by being exclusively fresh-water in their habitat. Although none of the genera inhabiting the Eastern Hemisphere are common to the Western, these fish inhabit the rivers of Tropical Africa, Madagascar, Syria, Palestine, and Tropical America, while a single genus is found in India. From the other members of the present group, the chromids may be distinguished by the absence of false gills. In appearance they are not very unlike wrasses, having a single dorsal fin, of which the anterior portion is spiny, the scales generally ctenoid, and the lateral line more or less markedly interrupted. In regard to diet, they display considerable variation, some forms being entirely carnivorous, whereas others are as distinctly vegetable feeders. Most are relatively small fishes, although the balti of the Nile, which belongs to *Chromis*, grows to twenty inches. Of the genera, *Etroplus* is Indian, *Chromis* and *Hemichromis* are African and Syrian, and *Paretroplus* Malagasy.

SUB-ORDER II.—LOPHOBRANCHII.

This and the following sub-order include a small number of peculiar fishes which may probably be regarded as highly specialised offshoots from the primitive stock of the Acanthopterygii, neither of them having a duct to the air-bladder. The Lophobranchii take their name from the form of the gills, which consist of small rounded tufts arising from the gill-arches; the gill-apertures being small, and the operculum or gill-cover comprising only a single plate-like bone. All these fishes have the body enclosed in a many-jointed shield of bone, and the mouth is produced into a toothless tube. Another peculiarity is to be found in the exceedingly feeble development of the muscles.

Family *Solenostomatidæ*.

The first family of the sub-order is formed solely by the members of the genus *Solenostoma*, which are few in number and small in size, and inhabit the Indian Ocean. These fishes have the fins well developed, no soft rays to the first dorsal, wide gill-apertures, and the muzzle greatly elongated. The body is much compressed and the tail very short; the soft dorsal and anal fins arising opposite one another from elevations of the hinder part of the body, while the pelvic pair, which are seven-rayed, are situated below the first dorsal, and in the female are united to the chest by their outer edges to form a receptacle for the eggs. None of these fishes have an air-bladder.

Family *Syngnathidæ*.

The second family of the group is represented by the pipe-fishes (*Syngnathus*, *Siphonostoma*, etc.), and the still more bizarre sea-horses (*Hippocampus* and *Phyllopteryx*), the latter differing from the former in having the tail prehensile, and employing it as an anchor. These fishes are distinguished from the first family by the aperture of the gill-chamber being reduced to a very minute opening at the hinder upper angle of the operculum, and by the loss of the first dorsal and pelvic fins. In certain cases some of the other fins are likewise aborted. The pipe-fishes have the body exceedingly elongated, whereas in the sea-horses it is shorter and deeper, while spiny leaf-like processes arise from the ridges on the head and back. Many of these fish have special structural modifications for the purpose of protecting the eggs, as is also the case with some of the *Solenostomatidæ*. Thus, the females of *Solenostoma* are provided on the lower surface of the body with a roomy pouch, formed by the adherence of the pelvic fins to the skin of the abdomen. The inner walls of this pouch are furnished with long filaments, which aid in keeping the egg in position; and it is probable that after the fry are hatched they are retained for some time by attachment to the walls of the chamber. In the typical pipe-fishes (*Syngnathus*) the care of the family falls to the share of the males, which are provided with a long pouch on the under surface of the tail,

Fig. 18.—PIPE-FISH.

formed by a fold of skin arising on each side, and the two meeting in the middle line. The manner in which the eggs are conveyed into this pouch appears to be unknown, but when once there they are completely enclosed by the junction of the edges of the two folds of skin, and thus remain till they are hatched into minute eel-like pipe-fish, which soon make their way into the water by bursting open the folds of the pouch. In the sea-horses the development is carried one stage further, the nursing-pouch being closed along the middle line, so as to communicate with the exterior only by means of a small aperture at the anterior end, through which the eggs are by some means or other introduced, and by which in due course the young make their escape. Certain pipe-fishes (*Doryichthys*) differ from the ordinary forms in that the males have the pouch placed beneath the abdomen instead of under the tail; and it is remarkable that in some allied genera (*Nerophis*) the eggs are simply attached to the lower surface of the abdomen of the male without the development of any pouch.

Both the *Solenostomatidæ* and *Syngnathidæ* are feeble swimmers; they generally frequent coasts well protected by sea-weed, to which the species provided with prehensile tails attach themselves by means of that useful appendage. In swimming, they generally maintain themselves in a more or less nearly vertical position. Writing of the sea-horse, Dr. Bashford Dean says that, "in spite of its many structural oddities, its genetic kinship with the stickle-backs cannot be doubted. Yet to have attained its present form, its evolution must have carried it along a widely divergent path. It may, in the first place, have fused the lines of its metameral scales, dividing off the surface of its elongate body in sharp-edged rectangles, whose corners have become produced into spines. At this state of evolution its appearance might well be represented by that of the kindred pipe-fish. To secure more perfect anchorage in its algous feeding-ground, its body-terminal must now have discarded its fin-membranes and become prehensile, probably the most remarkable adaptation in the entire class of fishes, since it causes metameral organs to change the plane in which they function from a horizontal to a vertical one."

SUB-ORDER III.—PLECTOGNATHI.

The spine-clad globe-fishes, of which dried specimens are so frequently exhibited in old curiosity shops, may be taken as a familiar example of this small sub-order, which, like the last, includes highly modified and specialised forms. All these fishes have a narrow mouth, and some of the bones of the upper jaw fused together, while in some of them the jaws are produced into a beak-like form. They have but few segments in the back-bone, and whereas the bones of the head are fully hardened, those of the rest of the skeleton are comparatively soft. In form, the gills are pectinate; the gill-apertures being very small, and placed in advance of the pectoral pair of fins. If the pelvic fins persist they are reduced to mere spines; the spinous dorsal, too, is more or less rudimental, although the soft dorsal is generally well developed and situated far back, immediately over the anal. Very various is the covering of the body, the skin in some forms being naked, while in others it is dotted over with long spines; in others the whole head and body is invested in a complete cuirass of true bone, while in others there are roughened scales. All, however, agree in the absence of a duct to the air-bladder.

The first family of the Plectogathi is represented by the file-fishes (*Balistes*, etc.) and the strange coffer-fishes (*Ostracium*). In these fishes there are a few separate teeth in the jaws, and traces of the spinous dorsal and pelvic fins usually persist. In form, the body may be either compressed or angulated, and the muzzle is rather elongated; the skin being either spiny or rough, or replaced by a bony armour. Their chief habitat is the tropical oceans, although some range into cooler seas. The Oriental genus *Triacanthus* belongs to a sub-family characterised by the presence of roughened scale-like plates on the skin, and the retention of from four to six spines in the first dorsal fin. On the other hand, *Balistes* is included in a sub-family in which there are never more than three spines in the fin last mentioned; while the pelvic fins are absent, or indicated only by a swelling on the lower surface of the body; the compressed body being clothed with scale-like plates capable of being moved, or with a roughened skin. There are several genera in this group, and the flesh of certain kinds is poisonous. *Balistes* itself, which is furnished with powerful cutting teeth in the front of the jaws, browses upon living coral, or eats through the shells of molluscs in order to get at the animal within. The angulated bony carapace—composed of hexagonal plates joined together like mosaic—sufficiently distinguishes the coffer-fishes (*Ostracium*), which constitute a sub-family by themselves.

Family *Balistidæ.*

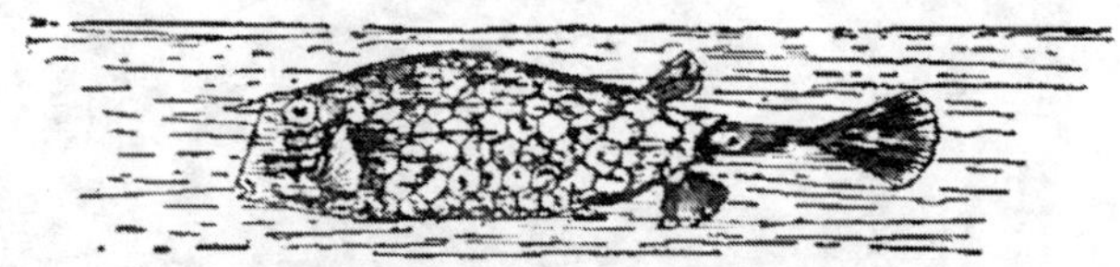

Fig. 19.—COFFER-FISH.

The second family includes the globe-fishes and their near allies the sun-fishes, in both of which the bones of the jaws are welded together so as to form a cutting parrot-like beak of great power. The teeth are modified into large dental plates tightly adherent to the jaws, and consisting structurally of a number of very thin parallel laminæ, arranged like the leaves in a book. These fishes are mostly inhabitants of the hotter seas, although a few have taken to a fresh-water existence. The one Oriental species of *Triodon* alone represents the first sub-family, and has the skin of the lower surface dilated into a large, inflatable sac; the dental plate of the upper-jaw being divided in the middle, while that of the lower is single. Spiny bony plates, which do not overlap, clothe the body, and the tail-fin is forked. The globe-fishes (*Diodon*, *Tetrodon*, etc.) form the second sub-family, and have the more or less shortened and rounded body covered with spines, while there is a distinct tail and caudal fin, and the distensible throat can be inflated with air. The different genera are chiefly distinguished from one another by the conformation of the dental plates, and the size and distribution of the spines. Dr. Günther writes, that "these fishes have the power of inflating their body by filling their distensible œsophagus with air, and thus assume a more or less globular form. The skin is then stretched to its utmost extent, and the spines protrude and form a more or less formidable defensive armour, as in a

Family *Diodontidæ.*

Fig. 20.—GLOBE-FISH.

hedgehog; therefore they are frequently called sea-hedgehogs. However, it is probable that the spines are a protection not only when the fish is on the surface and able to take in air, but also when it is under water." The third sub-family of the *Diodontidæ* includes only the two species of sun-fish, *Orthagoriscus*, specimens of which at times grow to as much as seven feet in length. Having the body excessively compressed and deep, with a very tall dorsal and anal fin placed one above the other at the hinder end, the sun-fishes are especially characterised by the short, deep, and truncated tail, of which the fin is confluent above with the base of the dorsal, and below with that of the anal. There is no dilatable sac beneath the skin, which may be either rough or smoothly tesselated; and externally the pelvic fins and internally the air-bladder are absent. Sun-fish are pelagic forms, generally swimming in a vertical position near the surface of the water. Both kinds seem to feed chiefly on shell-fish.

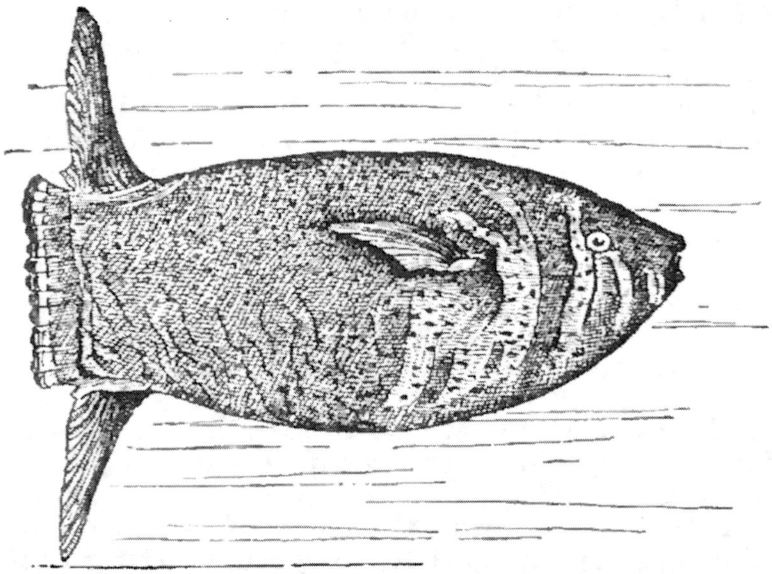

Fig. 21.—Common Sun-Fish.

SUB-ORDER IV.—ANACANTHINI.

The members of this comparatively small, although highly important sub-order are distinguished from the Acanthopterygii by the pelvic and median fins being, as a general rule, devoid of spines and composed of soft jointed rays. When present at all, the pelvic fins are invariably either thoracic or jugular in position; and in those forms furnished with an air bladder, this has no communication with the œsophagus.

The first four families of the sub-order form a section known as the Gadoidei, and are characterised by the normal and symmetrical form of the head and body. The family of the *Lycodidæ* includes several genera of blenny-like fish characterised by the union of all the median fins, and by the pelvics, when present, being small, jugular, and articulated to the pectoral arch. Most of these fishes are inhabitants of the seas in the neighbourhood of the two poles. Passing by the family with the bare mention that *Lycodes* and *Gymnelis* are two of the best-known genera, we turn to the much more important cod family. In these the caudal fin is generally distinct from the others, but when it is united therewith, the first dorsal is divided, so that three dorsals are produced. Generally the pelvic fins —which are jugular—are well developed, but in those instances where they are filamentary, the first dorsal is double. There may be either a single or a double anal. As regards their internal anatomy, it will suffice to say that the cods generally have an air-bladder; while as their

Family *Lycodidæ*.

Family *Gadidæ*.

external form is so familiar, it will not be necessary to say more than that the scales are small and the lateral line distinct. Cod are for the most part inhabitants of comparatively shallow seas of the cooler portions of the Northern Hemisphere, although there are some widely distributed deep-sea forms, and a very few live in fresh water. All the members of the family are edible ; and as they are particularly suitable for salting, their value as a food-supply is very great, although the taste and quality of their flesh is far inferior to that of many other fish. In the typical genus *Gadus* are included the greater number of the larger and more valuable species, such as the common cod (*G. morrhua*), the haddock (*G. æglefinus*), the whiting (*G. merlangus*), the pollack (*G. pollachius*), and the coal-fish (*G. virens*). In all of these there are three dorsal and two anal fins ; and whereas teeth are developed on the vomerine bones of the palate, the palatines are toothless. Most, although not all, have a barbel on the chin. In the allied group of the hakes (*Merluccius*) this barbel is wanting, while the number of dorsal fins is reduced to two, and there is but a single anal ; the pelvic fins being strong, and broad at the base, and teeth being present alike in the jaws and on the vomer. The large fresh-water cod known as the burbot (*Lota vulgaris*) is found both in Europe and in North America, and has the same number of fins as the hakes, but the body is longer, the head flatter, and the chin bears a barbel. Nearly allied are the marine lings (*Molva*), distinguished by having several large teeth on the vomer and in the lower jaw. In the rocklings (*Motella*) the first dorsal fin merely forms a fringe, partly concealed in a groove ; and there are barbels—varying in number with the species—to both jaws. Some members of this genus are remarkable on account of their southern habitat, being found in the seas of New Zealand and the Cape.

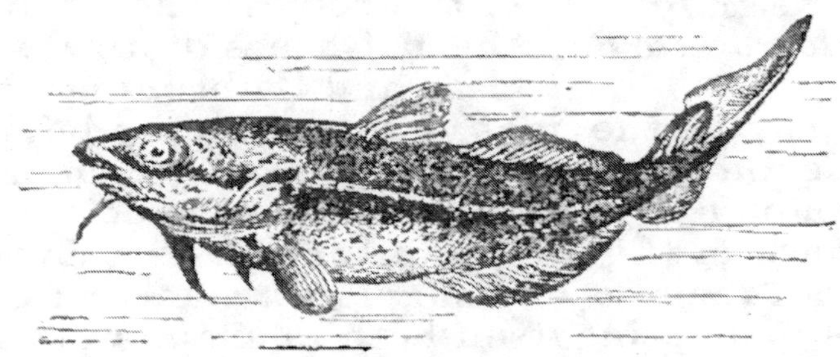

Fig. 22.—COMMON COD.

Family *Ophidiidæ*.

Although most familiarly known by the sand-eels, the chief interest in the family *Ophidiidæ* centres round the blind cave-fish from the caves of Cuba. In none of the tribe are the pelvic fins fully developed, and in some they are wanting ; while there is no distinct first dorsal or first anal, and the caudal fin is in most cases not distinct from the other median fins. The two small fresh-water fishes constituting the genus *Lucifuga* are sufficiently distinguished by the absence of eyes ; but they have a near ally in the marine *Brotula*, which possesses fully developed visual organs. There are, however, blind deep-sea types, such as *Typhlonus*. All these retain pelvic fins, which are jugular in position ; but in the typical *Ophidium* these are replaced by long filaments. Very interesting are the somewhat eel-like small parasitic fishes constituting the genera *Encheliophis* and *Fierasfer*, which frequent the breathing-chambers of sea-cucumbers, the interior of bivalve molluscs, and other safe positions in living animals. They have no pelvic fins, and the vent is situated quite close up to the throat. On the other hand, in the sand-launces, or sand-eels (*Ammodytes*), while pelvic fins are absent, the position of the vent is normal. These fish—which love to bury themselves in the sand—have elongated bodies, on which the low dorsal fin extends from a little distance behind the head to the tail, while the anal occupies almost all the hinder half of the lower surface.

Of comparatively little importance is the small marine family typified by the genus *Macrurus*. Their chief character is that the body terminates behind in an elongated, tapering, compressed tail, without an expanded caudal fin, and is coated with scales, which may be either striated, keeled, or spined. Some of the numerous species measure as much as a yard in length.

Family *Macruridæ.*

The last family of the sub-order is that of the flat-fishes, which forms a section to itself, known as the Pleuronectoidei, and characterised by the unsymmetrical conformation of the head and anterior portion of the body in the adult. This strange modification renders the flat-fishes quite distinct from all other members of the class, and by bringing the two eyes to one side of the body—it may be the right or it may be the left—enables them to rest with the other side on the bottom of the sea. Generally, too, they swim in this position, although it is believed that some of the less modified types swim, at least at times, in the normal manner. In this type of fish we have, as Dr. Bashford Dean remarks, "a singular instance of environmental evolution, the flattened body adapting itself both in shape and colour to its bottom-living. Its entire side—not the ventral region, as in the rays—is flattened to the bottom. The unpaired fins now become of especial value; they increase in size, and their undulatory movements enable the fish to swim rapidly yet retain its one-sided position; ventral fins become useless and degenerate. The further adaptations of the flat-fish include its pigmentation only on the upper or light-exposed side, in this giving one of the most remarkable cases of adaptation known among vertebrates." Among the rather numerous genera constituting this family, the one in which the adaptation is least developed is *Psettodes*, represented by a species whose distribution extends from China to the west coast of Africa. In this fish the dorsal fin, which in the other types commences at, or in front of the eye, begins on the neck; the eyes being either on the left or the right side. The two species of halibut (*Hippoglossus*) mark one step in advance, the dorsal fin starting above the eye, although the jaws are still of nearly equal development on both sides. More specialised is the genus *Rhombus*, which includes the turbot, brill, and mary-sole. Here the dorsal fin commences on the snout, and the eyes are situated on the left side of the body; the scales being either minute or wanting. All these fishes have teeth on the vomerine bones of the palate, but since the so-called top-knot of the Mediterranean and the Channel has an edentulous vomer, it is referred to a genus apart, under the name of *Phrynorhombus*. Omitting mention of a number of other less familiar genera, brief reference must be made to *Pleuronectes*, so well known in the shape of the flounder and the plaice. In these fish the dorsal fin starts above the eye, and the narrow mouth is very unsymmetrical, having its teeth much more developed on the blind than on the coloured side. There are no teeth in the palate, and the eyes are generally on the right side, scales being small or wanting. Lastly, the soles (*Solea*)

Family *Pleuronectoidæ.*

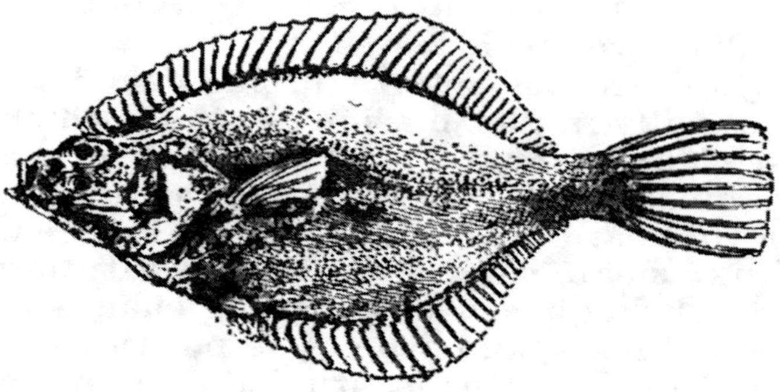

Fig. 23.—THE FLOUNDER.

are right-eyed fishes, with the upper eye somewhat in front of the lower one, and the narrow mouth twisted round to the left side; the dorsal fin, which is distinct from the caudal, starting on the snout.

SUB-ORDER V.—PHYSOSTOMI.

Section A.—Apodes.

The bony fishes forming the present group are broadly distinguished from all the foregoing by the possession of a duct to the air-bladder when present; such duct opening either into the œsophagus or the stomach. To this leading and all-important internal feature of the group it may be added, that externally all these fishes have the pelvic fins situated far behind the pectoral pair, whence they are described as abdominal in position. If the skull be examined, it will be found that, as a general rule, the parietal bones meet in the middle line. The rays supporting the fins are mostly soft, although the first in the pectoral pair and dorsal are spiny. Most of these features are primitive—a duct to the air-bladder being found in the succeeding sub-orders of the Teleostomi, which are clearly low types—and it may accordingly be inferred that the Physostomi are inferior in their organisation to the groups in which the air-bladder is unprovided with a duct. The section named above includes three families of eel-like fishes, but as the features by which this section differs from those that follow are deep-seated and would require a considerable amount of technical language for their adequate explanation, they cannot be described on this occasion.

The Eel-Tribe.—Family *Murænidæ*.

The *Murænidæ* are all characterised by their snake-like bodily form, but as this form is common to the other two families included in the section, other features have to be relied on for the definition of the group. Unfortunately, many of these features can only be observed by an examination of the skeleton or internal soft parts. Externally eels are characterised by the absence of the pelvic pair of fins, and in some forms the pectorals are likewise wanting. If the dorsal and anal fins are developed, these either form with the tail a continuous fringe, or are merely separated by the projecting extremity of the latter. The skin is either bare, or contains minute rudimental scales. The backward position of the vent is likewise a characteristic feature of the family. More important is the structure of the upper jaw, of which the front portion of the margin is formed by the premaxillæ, while the sides are constituted by the maxillæ, which are well provided with teeth. Equally important is the circumstance that posteriorly the skull has no connection with the pectoral arch, which is attached solely to the vertebræ of the neck. Of the soft parts, it will suffice to state that there are no ducts to the reproductive organs. Whereas some members of the family are exclusively marine, others pass a considerable portion of their existence in fresh waters. Among the former are the brightly-coloured and frequently gigantic species constituting the genus *Muræna*, some of which grow to fully eight feet in length. They have no paired fins, although the median ones are well developed; and save for the presence of the latter, are exceedingly like large snakes. In all the skin is naked, and in many the teeth are very large and powerful. A peculiar feature is the presence of two pairs of external nostrils, of which the foremost are tubular, while the hinder pair are also of a similar type in certain species. There are many representatives of the genus from tropical and temperate seas, some of which ascend tidal rivers. All are highly predaceous. The so-called glass-eels (*Leptocephalus*) are larval forms of the members of the present family. Although occasionally brought by currents to the surface, they live at great depths in the sea. Before turning into the adult form they undergo a distinct metamorphosis. Nearly allied are the five representatives of the genus *Gymnomuræna*, which inhabit the Pacific and Indian Oceans, and have the median fins represented by mere rudiments near the extremity of the tail. From both these genera the true eels (*Anguilla*) may be easily distinguished by the retention of the pectoral fins, which are placed close to the head, and have the narrow gill-openings just behind their roots. The two jaws are approximately equal in length; the skin contains a number of rudimental scales; and the teeth are small and arranged in the form of bands. Eels are so familiar to all that they need no further description. Before companies were so careful in filtering their water as at present, eels would, not unfrequently, enter the service-pipes, where they would remain until the passage became completely choked, owing to their increase in size. Eels occur in the fresh waters of all parts of the world where the temperature is not permanently below the freezing point. Reams of paper have been spoilt in discussing their breeding-habits, which long remained a mystery. It is, however, now ascertained that eels breed only in the sea, and that the reproductive process seems to be fatal to their existence; such individuals as are confined to fresh waters being sterile. In autumn such adults as are enabled to find a passage make their way to the ocean, whence they never return; while in spring the elvers, or young eels, ascend the rivers, frequently in enormous numbers. On such migrations scarcely any obstacles will stay their advance, and they have even been known to circumvent a barrier by leaving the water and making a detour over moist rocks or marshy ground. Thus St. John writes that in a Scotch river when the elvers "came to a fall that they could not possibly ascend, they wriggled out of the water, and gliding along the rock, close to the edge where the stone was constantly wet from the splashing and spray of the fall, they made their way up till they got above the difficulty, and then again slipping into the water, continued their course." Writing of eel-migrations in the Thames, Jesse observes that this takes place in May. "The young eels are about two inches in length, and they make their approach in one regular and undeviating column of about five inches in breadth, and as thick together as it is possible for them to be. As the procession generally lasts two or three days, and as they appear to move at the rate of nearly two miles and a half an hour, some idea may be formed of their enormous number." The largest eels occur in Oceania, where examples measuring as much as ten feet in length have been recorded. From the true eels the marine species included in the genus *Conger* differ by the total want of scales, as well as by the larger mouth, the presence of an outer series of cutting teeth in the jaws, and the more forward extension of the dorsal fin. At least four species of conger are known, among which *C. vulgaris* is almost

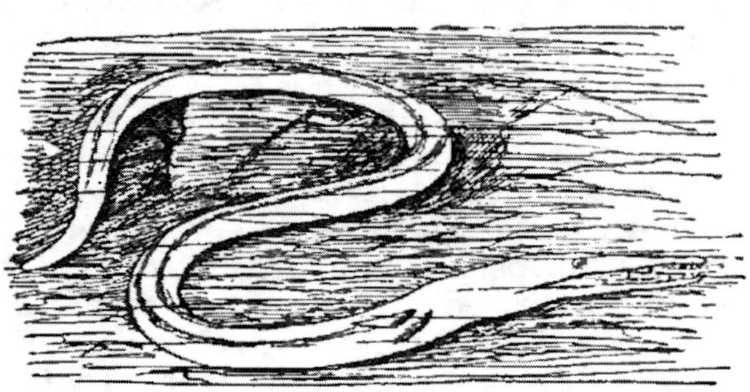

Fig. 24.—Serpent-Eel.

cosmopolitan in distribution. Congers are found at moderate depths on rocky bottoms, and are extremely voracious, taking at night almost any kind of bait. Eight feet is not an uncommon length for one of these eels. There are also deep-sea congers, such as *Synaphobranchus* and *Saccopharynx*, living at depths down to two thousand fathoms; the former being characterised by the union of the gill-openings to form a median slit on the under surface of the fore-part of the body, and the latter by the soft and spongy texture of the flesh of the body. An allied group is formed by the numerous tropical species of *Ophichthys*, in which the nostrils are situated in the lips, and the extremity of the tail is free and finless.

Family *Symbranchidæ*.

There are many other generic representatives of the *Murænidæ*, but we pass on to briefly notice the small family of the *Symbranchidæ*, which takes its name from the gill-openings forming a transverse slit on the lower surface. In these eels the median fins are wanting, and the paired fins rudimental, while the margin of the upper jaw is formed solely by the premaxillæ. The air-bladder, too, is wanting; but ducts are present to the reproductive organs. Most of the members of the family are fresh-water forms from Tropical America and Asia, but the Tasmanian and Australian genus *Chilobranchus* is marine. The Indian *Amphipnous*—in which the gills are much reduced—is remarkable for the possession of an additional breathing-organ in the form of a lung-like sac on each side of the body close behind the head.

Family *Gymnotidæ*.

The third and last family of the section is represented by certain fresh-water eels from Tropical America, which are arranged in five genera. From the *Murænidæ* these eels may be distinguished by the absence or rudimental condition of the dorsal fin, the great elongation of the ânal, and the general absence of the caudal, fin, the tail terminating in a point, and being as fragile as that of the blind-worm. The vent is placed close to the throat, the reproductive organs have ducts, and the pectoral girdle is connected with the skull. The chief interest of this family is concentrated on the electric eel (*Gymnotus electricus*), from the fresh-waters of the Guianas and Brazil, which attains a length of six feet, and is provided with electric organs very similar in structure to those of the electric ray described in the sequel, and capable of inflicting equally powerful shocks. Most books on natural history copy from Humboldt a wonderful account of the capture of these eels by means of horses driven into the waters they frequent, but there is only too much reason to believe that the whole story is a pure fiction, although not an intentional one, on the part of the illustrious traveller. It is high time that it should be forgotten.

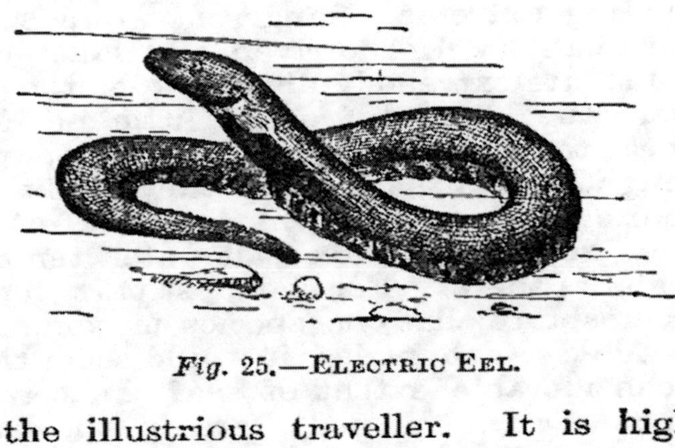

Fig. 25.—Electric Eel.

Section B.—Nematagnathi.

The second section of the Physostomi includes only the cat-fishes or sheath-fishes, typified by the huge wels (*Silurus glanis*) of the larger rivers of Eastern Europe, which is the sole European representative of this immense family. Apart from the structural features distinctive of the section, the cat-fishes are characterised by the skin of the body being either naked, or protected by bony plates of variable size, scales being invariably wanting.

Cat-fishes.—Family *Siluridæ.*

In all, the mouth is provided with barbels, or feelers, frequently of great length, and it is from the presence of these highly sensitive organs that the name of cat-fish is due. Many of them have the bones of the hinder region of the skull ornamented with a rough tubercular sculpture, and there is frequently a large shield, similarly sculptured, covering the upper surface of the neck and shoulders. Often, too, the front of the dorsal fin is armed with a long, powerful, and sometimes poisonous, spine, which in some forms can be raised or depressed by the aid of a kind of trigger-like arrangement connected with the spines of the vertebræ of the neck. Very often there is a fatty dorsal fin, and there is also a rayed dorsal. In the skull the margin of the upper jaw is mainly formed by the premaxillæ ; but a more important character is to be found in the absence from the gill-cover of the bone technically known as the subopercular. The air-bladder, which may be bony, is very generally present, and is then connected with the internal ear by means of minute bones. Cat-fishes are ugly creatures, with large ungainly heads. small eyes, and the aforesaid long barbels. Some, like the Oriental *Bagarius yarelli*, grow to a length of a couple of yards, and have huge ugly mouths, opening nearly the full width of the head. In habits they are sluggish, and dwell for the most part on the bottom of muddy rivers, lakes, or ponds, where their barbels probably play a large part in enabling them to find their way about. They are remarkably tenacious of life, and the writer once found it absolutely impossible to kill some of these fish, caught while he was quarantined on board ship in the Rio de la Plata. All these fishes should be handled with extreme caution, as the spines of many of them are capable of inflicting extremely dangerous wounds. Their flesh, although eatable, is of poor quality. In the rivers and lakes of India and other Oriental countries, cat-fish are extremely abundant, as they also are in those of South America, where the shores of every little pond is strewn with their skulls. They appear to inhabit ponds or lakes liable to be dried up in seasons of unusual drought, and at such times they doubtless are enabled to survive by burying themselves deep down in the mud. Although the majority are fresh-water fishes, some will enter salt water temporarily, while others are permanent residents there. For the most part they keep near the coasts, but from the circumstance that one species is common to the rivers of India and some of the Malayan countries, it would seem that certain kinds occasionally traverse a considerable extent of sea. In certain forms, like the members of the genus *Arius*, the males are in the habit of taking charge of the nursery arrangements, by carrying the eggs about with them in their mouths. Since the family comprises considerably more than a hundred distinct genera, it is obviously impossible to give any adequate account in a work of the present nature. It is sub-divided into several sections, in the first of which the dorsal and anal fins occupy the greater part of the length of the body, the

African and Asiatic genus *Clarias* being an example of this section. To the second section belongs the typical *Silurus*, of which there are five species, from the temperate regions of Asia and Eastern Europe. Here the rayed portion of the dorsal fin is much reduced in length, and, if present at all, confined to the hinder region of the back, while the fatty dorsal is also small or wanting. On the other hand, the anal is long, occupying nearly the whole of the caudal region. The third group is small, and of little importance; but the fourth is a very large one, and includes the Nilotic *Bagrus* (represented by the bagad), the South American *Pimelodus*, the widely spread *Arius*, the gigantic Asiatic *Bagarius*, and a host of others. In this group the short-rayed dorsal does not include more than a dozen rays, and is placed far back on the body; the fatty dorsal is present, although often small; and the anal is much shorter than the caudal portion of the backbone. If barbels are present on the nose, they belong to the hinder of the two pairs of nostrils. Passing over the fifth group, and likewise omitting mention of the seventh and eighth, attention may be directed to the sixth, on account of its including a number of South and Central American forms in which the body is invested in a more or less complete armour, formed of large plates of bone. As examples, may be mentioned the short and deep-bodied *Callichthys*, and the long and slender *Loricaria* and *Hypoptopoma*, all three of which are abundantly represented in the Amazons.

Fig. 26.—THE WELS.

Section C.—Plectispondyli.

The third section of the Physostomi is an important one, as containing the large family of the carps, together with two other family groups. In both the Nematognathi and Plectispondyli the first four vertebræ in the neck are specially modified and united into a single mass; but the subopercular bone, which, as already mentioned, is wanting in the gill-cover of the former section, is present in that of the latter.

Family *Cyprinidæ*.

Although the numerous members of the large fresh-water family of the carps come under the designation of "coarse-fish," yet, owing to its cheapness, their flesh affords an important article of food among certain races and classes, while many of the species afford sport to those anglers who do not aspire to the highest grade of their pastime. All the carps have naked heads and toothless sucking mouths; such teeth as they may possess being confined to the pharyngeal bones of the throat. Usually the body is covered with scales, but if these are wanting the skin is naked. Some kinds are provided with false gills of a glandular type; and the air-bladder, when present, is large, and may be divided either longitudinally or transversely into two portions. When longitudinally divided, it has a bony capsule. In no carps is there a fatty dorsal fin; but the mouth often bears short barbels. Carp are unknown both in Central and South America and Australasia, but are elsewhere almost universally distributed. Their distribution is thus coëxtensive with the Arctogæic realm, as defined in the introductory part of the section on mammals. Unlike the cat-fish, the carps prefer clear water; and while the majority subsist on a mixed diet, some prefer animal substances; some others confine themselves more or less exclusively to food of a vegetable nature. Although the family approaches the *Siluridæ* in point of numbers, the importance of its members claim for it a somewhat fuller notice.

The typical sub-family *Cypridinæ* is characterised by the air-bladder being divided by a transverse constriction into two chambers, and not invested in a bony capsule. With the exception of the Oriental genus *Homalopterus*—in which they are increased to three, and the air-bladder is wanting—the number of pairs of barbels does not exceed two, but one or both of these may be absent. Of the various genera of this sub-family, the typical *Cyprinus* includes a small number of species from the fresh waters of temperate Asia and Europe, the common *Cyprinus carpio* having been originally introduced to the latter continent from the former. In common with certain other genera, *Cyprinus* generally has the short anal fin provided with five or six branching rays; but it is specially characterised by the lateral line occupying the middle of each side of the tail, and by the dorsal fin having its front edge placed immediately above the pelvic pair, and including one serrated bony, and more than nine branching rays. The blunted muzzle carries two pairs of barbels; and the teeth form a complete triple series, the outermost of which are adapted for crushing. From this genus, *Carassius*, which includes the crucian carp of Europe and the gold-fish of China and Japan, differs by the absence of barbels. Nearly allied is the very large Old World genus *Barbus*, typified by the common European barbel, but also well known in the person of the huge mahasir (*B. tor*), which affords such excellent sport with rod-and-line from Kashmir to Ceylon. The members of this genus have the mouth arched, and are provided with false gills; the barbels may be either four, two, or none, and the scales are very variable in size, while the form of the body is often less deep than in *Cyprinus*. Of the mahasir, or mahseer, General Macintyre writes, that "on the back its hue is a dark olive-green, shaded off—on the sides of a well-conditioned fish—into a golden orange, which merges into pale pink and silvery-white below. It has rather large toothless jaws, lined with a very tough membrane, so it requires to be struck pretty hard to be properly hooked. When I say struck, I mean that after the fish has hooked itself, as it will do by its own weight, a good pull without a jerk is necessary to drive home the barb into its leathern jaws. Owing to this toughness of mouth, a mahasir when fixed is seldom lost unless it breaks the tackle. This a big fish will often do in its first plunge, when it sometimes has a way of lashing its tail over the line. That crisis being safely over, if your tackle is trustworthy, landing your fish is usually only a matter of time and patience. Its strong teeth are set far back in its gullet, and the stoutest tackle has a poor chance if it gorges your lure beyond them. It cannot be easily clipped, as its large round scales are so hard that the sharpest gaff will glance off them. When running a mahasir after it has been finely hooked, I have never known it leap from the water, and I think it rarely does so, but its long and rapid rushes quite equal, if they do not surpass, those of any salmon of a similar size. As regards its

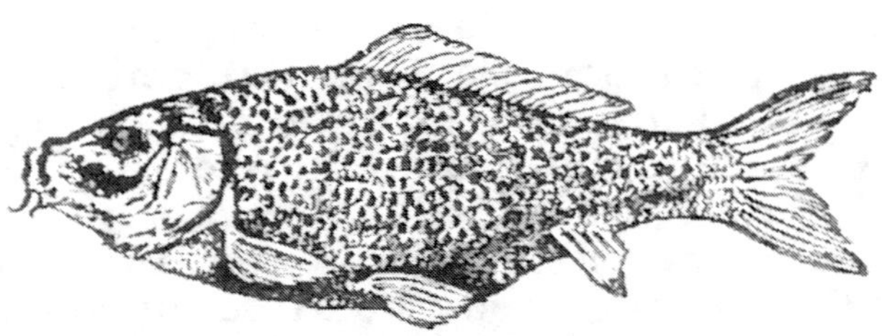

Fig. 27.—COMMON CARP.

weight, I am well within the mark when I state that the mahasir reaches nearly, if not quite, 100 lbs. The largest mahasir I ever heard of as having been taken with a trolling bait was 93 lbs.; and with fly, and that turned the scale at 62 lbs. But such monsters as these are very seldom landed with the rod."

Nearly allied are the two species of gudgeons, constituting the genus *Gobio*, which differ from the carps in that the pharyngeal, or throat-teeth, are arranged in one or two series instead of forming three rows. In these familiar fish the whole of the body is invested with scales of moderate size, and the mouth, which is inferior in position, has the bones on its upper margin protrusile, and there are two barbels. Gudgeon are found on the pebbly beds of clear streams, where they feed on minute aquatic animals.

The numerous kinds of so-called white fish, such as the dace, roach, and chub, belong to the genus *Leuciscus*, and, in common with certain other genera, differ from the foregoing types in the conformation of the anal fin, which is either of moderate length or short, includes from eight to eleven branching rays, and does not extend so far forwards as the line of the hinder edge of the dorsal. In the preceding forms the same fin usually has only five or six branched rays. The white fish have no barbels, neither is there a cutting edge to their jaws; while the throat-teeth are arranged in one or two rows, and the dorsal fin is short, and without a bony ray. White fish are found throughout the fresh waters of the cooler portions of the Northern Hemisphere, but their species are more numerous in Europe and Asia than in America. Their form and habits are sufficiently familiar to all. Nearly allied to the white fish is the golden-coloured tench, which represents a genus (*Tinca*) distinguished by the presence of a pair of barbels to the mouth, the slight extent to which the tail is notched, and the minute size of the scales. In this fish the lateral line is complete, and runs nearly in the middle of each side of the tail, as it does in such of the white fish as have it fully developed. Certain allied fishes from the Old World, constituting the genus *Chondrostoma*, may be recognised by the sharp cutting edge of the lower jaw, which is sheathed in horn. None of these fishes are British, as is also the case with the so-called bitterlings (*Rhodeus*), of which there are four species. The breams (*Abramis*) bring us, however, to another genus with an English representative. In this and certain other genera of the carp tribe, the anal fin is considerably elongated, and some portion at least of the lower border of the abdomen is compressed to such an extent as to form a sharp keel-like edge. In the bream the short and spineless dorsal fin is situated over the space between the pelvics and anal, the scales are of moderate size, and the lateral line runs somewhat below the middle line of the tail. As in the white fish, the bones of the upper jaw are capable of protrusion, and some members of the genus present the remarkable peculiarity of being "underhung," that is to say, they have the lower jaw somewhat longer than the upper. Passing over several allied species, mention must be made of the beautiful pearly little fish known as bleak (*Alburnus*), of which there are a considerable number of species inhabiting the fresh waters of Europe and Western Asia. In addition to the silvery lustre from which they take their name, these little fishes are specially characterised by the slender form of their gill-rakers, which are placed close together; the body being rather slender, the lateral line running somewhat below the middle of the tail, and the lower jaw somewhat exceeding the upper in length. Formerly the scales of the bleak were employed for making artificial pearls, the pearly matter being washed off, and afterwards deposited in the inner side of thin glass balls, of which the small aperture was finally closed with wax. An account of this manufacture will be found in a small work on British fishes by Frank Buckland. On account of the almost vertical position of the cleft of its up-turned mouth, mention must be made of the sichel of Eastern Europe, which forms a genus *(Pelecus)* sufficiently distinguished by this one characteristic.

The rare and local British fish known as the spiny loach (*Cobitis tænia*) is the typical member of the second sub-family (*Cobitinæ*) of the carp tribe; a group which includes several other genera of loaches, all confined to the fresh waters of Europe and Asia. In all the members of this sub-family the air-bladder is enclosed, either completely or partly, in a bony capsule, and none possess false gills. The body, too, never has the deep form characteristic of the carps, and in some groups is much elongated. Barbels, varying in number from six to twelve, are always present, and the mouth is inferior in position, with fleshy lips. Whereas the pelvic pair may be wanting, the median fins are devoid of spines, the number of rays in the dorsal being variable, but those of the anal always few. The tail-fin is rounded, and the scales, if present, are small, and buried in the mucus of the skin. One genus from the Oriental countries is peculiar in possessing scales on the top and sides of the head. The spiny loaches, of which there are at least three species, take their name from the presence of a pair of forked spines below the eyes; such spines being capable of erection at the will of their owners. In the large genus *Nemachilus*, which includes the common loach (*N. barbatulus*) of every English stream, the spines below the eyes are wanting, and the upper jaw alone is furnished with barbels, of which there are three pairs. The third European genus, *Misgurnus*, includes the giant loach of Europe, and three other species; its distributional area including Europe and Asia north of the Himalaya. In this genus there are either five or six pairs of barbels, two of which arise from the lower jaw. Many other genera are found in the Oriental countries, and it is noteworthy that whereas the European forms are inhabitants of clear running waters, these latter dwell in tanks, where they bury themselves in the mud at the bottom. All, however, agree in that their food is composed exclusively of animal substances.

Family *Kneriidæ.*

In the fresh waters of Tropical Africa the place of the loaches is taken by the two species of the genus *Kneria*, which form a family by themselves, distinguished from the *Cyprinidæ* by the absence of throat, or pharyngeal teeth, the simple, undivided form of the air-bladder, and the absence of barbels.

Family *Erythrinidæ.*

Of far more importance than the last is the very extensive family of fresh-water fishes commonly known as characinoid fishes, but which might perhaps be termed the southern carps. Their distribution is indeed largely complementary to that of the *Cyprinidæ*, since they are confined to Central and South America, and Africa south of the Sahara; carps being absent from the former countries, although present in the latter. This peculiar geographical distribution is one among many instances of the close affinity existing between the faunas of these two areas. The explanation of the absence of the *Cyprinidæ* from South America may possibly be that the characinoids entered Africa at the time when that country was in communication with South America, whereas the carps did not come in till that communication was severed. If that be so, the *Cyprinidæ* must have come into Africa at the same time as many of the large mammals, such as hippopotami, giraffes, rhinoceroses, elephants, and antelopes. From the *Cyprinidæ* the present family is broadly distinguished by certain peculiarities in the structure of the skull, and by the number of upper pharyngeal bones being one or four, in place of two. The margin of the upper jaw is also different, in that it is formed in front by the premaxillæ, and by the maxillæ at the sides, instead of entirely by the former bones. Barbels, too, are wanting; but whereas the head is as devoid of scales as in the *Cyprinidæ*, the jaws may be either smooth or furnished with powerful teeth. In such an extensive family, it is but little use referring to genera by name, when their distinctive features cannot be described. It may be mentioned, however, that the African and the American genera are distinct from one another, and that the typical *Erythrinus* is from America. Two genera—of which *Hydrocyon* is African, and *Cynodon* Tropical America—are, however, noteworthy on account of the large size and predaceous habits of some of their representatives. Two species of the former genus are abundant in the Nile, where they grow to about four feet in length, and are respectively known by the Egyptians by the names of *Kelb-el-bahr* and *Kelb-el-moyeh*.

Section D.—Haplopomi.

Family *Cyprinodontidæ*.

In this fourth section of the Physostomi the first four vertebræ of the backbone are distinct from one another, and unmodified; the supraoccipital bone of the skull extends forwards to separate the two parietals, and the full number of bones is developed in the gill-covers, or operculum. The pharyngeal bones, too, are separate, and in the upper jaw are three or four in number, and directed forwards. The first family of the section is that of the *Cyprinodontidæ*, which includes a considerable number of genera of small fishes ranging over America, Africa, Asia, and the south of Europe, and inhabiting alike salt, brackish, and fresh water. With a mouth devoid of barbels, these fish are easily recognised by the scales extending on to the head, as well as by the absence of a fatty dorsal fin, and the backward position of the rayed dorsal. As in the carps, the margin of the upper jaw is formed entirely by the premaxillary bones. The third upper pharyngeal bone is enlarged, and teeth are present, not only on the pharyngeals, but likewise in the margins of the jaws. Whereas some cyprinodonts feed on living animals, others seek their food in mud. The males, which are much inferior in size to their partners, include some of the smallest of all living fishes; and most species produce their young in a living condition. In a family so extensive, it is difficult to select genera for special mention. The typical *Cyprinodon* has a very wide distribution, and is represented by seven species from the countries bordering the Mediterranean. Some of its members are remarkable for inhabiting springs or pools almost saturated with salt, while others are found in springs of very high temperature. Perhaps the most noteworthy forms are the species of the genus *Anableps* from Tropical America, in which the eyes are divided by a horizontal line into an upper and a lower half. The convexity of the lens differs in these two halves, the upper half being suited to vision in air, and the lower in water. This enables the fish to see perfectly in both media when swimming near the surface of the water, with one half of the eye below, and the other above, the surface. A good account of the habits of these curious fishes has been recently published in the *Field* newspaper. It may be mentioned that, according to an American writer, the name of the family should be changed from *Cyprinodontidæ* to *Pæciliidæ*.

Family *Amblyopsidæ.*

Nearly allied to the last are two genera of small North American fishes, in one of which (*Amblyopsis*) the eyes are wanting, while in the second (*Chologaster*) they are very minute. The one is represented by the well-known blind fish from caves and other subterranean waters, while the single species of the latter is found in the rice-fields of the Southern States, although very rare. *Chologaster* has no pelvic fins, but these may or may not be present in *Amblyopsis*, as is also the case with *Cyprinodon*. The blind fish, which grows to a length of about five inches, is quite colourless, and when the dark waters of their habitat are artificially illuminated these fishes have a weird and ghostly appearance.

Families *Umbridæ and Esocidæ.*

Of the other two families of the section, the first is an unimportant one, represented by one species of the single genus *Umbra* from Austria and Hungary, and a second from the United States. Small in size, these fish are very similar to the *Cyprinodontidæ*, from which they may be distinguished by the lateral margin of the upper jaw being formed by the maxillæ. Although likewise represented only by a single genus (*Esox*), the pikes are a much more important and better-known family, the common European species (*E. lucius*) being well known to all. Pike are inhabitants of the fresh waters of North America, Temperate Asia, and Europe, but are more numerously represented in the Western than in the Eastern Hemisphere, six species being exclusively American, whereas the common pike ranges over all three continents. In these fishes the margin of the upper jaw is formed in the same manner as that of the umbrers; but the absence of scales on the head serves to distinguish them from all other members of the section. Their elongated, "pike"-like form, their large size, and their voracious habits, are familiar features of the family; but it may be added that there are no barbels to the mouth, while there is no fatty fin, and the dorsal occupies the position of the fatty fin of the *Salmonidæ*. Summarising some of the accounts which have been given of the voracity and fierceness of the pike, the editor of this volume writes as follows:—"It has been known to attack a man when its retreat has been cut off, to bite the legs of bathers, and to snap at the fingers of persons cooling their hands in the water; and when pressed with hunger, to fight an otter for the possession of a carp. Its strength and endurance have often been demonstrated in the destruction of strong tackle, and in its power to survive—without apparent inconvenience—with hooks and wires mingling with its anatomy. Captain Brown gives an instance of a pike being caught which had a strong piece of twisted wire projecting from its side. It was in excellent condition, and on being opened, discovered in its stomach a double eel-hook, much corroded, and attached to the protruding wire. Another pike, when caught in the River Ouse, was found in possession of a watch with a black ribbon and seals attached—property which, it was afterwards discovered, had belonged to a

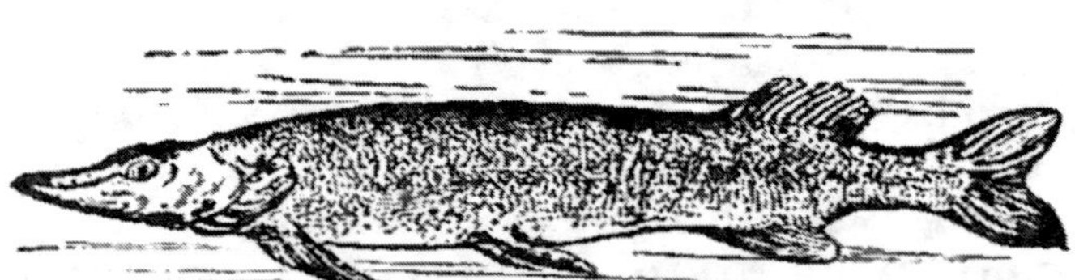

Fig. 28.—COMMON PIKE.

gentleman's servant who had been drowned. The pike has often been caught with portions of tackle broken from the line in former engagements hanging from its mouth. Its rapacity is extraordinary. Eight hundred gudgeon are said to have been consumed in three weeks by eight pike of not more than five pounds weight each."

Section E.—Scyphophori.

Family *Mormyridæ.*

The next family of the Physostomi comprises a few fishes from Tropical Africa which appear to have no very near relations, and are consequently regarded as forming a sectional group by themselves. The chief characters of the section are derived from the bones of the skull, in which the parietals are separate alike from one another, and from the supraoccipital; while the pterotic bones, which are situated on the outer sides of the parietals, are large, funnel-shaped, and contain a cavity closed by a lid. The full series of bones are developed in the gill-cover, and in the back-bone the four first joints are separate and unmodified. As a family, the *Mormyridæ* are characterised by the naked head, the want of barbels, the slit-like opening of the gills, the simple air-bladder, and the absence of a fatty fin on the back. The front portion of the margin of the upper jaw is constituted by the premaxillæ, which are united together; but the sides are formed by the maxillæ. All these fishes are dwellers in fresh water. The typical genus is *Mormyrus*, from which some writers distinguish certain species under the name of *Mormyrops*, other members of the family being included in *Gymnarchus*, which is characterised by the complete disappearance of the pelvic, anal, and caudal fins, the tail terminating in a point. Many of the species of *Mormyrus* have the muzzle more or less elongated and beak-like, but *M. petersi* has the extremity of the lower jaw produced into a large, conical, fleshy appendage of great relative length. *Gymnarchus*—of which there is only one species—is, on the other hand, a large eel-like fish, growing to a length of a couple of yards.

Section F.—Isospondyli.

The sixth and last section of the Physostomi is the largest and most important of all, including—in addition to many other groups—the families of the herrings and salmon, whose numerous representatives are so highly valued as food.

Family *Notopteridæ.*

These fishes are the most generalised of all the Physostomi, and consequently make the nearest approach to the under-mentioned ganoids. In all of them the two parietal bones are separate, and the so-called symplectic bone, which is wanting in the preceding family, is here present. As in the latter, the anterior segments of the vertebral column are of the simple, unmodified type; but both the upper and the lower pharyngeal bones are separate. The first representative of the section is the genus *Notopterus*, which constitutes a family by itself, and includes several species from the Oriental countries and West Africa. None of these fishes have a fatty dorsal fin or barbels, but many of them possess a short and tall dorsal fin, situated far back on the body, and standing up in such a conspicuous manner as to give rise to the name of "feather-back." A better character is, however, to be found in the backward continuation of the anal fin to form a fringe surrounding the tail. There are many other structural peculiarities in these fresh-water fishes, but it will suffice to mention that the air-bladder is divided into a number of compartments, and furnished at each end with a pair of prolongations, so that it presents some resemblance to a shark's egg in form. More important, on account of their peculiar geographical distribution, are the small fresh-water fishes from the Southern Hemisphere, forming the genus *Galaxias*, and typifying a family by themselves. They have the base of the skull single, the pterotic bones solid, and the tail forked or rounded, while there are neither scales, barbels, or a fatty fin, the dorsal being situated directly over the anal fin. The eggs of the female are discharged into the cavity of the abdomen, as in the last family, from which these fishes differ by the simple structure of the air-bladder. The typical *Galaxias* has long been known from the extremity of South America, Australia, and New Zealand (where, from their spotted coloration, they were formerly known as trout), but it is only recently that a species has been recorded from the Cape. The New Zealand *Neochanna*—of which the known specimens have been found buried in mud far away from water—differs by the lack of the pelvic fins.

Family *Galaxiidæ*.

This family is noteworthy on account of its containing the largest fresh-water bony fish, the huge *Arapaima gigas* of the Guianas and Brazil, which attains a length of fully fifteen feet, and a weight of four hundred pounds. As a family, the arapaimas are distinguished from the *Galaxiidæ* by generally possessing three, instead of two, upper pharyngeal bones. The body of these fishes is invested with unusually large scales, marked with a kind of mosaic-like sculpture, but the head is devoid of scales, and protected by large roughened, ossified plates. Wide openings of the mucus canal constitute the lateral line, and the long dorsal fin is placed immediately over the anal—to which it is almost similar—very far back on the body. Indeed, so far back are these fins, that they sometimes coalesce with the caudal. The openings of the gills are wide, and both the premaxillæ and maxillæ enter into the formation of the margin of the upper jaw; but there are no false gills. Whereas some forms have the air-bladder simple, in others it is composed of cells. Allusion having been already made to *Arapaima*, we pass on to the typical *Osteoglossum*, of which there is one species from South America, and a second from Borneo and Sumatra, while the other two are inhabitants of Australia. A pair of barbels to the lower jaw, and the obliquity of the cleft of the mouth, are sufficient to distinguish these large fishes from *Arapaima*. The flesh is of excellent quality. The last genus, *Heterotis*, is African, and differs from the other two in having only two upper pharyngeal bones—thereby resembling the *Galaxiidæ*—and its air-bladder is cellular. The one species is common to the Nile and the rivers of West Africa.

Family *Osteoglossidæ*.

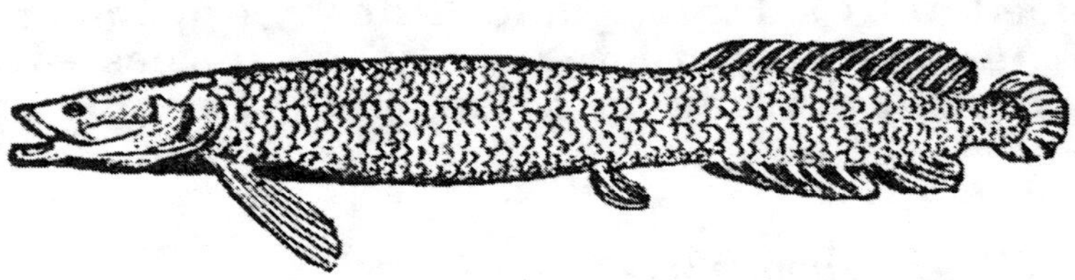

Fig. 29.—ARAPAIMA.

A fresh-water fish from North America known as the moon-eye (*Hyòdon tergissus*), and a small fish (*Pantodon bucholzi*) remarkably like a cyprinodont, from West Africa, severally represent two families. From the foregoing families of the section, these two groups are distinguished by the under-mentioned characters. The pterotic bones are of normal conformation; there are four separate upper pharyngeal bones, of which the third and largest is directed forwards; and the base of the skull is double. All these features are common to the remaining families of the section. In the *Hyodontidæ* the two parietal bones are united together, and the bony structure supporting the tail-fin is preceded by two true caudal vertebræ. Whereas in the moon-eye the tail is deeply forked, in *Pantodon* it terminates in a point.

Families *Hyodontidæ* and *Pantodontidæ*.

A long slender fish from the seas of Australia, Japan, and South Africa, known as the beaked salmon (*Gonorhynchus greyi*), likewise constitutes a separate family, distinguished from the last two by the presence of barbels to the mouth, and the absence of true caudal vertebræ. The beaked salmon varies from a foot to a foot and a half in length, and is often found in sandy bays. Its flesh is eaten.

Family *Gonorhynchidæ*.

The three families now to be mentioned include marine fishes, of which the majority are deep-sea or pelagic in their habitat, while many are remarkable for the development of special phosphorescent organs, by the aid of which they find their way in the dark ocean abysses. From the preceding family, the *Scopelidæ* are distinguished by the absence of barbels, and of spines on the scales (when the latter are developed), and the presence of a small fatty fin posterior to the dorsal. Whereas some forms are scaled, others are naked; but all are characterised by the wide gill-opening, the possession of false gills, the absence of an air-bladder, and the formation of the margin of the upper jaw by the premaxillæ alone. A peculiarity of these fishes is the extreme shortness of the intestine. The typical genus *Scopelus* includes fishes of normal form, with rows of phosphorescent spots on the lower side of the body; but in *Ipnops* the whole body is exceedingly long and slender, and the upper surface of the flattened head occupied by a large luminous organ. Other genera are *Saurus*, *Paralepis*, *Plagyodus* (in which the body is naked, and the jaws are armed with large tusks), and *Gymnoscopelus*, in which scales are likewise wanting. Of the other two families it will be unnecessary to give all the characters, but it may be mentioned that in the *Sternoptychidæ* the fatty fin is either very small or rudimental, while there are no barbels, and the body may be either naked or covered with thin deciduous scales, while the maxillæ enter into the margin of the upper jaw. On the lower parts, light-organs are developed. One of the best-known forms is the somewhat elongated *Photichthys*, from which the allied *Chauliodus* differs by the large size of its teeth. On the other hand, the typical *Sternoptyx* has the body deep and compressed, and the tail short. The *Stomiatidæ* differ by the presence of a long barbel attached to the hyoid bone, which depends from the lower jaw, the fatty fin being often totally wanting. *Astronesthes*, which is one of the genera with a small fatty fin, has a large head, and jaws armed with powerful teeth. *Stomias* and *Echiostoma* both lack the fatty fin, but whereas the former has the body covered with minute scales, in the latter the skin is naked, and the small pectoral fins have some of their rays prolonged into thread-like filaments. At times the deep-sea fishes of the present group are met with floating in a helpless inert condition on the surface of the ocean; but they are generally only obtained by

Families *Scopelidæ*, *Sternoptychidæ*, and *Stomiatidæ*.

dredging. When brought to the surface, owing to the sudden diminution of pressure, their eyes start out of the sockets, the scales stand erect, and the flesh is loose and fragile, so that the preservation of specimens is frequently a matter of considerable difficulty.

Families *Chirocentridæ* and *Bathythrissidæ*.

These two unimportant families, severally represented by a single type, may be distinguished from the preceding members of the Isospondyli by the circumstance that the supraoccipital bone of the skull extends forwards so as to separate the two parietals from one another. And in this feature they agree with the members of the following families of the section, except for a few aberrant types of two. The first family is represented by the dorab (*Chirocentrus dorab*), of the Malayan and Red Seas, and is distinguished by the possession of but one caudal vertebra. The dorab is a large elongated fish, with a deeply-forked tail, no fatty fin, an up-turned muzzle, powerful teeth, and a sharply-keeled and serrated under surface. In length it is stated to grow to as much as twelve feet. Very different is the deep-sea *Bathythrissa dorsalis* of Japan, in which the body is deep and oblong, with the under surface rounded, the head naked and without barbels, and the dorsal fin so much elongated as to occupy nearly the whole length of the back, a fatty fin being wanting. This fish forms an exception to the generality of the members of the sub-order in lacking an air-bladder.

Herrings.—Family *Clupeidæ*.

The familiar "red-herring," in its natural condition, is the type of a family of mostly marine and littoral fishes whose importance as a food-supply can scarcely be overrated. Limits of space, unfortunately, allow of only a very inadequate notice of the group. Dr. Günther writes "that the family of herrings is probably unsurpassed by any other in the number of individuals, although others comprise a much greater variety of species. The herrings are principally coast fishes, or at least do not go far from the shore; none belong to the deep-sea fauna, scarcely any have pelagic habits, but many enter or live in fresh-waters communicating with the sea. They are spread over all the temperate and tropical zones." With the exception of one genus, agreeing with the *Chirocentidæ* in the structure of the skull and presence of a single caudal vertebra, the *Clupeidæ* are specially characterised by the want of a fatty fin, and the general presence of small plates of bone on the lower surface of the body, which is usually sharp and often serrated. The head is devoid of barbels, and usually also of scales, but the body is always fully scaled, although the lateral line is generally wanting. The margin of the upper jaw is formed in part by the premaxillæ, and in part by the maxillæ; each of the latter bones consisting of three distinct elements. Usually the gill-openings are complete, and the operculum comprises the full number of elements. The rays of the short dorsal fin are few and weak, although those of the anal may be numerous. The air-bladder is comparatively single, and most members of the family are furnished with false gills. In the typical genus *Clupea* the two jaws are sub-equal in length, the eyes have fatty lids, and the body is compressed, with the abdomen serrated inferiorly as far forwards as the chest. The cleft of the mouth is of moderate width, and if teeth are present at all, they are rudi-

Fig. 30.—THE HERRING.

mental and deciduous. The anal fin is of moderate length, with less than thirty rays, the dorsal fin is placed above the pelvic pair, and the caudal is deeply forked. Among over half a hundred species, we may name the common herring (*C. harengus*), the spratt (*C. sprattus*), the alliceshad (*C. alosa*), the shad (*C. finta*), the American mossbanker (*C. menhaden*), and the pilchard or sardine (*C. pilchardus*). Herrings, as is well known, are gregarious and carnivorous fishes, going about in huge shoals, the presence of which is often indicated not only by the appearance of the surface of the water, but by the flocks of sea-birds which hover overhead in search of prey. The shoals appear to approach the coasts solely for the purpose of spawning, after which they retire to deeper water. Australia is the home of certain fresh-water herrings forming the genus *Diplomystus*, and characterised by having plates of bone behind the head similar in character to those on the under surface. Another and larger genus (*Engraulis*) is typified by the Mediterranean anchovy, and is characterised by the prolongation of the nearly conical snout beyond the tip of the lower jaw, and by the eyes being covered with a continuous skin. The Mediterranean species, either preserved whole, or made into a paste, affords the piquant anchovy of commerce. The only other type that can be mentioned here is *Elops*, which is peculiar in that the parietal bones of the skull are in contact, and also for the possession of two caudal vertebræ. There are two species from the warmer seas, in both of which the space between the two branches of the lower jaw is protected by a thin plate of bone, while the lower surface of the body is rounded and smooth.

Families *Alepocephalidæ* and *Haplochitonidæ*.

Very brief notice must suffice for two small and unimportant families now generally placed between the closely allied groups of the herrings and salmon. The *Alepocephalidæ* resemble *Elops*, and thus the *Salmonidæ*, in having two caudal vertebræ, but differ from the former, and thereby agree with most of the latter, in that the two parietal bones of the skull are separated by the supra-occipital. They lack, however, the fatty fin of the latter, and barbels are wanting to the head, which is likewise devoid of scales, as is sometimes also the body. Both pairs of jaw-bones enter into the formation of the margin of the upper jaw, and the stomach lacks the blind appendage, or cæcum, characterising that of the herrings. In the typical genus *Alepocephalus* the body is covered with thin scales, but in *Xenodermichthys* these are replaced by fine nodules. Two other genera are known. The trout-like fish from the rivers of Chili and the southern extremity of South America and the Falklands known as *Haplochiton*, together with the allied Australian genus *Prototroctes*, represent the second of the two families now under consideration; the first of these resembling a scaleless trout, whereas in the second the body is scaled and the jaws are armed with minute teeth. These fish differ from the families last noticed in possessing a small fatty fin. In this respect they resemble the *Salmonidæ*, from which they may be distinguished by the fact that the maxillæ do not enter into the formation of the margin of the upper jaw.

Salmon Tribe.—Family *Salmonidæ*.

From the other allied families the *Salmonidæ* may be distinguished by the possession of a small fatty fin between the dorsal and the tail, coupled with the circumstance that the margin of the upper jaw is formed in front by the premaxillæ and at the sides by the maxillæ. The inferior aspect of the body is rounded; and whereas the skin of the head is invariably naked, the body is generally clothed with scales. The *Salmonidæ* are in the main restricted to the cooler portions of the Northern Hemisphere, although one genus is found in the fresh waters of New Zealand. Whereas some kinds spend the whole of their time in fresh water lakes or rivers, others descend periodically to the sea—or, as it is perhaps more correct to say, ascend rivers from the sea for the purpose of spawning. Certain kinds are, however, permanently marine, most of these being deep-water fishes, although the members of two genera are pelagic. On account of the large size of many of the species, coupled with the superlatively excellent quality of their flesh, the *Salmonidæ* are commercially one of the most valuable families of fishes. It appears that the "salmon-colour" characterising the flesh of some of the species is due to the pigment derived from the crustaceans on which they feed; the action of the gastric juice turning such pigment red in the same manner as boiling. Volumes have been written on the life-history of the *Salmonidæ*, and the question as to the number of species of fresh-water trout and charr; and many pages of this work would be necessary to give even a full outline of the subject. As it is, little more than a bare mention of the leading genera and species can be attempted. It should, however, be mentioned that whereas the adults are usually silvery, or spotted with black and red, the immature fish pass through a stage—the "parr"—when they are marked by dark transverse bars. In certain fresh-water kinds these immature markings may, however, be retained individually during the whole of life. There are also sexual or seasonal differences in the adult fish; as exemplified by the hooked lower jaw of the male salmon in the spawning season. The genus *Salmo*, which includes the common salmon (*S. salmo*), and the various species or varieties of trout and charr, has the dorsal fin situated nearly or immediately above the pelvic pair, the scales small, and well-developed teeth in the jaws, and likewise on the vomerine and palatine bones and tongue; while the anal fin never includes more than fourteen rays, and the intestine is furnished with a large number of small blind appendages or cæca. Moreover, the mouth is so deeply cleft, that its opening extends at least as far back as the eye. Southwards, the range of this large genus does not extend beyond the Atlas and Hindu Kush in the Eastern Hemisphere, or the rivers flowing into the head of the Gulf of California in the Western. In the various kinds of true salmon and trout the whole length of the bone known as the vomer carries teeth during some period of life. On the other hand, in the mostly smaller and more brilliantly-coloured charr the vomerine teeth are restricted to the head of that bone. The largest member of the charr group is the Danubian hucho (*S. hucho*), which rivals the salmon in size. The migratory species, which periodically ascend the rivers of North America and Asia flowing into the Pacific in incredible numbers, form the genus *Onchorhynchus*, distinguished by the possession of more than fourteen rays in the anal fin. A third genus (*Osmerus*) contains the three species of smelt, and is to some extent intermediate between *Salmo* and *Onchorhynchus* on the one hand, and *Coregonus* on the other. They are, however, peculiar, on account of the small size and number of the cæcal appendages to the intestine, while their eggs are relatively small. As examples of the large and mostly fresh-water genus *Core-*

Fig. 31.—THE SALMON.

gonus, may be mentioned the vendace (*C. vandesius*), the pollan (*C. pollan*), and the powan (*C. clupeoides*), all of which are British. Like smelts, these fish have small eggs; but then they have a great number of blind appendages to the intestine, and if any teeth remain in the adult, they are usually restricted to the tongue, while even in the young state these organs are minute. The cleft of the mouth is always much less deep than in the *Salmo*, while the forking of the tail is more strongly marked. In common with the grayling, these fishes differ from the other members of the family in that the two parietal bones meet together for a short distance in the middle line in advance of the supraoccipital. The genus extends over a considerable portion of Northern Europe, Asia, and America; and its very numerous members are for the most part permanent inhabitants of fresh water. The grayling (*Thymallus*), which have a geographical distribution very similar to that of *Coregonus*, differ from that genus by the taller and longer dorsal fin, in which the number of rays varies from thirteen to twenty-three. The mouth, too, has a smaller cleft; while the blind appendages of the intestine are much less numerous, and teeth are present in the jaws, and on the palatines and the head of the vomer, although wanting from the tongue. Although ranging from Lapland to Venice, and from England to Russia, the grayling is a very local fish, which is unknown in Ireland; and it appears that only under certain conditions will it thrive and multiply in a river. A writer in *Land and Water* for 1868 remarks, that "there is one singular peculiarity about the grayling that distinguishes it from all other species of *Salmonidæ*, and that is its remarkable odour. It resembles more than anything else the smell of a freshly-cut cucumber; by this criterion it may be immediately detected. Some authorities assert that the smell of this fish resembles thyme, but I cannot endorse this, or perceive the slightest affinity."

A small family is represented by the North American fresh-water *Percopsis guttata* and the allied *Columbia transmontana*, which, although possessing the structural features of the *Salmonidæ*, assimilate in the nature of the scales and the bones of the mouth to the perch tribe. **Percopsidæ.**

SUB-ORDER VI.—ÆTHEOSPONDYLI.

This and the next subordinal group of the Actinopterygii are now respectively represented only by a single North American genus, although both were abundant during earlier epochs of the earth's history. To understand fully their relationship to other fishes it is essential to take the extinct forms into consideration, but as this is impossible here, their general structural features can be only very slightly touched upon. The present sub-order is now represented only by the three species of bony pike (*Lepidosteus*) from the fresh waters of North America, which typify the family *Lepidosteidæ*. These fishes, some of which measure fully six feet in length, have the head covered with bony plates, and the whole body invested with a coat of hard, shining, quadrangular scales, which articulate together by means of a peg and socket. The long head is depressed, with the jaws well-armed with teeth; and the body is elongated, with the anal and dorsal fins—which have no spines—placed near the tail, and the latter of the so-called abbreviate

Fig. 32.—Bony Pike.

heterocercal type. In the skeleton, the vertebræ are unique among living fishes in that the articular surfaces of their bodies form a cup behind and a ball in front. The air-bladder has a duct, and the nerves supplying the eyes where they meet one another in the middle line give off interlacing fibres, and there are remnants of a spiral valve in the lining membrane of the intestine. Bony pike, which are abundant in many of the North American rivers, are very analogous in their habits to true pike, feeding upon other fishes.

SUB-ORDER VII.—PROTOSPONDYLI.

The single existing family (*Amiidæ*) of this once abundant subordinal group is now represented by the bow-fin (*Amia-calva*) of the fresh waters of the United States. This fish, while agreeing with the bony pike in the conformation of the optic nerves supplying the eyes, differs in the fuller development of the spiral valve in the intestine, and in the simpler form of the bodies of the vertebræ, which are disc-like. Although the scales are coated with ganoin, they differ from those of the bony pike in being thin, rounded, and deeply over-lapping. A peculiar feature of the bow-fin, and the one from which it takes its vernacular name, is the great length of the dorsal fin, which occupies more than half the entire length of the back, and posteriorly is separated only by a notch from the tail-fin; the latter being of the abbreviate heterocercal type. The bow-fin grows to a length of about a couple of feet, and is a carnivorous fish, exceedingly abundant in some of the North American lakes. It feeds not only on other fishes, but likewise on various invertebrate animals, and can exist for a considerable time out of water. Its favourite haunts are the dense masses of floating vegetation fringing the North American lakes, among which it lays during the month of May a host of minute eggs.

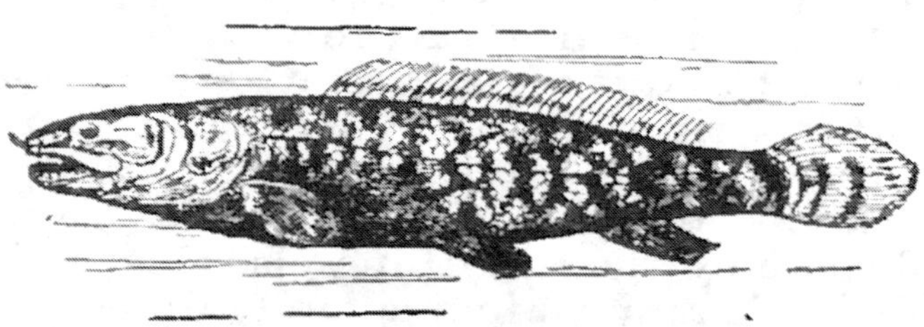

Fig. 33.—BOW-FIN.

SUB-ORDER VIII.—CHONDROSTEI—STURGEONS.

The title of royal fish bestowed on the common sturgeon would seem to indicate that it has some special claim to superiority over the other members of the finny tribe. This, however, is not the case, the title being due to the circumstance that all such fish, according to an act of Edward II. which appears to be still in force, belong of right to the crown. The enactment runs that "the king shall have wreck of the sea throughout the realm, whales, and great sturgeons, taken in the sea or elsewhere in the realm, except in certain places privileged by the king." From all the other subordinal groups of the Teleostomi, the sturgeons and their extinct allies are broadly distinguished by the greater relative number of the dermal rays in the dorsal and anal fins, which exceed the bony or cartilaginous elements pertaining to the true skeleton by which they are supported, instead of these two elements being numerically equal. As regards the optic nerves and the lining membrane of the intestine, the sturgeons resemble the preceding sub-order. All the members of the sub-order have a persistent notochord and a cartilaginous skeleton, but the tail may be of either the heterocercal or the diphycerca, type. It might be thought that the bony shields investing the head, and the longitudinal rows of prominent bony tubercles or plates frequently present on the otherwise entirely naked skin, would form a distinctive feature of the group. As a matter of fact this is not so, seeing that a number of extinct fishes now classed with the sturgeons have a complete coat of ganoid scales. Still, however, as distinctive of the existing forms—with which alone we are concerned here—the presence of these shields or plates, or both, coupled with the absence of scales (save in one family on part of the tail) are very distinctive. Existing sturgeons may be classified in two families, in both of which the tail is heterocercal.

Family *Polyodontidæ*.

The first of these is represented only by two genera, each with a single species, and its distinctive features are to be found in the presence of minute teeth in the jaws throughout life, as well as of a median series of unpaired bony shields in the armour of the head, and likewise by the skin—save for a few minute stellate ossifications—being naked all over the body, although there may be a few scales on the upper lobe of the tail. The typical *Polyodon folius*, from the Mississippi basin, is a comparatively small fish, apparently not exceeding about six feet in length, characterised by the upper jaw terminating in an enormous shovel-like beak, furnished with soft thin margins, and equal to fully one quarter the entire length of the fish. Vastly larger is *Psephurus gladius* from some of the great Chinese rivers, which grows to something approaching twenty feet, and has a much more slender beak. Both these fishes have minute eyes, and appear to grovel in the mud in the river bottom in search of their food. The occurrence of two such closely allied forms in the rivers of North America and China is paralleled by the instance of the American and Chinese alligators, and likewise the two kinds of giant salamander (*Megalobatrachus* and *Cryptobranchus*), all these examples indicating the close affinity between the fauna of North America and that of North-Eastern Asia.

Family *Acipenseridæ*.

The members of the second family of the group differ from the *Polyodontidæ* by the disappearance of the teeth in the adult, and likewise by the bare skin of the body being traversed by five longitudinal rows of large elevated bony plates. The median series of shields is also wanting on the head, and the under surface of the muzzle is provided with two pairs of flexible barbels, of which there is no trace in the first family. All the members of the family are restricted to the temperate parts of the Northern Hemisphere, and all are largely fresh water in their habits, some being exclusively so, although others ascend the larger rivers only for the purpose of spawning, after which they return to the ocean. Whereas the typical members of the family belong to the genus *Acipenser*, certain fresh-water kinds from the basin of the Mississippi and Central Asia form a genus apart, under the name of *Scaphirhynchus*, one of their distinctive features being the production of the muzzle into a shovel-like beak very similar to that of *Psephurus*. Of the typical genus, the largest species is the huso (*Acipenser huso*) of the Russian rivers and inland seas, which occasionally attains the enormous

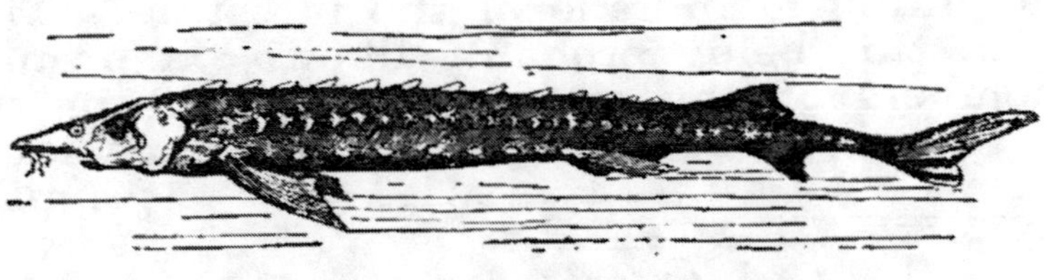

Fig. 34.—COMMON STURGEON.

length of four-and-twenty feet. The smallest is the sterlet (*A. ruthvenus*), whose length is only about three feet, while the common species (*A. sturio*) is intermediate between the other two. The sterlet claims pre-eminence on account of the excellent quality of its flesh, while the roe of all the larger species affords caviare, and the air-bladder isinglass. Frank Buckland writes that "sturgeons seek their food chiefly among the mud at the bottom of rivers, and their head is admirably adapted for the purpose. The elongated snout, protected by broad plates, ploughs up the mud as a hog does the ground; and it is probably from this habit they got the name of sturgeons, from the German, *stören* (which means to rake up, poke, or stir). A little way behind the point of the snout, and on the under side, is placed a series of worm-like tentacles, or feelers, the office of which is to examine the objects turned up by the snout; and in rear of these comes the sucker-like mouth, ready to receive what is thus provided." In reference to the last sentence, it may be suggested that the use of the tentacles may be to attract other fishes within range of the mouth.

ORDER II.—CROSSOPTERYGII.

FRINGE-FINNED GANOIDS.

Africa is a country where several ancient types of animal life that have disappeared from other regions of the globe still linger on, and a remarkable instance of this survival is afforded by two fishes from the fresh waters of that continent. One of these is the bichir (*Polypterus bichir*) of the Nile and its tributaries, as well as the rivers of the west coast, and the other the reed-fish (*Calamoichthys calabaricus*) of the fresh waters of Old Calabar on the west coast. In the structure of their fins, and likewise in the hard quadrangular ganoid scales with which the body is covered, these strange fishes resemble a host of ancient types which were widely spread over the fresh waters of the globe during the Palæozoic epoch. Their essential difference from all other living representatives of the sub-class Teleostomi is, however, to be found in the structure of the fins, seeing that scales of a similar nature are met with in the bony pike already described. In all these fishes the pectoral and pelvic fins consist internally of a jointed longitudinal axis, from which proceed a larger or smaller number of divergent rays belonging to the dermal system. On the under surface of the lower jaw there is at least one pair of jugular plates occupying the space left between its two branches. The nerves supplying the eyes when meeting one another in the middle line give off interlacing fibres, and another primitive feature is the presence of a spiral valve in the lining membrane of the intestine. The air-bladder is provided with a duct, this being probably likewise a primitive character. Both the living members of the order are included in the family *Polypteridæ*, which is characterised by the replacement of the primitive notochord by bony vertebræ, as well as by certain features of the skeleton which need not be noticed here. The tail is very short, and terminates in a diphycercal fin; and the dorsal fin is peculiar in being split up into a number of finlets, severally supported by a spine in front, such finlets varying in the type genus from eight to eighteen in number.

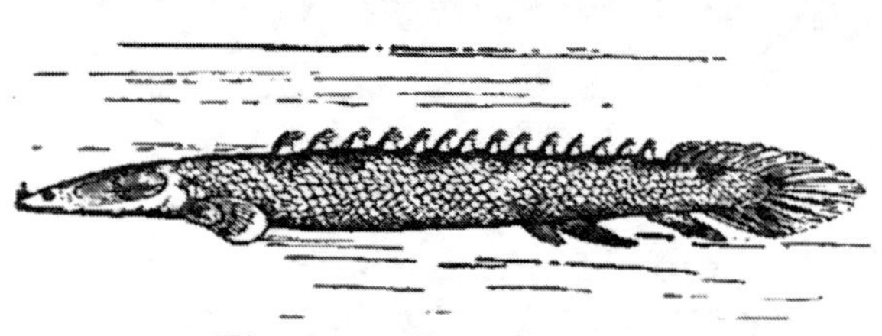

Fig. 35.—THE BICHIR.

The anal fins are situated very far back on the elongated body, so as to be separated by only a short distance from the caudal. It is only in the pectoral fins that the lobate structure is visible externally, each of these consisting of a central scaled portion, surrounded on the free margins by a fringe of rays. The bichir, which grows to a length of four feet, is characterised by the moderate elongation of the body, and the presence of well-developed pelvic fins. These last are wanting in the much smaller reed-fish, which takes its name from the excessive attenuation of the body. Information is much wanting as to the life-history of these fishes, although it is known that they lay small eggs. If we may judge from the analogy of the Australian lung-fish, which has a similar type of fins, it is, however, probable that they are comparatively slow and sluggish in their movements, and live on, if not in, the mud at the river bottoms. In the late larval state, *Polypterus*, at any rate, develops a large external gill on each side, projecting backwards from the gill-opening. In addition to the fringing dorsal fin, the tubular nasal openings may be noticed as peculiar characters of the existing forms. It may be added that some authorities like Dr. Steindachner recognise more than a single species of bichir, one of them being named *Polypterus lapradei*.

SUB-CLASS IV.—ELASMOBRANCHII.

Sharks and Rays.

The dreaded sharks are the types of a fairly large sub-class of fishes, which also includes the smaller but very similar dog-fishes, as well as the more aberrant saw-fishes, and the skates and rays. The latter are, indeed, so unlike sharks in general appearance, that it is probable their affinities to the latter are not generally recognised. Nevertheless, the two groups agree in all essential structural features, and are evidently very nearly allied. Perhaps the most characteristic feature of the sub-class, and the one from which it derives its title of Elasmobranchii, is the conformation of the gills and their apertures. Everybody knows the five vertical slits on each side of the neck of a dog-fish. These are the apertures leading into the gill-chambers; and in the latter the gills themselves are attached by their margins to the skin. It will not fail to be noticed that in this type of structure there is nothing comparable to the gill-cover or operculum of the bony fishes and their allies. Still there is a very important point of connection between the Elasmobranchii and the Teleostomi; this being a feature whereby these two sub-classes are broadly distinguished from the Dipnoi and Holocephali. To explain this peculiarity in detail requires the use of a number of technical terms; and it must suffice to state that it is connected with the manner in which the suspending apparatus of the lower jaw is attached to the skull; the attachment in this case being movable, whereas in the other two sub-classes it is immovably fixed. It has been said above that the number of gill-slits in a dog-fish is five, and this number is very characteristic of the order generally. Still, however, there are a few exceptions, and the number of slits may be increased to six or even seven on each side of the neck.

Although the structure of the breathing apparatus alone is sufficient to distinguish the Elasmobranchii from all other fishes, it is advisable to glance at some of the other leading structural features of their organisation. And here it may be mentioned that we allude only to the living forms, and that some extinct groups do not agree in all respects with the characteristics of the sub-class as defined from the former alone. From the typical bony fishes, the Elasmobranchii are distinguished internally by the cartilaginous nature of the skeleton; such hardening as takes place in this framework being due to the deposition of calcareous matter in the cartilage, and not to the replacement of the latter by bone. In consequence of this want of development of bony structures, the primitive cartilaginous skull persists throughout life; and the functional jaws are bars of cartilage, which do not correspond with the bony jaws of higher creatures. Teeth of the ordinary structure are developed on these spurious jaws; and such hard structures as exist in the skin likewise partake of the nature of teeth, and are, therefore, very distinct from bone. Of this kind are the fine granules found in the skin of sharks, and the larger pustules, cones, knobs, or spines occurring on that of many kinds of rays, where they are often arranged in a number of isolated prominent ridges on different parts of the back. From this remarkable absence of bone in the group, the name of boneless fishes would not be an inappropriate name for the sharks and rays. Owing to the number of minute tooth-like structures embedded in its surface, shark-skin forms an admirable polisher; and as it also affords a firm hand-hold, it is likewise used for covering sword-hilts.

In their internal structure the Elasmobranchii show a decidedly primitive type, in that where the two nerves supplying the eyes meet, there the fibres interlace to form a chiasma. The formation of a spiral valve by the lining membrane of the intestine also seems to be a primitive feature. In no member of the group is an air-bladder ever developed. Unlike ordinary fishes, sharks lay a small number of eggs, each of which is of large size, and is entirely separate from the other. Generally these eggs are invested in a hard, horny envelope, which is of an oblong shape, and furnished at each angle with a curling tendril, by means of which they become moored to the stems of sea-weeds or other submarine objects, where they remain till the young come forth. The empty envelopes are frequently to be found thrown up on the beach, and are commonly known as sea-purses. In certain species the eggs are, however, retained within the body of the female parent until hatched, so that the young are born alive. While within the shell, young sharks and rays are provided with external gills, and thus resemble tadpoles, but these gills are always lost before birth. The upper surface of the head in many members of the group is furnished with the organs known as spiracles.

As regards the internal skeleton of the fins of the Elasmobranchii, it will suffice for our present purpose to state that the supporting cartilages are arranged somewhat in the form of a fan made up of flattened divergent rays, at the base of which are certain other short cartilages. To the homologies of these latter it is unnecessary to refer in this work. In a few living sharks powerful spines—whose structure is also comparable to that of teeth—form the front portion of the dorsal fins, such spines being loosely inserted in the flesh, without any basal connection with the vertebræ. The pelvic fins are situated a long distance behind the pectoral pair; and in the males the supporting axis of each of the former is developed, as in the Chimæroids, into a long conical clasper. The tail-fin is of the heterocercal type, with its upper lobe—which is traversed by the extremity of the back-bone—greatly developed at the expense of the lower one. As all are aware who have ever seen a shark turn over on its back to seize its prey, in most members of the class the mouth is situated on the lower aspect of the head, some considerable distance behind the tip of the muzzle. And a cruel mouth it is in the case of ordinary sharks, where it is lined with row after row of sharp triangular teeth, of which the outermost stand upright in readiness for immediate use, whereas those of the innermost rows are recumbent, and not destined to see active service until those near the margins have been worn out and shed. Some sharks, like the Port Jackson species, have, however, the mouth placed in the ordinary position at the extremity of the muzzle, while the teeth—except a few at the front of the jaws—have low flattened, crowns, and form a mill-like pavement adapted to grinding the shells of molluscs and crabs. Rays, too, have pavement-like teeth of a still more markedly crushing type, although in the males of certain kinds the individual denticules are cusped.

Sharks include the most predaceous and most dreaded of all fishes, and many of the rays are likewise formidable monsters, which have the power of inflicting terrible wounds by means of the poisonous spines arming the whip-like tail. Bodily size is, however, by no means a criterion of offensive power among the members of the sub-class, since the largest of all sharks, namely, the basking-sharks, are harmless species, whose terminal mouths are armed only with feeble teeth, and whose food consists chiefly of various invertebrate animals. Skates and rays, which are bottom-haunting creatures, likewise feed on invertebrates, their grinding teeth being specially adapted for crushing shells. Although many kinds ascend tidal rivers for considerable distances, while a few have become adapted—probably owing to physical alterations on the earth's surface—to a fresh-water mode of life, the Elasmobranchii in general are marine fishes. Although, as already stated, the rays are found on the sea-bottom, while some sharks are met with at great depths, the majority of the latter group are essentially pelagic creatures, pursuing their prey at or near the surface of the open sea. The abundance of food to be met with in the neighbourhood of frequented harbours renders these fishes generally more numerous in such localities than elsewhere.

Order I.—Selachii.

SUB-ORDER I.—ASTEROSPONDYLI.

As all the existing members of the sub-class are placed in a single ordinal group, it will be unnecessary to enter into the consideration of the features by which that order is distinguished from the extinct groups now included among the Elasmobranchii. It will accordingly suffice to point out the distinctive features of the sub-order Asterospondyli, which includes the greater number of the sharks. The group takes its name from the structure of the bodies of the vertebræ, which in section show a star-like arrangement of the calcareous plates forming their internal support, such radiating plates being considerably more numerous than the circular ones running parallel to the outer surface. The members of this sub-order are characterised externally by the long and nearly cylindrical body, the powerful rudder-like tail, the presence of an anal fin, the moderate dimensions of the pectorals, and the small size or absence of the spiracle. In consequence of the divergence of the two branches of the jaws, the teeth form oblique rows, and at least the teeth in the front of the jaws are sharp-pointed, their general form being a much flattened cone, with or without lateral cusps at the base.

In the family typified by the formidable blue shark there are no spines to the fins; the first dorsal fin is placed immediately over the space separating the pelvics from the pectorals, the teeth have hollow crowns, and are generally sharp-pointed, the mouth is inferior, the skin is of the shagreen type, and the eyes are furnished with a nictitating membrane, which fulfils the function of an eye-lid. The limits of our space forbid giving the distinctive features of the various genera included in this family. The blue shark (*Carcharias glaucus*) is the most familiar representative of the type genus, while the strange-looking hammer-headed sharks form another genus (*Sphyrna*), distinguished from all other fish by the peculiar flattening and lateral expansion of the muzzle into a pair of projecting lobes, each bearing an eye at its apex. These sharks grow to a length of about fifteen feet, and are fairly abundant in the warmer seas. The genus *Galeus*, in which the head is of normal form, includes small sharks, represented in British waters by the tope (*G. canis*). Other small British sharks known as hounds (*Mustelus*) differ externally by the more blunted form of the muzzle. Unlike the species of *Carcharias*, these sharks haunt the bottom of shallow seas, where they feed on shell-fish, crabs, etc. They produce living young. Stories of the ferocity of the various kinds of large carnivorous sharks are so numerous that it is difficult to make a selection. The following anecdote by the well-known writer, Mrs. Bowdich, is, however, of special interest, as illustrating the indifference to the near presence of these terrible monsters which seems to become habitual to the natives of many of the warmer coasts. "Sharks abounded at Cape Coast," writes this lady, "and one day, as I stood at a window commanding a view of the sea, I saw some of the inhabitants of the town bathing, and the sharks hastening to seize upon them—they being visible from always swimming with part of their dorsal fin out of water. I sent to warn the men of their danger, and all came ashore except one, who laughed at the caution of his companions. A huge shark was rapidly approaching, and I sent my servant again, and this time armed with half a bottle of rum to bribe the man to save himself. It was too late. The murderous creature had seized him, and the water around was dyed with his blood. A canoe was despatched to bring him ashore, but a wave threw him on to the beach, and it was found that the shark had taken the thigh-bone completely out of the socket. The man, of course, expired in a few minutes. Accidents were often happening, and always fatal, and yet the negroes, who

Family
Carchariidæ.

Fig. 36.—BLUE SHARK.

seldom think beyond the present moment, could not be dissuaded from bathing. A man walking in the sea up to his knees was dragged away by one almost before my eyes."

Family *Lamnidæ*.

From the *Carchariidæ* the members of the allied family *Lamnidæ* differ by the solid crowns of the fully developed teeth as well as by the absence of a nictitating membrane to protect the eye. The typical representative of the family is the well-known porbeagle (*Lamna cornubica*), a species widely spread in the seas of the Northern Hemisphere, where it feeds on fishes, which are bolted whole. It seldom grows to more than about ten feet in length, and is believed to produce its young alive. Far larger is the gigantic *Carcharodon rondeletii*, which may attain the enormous length of forty feet, and is in truth the giant of the carnivorous sharks. It has huge, flattened, triangular teeth of great depth ; but as teeth of similar type, although of much larger dimensions, are met with in various superficial deposits, as they are also in some of the ocean abysses, it is evident that the living species is only an unworthy representative of its ancestors. It is, however, quite large enough, and we may be thankful that its still more gigantic predecessors have disappeared from the scene. Much smaller, and with a different type of teeth, are the two species of the allied genus *Odontaspis*. Next comes the thresher or fox-shark (*Alopecias vulpes*), a species growing to a length of about fifteen feet, and easily recognised by the excessive development of the upper lobe of the tail, which forms more than half the total length of the creature. It has feeble teeth, and feeds on mackerel and other fish, which it drives together by striking the surface of the water with its tail, whence the name of thresher. Sailors state that threshers also harass whales by jumping up in the air, and dealing them sounding "whacks" with their tails in their descent. But this naturalists, who are for the most part an incredulous race, stoutly refuse to believe. However, we think that, as in the case of adders swallowing their young, popular observation is more likely to be in the right than conclusions drawn from the study of museum specimens. To the same family belongs the gigantic basking-shark (*Cetorhinus maximus*) of the North Atlantic, commonly met with off the west coast of Ireland, and attaining a length of fully thirty feet. This shark, which has very minute teeth, is characterised, among other features, by the small size of the anal and second dorsal fins, and the large dimensions of its gill-slits. It is a somewhat sociable species, floating motionless on the surface of the sea in calm sunny weather. On account of the large quantity of excellent oil yielded by its liver, it is a regular object of pursuit.

Family *Rhinodontidæ*.

Another species (*Rhinodon typicus*), commonly known by the same vernacular name as the last, forms a family by itself, being distinguished from all the foregoing members of the order by the terminal position of the mouth, which is of huge size, and somewhat reminds us of an open square-topped bag. The eyes are extremely minute, the teeth feeble, and the whole body much depressed, with the first dorsal fin relatively small, and placed behind the highest point of the back, nearly above the pelvic pair. Still smaller is the second dorsal, which is situated near the tail, just over the anal. In spite of its huge dimensions, fifty feet or more, this shark is a perfectly harmless creature. It probably feeds on small fishes and various invertebrate animals. It appears to be confined to the Indo-Pacific seas, where it is common in the neighbourhood of the Seychelles.

Family *Scylliidæ*.

The dog-fishes and allied members of this family differ from the foregoing sharks with the mouth terminal by the backward position of the second dorsal fin which occupies a position immediately over, or behind the line of the pelvic pair. The teeth, of which several series are generally in use, are of small size, the eye lacks the nictitating membrane, and spiracles are present on the head. The dog-fishes, of which there are two species from British waters, form the genus *Scyllium;* most of the species having their skins elegantly spotted. Much larger is the Indian zebra-shark (*Stegostoma*), growing to some fifteen feet in length, and taking its name from its zebra or tiger-like coloration. Mention must also be made of the sharks of the genus *Crossorhinus*, from Japan and Australia, not only on account of the circumstance that they are deep-water forms, but likewise from the presence of leaf-like outgrowths of the skin of the sides of the head ; such appendages being probably for the purpose of attracting prey within reach of the jaws.

Family *Cestraciidæ*.

The Port Jackson shark, together with three allied species, form the genus *Cestracion* (or more properly, *Cestracium* [1]), which now alone constitutes a family easily recognised by the peculiar character of the dentition, and likewise by the presence of a spine in the front portion of each dorsal fin. Whereas in the forepart of both jaws the numerous rows of teeth are sharp and cusped, on the sides and hinder region they form a pavement-like structure, arranged in oblique rows ; the teeth in some of these rows being much larger than in the others. The mouth is situated at the extremity of the muzzle, and the eye is unprovided with a nictitating membrane. These sharks, which do not grow to more than about five feet in length, are widely distributed in the warmer seas. Although we are still very ignorant as to their life-history, it is known that their food is principally composed of shell-fish, and also that their eggs are unlike those of other members of the order, their enveloping membranes being twisted into the form of a screw.

Fig. 37.—Port Jackson Shark.

Family *Notidanidæ*.

The two genera of sharks constituting this small sub-family stand apart from the other members of the sub-order in regard to the manner in which the jaws are articulated to the cranium, while externally they are readily distinguished by the number of gill-clefts being increased from the normal five to either six or seven, and also by the single dorsal fin. There is no spine to the latter, and the teeth are cusped, and form several series. The typical genus *Notidanus* includes four species, characterised by the simple gill-slits and the complicated structure of the teeth, which consist of an elongated base

[1] The name of the family is commonly given as *Cestraciontidæ*, but it should be as written here.

carrying a large number of cusps, these latter gradually diminishing in height from one end of the tooth to the other. The notochord remains in its original condition throughout the greater part of the backbone. These sharks, which may grow to about fifteen feet in length, are to be found in most of the warmer seas. In the second genus, *Chlamydoselache*, which is represented only by a single species from the Japanese seas, the six gill-slits have frill-like expansions of skin on their margins, the teeth are of simpler structure, and the body is so long and slender as to be almost eel-like.

SUB-ORDER II.—TECTOSPONDYLI.

In this sub-order—which includes the spiny dog-fishes, saw-fishes, and the rays—the vertebræ, when fully developed, have their calcareous plates so arranged that in cross-section the circular ones predominate over those that radiate from the centre to the circumference. None of the members have an anal fin, but the spiracles are large. In the rays the body is characterised by its extreme depression, and the pectoral fins are developed into huge flaps bordering its sides.

Family *Spinacidæ*.

While agreeing with the other members of the sub-order in the structure of the vertebræ, the species forming the family *Spinacidæ* are externally like sharks. The gill-clefts are small and lateral in position, the spiracles are situated behind the eyes, and there are two dorsal fins, which may be furnished in front with spines. In addition to the typical genus *Spinax*, the family includes the spiny dog-fishes (*Acanthias*), taking their name from the presence of spines to the dorsal fins, and likewise the Greenland shark (*Læmargus*). Whereas the spiny dog-fishes do not exceed about four feet in length, the latter species grows to as much as fifteen, and has no spines to the fins of the back. It has a peculiarly tuberculated skin ; and whereas the upper teeth are small, those of the lower jaw are taller, and have their tips bent to one side. Nearly allied is the spiny shark (*Echinorhinus*) of the Atlantic and Mediterranean, in which the upper and lower teeth are alike.

Family *Squatinidæ*.

The monk- or angel-fish (*Squatina vulgaris*) is the sole member of a family which serves to connect the last with the true rays. This ugly fish has a depressed skate-like body, but a nearly terminal mouth, and the pectoral fins not connected at their bases with the head. The conical teeth are sharply pointed, the gill-slits are lateral, the skin is tuberculated, and the dorsal fins, which have no spines, are placed on the tail. The monk-fish reaches a length of fully five feet, and is found in nearly all seas.

Families *Pristiophoridæ* and *Pristidæ*.

The production of the extremity of the upper jaw into a long, flattened bony process, armed on each side with sharp quadrangular teeth set in sockets, serves at once to distinguish the saw-fishes from all their kindred. They form two genera—*Pristiophorus* and *Pristis*—each of which is regarded as representing a family by itself, although such a division certainly seems somewhat superfluous. The members of the first genus are relatively small fishes from the seas of Australia and Japan, characterised, among other features, by the lateral situation of the gill-slits, and the possession of a pair of tentacles arising from the middle of the jaw, and projecting far beyond the teeth. In the second genus, of which various members range through all the warmer seas, the gill-slits are placed on the inferior aspect, and there are no tentacles to the saw. Saw-fishes of this genus grow to twenty feet or more in length, when their offensive weapon may measure as much as a couple of yards. They are some of the most terrible and cruel members of the whole order, using their formidable saw for the purpose of ripping open the bodies of their victims by a lateral stroke, and then feeding greedily on the intestines and torn flesh. Even bathers in fresh waters are by no means exempt from their attacks, as these fishes frequently ascend large rivers to a considerable distance.

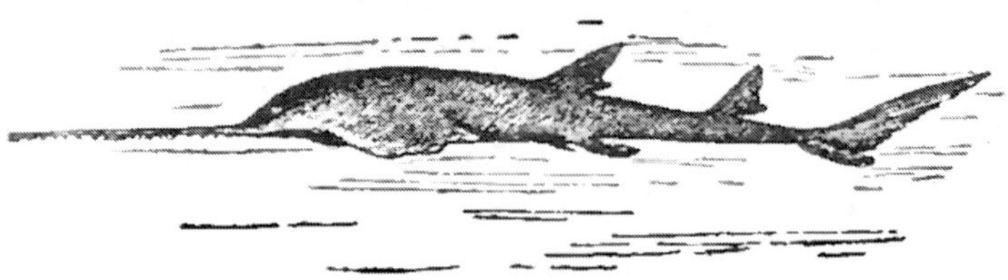

Fig. 38.—SAW-FISH.

Family *Rhinobatidæ*.

The genera of beaked rays constituting this family differ from all the preceding groups by the much greater development of their pectoral fins, which extend forwards to join the head, the portion of the head and body thus surrounded by fins being technically termed the disc. In these and the other rays referred to below, the dorsal fins are shifted backwards to the more or less whip-like tail, and the gill-slits are placed inferiorly, as is generally the mouth. The *Rhinobatidæ* are specially distinguished from their kindred by the moderate development of the pectoral fins, of which the portion furnished with cartilaginous rays does not extend forwards to the beak; and the long tail, which is marked on the sides by a fold of skin, carries two large dorsal fins. In addition to the typical genus *Rhinobatis*, which includes a considerable number of species from all the warmer oceans, the present family comprises the Australian *Trigonorhina* and the two species of *Rhynchobatis*, from the hottest regions of the Indian Ocean. The last-named is remarkable for the beautiful structure of its teeth, which form a compact pavement, with a prominent ridge in the middle line of one jaw fitting into a corresponding depression in that of the other, and also having undulations at the sides. From six to eight feet is a common length for these rays. Like the skates and rays of the following families, the members of these genera are somewhat sluggish fishes, living near the bottom in water of moderate depth, and flapping lazily along when in movement by the aid of their huge pectoral fins, the tail acting merely as a rudder. When at rest, the colour of the upper surface of a ray's back is so like the sand or mud on which the creature rests that it often requires a practised eye to detect its presence. The ridges of tubercles found on the backs of some species probably increase the resemblance by simulating lines of small stones on the sand. The food of rays consists of shell-fish and various crustaceans, whose hard shells are instantaneously ground up by the powerful mill-like jaws. In seizing their prey, these fish throw themselves right above it, so as to be able readily to convey it to the mouth, which is situated on the lower surface of the head some considerable distance behind the muzzle.

Family *Raiidæ*.

The second family of rays includes the genera *Raia*, *Psammobatis*, and *Platyrhina*, in all of which the disc is very broad, with its rayed portion extending as far forwards as the muzzle, while the tail is marked on each side by a fold. Very generally the skin is roughened by tubercles, which may terminate in spines. To the typical genus belongs the common thornback skate of the British seas, in which the two sexes are distinguished by the structure of the teeth, those of the female forming a comparatively smooth pavement, whereas those of the male—although still arranged in the same manner—are cusped. In other species of the same genus sexual differences display themselves in other parts of the body. Skates of this genus are more abundant in northern than in tropical seas, and some of them range considerably farther north than any other members of the group. The flesh of all is largely used as food.

Fig. 39.—THORNBACK SKATE.

The presence of an electric organ, composed of vertical prisms, between the head and the pectoral fins, serves to differentiate the numerous kinds of electric rays from the other representatives of the group. The body of these fishes forms a broad, smooth disc, covered with a naked skin ; the tail has a longitudinal fold on each side and a caudal fin, and there is generally a rayed dorsal fin. The vertical prisms of the electric organ are divided by a number of horizontal partitions into separate cells, each filled with a translucent substance somewhat resembling jelly in appearance. The currents produced by this singular structure are precisely similar to those from a galvanic battery ; and in fishes of moderate dimensions are sufficiently powerful to disable even human beings. The typical genus *Torpedo* includes half a dozen species from the Indian and Atlantic Oceans, some of which are also abundant in the Mediterranean, while one occasionally wanders to the southern shores of Britain. From the warmer seas there are also several other genera belonging to this family, such as *Astrape*, *Discopyge*, *Hypnus*, *Narcine*, and *Temera*, severally distinguished by the conformation and position of the fins.

Family *Torpedinidæ.*

The largest and most hideous of all the skates are the so-called eagle-rays, several of which are popularly known as devil-fish. In the five genera included in this family the pectoral fins obtain an enormous development, in consequence of which the disc becomes greatly widened. Along the sides of the head the pectoral fins are, however, interrupted ; their anterior extremities forming small finlets on the muzzle, known as cephalic fins. In some of the genera these cephalic fins are modified to form a pair of horn-like structures projecting forwards on each side of the muzzle, the function of which is to assist in capturing and conveying to the mouth the prey. In all, the tail forms a long, tapering, whip-like organ. When the mouth is armed with teeth, these take the form of a pavement, which in the typical genus *Myliobatis* is perfectly smooth, and composed of a number of oblong and hexagonal plates, fitted closely together at their edges, and with their grinding surface like polished ivory. Several widely-spread species are included in the typical genus, two of which are visitors to the British coasts. Most of them have a barbed spine to the tail, and with this, when caught, they lash out

Family *Myliobatidæ.*

violently, and thus inflict severe wounds. In comparison with the electric rays—in which the width of the disc seldom exceeds from two to three feet—these fishes are giants, their length being at times as much as fifteen feet. The tropical devil-fishes forming the genera *Dicerobatis* and *Cephaloptera* are, however, still more gigantic, some examples measuring nearly twenty feet across the disc, and weighing considerably more than a thousand pounds. In *Dicerobatis* the truncated muzzle is armed with a formidable pair of horns, the mouth is inferior, and has both its jaws furnished with teeth. On the other hand, in *Cephaloptera*, the position of the mouth is terminal, and there are teeth only in the lower jaw. Of these ungainly monsters, Mr. S. Ward, in a letter quoted by Dr. Percival Wright, describes his experiences in the Seychelles as follows:—"Coming home, we passed close to an enormous *diable-de-mer* floating quietly about. We changed from the pirogue to the whale-boat, which I had scientifically fitted up for the *grosses poissóns*, and went alongside of him, driving a regular whale-harpoon right through his body. The way he towed the whaler was beautiful, but we would not give him an inch of line, and he had to succumb to a rather protracted lancing. His size will give you an idea of his strength in the water—forty-two feet in circumference. We got him awash on the beach, but the united strength of ten men could not get him an inch farther, so we were obliged to leave him there. By this time the sharks will not have left much of him; they have not had such a meal for a long time. The fishermen say that, when alive, the sharks do not molest the *diable-de-mer*, whose offensive weapons consist of their enormous flexible sides (one can hardly call them fins) with which they can beat almost any shark to death. As a rule, when harpooned, they endeavour, like other rays, to bury themselves in the sand, and if they succeed in doing this, no line can ever haul them out of it—their flat bodies act on the principle of an enormous sucker. Another curious fact about them is that when harpooned, they swim sideways, edge-on, in order to avoid exposing too broad a surface to the enemy. They never do this unless harpooned." Other genera are *Aëtobatis* and *Rhinoptera*, both distinguished by the dentition and the position and form of the fins. Whereas the former of these has but a single species, the latter possesses several.

Family *Trygonidæ.*

The last existing representatives of the Elasmobranchii are the formidable and dreaded sting-rays, which are typified by the genus *Trygon*, but also include *Pteroplatea*, *Urogymnus*, and *Urolophus*. In species the typical genus is very numerous, some of these having a very wide geographical range. They are mostly tropical, and attain their maximum development in the Atlantic Ocean and the Indian seas. It is remarkable that certain species inhabiting the eastern districts of Tropical America have become accustomed to a fresh-water existence, and are now restricted to certain inland lakes. All these fishes are distinguished by the excessive development of the fore-part of the pectoral fins, which are so extended as to encircle the muzzle, and thus complete the disc. The whip-like tail is distinctly marked off from the body, and generally bears a poisonous serrated spine; and in many kinds the median fins—which are never large—are replaced by similar spines. These armed rays are some of the most dangerous of all fishes.

SUB-KINGDOM I.—VERTEBRATA.

CLASS VI.—CYCLOSTOMATA.

BY R. LYDEKKER, B.A., F.R.S., V.P.G.S., &c.

LAMPREYS AND HAG-FISHES.

As indicated by the name hag-fishes, which is popularly applied to the members of one of the two families, the animals now to be considered are commonly regarded as fishes. Popular natural history and scientific zoology take, however, very different estimates of the mutual relationships of organised beings; and zoologists are now pretty well agreed that, although they were formerly admitted within its limits, lampreys and hag-fishes have no real claim to be included in the class Pisces. Consequently, they are now regarded as forming a class by themselves—the Cyclostomata. This class includes the last group of animals now termed true Vertebrata; the lancelets, which were likewise formerly regarded as fishes, being now considered as the highest of the Protochordata or semi-Vertebrates. The essential features by which the members of the lamprey group are broadly distinguished from the higher classes of the Vertebrates are the complete absence of jaws, the single—instead of double—aperture of the nostrils, and the rasping tongue. Round-mouths—the English equivalent of Cyclostomata—is a name which well expresses the first of these three distinctive features; but, in allusion to the second characteristic, the alternative name of Monorhina has likewise been proposed for the class. Whichever name may be selected, there can be no doubt as to the right of the lamprey group to constitute a class by itself. Had we these living forms alone to deal with, there would be no need to sub-divide the class into groups of higher rank than families. It happens, however, that there are certain extinct, somewhat fish-like creatures, which there is considerable reason for regarding as more or less distantly related to the modern lampreys. Consequently, it is necessary to make the latter into a sub-class by themselves; and for this sub-class the name of Marsipobranchii has been selected. This name refers to the circumstance that in the lampreys and hag-fishes the gills form a series of pouches on the sides of the neck, on which they usually open by round apertures coincident in number with the pouches. Either six or seven is the number of pairs of gill-pouches, in which there are no supporting gill-arches. The sucking-mouth, which occupies the extremity of the muzzle, is of circular form, with its more or less lip-like margin sustained by a system of internal cartilages. The skin of the body is soft, and unprovided with scales; but the upper and lower surfaces of its hinder half bear well-developed fins in the middle line, which are supported by vertical rays of cartilage. Paired fins—corresponding to those of fishes and representing the limbs of the higher Vertebrates—are, however, conspicuous by their absence; this lack of limbs forming, indeed, a characteristic of the class rather than a feature of the sub-class. Internally, a lamprey lacks all traces of ribs, and the vertebral column is either represented by the primitive notochord alone, or by that structure surrounded by a series of calcareous rings. In reality, therefore, a lamprey has only the very remotest claim to be called a vertebrate animal; but since some of the sharks are in a very similar predicament as regards the differentiation of their backbones, this deficiency can scarcely be regarded as a bar to the title. The heart of a lamprey is decidedly of a lower type than that of a fish, since it lacks the chamber at the front end technically designated the *bulbus arteriosus*. The digestive tract is peculiar in being quite simple and straight; and the organs of reproduction discharge their products directly into the general cavity of the body. The function of teeth is discharged by a variable number of horny plates or cusps.

Lampreys.—Family *Petromyzidæ*.

As a family, the lampreys are distinguished from the hag-fishes by undergoing a metamorphosis, and by the nostril terminating behind as a blind sac without perforating the palate. In the adult form rasping horny teeth cover the tongue, and teeth of similar structure are present above and below the mouth, as well as in the surrounding adhesive disc, while the aperture of the nostril is situated near the middle of the head, and there are well-developed eyes. The gill-pouches are seven in number, and each opens by a separate aperture on the side of the neck; but internally those of each side have only a single opening into the pharynx, their ducts uniting to form one tube. On the other hand, the larvæ, which were long regarded as distinct creatures, under the name of *Ammocœtes*, have an undivided median fin, and toothless mouth. All the members of this family lay very small eggs, and the lining membrane of the intestine forms a spiral valve. The true lampreys, or those included in the genus *Petromyzum*, appear to be four in number, and have a wide range in the Northern Hemisphere, one extending as far south as the west coast of Africa. In this genus the hinder of the two fins on the back is continuous with the tail-fin; the rasp-like teeth on the tongue are serrated; and on the upper side of the mouth there is either a transverse horny ridge bearing one two-cusped, or two separate teeth situated close together. The largest form is the sea lamprey (*P. marinum*), which is not unfrequently as much as three feet in length, whereas the common river lamprey (*P. fluviatile*) does not reach a couple of feet. Lampreys live chiefly or entirely on the flesh of fishes, to whose bodies they attach themselves by their adhesive discs, and then rasp off the flesh with their horny dental organs. All ascend rivers for the purpose of breeding, and the larvæ of some kinds remain in fresh water until they develop into the adult form. At the breeding season some lampreys ascend the rivers of the Northern Hemisphere in vast shoals. They deposit their eggs in furrows excavated in the river bottom. Another genus (*Mordacia*) is represented by a species found in localities as remote from one another as the coasts of Tasmania and Chili, and differs in that the teeth above the mouth are arranged in two three-cusped groups. In the allied genus *Geotria*, of which one species is found in South Australia, and the second in Chili, the hinder fin on the back is distinct from the tail-fin. The last genus is the little-known *Exomegas*, from the Argentine coast.

Hag-Fishes.—Family *Myxinidæ*.

In this family the nostril is extended backwards to perforate the palate, and its front aperture is placed close to the muzzle. Two pairs of barbels decorate the sides of the muzzle, the mouth has no lip-like structure, a single tooth occupies the middle of the palate, and the teeth on the tongue are arranged in a double comb-like series. Each gill-pouch opens by a duct of its own into the pharynx, and the external apertures of the pouches are situated a considerable distance behind the head, instead of close to it. The eggs differ from those of the lampreys by their relatively large size, as well as by having a horny coating furnished with tendrils for the purpose of attachment to submerged objects. The young are hatched in a fully-developed state, and undergo no metamorphosis. In the members of the typical genus *Myxine* there is only one gill-aperture on each side of the body, but this gives rise to six ducts leading to the gill-pouches. On the other hand, in the genus *Bdellostoma* each of the six or more gill-pouches communicates directly with the exterior by a separate aperture. Whereas the members of the first genus have a wide geographical range, the two representatives of the second appear to be confined to the coasts of the South Pacific. All are exclusively marine, and they have been taken at great depths. They are blind, and to a large extent parasitic, so that they may be regarded as degraded types; and they have the habit of secreting a vast quantity of stiff slime. Like the lampreys, they feed on the flesh of fishes, the various members of the cod tribe being their especial favourites. They do not, however, content themselves by hanging on to the surface of the body, for which the structure of the mouth is less suited, but actually bore their way into the flesh of their unwilling hosts.

SUB-KINGDOM I.—VERTEBRATA.

CLASS VII.—PROTOCHORDA.

By W. Garstang, M.A., F.Z.S.

SUB-CLASS I.—CEPHALOCHORDA.

The group Cephalochorda contains a number of small marine animals which resemble fishes in many respects, but are much more lowly organised than even the simplest of the finny tribe. They breathe like fishes by taking water into their mouths and passing it out through a series of slit-like holes in the sides of their throats (gill-slits). The number of these gill-slits is much greater than in fishes, frequently amounting to more than a hundred. A supporting rod, the notochord, the forerunner of the backbone of higher forms, extends along the back of the animal from head to tail, and the tubular nervous system lies above it. There are no true side-fins, but a pair of ridges along the under side of the body of the young animal possibly represents them. In the very young animal the gill-slits open directly to the outside, but at an early period the fin-like ridges, which have just been mentioned, close over the slits and unite with one another on the under side of the body, leaving merely a small hole or water-pore for the outflow of the water. These little animals are capable of extremely rapid movements, wriggling their lancet-shaped bodies from side to side after the manner of an eel. They have no jaws, and depend for their food upon the microscopic plants and other organisms contained in the stream of water constantly passing through their mouths. This current of water is set up by the action of innumerable fine whip-like lashes which beset the sides of the gill-slits, and by their united action drive the water outwards into the surrounding water-cavity, and so to the exterior through the water-pore. New water is constantly streaming into the mouth to take the place of the water driven out, and the food-particles it contains are incessantly extracted from it by means of the slimy coating of the walls of the throat, to which they adhere. Another set of microscopic lashes then drives the entangled food-particles down the proper channel to the animal's stomach, where they are digested in the ordinary way.

The lancelet (*Amphioxus lanceolatus*) is the only representative of the group in the Mediterranean and North Atlantic seas. It is a semi-transparent little creature, from one to two inches in length, compressed from side to side, pointed at both ends, provided with a circle of small stiff tentacles round the mouth, and with a distinct tail-fin behind. It lives in shallow water, in beds of loose sand, into which it burrows with lightning-like rapidity. It lies obliquely on its back in its sandy bed, its head and mouth alone protruding

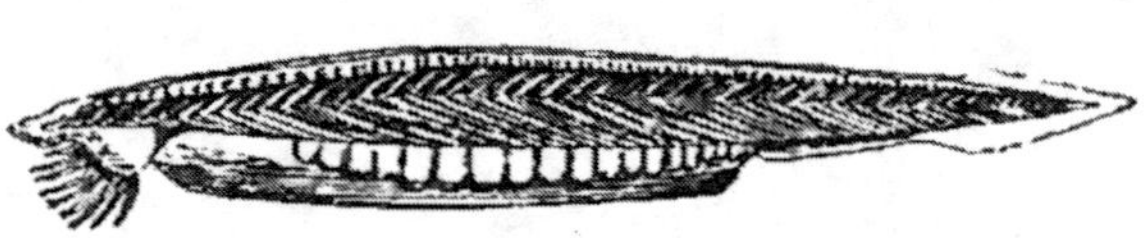

Fig. 1.—The Lancelet (*Amphioxus lanceolatus*).

above the surface. These habits clearly provide the reason why the delicate gill-slit region of the body should be protected from injury and enclosed within a special chamber, formed by the union of a pair of fin-like ridges.

Other representatives of the group, closely resembling the European lancelet, are found in shallow seas all over the world. A peculiar type (*Asymmetron lucayanum*), which possesses a slender backward prolongation of its tail, is found in the Bahamas, where it may be taken swimming freely at the surface of the sea at night, or in the day-time buried in the coral sand.

SUB-CLASS II.—UROCHORDA OR TUNICATA.

This group of exclusively marine animals is closely related to the Cephalochorda, although its various representatives are very unlike Amphioxus in their final shape and appearance. They agree with Amphioxus, however, in having similar organs for breathing and feeding, and in having a similar tubular nervous system and supporting rod along the back of the body. Unlike Amphioxus, however, the primitive backbone or notochord of Tunicata is confined to the hinder part of the body, which is in the form of a well-marked tail like that of a tadpole. The body also possesses the power of producing a gelatinous envelope or tunic called the test, which clothes the animal either loosely as in Appendicularians, or closely as in all others. The group consists of two principal sections, which may be called the Tailed and Tailless Tunicata.

The members of the first section (Appendicularians) are free-swimming, and retain their tails with the nerve-cord and notochord during their whole career. They are very small and inconspicuous creatures, the body being about the size of a small pin's head, and the tail less than a quarter of an inch in length, and the whole animal is of glass-like transparency. The tunic is thin, and forms a delicate "house" in which the Appendicularian swims about, and from which it can escape when attacked by its enemies. These creatures can often be caught at the surface of the sea round our coasts by the use of a fine muslin net.

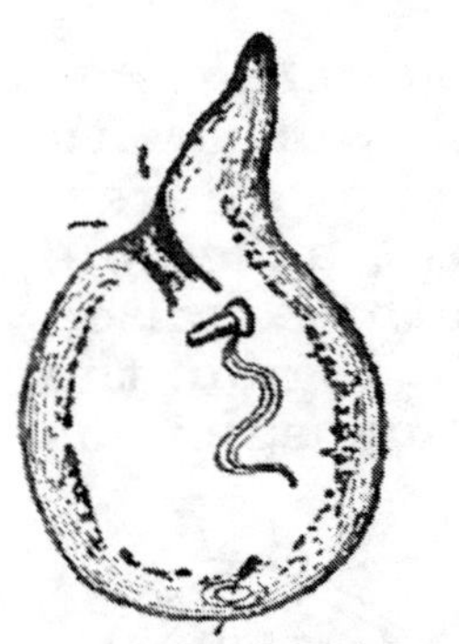

Fig. 2.—An Appendicularian (*Oikopleura*). In its house.

The members of the second section, the Tailless Tunicata, are tailed only in their early stages. After a brief free-swimming career they lose their tails, like the tadpoles of the common frog, and grow up into soft back-boneless animals of a quite different appearance. Some of these tailless forms retain, or regain, their free-swimming habits, and usually acquire a barrel-like shape and a number of hoop-like muscle bands, by the contractions of which they drive themselves through the water (Salps), or they may form definite colonies and float idly about at the mercy of the waves (Pyrosoma). The majority of the Tailless Tunicata, however, become permanently attached to rocks, stones, and sea-weeds on the sea-bottom, and are especially abundant between tide-

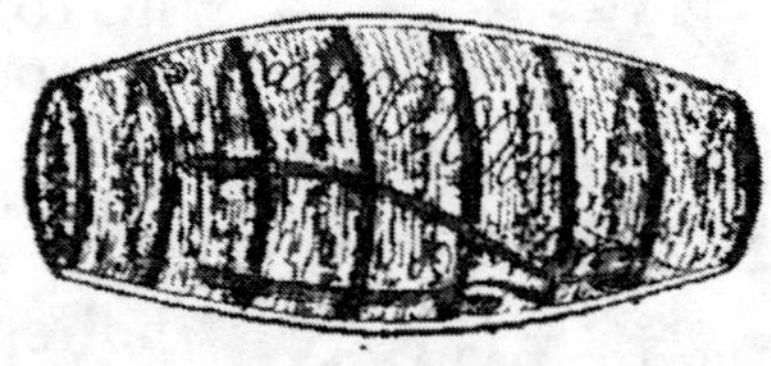

Fig. 3.—Doliolum Tritonis.

marks round our shores. They are known as Ascidians or sea-squirts, and they may be either solitary or colonial. The solitary forms are sac-shaped, leathery creatures fastened at the base, and possessing a mouth at the opposite

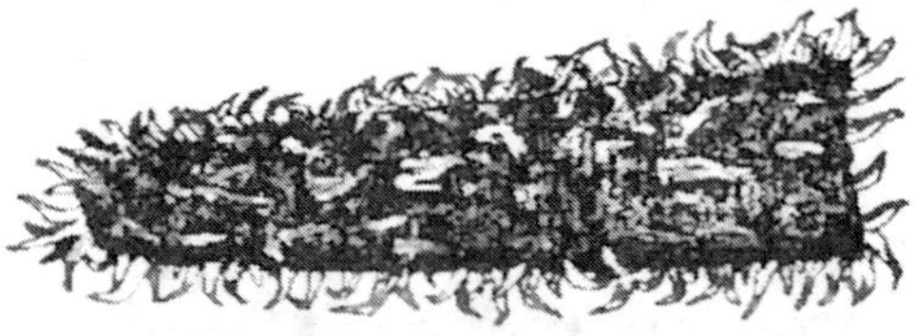

Fig. 4.—PYROSOMA.

Fig. 5.—COMMON SEA SQUIRT (*Ascidiella aspersa*).

Fig. 6.—BOTRYLLUS.

end. There is also another opening by which the water from the gill-slits is passed out of the body. The colonial forms are smaller in size, and are united together into irregular or star-shaped clusters usually brightly coloured.

CLASS VIII.—HERMICHORDA or ENTEROPNEUSTA.

THE commonest representative of this group is the remarkable *Balanoglossus*, an animal which combines the creeping mud-burrowing habits of a worm with some of the organs especially characteristic of vertebrata. The body is divided into three parts, a flexible tongue-like proboscis in front of the mouth, a raised collar behind it, and a long cylindrical hind-region, the sides of which are perforated by numerous inconspicuous gill-slits. In the back of the collar of *Balanoglossus* a short tubular nerve-cord is found like that of vertebrata. In its young condition *Balanoglossus* is a small transparent creature, about one-tenth of an inch in length, remarkably similar to the free-swimming larval form of star-fishes and sea-cucumbers.

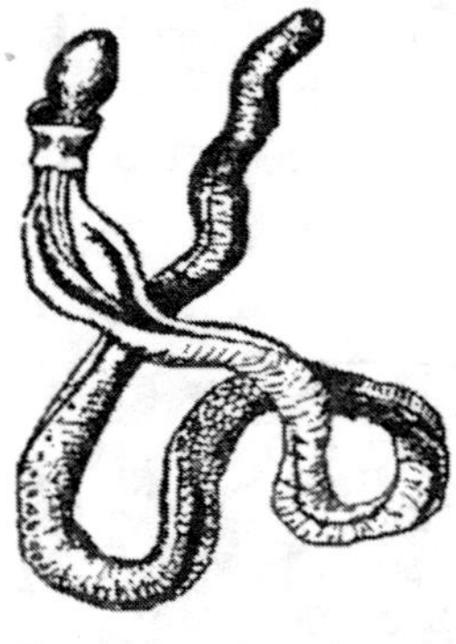

Fig. 7.—BALANOGLOSSUS SARNIENSIS.

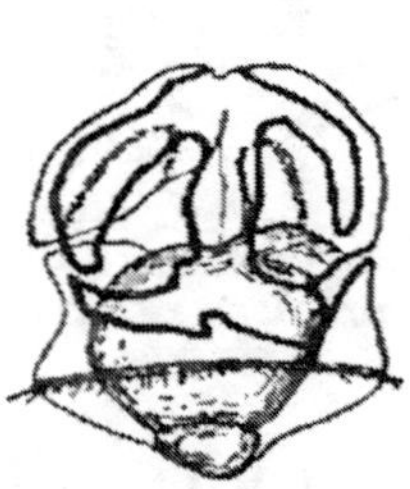

Fig. 8.—TORNARIA.

Balanoglossus has only once been taken on the coast of the British Isles, but is not uncommon on the shores of the Channel Islands and other parts of the world. *Balanoglossus sarniensis*, found in the Channel Islands, varies from one to three feet in length, and is difficult to obtain in a perfect condition, owing to its softness and fragility. The young form, *Tornaria*, may be found in the autumn months free-swimming at the surface of the sea off the southern shores of Great Britain.

SUB-KINGDOM II.—ARTHROPODA.

CRUSTACEA, INSECTA, &c.

BY W. F. KIRBY, F.L.S., F.E.S., &c.

THE *Arthropoda* (otherwise called *Articulata* or *Annulosa*) include an enormous number of animals with an external skeleton, or, at least, a thickened integument to which the muscles are attached; and a body divided into segments, and furnished with jointed organs for locomotion, etc. Many of them undergo a metamorphosis, passing through several dissimilar stages before reaching the perfect state in which they become sexually mature, and capable of reproducing their kind. The sexes are generally distinct. They breathe by tracheæ, or by gills, and the nervous system consists of a series of ganglia, of which the largest, situated in the head, are considered to correspond to the brain. The blood is usually white.

The following classes may be grouped under this heading :—

Classes of Arthropoda.

I. CRUSTACEA (Crabs, Lobsters, Shrimps, etc.).
II. ARACHNIDA (Spiders, Scorpions and Mites).
III. MYRIOPODA (Centipedes and Millepedes).
IV. PROTRACHEATA.
V. INSECTA (Insects).

The characters of these classes are noticed in their places, and to enumerate them here would be repetition. It must not be forgotten that all organic beings show complicated affinities all round, and that no linear arrangement can possibly be natural, and, therefore, we can only follow what appears to be a fairly natural sequence, always remembering that by laying stress on some characters we are necessarily ignoring others of perhaps equal or greater importance; and sometimes widely separating creatures which, when looked at from a slightly different point of view, are seen to be closely allied.

Space at disposal necessarily limits this article to a brief sketch of a vast subject; but care has been taken to preserve a certain proportion in allotting the space to the different sections of which it is composed, and the information given, though far from exhaustive, will be found to be useful and instructive. The selection made is that of the most important and interesting groups into which these animals have been divided. These are dealt with in the order given above, and are illustrated by numerous original drawings reproduced in most cases life size.

CLASS I.—CRUSTACEA.

THE *Crustacea* may be considered as the marine representatives of the Insects; for although a few insects are marine, and some *Crustacea* are found on land or in fresh water, yet an overwhelming preponderance of the *Crustacea* are exclusively marine. In the perfect state they are covered with a hard jointed shell. Sometimes the head is united with the thorax, as in the class *Arachnida*, but it is more often separated. Being water animals, or living with few exceptions in damp places on land, they breathe with gills. They have generally two eyes, two pairs of antennæ, three pairs of jaws, three pairs of foot-jaws, the two outer pairs of which often serve the purpose of legs, and five pairs of legs. Most of the species undergo a peculiar metamorphosis, like that of the Barnacles, which has led to the latter being now classed as retrograde *Crustacea*. These larval forms are generally called *Nauplius*, or *Zoea*, these names having been given to them when they were first discovered, and were supposed to be perfect organisms. They have large eyes, and curious bifid appendages terminating in long bristles, and utilised as swimming feet. The *Nauplius*-form (compare *Fig.* 5) shown by many *Crustacea* on emerging from the egg, is oval, with a single eye, and it gradually acquires three pairs of limbs. In the *Copepoda* and *Ostracoda* it passes gradually into the perfect state by successive moults; but in the *Siphonostoma* it undergoes a retrograde metamorphosis, losing the eyes, and limbs, as locomotive organs. This form of larva is seldom met with among the *Decapoda*. The *Zoea*-form of larva has seven pairs of jointed appendages, of which the foot-jaws are very large; and two large eyes. (See *Fig.* 1.) When the *Zoea* was first discovered, it was thought to be a creature of the greatest rarity and interest, and it is amusing to read in the old books of the capture of single specimens of a *Zoea* at intervals of years, in distant parts of the globe. Now they are known to be simply the larval forms of many of our commonest *Crustacea*. Similar unexpected discoveries perhaps still exist, in the case of other, as yet unsuspected, inhabitants of our globe.

Larval Forms of *Crustacea.*

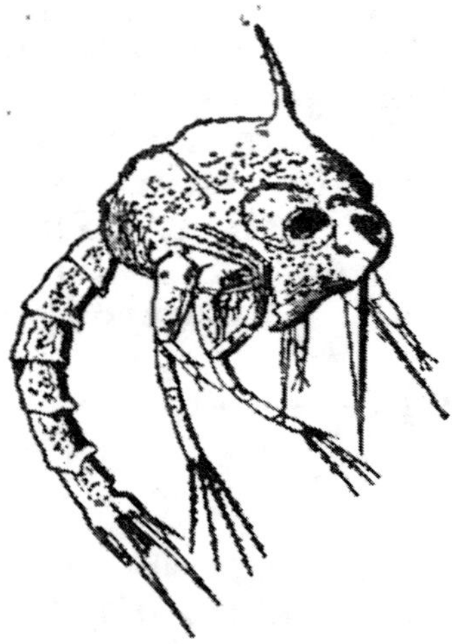

Fig. 1.—ZOEA-LARVA OF SPIDER-CRAB (*Maia Squinado*). Magnified.

Crustacea are carnivorous or omnivorous, and some of the smaller kinds are parasitic. Some *Crustacea* are of very small size, while others are the largest of known *Arthropoda*. Their average size is considerably above that of insects. There are probably no species which can be considered actually injurious to man; but many are of considerable economic importance. Crabs, shrimps, lobsters, prawns, and crayfish are the only *Arthropoda* which form staple articles of diet among civilised nations at the present day, though there is no reason why locusts and large wood-feeding grubs and caterpillars should not be eaten. Locusts have always been relished in the East; and the Cossus, which was probably the larva of some large beetle, was considered a dainty by the Romans. However, with the exception of cheese-maggots and cheese-mites, both of which are probably less wholesome than the insects just

Edible *Arthropoda.*

mentioned, Europeans turn from insects, etc., with disgust, while eating crabs and shrimps without hesitation. Food is more a matter of fashion than of anything else, after all.

A most ingenious theory has lately been propounded by Mr. H. M. Bernard, in his work on the *Apodidæ*. He considers the *Crustacea* to have originated from the *Annelida*, and that the earliest *Crustacea* were simply *Annelida* with the head bent down under the body; but this is a matter on which only specialists are entitled to express an opinion. Nevertheless, we may begin the *Crustacea* with the *Entomostraca*, as the group nearest approaching to the *Annelida*. We may add that the *Pycnogonida*, which we have included with the *Arachnida*, have been placed by some authors in the *Crustacea*, while others have regarded them as forming a distinct class of *Arthropoda* by themselves.

SUB-CLASS I.—ENTOMOSTRACA.

This large section is only retained as a matter of convenience to include the smaller *Crustacea*, many of which exhibit forms which have little resemblance to the more typical *Crustacea*. It includes most of the parasitic species. The *Cirripedia* are sometimes treated as an additional order of *Entomostraca*.

Order I.—Phyllopoda.

The *Phyllopoda* have received their name from their leaf-like swimming legs, of which there are four pairs, or more. Sometimes more or less of the animal is covered by a bivalve shell, somewhat as in the *Ostracoda*, or by a

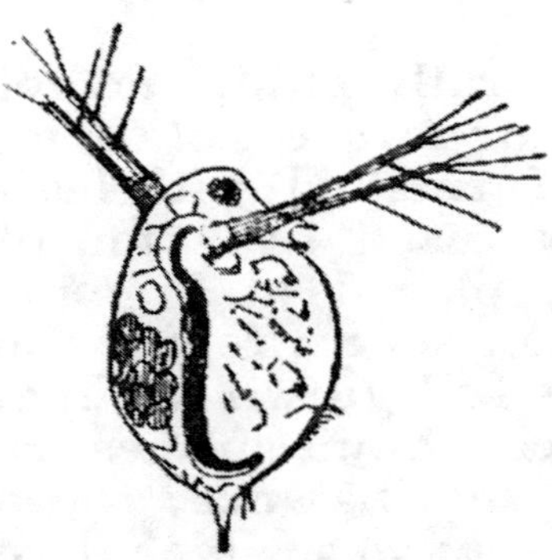

Fig. 2.—Water-Flea (*Daphnia pulex*). Magnified.

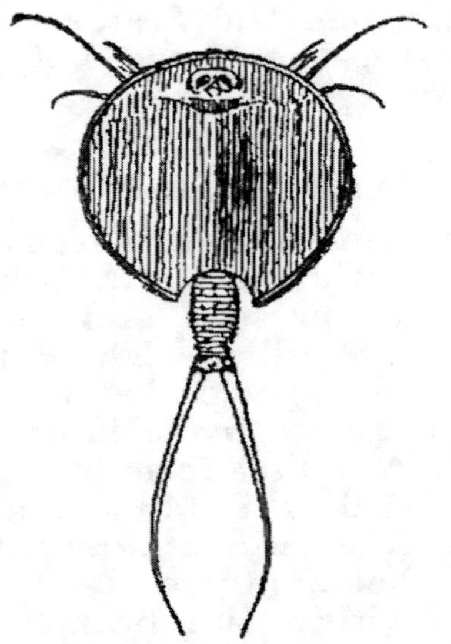

Fig. 3.—*Apus cancriformis*. Nat. size.

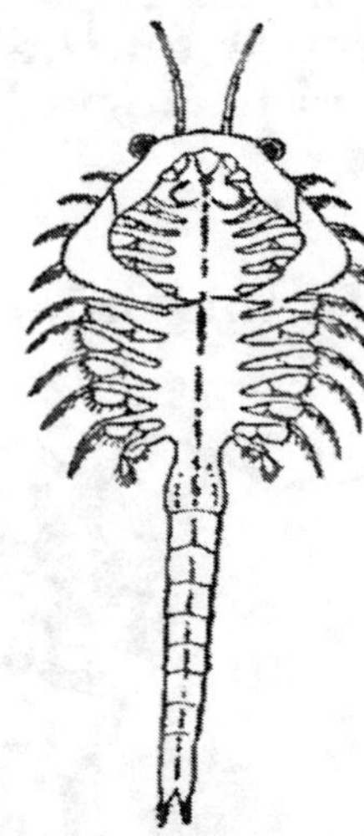

Fig. 4.—Brine Shrimp (*Artemia salina*). Magnified.

solid carapace; in other cases this is wanting. Some are marine, while others inhabit fresh water. They have usually two eyes, which, however, are sometimes contiguous. Three families of this order may be briefly noticed. The

Daphniidæ, or water-fleas are small *Crustacea* which abound in fresh water. They are of a compressed oval form, and are partly covered by a thin, transparent bivalve shell. The first pair of antennæ is small, but the second very large, bifid at the extremity, and set with long hairs, which serve as the principal organs of locomotion. The eyes are fused into one large one, near which is often another small one. They have from four to six pairs of swimming legs. They are very favourite objects with microscopists, being abundant, and admitting of easy observation. In the *Apodidæ* the body is covered with a shield-shaped carapace, and there are two contiguous eyes, and from 30 to 40 pairs of gill-feet. *Apus cancriformis*, Schäff., is a brownish yellow species, about two inches long, which is found in ponds. The large, oval carapace covers all but the last few segments of the body, which ends in a flat double tail, on each side of which a long bristly appendage is visible. This family is of interest as having formed the subject of Mr. Bernard's memoir, already alluded to, in which he connects the *Annelida* with the Trilobites through the *Apodidæ*. The *Branchipodidæ* have no shell, but a strongly-segmented body, stalked eyes, and a long tapering tail, ending in a flat pair of flattened appendages set with bristles. The most interesting species of this family is the brine shrimp, *Artemia salina* (Linn.), which is of a pink colour, and about half an inch long. It is more shrimp-like in appearance than any other species of Entomostraca which we have mentioned, and is only found in brine pits, appearing to prefer the most concentrated brine.

ORDER II.—OSTRACODA.

In the *Ostracoda* the body is not segmented, and is entirely covered by a bean-shaped bivalve shell. There are four antennæ set with bristles, and one or both pairs are used for swimming and grasping. There are five pairs of other appendages, of which the first, second, often the third, and sometimes even the fourth, serve the purpose of jaws, and only the last pair or pairs perform the office of legs.

ORDER III.—COPEPODA.

In this order there are ten swimming-legs at most, generally bifid, and set with hairs and bristles. One or two sessile eyes are present, and the mouth is furnished with leaf-like gills. The large eye possessed by some of the species led to their being placed in a genus *Cyclops* by Müller. They commence life in the *Nauplius*-form, to which the full-grown animal still exhibits a strong resemblance. Some species are free, and others parasitic ; as, for instance, those belonging to the family *Notodelphyidæ*, which live within the branchial cavity of *Ascidia*. A few species like these are marine, but the majority of the *Cyclopidæ* live in fresh water, one species, *Canthocamptus alpestris* (Vogt), being found in the glacier waters of the Aar in Switzerland, at an elevation of 8,500 feet. The family *Argulidæ* includes some species which are parasitic on the carp, and which are known as "carp lice."

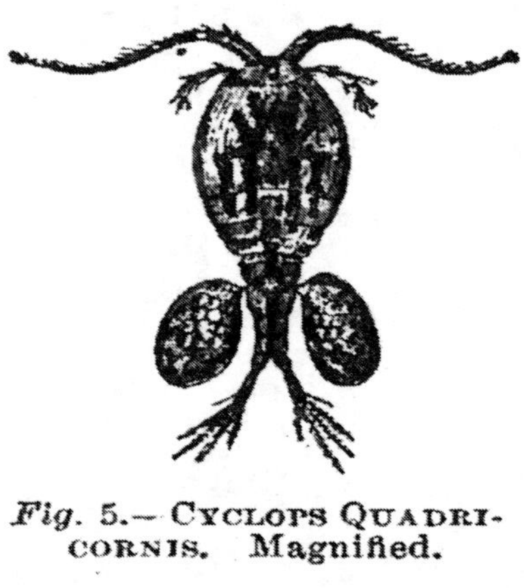

Fig. 5.—CYCLOPS QUADRICORNIS. Magnified.

Order IV.—Cirripedia.

By recent authors the *Cirripedia* have been treated as a section of the *Crustacea*, from which, however, they differ so much when adult, that they were formerly regarded as a separate class. In their perfect state they are fixed immovably by their heads to a rock, or some other object submerged in the sea, and are without antennæ, eyes, or any means of locomotion. Their bodies are enclosed more or less completely in a calcareous shell, formed of several parts, which led to the earlier naturalists regarding them as *Mollusca*, and their shells were called Multivalves by collectors, in opposition to Univalves and Bivalves. In the larval stages they are provided with antennæ, eyes, and swimming-feet, the last of which become modified into short, jointed, cirrhated appendages, of which there are usually six pairs, and which are used to capture prey. They are generally hermophrodite. All the species are marine. A peculiar interest attaches to these animals, owing to their having formed a special object of study with Charles Darwin, who published an elaborate monograph upon them in 1851 and 1854. There are several sub-divisions of the *Cirripedia*, many of which live parasitically on various *Crustacea*, *Mollusca*, or on other *Cirripedia*. The only two families which we shall notice here are the *Balanidæ* and the *Lepadidæ*.

Fig. 6.—Acorn Barnacle (*Balanus balanoides*). Nat. size.

Acorn Barnacles (*Balanidæ*).

The *Balanidæ* or acorn barnacles attach themselves to the rocks, often between tide-marks, after the manner of a limpet; but they can always be distinguished from true *Mollusca* by their multivalve shells. The *Lepadidæ*, on the other hand, fix themselves by a fleshy stalk to any suitable object, from which they hang. Some of the larger marine animals are often chosen by them; and they frequently attach themselves in great numbers to the bottoms of wooden ships, which require to be periodically freed from such appendages. There was a curious belief in the Middle Ages that the bird known as the barnacle goose was born from hanging barnacles, and a common barnacle was named *Lepas anatifera* by Linnæus on this account. Old traditions of this description, when investigated without prejudice, almost always prove to contain some germ of truth; but it is difficult to imagine in what curious error the story of the barnacle goose could have originated.

Goose Barnacles (*Lepadidæ*).

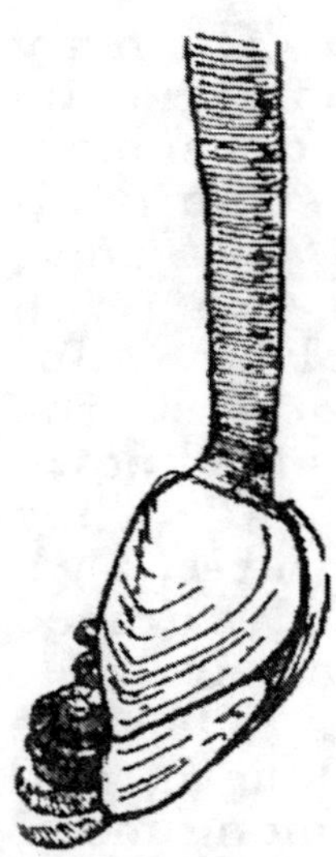

Fig. 7.—Goose Barnacle (*Lepas anatifera*). ½ Nat. size.

SUB-CLASS II.—MALACOSTRACA.

The *Malacostraca*, which include all the higher *Crustacea*, are normally composed of 20 segments; 13 segments, each bearing a pair of jointed appendages, composing the head and thorax; 6 abdominal segments, also frequently bearing jointed appendages; and a tail-piece. They have two antennæ, and two or four eyes. They differ very much in shape and appearance, but include nearly all the *Crustacea* which fall under ordinary observation.

ORDER I.—ARTHROSTRACA.

The *Arthrostraca* are small or moderate-sized *Crustacea*, with two compound eyes, which are not stalked. There are two pairs of antennæ, three pairs of jaws, and one pair of foot-jaws attached to the head. The thorax usually consists of seven segments (rarely less), each bearing a pair of legs. The abdomen likewise generally consists of six segments bearing legs, and a terminal segment, but is sometimes much modified and aborted.

The *Arthrostraca* are divided into two sub-orders, and these again into numerous families.

Sub-Order I.—Isopoda.

In the *Isopoda* the head is distinctly separated from the thorax. The body is broad, and somewhat arched, and there are usually 7 thoracic segments bearing legs; but the abdomen is short and often imperfectly developed, bearing lamellated gill-feet. In some families, such as the *Bopyridæ* and *Cymothoidæ*, which are parasitic on other *Crustacea*, or on fishes, the legs are armed with claws. But the most familiar family of the *Isopoda* is the *Oniscidæ*, which includes the creatures known as "wood-lice," "sows" or "sow-bugs." They are short, broad, brown scaly creatures, with conspicuous antennæ, and a body arched above, and flattish below. Some are able to roll themselves up into a ball. They are about half an inch or less in length, and are found in damp, dark places among moss, under the loose bark of trees, or in cellars. One large species, over an inch in length, *Lygia oceanica* (Linn.), is marine, and is met with running over rocks between tide marks. As I have already mentioned elsewhere, a specimen which was found running along a tow-rope in Dublin Harbour during the Colorado Beetle scare some years ago, was secured and announced in the papers as the dreaded Colorado Beetle just landing from America!

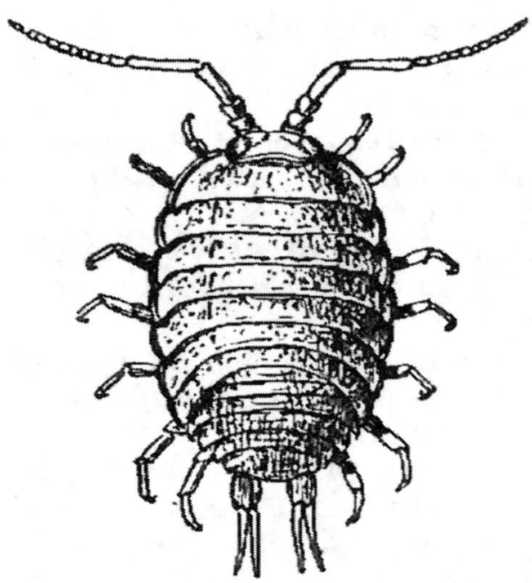

Fig. 8.—LYGIA OCEANICA. Nat. size.

Sub-Order II.—Amphipoda.

In the *Amphipoda*, the head and the first thoracic segment are fused together, and the body is laterally compressed, and strongly arched. There are always seven pairs of legs, and the abdomen and its appendages are also well developed in some families, the hinder segments bearing long legs adapted for leaping. This description applies best to the *Gammaridæ*, one or two of which, that live in fresh water, grow to the length of half an inch. The greater part of the *Amphipoda*, however, are marine, and differ considerably in size, shape, and habits. Some swim freely in the water, and others burrow into woodwork. Many are in the habit of attaching themselves to various marine animals; and one family, *Læmodipodidæ*, in which the abdomen is rudimentary, is truly parasitic. One curious genus, *Cyamus* (Lamarck), which is parasitic on whales, has strong hooked appendages at both ends of the body; and the species are known as Whale-Lice. We have figured *C. ovalis* (Roussel).

Fig. 9.—WHALE-LOUSE (*Cyamus ovalis*). Nat. size.

ORDER II.—THORACOSTRACA.

The present order agrees with the last in the number of segments, but is distinguished from it by having more or fewer of the thoracic segments united with the head by a common shell, or carapace, and there are usually two compound stalked eyes. We find no true parasites in this group, though some of them seek the society of other animals for the sake of food and shelter, as in the case of the small crab which takes up its residence in the shell of the *Pinna*.

Sub-Order I.—Cumacea.

Includes small marine species, with sessile eyes, and a long, slender abdomen.

Sub-Order II.—Stomatopoda.

This order is now restricted to the single family *Squillidæ*, which are marine *Crustacea* resembling large prawns, three inches or more in length, with the cephalothorax slender, a large tail-fin, and the second pair of foot-jaws developed into an enormous claw, which has led to one of the common species being called *Squilla mantis* (Rondel), on account of the shape and attitude of its legs very closely resembling the predaceous legs of the *Mantidæ* among the *Orthoptera*. This species swims strongly, and is eaten in Italy, where it attains a length of six inches; in the British seas it does not exceed $4\frac{1}{2}$ inches in length.

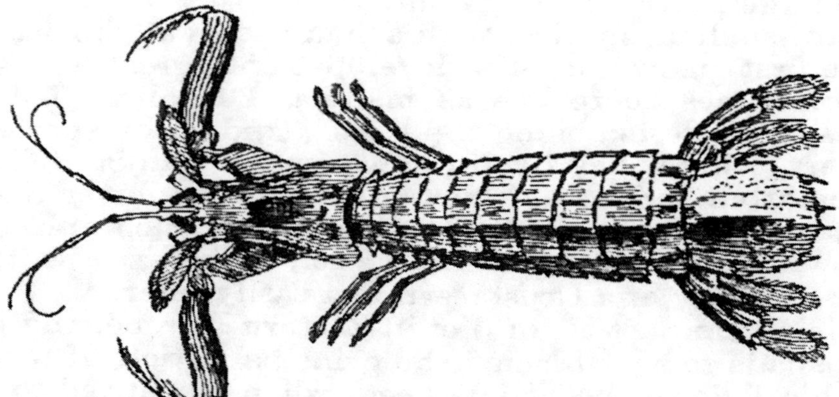

Fig. 10.—SQUILLA MANTIS. $\frac{1}{2}$ Nat. size.

Sub-Order III.—Schizopoda.

These are slender shrimp-like *Crustacea*, with a large soft shield covering the cephalothorax, and even part of the abdomen. The legs and gill-feet are bifid, and similarly formed. They swim in large shoals in the open sea, and are among the numerous surface-animals which form the food of whales.

ORDER III.—DECAPODA.

This extensive order is the most important among the *Crustacea*. The species which it includes have a hard calcareous shield, which generally covers the head and thoracic segments, as well as more or less of the abdomen. Under this shield lie the gills. There are two faceted stalked eyes, between which frequently projects a strong spine. They have usually three pairs of jaws, three pairs of thoracic gill-feet, and five pairs of walking legs, from which they derive their name. They may be divided into three sub-orders —the *Macrura*, or lobsters, prawns, and shrimps; the *Anomura*, or hermit crabs; and the *Brachyura*, or crabs.

Sub-Order I.—Macrura.

In the *Macrura* the abdomen is largely developed, and the first five (or more rarely, four) segments bear walking legs. There is a large flattened triple fin at the extremity of the abdomen, formed by the terminal segment, and a leaf-like appendage attached on each side to the one preceding.

Shrimps and Prawns.

The *Crangonidæ* are moderate-sized *Crustacea* with semi-transparent bodies, a thin horny carapace, the outer antennæ with a large moveable scale at the base, and sometimes a very strong ridged spine between the eyes. The first three pairs of legs are generally chelate (pincer-like). The species generally live in shoals in shallow water, near the shore, where they are captured by waders in specially-constructed nets. Most of the species are marine, such as the shrimps and prawns; some are found in fresh water lakes and rivers; and one or two blind species in caves. Some species, in which the skeleton is universally soft, inhabit the large shells of the *Pinna*.

Lobsters.

The *Astacidæ* are large hard-shelled species, with a small scale at the base of the outer antennæ. The first pair of legs is developed into great claws. The gills are numerous; sometimes there are as many as 20 pairs. They inhabit the sea, where they live in clefts among the rocks; and other species are found in lakes and rivers, where they live in holes in the banks. The two representative species of this family are the lobster and the river crayfish. Some years ago a detailed monograph on the crayfish was published by the late Prof. Huxley, to which those who wish to study the anatomy of a Crustacean can easily refer.

Crayfish.

The crayfish forms a very important article of diet in Eastern Europe, and is recorded in the Esthonian ballads to have formed the principal article of food of their mythical hero, the Kalevi poeg, when he retired to a hermitage on the banks of a river, after a disastrous war. He used a tall fir-tree torn up by the roots, as an angle, and baited it with the body of a dead mare. (See my "Hero of Esthonia," i., p. 140.)

Spiny Lobsters.

In the *Palinuridæ*, or Spiny Lobsters, the outer pair of antennæ are much thickened at the base, but are destitute of a scale. The legs are short and all end in simple claws; the abdomen is broad. These animals resemble lobsters in size and appearance, but the shell is very hard and spiny. They are numerous in the Mediterranean, but are not common in the colder seas of Northern Europe.

Sub-Order II.—Anomura.

This section is often included with the *Macrura*, but may conveniently be treated separately. The abdomen is more or less reduced; it is soft, and its appendages are rudimentary; the hinder legs are also frequently much reduced. The front pair of legs is armed with strong pincers, and the outer antennæ are long. The animals generally burrow in the sand, or live in the shells of molluscs. They are more abundant in warm countries than in cold.

The following are the two most interesting families:—

Robber Crabs.

In the *Birgidæ* the abdomen is hard above, and pouch-shaped at the extremity. The cephalothorax is broad, and angulated in front. The type of this family, *Birgus latro* (Herbst), is a very large Crustacean, measuring over two feet in length; it is of a blue colour. It is common in the Eastern Archipelago. It is amphibious, and is said to climb trees in search of cocoa-nuts, which it is strong enough to denude of the husk, when it contrives to force in the eye-hole, and to extract the contents with its pincers.

Hermit Crabs.

The *Paguridæ*, or Hermit Crabs, have a very soft abdomen, and take up their abode in empty univalve shells. Several common species inhabit our shores, and may often be seen ensconced in whelk-shells, etc., into which they retreat as far as possible on the least appearance of danger. In Tropical countries they grow to a much larger size; and some of them are land-animals, and inhabit land-shells, such as *Helix* and *Bulimus*.

Sub-Order III.—Brachyura.

This section includes the Crabs proper, in which the cephalothorax is short and broad; and the short abdomen, which has usually no tail-fin, and is narrow in the male and broad in the female, is curved under the cephalothorax. In the males there are one or two pairs of abdominal feet, and in the females five.

Fig. 11.—Spider Crab (*Maia Squinado*).

The *Porcellanidæ* are represented in England by one or two species, the commonest of which is the Porcelain Crab, *Porcellana platycheles* (Tennant), a polished flattened crab, of a reddish brown colour, with very large broad claws. It is nearly round, and about two inches in length; and is common under stones near low-water mark.

The Spider Crab, *Maia Squinado* (Linn.), is the representative of another family. (See *Fig.* 11.) It is a large oval crab sometimes measuring 8 inches in length and 6 inches in breadth. It is covered and margined with strong sharp spines, two of which project in front. It is an active sea-scavenger, and most of our readers will remember the amusing account in "Glaucus" of "Maia Squinado, Esq.," sitting at the bottom of the boat, twiddling his feelers. It creeps, but does not swim. The young form of the larva is represented on an earlier page (*Fig.* 1.) There are a great many other crabs, both British and foreign, differing very much in size, shape, and habits. Some are smooth, others rough, spiny, or hairy. Some are round, others oval. Many small crabs and some larger ones are common running over the sand, or among seaweed, or in rock-pools between tide-marks; others, like the large Edible Crab, *Cancer pagurus* (Linn.), are inhabitants of deep water, and some are good swimmers.

Among foreign crabs we may mention the genus *Pinnotheres* (Latr.), which lives in pairs, in large shells, such as *Pinna*, from which they derive their name. The land-crabs of tropical countries are large crabs which live almost entirely on land. They burrow in the ground, and are able to run with extraordinary swiftness. One genus, with very large claws, has been called *Gelasimus* (laughable) from the ridiculous appearance which it presents when chasing along brandishing its great claws, only one of which is fully developed, over its body.

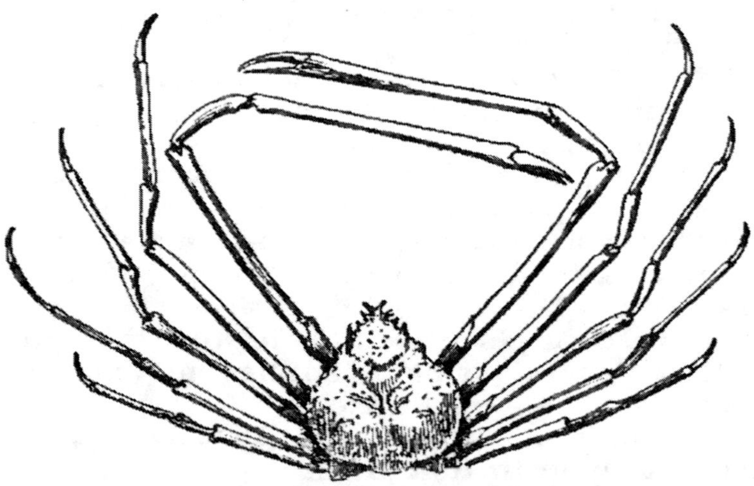

Fig 12.—GREAT JAPANESE CRAB. (*Macrocheira Kämpferi*).

One of the largest known *Crustacea* in expanse is *Macrocheira Kämpferi* (De Haan), a Japanese crab, not very remotely allied to the Spider Crabs, which has a compact, slightly oval body rather less than a foot long, but with enormously long, though comparatively slender legs, four or five feet in length. Two fine specimens may be seen in the public Insect Room at the Natural History Museum, South Kensington, where Crustacea are exhibited as well as Insects.

SUB-CLASS III.—GIGANTOSTRACA.

ORDER XIPHOSURA.—KING-CRABS.

IN the king-crabs, *Limulus* (Müller), the upper part of the body is covered by two great horny shields, the first covering the cephalothorax and curved backwards at a sharp angle on each side, and the second smaller, covering the abdomen, and set with several strong, sharp projections on the sides, pointing obliquely backwards. Beyond this is a sharp horny spine not jointed, and at least as long as the rest of the body. The antennæ, jaws, and gill-feet all resemble legs, and all terminate in pincers except the last pair. Two compound and two simple eyes are present. The legs are short, and are entirely covered by the shields. The few living species known are found in the East and West Indies, and on the East coast of North America, living in shallow water, or running over and burrowing in the sand. The species figured, *Limulus moluccanus* (Clusius), has larger spines than the others. The *Limulia* sometimes attain a length of two or three feet. They are the last survivors of a great group of Crustaceans, now only imperfectly known by their fossil remains. Three other orders, now wholly extinct, are referred to the *Gigantostraca:* the *Merostomata*, the *Hemiaspida* and the *Trilobita.* Some authors have recently proposed to regard *Limulus* as more nearly allied to the *Arachnida* than to the *Crustacea;* but its external resemblance to the latter is certainly far more obvious.

Fig. 13.—King-Crab (*Limulus moluccanus*). Reduced.

SUB-CLASS IV.—PYCNOGONIDA.

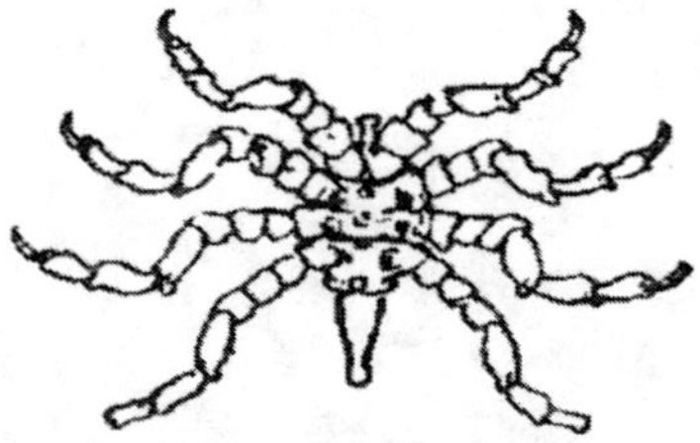

Fig. 14.—*Pycnogonum litorale*, Müller. Nat. size.

These are sluggish animals, found among seaweeds on the sea-shore, and somewhat intermediate between *Arachnida* and *Crustacea.* The front of the body consists of four well-marked segments, the first of which is formed of three fused together, each bearing a pair of long, jointed legs, and the abdomen is very small. They are provided with a long suctorial proboscis. In their young state, they are parasitic on *Hydractiniæ*, and are provided with three additional pairs of limbs, which was short or wanting in the adults.

CLASS II.—ARACHNIDA (SPIDERS, SCORPIONS, AND MITES).

This rather extensive group of animals is generally recognisable by a few salient characters. The head and thorax, instead of being separated, as in insects, are usually fused together into a single mass, called the cephalothorax; there are two pairs of jaws, one pair of which are sometimes regarded as modified antennæ; from two to twelve simple eyes, variously arranged in different species; and usually eight pairs of legs, all situated on the cephalothorax. The abdomen is without limbs, and is most frequently separated from the cephalothorax. The sexes are distinct, except in the *Tardigrada*. Most of the animals comprising this class are carnivorous; but among the mites, many feed on vegetable, as well as on animal substances; and some species are parasitic, and often subcutaneous, giving rise to, or accompanying various diseases, such as itch, mange, Plica Polonica, dysentery, etc., in man and beast. The *Arachnida* may be classed in three main divisions.

Order I.—Scorpionidea (Scorpions).

The scorpions are well known by their curved foot-jaws, cleft at the end like the claws of a crab, which they much resemble; and their long jointed tail ending in a sharp and venomous sting. They are generally of a black or yellow colour, and differ very much in shape and size, some being small and slender, and not more than a couple of inches in

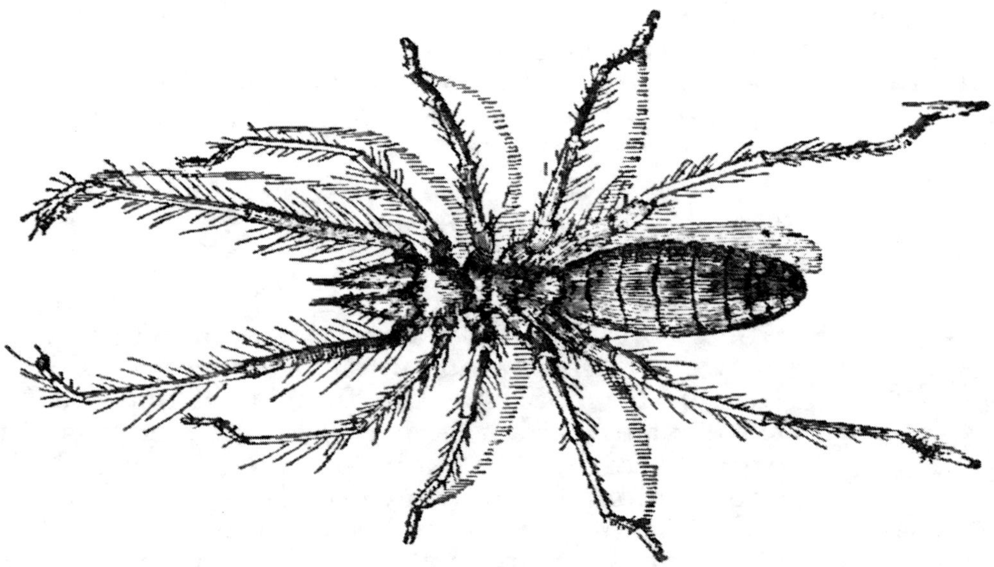

Fig. 15.—Galeodes arabs, Koch. ½ Nat. size.

length; and others being much shorter and thicker in proportion, and attaining to a length of 8 or 9 inches. They are not British, though several small species are met with in the South of Europe. They are found under stones, under the bark of trees, in holes in walls, etc., and are only active at night. The effects of the sting differ very much in different species, irrespective of size, as it appears. That of many species is probably not very much more severe than the sting of the wasp; but that of others is liable to cause great pain and suffering, and sometimes death. Scorpions are viviparous, and the young are carried about by the mother on her back for some time after birth. There is an old story, which has been recently revived, that when a scorpion is surrounded by a ring of fire, it will sting itself to death; and the same result is said to ensue if a drop of irritating fluid, such as whisky, is allowed to fall on its back.

ORDER II.—SOLPUGIDÆ.

These are large animals, resembling spiders, but with the head and thorax separated, and the abdomen segmented; the legs are very hairy. They are not numerous in species, and are chiefly found in warm countries. They inhabit sandy places, and although frequently called *Solifugæ*, the majority of the species are most active by day. One species is *Galeodes araneoides* (Pallas), which is common on the Lower Volga; it is about two inches long, and is much dreaded on account of its very painful bite. They hide themselves in the sand and among plants, from whence they rush upon their prey. They will sometimes kill lizards and birds, but their commonest food appears to be grasshoppers. They are sometimes very troublesome to camels by their bite. The North African species, which we have figured, *G. arabs* (Koch)—(*Fig.* 15)—is one of the largest known; it is of a yellowish colour.

ORDER III.—PSEUDOSCORPIONIDEA (BOOK-SCORPIONS)

These are small, but not microscopic, animals, with the abdomen united to the cephalothorax, but distinctly jointed, and with very long curving foot-jaws, cleft at the end. They resemble very small tail-less scorpions, and are frequently found among old books and papers, where they feed on mites and other small creatures. They are often seen clinging to the legs of flies, but rather, perhaps, as a convenient means of transport from place to place, than with the intention of preying on the flies themselves. The number of species is not very large; the typical genus is *Chelifer* (Latr.).

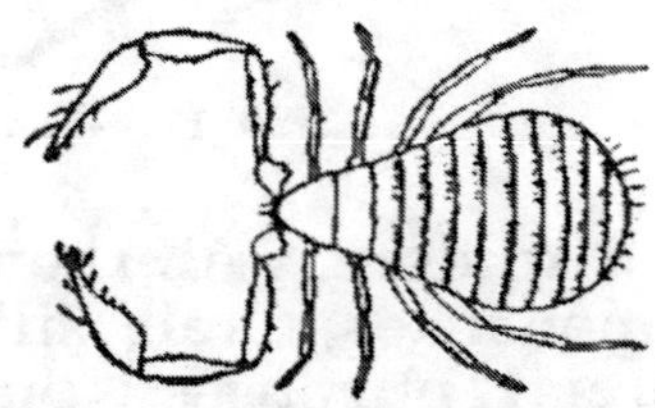

Fig. 16.—BOOK-SCORPION (*Chiridium musæorum*, Leach). Magnified.

ORDER IV.—PEDIPULPI (FALSE SCORPIONS).

These are large tropical creatures, an inch or more in length, resembling spiders, but with a jointed abdomen, large pincers like a scorpion, long hairy legs, of which the first pair are much longer and slenderer than the others, and no tail, or else a short one, not terminating in a sting. They are much dreaded by the natives of the countries in which they are found, but whether their claws are venomous does not seem to have been positively ascertained. The typical genus is *Phrynus* (Latr.).

ORDER V.—PHALANGIIDA (HARVEST-MEN).

These are small spider-like animals, with enormously long slender legs. The abdomen is segmented, there are no spinning glands, and the maxillary palpi end in a single claw, while the mandibles are jointed. They breathe by tracheæ. They feed on *Aphides* and other small insects by night. (See *Fig.* 17).

ORDER VI.—ARANEIDA (SPIDERS).

THE Araneida, or Spiders, are a very extensive group, with the usually unjointed abdomen well separated from the cephalothorax; strong mandibles; spinning glands; and breathing with lungs and tracheæ or with tracheæ alone. There is a variable number of eyes. They have been divided into many families differing much in habits. They are very ferocious, and will often kill and eat each other, but are much exposed to the attacks of birds and carnivorous insects, many sand-wasps provisioning their nests chiefly

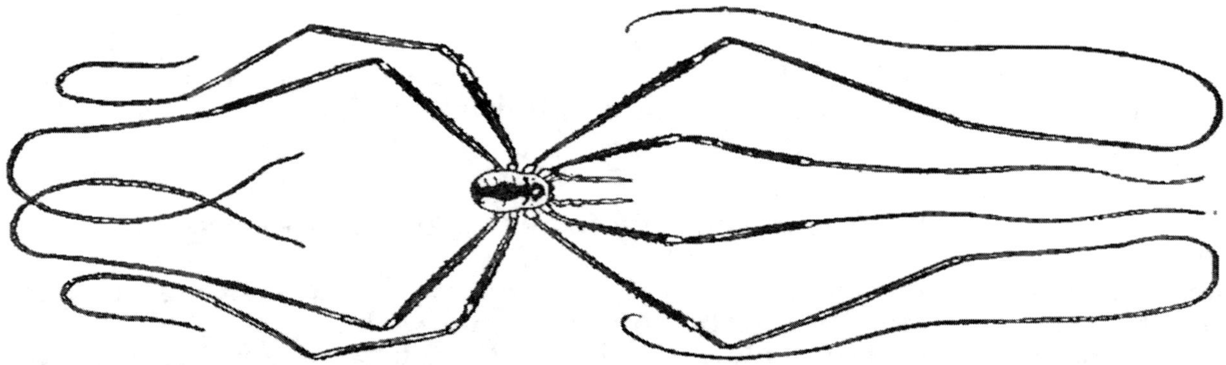

Fig 17.—HARVEST MAN (*Liobunum religiosum* Simon). Nat. size.

with spiders. As they cannot be domesticated, owing to their cannibalistic propensities, their silk cannot be collected in sufficient quantities for commercial purposes; but spider's web has been recommended as a useful application to stop bleeding. There are many kinds of spiders in various countries the bite of which is said to be dangerous to man.

FAMILY I.—THERAPHOSIDÆ.

This family is distinguished from all the remaining spiders by the possession of four lungs and only four spinnerets (except in *Atypus*, etc., which have six); the remaining spiders having only two lungs (or two lungs and sometimes two tracheæ also) and six spinnerets. These characters are sometimes used to separate the spiders into two main sections, the *Tetrapneumones*, including only the *Theraphosidæ* (formerly called *Mygalidæ*), and the *Dipneumones*, including the remaining spiders.

The *Theraphosidæ* are further remarkable for their large size, very hairy legs and bodies, and hard polished poison-fangs. Some of the larger species attain a length of from two to four inches, and spin a dense white web, in which birds as large as finches are sometimes entangled. This was first recorded by Madame Merian two centuries ago. It was doubted, but has since been confirmed by Bates in his "Naturalist on the Amazons," i. pp. 160-162; and by other observers. Bates further adds that the hairs of these large spiders are excessively irritating to the skin; and lastly, "Some Mygales are of immense size. One day I saw the children belonging to an Indian family who collected for me, with one of these monsters secured by a cord round

Bird-catching Spiders.

its waist, by which they were leading it about the house as they would a dog." The amount of valuable scientific and general information collected by Bates during his eleven years of travel on the Amazons was very extensive, and it is much to be regretted that though part was published in his book, and in various essays shortly after his return to England, a great deal must have died with him.

The *Theraphosidæ* also include smaller spiders, which construct nests in the ground provided with a round trap-door, which fits down over it in such a manner as to completely close and conceal it. Trap-door spiders are plentiful in many parts of the world, including South France; but our only British representative of the family, *Atypus sulzeri* (Latr.), constructs a tubular gallery in the ground, about half an inch in diameter, in which the female deposits her eggs, but which is not closed with a trap-door. The spider itself is about half an inch in length.

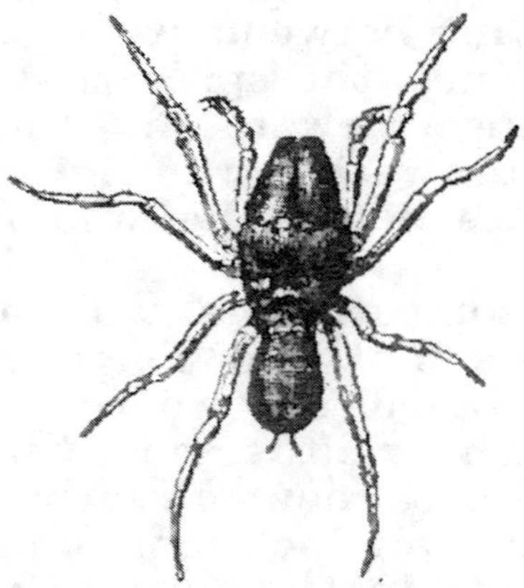

Fig. 18.—(*Atypus sulzeri.*) Twice nat. size.

Turning now to the remaining spiders, it will, perhaps, be sufficient to illustrate them by noticing a few of the more interesting and representative groups and species.

Hunting-Spiders.

The *Salticidæ*, or hunting-spiders do not construct a web, except as a resting-place at night or when moulting their skins, and as an egg-sac, but capture their prey by leaping on it, connecting themselves, however, with the spot they have quitted by drawing out a thread behind them as they leap. The cephalothorax is arched, and they have eight eyes. Their legs are rather short and stout. Several species, both British and foreign, resemble ants, a resemblance which is probably protective to themselves rather than designed to mask their approach from their prey.

The *Lycosidæ*, or wolf-spiders are similar in some of their habits to the last family, but generally pursue their prey by running, not by leaping. Their cephalothorax is arched, but narrowed in front. They have eight eyes arranged in three or four transverse rows, and their legs are long and hairy. The egg-pouch of the female is carried about with her attached to the end of her body till the young hatch, when they climb on her back. Some species carry their egg-sac in their mandibles.

Tarantula.

To this family belongs the famous spider *Lycosa tarentula* (Linnæus), the bite of which was supposed in Italy to produce a fit of melancholia, that could only be cured by the tune known as the Tarentella. The nests of some of these spiders are hardly less curious than those of the trap-door spiders; that of a North American species, *Lycosa arenicola* (Scudder), figured in Comstock's "Manual for the Study of Insects," p. 41, makes a structure resembling a high bird's-nest, or small turret, over the entrance to the tube. Some of the *Lycosidæ* frequent water, and are able to pursue their prey on or in it; and *Dolomedes fimbriatus* (Clerck) actually constructs a small raft on which it sails about.

The *Thomisidæ*, or crab-spiders, have small eyes arranged in two rows, and long sprawling legs, like those of a crab. Their colours are usually protective, being grey or brown in the case of tree-frequenting species, and green or yellow in the case of those which conceal themselves in flowers.

The *Uloboridæ* are an unimportant family in England; but Comstock quotes from Dr. Wilder the following curious account of the use of the triangular web of *Hyptiotes cavatus* (Hentz), a common species in the United States:—"Its web is most often found stretched between the twigs of a dead branch of pine or spruce. At first sight this web appears like the fragment of an orb web, but a little study will show that it is complete. . . . It consists of four plain lines corresponding to the radiating lines of an orb web, and a series of double cross lines. . . . From the points where the radiating lines meet, a strong line extends to one of the supporting twigs. Near this twig the spider rests, pulling the web tight so that there is some loose line between its legs. When an insect becomes entangled in one of the cross lines, the spider suddenly lets go the loose line, so that the whole web springs forward, and the insect is entangled in other threads. The spider then draws the web tight, and snaps it again. This may be repeated several times before the spider goes out upon the web after its prey."

Garden-Spiders.

The *Epeiridæ*, or garden-spiders, are large and handsome spiders, with a rounded abdomen, and moderately long hairy legs, the first pair longest. They have eight eyes irregularly arranged in two rows. They spin circular webs, and await their prey either near the centre of their web, or in a place of concealment close by. The commonest species, *Epeira diadema* (Clerck), is nearly an inch long, and has a green abdomen marked with white or yellow spots in the form of a cross. One North American species, *Argiope riparia* (Walckenaer), is recorded to make a large egg-sac, in which the young pass the winter; only those emerging from it in spring which have not been devoured by their fellows in the interval. Other species have the same curious cannibal habit.

The *Gastracanthidæ* are a very curious family of exotic spiders, with hard, horny, angular bodies, and sometimes with a long curved spine projecting on each side at the extremity of the abdomen. They are often of very varied colours. Many writers include them in the *Epeiridæ*. The species figured is *Gastracantha fornicata* (Fabr.). It is reddish (probably yellow when alive), with the head, thorax, and some round spots on the abdomen, blackish; and it inhabits Ceylon, Java, and Australia.

Fig. 19.—(*Gastracantha fornicata.*) Nat. size.

To the *Agelenidæ*, a large family in which the eyes are arranged in two curved transverse rows, belong our common house-spiders, which are too well-known to need description, and which spin their cobwebs wherever they are left for a day or two undisturbed. Another very interesting species is the water-spider, *Argyroneta aquatica* (Linn.), which dives beneath fresh water, enclosed in a shining bubble of air entangled in the hairs of its body, and constructs a silken subaqueous dome, which it fills with air like a diving-bell, in which it waits for prey, hibernates, and deposits its egg-cocoons.

To the allied family *Theridiidæ* belong several large and handsomely-coloured spiders found in Southern Europe, New Zealand, and elsewhere, which are much dreaded on account of their poisonous bite.

Order VII.—Acarina (Mites and Ticks).

This large order includes a great variety of creatures. Most of them are very minute, and many are almost microscopic. The cephalothorax and abdomen are fused together, the body forming a compact, rounded, or oval mass; the sexes are separate, and sometimes very different in appearance; the mouth is formed for biting or sucking, and there are nearly always eight legs in the perfect state, but often six only in the earlier stages. The *Phytopti* have usually only four. Many of the species are more or less bristly. Some feed on plants, and others on decaying animal and vegetable substances. A considerable number are parasitic.

The *Bdellidæ* are mites of a bright red colour, with a long snout, and long palpi, which are generally elbowed, and have the appearance of antennæ. Some are found among moss, and others on the sea-shore; while others, again, are parasitic on various insects. The number of eyes varies, and in some cave-frequenting species, the eyes are obsolete.

Insect-Mites (*Gamasidæ*).

The *Gamasidæ* are a family of mites, many of which are parasitic on insects, and others on warm-blooded animals. They are without eyes, the mandibles are pincer-like, and the legs are hairy, and furnished with two claws. The first or second pair of legs are frequently much thicker than the others; and the immature mites have only six legs. The species of *Gamasus* (Latr.) infest different kinds of insects, especially the black dung-beetles belonging to the genus *Geotrupes* (Fabr.), and its allies; and they are also numerous on humble-bees. They may often be found running over these insects; but there are other mites infesting beetles which are attached to their host by a thread; these belong to the genus *Uropoda* (Latr.). Other mites of this family attack warm-blooded animals, and are very numerous among poultry and caged birds, and sometimes become troublesome to man by transference.

Marine Mites (*Halacaridæ*).

The *Halacaridæ* are a small family of mites, living habitually under the sea, having either a stiff, or a more or less rigid, cuirassed skin, and with their legs springing from the inner margin of the body. They are found among sea-weeds in rock-pools, or are brought up, sometimes in large numbers, by the dredge. The body is oval, the snout more or less produced, and the palpi rather long.

Fresh-Water Mites (*Hydrachnidæ*).

The next family we have to consider is that of the *Hydrachnidæ*, or fresh-water mites. These are round, or, more rarely, oval, and are generally smooth and velvety, and of a red, black and red, or purple colour. Most of them have only six legs when immature. They have a hook at the extremity of the palpi, and are in the habit of attaching themselves to various water-animals.

Ticks (*Ixodidæ*).

The *Ixodidæ*, or ticks, are among the largest and most troublesome of the whole group. They are usually of an oval form, and have a tough skin, and a mouth fitted for sucking. Some are provided with eyes, and others are blind. They live on grass and herbage, and the usual habit of the female is to attach herself to any warm-blooded animal, pierce the skin, and suck the blood till she is gorged, when she falls off. They are sometimes very troublesome in summer and autumn, even in England; but in hot countries they are often a terrible pest, especially in the Southern States of America, and in some parts of South America, where they are particularly troublesome to cattle.

In Brazil they are said to have been introduced. This has been doubted; but it is not unlikely that a particularly troublesome species may be carried from one country to another, or introduced into districts in which it was previously unknown. For a tropical country, Jamaica is remarkably free from noxious creatures; and it is only of late years that ticks have multiplied in the island to such an extent as to make it highly unpleasant to venture among the herbage at all. This is attributed to the introduction of the mongoose, which was imported to destroy rats, and which is said to have carried the ticks over the whole island. The largest known ticks, which sometimes attain a length of nearly an inch, are those which are found occasionally upon the tortoise. *Argas persicus* (Fisch.) was said by travellers to produce fatal injuries by its attacks, and to abound so much in some parts of Persia as to lead to the abandonment of whole villages; but these reports are now believed to have been much exaggerated.

The *Oribatidæ* are dark-coloured, hard, shiny mites, found among moss and vegetable refuse; but when they are older, they feed on various small insects. The front of the body is often produced into a broad, triangular shape, and, as in many other mites, the palpi are frequently so largely developed as to resemble antennæ in appearance.

Gall-Mites (*Phytoptidæ*).

The *Phytoptidæ*, or gall mites, are an extremely large group, concerning which much has been written of late years. They are very long, microscopic mites, usually with only four legs visible at the anterior end of the body. They produce small galls on the leaves of various plants, sometimes conical, as on the lime trees, and sometimes rounded, as on the vine. These galls may be distinguished from insect-galls by having a small opening at the base.

Itch-Mites (*Sarcoptidæ*).

The *Sarcoptidæ*, or itch-mites, are a family of parasites which, not content with sucking blood, burrow under the skin of warm-blooded animals, causing, by their irritation, diseases known as the itch or mange. Various species have also been observed on patients suffering from Polish Plait (*Plica polonica*), and whether they actually cause this disease or not, they doubtless aggravate it. The itch-mites are round, with short, bristly legs, and most mammals seem to be more or less subject to their attacks. In birds, they frequently attack the feet. They are most active at night, and the troublesome itching they cause is consequently worst then. There are two principal forms of the disease in man, one common in most parts of the world, caused by *Sarcoptes scabiei* (Latr.), while the other, *S. scabiei-crustosæ* (Murray), which is far worse, is almost confined to Northern Europe. The itch has often been a great pest during the hardships of a campaign, and the survivors of Sir John Moore's force, in the Peninsular War, were greatly affected by it. Before the cause was discovered, it was regarded as a most formidable disease, and Dr. Russell informs us that in the last century it was more dreaded at Aleppo than the plague itself. But in recent years, the use of sulphur baths has proved to be an easy and efficacious method of getting rid of at least the milder forms of this complaint.

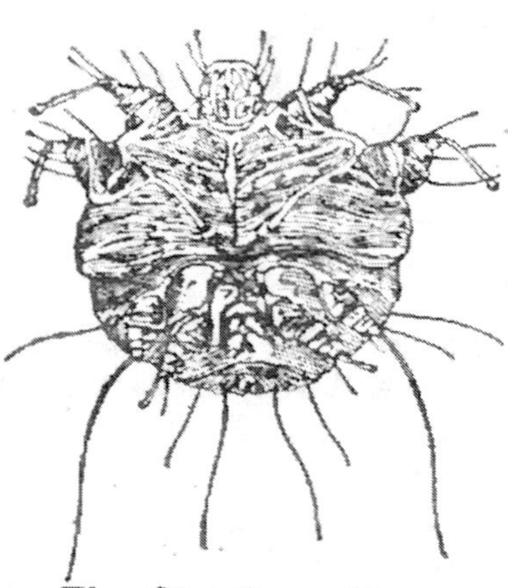

Fig. 20.—ITCH-MITE (*Sarcoptes scabiei*). Under-surface of male. Magnified.

Two other families of parasitic mites may be briefly mentioned. These are *Myobiidæ*, small, oval mites, not unlike lice in shape, which infest mice and other small mammals, and birds; and *Demodicidæ*, the few species of which are long, tapering, microscopic mites, infesting the hair-follicles of man and other animals. In man, the common *Demodex folliculorum* (Simon) often occurs on the face, where its presence is indicated externally by a black speck; but as it is a parasite of very small size and stationary habits, its presence does not cause anything like the same annoyance as that of *Sarcoptes scabiei*.

The *Trombidiidæ* are a family of brown, or bright scarlet mites, which are in the habit of attaching themselves to insects, to which they cling so tightly that they may often be seen in numbers attached to Museum specimens. They attack flies, sawflies, and other insects, but are most conspicuous when attached to the wings of dragonflies in more or less symmetrical rows. Some very large species, measuring nearly half an inch in length, are often found pinned in miscellaneous collections of insects, etc., from Africa and the East Indies.

"Red Spiders" (*Tetranychus*).

The *Tetranychidæ* are allied to the last family, but are plant-feeders. The two best known species are that great pest in hothouses, the "Red Spider" (*Tetranychus telarius*, Linn.), which, however, is not a spider, but a mite; and the harvest bug (*T. autumnalis*, Shaw), which burrows into the skin, causing great inconvenience; while in the case of allied tropical species, suppuration and ulceration may result in extreme cases. However, most of the species of this family are harmless, living on plants, or under stones, and not attacking animals.

Cheese-Mites, etc. (*Tyroglyphidæ*).

The last family we have to notice, the *Tyroglyphidæ*, includes several of the most typical mites, such as the cheese-mites and the sugar-mite. *Tyroglyphus siro* (Linn.), the commonest of the former, abounds in cheese, causing a kind of dry rot; and the dust from such a cheese, when placed under the microscope, generally proves to be full of mites. They are harmless when swallowed, nor do they attack the skin. Other mites, belonging to the genus *Cheyletus* (Latr.), with large claw-like palpi, feed on cheese-mites, etc. Very small mites, belonging to the genus *Tyroglyphus*, are among the most destructive pests in collections of insects. The sugar-mite (*T. sacchari*, Cameron), abounds in unrefined sugar, and is sometimes the cause of a complaint known as "grocer's itch." Now, however, almost all sugar brought into the market is more or less refined, and no longer liable to the attacks of mites. Most of the *Tyroglyphidæ* are harmless, some feeding on dried vegetable or animal substances, while others are carnivorous, feeding on insects; and others, again, are, or may accidentally become, parasitic. Cases of dysentery have sometimes been attributed to the presence in the intestines of mites belonging to this family, which had been accidentally swallowed.

ORDER VIII.—TARDIGRADA.

These are small mites found among moss and seaweed. The cephalothorax and abdomen are fused together; the body is broad, with four indistinct rings on the body. The sexes are not separate. The position of this group is still doubtful.

ORDER IX.—LINGUATULIDA.

These are worm-like parasites, with jointed bodies and separate sexes. They are curiously intermediate between parasitic worms and *Arthropoda*, but they are now referred to the *Arachnidæ* as an aberrant group. In their embryo state, they have two pairs of short, two-jointed legs, with two strong claws, and two hooks at the mouth. In their sexually mature condition, they have four hooks at the mouth, but no legs. They are met with in the encysted larval conditions in the lungs and liver of the horse, dog, wolf, hare, and rabbit, as well as in snakes, crocodiles, and fish ; and occasionally in man. In their mature form, they inhabit the frontal sinuses of the hare, rabbit, and horse.

CLASS III.—MYRIOPODA (CENTIPEDES AND MILLEPEDES).

THIS is the most worm-like class of the sub-kingdom *Annulosa* in the perfect state of the animals included under it. The head is well differentiated from the rest of the body, and is provided with one pair of antennæ, and three (more rarely, two) pairs of jaws. The thorax and abdomen are not differentiated, except into segments. They undergo a reversed and very imperfect metamorphosis compared to that of insects, for whereas insects begin with a worm-like body, sometimes provided with as many as twenty-two legs, and end with only six, the *Myriopoda* sometimes begin with only six legs, and continue to increase both in number of joints and number of legs, till they have reached their full growth, in which they are generally long and worm-like. Hence they are called *Myriapoda* or *Myriopoda* (either form of the word being equally correct); and they are sub-divided into two principal orders, the *Chilopoda* which are generally called centipedes or hundred-feet; and the *Chilognatha*, which are generally called millepedes or thousand-feet.

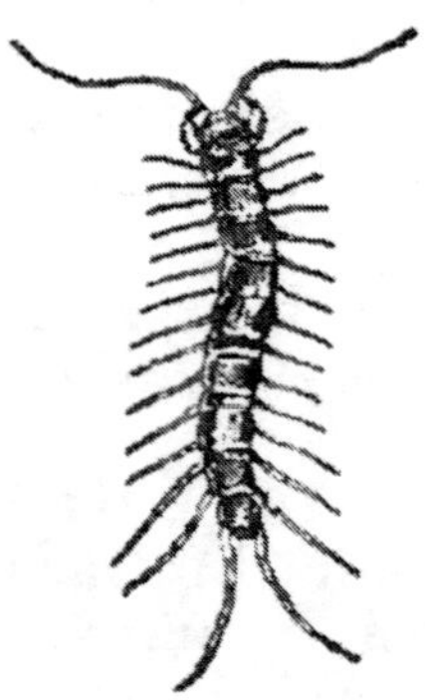

Fig. 21.—(*Lithobius forficatus.*) Nat. size.

ORDER CHILOPODA (CENTIPEDES).

The centipedes are carnivorous, and are provided with perforated foot-jaws, connected with a poison-gland. The body and jaws are generally rather flattened, and there is never more than a single pair of legs on each segment. The head is divided into two regions, provided with two pairs of maxillæ, behind which spring the great foot-jaws.

The *Scutigeridæ* are distinguished from the other families of *Chilopoda* by having the two pairs of mandibles united, and by the long antennæ, legs, and abdominal appendages, which has led to the common South European species being called *Scutigera araneoides* (Pall.), from its fancied resemblance to a spider. It is about an inch long, the antennæ being at least as long as the body, and the last pair of legs twice as long ; the other legs are comparatively short in front, but increase rapidly in length till they are nearly as long as the body. The proportions of the limbs, etc., however, vary considerably in different species; the legs are very brittle. These centipedes feed on insects, and are very active. Most of them are inhabitants of warm climates (the family is unrepresented in England), and the colour is usually greenish when alive, but is liable to change rapidly after death. They have only sixteen joints, and are provided with compound eyes instead of ocelli.

The *Lithobiidæ* are represented in Britain by *Lithobius forficatus* (Linn.), which has two clusters of ocelli, fifteen pairs of legs, increasing in length hindwards, and long antennæ, with more than forty joints. It is a repulsive-looking, reddish-brown creature about an inch long, with a comparatively broad body. It is very active in its movements, and feeds chiefly on worms; and is often unearthed by digging in garden-mould or in a dung-heap. (*Fig.* 21.)

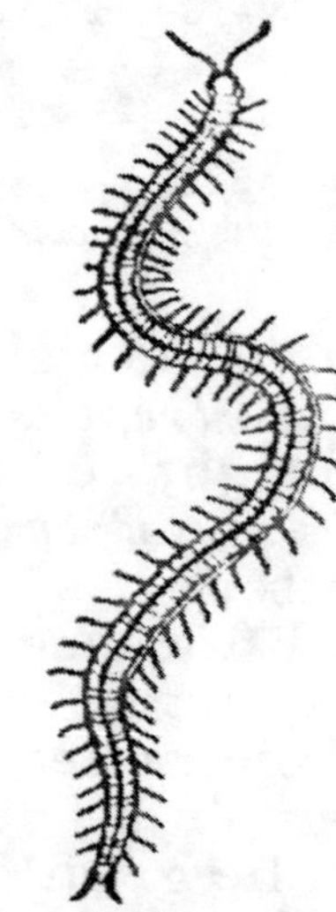

Fig. 22.—Electric Centipede (*Linotænia crassipes*, Koch.) Magnified.

The *Scolopendridæ* generally have four simple eyes on both sides, antennæ with about twenty joints, and usually twenty-one pairs of legs. The body is often very broad and flattened. The family is represented in South Europe, and the species are often of considerable size, sometimes measuring more than a foot in length. Their bite is as painful and dangerous as that of a scorpion, though they are sometimes used as an article of food by the natives of the countries where they are numerous. They are generally of a brown or reddish colour, or banded with green and yellow. In Britain we have only one small blind yellowish species of the family, *Cryptops hortensis* (Leach), which is harmless.

The *Geophilidæ* are very long slender centipedes, with fourteen-jointed antennæ, neither compound eyes nor ocelli, and from thirty-one to one hundred and seventy-three leg-bearing segments, each provided with a pair of rather short legs. They are nocturnal creatures, of a whitish or yellowish colour, and are remarkable for emitting a pale phosphorescence which has led to their being called electric centipedes. They are found in Britain as well as in warmer countries.

Order Chilognatha (Millepedes).

The millepedes are distinguished from the centipedes by their feeding chiefly on vegetable matters; and, consequently, they have imperforate foot-jaws, and are not venomous. Their bodies are generally convex above, and more or less flattened beneath; and while the first three segments behind the head, corresponding to the thorax in insects, bear only one pair of legs each, the remaining segments bear two pairs. The head of the millepede is composed of a single segment only. They vary much in size; and dead specimens become extremely brittle, the segments separating at the least touch.

The *Polyzoniidæ* are semi-cylindrical creatures, with small heads, and from 30 to 100 or more joints, and capable of rolling themselves up spirally. The mouth-parts are modified into a sucking proboscis. The best known species, *Polyzonium germanicum* (Brandt), is about two-fifths of an inch long.

The most familiar representatives of the millepedes in European countries are perhaps the *Julidæ*. They have a large head, and a long, cylindrical body composed of upwards of 30 segments, which can be rolled up spirally. They are either eyeless, or furnished with aggregations of ocelli. They are called snake-millepedes, and are very injurious in fields and gardens, feeding on roots and tubers, like wireworms. Our species are of small size, measuring from half an inch to nearly two inches in length, and are mostly of a dull bluish-black or lead colour. In tropical countries, some species grow to the length of a foot or more; and they are described as creeping about the branches of the trees in the damp African forests. Unlike the centipedes, the millepedes are very sluggish creatures, and move very slowly, notwithstanding their numerous legs. The species figured, *Spirostreptus pyrocephalus* (Koch), inhabits South Africa. It is black, with a bright red head, and is about four inches long.

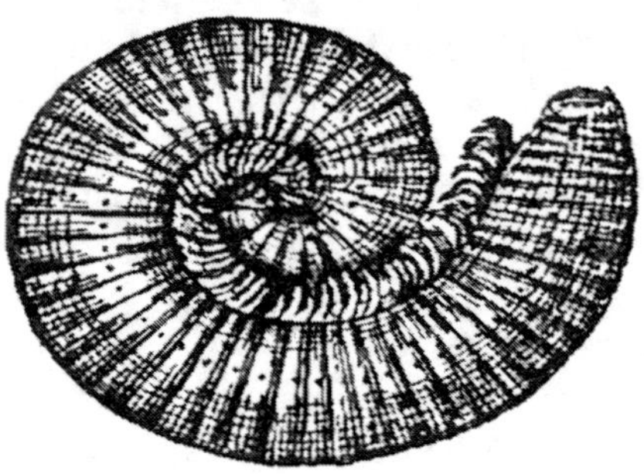

Fig. 23.—MILLEPEDE (*Spirostreptus pyrocephalus*, Koch.).

The *Polydesmidæ* much resemble the *Julidæ* in habits, but are more flattened, and the three single pairs of legs are placed on the second, fourth, and fifth segments, instead of on the second, third, and fourth. They are very hard, but very brittle. The British species are small; but some of the foreign ones attain to a considerable size. They are composed of about 20 segments. Some species belonging to this family have been met with in the great caves of Moravia and Carinthia. All are blind.

The *Polyxenidæ* are very small, whitish millepedes, not exceeding one-third of an inch in length in the largest species, and composed of only 9 or 10 segments. The head is well-marked, and they are provided with two clusters of ocelli. They are found under fallen leaves.

The *Glomeridæ* are composed of from 10 to 13 segments above, but each segment composed of four divisions below, an arrangement which enables the animal to roll itself up like a ball. They are short and broad, and much resemble wood-lice in shape, size, and appearance.

CLASS IV.—PROTRACHEATA.

THIS class includes the single family *Peripatidæ*, the typical genus being *Peripatus* (Guilding). The few known species resemble caterpillars in appearance; but have two rather long antennæ, and soft, cylindrical bodies, indistinctly divided into from 13 to 40 segments, each bearing a pair of imperfectly-jointed feet, armed with two small claws. They are viviparous, and are found under leaves and among rotten wood. The body is capable of great extension and retraction. When first discovered, they were supposed to be *Mollusca*, but were afterwards found to have more resemblance to the *Myriopoda*. There is a well-developed tracheal system, opening by inconspicuous stigmata placed irregularly over the body. The known species are found in South Africa, and in various parts of the West Indies and South America, as well as in Australia and New Zealand. *Peripatus iuliformis* (Guilding), from the Island of St. Vincent, is about two inches long. (See *Fig.* 24).

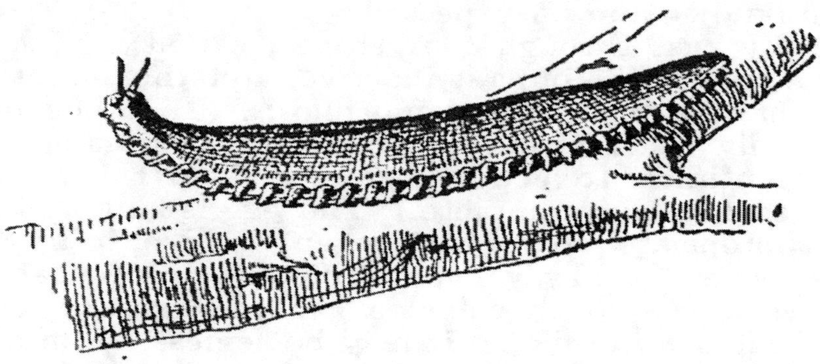

Fig. 24.—*Peripatus iuliformis* (Guild.).

CLASS V.—INSECTA.

Number of Species of Insects.

INSECTS are by far the most numerous class of animals which inhabit the globe at the present time. The actual number of species on our lists cannot be much less than 300,000; and many thousands of new species are described every year. In this country alone we have between 12,000 and 13,000 species, although our fauna is exceedingly poor, not only as compared with that of tropical countries, but even in comparison to that of Continental Europe. Only a few families and orders of insects are at all adequately known at present, and those only as existing in the best-explored countries. The late Professor Riley estimated the probable number of existing species of insects at possibly ten millions; and such estimates are generally far below the mark. The alternative estimate of two millions, which is put forward by some entomologists, seems to me to be ridiculously low, when we consider that the world has been so badly explored that we are not yet acquainted with a dozen species of *Phasmidæ*, or stick-insects, from Madagascar, an island which has been visited by many collectors, while the *Phasmidæ* are not a group of small and obscure insects, but one which includes many very handsome and conspicuous species, and to which belong the largest of all known insects.

To take another illustration, Mr. E. Ernest Green is now working at a monograph of the *Coccidæ*, or scale-insects, of Ceylon. Very few species were previously known from that island, and he will probably be easily able to multiply them at least by ten.

Nevertheless, insects, like the plants on which they feed, are becoming rapidly exterminated in nearly all parts of the world by cultivation, clearing of forests, drainage, etc.; and there is good reason to believe that a large proportion of the insects now existing will become extinct before they ever find a place in our museums at all. The extermination of small animals proceeds *pari passu* with that of larger ones; but is rarely noticed, as their existence is, for the most part, unknown and unsuspected.

Extermination of Species.

Insects generally pass through four stages, called egg, larva, pupa, and imago. In some orders, the pupa is inactive, and the insect is then said to have a perfect metamorphosis. In other orders, the pupa only differs from the larva by possessing wing-cases, and continues to feed as before. Then the metamorphoses are said to be incomplete. The egg is laid by the parent insect on or near the appropriate food of its progeny, which, in insects with perfect metamorphoses, is nearly always very different from that of the perfect insect. The larva is frequently called a grub, maggot, or caterpillar, and is generally more or less worm-like. It may be legless, or may possess several pairs of legs, as well as the six pairs analogous to those of the perfect insect. In insects with imperfect metamorphoses, the larva and pupa much resemble the perfect insect; and their food is frequently nearly similar. When insects reach their final stage, they generally acquire wings, and become capable of perpetuating their species. There are, however, numerous insects which never acquire wings; and in other cases the wings are undeveloped in one sex, generally the female.

Metamorphoses of Insects.

In the perfect state, an insect consists of a number of rings, called segments, or somites, agglutinated into three masses, called the head, thorax, and abdomen, which can generally be well distinguished. The head is considered to consist of a number of somites, just as the skull of vertebrate animals is thought to consist of a number of modified vertebræ. The head contains several of the most important organs of the senses, such as the compound facetted eyes on each side of the head; the antennæ, two long jointed organs, often feathered, or knobbed at the extremity, which are generally inserted in front between the eyes; the ocelli, stemmata, or simple eyes, of which there may be one, two, or three, on the crown of the head; and the mouth, which is either furnished with mandibles for biting, or a proboscis for sucking. There are also two pairs of jointed organs projecting in front of the mouth, called labial and maxillary palpi; but one or other pair is frequently wanting.

Head of Imago.

The three segments behind the head are called the thorax. Each of these bears one pair of legs beneath, and the second and third pairs bear the wings at the sides; for most insects have four wings and six legs in the perfect state. The legs are composed of several parts, called the coxæ, or hips; the trochanters, or hinge-joints; the femora, or thighs; the tibiæ, or shanks; and the tarsi, or feet. The tarsus is composed of five or fewer joints, known as the joints of the tarsi. The abdomen is composed normally of nine segments, exclusive of some smaller ones at the extremity in connection with the appendages of the generative system; but there are often fewer visible. Insects breathe by tracheæ, tubes which open by spiracles on the sides of the body. Many insects are furnished with stridulating organs in the abdomen, while others stridulate by means of various structures on their legs and wings; and in some insects the organs of hearing are situated on the legs.

Thorax.

The wings of insects are furnished with a ramifying system of tubes, called nervures. When the insect emerges from the pupa its wings are small and limp; but first fluid and then air is pumped through these tubes, and the wing quickly grows to its proper size and dries. These nervures differ much in arrangement in different insects, and are very useful in classification. The front of the wing is called the costa, the part nearest to the body the base, the part opposite to the body the hind margin or outer margin, and the part opposite the costa the inner margin. The extremity of the costa is called the tip, and that of the inner margin the hinder, or in the hind-wings the anal, angle. But these divisions shade imperceptibly into each other in insects with rounded wings. Between the bases of the fore-wings we sometimes find a triangular plate called the scutellum. The hind-wings are often smaller, rounder, and of a different consistency to the fore-wings, but when the fore-wings play the part of wing-cases, under which the hind-wings are folded, the latter are often much larger. Many insects possess the power of leaping, in which case the hind legs are often very long, or the coxæ and femora are much thickened.

Wings.

Insects are divided into several large orders, of which the following are the principal ones :—

I. Coleoptera (Beetles).—Insects with mandibles ; fore-wings (called elytra) horny or leathery; wings membranous, folded and doubled beneath them.

II. Orthoptera (Grasshoppers, etc.). — Insects with mandibles ; fore-wings (called tegmina) leathery; hind-wings folded fan-like beneath them.

Orders of Insects.

III. Neuroptera (Dragonflies, etc.).—Insects with mandibles (sometimes very imperfectly developed ; wings with many nervures ; membranous and naked, or clothed with hairs.

IV. Hymenoptera (Bees, Wasps, Ants, etc.).—Insects with mandibles, and often a proboscis ; wings membranous, rather small, with few nervures ; the fore and hind-wings often connected together by a series of little hooks.

V. Lepidoptera (Butterflies and Moths).—Insects with a sucking proboscis, and membranous wings clothed with scales.

VI. Hemiptera (Bugs and Froghoppers).—Insects with a sucking proboscis, fore-wings leathery or membranous (or membranous only at the tips) ; hindwings membranous.

VII. Diptera (Flies).—Insects with a sucking proboscis, and only one pair of membranous wings.

The first four orders are sometimes called *Insecta Mandibulata*, and the three last *Insecta Haustellata*.

Fuller characters for these orders will be given in their places. There are also some groups of insects (chiefly apterous) which will not fit very well into any of these orders, and which will be noticed separately.

Order Coleoptera (Beetles).

The *Coleoptera* are physically among the most highly organised insects, although they cannot compare with the *Hymenoptera* in intellectual development. They are distinguished by having four wings, the first pair of which, called elytra, are of a horny or leathery consistency, and when closed, form covers for the true wings, which are membranous, and are folded beneath them like a fan, but with the end doubled back. They undergo a perfect metamorphosis, the pupa being what is called necromorphous, or corpse-like, because, although inactive, it is not enclosed in a single tight-fitting integument, like that of a butterfly or moth, but is furnished with separate though immovable sheaths for the antennæ, legs, etc. The mouth of the perfect insect is mandibulate, or furnished with strong jaws or mandibles.

Number of Species.

Beetles are very numerous. We are probably at present acquainted with at least 150,000 species; and although they have been more carefully collected than most other orders of insects, there are, doubtless, enormous numbers which yet remain to be discovered. In Britain we have in round numbers about 3,000 species. They feed on all kinds of animal and vegetable substances on land, in the water, and on the seashore; but very few are parasitic on other insects. They vary in size from an almost invisible speck to six inches in length, or with expanded legs and antennæ much more. Many of the plant-feeding beetles, as the wire-worms, the chafers, the Colorado potato-beetle, the turnip-fly, etc., are extremely destructive to our crops; but the carnivorous beetles, such as the ground-beetles, the tortoise-beetles, the lady-birds, etc., are very useful in destroying other injurious insects; and the grubs of some of the large wood-feeding beetles are esteemed a great delicacy in some countries; indeed, it is far more probable that the Cossus of the Romans was the larva of some large Lamellicorn or Longicorn beetle than that it was the repulsive foul-smelling larva of the goat-moth, although Linné applied the name to the latter insect.

Classification.

In the classification of beetles, the structure of the antennæ, wing-cases and legs is of primary importance. The neuration of the wings, which is important in some orders of insects, is not much used in *Coleoptera*. It should, perhaps, be noted that the wings are sometimes wanting, when the elytra are sometimes free, and sometimes soldered together at the middle line where they meet, which is called the suture. Sometimes both wings and elytra are absent, either in both sexes, or in the female only, as in that of the glow-worm. In some beetles there is a triangular space, let in, as it were, between the bases of the elytra; this is called the scutellum. In some families the anal appendages are useful in classification, while in others the structure of these parts is so uniform that it is not worth noting in this connection. Ridges on the body or elytra are called carinæ, and circular pits (very conspicuous and numerous in some species) are called punctures.

The first large group of the beetles is that of the *Geodephaga*, or carnivorous ground-beetles, which are divided into two main families, the *Cicindelidæ*, or tiger-beetles, and the *Carabidæ*, or ground-beetles proper. They are hard-shelled oval beetles, with long slender legs and antennæ, and five-jointed tarsi on all the legs.

Tiger-Beetles.

The tiger-beetles have a small moveable hook at the end of the maxillæ, large heads, with very prominent eyes and strong jaws, and very long and slender legs and antennæ. The front tibiæ are not notched on the inner side. We have but one British genus, of which the green tiger-beetle, *Cicindela campestris* (Linn.), is the commonest species. It is found in sandy places, where its larva constructs a pitfall for other insects, very much resembling that formed by an ant-lion. The perfect insect is bright green, with white markings, and coppery legs and under-surface. It feeds on other insects, and runs and flies in the sun with great activity. Some of the foreign species are very handsome. Some genera frequent trees. We have figured a large green Chinese species, *C. Chinensis* (Linn.), with black and white markings.

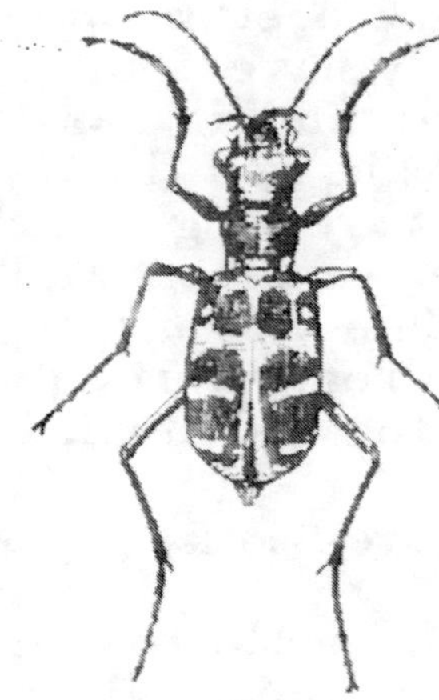

Fig. 25.—TIGER-BEETLE (*Cicindela Chinensis*, Linn.).

In the *Carabidæ* the legs and antennæ are less slender, the front tibiæ being sometimes flattened, and often furnished with a conspicuous notch on each side, and the head is smaller and eyes less prominent; the maxillæ have no moveable hook at the tip. They are much more nocturnal in their habits than the tiger-beetles, though many species may be met with by day. The species of the typical genus *Carabus* (Linn.) are rather large beetles, many of them measuring an inch or more in length. The elytra are well developed, and moveable, but the wings are absent. They are long beetles, of a black or bronzy colour, and some species are beautifully metallic. One of the most conspicuous of these is the golden-green *Carabus auratus* (Linn.), a common garden insect abroad, but rare in England, though it is not unfrequently imported with vegetables. Some of the smaller species of this group—genus *Bembidium*, (Latr.), etc.—are found in marshy places, though they are not quite aquatic in their habits.

Ground-Beetles.

We have figured *Zabrus gibbus*, a blackish insect half an inch long, with red legs and antennæ; which, contrary to the usual habit of the family, is destructive to growing corn, attacking the ears at night. The Bombardier beetles, belonging to the genus *Brachinus* (Weber), are reddish beetles, about one-third of an inch long, with blue-black elytra, much broader than the thorax. They lurk under stones, and when alarmed, discharge an acid fluid which volatilises into smoke with a slight explosion.

Fig. 26.—ZABRUS GIBBUS.

Among the foreign *Carabidæ* the most remarkable is the fiddler beetle *Mormolyce phyllodes* (Hagenbach), a reddish-brown beetle, about two inches in length, with very broad elytra. The shape of the beetle is really something like that of a fiddle. It is a native of Java.

The next group, the *Hydradephaga*, or water-beetles, have the two front pairs of legs near together, and the hinder pair more widely separated, and widened, flattened, and fringed with hair, so as to form a pair of oars. They are divided into two main families, the *Dytiscidæ* and the *Gyrinidæ*. The species of *Dytiscus* (Linn.) are large smooth or furrowed olive-brown beetles, an inch in length, and nearly half as broad. Their larvæ are long white grubs, with very strong jaws, and both the larvæ and the beetles are very voracious, destroying great numbers of water-animals, and are even very destructive to fish fry. The beetles quit the water at night and fly about, returning to the water for the day. Sometimes they will dash themselves against a pane of glass, mistaking it for water. There are numerous smaller species of this family, more variegated in their colours; but the *Gyrinidæ*, of which there are only a few species in England, are more likely to attract

Carnivorous Water-Beetles.

attention by their habit of spinning round in circles on the surface of the water, which has given them the name of whirligig beetles. They are blue-black beetles, about one-third of an inch long, with reddish legs and antennæ. They have four eyes (each eye being divided in two, an upper and a lower one), and it has been suggested that the upper eyes are intended for use in the air, and the lower ones for use below the surface of the water. The front legs are long and slender, but the two hinder pairs, as well as the antennæ, are very short and stout.

Rove-Beetles.

The *Brachelytra* are a very extensive family of beetles, distinguished by the very short square-cut elytra, which do not nearly reach to the extremity of the abdomen, but which cover the ample wings, which are folded beneath them. They are often called "Rove-Beetles," owing to some of the larger species, such as *Ocypus olens* (Linn.) being found running about in search of dung or carrion. The beetle to which we have referred is a black, foul-smelling beetle with strong jaws, which lifts up its head and tail when molested, and is known in many parts of the country by the name of the "Devil's Coach-Horse." In

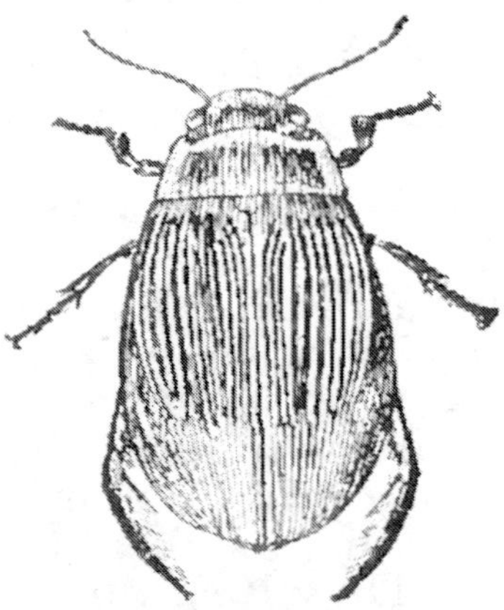

Fig. 27.—Dytiscus marginalis.

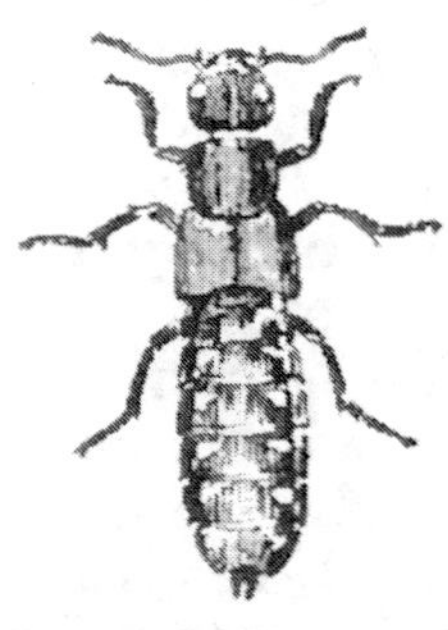

Fig. 28.—Staphylinus cæsareus.

Fig. 29.—Necrophorus vespillo.

Ireland it is regarded as a diabolical creature, which it is a meritorious action to kill. We have figured *Staphylinus cæsareus* (Cederh.), a black species with red legs and tegmina, and the thorax and segments of the abdomen partly bordered with silky yellow or golden pubescence. Most of the species of *Brachelytra* are much smaller than either of those just mentioned. Their habits are very varied. Many species may be found among moss or flowers, and others again live in ants' nests.

The next group, the *Necrophaga* or *Clavicornia*, is tolerably numerous in species, though less so than the last, and is chiefly distinguished by the conspicuous knobs at the end of the antennæ. Most of the species feed on decaying animal or vegetable substances (carrion, fungi, etc.), and some of those belonging to the genera *Dermestes* (Linn.), *Anthrenus* (Geoffr.), and their allies, are very destructive to hams, dried skins, etc. *Dermestes lardarius* (Linn.) —the "Bacon Beetle")—is black, banded with grey, and spotted with black; it is about a third of an inch long. The beetle and its hairy larva are too familiar objects to many housekeepers.

The burying beetles, which belong to this section, are larger insects, half an inch or more in length, and are black, with orange-red bands on the elytra. They are remarkable for their habit of interring the bodies of small animals, such as mice or birds, which they may find lying about, by scooping out the earth underneath, dragging and stamping them down, and covering them up. The females are buried with the carcase, on which they deposit their eggs, and then make their way back to the surface. We have figured *Necrophorus vespillo* (Linn.), one of the commonest species.

Burying-Beetles.

There is a group of beetles allied to, and sometimes included in, the *Necrophaga*, called, from their aquatic habits, the *Philhydrida*. The largest species, *Hydrous piceus* (Linn.), is a shining black beetle, longer, narrower, and more convex than the species of *Dytiscus*, from which its short-clubbed antennæ and much longer hind legs will at once distinguish it. It is sometimes called the great water-beetle.

Great Water-Beetle.

The *Lamellicornes* or chafers form a very interesting and important group of beetles, but are not very numerous in Europe. They are distinguished by the structure of their antennæ, which are short, and furnished at the extremity with a series of flat plates, which spread out like a fan. They feed on plants or dung, and some species are very destructive. They are stout, round, or oblong beetles of considerable size. Many of the species are black, but others exhibit much variety of colour. There are many large species among them, and they are frequently furnished with great horns, largest in the males, and often assuming very strange shapes, on different parts of the head and thorax.

Chafers.

The dung-beetles or *Scarabæidæ* (a name sometimes applied to all the *Lamellicornes*) are generally black and shining, though sometimes inclining to greenish or purple, especially beneath. They have strongly toothed and flattened legs for digging. Some species, like the Egyptian sacred beetle, form pellets of dung which they roll to a suitable place, and in this deposit their eggs. This insect, *Scarabæus sacer* (Linn.), is common throughout the Mediterranean region, and is black, with a broad flat head, with a vertical spine in the middle, and strongly dentated on the front curve. There are a number of species of more or less similar appearance and habits, several of which are represented on Egyptian monuments.

Dung-Beetles.

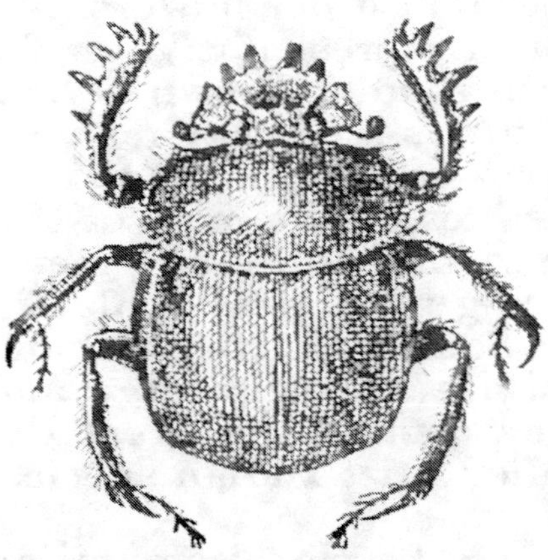

Fig. 30.—THE EGYPTIAN SACRED BEETLE (*Scarabæus sacer*, Linn.).

Our common black dung-beetles belong to the genus *Geotrupes* (Fabr)., and have a much smaller head than the sacred beetles. They fly in a straight line in the evening, as in the time of Shakespeare, who speaks of the "shardhorn beetle with his drowsy hum." They are frequently much infested with mites. The smaller dung-beetles of the genus *Aphodius* (Illiger) are more numerous in species, and more various in colour. They resemble very small cock-chafers in appearance, and may often be seen flying about dung in the sunshine.

The *Melolonthidæ* include the true cock-chafers, Our species, *Melolontha vulgaris* and *hippocastani* (Fabr.) are about an inch long, and are reddish-brown above, and black beneath, more or less clothed with whitish pubescence; the abdomen ends in a blunt projection. They are very destructive insects. The larva, which is called the white grub, lives in the ground for three years, feeding on the roots of plants; and the beetle feeds on the leaves of trees. A similar but smaller species, *Rhizotrogus solstitialis* (Linn.), is common in many places, flying round trees in the evening.

Cock-Chafers.

The *Dynastidæ* include the largest and most strangely-shaped of the *Lamellicornes*, but they are not British, though one or two species are found in the south of Europe. The larvæ feed, like those of the stag-beetles, in the wood of trees. The largest species are found in South America, the males of the Hercules beetle, *Dynastes hercules* (Linn.), and one or two other species, having a huge horn, nearly as long as the rest of the body, projecting from the front of the thorax, and curving downwards to meet a similar horn which projects from the front of the head, and curves upwards. It is black, with greenish-grey elytra, and is represented of half the natural size in the accompanying illustration.

Fig. 31.—HERCULES BEETLE (*Dynastes hercules*).

To the *Cetoniidæ* belong the great Goliath beetles of Africa, probably the bulkiest, but not the largest of all beetles. They are black, brown, or reddish, with longitudinal white bands on the thorax. Our most familiar representative of this family is the rose-chafer, *Cetonia aurata* (Linn.), the beautiful, round, green, white-spotted beetle which we so often find nestling in roses and other flowers.

Rose-Chafers.

The stag-beetle, *Lucanus cervus* (Linn.), is the typical representative of the important family of the *Lucanidæ*. It is black, with reddish-brown elytra, and the large males are often two inches long, having very large branching mandibles; in the females the mandibles are comparatively small. The mandibles of the male of this and other species of *Lucanidæ* vary very much in size and in development, but conform to certain recognised patterns, commencing with small males in which the mandibles are scarcely more developed than in the female, and proceeding to the largest males, in which the mandibles are very large and branched. However, our common stag-beetle never attains the great development of mandibles which is noticed in some allied East Indian species. As already mentioned, the larvæ feed in the wood of trees.

Stag-Beetles.

The *Serricornes* are another group of plant-feeding beetles, comprising (besides others) the two important families of *Buprestidæ* and *Elateridæ*. These are long and narrow beetles with hard integuments, and generally with more or less pectinated antennæ. The *Buprestidæ* have no power of leaping, but many of the foreign species are remarkable for their brilliant golden-green colour; and as they often measure nearly two inches in length they form very conspicuous objects in collections of foreign insects. The British species are not remarkable, but the larvæ of the next family, the *Elateridæ*, or click-beetles, are too well known to all agriculturists as wire-worms. The beetles are often found in corn, flowers, etc.; they are about half an inch long, and of various subdued colours. The hinder angles of the thorax are rather pointed, and on the under-surface there is a strong spine pointing backwards and fixed in a groove. If the insect is placed on its back it bends its body, and uses this apparatus to enable it to leap up with a clicking sound.

Click-Beetles and Wire-Worms.

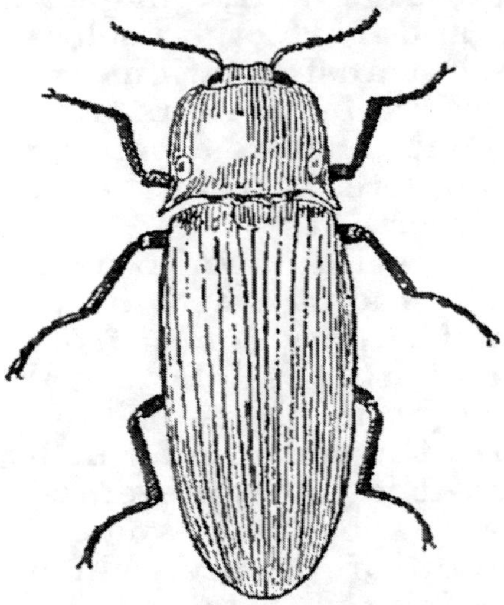

Fig. 32.—THE FIRE-FLY (*Pyrophorus noctilucus*, Linn).

Some of the larger foreign species of *Elateridæ* rival the *Buprestidæ* in size; but though sometimes green, rarely exhibit the same brilliant metallic colouring. However, some of the larger species are luminous, the species of *Pyrophorus*, (Ill.), being the well-known fire-flies of Mexico and the West Indies. Some of these emit two different-coloured lights from different parts of their body. Their body-colours are not conspicuous; the species figured, *Pyrophorus noctilucus* (Linn.), is brown.

Fire-Flies.

The *Malacodermi* are another group, in which the form is generally long and narrow, the integuments unusually soft, the elytra being leathery rather than horny, and the thorax often rounded above. They are active insects, and of carnivorous habits. The most interesting beetles of this section are the glow-worms, in which the females are apterous. In our common yellowish green glow-worm, *Lampyris noctiluca* (Linn.), both sexes of which are here figured, the female, which is apterous, is most luminous; and is frequently noticed shining like a spark on a grassy bank or under a hedge. An allied species is common on the Continent, and may be seen flying about in the evening like little sparks; but the Italian fire-fly, which is also a *Lampyris*, and which is not found north of the Alps, is far more brilliant.

Glow-Worms.

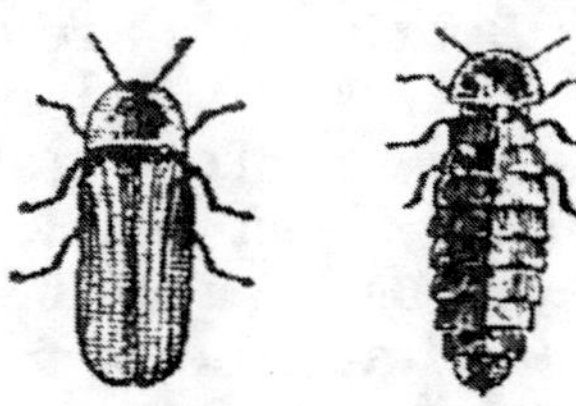

Fig. 33. *Fig.* 34.—GLOW-WORMS (*Lampyris noctiluca*, Linn.).

In almost all the beetles, which we have hitherto been considering, the tarsi are five-jointed on all the legs; but we now come to the large group of *Heteromera*, in which the two front pairs of legs have five-jointed tarsi, but there are only five joints to the hind tarsi. Another peculiarity of this group is that the antennæ are generally moniliform; that is, consisting of a series of rounded joints looking like a string of beads. They are generally of a black colour, and many of the species have much resemblance to the *Carabidæ*, from which either of the characters mentioned will at once distinguish them.

The *Heteromera*, though rather numerous, need not detain us very long, but we may mention three or four of the more interesting species. The cellar-beetles, which belong to the genus *Blaps*, are hard, wingless beetles nearly an inch long, with the body ending in a point, and of the colour of an unpolished boot. Black as they are, they are not the "black-beetles" of our housekeepers, this

Cellar-Beetles.

scientific term being reserved for the reddish-brown cockroaches, which do not agree with either the adjective or the noun.

Meal-Worms and Oil-Beetles.

Another beetle common in houses is *Tenebrio molitor* (Linn.), a narrow, dark brown beetle about half an inch in length, which is better known in its larval state as the meal-worm. Out of doors the oil-beetles, of the genus *Meloe* (Linn.), are familiar objects, and can hardly be mistaken for anything else. They are large, soft, sluggish, blue-black beetles, with short, soft, and perfectly useless elytra, and are found clinging to blades of grass. Their transformations are extremely remarkable, for they pass their early stages in bees' nests, and undergo two or three transformations into larvæ and pupæ before assuming the perfect state, which even then is sufficiently incomplete, as they never develop wings, except in the rudimentary form above described.

Blister-Beetles.

The blister-beetle, *Cantharis vesicatoria* (Linn.), is too well-known to need description. It is found in the south of England, but is too rare with us to be of any commercial value; the chief supply comes from Southern Europe. An ash tree loaded with these beautiful metallic green beetles is a splendid sight in the sunshine. *Mylabris* (Fabr.) is a rather large genus of *Heteromera*, the species of which are used for blistering purposes in some countries, but it is not represented in Britain. They are black beetles, with yellow or tawny spots and bands.

Weevils.

The *Rhynchophora*, or weevils, are a very large group of beetles, which may easily be distinguished by the apparently four-jointed tarsi on all the legs; by their very hard integuments, and by the structure of their head and antennæ. The head is produced into a long snout, towards the end of which the short, angulated, and generally clubbed antennæ project on each side. Most of our British species are of small size; but among the foreign beetles we find the large and beautiful metallic green diamond-beetles, and the palm-weevil of the West Indies, a large reddish-brown beetle an inch and a half long, the wood-feeding grub of which is considered a great delicacy. The nut-weevil, *Balaninus nucum* (Linn.), is a small brown beetle, with the elytra varied with grey. It is about $\frac{3}{8}$ of an inch in length, and is represented somewhat above natural size in the accompanying wood-cut. It exhibits the peculiar structure of the rostrum and antennæ very typically. The *Scolytidæ* have the head less prolonged than usual among the weevils, and are extremely destructive to trees, eating galleries through the wood in all directions.

Diamond-Beetles.

Fig. 35.—The Nut-Weevil (*Balaninus nucum*, Linn.).

Long-Horned Beetles.

The *Longicornes*, or long-horned beetles, are an extensive group, with apparently four-jointed tarsi, long slender antennæ, often as long and sometimes many times longer than the body; not clubbed at the extremity, but with a long and thick basal joint. The eyes are generally more or less constricted in the middle, at least on one side, and are sometimes completely divided, as in the *Gyrinidæ*. They are generally insects of large size with long bodies, and their larvæ feed in the wood of trees. They are very numerous in warm climates; but most of our British species are either of small size, or are scarce. Others, which are not considered indigenous, are frequently imported into England with timber. One of the commonest and most beautiful of our larger species is the musk-beetle *Aromia moschata* (Linn.), which is common in most parts of the country, and is often found resting on the trunks of willows, in which the larvæ feed, in the daytime. It exhales a strong but agreeable odour, contrary to the habit of most other beetles, many of which discharge an extremely offensive liquid when touched. It is of a bright green colour, and often exceeds an inch in length.

This species belongs to the *Cerambycidæ*, the typical family of the *Longicornes*; but the largest and bulkiest species belong to the *Prionidæ*, which are brown or reddish-brown beetles frequently three inches long. Our single native species, *Prionus coriarius* (Linn.), is rather scarce. It is about the length of the musk-beetle, but much stouter, and of a brown colour. We have figured both sexes of *Acanthocinus ædilis* (Linn.), which has longer antennæ in the male than any other British species. It is rather scarce with us, being found chiefly at Rannoch, in Scotland, in the pine forests. It is reddish-brown with grey pubescence, and four yellowish spots on the thorax. It belongs to the family of the *Lamiidæ*, which is distinguished by the large head, and almost vertical face.

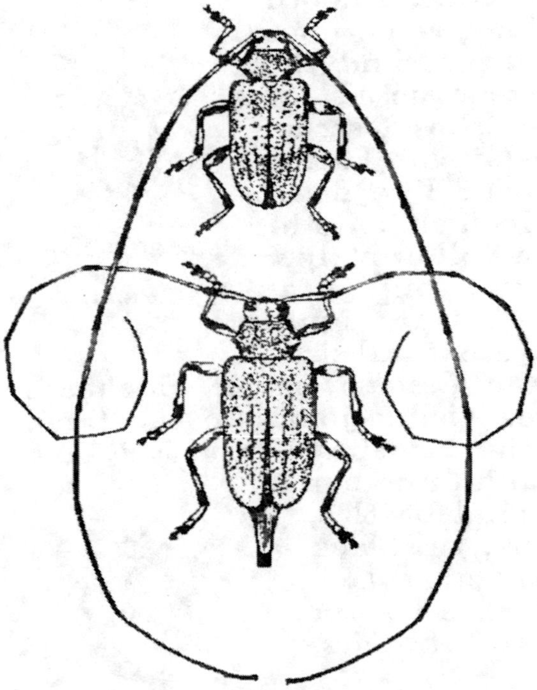

Figs. 36, 37.—*Acanthocinus ædilis*, Linn.

Plant-Feeding Beetles.

The last group of the beetles with apparently four joints to the tarsi is that of the *Phytophaga*, or plant-feeding beetles *par excellence*. They are round or oval beetles, of small or moderate size, and of various colours, many being of a brilliant green. The antennæ are generally rather short, and not elbowed, or set on a rostrum, and this alone will generally distinguish them from the beetles of the two preceding groups.

Colorado Potato-Beetle.

This group includes several very injurious species, among others the Colorado potato-beetle, and the turnip-beetles. The Colorado Potato-beetle, *Leptinotarsa decemlineata* (Say), is a native of the Western States of America. It is about half an inch long, and of a yellowish colour, with eighteen black spots on the thorax, and ten black stripes on the wing-cases; the larva is red, spotted with black. Our figure is somewhat above natural size. Some years ago this beetle began to spread eastwards from its haunts in the Rocky Mountains, where it used to feed on a wild species of potato; and to attack the cultivated plant. It soon spread over the whole of the United States, and there is no efficient way of arresting its ravages but by the free use of "Paris Green," a dangerous compound of arsenic. Great fears were expressed lest it should spread to Europe, and special measures were taken by all the principal Governments to guard against its invasion. Nevertheless, in addition to a few isolated instances of its occurrence in various countries, a whole colony was dis-

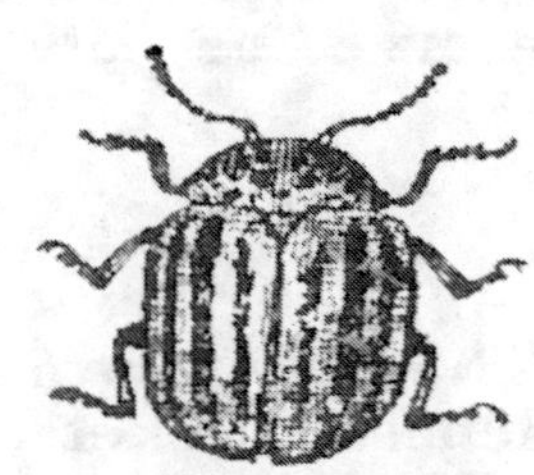

Fig. 38.—COLORADO BEETLE (*Leptinotarsa decemlineata*, Say).

covered many miles from the sea-coast in some potato fields at Mülheim-on-Rhine, nearly opposite Cologne. The fields were at once ploughed up, drenched with petroleum and burned over; and the pest was fortunately stamped out. The scare has now subsided, but it is all the more necessary for us to be prepared to take equally prompt and energetic measures if the Colorado beetle should happen to make its appearance among us, as is always possible enough, perhaps at some out-of-the-way place where it is least expected.

Among the largest and most conspicuous of the foreign species of this group are the species of the genus *Sagra* (Fabr.), which are found in the East Indies and Africa. They are long, smooth beetles, of a brilliant green colour, sometimes varied with coppery red, or purple, and the hind femora are of very large size, being constructed for leaping. These beetles are an inch long, but the destructive turnip-beetles, belonging to the genus *Phyllotreta* (Latr.), have also thickened hind femora, and skip about like fleas. They are oval, and less than a quarter of an inch in length. The elytra are bronzy black, and marked with a yellow stripe. They are often called "Turnip Flies," but turnip flea-beetles would be a more appropriate term. Our figure of *Phyllotreta nemorum* (Linn.) is somewhat above natural size.

Turnip-Beetles.

Fig. 39.—Phyllotreta nemorum.

The last of the great group of beetles are the *Pseudotrimera*, which are small species, distinguished by having only three visible joints to the tarsi. The best known of these are the lady-birds (*Coccinellidæ*), of which there are a considerable number in England. They are small round beetles, and the elytra are mostly red with black spots, or black with red or yellow spots. The head and thorax are black with white markings. They are very useful insects, for they are carnivorous, and destroy large numbers of *Aphides*, or plant-lice.

Lady-Birds.

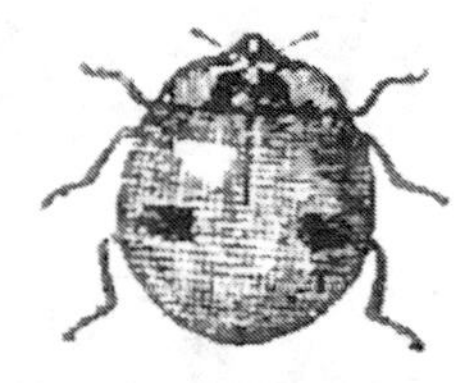

Fig. 40.—LADY-BIRD (*Coccinella bipunctata*).

We have figured the typical form of one of the commonest species, *Coccinella bipunctata* (Linn.), slightly magnified. It is very variable, and the elytra are sometimes almost black, instead of being red, with a black spot on each, as in our figure.

Other families of this group are the *Trichopterygidæ*, the smallest of all beetles, and if we except some of the egg-parasites among the *Hymenoptera*, almost the smallest insects known. They are little black beetles, with long, slender, clubbed antennæ, and are found among decaying vegetable refuse.

Other species belonging to the *Pseudotrimera* are found in fungi, and others, again, inhabit ants' nests, where, it has been suggested, they may be preserved as pets.

ORDER ORTHOPTERA (CRICKETS, LOCUSTS, ETC.).

The Order *Orthoptera*, or straight-winged insects, includes the earwigs, cockroaches, crickets, grasshoppers, locusts, etc. These are all insects with strong jaws, instead of a proboscis, and differ from the other mandibulate orders by the fore-wings (which are called in *Orthoptera* not elytra, but tegmina) being generally of a different consistency to the others throughout, and leathery, rather than horny, as in the *Coleoptera*. They also differ from the *Coleoptera* in the hind-wings being folded lengthwise, and not doubled back at the tips, except in the earwigs and cockroaches, which some authors consider to form two separate orders, distinct from the *Orthoptera*.

Metamorphoses.

In the *Orthoptera* the metamorphosis is incomplete, there being no inactive pupa-state. The larva resembles the perfect insect, except in size, and in the absence of wings. During the period which elapses between the last two moults, the insect possesses short wing cases which enclose the undeveloped wings, and this stage is considered to correspond to the pupa-state of insects with complete metamorphoses. The insect is, however, as active and voracious as in the larva state, and is frequently termed a "nymph" by those who restrict the term "pupa" to insects with complete metamorphoses. In the perfect insect the antennæ are usually slender, with well-marked joints, and are sometimes of great length.

Habits.

The bulk of the *Orthoptera* are plant-feeding insects, but the *Mantidæ*, or praying insects, are carnivorous, and the earwigs and cockroaches will eat decaying animal as well as vegetable substances. This order contains no parasitic insects, and scarcely any which are *directly* harmful to man, but the *economic* injury occasionally caused by locusts in many countries probably far exceeds that due to the ravages of all other insects put together. These insects are generally voracious in all their stages after leaving the egg.

The *Orthoptera* are one of the least numerous orders of insects in species, though most abundant in individuals, and are very poorly represented in cold countries. In England we have only about sixty species, including casual visitors, and introduced species.

Earwigs (*Forficulidæ*).

The *Forficulidæ*, or earwigs, much resemble the *Staphylinidæ* among the *Coleoptera*, and were actually included in the *Coleoptera* by Linnæus. Their tegmina are very short, and the large transparent wings are folded beneath them, so as to be quite invisible when closed, except the projecting tips of the opaque part of the costa, which are of about the same colour and consistency as the tegmina. At the end of the body there is always a peculiar appendage like a forceps, which is more developed in the male than in the female, and which is said to be used for folding and unfolding the wings. Many species, however, are apterous, and others, though provided with ample wings, are never seen to fly, though they may possibly use them only in the darkness of night; others, however (chiefly small species) fly about by day. They are fond of concealing themselves in any sort of crevice, and some flowers, such as dahlias and sunflowers, are greatly infested by them. They have sometimes been known to creep into the human ear, and there is no doubt that their popular name has originated in this manner. They are generally dull reddish-brown, unattractive-looking insects, though one or two East Indian species are of a rich purple. They measure from half an inch to rather over an inch in length; the antennæ are generally of moderate length, and the legs are short. We have figured a brown apterous species, which has been introduced into most parts of the world, and is occasionally found in England.

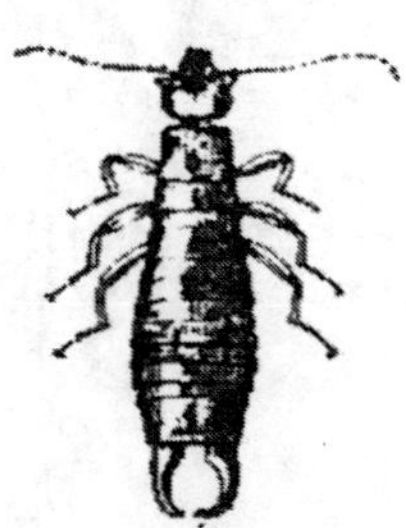

Fig. 41.—EARWIG (*Anisolabis maritima*).

The *Blattidæ*, or cockroaches, are another very isolated group. These are oval insects, generally more or less flat, with a round or oval thorax, under which the small head is often quite hidden. The antennæ are slender, and moderately long, and the legs are very spiny. Many species are apterous, at least in the females; but the majority are winged, the wing-cases being of a parchment-like consistency, and generally more or less overlapping; the wings are transparent. They are nocturnal insects, feeding chiefly on decaying vegetable matter; but many are carnivorous, our domestic species being particularly fond of bed-bugs. The eggs are deposited in a capsule, and the female may often be seen running about with the capsule projecting from her body. They are nearly always of dull colours, such as grey, reddish-brown, or black. Three species commonly infest our houses, all of which appear to have been imported insects, like most of our household pests. The first and smallest of these is *Phyllodromia germanica* (Linn.), a pale brown, winged insect, about half an inch long. It is sometimes found in bakeries. The female is said to open the egg-case to allow of the escape of the young. In America, where it is much commoner than with us, it is called the croton bug, and is said to frequent the neighbourhood of water-pipes. Our common cockroach, *Blatta orientalis* (Linn.), a reddish-brown insect, with fully developed wings in the male, but only rudimentary wings in the female, is generally called "the black beetle," though it is neither black nor a beetle. Another species, *Periplaneta americana* (Fabr.), which is winged in both sexes, is redder; the thorax is yellowish-grey, with a large black mark in the centre; it expands nearly two inches across the wings, and is not uncommon in warehouses. Cockroaches of various species abound on board ship; and apart from one or two small indigenous species (found not in houses, but in woods and fields), many others, besides those which we have mentioned, may be met with in the docks, and elsewhere, some of which may perhaps succeed in establishing themselves in this country. Even specimens belonging to the genus *Blaberus* (Serville), which includes the great broad-winged species called "drummers" in the West Indies, have been met with occasionally. These are yellowish-grey, with a large black mark on the middle of the thorax, and measure at least three inches across the wings; but the largest of all the cockroaches belong to the genus *Megaloblatta* (Dohrn), found in Mexico and South America. They have longer and narrower wings in

Cockroaches (*Blattidæ*).

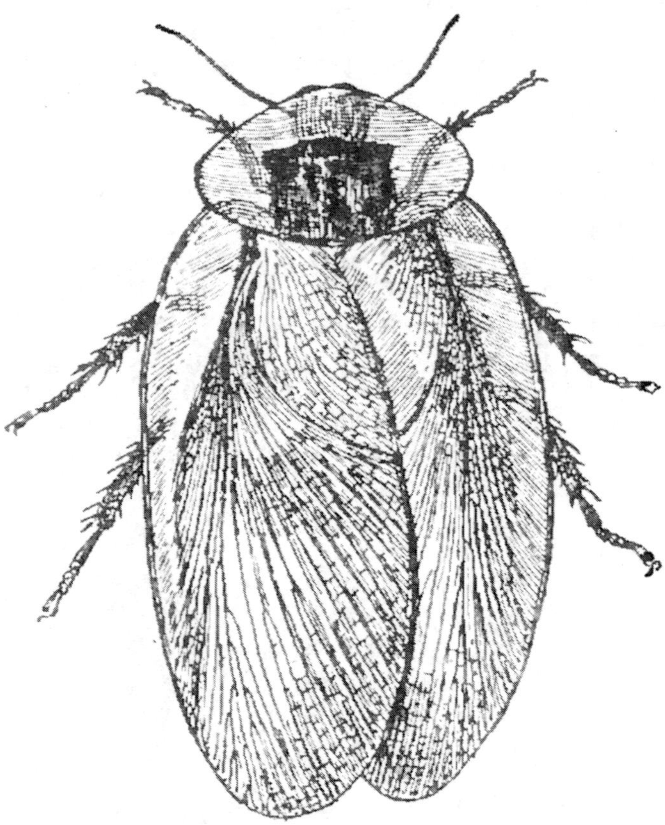

Fig. 42.—DRUMMER COCKROACH (*Blaberus giganteus*, Linn.).

proportion than *Blaberus*, measuring fully six inches in expanse, and are of a dark reddish-brown colour.

The late Mr. H. N. Moseley, in his "Notes of a Naturalist on the *Challenger*" (pp. 592, 593), gives the following amusing account of the cockroaches on board ship :—"The first cockroaches apparently came on board at St. Vincent, Cape Verdes, for a large one of these insects was caught by one of the lieutenants on his bed soon after we left that port. Cockroaches soon became plentiful on board, and showed themselves whenever the ship was in a warm climate. A special haunt of a swarm of them was behind the books in the chemical laboratory, from which Mr. Buchanan in vain attempted to evict them. At one period of the voyage, a number of these insects established themselves in my cabin, and devoured parts of my boots, nibbling off all the margins of leather projecting beyond the seams on the upper leather. One huge winged cockroach baffled me in my attempts to get rid of him for a long time. I could not discover his retreat. At night he came out and rested on my book-shelf at the foot of my bed, swaying his antennæ to and fro, and watching me closely. If I reached out my hand from bed to get a stick, or raised my book to throw it at him, he dropped at once on the deck, and was forthwith out of harm's way. He bothered me much, because, when my light was out, he had a familiar habit of coming to sip the moisture from my face and lips, which was decidedly unpleasant, and awoke me often from a doze. I believe it was with this object that he watched me before I went to sleep. I often had a shot at him with a book or other missile as he sat on the book-shelf ; but he always dodged and escaped. His quickness and agility astonished me. At last I triumphed, by adopting the advice of Captain Maclean, and shooting him with a pellet of paper from my air-gun, a mode of attack for which he was evidently unprepared ; but I was taken to task for discharging the air-gun in my cabin, because it made a noise just like the sharp crack of a spar when broken by the force of the breeze, and created some excitement on the upper deck, where the sound was plainly heard."

Cockroaches on the *Challenger*.

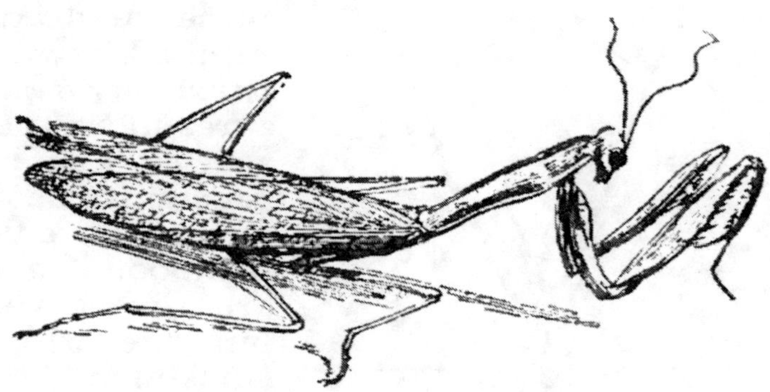

Fig. 43.—Mantis religiosa.

Turning now to the more typical *Orthoptera*, we commence with the *Mantidæ* or praying insects, which are not British, though one or two species are common in Southern Europe. They are generally green, yellow, or brown (very rarely blue), with ample wings, which are generally transparent; the tegmina are likewise broad, and are opaque, at least along the costa. They are usually insects with long slender bodies and slender legs ; the front pair of legs, however, is large and strong, and the lower surface of the tibia is furnished with a row of very strong curved spines, which close against the femora, which are also sometimes denticulated or knobbed. They are carnivorous and very predatory insects, and usually sit with the forepart of the body and the fore-legs raised on the watch for prey. This position has caused them to be looked upon with superstitious reverence ; and it was said that if

Praying Insects (*Mantidæ*).

children had lost their way they had only to ask a Mantis, which would immediately extend one of its front legs in the desired direction. Some idea of their real propensities, however, may be gathered from the following anecdote: A male and female Mantis were once observed courting, when the female suddenly chopped off the head of her mate and devoured it. This incident was followed by their union, after which the female devoured the body of her unfortunate partner. But it should be mentioned that in most insects (subject, however, to exceptions) the female is much larger and, as a rule, less brightly coloured than the male. We have figured a green European species of Mantis. (*Fig.* 43.)

Stick Insects (*Phasmidæ*).

The *Phasmidæ* are another group of *Orthoptera*, which are wholly unrepresented in England, though a few small species belonging to the typical genus *Phasma* (Illiger) are found on the northern shores of the Mediterranean. These are apterous insects, about two or three inches long, and with short antennæ, though the generic name is frequently misapplied to a South American genus with long antennæ, and large, brightly-coloured wings. The *Phasmidæ*, or stick insects, have long slender legs and bodies, and are exclusively vegetable feeders. Although the legs are spiny in many species, they are not raptorial, as in the *Mantidæ*. A great number of species are apterous, and of a brown or yellowish colour, perfectly resembling pieces of dead stick in appearance. The largest insect known is a species from Borneo, *Phryganistria serratipes* (Gray), the female of which measures more than a foot in length. Other apterous species, about nine inches long, and half an inch broad, are flattened rather than rounded, and are of a green colour, perfectly resembling shoots of bamboo. In the winged *Phasmidæ* the tegmina are always very short, and frequently scale-like; but the wings are often very ample, and are thickened along the costal area, which really answers the purpose of tegmina in protecting the delicate fan-like wings. Many of the Australian *Phasmidæ* measure six or seven inches in expanse, and are most beautiful insects, with large pink, blue, or green wings. There is a smaller green species in the Pacific Islands, *Lopaphus cocophages* (Newp.), about five inches long, which is extremely destructive to the cocoanut trees. It has odd little rudimentary red wings not more than an inch long; and shares with other species of *Phasmidæ* the habit of ejecting a disagreeable fluid when alarmed. This particular insect is said to be able to shoot it a distance of five feet, and the fluid is so acrid that it is liable to cause blindness if it reaches the eyes.

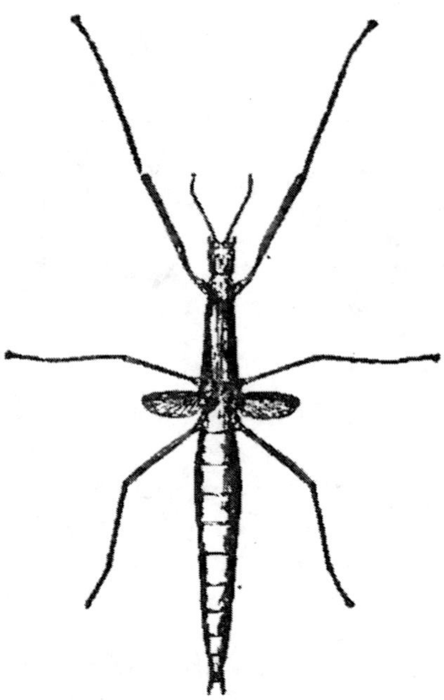

Fig. 44.—Stick Insect *Lopaphus cocophages*). $\frac{1}{3}$ Nat. size.

Crickets (*Gryllidæ*).

The next family, the *Gryllidæ*, or crickets, agrees with the remaining groups in having the hind femora much thickened, and adapted for leaping. The antennæ are long and slender, the tegmina rest flat on the back, and are frequently curved downwards at the sides, but are never roof-like, and the head is large and vertical, with prominent eyes. The legs are generally strongly spined, and the ovipositor of the female is short and straight. In the male the tegmina are differently formed from the female, exhibiting a bare space covered by strong veins, which are roughened beneath like a file, so as to produce a chirping sound when the tegmina are rubbed over one another. The females are mute, as in most other Orthopterous insects.

We have three conspicuous kinds of crickets in this country, of which the best known is the pale brown house-cricket, *Gryllus domesticus* (Linn.). It is very similar in its habits to the cockroach, but is a much less disgusting insect, both in appearance, and because it does not possess the foul odour of the cockroach. It is, however, a destructive insect, and is very fond of moisture; and this is the reason why it sometimes eats holes in wet clothes left hanging at the fire to dry during the night; though I have sometimes heard that "it was out of spite against the maid, who was in the habit of killing them." Many persons have a superstitious dislike to injure crickets; and I lately heard of an attack of toothache being attributed to the murder of a cricket. The field-cricket, *Acheta campestris* (Linn.), is rather larger and stouter than the house-cricket, and is of a nearly black colour, except the tegmina, which are brown. It is a very destructive insect, feeding on the roots of plants; but has become exterminated by cultivation, and is now very rare in England, though it and several other closely-allied species are abundant in most parts of the world. The mole-cricket, *Curtilla gryllotalpa* (Linn.), is a brown insect two inches long, which represents a small section of crickets in which the front legs are very broad and flat, resembling those of a mole, and are used for burrowing in a similar manner. It does much mischief by destroying the roots of plants, and is a common insect, though seldom seen above ground.

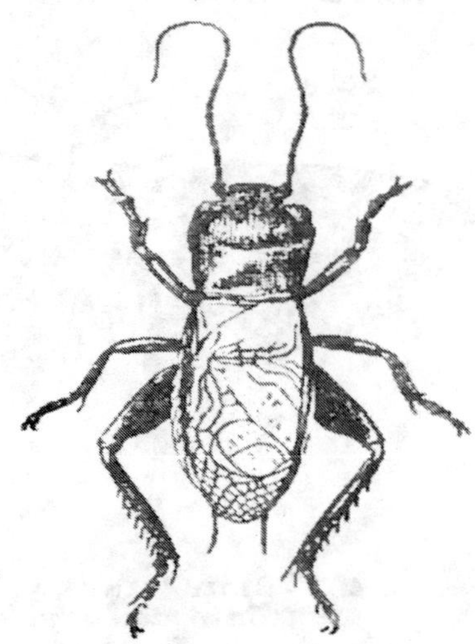

Fig. 45.—FIELD-CRICKET (*Acheta campestris*).

Long-Horned Grasshoppers (*Phasgonuridæ.*)

The *Phasgonuridæ*, or long-horned grasshoppers, are a large group divided into numerous sub-families, which resemble the crickets in many respects, having large heads which frequently slope inwards and downwards, and long or very long antennæ. The tegmina, however, are generally roof-like, and the colour is most frequently green, though sometimes brown. The ovipositor of the female is long, compressed, and curved upwards at the end. The legs are generally less strongly spined than in the crickets. The typical species of this family is known as the Great Green Grasshopper, and is not uncommon in the south of England, where it can easily be recognised by its large size (three inches or more in expanse of wing), bright green colour, very long antennæ, and in the female its long ovipositor. Some of the North American species of this family are called "Katydids." their chirping having been read into the words, "Katy did, Katy did, Katy didn't, she did, she didn't," and so on.

Some insects belonging to foreign sub-families of this group are of very large size, measuring six or eight inches in expanse ; and some are remarkable for their broad flattened thorax, or for their disproportionately long hind legs. Others, which are found in the deserts of Africa, are bulky apterous insects, on the large fore-legs of which the curious auditory organs which many Orthopterous insects possess in this odd situation are very conspicuous, opening either in a large oval depression, or in a mere slit.

The last family of the *Orthoptera*, the *Locustidæ*, which comprises the true locusts and grasshoppers, may be distinguished at once by the short antennæ.

Locusts and Grasshoppers (*Locustidæ*).

The ovipositor is inconspicuous, and the hind legs are long and slender, the hind tibiæ being generally furnished with a double row of spines above. Our common grasshoppers leap rather than fly, but the locusts, some of which visit us occasionally, though they probably never breed here, are very strong on the wing. The body and tegmina are generally brown, but the wings are often red, blue or green. The most destructive species in Asia and Africa are about five or six inches in expanse; but the largest South American locusts measure nearly a foot across the tegmina. In some of the earlier sub-families, the antennæ are very broad and flattened, but in the more typical species they are cylindrical. These chiefly inhabit the warmer parts of Asia and Africa. Destructive locusts are not always large; for instance, those which ravage Cyprus and the United States are small species, not expanding more than a couple of inches across the wings. Species of about the same size, with blue and red wings, are common on the Continent, in pine forests, and vineyards, etc.; and the blue-winged grasshopper, *Œdipoda cœrulescens* (Linn.), is said to be sometimes found in England.

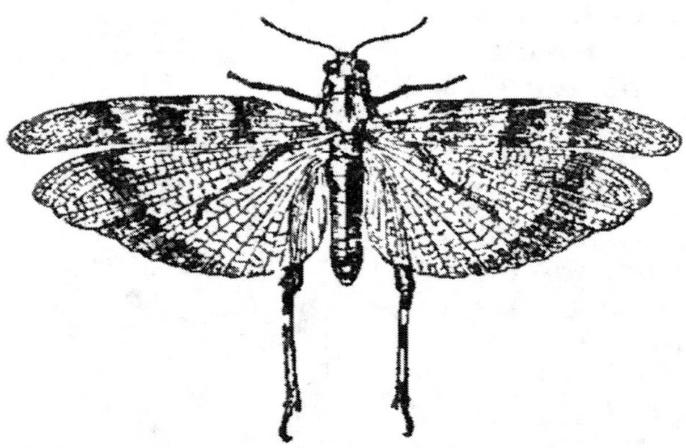

Fig. 46.—Blue-winged Grasshopper (*Œdipoda cœrulescens*).

Locusts are equally destructive in all their stages after quitting the egg, for the young locusts can leap, though not fly, and they advance across the country in vast hordes in this manner, before they acquire their wings, and they have no quiescent pupa stage. No one can form any conception of the meaning of an invasion of locusts who has not actually seen one; and at present, schemes are in progress for checking their ravages in Natal by the use of specially constructed guns and mortars, in addition to other means. In America and Australia the term "locust" is frequently but improperly applied to the *Cicadidæ*, which belong to quite a different order of insects.

Order Neuroptera (Lace-winged Insects).

Linnæus applied the term *Neuroptera*, or Nerve-wings, to an Order including a number of conspicuous insects of rather large size. They have strong jaws, four wings, similar in texture, and generally covered with a network of very numerous nervures; incomplete metamorphoses, and carnivorous habits.

Several very discordant groups are included under the term *Neuroptera*; and although we have treated of the *Trichoptera*, *Mallophaga*, *Thysanura*, and *Collembola* separately, many groups besides these are regarded by some authors as forming distinct orders.

Although the size and importance of the dragonflies indicate them as the true types of the Linnean *Neuroptera*, yet they have sometimes been united with the *Orthoptera* under the absurd term *Pseudo-neuroptera*. But the dissimilarity of their wings is quite sufficient to preclude their being classed in the same order as the *Orthoptera*; while if they were, the name *Orthoptera* would have to be abolished, being of post-Linnean date, and its contents transferred to the *Neuroptera*. The dragonflies are frequently called *Odonata*.

Dragonflies (*Odonata*).

They are generally slender-bodied insects, with long, moderately broad wings, and a large head, the greater part of which, however, is occupied by the two large compound eyes. Their wings are generally colourless, but in some species are very brightly coloured, in whole, or in part, with iridescent purple, blue, green, or scarlet. The commonest pattern, where any exists, and which reappears in several distinct families, is a broad purplish-brown band across the middle of both pairs of wings. They are predaceous insects in all their stages. The larva and pupa are brown, and live in fresh water; the pupæ can be distinguished by their conspicuous wing-cases. When the pupa is matured, it leaves the water, climbing up a reed, or some other convenient support, and then splits down the back, to allow of the emergence of the perfect insect.

Metamorphoses.

The neuration in some of these insects is often very complicated, the network forming many thousands of cells in each wing in some species, while others exhibit comparatively few nervures. They are divided into several families and sub-families, of which we will notice two or three. In the *Libellulidæ*, the triangular (or more rarely, quadrilateral) space near the base of the wing, from which several of the principal longitudinal nervures of the wings start, is differently shaped in the fore and hind wings, and the eyes are contiguous, but rarely united by a long suture. This family takes in the greater part of the moderate-sized dragonflies with rather stout bodies, the commonest of which, *Libellula depressa* (Linn.), which may often be seen flying over water, has transparent wings three inches in expanse, and a flattened and rather short and broad body, which is blue in the male, and yellow in the female. We have figured a common South American species of this family, *Trithemis umbrata*, (Linn.). The *Gomphidæ* resembles the *Libellulidæ*, but the eyes are distinctly

Family *Libellulidæ*.

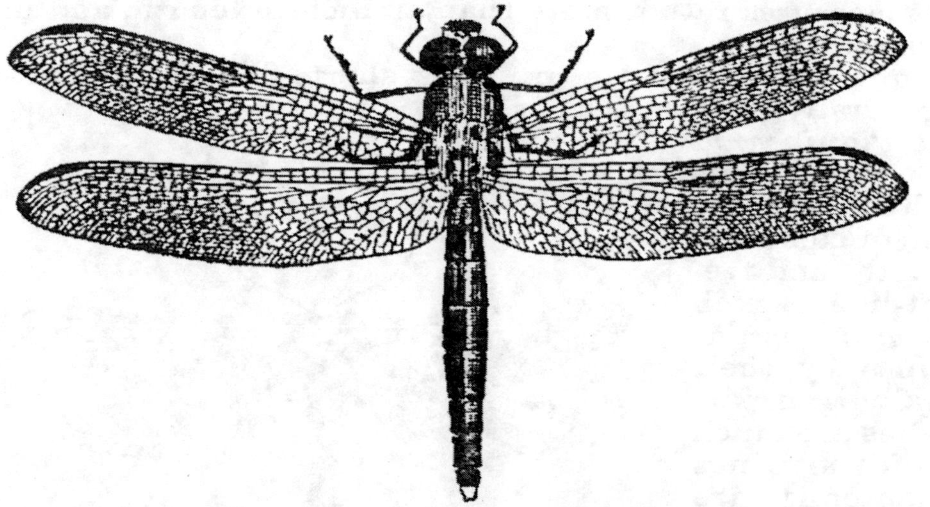

Fig. 47.—DRAGONFLY (*Trithemis umbrata*). Nat. size.

separated. The *Æschnidæ*, which perhaps attract more notice than any other dragonflies, measure three or four inches in length, and also across the wings, and have a long narrow triangle, crossed by several nervures, on each wing, shaped nearly alike on all the wings, and very large eyes, which are contiguous, being only separated by a small suture on the top of the head. The wings are transparent, tinged with brown in one species; and the bodies are elegantly marked with blue, green, and yellow, on a brown or black ground; but these colours generally fade in a short time after death.

Family *Æschnidæ*.

The *Agrionidæ* have slender bodies, small and inconspicuous triangles on the wings, and wide heads, with the eyes far apart; in fact their heads are something like those of the hammer-headed shark on a small scale. Some of the larger European species, measuring upwards of two inches across, have beautifully coloured wings, and frequently blue or green bodies. Two species are common in England, one with purplish wings, and the other with a purplish band, resembling our figure 47, but with a longer and more slender body Some of the foreign species are far more brilliantly coloured, the common Indian *Neurobasis chinensis* (Linn.) having bright green or blue hind wings Several of the American species of *Hetærina* (De Selys), and allied genera, are transparent, with a bright scarlet patch at the base of the wings, which are otherwise transparent. Our two British species of *Agrion*, already mentioned, are fond of flying over ponds or slowly-flowing streams. These coloured species belong to the family *Agrioninæ*, and have more cross-nervures on the costa before the middle of the wing than the other sub-family *Cœnagrioninæ*, in which there are only two. The latter sub-family includes a considerable variety of species, all slender, but among them are the largest and the smallest dragonflies known. The largest are South American species, six or seven inches in length and expanse, with long transparent wings, tipped with black or yellow; the smallest are the little slender-bodied, transparent-winged dragonflies which are so abundant among reeds and rushes. The type of this sub-family is *Cœnagrion puella* (Linn.), which has a long body prettily marked with blue and black. It measures rather more than an inch in length, and in the expanse of its transparent wings.

Family *Agrionidæ*.

In all the true dragonflies the antennæ are very short, filiform, and inconspicuous, and are generally only three-jointed; but in the *Planipennia* we meet with insects in which the antennæ are often of considerable length, and frequently clubbed. The ant-lions, which belong to the family *Myrmeleonidæ*, much resemble dragonflies by their long, narrow, and generally transparent wings, but their bodies are much shorter, the neuration of the wings is dissimilar, and the antennæ are short and clubbed. The ant-lions are not British, though several species are found in Southern Europe; their larvæ have strong jaws, and hide themselves at the bottom of pitfalls,

Ant-Lions (*Myrmeleonidæ*).

Fig. 48.—*Ascalaphus Kolyvanensis, Laxm.* Nat. size.

which they dig in sandy soil, to entrap the ants and other insects on which they feed. The *Ascalaphidæ* are another family not represented in Britain, but which has also several representatives in Southern Europe. It is distinguished by its very long, clubbed antennæ. In the typical genus *Ascalaphus* (Fabr.), the wings are black and yellow, and broader and shorter than in the *Myrmeleonidæ;* but in many of the allied tropical genera, the wings are longer, narrower, and mostly transparent. A third allied family, the *Nemopteridæ*, not British, and not extending so far south as the others, being confined in Europe to the shores of the Mediterranean, has rather short and slender antennæ, broad, oval, black and yellow fore-wings, and very long and narrow hind-wings, looking, when the insect is held head upwards, almost like a pair of stilts. The fore-wings measure about an inch and a half in expanse, but the curious narrow hind-wings are nearly two inches long.

Family *Ascalaphidæ.*

Family *Nemopteridæ.*

The most interesting British species of *Planipennia* belong to the *Chrysopidæ*, or lace-winged flies, which have bright green bodies, long slender antennæ, golden eyes, and transparent, delicately reticulated wings, rarely exceeding an inch in expanse. Their larvæ are very useful in gardens by destroying the *Aphides*, or plant-lice.

Lace-winged Flies (*Chrysopidæ*).

The *Ephemeridæ*, which are generally called May-flies, or Day-flies, fly over streams in summer. They have long, slender antennæ, slender bodies, ending in two or three long filaments, broad fore-wings, about an inch and a half in expanse, and very small, or undeveloped hind-wings. Their larvæ are aquatic, and take several months to arrive at maturity; but the perfect insects live a very short time. They are insects of dull colours, brown, greenish, dull grey, or whitish; and on the Continent there are several white species which emerge from the water after sunset, and perish before sunrise. In the evening they swarm in at the open windows of waterside houses to the lights in great numbers. In the morning the ground near the rivers where they breed is covered with their dead bodies, lying in heaps.

May-Flies (*Ephemeridæ*).

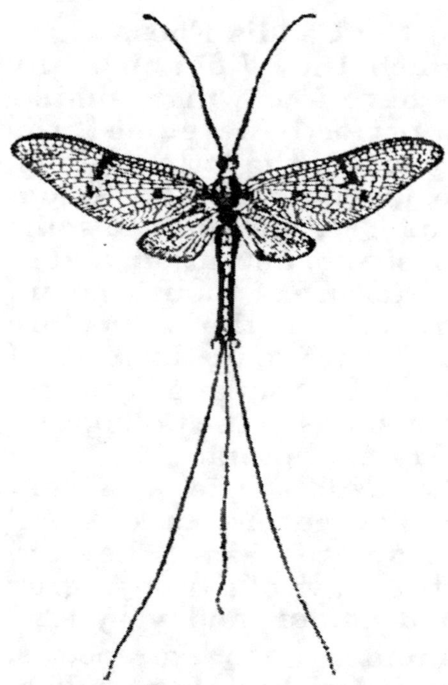

Fig. 49.—May Fly (*Ephemera vulgata*, Linn.).

The *Perlidæ* is another family of brown *Neuroptera*, with well-developed hind-wings, large heads, and two long filaments at the end of the body. Their larvæ likewise are aquatic.

Stone Flies (*Perlidæ*).

The *Termitidæ*, or white ants, are fortunately not British, and it is to be hoped that they will never succeed in getting a footing in this country. The males and females have long and rather narrow wings, and short, stout bodies; the workers are wingless, and have very large heads, and powerful jaws. They are very similar to ants in their habits, and shun the light, always living either in

White Ants (*Termetidæ*).

large nests, or forming galleries in wood, which they eat away from the inside.

Family *Psocidæ.*

Some of the remaining families of *Neuroptera* contain very small species. Among the *Psocidæ*, some are winged, and others are apterous. The species most often seen is *Atropos pulsatoria*, a small white apterous insect, which is frequently met with in neglected collections of insects, and is often called a mite. It is active, and sufficiently large to be seen running about. It has been stated on good authority to produce a ticking sound, but this appears almost impossible in the case of so small and soft a creature.

Fig. 50.—*Thrips cerealium:* Magnified.

Family *Thripidæ.*

The *Thripidæ* are very small insects, which are sometimes placed in a distinct order, under the name of *Thysanoptera*. They have rather long narrow wings, with very long fringes, and sometimes cause much injury to plants, especially in greenhouses, where the most troublesome species have received the name of the "black fly." Tobacco smoke is recommended for their destruction. The species figured, *Thrips cerealium* (Hal.), infests the ears of wheat.

Order Trichoptera.

Caddis Flies (*Trichoptera*).

The Trichoptera, or hairy-winged insects, include the Caddis Flies, which were formerly placed with the Neuroptera, from which they differ in many important particulars. The insects have four wings, similar in texture. The mouth parts are imperfectly developed, the antennæ and legs are long and slender, and the latter spined, and the metamorphoses are complete, and aquatic. The Trichoptera, especially some of the smaller species, have much resemblance to some of the *Pyralidæ* and *Tineidæ* among the Lepidoptera, in shape, neuration, and in the structure of their legs and antennæ, but the wings are clothed with hair instead of scales. The pupæ are necromorphous, as in the Coleoptera and Hymenoptera.

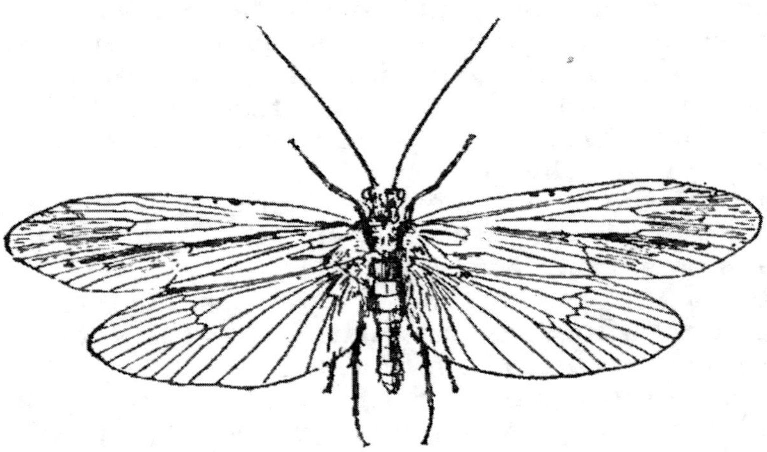

Fig. 51.—Caddis Fly (*Phryganea grandis*). Nat. size.

The Caddis Flies are very dull-coloured insects, of small or moderate size. They are nearly always of a brown, grey or buff colour, and very few, even among the foreign species, are varied with white, purplish, or yellow. The largest British species, *Phrygane a grandis*, (Linn.) measures about an inch and a half across the wings. Some of the smaller species have very long antennæ, several times as long as the body. These insects are chiefly remarkable for the habits of the larvæ.

The caddis worms, as they are called, live in ponds and ditches, and make themselves cases of stick, or small stones and shells, bound together, and lined with silk, and in these they live, and undergo their metamorphoses.

Wingless Insects, allied to Neuroptera.

There are three groups of wingless insects, which are sometimes classed with the Neuroptera, and are sometimes treated separately. They are as follows :—

The Mallophaga are placed by some authors with the Anoplura, or true lice, as an aberrant family of Hemiptera, but others place them with the Neuroptera, and others again treat them as a distinct order.

Bird Lice (*Mallophaga*).

They much resemble the lice, but differ from them in possessing well-developed mandibles. They have large flattened bodies, large heads, and rather short legs. They infest different species of birds, feeding on the soft part of the feathers near the quills. Most of them are of rather small size; the largest, which are nearly half an inch in length, infest the eagles, vultures, and albatrosses.

The Thysanura and Collembola are two small orders or sub-orders of wingless insects, which have long, jointed antennæ, and six legs, but undergo no metamorphoses. The Thysanura have an apparatus for leaping at the end of the body, and are frequently called spring tails. The best known, however, is the silver fish, *Lepisma saccharina* (Linn.), a silvery-grey insect, about half an inch long, often found in crevices in dark corners in houses, where it darts about with great activity when disturbed.

Spring Tails (*Thysanura*).

Silver Fish.

ORDER HYMENOPTERA (BEES, WASPS, ANTS, ETC.).

Structure and Metamorphoses.

In this Order we find insects with four wings, which are generally long and narrow, and frequently clothed with short hairs, only visible under the microscope. The fore and hind wings are often linked together by a row of small links, which has suggested the name of the order. The veins of the wings are never very numerous, nor is the neuration complicated. In many families, however, the females and sometimes both sexes are wingless, and in others there is a race of imperfectly developed females, called neuters or workers, which are frequently wingless. The ovipositor of the female is modified either into a sting, or into a boring apparatus, which, in the latter case, is sometimes of great length. There are usually three ocelli, or simple eyes on the vertex in addition to the two large lateral compound eyes. The metamorphoses are complete, and the pupa is inactive, and necromorphous, as in Coleoptera, the limbs being encased in separate immovable sheaths. The pupa is usually enclosed in a cocoon.

The Hymenoptera include a large number of insects, which, though very diversified in form and habits, have still such a strong family likeness that they cannot easily be mistaken for insects of any other order. Some are vegetable-feeders, like the saw-flies, the larvæ of which so much resemble caterpillars that they have been not inaptly termed "false caterpillars"; the larvæ of the wood-wasps burrow in the wood of trees; the gall-flies form excrescences called galls on various plants, especially on the oak and rose, though many of the smaller species are parasitic ; the groups generally classed together roughly as ichneumons, though they really include several very distinct families, are parasitic on other insects ; the burrowing and solitary wasps are carnivorous, the social wasps and the ants are omnivorous, and the bees feed on the pollen and honey of flowers.

Habits.

The ants, bees, and wasps, and the termites, or white ants, which greatly resemble them, but which belong to the order Neuroptera, far surpass all other animals in intelligence, and are the only creatures known to scientific men which have developed any phases of social life and civilisation at all resembling our own, and this is especially true of the ants.

The Hymenoptera are probably the most numerous of all insects in number of species, for although only 36,000 species have yet been described, a much smaller number than either the Coleoptera or Lepidoptera, yet we have considerably more than 3,000 species in England, a greater number than is known of any other order, and fully half of these belong to the parasitic groups, which only one or two entomologists have taken the trouble to study at all, and many of which are of very small size, some, indeed, being the most minute of all known insects, and there is no reason to doubt their being proportionately as numerous in other countries as in our own.

Number of Species.

The Hymenoptera are divided into two principal sections : the Terebrantia, or Boring Hymenoptera, in which the ovipositor is modified into a boring apparatus; and the Aculeata, or Stinging Hymenoptera, in which it is modified into a sting. In the Terebrantia the trochanter, or small hinge-joint which separates the coxa, or hip, from the femur, or thigh, is generally double, while in the *Aculeata* it is generally single ; but this is not an invariable character.

Boring Hymenoptera (*Terebrantia*).

The first division of the *Terebrantia* consists of the *Serrifera*, including the families *Tenthredinidæ* and *Siricidæ*, or saw-flies and wood-wasps.

The *Tenthredinidæ* are divided into several sub-families, in some of which the antennæ are short, and strongly clubbed at the end, like those of a butterfly. The commonest of these species in England is *Trichiosoma lucorum* (Linn.), which is a blackish hairy insect, measuring rather more than an inch in expanse, with transparent wings bordered with brown. The twenty-two-legged larva feeds on hawthorn, and constructs a very solid brown egg-shaped cocoon. It belongs to the sub-family *Cimbicinæ*. Another very interesting sub-family is that of the *Perginæ*, which are found in Australia, and have short, club-shaped antennæ ; the species are mostly black and yellow, and smaller than *Trichiosoma*, though some of them are greenish, and about the same size. Their black larvæ have only six true legs, no prolegs being developed, and they feed gregariously on gum-trees (*Eucalyptus*). In some species, the female is said to tend the young larvæ after they are hatched, an unusual habit, except in the case of social insects. The number of joints of the antennæ varies in the

Saw-Flies (*Tenthredinidæ*).

Habits of *Perga*.

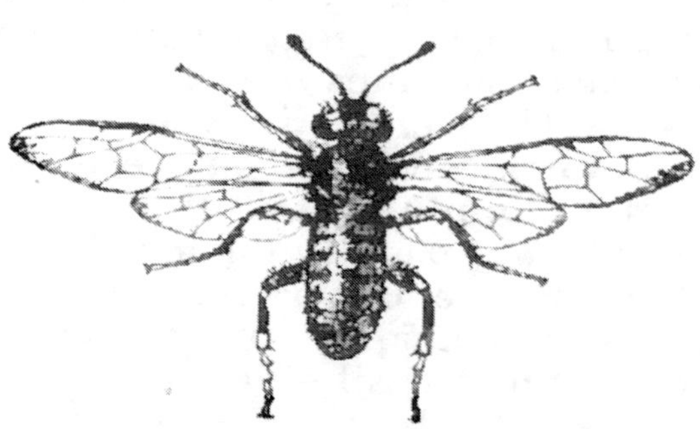

Fig. 52.—SAW-FLY (*Trichiosoma lucorum*). Nat. size.

Tenthredinidæ, but is most frequently nine, especially in the more typical sub-families, in which the joints are long, cylindrical, and well-marked. In one sub-family, however, the short, thick antennæ are composed of only three well-separated joints; the scape, a short joint, and a long terminal one composed of several fused together. Sometimes this third joint is bifid, each antenna being thus double nearly to the base.

Antennæ of Saw-Flies.

Our fruit-trees often suffer severely from the attacks of the larvæ of various saw-flies. Those best known to ordinary observers are probably the small greenish or yellowish black-dotted larvæ which frequently strip our gooseberry and currant bushes of all their leaves, and which develop into small black and yellow four-winged flies about half-an-inch in expanse, belonging to various species of the great genus *Nematu* (Panzer.). But these bushes are liable to the attacks of the larvæ of saw-flies belonging to other sub-families than the *Nematinæ*, and also by the larvæ of various Lepidoptera and other insects.

Saw-Flies injurious to fruit trees.

The *Siricidæ*, or wood-wasps, burrow in the larva state in timber, with which they are frequently imported into this country. The commonest and most conspicuous species is *Sirex gigas* (Linn.), a very formidable-looking insect, the large females of which sometimes measure nearly two inches across the wings, though many specimens are much smaller; for wood-feeding insects, as a rule, vary very much, both in size, and in the length of time which they require to reach maturity. It is black and yellow, and the female has a stout ovipositor projecting behind the body for about one-third of its length. The abdomen of the male, on the other hand, terminates in a rectangle. These insects will sometimes emerge from planks of deal or pine, which have been built into the floors or fittings of a house, and make a loud buzzing, which has sometimes led to their being mistaken for hornets, but they are really quite harmless.

Wood-Wasps (*Siricidæ*).

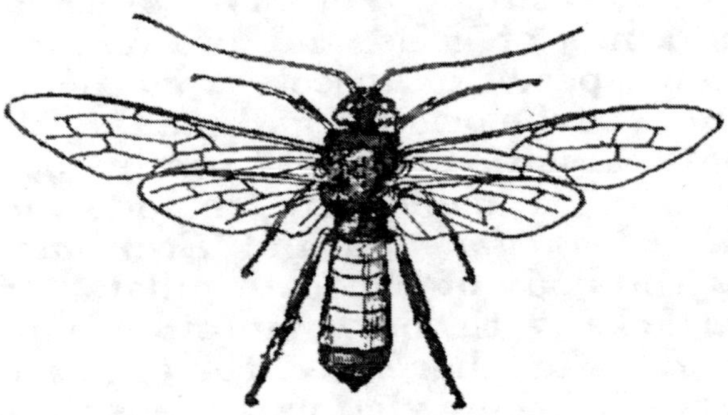

Fig. 53.—Sirex gigas. Male. Nat. size.

The *Gallicolæ*, or gall-flies, are far better known by the galls which grow upon the leaf or stalk in which they have deposited their eggs than by the flies themselves, which are generally small shining black or reddish insects, with long antennæ and transparent wings, with the very

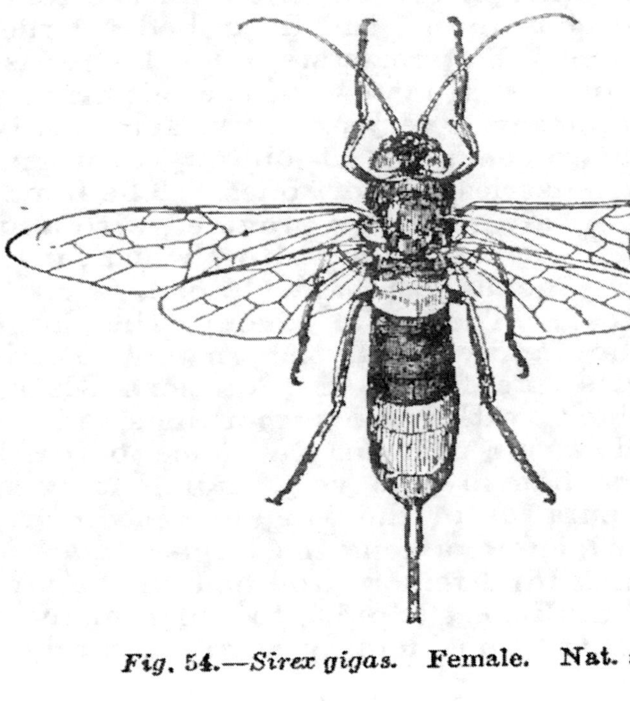

Fig. 54.—Sirex gigas. Female. Nat. size.

few nervures visible on the fore-wings forming one large cell near the centre. The abdomen is short, slightly compressed, and much elevated. A common British species is figured. It is hardly necessary to remind our readers that the principal ingredient in ink is obtained from the galls of a Levantine species of *Cynips*. Some of our own galls are not unlike a cherry, or other fruit; and there are foreign galls which are much larger and more tempting in appearance; some of these are called "Apples of Sodom."

Gall-Flies (*Gallicolæ*).

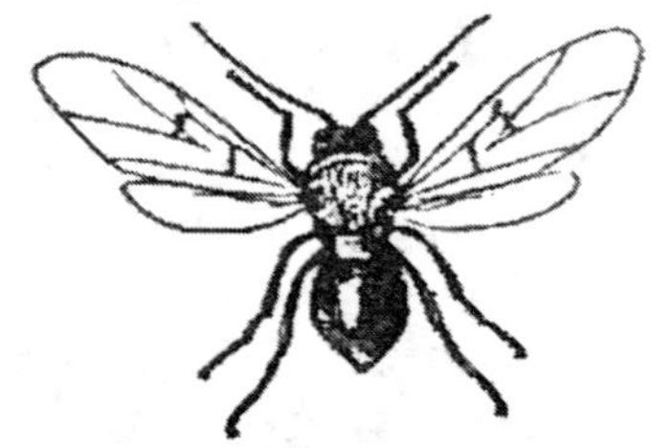

Fig. 55.—GALL-FLY (*Cynips kollari*, Hart.). Slightly magnified.

Many of the gall-flies appear at different seasons of the year in two different forms, one in which the sexes are separate, while the other consists exclusively of females, or rather of individuals capable of self-reproduction. Sometimes one form is winged, and the other apterous and subterranean. It is needless to say that until their habits were discovered, the two broods were regarded as belonging not only to different species, but to distinct genera. Another noteworthy circumstance relative to galls is their extreme liability to attacks of parasites. You may collect a very large quantity of some kinds of galls, and breed hundreds of specimens of different species of insects from them, and yet never obtain a specimen of the original gall-maker; all will be parasites, and not a few will be a small parasitic species of *Cynipidæ*.

Gall-Parasites.

The *Entomophaga*, or truly parasitic groups of Hymenoptera, include the families *Chalcididæ*, *Proctotrypidæ*, *Braconidæ*, *Ichneumonidæ* and *Evaniidæ*. The female usually pierces the body of the caterpillars, or other victims which she attacks, with her ovipositor, and lodges an egg in each wound. In other cases, the eggs are deposited on the eggs or larvæ of their victims. Eggs thus attacked never hatch; but ichneumoned larvæ generally attain their full growth, and then die, when the larvæ of the parasite, which have been feeding on it all the time, often emerge from it, and form their own cocoons round the dead body of the caterpillar. In other cases, the larva assumes the pupa-state, and the parasites pupate within it, emerging from the pupa-skin instead of the butterfly.

Parasitic Hymenoptera (*Entomophaga*).

The *Chalcididæ* are a very extensive family, divided into many sub-families. The antennæ are generally 13-jointed, consisting of a long basal joint and a series of short ones. The females are generally provided with a long or short ovipositor, which, in the genus *Leucospis* (Fabr.), is curved over the back. These are among the largest species of the family, and though not British, several species are found in Southern Europe. They are black, with yellow markings, and resemble small wasps, but may at once be distinguished from them by the very rudimentary and incomplete neuration of the wings. *Leucospis* and several other genera among the larger *Chalcididæ* have very thick hind femora, toothed on the under-surface.

Family *Chalcididæ*.

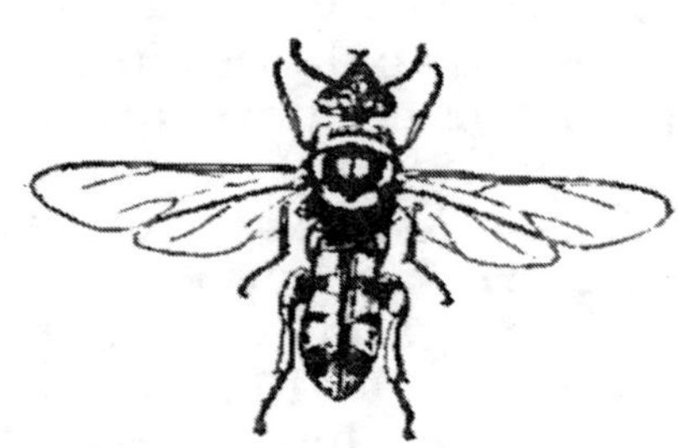

Fig. 56.—*Leucospis grandis.* Nat. size.

The genus *Callimome* (Spin.), to which many species which are parasitic in galls, belong, are considerably smaller, rarely measuring more than about half an inch across the wings. They are, however, by no means inconspicuous insects, being of a bright metallic green, or cupreous; and the female has a long straight ovipositor.

The pupæ of the *Chalcididæ* are naked, but those of the next family, the *Proctotrypidæ*, are enclosed in cocoons. The body, which is usually stout in the *Chalcididæ*, is slender in the *Proctotrypidæ*, and the wings are almost destitute of any trace of neuration. Most of them are egg-parasites, and some are among the smallest of known insects, being barely visible even to the most practised eye, except as a mere speck on a window-pane. The smallest of all belong to the sub-family *Mymarinæ*, and Mr. F. Enock, who has paid special attention to them, calls them "fairy flies." They have very narrow oval or battledore-shaped wings, fringed round with long hairs; and one or two of them are aquatic in their habits, probably attacking the eggs of some water-insect.

Family *Proctotrypidæ*.

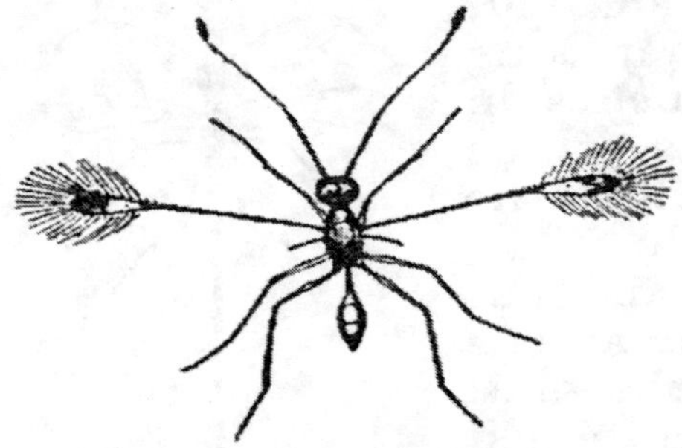

Fig. 57.—FAIRY FLY (*Mymar pulchellus*, Curt.). Magnified.

The *Braconidæ* and *Ichneumonidæ* include the greater part of the remaining parasitic Hymenoptera. The neuration, though still not very complicated, extends over the greater part of the forewings; and the antennæ are generally long and slender. In the *Braconidæ* there is one small joint beyond the scape of the antennæ, but in the *Ichneumonidæ* there are always two. In the *Ichneumonidæ* we often find an open space towards the middle of the forewings, in which the principal nervures of the wing centre; this is called the areolet. In some genera of these two families, the ovipositor is concealed; but in some of the larger *Ichneumonidæ* belonging to the sub-family *Pimplinæ*, the ovipositor, which is usually composed of three separate filaments, is of great length, being intended to reach the larvæ of wood-boring insects. *Rhyssa persuasoria* (Linn.), which attacks the larva of *Sirex gigas* in its wooden galleries, is black with yellow markings, and is one of the largest of the British *Ichneumonidæ*, measuring nearly two inches across the wings, and nearly three inches from the head to the extremity of the ovipositor, which is nearly twice as long as the rest of the body. But in some of the allied foreign species, the ovipositor is much longer, not measuring less than six or eight inches in length.

Family *Braconidæ*.

Family *Ichneumonidæ*.

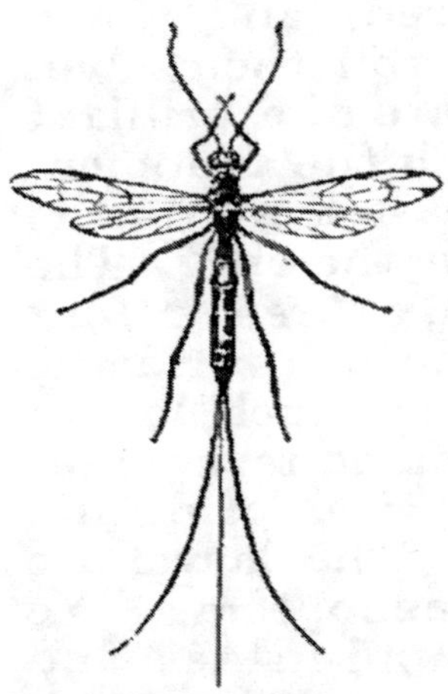

Fig. 58.—ICHNEUMON FLY (*Rhyssa persuasoria*). ½ Nat. size.

The *Evaniinæ* are a small family of parasitic insects, remarkable for their peculiar forms. The abdomen is attached to the upper part of the metathorax, which gives the whole insect a very peculiar appearance. The species of the genus *Evania* (Fabr.) are parasitic on the egg-capsules of cockroaches, and are found all over the world, though for some reason or other they are extremely rare in England. They are small black insects, measuring about three-quarters of

Family *Evaniidæ*.

an inch across the expanded transparent wings, with a very small petiolated abdomen, so small that it hardly appears to belong to the insect; and long sprawling legs, with very long black or red hind femora, much longer and thicker than the abdomen of the insect. Another genus of this family, *Pelecinus* (Latr.), is of a very different size and shape, but is not less remarkable. The species are black and shining, and measure an inch and a half across the rather long wings. The whole insect, however, is three inches in length, on account of the great length of the joints of the abdomen, which looks like a telescope, except that the joints are of equal thickness. Such is the female. The male, which is very rarely seen, is much smaller, and has the abdomen very differently formed; it is slender at the base, and gradually thickened into an oval club at the end. Here we see that instead of the ovipositor being lengthened in the female, the whole abdomen has been inordinately lengthened instead. This genus is not British, but is common in North America, and other parts of the world.

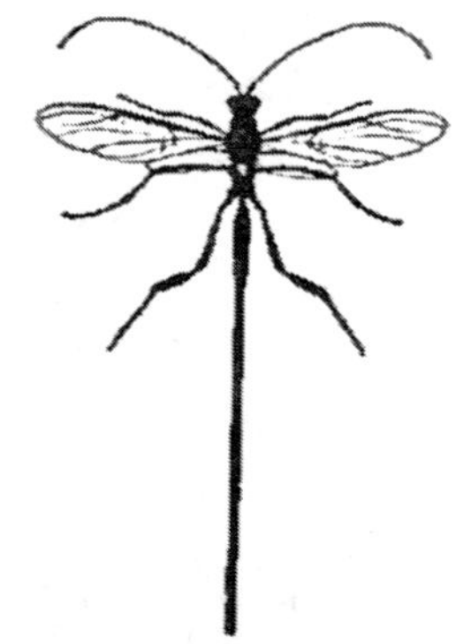

Fig. 59.—*Pelecinus polilurator*, Linn. Reduced.

We now come to the important section of the Hymenoptera Aculeata, which are not only more familiar insects than the *Terebrantia*, but have been much more studied by entomologists, though not to anything like the same extent as the two favourite orders of *Coleoptera* and *Lepidoptera*.

Stinging Hymenoptera (Aculeata).

The first section, the *Tubulifera*, includes only one family, the *Chrysididæ*, or ruby-tailed wasps, which hold an intermediate place between the two great sections of the Hymenoptera, being armed with a rudimentary sting. They are small insects, generally expanding less than an inch across the transparent wings. Their bodies are very hard, and very strongly punctured, and when alarmed, they double their bodies together, and sometimes roll themselves up into a ball. Most of the species are of a brilliant metallic green (more rarely blue), with the abdomen, which is more or less smooth, at least towards the tip, often purple or fiery-red towards the end. The abdomen is usually composed of only three or four segments visible above, and is more or less retractile under the first, which is usually very much longer than the others; the last dorsal segment terminates in a row of strong teeth, varying in size, form, and number according to the species. The larvæ are parasitic in the nests of other Hymenoptera. We have figured *Stilbum amethystinum* (Fabr.), a large species found in Asia and Africa, which is sometimes blue and sometimes green.

Ruby-Tails (*Chrysididæ*).

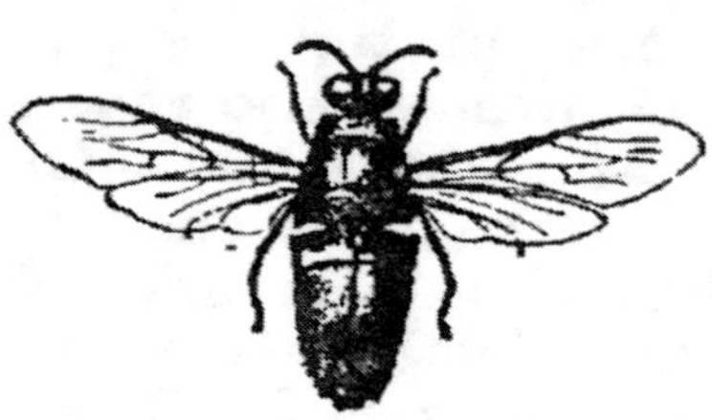

Fig. 60.—Ruby-Tail (*Stilbum amethystinum*). Nat. size.

The first section of the true Hymenoptera Aculeata is that of the *Heterogyna*, or ants. They are social insects, and consist of limited numbers of winged males and females, and of numerous wingless and imperfectly developed females, called workers, or neuters. In all Hymenoptera the female is the predominant sex, but this is pre-eminently the case in the social species. When the ants swarm, the males and females fly away and pair, after which the great bulk of them perish. The females shed their wings,

Ants (*Heterogyna*).

and those which are sufficiently fortunate to return to a nest of their own species, become the future mothers of the community, and devote all their energies to egg-laying. The wings of ants are rather long and large, and the two principal nervures generally cross obliquely about the middle of the fore-wings, and beyond this, a large, closed cell is formed in some genera. Ants are divided into three principal families. The *Formicidæ* bite, but do not sting, and have only one node on the petiole of the abdomen. In the *Poneridæ*, the node is formed by the first segment of the abdomen, which is frequently nearly as large as the others, but is completely detached from them; and in the *Myrmicidæ* there are two small nodes forming the petiole of the abdomen. Both these last families sting as well as bite. The most familiar examples of the first and last families are the wood ant, *Formica rufa* (Linn.), a large, smooth, reddish ant, which forms large mound-nests in woods; the much smaller red ants of the genus *Myrmica* (Latr.), which infest our gardens; and the minute yellow house-ant, which is so troublesome and difficult to get rid of wherever it effects a lodgment. Our British representatives of the *Poneridæ*, or "wicked ones," are small and insignificant; but to this family belong some of the largest known ants, such as the great black *Dinoponera grandis* (Guér.) of Brazil, which measures upwards of an inch in length. In some of the larger species of *Myrmicidæ*, belonging to the genera *Odontomachus* (Latr.), *Myrmecia* (Fabr.), etc., the jaws are very long, and armed with formidable teeth. We have figured a large red and black Australian ant, *Myrmecia forficata* (Fabr.).

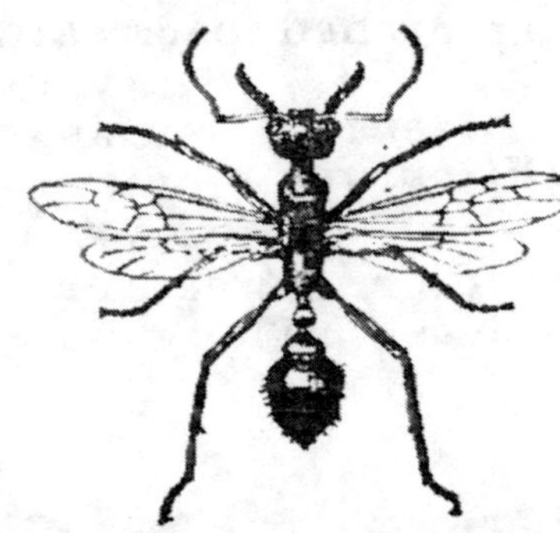

Fig. 61.—ANT (*Myrmecia forficata*). Nat. size.

We have no space here to discuss the habits of ants, but those of our readers who are interested in their wars, slave-raids, agriculture, cattle and pets, will find ample information in the works of Huber, Kirby and Spence, Moggridge, Lubbock, M'Cook, and others.

Sand Wasps (*Fossores*).

The *Fossores*, or sand wasps, are a large group of insects consisting of winged males, and winged or apterous females, which are solitary in their habits, and generally dig holes in the ground, which they fill with insects or spiders which they have paralysed but not killed with their sting, and which remain as a store of fresh provision for the larvæ of the wasps. The wings of the burrowing wasps are not folded longitudinally when at rest; the abdomen is often petiolated; the legs are usually very spiny or hairy, and the prothorax is transverse, the sides not being arched backwards to the base of the wings, as in the true wasps. We notice here some of the principal families only.

Families of *Fossores*.

The *Mutillidæ* have winged males, and very hairy apterous females, and are sometimes improperly called "solitary ants." They are very numerous in the warmer parts of the world, and we have two or three species in Britain, though they are not very common. The *Thynnidæ* are another family with apterous, but nearly naked females; they are almost confined to Australia and South America. In both the above families the legs are very hairy. The *Pompilidæ* have long spiny legs, and the abdomen is shortly petiolated. Among them we find the largest Hymenopterous insects known, some of which measure upwards of three inches across the wings. Some of the species of *Mygnimia* (Smith) are conspicuous by their beautiful green or purple iridescent wings. The last family we can notice is the *Sphegidæ*, which are remarkable for the long petiolated abdomen, and for the brilliant metallic green of some of the Indian and African species of *Chlorion* (Latr.), etc. In these, however, the wings are generally transparent, or are at most only bordered with brown. *Pelopæus spirifex* (Linn.) is a black and yellow species, common in the warmer parts of the Old World.

Fig. 62.—SAND WASP (*Pelopæus spirifex*). Nat. size.

Wasps (*Diploptera*).

The *Diploptera*, or true wasps, may be distinguished by the fore-wings being longitudinally folded in repose, and by the prothorax being arched backwards to the base of the wings. The species are solitary or social; and the former generally construct small nests or cells, which they provision with insects. The social wasps, belonging to the typical genus *Vespa*, are too well known to need description; they construct large nests in the ground or in trees, but their habits are less interesting than those of the ants and bees. The nest is, however, always commenced by one queen, which has survived the winter; and its extension is afterwards carried on by her progeny. The bulk of the inhabitants consist of neuters, though males and females are also produced; the latter assist the mother in carrying on the work of the nest, for, unlike bees, more than one perfect female is allowed to live in a wasp's nest at the same time. At the end of the season, the whole community dies off, except a few queens, which perpetuate the brood next year; and hence every wasp destroyed in spring means the destruction of a possible nest. We have six species of *Vespa* in England, all very similar, except the hornet, which is twice as large as the others, but lives in smaller communities. It is much scarcer, too, and rarely stings except under provocation. The largest known species of *Vespa* are found in India, China, and Japan.

Fig. 63.—HORNET (*Vespa crabro*). Nat. size.

Bees (*Anthophila*).

The last family of the Hymenoptera is that of the *Anthophila*, or bees. They are generally short, hairy insects, though some genera are almost naked, such as the curious wasp-like parasitic bees of the genus *Nomada* (Fabr.), which are mostly black and red, in various proportions, with yellow markings.

Many of the solitary bees of the large genus *Andrena* (Fabr.) appear in spring, sometimes as early as January or February, and make nests in the ground. Some are very peculiar in their habits, such as the leaf-cutter bees, *Megachile* (Latr.), and the carpenter bees, *Xylocopa* (Latr.), which are common abroad, but are not known in England, and have deep violet-coloured wings; while there are other bees which form their nests in old walls. The humble-bees, *Bombus* (Fabr.), make their nests in the ground,

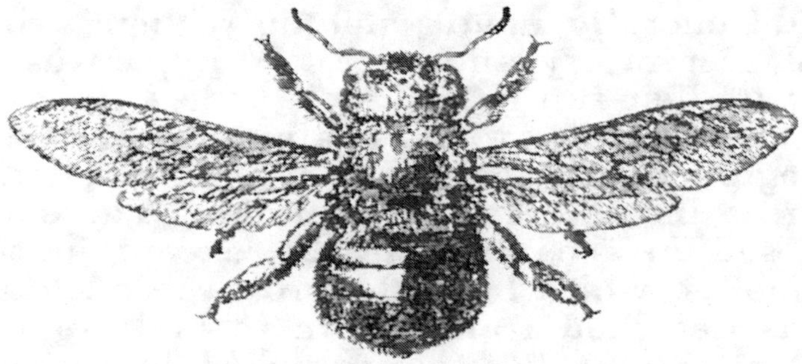

Fig. 64.—CARPENTER BEE (*Xylocopa violacea*, Linn.). Nat. size.

Fig. 65.—HIVE-BEE (*Apis mellifica*). Nat. size.

and live in small communities, consisting, like the hive bee, of males, females and workers, all winged.

Apis mellifica (Linn.), the hive-bee, closes our list of the Hymenoptera. The genus *Apis* occupies a rather isolated position among the bees, and may be recognised at once by the very long narrow costal cell, which extends almost to the tip of the fore-wings. The species of *Apis* are not numerous; but apart from the common hive-bee, ten or twelve others are met with in different parts of the world.

ORDER LEPIDOPTERA (BUTTERFLIES AND MOTHS).

General Characteristics.

The Lepidoptera, or scale-winged insects, have four wings, clothed with scales, which look like fine powder, and easily rub off, but which exhibit a great variety of form under the microscope. The colour of the insects is due partly to pigment, and partly to refraction from the edges of the scales, which sometimes produces the most brilliant iridescent changes, as in some of the blue Morphos of Tropical America, and in the widely-dispersed genus *Apatura* (Fabr.), to which our own Purple Emperor belongs. The antennæ are long and many-jointed, and one pair of palpi, at least, is more or less conspicuous. There is also a long proboscis for imbibing the nectar of flowers, or moisture from trees or the ground. In some of the hawk moths this is of immense length, nearly reaching a foot in the largest South American species; but in some groups of moths, as in many of those classed under the heading of *Bombyces*, it is often so slightly developed as to be practically obsolete.

Eggs.

In Lepidoptera the metamorphoses are complete, the insects passing through four stages. The female lays her eggs on a plant suitable for the nourishment of her brood. These are laid singly or in clusters, and are frequently covered with a kind of cement, or else with down from the body of the mother. They are of various shapes and sizes, and are often ribbed or fluted.

From the eggs emerge the larvæ, or caterpillars, which are usually provided with sixteen legs: six horny legs, corresponding to the true legs of the perfect insect; eight fleshy legs, called prolegs; and a terminal pair, called claspers. In the larvæ of the *Geometridæ*, and in the early stages of those of many other moths, the first three pairs of prolegs are obsolete, and the larvæ arch the back at every movement, and are then called "loopers." Caterpillars are very voracious, and generally moult, not only their skins, but the lining of part of the internal respiratory and digestive apparatus as well, more than once before arriving at their full growth.

Larva, or Caterpillar.

The next stage is that of the pupa or chrysalis, which is almost motionless, being encased in a tight-fitting integument, on the upper half of which the outlines of the perfect insect may be observed. These are not, however, enclosed in separate sheaths, except in the case of some hawk-moths, which have the proboscis enclosed in a sheath which is detached from the main body of the pupa. The pupa takes no nourishment, and it is either attached by threads to a leaf,[1] etc, as in the case of most butterflies, or enclosed in a cocoon, formed of silk in those species in which it is constructed on or above the ground, and of agglutinated earth in most instances in which it is subterranean. In due time the perfect butterfly or moth quits the pupa-case; its wings, which are at first soft and limp, soon expand to their full size; the limbs of the insect dry in the sun and air, and it flies away to join its comrades, and to reproduce its kind. Most species, on emerging from the chrysalis, discharge a fluid, which in former times, when they happened to be particularly numerous, and when everything unusual was attributed to miraculous causes, sometimes gave rise to the notion that a rain of blood had fallen.

Pupa, or Chrysalis.

Entomologists in England have generally agreed to call the first few families of Lepidoptera butterflies, and the remainder moths; but there is no such distinction on the Continent, where they are generally called by words corresponding to day-butterflies and night-butterflies. Butterflies are broad-winged insects, often adorned with bright colours, and with comparatively slender bodies. The antennæ are almost invariably thickened into a knob at the extremity, a peculiarity which is not very common in other insects, though we meet with it in some saw-flies, flies, the ant-lions, and other allied families of *Neuroptera*, and in many beetles, etc. Hence the butterflies are often called *Rhopalocera*, or club-horns. They fly by day, and seldom, unless disturbed, at dusk or at night, though some Tropical genera are twilight-fliers, or frequent the deep gloom of thick forests. Moths, on the other hand, have the antennæ of various shapes, sometimes thickened in the middle, or before the end, but almost never clubbed at the extremity, and generally thread-like or comb-like. Most moths fly at night, or, at least, not before dusk, though a few are day-fliers, and may be seen frequenting flowers, among butterflies. Many of them have stout bodies, and are of dull or subdued colours. Butterflies often rest with the wings raised over the back, an attitude rarely assumed by moths. The latter, however, more frequently rest with all their wings spread out flat, while in the stout-bodied moths the fore-wings often more or less cover the hind-wings when at rest, and are sometimes

Rhopalocera, or Butterflies.

[1] In the *Nymphalidæ* the pupa is suspended freely by the tail; in the other families of butterflies (except in the *Hesperiidæ*) it is generally attached by the tail, and by a girth round the body as well.

sloped roof-like, the hind-wings frequently folding together like a fan, which is never the case in butterflies.

Moths.

Moths are much more numerous in proportion than butterflies, especially in temperate climates. Tropical America produces more than half of all the known butterflies ; in the tropics of the Old World they are much less numerous. England is poor in butterflies, producing only 60 or 70 species out of the 300 European species, as against 2,000 British moths. The richest countries in Europe for butterflies are those lying round the central ranges from the Pyrenees to the Balkans ; but the numbers rapidly diminish, both north and south. Sweden produces about twice as many species of butterflies as Britain ; but Andalusia is not richer than Sweden, and North Africa is much poorer. Nevertheless, both butterflies and moths are to be met with (though, of course, their number is but few), not only in Lapland, but everywhere in Greenland where any vegetation will grow. Iceland, though producing many moths, is the only important country in which it is believed that no butterflies are to be met with.

In the wings of butterflies, the front edge is called the costa, the outer edge the hind margin, the hinder edge (which, in the hind-wings, is parallel to the abdomen) the inner margin, and the side nearest to the body of the insect the base. The nervures of the wings are useful in classification. The principal nervures which run from the base are the costal, subcostal, median, submedian, and internal nervures. The nervures which do not start from the base are called nervules. A wide space, which extends from the base towards the middle of the wing, between the subcostal and median nervures, is called the discoidal cell. The subcostal nervure divides into two branches on the hind-wings, and generally into from three to five on the fore-wings ; and the median nervure always divides into three. These branches are either called branches of the subcostal and median respectively, or subcostal and median nervules. The discoidal cell is closed at the extremity by short nervules, called discocellular nervules ; and from the end of the cell one or two nervules (called discoidal nervules) run to the extremity of the wing. In some butterflies one of the discocellular nervules is absent or imperfectly formed, leaving the wing open from the base to the hind margin. In such a case the discoidal cell is said to be open ; but otherwise it is called closed. The internal nervure is absent in some families of butterflies.

Family *Nymphalidæ.*

The first family of butterflies, the *Nymphalidæ*, includes about half the entire number of species, and may be known by the first pair of legs being always more or less imperfect, especially in the males. The pupa, when attached to anything (for in exceptional cases among the *Satyrinæ* it is placed on the ground), is suspended freely by the tail. The larvæ are cylindrical, and are generally furnished with bristles, spines, or long filaments, or are naked, with a bifid tail. Sometimes they have horny projections on the head.

—Sub-Family *Danainæ.*

The *Nymphalidæ* are divided into several sub-families The *Danainæ* are chiefly an Old World group, and the best-known species is *Limnas chrysippus* (Linn.), a tawny butterfly, about three or four inches across the wings, with an oblique white bar across the tip of the fore-wings, and a curved row of small black spots on the middle of the hind-wings. It is common throughout Africa and Southern Asia, and extends into South-Eastern Europe. Another section of this family is represented by the East Indian genus *Euplœa* (Fabr.), and its allies. Many of these are butterflies of a rich velvety black or brown, with bluish-white spots towards the extremity of the long, broad, rounded wings, and also in the middle. They are often flushed with rich purple. The *Danainæ* are butterflies with very tough integuments, and exhale an odour which is supposed to render them distasteful to birds.

Mimicry in Butterflies.

Many other butterflies and moths resemble them externally, and are believed to share in their immunity from persecution. This phenomenon is called "mimicry," and is exhibited in the greatest perfection by *Limnas chrysippus*, the pattern and colours of which are more or less accurately reproduced in at least a dozen butterflies and moths, belonging to different families; but in several instances in the female only, the male exhibiting the normally and frequently very different colouring of its proper genus. The larvæ of the *Danainæ* are usually provided with several pairs of long fleshy filaments, and feed on *Aristolochiæ*.

Sub-Families *Ithomiinæ and Heliconinæ*.

Of the remaining sub-families, several are entirely exotic, and two, the *Ithomiinæ* and *Heliconinæ*, are American butterflies with long rounded wings and slender bodies, which have sometimes been compared to dragonflies. They are butterflies generally measuring from two to four inches across the wings, which are often black, with red or yellow markings, or yellow with black markings. The typical species of the *Ithomiinæ*, however, often have transparent wings, with only brown borders, and a brown band at the end of the discoidal cell.

Sub-Family *Acræinæ*.

The *Acræinæ* are another long-winged sub-family of butterflies, chiefly found in Africa and America. The African and the few Eastern species are generally red or tawny, with black spots, and sometimes partly transparent; but the American group usually has black markings on a tawny ground, or radiated tawny markings on a dark ground, especially on the hind-wings.

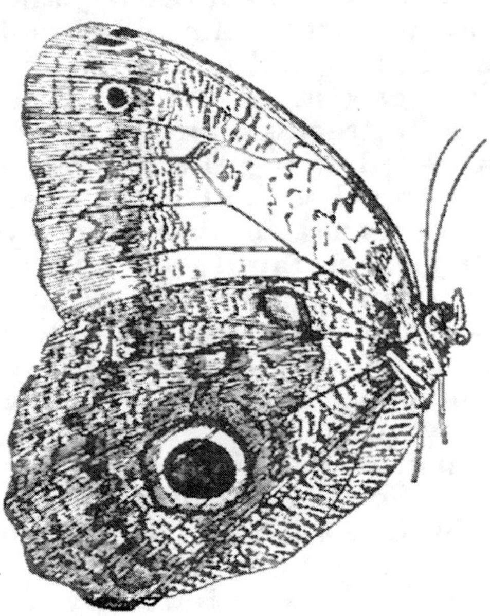

Fig. 66.—Caligo teucer. Reduced.

Sub-Families *Morphinæ and Brassolinæ*.

Two more sub-families of large butterflies are chiefly South American. These are the *Morphinæ* and *Brassolinæ*. The typical species of *Morpho* (Fabr.) measure from three to eight inches across the wings, and many of them are of a brilliant azure blue; others are black, with a broad blue band through the wings; while others, including some of the largest and longest-winged species, are brown or orange. These are all American; but there is a greater variety of genera, though much smaller, and more varied in colour, in the East Indies. On the under-surface they are always marked with large eye-spots, as in the *Satyrinæ*. The *Brassolinæ* are large brown or tawny butterflies (rarely dull blue), which are entirely confined to Tropical America. They have generally one large eye-spot on the under-side of the wings, and traces of one or two more;

and, like some of the Tropical *Satyrinæ*, they are twilight-fliers, although true butterflies. The accompanying figure represents the under-surface of the wings of *Caligo teucer* (Linn.), a common South American species belonging to the sub-family *Brassolinæ*. The expanded wings of this butterfly measure five or six inches from tip to tip.

Sub-Family *Satyrinæ*.

The two remaining sub-families, the *Satyrinæ* and the *Nymphalinæ*, contain many of our commonest and most familiar British butterflies. The *Satyrinæ* are brown or tawny butterflies, such as the meadow brown, of moderate or rather small size, and are nearly always adorned with eye-spots, at least on the under-surface of the wings. The wings are rounded, and there is usually at least one eye-spot towards the tip of the fore-wings, and two or three towards the borders of the hind-wings.

Sub-Family *Nymphalinæ*.

The typical *Nymphalinæ* may be known from the foregoing sub-families, except the *Morphinæ*, by the open wing-cells, and often by the more or less dentated wings. This is a very large group of large or moderate-sized butterflies, and includes the tortoise-shells, peacock, red admiral, fritillaries, purple emperor, and white admiral, among our British butterflies, which are described in full in every book on the subject.

We have figured *Kallima inachis* (Boisduval), a butterfly found in North India, which is remarkable for its resemblance to a dead leaf. It measures three inches across the wings, which are dull blue above, with a broad orange band with a transparent spot in the middle, on the fore-wings. The under-surface is brown, with a dark line running from the tip of the fore-wings to the end of the lobe on the hind-wings. This line represents the midrib of the leaf, and the butterfly is shaped and lined and mottled in such a manner as to increase the deception. There is a case of such butterflies mounted, with leaves, in the hall of the Natural History Museum at South Kensington; and the butterflies and leaves can hardly be distinguished from one another. Our figure shows a butterfly on one side of a twig, and a leaf on the other.

Fig. 67.—Dead-Leaf Butterfly (*Kallima inachis*). Reduced.

Family *Lemoniidæ*.

The *Lemoniidæ* are a large family of small, brightly-coloured butterflies, which are most numerous in South America, and least so in Europe and Africa. The females have perfect legs, but the fore-legs of the male are imperfectly developed. The only European species is *Nemeobius lucina* (Linn.), the Duke of Burgundy Fritillary, a brown butterfly about an inch in expanse, with rows of tawny spots on the wings.

Family *Libytheidæ.*

The *Libytheidæ*, which some entomologists consider to be a sub-family of the *Lemoniidæ*, are distinguished by their very long palpi (much longer than in any other butterflies, except one or two *Nymphalinæ*), and by their brown, dentated, tawny-spotted wings, which gives them a superficial resemblance to some small species allied to *Vanessa*. The only European species is here figured.

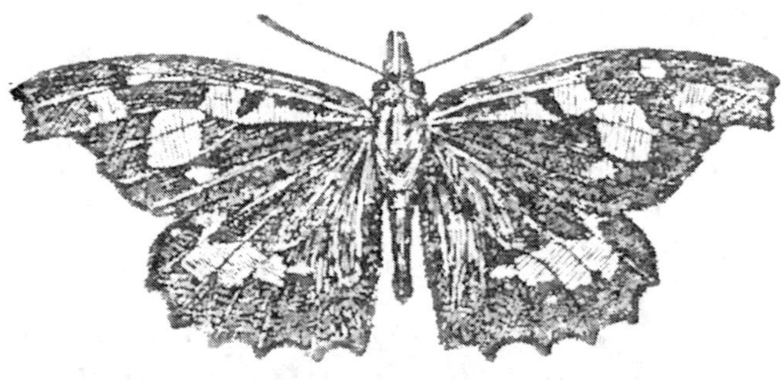

Fig. 68.—*Libythea celtis.* Nat. size.

Family *Lycænidæ.*

The *Lycænidæ* are a large family of small or moderate-sized butterflies, differing little structurally from the *Lemoniidæ*. They are, however, more of an Old World group, although many are found in America, too. Our species are known as hairstreaks, blues, and coppers. The hairstreaks are brown or blue butterflies, with white lines on the under-side of the wings, and a short tail. The green hairstreak, however, *Callophrys rubi* (Linn.), is tailless, and the under-side of the wings is green. There are a large number of brown or blue species allied to the hairstreaks in Tropical America, some measuring as much as two inches across the wings. The blues, which belong to the genus *Polyommatus* and its allies, are small butterflies, usually without tails, and generally with rows of ocellated spots on the under-side of the wings. Towards the hind-margins we often find a row of red spots above or below. The females of the blues are often brown, and in some species of the group both sexes are brown. They generally measure a little more than an inch in expanse. One species, *Lampides bæticus* (Linn.), has a short tail and a streaked under-side; but in England it is only occasionally met with on the south coast. The coppers are a very handsome group of butterflies, distinguished by the brilliant coppery red of many of the species, several of which formerly inhabited England; but they are all now believed to be extinct with us except the small copper, an insect with the coppery wings bordered and spotted with black. Some of the other species are shot with purple.

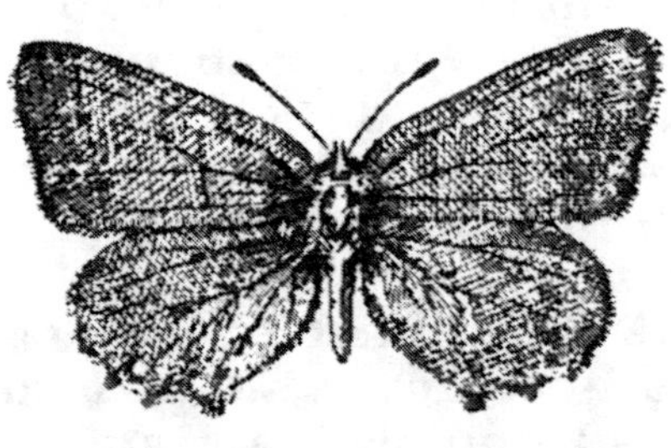

Fig. 69.—Green Hairstreak (*Callophrys rubi*). Nat. size.

Family *Pieridæ.*

The *Pieridæ* are a large group of middle-sized butterflies, most of which are white or yellow. All the legs are fully developed in both sexes; and they can most readily be distinguished from the next family by possessing an internal nervure to the

Fig. 70.—Orange Tip (*Euchloe cardamines*). Nat. size.

hind-wings. To the *Pieridæ* belong our garden whites, clouded yellows, orange tip, and brimstone butterflies, etc. The largest butterflies of this family are the great East Indian orange tips of the genus *Hebomoia*, Hübner. They measure five or six inches across the wings, which are much shorter and broader in proportion than in our common orange tip, *Euchloe cardamines* (Linn.), which is one of the prettiest and most admired of our vernal insects.

The *Equitidæ*, or swallow-tails, are a family of very handsome butterflies, many of which possess the long tails to the hind-wings from whence they derive their English name. Our only British species is the well-known swallow-tail butterfly *Eques machaon* (Linn.), at present almost confined, with us, to the fen districts of Norfolk, though formerly much more abundant. It is black and yellow, with a large red spot on the lower part of the hind-wings, and measures about four inches in expanse. The green caterpillar, with black spots and bands, and a retractile fork on the neck, feeds on fennel, carrot, and other umbelliferous plants. We have figured an allied species, *Eques alexanor* (Esper.), distinguished by the continuous black band near the base of the wings, which is found in the mountains of South Europe. To this family belong the great bird-winged butterflies, *Ornithoptera* (Boisd.), of the East Indies and the Eastern Archipelago. They share, with the *Morphinæ*, the distinction of being among the largest butterflies in the world, measuring from three to nine or ten inches in expanse; but usually about six or seven. They are long-winged butterflies, with black fore-wings and yellow hind-wings; or with large green, blue, or orange longitudinal bands on the dark fore-wings, and the hind-wings mostly of the colour of the bands. The larvæ are covered with rather long and thick fleshy spines, but have always the retractile fork on the neck, which is one of the most characteristic marks of the *Equitidæ*. Another interesting genus is *Parnassius* (Latr.). These are satiny-white butterflies, slightly transparent towards the edges, with black spots, and generally also round red spots, more or less centred with white, on the hind-wings, at least. They are mountain butterflies, and are most numerous in Central Asia; though three species inhabit the Swiss Alps, the commonest being *Parnassius apollo* (Linn.), which must be well known to everyone who has ever collected butterflies in Switzerland. These might easily be mistaken for *Pieridæ*, but that the inner margin of the hind-wings is not gutter-shaped, as it generally is in the *Pieridæ*, and the internal nervure, which is very conspicuous in the *Pieridæ*, is wholly absent in all the *Equitidæ*.

Fig. 71.—SWALLOW-TAIL (*Eques alexanor*). Nat. size.

Family *Hesperiidæ* (Skippers).

The last family of butterflies, the *Hesperiidæ*, has six perfect legs in both sexes, but differs very much from any of the preceding groups. The head is broad, the antennæ are set widely apart, and are generally hooked at the tips, the body is rather stout, and the flight is short and jerky. Our species have somewhat triangular fore-wings, and rounded hind-wings, and are brown and tawny; black, tesselated with square white spots; or brown, with dull greyish and rather indistinct spots. The *Hesperiidæ* are very numerous in South America, but less so in the Old World. They are mostly of small size, the largest being a dull blue West African species, *Rhopalocampta iphis* (Dru.), which measures about four inches across the wings. They form a transition to the moths; many species sit with the wings expanded, instead of raising them over their backs; and they often make a rough sort of cocoon in a leaf. The Grizzled Skipper, *Hesperia malvæ* (Linn.), here figured is a small black and white butterfly not uncommon in England.

Fig. 72.—GRIZZLED SKIPPER (*Hesperia malvæ*). Nat. size.

Heterocera, or Moths.

The *Heterocera*, or moths, are divided into a great number of families, which are loosely classed together under various headings; but the classification of moths is still in an unsatisfactory state, and though many groups of families, large and small, are perfectly natural, others are ill-defined and unsatisfactory. The old group *Sphinges* is now quite given up, including, as it did, three totally distinct sections, the hawk-moths, clear-wings, and burnets. The *Bombyces* include a number of very discordant families, for which no definite collective characters can be found, such as the tigers, footmen, eggars, emperor moths, swifts, etc. The *Noctuæ*, or night-flying moths proper, are more compact, though even here there is a difficulty in determining whether many genera belong to this group, or to the *Bombyces*. The *Geometræ* are a compact group, and so to some extent are the remaining groups. We will now consider the moths more in detail.

Of the families classed under *Sphinges* and *Bombyces*, most of the species have short, stout, and often tufted bodies, large wings, and pectinated, or sometimes fusiform antennæ. The larvæ have sixteen legs, and generally spin cocoons, though some pupate in the ground. Many beautiful day-flying moths belong here, some of which were formerly classed as butterflies. Among these are the bright green black-striped *Uraniidæ* of South America, three inches in expanse, with long tails on the hind-wings like swallow-tail butterflies. More familiar to us are the burnets (*Zygænidæ*), moths with long fore-wings about an inch and a half across, with long pubescent bodies, and blackish bronzy fore-wings, with five or six crimson spots, and red hind-wings. They are found in meadows, flying heavily from flower to flower in the daytime. The tiger moths (*Arctiidæ*) are larger, and very brightly coloured moths, and more nocturnal in their habits as a rule. The commonest, *Hypercompa caia* (Linn)., has brown fore-

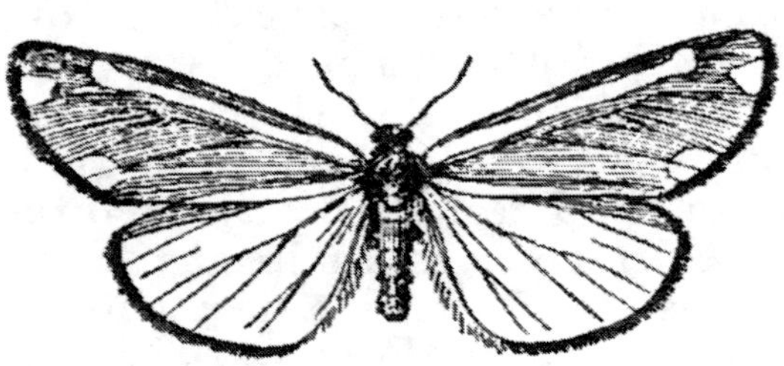

Fig. 73.—CINNABAR MOTH (*Hiposrita jacobæa*). Nat. size.

wings, with interlacing white markings, and red hindwings with large bluish black spots. Its caterpillar, which is often called the woolly bear, is common in gardens, and is covered with long reddish-brown hair, partly tipped with white. It feeds on all sorts of low plants, and when disturbed, rolls itself up into a ball, and drops among the herbage. Bred specimens of the moth are peculiarly liable to vary, some of the specimens being quite black; but those reared in a state of nature are much less variable.

The *Liparidæ* are another family of stout-bodied *Bombyces.* Many of the species are white, like the gold-tail and brown-tail moths, which are common on hedges, and receive their names from the tuft of wool at the end of the body, which the female uses to cover her eggs. They measure rather more than an inch across the wings, and the larvæ are gregarious, and are often very destructive.

Some of the families of moths classed as *Bombyces* have slender bodies and long wings. The *Lithosiidæ* are a group well represented in Europe. They generally have oblong greyish fore-wings, with a yellowish streak on the costa, and slate-coloured hind-wings: they measure about an inch and a half in expanse, and their larvæ feed on lichens. The cinnabar moth, *Hipocrita jacobææ* (Linn.), is more brightly coloured, being black and red, like the burnet moths, though the antennæ and the pattern of the wings are quite different. It is not rare in Britain. The South American family *Dioptidæ* includes larger moths, with more rounded wings, and more varied in their colours. Some of them are partially transparent; and many, except in their simple or slightly pectinated antennæ, resemble butterflies of the sub-family *Ithomiinæ.*

The *Cyllopodidæ* are another South American family of rather small moths, rarely measuring more than an inch and a half across the wings, which are remarkable for their strongly contrasted black and yellow colour.

The *Psychidæ* are a family of small grey or, more frequently, smoky-black moths, remarkable for their thick, hairy bodies, and strongly-pectinated antennæ. They rarely reach an inch in expanse, and are found flying among long grass in the daytime. The larvæ construct a case of bits of vegetable matter, in the same way as the larvæ of the caddis-flies, and the females are wingless, and in some instances, legless also, in which latter case they never quit the dwelling which they have inhabited as larvæ and pupæ. The species figured, *Chalia furva* (Borkhausen), is rather scarce in England.

Fig. 74.—Chalia furva. Nat. size.

Among the largest moths are the *Saturniidæ,* to which our emperor moth, *Saturnia pavonia-minor* (Linn.), belongs. The emperor moth measures two and a half to three inches across the wings, which are light brown, varied with orange in the male, and of a soft grey in the female; in the middle of each wing is a large round eye-spot. The green, red-spotted larva feeds on heath, and makes a flask-like cocoon.

All the moths of this family have stout and often short bodies, pectinated antennæ, and ample wings, with a more or less developed eye-spot or transparent mark in the middle of each. Some are green or brown, with long tails on the hind-wings; but the largest of all, the Indian Atlas Moth, which sometimes measures a foot in expanse, has tawny brown fore-wings, with festooned black and white lines, between which is a large talc-like spot on each wing, of very irregular shape.

Most of the silk-producing moths of any commercial value belong either to the *Saturniidæ* or the *Bombycidæ.* The common mulberry silk-worm moth, *Bombyx mori* (Linn.), the type of the *Bombyces,* is too well known to need description here.

The *Lasiocampidæ* are stout-bodied moths with strongly pectinated antennæ, and hairy caterpillars. They are generally of a brown or yellowish colour, and the wings are sometimes dentated, but never tailed. It includes the oak-eggar, drinker moth, lappet, lackey moth, and other familiar British species. The lackey moth, *Clisiocampa neustria* (Linn.), is remarkable for the habit of the female in laying her eggs in a ring round a slender twig. All the larvæ of this family are very hairy.

Fig. 75.—Lackey Moth (*Clisiocampa neustria*). Nat. size.

Three families of *Bombyces* are remarkable for their larvæ feeding in the trunks of trees, or on the roots of grasses; as well as for the abnormal neuration of the perfect insects. The goat-moth, *Trypanus cossus* (Linn.), belonging to the family *Zeuzeridæ,* is a broad-winged greyish-brown coarsely-scaled moth, in which the discoidal cell of the wings is divided by additional nervures, which are obsolete in most Lepidoptera. Its dark red, foul-smelling, naked larva is very destructive to old willows, and takes three years to arrive at maturity.

The *Castniidæ* are a South American group of stout-bodied moths, with rather short and broad wings, measuring from two to six or seven inches in

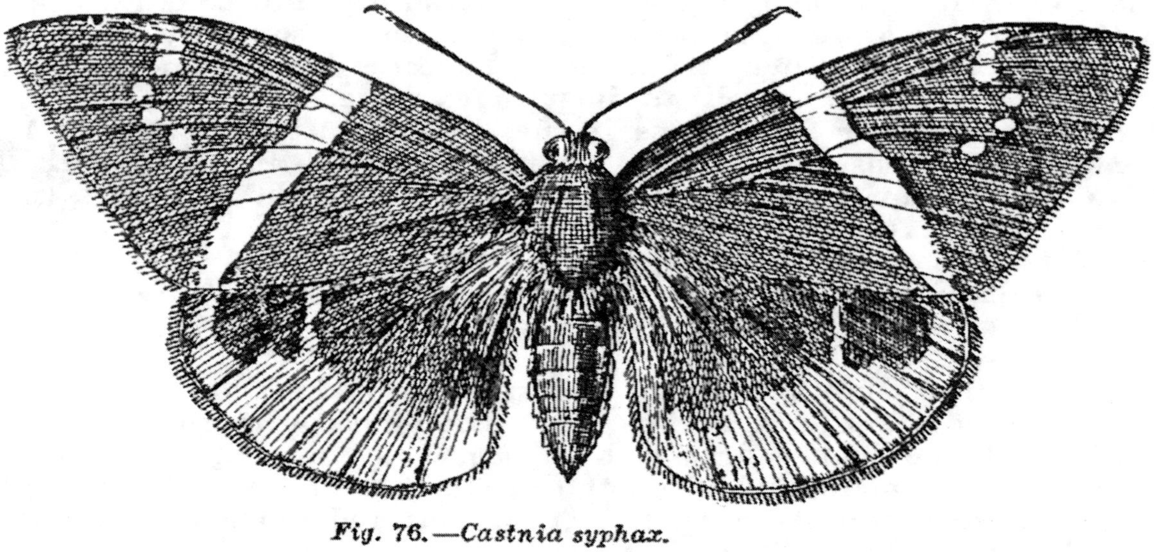

Fig. 76.—*Castnia syphax.*

expanse. The antennæ are very thick, and rather tapering at the ends They are brightly-coloured insects, and fly by day. They somewhat resemble large *Hesperiidæ,* and were classed as butterflies by all the older writers. The cells of their wings are sub-divided, as in the *Zeuzeridæ,* and hence we notice them now, though their natural position is near the beginning of the moths. The species figured, *Castnia syphax* (Fabr.), is black, with white markings on the fore-wings and a red border to the hind-wings.

Our swift moths (*Hepialidæ*) have rather long wings and very short antennæ. They exhibit many remarkable peculiarities; the wings are separated at the base, the connecting link between them being not by a bristle, as in many moths, but by a long lobe. The fore and hind-wings have similar neuration, and the hind-legs of the males are more or less aborted in some of the species. The ghost moth, *Hepialus humuli* (Linn.), is common in every meadow, where the male, which is white on the upper-side of the wings, and brown below, flies at dusk with a peculiar hovering motion. The female has yellow fore-wings blotched with red, and the hind-wings and under-surface are brown. The European swifts feed on the roots of plants, but there are some splendid green Australian species, measuring four or five inches across the wings, the larvæ of which feed on the wood of trees. Owing to the unusual neuration and mode of connection of the wings in the *Hepialidæ*, Professor Comstock has recently proposed to associate this family with the *Micropterygidæ*, a family which used to be placed among the *Tineæ*, and to treat them as forming a primary division (in fact, a sub-order) of the order Lepidoptera. In this innovation he has since been followed by other authors.

Fig. 77.—GHOST MOTH (female) (*Hepialus humuli*). Nat. size.

The *Noctuæ* are a large group of stout-bodied moths. To it belong many of the moths which we see flying over flowers, or about a candle in the evening. Most of our species measure from one to two inches in expanse, and many are of dull colours. Some have metallic spots, or letter-like markings, like the burnished brass moth, *Plusia chrysitis* (Linn.), which has large bronzy-green markings on its brown fore-wings; or the violet-grey gamma moth, *Plusia gamma* (Linn.), a very common day-flying species, with a white mark resembling the Greek letter γ on each of its fore-wings. Others are brown, with black streaks and dashes on the wings, like the heart-and-dart moth, *Agrotis exclamationis* (Linn.). The larvæ of the dart moths are often very destructive, as they live just below the surface of the ground, where they eat through the roots of plants. There are many closely-allied species, and the Americans call them "cut-worms."

Fig. 78.—BURNISHED BRASS MOTH (*Plusia chrysitis*). Nat. size.

If we toss about a heap of hay, or disturb the leaves of a strawberry-bed, we are very likely to start a specimen of one of the common yellow under-wing moths, *Triphæna* (Hübn.), which, after a short headlong flight, will settle again, and soon disappear. In these moths the fore-wings are brown, and comparatively long and narrow, and the hind-wings are very broad, and of a bright yellow, with a black border. In tropical countries other yellow underwinged butterflies are found, *Ophideres* (Boisd.), measuring three inches across the wings. They are remarkable for having the proboscis modified into a kind of boring instrument, with which they pierce the skin of oranges, and suck out the contents.

Geometræ.

We now come to the *Geometræ*, or land-measurers, which may always be distinguished (if the transformations are known) by the larvæ only possessing ten legs, the first three pairs of prolegs being obsolete. When they walk they fix themselves by the last pair of prolegs and the claspers, stretch out their bodies, fix themselves firmly by their true legs, and then draw up the four hinder legs, and repeat the process. Thus, the body of the caterpillar is arched into a loop at every step, and these caterpillars are often called "loopers" on that account. This performance, though it takes a long time to describe, is nevertheless comparatively rapid, and the larvæ are able to make as good progress as other caterpillars with the full complement of legs. These curious larvæ often fix themselves, as described, by the claspers and hind pair of prolegs, and stretch their bodies straight out, when they look for all the world like little bits of green or dried twigs.

Most of these moths have slender bodies and broad wings. They are frequently adorned with bright colours, and the fore and hind-wings are, more or less similar in markings; some species, however, have short, thick, hairy bodies, and resemble *Bombyces*, except in their larvæ. In several brown species, which appear during the winter, the females have only rudimentary wings. One of the commonest of the *Geometræ* is the magpie moth, *Abraxas grossulariata* (Linn.), which is found among gooseberry and currant bushes, on the leaves of which the larvæ feed. It measures an inch and a half across the wings, which are white, with black and yellowish spots.

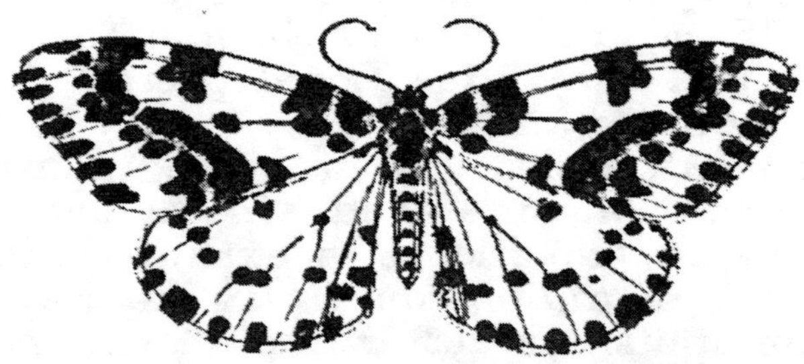

Fig. 79.—Magpie Moth (*Abraxas grossulariata*). Nat. size.

The next group of moths, the *Pyrales*, have long slender legs and antennæ, slender bodies, and large wings, the fore-wings being generally triangular, and the hind-wings rounded. They are of rather small size, rarely much exceeding an inch in expanse, and are often white, grey or yellow. Two of the best known species, the small magpie, *Botys urticata* (Linn.), which is white, marked with large black spots; and the mother-of-pearl, *B. verticalis* (Linn.), are common among nettles. Some of the smaller white and brown species are found among reeds, the larvæ feeding on water plants; other small species of this family, which frequent hill-sides and mountains, are black, with or without white lines or spots; or are beautifully marked with purple and gold.

Fig. 80.—Small Magpie Moth (*Botys urticata*). Nat. size.

The foregoing butterflies and moths mostly include species of comparatively large size, and are therefore often called Macro-Lepidoptera. The succeeding families mostly include small moths. The first group of these is the *Crambi*, which were frequently included in the *Pyrales* by the older entomologists. They are small moths, generally not much exceeding an inch in expanse, with long narrow fore-wings, and broad hind-wings. The best known representatives of this group are the grass moths, belonging to the genus *Crambus* (Fabr.), which have long palpi, like a snout, yellowish white-streaked fore-wings, and broad brown hind-wings. In some species, as in *C. ericellus* (Hübner), this white streak is very conspicuous. In walking through long grass, we often disturb these moths, which fly a short distance and then settle again on a stalk, head downwards, with their wings folded round them in almost a tubular form.

Fig. 81.—GRASS MOTH (*Crambus ericellus*). Nat. size.

The *Tortrices*, or bell moths, generally have broad, short fore-wings, cut off straight at the ends, and rounded hind-wings. They sit with their fore-wings flat, meeting over their backs, and covering the hind-wings, and in this position somewhat resemble a bell in shape, whence their popular name. There are about 300 British species of this group, some of which are very destructive. One of the best known and most easily recognised is the green oak tortrix, *Tortrix viridana* (Linn.), which has green fore-wings with a yellow costa, and brown hind-wings. If an oak-branch is struck or shaken, we may often see a whole shower of these conspicuous little green moths come fluttering down. They measure rather less than an inch in expanse. The larvæ are also green, with a brown head; they live between rolled-up leaves of the oak, and if alarmed, drop themselves a little way down by a thread, and climb back as soon as the danger appears to be over.

Fig. 82.—GREEN OAK TORTRIX (*Tortrix viridana*). Nat. size.

Other *Tortrices* feed, in the larva state, in flower-heads, and others, again, in fruits. Different species of the genus *Carpocapsa* (Treitschke) feed in acorns, beech-nuts, plums, etc.; but perhaps the most injurious of all is the codling moth, *C. pomonella* (Linn.), the pink larva of which feeds in apples and pears. The moth is grey, with darker lines, and some coppery markings towards the tip. It measures about three-quarters of an inch in expanse. It has been introduced into all parts of the world, and is everywhere as destructive as in England.

The *Tineæ* are a very large group of small moths, numbering in Britain alone upwards of 600 species. Very few exceed an inch in expanse, and the greater number are much smaller. They are divided into a great number of families, which differ very much in structure and habits, but they may generally be easily recognised by their small size and long narrow wings, with very long fringes. Some of them feed in cases or galleries, like many species of *Tineæ* (Linn.), to which genus the true clothes-moths, the corn-moth, and other highly destructive insects belong. Others feed on fungi, like *Tinea fulvimitrella* (Sodoffsky), a purplish-brown moth with white spots, which is a woodland insect, and not found in houses. Some have very long antennæ, like the beautiful delicate bronzy moths of the genus *Adela* (Latr.), which we find flying about bushes in spring. The small ermine moths of the genus *Hyponomeuta* (Latr.) are white or lead-coloured moths, with rows of black spots on the fore-wings; and their larvæ web over and devour our hedges and apple-trees, for they are gregarious, and often very destructive.

Fig. 83.—*Tinea fulvimitrella*. Nat. size.

Many entomologists regard the *Hyponomeutidæ* as more closely allied to the *Bombyces* than to the *Tineæ*. Many *Tineæ* mine the leaves of grasses, and this habit is characteristic of the *Elachistidæ*. Others, like the *Nepticulidæ*, a family which includes the smallest moths known, make long galleries or mines, as they are called, between the membranes of a leaf. These may often be found on leaves of bramble, nut, etc.; but such mines are not always due to the larvæ of *Tineæ;* for this habit is shared by other insects. Thus there is a very common mine on holly leaves which is produced by the larva of a two-winged fly. Some larvæ which feed in a similar manner produce a blotch on the leaf, and not a mine. One of the commonest of these blotches is that formed by the larva of the beautiful delicate little *Gracilaria syringella* (Linn.) on the leaves of the lilac.

The *Pterophoridæ*, or plume moths, are now considered by most authors to be allied to the *Pyrales.* They are very delicate insects, with long, slender bodies and legs, and long wings, measuring an inch or less in expanse, and cleft almost to the base into separate feathers, two on the fore-wings, and three on the hind-wings. The largest, commonest, and most conspicuous among them is the white plume moth, *Pterophorus pentadactylus* (Linn.). Its larva feeds on *Convolvulus*, and it may often be seen floating about weedy places, strawberry beds, etc., looking like a snow-flake. Strawberry beds are a favourite resort of many insects, probably for purposes of concealment.

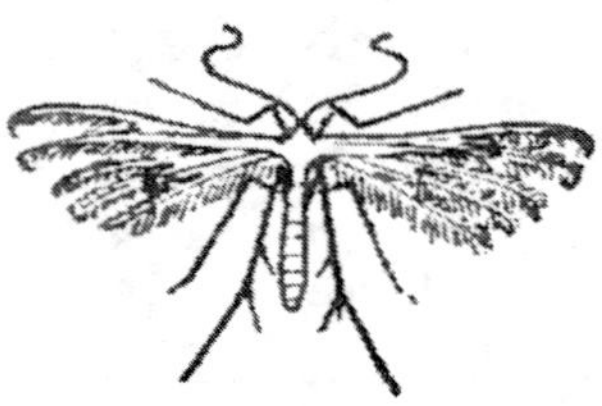

Fig. 84.—WHITE PLUME MOTH (*Pterophorus pentadactylus*).

The last family of moths, the *Alucitidæ*, which forms an isolated group, is represented in England by the twenty-plume moth, *Alucita hexadactyla* (Linn.). Its larva feeds in the buds of the honeysuckle. The moth is grey, with broad wings about two-thirds of an inch in expanse, and it is often noticed on windows, walls, etc., sitting with its wings spread out flat, and looking like one of the smaller Geometræ. But on a closer inspection we find that each wing is split up into six separate feathers, which distinguishes it at once from any other moth found in this country.

Fig. 85.—TWENTY-PLUME MOTH (*Alucita hexadactyla*). Nat. size.

ORDER HEMIPTERA (BUGS AND FROG-HOPPERS).

This is a somewhat extensive order of insects, with four wings, of which the front pair, or tegmina, are usually of a stouter consistency than the hind-wings. They are divided into two main sections. In the first, the Hemiptera Heteroptera, or true bugs, the tips of the tegmina are usually transparent, and veined; but in the Hemiptera the fore-wings are nearly of the same consistency throughout. In many large groups of Hemiptera, however, the fore-wings are transparent and veined, like the hind-wings; but all the insects belonging to both sections of the order may be known by their strong sucking proboscis, and the absence of mandibles. The metamorphoses are incomplete.

Sub-Order Heteroptera.

Bugs.

Sub-Order Heteroptera (*Bugs*).

The word bug is derived from the Arabic, and has nothing etymologically to do with bogy, with which it is popularly associated. It suggests an ugly, foul-smelling, wingless insect, which sucks blood, hides itself in crevices, and shuns the light. In America, however, the word has come to be extended to insects in general. Entomologically it is applied to the insects belonging to the sub-order Heteroptera, only some of which suck blood, the greater number feeding on the juices of plants; and these are as beautiful and varied in form and colour as the beetles; or more so, in proportion to their numbers, and they are mostly diurnal insects. These insects may easily be recognised, not only by the characters mentioned above, but by the peculiar structure of the antennæ, which, though generally of considerable length, are composed of a very few long and well-separated joints—generally four or five.

The *Scutellridæ*, or shield-bugs, are those which most resemble beetles, and would be easily mistaken for them at first sight. But the hard convex wing-covering is not formed by wing-cases meeting on their inner edges, as in beetles, but consists of an inordinate development of the appendage to the thorax called the scutellum, under which not only the wings, but the tegmina also, which in such cases differ little in consistency from the wings, are completely hidden. These bugs are not numerous in Europe, but in tropical countries they are often as large as a cockchafer, and of brilliant colours. *Callidea perplexa* (Hope), here figured, is a common East Indian species, of a brilliant green or purple, with black spots.

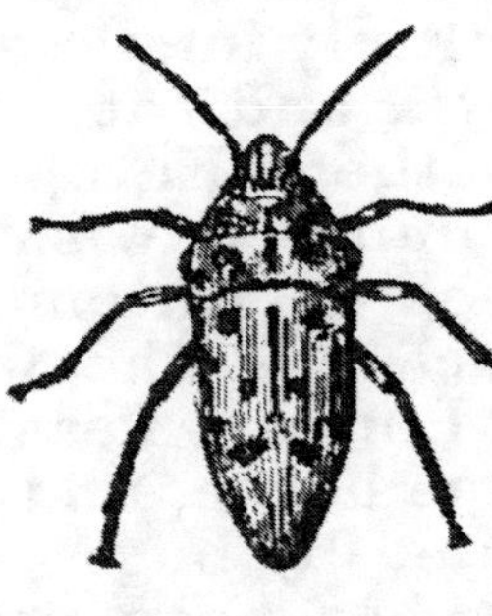

Fig. 86.—Shield-Bug (*Callidea perplexa*). Nat. size.

In the family *Pentatomidæ*, the body is still short, broad, and bulky in many of the species, but the scutellum, though still of considerable size, is a long structure, differing in shape, separating more or less of the basal portion of the tegmina, when the wings are closed. Beyond its extremity, the membranous portion of the over-lapping tegmina is generally visible. Several brown or grass-green species belonging to this family are not uncommon in England In many species, especially foreign ones, the front of the thorax expands into a kind of spine or horn on each side, often of considerable length.

Fig. 87.—*Acanthosoma griseum.* Linn. Nat. size.

Some species of *Pentatomidæ* are carnivorous as well as herbivorous, and will attack caterpillars and other soft insects, and suck out their juices. *Acanthosoma griseum* (Linn.), which is common in England on birch, is an oval insect, about a third of an inch long. The thorax is angulated in front, and the colour is reddish-ochreous or greenish, finely punctured with black; at the base of the scutellum is a black patch. Like some of the earwigs and Australian sawflies, the female of this species has been observed to watch over her newly-hatched young like a hen, and it is said that, as in the case of the crocodiles, and some other animals, her vigilance is chiefly required to guard them against the attacks of the male.

The species of this family are more numerous in America than in England, and they are called "stink bugs" in the former country, on account of the offensive odour which many of them emit.

There are a great variety of other flower-frequenting bugs belonging to various families, but the European species are mostly of small size, though often prettily coloured. The scutellum is generally much smaller than in the *Pentatomidæ*, and the body is more oval; the legs and antennæ are often long and slender, remarkably so in some species; and occasionally the antennæ are clubbed. In some of the large foreign species belonging to the family *Harpactoridæ*, the thorax is often curved forwards on each side, and toothed in front, while the antennæ and tibiæ are often lobate, and the hind-femora much thickened and dentated.

Plant-Bugs.

Among the carnivorous land-bugs, two families are specially notable. One of these is the *Cimicidæ*, the type of which, and, indeed, of the whole sub-order Heteroptera, is the common bed-bug, to which we have already alluded. It is of a reddish-brown colour, broad, flattened, with very slight rudiments of wings (which are said occasionally to become fully developed in hot climates), and measures less than a quarter of an inch in length when full grown; but the larval forms, which are, of course, much smaller, are equally fond of blood, though they must be capable of subsisting on other food, as they have been known to multiply in empty houses. Very similar species are found attacking pigeons, fowls, and bats. This insect has always been common throughout Africa and Southern Europe, but was scarcely known in England till it was introduced in numbers with foreign timber after the Fire of London. (See my "Text-Book of Entomology," p. 204.) It has many enemies, including the cock-roach and the wheel-bug; and I have been informed that in the poor parts of London, fleas and bugs do not generally exist in equal numbers in the same house, and that, as a rule, it is the cleaner houses which are most infested by bugs. Can it be that fleas will attack bugs? I am not aware that this has been previously observed or surmised; but, as fleas are known to attack caterpillars, it does not seem by any means impossible.

The Bed-Bug.

The *Reduviidæ*, or wheel-bugs, are a family of rather large bugs, with a large head, contracted behind into a neck, prominent eyes, two ocelli, rather short antennæ, and a curved proboscis or rostrum. The type of the family is the masked-bug, *Reduvius personatus* (Linn.), the larva and pupa of which cover themselves with particles of dust, apparently in order to creep upon their insect prey unnoticed. This species is not uncommon in outhouses, and is a blackish or dark brown insect, two-thirds of an inch long, and very hairy, especially on the head, antennæ, and legs. There is a whitish line on the membrane-suture of the tegmina. This species is rarely found in houses; but, as already mentioned, it preys on the bed-bug, as well as on flies, etc. Its own bite is said to be as painful as the sting of the bee, which may well be the case, considering its comparatively large size; but it does not appear to attack man or the higher animals habitually. There are, however, other and much larger species of the same family that are great pests to both man and beast in the Southern States of America, Chili, and other parts of the world.

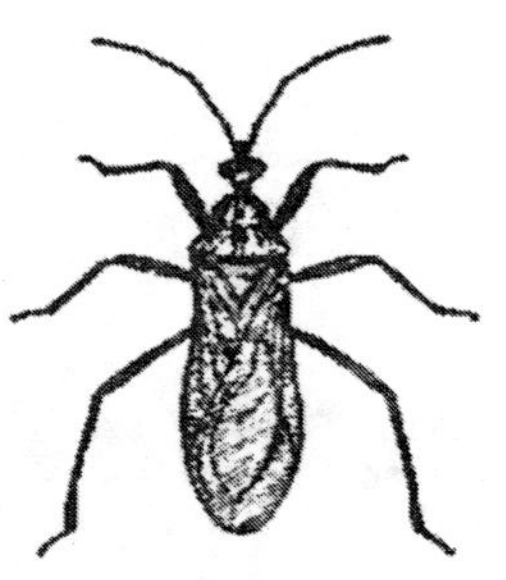

Fig. 88.—MASKED-BUG (*Reduvius personatus*). Nat. size.

Many bugs, including several of this family, are usually apterous, but acquire wings occasionally ; while in some species, two forms are habitually met with, in one of which the wings are more or less rudimentary, while in the other they are fully developed.

Hitherto we have been discussing land-bugs, but several families of the Heteroptera are aquatic, and among them we find the largest species of the sub-order.

Water-Bugs.

The first family includes the *Hydrometridæ*, the water-measurers, which are long, narrow, black insects, often with fine silvery pubescence. They have very long middle and hind-legs, and the front-legs are directed forward. Here, too, we meet with both winged and apterous adult individuals of the same species. They measure from one to three-quarters of an inch in length, and are found running rapidly on the surface of the water, and feeding on small insects. They can also dive when alarmed. One genus of this family, *Halobates* (Esch.), is found running on the surface of the open ocean in various regions of the tropics.

Water-Scorpion.

The *Nepidæ*, or water-scorpions, have an oval and rather flattened body, terminating in a breathing tube of nearly half its length, and the front pair of legs have thickened femora, and project forwards in such a manner as to suggest the pincers of a scorpion. Our British species, *Nepa cinerea* (Linn.) is a brown insect, nearly an inch long exclusive of the spiracular tube, and is found in muddy, stagnant pools.

Ranatra linearis (Linn.) is an insect allied to the last, and belonging to the family *Ranatridæ*. It is, however, very long and narrow, and of a lighter yellowish-brown colour. The middle and hind-legs are very long and slender, and the front pair are much longer and less thickened than in *Nepa*. It measures nearly three inches in length, of which the abdominal breathing-tube occupies nearly half. It is not a very common insect in England, and creeps about at the bottom of stagnant water.

The largest Heteroptera belong to the family *Belostomatidæ*, which is not British, though common in most of the warmer parts of the world. They are oval insects, with the legs flattened, especially the front femora. The insects sometimes measure four and a half inches in length, and six inches or more in expanse of wing. They are of a yellowish-brown colour. In the evening they leave the water, and fly about. This is a common habit with many water-insects, which enables them to migrate from one place to another, if the ponds in which they live dry up. In America, where one or two species are common, they are sometimes attracted in large numbers by the electric light. They feed on small fish, frogs, etc., as well as on water-insects.

Water-Boatmen.

The water-boatmen (*Notonectidæ*) are represented in England by one or two yellowish species, about half an inch long, with flattened hind-legs fringed with hairs, and which stand out from the body in the position of oars. They are used in a similar manner, for the insects float on their backs, and row themselves about with them. *Zaitha aurantiaca* (Leidy) is a light brown North American species.

Among the remaining water-bugs are the *Corixidæ*, which are not unlike the *Notonectidæ*, but are smaller, much broader in proportion, especially the head, and more obtuse behind. They are brown or black, glossy, with yellowish striæ above.

A friend once showed me an absurd error with respect to the term water-boatmen, which is frequently applied to different species of water-bugs. It occurred in connection with the habits of some South American birds, in an ornithological work, the name of which I have forgotten, and ran something like this :—"They feed on the eggs which the fishermen lay on the banks of the streams, in clusters of six lines long by three broad." If I remember right, the passage was translated from the French, and I have little doubt that in the original some expression was used equivalent to "water-boatmen." It reminds me of another story which I read in the translation of a Russian book of travels, in which an elephant was described as seizing an object with his tail, instead of his trunk. I have also heard of a translation of a German book, in which a naturalist on shipboard, who wanted to shoot a bird, was described as taking down the back-shutters, instead of the breech-loader.

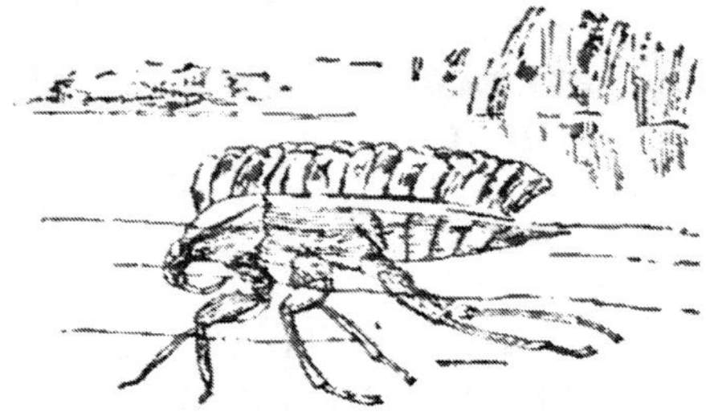

Fig. 89.—WATER-BUG (*Zaitha aurantiaca*), WITH EGGS. Nat. size.

SUB-ORDER HOMOPTERA (FROG-HOPPERS, PLANT-LICE, ETC.).

Sub-Order *Homoptera.*

A great number of insects are classed under this sub-order, which we have already briefly defined. They do not emit any foul odour like the Heteroptera ; their antennæ are generally very short ; and they are exclusively plant-feeders. Some of them supply us with useful products, such as shell-lac and cochineal, while others are among the most injurious insects which infest our gardens and greenhouses.

Family *Cicadidæ.*

The Homoptera are divided into several very distinct families, of which the first is the *Cicadidæ.* They are large, wedge-shaped insects, with a broad head, large eyes, a pointed body, with a short ovipositor in the female, and broad wings, which are generally, but not always, transparent. When at rest, the wings are folded roof-like over the body, and generally extend considerably beyond the abdomen. They are difficult insects to classify, as the most tangible characters available for the purpose are to be found in the drums of the males. These organs are found on each side of the abdomen, and are visible above in some genera, while in others they are covered by a flap. On the under-surface they are always covered by two flaps, called the opercula, which are sometimes very short, small, and rounded, and in others are very large, and extend nearly to the end of the abdomen. In the Australian genus *Thopha*, amongst the opercula are extended over the sides of the abdomen, as well as beneath. In *Tibicina* (Latr.), there are no covers at all on the upper surface of the abdomen ; and in *Zammara* (Amyot), the rims of the openings are slightly raised, giving them something of a pitcher shape. It has been proposed to divide the *Cicadidæ* into two sub-families, according to whether the drums are open or closed above ; but I find, not only that the upper abdominal covers differ very much in completeness or absence, but that many genera, otherwise closely allied, run in pairs, one with closed, and one with open tympana.

The sounds made by these insects have always made them celebrated, and they are among the noisiest denizens of the tropical forests. They are, however, difficult to capture, as they are not easily seen, and their flight, when disturbed, is very sudden and rapid. This is chiefly a tropical family, and the largest known species, *Pomponia imperatoria* (Westwood), which inhabits the Malay Islands, measures nearly eight inches in expanse. Several species are found in Southern Europe, and their song was greatly admired by the Greeks. In Northern Europe they are scarce, and we have but one small species in England, which is very far from common, and is almost confined to the New Forest, though it has once been met with near Haslemere. This species is *Melampsalta montana* (Scop.), and measures rather less than two inches in expanse. It is brown, with reddish markings on the thorax; and the principal wing nervures towards the base, and the incisions of the abdomen are of the same colour. It belongs to a very extensive genus of rather small species, in which the basal cell of the tegmina is long and narrow, and emits one bifurcating longitudinal nervure from its extremity, instead of two separate ones. This genus is represented by numerous, but usually comparatively small, species, in most parts of the world, and is especially numerous in Australia; and it is at present the only genus of *Cicadidæ* which is known to occur in New Zealand.

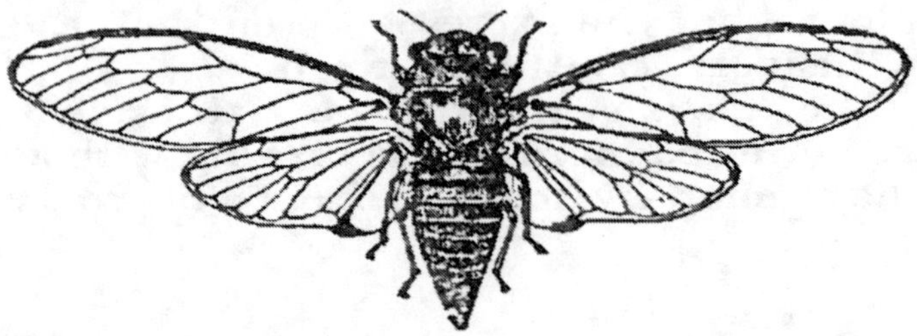

Fig. 90.—*Melampsalta montana* Nat. size.

The *Cicadidæ* vary from the general character of the Homoptera in the tegmina and wings being of uniform consistency, though the tegmina are always larger, and have a more elaborate neuration. They are insects with imperfect metamorphoses, and in countries where they are common, the empty pupa-skin may often be seen attached to trees by its strong claws, with a large hole in the back, through which the insect has emerged.

Family *Fulgoridæ*.—Lantern Flies.

The *Fulgoridæ* are an extensive and varied family, differing from the *Cicadidæ* in many particulars. There are only two ocelli, instead of three; the tegmina and wings are opaque, and generally differ considerably in consistency; the antennæ are inserted on the sides of the head and below the eyes; and the larvæ, and in many cases the perfect insects, are frequently covered with a white waxy exudation, which we seldom observe in the *Cicadidæ*, and then only to a trifling extent. This family is divided into several sub-families, of which we will mention some of the most interesting.

The *Fulgorinæ*, or true lantern and candle-flies, are exotic insects of rather large size, and are remarkable for having the front of the head produced into a long horn or excrescence, differing considerably in size and shape. The largest species is the lantern-fly of South America, *Fulgora laternaria* (Linn.), which often measures more than four inches in expanse. It is of a greenish-yellow colour, with a large eyelike spot on the hind-wings; the head is produced into a great hollow appendage, slightly bent downwards, and then continued forward. The candle-flies of the East Indies, *Hotinus candelarius* (Linn., etc.), are also large insects, measuring two or three inches in expanse. In the species we have mentioned, the tegmina are black and green, spotted

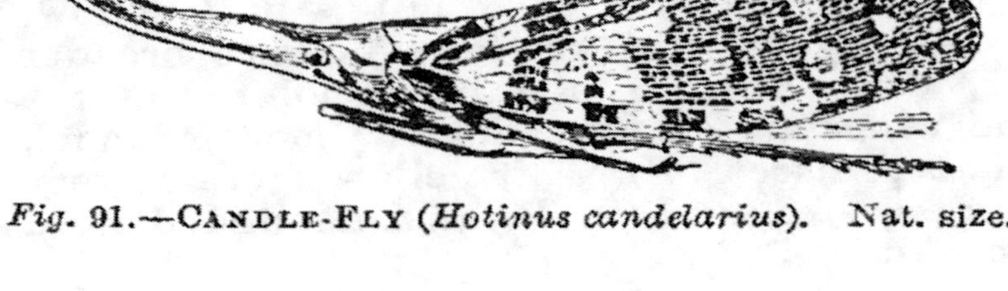

Fig. 91.—Candle-Fly (*Hotinus candelarius*). Nat. size.

with yellow, and the hind-wings are yellow, bordered with brown. There is a long and somewhat recurved horn on the head. Other species of this family are varied with blue or red, and the horns are of different colours and shapes; yellow or green, and pointed; dentated; white, with a red knob at the extremity; rather short, and trifid at the end, etc. Most of the species are East Indian or South American; a few are African.

The *Lystrinæ* are also tropical species of considerable size and bright colours, but the excrescence on the head is absent. They are chiefly, but not exclusively, South American.

The *Flatinæ* are another extensive tropical group, in which the tegmina are bordered more or less broadly with a row of oblique or transverse nervures. They generally measure from one to two inches in expanse. The tegmina are frequently green, sometimes prettily spotted with red, and are oval or angulated at the tips, and not much longer than the wings, which are generally light brown, grey, or white, and sub-hyaline. The species figured, *Flata circulata* (Guérin), is pale grey, with black markings. It is a native of Java.

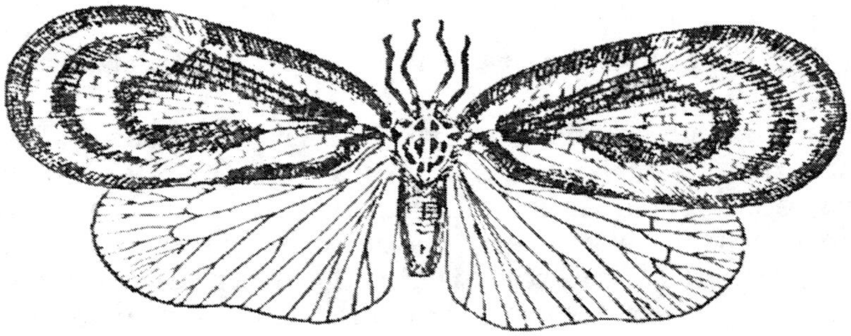

Fig. 92.—Flata circulata. Nat. size.

Most of the European *Fulgoridæ* are small insects. The *Delphacinæ*, which measure about one-sixth of an inch in length, have comparatively long antennæ, with the joints much thickened, and the last ending in a bristle. The hind-legs are very long, and strongly spined at the end of the tibiæ; they are generally of a yellow colour. The head is broad, and the face more or less keeled. They are generally found on grass in damp places, and many species are dimorphic, exhibiting both winged and subapterous forms.

The *Derbinæ* are a small exotic sub-family, with very short, oval bodies, comparatively long antennæ, unarmed legs, and long narrow wings, an inch in expanse, and shaped more like those of a *Tipula* or a *Pterophorus* than those of other homopterous insects.

In the *Cercopidæ*, the antennæ are placed between the eyes, just under the vertex; the scutellum is rather small, and the hind tibiæ are usually armed with from one to three spines, and a crown of stronger ones at their extremity.

This family includes the true frog-hoppers, the most conspicuous species of which is *Triecphora vulnerata* (Illiger), which is not unlike a small beetle in appearance. It is black, and measures about three-quarters of an inch across the long, oval, horny tegmina, which are black, with bright red markings; the wings are subhyaline. It is not uncommon in England. *Aphrophora alni* (Fall.) is about the same size, but is dull yellow, with brown markings on the elytra, which are broader than in *Triecphora vulnerata*, and more pointed at the tips; the hind-wings are also broader and more rounded than in the latter insect. Its soft yellow larva is very common on grass, etc., and is always surrounded by a mass of froth, called popularly "cuckoo-spit."

Fig. 93—Triecphora vulnerata. Nat. size.

Family *Jassidæ*.

The *Jassidæ* differ from the *Cercopidæ* in the hind tibiæ having a row of spines below. They are small yellowish insects, most of which are placed by Mr. G. B. Buckton, in his "Monograph of the British *Cicadæ*," under the genus *Deltocephalus* (Burm.).

Family *Membracidæ*.

The *Membracidæ* are remarkable for the thorax being produced into a long horn or spine, which is frequently recurved over the abdomen. The genus *Centrotus* (Fabr.), represented in England by *C. cornutus* (Linn.), is very numerous in species, which are generally of a black or brown colour, with paler wings and tegmina, the sides of the thorax projecting to a more or less sharp point, and a long spine, broad at the base, and narrowing behind, projecting from the thorax over the back. They are insects of small size, rarely reaching a quarter of an inch in length. Among the foreign species, the forms of the horn in this family are frequently very remarkable. In one genus, *Umbonia* (Burm.), the species are yellow, streaked with red, and the whole insect is shaped exactly like the thorn of a rose tree. These are found in Tropical America. Respecting the North American species, Prof. Comstock remarks, "In some cases the prothorax is elevated above the head, so that it looks like a peaked nightcap; in others it is shaped like a Tam-o'-Shanter; and sometimes it has horns, one on each side, which have given one species the name of the buffalo tree-hopper." In others, again, the horn of the prothorax is nearly vertical, larger than the whole of the rest of the insect, and recurved and bifid at the extremity, and in some species from Tropical America, belonging to the genus *Bocydium* (Latr.), the horn separates into a number of little balls, each of which again throws off a small spine.

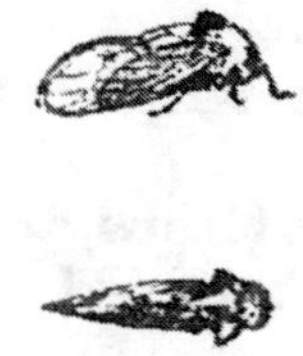

Fig. 94.—*Centrotus cornutus.* Nat. size.

The remaining families of Homoptera which we have to notice are all plant-feeding insects of small size, in which the proboscis appears to issue from between the front-legs, if present at all. The antennæ, when present, are usually long and slender, and the tarsi are one or two-jointed.

Family *Psyllidæ*.

The *Psyllidæ* are short, broad insects, which have been compared to minute Cicadas. The hind legs are thickened, and the antennæ terminate in two bristles. They leap about on plants, and many of the species produce galls. They resemble the *Aphidæ* in discharging a sweet fluid, which attracts ants, and their larvæ are covered with a white cottony exudation. They are provided with three ocelli. The wings are transparent.

Family *Aphididæ*.—Plant-Lice.

The *Aphididæ*, which are often called plant-lice, smother-flies, or blight, have slender legs, not fitted for leaping; the antennæ are long and slender, not terminating in a double bristle; the ocelli are absent, and the wings are transparent. There is a most curious alternation of broods in these insects, some forms being winged, and with separate sexes, and others winged or apterous, and capable of producing their kind for an indefinite number of generations before a sexual brood is again developed. Some produce galls, but the greater part feed on the leaves of trees. Sometimes one generation will live on one tree, and the next migrate to another, a future generation returning to the original food-plant. In fact, the anomalies of these insects are endless, and it would require volumes to epitomise even the comparatively little which has already been discovered with reference to their habits and transformations. They are small insects, but some are capable, like the *Phylloxera* of the vine, of ruining or crippling a vast industry over a considerable portion of the world. They exude a sweet liquid known as honey-dew, of which ants are extremely fond ; and to ants they bear the relation of milch-kine, and are frequently protected and tended by them accordingly. In some cases the ants are even said to superintend the breeding of the various broods.

The *Aleyrodidæ* are a small family, of which the perfect insects resemble very small moths, covered with a whitish powder. One or two species are very destructive to cabbages and tomatoes.

Family *Coccidæ.*—**Scale-Insects.**

The *Coccidæ*, or scale-insects, differ much from all other insects. The male has no rostrum, and only two wings, but possesses anal setæ, and the wingless, short-legged female settles herself permanently down on a leaf or twig, and forms a scale-like covering for her own eggs. Some of these furnish useful products, such as cochineal, but others are highly injurious. One species, *Icerya purchasi* (Maskell), caused great damage in California; but by the advice of the late Prof. C. V. Riley, an Australian lady-bird, *Novius cardinalis* (Muls.), was introduced into the country, and has since been effectual in keeping the ravages of the *Icerya* within bounds. Many of the *Coccidæ*, especially the larval forms, are covered either with a white cottony substance or with large plates of white wax, which in some cases has a commercial value.

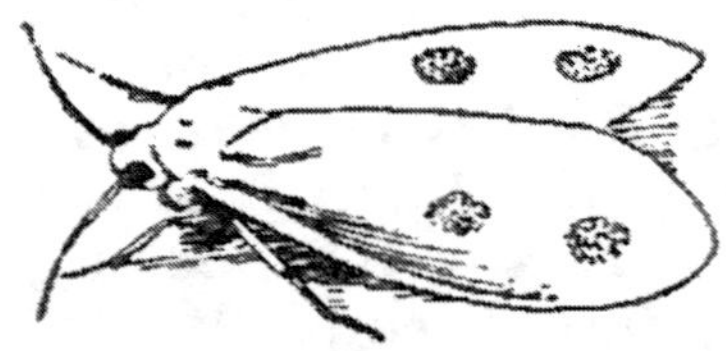

Fig. 95.—Aleyrodes proletella, Linn. Magnified.

Order Anoplura.

The true lice, which are wingless insects, parasitic on mammals, and furnished with a sucking proboscis, are sometimes regarded as a sub-order of Hemiptera. Three species at least infest man in European countries, and, besides the discomfort and annoyance which they occasion, are either the cause of, or accompany various diseases. They multiply very rapidly, but can usually be destroyed or kept away by ordinary attention to cleanliness. In warm countries, or, indeed, in any community where cleanliness is neglected, they are universally prevalent. There has been much controversy as to whether the lice infesting different races of mankind are to be regarded as distinct species, or only as slight varieties. Even the two species of lice which infest the head and clothes respectively, *Pediculus capitis* (Linn.), and *P. vestimenti* (Nitsch), although certainly distinct, are so much alike that they can hardly be distinguished from each other. The third species, the crab louse, *Pthirius inguinalis* (Leech), belongs to a distinct genus, and is much smaller, broader, and shorter than the others.

Order Diptera (Flies).

The Diptera, or Flies, differ from other insects in possessing only two wings throughout the whole of the Order, the hind-wings being represented only by two knobbed appendages like drumsticks, which are known as halteres or poisers. They are furnished with a proboscis, with which they imbibe their food, which consists, in the perfect state, of liquid substances only. They undergo a complete metamorphosis, their larvæ being footless maggots, which pass the pupa state in a barrel-shaped integument formed of the dried skin of the larva. In the larval state, many species live in water, some in the ground, others on plants, sometimes forming galls, while others feed on carrion, dung, etc.; and others, again, are parasitic on various animals, neither vertebrate nor invertebrate animals being secure from their attacks. They probably form one of the largest orders of insects, but have been so little studied that only 28,000 species were described up to 1892, of which between 2,000 and 3,000 inhabit the British Islands. The Flies are divided into two principal sections, and the Aphaniptera, or fleas, are now usually regarded as forming a third main section of Diptera rather than a separate order.

General Characteristics.

The body is not generally very hairy, and the wings are usually destitute of hair or scales, generally transparent, and with very few nervures, most of which are longitudinal. The Aphaniptera have the barest rudiments of wings, while some genera of Diptera are provided with small additional lobes at the base of the wings, which are usually called alulæ.

Diptera Nemocera (Gnats and Crane-Flies).

The insects belonging to this group are generally slender-bodied flies, with the antennæ long, or of moderate length, and composed of six joints and upwards. The palpi have from three to six joints. They frequently undergo their metamorphoses in the water or in the ground ; and none of the species of this section are parasitic, or even carnivorous, in the larval stage, though the females of certain families will suck blood in their perfect state.

The *Cecidomyiidæ*, or gall-gnats, with which we will commence our notice of the Nemocera, are very small, gnat-like insects, with long moniliform or cylindrical antennæ, often set with whorls of hairs, and comparatively broad, iridescent wings, with from two to five longitudinal nervures only, and these frequently not all clearly defined. Their bodies are clothed with long hairs. The larvæ are very various in their habits, many of them causing galls on various trees and plants, especially willows, while others live in bulbs, fungi, rotten wood, under bark, or in fir-cones. One or two species are at times very destructive to wheat, especially the wheat-midge and the Hessian-fly, *Diplosis tritici* (Kirb.), and *Cecidomyia destructor* (Say.). The latter has only lately been recognised as a British species. It attacks the stems of the wheat, which crack and bend over, and this appearance furnishes the easiest and most reliable evidence of the presence of the pest among the wheat. Its ravages are, however, much checked by the attacks of various small parasites belonging to the Hymenopterous family *Chalcididæ*.

Family *Cecidomyiidæ*. —Gall-Gnats.

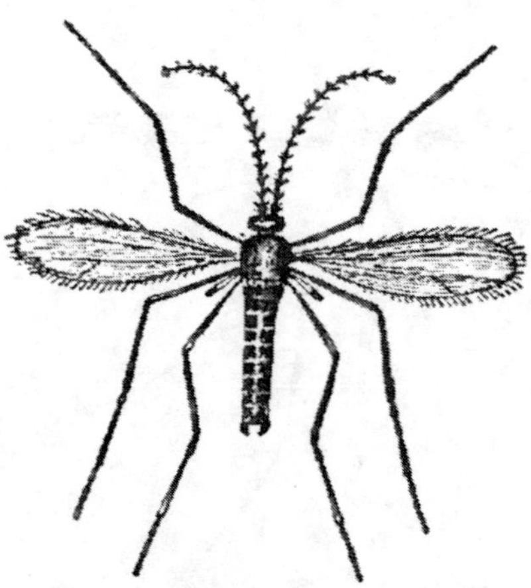

Fig. 96.—Hessian-Fly (*Cecidomyia destructor*). Magnified.

Besides the true gnats or mosquitoes (*Culicidæ*), some of the species belonging to several other families of this section of Diptera are extremely troublesome, the females sucking the blood of men and animals. These are the sand-flies (*Simuliidæ*), and also the *Chironomidæ* and *Psychodidæ*. The larvæ of all these families, except the *Psychodidæ*, live in water. The *Culicidæ* and *Chironomidæ* have more or less plumose antennæ in the males, which may often be seen on our windows. The transformations of the common gnat are very curious, and have often been described. The female gnat lays her eggs in a compact, boat-shaped mass, which floats on the surface of the water. The larva swims head downwards, having a respiratory tube at the hinder extremity of the body, through which it breathes. The pupa is of a different form, and swims head upwards, the upper end of the body, which is much thickened, being now provided with respiratory organs. When it has arrived at maturity, the skin of the upper end of the pupa splits, and the gnat gradually disengages itself, steps out on the surface of the water, and flies away. The *Simuliidæ* have short, broad wings, comparatively short and stout antennæ, and spotted legs, in which the first joint of the tarsi is as long as the remaining joints. The larvæ and pupæ live in water, where they form small cases, which they attach to grass-stems, weeds, stones, etc. Our British species are harmless, or nearly so ; but in many countries, as in the Banat of Hungary, for example, they form a terrible pest. The *Psychodidæ*, the last of this group of blood-sucking families which we shall notice, resemble small moths, and sit on the underside of leaves, or run actively over them. The principal blood-sucking species in this family is *Phlebotomus papatasii* (Scopoli), which inhabits the south-east of Europe. It is a small, hairy, yellowish-brown fly.

Gnats and Sand-Flies.

Next to the gnats and gnat-like flies, the most familiar insects belonging to the Nemocera are the *Tipulidæ*, which are generally called crane-flies, or daddy longlegs. These are flies with long, narrow, transparent or mottled wings, expanding from one to two inches ; a long pointed snout, on each side of which are moderately long antennæ ; and a long slender body, generally greyish-brown, but sometimes banded with yellow, and terminating, in the female, in a short horny point. They have very long slender legs, which break off at the least touch. They are easily disturbed when we are walking through the meadows, when they flit a few feet, and settle again with their wings extended. They frequently fly into rooms at night, being easily attracted by a light. Their grubs live in the ground, and feed on the roots of grass, frequently causing whole fields to wither and turn brown, as if parched up with drought. The smaller insects of this rather extensive family resemble gnats in size and general appearance, and some of them appear during the winter months. The species figured, *Pachyrhina crocata* (Linn.), is a rather handsome black and yellow insect, and is found in woods.

Family *Tipulidæ*.—Crane-Flies.

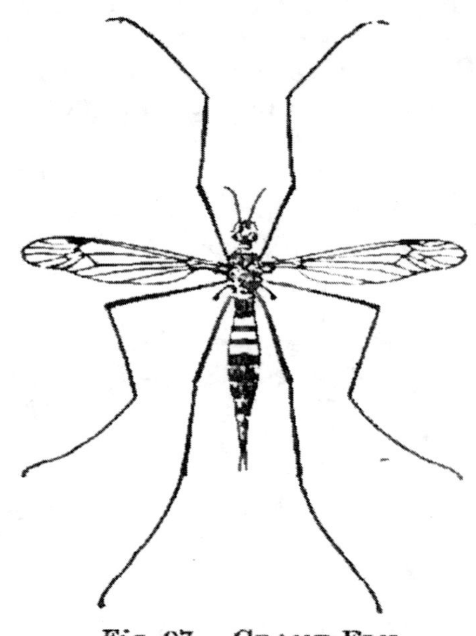

Fig. 97.—Crane-Fly (*Pachyrhina crocata*). Nat. size.

DIPTERA BRACHYCERA (FLIES).

The flies of this section are generally stouter than those of the last, and may be distinguished from them by their very short antennæ, which generally consist only of three joints (never more than six), and often terminate in a long bristle ; the palpi, too, consist of one or two joints only.

Family *Stratiomyidæ*.

The *Stratiomyidæ* are a family of small or moderate-sized flies of sluggish habits, which are often to be met with on flowers. Some are rather pretty black or black and yellow flies, often with spines on the scutellum. Many of their larvæ live in water or mud.

Family *Tabanidæ*.—Gad-Flies.

The *Tabanidæ*, or gad-flies, are large flies with stout bodies and a very strong proboscis. They vary in length from an inch downwards, and are frequently very troublesome in the woods and fields, by sucking the blood of men and animals. Some are of a plain brown colour, but others are rather pretty, being clothed with golden hair, while others are banded or marked with reddish-yellow. The larvæ are harmless, living in damp situations, among fallen leaves, etc.; and, as usual, it is only the female flies which suck blood.

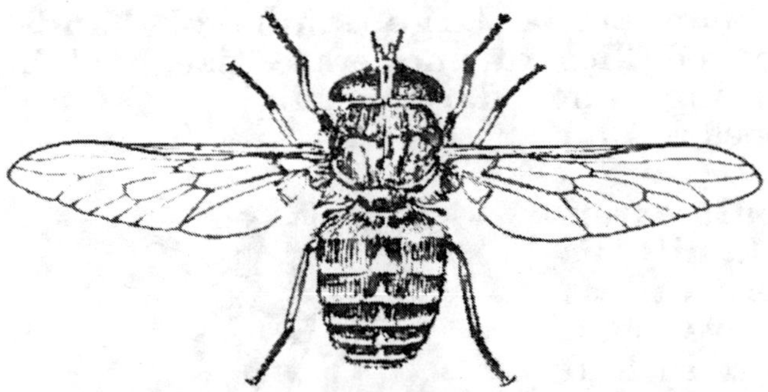

Fig. 98.—GAD-FLY (*Tabanus bovinus*). Nat. size.

We have been speaking here chiefly of the genus *Tabanus* (Linn.), the largest British species of which, *T. bovinus* (Linn.), is here figured ; but there are several other equally troublesome genera of this family, such as *Chrysops*, with its variegated wings and beautiful large golden-green eyes ; and *Hæmatopoda* (Meigen), which contains dull-coloured species, with longer and slenderer bodies than *Tabanus* and its allies. The species of *Hæmatopota* are particularly troublesome in the neighbourhood of woods, especially in rainy weather, one of the Linnean species being actually named *pluvialis* (rainy).

Fig. 99.—*Hæmatopota pluvialis.* Nat. size.

Family *Asilidæ*.—Robber-Flies.

The next family of interest is that of the *Asilidæ*, which are large flies, often measuring an inch or more in length, which feed, in the perfect state, on other insects. They have long and narrow wings, and long bodies, but their comparatively short and thick legs render it impossible for the most careless observer to mistake them for *Tipulidæ*. A handsome black and yellow species, *Asilus crabroniformis* (Linn.), is not rare. So far as is known, the larvæ feed on vegetable substances, either under the surface of the ground, or in the wood of trees ; but the transformations of most of the species of this family still remain to be discovered. Most flies which are either carnivorous or blood-suckers in their perfect state are vegetable-feeders in their early stages ; but some of the exotic family *Midaidæ*, the perfect insects of which are carnivorous, also feed on insects in the larva state, while the larvæ of others live in rotten wood. In the latter case, however, it is possible that they feed on other insects which live *in* the wood, and not *on* the wood itself.

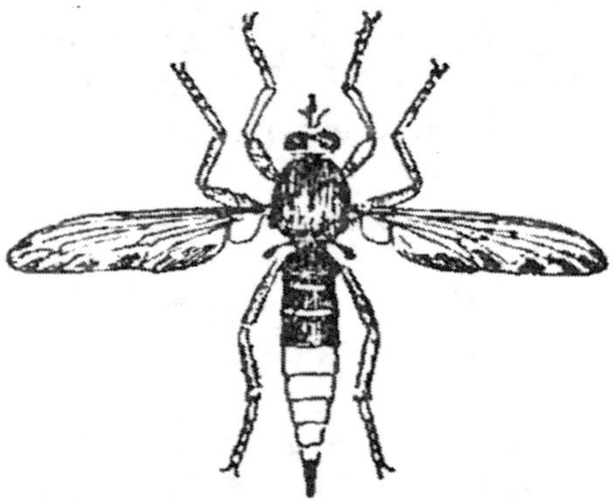

Fig. 100.—*Asilus crabroniformis.* Nat. size.

The species of the family *Empidæ* much resemble the *Asilidæ* in habits, but are smaller, and frequent woods rather than open places. They will, however, feed on vegetable as well as animal substances, and their larvæ live in loose earth.

The *Bombyliidæ*, or bee-like flies, are another interesting family. They are moderate-sized hairy flies, much resembling bees, but with a long straight proboscis, with which they suck the honey of flowers. The larvæ are parasitic on the earlier stages of other insects.

The *Syrphidæ* are a large family of handsomely-coloured flies of moderate size, which are remarkable for their curious hovering and darting flight. Many of the species resemble wasps and bees; and their larvæ live on decaying animal or vegetable substances, and frequently in foul water. The most interesting species of this family is *Eristalis tenax* (Linn.), a blackish fly, more or less clothed with tawny hair, and rather more than half an inch long. Its larva is often found in foul water, and is called the rat-tailed grub, from a long respiratory appendage at the end of the body. This species appears to have given rise to the widespread belief that bees might be reared from dead carcases, as we find recorded in the story of Sampson; in the "Georgics" of Virgil, and in many other old writings. Wasp-like flies of similar habits have also given rise to the idea that wasps or hornets were, or might be, bred from the carcases of horses.

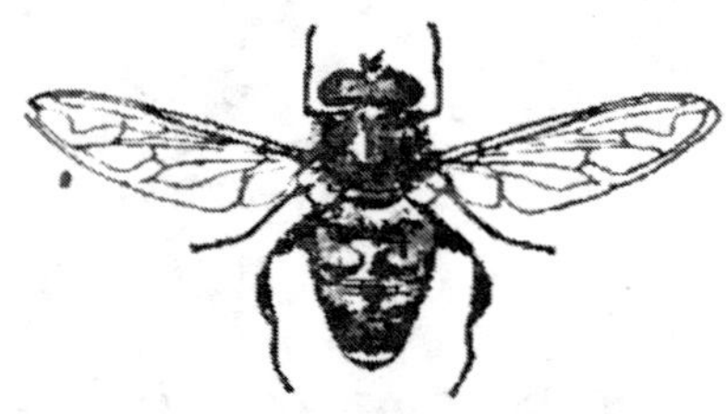

Fig. 101.—*Eristalis tenax.* Nat. size.

The *Œstridæ*, or bot-flies, are chiefly remarkable for being parasitic in mammalia. Recent statistics have shown that the amount of damage caused by the following species to cattle in England alone is quite astounding. *Hypoderma bovis* (Linn.) is a black hairy fly, varied with whitish and yellowish, which attacks oxen; it is about half an inch in length. The flies themselves are very rarely seen, unless when reared. Other species of this family live in the nasal fossæ of sheep and deer; in the stomach of the horse; and in various other situations. They have sometimes been known to attack man, especially in warm countries; but whether any species of this family habitually attacks man is doubtful. Hypodermic dipterous parasites which infest man belong, as a rule, to some section of the immense family *Muscidæ*, which we have now to consider.

Family *Œstridæ*. —Bot-Flies.

The *Muscidæ* include nearly half the known *Diptera*, and have nearly all more or less resemblance to the common house-fly, which is the type of the whole order. The antennæ are always three-jointed, with the third joint compressed, and bearing a bristle on the back, which is often plumose. The proboscis is always present, and is usually membranous, rarely horny; the palpi

Family *Muscidæ*.

are unjointed, and the abdomen has from four to seven joints, and is generally soft. The larvæ are footless maggots, and are either parasitic, or live on decaying animal and vegetable substances. The *Muscidæ* are divided into two main sections: the *Muscidæ Calypteræ*, in which the appendages called alulæ, or winglets, are present; and the *Muscidæ Acalypteræ*, in which they are absent or rudimentary. (The alulæ must not be confounded with the halteres, or poisers, which are drumstick or battledore-shaped organs, which are considered to correspond to the hind pair of wings in four-winged insects.) Each of these two sections is divided into several large sub-families, the more interesting of which we will now proceed to consider.

The *Tachininæ* are a sub-family remarkable for the very bristly abdomen of most of the species. The larvæ are parasitic on various species of Lepidoptera, and the flies, which are rather numerous in genera and species, are frequently found on the flowers of wild carrot, and other *Umbelliferæ*. A species of this sub-family has been reared from a nest of the gregarious larvæ of a West African moth of the genus *Anaphe*, and is here figured.

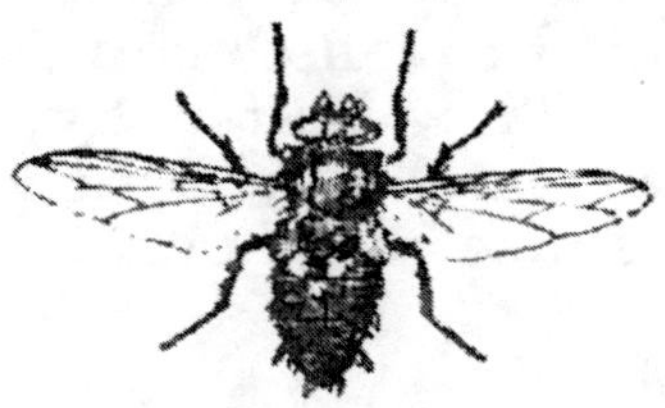

Fig. 102.—*Tachina*, sp. Twice nat. size.

The typical sub-family of the *Muscinæ* includes a large number of our most familiar flies; and among them the true house-fly, *Musca domestica* (Linn.), which is blackish, more or less varied with grey, and with the base of the abdomen reddish; it is about one-third of an inch long. The various organs of this insect: the compound facetted eyes, the proboscis, and the peculiarly complicated foot, all form interesting microscopic objects, and have often been described and figured in books on natural history. It is now believed that the pads of the foot do not support the insects when walking on a ceiling or window-pane by performing the office of suckers, but that they exude a viscid fluid which enables the insects to adhere to a smooth surface. The larvæ of *Musca domestica* live in dung, or in any sort of animal or vegetable refuse; and owing to the much greater cleanliness of our houses and enclosures, to what was the case formerly, flies are not nearly so numerous and troublesome as was the case even thirty or forty years ago. They do not bite or sting, but there is a greyer fly, *Stomoxys calcitrans* (Linn.), which comes into houses in wet weather, and bites sharply. Its pupæ have been found in horse-dung, in which the larva very probably feeds. But any flies can convey the infection of diseases which can be communicated in this manner, even those which do not bite; and ophthalmia is frequently thus communicated in Egypt; and the bite of flies that have been feeding on putrid substances is still more dangerous. The mosquitoes in the East Indies are even said to convey the germs of a small blood-parasite from one person to another in this manner. At the best, therefore, flies are undesirable visitors in our houses; but they are not allowed to increase indefinitely, but are liable to various natural checks. They are frequently seen in autumn plastered to the windows by a white fungus, which has spread over and round them till it has killed them. They are also frequently seen with the curious little creatures called false scorpions (belonging to the Arachnide family *Cheliferidæ*) clinging to their legs. These resemble microscopic scorpions without the tail, but it is doubtful if they are really injurious to the flies, which, it has been suggested, they may use as winged steeds to carry them to fresh fields and pastures new.

House-Flies.

The house-fly is most common in summer and autumn, but there are other flies very similar to it in size and colour, belonging to the sub-family *Anthomyinæ*, which are common in houses earlier in the year, and are commonly called house-flies. It is perhaps hardly necessary to say that although many genera and species of flies are common in houses, either habitually or casually, none of them ever grow after assuming the perfect state ; and it would, consequently, be an absurd error to suppose that the small flies are the young of the large ones, even though individuals of the same species may vary a little in size within narrow limits.

Other larger flies are common in our houses, with brown bodies and blue or purple abdomens. They are generally called blue-bottle flies, and their grubs feed on meat, or carrion. A smaller and prettier species, the green-bottle, *Lucilia cæsar* (Linn.), is more frequently observed out of doors. Linnæus is reported to have said that the progeny of three blow-flies could devour the carcass of an ox as quickly as a lion could. The Tse-tse fly, *Glossina morsitans* (Westwood), which destroys horses and cattle in South Africa, is another species of this sub-family ; it is about the size of a bee.

Muscidæ Acalypteræ.

This is another large section, divided into several sub-families, mostly of small size. Some of them feed on dung, like the conspicuous yellow fly, *Scatophaga stercoraria* (Linn.); others, as the sub-families, *Ortalinæ*, *Trypetinæ*, and *Agromyzinæ*, feed on plants ; some in the heads of flowers, and others mining the leaves of trees, like the *Tineæ* among the moths. Most of the flies of this section are small and slender, and many have very prettily variegated wings. The best known species is perhaps *Piophila casei* (Linn.), a rather slender, black, hairy fly, the larvæ of which feed on cheese or bacon. It belongs to the sub-family *Piophilinæ*.

Fig. 103.—Swallow Fly (*Ornithomyia avicularia*, Linn.). Nat. size.

Fig. 104.—Sheep Tick (*Mallophagus ovinus*, Linn.). Nat. size.

Diptera Homaloptera.

This section contains only two families, the *Hippoboscidæ* and *Nycteribiidæ*, which include a few species with a rather horny integument, and very hairy, sprawling legs. They are parasitic on various mammals and birds ; and some of the species, such as the sheep tick, *Melophagus ovinus* (Linn.), are apterous.

Diptera Aphaniptera.

This section includes the fleas, which are too well known to need description. The species are not well-defined, and it is not clear how far those which are found on different animals are really distinct.

Fleas.

They are all remarkable for their great powers of leaping; and they possess the merest rudiments of wings. They sometimes form colonies on the ground, especially in warm countries, and have been observed to attack caterpillars, so that their food is not confined to the blood of mammals or birds. They are probably quite as ready to attack any soft-bodied animal which comes in their way. I have already suggested (anteà, p. 596) that it is possible that they may even attack the common bed-bug, and exterminate it in houses where they are sufficiently numerous. In America it is said that the common house-flea is the dog-flea, the human flea being much less common.

SUB-KINGDOM III.—MOLLUSCA.

SNAILS, ETC.

By B. B. Woodward, F.L.S., F.G.S., Etc.

The sub-kingdom Mollusca includes such well-known creatures as the whelk, the oyster, the garden snail, and the octopus. It may be roughly characterised as comprising soft-bodied animals that are usually possessed of a hard shell into which they can withdraw for protection. The forms of its different members are as varied as the different conditions of life to which they have become adapted; for some live in the open sea, others hide in its depths; some live in rivers or swift-flowing streams and even torrents, or abide in still lakes and ponds; others, again, are adapted for life on dry land, and, though mostly lovers of moist, shady spots, will some of them rejoice in sun-baked rocks, or live in arid spots where vegetation is scanty. Indeed, save for the frozen polar regions and snow-capped mountain summits, or desert wastes—such as the Sahara—there is no spot on the surface of the globe, nor, unless it be certain of the extreme depths, any point on the sea bottom, without its representative mollusc. But it is in the tropical regions and oceans that they most abound. Their mode of life is as varied as their habitat: some are strong swimmers, others only float in the water; some crawl on land or under water, others burrow in the mud or sand, or even into hard rocks, whilst a few live in the tissues of other animals; others, again, attach themselves to different objects more or less permanently; this is especially the case with the shore dwellers, who have to withstand the action of currents, the sweep to and fro of the tides, or the violence of storm-tossed waters. Their food, too, differs, some being carnivorous and even cannibals, others strict vegetarians, whilst many prefer a mixed diet. Those that burrow, or are attached, generally feed on microscopic organisms, which they obtain from the mud or the water; whilst the parasites, as all the world over, dine at the expense of their hosts.

Owing to the great variations in form, and even in structure, which conformity to these widely different requirements of life has brought about, it is impossible to draw up any satisfactory definition of a mollusc which shall be fairly applicable to even the majority of the larger groups. Nevertheless, certain characters they do possess more or less in common. The shell, though not universally present, is on the whole, perhaps, the most conspicuous feature, although not the most important part of the animal. They have also a well-developed muscular system, of which that portion pertaining to the foot, or organ of locomotion, is the most prominent. There is a distinct nervous system; a heart and circulatory system with its associated organs of respiration; an alimentary system, or set of organs for preparing and digesting the food; an excretory system; and reproductive organs.

The shell in the majority of Mollusca consists of a single more or less coiled tube (as in the whelk and snail), and hence they are termed univalves; in the oyster and other bivalves the shell is in two pieces; whilst in the coat-of-mail shells, chitons, there are eight little overlapping shelly plates. The shell is composed mainly of carbonate of lime, with the admixture of an organic substance known as *conchiolin*, which is very similar to chitin, the horny material forming the hard parts of insects. It is generally divisible into layers exhibiting differences of structure. The outermost, called the *periostracum*, largely and often entirely consists of conchiolin; it varies greatly in appearance, being sometimes smooth and shiny, at others rough and coarse, frequently it is fibrous. In many forms it readily rubs off, in others it is firmly united to the true shell beneath. The term *epidermis*, which has been misapplied to this layer, should be reserved exclusively for the outermost layer of the skin of the animal itself. Of the shell proper the main layer is usually either porcellaneous or crystalline in structure, and in certain cases, such as *Pinna*, it is prismatic. The innermost layer is frequently pearly (nacreous), and in some, like the fresh-water mussels or the pearl oyster, it is the thickest of all. The iridescent play of colours, for which mother-of-pearl is noted, results not so much from any fine microscopic sculpturing of the surface as from the breaking up and refraction of the light that falls on them by the extremely thin films of which the pearly layer is built up. Yet another quality of shelly matter is that which is deposited when a damage in the shell has to be made good, or an unoccupied space requires to be filled up. Very similar, too, is the calcareous material of which the trap-door (operculum) closing the mouth of some shells is formed. These different layers of shelly matter are secreted by a series of special cells near the margin (*collar*) of the tough muscular skin (*mantle*) that envelops the greater portion of the animal's body, the outermost layer by the cells nearest the margin, the next one by those further in, and so on. The shell, therefore, increases in size by the addition of fresh material to its free edges, the whole being subsequently thickened and strengthened by further deposits on the inner surface. The successive additions along the growing edge generally leave ridges or marks parallel with it, that are known as *lines of growth*. The deposition of shell does not go on continuously; every now and again there comes a period of rest, and these rest-periods are frequently indicated by the occurrence of a stronger ridge or mark. The different details of sculpturing on the surfaces of the shell, striæ, ribs, spines, etc., are all the products of corresponding irregularities on the margin of the mantle, and were, when first formed, situated on the growing edge. Pearls result from the coating over with nacre of any irritating object that may have got between the mantle of a pearl-producing mollusc and its shell—a fact taken advantage of by the ingenious Chinese who introduce small metal images. More often, perhaps—and certainly it is the case with the finer examples—they result from a diseased condition of the cells that secrete the nacre.

The muscular foot, which is generally an organ of locomotion, takes various forms in the different groups of Mollusca: the univalves (snails and whelks) creep along by its means; the bivalves employ it to burrow with; in the cuttle-fish it is drawn out into the arms; in other Mollusca it is transformed into fins to swim with; whilst in some, like the oyster, it has ceased to be employed, and has degenerated into a mere rudiment. Most of the muscles of the body are concerned with the extension or retraction of the different organs of the body, and do not here need special enumeration.

The nervous system of Mollusca acquires peculiar importance in that it is the last feature to be influenced by the modifications of the organism, and hence is of extreme value in tracing relationships of the parts. Its principal elements comprise a series of paired nerve centres or ganglia; of these one pair, the *cerebral ganglia*, lying above the œsophagus, sends off nerves to (*innervates*) the head, eyes, and the special organs of sense; another pair, the *pedal ganglia*, situated below the œsophagus, innervates the foot; whilst the *pleural ganglia*, lying one on each side just above the pedal ganglia, form the third pair. These several ganglia are united by nerve cords, so that the whole usually forms a ring or collar round the throat. A nerve cord runs, also, from each pleural ganglion back into the visceral mass, innervating the viscera and various organs: these two ultimately joining form what is known as the *visceral commissure*. Sometimes these two cords cross over each to the opposite side of the body before uniting, and the loop becomes a figure of 8. Various sense organs are present in the Mollusca. Many of these are situated on the integument, and are probably, like the tentacles, organs of touch. Eyes are found in most forms, sometimes very perfect organs, as in the cuttle-fish; in snails generally they are less well-developed, and placed near the base of the horns, or on the summit of a special pair: the bivalves being headless, have usually no eyes; when visual organs are present they occur in some part of the margin of the mantle and are numerous. In the case of one or two molluscs, eyes are developed over the back. From their discrimination of certain food, some Mollusca appear to be capable of tasting, and they certainly can smell. The seat of the olfactory sense is believed to vary, and sometimes to reside in a tentacle, at others to be traced to a special organ called an *osphradium*, which in marine snails is situated close to the gills and resembles them somewhat in appearance. That molluscs can hear is inferred, rather than known, from the presence of *otocysts*, small cavities filled with fluid in which grains of shelly material float. These otocysts are situated close to the pedal ganglia and supplied by nerves from the cephalic ganglia.

The most important feature in connection with the digestive system of Mollusca is the armature of the mouth, and consists of a horny jaw or jaws, and the *radula*, as it is called. Both, however, are wanting in the bivalves and in a few other isolated forms.

The cuttle-fish have a pair of jaws, upper and under; the common snails and limpets, a single upper jaw; but the majority of the univalve Mollusca have a pair of jaws, right and left. The *radula* is characteristic of the Mollusca. It consists first of a ribbon-like horny, or chitinous, transparent, yellowish membrane lying on the floor of the mouth, and passing over two cartilages, to which it is attached by special muscles. On the surface of this membrane are set a series of minute, recurved teeth, also formed of very dense, hard chitine. In a few instances there is but a single row of teeth, one behind the other; usually there are several, sometimes a great many, side by side, and row upon row, each tooth repeating the form of the corresponding one in the row immediately in front of it. Only those teeth near the front are in use, the muscles attached to the basal membrane pulling that portion of the radula backwards and forwards over the cartilages, so that the teeth act very much after the manner of a chain-saw, and rasp off portions of the food.

The cartilages, too, which are attached by one end to the floor of the mouth, can be worked backwards and forwards by special muscles, and so bring the teeth into play. The action of the tongue thus formed can be well seen in a common pond snail, as it slowly crawls up the glass-side of an aquarium, clearing off the microscopic plant-growths as it goes. Of course the teeth in front soon wear away and drop off, so that further and further portions of the radula have to be brought into use as required. The portion of the radula held in reserve for this purpose is stowed away in a kind of pocket (the *radula sac*), situated at the back of the mouth and immediately under the œsophagus. At the extreme end of this radula sac a special set of cells, in the substance of its wall, are engaged in forming fresh teeth, so that a constant supply is being manufactured ready to be moved forward in place of the worn-out ones. When the reserve supply needed is very great the radula is of great length, and the radula sac, correspondingly long, has to be stowed away amongst the other organs of the body. This is especially the case in the limpet and the periwinkle, which last has proportionately the longest known radula of any mollusc. As a rule, in each transverse row of teeth there is a symmetrical central one called the *median* or *rachidian* tooth; on either side of this the teeth are unsymmetrical, and their shape changes as they are traced outwards from the centre, but each one pairs exactly with the corresponding tooth on the opposite side of the median one. Generally the first few near the median more or less resemble each other, and are succeeded rather abruptly by smaller ones, so that the whole radula appears divided into three longitudinal tracts. The middle tract is then termed the *rachis* and the teeth on it the *median* and *admedian*, whilst the outer tracts are styled *pleuræ* and their teeth *uncini*. Sometimes between the admedian and the uncini there is a conspicuous tooth differing from either, which may be termed the *lateral* or *capituliform* tooth. The shapes and patterns of these teeth (Fig. 1) and their arrangement are so characteristic in the different genera as to form valuable aids to classification, though, since they are apt to vary in the young and adult state of the same individual, they do not furnish an unerring clue to the identity of species. A formula has been invented for expressing the number of teeth in each transverse row thus :—

1·1·1 signifies that there is a median, with a single lateral on either side ; 2·1·1·1·2 has in addition 2 uncini on either side. When the uncini are very numerous the sign ∞ (= infinity), or, better still, x is employed, thus ∞·1·4·1·4·1·∞,

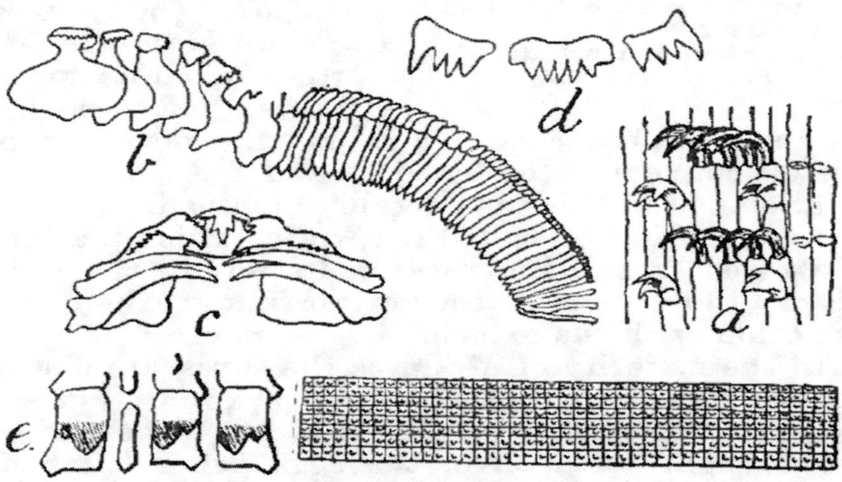

Fig. 1.—RADULÆ.
A, Docoglossa (*Patella vulgata*).
B, Rhipidoglossa (*Trochus cinerarius*).
C, Tænioglossa (*Cypræa Europæa*).
D, Rhachiglossa (*Buccinum undatum*)—Whelk.
E, *Achatina fulica*.

or x ·1·4·1·4·1· x, is the formula for certain kinds. Further allusion to these will be made when treating of the different groups.

All the Mollusca have a circulatory system, with a heart as the central organ, which propels the blood through the body. The heart lies in a cavity, known as the *pericardium*, and receives from *auricles*, usually two in number and lying one on each side of it, the blood that has been aerated in the gills. This blood is driven by the heart through a series of arteries, whence it passes in most Mollusca through a series of cavities amongst and between the various organs and muscles of the body; hence it finds its way back, for the most part through veins, to the gills, but some passes direct to the heart without aeration and thence circulates again. The blood is often colourless, or is slightly bluish, from the presence of an albuminoid (*hæmocyanin*) containing copper; sometimes it is red, and contains the same colouring matter (*hæmoglobin*) as the blood of vertebrates.

The gills have been so largely employed in classifying Mollusca that it is impossible to omit a brief description of their main features. The simple or primitive form of gill has been aptly compared to a plume, in that, like an ostrich feather, it consists of a main axis or shaft, from which, at short intervals, filaments are given off in pairs. The axis of the gill contains, on opposite sides, the vessels that convey the blood to the smaller passages in the filaments and carry it off again to the heart after it has been aerated in them. Increase in the surface of aeration is obtained either by the lengthening of the filaments, or by the union and flattening out of each pair into a small leaf-like expansion. The former is the *Filibranchiate*, or *Pectintinibranchiate* (comb-gilled), the latter the *Scutibranchiate*, or *Aspidobranchiate* (both meaning shield-gilled), or *Foliobranchiate* (leaf-gilled) condition (Fig. 2). Further modifications take place in the gills of bivalves, but these will be treated of later on. In the Foliobranchiate, and in the more complicated forms of gill, the vessels conveying the blood to and from the gill have their positions with relation to the axis considerably modified.

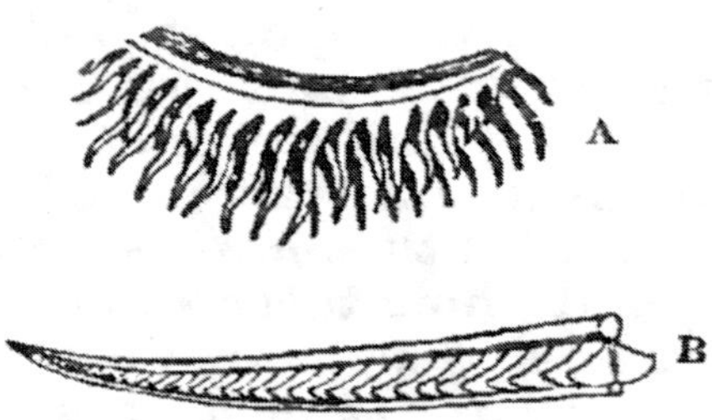

Fig. 2.—DIAGRAM ILLUSTRATING THE TWO TYPES OF GILL STRUCTURE.
A, Pectinibranchiate.
B, Foliobranchiate.

A pair of organs called *nephridia*, which play the part of kidneys and free the blood from impurities on its way to the gills, lie in the region of the heart; they open into the pericardium on the one hand, and communicate on the other with the exterior.

In the majority of Mollusca the sexes are distinct, but in the land snails, the sea slugs, and their allies, the sexes are united in each individual. Most Mollusca are oviparous; that is to say, lay eggs. In a few instances the young are brought forth alive, the eggs being hatched within the body of the parent; whilst in numerous other cases, notably the bivalves, the eggs are retained within the parent shell till hatched. The land snails lay separate eggs, which have each a tough outer layer or case, or even a regular shell like a bird's egg. There is one West African snail whose egg is as large as that of a pigeon, and has nearly as thick a shell. The fresh water and marine snails deposit their eggs generally in clusters, adhering together either in a mass, or spread out in a ribbon. Sometimes each egg is enclosed in a tough albuminous capsule, as in the case of the whelk and the cuttle-fish.

The early stages in the development of the young Mollusca are the same as in all other animals. The original single cell splits up into many cells, till it looks like a mulberry. These cells next arrange themselves in a single layer, so as to form a hollow ball; one side then becomes folded in, so that a double layer of cells results, enclosing a cavity which ultimately becomes the digestive tube; other cells arise between the two layers, that subsequently form the various organs and the muscles of the young animal. Meantime there arises a swimming organ, which is peculiar to the young mollusc; this is called the *velum*. It begins as a ridge, fringed with fine hairs (*cilia*), encircling that part of the head of the embryo which lies in front of the mouth, and it finally expands into a sort of disc, which is drawn out into lobes or into fingers. This is known as the *veliger stage*, and is further marked by the formation of the young shell and the first appearance of the foot. The young shell is always a simple coil, even in those forms which, when adult, have a straight shell, or discard their shell altogether. As the young snail grows up the velum disappears.

The molluscan sub-kingdom is divided into five classes:—

I. AMPHINEURA.
II. PELECYPODA, or LAMELLIBRANCHIATA.
III. SCAPHOPODA.
IV. GASTROPODA.
V. CEPHALOPODA.

Formerly the sea-butterflies PTEROPODA were considered to form a class by themselves: they are now, however, known to be only very greatly modified forms of Gastropoda.

CLASS I.—AMPHINEURA.

The Amphineura are in many respects the most primitive of all the Mollusca. They are literally symmetrical; that is to say, if the body were divided down the middle from head to tail, structures found on one side of the body would be seen to be repeated on the other.

The elementary canal is not bent, the hinder end opening at the opposite extremity of the elongate body to the mouth. The nervous system consists of two lateral and two ventral nerve trunks, which start from the cerebral ganglia and are connected together at intervals by numerous transverse nerve cords. The class is divided into two orders:—POLYPLACOPHORA and APLACOPHORA.

ORDER I.—POLYPLACOPHORA.

The Coat-of-Mail Shells, or Chitons (Fig. 2), are readily distinguished by being alone amongst the Mollusca in possessing a shelly covering of many pieces called the *lorica*. There are eight plates or valves in all on the back of the animal, fitting one over the other like the tiles on a roof. Generally the lorica is surrounded by a leathery *girdle*, so called, which helps to unite the several plates, and which, though sometimes naked, is usually studded with scales or beset with spines.

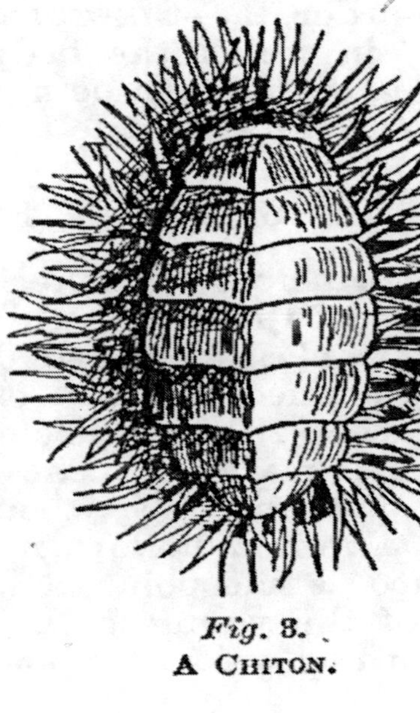

Fig. 8.
A CHITON.

In some forms the animal is very long in the body and the shelly plates are placed at intervals. The animals, which are vegetable feeders, may be found clinging, like limpets, to the under surfaces of rocks and stones at low tide, and when detached will coil up much after the fashion of the well-known wood-louse. The muscular foot extends the whole length of the under surface of the body; the end of the snout is just visible; there are no tentacles. A row of small gills is seen along each side of the body under the edge of the mantle. A remarkable feature in the shell of many chitons calls for special mention. The outer chitinous layer of the valves is perforated for the passage of sense organs, which, in the family Chitonidæ, are in part converted into eyes.

The Polyplacophora are divided into families as follows, according to details of sculpturing, etc., of the valves:—Lepidopleuridæ, Ischnochitonidæ, Mopaliidæ, Acanthochitidæ, Cryptoplacidæ, Chitonidæ.

Order II.—Aplacophora, or Solenogastra.

The Aplacophora, which are carnivorous, are so modified that they scarcely resemble molluscs at all. The body is worm-like and there is no trace of shell, but the much thickened outer skin contains shelly spicules, which probably represent the spines and scales of the Polyplacophora. The foot is extremely reduced, or altogether wanting. The gills are in a chamber at the latter end of the body, into which chamber also the excretory orifices open. Their blood is red. Two sub-orders are distinguished:—

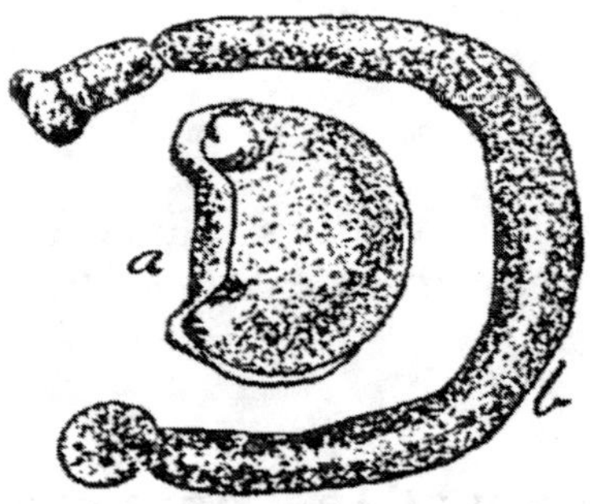

Fig. 4.
a, Neomenia.
b, Chætoderma.

Sub-order 1.—Neomeniina, in which the foot is reduced to a ridge sunk in a groove along the ventral side of the body.

The radula is of the usual many-toothed order, or wanting. There are four families:—Neomeniidæ, Proneomeniidæ, Dondersiidæ, and Parameniidæ.

Sub-order 2.—Chætodermatina, represented by a single genus *Chætoderma*, in which the body is extremely long and cylindrical; the foot is wanting, its position being merely indicated by a groove; whilst the radula is represented by a single tooth.

CLASS II.—PELECYPODA, or LAMELLIBRANCHIATA.

The principal characteristic of this class is the division of the shell into two halves, the *valves*, which lie on either side, right and left, of the animal: hence the class at one time received the name of Bivalvia. These valves are usually connected by an elastic, chitinous *ligament*, and are further kept in place, when the shell is closed, by a series of interlocking teeth that project from their margins. The shell is closed by powerful adductor muscles, but opens spontaneously, when the muscles relax, by the action of the ligament. Each valve is a hollow, irregular cone, the apex of which, termed the *beak* or *umbo*, is the point at which growth began, and is in fact formed by the valve of the young shell. In very good specimens, when the umbones are not worn or eroded, the two valves that were formed by the animal ere it issued from the egg can be seen crowning the umbones; they generally differ in shape and marking from the portion subsequently formed and are called the *prodissoconch*.

The umbo is generally curved more or less to one side, and usually points towards the head, or anterior end, when the shell is said to be *prosogyre*, in contradistinction to those in which the umbones are straight, *orthogyre*, or are directed backwards, *opisthogyre*. More often than not the two valves are of equal size and shape, and the shell is *equivalve*, as in the cockle; sometimes, however, as in the oyster, one valve is smaller than the other, and the shell is *inequivalve*. The bivalves are all more or less *inequilateral;* that is to say, if a line be drawn from the umbo to the ventral margin of the valve the portion on one side of that line, usually the front one, will be found to be smaller than that on the other. When the shell is shut it is said to be *close*, if the valves fit accurately; and to *gape*, if openings be left. The ligament is made up of two elements: an external horny, non-elastic layer, or ligament proper, and an inner, fibrous layer, the *resilium*, which imparts elasticity to the whole. The latter is sometimes separated from the outer layer and situated in a pit, *resilifer*, in the margin of the shell, or even borne on a process projecting into the interior. This resilium was formerly known under the misleading name of *cartilage*. The margin of the shell, on which the ligament and the teeth that lie close to it are situated, is termed the hinge line: it is sometimes expanded inwards and forms a sort of platform, the *hinge plate*, on which the teeth are placed. The central teeth, under the umbo, are termed *cardinal*, those on each side *lateral* teeth: frequently some one or other of these, and sometimes all, are wanting. The mode of origin of these teeth is a matter of extreme interest and importance, but is too special a subject to be followed out here. On the interior of the shell in each valve are impressed markings or *scars*, which indicate the points of attachment of the muscles. Firstly,

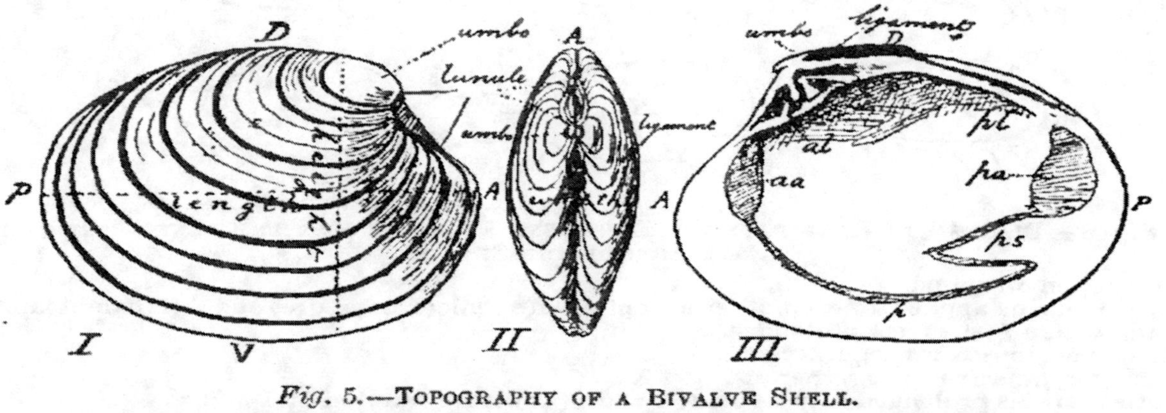

Fig. 5.—TOPOGRAPHY OF A BIVALVE SHELL.
I. Exterior of right valve. II. Dorsal view of both valves.
III. Interior of right valve.
A, Anterior or front. P, Posterior or hinder end. D, Dorsal area or back. V, Ventral area or under margin. *c*, Cardinal teeth. *al*, Anterior lateral teeth. *pl*, Posterior lateral teeth. *aa*, Scar of anterior adductor muscle. *pa*, Scar of posterior adductor muscle. *p*, Pallial line. *ps*, Pallial sinus.

there are in the majority of shells—*e.g.*, the fresh water mussel—two large impressions in each valve, one near the front, the other near the hinder, margin; these are the scars of the *adductor muscles* that close the shell. In some forms, like the oyster, only one such, the hinder one, remains. Bivalves with two adductor scars in each valve are termed *Dimyaria*, the others *Monomyaria*. The reduction and disappearance of the anterior adductor may be accounted for by the more rapid growth of the latter half of the body, which thus tends to bring the two muscles and the hinge into line, when the anterior adductor, being less and less required, is proportionately reduced and ultimately disappears. In *Pinna* the hinge is reduced to the lowest limit instead. Running from one adductor scar to the other in the Dimyaria, and at a short distance from the ventral margin of the shell, is a shallow groove, the *pallial line*, which marks the attachment of the muscular mantle. In a large group of the bivalves this line, instead of running in a continuous curve, makes, shortly before it reaches the hinder scar, a sharp bend back towards the centre of the valve, forming a bay or sinus called the *pallial sinus*. Its presence indicates that the animal had retractile breathing tubes or *siphons*, and to these further allusion will be made later on. Other small scars of lesser importance are generally present. The terms employed in designating the different parts will best be gathered from the accompanying diagrams (Fig. 5).

No bivalve mollusc possesses a head, and hence the term *Acephala*, or its equivalent *Lipocephala*, has sometimes been applied to the class. The animal is enclosed between the two lobes of the thin mantle, one lying on either side of it immediately under the shell. These lobes are attached along the back and reach out to the margin of the valves. In the more primitive forms the mantle margins are quite simple, and open from the front round the ventral edge to the back; but many different modifications take place in the higher forms. Instead of the margins being simple, there may be folds,

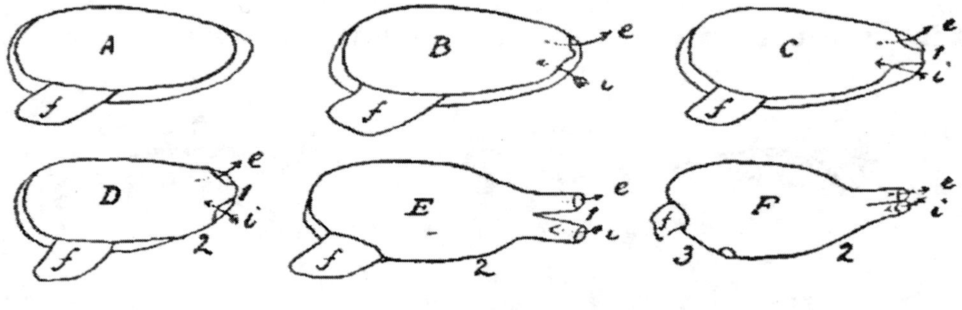

Fig. 6.—Diagram to Illustrate the Different Forms of Mantle Opening and the Formation of the Siphon.

A, Mantle open all round.
B, Mantle margins applied to each other except at *e* (exhalent aperture) and *i* (inhalent aperture) and where *f* (the foot) protrudes.
C, Mantle margins grown together at 1.
D, Mantle margins grown together at 1 and 2.
E, Mantle margins prolonged into siphons, *e* and *i* (as before), united at 1 and 2.
F, Siphons united, also mantle margins at 2 and 3.

thickenings, protuberances, tentacles, various glands, and even eyes. Nor are the margins always free; indeed, in extreme cases, they are united nearly the whole way round. There are various stages (Fig. 6): counting the open one as the first, in the second the currents of water, instead of being drawn in all the way round, the edges of the mantle are kept close together except where the foot protrudes and at two points at the hinder end, one of which (*i*) serves to admit the fresh water to the gills and food to the mouth, and is called the *inhalent aperture,* whilst the other (*e*) allows the fouled water to escape and is termed the *exhalent aperture.* In the next stage the edges of the mantle are united permanently at the point between these two openings, and in the fourth at a second point below the inhalent aperture. In the fifth stage the margins of these apertures have grown out into tubes (*siphons*), and the remaining portions of the mantle margins have united all round, except where the foot is protruded. Finally, the two siphons become united externally. In these cases there is frequently a fourth small aperture left in the ventral margin. The siphons, the ends of which are frequently fringed, can be wholly or partly withdrawn ; and it is to make room for them within the shell that the pallial attachment is set further back at that point, giving rise to the pallial sinus already spoken of. The proportionate length of the siphons forms a rough index to the burrowing habits of the animal, since the longer the siphons and the more complete the union of the mantle margins, the deeper the mollusc can burrow into the mud or silt and still inhale clear water from above.

The gills lie underneath the mantle, one on either side, in the space between the latter and the body of the animal. In structure these organs vary progressively from a very simple to an extremely complicated form, and since their features have been made the basis whereby this difficult group is classified, it is necessary briefly to describe them. In the more primitive bivalves the gill is of the foliobranch type (see ante, p. 614); but in the higher Pelecypods they are filibranch, only the filiments of each of the two rows, instead of running separate, have an arrangement whereby they interlock and form a continuous membrane, like the web of a feather. The mechanism by which this is brought about is extremely simple. At regular intervals on either side of each filiment are little patches of stiff hairs which interlock with the corresponding ones on the two neighbouring filiments, just as two brushes can be made to do; these are known as the *ciliated junctions* (Fig. 7 E). Moreover, the two membranes *lamellæ* thus arising do not simply depend from the axis, but their edges are folded upwards—that of the outer one outwards, that of the inner, inwards, making a W in section as shown at B, Fig. 7.

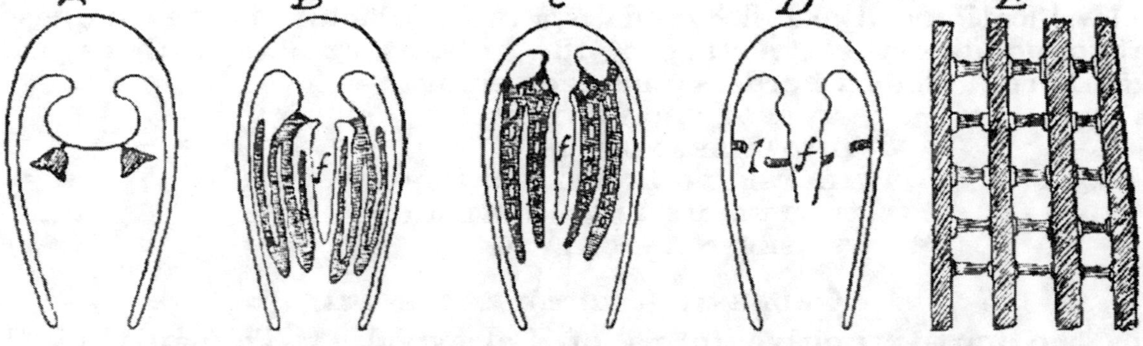

Fig. 7.—DIAGRAM ILLUSTRATING SUCCESSIVE DEVELOPMENT OF PELECYPOD GILLS.
A, Protobranch (or Foliobranch). B, Filibranch.
C, Eulamellibranch. D, Septibranch. E, Diagram of Ciliated Junctions.

A further complication of structure ensues when junctions, called *interlamellar junctions,* are formed between the dependent part of each filament and its reflected portion. In a more advanced stage still both the ciliated and the *interlamellar junctions* become solid connections, so that the whole structure presents a spongy appearance, whilst the reflected ends of the filaments, uniting with the walls of the mantle and foot, subdivide the pallial chamber (C, Fig. 7). One further development remains to be mentioned, in which the gills have become converted into a sort of party wall. The following diagrammatic drawings will make these various stages more clear (Fig. 7).

The muscular foot is a prominent feature in most bivalves, lying in the middle line towards the front of the body. It is actuated by special muscles, and is principally of service in forcing a way for the creature into the sand or mud; in a few it is a creeping organ; whilst the cockles, by its means, take extraordinary leaps. In some forms it is greatly reduced, or altogether wanting. Towards the back of the foot is situated the apparatus for spinning the horny threads by which many bivalves anchor themselves to stones, seaweed, etc. The common mussel is a familiar example, and the bunch of threads is known as the *byssus*. The animal generally has the power of rejecting its byssus at any time and spinning a fresh one.

The mouth is situated a little behind and beneath the front adductor muscle; it is unarmed, neither jaw nor radula being present. It is flanked on either side by a pair of twin, triangular lobes, the *labial palps*, which are in a line with, and in front of, the gills. Their function apparently is to collect, and possibly to taste, the food before it passes into the mouth. A short œsophagus leads to the stomach at the base of the foot, whence the intestine, more or less coiled, leads off, and, after passing through the pericardium, terminates beneath the hinder adductor muscle, at the base of the exhalent siphon.

The heart, in addition to the ventricle, which frequently encircles the alimentary canal, has usually two auricles. The nervous system is symmetrical, and consists typically of three pairs of ganglia:—The cerebro-pleural, resulting from the fusion of the cerebral and pleural ganglia, lying above the œsophagus; the pedal ganglia, which are situated in the foot, near its base; and the visceral ganglia, placed close to the posterior adductor muscle. These ganglia are connected by nerve cords, and supply nerve fibres to the various organs. The remaining anatomical features call for no comment here.

The classification of the Pelecypoda is a most difficult and vexed question; but that founded on the structure of the gills, as explained above, will be employed here. The five orders thus created are:—

I. PROTOBRANCHIATA.
II. FILIBRANCHIATA.
III. PSEUDOLAMELLIBRANCHIATA.
IV. EULAMELLIBRANCHIATA.
V. SEPTIBRANCHIATA.

ORDER I.—PROTOBRANCHIATA

Contains the most primitive forms of Pelecypoda. The gills are foliobranchiate in type, and the mantle margins generally open. The foot has a creeping disc on its ventral surface.

Two families are included in this order—the NUCULIDÆ and the SOLENOMYIDÆ. To the former belong the little nutshells (*Nucula*), small triangular shells of a plain brown exterior and pearly interior, provided with a series of fine transverse teeth in the hinge, calling to mind a comb, with the resilium borne in a small triangular pit in the middle. The umbones are directed backwards. Their close allies, *Leda* and *Yoldia*, are elongate, and have fewer and more prominent teeth, and a more prominent ligament pit. The family is one of the oldest known, dating back to the earliest geological times, and its modern representatives are found in all seas.

The SOLENOMYIDÆ comprise a single genus *Solenomya*, and are remarkable for being without teeth in the hinge, and in having the periostracum greatly prolonged beyond the margin of the valves. The typical species, *S. togata*, is found in the Mediterranean. The genus also occurs on the east coast of North America, the Antilles, Patagonia, New Zealand, and Australia.

ORDER II.—FILIBRANCHIATA.

In this order the gill filaments are dependent and reflexed with ciliar, but no interlamellar junctions. The animal generally spins a strong byssus. Four sub-orders are distinguished :—

Sub-order 1.—ANOMIACEÆ, whose typical genus *Anomia* is well-known by the common *A. ephippium*, found on our shores. The shell is very variable in shape, but the right valve is generally the flatter of the two, since it is moulded to the surface of the object the animal is attached to. The strong byssus, by which it holds on consists of a shelly "plug," instead of a bundle of threads, and passes through a notch in the right valve near the umbo. When quite young the notch is in the ventral margin of the valves, as in the next group, but the shell subsequently grows round it. There are no teeth in the hinge ; only a single adductor muscle, the posterior one, is present in the adult ; and the heart projecting into the pallial cavity lies almost without the body. The Saddle oyster, *Placuna sella*, also belongs to this group.

Sub-order 2.—ARCACEA, of which the Noah's Ark-shells are the type (Fig. 8), have hinge-teeth like *Nucula;* but the ligament is external, extends forward in advance of the umbones, and spreads over the wide space between the two beaks, frequently obtaining additional hold by grooves in the shell. In Arca there is often a strong and sometimes shelly byssus, which passes through an opening in the ventral margin of the shell. The two adductors are nearly equal in size. The mantle margins are entirely open. The genera *Pectunculus* and *Limopsis* have much rounder shells ; the teeth are far fewer, and less comb-like than in *Arca*.

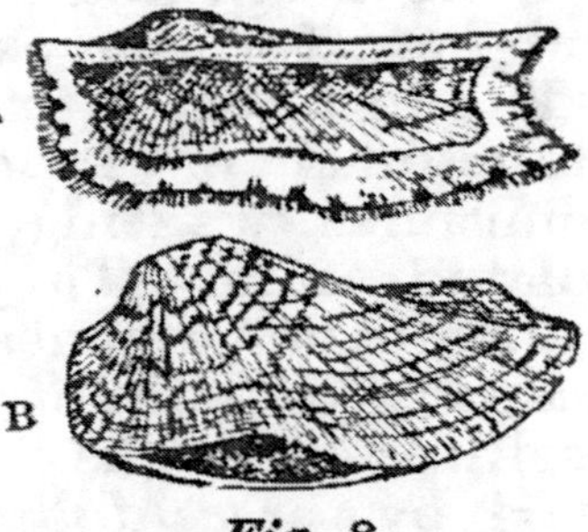

Fig. 8.
A, ARCA NOÆ.
B, ARCA ZEBRA.

All three genera are represented on our coasts, and have a wide distribution ; whilst *Arca* dates back to almost the earliest geological times.

Sub-order 3.—TRIGONIACEA, represented by a single family, TRIGONIIDÆ, having one genus *Trigonia*. This genus, now confined to the Australian seas, was in geological times very widely distributed. The living species are beautiful pearly shells, roughly triangular in shape and externally ribbed, after the manner of a cockle-shell. The right valve bears two cardinal teeth, the left four. These teeth are transversely grooved. There is no byssus.

Sub-order 4.—MYTILACEA is so well known through its representatives the common marine mussel, *Mytilus edulis*, and the Horse-mussel, *Modiola modiolus*, as to need no further description. The genus *Mytilus* is world-wide in its distribution: *Modiola* is chiefly tropical.

The genus *Crenella* is interesting on account of its hinge margin, which is crenulated behind the ligament. *Lithodomus*, the Date-shell, so called from its resemblance in external shape to a date-stone, is an interesting example of adaptation to habitat. It perforates corals and the hardest rocks, forming for itself a long, narrow burrow into which it exactly fits.

The fresh-water genus *Dreissensia*, introduced into this country from the Baltic on timber, may be placed here rather than with the fresh-water mussels, despite certain of its anatomical features, till its true affinities shall have been determined.

Order III.—Pseudolamellibranchiata.

In this division, to which the oyster belongs, the mantle is entirely open; the foot is but little developed, and the gill filaments are reflected and joined by interlamellar connections. The order is further subdivided into Aviculacia, Ostreacea, Pectinacea.

Fig. 9.—Avicula Hirundo.

Sub-order 1.—The Aviculacea, or swallow shells, are so called from the fancied resemblance presented by representative forms, when the two valves are spread open, to a flying bird (Fig. 9).

They are extremely pearly shells, indeed the pearl oyster of commerce is a conspicuous example, the nacreous layer being the thickest; the middle layer of the shell is prismatic and consequently brittle; the periostracum is very thin. In shape they are inequivalve; the hinge is long and straight, with few and obscure teeth, or none at all, and the hinge line is usually produced on either side of the umbones, forming expansions, technically known as ears.

The ligament is external, and placed in a groove or grooves. The posterior adductor is very large; the anterior, situated close to the umbo, is small, or sometimes wanting; the pallial line is represented by a chain of small isolated scars. They spin a strong byssus, which issues through a notch in the right valve beneath the front ear. They dwell in temperate or tropical seas, and in point of geological time are found right back to almost the earliest fossiliferous rocks. The principal genera are *Avicula*, *Meleagrina* (the pearl oyster), *Malleus* (the hammer-headed oyster), *Perna*, in which the ligament is crumpled into numerous folds, occupying transverse grooves in the thick hinge, and the common *Pinna*.

Sub-order 2.—The Ostreacea, of which the oyster (*Ostrea*) is the type, present some points of great interest other than gastronomic. The mantle margin is double and finely fringed, forming the so-called "beard." The foot is reduced to a rudiment, and there is no byssus. The anterior adductor in the adult is entirely wanting; but in the embryo, that, as in all bivalves, is the first of the two adductors to be formed, the posterior developing later and persisting, whilst the former disappears. The stage in which both are present has not yet been seen in the European oyster. Traces of teeth are sometimes to be observed. Oysters are world-wide in their distribution, if Arctic seas be omitted.

Sub-order 3.—The Pectinacea are best known by the scallop (*Pecten*), of which there are numerous species, many of them most beautifully coloured and marked. As in the oyster, the mantle margins are double and fringed, but in addition, there is a row of conspicuous round black eyes. Most of the pectens spin a byssus when young, and some do habitually; whilst many not only remain free but move about, progressing through the water by rapidly opening and closing their valves. With few exceptions the *Pecten* shells are ornamented with radiating ribs. The genus *Lima* resembles pecten, but is more elongate and not so equilateral.

The thorny oyster (*Spondylus*) is ornamented, as its popular name suggests, with spines and other shelly prominences. The *Spondyli* attach themselves to various objects, sometimes slightly by a few spines, sometimes by the whole surface of a valve. Two curved teeth in each valve so interlock with corresponding sockets in the other that it is impossible to separate them without damage. The big Water Spondylus in its growth leaves cavities in the shell substance which retain sea water.

ORDER IV.—EULAMELLIBRANCHIATA.

In this order is included the great majority of the bivalves. The gills have complete interfilamentary and interlamellar junctions. Both adductors, with few exceptions, are present. The hinge teeth are few and strong.

The following seven sub-orders may conveniently be distinguished:—SUBMYTILACEA, TELLINACEA, VENERACEA, CARDIACEA, MYACEA, PHOLADACEA, ANATINACEA.

Sub-order 1.—SUBMYTILACEA. The Submytilacea are generally devoid of siphons, and hence the pallial impression is simple. They are more nearly related to the Mytilacea than to the Pseudolamellibranchiata just described; indeed the Dreissensiidæ and the fossil Modiolopsidæ are by some included in the Mytilacea, and the Unionidæ and Ætheriidæ placed close to them.

The UNIONIDÆ include, amongst others, the fresh-water mussels familiar to all. The young, as soon as they leave the parent shell, attach themselves to passing fish, and, becoming buried in the skin, pass a short period of their lives as parasites. This stage of the young mussel, till its true nature was ascertained, was called *Glochidium*.

The ÆTHERIIDÆ include *Ætheria*, the fresh-water oyster of the Nile, that has a remarkable cellular shell, the layers on the inside looking like blisters. The corresponding South American form, *Mulleria*, has only a single (posterior) adductor, and looks yet more like an oyster.

The CYRENIDÆ, another fresh-water family, are represented in the British Isles by the genera *Cyclas* and *Pisidium*. Formerly there was a third genus, *Corbicula*, which spread all over Europe and Siberia, but is now confined to warmer climes.

The Cyrenidæ have equivalve, subtriangular shells with brown periostracum. The hinge has two or three cardinals, and laterial teeth are present, which in *Corbicula* are striated; the ligament is external. The siphons are short.

Amongst the marine forms belonging to this group are the CARDITIDÆ, stout, equivalved, heart-shaped shells, generally with radiating ribs like the Cockles, and having a strong hinge with one or two oblique cardinal teeth and one or two laterals; the ligament is external. One member of the family, *Cardita concamerata*, is remarkable for the curious egg-pouch, formed by an infold of the ventral margin of the mantle and shell. The Carditidæ are principally inhabitants of southern waters, but are represented in the Mediterranean.

The ASTARTIDÆ, on the other hand, are northern forms. Their shells are rather flattened, subtriangular, or ovoid in outline, marked with concentric ribs, and covered with a thick brown periostracum. There is a strong hinge with two or three cardinal teeth in each valve; the ligament is external.

The CRASSATELLIDÆ, another family of southern range, have a much longer shell, generally subtriangular and concentrically ribbed; there is a distinct lunule; the hinge is furnished with two or three cardinals in each valve; the resilium is lodged in a pit between the teeth.

The ARCTICIDÆ are best known by the *Arctica* [=*Cyprina*] *Islandica* of our own northern shores. It has a strong, fairly globose shell, with prominent umbones, covered with a rough brown periostracum; there is no lunule. The ligament is external; the hinge teeth well developed, and, like those of the Veneracea, there are two cardinal teeth, two posterial laterals, and two feeble anterior laterals in each valve. Another genus, *Libitina*, is found in the Red Sea and Indian Ocean; it is an oblong shell with very long, straight, posterior teeth. Another member of the group is *Coralliophaga*, which, in external form, closely resembles *Lithodomus*, already alluded to under Mytilacea.

The ISOCARDIIDÆ, or heart-cockles, which were formerly associated with the preceding, have very globose shells, and very prominent, widely separated, spiral umbones. The ligament which follows the umbones in their growth is split in front and curved out on either side.

A contrast to the foregoing is offered by most of the LUCINIDÆ, which have very round, but rather depressed, and generally white shells, with small umbones. The teeth, when well developed, comprise two cardinal and one lateral in each valve; the ligament is internal and very large. There is generally, in addition to the usual muscular scars on the interior, the mark of a muscular attachment running obliquely right across the valves. The foot is long and cylindrical. The UNGULINIDÆ, with a single genus *Ungulina*, are closely allied.

The three remaining families, KELLYELLIDÆ, ERYCINIDÆ, and GALEOMMIDÆ are small shells, which have the common characteristic of a foot adapted for creeping; many of them when thus crawling spread the valves wide open. The mantle is generally more or less reflected over the shell, and in *Ephippodonta* and *Clamydoconcha* it completely and permanently envelopes the valves.

Sub-order 2.—TELLINACEA. These have very long siphons, which are not united; the pallial sinus is correspondingly deep; the foot is large and flattened.

In the type family TELLINIDÆ, or sunset shells, the shell is generally very elongate, sometimes smooth and polished, sometimes marked with concentric ribs, and oblique and gaping behind. There are two cardinal and two lateral teeth, one anterior and one posterior, in each valve; the ligament is external. The Tellinidæ are world-wide in their distribution, but the finer specimens come from tropical seas.

The SCROBICULARIIDÆ are Tellinæ in which the ligament is internal; they love the mud of estuaries to dwell in, and obtain their food from it.

The PSAMMOBIIDÆ resemble the Tellinidæ both in shell and animal. The former, however, is more equivalve, less twisted, and gapes more widely behind. The hinge plate is broader and there are no lateral teeth. As their name indicates, they are sand dwellers. A few occur on the British coasts, but the finer examples come from the Pacific and Indian Oceans.

The DONACIDÆ, or wedge shells, are very inequilateral, the front portion being much longer than the truncated hinder part. The exterior is usually smooth, the umbones are directed backwards, and the margins of the valves are usually very finely crenulated, whilst the pallial sinus is deep. There are two or three cardinals and two laterals, one anterior and one posterior, in each valve.

The TANCREDIIDÆ have very similar shells to the Donacidæ.

The MACTRIDÆ are a large and widely-distributed family dwelling in sand. The shell is equivalve and somewhat triangular; commonly smooth and white, with a trace of periostracum. The hinge is usually marked by the conspicuous internal resilium lodged in a deep pit; but in some forms the whole ligament is external. The hinge-plate is well developed; the teeth vary somewhat, typically there is a Λ-shaped cardinal tooth in each valve in front of the resilifer, and single anterior and posterior lateral teeth in the right valve fitting into double ones in the right one.

The CARDILIIDÆ are very similar in their shell to the preceding, and are probably closely allied to them, but their anatomy is still unknown.

The MESODESMATIDÆ resemble the Mactridæ in their anatomy, but the siphons are not united, the shell usually is more like that of *Donax* with umbones directed backwards.

Sub-order 3—VENERACEA. These have usually short siphons, and therefore a moderate pallial sinus. The shells of the principal family, VENERIDÆ, are remarkable for the elegance of their forms and colours. Their texture is very hard and procellaneous, the exterior is frequently smooth and highly polished, sometimes ornamented with V-shaped lines of colour, sometimes with concentric grooves, whilst a few have projecting plates or spines (Fig. 10). The margins are closed, and often crenulate. The siphons are more or less united. The ligament is external, and there is a well-marked lunule; the hinge is strong, and consists of three well-developed cardinal teeth in each valve, two out of the three appearing double; the laterals are variable.

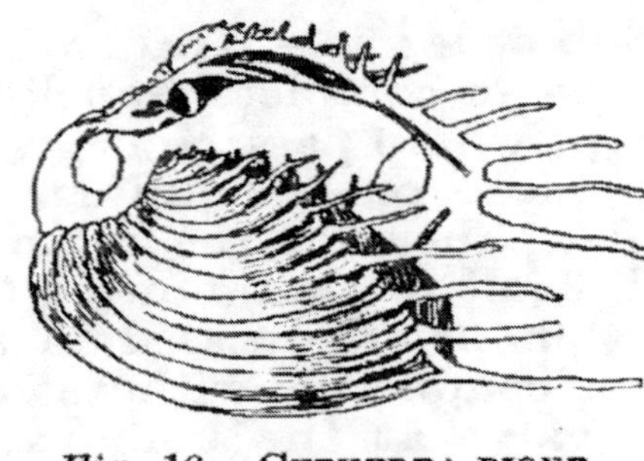

Fig. 10.—CYTHERRA DICNE.

The PETRICOLIDÆ, which occupy burrows in limestone, are very elongate; in their shape and external markings they closely resemble the well-known rock-borer *Pholas*, though they are readily distinguished by the possession of three cardinal teeth in each valve.

The GLAUCOMYIDÆ, which are fresh, or brackish-water forms, have very long siphons, and live buried in the mud of estuaries in India, China, and the Eastern Archipelago. The shell is shaped like *Mya*.

Sub-order 4.—CARDIACEA comprises the cockles and their allies. The shell is heart-shaped, with an internal ligament, and there are one or two cardinals in each valve; whilst the right valve usually carries two anterior and two posterior laterals, which receive the corresponding single teeth of the left valve. The siphons are short and deeply fringed; the foot very long and slender.

The cockles, CARDIIDÆ, live buried in sand or sandy mud, and in some species with a prickly shell the size and number of the spines is dependent on the nature of the sea bottom, the spines being fewest in those which bury in the firmest silt. The shells of the genus *Hemicardium* are the most peculiar in shape of almost any bivalve, for they are much shorter than wide or thick.

The "giant clam" (*Tridacna*), and the bear's-paw (*Hippopus*), so commonly used to make shell-baskets, form the family TRIDACNIDÆ. In these no anterior adductor is present in the adult, nor are there any siphons. The shell is ornamented with radiating ribs, and the margins are deeply indented. The hinge has a single cardinal in each valve, and two posterior laterals in the right, one in the left valve. *Tridacna* is the largest bivalve known, either recent or fossil, *T. gigas* attaining 2 ft. in length. It lives in coral reefs moored by its huge byssus, which issues through the large notch in the valves in front of the umbones. The animal is most gaudily coloured, rivalling the corals amongst which it dwells. Large dull pearls are sometimes found in it. *Hippopus*, on the other hand, has a close-fitting shell, through it spins a small byssus. It, too, is a reef-dweller.

The CHAMIDÆ, which resemble oysters in external appearance, and in being attached, are inequivalve, with sub-spiral umbones and external ligament. The shell is rough, and generally ornamented with frills, or flat shelly projections. Sometimes one valve is attached, sometimes the other; the hinge teeth consist of two cardinals in the attached, and one in the free valve, with traces of laterals. They inhabit tropical seas.

Sub-order 5.—MYACEA. The shells of this group gape more or less widely, and never completely enclose the animal. The mantle margins are united, except where passage is given for the foot, and at the siphons, which are long and more or less united. The hinge is degenerate. The typical family, *Myidæ*, includes the common *Mya* or "gaper" of our coasts. The animal is difficult to obtain owing to its habit of burrowing a foot down in the mud. Its siphons are encased in an extension of the horny periostracum, and are never completely withdrawn into the shell. The hinge is peculiar: from the left valve at the umbo a spoon-shaped process projects that carries the resilium, the corresponding attachment in the right valve being underneath the umbo, the hinge plate being folded quite back. Traces of the cardinal teeth are sometimes visible.

In the SOLENIDÆ, or razor-shells, the shell is usually very elongate and open at either end. The ligament is external, the hinge teeth are small, usually two or three in each valve. The foot is long and cylindrical; the siphons short, and mostly united. The family is world-wide in its distribution. The common *Solen* of the English shores is known to all. The razor-fish live deeply bedded in sand or mud, into which they force themselves by means of their powerful foot. By some the Solenidæ are placed as a separate group nearer the Tellinidæ.

The SAXICAVIDÆ resemble the Myidæ, but the gills extend into the cavity of the inhalent siphon. The genus *Glycimeris* also resembles *Mya* in its habitat; but the members of the typical genus *Saxicava* bore into hard stone, and are generally found in colonies, honeycombing the rocks with burrows sometimes 6 in. in depth, nor do they scruple to drill through their neighbours should they lie in their path. They are anchored in their crypts by a byssus. The shell is elongate and when young has two teeth in each valve; these disappear in the adult. It is one of the most widely distributed of all bivalves, and varies a great deal in shape.

The GASTROCHÆNIDÆ have wedge-shaped shells that gape widely in front; the anterior adductor scar is smaller than the posterior; the pallial sinus is deep; the gills are as in *Saxicava;* the siphons naked and united. The ligament is external; sometimes a single cardinal tooth is present. Some members of the family line their burrows with a shelly tube, to which, however, they are in no way attached.

Sub-order 6.—PHOLADACEA. In this are included the *Pholas*, or piddock, known to every sea-side visitant, the ship-worm, and their allies. The Pholadidæ have white, brittle shells, roughened like a file on the outside; they are generally elongate and gape at both ends widely; but in one genus, *Jouanettia*, the two valves form an almost spherical shell, with one small aperture. There is no hinge properly speaking, or ligament, the hinge plate being bent back over the umbo and the anterior adductor muscle carried with it so that it lies without the shell. It is by the action of this muscle that the valves are opened, the posterior adductor serving to close them. The little curved, shelly process that arises from beneath the umbo in each valve and projects into the interior serves the purpose of muscular attachment. The animals, which are phosphorescent, have long, united siphons; the mantle margins are united, except in front, where the large foot, that fills up the opening in the shell, protrudes. The adult animal has additional shelly plates on the back on either side of the umbones. The common *Pholas* of our shores bores into rocks, the burrows lying parallel to one another; but some species bore into floating wood across the grain.

The TEREDINIDÆ, or ship-worms, have two very small valves widely gaping at both ends, that are borne at the extreme anterior end of the long cylindrical animal. The greater portion of the creatures' length (ordinarily they are a foot long, and sometimes two and a half feet) is taken up by the gills and the fleshy siphons. These last are united to within a short distance of their extremities. At the point where they separate two little shelly *pallets*, or *styles*, are found. The true ship-worms bore into timber with the grain, and become so abundant where they once settle that they soon honey-comb and destroy the stoutest balks. Their burrows are lined with shell and sometimes show cross partitioning. One species bores into cocoa-nuts and other woody fruits floating in tropical seas. The tube of the giant *Teredo* is often a yard long and two in diameter; it burrows in sand and in the roots of mangroves.

Sub-order 7.—ANATINACEA. In the gills of this group the outer lamella on each side is directed upwards instead of downwards, and its free edge is not reflected. The margins of the mantle are largely united. The shell is usually thin, and pearly within, frequently strengthened at the umbo by a buttress. The hinge rarely has any teeth; the ligament is generally internal, and more or less divided by a shelly portion or *ossicle*. The principal families are:—PANDORIDÆ, CHAMOSTREIDÆ, VERTICORDIIDÆ, LYONSIIDÆ, ANATINIDÆ, PHOLADOMYIDÆ, and CLAVIGELLIDÆ. The Pandoridæ are represented in British seas by *Pandora*, in which the right valve is flat, whilst the left is convex; the shell is also very inequilateral. There are two diverging resilium grooves at the hinge. It lives buried in sand.

The single species *Chamostrea albida*, found off the coast of New South Wales, constitutes the family CHAMOSTRÆIDÆ. It has a thick, pearly shell; the right valve, by which it is attached, is deep and strongly keeled; the left valve is flat, with a conical tooth in front of the resilifer; the ossicle is extremely large.

The VERTICORDIIDÆ and LYONSIIDÆ are deep-water forms not often met with.

The ANATINIDÆ have extremely thin shells, sometimes granular on the surface, and gaping behind. The genus *Thracia* is British.

The PHOLADOMYIDÆ, represented to-day by a single species, *Pholadomya candida*, in the West Indies, was formerly an abundant group. The shell is oblong and equivalve, gapes behind, and is ornamented with obscure radiating ribs. The ligament is internal, and there is one tooth in each valve.

The CLAVIGELLIDÆ are in some respects the most interesting members of the group. One genus, *Clavigella*, bores into rocks, the left valve becomes attached to the wall of the burrow, the right remaining free; the passage to the exterior, occupied by the siphons, has a shelly lining, which projects freely on the exterior and terminates in two or more frills.

The other principal genus *Brechites* [=*Aspergillum*], known as the watering-pot shell, burrows in sand, lining the burrow with a shelly tube, into the wall of which the valves of the young shell are built. The free end of the tube is also frilled. The adductor muscles not being required are aborted. When the animal is full grown the bottom of the tube is closed with the familiar perforated plate, secreted by the fringed foot. It occurs only in the tropical seas.

ORDER V.—SEPTIBRANCHIATA

Contains two families—POROMYIDÆ and CUSPIDARIIDÆ—principally interesting on account of the modification of the gills to form a transverse septem as already described (ante, p. 620). The POROMYIDÆ are rounded shells with a single tooth in each valve. The siphons are fringed. The CUSPIDARIIDÆ are represented in British waters. The shell is beaked behind, and the valves are closed except at the end of the beak through which the fringed siphons protrude. There are no teeth in the hinge.

CLASS III.—SCAPHOPODA, OR SOLENOCONCHA.

The Elephant's-tooth shells belong to a small but very distinct class of low organisation. The shell is long, slightly curved, and tapers almost to a point, resembling in external appearance a miniature elephant's tusk. It is, of course, quite hollow, and there is an opening at each end; the one at the small end is generally notched on the ventral, *i.e.*, the convex side. Sometimes the shell is finely striated lengthwise. The animal is symmetrical. The margins of the mantle are united beneath, forming a long tube open at either end; a barrel-shaped prominence or snout represents the head, and the mouth at its extremity is surrounded by leaf like tentacles.

The formula of the radula is 1·1·1·1·1. The alimentary canal is doubled on itself, and terminates about the middle of the ventral side, opening into the mantle cavity, which latter has its efferent opening at the apex of the shell. There are no gills properly so called, but their function is probably taken by a double row of retractile filaments, each terminating in a knob-like thickening, that encircle the base of the snout. The heart is quite rudimentary. The foot lies under the snout, and is a long, cylindrical body directed forwards and terminating in three lobes. The nervous system

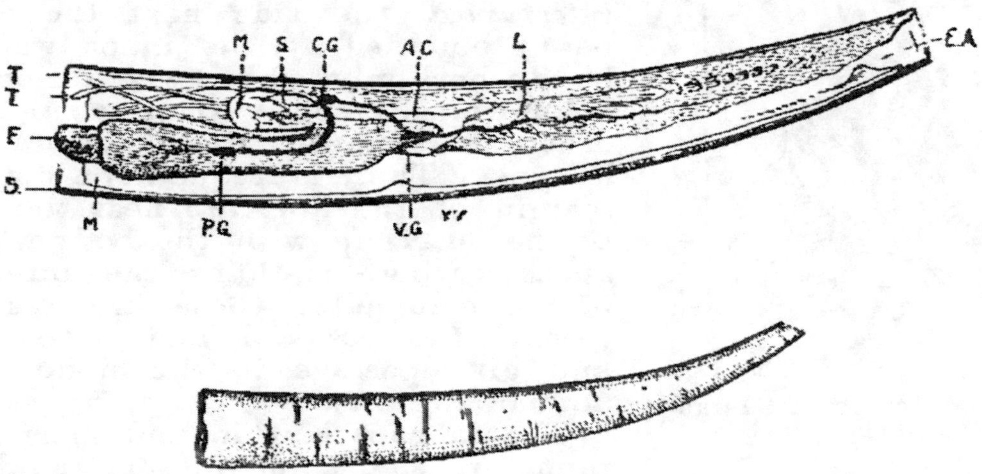

Fig. 11.—DENTALIUM SHELL AND DIAGRAM OF ANATOMY.

AC, Ailmentary canal. F, Foot. M', Mantle. S'. Shell.
CG, Cephalic ganglia. L, Liver. PG, Pedal ganglia. TT, Tentacles.
EA, Efferent aperture. M, Mouth. S, Snout. VG, Visceral ganglia.

is simple and resembles in general arrangement that of the Pelecypoda already described (p. 620), except that the cerebral and pleural ganglia are not fused. The Scaphopoda live in mud, and feed on the small organisms they find in it.

CLASS IV.—GASTROPODA.

In this class are included mollusca like the snail, whelk, etc., that have a distinct head, and, along the underside of the body, a muscular foot on which they creep; whilst the visceral mass situated above is sometimes naked, but more often covered with a shell, composed of a single piece.

The organs of the body are asymmetrical, *i.e.*, those on one side of the body are not matched by corresponding ones on the other.

The shell is essentially a longer or shorter hollow cone. In some, such as the limpet, it is a simple cone, but in by far the greater number it is an elongated cone, coiled round and round spirally, each coil forming a *whorl*, the last being the *body-whorl*. Nearly all spiral shells are *dextral*; that is to say, when placed with the mouth uppermost, and the apex directed away from the observer, the mouth lies to the right hand of the axis of the shell. Some are wound in the opposite direction, and are sinistral. Reversed varieties of shells normally dextral, or sinistral, are met with.

The axis or *columella* of the shell is sometimes hollow or *umbilicated* (the hollow itself being called the *umbilicus*), sometimes the whorls are closely coiled, and solid pillar of shell results. The *apex* or extreme top of the shell generally differs in markings and other features from the rest, and offers important characters. This *nucleus* or *protoconch* is the portion formed in the egg, hence it is also known as the *embryonic shell.*

The spiral channel formed by the junction of the whorls is termed the *suture*. A spiral line traced along the whorls midway between the sutures would mark the *periphery*. The *mouth* or *aperture* has sometimes quite a circular margin (*peristome*) when it is said to be continuous; more often it is *interrupted*, the side next the columella being bounded by the inner wall of the body-whorl only, when the exterior portion is known as the *outer lip* or *labrum*, and the other side as the *inner*, *columella lip* or *labium*. There is frequently a notch in the margin of the aperture near the junction of the outer lip with the body-whorl, and another where it joins the anterior end of the columella: these are respectively termed the *posterior* and *anterior canal*, and give passage to the siphons of the animal (Fig. 12).

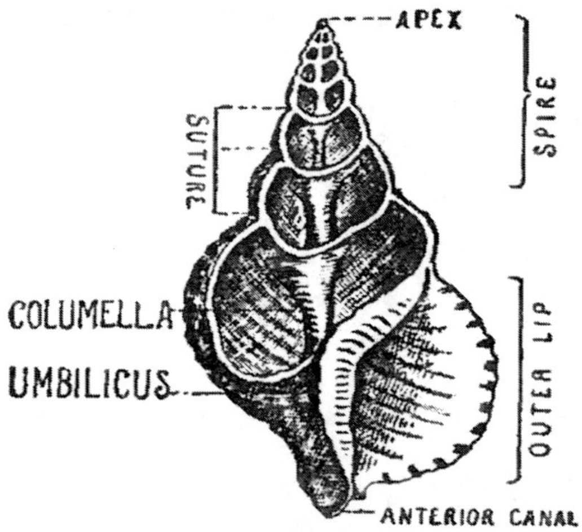

Fig. 12.—Topography of a Gastropod Shell.

The labrum is thin and sharp in most immature shells, and in some adult forms; but more frequently it is either thickened, or curved outwards (reflected), or curled inwards (inflected), or expanded, or fringed with spines. When these thickenings or expansions occur periodically during the growth of the shell they form conspicuous transverse markings on the whorl termed *varices*.

The exterior of the shell is also more frequently than not ornamented with either spiral lines or ridges running in the direction of growth, or with transverse markings coinciding with the "lines of growth," or with both.

Many Gastropods, like the periwinkle, close the aperture of the shell when they retire with a horny, or shelly trap-door, the *operculum*. It is developed in the embryo within the egg, and to its inner surface are attached strong muscles that hold it firmly in place. The following figures (Fig. 13) give some idea of the principal forms.

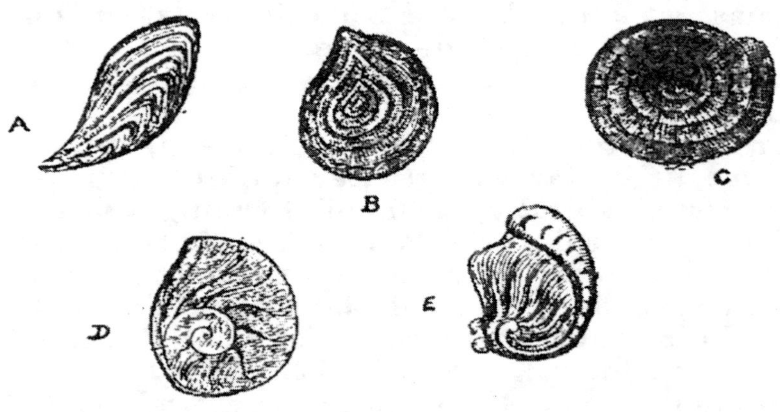

Fig 13.—Principal Forms of Opercula.
A, Unguiculate or claw-shaped. B, Concentric. C, Multispiral. D, Paucispiral. E, Articulate.

The head of the animal bears either a single pair or two pairs of tentacles, beneath which, quite in front, the mouth is situated. Of the armature of the mouth mention has already been made (ante, p. 612-14).

The visceral mass is externally covered by the mantle, which is in one piece. Towards the front, and a little to the right side, there is, under the edge of the mantle, a cavity in which are placed the gills or gill, whilst into it also the excretory duct and the terminal end of the digestive tract open. The mantle margin is sometimes prolonged in front of this cavity into a respiratory siphon: a posterior exhalent siphon is likewise present in certain forms.

Originally, in all probability, the animal, like the Amphineura, had a straight alimentary canal, terminating behind with a gill on either side of the opening; but, through the operation of causes which need not here be discussed, the alimentary canal first became arched, then its hinder portion was tucked-under, so to speak, whilst subsequently the visceral mass became twisted, the hinder portion, with the gills, being forced round by the right side to the front, so that in its final stage what had been the left gill is, in the typical gastropod of to-day, now on the right side, whilst the right one has passed over the neck to the left side. This last, however, is wanting in the majority of Gastropoda.

In the process of this torsion the visceral nerve-loop became twisted into a figure of 8, and, though in one great group the body is again untwisted, traces of its former contortion can still be traced in the nerve-loop.

The Gastropoda are divided first into two sub-classes: A, Streptoneura, in which the visceral nerve-loop forms a figure of 8; and B, Euthyneura, in which the loop is not thus twisted.

SUB-CLASS A.—STREPTONEURA.

To this section the name Prosobranchiata has also been applied, since the gills are in advance of the heart. There is only a single pair of tentacles, the eyes being situated on prominences near their bases. The sexes are usually distinct.

They are further sub-divided, according to the structure of their gills, into Scutibranchiata and Pectinibranchiata.

ORDER I.—SCUTIBRANCHIATA

(Sometimes called Diotocardia because the heart has two auricles) comprises the Limpets, Keyhole Limpets, Ormers, and Top-Shells.

For convenience they are further sub-divided, according to the arrangement of the teeth on the radula, into Docoglossa and Rhipidoglossa.

Sub-order 1.—The DOCOGLOSSA, or limpets, are characterised by their simple conical shell without any operculum. The animals adhere by the sucker-like foot to rocks between tide-marks. There are three families:—The ACMÆIDÆ in which there is but one true gill. The genus *Scurria* has in addition a series of leaflets arising from the mantle in a circle between it and the foot, that also serve for the purpose of respiration, and are known as pallial gills. The PATELLIDÆ, to which the common limpet belongs, have a circlet of pallial gills, but nearly all trace of the ordinary gill has disappeared. The LEPETIDÆ, going a step further, have neither ordinary nor pallial gills, nor have they any eyes.

Sub-order 2.—RHIPIDOGLOSSA. The radula of this group is very distinctive. The teeth are numerous and weak, the large number of uncini being especially remarkable.

The FISSURELLIDÆ, called keyhole limpets on account of the aperture in the shell that communicates with the pallial chamber, where the two gills are. In *Emarginula* the "keyhole" takes the form of a notch in the edge of the shell.

The PLEUROTOMIDÆ, or slit-shells, have conical, spiral shells with a notch in the outer lip at the periphery. The typical genus *Pleurotoma* is one of the rarest of living sea-shells (only a few specimens have ever been dredged), but they include one very fine example measuring over 6 in. in height (Fig. 14). There are two gills and the mantle is slit in front. The shell is pearly within, and there is an operculum.

Fig. 14.—PLEUROTOMARIA ADANSONIANA.

The HALIOTIDÆ, or ormers, have an ear-shaped, flat, spiral, pearly shell, with a row of perforations, a very wide aperture, and no operculum. The animal has two gills, of which the right one (left in position) is the smaller.

In the families next succeeding the mantle is entire, there is no slit or perforation in the shell, and only one gill remains, the (originally) left one.

The TROCHIDÆ have spiral shells of conical form, and very largely composed of nacre; they are frequently used for necklaces after the non-pearly outer coat has been removed. Some of the smaller examples are common on our coasts, but the finer and more handsomely coloured ones all come from tropical seas. The operculum is circular, horny, and spiral.

The STOMATIDÆ are for the most part pearly shells with a minute spire and large aperture; the operculum is like that of the Trochidæ.

The DELPHINULIDÆ are flat-topped, spiral shells, having few whorls; the umbilicus is wide and the angles of the whorls rough or spiny; the interior is pearly. They occur in tropical seas.

The CYCLOSTREMATIDÆ are small, sometimes minute, nearly discoidal shells, with cross-ribbing on the whorls. They are not pearly within.

The TURBINIDÆ include large and very pearly shells, much used as ornaments. They have a moderate number of rounded whorls, sometimes very richly coloured. The operculum is calcareous, and sometimes very thick and heavy, with the outer surface frequently beautifully sculptured or coloured: one kind, called cat's-eyes, has been used for necklaces. The Turbinidæ are tropical forms.

The NERITOPSIDÆ have solid shells much resembling *Natica* in shape. There is only one living species known.

The NERITIDÆ have solid and rather globular shells of not many whorls and very short spire, or none at all; the columellar lip is crenulate or toothed, and the shelly operculum is articulated. The genus *Neritina* occurs both in the sea and in fresh water.

The TITISCANIIDÆ are shell-less: one species only is known, which comes from the Pacific.

The PROSPERPINIDÆ, HELICINIDÆ, and HYDROCENIDÆ are terrestrial members of the sub-order, in which the gill is absent and the gill cavity transformed into a pulmonary chamber, as in the snail. The shell is more or less globular, and mostly of a yellow tint. All three are tropical families, and occur, the first two in the New World, the last in the Old.

ORDER II.—PECTINIBRANCHIATA

(Sometimes termed Monotocardia, the heart having only one auricle).

In this order, which includes the majority of the marine Gastropods, only one gill remains, the (originally) left one. The greater number, moreover, are monopectinate; that is to say, the gill has only one row of filaments.

The Pectinibranchiata are further divided into sub-orders according to the characters of the radula.

Sub-order 1.—GYMNOGLOSSA. Under this are grouped some more or less parasitic Mollusca which have no radula. The arrangement is artificial but convenient. Two families are distinguished, both of universal distribution:—EULIMIDÆ and PYRAMIDELLIDÆ. The former are mostly high-spired, very glossy; small white shells, with slightly bent axis; at times furnished with an operculum. Some species are found crawling in the stomachs of sea-cucumbers (Holothuria), others affix themselves to the exterior of the same creatures by means of the long proboscis, which is thrust through the skin of the host. The genus *Stylifer* has a glassy, globular shell, and lives amongst the spines of Echinoderms or buried in the skin of star-fish. The Pyramidellidæ form the preceding family by the occurrence of plaits or folds on the columellar, and by the fact that the protoconch is sinistral, whilst the rest of the shell is dextral and the axis of the former inclined at a considerable angle to that of the latter.

Sub-order 2.—PTENOGLOSSA. Two families are associated, probably provisionally, under this sub-order, having but one feature in common, viz., the radula contains a great number of similar teeth in each row, the largest being at the outer edges.

The IANTHINIDÆ, or purple sea-snails, float about in mid-ocean. Their violet shells are thin and translucent; the animal has a distinct snout; the eyes are generally wanting. Two plume-like gills are present. At certain seasons a membranous float or raft, full of air cells, is secreted by the animals, the egg-sacs are attached beneath, and when the whole is complete it is cast adrift. They seem to be gregarious, and stray parties brought by the Gulf Stream are frequently stranded on our western shores.

The SCALARIIDÆ, or wentle-traps, are high-spired shells, with the whorls often only united by the prominent varices that occur at regular intervals and impart to the shell its most characteristic feature. The aperture is circular, the operculum horny and spiral. The animal has a retractile snout. The Scalariidæ are carnivorous snails and widely distributed. Four species are British.

Sub-order 3.—TÆNIOGLOSSA. To this the greater part of the Pectinibranchiata belongs. The radula usually has the formula 2·1·1·1·2. The various families may be conveniently taken in the following order, but the position in the group of the first two is still undecided.

The SOLARIIDÆ, called "stair-case shells," from the appearance of the whorls as seen within the open umbilicus of *Solarium*, comprise forms having, for the most part, depressed shells with wide and deep umbilicus. The opercula vary in the different genera.

The HOMALOGYRIDÆ include one genus—*Homalogyra*—which has a very small, flat, coiled shell with circular operculum. The animal has no tentacles, and the eyes are not on stalks; the front of the foot is lobed and covered with fine hairs.

The NATICIDÆ have, for the most part, very stout, globular shells in which the umbilicus is sometimes open, sometimes more or less completely filled up with a shelly deposit termed the *callus*. The operculum is either horny or shelly. The animal of *Natica* is blind and has an extension of the fore-part of the foot that projects over its head when the animal is crawling; extensions of the side of the foot also partially envelop the shell. The Naticas prey on bivalves, boring a small hole right through the shell. Several species are British.

The Lamellariidæ have a delicate shell over which the mantle is reflected to a greater or less degree. The aperture is very large and rounded, and there is no operculum.

The Trichotropidæ have a conical shell; the whorls are keeled, and the periostracum, where it covers these, is fringed with hairs. They are northern forms and come from moderately deep water. The operculum is short and claw-shaped.

The Naricidæ have shells shaped like *Natica*, but covered with a velvety periostracum, whilst the shell itself is marked with spiral and transverse ridges, forming a kind of network sculpturing. The operculum is thin and horny.

The majority of the Xenophoridæ may be recognised at once by their curious habit of building into their own shells those or parts of others, stones, corals, or whatever may happen to be lying on the sea-bottom where they dwell (Fig. 15).

Fig. 15.—Xenophora.

The shell in the Capulidæ is limpet-like. In *Capulus*, the cap-of-liberty shells, it has a little curly apex; whilst in the cup-and-saucer limpets (*Crucibulum*, etc.) there is an internal shelly projection which serves for muscular attachments.

The Hipponicidæ have also limpet-like shells, but the mouth is closed by an accurately-fitting shelly plate attached to some fixed object. This plate is secreted by a kind of second mantle that envelopes the under surface of the animal and represents the foot, of which there is none properly so-called. A great horse-shoe-shaped muscle holds the shell to its base.

The four next families are all dwellers on the land, and in place of the gill, which is not developed, the pallial cavity is converted into a lung, as in the common snail. The animals have a distinct snout.

The Truncatellidæ and Ariculidæ are diminutive forms with cylindrical, many-whorled shells having a blunt apex, and closed with a spiral operculum.

The Cyclostomatidæ have spiral shells, sometimes top-shaped, sometimes globose, closed by a spiral operculum. One species of *Cyclostoma* is found on our chalk downs.

The Cyclophoridæ vary much in the shape of their shells, some having high spires, whilst others have none at all. The mouth is always circular, and closed with a tightly-fitting operculum, in which the nucleus is generally central. To enable the creature to breathe, when fast shut in its shell, there is often either a notch in the peristome or an aperture a short distance from the margin, that is occasionally prolonged into a tube. A few examples occur in Southern Europe, but the majority are found in the tropical regions of the Old World.

The succeeding five families are all fresh or brackish-water forms.

The ASSIMINIDÆ are small, high-spired shells that live in brackish waters, near the mouths of large rivers through Europe, Asia, and in the Antilles. One species is still to be found in ditches beside the mouth of the Thames, but is rapidly becoming extinct.

The AMPULLARIIDÆ dwell in tropical lakes and rivers. They have globular shells, with greenish periostracum, and closed with a horny or shelly concentric operculum. In some species the shell is sinistral. The animal of *Ampullaria* has a double respiratory chamber—one portion for breathing air, the other for respiring water.

The VALVATIDÆ, in which there is but a single genus *Valvata*, are restricted apparently to the northern hemisphere. Two species occur in Britain. The shell is flat, or moderately spired, and furnished with a many-whorled operculum fitting the circular mouth.

The VIVIPARIDÆ have two common British representatives, known as the banded water-snails. The shell is high-spired with rounded whorls, the mouth is oval, and the operculum horny.

The right tentacle of the males is shorter than the left, and has a deformed look. The eggs are usually hatched within the parent. The family is confined to the northern hemisphere, except in Africa, where it extends to the head-waters of the Nile.

The PALUDESTRINIDÆ are miniature editions, so to speak, of the preceding; but the tentacles are not modified. The operculum is calcareous in *Bythinia*. They are world-wide in their distribution, and there are several British representatives.

The RISSOIIDÆ are minute marine shells, very similar to the preceding; they are abundant everywhere. The LITIOPIDÆ and JEFFREYSIIDÆ are closely allied to the Rissoiidæ.

The LITTORINIDÆ, or Periwinkles, both the common one with its round, banded shell and short, sharp spire, and the yellow one without any spire, are too well known to need description. Some of the species have spiral ridges on the shell. *Pagodus* has a conical shell with tubercles or spines. The operculum in this family is horny and spiral.

The FOSSARIDÆ are closely allied and very similar to the Littorinidæ.

The MELANIIDÆ and PLEUROCERIDÆ have as a rule very high-spired shells covered with a brown periostracum; the mouth is simple, and the spiral operculum oval. The whorls are sometimes smooth, sometimes ornamented with spiral ridges and lines of tubercles, or a row of spines near the suture. They are exclusively fresh-water forms.

The CÆCIDÆ, sole genus *Cæcum*, are strange little curved shells without any markings. The young shell is coiled, but the creature, as it grows, breaks off successive portions and blocks up the end with a shelly plate, so that the whole shell is never found in the adult. It has a horny, spiral, circular operculum. Two species occur in Britain.

The TURRITELLIDÆ, or screw-shells, have long, slender, pointed shells of a great many whorls, more or less keeled, or ornamented with spiral ridges; the aperture is small, the lip simple, and the operculum horny, many-whorled, and covered with short hairs. The family has a world-wide distribution. One species of *Turritella* is British.

The VERMETIDÆ, when young, often have a neatly-wound spiral shell like Turritella, but in the more mature and the adult state this straggles off into an irregular circular tube much resembling those of certain marine worms. The shells are attached to each other in masses or to other objects. The foot of the animal is plug-like and quite useless for crawling. In the genus *Tenagodes* the tubular shell is fissured for almost its whole length.

The CERITHIIDÆ have long shells like the Turritellidæ, but the mouth is not so round and is interrupted by the anterior and posterior canals, the former of which is usually bent to the left. The operculum is horny. The whorls are generally sculptured, or ornamented with ribs, tubercles, or spines. They occur in all parts of the world and dwell in the shallow waters of coasts and estuaries, some even advancing up the rivers into fresh waters. There are three British species.

The wing-shells, STROMBIDÆ, APORRHAIDÆ, and STRUTHIOLARIIDÆ, are noted for their strong shells, with very short spire and widely expanded outer lip, which is often drawn out into curved spines. The fountain-shell, *Strombus gigas*, of the West Indies, the scorpion-shells, *Pterocera*, and the pelican's-foot shell, *Aporrhais*, are familiar examples. The operculum, which is rudimentary in all, is horny and claw-shaped: in the Strombidæ its outer edge is serrate.

In the CYPRÆIDÆ, or cowries, the outer lip of the adult shell is curled inwards, blocking still further the already narrow aperture, which is, moreover, edged with numerous fine teeth, whilst the short spire is almost, if not quite, concealed. The young shell, on the other hand, has a distinct spire and thin, sharp lip. The mantle when the animal is crawling is greatly extended, enveloping the shell, which thus acquires that beautiful polished surface for which the cowries are noted.

The DOLIIDÆ are, for the most part, large, thin, and rather globose shells, the fragile whorls of which are strengthened by their walls being corrugated. In *Pirula* the shell is stouter, and furnished with a long anterior canal. There is no operculum. They are denizens of tropical seas.

The CASSIDIDÆ, or helmet-shells, resemble the preceding, to which they are closely allied, and with which they are found. Their shells, however, have the margin of the outer lip inflected, or thickened and crenulated, and they furthermore possess a fan-shaped, horny operculum. The under-layers of the shell in *Strombus*, *Cypræa*, and *Cassis* being of a different colour to the upper ones, these shells lend themselves especially to the art of the cameo engraver: the best results are generally those obtained from the *Cassis rufa* of West Africa.

The LOTORIIDÆ are best typified by the great triton-shell (Fig. 12), which the sea-gods in mythical pictures are represented blowing. It is a fine large shell, with slender pointed spire and numerous varices, resulting from the formation of periodic mouths. The aperture is large and oval, whilst both inner and outer lip are denticulate. The periostracum in this family is usually stout and fibrous: the operculum is horny and claw-shaped.

The most highly specialised of all the Tænioglossa are certain pelagic forms formerly placed in a separate group, and called Heteropoda or Nucleobranchiata. The animals are remarkable for their transparency, all the various organs being perfectly visible even through the shell. They swim upside down in the water, the flattened foot acting as a fin. Two families are distinguished:—

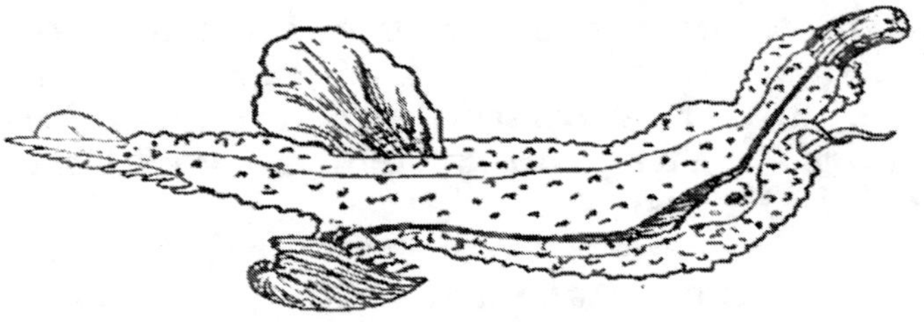

Fig. 16.—CARINARIA.

The ATLANTIDÆ have convolute shells, which in *Atlanta* is flat, and furnished with a single remarkably deep keel at the periphery, and in *Oxygyrus* is globose, and provided with many small keels.

The PTEROTRACHÆIDÆ, as a rule, have neither mantle, shell, nor tentacles; in *Carinaria* (Fig. 16), however, there is a cap-shaped, transparent, glassy shell covering the small visceral mass. The animals are carnivorous.

To the Tænioglossa, also, in all probability, belong the families CHORISTIDÆ, ADEORBIDÆ, SEGUENZIIDÆ, and OOCORYTHIDÆ.

Sub-order 4.—RACHIGLOSSA, Mollusca with long retractile proboscis. The formula for the radula is 1·1·1; the laterals, however, are often wanting.

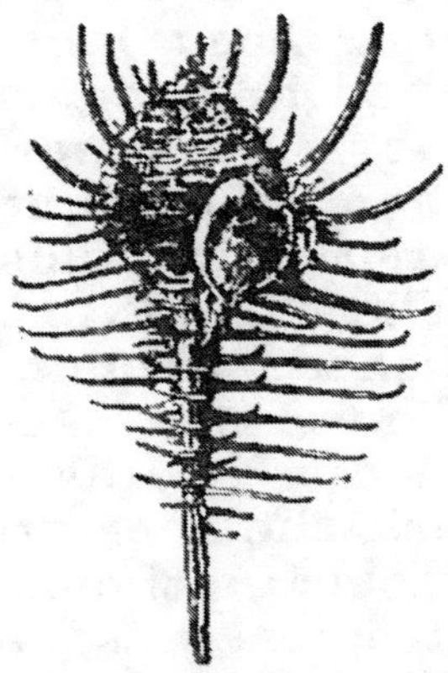

Fig. 17.
MUREX TENUI-SPINA.

The MURICIDÆ are a numerous family, chiefly familiar by the many examples of the spiny species of *Murea* that adorn some people's houses. Their shells have moderate spires and generally a large body-whorl; the mouth is furnished with both anterior and posterior canals, the former often being of great length, and a horny operculum. They are usually more or less spirally ribbed, whilst *Murex* has numerous strong varices frequently ornamented with spines of great length, which, in the Venus' Comb (Fig. 17), extend the whole length of the anterior canal. The dog-periwinkle, *Purpura lapillus*, so common on our coasts, belongs to this family.

The CORALLIOPHILIDÆ live amongst masses of coral; *Magilus*, indeed, becomes buried in them, and forms a tubular shell to keep pace with the coral as it grows. The young *Magilus*, before it becomes fixed, and the other members of the family resemble Purpura, both in shell and animal, but have no radula.

The COLUMBELLIDÆ are small fusiform shells resembling *Strombus* in shape; but the lip, instead of being expanded, is thickened and dentate within; the aperture is narrow and the anterior canal short.

The NASSIDÆ, or dog-whelks, have a shell like the common whelk, only smaller; the outer lip is thickened and dentate; the columella lip is thickened with a callus; the operculum is horny; the wide, thin foot of the animal is divided behind into two tails. *Nassa reticulata* is very common on our coasts.

To the BUCCINIDÆ belong the common whelk and its allies. The siphon is rather long and allows the animal to burrow in the mud in search of the bivalves on which it feeds, boring a neat little hole in their shells and rasping out its victim with the radula in its long, retractile proboscis. The foot is large and thin; the operculum horny and oval; a scanty, rough periostracum is found on fresh specimens, but soon rubs off.

The TURBINELLIDÆ have generally pear-shaped, solid shells, usually with shelly plaits or folds on the columella; the anterior canal is fairly long. They are for the most part tropical forms. To this family belongs the largest known Gastropod, *Semifusus proboscidiferus*, which attains 2 ft. in length. It comes from Australia.

The FASCIOLARIIDÆ have elongate fusiform shells; the spire is generally high and pointed and the anterior canal long. The columella bears several shelly plaits or folds; the lip is simple, and the horny operculum bluntly claw-shaped. The whorls are frequently ornamented with tubercles arranged spirally, and with spiral striæ. The members of this family, also, chiefly inhabit southern seas.

The MITRIDÆ are more cylindrical shells than the preceding, with more or less acute spire and narrow aperture, without operculum; the columella bears several folds, of which the hindermost, *i.e.*, the one furthest from the well-marked anterior canal, is the largest. The Mitridæ are tropical shells, the best-known examples being, perhaps, *Mitra episcopalis*, which is white, with squarish, red spots arranged in rows.

The VOLUTIDÆ include some of the finest of the tropical shells. The animal has a long foot and a wide, flat head; the shell varies, being spindle-shaped in some, and greatly swollen in others; in all, however, the aperture is large, the outer lip slightly turned out, the margin simple, notched for the siphon at the anterior end next the columella, which ends in a point, and bears several folds. The protoconch is set obliquely.

The MARGINELLIDÆ have oval, or sub-conoidal, shells that are shining and polished, without operculum.

The HARPIDÆ include but a single genus, *Harpa*, to the shell of which the periodic mouths impart its characteristic lirate appearance. The spire is short, the aperture wide, lip simple, with anterior siphonal notch; there are no folds on the columella, nor is there any operculum. The Harps are found in tropical seas, and so, too, are olives, which come next.

The OLIVIDÆ, or olives and rice-shells, in point of polished surface and in colour-markings, are equal to the cowries. They are more or less cylindrical, with a short spire and long, narrow mouth; the columella is callous, and bears several plaits towards the anterior extremity· an operculum is sometimes present.

Sub-order 5.—TOXOGLOSSA. The radula normally has the formula 1·0 1, and the teeth are large.

The CANCELLARIIDÆ include but one genus, *Cancellaria*, so named from the cancellate, or cross-marked sculpturing of the shell, which is oval, or turreted, with anterior siphonal notch; the columella is strongly plicate; the operculum is wanting.

The PLEUROTOMIDÆ include a great number of spindle-shaped shells, most of which bear a characteristic notch in the outer lip, and a marked anterior canal; the columella is smooth; the operculum is not always developed.

The CONIDÆ are too universally known to require description, their conical shells, with long, narrow apertures, are only approached in form in one or two exceptional instances by members of other families. The operculum, when present, is very small, and almost rudimentary. Perhaps the most remarkable feature about the animal lies in its radula, the teeth of which are proportionately large, are barbed, and perforated by a duct leading to a poison gland. This character has not been observed in any other group. The cones are essentially tropical inhabitants. The varied markings of their shells are completely concealed during the lifetime of the occupant by the tough periostracum in which they are enveloped.

The TEREBRIDÆ, or auger shells, are extremely long and slender, with many whorls, which are sometimes smooth but often ribbed; the mouth is oblique, with simple, thin lips and large anterior notch; the columella is without folds. The horny operculum is bluntly claw-shaped. The sole genus, *Terebra*, is entirely confined to tropical seas.

SUB-CLASS B.—EUTHYNEURA.

Gastropoda, in which the visceral nerve-loop, with one exception, is not twisted into a figure of 8, and in which the nerve ganglia are brought closer together around the œsophagus. The twist in the visceral mass is not so great as in the preceding sub-class, and the pallial cavity with its accompanying organs lies on the right side of the body. The head generally bears two pairs of tentacles; the radula is usually composed of rows of uniform teeth on either side of a central one; and the sexes are united in each individual.

The Euthyneura are divisible into two orders—Opisthobranchiata and Pulmonata.

ORDER I.—OPISTHOBRANCHIATA.

In this group the heart is placed in front of the gills. The order is subdivided into Tectibranchiata and Nudibranchiata.

Sub-order 1.—TECTIBRANCHIATA. The animal possesses a shell usually more or less completely concealed by the folds of the mantle and skin. For convenience this sub-order is further divided into three groups—Bulloidea, Aplysioidea, and Pleurobranchoidea.

A.—BULLOIDEA.

The Bulloidea have a well-developed shell, external or internal (Fig. 18 A-C); the head is generally devoid of tentacles, and the skin of the upper part is produced into a broad disc. In many the stomach is armed with shelly plates for crushing the shells of their prey.

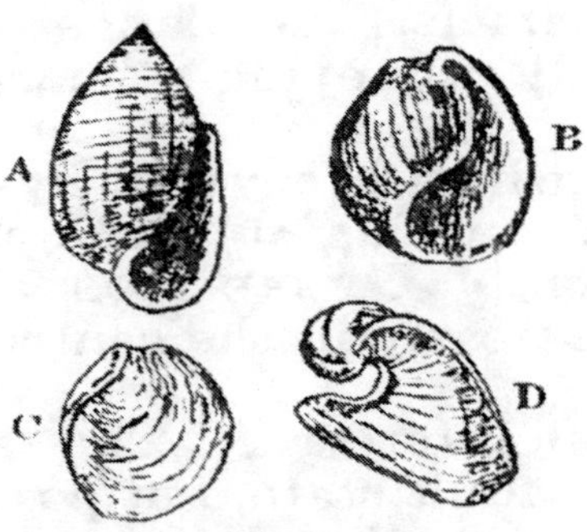

Fig. 18.—TECTIBRANCHS.
A, Actæon.
B, Bulla.
C, Philine.
D, Dolabella.

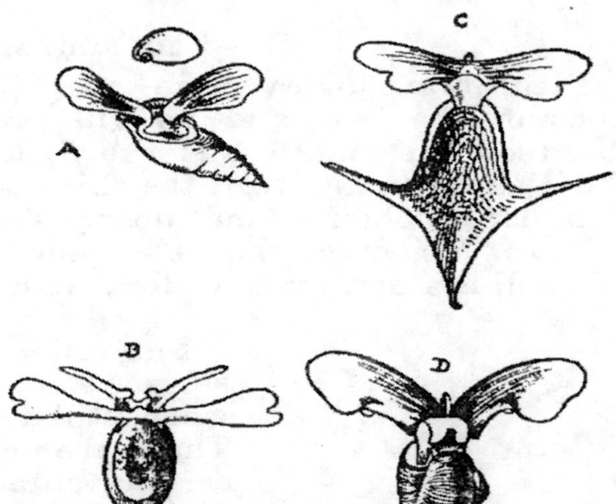

Fig. 19.—PTEROPODS.
A, Spiralis. C, Cleodora.
B, Eurybia. D, Limacina

The genus *Actæon* is distinctly streptoneurous and thus forms a connecting link between the Streptoneura and Euthyneura. It has an ovate, spired shell, with pointed apex and a narrow aperture that widens out in front. The horny operculum is elliptical in shape.

In the genus *Tornatina* the shell is cylindrical, the apex of the short spire being sinistral; in *Volvulella* the spire is no longer raised, the shell being convolute, *i.e.*, wound on itself like a measuring tape; in *Bulla* and *Bullinella* [=*Cylichna*] it is involute, *i.e.*, the spire is sunk, leaving an aperture, whilst the columella is less pronounced; in *Scaphander* the latter has disappeared and the shell is without any central axis, the whole interior being visible from the front; in *Philine* this is carried still further, the shell, which is internal, being widely open—unrolled, as it were.

To the Bulloidea is now referred that section of the old class Pteropoda, or sea-butterflies, in which the animal retains its shell in the adult state.

The chief peculiarity of the Pteropoda lies in the conversion of the foot into a pair of wing-like fins. Their shells vary greatly in shape, whilst their general appearance will best be understood from the foregoing figures (Fig. 19).

The following families are referred to the Bulloidea:—Actæonidæ, Tornatinidæ, Scaphandridæ, Bullidæ, Aplustridæ, Ringiculidæ, Gastropteridæ, Philinidæ, Doridiidæ, Runcinidæ, Oxynoidæ, Limacinidæ, Cymbulidæ, Cavolinidæ.

B.—Aplysioidea.

In the Aplysioidea the shell is either very greatly reduced or wanting altogether; the head carries two pairs of tentacles.

The Aplysiidæ, or sea-hares, have large bodies of greenish or olive-green hue, with a pair of lappet-like extensions of the foot folded over the back; the shell, concealed beneath the mantle-folds, is thin, covered with a horny periostracum, triangular in shape, and flexible when first removed from the animal (Fig. 18 D).

The shell-less sea-butterflies are now placed with this group, which includes the following families:—Aplysiidæ, Pneumonodermatidæ, Clionopsidæ, Clionidæ, Notobranchæidæ, and Eurybiidæ.

C.—Pleurobranchoidea.

The Pleurobranchoidea have two pairs of tentacles, no lappet-like extensions of the foot, and no gill cavity, the gill occupying a narrow space between the mantle and the foot.

In the Pleurobranchidæ, the thin flexible shell which is covered by the mantle is large, oblong, and nearly flat, with the nucleus at the hinder margin. In *Umbrella*, the sole genus in the family Umbrellidæ, the external shell is a flat, circular disc, with the nucleus nearly in the centre.

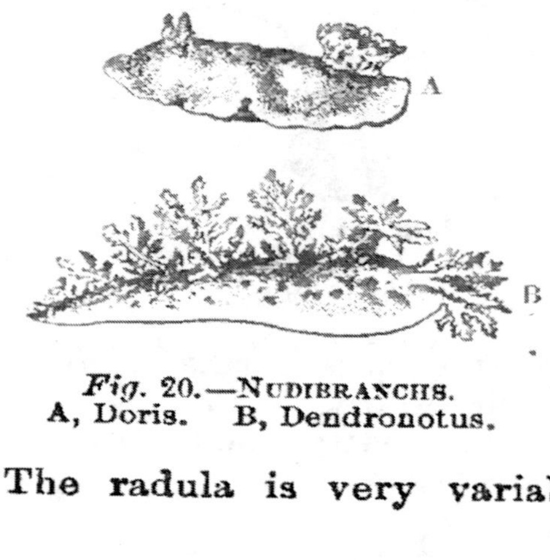

Fig. 20.—Nudibranchs.
A, Doris. B, Dendronotus.

Sub-order 2.—Nudibranchiata. The sea-slugs are shell-less in the adult state, but possess when still in the egg both shell and operculum. There are no true gills; their place is taken by certain tentacle-like organs that sometimes are placed in a cluster near the end of the body (Fig. 20 A), and sometimes ranged in rows down the back (Fig. 20 B). These "branchial leaflets," "dorsal appendages," or "cerata," as they are variously styled, frequently bear a striking resemblance both in form and colour to some other marine object, such as a cluster of zoophytes or small sea-weeds, etc. The radula is very variable, sometimes there are many teeth in each transverse row, sometimes the whole radula consists of a row of single teeth, one behind the other. In one group, the Elysioidea, the worn-out teeth as they drop off are saved up in a little pouch in front of the mouth.

The Nudibranchiata are divided into Elysioidea, Tritonioidea, Æolidioidea and Doridoidea.

Though they occur on every sea-coast they are not forms often met with by the ordinary student, and hence will not be discussed in further detail.

ORDER II.—PULMONATA.

In this order are included the vast majority of the land Mollusca (both snails and slugs) and of the fresh-water snails, besides three genera, representing a like number of families, of marine Gastropods. In all, the gills have entirely disappeared, and the pallial cavity has been converted into a breathing organ. The free edge of the mantle has been united to the skin of the neck and back, leaving only a small contractile aperture, whilst on the roof of the chamber thus formed respiration is effected by means of a branching net-work of blood-vessels that surround and lead to the heart, which lies with its auricle to the front. In the marine forms sea water is admitted into this cavity, in the others air is drawn in and then expelled. With one exception no operculum is present in the adult.

The Pulmonata are divided into—BASOMMATOPHORA, or those in which the eyes are placed at the base of the tentacles, and STYLOMMATOPHORA, in which the eyes are borne on the ends of tentacles.

Sub-order 1.—BASOMMATOPHORA. These have one pair of tentacles, which are not retractile, and the eyes are placed at their bases. All have an external shell, and, in the egg, an operculum, which is subsequently lost, except in *Amphibola*.

The AURICULIDÆ greatly resemble the Actæonidæ—from which in all probability they have descended—in the shape of their shells as well as in certain points in their anatomy. The shell is oval in outline, with a prominent spire and large body-whorl, whilst the aperture is long, narrow behind, and widening out in front. There are two or three strong folds on the columella; the margin of the outer lip is thickened and often more or less toothed on its inner side. They especially frequent salt marshes and damp spots within reach of the waves. The smallest British land-shell, *Carychium minimum*, is, however, found inland everywhere in damp spots at the roots of grass.

The OTINIDÆ are closely related; their shells are auriform. They occur between tide-marks, and one species is British.

The AMPHIBOLIDÆ are represented by a single genus, *Amphibola*, which has a globular, spiral shell, with an uneven surface, looking as if it had shrivelled. The operculum is horny and sub-spiral. They live by the margins of the sea in the Indian Ocean, Australia, New Zealand, and the Pacific Islands.

The SIPHONARIIDÆ have limpet-like shells, only distinguishable from those of the true Patellidæ by the slight, channel-like depression on the interior that marks the position of the opening into the respiratory chamber. Like the limpets they are found clinging to rocks at low water, but do not occur in the colder seas.

The CHILINIDÆ are fresh-water forms that occur in South America. The single genus *Chilinia* has a globose shell with wide aperture, a thickened columella with one or two strong folds; the exterior is ornamented with zigzag lines and spots of colour.

The LIMNÆIDÆ include our commonest pond-snails, *Limnæa* and *Planorbis*, as well as the little fresh-water limpet, *Ancylus*, with a few other allied genera. A characteristic feature of their shells is that their surface looks as if it had been beaten with a hammer.

The Limnæidæ are amongst the most widely distributed of Mollusca, being found from arctic to tropical climes, whilst *Limnæa* can even live in hot springs where the water attains a temperature of 104° F. The shells of *Limnæa* vary from very high to very short spired forms, but all have a very large body-whorl. The genus *Planorbis*, or the flat-coil shells, are really sinistral forms. *Ancylus* is found clinging to stones in swift-flowing streams.

The PHYSIDÆ are sinistral forms, and have very thin, globular, horn-coloured, and glossy little shells.

Sub-order 2.—STYLOMMATOPHORA. The Stylommatophora have, as a rule, two pairs of tentacles, which can be withdrawn into the body by a process of inversion, and carry their eyes on the summits of the upper pair. They are all terrestrial forms and have an external spiral shell, except the slugs, in which it is reduced to an internal shelly plate, or is wanting altogether. The slugs do not constitute a group by themselves, but belong to different families.

The land-snails occur in all climes and at all altitudes where life is possible, and include innumerable forms which have been variously divided into a great number of families and sections; the following, however, may be taken as constituting the principal groups:—

The ONCHIDIIDÆ are slug-like animals, entirely devoid of any shell, that live close down to the margin of the sea. Only one pair of retractile tentacles, bearing the eyes, is present. Certain species are also furnished with eyes on the back. There is a British representative found locally on the coasts of Cornwall and Devon.

The VAGINULIDÆ are shell-less slugs, unrepresented in Europe. Only one genus, *Vaginula*, is distinguished.

The ATHORACOPHORIDÆ, with a single genus, *Athoracophorus*, have a small, flat, internal, shelly plate. The lower pair of tentacles is wanting. They are found in New Zealand, New Caledonia, and the New Hebrides.

The SUCCINEIDÆ include snails, in some of which the shell is external, whilst in others it is internal. The lower pair of tentacles is either little developed or wanting. The type genus *Succinea*, or the amber-snails, are world-wide in their distribution, and have pretty little delicate, amber-coloured, glossy, spiral shells. Two or three species are British. *Hyalimax* is one of the slug-like members of the family found in the Mascareigne and Nicobar Islands.

The ACHATINELLIDÆ occur in the Sandwich Islands. They are prettily marked, and very variable little high-spired shells, that are sometimes dextral and sometimes sinistral.

The ACHATINIDÆ include at the same time some of the largest and of the smallest land-snails. The type genus *Achatina* is confined to Africa and its islands, although one species has been introduced into the Botanical Gardens in India. It has a high-spired shell, usually with a large body-whorl. The largest species attains 7 in. in length, and lays an egg as large as a pigeon's, with a calcareous shell. *Stenogyra* has a very long and narrow, many-whorled, glossy shell; some species are nearly an inch in length. *Cæcillianella* is very small and lives underground. It is, as its name implies, blind. One species occurs in England.

The PUPIDÆ have many-whorled (more or less cylindrical) spiral shells, often strongly striated and frequently sinistral.

The genus *Pupa*, the chrysalis-shells, is represented in Britain, as also is *Clausilia*, in which the shell is very long and sinistral. The latter is remarkable for possessing a curious little valve, the *clausium*, which is attached within the shell by a spiral elastic stalk to the columella, and closes automatically behind the animal when it retires (Fig. 21).

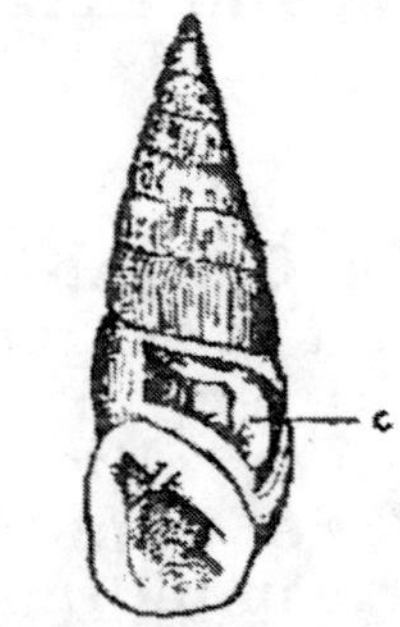

Fig. 21.—CLAUSILIA, showing clausium (c) in position.

The CYLINDRELLIDÆ, which are confined to America and the West Indies, have exceedingly long, many-whorled shells, with circular aperture: the last whorl often stands out from the rest.

The BULIMULIDÆ occur in America, Southern Asia, and Polynesia. With the exception of the slug-like genus *Peltella*, they have external high-spired shells.

The ORTHALICIDÆ are an American family, whose single genus *Orthalicus* has a shell in external shape resembling that of *Bulimulus*.

The HELICIDÆ comprise an enormous number of forms:—High-spired shells as in the genus *Bulimus*, which is confined to South America and the West Indies; or as in the gaudily-painted shells of the Philippine genus *Helicostyla* and our own *Cochlicella*; shells with short spire or no spire at all, as in the big genus *Helix*, of which the garden snail is an example.

The family THYROPHORELLIDÆ has been created to receive one small species, *Thyrophorella Thomensis* (Fig. 22), from the Island of St. Thomas, Gulf of Guinea.

The unique feature about the shell, which is a flat, spiral one, consists in the prolongation of the upper half of the peristome beyond the aperture and the formation of a hinge allowing this projection to close over the mouth and thus act like an operculum when the animal retires.

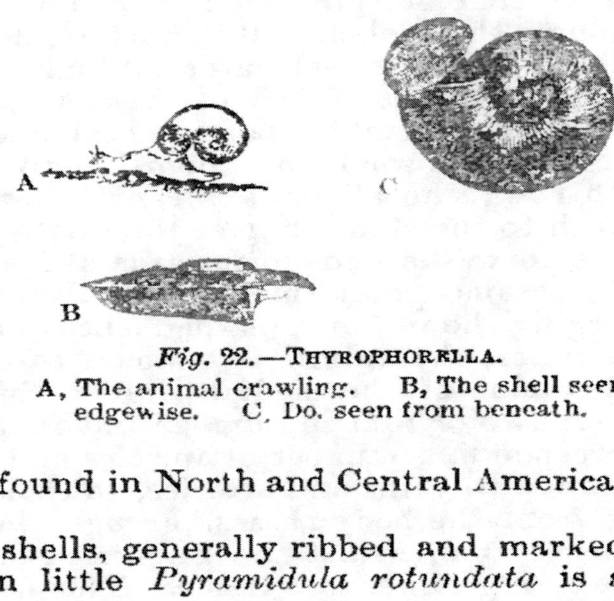

Fig. 22.—THYROPHORELLA.
A, The animal crawling. B, The shell seen edgewise. C, Do. seen from beneath.

The ARIONIDÆ are slugs whose shell is represented by a few calcareous grains beneath the mantle. The big black slug *Arion ater* is a type.

The PHILOMYCIDÆ are shell-less slugs found in North and Central America, Eastern Asia, and Java.

The ENDODONTIDÆ have flatly-coiled shells, generally ribbed and marked with little red patches. The common little *Pyramidula rotundata* is a British example.

The LIMACIDÆ are slugs with small, internal, shelly plate. The majority of the British slugs belong to this group.

The ZONITIDÆ have external shells, often very thin and shining. The peristome is sharp. The cellar-snail, *Vitrea cellaria*, is one of several British examples.

The TESTACELLIDÆ and SELENITIDÆ are the most highly specialised of the Stylommatophora and are almost all voracious carnivores. *Testacella* looks like a slug with a tiny shell at the end of its tail. It is a worm-eater and follows its prey in their burrows, hence it is seldom seen though fairly abundant in England. Other members of the group have shells of varying sizes and shapes.

CLASS V.—CEPHALOPODA.

THE Cephalopoda include not only the most highly organised Mollusca, but also the largest of them all, some forms, it is calculated, exceeding 50 ft. in total length. The pearly nautilus has an external shell, the cuttle-fish and its near allies have internal shells, whilst the octopus has none at all.

The Cephalopoda are symmetrical animals, the two halves of the body corresponding in structure. The visceral mass is large and often elongated. The head, on either side of which there is a large and well-developed eye, is more or less distinct, and is surrounded by the foot, which has in fact grown around the head and has developed, or been drawn out into, eight or ten long processes called *arms*.

In the majority of living forms these arms are furnished with rows of suckers or hooks. The upper part of the back of the foot has grown out into two fleshy lobes, the free, outer edges of which can be applied to each other so as to form a tube, known as the funnel, or siphon, that communicates with the mantle-cavity. Sometimes the edges of these lobes have grown together and form a complete tube. The bell-shaped mantle which envelopes the body is extremely tough and muscular.

The mantle-cavity is on the under side towards the back of the body, and the water for respiration is taken in at its open end and then discharged through the siphon. By the forcible expulsion of water in this way these animals can dart backwards through the water with great rapidity.

The mouth is placed in the centre of the arms; it is furnished with two jaws which resemble a parrot's beak and which are moved by powerful muscles. The radula is small in proportion to the animal, and has but few teeth in each row; the alimentary canal runs in an almost straight line from the mouth to the stomach near the further end of the body, thence the intestine leads forwards and downwards and terminates in the mantle-cavity. Just at the same point the ink-bag also opens into the mantle-cavity. By discharging the ink or sepia-pigment contained in this gland, and thus clouding the water, the animal is enabled to cover its retreat from an enemy. On either side of the median line, within the pallial-cavity also, are the gills, either two or four in number and foliobranchiate in type. The heart has a corresponding number of auricles and a ventricle, whilst the blood is largely confined to veins and arteries, so that nearly the whole of the blood returning from the body passes through the gills. The nervous system is highly concentrated, whilst the ganglia around the œsophagus are fused together into a ring of nervous tissue. This nerve-collar in *Nautilus* is partly, and in the other Cephalopoda completely, enclosed by a cartilage called the *cephalic cartilage*. There are other cartilages present, except in *Nautilus*, in different parts of the body, that serve as points of attachment for the larger muscles.

The faculty which Cephalopods possess of changing their colour is one of considerable interest. Scattered over the surface of the body, and just beneath the outer layer of the skin, are a number of pigment cells called *chromatophores*, and it is by the contraction and expansion of these, which are partly under the control of the animal, that the changes of colour are effected.

The class is divided into two orders, according to the number of gills present, viz.:—Tetrabranchiata and Dibranchiata.

Order I.—Tetrabranchiata

Is represented at the present day by a single genus *Nautilus*; but in past times there were many other very strange forms whose shells were either uncoiled or curved or quite straight.

The shell of *Nautilus* is entirely external and coiled forwards over the animal's back; the aperture of the shell of the male is proportionately wider than that of the females. Its outer layer is porcellaneous, the inner nacreous. Inside, when neatly cut in half, it is seen to be divided off by a number of shelly partitions into a series of chambers (Fig. 23). The reason for these lies in the fact that the animal does not occupy the hinder part, which it shuts off each time that growth compels it to construct a wider and more commodious portion in front. The first chamber of all, or protoconch, being horny, is never preserved in the Nautiloidea. Running right through these chambers to the last one is a small tube, the walls of which are pervious and lined with a black horny layer. It is occupied by a backward extension of the mantle called the *siphuncle*. What the function of this siphuncle may be is still unknown, nor is it yet ascertained for certain whether the untenanted chambers are filled with gas or water, though the latter appears more probable.

Fig. 23.—Nautilus.

The animal of *Nautilus* is rare, and differs conspicuously from other Cephalopods in that it has no long arms furnished with suckers; the mouth is, instead, surrounded by numerous suckerless tentacles which can be retracted into special sheaths. The margins of the lobes which form the funnel are not united. There is no ink-bag. The gills are four in number.

The eye is remarkable for being of the simplest description: it consists of a cup-shaped depression lined by the retina and covered with an outer layer of the skin, save for one small aperture in the centre. The sea-water fills the cavity when the animal is alive, and the whole apparatus must work on the principle of a pin-hole camera.

Four species of *Nautilus* are known—from the Gulf of Persia, the Indian Ocean, the China Sea, and the Pacific Ocean.

To the Tetrabranchiata probably also belongs the fossil group Ammonea, in which the shell was external and of various shapes, but retained the protoconch.

Order II.—Dibranchiata

Characterised by the possession of a single pair of gills. The funnel is complete. The eye is highly developed, having both lens and cornea. The shell, when present, is internal.

Sub-order 1.—Decapoda. The members of this sub-order have ten arms. Eight of these, often shorter than the body, are tapering and armed with rows of suckers. Each sucker, or *acetabulum*, is on a short stalk or pedicle, and strengthened by a horny rim which is frequently toothed. The horny rim is sometimes replaced by a hook which is retractile like the claw of a cat. The other two arms, called the "prehensile tentacles" or "tentacular arms," placed one on either side, are longer than the rest and cylindrical in form, with expanded ends armed with suckers, or with hooks. Just beneath the expanded tips there is sometimes an arrangement of suckers enabling the two to lock together and act in concert. These arms are retractile, and in the cuttle-fish can be withdrawn into special pouches.

The shell is concealed beneath the mantle on the side of the body opposite to the pallial cavity. It is generally more or less rudimentary, but is most developed in the cuttle-fish (*Sepia*) in which the "cuttle-bone" or "sepion" occupies the whole length and nearly the width of the body. In another form, *Loligo*, the shell is reduced to a horny "pen" or "gladius." *Spirula* (Fig. 24), however, has a spirally-coiled chambered shell in which the whorls are widely separated. This shell lies in the hinder extremity of the body, and, in the few specimens of the animal that have been obtained, is not completely concealed by the mantle, though whether this is the natural state or due to injury is not yet clearly ascertained. It is thus strikingly different from the shells of other living Decapoda; the gap between them is, however, supplied in fossil forms. In some of these, the Belemnites, the apex of the shell is enclosed in a calcareous sheath called the *guard*, or by quarrymen "thunderbolts." The shell of Spirula is common enough and frequently cast up on our shores, but the animal is an inhabitant of deep water and rarely obtained. The other members of the group frequent the open sea, and often have lateral expansions of the mantle that act as fins.

Fig. 24.—Spirula. The position of the shell is indicated as if seen through the skin.

The Decapoda are divided into two sections:—Oigopsida, in which the sea-water has access to the space between the cornea and lens of the eye, and Myopsida, in which the cornea is entire and water is not admitted.

The following are the principal families:—A, Oigopsida—Families—Thysanoteuthidæ, Ommastrephidæ, Onychoteuthidæ, Gonatidæ, Chiroteuthidæ, Cranchiadæ, Spirulidæ, and the fossil Decapods with "guarded" shells. B, Myopsida—Families—Sepiolidæ, Sepiadariidæ, Idiosepiidæ, Sepiidæ, and Loliginidæ.

Sub-order 2.—Octopoda. The members of this sub-order have short bag-like bodies without tentacular arms, only the eight tapering ones, which are always longer than the body, and the suckers of which have no horny rings. In many the arms are connected by a web, the *umbrella*, which may exist only at their base or extend almost to their tips, as in *Cirroteuthis;* it is probably of assistance in swimming.

There is no shell except in the famous "Paper-Nautilus" (*Argonauta*), and then it is not a true shell but a secondary one. This is carried by the females only, and is formed after the animal is hatched. It consists of a thin, white, perfectly open shell, which is slightly coiled towards the back; its corrugated walls are formed of three layers—the outer ones prismatic, the inner fibrous. The animal nestles in the boat-like shell, which is in nowise attached to the body, and holds it in place with the two front arms. The ends of these arms are curved round and sustain thin membranes, *vela*, which cover the exterior of the shell on either side (Fig. 25). Whether the mantle takes part in the secretion of this shell, or whether it is wholly formed by the "vela," is not yet quite clear; its function, however, is probably less to protect the animal than to serve as a receptacle for the eggs.

Fig. 25.—ARGONAUT.

The following families are included in the Octopoda:—Cirroteuthidæ, Amphitretidæ, Argonautidæ, Tremoctopodidæ, Allopsidæ, and Octopodidæ.

SUB-KINGDOM IV.—BRACHIOPODA.

LAMPSHELLS, ETC.

BY F. A. BATHER, M.A., F.G.S., ETC.

THE Brachiopoda are marine animals which, like some Mollusca, form external shells; but they differ from the Mollusca in many points.

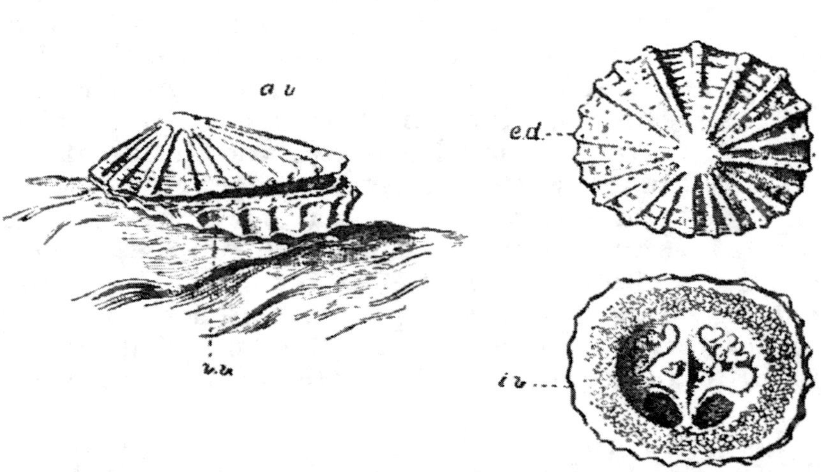

Fig. 1.—A SESSILE BRACHIOPOD (*Crania*); attached to a piece of oyster-shell; *d.v.*, dorsal valve; *v.v.*, ventral valve; *e.d.*, exterior of dorsal valve; *i.v.*, interior of ventral valve. Twice natural size.

The shell consists of two valves, which lie on the back and front of the animal, not on its sides as in bivalve Mollusca. Each valve is symmetrical in itself, which is very rarely the case in Mollusca; but one valve is nearly always larger than the other. By this larger valve the adult animal is usually attached to rocks or other objects, either by the direct growth of the valve to the rock (*e.g.*, *Crania*, Fig. 1), or, as is more usual, by means of a

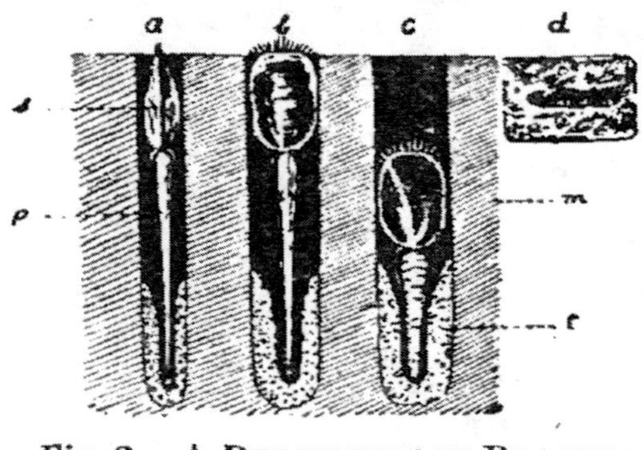

Fig. 2.—A PEDUNCULATE BRACHIOPOD (*Lingula*) The animal lives in the mud (*m.*) in a tube, the bottom of which is lined with cemented sand-grains (*t.*). The shell (*s.*) is attached to this by a peduncle (*p.*), which can contract. *a.* and *b.*, the peduncle outstretched; *c.*, the peduncle contracted; *d.*, the opening of the tube from above. Greatly reduced.

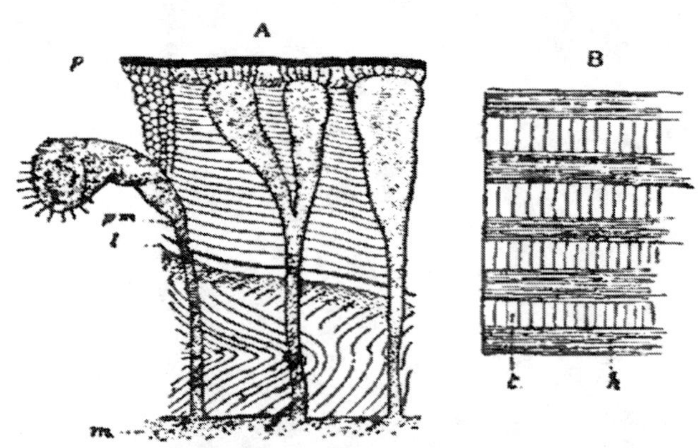

Fig. 3.—Shell structure of, *A*, a calcareous shelled Brachiopod; *B*, a horny shelled; *m.*, mantle, which sends processes (*p.m.*) through the prisms of carbonate of lime that make up most of the shell; *p.*, outer imperforate layer; *l.*, line of growth; *h.*, horny layers; *c.*, calcareous layers with vertical canals. Greatly magnified.

long muscular stalk, called the peduncle (Fig. 2). This larger valve is therefore often called the "peduncle valve"; by English writers it is called the "ventral valve," although in the natural position of stalked forms it is always the uppermost. The smaller valve is called the "brachial" or "dorsal" valve. In microscopic structure, also, the shell differs from that of the Mollusca (Fig. 3). The two valves may be united by a hinge at the hinder, or umbonal end (ARTICULATA, Fig. 4), or they may not (INARTICULATA, Fig. 5).

The shell-valves are lined by two mantle-folds, or extensions of the body-walls, which contain prolongations of the body-cavity; and in them the generative products are formed. The free margins of the mantle-folds are beset with bristles (setæ, shown at *b.* in Fig. 2). Muscles pass across the body of the animal from one valve to the other; they serve to open and to close the valves, and to move them sideways. The imprints of these muscles on the shell are important in the study of fossil brachiopods (Fig. 5).

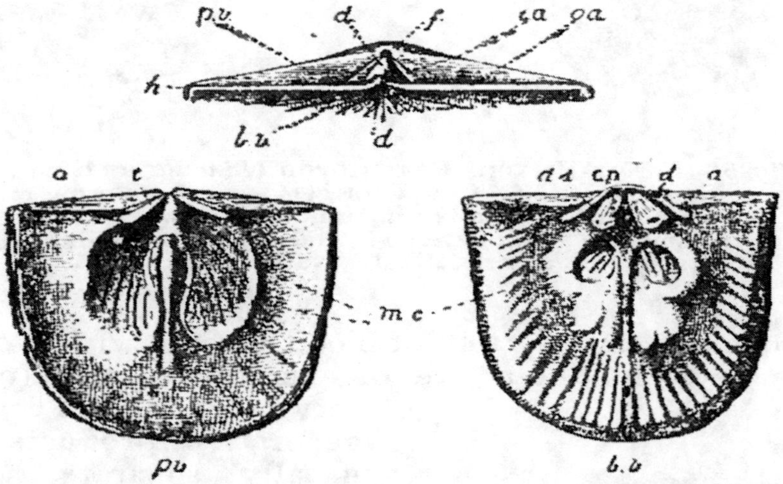

Fig. 4.—A HINGED BRACHIOPOD (*Rafinesquina alternata*). The upper figure shows the hinge from outside; the lower figures show the inside of the valves. *p.v.*, peduncular or ventral valve; *b.v.*, brachial or dorsal valve; *h.*, hinge-line; *d.*, deltidium; *f.*, foramen; *a.*, area; *i.a.* and *o.a.*, its inner and outer portions; *t.*, tooth; *d.s.*, socket in which tooth works; *c.p.*, cardinal process; *m.c.*, muscle scars. Two-thirds natural size.

The viscera (Fig. 6) lie near the hinder umbonal part of the shell, and the mouth is directed towards the fore-part or opening of the shell. Around the mouth is a somewhat horseshoe-shaped disc, bearing ciliated tentacles, and called the lophophore (tuft-bearer). It is often produced into two processes or "arms," which fill the fore-part and sides of the shell-cavity, and are often spirally coiled. From these "arms" is derived the name "Brachiopoda" (βραχίων, an arm, and πούς, a foot); they are often supported by a calcareous skeleton, the shape of which is of great importance in classifying fossil forms. The movement of the cilia of the lophophore serves to drive to the mouth currents of water containing food-particles. A lophophore is also found in the Bryozoa, and in a few other sessile marine animals (*Phoronis*, *Rhabdopleura*, *Cephalodiscus*). The mouth leads to a slightly-coiled intestine, which may have an anus (Tretenterata), or may not (Clistenterata).

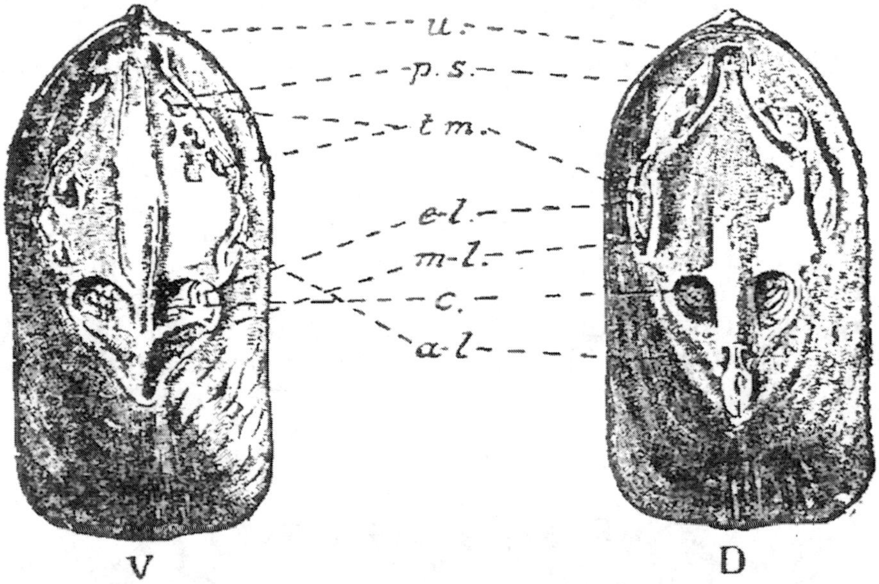

Fig. 5.—A Non-Hinged Brachiopod (*Lingula anatina*). Interior of ventral (*V.*) and dorsal (*D.*) valves, showing muscle scars, named as follows: *u.*, umbonal; *p.s.*, parietal; *t.m.*, transmedian; *e.-l.*, externo-lateral; *m.-l.*, medio-lateral; *c.*, central; *a.-l.*, antero-lateral. Natural size.

The Brachiopoda possess a system of blood-vessels, with a contractile heart, a distinct nervous system, and a pair of excretory organs (nephridia), which serve also for the transmission of the generative products. The sexes are usually separate, but *Lingula* is hermaphrodite.

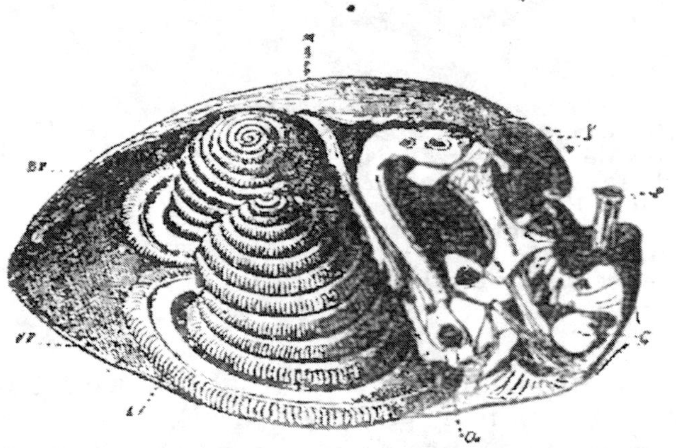

Fig. 6. — Internal organs of a Brachiopod (*Rhynchonella psittacea*). *p.*, peduncle; *D.V.*, dorsal valve, and *V.V.*, ventral valve, of the shell, which are broken away on one side, exposing—*L.*, lophophore; *M.*, median partition; *Oe.*, oesophagus, leading from a mouth between the coils of the lophophore to the stomach, *S.*; *C.*, the coecum, or blind end of the gut, which has no anus.

The Brachiopoda are found in seas all over the world, and usually at depths of less than 100 fathoms, but they have been dredged at a depth of 2,900 fathoms. A few (*e.g.*, *Lingula*, Fig. 2) bury themselves in mud; but most attach themselves to rocks. They occur in great numbers wherever found. Their shells, which are easily preserved, abound in strata of all ages, so that a knowledge of them is of great assistance to the geologist.

The simplest form of Brachiopod known occurs in the Lower Cambrian rocks of America, and is called *Paterina* (Fig. 7). Its valves are oval in outline, with one side truncated by a straight hinge-line. Concentric lines of growth run parallel to the curved margin of the shell, and up to the hinge-line, whence we see that at all stages of its growth the shell was of the same shape. A very large number of the genera of the Brachiopods pass through a stage in early youth in which both valves, or, more generally, the dorsal valve alone, are of the same shape as the adult *Paterina.* But during growth, changes in the shape of the valves take place, chiefly produced by the enclosure of the peduncle in the walls of the ventral valve, and by the formation of a definite hinge. In the simple types of Brachiopoda, such as *Paterina* and *Lingula* (Fig. 5), the peduncle passes out freely between both of the valves ; such forms are known as ATREMATA.

Fig. 7.—THE ANCESTOR OF THE BRACHIOPODA (*Paterina*). Enlarged.

Next, the peduncle-opening is restricted to the ventral valve, where it lies in a slit, which may become transformed into a round opening by growth of shell substance, a stage that is still seen in the modern *Discina* and *Discinisca* (Fig. 8). Such forms are known as NEOTREMATA. The two orders, *Atremata* and *Neotremata*, are equivalent to the old order, *Inarticulata* or *Tretenterata.*

In the next order, the PROTREMATA, the peduncle lies at the apex of a triangular fissure (delthyrium). This is partially closed in early life by a single shelly plate (pseudo-deltidium), as in *Clitambonites* (Fig. 9). This plate is secreted by the peduncle and posterior part of the body itself, and lies towards the apex of the delthyrium. In the adult, the pseudo-delthyrium becomes fused to the ventral valve, and often decreases in size.

The last order is the TELOTREMATA, in which the delthyrium becomes closed by the development of a pair of shelly plates (deltidial plates). These are

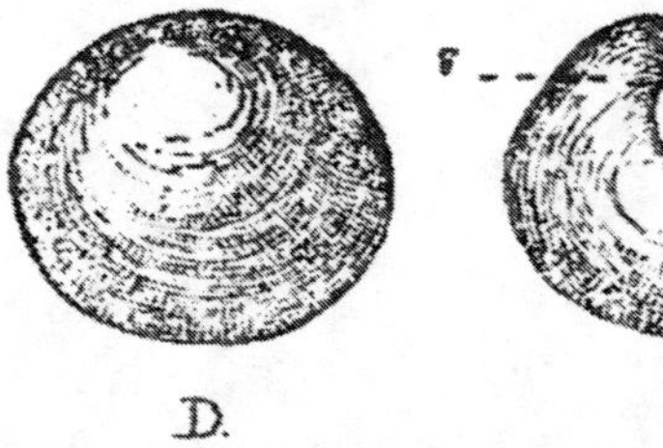

Fig. 8.—*Discinisca. D.*, dorsal, and *V.*, ventral, valve ; *F.*, peduncle slit. Natural size.

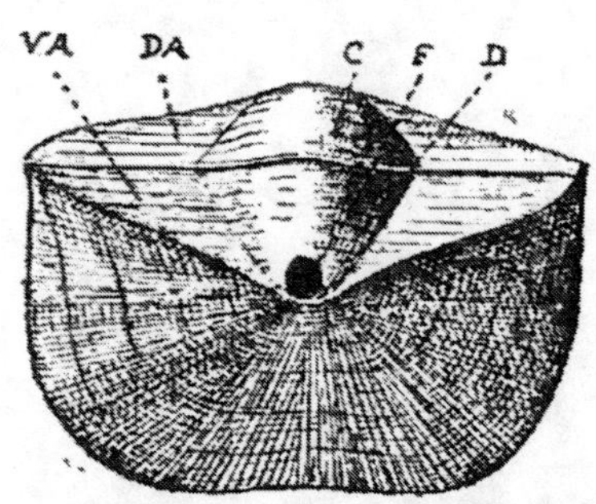

Fig 9.—*Clitambonites adscendens. F.*, foramen for peduncle ; *D.*, deltidium of ventral valve; *C.*, deltidium of dorsal valve (chilidium) ; *V.A.* and *D.A.*, areas of ventral and dorsal valves. Natural size.

secreted by the edges of the mantle, and may fuse, either in the adult or from their earliest appearance, to form a single plate (deltidium). (See Fig. 10.) Some of the earliest forms of this order are the *Rhynchonellidæ*, which occur early in palæozoic times. Subsequently, we find two main branches of the order, in which the lophophore is borne either by simple loops of shelly substance (*e.g.*, *Terebratula* and *Magellania*), or by coiled spires (*e.g.*, *Spirifer* and *Atrypa*) respectively (Fig. 11). The two orders *Protremata* and *Telotremata* together correspond to the old order, *Articulata* or *Clistenterata.*

The Brachiopoda, which were formerly very numerous, both in genera, species, and individuals, are now represented by a little over a hundred species, distributed among some fifteen or sixteen genera.

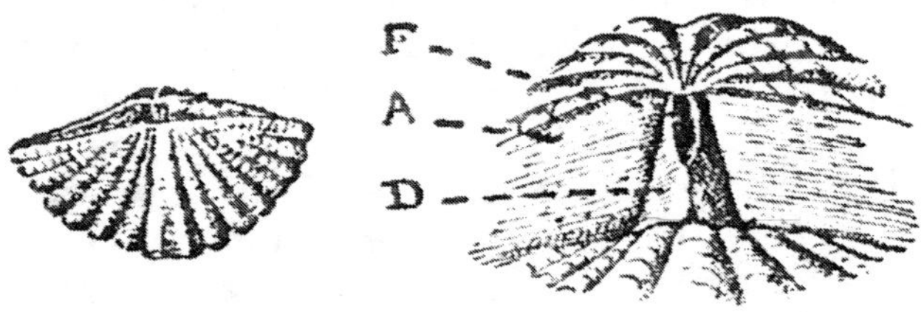

Fig. 10.—*Spirifer sulcatus.* A specimen, natural size, and an enlargement of the middle part of the hinge-area (*A.*) of the ventral valve, showing the delthyrium almost closed by two deltidial plates (*D.*), so that only a small foramen (*F.*) remains.

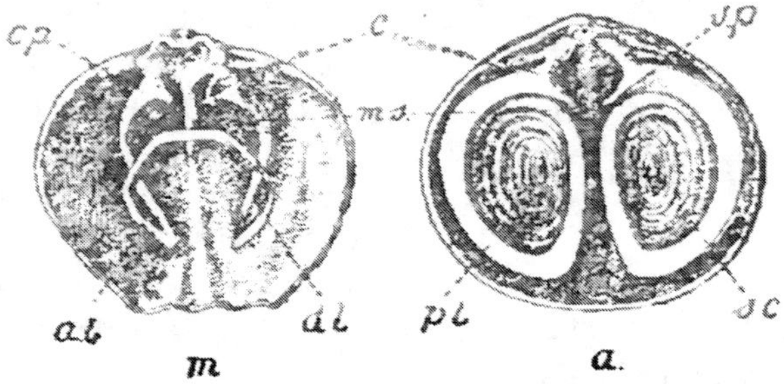

Fig. 11.—Lophophore supports in *Magellania* (*m.*) and *Atrypa* (*a.*). *m.s.*, median septum; *c.*, crura; *c.p.*, crural processes; *j.p.*, jugal processes; *d.l.*, descending lamella *a.l.*, ascending lamella; *p.l.*, primary lamella; *s.c.*, spiral coils.

The Brachiopoda have often been grouped together with the other forms that have a lophophore (Bryozoa, etc.) under the name Molluscoidea (mollusc-like). But, while they certainly are not related to the Mollusca, it is very doubtful how far they are allied to these other forms. It is therefore safer to keep them as a separate group of the animal kingdom.

SUB-KINGDOM V.—ECHINODERMA.

STAR-FISH, ETC.

By F. A. Bather, M.A., F.G.S., Etc.

This is one of the main groups of the animal kingdom, and the animals contained in it, such as the star-fish (Figs. 1, 2), brittle-stars (Figs. 5, 6), sea-urchins (Figs. 7, 8), feather-stars (Figs. 13, 15), and sea-cucumbers (Figs. 9-12), are well marked off from all other animals by certain well-defined characters. The first is the feature that has suggested the name of the group, namely, the deposition in the lower layers of the integument of a crystalline deposit of carbonate of lime. This may be in the form of minute spicules (Fig. 11, *s*), of separate plates, or of larger plates and ossicles closely joined together into a more or less rigid test (Figs. 7 and 13). In all cases it is characterised by its trellis-work structure, and by the ease with which it may be split in certain definite directions. Such deposition of carbonate of lime may also take place among the internal organs of the animal.

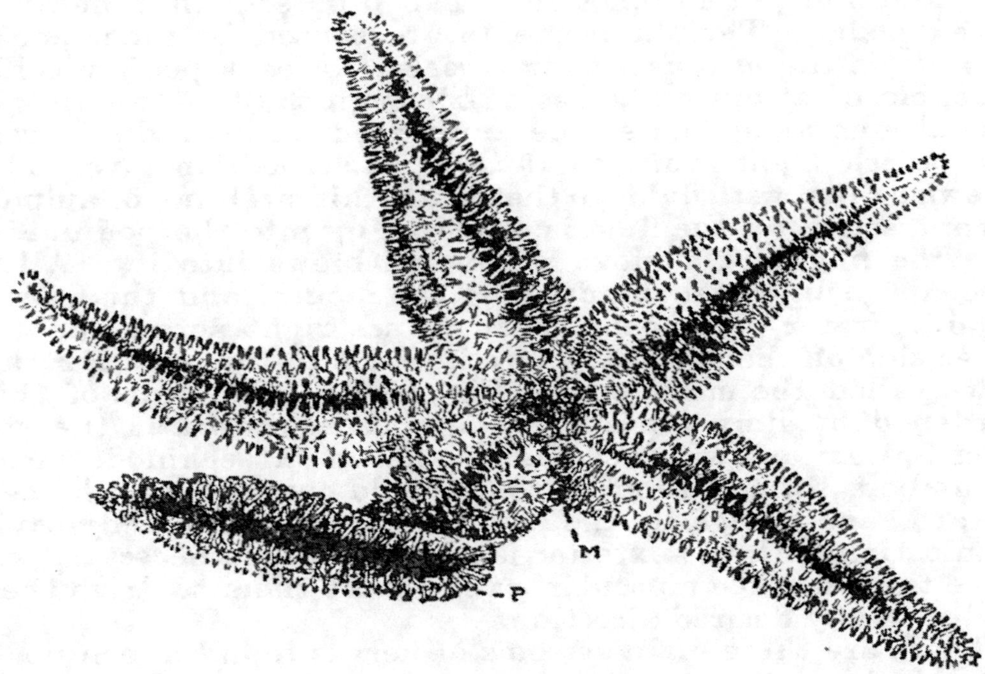

Fig. 1.—A Star-fish (*Asterias rubens*) from Upper Surface.
Two thirds natural size.

The second feature is the radiate structure so obvious in the ordinary star-fish (Fig. 1). The number of rays is generally five, and the external and internal organs of the animal are variously affected in the various classes of echinoderms by this five-rayed symmetry. The Echinoderma resemble the Mollusca, the Arthropoda, the Vertebrata, and many other groups, in possessing a separate gut, shut off from the rest of the body-cavity, as well as a system of branched tubes which convey blood through the body; and in these respects they differ from the jelly-fish, with which their radiate symmetry has often caused them to be allied.

A system of tubes conveying water from the exterior throughout the body, and serving as a hydraulic system, is characteristic of the echinoderms. On the under side of the rays in a living star-fish may be seen a number of small cylindrical processes which wave about gently like trees in a wind (Fig. 1, P). They lie in each ray along two rows with a clear space between, as trees on either side of an avenue; hence the whole band of them in each ray is called an ambulacrum (garden-walk). In the sea-urchin similar rows of the tube-like processes are seen passing from the summit down to the base, dividing the test into five equal portions. In the star-fish and sea-urchin these processes end in sucker-like discs. The tubular process can be extended to a considerable length and its disc attached to some neighbouring object. The contraction of the process then draws the animal along; hence in these animals the processes are called tube-feet. Similar processes occurring in the brittle-stars and crinoids have no suckers at the end, and serve only for purposes of respiration and not for locomotion. The processes in general may therefore be called podia. Their movements are caused by the squeezing of water into them from the internal water-vessels; for each podium is like an indiarubber tube, closed at one end, passing through the test to join with one main tube which runs along under the ambulacrum in a radial direction (Fig. 3, W), and before it joins this radial canal, each podium gives off a small swelling likewise filled with fluid, so that when this swelling, or ampulla (Fig. 3, Amp.), is contracted, all the fluid is squeezed up into the podium, and pushes it out like the finger of a glove when one blows into it. All the radial canals meet in a ring-canal surrounding the mouth, and this is connected with the outside water by a canal that passes right across the body-cavity to the other side of the animal, where it opens to the exterior through a sieve-like plate called the madreporite (Fig. 1, M). The walls of this canal are often hardened by limy deposits, whence it is known as the stone-canal. Some such system of water-canals occurs in all echinoderms, but in the sea-cucumbers the madreporite that should connect it with the exterior is sunk inward, and hangs in the fluid of the general body-cavity. Direct communication with the exterior is perhaps not so necessary with these animals since their flexible muscular walls enable them to drive the fluid of the body-cavity in any desired direction.

There are three main systems of nerves found in echinoderms, one supplying the skin, the podia, and the gut, and consisting of a nerve-ring round the mouth, with radial nerves passing from it beneath the ambulacra; the second, with a similar arrangement, but placed deeper, and supplying the internal muscles of the body wall; the third, which is best seen in crinoids, starts from the other side of the body, opposite to the mouth, and supplies the muscles that work the arms and stems.

In the star-fish the generative glands are orange-coloured tubes somewhat branched and knotty, which pass down the sides of the rays and communicate with the exterior at the angles between the rays (Fig. 2, G); they have a similar position in the sea-urchins; in crinoids they extend right down the arms, at the extremities of which the generative products are produced. In the sea-cucumber, however, there is but a single much-branched generative gland.

The echinoderms now living are divided into five classes—Asteroidea, star-fish; Ophiuroidea, brittle-stars; Echinoidea, sea-urchins; Crinoidea, sea-lilies, feather-stars; and Holothuroidea, sea-cucumbers. There are two extinct classes—first, the Cystidea, which are closely allied to the ancestors of all echinoderms; and second, the Blastoidea, which are perhaps nothing more than an offshoot from the crinoids. In the star-fish and brittle-star the mouth (see Fig. 6) is in the centre of the under side of the body, directed towards the sea-floor; while the anus (Fig. 2, As), when it exists, is on the other side and directed upwards. In a regular sea-urchin (Fig. 7) the mouth and anus are in a similar position, but in the irregular sea-urchins (Fig. 8) the body has become somewhat elliptical in shape and the mouth has moved a little forward; while the anus has moved down from the top of the body to its lower surface, so that both mouth aud anus lie on the under surface at either end of the long axis. In a holothurian (Fig. 9) the body is cucumber-shaped, with the mouth at one end and the anus at the other, and the animal usually crawls along on one side of its body. In the crinoids both mouth and anus are on the upper surface of the body, the mouth usually in the centre (Fig. 15, M) and the anus (Fig. 15, As) a little on one side, and both are directed upwards; while the opposite or under side of the body is prolonged into a stem (Figs. 13, 14) by which the animal is generally attached to the sea-floor or some other object.

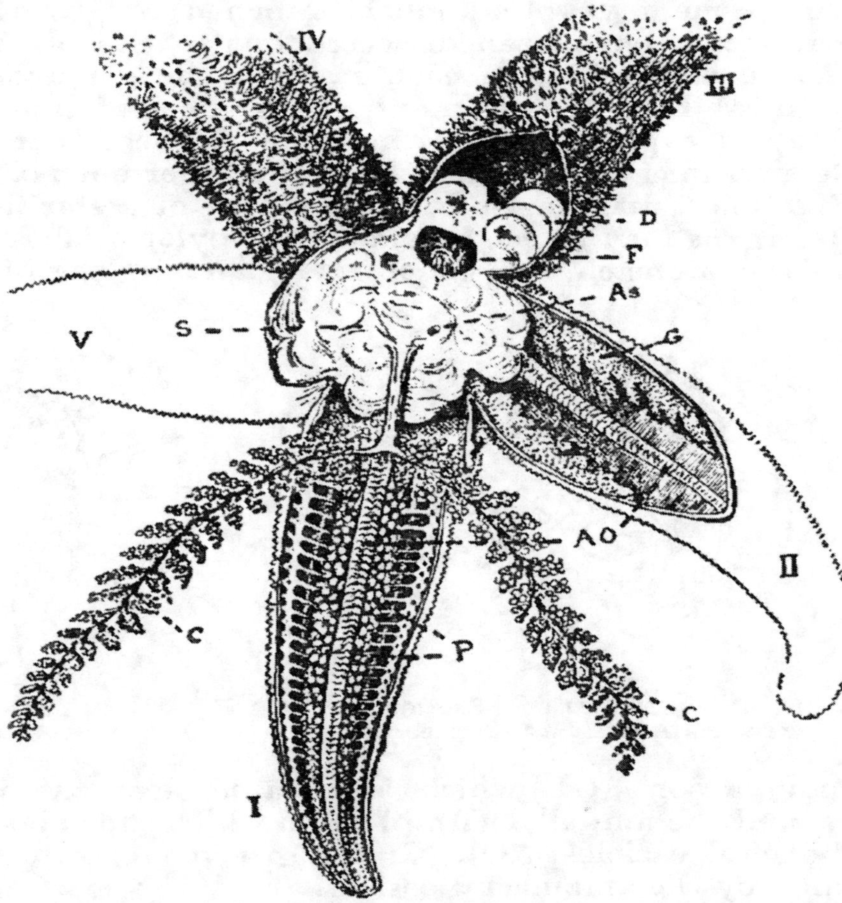

Fig. 2.—DISSECTION OF COMMON CROSS-FISH (*Asterias rubens*
Two-thirds natural size.

Echinoderms cannot live on land, since they require water to work their hydraulic apparatus, neither can they live in fresh water, where they would not find enough lime-salts from which to build their skeletons: in the sea, however, they have a universal distribution. Hence their calcareous remains have often been preserved as fossils, and are found in the rocks from the earliest period in which animals are known to have existed. Echinoderms move little from place to place during adult life; many of them, however, have rather larger powers of locomotion in the larval stage, and the free-swimming larvae are occasionally carried to considerable distances by ocean-currents.

ASTEROIDEA (Star-fish).

The common cross-fish, *Asterias rubens*, is perhaps the commonest example of an echinoderm, known to all visitors to the sea-side. Fig. 1 shows it from the upper surface, one of the arms being slightly turned over so as to show the ambulacral grooves with the tube-feet (P) on either side. Towards the middle of the body, at the junction of two of the rays, is seen the madreporite (M). These two rays are known as the bivium, while the other three rays form the trivium. A line drawn between the two rays of the bivium, through the madreporite and down the central ray of the trivium, would divide the star-fish into two equal and symmetrical portions. In Fig. 2 the same animal is shown, also from the upper surface, but partly dissected. In the ray marked IV. the rough spiny skin has been left on, while it has been removed over the middle of the body from portions of rays II. and III., and from the whole of the upper surface of the ray marked I. In the middle is seen the stomach (S), which sends into the rays the pouch-like extensions (D). At F part of the roof of the stomach has been removed to show the folded arrangement of its walls. Near the centre is the anus (As). From the stomach there pass down in the rays blind, much-branched outgrowths (C), known as pyloric caeca, which have been dissected out in the ray marked I. Underneath these, on either side of each ray, are the generative glands (G), which are seen in ray II. In rays I. and II. the central line of plates (Ao) separating the ray is exposed. On either side of these there are shown in ray I. the little swellings or ampullae (P) at the inner ends of the tube-feet.

Fig. 3 is a diagram showing the arm of a star-fish in section. Here the same organs may be seen, namely, the pyloric caeca (PC), the blind processes from the stomach, the generative glands (G), which open to the exterior

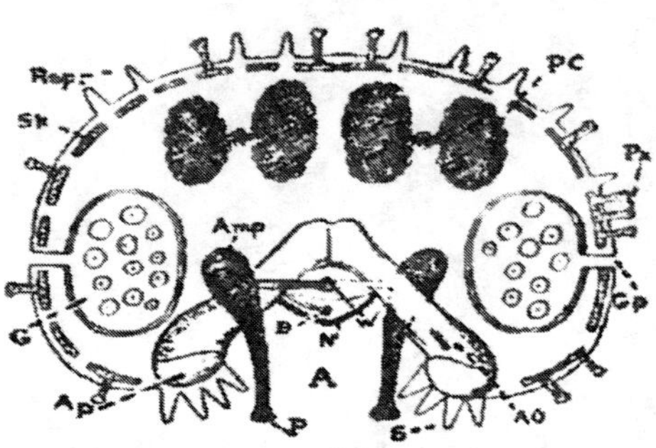

Fig. 3.—DIAGRAMATIC CROSS SECTION OF STAR-FISH ARM. Natural size.

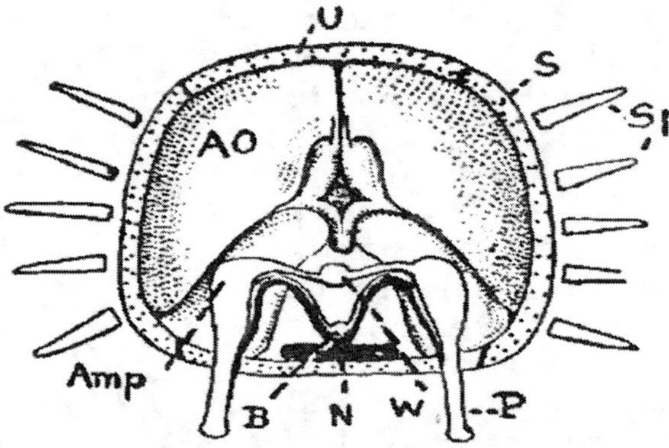

Fig. 4.—DIAGRAMATIC CROSS SECTION OF OPHIURID ARM. Much enlarged.

through a pore (GP) which is situated near the junction of two adjacent rays, and the ampullae (Amp), from which the tube-feet (P) pass through the ambulacral ossicles (AO). In the groove (A) on the under side of the arm, formed by the ambulacral ossicles and lying between the tube-feet, there are shown the following structures: close to the surface, the radial nerve (N); below this, the radial blood-vessel (B); and below this again, the radial water-vessel (W). All of these give off side branches, those from the latter going to the ampullae. The arm is encased in an external skeleton of irregular limestone plates (SK); some of these support spines (S), and others support curious kinds of spines with branched heads, known as paxillae (Px). Between the plates there pass out thin-walled processes (Rsp), which serve for respiration by bringing the fluid of the body-cavity into the proximity of the outer water. Besides the paxillae, there occur on the outer surface of a star-fish, as well as on that of a sea-urchin, small pincer-like organs called pedicellariae. These resemble little pincers supported at the end of a movable stalk, and they have probably been evolved from the smaller spines that cover the test of these animals. They move with extreme rapidity, and catch hold of any minute object that is brought into contact with their inner surfaces. They are variously supposed to hold small particles of food, to clean the test of dirt, and to catch hold of fronds of sea-weed for the steadying of the animal; while the fact that in the sea-urchin they are sometimes provided with poison-glands seems to show that they serve also as weapons of offence. At the extremity of each arm is a single tube-foot, with no

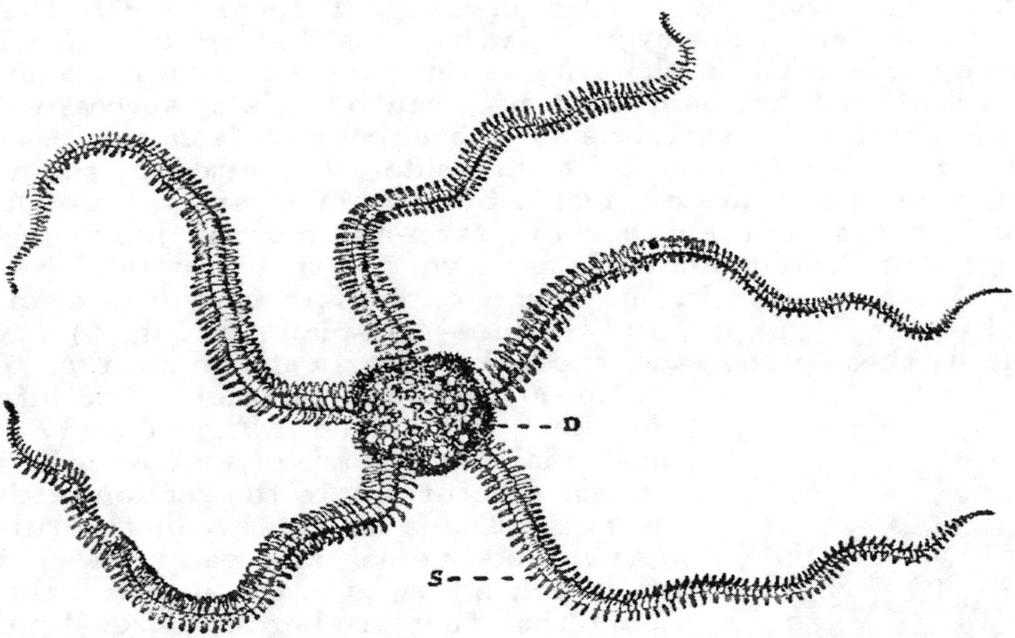

Fig. 5.—A Brittle-star (*Ophiopholis aculeata*). Two-thirds natural size.

sucker at the end: this is always stretched straight out, and is known as the unpaired tentacle. Immediately above it is a small eye coloured with red pigment, and protected by small tentacles.

Star-fish are sluggish animals, rarely moving of themselves, and staying for days in the same position. They can, however, travel at a fair pace when disturbed. When turned over on their backs, they are able to right themselves, but some of them, which have very stiff skeletons, take much longer over the process than those that are able to twist their arms about in acrobat fashion. They are, like most echinoderms, a sociable class, living usually in swarms. Some species of shallow-water forms have been observed to pair during the breeding season. They are voracious animals, eating all kinds of food, and taking plenty at a time. The stomach can, in most cases, be extruded through the mouth, and can enfold such articles of food as an oyster; star-fish are, in fact, dangerous enemies to oysters, and also attack the bait of fishermen, whence they are regarded by that class with a holy horror, and the cross-fish sometimes is called by them "Devil's fingers." To their credit it must be said that they serve as the scavengers of the sea, and that they make excellent manure.

OPHIUROIDEA (Brittle-stars).

The brittle-stars and sand-stars, which may often be found hiding under the rocks, or in the sea-weed, or in pools at low tide, resemble the ordinary star-fish in having five distinct arms. These, however, as shown in Fig. 5, are long and serpent-like, and are attached to a relatively small body or disc (D, in Fig. 5). There are other differences, as may be seen by a comparison of the section shown in Fig. 4 with that of the star-fish in Fig. 3. Here it is seen that the digestive and generative systems do not extend to the arms but are confined to the body. The arms are cylindrical and have no groove on the under side, such as exists in star-fish, but they have little openings through which the tube-feet P pass. In this class, however, it is the arms that are used for locomotion and not the tube-feet, so that the latter have no terminal suckers. The greater part of each arm is formed by a central axis of successive calcareous ossicles not unlike the vertebræ of a backbone. Each arm-ossicle (AO) is composed of two parts—one on either side and united in the middle line. The successive ossicles are connected by pairs of straight, muscular bundles, and articulate with one another by tenon-and-mortise joints, according to whose degree of development the arms vary in their power of coiling. The arm-ossicles are encased in the tough outer skin of the arm, in which are developed plates (U, upper, and S, side—arm-plates in Fig. 4). Spines (Sp) are borne by these plates, and these are clearly shown in Fig. 5 (S); they aid the animal in locomotion. The integument of the disc, as shown in Figs. 5 and 6, also bears small plates which are often covered with minute spines. Returning to the section of the arm, we see on its under side between the tube-feet, the nerve, blood-vessel, and water-vessel, which give off branches just as in the star-fish, the difference being that they are here enclosed by the integument of the arm. The mouth is shown in Fig. 6 on the under surface of the disc. Around the mouth are a number of short, flat processes, the mouth papillæ, which serve as strainers. Inside the mouth are seen the five tooth-plates.

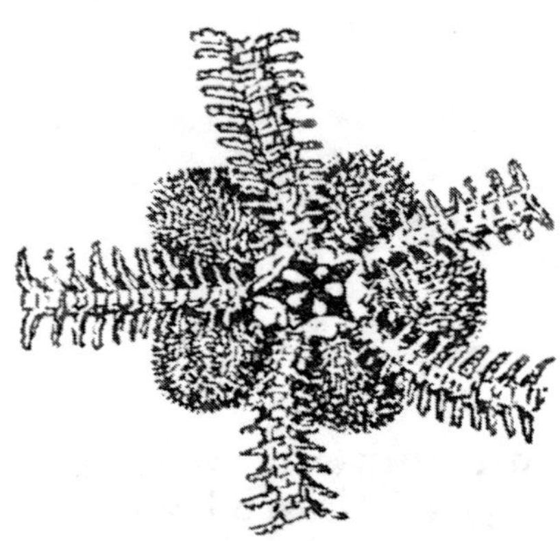

Fig. 6.—UNDER SURFACE OF OPHIURID BODY (*Ophiopholis aculeata*). Natural size.

Ophiuroids are found in all seas, usually occurring in quantities. They are most abundant in the rock-pools of the tropics. They gather their food to them by sweeping their arms over the sea-bottom, and thus conveying any suitable substances to the mouth. Figs. 5 and 6 represent a daisy brittle-star, *Ophiopholis aculeata*, which occurs all round the British coast. The colloquial name is due to the resemblance to a daisy caused by the intermingling of spines and plates on the surface of the disc. The popular name, brittle-star, applied to the ophiuroids is due to their fragile nature and their habit, so distressing to the collector, of breaking themselves into small portions when touched.

Echinoidea (Sea-urchins).

The sea-urchins are the best known and most numerous of echinoderms. They are divided into two groups—regular and irregular sea-urchins. Fig. 7 shows the test of a regular sea-urchin, *Cidaris papillata*, which is called the Piper from the supposed resemblance of its spines to the drones of a bagpipe. In the figure most of the larger spines have been removed, but three or four have been left on (S). Several of the plates of the test are seen to bear a rounded tubercle (T), and it is to these that the large spines are attached by a ball-and-socket joint, which is surrounded by muscles that can move the spines in any direction. The bases of the large spines are protected by smaller spines (s^1)—see figure—which are similarly attached to smaller tubercles. The spine-bearing tubercles do not cover the whole test, but are disposed chiefly in five broad zones, interambulacra (IA), which extend from one pole to the other. Alternating with these are the narrower ambulacra (A). In these can be seen the holes through which the tube-feet pass. At the summit of the test, where these zones converge, is a star-shaped space covered with membrane, and in the middle of this is the anus. Regularly placed round this, at the summit of the interambulacral zones, are five conspicuous plates, each pierced by a hole (G), which is the duct of the underlying generative gland. One of the plates (M) is also pierced by a number of small water-pores, and is the madreporite. Outside these five plates, and alternating with them, are five other plates, each at the top of an ambulacrum, and each pierced by the unpaired tentacles which terminate the water-canals, and represent the unpaired tentacles near the eye at the end of the star-fish arms. These plates, marked O, are therefore called oculars; in a few cases they do actually bear eyes. The mouth is at the other pole of the body, and is therefore not shown in the figure. It is surrounded by an elaborate arrangement of teeth, found in all regular urchins, and compared by Aristotle to a lantern. The gut, which passes from the mouth, coils round inside the test. Such a sea-urchin as *Cidaris*, or the common egg-urchin, *Echinus*, shows most clearly the five-rayed symmetry that has been impressed upon the echinoderms. In the irregular sea-urchins, however, one of which, *Echinocardium cordatum*, is shown in Fig. 8, the animal has become elongated along one of the axes so as to have a superficial two-sided symmetry. This is connected with constant movement in one direction, and such modification is found among those urchins that live on muddy bottoms, and especially in those from considerable depths. Not only is the test elongated, but the mouth moves forward to the

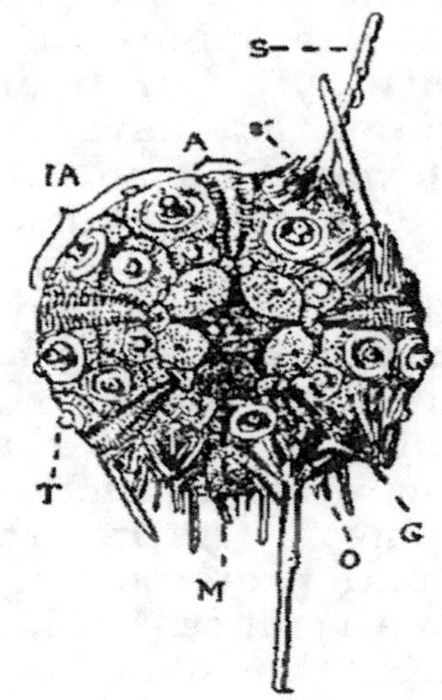

Fig. 7.—A Regular Sea-urchin (*Cidaris papillata*). One-half natural size.

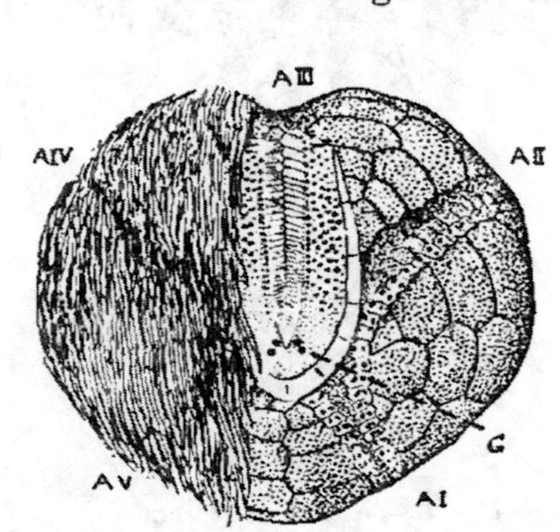

Fig. 8.—Irregular Sea-urchin (*Echinocardium cordatum*). Two-thirds natural size.

front margin, while the anus moves downwards to the hinder margin, and eventually comes to lie on the under side of the test. These heart-urchins, as they move along through the sand and mud, scoop it up into their mouths, and pass it through the gut, extracting from it on its passage such nutriment as the minute organisms in it can afford. Urchins of this type have short delicate spines, as shown on the left side of Fig. 8. They move almost entirely by stretching out their long tube-feet. It is, perhaps, the hair-like spines that have caused the urchin here figured to be popularly known as Mermaid's head, Child's head urchin, and Hair sea-egg.

The sea-urchins, like the star-fish, have pedicellariæ. In the regular urchin locomotion is chiefly effected by means of the spines, which are used like crutches; they can also be used like chop-sticks for prehension. The spines also serve as organs of protection, but their efficacy varies much in different forms. In *Diadema setosum* the spines reach a length of 10 in., and are so fine that one is pricked by them before one can see them. A few urchins, such as *Asthenosoma urens*, have poison-glands attached to their spines. On the other hand, the large spines of the Piper appear to be very small protection against its natural enemies, fish and star-fish; it is only the small spines that have any defensive value, and they are placed for this purpose near the main openings and organs of the body. Some sea-urchins cover themselves with dead shells, sea-weed, and similar objects, which they hold on by their tube-feet and so move about unobserved. Other sea-urchins do not move about but live in holes in the rocks, which in some cases they can be proved to have bored for themselves. The sea-urchins here figured have a rigid test; but there are others in which the plates are not so closely joined together, and the test is flexible. Fossil examples of such leathery urchins have long been known from the Chalk, but were not found in the living state before the dredging expedition of the *Porcupine*. The regular sea-urchins breathe by ten thin-walled extensions of the body-cavity which are protruded around the mouth. In the irregular urchins some of the tube-feet are modified for respiration.

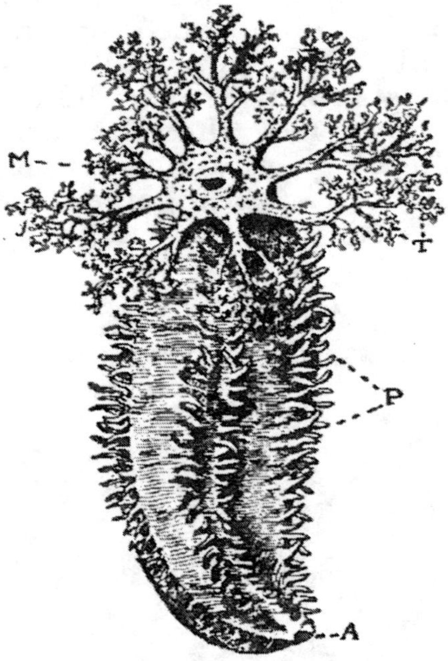

Fig. 9.—A Sea-cucumber (*Cucumaria planci*). Natural size.

Sea-urchins live on both animal and vegetable food, and even on one another. They themselves are often eaten by fish, and some are thought delicacies by man. The ovaries, when in the spring they are full of eggs, are said to equal the best fish-roe.

Holothuroidea (Sea-cucumbers).

A typical example of the sea-cucumber, *Cucumaria planci*, is represented in Fig. 9. The body, as already said, is elongated, with a mouth (M) at one end, and an anus (A) at the other. Around the mouth is a fringe of branched tentacles connected with the water-vascular ring. Two of these tentacles, those in the direction of the letter M, are shorter than the others. Five rows of tube-feet pass from the mouth to the anus, and under them lie radially-disposed nerves and muscles. In no holothurian, however, does the radial arrangement affect any portion of the digestive or generative systems. In most other echinoderms, it will be remembered, a canal passes from the water-vascular ring, and opens to the exterior by a madreporite. In a few holothurians of primitive structure this is similarly the case, but in *Cucumaria*, as in most, the connection with the exterior is lost, and the canal with its madreporite hangs down into the body-cavity. The skin is leathery, and contains a comparatively small amount of calcareous matter. What there is occurs usually in small spicules, which assume very definite shapes, such as anchors in *Synapta*, or wheels in *Chiridota*. Such spicules are represented in Fig. 11 (S^1 and S^2). In such forms as *Psolus*, however (Fig. 10), the spicules increase in size so as to form a plated integument; there may also often be a ring of calcareous plates round the gullet and round the anus (M and As in Fig. 10). The tentacles of *Cucumaria* and some other forms are used like a net to intercept floating organisms in the surrounding water. Many holothurians take a good deal of sand into the gut and the intestines; those that live near coral reefs generally contain fragments of coral. They usually attach themselves by their tube-feet to rocks or sea weed, and wave the tentacles around. The food-laden tentacles are thrust one after the other into the circular mouth. Some curious modifications of form have taken place among the Holothuroidea. In *Psolus* the animal has become flattened, and the tube-feet restricted to three out of the five ambulacra, and by these three the animal creeps about or holds itself fixed to the rock. The species shown in Fig. 10 is one of those that were dredged by the U.S. steamer *Albatross*, and occurs near the Cocos Islands at a depth of 66 fathoms, adhering to the rocks like a limpet. It represents a highly specialised form of the genus.

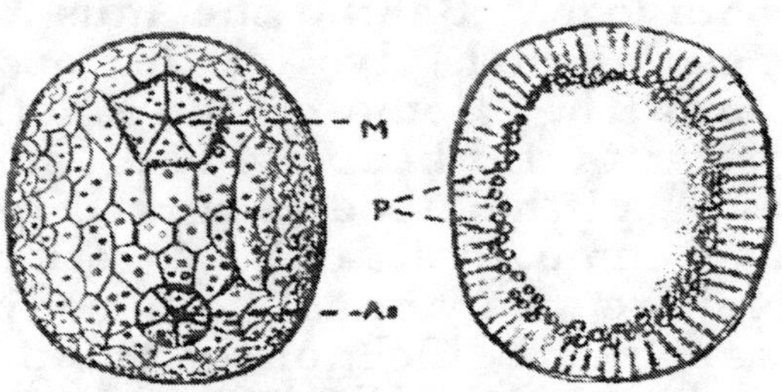

Fig. 10.—PLATED HOLOTHURIAN (*Psolus diomediae*). 3-2 natural size

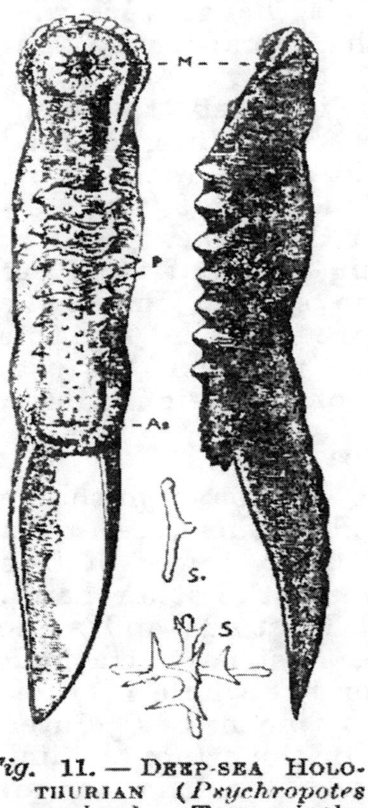

Fig. 11.—DEEP-SEA HOLOTHURIAN (*Psychropotes raripes*). Two-ninths natural size.

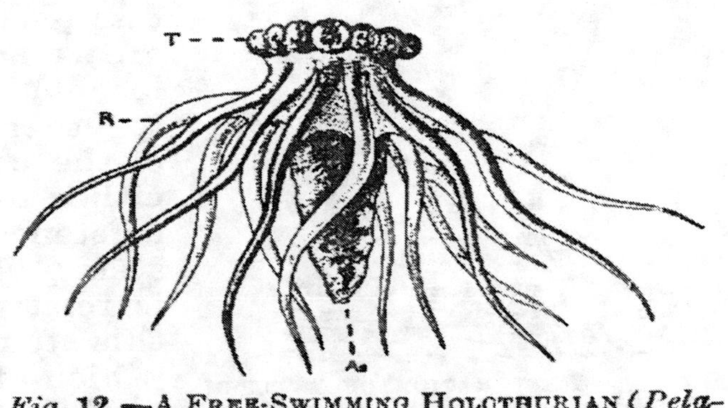

Fig. 12.—A FREE-SWIMMING HOLOTHURIAN (*Pelagothuria natatrix*). One-half natural size.

The tube-feet (P) are seen on its under side, forming a somewhat irregular ring. The curious form, *Psychropotes raripes*, shown in Fig. 11, is one of the deep-sea forms known as Elasipoda. It also was dredged by the *Albatross*, and comes from a depth of 1,573 fathoms, south of Cape San Francisco. The left-hand figure shows the under side of it, with the mouth

(M) at the anterior end, and the anus (As) at the posterior. The row of tube-feet passes down the middle of the under surface, between the mouth and anus. On either side of these tube-feet, and well seen in the side-view, is a row of podgy stumps, by which the animal moves as a centipede moves by its legs. Behind the anus a part of the body is prolonged into a flat tail. These animals live on the ooze of the abyssal ocean, gorging themselves therewith. Some of the holothurians that live in the sand of the deep sea, by constantly keeping both mouth and anus above the surface of the mud, have had their bodies curved in U-fashion, and in one genus the two openings have come to lie close together at the top of a thick stalk, so that one may compare the animal to a conjuror's bottle with a divided mouth. A yet stranger modification of the holothurian type is the beautiful *Pelagothuria*, represented in Fig. 12; this lives in the East Pacific on the surface of the ocean. It has no calcareous spicules, and the longitudinal muscles are mostly changed into a jelly tissue. Around the mouth is a circlet of short tentacles (T); and from these radiate thirteen to sixteen long feelers (R), the bases of which are united by a web forming a disc, by which the animal swims in much the same way as a floating jellyfish. The rest of the body, with the anus (As) at the end of it, hangs vertically downwards. In life the semi-transparent body is tinged a purplish red.

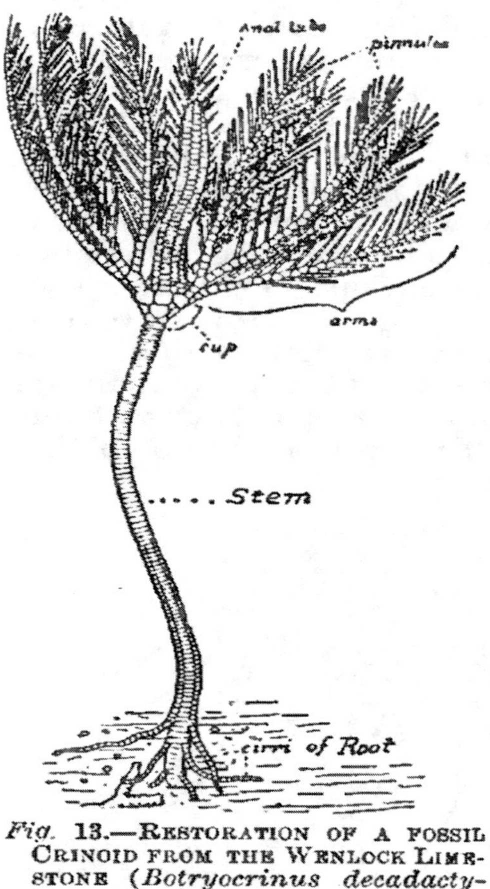

Fig. 13.—RESTORATION OF A FOSSIL CRINOID FROM THE WENLOCK LIMESTONE (*Botryocrinus decadactylus*). Two-thirds natural size.

Holothurians are of interest to men, especially Chinamen, as furnishing a food known as Trepang, which ranks with edible birds' nests among the delicacies of the celestial table. The fishing for this takes place in the East Indies and along the Barrier Reef of Australia. Only those species that have few calcareous spicules are of value for this purpose, while others are rejected because, when caught, they get rid of all their insides.

CRINOIDEA (Sea-lilies).

The echinoderms that we have hitherto discussed have all availed themselves, to a greater or less extent, of their power of free locomotion. The crinoids, on the other hand, together with the extinct blastoids and some of the cystids, are for the most part attached, either during youth or for the whole of their existence, to the sea-floor by means of a jointed stem (Fig. 13). The body of the crinoid, which is relatively small, is placed on the top of this stem, and from it there extend long arms which are usually branched and often provided with yet smaller branches regularly arranged along them, and called pinnules. Each of the pinnules, or each of the finer divisions of the arms, is provided on the upper side with a groove, carpeted by the minute rapidly waving processes known as cilia. These constantly drive a stream of water down the groove towards the main arm, which is provided with a similar groove. The water itself passes down the arms towards the body, and is then carried down five similar grooves, one leading from each arm to the mouth, which is placed at or near the centre of the upper surface of the body. The stream of water, containing numerous animalculae and food particles, passes through the mouth into the gut, which is coiled round the inside of the body, and passes out again at the anal opening. This latter is often raised on a small eminence or papilla (Fig. 15, As). In some forms, especially in some extinct genera, this papilla was extended into a long tube, so that the excrement was carried far away from the food-grooves of the arms (Fig. 13). Ranged along the sides of the food-grooves are the tube-feet, which, however, are not provided with suckers, but probably serve as respiratory processes. The small size of the body is perhaps to be accounted for by the fact that the generative glands do not develop within the body, but extend along the arms underneath the food-groove into the pinnules. Here the generative products become ripe and swell up the pinnules, from which they ultimately burst. The calcareous case that encloses the organs of the body is known as the calyx; it may be regarded as composed of a cup supported like a wine-glass on a stem, from the edges of which cup the arms originate; while it is covered by a lid in which are the openings for the mouth and anus. The lid is pierced by pores which put the water-vascular system in connection with the exterior. These may either be dispersed over the surface of the lid, or, as in other echinoderms, collected in one plate—the madreporite. This plate, when it exists, lies between the mouth and the anus. In the crinoids now living the cup is composed of only two or three circlets of plates, with no more plates than five in each circlet, and in many cases the two lower circlets are hardly to be distinguished. In some ancient crinoids, however, the organs of the body take up much more room, and to accommodate them the cup had an increase in size. This was effected, not by the plates becoming larger, but by the lid being, as it were, raised up the arms, so that the lower plates of the arms were included in the walls of the cup. At the same time, further plates were intercalated between the arms and their branches, binding them all into a plated integument, which looked like a tesselated pavement.

The stem is perhaps the most interesting part of the crinoid anatomy. All echinoderms, and many other animals, including, oddly enough, some which are generally reckoned by zoologists among the ancestors of the Vertebrata, have in their youngest stages a small process or lobe extending in front of the mouth, by which lobe they are accustomed to attach themselves as though by a sucker. In many cases the attachment lasts but a short period; but in the crinoids, at all events, it persists for some time, and the lobe becomes extended, while rings of calcareous substances are deposited in its integument. The increase of these rings in number and in size gradually produces a stem or column formed of superposed ossicles, perforated by a canal which is an extension of the original body-cavity. In the crinoids this canal contains extensions of blood-vessels and also of a sheath of nervous substance surrounding the blood-vessels. These extensions pass from a central five-chambered organ placed at the bottom of the cup, just at its junction with the stem. From this strands of the same nervous substance also pass in criss-cross fashion through all the plates of the cup, and finally join

Fig. 14.—STALKED LARVA OF THE FEATHER-STAR (*Antedon rosacea*) Eight times natural size.

together and pass up the ossicles of the arms. These are motor nerves, and the central organ controls the movements of the arms, the stem, and all appendages of the crinoid.

Although crinoids are typically fixed by this stem, and although the ancestors, at least, of all crinoids have been fixed by such a stem, still there are some, both living and extinct, in which the stem has entirely or almost entirely disappeared, leaving the crinoid with powers of free locomotion. There are some four or five living genera in which this has taken place; the most familiar instance is the rosy feather-star of our own seas, shown in Fig. 15. In its younger stages, however (see Fig. 14), the animal is provided with a stem. From this it ultimately breaks off, retaining but a few of the ossicles. These ossicles become fused together, and form a thick knob at the base of the cup. From this knob, which is called the centrodorsal, there pass small branches called cirri (C, Fig. 15); by these cirri the animal can hold on to stones or other objects at the bottom of the sea, so that, although able to move at will, it can save itself from being swept away by storms or currents. Fig. 15 shows one of these creatures in the act of crawling away from the stone to which it was attached. The arm towards the spectator is stretched out and slightly curved back, the pinnules at its extremity being bent right back like the barbs of a fish-hook. By these it will hook on to the rough surface of the sea-floor, and the arms will then bend and the animal be dragged along. At the same time the opposite arms are bent downwards and their pinnules are pushed in the opposite direction. This shortening of the stem and power of locomotion has been a gradual development. The *Pentacrini*, which are among the commonest of living stalked crinoids, have their stem beset at intervals with whorls of cirri. The joints of the stem just below each whorl are not muscular, but brittle, so that the crinoid can easily break its stem at those joints, and after moving away a short space, can again affix itself by the whorl of cirri remaining at the broken end. In this way *Pentacrini* have been found attached to telegraph cables but a short time after they had been laid down.

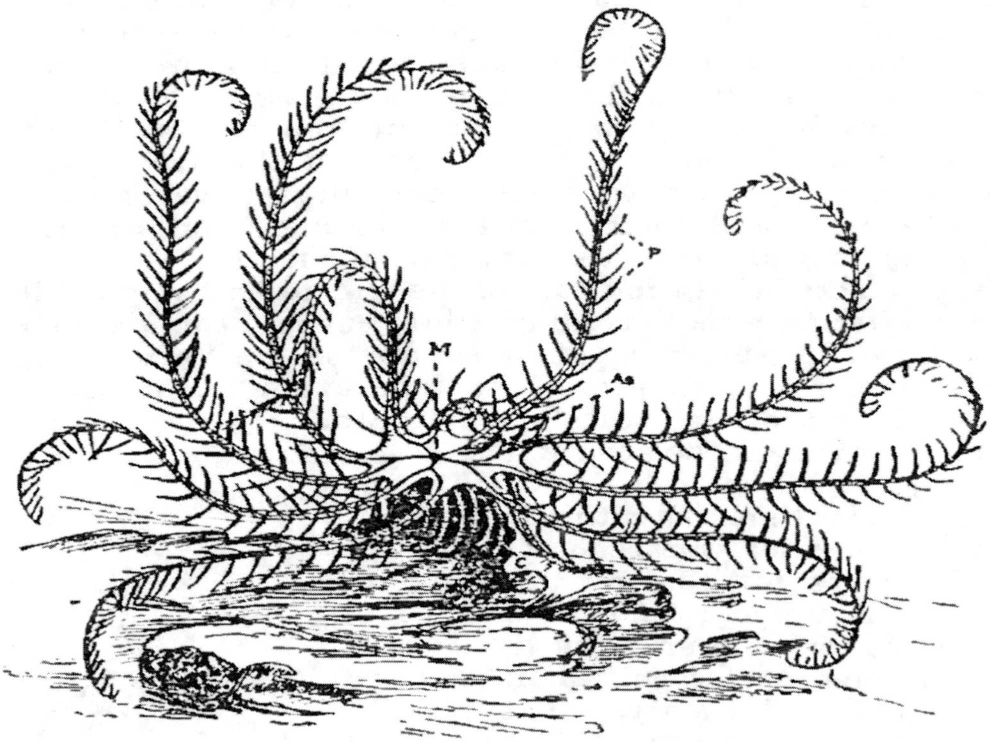

Fig. 15.—A FEATHER-STAR CRAWLING (*Antedon rosacea*). Natural size.

SUB-KINGDOM VI.—BRYOZOA
[Or POLYZOA].

MOSS ANIMALS.

By R. Kirkpatrick.

If the sea-weeds and shells cast up on the sea-shore be carefully examined, some of these objects will probably be found overgrown by encrustations and patches, which, viewed through a lens, resemble fine lacework or tracery of varying pattern. Probably, also, some of the supposed sea-weeds themselves will, on closer inspection, prove to be wholly different from plants, and to be, in fact, Bryozoa. One of the commonest of these plant-like animals is the Sea Mat or Broad-leaved Hornwrack (*Flustra foliacea*), (Fig. 1), found all round the shores of Great Britain, growing in shallow water, attached to shells and rocks. It is often found in abundance amongst the sea-weeds cast up on shore, especially after a gale.

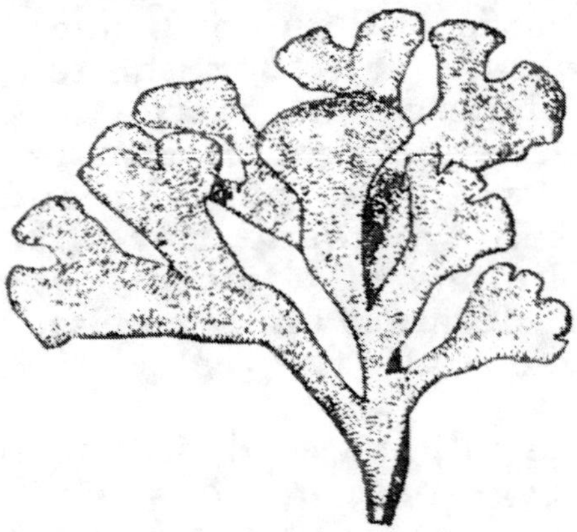

Fig. 1.—Flustra Foliacea.

The Sea Mat forms thin brown strap-shaped or fan-shaped fronds, expanding upwards from a flat, narrow stem to a height of four to six inches, and branching in one plane. A very fine reticulate pattern is visible on both surfaces. Under a low magnifying power this appearance (Fig. 2) is seen to be due to the raised margins of oblong boxes arranged in longitudinal rows; two spines rise from the margin on each side of the rounded and expanded upper end, and frequently a fifth spine between and above the lateral pairs. The front of each box is covered with a roof of membrane. On examining a fresh leaflet in sea-water, crowns of very slender tentacles will be seen to be extruded through the upper ends of the front of the boxes, a thin, horny, semi-circular lid being pushed up during the process; on the slightest alarm the tentacles are rapidly withdrawn. It is also possible to see a bent tube beneath the membranous roof. Each box or cell (Fig. 2) is the home of a polypide, which has formed the cell. The tentacles of the polypide arise in a circle from a platform, in the centre of which is an orifice, the mouth.

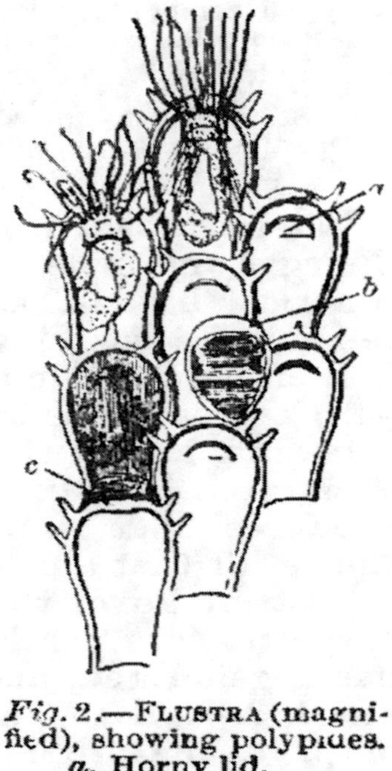

Fig. 2.—Flustra (magnified), showing polypides.
a, Horny lid.
b, Avicularium.
c, Egg capsule.

The circle of tentacles surmounts a conical proboscis, which, together with the tentacles, can be completely withdrawn into a sheath cavity, over which there falls a horny lid. The proboscis is merely a part of the cell wall, which always remains flexible and capable of being rolled in or out. The horny lid is a specialised fold of the wall, and is characteristic of the order of Bryozoa (*Chilostomata*, lip-mouthed) to which Flustra belongs. A glove-finger, with a hole in the top, surrounded by a crown of bristles to represent the mouth and tentacles, will convey an idea of the arrangement of the tentacular sheath; when the top is rolled in, a fold or lid must be supposed to fall over the cavity thus formed. The tentacles are hollow, and each is provided with a double row of cilia, by whose motion currents are set up, which converge to the mouth. This opening leads into a pharynx and gullet (Fig. 3), and the latter opens into the stomach, which forms the bend of the bent tube; the stomach is continued into the intestine, which opens to the exterior outside the circle of tentacles. The U-shaped intestinal tract is suspended in the cavity of the cell, and is separated from the walls by a space filled with fluid and continued up into the interior of the tentacles; the latter organs thus have a respiratory function, since the peri-visceral fluid is brought into close proximity to the sea-water. Further, the tentacles are sensory organs capable of perceiving tactile and, perhaps, other sensations. A nerve ganglion is situated at the upper end of the cell between the pharynx and intestine. In the walls of each cell are round sieve-like areas, through which the inner linings of adjacent cells become continuous, so that an organic and, perhaps, nervous continuity exists between all the cells of a colony.

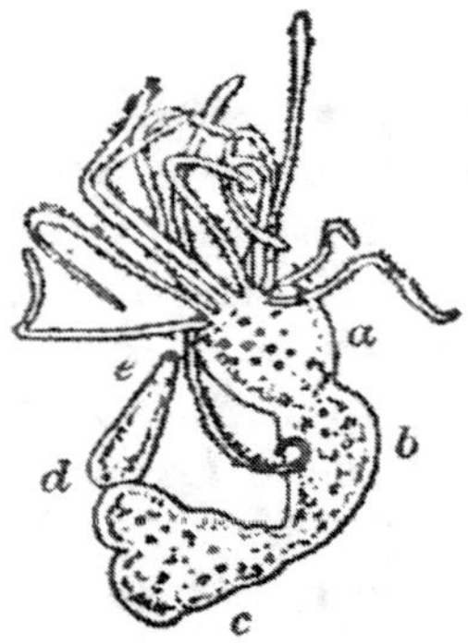

Fig. 3.—FLUSTRA. Polypide removed from cell.
A, Pharynx.
B, Gullet.
C, Stomach.
D, Intestines
E, Vent.

Passing down from the stomach to the base of the cell is a cord, in which the eggs and male cells are formed. The fertilised eggs pass up to a hemispherical brood-chamber, which forms a hood over the top of some of the cells, and there develop into embryos, which swim away from the parent. The embryos are minute, nearly spherical, bodies, flattened at each pole, and with a broad zone of cilia round the equator. At one pole is the mouth and intestine, and at the other a flattened disk, wherewith the embryo, after a short free life, fixes itself, and gives rise to the first polypide; the latter produces buds which develop, and in their turn produce other buds, with the result that a colony is formed.

Scattered over the surface of the frond, and interpolated among the ordinary cells, are small oval shallow cells with large thick lids; here the polypide has degenerated, and a muscular apparatus for opening and shutting the lid alone remains. The purpose served by these modified cells is the retention of prey, and probably the motion of the lid also serves to frighten away undesirable intruders. In some species of Bryozoa these metamorphosed cells have an extraordinary resemblance to birds' beaks, and hence were named "avicularia" (*avicula*, a bird's beak), this name being applied to all such cases of metamorphosis, whatever the shape of the modified cell may be.

In all Bryozoa we find an approximately U-shaped intestinal tract contained in a sack or box. The mouth is either surrounded by a circular or horseshoe shaped crown of tentacles, or the area surrounding the mouth is drawn out into processes provided with tentacles, and the vent opening is on about the same level as the mouth opening. Further, all Bryozoa (excepting the doubtful Phoronis) produce buds, which (excepting in Loxosoma) remain connected so as to form colonies. The colonies vary greatly in their composition, texture, and outward appearance. They may be stony, horny, and flexible; gelatinous, fleshy, or like leather or paper. They may form crusts and patches, hard or flexible leaves, bushy or shrubby growths, stony nodules, branches or plates, shapeless fleshy masses, etc. In all, we have as the unit the polypide in its cell. Often the same species occurs as a crust, or in plates of single or double lamellæ, the identity being revealed by the characters of the individual cells composing the colony. A few typical and interesting species will now be briefly referred to.

The Birds' Head Coralline (*Bugula turbinata*, Figs. 4, 5) forms brownish horny tufts about two inches in height; the branches, which are arranged spirally round the stem, are very slender. The cells are boat-shaped, and expand at the upper end. The upper three-fourths of the front surface is membranous, the rest of the cell being composed of hard, horny material. At the upper part of the membranous area is the lid, which is pushed up when the tentacles are extruded. The animal owes its popular name to the remarkable avicularia which arise from the edges of the cells; these organs consist of a short stalk, a curved head and beak, and a horny mandible. The "head" is filled with powerful muscles, which keep the mandible continually snapping, the whole presenting a ludicrous resemblance to a bird's beak (Fig. 5).

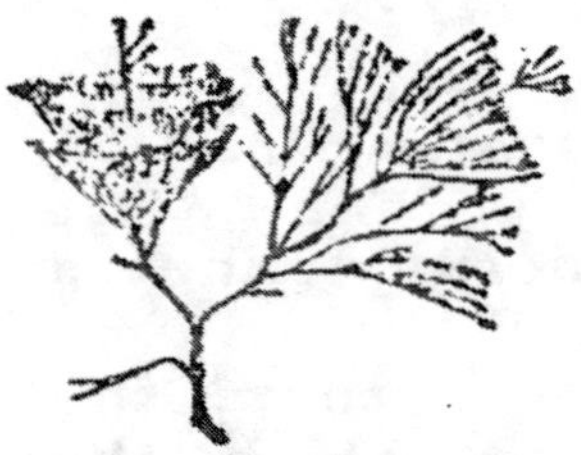

Fig. 4.—BUGULA TURBINATA.

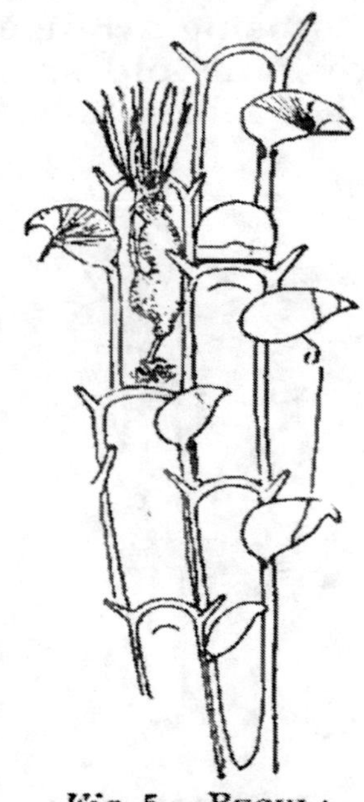

Fig. 5.—BUGULA (magnified). A, Avicularia.

In the Creeping Coralline (*Scrupocellaria reptans*) a further modification of the cell is seen. At the back of each ordinary cell is a very minute tubular cell known as a vibraculum (bristle cell), with a cleft at the top in which a long fine bristle is hinged. Sometimes the bristles are all kept moving together like oars, or, again, individual bristles may sweep round the front of the cells to clear away *debris* or frighten trespassers. The cell and its contained polypide are here reduced to a tubular cell and muscular apparatus, while the lid of the ordinary cell has become lengthened out and changed into a bristle.

Bryozoa are perhaps most commonly met with in the form of crusts and patches on stones, shells, and sea-weeds. The Lepralia of Pallas (*Lepralia pallasiana* (Figs. 6, 7) forms circular reddish-white or vitreous patches on shells, etc. The cells are arranged in radiating lines, each cell being a stony box with a punctured pattern on the front surface. At the outer end of the front surface is a square aperture, surrounded by an elevated rim and closed by a horny lid. One of the cells in the figure shows a lid partly pushed up by the tentacles of the polypide in the interior.

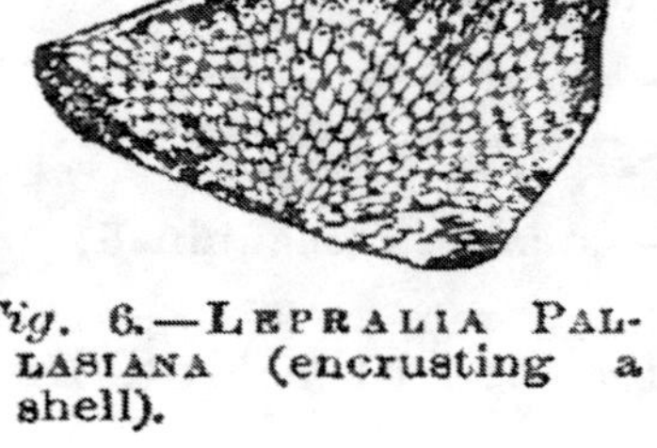

Fig. 6.—LEPRALIA PALLASIANA (encrusting a shell).

All the species hitherto referred to belong to the order Chilostomata (lip-mouthed), which is characterised by the presence of the horny lid covering the tentacle sheath. A second order, the Cyclostomata (circular-mouthed), commonly form white circular or fan-shaped stony crusts, plates, or branches, the component cells being tubular, and without horny lids. The tubes are frequently arranged in single or double rows. In a third order, the Ctenostomata (comb-mouthed), the colonies are horny or fleshy, never stony. When the tentacles are extruded, a comb-like circle of fine bristles is seen arising from the proboscis near the base of the tentacles; when the tentacles are retracted the bristles form a kind of operculum. The gelatinous Alcyonidium, so called from its resemblance to the zoophyte Alcyonium ("dead men's fingers"), forms fleshy masses or long cylindrical branches. The polyps, which are embdded near the surface, extrude their tentacles when undisturbed. The Nit Coralline (*Amathia lendigera*) forms little dark brown bushy tufts, the cells being arranged on the branches in double rows of small horny cylinders like Pan's-pipes.

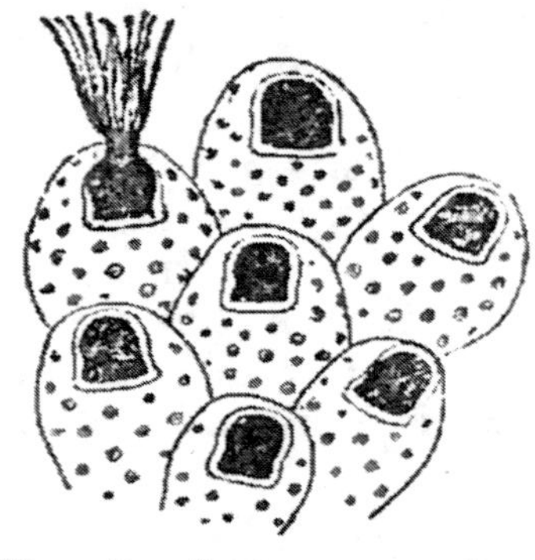

Fig 7.—LEPRALIA PALLASIANA (magnified).

The three orders above mentioned are included in one group, the Infundibulata (*infundibulum*, a funnel), in which the tentacles form a funnel-like circle round the mouth. The rest of the Bryozoa are included under the group Lophopoda (crest foot), in which the tentacles are arranged in a horse-shoe shaped zone round the mouth. Nearly all the fresh-water Bryozoa belong to this group. *Lophopus crystallinus* (Figs. 8, 9) is found in the form of little jelly-like blobs on the stems of Duck-weed (Fig. 8). The polypides can be seen as yellowish red streaks in the interior of a blob; when the horse-shoe plumes of tantacles are expanded the animal presents a beautiful appearance. *Lophopus* and other fresh-water Bryozoa commonly propagate themselves by means of peculiar internal buds, termed "statoblasts" (Fig. 10), which arise in the cord passing from the stomach to the base of the cell.

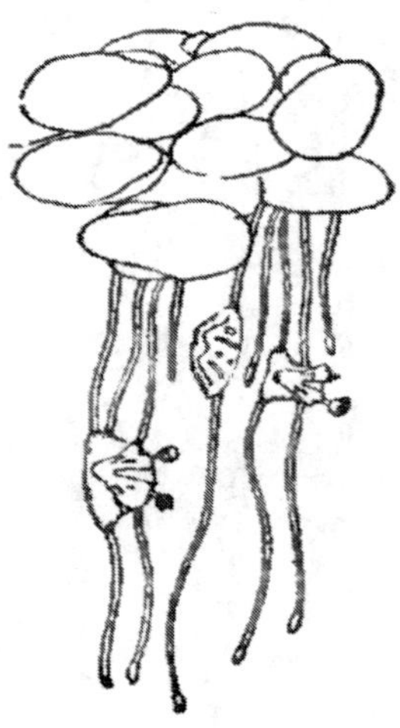

Fig. 8.—LOPHOPUS CRYSTALLINUS ON DUCK-WEED.

In *Lophopus* each statoblast is a flat, elliptical, seed-like body about $\frac{1}{70}$ in. in diameter, pointed at each end, and with a dark-brown oval centre surrounded by a broad band with a reticulate pattern. In the autumn the central part opens like a watch, and a young polypide half emerges and forms the nucleus of a colony. The remarkable *Cristatella mucedo* forms pale-green worm-like colonies averaging about an inch in length and one-sixth of an inch in breadth; the animal creeps about on the stems of water weeds. The polypides are arranged in

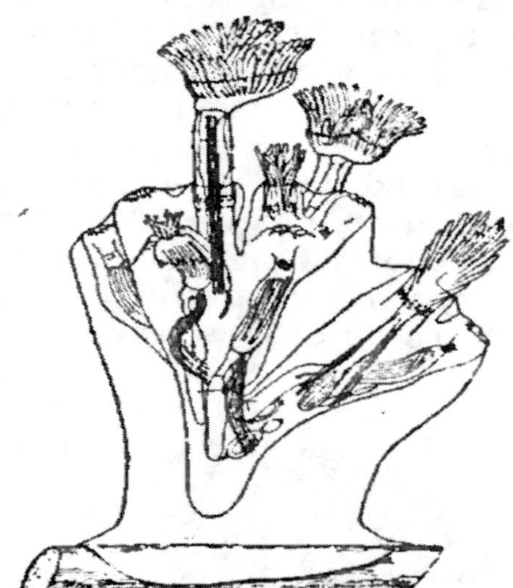

Fig. 9.—LOPHOPUS (magnified)

three concentric series on the upper convex surface, the lower flat surface, on which the colony moves along, being devoid of polyps. The statoblasts are provided with a double circle of long slender spines, ending in recurved hooks. *Alcyonella fungosa* is a species commonly found in streams and ponds in the form of brown clumps and nodules on floating timber, stems, sticks, etc.

In the Pedicellinidæ, which are mostly marine, the polypides are stalked, the stalks arising from a creeping stolon; the tentacles, which form an almost complete circle round the mouth, are not capable of being retracted into a sheath. In the aberrant genus, *Rhabdopleura*, the platform round the mouth is drawn out into two long tentacle-bearing arms. In *Cephalodiscus*, dredged up in the Straits of Magellan by the *Challenger*, the oral platform is drawn out into twelve processes—six on each side, armed with plumes of tentacles; the colony, which resembles a branching, spiny, gelatinous sea-weed, is permeated by canals along which the polypides can wander freely. In most of the Lophopoda a lobe projects over the mouth; the presence or absence of this character was made use of by Allman for the purpose of classifying Bryozoa into two groups —Phylactolæmata (guarded throat) and Gymnolæmata (unprotected throat).

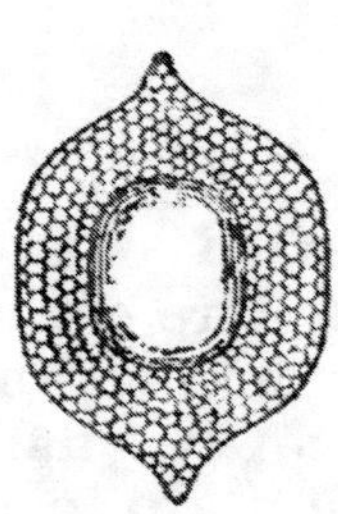

Fig. 10.—STATOBLAST OF LOPHOPUS (magnified).

The Bryozoa are found in the Palaeozoic rocks, and occur in great abundance in the Chalk, the Cyclostomatous group prevailing in the earlier formations. A classification is here appended for reference :—

Sub-class I.—Infundibulata—with a circle of tentacles. *a*, Chilostomata—with a horny lid shutting down over the tentacle sheath (Flustra, Bugula, Lepralia, etc.). *b*, Cyclostomata—all calcareous; without a horny lid; without avicularia (Crisia, Tubulipora). *c*, Ctenostomata—with a circle of bristles forming a kind of operculum; never calcareous (Amathia, Alcyonidium, etc.).

Sub-class II.—Lophopoda—with horse-shoe shaped plume of tentacles or arm-like processes bearing tentacles (Alcyonella, Pedicellina, etc.).

[*Note*.—The name Polyzoa is often used by English zoologists in place of Bryozoa, but the latter term, definitely employed as a class name by Ehrenberg in 1834, apparently has greater claims to acceptance. Bibliography — Johnston's "British Zoophytes;" Hincks' "British Marine Polyzoa;" Allman's "Fresh-water Polyzoa;" "Encyclopædia Britannica," Polyzoa (Lankester).

SUB-KINGDOM VII.—VERMES.

THE WORMS.

BY R. I. POCOCK.

To give a concise diagnosis of the Vermes is a matter of no small difficulty, for the different classes that are discussed in this chapter are merely grouped together for the sake of convenience, since they present few features in common to justify their association, apart, that is, from the negative fact that they do not possess the characters by which the rest of the sub-kingdoms may be recognised. From the Echinoderms (star-fish, sea-urchins, etc.) and Cœlenterates (corals, jelly-fish), for example, they may be distinguished by beng bi-laterally and not radially symmetrical; bi-laterally symmetrical anmals being those in which the right and left halves of the body are alike. From the Arthropoda (insects, spiders, etc.) they may be recognised by the abisence of jointed limbs and of limbs modified to act as jaws; from the Chordata (Vertebrates and Ascidians) by the absence of the cartilaginous doirsal chord (notochord) and of slits in the walls of the gullet; and from the Mollusca (snails, cuttle-fish, mussels) by the absence of the gland for producing the shell, and of the muscular foot, which subserves locomotion. In addition, however, to these negative features, it may be said that the body is soft, usually long, and often jointed; the alimentary canal, when present, usually traverses it from end to end; but in the lowest forms it has no posterior outlet, and in some of the parasitic species has entirely disappeared. In the simpler types the nervous system consists of two chords, one running along each side of the body, and uniting in the head to form the brain, which is placed just above the gullet. But in the higher groups these chords are united throughout their length, and form a double chain, traversing the body from end to end beneath the alimentary canal. In the higher forms, again, there is a highly developed circulatory system, consisting of longitudinal and transverse vessels, but no such organs have been observed in the less highly organised types. Very characteristic, too, of all the classes are the excretory vessels, consisting of tubes that open to the exterior, and at their inner end communicate with the body cavity.

A bond of union, however, between some of the classes, which in the adult stages are very dissimilar, may perhaps be sought in the similarity that is observable in their larval forms. For example, in the groups known as Polychæta, Gephyrea, Nemertinea, and Turbellaria, in addition to some others of less importance and extent, the young is an active larva furnished with *cilia*, or vibratile hairs, arranged in one or more definite belts around the body, by the movement of which it is enabled to swim freely through the water. These groups would thus seem to have at least a common starting-point in development, from which they have diverged in different directions.

But too much stress must not be laid upon this circumstance, seeing that other marine groups of invertebrated animals, like the Mollusca and Hemichordata, may also be developed from ciliated larvæ not very different in structure from those that are met with in the Vermes.

The Vermes may be divided into the following six classes :—1. Annelida (earthworms, leeches, etc.); 2. Gephyrea; 3. Nematohelminthes (thread-worms); 4. Rotifera (wheel-animalcules); 5. Nemertinea; 6. Platyhelminthes (flat-worms).

THE RINGED WORMS.

Class Annelida.

To this class belong those highly specialised worms whose organisation has been briefly referred to above. The body consists of a series of rings or segments, each of which is substantially similar to the one behind and the one in front of it. The alimentary canal traverses the body from end to end, and beneath it lies the nerve-chord, consisting of a double thread united in each segment to form a ganglion or swelling, and connected in front with the brain, one of the threads passing on each side of the œsophagus. Each segment, too, typically contains a pair of excretory tubes or nephridia, and the circulatory system consists of longitudinal vessels, connected by transverse branches. The most highly organised members of this class, namely, the Chætopoda, are structurally not very far removed from the Arthropoda (crustaceans, insects, centipedes, etc.). The chief distinctions between the two groups are, however, three in number. In all the Arthropods, except *Peripatus*, the legs are jointed, and at least one pair of them has become modified to act as jaws. But in the Chætopoda, although there may be distinct leg-like processes, these are never jointed, and the jaws, when present, are merely horny teeth developed in the mouth. Again, in the Arthropods the walls of the heart, or dorsal blood-vessel, are perforated by slits, by means of which the blood makes its way back to that organ, whereas no such slits are present in the corresponding blood-vessels in the Annelids. The Annelida are divisible into the Chætopoda and Hirudinea.

The Bristle-Footed Worms—Sub-Class Chætopoda.—At the head of the Vermes stand the species known as the Bristle-Footed Worms or Chætopoda, which in many details of their organisation approach the Arthropoda. For example, in the typical members of the class the body consists of a series of approximately similar segments, each of which is furnished at the sides with two rows of bristles, and very often with limb-like prominences, known as a parapodia. There is a distinct head, bearing above the mouth, a prostomium or kind of enlarged upper lip, and often furnished in addition with one or more pairs of tentacles. The alimentary canal traverses the body from end to end; and beneath it lies the double nerve chord, which is in front connected with the brain, placed in the head above the mouth.

Leaving aside for the moment some of the less important types, the Chætopoda may be said to fall into two orders, known as the Polychæta and the Oligochæta.

The Polychæta have a conspicuous head, usually bearing feelers and gills, and the segments of the body are furnished at the sides with limb-like processes, usually supplied with a rich armature of bristles.

Nearly all the species are marine, and many of them are of considerable size and great beauty. According to structure and mode of life, they are divided into two sub-orders—(1) the SEDENTARIA or TUBICOLA and (2) the ERRANTIA.

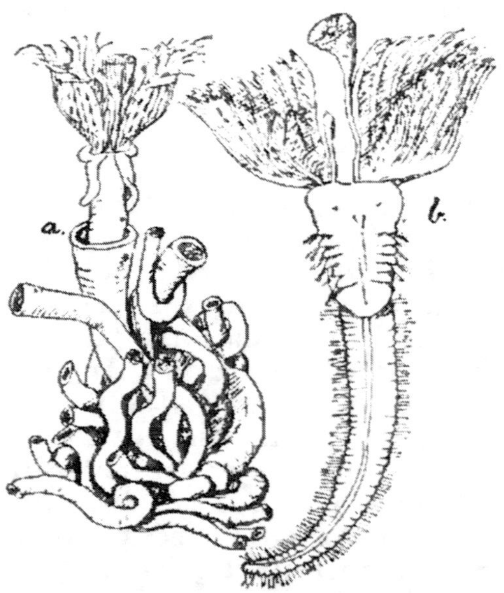

Fig. 1.—TUBE-MAKING ANNELID (*Serpula contortuplicata*).
a, Group of tubes with worm protruding.
b, Worm removed from tube.

The typical members of the Sedentaria live in tubes of sand, mud, or pieces of shell glued together by the slimy secretion of their skins, or composed of a dense, shelly, chalk-like substance. The worm known as *Terebella* constructs a dwelling-place of the former kind, gathering together the particles by means of long flexible tentacles placed on its head; while tubes of cement are built by such forms as *Serpula* and *Spirorbis*. The latter is the maker of those tubes so much resembling a snail-shell, which are common on our coasts; while *Serpula* makes the long, sinuous, serpent-like tubes which may be often found in interlacing clusters encrusting stones and shells of various kinds. When undisturbed these worms may be seen protruding from their tubes and waving in the water their gills and tentacles, which are affixed to the head, but upon the slightest alarm they shoot back like a flash out of harm's way, and remain securely concealed within their homes until the danger is overpast. To render itself still safer within its retreat, the worm called *Serpula* has one of its tentacles transformed into a veritable stopper, which exactly fits the mouth of the tube and completely closes it up when the worm has withdrawn itself.

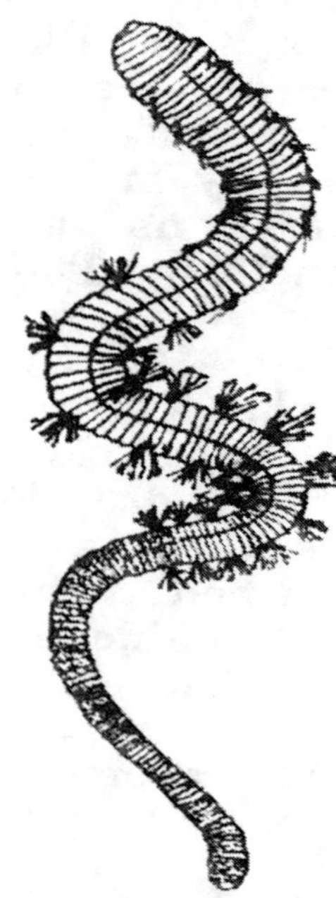

Fig. 2.—LUG-WORM (*Arenicola marina*).

Although differing from the *Serpula* and *Terebella*, and approaching the Errant Polychæta in many characters, the common Sand-worm or Lug-worm (*Arenicola marina*), so much sought for on our coasts as bait, also belongs to the group of Sedentaria. In this species the gills are represented by plumes situated on the middle segments of the body. At low water on the sandy shores of northern Europe the Lug-worm may be found at times in great quantities, the position of its burrows being easily detected by the little heaps of sand that accumulate at the entrance. For, like the Earth-worm, the Lug-worm swallows large quantities of sand, in order to extract for its nourishment any organic matter it may contain; and it comes to the surface to unburden its body of the sand that has passed through it.

To the section Errantia belong the most highly-organised species of the class. They lead a free predatory life, wandering hither and thither in search of food, which consists almost exclusively of animals more defenceless than themselves. For this purpose they are fitted with organs of locomotion in the form of prominent limb-like, bristle-bearing, processes (parapodia); the conspicuous head is supplied with tentacles of various kinds, and generally with eyes, while the gullet, which is protrusible, is armed with horny teeth. Many of these worms are of large size and are composed of a long series of segments, a species, for example, named *Eunice gigantea*, is said to have over 400 of them, and to be upwards of four feet in length. But one of the commonest forms upon our coast, known as the Sea-mouse (*Aphrodite aculeata*), is a very different looking animal, with a short, broad, more or less oval body, convex above and flat below, like that of a Slug. Its sides are ornamented with the most beautifully iridescent hairs, and with barbed retractile spines, which serve as a protection against carnivorous fish or other enemies.

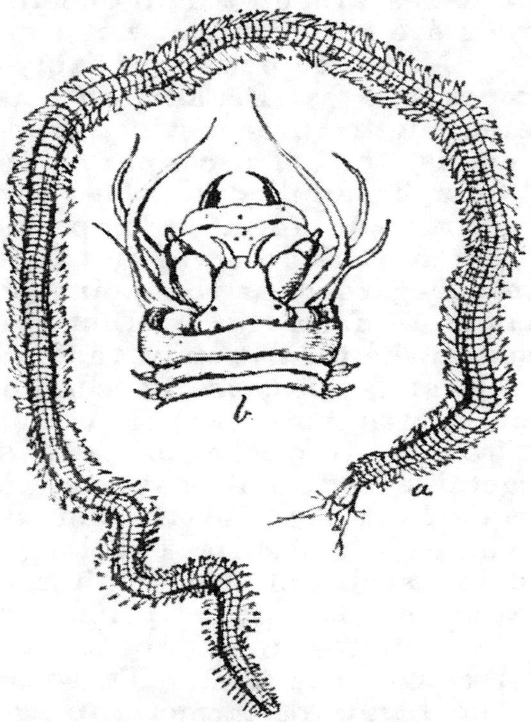

Fig. 3.—THE PEARLY NEREIS (*Nereis margaritacea*).
a, Entire worm.
b, Head with jaws, feelers, and eyes.

An interesting feature connected with some of these Bristle-worms, is that their method of development takes place by means of what is called an alternation of generations. In *Autolytus*, one of the Syllidæ, for example, the worm that is hatched from the egg and grows to maturity is a neuter, and is consequently quite incapable of reproducing its kind in the ordinary way. But the difficulty is overcome by the formation of a new worm, the hinder end of the old one breaking off and turning either into a male or a female. In some cases more than one individual is produced at a time by this process of division, so that before they sever themselves from the parent stock a regular chain of worms is formed. In another member of this family, namely, the Branched Syllis (*Syllis ramosa*), which lives in certain sponges, new individuals are produced as lateral branches, as well as one behind the other. Very exceptionally in the Polychæta the young are born alive. In the majority of cases the eggs give rise to a free swimming larva, the *Trochophore* or *Trochosphere*, characterised by the presence of one or more belts of long vibratile cilia encircling the body. According to the number and disposition of these belts the larvæ have been named; those that possess several of them being known, for example, as *Polytrochous*. Sometimes there is but one belt, which may be in the middle of the body (*Mesotrochous*), or in front of the mouth (*Monotrochous*), while not infrequently the *Monotrochous* larva has a second belt surrounding its posterior end, when it is known as *Telotrochous*. Sometimes, again, there is no definite belt (*Atrochous*), the larva being uniformly covered with short cilia, bearing, in addition, a special tuft of them at the front end of the body. Somewhat similar larvæ are found in other groups of Vermes, and are of special interest, as showing possible relationship between them and the Annelida.

The second order of Bristle-footed worms is named Oligochæta, on account of the relatively poor development of the armature of bristles as compared with the Polychæta. In other respects they are less highly organised, as is shown by the absence of tentacles and gills and teeth, and by the fact that the sexes are united in one individual. The best-known members of this order are the familiar earth-worms, belonging to the families *Lumbricidæ*, etc. Most people are probably of opinion that but one species of this animal occurs in Great Britain; but, as a matter of fact, there are about twenty belonging to three distinct genera. Another popular belief connected with them is, that if a couple of specimens be cut in two, and the head end of one be applied to the tail end of the other, the two parts will grow together and form a complete individual. In fact, the curious swelling which may be observed in the fore part of the body of a full-grown worm is often regarded as the point of union of two such separate pieces. As a matter of fact, this swelling, called the *clitellum* or *cingulum*, is an organ used in the formation of the cocoons in which the eggs are laid.

Although occasionally seen on the surface of the ground during the day-time, Earth-worms are for the most part strictly nocturnal and subterranean, burrowing into the soil in all directions, and devouring any animal or vegetable refuse it may contain. In connection with food they swallow large quantities of earth, and when this has passed through their bodies, it is voided at the surface of the ground, forming the so-called vegetable mould. During spells of dry weather they bury themselves deep in the earth in search of moisture, without which life is an impossibility; and in the winter months they descend to the lower layers of the soil so as to be out of reach of the frost. These animals are subjected to ruthless persecution at the hands of farmers and gardeners on account of their propensity for pulling shoots of young corn and blades of grass beneath the surface. But it is doubtful if the harm done in this respect is not more than counteracted by the benefit that plants derive from the ceaseless tunnelling of the soil, the loosening of its particles, and the porterage of the lower layers to the surface, to be deposited as castings. In fact, so extensively is this work carried on by earth worms, that Mr. Darwin has compared their action to that of a plough, and adds that it is doubtful whether many other animals have played so important a part in the history of the world. Earth-worms are found in all parts of the world in spots suitable for their existence, and in some countries they reach an enormous length as compared with the common species with which we are familiar. In South Africa, for instance, there is a species called *Microchæta Rappi*, which attains a length of about five feet. It is, however, by no means frequently seen, rarely appearing on the surface, and then only after heavy rains.

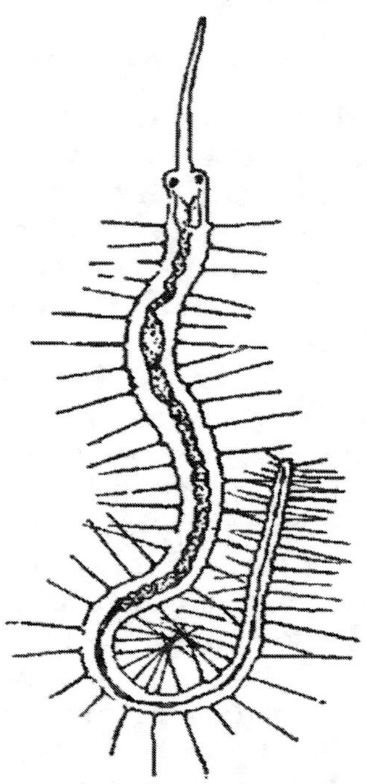

Fig. 4.—SNOUTED NAIS (*Nais proboscidea*).

Other worms, however, besides the earth-worms, belong to the Oligochæta. Many representatives of this group live in fresh water streams and ditches, as well as in the sea. For example, the common *Tubifex rivulorum*, a long, slender, reddish worm, may be found in quantities in the muddy bottom of ponds, where it constructs long tubular burrows. When undisturbed it has the peculiar habit of projecting the hinder part of its body from its burrow and waving it incessantly in the water. But one of the best known of these aquatic worms is the species called *Nais proboscidea*, which has long hair-like bristles jutting out from the sides of its body, and a proboscis-like feeler projecting from the forepart of its head. This worm may be regarded as more highly organised than the earth-worm, as is indicated by the presence of a couple of eyes upon its head. Like some of the Polychæta, too, it possesses the power of reproducing by fission. Between two of the segments in the posterior half of the body a mass of tissue appears, and from the front part of this a new tail is formed for the original piece bearing the head, while from its hinder part a new head develops for the part that was primarily the tail-end of the parent form. It not infrequently happens that several new worms start almost contemporaneously in this way one behind the other, and before the severance between them is effected, they appear as a chain of individuals, exactly as described above in the case of *Autolytus*, one of the Polychæta.

In addition to the Polychæta and Oligochæta a third group, called Archiannelida, is now referred to the Chætopoda, in spite of the fact that the integument bears no bristles, and the only external signs of segmentation are shallow grooves in the skin and serially arranged rows of cilia (fine hairs). The head is furnished with tentacles, but there are no parapodia. This group, lying in some respects midway between the Chætopoda and the Flatworms of the sub-class Turbellaria, contains several marine forms, of which the best known are *Protodrilus* and *Polygordius*. The young of the Archiannelida are developed from Trochophore larvæ of the type known as Telotrochous (see p. 673).

Usually now regarded as aberrant members of the class Chætopoda are the remarkable species belonging to the genus *Myzostoma*, of the family Myzostomidæ. These degraded creatures live parasitically upon the Sea-lilies (Crinoidea), their presence giving rise to tumours or various irregularities of growth. The body is oval and flattened and unsegmented, and its margins are produced into a number of short, prehensile filaments ; while on the lower surface near the edge are four pairs of suckers, and on the inner side of these five pairs of conical, foot-like processes, each of which is provided with a pair of retractile bristles. But in spite of the anomalous structure of the adult, these parasites are developed from free-swimming larvæ furnished with ciliated bands, and calling to mind the Trochophore of the Annelida.

THE LEECHES—SUB-CLASS HIRUDINEA.—The Leeches, or Hirudinea (Latin, *hirudo*, a leech), sometimes called the Discophora (disc-bearers), on account of the suckers with which they are furnished, are not unlike earth-worms in general appearance, and also in many points of structure. The integument is divided by shallow transverse grooves into a multitude of rings, a varying number of which (five to three) correspond to each true segment of the body. There are no bristles nor organs of locomotion in the form of parapodia, movement from one spot to another being effected by means of swimming or by crawling, with the aid of the suckers, after the manner of the "looper" caterpillars. There is always a large sucker situated at the hinder end of the body, and usually a second at the opposite extremity, with the mouth placed in its centre.

The Leeches are divisible into two families—the *Gnathobdellidæ*, or jaw-bearing species, and the *Rhynchobdellidæ*, or proboscis-bearing species. Of the Gnathobdellidæ, the medicinal leech (*Hirudo medicinalis*) is a well-known example. This animal is usually of a blackish colour, and ornamented with longitudinal bands of yellow spots. It is somewhat scarce in England, and in the days when blood-letting was extensively practised by doctors the demand for it was met by the importation of large quantities from the Continent, where it is not only more abundant than with us, but was artificially cultivated on a large scale in especially-constructed tanks. The power of these animals to pierce the skin and draw blood, upon which their value as blood-letters depends, is due to the presence in the mouth of three semi-circular jaws, each of which is studded with a series of minute horny teeth. By means of a set of powerful muscles these jaws are capable of being worked backwards and forwards after the manner of a saw, while by aid of the sucker, the mouth is kept closely applied to the wounded spot and the blood is drawn into the worm's stomach. This is a capacious sac, consisting of no fewer than eleven pairs of pouches, capable of considerable distention, and occupying the greater part of the space between the walls of the body. When the leech has pumped itself full of blood, but not before, it relaxes its hold; and it has been affirmed that the amount thus imbibed will be sufficient for a whole year.

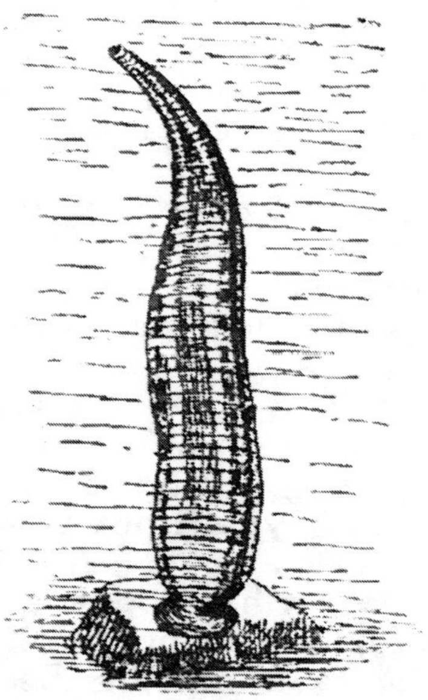

Fig. 5. — MEDICINAL LEECH (*Hirudo medicinalis*).

In a natural state these leeches are found in ponds, marshes, or sluggish brooks with a bottom of mud or clay. Out of water they cannot live for any length of time, since they speedily succumb to the drying effects of the atmosphere. During the day, especially if the weather be warm and bright, they may be seen swimming about with liveliness, but in cold or dark days and at night-time they lose their activity, and remain curled up with head and tail closely applied. In the autumn they bury themselves deep in the mud. Their food consists of the blood of fishes or aquatic amphibians, or of terrestrial vertebrates, that visit their haunts to bathe or drink. Like earth-worms, leeches are hermaphrodite, and after pairing in the spring they creep up the banks of the pond or ditch above the surface of the water and dig burrows in the soft damp soil, and in these, like the earth-worms again, they construct for the reception of their eggs elliptical cocoons, formed of a secretion from certain skin-glands, which afterwards hardens. Externally, the cocoons are covered with a layer of spongy material, while the inside is filled with albumen, in which the small eggs, usually about twenty in number, are embedded. When the eggs are hatched, the young float in the albumen, and obtain their nourishment from it. Upon quitting the cocoon after several weeks' residence therein, the young leeches resemble their parents in form, though they are not dark-coloured. Growth, however, is a slow process, maturity not being reached until five years have passed, and life enduring, under favourable conditions, for about twenty years.

A far commoner species in England than the medicinal leech is the so-called Horse-leech (*Aulostomum gulo*), which may be distinguished from the former by the absence of the bands of yellow spots, the skin being of a uniform greenish-black, and by the fact that its jaws are furnished with fewer and blunter teeth. This difference of dentition is evidently correlated with the difference in the feeding habits of the two animals, the food of the Horse-leech, in spite of its name, consisting of such soft-bodied creatures as earth-worms and snails.

It must not be supposed, however, that all leeches are inhabitants of fresh water. In many countries, indeed, especially in the tropics, land leeches are abundant, as many a traveller knows to his cost. They inhabit jungle and forest land, where the vegetation in the wet season is saturated with moisture; but in the dry season they entirely disappear, presumably burying themselves deep in the earth. According to the accounts of those who have had practical experience of them, these animals are a terrible plague. Gifted with the power of perceiving the presence of prey at some distance, they hasten towards it in crowds from all quarters, or collect in the herbage bordering the forest paths, with head extended, ready to seize hold of any passing man or beast. To protect themselves from their attacks, Europeans are compelled to wear leather or closely-woven cloth gaiters, tied tightly round the knee, while the natives rub their bare legs with oil or lemon juice.

The leeches of the second family (the Rhynchobdellidæ) differ from those belonging to the Gnathobdellidæ, that have been hitherto discussed, in having the front of the body furnished with a protrusible proboscis at the end of which the mouth is situated. To this family belongs the fresh water leech *Clepsine*. This animal is yellow, grey, or whitish in colour, occurs on the leaves of plants or on the lower side of stones, and feeds apparently upon water-snails and the young of fresh water mussels. The eggs, in number about 200, are not embedded in albumen as is the case in the medicinal leech, but are of larger size and contain their own food-yolk. They are laid in flattish cocoons which are attached to some stone or water-plant, and the leech curls itself round the cocoon to protect it. Moreover, when the young are hatched, the mother still continues to look after them, carrying them about with her attached to the lower surface of the body.

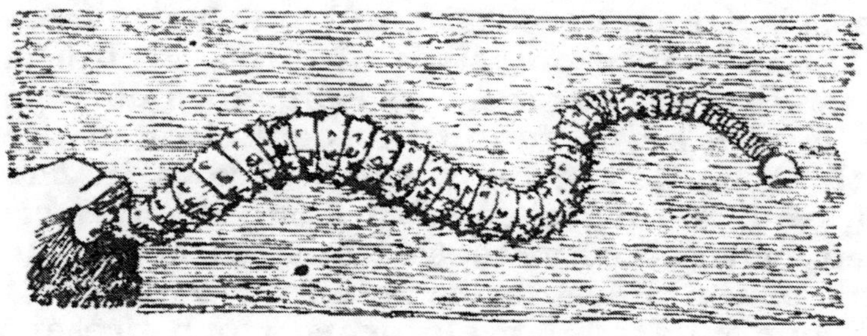

Fig. 6.—Warty Skate-leech (*Pontobdella muricata*).

Also belonging to this family is the Warty Sea-leech (*Pontobdella muricata*) which is common on our coasts, and may be readily recognised by its greenish grey colour, cylindrical body, and tough knobby integument. It is found mostly on fishes of the skate tribe, and hence is sometimes called the skate-sucker.

THE GEPHYREAN WORMS.

Class Gephyrea.

The worms of this class are all marine, and although more or less cylindrical in shape, show scarcely any traces of segmentation. The front of the body is furnished with a large proboscis, and the integument is covered with warts.

The species fall into two well-marked orders known as the Chætifera and the Achæta. The Chætifera, or bristle-bearing Gephyrea, show strong indications of affinity with the Chætopoda, and are by some authors considered to belong to that class. In the young the body is partially segmented, and in the adult is furnished below with a pair of hooked bristles. The alimentary canal terminates at the hinder end of the body, and the proboscis, which is ciliated and often of enormous length as compared with the size of the animal, appears to be nothing but an enlargement of the prostomium or region in front of the mouth, the latter being situated at its base. The best-known members of the group are *Bonellia*, *Echiurus*, and *Thalassema*. They are to be found at the bottom of the sea or beneath stones in pools, and appear to be gifted with but little activity.

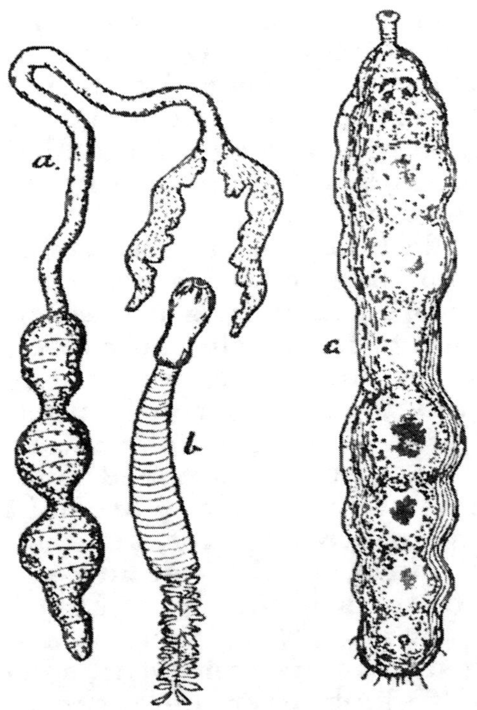

Fig. 7.—Gephyrean Worms.
A, *Bonellia viridis* (with proboscis distended).
B, *Priapulus caudatus*
C, *Echiurus*.

The Achæta have no bristles, as their name indicates; there is no sign of segmentation at any period of life; the alimentary canal is twisted upon itself, and terminates in the front half of the body; and the proboscis carries the mouth at its tip, and can be retracted inside the body by muscles specially set apart for the purpose. In some of these worms—in those, for example, known as *Sipunculus*, *Phascolosoma*, and *Phymosoma*—the tip of the proboscis is furnished with a circlet of tentacles surrounding the mouth. These animals live on the sea-bottom in deserted univalve shells, closing up the mouth of the shell with sand grains cemented together with slime, but leaving an aperture just large enough to allow the extensible proboscis to be thrust in and out with ease. A British representative of this group is *Sipunculus bernhardus*. A still more curious form is *Priapulus*, found in deep water in the North Atlantic. This worm burrows in the sand, and is furnished with a stout probocis armed with horny teeth, but without the circlet of tentacles observable in *Sipunculus*.

In both groups of the Gephyrea occur ciliated larval forms which present a close resemblance to the Trochophore of the Polychæta.

THE THREAD-WORMS.

Class Nematohelminthes.

As implied by their name, the worms of this class are mostly long, slender, and more or less thread-like. The body is usually pointed at both ends, and it presents at most but slight external indications of segmentation, and none of that serial repetition of internal organs which is so characteristic of the highly organised Annelida. The skin, moreover, instead of being furnished with bristles or the delicate hairs known as cilia, is protected by a smooth and relatively tough cuticle. In all the typical members there is a distinct alimentary canal traversing the body nearly from end to end, and there is an excretory system, consisting of tubes lying lengthwise, which communicate with each other in the fore part of the body and open upon its lower surface by a single pore. The sexes are generally distinct.

Although a large majority of the species of this class are parasitic, spending the whole or part of their lives within the bodies of other animals, a few, nevertheless, are to be found on plants, on fresh water or damp earth, or even in the sea. But amongst the parasitic forms we meet with species that are free during a part of their existence; that is to say, either during the immature stages of life or after maturity is attained. Such species as these thus show an interesting gradation in habit between those kinds that are wholly independent and those that live permanently in other organisms.

One of the best known of the free living species is the Vinegar or Paste-eel (*Anguillula aceti*), which feeds upon the minute fungi found growing in these substances. Allied forms, known as *Leptodera* and *Pelodera*, occur in water or damp earth; but, unless supplied with plenty of nitrogenous food in the form of decaying animal or vegetable matter, they remain in the larval stage, a supply of food of this nature being necessary for the attainment of maturity.

Before passing to the most interesting members of this class, namely, those that are parasitic in animals, and especially in mankind, brief reference may be made to a couple of species which infest plants and are of considerable economic importance on account of the damage done by their agency to corn crops and vegetables of the turnip kind. Adult examples of the Wheat-eel (*Tylenchus tritici*) attack developing ears of wheat, converting them into a kind of gall. Here the young are hatched, ultimately reaching the ground by the falling of the grain. They are then set free in the moist earth, and wander hither and thither in search of the young shoots of growing corn. If successful in their quest they ascend the stalks, and, finally reaching the summit, take up their abode in the blossom of the wheat; and, nourishing themselves upon it, arrive at maturity and then produce new generations. The second vegetable pest to be noticed is the Turnip Thread-worm (*Heterodera schachti*), which gives rise to swellings on the roots of the sweet turnip or sugar-beet. These swellings are caused by the expansion of the female worm into a spherical body owing to the quantity of nourishment she absorbs. Here the eggs are laid, and after being retained for a time in a special brood-pouch, pass to the outer world, and undergo the first stages of their development. Subsequently the females bore their way into the turnip roots by means of a special instrument with which the throat is fitted for the purpose.

Passing now to the species that live parasitically in other animals, we find the simplest life-history in such kinds as *Ascaris lumbricoides* and *Oxyuris vermicularis*, known to medical men respectively as the "round-worm" and the "thread-worm," and occurring not infrequently in the human intestine, especially during childhood. The eggs of these worms are discharged from the alimentary canal of their host, and make their way back again through the mouth in connection with food or impure water. In addition to mankind, species of thread-worms allied to those just mentioned infest the intestines of horses, pigs, dogs, cats, and a variety of other animals.

In addition, however, to the alimentary canal, other organs of man are liable to the attacks of various Thread-worms. The Guinea or Medina-worm (*Dracunculus medinensis*), for example, reaches maturity in the subcutaneous tissue of man in the tropical countries of the Old World, measuring, when adult, many inches in length. It is usually extracted by being carefully wound round a small roller, an operation which often occupies several days. owing to the precautions that are taken not to fracture the animal. But if allowed to remain beneath the skin, the worm effects its escape to the outer world through the abscess to which its presence gives rise. Then the young with which the females are laden make their way into fresh water streams or lakes, and falling in with minute water-fleas of the family Cyclopidæ, bore their way into the interior of these crustaceans, which are swallowed by mankind in connection with drinking-water; and so, by means of an intermediate host, the young Guinea-worms are introduced into their final place of abode. A similar transference of parasitic worms from one host to another is of common occurrence in this, as in other, groups of entozoic vermes, and we meet with it again in another thread-worm (*Filaria sanguinis-hominis*) which, in various parts of the Old World, infests the blood system of man, giving rise, by the stoppage of the circulation in the small vessels, to the disease known as elephantiasis. In this case the embryos are sucked from the vascular system by mosquitoes or other suctorial diptera, and so become scattered abroad, making their way in all probability back again into the human body along with drinking water.

To the genera *Gordius* and *Mermis* belong the horse-hair worms, so named on account of their length, slenderness, and colour, which recall the form of a long hair from a horse's mane or tail. In *Gordius*, which is found in fresh water streams and ponds, the alimentary canal is functionless and the mouth closed. The eggs, deposited in clusters and glued together by an adhesive substance, sink to the bottom of the water, and there remain until the hatching of the young. These are armed in front with a sharp proboscis and circles of hooks, by means of which they bore their way into the bodies of aquatic insect larvæ, such as gnats and mayflies, and there remain encysted until the host is devoured by a fish or carnivorous insect. Thus introduced into the alimentary canal of a fresh host, the young *Gordius* subsequently penetrate into the body-cavity, and undergo the semi-final stages of their development, acquire the form characteristic of the adult, and then making their escape into the water become fully adult (see Fig. 8, *b*). The other hair-worm known as *Mermis* lives in damp earth. Here the eggs are laid, and the young penetrate the skin and take up their abode in the bodies of caterpillars or other insects, whence, after a prolonged residence, they escape again to the ground, become mature, and lay their eggs.

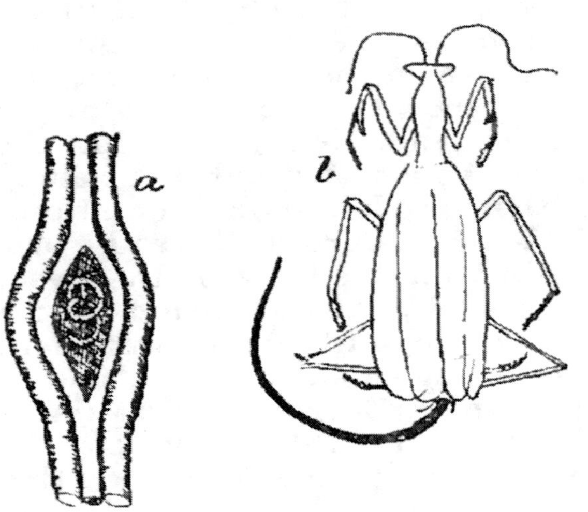

Fig. 8.—THREAD-WORMS.
a, Trichinosis-worm (*Trichina spiralis*) encysted in muscle.
b, Horse-hair worm (*Gordius*) escaping from an insect (*Mantis*).

The descriptions that have hitherto been given of the life-histories of the parasitic thread-worms deal with species which lead a free existence, at all events during a part of life. But the last of the species that we have space to notice is of special interest, not only on account of its being one of the most dangerous of parasitic worms to mankind, but also because it spends the whole of its existence within the bodies of two hosts, carrying the parasitic habit to a greater extreme than is met with elsewhere in the group. This is the worm called *Trichina spiralis*, which gives rise to the dreaded disease trichinosis. In the adult or sexually mature stage this worm lives in the intestine of various carnivorous mammals, man being amongst the number. But the minute young, which are born alive, instead of making their way to the outer world in connection with excrementitious matter, bore through the wall of their host's alimentary canal and entering the blood-stream are carried by the circulation to various parts of the body, ultimately coming to a standstill in the muscles. Here the little creatures begin to grow and form for themselves a protective capsule or cyst between the fibres of the muscular tissue. Meat infested with these encysted worms is said to be "trichinised" (Fig. 8, *a*). In this state the Trichinæ remain without attaining maturity until the meat in which they have taken up their abode is eaten by another animal, whereupon the action of the digestive juices of the new host, dissolving away the muscular fibres and the capsule, set free the worms, which in their new surroundings quickly become adult, and each female gives birth to thousands of new individuals. Man as a rule contracts "trichinosis" through eating "trichinised" pork in an underdone state. But, happily, since the discovery of the source of infection some fifty years ago, and the introduction of stringent laws against the sale of unhealthy pork, the disease has become far less common than in former times.

Usually classified with the thread-worms, though differing from them in the absence of mouth and alimentary canal, and in other anatomical details, are the parasitic-worms, known as *Echinorhynchus*, belonging to the group Acanthocephali. These two names—the former meaning "spiny-beaked" and the latter "thorny-headed"—refer to the presence on the worm's head of a retractile proboscis, armed with rows of backwardly directed hooks. The various species of *Echinorhynchus* are internal parasites, the mature stages being found in vertebrata of different kinds, and the immature stages in certain invertebrated animals. For example, a species known as *Echinorhynchus gigas*, which infests the alimentary canal of the pig, passes the earlier part of its life in the intestine of the larvæ of various kinds of chafers, such as the cock-chafer (*Melolontha vulgaris*) or the rose-chafer (*Cetonia aurata*). The migration from the one host to the other is effected in the following manner:—The embryos of the worm, invested in a protective membrane, after passing out of the pig's alimentary canal in connection with excrementitious matter, are devoured by the beetle-larvæ along with their food. In the stomach of the new host the investing membrane becomes dissolved, and the worm, thereby set free, bores into the intestinal walls of the larvæ. These in turn are rooted up and swallowed by the pigs, and the young Echinorhynchi thus become transferred again into the

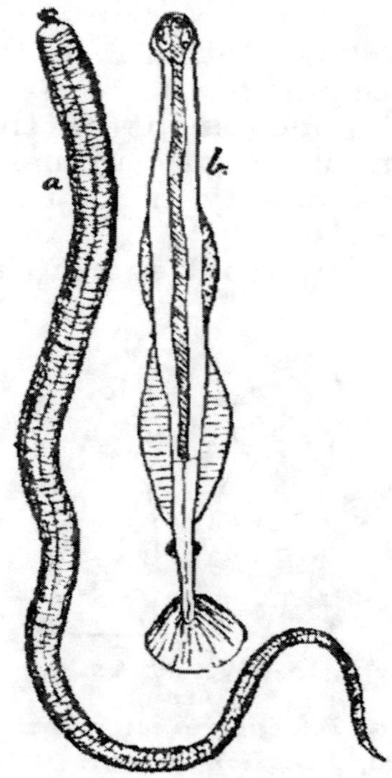

Fig. 9.
a, *Echinorhynchus gigas*.
b, *Sagitta bipunctata*.

alimentary canal of the animal from which they set out. The migrations of other species is substantially similar to that of *E. gigas*. For instance, *E. polymorphus* lives as a mature animal in the intestine of ducks or other water-fowl, while in the immature stage it occurs in the little fresh-water crustacean (*Gammarus pulex*). This amphipod (*G. pulex*) is also, in conjunction with the fresh-water wood-louse (*Asellus aquaticus*), the intermediate host of two other species, *E. angustatus* and *E. proteus*, which, when mature, infest the alimentary canal of fresh-water fish. Instances of the occurrence of worms of this group in mankind have been recorded, but, happily, such cases are rare.

Although, probably, more nearly related to the Thread-worms than to any other group in the animal kingdom, the Arrow-worm (*Sagitta*) presents so many peculiarities of organisation that its true systematic position is still a matter of doubt, and it forms the sole type of an order known as Chætognatha. This name, meaning "bristle-jawed," is given to it in allusion to the fact that the head is armed with a number of strong, movable, horny spikes which act as jaws. The body is long, slender, and unsegmented, with a rounded, blunt head, bearing eyes, and a narrow-pointed tail; but the tip of the tail and the sides of the body in its hinder half are furnished with horizontally-projecting fins (Fig. 9, *b*).

The Arrow-worms, so called from their arrow-like shape, are not parasitic like the Thread-worms, but are to be found swimming in numbers on the surface of the ocean in all parts of the world.

THE WHEEL-ANIMALCULES.

Class Rotifera.

The Rotifera, or "Wheel-animalcules," as they were formerly called, on account of the appearance in the water of a rapidly rotating wheel, to which the movement of the circlet of hairs on their heads gives rise, are all small, aquatic animals, varying in length from $\frac{1}{8}$ to $\frac{1}{500}$ of an inch, and found universally in marine and fresh water, but most abundantly in stagnant pools.

The front end of the body is usually broader than the opposite extremity, and is shaped like a disc, the trochal disc, which is fringed with long vibratile hairs or cilia. By means of the currents of water set up by the movement of these cilia, particles of food are swept into the mouth, a wide aperture placed in the middle or at the sides of the trochal disc. The mouth passes into the stomach, which is supplied with a complicated armature of teeth, and by means of these the food is crushed and divided. In the females the alimentary canal passes right through the body, but in the males, strange to say, it has ceased to be functional, and is reduced to a solid chord-like organ. Apart from the cilia of the trochal disc, the integument of the body is smooth, and the only signs of segmentation that it presents are a few weak wrinkles. The tail-end, or the foot, as it is called, varies considerably in structure according to the habits of the species. In some forms that are

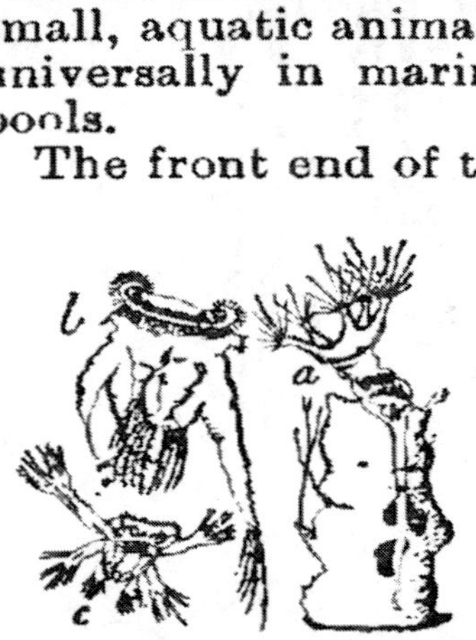

Fig. 10.—Wheel-Animalcules.
a, *Floscularia coronetta.*
b, *Pedalion mirum.*
c, *Hexarthra polyptera* (after Hudson).

fixed (*Floscularia*), it ends in an adhesive disc or cup, and is not wrinkled nor retractile; but in most of the free-living species the foot is retractile within the body and terminates in a couple of nippers which serve to anchor the body in place. In other forms (*Pedalion* and *Hexarthra*), the body is provided with pairs of limb-like processes, ending in a fan-shaped tuft of cilia. These two are free-living forms, skipping through the water by means of their limbs and swimming by means of the ciliary wreath.

The habitat of the "Wheel-animalcules" is tolerably varied. They may be found in ditches, gutters, ponds, and streams; sometimes attached to stems and leaves of plants; sometimes creeping upon them; sometimes roving through the water. Some species, again, are parasitic. A species, for instance, named *Drilophaga bucephala*, holds by means of its jaws to a water-worm, *Lumbriculus*, and sucks the animal it clings to. Again, *Callidina parasitica* is always found adhering to the limbs of the fresh-water shrimp (*Gammarus pulex*), and merely creeps about the body of its host. And lastly, the genus named *Albertia* furnishes an instance of internal parasitism, its species, *vermiculus*, being found living in earth-worms and slugs.

The true position of the Wheel-animalcules amongst the Vermes is one of some doubt. But it is important to notice the resemblances that exist between them with their wreath of cilia and the Trochophore larvæ of the Polychætous Annelids.

NEMERTINE WORMS.

CLASS NEMERTINEA.

Although the members of this division are but little known to the ordinary public, many of them, so far as length is concerned, are the most striking of all Vermes. There is, however, a most astonishing difference in size between various species, for while some of those belonging to the genus *Lineus* may attain a length of several yards, the species of other genera are comparatively of quite insignificant dimensions. In other respects, however, there is a close similarity between the various members of the class, the structural characteristics of which may be briefly summarised as follows:—The body is not segmented, and its integument is covered externally with cilia. At the front end a head-region may be distinguished by the presence of eyes and of a pair of ciliated pits, which are probably sense organs of some kind. On the lower side of the head opens the mouth, and this leads into a spacious alimentary canal which traverses the body from end to end. But in addition to the mouth, the head is also furnished with a second aperture, from which a retractile proboscis can be shot forth. This proboscis is one of the most characteristic features of the Nemertines. When retracted it rests in a special sheath lying along the back, above the alimentary canal, and reaching sometimes to the hinder end of the body. In this state the proboscis has been compared to the finger of a glove that has been turned outside in within the part that covers the hand, the latter representing the sheath; but when protruded, the organ is comparable to the finger of the glove in its normal situation. This type of proboscis is of not uncommon occurrence in the Vermes, and from its method of protrusion and retraction is often called an "introvert." The nervous system consists of a pair of chords, one running along each side of the body and uniting at its fore end with the brain, which lies above the alimentary canal and beneath the proboscis-sheath—or rather round the proboscis-sheath like a ring, for the right and left halves of the brain are joined together by a transverse band which passes above this sheath. The only other organs that need be noticed are the paired nephridia or excretory organs situated in the front part of the body and the thin blood-vessels, sometimes containing red blood, which lie just above and at the sides of the alimentary canal and unite at the anterior and posterior ends of the body.

In most Nemertines the sexes are distinct, and, as a rule, the young are produced from eggs that are deposited by the mother either singly or in gelatinous clusters; some forms, however, such as *Monopora vivipara*, retain the eggs until the development is far advanced and the young are born alive. In many species again, as in *Lineus*, the young goes through a striking metamorphosis, the egg giving rise to a free-swimming ciliated larva known as the *pilidium* and consisting of an upper bell-shaped part, from the lower rim of which spring a pair of lobes. Within this larva the young Nemertine is gradually formed, and when sufficiently advanced to lead an independent life it breaks free from its pilidium-case and deserts it. In other cases the development is less complicated, conditions in different species having been observed, which lead from the complete metamorphosis by means of the pilidium to the direct development of such species as *Tetrastemma* and *Malacobdella*.

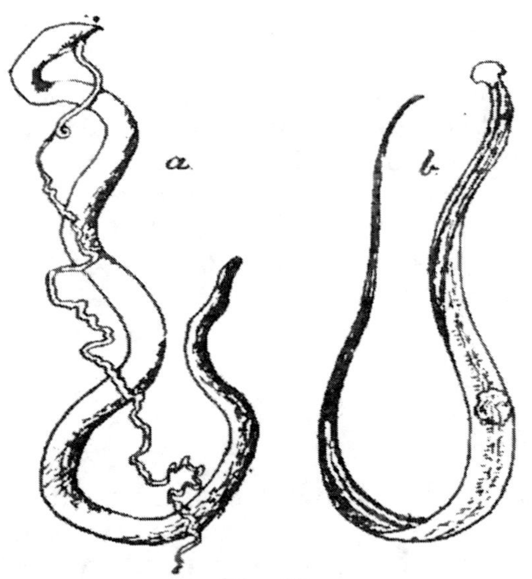

Fig. 11.
a, Nemertine Worm.—*Lineus marinus* (with proboscis protruded).
b, Land Planarian (*Bipalium kewense*).

The class is usually divided into two orders, the Enopla and the Anopla, the difference between the two consisting in the presence of stylets on the proboscis in the former and their absence in the latter. To the Anopla belong such genera as *Polia* and *Lineus*, and to the Enopla or Hoplonemertinea, *Malacobdella*, *Tetrastemma*, and *Geonemertes*.

All Nemertines appear to be carnivorous, feeding upon annelids or other soft-bodied living organisms. The great majority of the species are marine, occurring for the most part amongst sea-weeds and coral rocks, in shallow water; a genus, however, called *Pelagonemertes* is found in the open sea. Of the marine forms *Malacobdella*, which was originally regarded as nearly allied to the Leeches, lives parasitically upon bivalved Mollusca of the genera *Mya*, *Venus*, and *Cypridina*. The genus *Tetrastemma* is interesting for the reason that some of its species are marine, some fresh water, and some terrestrial, one fresh-water species having been found in England, another (*T. aquarum-dulcium*) in North America; the two known land species being from Rodriguez (*T. rodericanum*) and the Bermudas (*T. agricola*). The rest of the land species are furnished by the genus *Geonemertes*, which has a representative (*G. australiensis*) in Australia, another in New Zealand (*G. novæ-zelandiæ*), a third in the Pelew Islands (*G. palaensis*), and a fifth, which has probably been introduced, in Germany; all these land species are found in damp spots beneath logs, stones, etc.

FLAT-WORMS.

CLASS PLATYHELMINTHES.

Many of the worms of this division have been greatly modified by a parasitic life, have lost all trace of the mouth and alimentary canal, and in the case of the Tape-worms have acquired a rich segmentation of the body, which, as will be explained, is subservient to the process of reproduction; but the forms that lead a free existence, and may be looked upon as the primitive members of the class, approach the Nemertines in many points of structure, though, on the whole, they are much less highly organised, there being no distinct vascular system, no dorsal proboscis and sheath, and the alimentary canal, when present, has no posterior outlet.

THE PLANARIAN WORMS—SUB-CLASS TURBELLARIA.—To this sub-class belong the free-living flat-worms alluded to above. The flattish unsegmented body is either short and broad or long and slender, and, as in the Nemertines, its integument is covered with cilia. The mouth, which varies much in position, being sometimes placed at the front end of the body and sometimes in the middle of its lower surface, leads into a muscular pharynx, and this usually passes into a spacious digestive tract, upon the structure of which the classification of the group is based. In the first section, named RHABDOCŒLA, for example, the alimentary canal consists of a single undivided pouch. In the DENDROCŒLA, on the other hand, the stomach is branched, being divided into three (Tricladida), or a very large number of branches (Polycladida), while in the section known as ACŒLA there is no true intestine, the alimentary canal being merely represented by the mouth and the muscular pharynx or gullet which immediately follows it. In some cases, as represented in our figure of *Bipalium kewense*, one of the land Planarians, the pharynx is capable of protrusion through the aperture of the mouth, and of acting as a sucker. The nervous system is well developed, and consists of a bilobed mass or ganglion placed in the head, and from this a pair of widely-separated chords pass backwards to the hinder end of the body, and others go to supply the head and eyes, of which there are sometimes many, though more usually only one or two pairs. Sometimes, too, ears of a simple kind are found.

The habitat of Planarian worms is tolerably varied, some species being found in the sea, others in fresh water, and others, again, on the land. Most of them are free living. A few, however, have taken to a parasitic life, two of the Rhabdocœla, named *Graffila* and *Anoplodium*, occurring respectively upon Mollusca of the snail-kind and upon Sea-cucumbers, while *Bdellura*, a Triclad Dendrocœl, lives on the king-crab. All the members of the Polyclad Dendrocœls are marine, and in this group we meet with a metamorphosis in the development, the young Planarian, known as Müller's larva, being furnished with eight ciliated processes arranged round the middle of its body. Thus equipped it leads a free life, circling about in the water. In other members of the class the development takes place without the intervention of active larval forms. Usually the method of reproduction offers nothing worthy of special comment; but one of the Rhabdocœls, known as *Microstoma*, presents an alternation of generation such as has been described in the case of some Annelids (*e.g.*, *Nereis*). The hinder portion of the body becomes divided by a partition from the front portion;

each part then again divides into two, the process being repeated until there may be as many as eight, sixteen, or thirty-two divisions. Each division acquires a mouth, and when each is sexually mature, the chain breaks up into a number of separate individuals, which lay eggs, these ultimately giving rise to sexless individuals, which can only reproduce by fission.

Many Planarians are elegantly coloured, presenting either a tolerably uniform vivid tint, or considerable diversity of pattern. Two species, namely, *Vortex viridis* and *Convoluta schultzii*, the former belonging to the RHABDOCŒLA and the latter to the ACŒLA, are noteworthy in this connection as being coloured with chlorophyll, the material which imparts to plants their characteristic green tint, and which enables them under the influence of sunlight to break up carbonic acid gas into its constituent chemical elements, oxygen and carbon. Both of these Planarians are of small size, measuring less than half an inch in length. Many other kinds are, however, much larger than this, one of the terrestrial species, *Geoplana australis*, from New Zealand, being upwards of a foot long.

The acquatic forms swim by means of the undulatory movement of the body, aided by the sweeping action of the multitude of cilia which clothe the integument. The terrestrial forms progress in the same manner, preserving their moisture by the copious secretion of slime. Avoiding the light and living under stones and logs of wood during the daytime, they venture forth at night from their dark humid haunts, and crawl about with the sensitive head raised and gently swayed from side to side to feel the way. Their food consists of earth-worms and defenceless insects, the soft parts of which are imbibed by means of the gullet, the prey being securely held the while by the slimy coils of the Planarian. The figure of the Planarian (*Bipalium kewense*) on page 684, represents one of these terrestrial leech-like species, which is recognisable by the peculiar shape of its head. It was first obtained in Kew Gardens, and has been introduced into many parts of the world in connection with imported exotic plants.

THE TAPE-WORMS—SUB-CLASS CESTODA.—Almost all the members of this class live, when mature, as parasites in the alimentary canal of carnivorous vertebrated animals; but during the younger stages they occur in different parts of the body of animals of many kinds, including ticks, fresh-water shrimps, molluscs, and water-worms, as well as fish, rabbits, pigs, etc. Unless, in fact, the worm is able to change its host it is quite unable to reach the adult state. The truth of this is well illustrated in the case of one of the commonest of mankind's Tape-worms, known as *Tænia solium*, which may be selected as a convenient type to illustrate the life-history and the structure of the other members of the class.

Upwards of three yards in length, this worm floats in the intestinal juices, maintaining a firm hold of the inner wall of the gut by means of its minute pin-sized head, which is furnished for the purpose with a circlet of five hooks and four strong suckers. Immediately behind the head comes a narrow part, called the neck, which is unjointed and only about half an inch long. This is continuous with the rest of the body, which gradually expands into the characteristic tape-like form, and becomes divided into a vast number of segments. At first imperfectly defined, these segments become longer and longer and more and more distinct as they pass from the neck to the posterior end, the last ones alone being what is called "ripe" and ready to break off from the parent stock. The worm is furnished with a well-developed muscular system, consisting of fibres that run lengthwise throughout the body, and of others that pass from wall to wall of the segments. It also possesses a nervous and excretory system, the former represented by a ganglion in the head, whence a pair of nerves run backwards along each side of the segments to the end of the body. The excretory organs consist of a circular canal lodged in the head, from which spring four branches, one corresponding to each sucker ; two of these traverse the sides of the body, and, becoming united in the last segment, open by a common aperture on its hinder edge. They are also put into communication with each other in each segment by means of a transverse canal, which runs along its posterior border. Of mouth and alimentary canal there is no vestige, the animal gaining its nutriment by absorbing the fluids in which it floats.

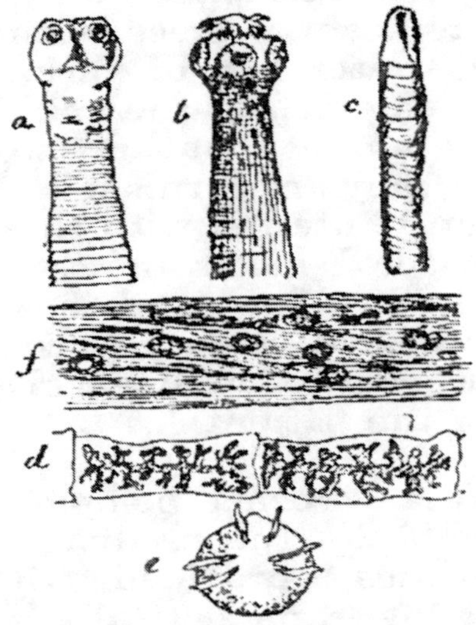

Fig. 12.—Tape-worms.
a, Head of *Tænia saginata.*
b, Head of *Tænia solium.*
c, Head of *Bothriocephalus latus.*
d, Ripe Segments of *Tænia solium*
e, Hooked Embryo of *Tænia solium.*
f, Measly Pork infested with Cysticercus.

A Tape-worm is unable to propagate its kind within the host in which it is lodged. But each segment contains a complete set of organs necessary for the purpose, and when it is ripe and breaks off in the manner mentioned above, it is found to be charged with eggs. Such a segment, called a *proglottis*, makes its way to the exterior, and, bursting, sets free the eggs, which are thus disseminated. Sooner or later some of them, in connection with food or water, are swallowed by a pig. Each egg is then hatched and gives rise to the young known as the *proscolex*, a minute organism provided with three pairs of hooks (Fig. 12, *e*). By means of its armature, the *proscolex* bores it way through the coats of the pig's alimentary canal and enters its blood-vessels. It is then carried by the blood stream to some such organ as the brain, lung, muscles, etc., where it ultimately becomes lodged. Then growth sets in in earnest, the proscolex loses its hooks, and, enlarging, becomes converted into a bladder. Pork thus infested is technically called measly (Fig. 12, *f*). At one point of the bladder a deep depression arises, and at the bottom of this the hooks and suckers of the tape-worm head are developed; the depression is then pushed outwards until it becomes a process, carrying at the tip the head which is thus formed outside in. But beyond this stage, known as the *Cysticercus* or *Bladder-worm*, the parasite cannot pass without again changing its host. This is effected when the meat of an infested pig is eaten in an uncooked state by a human being, whereby the Cysticercus is introduced into the alimentary canal, the bladder is digested, and the head or *Scolex*, attaching itself to the wall of the intestine, starts growing in length, until it assumes the adult form and breaks up into proglottides.

Another tape-worm, common in man, and presenting the same cycle of development as *Tænia solium*, with the exception that oxen are the intermediate hosts, is *Tænia saginata*, which is larger than the one just described, and may be at once recognised from it by the absence of the circlet of hooks on the head (Fig. 12, *a*).

A third species that infests mankind, but is of more frequent occurrence in Central Europe than in England, is the cleft-headed or Broad Tape-worm (*Bothriocephalus latus*), which is said to attain a length of 30 ft. The head has neither hooks nor protuberant suckers, but is furnished on each side with a deep groove (Fig. 12, *c*). The intermediate hosts of these worms and of their allies, which live in water-birds, are fresh-water fish of various kinds, and an interesting fact connected with their development is the ability of the larvæ to live for a while an independent life, swimming about in water by means of a set of vibratile hairs or cilia with which they are furnished.

It must not, however, be supposed that man is only infested with these parasites in their sexual stage. There is a kind, called *Tænia echinococcus*, found in dogs, which scatter the eggs broadcast with their dung; and these, if swallowed by man in connection with water or unwashed salad, are converted into embryos, which ultimately, making their way to the liver, give rise to cysts of large size, and often cause the death of the patient.

FLUKE-WORMS—SUB-CLASS TREMATODA.—The Flat-worms belonging to this section are characterised by having smooth (not ciliated), more or less leaf-like, shortish, unsegmented bodies, provided with two or more suckers, by means of which they adhere parasitically to the hosts they infest. According to the number of the suckers, these worms are divided into two sections, the *Polystomeæ* and the *Distomeæ*. The Polystomeæ have two suckers in the fore part of the body, and one large one or several smaller ones at the hinder end; not infrequently, too, they are armed with hooks for clinging. This rich equipment of organs for adhesion is explained by the fact that these creatures live mostly as external parasites upon various kinds of fish, and are thus constantly exposed to the danger of being washed from their moorings by the water. Their development also takes place directly and without any such curious metamorphoses as obtain in many of the entoparasitic worms. The following species may be cited as examples of this order:—*Cyclatella annelidicola* found upon annelidan worms; *Trochopus tubiporus* on the Gurnet; and *Aspidogaster conchicola*, which lives in the pericardial cavity of the fresh-water mussel. Perhaps the most remarkable form of all is the one known as *Diplozoon paradoxum*, the double-worm, which frequents the gills of minnow, gudgeon, etc. The young of this worm is ciliated and leads a free swimming life. It is furnished with two eye-spots and with a small ventral sucker and a dorsal papilla. In this stage it is known as the *Diporpa*. After a time the *Diporpæ* settle down upon the gills of their host, and two of them approaching each other unite, the one seizing the papilla of the other with its sucker, then with a dexterous twist the second similarly gets hold of the papilla of the first, and, growing together, the two become inseparably united (Fig. 13, *f*).

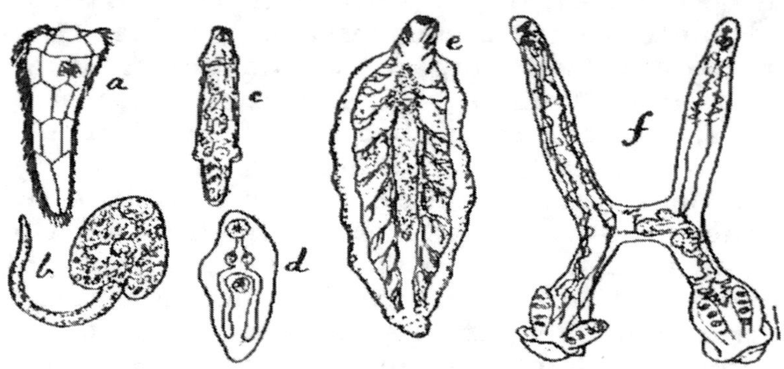

Fig. 13.
a-e, LIFE HISTORY OF THE LIVER FLUKE.
a, Free swimming larva; *b*, cercaria larva; *c*, redia larva; *d*, young fluke; *e*, adult fluke; *f* *Diplozoon paradoxum*.

The Distomeæ, as their name, meaning two-mouthed, implies, are provided with only two suckers, and have no clinging hooks; for, being internal parasites, they have no such special need of instruments for maintaining a secure hold as the more highly organised species of the previous group. Their development, too, is often complicated by the most extraordinary metamorphoses, and is accompanied by migrations from one host to another.

A well-known example of this section is the Liver-fluke (*Distoma hepaticum*), which lives parasitically in the liver of herbivorous mammalia—such as sheep. The worm is less than an inch long, and is broad and flat, wider in front than behind, and bearing on its front end a conical projection supporting the mouth, which is lodged in the centre of a sucker. The second sucker is situated on the ventral surface a short distance behind the first. The eggs of the Fluke enter the intestines of the sheep through the bile ducts, and are thence discharged with the droppings. Thereupon they hatch; but the embryo perishes, unless by chance it is carried or washed into some fresh-water pond or stream. If favoured by fortune in this particular, it swims actively about by means of its long cilia in search of the particular host in which it is forced for a while to sojourn. This host is the water-snail known as *Limnæus truncatulus.* Into the soft tissues of this mollusc the young Fluke bores its way, and after losing its cilia becomes converted into an oval sac known as the *Sporocyst.* Within this fresh individuals, known as *Rediæ*, are developed, the *Rediæ* being short cylindrical little worms, furnished, like the parent form, with mouth, gullet, and stomach. After making their way to the snails' liver, the *Rediæ* in turn take up the process of development, and give rise to individuals as different from themselves as they are from the ciliated embryo. These new forms, known as *Cercariæ*, somewhat resemble a tadpole in shape, consisting of a flattish, heart-shaped body, furnished with two suckers, a mouth, a forked alimentary canal, and produced behind into a long vibratile tail. These make their escape from the body of the snail, and, after swimming about for a time, settle upon some plant, and envelop themselves in a coating or cyst. In times of flood this takes place upon the grass blades of some overflowed meadow, and in this case there is a chance that the organism will be devoured by a grazing sheep, and will become lodged in the bile ducts of its new host, where the development into the adult Fluke will be completed (see Fig. 13, *a-e*).

To be regarded in all probability as degenerate Flat-worms are the minute organisms belonging to the *Dicyemidæ* and *Orthonectidæ*, which live as parasites, the former in the branchial veins of cuttle-fish and the latter upon Planarian and Nemertine worms and on sand-stars. They are ciliated vermiform creatures, without trace of body cavity or alimentary canal, the chief peculiarity of their organisation consisting in the fact that the solid body consists of a central mass, composed in the Dicyemidæ of one large nucleated cell, and in the Orthonectidæ of a cluster of cells, surrounded externally by a single layer of ectoderm cells.

SUB-KINGDOM VIII.

THE COELENTERATA.

SPONGES, CORALS, ETC.

BY HENRY M. BERNARD, M.A., F.L.S., ETC., AND MATILDA BERNARD.

THE Coelenterata are to be distinguished from all the animals hitherto described by the fact that the alimentary canal no longer runs through the body as a free tube suspended to its walls and surrounded by the body cavity. Animals in which such a closed alimentary canal is found are known as the Coelomata, on account of the spaces between the canal and the body wall. In contradistinction, the Coelenterata or hollow-bodied animals are called the Acoelomata, because the digestive sac fills up the whole body without leaving any spaces between the digestive layer and the body wall. The body is, in fact, a more or less simple sac into which the mouth opens.

The Coelenterata, while thus distinguished from all animals higher than themselves, are nevertheless associated with them owing to the multicellular composition of the body. As Metazoa, or many-celled animals, they differ from all lower animals or Protozoa, whose bodies are unicellular.

The Coelenterata may be divided into two groups—(1) the Sponges, and (2) the Cnidaria.

I.—THE SPONGES.

The Sponges, which are also known as the Porifera, on account of the pores that perforate their walls, are usually considered to be Coelenterates of a very simple kind. although many naturalists place them in a group by themselves.

The Sponges have been the subject of frequent discussion among naturalists from the time of Aristotle down to the present day. Aristotle was of opinion that they were animals, because they appeared to shrink when torn from the rocks, and thus seemed to show signs of sensation, but their real nature was altogether misunderstood by most of the earlier naturalists, some considering them to be plants, others congealed foam of the sea. Lamarck, even, imagined the apertures on the surface of a Sponge to be the mouths of cells occupied by small polyps something like the Coral polyps, which, however, could never be discovered in their homes. Peysonnel, on the other hand, considered a large worm which often lives in Sponges to be their "sole fabricant, the rest being mere nidus or excretion." About one hundred and fifty years ago the secret of Sponge life was revealed when the fact that water is drawn into the Sponge and expelled by it was established, but the various ways in which the currents of water pass through the body, and their relation to the life of the Sponge, were not accurately investigated until about seventy years ago, and are, indeed, still to a certain extent problematical.

In the Sponge we have the very simplest type of Metazoan or multicellular animal. The component cells of the body, which, in the higher Metazoa, lose much of their individuality, functioning in masses (as tissues or organs) for the good of the whole complex organism rather than as individuals for their own benefit, are comparatively little modified in the body of the Sponge, still acting individually almost more than collectively.

Constitution of the Sponge Body.

The body wall of a Sponge consists of two layers. The outer layer is of a gelatinous nature, and contains (1) cells which, like some of the unicellular animals such as the Amoeba (Fig. 1, p. 714), can change their shape, throwing out processes in various directions; and (2) needle-like bodies, called spicules, which are formed by cells and give firmness to the wall and support the apertures on its surface. The inner layer primarily consists of cells closely resembling another form of unicellular organisms, the collared Flagellata (Fig. 6, C, p. 718). Each of the collar cells in this layer is provided with the whip-like appendage which characterises the Flagellata, so that the whole inner surface of the wall of the simplest Sponge is lined with fine, waving whips. The presence of these "whip cells" at one time led naturalists to consider the Sponges as mere aggregates of unicellular animals.

The very simplest type of Sponge, such as the one depicted in Fig. 1, is a simple sac, generally more or less cylindrical, and attached by its narrowed base to a rock or some other surface. This sac, which opens above by a wide, circular orifice, the oscule, consists of an outer and an inner layer such as have just been described.

The water necessary to the life of the Sponge does not enter in at the oscule, which must not be considered as a mouth, but through multitudes of much smaller apertures or pores that perforate the wall. Within the cavity of the sac the collar cells of the lining layer draw in from the water, which enters at the pores and streams out at the oscule, small particles of nourishment, and for this reason this space has been called the "gastral cavity." All indigestible matter, together with the water containing it, is ejected through the oscule. The whips with which the collar cells are provided keep the water in constant motion, and help to draw it in through the pores and to eject it through the oscule.

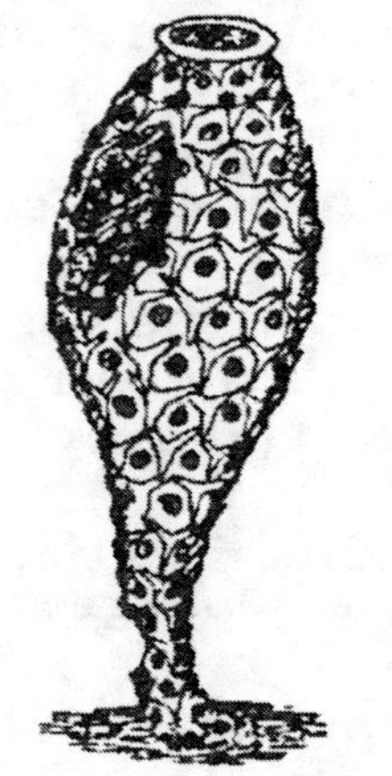

Fig. 1.—THE SIMPLEST TYPE OF SPONGE (*Ascetta*).

Other Sponges are less simple in structure, complexity being brought about by the thickening of the walls of the sac and by new arrangements of the whip cells.

In a rather more complicated type of Sponge, the wall is bulged out in the form of numbers of small radiating tubes. The wall of each of these tubes is perforated by pores through which the water is drawn by the action of the whip cells, and is passed on into the central cavity with which all the tubes communicate. It is finally ejected through the oscule, which has here the same position as in the simpler type of Sponge. In this second type of Sponge the collar cells line the tubes only, the central cavity being lined with flat cells.

In still more complicated types of Sponges with very thick walls an elaborate canal system arises, leading the water through the thick walls to the central cavity. The collar cells here no longer line either the central cavity or the canals, but form the lining of a great number of round chambers which may be called "whip chambers." The water, entering through the pores on the outer surface, passes through canals into these spherical chambers, the whips of the lining cells keeping it in movement and sending it on through other canals, which unite with those from other whip chambers to form large channels that finally open into the central cavity. When such a sponge is cut across and highly magnified we see, as in the diagram Fig. 2, an elaborate and repeatedly branched system of canals. The whip chambers unite the ramifications, which come from the outer surface (the incurrent canals), with those that lead to large trunks opening into the gastral cavity (the excurrent canals).

The Canal System.

Fig. 2.—DIAGRAM OF THE CANAL SYSTEM OF A SPONGE.

The above descriptions apply only to what may be regarded as single sponge individuals; but, by repeated budding, individual sponges may, in some cases, form colonies in which the individuals are no longer separately recognisable. This budding process giving rise to colonies is, however, not the only method of reproduction. In a Sponge whose life-history has been fully worked out, the process is as follows:—Eggs are produced at certain parts of the body-wall which, when fertilised, divide up and give rise to small oval embryos covered with cilia. These are either solid or are provided with a small central cavity. They escape from the parent through the oscule, and swim about for a short time, varying from a few hours to a day or two. During this time they change their shape, and spicules develop in their walls. When such an embryo attaches itself and becomes a sponge, the whip cells which clothed the outer surface and rowed the tiny creature about, come, in various ways, to line the interior and set up currents of water which bring in the necessary food.

Development of a Sponge.

Although the canal system is so essential to the life of the Sponges, and is so typically developed in the different kinds, its various modifications are apparently of little use in classification. Those who have made Sponges a special study prefer to group them according to the structure of the hard parts which support the outer layer of the body. These hard parts are either spicules or fibres, and are very rarely absent.

Classification of Sponges.

In the Calcareous Sponges, the skeleton consists of separate spicules of carbonate of lime. In the Siliceous Sponges, flinty spicules are found, which either remain separate or become united together to form networks or other supporting structures. There are, further, Sponges with skeletons composed of horny fibres, and besides the spicules or fibres secreted by the Sponge itself, foreign objects are sometimes appropriated to assist in the formation of the skeleton.

The spicules found in Sponges assume a vast variety of shapes, a few of which are given in Fig. 3. Some are like fine needles pointed at both ends, others have several rays, the number of these determining the classification of the Siliceous Sponges into those with six or four-rayed or uniaxial spicules. Other spicules, again, terminate either at one end or both in anchor-like projections, or else resemble thorny sticks; others end in lobes instead of points. The spicules either lie embedded separately in the Sponge tissue, giving it firmness, or unite in many different ways, forming rosette-like or plate-like structures or else delicate supporting frameworks. Several kinds of spicules may be found in the same Sponge. Besides strengthening the body, they also protect it, as is evident from their position. Spicules of the anchor type are frequently found projecting from the outer surface, especially round the oscules and pores, and, in some Sponges, spicules stand out like thorns all over the surface of the gastral cavity.

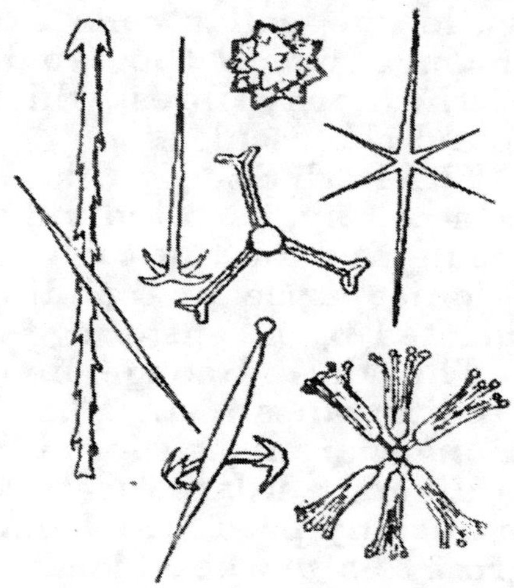

Fig. 3—Sponge Spicules.

The exceedingly fine and brittle nature of Sponge spicules causes them to penetrate any soft object that comes in contact with them. If some Sponges are handled carelessly, a burning irritation is set up by the fine points, which pierce and break off in the skin. One Sponge has on this account received the significant name of *Agelas noli tangere.* This peculiarity no doubt efficiently protects Sponges from many enemies which might prey upon them.

In size, Sponges vary greatly; some are minute objects only to be distinctly seen under the microscope, others form enormous masses several feet high.

By far the greater number of Sponges live in the sea; a few species of fresh-water Sponges, however, occur in our own rivers, lakes, and ponds, and many others are found in various parts of the globe.

A considerable number of marine Sponges are to be found in our own coasts, but these are less attractive in appearance than some of the tropical Sponges, especially those with elegant framework, produced by combinations of six-rayed spicules. The skeletons of the Venus's Flower Basket (Fig. 4, A), the Lacework Sponge, and Bird's-Nest Sponge are familiar objects in museums. Below the beautiful framework of the Sponge itself, a tangle of very fine threads resembling spun glass is to be seen. These are modified spicules, and by their means the Sponges anchor themselves in the mud. The Glass-Rope Sponge (Fig. 4, B) derives its name from the rope-like appearance of the anchoring threads, which are slightly twisted.

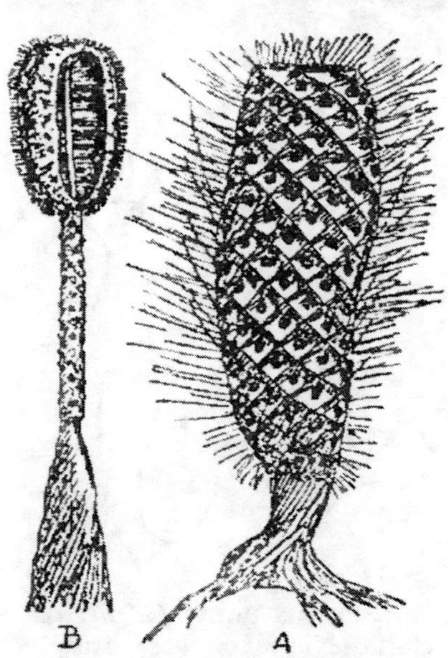

Fig. 4.—Six-rayed Sponges (*Hexactinellidæ*).
A, Venus's Flower Basket (*Euplectella*).
B, The Glass-Rope Sponge (*Hyalonema*).

Among the more massive Sponges is the Neptune's Cup, which may stand several feet high.

The Bath Sponge (*Euspongia officinalis*).

The most familiar of all Sponges, the Bath Sponge, has a skeleton of horny fibres. In a living condition, it forms large dark, often almost black masses, the surface of which is raised up into numberless conical prominences and broken through by large oscules; each oscule is surrounded by an iris-like membrane; fine pores are to be found opening on the surface between the conical prominences. Canal systems with whip chambers run through the entire mass, all the cavities and canals being lined with flat cells, while the collar cells are restricted to the whip chambers. The tissue through which the canal systems run receives firmness from the presence of the horny fibres, which are specially plentiful along the chief canals and round the oscules.

The Bath Sponge, like most of the other massive Sponges, may be regarded as a colony, each individual of which consists of a cavity opening through an oscule and of the canal system which finally leads into that cavity. Such colonies arise by budding; the reproduction of the colony is, however, effected by means of eggs which grow into free-swimming larvæ.

The Bath Sponge flourishes on the coasts of the eastern half of the Mediterranean, in the West Indies, the Bahamas, and Florida. The sponges are fished for either with harpoons or nets, or are obtained by means of divers, and are carefully prepared for the market. Large Sponges are also artificially produced from small pieces which, under favourable conditions, grow to a marketable size in the space of about seven years.

II.—The Cnidaria.

The Cnidaria, which form the other great division of the Coelenterata derive their name from the peculiar stinging cells with which they are provided. They have been divided into:—(1) The Hydrozoa, or water animals, to which all the Zoophytes or plant-like animals, and some of the Jelly-fish belong. (2) The Scyphozoa, which include most of the larger Jelly-fish, the Sea-anemones, and the Corals. (3) The Ctenophora or Comb-bearers.

The Hydrozoa.

A short account of one of the simplest and most easily accessible of the Hydrozoa will serve to give some idea of the essential features of the Cnidarian body. The Hydra is a small fresh-water Hydrozoan very common in ponds and aquaria. As it is from $\frac{1}{4}$ to $\frac{1}{2}$ an inch in length, it can easily be seen with the naked eye hanging from the under surface of some water plant or other submerged object, to which it has attached itself by a very simple kind of sucker at the lower end of the body. The free end terminates in a mouth at the tip of a prominence which is surrounded by a ring of long tentacles. Both the body and the tentacles are exceedingly contractile, so that while the whole animal, when retracted, appears like a gelatinous ball crowned with bud-like knobs, when fully extended its body is slender and the tentacles thread-like.

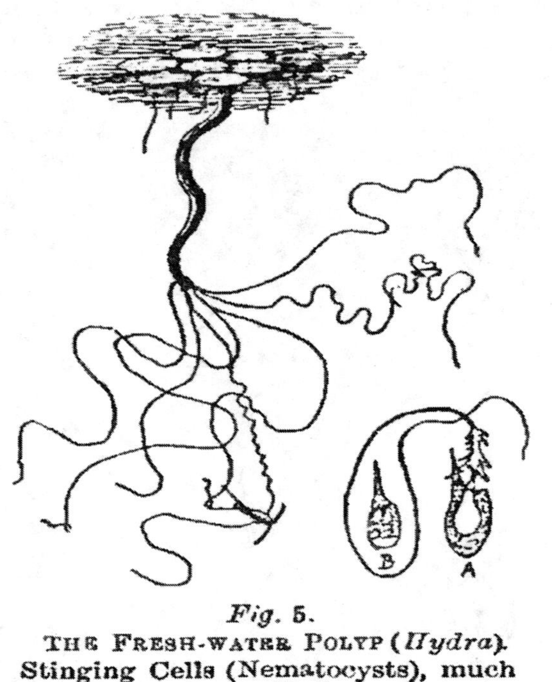

Fig. 5.
THE FRESH-WATER POLYP (*Hydra*).
Stinging Cells (Nematocysts), much magnified.
A, The vesicle with thread discharged.
B, The vesicle containing coiled thread.

The walls of the simple tube-like body of the Hydra consist of two layers of cells—an outer layer in contact with the surrounding medium, and an inner layer lining the tube-like interior or stomach cavity. Separating these cell layers there is a very thin intermediate or supporting (non-cellular) layer. This supporting layer by itself might be thought of as a kind of framework exactly corresponding with the shape of the body, for it penetrates even to the tips of the tentacles, which arise as outpushings of the body wall, and are therefore themselves tube-like. In this intermediate layer are found all the processes of the cellular layers which function as nerves and muscles. At the mouth, the outer and inner cell layers pass into one another ; this is an important point, because, as we shall presently see, the arrangement of the layers at the mouth forms one of the chief distinctions between the Hydrozoa and the Scyphozoa.

The cells of the outer layer of the Hydra body are chiefly remarkable for their stinging apparatus. The stinging cells contain minute vesicles (Fig. 5), many of them measuring not more than $\frac{1}{1500}$ of an inch, in which are coiled up stinging threads, which are very valuable weapons of attack and defence. Each of these stinging cells is provided with a minute projection, the cnidocil, and it appears that, when this is touched, the vesicle shoots out its long, coiled, barbed thread so rapidly that, delicate as it is, it is able to penetrate the body of any creature rash enough to approach too near. The poisonous effect of these weapons is shown by the fact that any small animal thus attacked appears to be paralysed ; the victim speedily ceases struggling to escape, and is drawn in by the tentacles to the mouth. It is said that each tentacle of a Hydra is provided with many thousands of such weapons, which are being constantly produced afresh, new cells taking the place of those which have been discharged.

The cells constituting the inner lining of the body are provided with fine hairs or whips, and are capable of changing their shape, and of sending out processes into the cavity of the body ; they are therefore called amoeboid cells. The simple crustacean or other prey which, caught and paralysed by the stinging tentacles, has been pushed through the mouth into the cavity of the body, is digested by the cells of this lining layer. Whatever cannot be assimilated is thrown out again at the mouth, the muscles of the body wall and the current of water kept up by the whips in the cavity assisting in this process.

The Hydra often reproduces itself by means of buds which grow out from the parent body, and when fully equipped for independent life, break off and attach themselves near the parent. But, at certain seasons, a large globular body forms at some part of the surface of the fully-grown Hydra. This represents an egg, and, when fertilised, separates from the parent and develops into a new Hydra.

The Hydra and its allies have a wonderful power of repairing injuries which the body may suffer. Almost any part of the body, if cut off, is able to reproduce the rest. Some naturalists have amused themselves by producing monstrous growths possessed of a large number of heads, and others have tried the experiment of turning the sac-like body inside out, and have even asserted that the Hydra is able to carry on its life activities in such a condition. It has, however, been proved that, under such circumstances, the Hydra either manages to regain its normal state or else dies.

In this account of the Hydra, which is also known as the Fresh-water polyp, in contradistinction to other marine polyps, such as the Sea-anemones, the Corals, and the Zoophytes, we have noticed some of the essential points in the structure of the Cnidarian body. Among these are the sac-like nature of the body, the digestion of food by the walls of the body cavity, the capture of prey, and defence against enemies, by means of the formidable stinging threads.

The Hydra we have described is not an entirely stationary animal; it can detach its disc and creep along by using alternately its tentacles and its disc, and sometimes even casts its body loose, using the expanded disc as a float and the tentacles for swimming. Most other Hydroids, however, unite to form stationary colonies, the young, which bud from each successive generation, remaining attached like branches, or by means of rootlets, to the original parent animal. Such colonies are often found encrusting empty shells, which they sometimes entirely cover with branched growths. One of them is represented in Fig. 6. Some of the members of this colony (A, A) bear a great resemblance to the Hydra, having the same tube-like body, surrounded at the free end by a crown of tentacles. But a large colony of such highly contractile creatures as the Hydra clustered together would be unmanageable, so, in these cases, their trunks are generally enveloped in a more or less stiff covering, which protects and supports the colony. The free ends of the individuals, with the mouths and tentacles, however, protruding from the open ends of the envelopes, contract and expand freely.

Hydroid Colonies —Zoophytes.

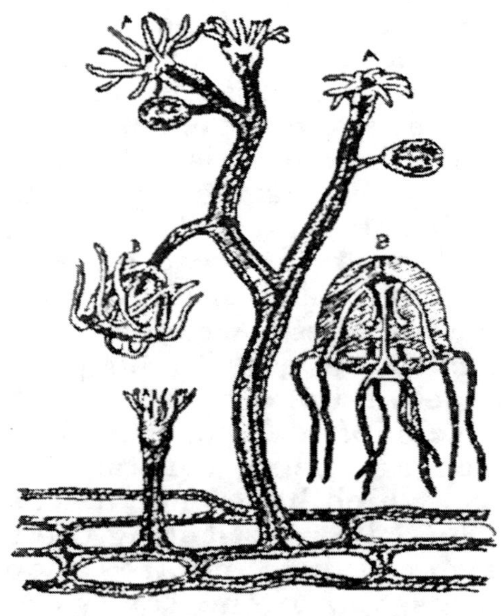

Fig. 6.—A HYDROID COLONY (*Bougainvillea ramosa*).
A, Hydra like individuals.
B, Medusoid individuals.

In the branched Hydroid figured, two important points are to be noticed. First, the gastral cavities of all the members of the colony are in communication with each other, so that, when one of them captures food, the superfluous nutritive fluid produced can be passed on to the other members through the communicating canals that run along the trunk and stems. Secondly, while most of the members of a colony are Hydra-like, and help to feed the whole, others (Fig. 6, B) are quite unlike the Hydra, differing both in the shape of the body and in the character of the tentacles. These, which are called Medusoid individuals on account of their resemblance to Medusæ or Jelly-fish, are the members in which the reproductive elements are produced. In some cases the medusoid buds remain attached to the colony, and send forth ciliated larvæ, which swim away and settle later to start fresh colonies; but, in the colony depicted, the medusoid individuals break loose, swim about freely, often greatly increasing in size, and after a time give rise to young forms which attach themselves as Hydroids.

Here, then, we have a most interesting phenomenon. These colonies of Hydroids are stationary like trees or bushes, and, as in the case of trees or bushes, it would be a disadvantage to them if their young grew up too close around them; they would crowd each other to death. In the vegetable kingdom there are many beautiful arrangements for securing the scattering of the seed, but surely none more beautiful than the method adopted by some of the Hyroids. The individuals selected to bear the young change their shapes, break off and swim away as minute Jelly-fish (Fig. 6, B), dispersing their young as they go.

Before giving any further account of these reproductive individuals, we must describe the Hydroid colonies a little more closely. They frequently resemble delicately branching trees or bushes, fine moss, or feathers, or sometimes form crusts over stones—hence the name of Zoophytes or animal-plants. Such growths are very common on our coasts, and are still popularly considered, on account of their plant-like appearance, to be sea-weeds; this deceptive appearance being heightened by the fact that the very minute polyps forming the colony are, in many cases, when contracted, entirely hidden within the protective framework. This common protective covering is sometimes of a horny nature and transparent, sometimes hard and chalky, and, round the bodies of the individuals of the colony, may take the form of cups into which the soft polyps can withdraw. The Campanularians received their name from their bell-shaped, protective cups. In the Sea-firs or Sertularia, the cups project from each side of the stalk; in the Plumularians, from only one side. In other forms, again, there are no protective cups. The Oaten straw coralline (Tubularia) resembles a number of closely-packed straws, from the ends of which the beautiful little crimson-tentacled polyps project.

Besides these colonies which invest themselves with hard, tubular coverings, there are others in which the chalky parts become so greatly developed as to form massive skeletons so like those of Corals that they were long classed as such. These Hydrocorallia are often found in coral reefs, and would be taken, by the uninitiated, for true coral. In one family, the skeleton of which exactly resembles that of a branched, pink coral, the similarity is even carried out in the structure of the polyp. This family has received the name of the Stylasteridæ, because of the central style or column which seems to imitate the columella of the true coral.

The Hydrocorallia.

Another family of the Hydrocorallia, the Millepora, affords an interesting example of the division of the life-work of a colony among its different members. We have already described colonies in which the feeding was undertaken by some of the members and the reproduction by others, but here we have a more remarkable distinction between the different members. If we examine a mass of skeleton of a Millepore, the minute apertures on its surface are often seen to be arranged in groups, one larger, central aperture being surrounded by a number of smaller ones. When the surface of such a skeleton is alive with polyps, the central tube is inhabited by a polyp shorter and thicker than its neighbours, with a mouth and a few knob-like tentacles (Fig. 7, A). From the smaller tubes, long slender polyps project, not provided with mouths, but only with tentacles (Fig. 7, B). The outer slender polyps keep up a constant waving motion, bending from time to time over the central polyp.

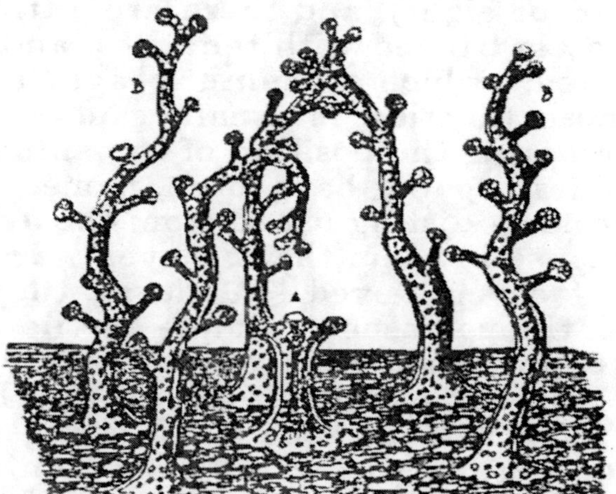

Fig. 7.—MILLEPORA.
A, Gastric individual.
B, Tentaculate individual.

With their tentacles, no doubt amply provided with stinging threads, they catch the food which, being themselves unable to eat, they pass on to the mouth of the central polyp. Within the body of this central polyp the food is digested, but not for itself alone, as the products of digestion, flowing along the many canals of the colony, feed all its members. There are no free swimming Medusæ connected with these Hydrocorallia.

Hydromedusæ. We return now to the reproductive individuals, which, in many Hydroid colonics, carry and distribute the eggs (Fig. 6, B). These, when seen swimming about independently, are so like the larger Jelly-fish belonging to the Scyphozoa that they were long mistaken for them. The general plan of the body, indeed, is very similar and is worth describing, especially in order to show what changes are necessary in the ordinary Hydra-like body to produce a swimming bell.

In all Medusæ the general shape of the body is due to the great thickening of the middle supporting layer in the body wall, which we described in connection with the Hydra. Instead of a long body like that of the Hydra, running like a tube from the mouth to the bottom of the gastric sac, we have one flattened out like an umbrella, the upper part of the umbrella corresponding with the former closed end of the tube, while the mouth is at the tip of a short stalk or handle to the umbrella. The transformation of the Hydra into the Medusoid can be imagined by supposing the mouth prominence between the tentacles to be pushed down into the body, which expands laterally, till the whole forms a bowl with the oral prominence rising up in its base; the tentacles take up positions on the rim of the bowl. The stomach lies partly in the mouth stalk or manubrium (handle) and partly in the body of the umbrella. Here it sometimes forms a cavity, and a number of canals run from it radially out, like spokes, to the edge of the umbrella, there to meet a canal which runs round the margin. When food is taken into the stomach the nutritive fluid derived from it passes through the radial canals to the circumferential canal and nourishes the whole body. The number of these radial canals in the Hydromedusæ is usually small (two, four, or eight), and these are little if at all branched. The margin of the body is fringed with tentacles, and carries the so-called "marginal bodies," some of which are minute bags (lithocysts) containing bodies called otoliths, whose function is usually said to be auditory, but is more probably that of regulating the position of the animal in the water. Other brilliantly coloured bodies, again, have been named "eye-spots." The Hydromedusæ were formerly distinguished from the Jelly-fish proper as "naked-eyed" Medusæ, because in them these "eyes" are exposed, whereas in the other Jelly-fish, or "covered-eyed" Medusæ, they are protected by a hood-like lappet of gelatinous tissue. Simple tactile organs are also found along the margin of the Hydromedusæ, round which a double nerve ring runs.

Another characteristic of the Hydromedusæ is the velum (veil), a thin, muscular membrane which hangs down from the margin of the umbrella, slanting inward toward the manubrium.

The swimming movements of these animals also deserve notice. The lower concave surface of the "umbrella" is supplied with a very thin layer of contractile tissue or muscle, by the contraction of which the umbrella is partially closed. This action, performed suddenly, drives the water out from under the umbrella and propels the Medusa along.

The eggs, in the Hydromedusæ, form along the radial canals, or on the inner walls of the manubrium, and give rise to ciliated larvæ which pass through the cavity of the umbrella into the open water, become attached, and, by budding, produce new Hydroid colonies. Such colonies again produce Medusoids, and so on. This process is a simple case of what is called alternation of generations. The Hydroid form has been called in German the "nursing" generation, as it does not itself produce the young, but brings to perfection the individuals which, when free, become the reproductive generation.

Although most Hydromedusæ are the products of a Hydroid colony, and their eggs develop again into such colonies, there are others which develop direct from forms in every respect like themselves, *i.e.*, the young ones no longer pass through any attached Hydroid stage. On the other hand, there are Hydroid colonies which never develop free medusoid forms to secure the dispersal of their progeny.

The Siphonophora.

Leaving the fixed Hydroid colonies and their free swimming members, we come to the one remaining group of the Hydrozoa, the Siphonophora, which consists of large Hydroid colonies, no longer attached, but floating freely about. These are very complicated creatures in which the Hydroid and Medusoid type of body is so curiously changed as to be scarcely recognisable, and in which also division of labour has reached an extreme point.

The Siphonophora are exceedingly striking and beautiful objects, only to be seen in tropical seas, where they delight the traveller by their exquisite shapes and brilliant colouring.

The colonies are not branched, but the many members are arranged round a central stalk. The cavities of all the members communicate as in the Zoophytes. The uppermost individual is turned into a kind of air-bladder for floating the colony, and then come a number of individuals turned into swimming-bells which drive the whole colony through the water. Beneath these locomotory individuals come nutritive individuals, which are often little more than stomach-tubes, reproductive individuals, frequently in clusters, and protective individuals, arranged in such a way as to overlap the nutritive and reproductive members of the colony. There are, further, tentacular individuals which are usually long filaments (sometimes called fishing lines). These are richly provided with stinging batteries, their function being to capture food for the colony and to defend it from its enemies.

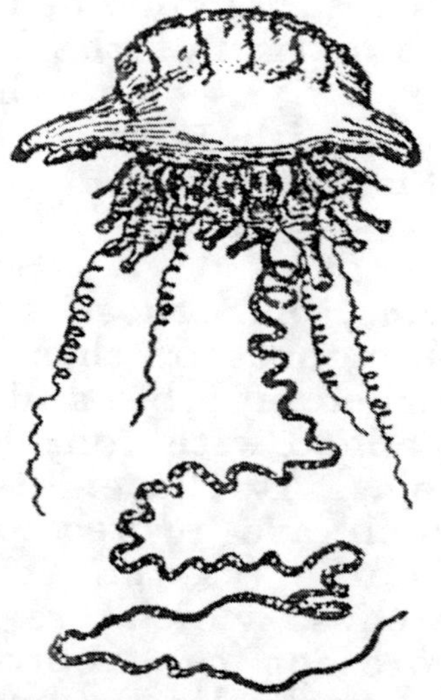

Fig. 8.—The Portuguese Man-of-War (*Physalia*).

In the simpler forms of Siphonophora the stalk is long, and the members of the colony project from it at intervals. Sometimes several pairs of swimming bells follow each other for a short way down the stalk, in other cases a single pair heads the colony. In other forms the stalk is much shortened, and a central air-bladder is surrounded by medusa-like swimming bells, the other members of the colony being crowded together beneath these. One of the best-known Siphonophora is the Portuguese Man-of-War, illustrated in Fig. 8. This is one of the most specialised forms. The large, crested, and exquisitely coloured air-bladder alone appears above the waves. This air-bladder secretes its own gas, and has an aperture through which some of its contents can be forced out. The feeding, reproductive, and other members cluster beneath the float, and several immensely long filaments, supplied with multitudes of stinging batteries, trail down into the water. The stinging powers of this Cnidarian are so great that adventurous people who have tried to capture a large specimen have narrowly escaped with their lives.

The Scyphozoa.

Turning now to the second great division of the Cnidaria, the Scyphozoa, we find that an important change has taken place in the simple sac or tube-like body. A tube has grown inward from the mouth into the body, forming a passage to the stomach (a simple kind of œsophagus); this, being an ingrowth from outside, is always lined with the outer layer of the body wall. All the Scyphozoa—*i.e.*, the Jelly-fish proper, the Anemones, and the Corals—are distinguished by the presence of this œsophagus from the Hydrozoa above described.

The Scyphomedusæ.

In the Hydrozoa we had single stationary polyps, stationary colonies, medusoid individuals which have broken loose from stationary colonies, and medusæ which no longer belong to any stationary form. In the Scyphozoa, also, we have single stationary polyps, colonies of polyps, and free-swimming medusæ. Taking the last of these forms, the Scyphomedusæ, first, we find not only that they are far larger and more important than are the Hydromedusæ, but that the thickening of the middle gelatinous layer of their body is even greater than in the Hydromedusæ. The gelatinous tissue is a mere network of connective tissue, the interstices of which are filled with water, which far exceeds in volume all the delicate body tissues of the animal. This is well illustrated by the fact that a Jelly-fish weighing 34 lbs., and measuring 7 ft. in diameter without its tentacles, when left to dry in the sun, in a few days lost $\frac{99}{100}$ of its original weight. It has also been stated that, when a large Jelly-fish is placed in the sun on blotting paper, nothing but the outline of its form has been found after a few hours have passed.

An English Jelly-Fish (*Aurelia aurita*).

These Scyphomedusæ differ from the Hydromedusæ in several ways. The margin of the umbrella is generally lobed, and there is no true velum; the mouth at the tip of the manubrium is often square. The cavity of the body is more complicated than in the Hydromedusæ, being divided up in various ways, and the radial canals are often richly branched. To the Scyphomedusæ belong, not only many lovely tropical forms, but those commonly seen floating in our own waters. In the commonest of these last (*Aurelia aurita*) the margin forms eight slightly marked off lobes and is fringed with very fine tentacles. The square mouth is edged with four long arms, which hang down into the water and catch prey. At the eight notches between the lobes are small sensory bodies which are protected in the way characteristic of the "covered eyed" Medusæ (as the Scyphozoa were formerly called). Four large coloured patches, which are very marked on the upper surface of the umbrella, represent the reproductive masses, beneath which the under surface of the umbrella is hollowed out into four pits. The water needed for aerating the tissues is thus brought into closer proximity to the reproductive elements.

A curious modification of the ordinary form is found in the Rhizostomæ or Root-footed Jelly-fish. The corners of the square mouth at the tip of the manubrium are prolonged into long oral arms. The edges of each of these fold together so as to form tubes. The mouth then closes and suckers are developed along the inner surfaces of the tubes, through which alone nourishment reaches the stomach. Very large prey, such as fish, is often captured by these Jelly-fish, and held fast by the oral arms while the nourishment is sucked out of it.

In many of these Jelly-fish, reproduction takes place by means of eggs which develop in the reproductive chambers. These eggs usually develop into Medusæ, but, in the large family of the Discophoræ, to which our own Jelly-fish belong, the larva which results from the egg is a small spherical body covered with cilia, and never grows into a Medusa direct. It attaches itself to a rock or sea-weed (Fig. 9, 1), develops tentacles, and lengthens out. Constrictions then begin to appear round its body: the first just below the tentacles, and others successively further down. The edges formed by the constrictions become lobed, and the little creature, usually not more than an inch long, soon has the appearance of a series of saucers with lobed margins piled one upon another, but increasing in size upward (Fig. 9, S). After a time the whole structure breaks up, each detached disc developing later into a Medusa, often of gigantic size. This curious process of a sexual multiplication is known as strobilation, each series of developing young being a strobila, which is the Greek for fir-cone.

Fig 9.—STROBILATION.
1, Larva. S, Strobila.

There is only one permanently attached form among these Medusæ. This is the Lucernaria, a very beautiful flower-like animal often found adhering to sea-weed.

The Anthozoa.

The Anthozoa or flower-like animals, which form the next group of the Scyphozoa, include the stationary Sea-anemones and the Corals, the living bodies of both of which are built on essentially the same plan. The body of the Sea-anemone, however, always remains soft, while that of the Coral proper develops a hard skeleton. For this reason the Sea-anemones have been called the Fleshy Corals, while one large division of the Corals is called the Stony Corals, on account of their stony skeletons. The Sea-anemones always remain single, while the Corals comprise both single and colonial forms.

The Sea-anemones (*Actinia*).

The Sea-anemone is a familiar object to most of us, as it is very plentiful on our rocky shores. Small, coloured, jelly-like masses are often to be seen adhering to the rocks at low tide, which, as soon as they are again covered by water on the return of the tide, expand in beautiful and brilliantly-coloured flower-like animals. Looking down upon an Anemone, the central mouth can generally be made out fringed with its tentacles. If the body were cut across a little below the level of these, we should find that it consisted of two tubes, one within the other. The inner tube is the stomach tube or œsophagus, lined with the outer skin, which, as above described, characterises all the Scyphozoa. It is united to the wall of the outer tube, which is the body wall of the Anemone, by a number of fleshy partitions, which, running right through the length of the body, divide it up into many compartments. The uppermost portion of each of these compartments runs up into a tentacle. These fleshy "septa" are infoldings of the inner layer of the wall of the sac-like body. They do not all arise at the same time, nor do they all project equally far into the body cavity. Only some of them run out far enough to connect the two tubes in the upper part of the body.

This dividing up of the body into compartments is one of the chief distinctions between the Sea-anemone polyp and the Hydra polyp. In many other respects the Sea-anemone closely resembles the Hydra. It has the same power of retracting its tentacles and reducing its whole body to a bud-like shape. It captures food with its tentacles, and digests it within its body cavity, throwing out at the mouth all that it cannot assimilate. It has also a limited power of motion, not, however, like the Hydra, using its tentacles for this purpose, but gliding along on its base.

The Anemone is still richer than the Hydra in stinging cells. It has been calculated that some Anemones possess as many as 43,000,000 of stinging cells in one tentacle, and in the whole body something like 6,450,000,000. The stinging cells in Anemones measure from $\frac{1}{350}$ to $\frac{1}{5000}$ of an inch, the thread being often twenty times as long as the cell, and more richly supplied with barbs than are those of the Hydra. These cells, too, in the Anemone, are not merely found in the outer skin, but form in great quantities in the gastric cavity.

The outer skin of the Anemone is not always smooth and jelly-like; it is often covered with wart-like protuberances, which sometimes secrete a sticky fluid. Some Anemones have, further, a circle of "eyes" placed like a necklace round the body. Each of these has a lens and simple optic nerve, but the latter is not connected with any other nerves. From time to time, as the Anemone grows, it is able to cast off its outer skin, after having formed a new one beneath it; the old skin can often be seen in a wrinkled, dead-looking condition encircling the base of the animal.

Although none of the Sea-anemones found on our own shores attain the size of some of the tropical specimens, they are very beautiful and well worthy of study. A few only can here be briefly described.

The Plumose Anemone (Fig. 10) and the Daisy Anemone are two of the English varieties of the Sagartiadæ, so-called after a tribe in the army of Xerxes, known for their practice of entangling their enemies by means of noosed ropes. All these Anemones possess, attached to the septa of the gastric cavity, tangled masses of stinging threads resembling tangles of white cotton. These they can at will shoot out of the mouth, and, in some cases, through apertures at the sides of the body, for the purpose of paralysing their enemies. In large

Fig. 10.—THE PLUMOSE ANEMONE (*Actinoloba dianthus*).

Fig. 11.—EDWARDSIA.

specimens these "acontia" may, when extended straight through the mouth, measure as much as six inches.

In the Plumose Anemone, which is flesh-coloured, pale orange, or clear white, the pillar-like body is surmounted by a widely-expanded, frilled disc edged with numberless fringe-like tentacles. When these Anemones move along on the disc small pieces are sometimes torn off and left behind. These pieces can develop into young Anemones; at other times young forms bud out from the parent.

The Daisy Anemone (*Sagartia bellis*).

In the Daisy Anemone the upper part of the body wall is studded with suckers, to which fragments of shell or gravel may become attached. In colour this Anemone varies greatly, almost all shades, from a delicate flesh colour to a deep chocolate or olive green, being seen in various specimens. The small tentacles are arranged in many rows, and may amount to 500. The Daisy Anemone is exceedingly prolific. Its young, which arise from fertilised eggs, are usually matured within the body cavity and thrown out at the mouth as minute but perfect Anemones. From 160 to 300 of such young are said to have been produced by a Daisy Anemone in a single day.

The Cloak Anemone (*Adamsia palliata*).

The Cloak Anemone is noted for being constantly found in company with the Hermit Crab, on the lip of whose borrowed shell it attaches itself. Two wing-like lobes grow out from the base of the Anemone, gradually surround the lip of the shell, meeting finally on the other side and forming the so-called "cloak." The Anemone no doubt profits by its chosen position, as it can feed on particles of the prey caught and torn up by the claws of the crab, and is borne along by him in his wanderings, sometimes thus travelling a mile or two out to sea, and enjoying constant change of water. If the shell chosen by this strange couple is too small for the Anemone, or gets broken, it can fabricate a shelly substance which makes good all defects.

The Opelet (*Anthea cereus*).

The Opelet, so called because its disc is habitually expanded, has long, emerald-green tentacles, which can coil round its prey. Large sea-weeds are often found studded with these beautiful flower-like creatures, which, in some parts of France, are appreciated as an article of food.

The Beadlet (*Actinia mesembryanthemum*).

The Beadlet is distinguished by brilliantly coloured beadlike vesicles set near the edge of the disc. These may be stinging batteries, for these Anemones are not provided, like the Sagartiadæ, with internal stinging threads. The Beadlet, which is also called the Strawberry Anemone, is the commonest of the red Anemones found on English rocks. It is very hardy, and has been known to live as long as thirty years in captivity, during that time giving rise to three hundred and thirty-four young Anemones.

The Dahlia Wartlet (*Tealia crassicornis*).

The Dahlia Wartlet has the surface of its body covered with small grey warts to which fragments of stone or shell adhere. This Anemone is scarcely less abundant on our shores than the Beadlet, and is very handsome, one variety having white tentacles, vividly contrasting with the crimson disc. It is particularly voracious, devouring shore crabs, limpets, and other molluscs, and even sea-urchins and fish.

The Cave-dwelling Anemone (*Sagartia troglodytes*).

The Cave-dwelling Anemone, though plentiful on our coasts, is very difficult to find, its colouring being wonderfully adapted to the sand or mud of the pools it inhabits. The black, white, and grey of the disc are arranged in delicate patterns, which have been compared with those on the feathers of a snipe. The purpose of concealment is further aided by fragments of shells, etc., attached to the suckers on its column.

The Crimson Pufflet (*Edwardsia carnea*).

In the Edwardsias (Fig. 11, p. 702) the body is much elongated, and the lower part is usually buried in the sand or mud. One of the best-known of these Anemones is the Crimson Pufflet, which often inhabits the old burrows of Molluscs in limestone rocks on the coast of South Devon, the beautiful crimson tentacles protruding from the mouth of the burrow.

Tropical Anemones.

On tropical shores there are many brilliantly beautiful varieties of Sea-anemones, some of which attain a very large size. *Actinia paumotensis*, found on the islands of the Paumotu Archipelago, is described by Dana as one of the most beautiful of all Anemones. It has a disc often 14 in. in diameter, "densely covered with large tentacles tipped with bright lake, the margin undulating so as to form numerous lobes, each of which has the appearance of being a separate Actinian, and the whole resembling a beautiful bouquet." Other tropical forms have been said to resemble brilliantly-coloured carpets covering the rocks. Some of these large, tropical Anemones are used as homes by other animals, which live within the stomach cavity. A fish some 3 in. long and very vividly coloured in striking contrast to its host, and a brightly-coloured prawn are almost always found thus associated with certain large Anemones on the great Barrier Reef of Australia, as recently described by Mr. Saville Kent. These curious lodgers emerge from their refuge from time to time to swim about in the sea, but dart back again into the mouths of their hosts when pursued by enemies. It has been supposed that this association may be of advantage to the Anemone as well as to the fish and the prawn. Animals are attracted to pursue these brilliant decoys and fall victims to the voracious Anemone, while the fish and the prawn live on the crumbs which fall from the feasts of their magnificent friends and protectors.

In the Corals proper, the polyps are essentially like the Sea-anemones, but are able to form a hard, protective framework for their bodies.

The Corals.

The soft, fleshy body first gives off upon the rock below it a quantity of chalky matter from its base, and thus forms a kind of pedestal for itself, which is called the foot-plate. From this, six hard ridges rise up into the body, given off by the fleshy parts of the base; six, at least, is the number first produced, other ridges arising later in the intervals between these. From the outer edges of these plates, phlanges may grow out till they meet one another, and make a hard ring supporting the ridges. Sometimes, too, a hard column arises from the centre of the foot-plate; this is called the columella. All over these hard ridges, rings, and columns, the basal skin of the soft body of the animal fits closely. This arrangement is doubtless protective, for, on being disturbed, the whole animal, which was perhaps seen a moment before as a beautiful Anemone, with expanded tentacles, collapses between the projections, and nothing is seen over them but a thin shiny skin.

Fig. 12 shows us the skeletons of two solitary corals which have thus built up their pedestals to a considerable height. The greater number of coral polyps, however, do not remain solitary, but are continually producing daughter polyps, whole families together forming great colonies, each member of which as it grows adds its own pedestal to the mass. All the stony corals seen in our museums are but the complicated skeletons, *i.e.*, the combined pedestals of polyps whose soft, jelly-like bodies have perished. In the living state these hard masses were covered by the flesh of the animal colony, as a thin layer of slimy matter. The individual Sea-anemone-like animals lurked in the cavities, rising and expanding their tentacles when in search of food, but drawing them back under shelter whenever threatened or disturbed.

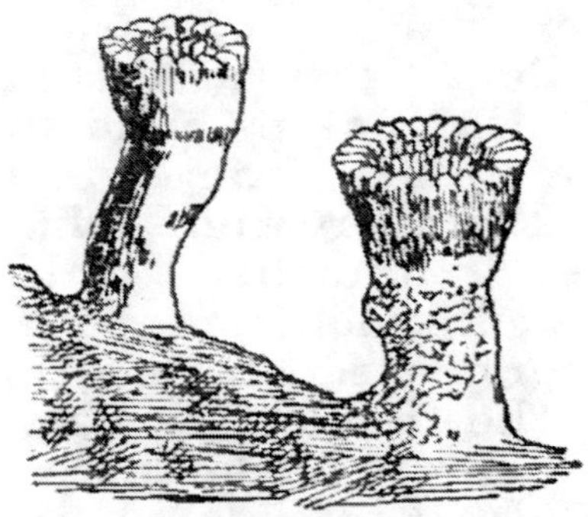

Fig. 12.—The Cup Coral (*Caryophyllia*).

Corals are usually grouped according to the number of divisions, compartments, or "rays" in their bodies, each compartment, as in the Anemone, running up into the hollow axis of a tentacle.

Six-rayed polyps have six tentacles or (approximately) some multiple of six, eighteen, twenty-four, forty-eight, and even more.

Eight-rayed polyps have eight tentacles or some multiple of eight.

The Six-rayed Corals (*Hexactinia*).

Most of the six-rayed polyps live in great colonies, their skeletons producing the chalky masses with which we are much more familiar than we are with the living animals. One important family of the six-rayed polyps, however, the Fungidæ, or Mushroom corals, consists of single individuals. The median slit seen along the surface of the Mushroom coral (Fig. 13) indicates the position of the mouth, while the many jagged ridges that radiate out from it and give the whole the appearance of an inverted mushroom are the hard, stony ridges and partitions over which the body of the polyp fits. When the polyp is expanded, all this skeleton is hidden from view by the beautifully coloured soft body, the whole surface being one mass of tentacles, often of a vivid green, tipped with white. With these tentacles, each richly provided with stinging cells, the huge polyp paralyses and masters its prey, using them also as weapons of defence against enemies. When disturbed, the whole animal sinks down among the toothed ridges, which project through without actually piercing the thin skin, and may well defy any enemy to touch him. These Mushroom corals, when young, are cup-like or cylindrical like other corals, and provided with a stalk ; as they grow, the sides of the cup get flatter and flatter until the whole becomes quite flat, or the bottom of the original cup rises even higher

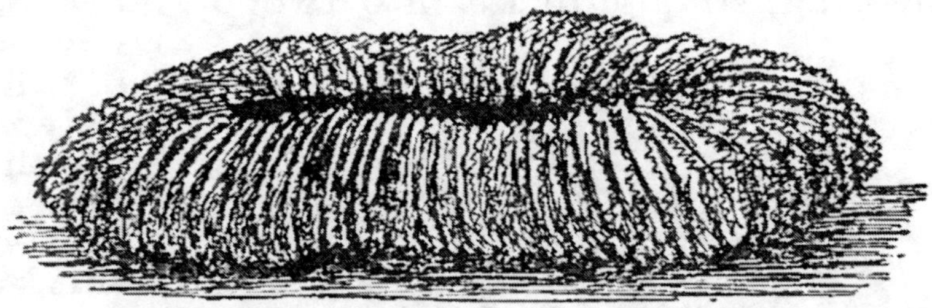

Fig. 13.—A Mushroom Coral (*Fungia*).

than the rim. The young, as a rule, bud from the under surface of the parent, then drop off, and lie loosely on the rock or sea-bottom. A branched form is known in which young Fungia drop from the tips of branches.

This branching condition, which is exceptional in the Mushroom corals, is the rule in nearly all other corals. By division or budding of various kinds an endless variety of colonies are produced. Sometimes, as among the Zoophytes, the polyps build up branched frameworks, from which at intervals they protrude, like flowers from a branched stalk. The form of such colonies depends upon the intervals separating the polyps, and the angle at which they branch out from the parent individuals. In Fig. 14, in the coral on the left, the polyps are far apart, in that on the right the budding is frequent and the polyps crowded. In this latter case the skeleton is penetrated in all directions with canals which, for a certain distance below the surface, carry food juice from polyp to polyp. The Madrepores, of which the coral to the right of Fig. 14 is an example, are amongst the most important builders of coral reefs and islands. Other coral colonies form waving plates, often beautifully frilled at the edges, the polyps usually projecting from the upper surface of the plate. The variety in form and structure of coral colonies is, indeed, almost endless.

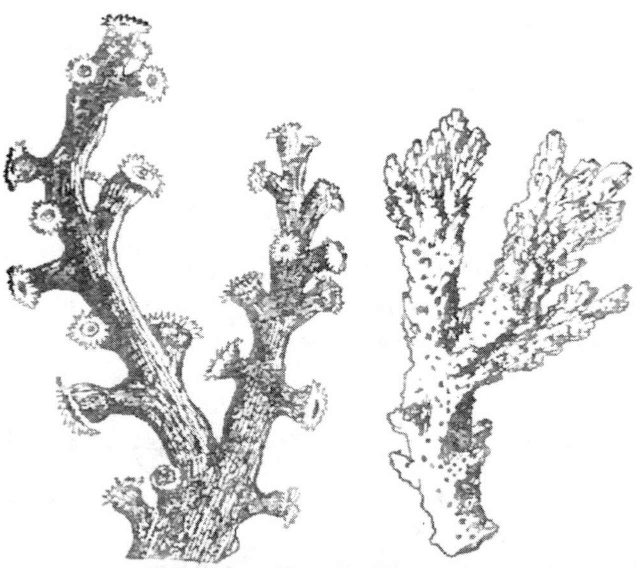

Fig. 14.—Coral Colonies.
Dendrosoma. Madrepora.

Entirely different coral forms are produced by polyps which, instead of budding, simply divide into two or more new individuals. In Fig. 15 we have a hemispherical mass, the surface of which is thickly set with star-like polyps; some are seen expanded, with the slit-like mouths in the centre of the disc, others are in a retracted condition. The star-like shape of the polyps in this kind of coral has obtained for it the name of star-coral. On such a mass a larger polyp is often found which has two mouths instead of one; a row of tentacles forms between the two mouths, this row then breaks up into two, and two polyps are seen on the surface where only one was before. In this case we have complete division of the individuals, for, while these outer changes have been going on, corresponding changes have been taking place below the surface, resulting in a more or less complete division of the original animal into two. In these colonies, the whole hemispherical mass, which may grow to an enormous size, is built up layer after layer, the

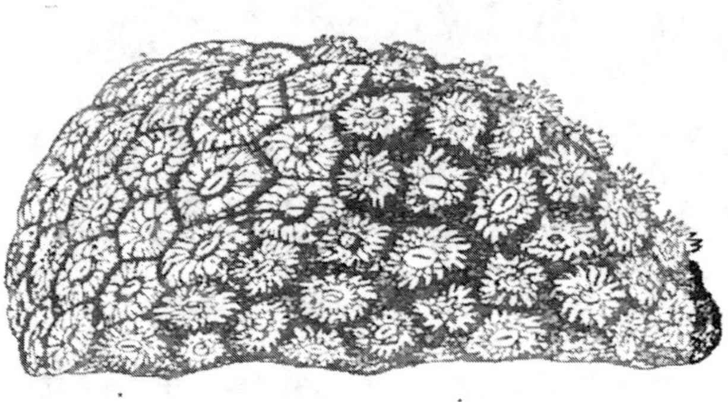

Fig. 15.—The Star Coral (*Astræa*).

living flesh of the colony never forming more than a thin layer over the surface.

The skeleton of the Brain Coral (Fig. 16), which is distinguished by the systems of ridges and furrows winding over its surface, is built up in successive layers like that of the Star Coral, but the polyps multiply in a different manner. Each long furrow denotes the former home of a large polyp, which formed a whole row of new mouths without dividing up into new individuals. Here, therefore, we have incomplete division of the individuals. This furrow was fringed by tentacles which rose above the ridges. After a certain stage of elongation of the polyp was reached, the body completed itself, as it were, with a new row of tentacles between two of the mouths, and so a new individual was started.

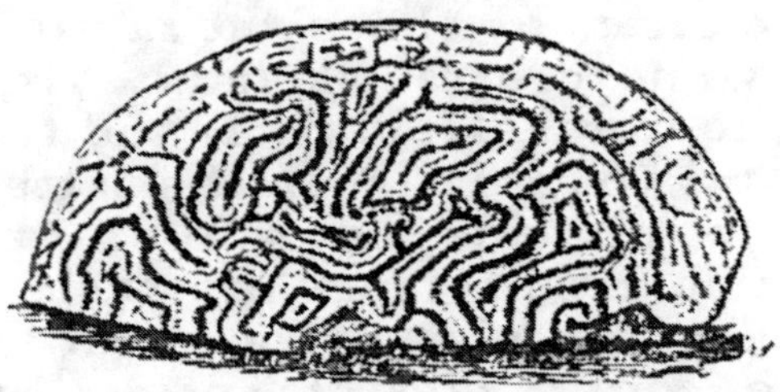

Fig. 16.—BRAIN CORAL (*Maeandrina*).

Development of Corals.

While budding and division play such a large part in increasing the number of polyps forming a colony, each new colony itself is started by another method of reproduction. Eggs, which form on the internal partitions or septa of the polyp, give rise to minute larvæ that swim about, first within the body of the parent, and then in the open water, sometimes for as long as two months. Then they attach themselves by one end to a rock or some other surface, and begin to assume the polyp shape, tentacles and mouth developing at the free end of the body, and the hard parts form as in the parent animal. Such polyps, by budding and division, found new colonies.

The Black Corals (*Antipatharia*).

All the skeletons we have as yet mentioned are more or less massive or stony, as is usually the case with the skeletons of the six-rayed polyps (hence the name stony corals), but some colonies of this division secrete horny instead of chalky skeletons. The skeletons of the Black Corals or Antipatharia form branching tufts or trees of horny substance. The surface of the branches appears smooth and polished, and, in some of the larger species, resembles ebony. These corals grow to a great height as single trunks, or as tree-like growths; sometimes the separate branches fuse to produce networks. In such coral skeletons there are none of the traces of the former presence of polyps such as we see on the surface of the stony corals, because the branched stem is merely the central axis of the living colony that produced it and once covered it with a soft crust. Out of this crust the individual polyps protruded at intervals. The hard, rod-like skeletons of the Black Corals are used by natives in various parts of the world for dagger handles, necklaces, or mouthpieces for pipes, on account of their toughness and susceptibility to polish.

The Eight-rayed Corals (*Octactinia*).

The eight-rayed polyps differ in several ways, too technical for us to enter upon, from the six-rayed polyps. The eight tentacles of the individual polyps are toothed or feathered, and form a more imposing crown than do the simple cylindrical tentacles of the six-rayed order. The hard parts produced by them, in the majority of cases, take the form of a central axis like that found in the Black Corals, but here of chalk or horn, or of chalk and horn alternately. The fleshy crust which covers the axis, and out of which the individual polyps protrude, is supported by chalky spicules or plates scattered through its substance (see Fig. 18). There are, however, massive forms produced by the eight-rayed polyps which have no central skeletal axis, such as the Blue Coral (Heliopora) and the Organ Pipe Coral (Fig. 17). In the latter, the polyps grow up side by side in separate tubes which result from the fusion of coloured chalky spicules. Those tubes, from which the coral takes its name, are, at regular intervals, joined together by platforms. It is from these platforms, where the interval between two tubes is considerable, that new buds arise to grow up alongside of the older polyps. Both the skeleton and the soft parts of this colony are of a deep crimson, the tentacles of the polyps being of an emerald green.

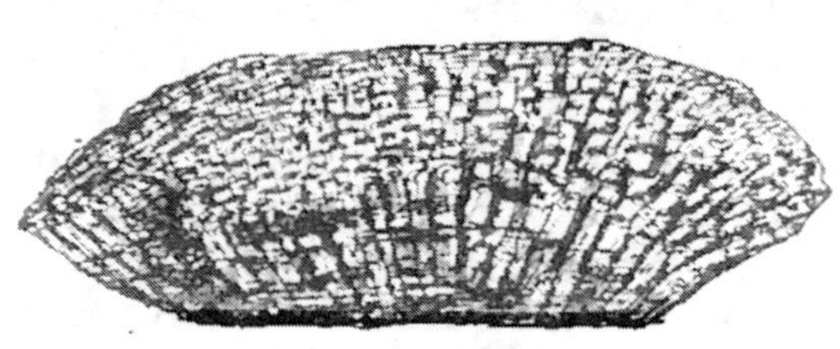

Fig. 17.—ORGAN-PIPE CORAL (*Tubipora musica*).

The coral we probably know best in its skeletal condition, the Red Coral of commerce, is also the product of one of the eight-rayed corals. Some idea of the structure of this coral in its living condition may be gained from the diagramatic section of it given in Fig. 18. The central hard (chalky) axis answers to the smooth red branch with which we are familiar. This is covered by a layer of soft tubes, some of which, in the illustration, are thrown back in order to reveal the hard axis, the grooved markings on which show where the canals ran. These tubes convey the nourishing fluid through the whole colony, receiving it from the polyps and giving it off through branches connecting them with the soft crust that lies over them. Throughout this crust star or plate-like spicules are scattered, which give it some degree of firmness. Three polyps are seen in the illustration: the one to the right has its fringed tentacles extended in search of prey, the middle one is in a retracted condition, and that to the left is cut across to show the partitions in the body. The soft bodies of these polyps are pure white, and the effect of their feathered tentacles, projecting here and there from the bright red crust, is very beautiful.

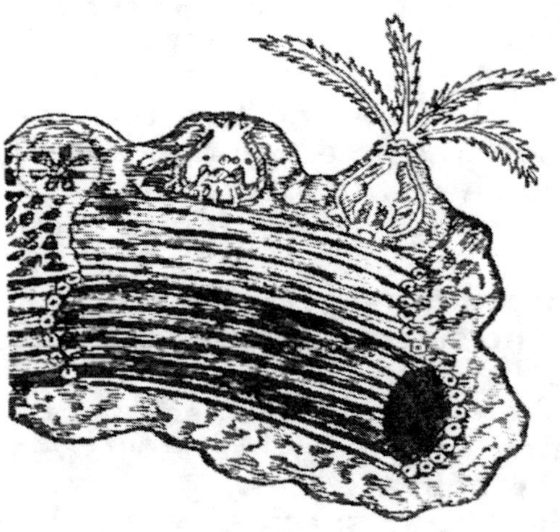

Fig. 18.—THE RED CORAL OF COMMERCE (*Corallum rubrum*).

These corals form tree-like growths often several feet high, and are very plentiful in the Mediterranean. Coral fisheries on an extensive scale are carried on, chiefly by Italians, off the coasts of Italy, Algiers, and Spain, the corals being dredged for with nets. The soft living crust is easily removed, and the axis, which takes a high polish, is used for ornamental purposes.

Though the two corals last described, the Organ Pipe Coral and the Red Coral of commerce, as well as a few other of the Octactinia, are rigid growths, in the majority of the eight-rayed corals, which have horny axial skeletons, the branches are not hard and stiff like those of the stony corals, but can wave about with the motion of the water, the brightly-coloured living jelly that covers them often glistening with metallic lustre. Sometimes the delicate branches unite to form networks, as in the Sea-fans (Gorgonia). In other cases fine branches stand out from a central shaft, and the whole colony resembles a feather with its barbs. Fig. 19 represents one of the Sea-pens belonging to this group. The lower end of the colony does not carry any polyps, but is buried in sand or mud. This is a peculiarly beautiful object when alive, especially in the dark, as waves of phosphorescent light sweep over the surface of the colony and make it glow with indescribable beauty. It is these graceful and vividly-coloured corals which form the chief adornments of the coral reefs, the solid rocks of which are derived from the harder and more massive skeletons produced by the six-rayed corals.

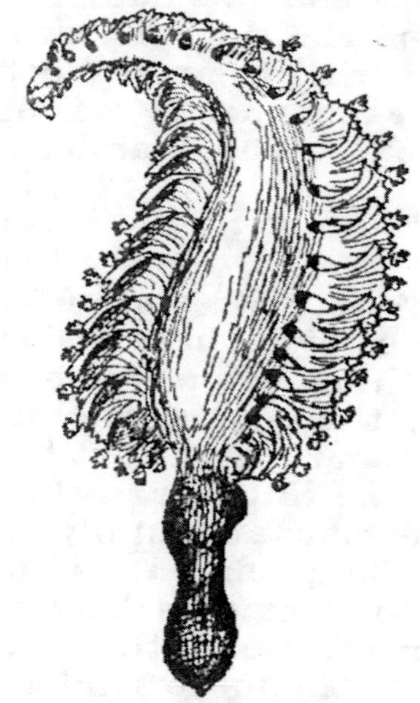

Fig. 19.—SEA-PEN (*Pennatula*).

The marvellous beauty of the banks covered with living corals in the Red Sea and elsewhere, where shallow water enables the traveller to feast his eyes on these exquisite growths, has often roused the enthusiasm of naturalists. They have been compared with fields or gardens of the choicest and most brilliantly-coloured flowers growing in the richest profusion, all the intervals between the larger growths being filled up with bright moss, which is itself composed of minute corals. Among the elegant flowering shrubs and bushes of this garden brilliantly-coloured fishes, glittering with metallic lustre, dart to and fro; Star-fishes, Sea-urchins, and Snails climb about among the branches, while transparent Crustaceans and Jelly-fish swarm in the crystal water around.

Coral Reefs and Islands.

Before quitting the Corals we must briefly recall the important part they have played in Nature in helping to build up the continents which we now inhabit, a process which can still be seen going on in the great coral reefs and islands of tropical seas. With the exception of a few unimportant forms, Corals are now restricted to regions within 30° on either side of the equator, the more important reef-building forms being able to carry on their life activities only in water above a certain temperature. Even within these latitudes corals are not found everywhere. They flourish best in the Indian Ocean, the Pacific Ocean, and the Carribean Sea, where the reef-builders are at work over thousands of square miles.

The Fringing Reef.

A coral reef is a bank of coral rock built upon the shallow sea-bottom immediately surrounding the shores of tropical lands. Where the land is edged by a reef, as in the island of Mauritius, the ordinary beach passes into a flat irregular bank terminating at a varying distance from land, in a ridge over which the sea continually breaks. This bank, which is called a "fringing reef," is almost entirely made up of the skeletons of colonies of corals, with which, however, are mixed the calcareous remains of myriads of molluscs, sea-urchins and crabs, and the tubes of the tube-dwelling worms which haunt every cranny and crevice of coral growths. At low tide broad expanses of the coral rock are to be seen just above water level, strongly contrasting with the usually steep shore of the land to which the reef forms a margin. At high tide, except when a retreating wave reveals a small portion of rock, the only sign of the presence of the reef is the line of breakers along its outer edge, where the shallow water suddenly passes into deep water, the outer side of the reef sloping steeply down to a great depth. Between this outer edge and the land a shallow basin or channel arises, and here the water is usually very clear, and brilliantly-coloured corals are seen covering the rocky bottom.

The Barrier Reef.

From such a "fringing reef" there arises, in process of time, a "barrier reef." The channel between the edge of the reef and the shore tends to widen, the corals along its bottom not flourishing so well as those along the outer edge. The water, too, in which they are condemned to live receives its chief additions from rivers or streams of fresh water washing down mud and sand from the land. The corals here, indeed, cannot grow fast enough to repair the continual disintegration which is going on. The coral colonies at the edge of the reef, on the contrary, grow luxuriantly, continually raising the level of the reef and carrying it out to sea. It seems at first sight strange that corals exposed to the full fury of the breakers should thus flourish; this is no doubt due to the constant supply of food in the shape of minute organisms which swarm in the open sea. Even the storms which often break up the coral colonies into fragments help on the work they are doing, as the broken pieces are thrown up on the reef and fill up all interstices left in it, rendering it thus only the more solid and complete. Even the fragments broken off can give rise to new colonies if only the living polyps retracted within their stony cells have escaped undamaged, and provided also that their new position is favourable in the matter of food.

Barrier reefs are found rising up like ramparts against the waves even as much as one hundred miles from the shores where they must have originated. They thus cover vast areas of the sea-bottom. The Great Barrier Reef off the N.E. coast of Australia is 1100 miles long, the distance from land of its outer edge being usually from 20 to 30 miles, and in places over 100 miles. Saville Kent computes the total area of this reef, built up by coral polyps, as at least 80,000 square geographical miles! Over the whole of this enormous area of coral rock, the water remains comparatively shallow, while the outer edge dips down almost suddenly into as much as 1000 fathoms. The whole surface of such a reef is covered, wherever the circumstances are favourable, with living masses of coral, while, in the large areas where the corals cannot flourish, the reef is a vast conglomerate, the sand and fine mud, swept about by the tides, filling up the interstices between the skeletons of original coral colonies.

Coral Islands and Atolls.

When reefs form round small islands, the edge of the reef rising a little above the water, a coral island is produced, enclosing a lake or lagoon out of which rises the original island. Such circular reefs are also found surrounding a clear lake of still water without any island in the middle; these latter are known as "atolls." These wonderful products of the coral polyps are a very marked feature of tropical seas, to the beauty of which they greatly add. The reef encircling an island or smooth lagoon becomes raised above the level of the surrounding sea by the *debris* washed up upon it; as a rule, however, it does not rise more than a few feet above the surface, the sea often dashing, at the narrower parts, over into the enclosed lagoon. In other cases, it may rise 10 or 12 ft. above high tide and may be covered with the rich verdure of the tropics, the wind and birds having supplied it with seeds as soon as it rose above the waves. The enclosed lake is often fringed with graceful palms, and the whole island, the product of minute coral polyps, becomes a fruitful habitation for man.

These different kinds of reef formations were all traced back by Darwin to fringing reefs, and accounted for by the subsidence of the land round which these reefs originally formed. A fringing reef would gradually become a barrier reef as the land on which it stood sank, and in the same way, a reef surrounding an island would be transformed, after subsidence of the island, into a circle of coral rock enclosing a lake. As long as the highest points of the land remained above water, the lagoon would contain islands, but, when the original land had entirely sunk beneath the waves, an atoll would result. In the case of a very large island, surrounded, as New Caledonia now is, by a barrier reef, the gradual sinking of the land would lead to the formation of a complicated archipelago of islands, like that of the Maladives to the west of Ceylon, where 12,000 small islands appear to represent a huge reef which must once have surrounded a vast island long since sunk beneath the waves. Darwin's theory of subsidence has, however, recently been disputed, and cannot be considered as fully established.

The Ctenophora.

The Ctenophora, which constitute the last division of the Cnidaria, are beautiful, almost transparent, marine creatures, either more or less round in form, or else flattened out in the shape of ribbons. Their relationship to the other groups is still a matter of uncertainty; they are often placed near the Hydrozoa. The animals belonging to this group move through the water, mouth downward, by means of swimming plates or "combs," from which they take the name of Ctenophora or Comb-bearers. Eight rows of these swimming plates run from pole to pole of the body, each plate consisting of a row of fine hairs or cilia connected at their bases, but capable of independent movement. The animal can, at will, move the plates either separately or collectively, and thus bring about slow locomotion in the direction opposite to the mouth, and, by the help of tentacles and other appendages, twisting and swaying movements can also take place. In the ribbon-like forms muscular contractions bring about serpentine movements.

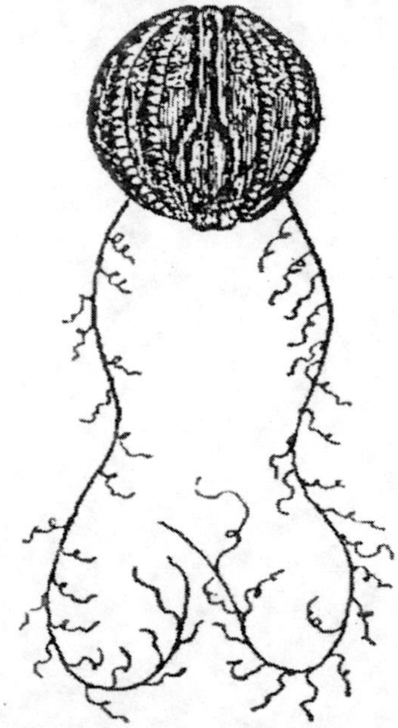

Fig. 20.—THE SEA GOOSEBERRY (*Cydippe*).

The mouth leads into a stomach, which, again, opens into a funnel that sends off eight vessels, which run, in meridians, down the sides of the body, just below the eight rows of swimming plates. The animal is usually provided with tentacles and with long "capturing filaments" (Fig. 20). These are not armed, like the tentacles of other Cnidaria, with stinging cells, but with small knobs on coiled stalks, which are called "adhesive" cells. These are not poisonous, but simply sticky, and when shot out at prey entangle it and prevent its escape. They differ from stinging cells also in the fact that they are not finally discharged from the body, but, when the prey is mastered, can be drawn in again, and are capable of functioning any number of times.

Another peculiarity of the Ctenophora is a sensory organ always found at the end of the body opposite to the mouth. This somewhat resembles a small weight borne on springs, and, as it is sensitive to the slightest oscillations of the body, seems to enable the animal to regulate its position in the water.

The Sea Gooseberry, depicted in Fig. 20, is a good example of a round Ctenophoran, the swimming plates and long capturing filaments being well developed. The best known of the ribbon-like forms is Venus's Girdle (*Cestus veneris*). The mouth lies at the centre of the long, transparent ribbon, which has no swimming plates, but is fringed with cilia. When alarmed, this Ctenophoran can roll up either or both ends of its body spirally, but, when undisturbed, passes through the water with a graceful, undulating motion. Its iridescent colouring makes it a peculiarly lovely object. Other Ctenophorans are barrel-shaped, or resemble Phrygian caps, and many are beautifully phosphorescent at night.

Most of the Ctenophora feed on small Crustaceans. Some, *e.g.*, the Beroidæ, are very voracious, devouring creatures of their own kind, and often larger than themselves, as the mouth is very wide, and the body distensible. They have even been known to swallow and digest fish.

All the Ctenophora multiply by means of fertilised eggs and ciliated larvæ, which only very gradually attain the adult form.

SUB-KINGDOM IX.—THE PROTOZOA.

ANIMALCULÆ.

By Henry M. Bernard, M.A., F.L.S., Etc., and Matilda Bernard.

The Protozoa, or first animals, are distinguished from all others by the fact that they are unicellular organisms, *i.e.*, the body of a Protozoan consists of a single cell, whereas the bodies of all other animals, or Metazoa, are built up of many cells. The one-celled Protozoan is capable of all the vital functions of feeding, moving, breathing, and reproducing itself. In the Metazoa, the greater number of the living cells of which the body is composed are stationary in relation to one another, and the vital activities of the whole have to be considered apart from the lives of the individual cells building it up. We accordingly find these cells arranged into organs and tissues, each specialised for some function necessary to the life of the whole.

The Protozoan, then, is a free-living cell essentially like the cells which, organised into great masses, build up the bodies of all other animals.

All the Protozoa are of microscopic size, and are therefore removed from ordinary observation. This is the more to be regretted since they compare favourably with other classes of animals in variety and beauty of form, and probably surpass all others in actual number of existing individuals. At least five thousand species of these minute creatures are known, swarming, at the present day, in salt and fresh water or in other animal organisms. There are, in addition, several thousand fossil forms, the latter representing, of course, only those Protozoa of past ages which were provided with a shell or skeleton capable of preservation. Countless millions of such shells form the chief constituent of vast areas of limestone rocks all over the world's surface, and, in some more or less transformed condition, enter into the composition of a large part of the earth's crust. Vast numbers, again, are daily being deposited on the sea-bottom to form the rocks of future ages. Nine-tenths of the ooze over the greater part of the North Atlantic consists of the shells of Protozoans, and one ounce of sand from the Naples shore yields no fewer than one and a half million of their shells or parts of such shells.

The Monera.

The very lowest of the Protozoa, that is, the very simplest of all animals, called the Monera, are mere microscopic particles of living jelly or protoplasm, in which, so far, no definite structure has been discovered. In all other Protozoa, however, some differentiation of the protoplasmic body has been found. Among many minute granular particles scattered about in the jelly, there is always one body (sometimes more than one) somewhat larger than the granules, and different in character from the rest. This usually rounded body is known as the nucleus.

The Rhizopoda.

The lowest of the nucleated Protozoa are the Rhizopoda or root-footed animals, a name given to them on account of their manner of moving by means of root-like prolongations of the body. The simplest of these Rhizopoda is the Amœba, which has been called the Proteus animalcule because of its constant changes of shape. These animalcules are to be found in most rain-water puddles and in ponds, and when seen under the microscope might escape observation as mere specks of clear jelly-like matter, yet the careful observer will find that each such speck is capable of moving about and feeding, and, indeed, can be proved to be living, carrying on all those functions which, taken together, we designate as life.

The Amœba.

If a Proteus animalcule is magnified about three or four hundred times the following important points can be noted :—(1) It is naked, *i.e.*, it has no cuticle or shell. (2) The surface layer of protoplasm, though not forming a skin, is clear and glassy, and completely envelops the more fluid and granular inner portion of the Amœba. (3) Among these granules can be seen the nucleus and foreign particles, taken in as food, the remains of such particles, and other bodies not understood. (4) Lastly, if the Amœba is carefully watched, a round space, like a bubble, appears, increases in size, and then instantaneously disappears, forming again at another spot. This is the contractile vesicle which is thought to collect the waste products of the body and to eject them when it contracts.

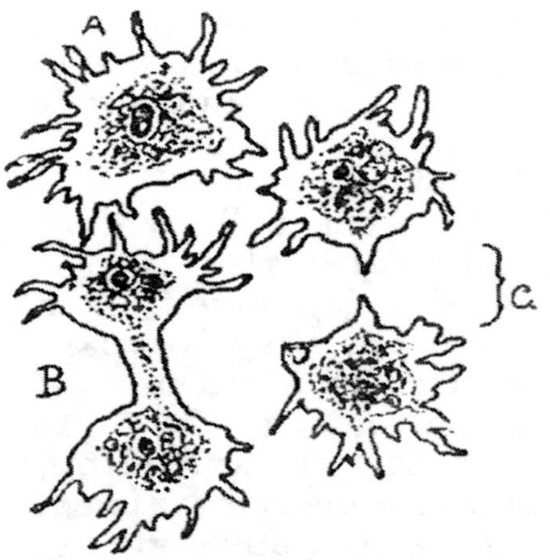

Fig. 1.—A, B, C.
A PROTEUS ANIMALCULE (*Amœba*) in three stages.

The Amœba is seen to change its shape slowly by protruding at certain points finger-like or knob-like processes which are called pseudopodia or make-believe feet. Its exceedingly slow movements over the surface of plants or other submerged objects, or through the water, are all made by the extension of pseudopodia in one direction and corresponding withdrawal on another side, the whole body seeming to flow on along its pseudopodia. If, in its course, it meets with minute plant cells suitable for food, it admits them into its body at any point, retains them within it for a time, while it evidently assimilates some nourishment from them, and then flows on, the indigestible remains of its meal being left behind. The manner in which the Amœba breathes cannot be seen, but the fact that it breathes is indisputable, for if the water in which Amœbæ are kept is deprived of its free oxygen, the assimilation of which is what is meant by breathing, the animals become rigid and lifeless.

When, in consequence of the nourishment derived from the assimilated particles, an Amœba has grown to a certain limit, its shape becomes that of a dumb-bell (Fig. 1, B), the nucleus divides into two, each end of the dumb-bell containing one of the new nuclei, the connecting part narrows more and more, and finally the two ends separate completely (Fig. 1, C), and each half (or "daughter") repeats the simple life activities of the original whole (or "mother"). These terms mother and daughter at first sight appear hardly justifiable, yet we now know that all reproductive processes, even in the highest animals, are but specialisations of this simple dividing up of living cells.

The Amœba has been described somewhat fully, as a simple type of the Root-footed animals. Many different kinds of Amœbæ have been distinguished, varying in the characters of the pseudopodia and in other respects, but they all agree in being single cells of granulated protoplasm, containing a nucleus, and moving and feeding by means of pseudopodia.

In the group next above the Amœbæ, the Foraminifera, the protoplasm of the central body is no longer naked. The animal assimilates from the water in which it lives the necessary material for surrounding itself with a chitinous or shelly covering, or perhaps it utilises its own waste products for this purpose.

The Foraminifera.

This shell, in some of the Foraminifera, is merely a delicate case within which the soft body lives. In others, grains of sand, or sponge spicules are obtained from without and embodied in the shell.

For the purposes of movement, the animal sends out pseudopodia into the surrounding water through the openings in its shell. The Foraminifera have been divided into the Perforate and the Imperforate, according as the pseudopodia protrude through small openings scattered all over the surface of the shell, or through only one or two large openings. The shells depicted in Fig. 3 are those of Perforate Foraminifera, while in Fig. 2 we have an Imperforate form, the egg-shaped Gromia. In this latter, the protoplasm streams out at one aperture, breaks up into numberless fine threads which, here and there, run together, forming thicker patches. The whole surface of the simple shell has also become covered with a thin layer of protoplasm. If any small plant cell or other particle suitable for food touches one of the pseudopodia, other threads flow together round it, and it is slowly drawn in towards the aperture and passed into the body. Such particles of food can often be seen, as in the illustration, within the body of a Gromia.

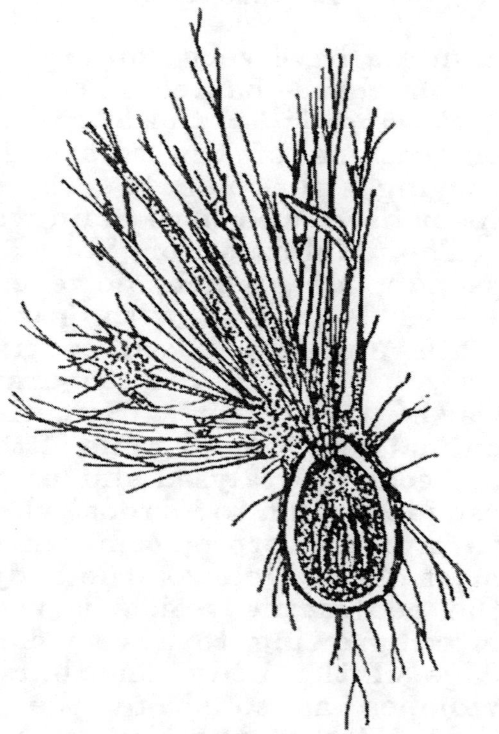

Fig. 2.—GROMIA OVIFORMIS.

The shells of the Perforate Foraminifera are very varied in form. Sometimes they consist of many chambers, for the protoplasm, as it grows, has not room in the one little chamber with which it at first surrounds itself, and adds another from time to time, each chamber, however, remaining in communication with the last by means of one or more minute apertures through which a thread or threads of protoplasm pass. The inner protoplasm can also stream out in all directions through the perforations in the sides of the shell.

A few of the many forms assumed by the shells of such Foraminifera are given in Fig. 3. Some are more or less flattened, like coins, and have therefore been called Nummilites (Fig. 3, A); others are flask-shaped (C); others again closely resemble the shells of the Ammonite or the Nautilus (B); in fact, such forms were long considered to be minute Molluscs. The shells of the Globigerina, or globe-bearers (D), help largely to build up Chalk. They are said to constitute almost one-third of the ooze covering vast areas of the sea-bottom in the North Atlantic. Milliolite shells (E) are the chief constituent of the stone of which the houses of Paris are built. Nummilitic limestones cover an enormous area of Central and Southern Europe, North Africa, West Asia, and India. All limestones indeed abound in the shells of Foraminifera, some species being found in the Coal formations also.

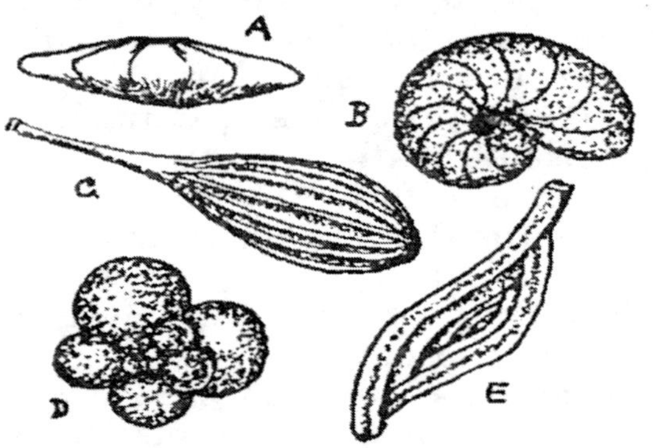

Fig. 3.—SHELLS OF FORAMINIFERA.
A, Nummulites.
B, Nonionina.
C, Lagena.
D, Globigerina.
E, Milliola.

The Foraminifera nearly all live in the sea, creeping along its bottom; but some float about. Young ones are produced by the breaking up of the protoplasm into small portions, which secrete their characteristic shelly covering before leaving the body of the parent. Some young Foraminifera have very simple single shells, but others are provided from the first with a three-chambered shell.

Passing from those Protozoa whose protoplasmic processes are mere protrusions of the soft body showing no definite shape, but constantly varying, we come to others in which these body processes are highly specialised, and here again we have naked and shelled forms.

The Heliozoa.

The Heliozoa, or Sun animalcules (Fig. 4), have straight, ray-like pseudopodia, which, however, are not rigid, but when brought in contact with particles of food, can contract or bend so as to draw them in towards the body. Sometimes a minute animalcule, touching one of the rays, appears to become paralysed and to glide down the pseudopodium to its root, where a protruding part of the protoplasm can draw in it. In most of the Heliozoa the body is naked, and the contractile vesicle is very conspicuous, often growing to a very large size at the edge of the body, and bursting with such violence as to shake the whole animal. Some idea of the size of these animalcules can be gained from the fact that four hundred of them set closely side by side would measure an inch. In spite of the formidable rays by which the Sun animalcule is surrounded, it often falls a prey to a simple Amœba, which either envelops the whole animalcule or tears out portions of its soft body.

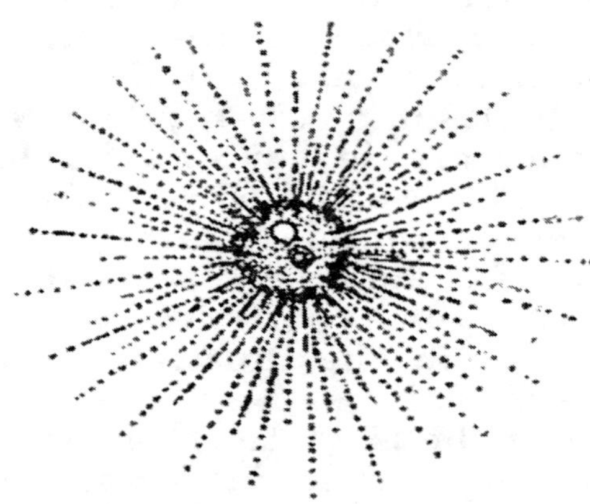

Fig. 4.—THE SUN ANIMALCULE (*Actinophrys sol*).

The Radiolaria.

Next in order above the Sun animalcules, and far more complicated in appearance on account of their elaborate skeletons, are the Ray animalcules or Radiolaria. In these the soft body is not, as in the Foraminifera, enclosed in an almost continuous outer shell, but the hard matter, usually of a flinty nature, derived from the surrounding water, takes the form of rods or spikes which pierce the soft body, and also often form some kind of protective framework around it. Another peculiarity of the Radiolaria is that the soft body is divided into an inner portion, containing the nucleus and enclosed in a gelatinous membrane called a capsule, and an outer portion which surrounds the other and is itself enclosed in a gelatinous envelope. The inner capsule is perforated so that the inner protoplasm can pass outward, while the outer protoplasm sends out radiating threads in all directions through the numberless fine perforations of its envelope.

A vast number of exquisite forms assumed by the skeletons of the Radiolaria were found in the dredgings made by the *Challenger* expedition. Some of these skeletons consist only of spines radiating from the centre which, however, are often beautifully sculptured or branched; in one form the number of the spines is always twenty, and these are arranged with absolute regularity at definite angles to each other. The whole animal often has the appearance of a spiny ball (Fig. 5, A). In other cases the hard rods, which

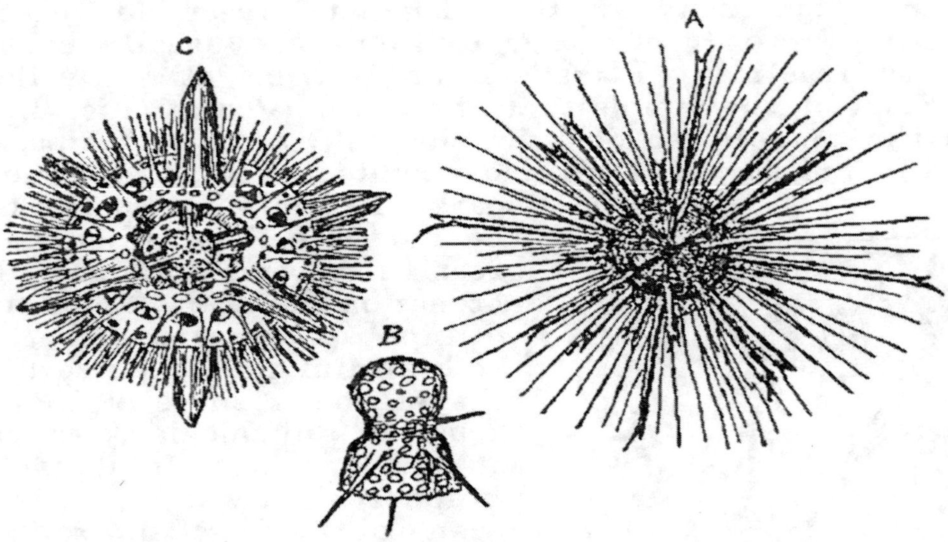

Fig. 5.—SKELETONS OF RADIOLARIA.
C, Actinomma. *B*, Lithomelissa. *A*, Acanthometra.

form the constituent elements of all these skeletons, may be arranged so as to form a framework or network outside the protoplasm with hexagonal apertures. Such a framework may be more or less round for a time, and then a second framework may be added below the first with a wide opening at its base—the whole having the appearance of a helmet ornamented at definite points with a few of the characteristic spines that pierce the inner protoplasm (B). Sometimes a whole series of fenestrated balls is produced, one outside the other (C), recalling the elaborate carved ivory spheres of the Chinese. In the illustration, some of the outer spheres have been broken through to show the inner structure. Such successive spheres are firmly united together by means of cross rods or of the characteristic spines.

The Radiolaria are all found in salt water, but, unlike the Foraminifera, float near the surface. Their skeletons form an important element in the rocks of Sicily and Greece; and the "Barbadoes earth," which is used for polishing, is mainly composed of the flinty skeletons of Radiolarians. Although there is little doubt that Radiolaria abounded in the seas where the great Chalk beds were deposited, they are not found in chalk; their siliceous skeletons probably having been dissolved and re-deposited as flint.

In the next division of the Protozoa, we find animals in which the protoplasmic processes of the body are still further specialised. They no longer send out indefinite pseudopodia for creeping slowly along on the surface of the ground, nor do they float free in the water, the protoplasm streaming out on all sides in fine rays. We now have only one or two processes adapted for locomotion through the water, and these are long and whip-like. These whips or "flagella," at the anterior end of the body, by their constant movement, drag it along rapidly through the water.

The Flagellata.

Some of the simplest of these Flagellata are so very like vegetable cells, that they were long excluded from the animal kingdom. It is, indeed, impossible to draw any very hard and fast line between the lowest plant and animal cells, and, as authorities are still more or less divided in opinion, such simple Flagellates may be regarded as belonging to a border land. One point in which many of the Flagellata resemble vegetable cells is colour. The Protozoa of other divisions are usually colourless and transparent, whereas many Flagellates are of a bright red, yellow, brown, or green. Some of the simplest of these animalcules (Fig. 6, A) as they dart across the microscopic field by the help of their whips, which, on account of the rapidity of their movements are for the time invisible, sparkle like minute emeralds. Some of the red Flagellata, when swarming in great numbers, produce large red patches on the sea. Other forms shine with phosphorescent light, and cause the beautiful glow often seen among the breakers on a shore at night. Thirty thousand animalcules are said to be contained in one cubic inch of such phosphorescent water.

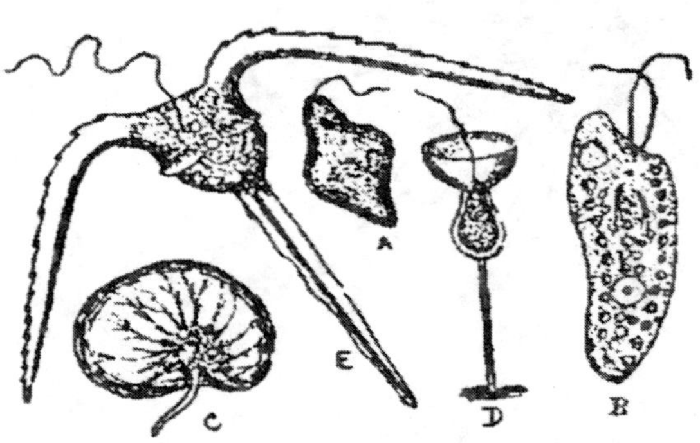

Fig. 6.—FLAGELLATA.
A, Euglena.
B, Chilomonas.
C, Noctiluca.
D, Monosiga.
E, Ceratium.

Some of the Flagellata are distinguished by a collar-shaped projection round the depression from which the whip-like appendage rises (Fig. 6, D), others by taking in food at one spot only of the body, *i.e.*, at the base of the chief whip (C). A shelly covering is present in some forms, in which it may resemble a cuirass or may be prolonged into several sharp, horn-like processes (E). These horny cases are often found in Chalk rocks.

Flagellate Colonies.

The Flagellata do not always, like the creatures we have hitherto described, lead independent lives, each individual feeding, moving, etc., on its own account. They are often found grouped together in colonies, the various individuals composing the colony being united by a common mass of protoplasm. The manner in which such colonies arise is interesting and important, inasmuch as, from this primitive grouping of single cells to form simple colonies, complex and highly organised colonies arose, culminating in the bodies of the higher animals, which are in reality gigantic colonies of countless living cells arranged into organs, each with its own special function to perform for the life of the whole. Single cells multiply in several ways, the simplest being that of the Amœba, which, creeping along the ground, parts into two daughter Amœbæ, each of which creeps on its separate way. In the case of free-swimming cells, like the Flagellata, separation into two might not be so easy, especially if the mechanism of locomotion is not very powerful as compared with the size of the body. In such creatures the cells, though actually dividing, need not finally separate, but may swim about in contact with one another; and, if successive generations of cells thus remain together, simple colonies arise. Several balls made up of flagellate cells are known, in which all the whips of the component cells are turned outward, and, by their movement, send the whole colony rolling along through the water. The best known of these is *Volvox globator*, which, on account of the bright green colour in its cells, is often claimed as a plant.

It is clear again that colonies may also arise by the dividing up of cells which are stationary. The daughter cells in this case may either grow up simply alongside of the parent, or may branch out from it. We are, however, fairly safe in assuming that all the higher animals arose from free-swimming, and not from stationary colonies, a stationary manner of life being but little conducive to progress. In Fig. 7, A, we see stationary colonies of Flagellata which, but for the stalk of attachment, somewhat resemble Volvox above mentioned. Another stationary colony is seen in the same figure (B), and is formed by the contiguous tubular sheaths of a number of flagellate cells, each provided with two whips. This colony forms folded, fan-like growths, the height of the whole structure being often not more than $\frac{1}{75}$ of an inch. Collared Flagellates also form colonies, sometimes being grouped together in flower-like bunches on stalks, as in Fig. 7, C, or floating about freely with the collars and whips projecting from a mass of common protoplasm. A colony of this latter sort has been named Protospongia, as it seems to foreshadow the arrangement of somewhat similar collared cells found in the Sponges.

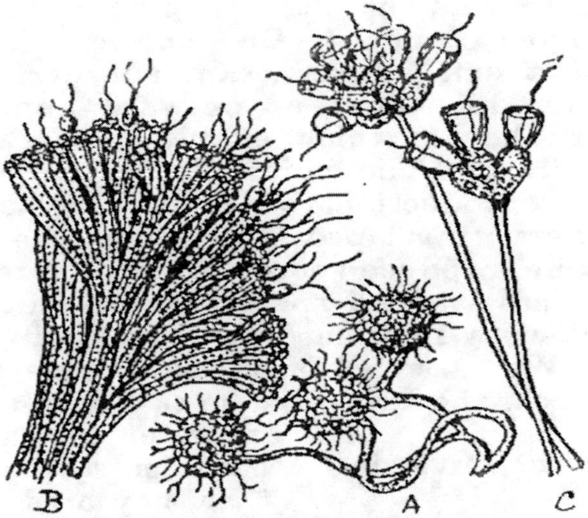

Fig. 7.—FLAGELLATE COLONIES.
A, Anthrophysa.
B, Rhipidodendron.
C, Codosiga.

Returning, however, to the Flagellata which remain single, *i.e.*, do not form colonies, reproduction takes place among them in several different ways. Some Flagellata simply break up into parts, like the Amœba, others detach only small pieces of their bodies, each piece developing into a new animal, a process which is called budding or gemmation; others, again, reproduce themselves by a kind of internal budding called spore-formation. The whole inside of the animal divides into a great number of minute "spores," each of which, after resting a while, grows into an animal like the parent. The Noctiluca (Fig. 6, C), for instance, which causes the marine phosphorescence already alluded to, may pass through a resting stage when it loses its whip and looks like a mere gelatinous ball (it is then said to be encysted). The protoplasm seems to collect in one part of the cyst and to break up into minute nodules. These nodules, which are called spores, raise up the outer surface into prominences, and finally, when mature, pass through the wall of the cyst, develop whips of their own, and swim about freely as young individuals known as "swarm spores."

Leaving now for a moment those Protozoa, which are rising higher and higher in the scale of organic life, we must notice a group which shows curious degeneration, the Gregarinæ. These creatures possess neither pseudopodia nor flagella: they can only move very slowly by a kind of contraction of the protoplasm just below the outer surface, which, being somewhat different from the rest of the body, we may call the "skin." These animalcules are all parasites, hence their degradation. They have managed to get into the bodies of animals higher than themselves, and are able to draw in as food, through the whole surface of the body, the juices of their "host" without any exertion on their own part. They are very common in the bodies of all classes of animals from the worms upward, each kind of Gregarina having its own special feeding ground in some part of a higher animal. One species, for instance, is only found in the gills of a small Crustacean, another in the liver of the Rabbit, and so on. The only kind of outward appendages ever found in these creatures are hooks which enable them the better to attach themselves to their victims. The chief life activity in these, as in most other parasites, is reproduction, which takes place by spore-formation. Two or more of the worm-shaped Gregarinæ fuse together, become encysted, and, after a time, produce spores, which are released by the bursting of the cyst. Each spindle-shaped spore develops into an independent individual, being supplied by its immediate surroundings with appropriate nourishment.

The Gregarinæ.

We pass on from these degenerate creatures to the highest of the Protozoa, the Infusoria, so-called on account of being found in infusions—*i.e.*, in water in which decaying animal or vegetable matter has been soaked, and in which it was at one time thought that they bred spontaneously.

The Infusoria.

In the Infusorians the protoplasm of the body shows more variety than in any other Protozoans. Not only is the outer surface of the body distinctly unlike the inner protoplasm, but it is more or less covered with very fine hairs or cilia (literally eyelashes), which promote its motion. It is sometimes provided with hooks or bristles as well, by means of which it can creep or hang on to other objects. At one definite spot there is a simple mouth, from which a depression often leads into the interior of the body. The mouth is usually encircled by cilia, which, by their rapid vibrations, keep up a kind of whirlpool, and bring particles of food within reach. As the food, which passes on into the body along the tube, is absorbed, definite streamings in certain directions can be made out in the granulated protoplasm. The indigestible portions of the food are, in some forms, ejected at a definite part of the body. The nucleus is not always round—it may be horse-shoe-shaped, or ribbon-like, or it may even resemble a string of beads. There are often several contractile vesicles.

The Infusoria are very plentiful in fresh water: they prey upon each other, and sometimes upon higher animals, such as Rotifers. Some are parasites.

There are Ciliated Infusorians and Tentacled Infusorians.

The Ciliated Infusorians are classed according to the arrangement of their cilia. These sometimes cover the whole surface of the body, as in the Slipper animalcule (Fig. 8, A), which is very common in pond water or in infusions of hay, and measures from $\frac{1}{96}$ to $\frac{1}{120}$ of an inch in length. In this Protozoan, the distinction between the outer part of the body and the inner granulated part is very clear, and the mouth and tube leading from it are very evident. In the outer "skin" a number of small oval bodies can be seen pointing outwards. These, which are known as trichocysts, are minute bags containing threads which can be shot out of them and are probably used as a defence against enemies. These structures recall the stinging threads of the Coelenterates, but are still more wonderful as the products of a single cell.

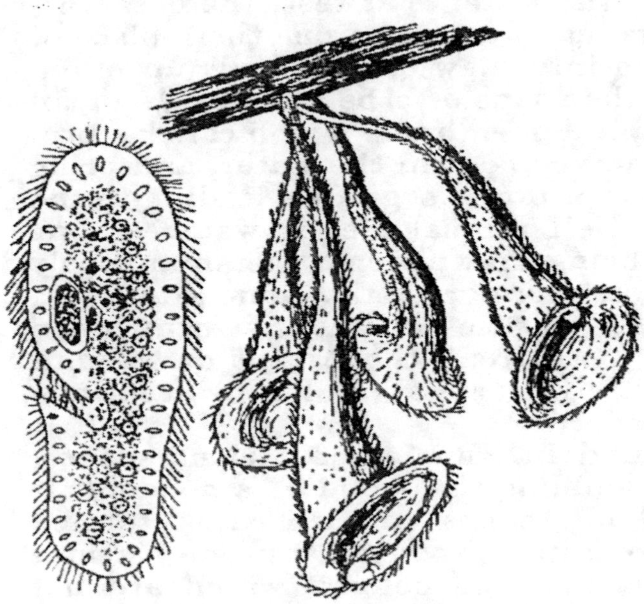

A B

Fig. 8.—CILIATED INFUSORIA.
A, Paramœcium.
B, Stentor.

In the next division of the Ciliated Infusorians, very fine cilia cover the surface of the body, while longer ones encircle the mouth. The Trumpet animalcules (Fig. 8, B), usually about $\frac{1}{20}$ of an inch in length, are found moving about freely in the water or attached, either singly or in groups, to some submerged object by the narrowed end of the body. The lower part of the body is sometimes protected by a kind of sheath or case. The wide opening at the free end which surrounds the mouth is fringed with long and strong cilia. In order to multiply, these Trumpet animalcules divide into two, a new mouth and oral fringe forming on the parent animal before division.

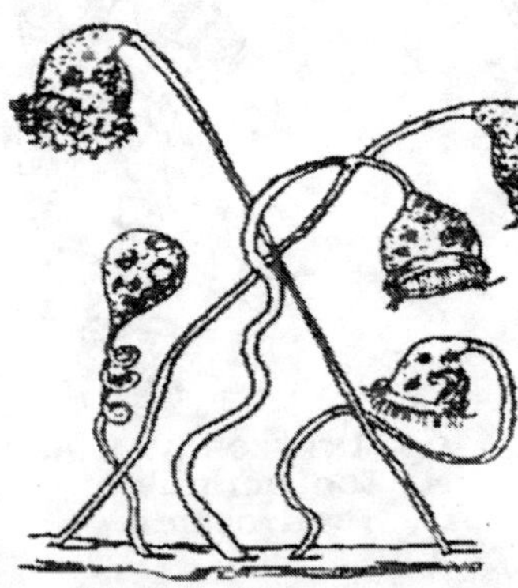

*Fig.*9.—GROUP OF BELL ANIMALCULES (*Vorticellidae*).

The Infusorians of the next division have smooth bodies, the cilia being usually confined to the region round the mouth; in some cases, however, a second band of cilia surrounds some other part of the body. Some of the attached Infusorians of this kind surround themselves with a slipper-shaped case of protoplasm, which helps to protect the soft part of the body, and can, when necessary, almost entirely cover it. As a rule, however, the mouth end, with its circle of cilia, protrudes from the aperture of the case in search of food. Other forms attach themselves by stalks which are contractile, and can, by coiling up spirally, quickly withdraw the animal from any threatening danger.

The Bell animalcules, when watched under the microscope, afford a very interesting example of the complexity of life and movement which may be attained by the single cell. When the water in which they are is, for any reason, in a state of disturbance, the minute gelatinous balls lie hidden close to the surface of some water weed at the ends of their tightly coiled stalks, and thus easily elude observation. But if the water is at rest, the observer, through the microscope, will see them gradually emerge from their place of refuge, one individual after another rising into view on its slowly uncoiling stalk, the ball lengthening and assuming the shape of a bell about $\frac{1}{300}$ of an inch in length. Long cilia, fringing a spiral membrane which can be protruded beyond the aperture of the bell, wave about in the water, and bring within reach particles of food that are swept down a groove leading to the inner protoplasm. As such a group of Bell animalcules is watched, one individual or another suddenly vanishes, being drawn down instantaneously by the contraction of its stalk, while others more gradually come into sight. These animalcules multiply by dividing lengthwise; the young form, when provided with its circle of cilia, breaks loose from the parent and swims about freely for a time before attaching itself by a stalk. Young are sometimes also produced within the parent as spores.

These beautiful creatures are often found in colonies of various shapes, some of the most delicate (Fig. 10, A) resembling the frond of a maidenhair fern. The stem is, in such cases, formed of protoplasm, produced by the various individuals of the colony, which are not always all alike. In the form illustrated spherical individuals without stalks are to be seen attached at the bases of the branchlets which carry the other individuals.

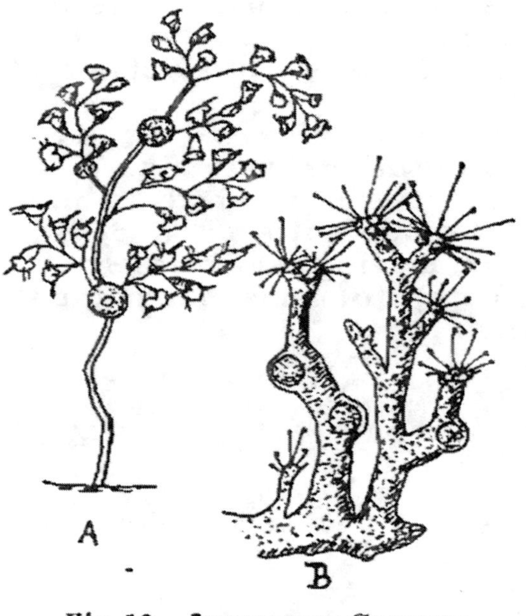

Fig. 10 —INFUSORIAN COLONIES.
A, Zoothamnium.
B, Dendrosoma.

In the fourth division of the Ciliated Infusorians the cilia are confined to the lower surface of the body, and are sometimes changed into bristles or hooks; these forms are much less attractive in appearance than those we have just described.

We come, in the last place, to the Tentacled Infusorians which are often to be found attached to pond weeds by long, straight stalks. The soft body is usually contained in a cup-like sheath, sometimes triangular in form, and terminates at the free end in one or more projecting knobs, ornamented with groups of stiff, hollow tentacles. The animal has no mouth, but feeds by means of these tentacles, the minute discs in which they end arresting and piercing the bodies of any small animalcules that come within reach. The soft parts of the victim are sucked up through the hollow tentacles and drawn into the body within the sheath. These stationary bodies give rise, by means of budding, to free young forms with cilia which swim about for a time, then attach themselves, lose their cilia, and develop tentacles like those of the parent form.

These Tentacled Infusorians sometimes form very complicated colonies consisting of creeping roots, from which rise trunks and branches (Fig. 10, B). Each branch and branchlet terminates in an individual with its radiating tentacles, but besides these tentacled members of the colony there are other spherical members, sometimes clustered together like bunches of berries, and within the protoplasm of the trunks there are capsules in which the young are produced and matured. So complicated are these beautiful colonies, in which a distinct division of labour takes place, that it is difficult to realise that they are nothing more than communities of Protozoans.

INDEX

B.

C.

D.

E.

F.

I.

J.

K.

N.

O

P.

Q.

R.

T.

U.

V.

W.

X.

Y.

Z.

THE END.

THE NATURAL HISTORY OF SELBORNE AND OBSERVATIONS ON NATURE. By GILBERT WHITE. With an Introduction by John Burroughs, 80 Illustrations by Clifton Johnson, and the Text and New Letters of the Buckland Edition. In two volumes. 12mo. Cloth, $4.00.

"White himself, were he alive to-day, would join all his loving readers in thanking the American publishers for a thoroughly excellent presentation of his famous book. . . . This latest edition of White's book must go into all our libraries; our young people must have it at hand, and our trained lovers of select literature must take it into their homes. By such reading we keep knowledge in proper perspective and are able to grasp the proportions of discovery."—MAURICE THOMPSON, *in the Independent.*

"White's 'Selborne' belongs in the same category as Walton's 'Complete Angler'; . . . here they are, the 'Complete Angler' well along in its third century, and the other just started in its second century, both of them as highly esteemed as they were when first published, both bound to live forever, if we may trust the predictions of their respective admirers. John Burroughs, in his charming introduction, tells us why White's book has lasted, and why this new and beautiful edition has been printed. . . . This new edition of his work comes to us beautifully illustrated by Clifton Johnson."—*New York Times.*

"White's 'Selborne' has been reprinted many times, in many forms, but never before, so far as we can remember, in so creditable a form as it assumes in these two volumes, nor with drawings comparable to those which Mr. Clifton Johnson has made for them."—*New York Mail and Express.*

"We are loath to put down the two handsome volumes in which the source of such a gift as this has been republished. The type is so clear, the paper is so pleasant to the touch, the weight of each volume is so nicely adapted to the hand, and one turns page after page with exactly that quiet sense of ever new and ever old endeared delight which comes through a window looking on the English countryside—the rooks cawing in a neighboring copse, the little village nestling sleepily amid the trees, trees so green that sometimes they seem to hover on the edge of black, and then again so green that they seem vivid with the flaunting bravery of spring." — *New York Tribune.*

"Not only for the significance they lend to one of the masterpieces of English literature, but as a revelation of English rural life and scenes, are these pictures delightfully welcome. The edition is in every way creditable to the publishers."—*Boston Beacon.*

"Rural England has many attractions for the lover of Nature, and no work, perhaps, has done its charms greater justice than Gilbert White's 'Natural History of Selborne.'"—*Boston Journal.*

"This charming edition leaves really nothing to be desired." — *Westminster Gazette.*

"This edition is beautifully illustrated and bound, and deserves to be welcomed by all naturalists and Nature lovers."—*London Daily Chronicle.*

"Handsome and desirable in every respect. . . . Welcome to old and young."—*New York Herald.*

"The charm of White's 'Selborne' is not definable. But there is no other book of the past generations that will ever take the place with the field naturalists."—*Baltimore Sun.*

BIRD-LIFE. A Guide to the Study of our Common Birds. By FRANK M. CHAPMAN, Assistant Curator of Mammalogy and Ornithology, American Museum of Natural History; Author of "Handbook of Birds of Eastern North America." With 75 full-page Plates and numerous Text Drawings by Ernest Seton Thompson. 12mo. Cloth, $1.75.

"'Bird-Life' is different from other books. It deals with birds that are familiar, or half familiar; it interests the ignorant reader at once, and it makes the relations between birds and men seem more intimate. The economic value of birds will be better appreciated after reading this book."—*Boston Herald.*

"Contains more information about birds, in the same space, attractively as well as concisely stated, than can be found in any other book with which we are acquainted. . . . A delightful, valuable, instructive, entertaining, beautiful book."—*Brooklyn Standard-Union.*

"Most heartily can 'Bird-Life' be commended. It is by a practical ornithologist, but it is simple and comprehensible. It is compact, pointed, clear. . . . The work is perfectly reliable. . . . The author uses every line to give information. A straightforward and very compact guide-book to bird-land."—*Hartford Post.*

"An intelligent consideration of the book will add to the reader's pleasure in his walks in field and wood, quicken his ear, make him hear and see things which before went unnoticed. . . . Gives the student an introduction to ornithology, which places him on the threshold of the entrance to the innermost circles of bird-life."—*Boston Times.*

"Mr. Chapman's book ought to be as greatly in demand in the average household as a history of one's country."—*Providence Journal.*

"A comprehensive book, one that is sufficient for all the ordinary needs of the amateur ornithologist. It is satisfactory in every detail, and arranged with a care and method that will draw praise from the highest sources. Every lover of outdoor life will find this book a delightful companion and an invaluable aid."—*Buffalo Enquirer.*

"A volume exceptionally well adapted to the requirements of people who wish to study common birds in the simplest and most profitable manner possible. . . . As a readily intelligible and authoritative guide this manual has qualities that will commend it at once to the attention of the discerning student."—*Boston Beacon.*

"Such a study as every intelligent reader will desire to make, even the busiest of them. . . . The author is in every way fitted for the task he has taken, and his book abounds in its facts of value, and they are pleasingly and gracefully told."—*Chicago Inter-Ocean.*

"An interesting mass of data collected through years of study and observation. . . . While accurate from a scientific point of view, it makes delightful reading for those who will soon be among the flowers and the fields."—*Philadelphia Inquirer.*

FAMILIAR FLOWERS OF FIELD AND GARDEN.

By F. SCHUYLER MATHEWS. Illustrated with 200 Drawings by the Author, and containing an elaborate Index showing at a glance the botanical and popular names, family, color, locality, environment, and time of bloom of several hundred flowers. 12mo. Library Edition, cloth, $1.75; Pocket Edition, flexible covers, $2.25.

"In this convenient and useful volume the flowers which one finds in the fields are identified, illustrated, and described in familiar language. Their connection with garden flowers is made clear. Particular attention is drawn to the beautiful ones which have come under cultivation, and, as the title indicates, the book furnishes a ready guide to a knowledge of wild and cultivated flowers alike.

"I have examined Mr. Mathews's little book upon 'Familiar Flowers of Field and Garden,' and I have pleasure in commending the accuracy and beauty of the drawings and the freshness of the text. We have long needed some botany from the hand of an artist who sees form and color without the formality of the scientist. The book deserves a reputation."—L. H. BAILEY, *Professor of Horticulture, Cornell University.*

"I am much pleased with your 'Familiar Flowers of Field and Garden.' It is a useful and handsomely prepared handbook, and the elaborate index is an especially valuable part of it. Taken in connection with the many careful drawings, it would seem as though your little volume thoroughly covers its subject."—LOUIS PRANG.

"The author describes in a most interesting and charming manner many familiar wild and cultivated plants, enlivening his remarks by crisp epigrams, and rendering identification of the subjects described simple by means of some two hundred drawings from Nature, made by his own pen. . . . The book will do much to more fully acquaint the reader with those plants of field and garden treated upon with which he may be but partly familiar, and go a long way toward correcting many popular errors existing in the matter of colors of their flowers—a subject to which Mr. Mathews has devoted much attention, and on which he is now a recognized authority in the trade."—*New York Florists' Exchange.*

"A book of much value and interest, admirably arranged for the student and the lover of flowers. . . . The text is full of compact information, well selected and interestingly presented. . . . It seems to us to be a most attractive handbook of its kind."—*New York Sun.*

"A delightful book and very useful. Its language is plain and familiar, and the illustrations are dainty works of art. It is just the book for those who want to be familiar with the well-known flowers, those that grow in the cultivated gardens as well as those that blossom in the fields."—*Newark Daily Advertiser.*

"Seasonable and valuable. The young botanist and the lover of flowers, who have only studied from Nature, will be greatly aided by this work."—*Pittsburg Post.*

"Charmingly written, and to any one who loves the flowers—and who does not?—will prove no less fascinating than instructive. It will open up in the garden and the fields a new world full of curiosity and delight, and invest them with a new interest in his sight."—*Christian Work.*

"One need not be deeply read in floral lore to be interested in what Mr. Mathews has written, and the more proficient one is therein the greater his satisfaction is likely to be."—*New York Mail and Express.*

"Mr. F. Schuyler Mathews's careful description and graceful drawings of our 'Familiar Flowers of Field and Garden' are fitted to make them familiar even to those who have not before made their acquaintance."—*New York Evening Post.*

CLIMBING IN THE HIMALAYAS. By WILLIAM MARTIN CONWAY, M. A., F. R. G. S., Vice-President of the Alpine Club; formerly Professor of Art in University College, Liverpool. With 300 Illustrations by A. D. MCCORMICK, and a Map. 8vo. Cloth, $10.00.

This work contains a minute record of one of the most important and thrilling geographical enterprises of the century—an expedition made in 1892, under the auspices of the Royal Geographical Society, the Royal Society, the British Association, and the Government of India. It included an exploration of the glaciers at the head of the Bagrot Valley and the great peaks in the neighborhood of Rakipushi (25,500 feet); an expedition to Hispar, at the foot of the longest glacier in the world outside the polar regions; the first definitely recorded passage of the Hispar Pass, the longest known pass in the world; and the ascent of Pioneer Peak (about 23,000 feet), the highest ascent yet authentically made. No better man could have been chosen for this important expedition than Mr. Conway, who has spent over twenty years in mountaineering work in the Alps. Already the author of nine published books, he has recorded his discoveries in this volume in the clear, incisive, and thrilling language of an expert.

"It would be hard to say too much in praise of this superb work. As a record of mountaineering it is almost, if not quite, unique. Among records of Himalayan exploration it certainly stands alone. . . . The farther Himalayas . . . have never been so faithfully—in other words, so poetically—presented as in the masterly delicate sketches with which Mr. McCormick has adorned this book."—*London Daily News.*

"This stately volume is a worthy record of a splendid journey. . . . The book is not merely the narrative of the best organized and most successful mountaineering expedition as yet made; it is a most valuable and minute account, based on first-hand evidence, of a most fascinating region of the heaven-soaring Himalayas."—*Pall Mall Gazette.*

"Mr. Conway's volume is a splendid record of a daring and adventurous scientific expedition. . . . What Mr. Whymper did for the northern Andes, Mr. Conway has done for the Karakorum Himalayas."—*London Times.*

"It would be difficult to say which of the many classes of readers who will welcome the work will find most enjoyment in its fascinating pages. Mr. Conway's pen and Mr. McCormick's pencil have made their countrymen partners in their pleasure."—*London Standard.*

". . . In addition to this, Mr. Conway is a man of letters, a student (and a teacher, too) of art, a scholar in several languages; one, too, who knows the Latin names of plants, and the use of theodolite and plane table. From him, therefore, if from any one, the world had a right to expect a book that should combine accurate observation and intelligible reporting with an original and acute record of impressions; nor will the world have any reason to be disappointed."—*London Athenæum.*

"With its three hundred illustrations we have seldom seen a volume which speaks to the eye and understanding so pleasantly and expressively on every page. . . . We have an exhaustive panorama of the Himalayan scenery, of the manner in which the rough marching was conducted, of ascents achieved under the most dangerous conditions, and of the troubles and humors of the shifting camps where the coolies rested from their labors."—*London Saturday Review.*

ACTUAL AFRICA; or, The Coming Continent. A Tour of Exploration. By FRANK VINCENT, author of "The Land of the White Elephant," etc. With Map and 102 Illustrations. 8vo. Cloth, $5.00.

This thorough and comprehensive work furnishes a survey of the entire continent, which this experienced traveler has circumnavigated in addition to his inland explorations. The latter have included journeys in northern Africa, Madagascar, southern Africa, and an expedition into the Congo country which has covered fresh ground. His book has the distinction of presenting a comprehensive summary, instead of offering an account of one special district. It is more elaborately illustrated than any book upon the subject, and contains a large map carefully corrected to date.

"Mr. Frank Vincent's books of travel merit to be ranked among the very best, not only for their thoroughness, but for the animation of their narrative, and the skill with which he fastens upon his reader's mind the impression made upon him by his voyagings."—*Boston Saturday Evening Gazette.*

"A new volume from Mr. Frank Vincent is always welcome, for the reading public have learned to regard him as one of the most intelligent and observing of travelers."—*New York Tribune.*

AROUND AND ABOUT SOUTH AMERICA: Twenty Months of Quest and Query. By FRANK VINCENT. With Maps, Plans, and 54 full-page Illustrations. 8vo, xxiv + 473 pages. Ornamental cloth, $5.00.

"South America, with its civilization, its resources, and its charms, is being constantly introduced to us, and constantly surprises us. . . . The Parisian who thinks us all barbarians is probably not denser in his prejudices than most of us are about our Southern continent. We are content not to know, there seeming to be no reason why we should. Fashion has not yet directed her steps there, and there has been nothing to stir us out of our lethargy. . . . Mr. Vincent observes very carefully, is always good-humored, and gives us the best of what he sees. . . . The reader of his book will gain a clear idea of a marvelous country. Maps and illustrations add greatly to the value of this work."—*New York Commercial Advertiser.*

"The author's style is unusually simple and straightforward, the printing is remarkably accurate, and the forty odd illustrations are refreshingly original for the most part."—*The Nation.*

"Mr. Vincent has succeeded in giving a most interesting and valuable narrative. His account is made doubly valuable by the exceptionally good illustrations, most of them photographic reproductions. The printing of both text and plates is beyond criticism."—*Philadelphia Public Ledger.*

IN AND OUT OF CENTRAL AMERICA; and Other Sketches and Studies of Travel. By FRANK VINCENT. With Maps and Illustrations. 12mo. Cloth, $2.00.

"Few living travelers have had a literary success equal to Mr. Vincent's."—*Harper's Weekly.*

"Mr. Vincent has now seen all the most interesting parts of the world, having traveled, during a total period of eleven years, two hundred and sixty-five thousand miles. His personal knowledge of man and Nature is probably as varied and complete as that of any person living."—*New York Home Journal.*